McCORMICK
ON EVIDENCE

*

McCORMICK ON EVIDENCE

Fourth Edition

By

John William Strong
General Editor
Rosenstiel Professor of Law, University of Arizona

Contributing Authors

Kenneth S. Broun
Henry Brandis Professor of Law, University of North Carolina

George E. Dix
A.W. Walker Centennial Professor of Law, The University of Texas

Michael H. Graham
Professor of Law, University of Miami

D. H. Kaye
Regents Professor of Law, Arizona State University

Robert R. Mosteller
Professor of Law, Duke University

E. F. Roberts
Edwin H. Woodruff Professor of Law, The Cornell Law School

Volume 2
Chapters 21–End
Appendices
Tables
Index

PRACTITIONER TREATISE SERIES®

WEST PUBLISHING CO.
ST. PAUL, MINN., 1992

COPYRIGHT © 1954, 1972, 1984, 1987 WEST PUBLISHING CO.
COPYRIGHT © 1992 By WEST PUBLISHING CO.
                    50 West Kellogg Boulevard
                    P.O. Box 64526
                    St. Paul, MN 55164–0526

Library of Congress Cataloging-in-Publication Data

McCormick, Charles Tilford, 1889–1963.
    McCormick on evidence / by John William Strong, general editor ;
contributing authors, Kenneth S. Broun . . . [et al.]. — 4th ed.
        p. cm. — (Practitioner treatise series)
    Includes index.
    ISBN 0–314–89311–3 (v. 1). — ISBN 0–314–89312–1 (v. 2)
    1. Evidence (Law)—United States. I. Strong, John William, 1935–
. II. Broun, Kenneth S. III. Title. IV. Series.
KF8935.M29 1992
347.73'6—dc20
[347.3076]   91–25824
                                                                CIP

ISBN 0–314–89312–1

WESTLAW® Overview

McCormick on Evidence offers a detailed and comprehensive treatment of the basic rules and principles of evidence law. To supplement the information supplied in this treatise, researchers can access WESTLAW. WESTLAW is a computer-assisted legal research service of West Publishing Company.

The law of evidence on WESTLAW includes case law, statutes, court rules and orders, administrative materials and commentary databases. To help research the law of evidence, a WESTLAW appendix is included in this edition. This appendix provides information on databases, search techniques and sample research problems so that you can coordinate WESTLAW research with this book.

THE PUBLISHER

*

Summary of Contents

Volume 1

TITLE 1. INTRODUCTION

TITLE 2. EXAMINATION OF WITNESSES

TITLE 3. ADMISSION AND EXCLUSION

TITLE 4. COMPETENCY

TITLE 5. PRIVILEGE: COMMON LAW AND STATUTORY

TITLE 6. PRIVILEGE: CONSTITUTIONAL

Volume 2

TITLE 8. DEMONSTRATIVE EVIDENCE

TITLE 9. WRITINGS

TITLE 10. THE HEARSAY RULE AND ITS EXCEPTIONS

TITLE 11. JUDICIAL NOTICE

TITLE 12. BURDEN OF PROOF AND PRESUMPTIONS

TITLE 13. ADMINISTRATIVE EVIDENCE

Appendices

*

Table of Contents

Volume 1

TITLE 1. INTRODUCTION

TITLE 2. EXAMINATION OF WITNESSES

TITLE 3. ADMISSION AND EXCLUSION

TITLE 4. COMPETENCY

TITLE 5. PRIVILEGE: COMMON LAW AND STATUTORY

Volume 2

TITLE 8. DEMONSTRATIVE EVIDENCE

TITLE 9. WRITINGS

TITLE 10. THE HEARSAY RULE AND ITS EXCEPTIONS

TITLE 13. ADMINISTRATIVE EVIDENCE

Appendices

Title 8

DEMONSTRATIVE EVIDENCE

Chapter 21

DEMONSTRATIVE EVIDENCE

Table of Sections

§ 212. Demonstrative Evidence in General [1]

There is a type of evidence which consists of things, e.g., weapons, whiskey bottles, writings,[2] and wearing apparel, as distinguished from

§ 212

1. See 4 Wigmore, Evidence §§ 1150–1169 (Chadbourn rev. 1972); C.J.S. Evidence §§ 601–622; Dec.Dig. Evidence ⇐188–195; Criminal Law ⇐404 (1–4); Trial ⇐28 and 375.

Demonstrative evidence, as a generic class, is not singled out for specific treatment by the Federal or Revised Uniform Rules of Evidence. As is stressed in the text infra at nn. 22, 23 demonstrative evidence is particularly likely to raise issues to which Rules 402–403 are applicable. The Federal Rules provide:

Rule 402. Relevant Evidence Generally Admissible; Irrelevant Evidence Inadmissible.

All relevant evidence is admissible, except as otherwise provided by the Constitution of the United States, by Act of Congress, by these rules, or by other rules prescribed by the Supreme Court pursuant to statutory authority. Evidence which is not relevant is not admissible.

Rule 403. Exclusion of Relevant Evidence on Grounds of Prejudice, Confusion, or Waste of Time.

Although relevant, evidence may be excluded if its probative value is substantially outweighed by the danger of unfair prejudice, confusion of the issues, or misleading the jury, or by considerations of undue delay, waste of time, or needless presentation of cumulative evidence.

The revised Uniform Rules are identical except for adaptation of Rule 402 to state use.

2. Writings, except insofar as they contain statements which the writing is offered to prove, are examples of the present

2

the assertions of witnesses (or hearsay declarants) about things. Most broadly viewed, this type of evidence includes all phenomena which can convey a relevant firsthand sense impression to the trier of fact,[3] as opposed to those which serve merely to report the secondhand sense impressions of others. Thus, for example, demeanor evidence, i.e. the bearing, expression, and manner of a witness while testifying,[4] is an instance of the type of evidence here considered, but the statements which he utters are not.

Evidence from which the trier of fact may derive a relevant firsthand sense impression is almost unlimited in its variety. As a result, the problem of satisfactorily labeling and classifying has proved a difficult one,[5] and it will be seen variously referred to as real, autoptic, demonstrative, tangible, and objective. For present purposes, the term "demonstrative" will be used to refer to the generic class, though it should be noted that some courts employ this term in a more limited sense.[6]

Since "seeing is believing," and demonstrative evidence appeals directly to the senses of the trier of fact,[7] it is today universally felt that this kind of evidence possesses an immediacy and reality which endow it with particularly persuasive effect.[8] Largely as a result of this potential, the use of demonstrative evidence of all types has increased dramatically during recent years, and the trend seems certain to continue in the immediate future. At the same time, demonstrative evidence remains the exception rather than the rule, and its use raises certain problems for a juridical system the mechanics of which are essentially geared to the reception of *viva voce* testimony by witnesses. Some of these problems are so commonly raised by the offer of demons-

subject. They have, however, developed rules of their own which are treated independently. See Ch. 22 (authentication) and Ch. 23 (documentary originals).

3. Schertzinger v. Williams, 198 Cal. App.2d 242, 17 Cal.Rptr. 719 (1961).

4. While demeanor evidence is analytically a type of demonstrative evidence, it is inseparably related to oral testimony and is thus treated elsewhere. See § 245, infra.

5. See, Michael & Adler, Real Proof, 5 Vand.L.Rev. 344 (1952); Nokes, Real Evidence, 65 L.Q.Rev. 57 (1949); Patterson, Types of Evidence, 19 Vand.L.Rev. 1 (1965); 4 Wigmore, Evidence § 1150 (Chadbourn rev. 1972).

6. I.e., as contrasted with "real" evidence. See discussion at note 25 infra.

7. While the great bulk of demonstrative evidence is directed to the sense of sight, each of the other senses may on occasion be appealed to. See, e.g., Ragusa v. American Metal Works, Inc., 97 So.2d 683 (La.App.1957) (hearing); People v. Kin-

ney, 124 Mich. 486, 83 N.W. 147 (1900) (taste); McAndrews v. Leonard, 99 Vt. 512, 134 A. 710 (1926) (touch); Rust v. Guinn, 429 N.E.2d 299 (Ind.App.1981) (smell).

8. Of the many articles emphasizing the point, the following may be cited: Belli, Demonstrative Evidence and the Adequate Award, 22 Miss.L.J. 284 (1951); Dombroff, Innovative Developments in Demonstrative Evidence Techniques and Associated Problems of Admissibility, 45 J.Air L. 139 (1980); Dooley, Demonstrative Evidence—Nothing New, 42 Ill.B.J. 136 (1953); Gamble, Using Demonstrative Evidence, 26 La.B.J. 215 (1979); Hinshaw, Use and Abuse of Demonstrative Evidence: The Art of Jury Persuasion, 40 A.B.A.J. 479 (1954); Hare, Demonstrative Evidence, 27 Ala.Law. 193 (1966); Kilroy, Seeing Is Believing, 8 Kan.L.Rev. 445 (1960); Knepper, Exhibits and Demonstrative Evidence, 30 Ins.L.J. 133 (1963); Lay, Use of Real Evidence, 37 Neb.L.Rev. 501 (1958); Perlman, Demonstrative Evidence, 33 Ky.S.B.J. 5 (1969); Spangenburg, The Use of Demonstrative Evidence, 21 Ohio St.L.J. 178 (1960).

trative evidence, and are so frequently made the bases of objections to its admission, that they deserve preliminary note.[9]

It has already been noted that evidence from which the trier of fact may derive his own perceptions, rather than evidence consisting of the reported perceptions of others, possesses unusual force. Consequently, demonstrative evidence is frequently objected to as prejudicial, a term which is today generally defined as suggesting "decision on an improper basis, commonly, though not necessarily, an emotional one." [10] A great deal of demonstrative evidence has the capacity to generate emotional responses such as pity, revulsion, or contempt, and where this capacity outweighs the value of the evidence on the issues in litigation, exclusion is appropriate.

Again, even if no essentially emotional response is likely to result, demonstrative evidence may convey an impression of objective reality to the trier. Thus, the courts are frequently sensitive to the objection that the evidence is "misleading," and zealous to insure that there is no misleading differential between objective things offered at trial and the same or different objective things as they existed at the time of the events or occurrences in litigation.[11]

Further, and apart from its bearing on the issues of the case, demonstrative evidence as a class presents certain essentially logistical difficulties for the courts. Since the courts are basically structured, architecturally and otherwise, to receive the testimony of witnesses, the presentation of demonstrative evidence may require that the court physically move to receive it, or that unwieldly objects or paraphernalia be introduced into the courtroom, actions which may occasion delay and confusion.[12] Finally, while oral testimony is easily incorporated into a paper record for purposes of appellate review, demonstrative evidence will sometimes be insusceptible to similar preservation and transmission.[13]

9. For an extended treatment of the objections commonly raised to demonstrative evidence, see Cady, Objections to Demonstrative Evidence, 32 Mo.L.Rev. 333 (1967).

10. See Fed.R.Evid. 403 advisory committee note.

11. See discussion at note 26 infra.

12. Ford v. Chicago, 132 Ill.App.3d 408, 87 Ill.Dec. 240, 476 N.E.2d 1232 (1985) (admission of motorcycle upheld as discretionary despite argument that large size of motorcycle and small size of courtroom caused jury to be overwhelmed).

13. E.g., Indiana Appellate Rules, Rule 7.2(A)(3)(b) provides as follows:

Exhibits—Physical Objects. Physical objects (except papers, maps, pictures and like materials) which, because of their nature cannot be incorporated in a transcript, shall not be sent to this Court

on appeal, but shall remain in the custody of the trial court below until the appeal is terminated. However, such objects shall be briefly named and identified in the transcript following the exhibit number therein. A photograph of such exhibits may be included in the transcript.

Some examples of demonstrative evidence are difficult if not impossible to accommodate under such a rule, which will sometimes raise the question whether non-record evidence may suffice to support a verdict. See § 216 infra. See also, Tuttle v. Miami Dolphins, Ltd., 551 So.2d 477 (Fla.App.1988) (appearance of plaintiff though not of record held to support jury finding of "wilfull" sale of alcohol to minor 6 years earlier; scholarly opinion suggests modern methods of preserving such evidence for record).

The cogency and force of the foregoing objections to the introduction of demonstrative evidence will obviously vary greatly with the nature of the particular item offered, and the purpose and need for its introduction in the particular case. Since the types of demonstrative evidence and the purposes for which it is sought to be introduced are extremely varied, it is generally viewed as appropriate to accord the trial judge broad discretion in ruling upon the admissibility of many types of demonstrative evidence.[14]

Despite its great variety, certain classifications of demonstrative evidence appear both valid and useful. First, like other evidence, it may be either direct or circumstantial. If a material issue in the case is whether an object does or does not possess a perceptible feature, characteristic, or quality, the most satisfactory method of demonstrating the truth of the matter will ordinarily be to produce the object so that the trier of fact may perceive the quality, or its absence, for himself. Thus, where a party seeks damages for the loss of a limb or for an injury leaving a disfiguring scar, exhibition of the person will constitute direct evidence of a material fact.[15] Similarly, exhibition of the chattel purchased in an action for breach of warranty will, at least if the quality or characteristic warranted is a perceivable one, constitute direct evidence on the issue of condition.[16] In these cases no process of inference, at least in the ordinary sense, is required.[17] Similarly, exhibition of a person to establish such facts as race[18] and age[19] may perhaps also be considered examples of demonstrative evidence of a direct sort, though the immediate perceptibility of these qualities may on occasion be subject to more doubt.

Demonstrative evidence may also be offered for its circumstantial value, i.e., as the basis for an inference beyond those facts which are perceivable. Such is the case when the exhibition of a person is made for the purpose of demonstrating his relationship to another, as in a filiation proceeding.[20] The use of demonstrative evidence is even more

---

14. E.g., the types of demonstrative evidence discussed in §§ 213–216 infra.

15. See Calumet Paving Co. v. Butkus, 113 Ind.App. 232, 47 N.E.2d 829 (1943) (exhibition of plaintiff's shoulder most satisfactory evidence of injury); Hendricks v. Sanford, 216 Or. 149, 337 P.2d 974 (1959) (exhibition "completely relevant" to show declivity in plaintiff's back). See § 215 notes 1–6 infra.

16. See, e.g., Woodward & Lothrop v. Heed, 44 A.2d 369 (D.C.Mun.App.1945) (breach of implied warranty on fur coat; "When the issue of fact is the condition of * * * an article, the introduction in evidence of the thing itself, to enable a jury to observe its condition, is competent and persuasive evidence.")

17. 4 Wigmore, Evidence § 1150 (Chadbourn rev. 1972).

18. See, e.g., White v. Holderby, 192 F.2d 722 (5th Cir.1951).

19. See, e.g., United States ex rel. Fong on v. Day, 54 F.2d 990, 991 (2d Cir.1932) ("it can hardly be doubted that [the jury] are at liberty to use their senses and draw an inference as to the person's age from his physical appearance"); State v. Dorathy, 132 Me. 291, 170 A. 506 (1934). But see Watson v. State, 236 Ind. 329, 140 N.E.2d 109 (1957) (appearance of defendant not alone sufficient to support finding as to age), noted in 15 Wash. & L.L.Rev. 290 (1958).

20. Many states hold that the trial court may, in its discretion, permit a child to be exhibited in a filiation proceeding for the purpose of showing a resemblance to the putative father. See, e.g., Judway v. Kovacs, 4 Conn.Cir. 713, 239 A.2d 556 (1967) (dictum); Glascock v. Anderson, 83

clearly circumstantial when articles of clothing worn at the time of his arrest by the defendant in a robbery prosecution are exhibited to the jury to demonstrate their conformity with the descriptions of the robber given by witnesses.[21]

The practical significance of the foregoing distinction lies in the fact that direct evidence, because of its eminently satisfactory character, will generally be admitted even where it is likely to occasion some prejudice or physical difficulty.[22] Thus, gruesome photographs which directly show a material fact have been held properly admitted in innumerable criminal cases, often without regard to their obvious capacity to inflame the jury.[23] The better view, reflected in some

N.M. 725, 497 P.2d 727 (1972), 1973 Wash. U.L.Rev. 245. The practice is by no means universally accepted. See 1 Wigmore, Evidence § 166 (3d ed. 1940); Annot., 40 A.L.R. 111, 95 A.L.R. 314.

21. See, e.g., Caldwell v. United States, 338 F.2d 385 (8th Cir.1964); Vanleeward v. State, 220 Ga. 135, 137 S.E.2d 452 (1964).

22. Rich v. Ellerman & Bucknall Steamship Co., 278 F.2d 704, 708 (2d Cir. 1960) ("Autoptic preference is always proper, unless reasons of policy apply to exclude it;" error to exclude photos of plaintiff's injuries). Cases are collected in 4 Wigmore, Evidence §§ 1157, 1158 (Chadbourn rev. 1972); Dec.Dig. Crim. Law ⬅404, Evidence ⬅188.

23. In some instances it is said that potential prejudice does not support the exclusion of material evidence. State v. Murphy, 610 S.W.2d 382, 385 (Mo.App. 1980) ("The only discretion a trial court has to deny admission of demonstrative evidence is if the evidence is both irrelevant to a material issue and also inflammatory or prejudicial"); State v. Bucanis, 26 N.J. 45, 138 A.2d 739 (1958) (conviction upheld though pictures were "more harmful than illuminating"); Wilson v. State, 247 Ind. 680, 221 N.E.2d 347 (1966) (gruesomeness not considered where evidence relevant). Even where a balancing of probative value against prejudice is approved in theory, see § 185 supra, admission is usually upheld. United States v. McRae, 593 F.2d 700 (5th Cir.1979), cert. denied 444 U.S. 862 (photos of "exploded head" of victim wife, alleged improperly admitted under Fed.R.Evid. 403; Rule 403 held not meant to "even out" evidence or unrealistically to "sanitize" trial); State v. Kelly, 122 Ariz. 495, 595 P.2d 1040 (App.1979) (balancing required, but no error to permit victim to display scars from wounds); Washington v. Commonwealth, 228 Va. 535, 323 S.E.2d 577 (1984) (accurate photo not inadmissible because gruesome or shocking, stating that exclusion for grue-

someness would provide incentive for extreme mutilation of victim). Where a balance is required and improperly struck, the resulting admission of prejudicial evidence may constitute only harmless error. State v. Banks, 564 S.W.2d 947 (Tenn.1978) (prejudicial effect of photos "far outweigh[ed] their probative value;" resulting error in admission harmless under circumstances). To date, federal constitutional guarantees have not been found implicated by even a serious imbalance. Thompson v. Oklahoma, 487 U.S. 815 (1988) (decided on other grounds) (Scalia, J., dissenting; "[Court has] never before held that the excessively inflammatory character of concededly relevant evidence can form the basis of a constitutional attack.")

Cases are collected in Annot., 159 A.L.R. 1413, 73 A.L.R.2d 769.

Where materiality is entirely lacking, of course, the admission of prejudicial demonstrative evidence is improper. See, e.g., State v. Bischert, 131 Mont. 152, 308 P.2d 969 (1957); State v. Clawson, 165 W.Va. 588, 270 S.E.2d 659 (1980) (admission of gruesome photos having "no probative value" held reversible error). But attempts to remove materiality by admitting or stipulating to the fact to be proved are rarely successful. See, e.g., United States v. Brady, 595 F.2d 359 (6th Cir.1979) (stipulation that victims died by gunshot did not eliminate materiality of photos of victims lying in pools of blood in bank; photos relevant to show killings occurred in course of robbery); People v. Mireles, 79 Ill.App.3d 173, 34 Ill.Dec. 475, 398 N.E.2d 150 (1979) (admission of photos of victim and wires with which she was strangled upheld where defendant admitted killing and pleaded insanity); State v. Taylor, 294 N.C. 347, 240 S.E.2d 784 (1978). But see Fortune, Judicial Admissions in Criminal Cases: Blocking the Introduction of Prejudicial Evidence, 17 Crim.L.Bull. 101 (1981).

recent decisions, is that the admission even of demonstrative evidence which directly portrays material facts calls for the exercise of judicial discretion.[24]

When circumstantial evidence is involved, in the present context as elsewhere, the trial judge will generally be viewed as possessing a broader discretionary power to weigh the probative value of the evidence against whatever prejudice, confusion, surprise and waste of time are entailed, and to determine admissibility accordingly.[25]

As with other circumstantial evidence, of course, demonstrative evidence offered for its circumstantial value may give rise to more than one inference. Thus introduction of a firearm taken from the defendant on his arrest and shown to be similar to that used in the commission of the offense charged may imply both that the defendant was the robber and that the defendant is a dangerous individual given to carrying firearms. If a permissible inference is present, admission will generally be upheld, a limiting instruction being deemed sufficient to prevent any untoward damage.[26]

Again, demonstrative evidence may be classified as to whether the item offered did or did not play an actual and direct part in the incident

Many older decisions hold preservation of decency in the courtroom to be a policy warranting exclusion of some autoptic evidence. See, e.g., Garvik v. Burlington, Cedar Rapids & Northern Railway Co., 124 Iowa 691, 100 N.W. 498 (1904); Guhl v. Whitcomb, 109 Wis. 69, 85 N.W. 142 (1901). Most modern authority, however, reverses the priorities. See, e.g., Jensen v. South Adams County Water and Sanitation District, 149 Colo. 102, 368 P.2d 209 (1962). But see Hammonds v. State, 355 So.2d 759 (Ala.Crim.App.1978).

24. People v. Gibson, 56 Cal.App.3d 119, 128 Cal.Rptr. 302 (1976) (photographs' potential for prejudice "substantially outweighed" probative value; error to admit); Commonwealth v. Chacko, 480 Pa. 504, 391 A.2d 999 (1978) (error to admit gruesome photos where not of "essential evidentiary value" required by "Pennsylvania rule"); State v. Hennis, 323 N.C. 279, 372 S.E.2d 523 (1988) (admission of photos reversible error under "totality of circumstances," including method of display); State v. Cloud, 722 P.2d 750 (Utah 1986) (gruesome photos "presumptively prejudicial").

Fed. and Rev.Unif.R.Evid. 403 provide exclusion for prejudice if "probative value is substantially outweighed by the danger of unfair prejudice * * * "

25. See, e.g., Bertram v. Harris, 423 P.2d 909 (Alaska 1967) (whiskey bottle found in defendant's car after accident; within trial court's discretion to exclude when fact testified to). See also, E.C. Hed-

din v. Delhi Gas Pipeline Co., 522 S.W.2d 886 (Tex.1975) (photos of dead animals killed in pipe leakage accident had "no relevance" in eminent domain case).

26. United States v. Cunningham, 423 F.2d 1269 (4th Cir.1970). See also United States v. Robinson, 560 F.2d 507 (2d Cir. 1977), cert. denied 435 U.S. 905 (a careful balancing of relevance versus prejudice; not error to admit; judge minimized impact by denying admission of the weapon itself, but opinion cites with apparent approval cases admitting the weapons). Absent proof of similarity, no permissible inference is raised. Compare Walker v. United States, 490 F.2d 683 (8th Cir.1974) (citing treatise). In Moore v. Illinois, 408 U.S. 786 (1972), the Court refused to set aside on due process grounds a murder conviction involving admission of a shotgun admittedly of a different gauge from that used in the killing, on the grounds that the due process claim had not been raised in the State courts and in any event no due process denial was shown.

An exception is generally made to the rule stated in the case of "mug shots" relevant to prove identification of a criminal defendant by a victim. In the event the photograph bears any indication suggestive of previous incarceration of the defendant, its admission will frequently be held to constitute error. Johnson v. Commonwealth, 2 Va.App. 447, 345 S.E.2d 303 (1986); Annot., 30 A.L.R.3d 908.

or transaction giving rise to the trial. Objects offered as having played such a direct role, e.g., the alleged weapon in a murder prosecution, are commonly called "real" or "original" evidence and are to be distinguished from evidence which played no such part but is offered for illustrative or other purposes.[27] It will be readily apparent that when real evidence is offered an adequate foundation for admission will require testimony first that the object offered is *the* object which was involved in the incident, and further that the condition of the object is substantially unchanged.[28] If the offered item possesses characteristics which are fairly unique and readily identifiable, and if the substance of which the item is composed is relatively impervious to change, the trial court is viewed as having broad discretion to admit merely on the basis of testimony that the item is the one in question and is in a substantially unchanged condition.[29] On the other hand, if the offered evidence is of such a nature as not to be readily identifiable, or to be susceptible to alteration by tampering or contamination, sound exercise of the trial court's discretion may require a substantially more elaborate foundation.[30] A foundation of the latter sort will commonly entail testimonially tracing the "chain of custody" of the item with sufficient completeness to render it reasonably probable that the original item has neither been exchanged with another nor been contaminated or tampered with.[31] It should, however, always be borne in mind that foundational

27. Smith v. Ohio Oil Co., 10 Ill.App.2d 67, 134 N.E.2d 526 (1956), note 34, infra.

28. See, e.g., State v. Moore, 645 S.W.2d 109 (Mo.App.1982) (admission of weapon not identified with either defendant or crime reversible error); Gencorp, Inc. v. Wolfe, 481 So.2d 109 (Fla.App.1985) (failure to offer evidence of unchanged condition of chattel "fatal" to admissibility). See also 7 Wigmore, Evidence § 2129 (Chadbourn rev. 1978). See generally, Graham, Relevancy and Exclusion of Relevant Evidence—Real Evidence, 18 Crim.L.Bull. 333 (1982) (including sample foundations).

29. See, e.g., Walker v. Firestone Tire & Rubber Co., 412 F.2d 60 (2d Cir.1969) (tire rim and tire; admission discretionary where exhibit not easily alterable); State v. Sugimoto, 62 Hawaii 259, 614 P.2d 386 (1980) (trial court has discretion to admit items, here a check, without complete chain of custody when item is identifiable and relatively impervious to change); State v. Fox, 212 Mont. 488, 689 P.2d 252 (1984). But cf. Cheek v. Avco Lycoming Division, 56 Ill.App.3d 217, 13 Ill.Dec. 902, 371 N.E.2d 994 (1977) (airplane engine which had been in hands of several mechanics who had worked on it and replaced parts not admissible). If the object offered is not claimed to possess any unique trait material to the suit, strict proof of identity is sometimes foregone. See, e.g., Isaacs v. National Bank of Commerce, 50 Wash.2d

548, 313 P.2d 684 (1957); see also Comment, 61 Nw.U.L.Rev. 472 (1966).

For a clear statement of the relativity of foundation requirements, see Loza v. State, 263 Ind. 124, 325 N.E.2d 173 (1975).

30. See People v. Irpino, 122 Ill.App.3d 767, 78 Ill.Dec. 165, 461 N.E.2d 999 (1984) (more elaborate foundation said required for items subject to alteration or tampering); State v. Decker, 317 N.W.2d 138 (S.D.1982) (distinguishing foundations required for "readily identifiable" and "relatively indistinguishable" objects). Chemical specimens are frequently recognized as raising possibilities of mistaken exchange, tampering, and contamination. See, e.g., Jones v. Commonwealth, 228 Va. 427, 323 S.E.2d 554 (1984) (strict chain of custody applies only to exhibits offered as basis for chemical analysis or expert opinion); Annot., 21 A.L.R.2d 1216. Business records are frequently seen to obviate problems in establishing a chain. See, e.g., United States v. Mendel, 746 F.2d 155 (2d Cir. 1984). On the relativity of foundations required for demonstrative evidence, see Giannelli, Chain of Custody and the Handling of Real Evidence, 20 Am.Crim.L.Rev. 527 (1983).

31. United States v. Howard–Arias, 679 F.2d 363 (4th Cir.1982) (chain of custody a variation of authentication required by

requirements are essentially requirements of logic, and not rules of art. Thus, e.g., even a radically altered item of real evidence may be admissible if its pertinent features remain unaltered.[32]

Real evidence consisting of samples drawn from a larger mass are also generally held admissible, subject to the foregoing requirements pertaining to real evidence generally, and subject to the further requirement that the sample be established to be accurately representative of the mass.[33]

Demonstrative evidence, however, is by no means limited to items which may properly be classed as "real" or "original" evidence. It is today increasingly common to encounter the offer of tangible items which are not themselves contended to have played any part in the history of the case, but which are instead tendered for the purpose of rendering other evidence more comprehensible to the trier of fact.[34] Examples of types of items frequently offered for purposes of illustration and clarification include models, maps, photographs, charts, and drawings.[35] If an article is offered for these purposes, rather than as real or original evidence, its specific identity or source is generally of no significance whatever.[36] Instead, the theory justifying admission of these exhibits requires only that the item be sufficiently explanatory or illustrative of relevant testimony in the case to be of potential help to the trier of fact.[37] Whether the admission of a particular exhibit will in

Fed.R.Evid. 901; chain need only establish improbability of exchange or tampering; State v. Nakamura, 65 Hawaii 74, 648 P.2d 183 (1982) (only reasonable certainty required); Scheble v. Missouri Clean Water Com'n, 734 S.W.2d 541 (Mo.App.1987).

32. See United States v. Skelley, 501 F.2d 447 (7th Cir.1974) (unlawful possession of counterfeit; admission of counterfeit bills all bearing identical serial numbers held proper to prove knowledge of counterfeit against general objection based upon change in color from green to blue).

33. Kunzman v. Cherokee Silo Co., 253 Iowa 885, 114 N.W.2d 534 (1962); Annot., 95 A.L.R.2d 681. See also People v. Porpora, 91 Cal.App.Supp.3d 13, 154 Cal.Rptr. 400 (1979) (admission of sample data to show percentage of Pacific Mackerel in defendant's catch proper where predicated on statistical showing that sample was representative); State v. Wilhelm, 59 N.C.App. 298, 296 S.E.2d 664 (1982), review denied 307 N.C. 702, 301 S.E.2d 395 (random sampling of "several" capsules out of 100 sufficient to establish defendant possessed over 100 barbiturates).

34. Smith v. Ohio Oil Co., 10 Ill.App.2d 67, 134 N.E.2d 526 (1956) (holding skeleton properly admitted to illustrate medical testimony and distinguishing between "real" and "demonstrative" evidence).

35. 3 Wigmore, Evidence § 790 (Chadbourn rev. 1970). But a map or photograph can easily figure in the history of a case and thus constitute real evidence. Goldner & Mrovka, Demonstrative Evidence and Audio–Visual Aids at Trial, 8 U.Fla.L.Rev. 185, 187 (1955).

36. See, e.g., Cohen v. Kindlon, 366 F.2d 762 (2d Cir.1966) (failure to establish authorship of sketch used for illustration held "of no consequence"); Intermill v. Heumesser, 154 Colo. 496, 391 P.2d 684 (1964) (admission of X rays of unidentified person testified to be "normal" upheld and "encouraged"). But an occasional trial judge will be found confusing illustrative exhibits with real evidence and rejecting the former. See, e.g., Hernke v. Northern Insurance Co., 20 Wis.2d 352, 122 N.W.2d 395 (1963).

37. See, e.g., Slow Development Co. v. Coulter, 88 Ariz. 122, 353 P.2d 890 (1960) (charts, etc., admissible to illustrate anything witness allowed to describe); McKee v. Chase, 73 Idaho 491, 253 P.2d 787 (1953) (excellent statement of theory of admission); People v. Chatman, 102 Ill.App.3d 692, 58 Ill.Dec. 315, 430 N.E.2d 257 (1981) (citing treatise). See also Dec.Dig. Witnesses ⊕252. A number of courts, while allowing illustrative exhibits, assert they are not "substantive" evidence. See, e.g.,

fact be helpful, or will instead tend to confuse or mislead the trier, is a matter commonly viewed to be within the sound discretion of the trial court.[38]

§ 213. Maps, Models, and Duplicates [1]

Among the most frequently utilized types of illustrative evidence are maps, sketches, diagrams,[2] models and duplicates.[3] Unlike real evidence, the availability of which will frequently depend upon circumstances beyond counsel's control, opportunities for the use of the types of demonstrative evidence here considered are limited only by counsel's ability to recognize them. The potential of these aids for giving clarity and interest to spoken statements has brought about their widespread use [4], which will undoubtedly continue in the future.

While all jurisdictions allow the use of demonstrative items to illustrate and explain oral testimony, there is some diversity of judicial opinion concerning the precise evidentiary status of articles used for this purpose. Thus, while most jurisdictions treat items used to illustrate testimony as fully admissible [5], a few have singled out such items for distinct treatment [6]. Of the various restrictions which have been

Sykes v. Floyd, 65 N.C.App. 172, 308 S.E.2d 498 (1983) (photos "clearly" not substantive evidence). The practical consequences of the latter view are discussed in §§ 213, 216, infra.

38. See, e.g., Smith v. Ohio Oil Co., 10 Ill.App.2d 67, 134 N.E.2d 526 (1956); Brown v. United States, 464 A.2d 120 (D.C.App.1983) (admission of demonstrative evidence primarily matter of discretion). The discretion, however, is not unlimited. See, e.g., Workman v. McIntyre Const. Co., 190 Mont. 5, 617 P.2d 1281 (1980) (abuse of discretion to reject sample traffic sign; demonstrative evidence inadmissible only where irrelevant or prejudicial).

§ 213

1. 3 Wigmore, Evidence §§ 790, 791 (Chadbourn rev. 1970); Dec.Dig. Evidence ⬅194 (duplicates, models and casts), ⬅358 (maps, plats and diagrams), Criminal Law ⬅404(1)–(2), Trial ⬅39, Witnesses ⬅252.

2. Cases involving maps, sketches and diagrams are collected in Annot., 9 A.L.R.2d 1044.

3. Cases involving models and duplicates in various contexts are collected in Annot., 69 A.L.R.2d 424 (models of sites in civil actions), 23 A.L.R.3d 825 (models of property taken by eminent domain), 58 A.L.R.2d 689 (models and charts of human anatomy in civil cases), 93 A.L.R.2d 1097 (similar, criminal cases).

4. See authorities cited § 212 n. 8 supra.

Though most commonly used to illustrate testimony, illustration may also benefit argument. See Louisiana–Pacific Corp. v. Mims, 453 So.2d 211 (Fla.App.1984) (stating use of charts in argument widely accepted, but holding new trial required where chart sent with jury as court's exhibit); West v. Martin, 11 Kan.App.2d 55, 713 P.2d 957 (1986) (stating use of demonstrative on opening to be encouraged, but finding no error in trial court's refusal where record unclear as to what would be used). The question is usually held discretionary with the trial court. Bower v. O'Hara, 759 F.2d 1117 (3d Cir.1985) (allowance of use of chart on closing argument held within trial court's discretion, but court cautions that such aids should not be used without prior notice to opposing counsel and opportunity to point out inaccuracies); Ray v. State, 527 So.2d 166 (Ala. Crim.App.1987) (discretionary to prevent counsel from drawing on blackboard during opening); Carson v. State, 751 P.2d 1315 (Wyo.1988).

5. See Annotations, 9 A.L.R.2d 1044, 69 A.L.R.2d 424.

6. The following variegated positions are to be noted: Crocker v. Lee, 261 Ala. 439, 74 So.2d 429 (1954) ("The use of a map * * * for illustration must be distinguished from its admission in evidence"); State v. Peters, 44 Hawaii 1, 352 P.2d 329 (1959)

imposed, the most supportable is that which limits jury access to illustrative items during deliberation.[7] There would appear to be no reason why this policy, even if adopted, necessitates denying "admission" to such items.

Even in the majority of jurisdictions where there is no apparent bar to, or restriction upon, their full admission, it is not uncommon for maps, models, etc., to be displayed and referred to without being formally offered or admitted into evidence.[8] While no absolute prohibition would appear to be justified concerning such informal use of illustrative items, numerous appellate courts have commented upon the difficulties created on appeal when crucial testimony has been given in the form of indecipherable references to an object not available to the reviewing court.[9] By the more common, and clearly preferable practice, illustrative objects will be identified by the witness as substantially correct representations and will be formally introduced as part of the witness' testimony, in which they are incorporated by reference.[10] When the record is not so perfected many courts have presumed that the illustrative items and testimony referring to them support the verdict, making it in the interest of both parties to clarify the record.[11]

("irregular" to admit sketch used for illustration); Livermon v. Bridgett, 77 N.C.App. 533, 335 S.E.2d 753 (1985) (no error to exclude maps where offer did not indicate limited illustrative purpose of exhibit); Chambers v. Robert, 160 N.E.2d 357 (Ohio App.1958) (stating illustrative sketch should not be admitted and that opponent is entitled, on demand, to an instruction that item is illustrative).

7. If an item is presented solely on the theory that it is a graphic representation of testimony, then to send it to the jury is arguably an invitation to the jury to give particular emphasis to the testimony illustrated. This argument has special force where the item is a chart summarizing testimony. See United States v. Soulard, 730 F.2d 1292 (9th Cir.1984) (summary charts allowable as aid to testimony and argument, but should not be admitted or sent to jury); Pierce v. Ramsey Winch Co., 753 F.2d 416 (5th Cir.1985) (charts and summaries used as "pedagogical" devices not evidence and should not be sent to jury room absent consent of all parties); Moore v. State, 788 P.2d 387 (Okla.Crim.App. 1990) (no undue emphasis where summaries not admitted or taken to jury room). Compare Baker v. Zimmerman, 179 Iowa 272, 161 N.W. 479 (1917) ("not important" whether illustrative item is formally admitted, but it should not be taken to the jury room).

8. See, e.g., Maxwell v. State, 236 Ark. 694, 370 S.W.2d 113 (1963); Grantham v. Herod, 320 S.W.2d 536 (Mo.1959); Traders & General Insurance Co. v. Stone, 258 S.W.2d 409 (Tex.Civ.App.1953) (model spine and nerve charts used but not offered; no error). But compare Handford v. Cole, 402 P.2d 209 (Wyo.1965) (error to allow reference to drawings before formally identified and introduced). And see State Farm Fire and Cas. Co. v. Sawyer, 522 So.2d 248 (Ala.1988) (duplicate stove displayed and referred to became "evidence" without formal admission; no error since appropriate foundation present).

9. See, e.g., Meglemry v. Bruner, 344 S.W.2d 808 (Ky.1961); Murray v. Gervais, 112 R.I. 768, 315 A.2d 750 (1974).

10. See Handford v. Cole, 402 P.2d 209 (Wyo.1965).

Correspondingly, the blackboard as a device for illustrating testimony and argument has been replaced by an easel with a large pad of paper on which drawings may be made and the sheets included in the record on review when appropriate.

11. For a discerning discussion of the consequences of this rule, see Tuttle v. Miami Dolphins, Ltd., 551 So.2d 477 (Fla. App.1988) (Pearson, J.). See also, Radetsky v. Leonard, 145 Colo. 358, 358 P.2d 1014 (1961) (presumption applied); Friedl v. Benson, 25 Wash.App. 381, 609 P.2d 449 (1980) (semble). Compare State ex rel. State Highway Commission v. Hill, 373 S.W.2d 666 (Mo.App.1963) (remanding for new trial where record hopelessly obscure).

Illustrative exhibits may often properly and satisfactorily be used in lieu of real evidence. As previously noted, articles actually involved in a transaction or occurrence may have become lost or be unavailable, or witnesses may be unable to testify that the article present in court is the identical one they have previously observed. Where only the generic characteristics of the item are significant no objection would appear to exist to the introduction of a substantially similar "duplicate." [12] While the matter is generally viewed as within the discretion of the trial court,[13] it has been suggested that it would constitute reversible error to exclude a duplicate testified to be identical to the object involved in the occurrence.[14] On the other hand, if there is an absence of testimony that the object to be illustrated ever existed the introduction of a "duplicate" may foster a mistaken impression of certainty and thus merit exclusion.[15]

Models, maps, sketches, and diagrams (as distinguished from duplicates) are by their nature generally not confusable with real evidence, and are admissible simply on the basis of testimony that they are substantially accurate representations of what the witness is endeavoring to describe.[16] Some discretionary control in the trial court is generally deemed appropriate, however, since exhibits of this kind, due to inaccuracies, variations of scale, etc., may on occasion be more

12. See, e.g., People v. Jordan, 188 Cal. App.2d 456, 10 Cal.Rptr. 495 (1961) (where real evidence unavailable, similar object may be admitted); Dawson v. Mazda Motors of America, Inc., 517 So.2d 283 (La. App.1987) (immaterial difference between duplicate and original does not bar admission of former); State v. Royball, 710 P.2d 168 (Utah 1985) (duplicate admission where real evidence lost or unavailable). Compare Carson v. Polley, 689 F.2d 562 (5th Cir.1982) (error to admit similar knife where jury not clearly informed of illustrative nature of exhibit). Similar results have been reached by admitting objects as real evidence on the basis of equivocal "identifications." See, e.g., Crosby v. State, 2 Md.App. 578, 236 A.2d 33 (1967) (unique gun "looking like" that used admitted); Isaacs v. National Bank of Commerce, 50 Wash.2d 548, 313 P.2d 684 (1957) (hose "believed" to be the hose in question admitted). But compare Alston v. Shiver, 105 So.2d 785 (Fla.1958) (error to admit axe handle 3 feet long to illustrate one 2 feet long).

13. See, e.g., State v. McClain, 404 S.W.2d 186 (Mo.1966). An even more permissive view is suggested by Finch v. W.R. Roach Co., 295 Mich. 589, 295 N.W. 324 (1940) (duplicate admissible if proponent introduces testimony from which similarity might be found).

14. Sherman v. City of Springfield, 77 Ill.App.2d 195, 222 N.E.2d 62 (1966) (error to exclude accurate duplicate where original unobtainable); Cincinnati, New Orleans & Texas Pacific Railway Co. v. Duvall, 263 Ky. 387, 92 S.W.2d 363 (1936) (error to exclude model of car step proved to be exact duplicate); Rich v. Cooper, 234 Or. 300, 380 P.2d 613 (1963) (error to exclude exact duplicates; dictum).

15. See Young v. Price, 50 Hawaii 430, 442 P.2d 67 (1968) (comprehensive discussion of problem). But see also, Davis v. Lane, 814 F.2d 397 (7th Cir.1987) (no error to admit demonstrative "shank" where evidence in conflict as to possession of shank by inmate).

16. See, e.g., United States v. D'Antonio, 324 F.2d 667 (3d Cir.1963) (blackboard sketch not to scale admissible); Hoffman v. Niagra Mach. & Tool Works Co., 683 F.Supp. 489 (E.D.Pa.1988) (no error in admission of mechanical model not shown to be identical to original); Martinez v. W.R. Grace Co., 782 P.2d 827 (Colo.App.1989) (scale model properly admitted despite conflicting testimony as to fairness and accuracy). But see Gallick v. Novotney, 124 Ill.App.3d 756, 79 Ill.Dec. 942, 464 N.E.2d 846 (1984) (model properly excluded where no testimony offered supporting model's accuracy with respect to critical fact shown).

misleading than helpful.[17] Nevertheless, when the trial court has exercised its discretion to admit, it will only rarely be found in error, at least if potentially misleading inaccuracies have been pointed out by witnesses for the proponent, or could have been exposed upon cross-examination.[18]

§ 214. Photographs,[1] Movies,[2] and Sound Recordings[3]

The principle upon which photographs are most commonly admitted into evidence is the same as that underlying the admission of illustrative drawings, maps and diagrams. Under this theory, a photograph is viewed merely as a graphic portrayal of oral testimony, and becomes admissible only when a witness has testified that it is a correct and accurate representation of relevant facts personally observed by the witness.[4] Accordingly, under this theory, the witness who lays the foundation need not be the photographer nor need he know anything of the time, conditions, or mechanisms of the taking.[5] Instead he need only know about the facts represented or the scene or objects photographed, and once this knowledge is shown he can say whether the

17. San Mateo County v. Christen, 22 Cal.App.2d 375, 71 P.2d 88 (1937) (engineer's model excluded; "while models may frequently be of great assistance * * * even when constructed to scale they may frequently, because of the great disparity in size * * * also be very misleading, and trial courts must be allowed wide discretion * * * "). State v. Lee, 9 Ohio App.3d 282, 459 N.E.2d 910 (1983) (use of anatomical dolls by child rape victim allowable within trial court's discretion despite anatomical inaccuracies of dolls).

18. See, e.g., Grandquest v. Williams, 273 Ala. 140, 135 So.2d 391 (1961) (not error to admit sketch and toy autos not to scale where witness pointed out inaccuracies and could have been further cross-examined); Arkansas State Highway Commission v. Rhodes, 240 Ark. 565, 401 S.W.2d 558 (1966) (inaccuracies not misleading where explained); Wooden v. State, 486 N.E.2d 441 (Ind.1985) (admission of non-scale drawing proper where jury informed of lack of scale).

§ 214

1. 3 Wigmore, Evidence §§ 790–798 (Chadbourn rev. 1970); Scott, Photographic Evidence (2d ed. 1969); C.J.S. Evidence §§ 709–716; Dec.Dig. Evidence ⟵359(1), 380, Criminal Law ⟵438.

2. 3 Wigmore, Evidence § 798(a) (Chadbourn rev. 1970); Dec.Dig. Evidence ⟵359(6); Paradis, The Celluloid Witness, 37 U.Colo.L.Rev. 235 (1965).

3. Dec.Dig. Evidence ⟵359(5), 380.

4. 3 Wigmore, Evidence § 790, at 218 (Chadbourn rev. 1970): " * * * the mere picture * * * cannot be received except as a non-verbal expression of the *testimony of some witness* competent to speak to the facts represented." State v. Smith, 27 N.J. 433, 142 A.2d 890, 899 (1958) ("Fundamentally, photographs are deemed to be pictorial communications of a qualified witness.") In the effort to establish photographs as accurately illustrative of the data observed by the witness, it is sometimes forgotten that the data itself must be relevant. Knihal v. State, 150 Neb. 771, 36 N.W.2d 109, 9 A.L.R.2d 891 (1949) (holding photos improperly received where foundation established only that photo correctly portrayed objects photographed but did not establish what objects were); Beattie v. Traynor, 114 Vt. 495, 49 A.2d 200, 204 (1946) ("A photograph * * * is merely a witness' pictured expression of the data observed by him * * * and its admission, when properly verified, rests on the relevancy of the fact pictured.").

5. Kooyumjian v. Stevens, 10 Ill.App.2d 378, 135 N.E.2d 146, 151 (1956) ("The witness need not be the photographer, nor need he know anything of the time or condition of the taking, but he must have personal knowledge of the scene or object in question and testify that it is correctly portrayed by the photograph"); People v. Riley, 67 Mich.App. 320, 240 N.W.2d 787 (1976) (foundation need not be laid by photographer; citing treatise), reversed on other grounds, 406 Mich. 1016, 289 N.W.2d 928.

photograph correctly and accurately portrays these facts.[6] Once the photograph is thus verified it is admissible as a graphic portrayal of the verifying witness' testimony into which it is incorporated by reference.[7] If the photograph fails to portray the relevant facts with complete accuracy, such as where changed conditions have been brought about by lapse of time or other factors, the photograph may still be admissible in the trial court's discretion if the changes are not so substantial as to be misleading.[8]

The foregoing doctrine concerning the basis on which photographs are admitted is clearly a viable one and has undoubtedly served to facilitate the introduction of the general run of photographs. It is doubtful, however, whether this theory should be pressed to its logical limits, as some few courts have done, by limiting photographs admitted on this basis to "illustrative" status and denying them "substantive" effect.[9] This distinction has been cogently criticized, and in any event does not seem to warrant the procedural consequences seen to flow from it.[10] A majority of jurisdictions have either rejected the distinction explicitly or ignored it altogether.[11]

The products of certain applications of the photographic process do not readily lend themselves to admission in evidence on the foregoing theory.[12] X-ray photographs are a common example, and are of course

---

6. State v. Purcell, 711 P.2d 243 (Utah 1985) (testimony of witness with competent knowledge of facts that photo accurately reflects those facts renders photo admissible); Rosenthal v. Weckstein, 19 Mass.App. Ct. 944, 473 N.E.2d 202 (1985) (photos correctly excluded where no testimony offered that they portrayed relevant facts correctly).

7. Finch v. W.R. Roach Co., 295 Mich. 589, 295 N.W. 324, 326 (1940).

8. Thompson v. Bohlken, 312 N.W.2d 501 (Iowa 1981) (sufficiency of testimony as to similarity of circumstances largely within trial court's discretion); Owens v. Anderson, 58 Wash.2d 448, 364 P.2d 14 (1961) (slight changes in scene go to weight). But seriously defective photography or radically altered conditions may warrant exclusion. Hammond v. United States, 501 A.2d 796 (D.C.App.1985) (photo of interior of car showing handgun visible where testimony indicated handgun not visible should not have been admitted; error held harmless); Jones v. Talbot, 87 Idaho 498, 394 P.2d 316 (1964) (drastically altered conditions; photos properly excluded); Stormont v. New York Central R. Co., 1 Ohio App.2d 414, 205 N.E.2d 74 (1964) (improper to admit photos so poor as to distort conditions).

9. See, e.g., Foster v. Bilbruck, 20 Ill. App.2d 173, 155 N.E.2d 366 (1959) (stating that photos stand on same footing as maps and models, and are not themselves evidence); Sykes v. Floyd, 65 N.C.App. 172, 308 S.E.2d 498 (1983) (photos illustrative only, but no error in failing to so instruct jury in absence of request).

10. See Gardner, The Camera Goes to Court, 24 N.C.L.Rev. 233, 245 (1956) (criticizing distinction). Procedural consequences of its recognition have included instructing the jury that the photo is illustrative only, and not sending photos to the jury room during deliberations. See § 213, supra.

11. See State v. Goyet, 120 Vt. 12, 132 A.2d 623, 631 (1957) ("* * * a photograph is admissible in evidence, not merely as a map or diagram representing things to which a witness testifies, but as direct evidence of things which have not been directly described by a witness as having come from his observation."). A majority of courts simply seems to ignore the distinction. See cases cited 3 Wigmore, Evidence § 792, note 1 (Chadbourn rev. 1970); Dec. Dig. Evidence ☞359.

12. Comment, Photographic Evidence—Is There a Recognized Basis for Admissibility? 8 Hast.L.J. 310 (1957) (noting that scenes photographed by infrared flash or by electronically triggered surveillance cameras are not seen by any potential witness.)

McCORMICK
ON EVIDENCE

*

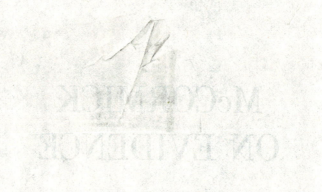

constantly admitted, despite the fact that no witness has actually viewed the objects portrayed.[13] The foundation typically required for X-rays is calculated to demonstrate that a reliable scientific process was correctly utilized to obtain the product offered in evidence. Earlier recognized only sporadically,[14] this same approach has in recent years found greatly increased acceptance as applied to various products of the photographic process. Under this doctrine, commonly referred to as the "silent witness" theory of admission,[15] photographic evidence may draw its verification, not from any witness who has actually viewed the scene portrayed on film, but from other evidence which supports the reliability of the photographic product. Most commonly, such evidence has been directed at establishing the validity of the photographic process by means of a foundation closely resembling that required for the admission of the products of other scientific processes.[16] However, it has been pointed out that other types of foundation may properly support the admission of "silent witness" evidence.[17] Today the "silent witness" doctrine affords an alternative route to the introduction of photographic evidence in virtually all jurisdictions.[18] However, since

13. See 3 Wigmore, Evidence § 795 (Chadbourn rev. 1970); Dec.Dig. Evidence ⊂⇒380.

14. People v. Bowley, 59 Cal.2d 855, 31 Cal.Rptr. 471, 382 P.2d 591, 595 (1963) ("We hold * * * that a photograph may, in a proper case, be admitted into evidence not merely as illustrated testimony of a human witness but as probative evidence in itself of what it shows."); People v. Doggett, 83 Cal.App.2d 405, 188 P.2d 792 (1948) (photos of defendants committing crime against nature; no other witnesses but photos admitted on basis of testimony by expert photographer that they were not composites or otherwise altered); State v. Matheson, 130 Iowa 440, 103 N.W. 137, 138 (1905) (" * * * the court takes judicial notice of the fact that by the ordinary photographic process a representation can be secured, sufficiently truthful and reliable to be considered as evidence with reference to objects which are in a condition to be thus photographed without regard to whether they have been actually observed by any witness or not.").

15. Among the substantial number of decisions relying expressly on the theory, the following may be cited: United States v. Bynum, 567 F.2d 1167 (1st Cir.1978); Fisher v. State, 7 Ark.App. 1, 643 S.W.2d 571 (1982) (comprehensively collecting authorities); Bergner v. State, 397 N.E.2d 1012 (Ind.App.1979) ("The 'silent witness theory' for the admission of photographic evidence permits the use of photographs at trial as *substantive* evidence, as opposed to merely demonstrative evidence. Thus, under the silent witness theory there is no need for a witness to testify a photograph accurately represents what he or she observed; the photograph 'speaks for itself' "); State v. Pulphus, 465 A.2d 153 (R.I.1983) (collecting authorities). See also Annot., 41 A.L.R. 4th 812.

16. See, e.g., United States v. Clayton, 643 F.2d 1071 (5th Cir.1981) and cases cited note 15, supra. Wigmore in fact treats some photographic products as scientific evidence, while conceding that the silent witness theory may be a "more satisfactory rationale." 3 Wigmore, Evidence § 795 at note 1 (Chadbourn rev. 1970).

17. McNeal, Silent Witness Evidence In Relation to the Illustrative Evidence Foundation, 37 Okla.L.Rev. 219 (1984). See also United States v. Stearns, 550 F.2d 1167 (9th Cir.1977) (admission of photos justified by circumstantial evidence without details of processing).

18. The two different theories of admissibility of photographs are reflected in these illustrations of authentication techniques in Fed.R.Evid. 901(b):

(1) *Testimony of witness with knowledge.* Testimony that a matter is what it is claimed to be.

. . .

(9) *Process or system.* Evidence describing a process or system used to produce a result and showing that the process or system produces an accurate result.

Of course, particular circumstances may dictate that only one theory is available.

the foundation required will generally be more elaborate than the relatively simple one sufficient under the traditional theory, resort to the latter remains preferable where circumstances permit.

The interest and vividness of photographs may be heightened by utilization of various techniques of photography, such as having the photographs taken in color, or having them enlarged so that pertinent facts may be more readily observed. While the use of these techniques clearly increases the number of factors subject to distortion, the basic standard governing admission of photos generally remains applicable.[19] Thus color and enlarged photographs have generally been viewed as admissible provided the photo represents the scene depicted with substantial accuracy.[20]

A somewhat more troublesome problem is presented by posed or artificially reconstructed scenes, in which people, automobiles, and other objects are placed so as to conform to the descriptions of the original crime or collision given by the witnesses.[21] When the posed photographs go no further than to portray the positions of persons and objects as reflected in the undisputed testimony, their admission has long been generally approved.[22] Frequently, however, a posed photograph will portray only the version of the facts supported by the testimony of the proponent's witness. The dangers inherent in this situation, i.e., the tendency of the photographs unduly to emphasize certain testimony and the possibility that the jury may confuse one party's reconstruction with objective fact, have led some courts to exclude photographs of this type.[23] The orthodox theory of photos as merely illustrated testimony, however, can be viewed to support the admission of any photo reflecting a state of facts testified to by a

See Saunders v. Commonwealth, 1 Va. App. 396, 339 S.E.2d 550 (1986).

19. See, e.g., Johnson v. Clement F. Sculley Construction Co., 255 Minn. 41, 95 N.W.2d 409 (1959) (color photos of personal injury admissible if accurate); Commonwealth Department of Highways v. Williams, 317 S.W.2d 482 (Ky.1958) (semble); State v. Clark, 99 Or. 629, 196 P. 360 (1921) (enlargements held admissible if not misleading). Nor does the presence of both factors together necessitate exclusion. See Commonwealth v. Makarewicz, 333 Mass. 575, 132 N.E.2d 294 (1956) (enlarged color photos held properly admitted).

20. See Annot., 53 A.L.R.2d 1102 (collecting cases on color photos); 72 A.L.R.2d 308 (enlargements). The following cases suggest that some failure to achieve exact reproduction is permissible: Green v. City and County of Denver, 111 Colo. 390, 142 P.2d 277 (1943) (color photos held admissible to show condition of putrid meat despite underexposure which made meat appear darker than it was.); State v. Smith,

27 N.J. 433, 142 A.2d 890 (1958) (color transparencies showing "bloody areas" admissible in trial court's discretion though witness testified pictures might "exaggerate on the red side").

21. Cases involving posed photos are collected in Annots., 27 A.L.R. 913, 19 A.L.R.2d 877. See also, Dec.Dig. Criminal Law ⊸438(k).

22. Langley v. State, 90 Okl.Cr. 310, 213 P.2d 886 (1950) (photos found illustrative of factual circumstances rather than party theory held properly admitted); Pollack v. State, 215 Wis. 200, 253 N.W. 560 (1934) (murder; photos of defendants in positions which they indicated they occupied at time of shooting). See also Note, 7 W. & M.L.Rev. 137 (1966) (collecting cases involving posed photos).

23. Martin v. State, 217 Miss. 506, 64 So.2d 629 (1953) (photos inadmissible where positions of persons shown was in dispute); Lynch v. Missouri–Kansas–Texas Ry. Co., 333 Mo. 89, 61 S.W.2d 918 (1933).

witness and the current trend would appear to be to permit even photos of disputed reconstructions in some instances.[24]

Motion pictures, when they were first sought to be introduced in evidence, were frequently objected to and sometimes excluded on the theory that they afforded manifold opportunities for fabrication and distortion.[25] Even those older decisions which upheld the admission of motion pictures appear to have done so on the basis of elaborate foundation testimony detailing the methods of taking, processing, and projecting the film.[26] More recently, however, it appears to have become generally recognized that, as with the still photograph, the reliability and accuracy of the motion picture need not necessarily rest upon the validity of the process used in its creation, but rather may be established by testimony that the motion picture accurately reproduces phenomena actually perceived by the witness.[27] Under this theory, though the requisite foundation may, and usually will, be laid by the photographer, it may also be provided by any witness who perceived the events filmed.[28] Of course, if the foundation testimony reveals the film to be distorted in some material particular, exclusion is the proper result.[29]

The "silent witness" theory of admissibility is as fully applicable to the motion picture as to the still photograph, and in fact many of the explicit applications of that theory have been with reference to movies.[30]

Both the "pictorial testimony" and "silent witness" doctrines previously discussed will readily be seen to be equally applicable to the

24. Tumey v. Richardson, 437 S.W.2d 201 (Ky.1969) (photos of posed accident scene admissible despite conflict in testimony as to material particulars). A number of courts have adopted the intermediate position that photos of partisan reconstruction are admissible if a pressing necessity is shown. State v. Oldham, 92 Idaho 124, 438 P.2d 275 (1968); State v. Ray, 43 N.J. 19, 202 A.2d 425 (1964). See also, Note, 47 Ky.L.J. 117 (1958) (arguing for freer admission of posed photos).

25. Gibson v. Gunn, 206 App.Div. 464, 202 N.Y.S. 19 (1923); Massachusetts Bonding & Insurance Co. v. Worthy, 9 S.W.2d 388 (Tex.Civ.App.1928) ("It is common knowledge that pictures showing a person in action may be made very deceptive * * *;" not error to exclude).

26. McGoorty v. Benhart, 305 Ill.App. 458, 27 N.E.2d 289 (1940) (motion pictures of malingerer admitted after laying of elaborate foundation).

27. Long v. General Electric Co., 213 Ga. 809, 102 S.E.2d 9 (1958) (motion picture held admissible on basis of foundation testimony by witness-photographer that it portrayed what he saw); Haley v. Hockey, 199 Misc. 512, 103 N.Y.S.2d 717 (Sup.Ct. 1950) (movie admissible upon identification of persons and actions filmed). See also, International Union, United Auto., Aircraft and Agr. Implement Workers v. Russell, 264 Ala. 456, 88 So.2d 175 (1956), affirmed 356 U.S. 634; Annot., 62 A.L.R.2d 686, 9 A.L.R.2d 921.

28. The witness through whom the foundation for introduction of motion pictures, as distinguished from stills, is laid must have been present when the pictures were taken. See Hare, Demonstrative Evidence, 27 Ala.Law. 193 (1966).

29. Powell v. Industrial Commission, 4 Ariz.App. 172, 418 P.2d 602 (1966) (films misrepresenting speed of actions portrayed inadmissible), vacated on other grounds 102 Ariz. 11, 423 P.2d 348; Utley v. Heckinger, 235 Ark. 780, 362 S.W.2d 13 (1962) (preferable not to have shown portion of film which accelerated portrayed action).

30. See authorities cited note 15, supra.

newer technology of the videotape,[31] despite the fact that the latter operates upon quite different principles. The videotape has several practical advantages [32] over the motion picture, and in fact seems largely to have displaced it as the common mechanism for presenting representations of motion to the trier of fact. While the admissibility of videotape evidence has sometimes been specifically provided for by rule or statute, such treatment is not a necessary precondition to reception of this type of evidence.[33]

Judicial discretion in the admission or exclusion of representation of action is constantly emphasized in the decisions,[34] and is perhaps largely attributable to the fact that the presentation of this kind of evidence will involve considerable expenditure of time and inconvenience. At the same time, however, when motion pictures are offered which reproduce the actual facts or original events in controversy, such as films of an allegedly incapacitated plaintiff shoveling snow or playing baseball,[35] or post-arrest films of an allegedly intoxicated driver,[36] the cogency of the evidence is such that the taking of considerable time and trouble to view the evidence would appear amply warranted.[37]

Somewhat more difficult questions are posed by moving pictures taken of an injured party pursuing ordinary day-to-day activities, offered for the purpose of bringing home to the trier of fact the

31. See, e.g., People v. Heading, 39 Mich.App. 126, 197 N.W.2d 325 (1972) (videotape admissible on same type of foundation as motion picture). See also, Annot., 60 A.L.R.3d 333.

See Cunningham, Videotape Evidence: Technological Innovation in the Trial Process, 36 Ala.Law. 228 (1975); Stewart, Videotape: Use in Demonstrative Evidence, 21 Def.L.J. 253 (1972). For an interesting suggestion as to the use of videotaping to insure availability of evidence in certain types of cases, see Peters & Wilkes, Videotaping of Surgery for Use as Demonstrative Evidence in Medical Malpractice Litigation, 16 Duq.L.Rev. 360 (1977).

32. See 2 Scott, Photographic Evidence § 714 (2nd ed. 1969) (Supp.1980). The significant advantages are said to include instant availability, ease of use, and inexpensiveness.

33. See, e.g., Ohio R.Civ.Pro., Rule 40.

34. Luther v. Maple, 250 F.2d 916 (8th Cir.1958) (no abuse of discretion despite appellate court's belief that admission had been unwise); International Union, United Auto. Aircraft and Agr. Implement Workers v. Russell, 264 Ala. 456, 88 So.2d 175 (1956), affirmed 356 U.S. 634 (question within discretion of trial court, reviewable only for gross abuse).

35. McGoorty v. Benhart, 305 Ill.App. 458, 27 N.E.2d 289 (1940); Lambert v.

Wolf's, Inc., 132 So.2d 522 (La.App.1961); McMiddleton v. Otis Elevator, 139 Mich. App. 418, 362 N.W.2d 812 (1984) (error to exclude videotape showing plaintiff's condition not as serious as claimed).

36. Lanford v. People, 159 Colo. 36, 409 P.2d 829 (1966) (motion picture of alleged drunk driver admissible though film disclosed defendant's declination to take sobriety test; extensive review of pertinent authorities); Lancaster v. State, 772 S.W.2d 137 (Tex.App.—Tyler 1988) (video of defendant in DWI prosecution minutes after arrest "particularly relevant, demonstrative, and compelling"). See also Durflinger v. Artiles, 727 F.2d 888 (10th Cir.1984) (videotape of confession minutes after occurrence). And see Annot., 60 A.L.R.3d 333.

37. Barham v. Nowell, 243 Miss. 441, 138 So.2d 493 (1962) (error to exclude motion pictures which in trial court's opinion were not "clear"); Wren v. St. Louis Public Service Co., 333 S.W.2d 92 (Mo.1960) (containing suggestion that if cogent motion pictures could not be satisfactorily viewed in courtroom, court should move to see them). But compare Douglas v. G.H.R. Energy Corp., 463 So.2d 5 (La.App.1984) (videotapes of debridement procedures performed on plaintiffs held inadmissible because "prejudicial" effect outweighed probative value).

implications and significance of the injury for which damages are sought.[38] With respect both to their relevance and to the possible objections which may legitimately be raised against them, these films are closely akin to bodily demonstrations of injuries in court.[39] Both species of evidence therefore ought to be governed by the same rule, to wit, both should be admissible only in the sound discretion, and under the strict control, of the trial court.[40]

A still different set of problems is presented by photographs or videotapes which do not portray original facts in controversy, but rather represent one party's staged reproduction of those facts. Here the extreme vividness and verisimilitude of pictorial evidence is truly a two-edged sword. For not only is the danger that the jury may confuse art with reality particularly great,[41] but the impressions generated by the evidence may prove particularly difficult to limit or, if the film is subsequently deemed inadmissible, to expunge by judicial instruction. The latter difficulty may be largely eliminated by a preliminary viewing by the court in chambers, and the decided cases suggest that this expedient is widely employed.[42]

Experiments and demonstrations must today be mentioned in the present context because of the frequency with which these are today filmed or taped so that the jury may observe the results rather than merely having them reported. While the fact of filming does not alter the basic principles applicable to experiments and demonstrations,[43] it does raise the additional problem that the evidence may be presented in such a way as to cause the jury to confuse the filmed event with the actual one in litigation. Thus, where the film or tape appears to

38. See Note, 33 S.Car.L.Rev. 577 (1982); Comment, 49 U.M.K.C.L.Rev. 179 (1981).

39. See Bannister v. Town of Noble, 812 F.2d 1265 (10th Cir.1987) (considering various concerns with such films). Compare the discussion of § 215, infra.

40. Though discretion is emphasized in the decisions, "day in the life" films seem generally to be admitted in the absence of factors which would render the evidence substantially misleading. See Bannister v. Town of Noble, supra note 39; Grimes v. Employers Mutual Liability Ins. Co., 73 F.R.D. 607 (D.Alaska 1977) (seemingly sound exercise of discretion in allowing film but excising certain segments); Strach v. St. John Hospital Corp., 160 Mich.App. 251, 408 N.W.2d 441 (1987); Barenbrugge v. Rich, 141 Ill.App.3d 1046, 96 Ill.Dec. 163, 490 N.E.2d 1368 (1986). More extreme examples include Arnold v. Burlington N.R. Co., 89 Or.App. 245, 748 P.2d 174 (1988) (upholding admission even though characterizing film as selective and self-serving); Roberts v. Stevens Clinic Hosp., Inc., __ W.Va. __, 345 S.E.2d 791 (1986) (upholding admission of professionally prepared video combining still photos, home videos, and recordings of deceased child). But see Transit Homes, Inc. v. Bellamy, 282 Ark. 453, 671 S.W.2d 153 (1984) (error to admit film where party pictured had already been quadriplegic before accident sued upon; prejudice clearly outweighed value).

41. See Sanchez v. Denver & Rio Grande Western Railroad Co., 538 F.2d 304 (10th Cir.1976), cert. denied 429 U.S. 1042 (stressing special scrutiny to be accorded motion picture showing reenactment of human conduct but holding motion picture admissible); French v. City of Springfield, 65 Ill.2d 74, 2 Ill.Dec. 271, 357 N.E.2d 438 (1976) (viewpoint of film may condition jury to accept party's theory; film inadmissible). Obviously, inclusion in a filmed reenactment of a material fact not supported by any evidence should result in exclusion of that portion of film. See Mills v. Nichols, 467 So.2d 924 (Miss.1985).

42. Wren v. St. Louis Public Service Co., supra note 37. Additional cases are collected in Paradis, The Celluloid Witness, 37 U.Colo.L.Rev. 235, 246 at n. 52 (1965).

43. See § 202, supra.

present a replication of the original event it will generally be required that the experiment be conducted under substantially similar circumstances.[44] Where the purpose of the evidence is not to present a graphic reproduction of the event and there is little chance of jury confusion this similarity requirement is not imposed.[45] Experiments intended to demonstrate the nature or capacity of physical objects are generally placed in this latter category, and films and tapes of such experiments have frequently been admitted.[46]

Sound recordings will sometimes be offered as an integral part of a motion picture, but a recording alone may of course also be probative of relevant facts. When a sound recording consists of spoken words, questions concerning the "best evidence" rule and the rule of completeness may be raised.[47] Where a sound recording itself does constitute the "best evidence," it is not uncommon to find a transcript of the recorded words offered to assist the jury in following the recording. Clearly such transcripts can serve a beneficial demonstrative function where no question exists as to the accuracy of the transcription, but serious theoretical and practical problems arise when a legitimate question is presented as to what words the recording contains.[48]

Sound recordings may also be offered as reproducing relevant nonverbal sounds, and when this is the purpose the considerations potentially affecting admissibility are substantially similar to those relating to motion pictures. Thus, the recording will generally be admitted if a witness testifies that the recording as played is an accurate reproduction of relevant sounds previously audited by the witness.[49] On occasion, too, sound recordings may be admitted upon a foundation analogous to that sometimes recognized for films taken by surveillance

---

44. Hale v. Firestone Tire & Rubber Co., 756 F.2d 1322 (8th Cir.1985) (admission of film held abuse of discretion where similarity of circumstances lacking); Carr v. Suzuki Motor Co., 280 Ark. 1, 655 S.W.2d 364 (1983) (semble); Ostler v. Albina Transfer Co., 781 P.2d 445 (Utah App.1989) (no error for trial court to exclude video of experiment not satisfying substantial similarity requirement).

45. Brandt v. French, 638 F.2d 209 (10th Cir.1981).

46. Nachtsheim v. Beech Aircraft Corp., 847 F.2d 1261 (7th Cir.1988) (video of operation of plane under icing conditions properly admitted as demonstration of principle); Gorelick v. Department of State Highways, 127 Mich.App. 324, 339 N.W.2d 635 (1983) (semble); Beers v. Western Auto Supply Co., 646 S.W.2d 812 (Mo.App.1982) (exclusion of filmed experiment not likely to confuse jury held abuse of discretion); Maskrey v. Volkswagenwerk Aktiengesellschaft, 125 Wis.2d 145, 370 N.W.2d 815 (App.1985). But compare Gladhill v. General Motors Corp., 743 F.2d 1049 (4th Cir.

1984) (videotape improperly admitted where demonstration "went well beyond" showing principle).

47. See Ch. 23 infra; § 56 supra.

48. See United States v. Robinson, 707 F.2d 872 (6th Cir.1983), appeal after remand 763 F.2d 778 (abuse of trial court discretion to allow use of transcript without foundation testimony of transcriber and independent determination of accuracy of transcript by court).

49. Wilms v. Hand, 101 Cal.App.2d 811, 226 P.2d 728 (1951) (recordings of dog noises emanating from veterinary establishment and alleged to be a nuisance); Ragusa v. American Metal Works, 97 So.2d 683 (La.App.1957) (recordings of factory noises; semble). But see Abernathy v. Superior Hardwoods, Inc., 704 F.2d 963 (7th Cir. 1983) (approving exclusion of sound portion of videotape and emphasizing amateur standing of recorder and his equipment). Cases dealing with the admissibility of sound recordings are collected in Annots., 58 A.L.R.2d 1024, 57 A.L.R.3d 746; Dec. Dig., Evidence ⚬⊐358(5).

cameras.[50] This will consist of a showing of the accuracy and completeness of the recording by scientific and corroborative evidence.[51]

§ 215. Bodily Demonstrations: Experiments in Court

The exhibition of a wound or physical injury, e.g., the injury sustained by a plaintiff in a personal injury action, will frequently be the best and most direct evidence of a material fact.[1] Not surprisingly, therefore, exhibitions of physical injuries to the jury are commonly allowed.[2] In most jurisdictions the matter is viewed as subject to the discretion of the trial court,[3] but has sometimes been said to be a matter of right on the part of the injured party.[4] Further, in those jurisdictions which hold the matter to be discretionary, a trial court is rarely reversed for permitting a bodily exhibition. Thus, when the exhibition is permitted no abuse of discretion is generally found present even though the injury displayed was particularly shocking,[5] or even

---

50. See note 15 supra.

51. United States v. Rengifo, 789 F.2d 975 (1st Cir.1986). In the unusual case of State v. Smith, 85 Wash.2d 840, 540 P.2d 424 (1975) the murder victim took the precaution of carrying a tape recorder with him while keeping an appointment with his murderer. The resulting tape of the event, found during the autopsy, was held admissible on the basis of scientific testimony and other evidence corroborating its accuracy and completeness.

§ 215

1. Calumet Paving Co. v. Butkus, 113 Ind.App. 232, 47 N.E.2d 829 (1943) ("There is no other class of evidence more satisfactory or convincing * * * than the production and inspection of the very object or person whose condition is being investigated * * * "); Chicago, Rock Island & Gulf Railway Co. v. De Bord, 62 Tex.Civ.App. 302, 132 S.W. 845 (1910) (exhibition of injuries proper; "evidence of a very high degree.") The significance of the exhibition, however, will vary with the issue to be proved. See Radosh v. Shipstad, 17 A.D.2d 660, 230 N.Y.S.2d 295 (1962) (exhibition of professional ice-skater in costume improper in breach of contract suit where issue was whether skater's weight at a prior time justified suspension).

2. See Annot., 66 A.L.R.2d 1334; Dec. Dig. Evidence ⟜192, Trial ⟜27. See note 15, § 212, supra.

3. See, e.g., Spaak v. Chicago & North Western Railway Co., 231 F.2d 279 (7th Cir.1956) (exhibition of injured foot; discretion of trial court not abused); Darling v. Charleston Community Memorial Hospital, 50 Ill.App.2d 253, 200 N.E.2d 149, 185

(1964), affirmed 33 Ill.2d 326, 211 N.E.2d 253 (1965) ("Permitting the plaintiff to exhibit the stump of his amputated leg is within the discretion of the court, and only if there be an abuse of discretion * * * would such be reversible error"; no abuse found). And see Hillman v. Funderburk, 504 A.2d 596 (D.C.App.1986) (trial court denied plaintiff permission to display injured breasts; no abuse of discretion though display would have been neither unduly prejudicial nor indecent).

Displays of prosthetic devices are similarly treated. Annot., 88 A.L.R.2d 1273.

4. Olson v. Tyner, 219 Iowa 251, 257 N.W. 538 (1934) (plaintiff stripped to the waist to display shriveled left arm dangling "as though suspended by a string;" " * * * appellee had the right to exhibit to the jury his arm to show the condition he was in"); Missouri, Kansas & Texas Railway Co. v. O'Hare, 39 S.W.2d 939, 941 (Tex.Civ.App.1931) (" * * * we think appellee had the right if he desired, to exhibit his injured arm to the jury;" but propriety of repeated exhibitions questioned.).

5. Slattery v. Marra Brothers, 186 F.2d 134, 138 (2d Cir.1951) (" * * * ordinarily it would seem that the very hideousness of the deformity was a part of the suffering of the victim, and could not rationally be excluded in assessment of his damages."); Beal v. Southern Union Gas Co., 66 N.M. 424, 349 P.2d 337 (1960) (not abuse of discretion in allowing plaintiff whose eyes, nose and ears were burned out to display injuries); Shell Petroleum Corp. v. Perrin, 179 Okl. 142, 64 P.2d 309 (1936) (not error to permit mother of little girl suing for injury to eye to remove girl's glass eye before the jury).

where the injury's nature or existence need not have been proved because admitted.[6]

The physical characteristics of a person may also constitute relevant evidence in a criminal prosecution. For example, the scars or physical condition of the victim may tend to prove the nature of an assault,[7] or a physical trait of a person may be relevant to prove or disprove the identity of the perpetrator of an offense.[8] Though some awkwardness is encountered in treating persons as exhibits,[9] bodily exhibitions for purposes such as those indicated are viewed as within the trial court's discretion and have frequently been allowed.[10] When the prosecution desires to exhibit traits of the defendant, the question has long been considered under the heading of self-incrimination and the demonstration allowed so long as it may be classed as "non-testimonial."[11] Similarly, it has generally been held that it is open to the defendant to display his physical characteristics to the trier of fact without incurring the necessity of taking the stand.[12]

Judicial opinion has been somewhat more divided concerning the propriety of going beyond the mere exhibition of an injury or physical

6. Stegall v. Carlson, 6 Ill.App.2d 388, 128 N.E.2d 352 (1955) (exhibition proper even where fact and nature of injury not disputed); Chicago, Burlington & Quincy Railway Co. v. Krayenbuhl, 70 Neb. 766, 98 N.W. 44 (1904) (rejecting contention that injury may not be displayed where admitted.) But compare Harper v. Bolton, 239 S.C. 541, 124 S.E.2d 54 (1962) (finding abuse in admission of plaintiff's removed and preserved eye where loss of eye was admitted); Curry v. American Enka, Inc., 452 F.Supp. 178 (E.D.Tenn.1977) (suggesting such demonstrations proper only where shedding light on a controverted fact; court refuses under any circumstances to compel unwilling jurors to feel plaintiff's "flesh," in this case his hands).

7. See, e.g., People v. Morgan, 191 Cal. App.3d 29, 236 Cal.Rptr. 186 (1987) (no error to allow alleged rape victim to appear before jury without being sworn to show retardation; "she was obviously the most compelling evidence on the issue" of consent); State v. Kelly, 122 Ariz. 495, 595 P.2d 1040 (App.1979) (exhibition of bullet entrance and exit wounds relevant to rebut claim of self-defense by defendant); State v. Black, 748 S.W.2d 184 (Mo.App.1988) (display of scars from knife assault relevant to charged offenses).

8. See, e.g., People v. Diaz, 111 Misc.2d 1083, 445 N.Y.S.2d 888 (1981) (person admissible as exhibit to disprove defense contention that person exhibited resembled description of perpetrator more than defendant) (interesting collection of precedents on persons as evidence). See also cases cited note 12, infra. But compare Commonwealth v. Hutchinson, 290 Pa.Super. 254, 434 A.2d 740 (1981) (no error to deny defendant permission to exhibit brother to jury in support of defense of mistaken identity; but court's discussion suggests circumstances where display would be proper).

9. See State v. Lopez, 157 Ariz. 23, 754 P.2d 352 (1988) (noting that adjustments must be made in such cases and upholding trial court's ruling permitting jury to look again at defendant's tatoos during deliberations); Haynes v. State, 180 Ga.App. 202, 349 S.E.2d 208 (1986) (semble).

10. Dec.Dig. Criminal Law § 404(1).

11. See section 124, supra.

12. United States v. Bay, 762 F.2d 1314 (9th Cir.1984) (holding defendant entitled to display tatooed hands without testifying on ground that "sauce for the goose is sauce for the gander"); People v. Perez, 216 Cal.App.3d 1346, 265 Cal.Rptr. 400 (1989) (defendant's tatooed hands potentially admissible as demonstrative evidence without testimony by defendant, but appropriate foundation required to demonstrate relevancy lacking); State v. Sanders, 691 S.W.2d 566 (Tenn.Cr.App.1984) (error to refuse defendant permission to stand before jury without testifying to demonstrate height). But compare State v. Wright, 473 So.2d 268 (Fla.App.1985) (discretionary to refuse defendant permission to display genitals to jury to demonstrate rape could not have taken place as testified by prosecutrix).

condition by having the injured person perform actions or submit to manipulation by a physician.[13] The dangers inherent in demonstrations of this latter type include undue emotional response on the part of the jury and the fact that manifestations of pain and impairment of function are easily feigned and difficult to test by cross-examination.[14] Nevertheless, this matter too is commonly left to the discretion of the trial courts, and that discretion is frequently exercised in favor of permitting the demonstration.[15] Occasional cases have, however, held the allowance of a particular demonstration to be an abuse of trial court discretion, a fact which may suggest that the tactic is a somewhat hazardous one for the party utilizing it.[16]

In addition to active demonstrations of physical injuries, in-court reenactment of material events by witnesses has been held permissible to illustrate testimony.[17]

Whether demonstrations in the form of experiments in court are to be permitted is also largely subject to the discretion of the trial judge.[18]

13. Annot., 66 A.L.R.2d 1382; Dec.Dig. Evidence ⊜192.

14. The possible objections to the practice are enumerated in Clark v. Brooklyn Heights Railway Co., 177 N.Y. 359, 69 N.E. 647 (1904) (criticizing demonstration, but holding matter discretionary).

15. Del Monte Banana Co. v. Chacon, 466 So.2d 1167 (Fla.App.1985) (demonstration where counsel struck at plaintiff's blind eye with a dagger upheld as within trial court's discretion, though caution in use of discretion urged on trial court; citing treatise); Wilson & Co. v. Campbell, 195 Okl. 323, 157 P.2d 465 (1945) (going beyond mere exhibition requires discretionary control by trial court; no abuse to allow cross-plaintiff to demonstrate numbness of injured leg by use of pins); Ensor v. Wilson, By and Through Wilson, 519 So.2d 1244 (Ala.1987) (upholding demonstration of 6–year old by sworn special education therapist, noting difficulty of demonstration of limitations on cognition without vocal expression or physical response). But discretion may equally be exercised in the opposite direction. Hehir v. Bowers, 85 Ill.App.3d 625, 40 Ill.Dec. 918, 921, 407 N.E.2d 149, 152 (1980) (no abuse of discretion to deny plaintiff opportunity to demonstrate limited range of motion in injured shoulder; "The allowance of such demonstrations by an injured party is generally frowned upon"). It may be noted that testimony as to pain and impairment of use is also subject to fabrication.

16. Peters v. Hockley, 152 Or. 434, 53 P.2d 1059 (1936) (abuse of discretion to permit demonstration calculated to make plaintiff cry out in pain.) It would appear that screaming by the party being manipu-

lated, though sometimes viewed as not prejudicial, is a factor likely to lead to reversal. See cases cited Annot., 66 A.L.R.2d 1382. If review is sought on this ground, however, it is critical for the objecting party to make an appropriate record. See Fravel v. Burlington Northern R.R., 671 S.W.2d 339 (Mo.App.1984), cert. denied 496 U.S. 1159 (court on appeal would not consider propriety of plaintiff's alleged cries and grimaces where record did not reflect these occurrences).

17. See State v. Anderson, 171 Mont. 188, 557 P.2d 795 (1976) (DWI prosecution; patrolman witness allowed to demonstrate manner in which defendant walked following arrest); State v. Page, 31 N.C.App. 740, 230 S.E.2d 433 (1976) (demonstration of events testified to by rape victim staged by victim and police officer "playing" defendant's role).

18. Lynch v. Missouri K.–T. Ry. Co., 333 Mo. 89, 61 S.W.2d 918 (1933) (admission of experimental evidence, whether experiment performed in or out of court, said to be "peculiarly within the discretion of the trial judge.") See also, Rex v. Duncan, [1944] 1 K.B. 713, Ct.Crim.App. (spiritualist medium, prosecuted under witchcraft statute, refused permission to summon departed spirits to courtroom); Coca-Cola Co. v. Langston, 198 Ark. 59, 127 S.W.2d 263 (1939) (witness offered to swallow teaspoon of ground glass; refusal to permit discretionary); Metropolitan Property & Liability Ins. Co. v. Shepherd, 166 Ga.App. 300, 304 S.E.2d 74 (1983) (in court demonstration of burning of piece of carpet within trial court's "broad discretion"); Otte v. Taylor, 180 Neb. 795, 146 N.W.2d 78 (1966)

Unlike experiments performed out of court, the results of which are generally communicated testimonially, in-court experimentation may involve considerable confusion and delay, and the trial judge is viewed as in the best position to judge whether the game is worth the candle.[19] Simple demonstrations by a witness are usually permitted, and may be strikingly effective in adding vividness to the spoken word.[20]

In addition to the limitations arising from the desirability of orderly and expeditious proceedings, in-court experiments are held to the same basic requirement of similarity of conditions which is applicable to experimental evidence generally.[21] This requirement may be particularly difficult to meet under courtroom conditions, and many proposed courtroom experiments have been held properly excluded on this ground.[22] Nevertheless, the well-planned courtroom experiment may provide extremely striking and persuasive evidence,[23] and the opportunities for utilizing such experiments should not be overlooked.

(physician allowed to swallow nembutal tablets at beginning of testimony and to testify an hour later he was not drowsy; discretion to permit upheld). Compare Schleunes v. American Casualty Co., 528 F.2d 634 (5th Cir.1976) (action on accidental death policy, with defendant claiming suicide; in view of sharp conflict in expert testimony, abuse of discretion to refuse to allow defendant's expert to demonstrate that rifle with which insured shot himself could not be fired without taking additional steps inconsistent with accidental firing); Monlux v. General Motors Corp., 68 Hawaii 358, 714 P.2d 930 (1986) (abuse of discretion to disallow test where conditions substantially similar and test would help resolve crucial question).

19. Hassebroek v. Norman, 236 Or. 209, 387 P.2d 824 (1963) (trial court refused to permit demonstration of child's toy which had injured plaintiff; "A request for a courtroom demonstration creates a problem peculiarly directed to the trial judge.").

20. Foster v. Devilbiss Co., 174 Ill. App.3d 359, 124 Ill.Dec. 600, 529 N.E.2d 581 (1988) (demonstration of flimsy nature of trigger guard held proper without showing of similarity of circumstances); Hamilton v. Pepsi Cola Bottling Co., 132 A.2d 500 (D.C.App.1957) (no abuse in permitting demonstration that pop bottles could be unsealed and resealed without detection); Geisel v. Haintl, 427 S.W.2d 525 (Mo.1968) (suit for personal injuries allegedly due to wobbly handrail; jurors held properly allowed to pull on scale previously used in out-of-court experiment to "see how much 25 pounds is").

21. See § 202 supra.

22. Burriss v. Texaco, Inc., 361 F.2d 169 (4th Cir.1966) (within trial court's discretion to refuse to permit re-enactment of fire on model of railroad yard where model was not to scale); Whitehurst v. Revlon, Inc., 307 F.Supp. 918 (E.D.Va.1969) (experiment to show inflammability of nail polish disallowed; conditions in court dissimilar to those of plaintiff's home); Pond v. Anderson, 241 Iowa 1038, 44 N.W.2d 372 (1950) (witness testified she overheard other end of a telephone; not abuse of discretion to disallow experiment whether witness could overhear remote end of call to phone on judge's desk since conditions dissimilar); Beasley v. Ford Motor Co., 237 S.C. 506, 117 S.E.2d 863 (1961) (proper to refuse experiment to show gasoline in contact with hot metal surface will not ignite; "A hot plate in the hands of the witness would hardly be comparable to the hot automobile motor * * * ").

Involving one or more members of the jury in the experiment can sometimes destroy similarity of circumstances. See Weinstein v. Daman, 132 A.D.2d 547, 517 N.Y.S.2d 278 (1987). And such involvement has been condemned for other reasons. Schaffner v. Chicago & North Western Transp. Co., 129 Ill.2d 1, 133 Ill.Dec. 432, 541 N.E.2d 643 (1989) (trial judge should have prevented such an experiment on his own motion; held harmless error under circumstances).

23. See United States v. Wanoskia, 800 F.2d 235 (10th Cir.1986) (perceptive opinion by Logan, J., noting potential value of such evidence).

§ 216. Views [1]

The courts, like the prophet, have sensibly recognized that if a thing cannot be brought to the observer, the observer must go to the thing. Venturing forth to observe places or objects which are material to litigation but which cannot feasibly be brought, or satisfactorily reproduced, within the courtroom, is termed a "view." While statutes or court rules concerning views are in effect in nearly all states,[2] it is frequently said that even without express statutory authorization there is an inherent power in the trial judge to order a view by the jury,[3] or, in a judge-tried case, to take a view personally.[4] This power extends to views of personalty,[5] realty, and to criminal[6] as well as civil cases.

Since a view is often time-consuming and disruptive of the ordinary course of a trial, the trial judge is in most instances vested with a wide leeway of discretion to grant or refuse a view.[7] It is to be noted, however, that a number of state statutes provide that in certain types of cases, notably eminent domain, either party is entitled to a view upon request as a matter of right.[8] Where the grant of a view is discretionary with the trial court, as is usually the case, factors which are commonly stated to be appropriate for consideration by the court in determining whether to a grant a view include the importance to the

§ 216

1. 4 Wigmore, Evidence §§ 1162–1169 (Chadbourn rev. 1972); Dec.Dig. Trial ☞28, Criminal Law ☞641.

2. See the rules and statutes collected in 4 Wigmore, Evidence § 1163, notes 7, 8 (Chadbourn rev. 1972).

3. Basham v. Owensboro City Railroad Co., 169 Ky. 155, 183 S.W. 492 (1916); State v. Black, 193 Or. 295, 236 P.2d 326 (1951) (inherent power of trial court to order view of stolen cattle unaffected by statute expressly sanctioning only views of realty); State v. Coburn, 82 Idaho 437, 354 P.2d 751 (1960) (view of automobiles, semble). Compare Steward v. State, 75 Nev. 498, 346 P.2d 1083 (1959) (holding a truck to be a "place" within meaning of statute authorizing views of places).

4. Bobrick v. Taylor, 171 Colo. 375, 467 P.2d 822 (1970). The judge's discretion is not, however, unlimited. See Jones v. Henderson, 513 So.2d 1020 (Ala.1987) (reversible error for judge to take view in bench trial with only one party notified and present).

5. See, e.g., cases cited note 3 supra. Even views of persons have sometimes been allowed. Nizer v. Phelps, 252 Md. 185, 249 A.2d 112 (1969) (view of personal injury victim in nursing home held permissible). Compare, however, Knight v. Landis, 11 Ga.App. 536, 75 S.E. 834 (1912) (holding views of personalty impermissible as a matter of "adopted common law," though stating that "no valid distinction" exists between views of realty and personalty). Compare Arnold v. Laird, 94 Wash.2d 867, 621 P.2d 138 (1980) (mistakenly assuming that views must be of realty, but upholding propriety of jury's viewing of defendant's dog "Blanket" on courthouse lawn as an "observation.")

6. Schonfeld v. United States, 277 Fed. 934 (2d Cir.1921); State v. O'Day, 188 La. 169, 175 So. 838 (1937) (trial court had power to order view in criminal case despite absence of statutory authorization).

7. Nearly every opinion stresses the discretion of the trial court. See, e.g., Hodge v. United States, 75 U.S.App.D.C. 332, 126 F.2d 849 (1942) (denial upheld as discretionary); Zipp v. Gasen's Drug Stores, Inc., 449 S.W.2d 612 (Mo.1970) (denial of view discretionary even where view would have been "helpful"); Bizich v. Sears, Roebuck & Co., 391 Pa. 640, 139 A.2d 663 (1958) (grant upheld); Dec.Dig.Trial ☞28(2). The trial judge's discretion extends to denying a view even though requested by both parties, Illinois Basin Oil Association v. Lynn, 425 S.W.2d 555 (Ky.1968); Floyd v. Williams, 198 Miss. 350, 22 So.2d 365 (1945), and also to the extent of the view. Meizoso v. Bajoros, 12 Conn.App. 516, 531 A.2d 943 (1987).

8. E.g., West's Fla.Stat.Ann. § 75.071; Ill.Rev.Stat.1988, ch. 47, ¶ 9.

issue of the information to be gained by the view,[9] the extent to which this information has or could have been secured from maps, photographs, or diagrams [10] and the extent to which the place or object to be viewed has changed in appearance since the controversy arose.[11]

The appropriate procedures to be followed in connection with views are widely regulated by statute. At common law, and generally in civil cases today, the presence of the trial judge at a view is not required,[12] the more common practice being for the jury to be conducted to the scene by "showers," expressly commissioned for the purpose.[13] Attendance at the view by the parties and their counsel is generally permitted though subject to the discretion of the trial judge.[14] In criminal cases, the rights of the defendant to have the judge present at the view, and to be present personally, are frequently provided for by statute.[15] Moreover, when testimony is taken at the view, or the view itself is deemed to constitute evidence, the right of the defendant to be present in all probability possesses a constitutional underpinning.[16]

---

9. Eizerman v. Behn, 9 Ill.App.2d 263, 132 N.E.2d 788 (1956) (denial of view of washing machine upheld; present condition of washer of little significance where issue was condition at earlier time).

10. Peake v. Omaha Cold Storage Co., 158 Neb. 676, 64 N.W.2d 470 (1954) (numerous maps and pictures in evidence; denial of view upheld as discretionary); State v. Holden, 75 Wash.2d 413, 451 P.2d 666 (1969) (semble). See also Zipp v. Gasen's Drug Store, Inc., 449 S.W.2d 612 (Mo.1970) (other evidence, including photographs, precluded "right" to have view).

11. Wimberly v. City of Paterson, 75 N.J.Super. 584, 183 A.2d 691 (1962) (denial of view not abuse of discretion where conditions changed and scene fully described by witnesses); Burke v. Thomas, 313 P.2d 1082 (Okl.1957) (denial proper within trial court's discretion where seasonal change of foliage had drastically altered scene.) Annot., 85 A.L.R.2d 512, collecting cases concerning effect of changed conditions upon propriety of granting view.

12. Sims Motor Transportation Lines, Inc. v. Foster, 293 S.W.2d 226 (Ky.1956) (attendance of trial judge at view in civil case discretionary); Yeary v. Holbrook, 171 Va. 266, 198 S.E. 441 (1938) (similar holding; review of earlier authorities concerning views).

13. On occasion, the trial judge will act as shower, Yeary v. Holbrook, 171 Va. 266, 198 S.E. 441 (1938), or appoint counsel for the parties to act as showers, Snyder v. Commonwealth of Massachusetts, 291 U.S. 97 (1934).

14. See, e.g., Pritchett v. Anding, 168 Ga.App. 658, 310 S.E.2d 267 (1983) (no abuse of discretion to refuse defendant's request to attend view with jury).

15. As to the trial judge's obligation to attend a view in criminal cases, see, McCollum v. State, 74 So.2d 74 (Fla.1954) (holding local statute made trial judge's attendance mandatory; extensive review of authorities); State v. Rohrich, 135 N.W.2d 175 (N.D.1965) (semble). Annot., 47 A.L.R.2d 1227 (necessity for presence of trial judge at view by jury in criminal case.)

Many states accord the defendant the right to be present at a view in a criminal case. State v. MacDonald, 229 A.2d 321 (Me.1967). Others hold the matter to be discretionary. Commonwealth v. Belenski, 276 Mass. 35, 176 N.E. 501 (1931).

16. In Snyder v. Commonwealth of Massachusetts, 291 U.S. 97 (1934) the Supreme Court held, four justices dissenting, that due process had not been denied a defendant who was refused the opportunity to be present at a view, even if it were assumed that the right of confrontation guaranteed by the Sixth Amendment is "reinforced" by the Fourteenth. Thus, even though the confrontation clause has now been held operative against the states by virtue of the Fourteenth Amendment, Pointer v. Texas, 380 U.S. 400 (1965), the defendant appears to have no federally guaranteed right to attend a view in every instance. The Court, however, carefully limited its holding in *Snyder* to the facts of that case. These included the fact that a view is not deemed evidence in Massachusetts, that no oral testimony was taken at the view, and that the judge, court reporter, and also defendant's counsel were

Statutory and constitutional considerations aside, the advisability of trial court attendance at views is strongly suggested by the numerous cases in which unauthorized comments, obviously hearsay,[17] have been made to the jury, or other improper events have occurred during the course of the view.[18] Presence of the trial judge would seem to afford the best guarantee available against the occurrence of events of this nature. On the other hand, where the trial judge is present to rule on admissibility, and provision for preparation of a proper record is made, there would appear no inherent vice in receiving testimony or allowing demonstrations or experiments during a view.[19] These practices, however, have often been looked upon with disfavor by appellate courts,[20] and some jurisdictions appear to hold reception of testimony or experiments during a view improper under any circumstances.[21]

Closely related to the above questions is the troublesome problem of what evidentiary status a view possesses. A large number of jurisdictions, probably a majority, holds that a view is not itself evidence, but is only to assist the trier of fact in understanding and evaluating the evidence.[22] This doctrine undoubtedly rests in large part upon the consideration that facts garnered by the jury from a view are difficult or impossible to embody in the written record, thus rendering review of

present. Compare State v. Garden, 267 Minn. 97, 125 N.W.2d 591 (1963) (holding defendant's constitutional rights violated by a view by jury in custody of sheriff, at which neither judge, court reporter nor defendant was present; "the substance of defendant's right is to know what transpired during the viewing.") See also Annot., 30 A.L.R. 1358; 90 id. 597.

In United States v. Walls, 443 F.2d 1220 (6th Cir.1971) the court, without reaching the constitutional issue of *Snyder*, and predicating its decision upon its supervisory authority, found reversible error in denying the defendant and his counsel the opportunity to attend a view.

17. 4 Wigmore, Evidence § 1167 (Chadbourn rev. 1972).

18. Scott v. Tubbs, 43 Colo. 221, 95 P. 540 (1908) (new trial required where petitioner entertained jury in saloon following view); Grand Trunk Western R. Co. v. Pursley, 530 N.E.2d 139 (Ind.App.1988) (improper ex parte experiment at view not attended by judge was error). Juett v. Calhoun, 405 S.W.2d 946 (Ky.1966) (error to allow jurors and party to ride together to view unaccompanied by officer.) Annot., 45 A.L.R.2d 1128.

19. State v. O'Day, 188 La. 169, 175 So. 838, 841 (1937) ("It would seem that it would be better to explain the locus by testimony on the scene * * * "); Williams v. Bethany Volunteer Fire Department, 307 N.C. 430, 298 S.E.2d 352 (1983) (view of fire truck moving with lights flashing and siren sounding held competent to illustrate testimony of witnesses, reversing court of appeals decision holding demonstration an improper experiment). For discussion of the question, generally favoring allowance of testimony and experiments at views, see Wendorf, Some Views on Jury Views, 15 Baylor L.Rev. 379, 394 (1963).

20. Yeary v. Holbrook, 171 Va. 266, 198 S.E. 441 (1938) (stating, "We do not approve the use of witnesses on a view * * *," but finding no reversible error under circumstances); Macon County Commission v. Sanders, 555 So.2d 1054 (Ala. 1990) (semble).

21. State v. Delaney, 15 Utah 2d 338, 393 P.2d 379 (1964) (statute authorizing views held not to authorize taking of testimony thereon); Brooks v. Gilbert, 250 Iowa 1164, 98 N.W.2d 309 (1959) ("recreation" of accident on view "never" permissible). A number of courts have found experiments during views involving the participation of jurors particularly offensive. See Cole v. McGhie, 59 Wash.2d 436, 367 P.2d 844 (1962) (citing numerous cases.)

22. Ernst v. Broughton, 213 Or. 253, 324 P.2d 241 (1958); Doherty v. Providence Journal Co., 94 R.I. 392, 181 A.2d 105 (1962); Kearns v. Hall, 197 Va. 736, 91 S.E.2d 648 (1956). The majority rule has been said to be "strictly applied" to bench trials. Belmont Nursing Home v. Illinois Dept. of Public Aid, 108 Ill.App.3d 660, 64 Ill.Dec. 260, 439 N.E.2d 511 (1982).

questions concerning weight or sufficiency of the evidence impracticable.[23] At the same time, however, this doctrine ignores the fact that many other varieties of demonstrative evidence are to some extent subject to the same difficulty, and further that it is unreasonable to assume that jurors, however they may be instructed, will apply the metaphysical distinction suggested and ignore the evidence of their own senses when it conflicts with the testimony of the witnesses. Commentators have uniformly condemned the downgrading of views to non-evidentiary status,[24] and a substantial number of courts holds a view to be evidence like any other.[25] The latter position appears to be the preferable one, at least when modified by the caveat that where the question is one of sufficiency, a view alone cannot logically be considered to constitute sufficient evidence of a fact the establishment of which ordinarily requires the introduction of expert testimony.

§ 217. Exhibits in the Jury Room [1]

Under modern American practice it is common to allow many types of tangible exhibits to be taken by the jury for consideration during the deliberations,[2] provided that the exhibits have been formally admitted into evidence.[3] The question whether a particular exhibit may be taken by the jury is widely viewed as subject to discretionary control by

23. As to the ability of the trial judge to direct a verdict or grant a new trial for insufficiency of evidence where a view has been had, see Keeney v. Ciborowski, 304 Mass. 371, 24 N.E.2d 17 (1939). Compare Beatty v. Depue, 78 S.D. 395, 103 N.W.2d 187 (1960) (holding view does not constitute evidence, but that reviewing court should consider fact view was taken in ruling upon sufficiency of evidence).

24. Hardman, The Evidentiary Effect of a View: Stare Decisis or Stare Dictis, 53 U.W.Va.L.Rev. 103 (1951); Hardman, The Evidentiary Effect of a View—Another Word, 58 U.W.Va.L.Rev. 69 (1956); Wendorf, Some Views on Jury Views, 15 Baylor L.Rev. 379 (1963).

25. Neel v. Mannings, Inc., 19 Cal.2d 647, 122 P.2d 576 (1942) (view was "independent" evidence); Chouinard v. Shaw, 99 N.H. 26, 104 A.2d 522 (1954) (jury, as "sensible" persons, expected to consider view along with other evidence); Moore, Kelly & Reddish, Inc. v. Shannondale, Inc., 152 W.Va. 549, 165 S.E.2d 113 (1968).

Some courts have finessed the problems of sufficiency-evaluation attendant upon holding a view evidence by holding also that a verdict or finding must be supported by evidence apart from the view. See In re State Highway Running Through Section

2, Township 12, Cass County, 129 Neb. 822, 263 N.W. 148 (1935). At least some states seem to recognize both evidentiary and non-evidentiary views. See Pritchett v. Anding, 168 Ga.App. 658, 310 S.E.2d 267 (1983) (distinguishing between "scene" and "evidentiary" views).

§ 217

1. 6 Wigmore, Evidence § 1913 (Chadbourn rev. 1976); Dec.Dig. Trial ⌐307, Criminal Law ⌐858.

2. See Dec.Dig. Trial ⌐307, Criminal Law ⌐858. Annot., 62 A.L.R.Fed. 950.

3. It is uniformly viewed as improper to permit the jury to take with it items not admitted.

Osborne v. United States, 351 F.2d 111 (8th Cir.1965); State v. Parker, 61 N.C.App. 94, 300 S.E.2d 451 (1983). However, it would appear that most courts hold that the unadmitted exhibit must have been of a potentially prejudicial nature to warrant reversal. United States v. Costa, 691 F.2d 1358 (11th Cir.1982) (error to allow unadmitted transcripts to go to jury, but error harmless where no prejudice accrued); Dallago v. United States, 427 F.2d 546 (D.C.App.1969) (unexplained presence of prejudicial record in jury room held reversible error).

the trial judge,[4] but in some jurisdictions jury access to at least certain types of exhibits is apparently made mandatory either by judicial holding or legislative enactment.[5]

The current practice extends, unlike that at common law,[6] to written exhibits generally except for those which are testimonial in nature, such as depositions, dying declarations in writing, etc.[7] The reason underlying this latter exception is that writings which are merely testimony in a different form should not, by being allowed to the jury, be unduly emphasized over other purely oral testimony in the case.[8] As an exception to the exception, however, written or recorded confessions in criminal cases, despite their obvious testimonial character, are in many jurisdictions allowed to be taken by the jury,[9] apparently on the theory that their centrality in the case warrants whatever emphasis may result.

The practice of allowing nontestimonial written evidence generally to be taken by the jury would appear to be supported by many of the same considerations which underlie the so-called "Best Evidence Rule."[10] Legal rights and liabilities are frequently a function of particular words and figures, and may be drastically affected by seemingly minor variations in phraseology.[11] Thus crucial documents, such as deeds, contracts, or ledger sheets may frequently be of vital help to the jury.[12] On

4. People v. Allen, 17 Ill.2d 55, 160 N.E.2d 818 (1959) (matter largely discretionary); Pakul v. Montgomery Ward Co., 282 Minn. 360, 166 N.W.2d 65 (1969) (within trial court's discretion to withhold exhibits from jury); Zagarri v. Nichols, 429 S.W.2d 758 (Mo.1968) (trial court has discretion to send admitted article to jury).

5. First Employees Ins. Co. v. Skinner, 646 S.W.2d 170 (Tex.1983) (statute held to make practice mandatory). See also McCaffrey v. Glendale Acres, Inc., 250 Or. 140, 440 P.2d 219 (1968) (exhibits are part of evidence and "should" go to jury room; dictum).

6. For explanation of the now obsolete common law practice limiting writings which could be taken to those under seal, see People v. Bartone, 12 Misc.2d 926, 172 N.Y.S.2d 976 (1958).

7. Tibbs v. Tibbs, 257 Ga. 370, 359 S.E.2d 674 (1987) (if testimony is given to jury in written form it is given undue emphasis); State v. Brooks, 675 S.W.2d 53, 57 (Mo.App.1984) ("generally, exhibits which are testimonial in nature may not be given to the jury"); State v. Buras, 459 So.2d 756 (La.App.1984) (applying statutory rule against jury consideration of contents of *any* written evidence). An occasional decision rejects the distinction. See United States v. DeCoito, 764 F.2d 690 (9th Cir.1985) (rejecting undue emphasis argument and holding proper jury access to

written prior consistent statements); State v. Snowden, 138 Ariz. 402, 675 P.2d 289 (App.1983) (tape recording of victim's call to police containing account of entire robbery).

8. See Tibbs v. Tibbs, note 7 supra; State v. Solomon, 96 Utah 500, 87 P.2d 807 (1939) (transcript of testimony at prior trial). The underlying principle is of course the same which underlies the frequently encountered prohibition against note-taking by jurors. See Annot., 14 A.L.R.3d 831.

9. People v. Caldwell, 39 Ill.2d 346, 236 N.E.2d 706 (1968) (containing extensive discussion and citing numerous authorities). See also Annot., 37 A.L.R.3d 238. But compare Franklin v. State, 74 Wis.2d 717, 247 N.W.2d 721 (1976) (holding practice improper). In a few states the practice is prohibited by rule or statute. See, e.g., Commonwealth v. Terry, 501 Pa. 626, 462 A.2d 676 (1983).

10. Whitehead v. Seymour, 120 Ga.App. 25, 169 S.E.2d 369 (1969) (indicating writings subject to the Best Evidence rule are appropriate for jury examination).

See generally Chapter 23 infra.

11. See Morgan, Basic Problems of Evidence 385 (1962).

12. See State of New Jersey v. Clawans, 38 N.J. 162, 183 A.2d 77 (1962) (subornation of perjury; sworn statement in con-

the other hand, where a writing is of only minor relevance, despatch to the jury may induce an emphasis upon it out of proportion to its intrinsic worth.[13]

The case for allowing the jury to take with it tangibles other than writings is somewhat weaker, at least if in-court examination of the tangible by the jury has been had. As noted in an earlier section, demonstrative evidence has peculiar force which arguably does not stand in need of yet additional augmentation.[14] Further, the relevant characteristics of many tangible exhibits are sufficiently gross as not to require the close perusal appropriate to writings, while at the other end of the spectrum there appears some anomaly in allowing independent jury inspection of tangibles the relevant features of which are so fine as to require expert exposition and interpretation.[15] Nevertheless, the sending of tangible exhibits to the jury room is today probably so well established as to be practically irreversible.

A major problem stemming from relatively free jury access to tangible exhibits other than writings is that of controlling jury use of them for purposes of experimentation. The general limitations upon the introduction of evidence of experiments obviously become largely meaningless if the jury is allowed to conduct experiments of its own devising in the jury room. In attempting to distinguish between proper and improper jury use of tangible exhibits, the most commonly drawn distinction is between experiments which constitute merely a closer scrutiny of the exhibit and experiments which go "beyond the lines of the evidence" introduced in court and thus constitute the introduction of new evidence in the jury room.[16] The decisions reached under the aegis of this rubric are perhaps not totally reconcilable.[17] Most courts,

flict with later testimony properly allowed in jury room).

13. See Rob–Lee Corp. v. Cushman, 727 S.W.2d 455 (Mo.App.1987) (proper exercise of discretion to refuse jury access to admitted exhibit containing warranty language which would have been irrelevant and misleading on issues).

14. Some courts, however, have viewed the persuasive character of demonstrative evidence as *supporting* jury access to it! See People v. Williams, 187 Cal.App.2d 355, 9 Cal.Rptr. 722 (1960) (not error to permit gruesome photos of victim to go to jury room where photos showed "more persuasively" than testimony what happened).

15. The view here suggested appears to find support in scattered decisions. See, e.g., People v. McElroy, 63 Ill.App.2d 403, 211 N.E.2d 444 (1965) (proper exercise of discretion to refuse to allow handwriting exemplars introduced and passed among jury to go to jury room; comparison properly to be made during reception of evidence); Commonwealth v. Datesman, 343 Pa.Super. 176, 494 A.2d 413 (1985) (ability of jury to consider exhibit without expert assistance considered in upholding submission of exhibit to jury).

16. Imperial Meat Co. v. United States, 316 F.2d 435 (10th Cir.1963); Williams v. State, 448 So.2d 49 (Fla.App.1984) (mistrial required where exhibit taken to jury room contained additional physical evidence unknown to parties).

17. Compare, e.g., the following holdings: Wilson v. United States, 116 Fed. 484 (9th Cir.1902) (prosecution for smuggling of opium "prepared for smoking;" whether opium so prepared was required to be proved by prosecution and could not be left to be ascertained by jury experiment in which opium was burned); United States v. Beach, 296 F.2d 153 (4th Cir.1961) (improper for jury to experiment with adding machines to determine noise level, that fact bearing upon credibility of witness in case); People v. Kurena, 87 Ill.App.3d 771, 43 Ill.Dec. 277, 410 N.E.2d 277 (1980) (experiments by jury with cardboard knife made by jury held "within the bounds of the

however, emphasize the immunity of jury-conducted experiments from adversary scrutiny as their preeminently objectionable feature.[18] Thus it would seem correct to say that jury experimentation is improper if reasonable grounds existed for an adversary attack on the experiment by the complaining party and, in addition, if nothing transpiring during the in-court proceedings rendered such an attack inappropriate. Specifically, experiments which are merely reruns of in-court experiments, or which use techniques of examination not markedly different from those employed during trial are not generally held to fall within the proscribed class.[19] On the other hand, jury experiments utilizing techniques or equipment substantially different from any employed in court tend to be held error, at least where counsel has not specifically acquiesced in the experiment, such as by arguing that the jury should be allowed certain tools.[20]

evidence"); Taylor v. Commonwealth, 90 Va. 109, 17 S.E. 812 (1893) (holding that where defendant introduced evidence that the firing pin of his rifle did not make marks on cartridge cases similar to those of murder weapon, jury properly disassembled defendant's rifle to detect tampering with firing pin). Cases involving experimentation by the jury outside the courtroom are collected in Annot., 31 A.L.R.4th 566.

18. United States v. Beach, 296 F.2d 153 (4th Cir.1961); Main v. Ballymore Co., 116 Ill.App.3d 1040, 70 Ill.Dec. 295, 449 N.E.2d 169 (1983) (improper to allow jury to take ladder to jury room where it was apparent to all that jury wanted to test it; jury testing not subject to "evidentiary constraints").

19. Taylor v. Reo Motors, Inc., 275 F.2d 699 (10th Cir.1960) (not improper for jury to dismantle and reassemble heat exchanger in jury room where essentially similar operation had been performed by experts in court); Geo. C. Christopher & Son, Inc. v. Kansas Paint & Color Co., Inc., 215 Kan. 185, 523 P.2d 709 (1974) (jury scraped paint samples with pocket knife; "An experiment or demonstration is proper when conducted by the jury with the use of exhibits properly submitted to it for the purpose of testing the truth of statements made by witnesses or duplicating tests made by witnesses in open court"). People v. Thorngate, 10 Mich.App. 317, 159 N.W.2d 373 (1968) (proper for jury to examine exhibits with magnifying glass); Torres v. State, 667 S.W.2d 190 (Tex.App.—Corpus Christi 1983) (mere examination of marijuana by jury not jury misconduct), reversed on other grounds 698 S.W.2d 677 (Tex.Cr.App.) And clearly no error will be found where the complaining party invited the experiment. People v. Harris, 84 A.D.2d 63, 445 N.Y.S.2d 520 (1981) (defense "hard-pressed to complain of experiment it had suggested").

20. United States v. Beach, 296 F.2d 153 (4th Cir.1961) (experiment with adding machine to ascertain level of noise produced held improper; court notes possible objections relating to accuracy to which experiment was subject); Jensen v. Dikel, 244 Minn. 71, 69 N.W.2d 108 (1955) (error for court to furnish tools for jury experiment in absence of express consent of parties); King v. Railway Express Agency, Inc., 94 N.W.2d 657 (N.D.1959) (introduction of ruler and string into jury room for purpose of experiment without consent of parties constituted error.)

For a suggestion of the possible problems involved in establishing that an improper jury experiment has in fact been performed, see State v. James, 70 Wash.2d 624, 424 P.2d 1005 (1967). See § 68 supra.

Title 9

WRITINGS

Chapter 22

AUTHENTICATION *

Table of Sections

* 7 Wigmore, Evidence §§ 2128–2169 (Chadbourn rev. 1978); Tracy, The Introduction of Documentary Evidence, 24 Iowa L.Rev. 436 (1939); Dec.Dig. Evidence ⟚369–382,

The subject of authentication is covered by Article IX of the Federal Rules of Evidence, which provides as follows:

Rule 901. Requirement of Authentication or Identification.

(a) General Provision.—The requirement of authentication or identification as a condition precedent to admissibility is satisfied by evidence sufficient to support a finding that the matter in question is what its proponent claims.

(b) Illustrations.—By way of illustration only, and not by way of limitation, the following are examples of authentication or identification conforming with the requirements of this rule:

(1) *Testimony of Witness With Knowledge.*—Testimony that a matter is what it is claimed to be.

(2) *Nonexpert Opinion on Handwriting.*—Nonexpert opinion as to the genuineness of handwriting, based upon familiarity not acquired for purposes of the litigation.

(3) *Comparison by Trier or Expert Witness.*—Comparison by the trier of fact or by expert witnesses with specimens which have been authenticated.

(4) *Distinctive Characteristics and the Like.*—Appearance, contents, substance, internal patterns, or other distinctive characteristics, taken in conjunction with circumstances.

(5) *Voice Identification.*—Identification of a voice, whether heard firsthand or through mechanical or electronic transmission or recording, by opinion based upon hearing the voice at any time under circumstances connecting it with the alleged speaker.

(6) *Telephone Conversations.*—Telephone conversations, by evidence that a call was made to the number assigned at the time by the telephone company to a particular person or business, if (A) in the case of a person, circumstances, including self-identification, show the person answering to be the one called, or (B) in the case of a business, the call was made to a place of business and the conversation related to business reasonably transacted over the telephone.

(7) *Public Records or Reports.*—Evidence that a writing authorized by law to be recorded or filed and in fact recorded or filed in a public office, or a purported public record, report, statement, or data compilation, in any form, is from the public office where items of this nature are kept.

(8) *Ancient Documents or Data Compilation.*—Evidence that a document or data compilation, in any form, (A) is in such condition as to create no suspicion concerning its authenticity, (B) was in a place where it, if authentic, would likely be, and (C) has been in existence 20 years or more at the time it is offered.

(9) *Process or System.*—Evidence describing a process or system used to produce a result and showing that the process or system produces an accurate result.

(10) *Methods Provided by Statute or Rule.*—Any method of authentication or identification provided by Act of Congress or by other rules prescribed by the Supreme Court pursuant to statutory authority.

Rule 902. Self–Authentication

Extrinsic evidence of authenticity as a condition precedent to admissibility is not required with respect to the following:

(1) *Domestic Public Documents Under Seal.*—A document bearing a seal purporting to be that of the United States, or of any State, district, Commonwealth, territory, or insular possession thereof, or the Panama Canal Zone, or the Trust Territory of the Pacific Islands, or of a political subdivision, department, officer, or agency thereof, and a signature purporting to be an attestation or execution.

(2) *Domestic Public Documents Not Under Seal.*—A document purporting to bear the signature in his official capacity of an officer or employee of any entity included in paragraph (1) hereof, having no seal, if a public officer having a seal and having official duties in the district or political subdivision of the officer or employee certifies under seal that the signer has the official capacity and that the signature is genuine.

(3) *Foreign Public Documents.*—A document purporting to be executed or attested in his official capacity by a person authorized by the laws of a foreign country to make the execution or attestation, and accompanied by a final certification as to the genuineness of the signature and official position (A) of the executing or attesting person, or (B) of any foreign official whose certificate of genuineness of signature and official position relates to the execution or attestation or is in a chain of certificates of genuineness of signature and official position relating to the execution or attestation. A final certification may be made by a secretary of embassy or legation, consul general, consul, vice consul, or consular agent of the United States, or a diplomatic or consular official of the foreign country assigned or accredited to the United States. If reasonable opportunity has been given to all parties to investigate the authenticity and accuracy of official documents, the court may, for good cause shown, order that they be treated as presumptively authentic without final certification or permit them to be evidenced by an attested summary with or without final certification.

(4) *Certified Copies of Public Records.*—A copy of an official record or report or entry therein, or of a document authorized by law to be recorded or filed and actually recorded or filed in a public office, including data compilations in any form, certified as correct by the custodian or other person authorized to make the certification, by certificate complying with paragraph (1), (2), or (3) of this rule or complying with any Act of Congress or rule prescribed by the Supreme Court pursuant to statutory authority.

(5) *Official Publications.*—Books, pamphlets, or other publications purporting to be issued by public authority.

(6) *Newspapers and Periodicals.*—Printed materials purporting to be newspapers or periodicals.

(7) *Trade Inscriptions and the Like.*—Inscriptions, signs, tags, or labels purporting to have been affixed in the

§ 218. General Theory: No Assumption of Authenticity

The concept of authentication, although continually used by the courts without apparent difficulty, seems almost to defy precise definition. Some writers have construed the term very broadly, as does Wigmore when he states that "when a claim or offer involves impliedly or expressly any element of *personal connection with a corporeal object,* that connection must be made to appear * * *." [1] So defined, "authentication" is not only a necessary preliminary to the introduction of most writings in evidence, but also to the introduction of various other sorts of tangibles. For example, an article of clothing found at the scene of a crime can hardly constitute relevant evidence against the defendant unless ownership or previous possession of the article is shown. Since authentication of tangibles other than writings,[2] has been treated elsewhere, however, the term authentication will here be used in the limited sense of proof of authorship of, or other connection with, writings.[3]

It is clear that the relevancy of a writing to a particular issue raised in litigation will frequently be logically dependent upon the existence of some connection between that writing and a particular individual.[4] If

course of business and indicating ownership, control, or origin.

(8) *Acknowledged Documents.*—Documents accompanied by a certificate of acknowledgment executed in the manner provided by law by a notary public or other officer authorized by law to take acknowledgments.

(9) *Commercial Paper and Related Documents.*—Commercial paper, signatures thereon, and documents relating thereto to the extent provided by general commercial law.

(10) *Presumptions Under Acts of Congress.*—Any signature, document, or other matter declared by Act of Congress to be presumptively or prima facie genuine or authentic.

Rule 903. Subscribing Witness' Testimony Unnecessary

The testimony of a subscribing witness is not necessary to authenticate a writing unless required by the laws of the jurisdiction whose laws govern the validity of the writing.

The corresponding provisions of the revised Uniform Rules are for all practical purposes identical.

§ 218

1. 7 Wigmore, Evidence § 2129 at 564 (Chadbourn rev. 1978).

2. See § 212 supra.

3. Though the connection necessary to establish relevancy will most frequently be authorship, it may in a given case consist of a variety of other relationships. In Bodrey v. Bodrey, 246 Ga. 122, 269 S.E.2d 14 (1980) the offered item was a love letter found by a wife in her husband's desk drawer. The court held that for purposes of the litigation the authorship of the letter was immaterial, and that the necessary connection was the wife's finding. See also, United States v. Sliker, 751 F.2d 477 (2d Cir.1984) (authorship of documents immaterial; authentication dependent upon connection with bank issuing checks).

4. R & D Amusement Corp. v. Christianson, 392 N.W.2d 385 (N.D.1986) (purpose of authentication is to establish relevancy); Fed.R.Evid. 901 Adv.Com.Note. As noted above, supra note 4, where the relevancy of a writing depends upon a connection other than authorship, it will sometimes be the case that the writing is authenticated without any showing as to its specific authorship. See, e.g., United States v. Helmel, 769 F.2d 1306 (8th Cir. 1985) (ledgers sufficiently shown to be records of illegal gambling operation held authenticated without proof of specific authorship); United States v. De Gudino, 722 F.2d 1351 (7th Cir.1983) (semble).

Y sues X for libel and attempts to introduce into evidence a writing containing libelous statements concerning Y, it will readily appear that the writing is relevant only if some connection between the writing and X exists, as where X authored or published it. The real question, however, is not whether such a connection is logically necessary for relevancy, but rather what standards are to be applied in determining whether the connection has been made to appear. In some instances testimony concerning a writing will be offered rather than the writing itself. Where this is permissible through the operation of the so-called "best evidence" rule or its exceptions,[5] is the requirement of authentication excused? The answer should necessarily be that it is not, for the connection between the writing and the individual is rendered no less logically significant because of the form of evidence concerning the writing.[6]

In the everyday affairs of business and social life, it is the custom to look merely at the writing itself for evidence as to its source. Thus, if the writing bears a signature purporting to be that of X, or recites that it was made by X, we assume, nothing to the contrary appearing, that it is exactly what it purports to be, the work of X. At this point, however, the law of evidence has long differed from the commonsense assumption upon which each of us conducts her own affairs, adopting instead the position that the purported signature or recital of authorship on the face of a writing will *not* be accepted as sufficient preliminary proof of authenticity to secure the admission of the writing in evidence.[7] The same attitude has traditionally extended as well to the authority of agents, with the result that if an instrument recites that it is signed by A as agent for P, not only must additional proof be given that A actually did the signing, but also of the fact that she was P's agent and authorized to sign.[8]

---

5. See Chapter 23, infra.

6. But see United States v. Cowley, 720 F.2d 1037 (9th Cir.1983), holding that where a witness testified that he received an envelope bearing a particular postmark there was no requirement of authentication, though such would have been required had the envelope itself been offered. Clearly, where the envelope itself was not offered, there was no necessity for the witness to testify that the tendered envelope was the same one received by him. But this connection is not the only one involved in the concept of authentication, and the court's holding must therefore be considered overbroad.

7. McGowan v. Armour, 248 Fed. 676 (8th Cir.1918) (letter bearing purported writer's signature, found in addressee's pocket, excluded); Continental Baking Co. v. Katz, 68 Cal.2d 512, 67 Cal.Rptr. 761, 897, 439 P.2d 889 (1968) ("We understand that in some legal systems it is assumed

that documents are what they purport to be unless shown to be otherwise. With us it is the other way around. Generally speaking, documents must be authenticated in some fashion before they are admissible * * * "); Idaho First National Bank v. Wells, 100 Idaho 256, 596 P.2d 429 (1979) (error to admit promissory notes without authentication); City of Randleman v. Hinshaw, 2 N.C.App. 381, 163 S.E.2d 95 (1968) (authentication of writing necessary to admission); Beltran v. State, 144 Tex.Cr.R. 338, 163 S.W.2d 211 (1942) (written confession purporting to be signed by accused); 7 Wigmore, Evidence § 2130, note 1 (Chadbourn rev. 1978); Dec.Dig. Evidence ⟐370(1).

8. Hill Aircraft & Leasing Corp. v. Cintas Corp., 169 Ga.App. 747, 315 S.E.2d 263 (1984) (citing treatise); Dec.Dig. Evidence ⟐370(5).

The principal justification urged for this judicial agnosticism toward the authorship of documents is that it constitutes a necessary check on the perpetration of fraud. Thus it is quite conceivable that the libelous writing previously adduced by way of example is not the work of X but of some third person who, for reasons of her own, wishes to embroil X in difficulties,[9] or to libel Y without suffering any adverse consequences. It is also possible that Y has fabricated the writing to provide herself with a cause of action.

Another possibility against which traditional authentication is sometimes suggested to guard is that of mistaken attribution of a writing to one who fortuitously happens to possess the same name, etc., as the author.

On the other side of the coin, requiring proof of what may correctly be assumed true in 99 out of 100 cases is at best time-consuming and expensive. At the worst, the requirement will occasionally be seen to produce results which are virtually indefensible.[10]

Thus, while traditional requirements of authentication admittedly furnish some slight obstacles to the perpetration of fraud or occurrence of mistake in the presentation of writings, it has frequently been questioned whether these benefits are not outweighed by the time, expense, and occasional untoward results entailed by the traditional negative attitude toward authenticity of writings.[11]

§ 219. Authentication by Direct Proof: (a) In General

The simplest form of direct testimony authenticating a writing as that of X, is the production of a witness who swears that he saw X sign the offered writing.[1] Other examples would be the testimony of X, the signer, acknowledging execution, or the admission of authenticity by an adverse party in the present action, either made out of court and

---

9. See Hughes v. Samuels Brothers, 179 Iowa 1077, 159 N.W. 589 (1916) (undertaker mailed business card of competitor to man whose wife was seriously ill).

10. Mancari v. Frank P. Smith, Inc., 72 U.S.App.D.C. 398, 114 F.2d 834 (1940), 26 Iowa L.Rev. 134, 15 So.Calif.L.Rev. 115 (plaintiff sued as a result of mention of his name in a widely distributed circular which purported to be issued by a manufacturer and a local retailer of shoes. Held, Judge Rutledge dissenting, that the trial court properly directed a verdict for defendant on the ground that the terms of the circular did not make a prima facie case of defendant's authorship).

11. See the quotation from Jeremy Bentham in 7 Wigmore, Evidence § 2148, p. 606 (Chadbourn rev. 1978); Alexander & Alexander, The Authentication of Documents Requirement: Barrier to Falsehood

or to Truth? 10 S.D.L.Rev. 266 (1973); Broun, Authentication and Content of Writings, 1969 L. & Soc.O. 611; Erich, Unnecessary Difficulties of Proof, 32 Yale L.J. 436 (1923); Strong, Liberalizing the Authentication of Private Writings, 52 Cornell L.Q. 284 (1967).

§ 219

1. Manifestly this is a sufficient authentication. Cottingham v. Doyle, 122 Mont. 301, 202 P.2d 533 (1949); Zodiac Corp. v. General Electric Credit Corp., 566 S.W.2d 341 (Tex.Civ.App.—Tyler 1978); Durham v. State, 422 P.2d 691 (Wyo.1967). Connections other than by signing may be similarly established. See United States v. Rizzo, 418 F.2d 71 (7th Cir.1969) (cards mailed to promote business of house of ill fame admissible where witness testified she had helped prepare "similar" cards for defendants).

reported by another witness or shown by the party's own letter or other writing, or in the form of the party's testimony on the stand.[2] It is generally held that business records may be authenticated[3] by the testimony of one familiar with the books of the concern, such as a custodian or supervisor, who has not made the record or seen it made, that the offered writing is actually part of the records of the business.[4]

§ 220. Authentication by Direct Proof: (b) Requirement of Production of Attesting Witnesses.[1]

Our rules about the production of subscribing witnesses are survivals of archaic law. They have their origins in Germanic practice earlier than jury trial, when pre-appointed transaction-witnesses were the only kind of witnesses that could be summoned or heard in court. When jury trial came in, the attesting witnesses at first were summoned along with the jurors themselves, and this practice seems to have lingered until the middle fifteen hundreds.[2] The rule in its modern common law form requires, when a document signed by subscribing witnesses is sought to be authenticated by witnesses, that an attesting witness must first be called,[3] or all attesters must be shown to be unavailable,[4] before

2. See Ch. 26 infra.

See Ch. 26 infra. And see Cathey v. Johns–Manville Sales Corp., 776 F.2d 1565 (6th Cir.1985) (admission of authenticity by same party in companion case before same court sufficient to authenticate letters).

3. Merely supplying the requirement that the books be identified as such, though other foundation proof may be required before the records will be accepted as evidence of the facts recorded under the hearsay exception for Business Records. See §§ 284–294 infra.

4. Rosenberg v. Collins, 624 F.2d 659, 665 (5th Cir.1980) ("Any person in a position to attest to the authenticity of certain records is competent to lay the foundation for the admissibility of the records * * * "); Miller v. State, 224 A.2d 592 (Del.1966) (church records; current pastor not preparing entries in question); State Dept. of Mental Health v. Milligan, 39 Ohio App.3d 178, 530 N.E.2d 965 (1988) (testimony of custodian of hospital records which included records prepared at other hospitals at which patient had been treated); Martin v. Martin, 755 S.W.2d 793 (Tenn.App.1988) (present custodian held competent to authenticate loan records of now-defunct bank). See § 312 infra.

§ 220

1. 4 Wigmore, Evidence §§ 1287–1321 (Chadbourn rev. 1972); Dec.Dig. Evidence ⟲374; C.J.S. Evidence § 739.

2. Thayer, Preliminary Treatise on Evidence 502 (1898).

3. If there are several attesters only one must be called. Sowell v. Bank of Brewton, 119 Ala. 92, 24 So. 585 (1898) (note); Allgood v. Allgood, 230 Ga. 312, 196 S.E.2d 888 (1973) (deed properly admitted though only one of two attesting witnesses testified; attestation said only to affect recordability); Shirley v. Fearne, 33 Miss. 653, 69 Am.Dec. 375 (1857) (deed with two attesters, though only one required by law). But the Chancery rule in England required the calling or accounting for all attesters, and a few American jurisdictions continued to impose the requirement in will cases. In re Estate of Coon, 154 Neb. 690, 48 N.W.2d 778 (1951); Swindoll v. Jones, 41 Tenn.App. 89, 292 S.W.2d 531 (1954). Cases concerning the requirement in will cases are collected in Dec.Dig. Wills ⟲303(4). For a collection of statutes affecting the question, see 4 Wigmore, Evidence § 1304 (Chadbourn rev. 1972).

4. Howard v. Russell, 104 Ga. 230, 30 S.E. 802 (1898) (semble: deed). But seemingly if there are more attesters than the law requires only the number required must be accounted for. Stemmler v. Crutcher, 719 S.W.2d 918 (Mo.App.1986) (testimony of two of three attesting witnesses sufficient to prove will where statute required only two witnesses to will). And if the attesting witnesses' identities cannot be ascertained, even proof of una-

other witnesses can be called to authenticate it.[5]

The requirement has no application where the foundation for introducing the document is the opponent's judicial admission [6] of its genuineness,[7] either by stipulation of the parties in writing or in open court, or under modern rules and statutes by the opponent's failure to deny the genuineness of the writing.[8] Though it has been suggested that extra-judicial admissions also, if in writing, might properly be held to dispense with the production of attesters, such American authority as exists seems to deny that extra-judicial admissions of any sort have this effect.[9]

The requirement is that the attesting witnesses be called before other authenticating witnesses are heard, but it is not required that the attesters give favorable testimony establishing the writing. So even if they profess want of memory [10] or even deny that they attested,[11] the writing may be established by other proof, and conversely if they support the writing, other proof may establish that it is not authentic.[12] Moreover, since the party calling the attester is required by law to do so, the prohibition upon impeaching one's own witness is held inapplicable.[13]

This requirement of calling particular persons, or accounting for them, to authenticate the writing is often inconvenient, and of doubtful expediency, and various exceptions have been carved out by the courts, as for ancient documents,[14] writings only "collaterally" involved in the suit,[15] and for certified copies of recorded conveyances, where the

---

vailability may be held unnecessary. Skaling v. Remick, 97 N.H. 106, 82 A.2d 81 (1951). Statutes defining "unavailability" are collected in 4 Wigmore, Evidence § 1310 (Chadbourn rev. 1972).

5. For a summary statement of the rule, see 4 Wigmore, Evidence § 1289 (Chadbourn rev. 1972).

6. As to meaning, see § 257 infra.

7. Jones v. Henry, 84 N.C. 320, 323 (1881) (stipulation of record, "defendants admit execution of bond" dispenses with producing attester); 4 Wigmore, Evidence § 1296 (Chadbourn rev. 1972).

8. See § 228 infra.

9. 4 Wigmore, Evidence § 1300 (Chadbourn rev. 1972).

10. Abbott v. Abbott, 41 Mich. 540, 2 N.W. 810 (1879); In Matter of Katz' Will, 277 N.Y. 470, 14 N.E.2d 797 (1938) (will may be established in direct opposition to testimony of subscribing witnesses); In re Ellis' Will, 235 N.C. 27, 69 S.E.2d 25 (1952); In re Estate of Farnsworth, 84 S.D. 675, 176 N.W.2d 247 (1970) (failure of attesting witnesses to recall execution does not preclude valid testamentary disposition).

11. Wheat v. Wheat, 156 Conn. 575, 244 A.2d 359 (1968); In re Estate of Lyons, 166 Ohio St. 207, 141 N.E.2d 151 (1957).

12. In re O'Connor's Estate, 105 Neb. 88, 179 N.W. 401, 12 A.L.R. 199 (1920), cert. denied 256 U.S. 690. In the Matter of Estate of Sylvestri, 44 N.Y.2d 260, 405 N.Y.S.2d 424, 376 N.E.2d 897 (1978).

13. Amerine v. Amerine, 177 Kan. 481, 280 P.2d 601 (1955); In re Warren's Estate, 138 Or. 283, 4 P.2d 635, 79 A.L.R. 389 (1931).

14. Smythe v. Inhabitants of New Providence Township, 263 Fed. 481, 484 (3d Cir.1920) ("the subscribing witnesses are presumed to be dead").

15. Steiner v. Tranum, 98 Ala. 315, 13 So. 365 (1893) (trover for horse: note given by plaintiff as evidence of his purchase, held "collateral"); Lugosch v. Public Service Railway Co., 100 N.J.L. 48, 126 A. 170 (1924) (writing offered to impeach, "collateral"). Compare Snead v. Stephens, 242 Ala. 76, 5 So.2d 740 (1941) where it was held that in a suit for destruction of plaintiff's mortgage lien on cotton by defendant's resale of the cotton, the mortgage itself was not collateral. The reversal of the judgment for plaintiff because of his

original is not required to be produced.[16] A more sweeping reform, generally effected by statute but on occasion by judicial decision, has been to dispense with the requirement of calling attesting witnesses except when the writing to be offered is one required by law to be attested.[17]

§ 221. Authentication by Direct Proof: (c) Proof of Handwriting [1]

A witness is placed on the stand. "Will you state whether you are acquainted with the handwriting of X?" "I am." "Will you look at this letter (or this signature) and tell me whether it is in the handwriting of X?" "It is." These or similar questions and answers are part of the familiar routine of authenticating writings, a routine which might be supposed to possess a rationale until note is taken of the qualifications typically required to be shown as part of his testimony by the witness through whom such a foundation is laid. These qualifications are minimal to say the least. Thus it is generally held that anyone familiar with the handwriting of a given person may supply authenticating testimony in the form of his opinion that a writing or signature is in the handwriting of that person.[2] Adequate familiarity may be present if the witness has seen the person write,[3] or if he has seen writings *purporting* to be those of the person in question under circumstances indicating their genuineness. Examples of the latter situation include instances where the witness has had an exchange of correspon-

failure to produce the subscribing witness to a writing the genuineness of which was not actually in doubt, illustrates the profitless aridity of the requirement.

16. Powers v. Russell, 13 Pick. (Mass.) 69, 75 (1832); 4 Wigmore, Evidence § 1318 (Chadbourn rev. 1972). Seemingly some courts would admit the original recorded deed, without calling subscribers under statutes providing that they "prove themselves." See Foxworth v. Brown, 120 Ala. 59, 24 So. 1, 4 (1898) and § 228 infra.

17. This is the apparent effect of Fed. R.Evid. 903, supra § 218, note 1. Statutes of similar import are collected in 4 Wigmore, Evidence § 1290 (Chadbourn rev. 1972). Even where an instrument's validity requires attesting witnesses, one state has eliminated any necessity for the testimony of such witnesses except where that testimony is specifically called for by statute. Alaska R.Ev. 903 (1979).

§ 221

1. See Berman, A Connecticut Commentary on Authenticating Private Documents, 28 Conn.B.J. 173 (1954); Tracy, Documentary Evidence, 24 Iowa L.Rev. 436 (1939); Dec.Dig. Evidence ☜378(4). See

also 20 Am.Jur. Proof of Facts 335 (bibliography).

2. See, e.g., Clark v. Grimsley, 270 So.2d 53 (Fla.App.1972) (family friend and frequent visitor familiar with decedent's handwriting competent); Apple v. Commonwealth, 296 S.W.2d 717 (Ky.1956) (lay witness' testimony of familiarity and identity warranted admission); Noyes v. Noyes, 224 Mass. 125, 112 N.E. 850 (1916) ("anybody familiar with a person's handwriting" may authenticate).

3. Auto Owners Finance Co. Inc. v. Rock, 121 Vt. 194, 151 A.2d 292 (1959). A single observation is frequently held sufficient. See United States v. Standing Soldier, 538 F.2d 196 (8th Cir.1976), cert. denied 429 U.S. 1025; State v. Bond, 12 Idaho 424, 86 P. 43 (1906); State v. Freshwater, 30 Utah 442, 85 P. 447 (1906). Further, the observation need not have been recent. See In re Diggins' Estate, 68 Vt. 198, 34 A. 696 (1896) (one observation, 20 years previously, apparently held sufficient). But a few states apply more rigorous standards. Compare Storm v. Hansen, 41 N.J.Super. 249, 124 A.2d 601 (1956) (lay identification "weak and unsatisfactory" at best; substantial familiarity required).

dence with the person,[4] or has seen writings which the person has asserted are his own,[5] or has been present in an office or other place where genuine writings of a particular person in the ordinary course of business would naturally be seen.[6] Finally, it is not required that the authenticating witness' identification be categorical in nature.[7]

The same assumptions which underlie lay witness authentication based upon familiarity with individual handwriting may be seen to justify another well-established doctrine, that of authentication by handwriting specimens or "exemplars." The common law limited the use of exemplars for comparison purposes to writings otherwise admissible in the case,[8] but this rule has generally been modified by rule or statute[9] to allow handwriting samples to be admitted solely for the purpose of comparison. Some conflict of authority exists concerning the standard by which the authenticity of such specimens is to be

4. Paccon, Inc. v. United States, 185 Ct.Cl. 24, 399 F.2d 162 (1968) (witness qualified to authenticate where he had seen 100 other documents purportedly signed by person over course of contract); Morgan v. First Pennsylvania Bank, 373 Pa.Super. 408, 541 A.2d 380 (1988) (familiarity gained through correspondence); Mack Financial Corp. v. Harnett Transfer, Inc., 42 N.C.App. 116, 256 S.E.2d 491 (1979) (familiarity through ordinary course of business).

5. Hershberger v. Hershberger, 345 Pa. 439, 29 A.2d 95 (1942) (witnesses had charged account of person with checks purporting to have been drawn by him, and he had not questioned them).

6. United States v. Kilgore, 518 F.2d 496 (5th Cir.1975) (witness would have seen documents initialed by purported author) (citing treatise). Hamilton v. Smith, 74 Conn. 374, 50 A. 884 (1902) (engineer who had frequently worked with maps signed by former town surveyor could authenticate latter's signature); Kinney v. Youngblood, 216 Ga. 354, 116 S.E.2d 608 (1960) (witness who had lived in apartment in defendant's home for three years and testified she knew his signature); Priest v. Poleshuck, 29 N.J.Super. 401, 102 A.2d 636 (1954) (bookkeeper competent to authenticate signature of employee); In re McDowell's Will, 230 N.C. 259, 52 S.E.2d 807 (1949) (granddaughter's identification of signature as that of grandfather with whom she lived held sufficient without testimony that witness "knew" handwriting of grandfather).

7. United States v. Barker, 735 F.2d 1280 (11th Cir.1984), cert. denied 469 U.S. 933 (authentication sufficient where witness testified that handwriting was "similar to Sarah's").

8. Doe v. Newton, 5 A. & E. 514 (1836); 7 Wigmore, Evidence §§ 1994, 2001 (Chadbourn rev. 1978). The earlier rule, while somewhat arbitrarily restrictive, had the advantage of eliminating certain troublesome questions concerning the creation and selection of exemplars. Under the rule here discussed these questions tend to recur. See United States v. Lam Muk Chiu, 522 F.2d 330 (2d Cir.1975) (exemplars prepared by defendant for litigation and not under court supervision, offered to show defendant had not authored incriminating letters; "objectionable as self-serving"); contra, United States v. Pastore, 537 F.2d 675, 35 A.L.R.Fed. 616 (2d Cir.1976) (exemplars prepared by witnesses for trial but not under court supervision held admissible to show witnesses had not endorsed checks as contended by defendant; self-interest of witnesses held not to bar admission). See also, Elliott v. United States, 385 A.2d 183 (D.C.App.1978) (defendant sent twin brother to furnish handwriting exemplars ordered by court).

A distinguishable type of problem is raised, unrelated to the reliability of the exemplar, when the exemplar would be inadmissible for some other reason. See United States v. Turquitt, 557 F.2d 464 (5th Cir.1977) (document introduced as exemplar suggested commission of earlier crime by defendant; held: admission improper where exemplar was cumulative and unnecessary as well as prejudicial).

9. State statutes and rules on the subject are collected in 7 Wigmore, Evidence § 2016 (Chadbourn rev. 1978). And see Fed.R.Evid. 901(b)(3) supra § 218, note 1.

determined.[10] Once admitted,[11] however, an apparent majority of jurisdictions hold that the genuineness of other offered writings alleged to be the work of the same author becomes a question for the trier of fact who may, but need not, be assisted in this task by expert comparisons.[12] Analogous holdings may be found in the relatively rarer cases of authentication by typing technique or word usage patterns (psycholinguistics), both of which, like handwriting identification, proceed on the basis of comparisons between the document in question and exemplars of known origin.[13]

Demonstration is available, if demonstration is thought to be needed, that evidence of the foregoing varieties is essentially meaningless in cases where the authenticity is actually disputed.[14] If a writing is in fact questioned no layperson is competent to distinguish a skilled forgery from a genuine writing. Certainly it is incredible that an unskilled layman who saw the person write once a decade before could make such a differentiation. In the event of an actual controversy over genuineness, both logic and good advocacy demand a resort to evidence of greater reliability and persuasiveness, principally, according to the prevalent view, the testimony of bona fide handwriting experts.[15]

The minimal qualifications required of the ordinary witness authenticating a writing by identification of handwriting are defensible only on the basis that no more than one in a hundred writings is questioned. The current permissive standards allow the admission of the general

10. Fed.R.Evid. 901(b)(3), supra § 218, note 1, requires only that exemplars be authenticated, and thus changed the preexisting law in many of the jurisdictions in which it has been adopted. Wellborn, Authentication and Identification Under Article IX of the Texas Rules of Evidence, 16 St. Mary's L.J. 371 (1985). And compare State v. Fortier, 427 A.2d 1317 (R.I.1981) (stating genuineness of exemplars required to be proved to trial court beyond a reasonable doubt in criminal case). Cases are collected in Annot. 41 A.L.R.2d 575.

11. See note 8 supra. Where the stated rule is followed the disputed document is sufficiently authenticated by being tendered for admission along with the authenticated exemplar. See State v. Haugen, 392 N.W.2d 799 (N.D.1986).

12. See, e.g., United States v. Woodson, 526 F.2d 550 (9th Cir.1975) (disputed documents properly admissible for comparison with exemplars by jury despite fact that expert witness for proponent testified to inability to draw conclusion as to common authorship). But compare Richardson v. State, 437 So.2d 1091 (Fla.1983) (jury not competent to make handwriting comparisons without aid of expert). Cases are collected in Annot., 80 A.L.R.2d 272. Of course, the jury is free to predicate a deci-

sion on handwriting comparisons even where authorship is denied in testimony. Veilleux v. Veilleux, 565 A.2d 95 (Me. 1989).

13. See, e.g., United States v. Clifford, 704 F.2d 86 (3d Cir.1983) (jury held competent to compare linguistic patterns of documents in evidence though expert testimony excluded); Forte v. Schiebe, 145 Cal. App.2d 296, 302 P.2d 336 (1956) (jury competent to compare typing samples). Cases are collected in Annot., 36 A.L.R.4th 598.

14. Inbau, Lay Witness Identification of Handwriting (An Experiment), 34 Ill. L.Rev. 433 (1939); Hilton, The Detection of Forgery, 30 J.Crim.L. & Criminology 568 (1939).

15. Handwriting comparisons for the purpose of determining authenticity has long been generally accepted as a proper subject for expert testimony. See § 207, notes 5, 20, supra. The claim of "scientific" status for the technique has, however, been trenchantly assailed. Risinger, Denbeaux, and Sax, Exorcism of Ignorance as a Proxy for Rational Knowledge: The Lessons of Handwriting Identification "Expertise," 137 U.Pa.L.Rev. 731 (1989) (conceding the difficulty of overturning the orthodoxy, but making practical suggestions for challenging such testimony).

run of authentic documents with a minimum of time, trouble, and expense. The latter argument, however, may prove too much since even greater savings in these commodities might safely be achieved by simply presuming the authenticity of writings for purposes of admissibility in the absence of proof raising a question as to genuineness.[16]

§ 222. Authentication by Circumstantial Evidence: (a) Generally

As has been seen there are various ways in which writings may be authenticated by direct evidence. Nevertheless, it will frequently occur that no direct evidence of authenticity of any type exists or can be found. Resort must then be had to circumstantial proof and it is clear that authentication by circumstantial evidence is uniformly recognized as permissible.[1] Certain configurations of circumstantial evidence have in fact been so frequently held to authenticate particular types of writings that they have come to be recognized as distinct rules, e.g., the ancient documents rule, the reply doctrine, etc. These more or less formalized rules are treated in succeeding sections.[2]

It is important to bear in mind, however, that authentication by circumstantial evidence is not limited to situations which fall within one of these recurrent patterns. Rather, proof of any circumstances which will support a finding that the writing is genuine will suffice to authenticate the writing.[3]

§ 223. Authentication by Circumstantial Evidence: (b) Ancient Documents [1]

A writing which has been in existence for a number of years will frequently be difficult to authenticate by direct evidence. Where the maker of an instrument, those who witnessed the making, and even those familiar with the maker's handwriting have over the course of years died or become unavailable, the need to resort to authentication by circumstantial evidence is apparent.[2] The circumstances which

---

16. Broun, Authentication and Contents of Writings, 1969 Law & Soc.Ord. 611; Levin, Authentication and Content of Writings, 10 Rut.L.Rev. 632 (1956); Strong, Liberalizing the Authentication of Private Writings, 52 Cornell L.Q. 284 (1967).

§ 222

1. See, e.g., Champion v. Champion, 368 Mich. 84, 117 N.W.2d 107 (1962) (authentication on basis of circumstantial evidence upheld); Walters v. Littleton, 223 Va. 446, 290 S.E.2d 839 (1982) (error to exclude medical bills properly authenticated by circumstances of receipt).

2. See §§ 223–226 infra.

3. United States v. Drougas, 748 F.2d 8 (1st Cir.1984); United States v. Sutton, 426

F.2d 1202 (D.C.Cir.1969); Cotton States Mutual Insurance Co. v. Clark, 114 Ga. App. 439, 151 S.E.2d 780 (1966); People v. Lynes, 64 A.D.2d 543, 406 N.Y.S.2d 816 (1978); McFarland v. McFarland, 176 Pa.Super. 342, 107 A.2d 615 (1954).

§ 223

1. 7 Wigmore, Evidence, §§ 2137–2146 (Chadbourn rev. 1978); Dec.Dig. Evidence ⚏372; C.J.S. Evidence §§ 743–752.

2. Louden v. Apollo Gas Co., 273 Pa.Super. 549, 417 A.2d 1185 (1980) (rule prevents difficulty or impossibility of authenticating ancient writings by ordinary means). When possible, of course, the authenticity of ancient documents may be

may, in a given case, raise an inference of the genuineness of an aged writing are of course quite varied, and any combination of circumstances sufficient to support a finding of genuineness will be appropriate authentication.[3] Facts which may be suggested as indicative of genuineness include unsuspicious appearance, emergence from natural custody, prompt recording, and, in the case of a deed or will, possession taken under the instrument. Age itself may be viewed as giving rise to some inference of genuineness in that an instrument is unlikely to be forged for fruition at a time in the distant future.

The frequent necessity of authenticating ancient writings by circumstantial evidence [4] plus the consideration that certain of the above facts probative of authenticity are commonly found associated with genuine older writings have led the courts to develop a rule of thumb for dealing with the question.[5] Under the common law form of this rule a writing is sufficiently authenticated as an ancient document if the party who offers it produces sufficient evidence that the writing is thirty years old,[6] that it is unsuspicious in appearance,[7] and further proves that the writing is produced from a place of custody natural for such a document.[8] The Federal Rules of Evidence and most state derivatives

proved by direct evidence. Kanimaya v. Choctaw Lumber Co., 147 Okl. 90, 294 P. 817 (1930).

3. See Gaskins v. Guthrie, 162 Ga. 103, 132 S.E. 764 (1926) (showing of particular fact not essential, if totality of circumstances afford finding of genuineness).

4. Wynne v. Tyrwhitt, [1821] 4 Barn. & Ald. 376, 106 Eng.Rep. 975 (rule founded on great difficulty of proving handwriting after lapse of time.) See also 7 Wigmore, Evidence § 2137 (Chadbourn rev. 1978).

5. See, e.g., Steele v. Fowler, 111 Ind. App. 364, 41 N.E.2d 678 (1942) ("When a document appears to be at least 30 years old and is found in proper custody, and is unblemished by alterations and otherwise free from suspicion, it is admissible without proof of execution."); Boucher v. Wallis, 236 S.W.2d 519 (Tex.Civ.App.1951) (semble).

6. The selection of 30 years is justified by Wigmore as being the normal period beyond which direct evidence of authenticity becomes practically unavailable. This justification however, would appear to support 30 years as a rough standard only and to fall short of warranting such quibbles as whether the period should be measured from execution to filing of action or introduction of evidence. See Reuter v. Stuckart, 181 Ill. 529, 54 N.E. 1014 (1899) (execution to introduction proper measure). Viewing the rule positively, existence for a substantial period of time less than 30 years might be viewed as raising an infer-

ence of genuineness, and to warrant flexible application of the rule. See Lee Pong Tai v. Acheson, 104 F.Supp. 503 (E.D.Pa. 1952) (26–year–old document admitted); Neustadt v. Coline Oil Co., 141 Okl. 113, 284 P. 52 (1929) (19 year-old document admitted under circumstances).

Age of a writing may be proved circumstantially by appearance and contents. Louden v. Apollo Gas Co., 273 Pa.Super. 549, 417 A.2d 1185 (1980); Kath v. Burlington Northern R. Co., 441 N.W.2d 569 (Minn.App.1989). The purported date of the document, while providing some evidence of age, is obviously not conclusive. In re McGary's Estate, 127 Colo. 495, 258 P.2d 770 (1953).

7. Stewart Oil Co. v. Sohio Petroleum Co., 202 F.Supp. 952 (E.D.Ill.1962) (alleged ancient document rejected as smacking of fraud); Apo v. Dillingham Investment Corp., 50 Hawaii 369, 440 P.2d 965 (1968) (misspelling of grantor's name and other irregularities; deeds excluded as suspicious); Muehrcke v. Behrens, 43 Wis.2d 1, 169 N.W.2d 86 (1969) ("When the instrument shows an alteration on its face it is the obligation of the party offering it to explain the alteration".); Roberts v. Waddell, 94 S.W.2d 211 (Tex.Civ.App.1936) (purported deed rejected because of mutilation and other reasons).

8. Matuszewski v. Pancoast, 38 Ohio App.3d 74, 526 N.E.2d 80 (1987) (requirement satisfied as to baptismal and marriage certificates found in Polish church

continue the rule but reduce the required documentary age to twenty years.[9] In addition to the foregoing requirements, some jurisdictions, if the writing is a dispositive one such as a deed or a will, impose the additional condition that possession must have been taken under the instrument.[10] The documents which may be authenticated under the rule here described, however, are not limited to dispositive instruments, and the rule has been applied to allow authentication of a wide variety of writings.[11]

In the case of a writing which purports to be executed by an agent, executor, or other person acting under power or authority from another, proof of the facts which authenticate the writing as an ancient document gives rise to a presumption that the person signing was duly authorized.[12]

It should be borne in mind that, despite the utility of the rule here discussed, it is merely a rule of authentication, the satisfaction of which does not necessarily guarantee the admission of the writing authenticated. Thus, it is sometimes forgotten that a writing may be proved perfectly genuine and yet remain inadmissible as being, e.g., hearsay or secondary evidence.[13] This source of confusion is compounded by a

where marriages and baptisms occurred). Compare Dartez v. Fibreboard Corp., 765 F.2d 456 (5th Cir.1985) (40 year old corporate memos inadmissible in absence of evidence that they were produced from expected locus, the corporate records).

9. Fed.R.Evid. 901(b)(3) supra § 218, note 1.

10. The concept underlying the possession requirement has more recently been reflected in statutory enactments creating presumptions of authenticity of aged documents which, in addition to the usual requirements for authentication, have been "acted upon" as genuine by persons having an interest in the matter. West's Ann.Cal. Evid.Code § 643. The strengthened inference of genuineness arising from the added circumstance of action on the instrument probably warrants treatment as a presumption. But such statutes need not be construed as rendering the raising of a presumption essential to admission, since the mere inference of authenticity should suffice for this purpose. See Devereaux v. Frazier Mountain Park & Fisheries Co., 248 Cal.App.2d 323, 56 Cal.Rptr. 345 (1967) (suggesting the conclusion here recommended on the basis of an arguably unnecessary flexible reading of the statute).

Conversely, failure to act may create suspicion sufficient to exclude. Hulihee v. Heirs of Hueu (K), 57 Hawaii 312, 555 P.2d 495 (1976) (not error to exclude ancient documents in bench trial where conduct of

grantor and grantee contradicted import of document).

11. See, e.g., United States v. Kairys, 782 F.2d 1374 (7th Cir.1986) (Personalbogen, or Waffen SS identity card, held properly authenticated as ancient document); Kirkpatrick v. Tapo Oil Co., 144 Cal. App.2d 404, 301 P.2d 274 (1956) (ledger entries); Trustees of German Township v. Farmers & Citizens Savings Bank Co., 66 Ohio L.Abs. 332, 113 N.E.2d 409 (App.1953) (old newspaper).

12. Wilson v. Snow, 228 U.S. 217 (1913) (deed of executrix; " * * * the ancient deed proves itself, whether it purports to have been signed by the grantor in his own right, as agent under power of attorney or—the original records having been lost— by an administrator under a power of sale given by order of court, not produced but recited in the deed itself"); Baumgarten v. Frost, 143 Tex. 533, 186 S.W.2d 982, 159 A.L.R. 428 (1945) (presumption recognized, but here receiver's assignment could not be presumed authorized where court's records intact and failed to show confirmation).

13. Town of Ninety–Six v. Southern Railway Co., 267 F.2d 579 (4th Cir.1959) ("The fact that an instrument is an ancient document does not affect its admissibility in evidence further than to dispense with proof of its genuineness"; ancient letter excluded as inadmissible hearsay); King v. Schultz, 141 Mont. 94, 375 P.2d 108 (1962) (" * * * ancient document rule does not change the basis for admission of evidence other than as to genuineness * * * ").

partial overlap between the requirements of the present rule and those of the distinct doctrine which holds that recitals in certain types of ancient instruments may be received as evidence of the facts recited.[14] The latter doctrine, however, constitutes an exception to the rule against hearsay and is quite distinct from the present rule concerning authentication. It is discussed in another place.[15]

The preferable and majority view is that satisfaction of the ancient document requirements will serve to authenticate an ancient copy of an original writing.[16] And a fresh certified copy of an instrument of record for thirty years will prove the ancient writing,[17] though perhaps with the additional qualification that before the copy can come in, the original documents rule must be satisfied by showing the unavailability of the original.[18] Admission of a writing as an ancient document does, however, dispense with the production of attesting witnesses.[19]

§ 224. Authentication by Circumstantial Evidence: (c) Custody [1]

If a writing purports to be an official report or record and is proved to have come from the proper public office where such official papers are kept, it is generally agreed that this authenticates the offered document as genuine.[2] This result is founded on the probability that the officers in custody of such records will carry out their public duty to receive or record only genuine official papers and reports, and thus it is the official duty to record and maintain the document, rather than the duty

14. The two doctrines are contrasted in Town of Ninety–Six v. Southern Railway Co., supra note 13. Numerous cases noting the distinction in connection with old maps and plats are found in Annot., 46 A.L.R.2d 1318 (admissibility of ancient maps and the like under the ancient document rule).

15. See § 323 infra.

16. Schell v. City of Jefferson, 357 Mo. 1020, 212 S.W.2d 430 (1948) (ancient copy of city plat, original not available, held improperly excluded, one judge dissenting); and see 7 Wigmore, Evidence § 2143 (Chadbourn rev. 1978) (supporting majority position and collecting older authorities). But some jurisdictions hold that the rule does not apply to copies. See Anderson v. Anderson, 150 Neb. 879, 36 N.W.2d 287 (1949) ("the rule applies only to original instruments * * * "); Solomon v. Beck, 387 S.W.2d 911 (Tex.Civ.App.1965) (examined copy of ancient instrument not admissible under rule).

17. See Hodge v. Palms, 117 Fed. 396 (6th Cir.1902); Solomon v. Beck, supra note 15. The certified copy of the long-recorded writing obviously has a stronger claim to

admissibility than the ancient unrecorded copy. See 7 Wigmore, Evidence § 2143 (Chadbourn rev. 1978).

18. Sudduth v. Central of Georgia Railway Co., 201 Ala. 56, 77 So. 350 (1917); Woods v. Bonner, 89 Tenn. 411, 18 S.W. 67 (1890); Emory v. Bailey, 111 Tex. 337, 234 S.W. 660, 662 (1921) ("on filing proper affidavit of loss," under statute). See § 240 infra.

19. See § 220 supra.

§ 224

1. 7 Wigmore, Evidence §§ 2158–2160 (Chadbourn rev. 1978); Dec.Dig. Evidence ⟊366, Criminal Law ⟊444.

2. United States v. Ward, 173 F.2d 628 (2d Cir.1949) (records from files of Selective Service, identified by custodian); Tameling v. Commissioner, 43 F.2d 814 (2d Cir.1930) (official assessment role shown to emanate from official custody admissible without further authentication); State v. Miller, 79 N.M. 117, 440 P.2d 792 (1968) (fingerprint record from F.B.I. file; stating rule in terms of above text). Fed.R.Evid. 901(b)(7) embodies the rule stated in the text.

to prepare it, which constitutes the document a public record.[3] Similarly, where a public office is the depository for private papers, such as wills, conveyances, or income tax returns, the proof that such a purporting deed, bill of sale, tax return or the like has come from the proper custody is usually accepted as sufficient authentication.[4] This again can be sustained on the same principle if it appears that the official custodian had a public duty to verify the genuineness of the papers offered for record or deposit and to accept only the genuine.

As is discussed in a subsequent section,[5] any need for testimonial proof of production from proper official custody is today frequently avoided by resort to certification procedures or "self-authentication." However, it is significant to note that such procedures are not exclusive or mandatory, and that proof of the facts necessary to secure admission of a public record may be made by any witness with competent knowledge.[6]

As is true with ancient documents, the question of the authenticity of official records should not be confused with the ultimate admissibility of such records. It is quite possible for a public record to be perfectly genuine, and yet remain inadmissible for some distinguishable reason, e.g., that it is excludable hearsay.[7]

Some question exists whether the rule which accepts, as prima facie genuine, documents which are shown to emerge from official custody

3. See United States v. Central Gulf Lines, Inc., 575 F.Supp. 1430 (E.D.La.1983) (documents prepared by foreign entities but required to be filed with U.S. government agency properly admissible as public records); Davis v. State, 772 S.W.2d 563 (Tex.App.—Waco 1989) (legal authority of state department of corrections to maintain records of judgments and sentences made documents admissible without certification by entering courts).

4. United States v. Olson, 576 F.2d 1267 (8th Cir.1978) (W–4E forms and tax returns purportedly filed by defendant; court dismisses suggestion forms filed by another D.D. Olson). Brooks v. Texas General Indemnity Co., 251 F.2d 15 (5th Cir.1958) (application for benefits produced from files of Veteran's Administration); Sternberg Dredging Co. v. Moran Towing & Transportation Co., Inc., 196 F.2d 1002 (2d Cir.1952) (letter report filed in compliance with statutory requirement and produced from official custody held improperly excluded; opinion by L. Hand, J.); Wausau Sulphate Fibre Co. v. Commissioner, 61 F.2d 879 (7th Cir.1932) (waiver bearing purported signature of taxpayer, from Bureau's files); Halko v. State, 58 Del. 383, 209 A.2d 895 (1965) (application for driver's license produced from official files admissible under local statutes). But compare State v. Stotts, 144 Ariz. 72, 695 P.2d 1110

(1985) (documents held not sufficiently authenticated by showing of retrieval from files of county attorney; "[I]t did not establish whether the County Attorney was a public office, whether the office had the authority to keep such records, whether the record was properly kept, nor whether the prosecutor had knowledge of these facts.").

5. See § 228 infra.

6. See United States v. Perlmuter, 693 F.2d 1290 (9th Cir.1982); Sunnyvale Maritime Co. v. Gomez, 546 So.2d 6 (Fla.App. 1989); State v. Thompson, 35 Wash.App. 766, 669 P.2d 1270 (1983). While the necessary testimony will most frequently be seen to be provided by the record's custodian, this also is not required. See Brien v. Wiley, 124 N.H. 573, 474 A.2d 1015 (1984) (error to exclude copies of public records made by party; any competent witness may provide necessary foundation).

7. See, e.g., Matthews v. United States, 217 F.2d 409 (5th Cir.1954) (statutorily required reports of sugar sales produced from government files properly identified but held inadmissible as hearsay); Wright v. Lewis, 777 S.W.2d 520 (Tex.App.—Corpus Christi 1989) (state counterparts to Fed. R.Evid. 901 and 902 concern authentication only and do not render hearsay admissible).

should be extended beyond the field of public duty and recognized as to writings found in private custody. Since the circumstances of private custody are infinitely more varied than those of public custody, a new rule in an already rule-ridden area seems inadvisable. No such rule, in fact, is needed, provided that, in their discretion, courts recognize that proof of private custody, together with other circumstances, is frequently strong circumstantial evidence of authenticity.[8]

§ 225. Authentication by Circumstantial Evidence: (d) Knowledge: Reply Letters and Telegrams[1]

When a letter, signed with the purported signature of X, is received "out of the blue," with no previous correspondence, the traditional "show me" skepticism of the common law trial practice[2] prevails, and the purported signature is not accepted as authentication,[3] unless authenticity is confirmed by additional facts.[4]

One circumstance recognized as sufficient is the fact that the letter discloses knowledge that only the purported signer would be likely to have.[5] Moreover, a convenient practice recognizes that if a letter has

8. Proof of private custody has frequently been so viewed. United States v. Black, 767 F.2d 1334 (9th Cir.1985) (production from defendant's custody sufficient authentication); Burgess v. Premier Corp., 727 F.2d 826 (9th Cir.1984) (semble); State v. Smith, 246 Ga. 129, 269 S.E.2d 21 (1980), on remand 156 Ga.App. 250, 274 S.E.2d 646 (possession of letter plus additional facts held sufficient to authenticate). Cf. People v. Manganaro, 218 N.Y. 9, 112 N.E. 436 (1916).

§ 225

1. 7 Wigmore, Evidence §§ 2148, 2153–2154 (Chadbourn rev. 1978); C.J.S. Evidence § 706b; Dec.Dig. Evidence ☞378, Criminal Law ☞444.

2. See § 218 supra.

3. Early v. State, 42 Ala.App. 200, 158 So.2d 495 (1963); Continental Baking Co. v. Katz, 68 Cal.2d 512, 67 Cal.Rptr. 761, 439 P.2d 889 (1968); Westland Distributing, Inc. v. Rio Grande Motorway, Inc., 38 Colo. App. 292, 555 P.2d 990 (1976) (stating rule as in text but admitting letter on basis of facts known to writer); State v. Golden, 67 Idaho 497, 186 P.2d 485 (1947). See also Harlow v. Commonwealth, 204 Va. 385, 131 S.E.2d 293 (1963) (unsigned telegram inadmissible without proof of authorship).

4. Greenbaum v. United States, 80 F.2d 113 (9th Cir.1935) (letter purporting to be signed for corporation by agent held authenticated by proof that person signing was agent of corporation and city of posting was the place of business of company);

Fuller v. State, 437 P.2d 772 (Alaska 1968), affirmed 393 U.S. 80 (telegram admissible where proved to have been paid for by occupant of room, and defendant was shown to have been occupant); Cotton States Mutual Insurance Co. v. Clark, 114 Ga.App. 439, 151 S.E.2d 780 (1966) (surrounding circumstances, including facts that letter was on defendant's letterhead and contract was on defendant's form, sufficient for authentication).

5. United States v. Lam Muk Chiu, 522 F.2d 330 (2d Cir.1975) (letters referring to prior agreement of defendant with narcotics informer); United States v. Sutton, 426 F.2d 1202 (D.C.Cir.1969) (notes suggesting defendant's plan for murder-suicide held authenticated where subsequent events observed by eyewitnesses followed note's predictions); Westland Distributing, Inc. v. Rio Grande Motorway, Inc., 38 Colo.App. 292, 555 P.2d 990 (1976) (letter disclosing knowledge unique to purported author and sent in response to phone conversation between addressee and purported author); People v. Munoz, 70 Ill.App.3d 76, 26 Ill. Dec. 509, 388 N.E.2d 133 (1979) (letter from jail bearing defendant's nickname and cell number and referring to facts then known to only four people held sufficient to authenticate; not necessary to disprove possible authorship by all others); State v. Milum, 202 Kan. 196, 447 P.2d 801, 803 (1968) ("Proof of the genuineness of a letter may be established when the contents themselves reveal knowledge peculiarly referable to a certain person * * * "); Champion

been written to X, and the letter now offered in evidence purports to be written by X and purports to be a reply to the first letter (that is either refers to it, or is responsive to its terms) and has been received without unusual delay, these facts authenticate it as a reply letter.[6] This result may be rested upon the knowledge-principle, mentioned above. In view of the regularity of the mails the first letter would almost invariably come exclusively into the hands of X, or those authorized to act for him, who would alone know of the terms of the letter. It is supported also by the fact that in common experience we know that reply letters do come from the person addressed in the first letter.

Considerations concerning reliability of the mails are significant only to demonstrate the likelihood that the purported author of the response did in fact receive the original communication. Thus, where receipt of the communication referred to in the reply can be established by other means, and the reply is timely received, these facts will be sufficient to authenticate.[7]

These same arguments apply to reply telegrams, but with a reduced degree of certainty. Some of the employees of the telegraph company, as well as the addressee, know the contents of the first telegram. Moreover, the instances of misdelivery of telegrams may be more numerous relatively than misdeliveries of letters. These considerations have led some courts to reject for reply telegrams this theory of authentication.[8] The contrary view, that the inference of authenticity of the reply telegram is substantial and sufficient,[9] seems more reasonable and expedient.

---

v. Champion, 368 Mich. 84, 117 N.W.2d 107 (1962) (knowledge of recipient's itinerary on European tour and of letters received at other points held circumstances indicating authenticity); State v. Porambo, 226 N.J.Super. 416, 544 A.2d 870 (1988) (letters revealing knowledge of extensive list of details of defendant's personal history); Casto v. Martin, 159 W.Va. 761, 230 S.E.2d 722 (1976) (typewritten memo relating details of complex business transaction known only to defendant; authentication sufficient where defendant did not deny authorship); Annot., 9 A.L.R. 984. After a letter is written a statement about its contents may identify the declarant as the writer. See Deaderick v. Deaderick, 182 Ga. 96, 185 S.E. 89 (1936). See Fed.R.Evid. 901(b)(4) supra § 218, note 1.

6. Winel v. United States, 365 F.2d 646, 648 (8th Cir.1966) ("* * * one of the principal situations where the authenticity of a letter is provable by circumstantial evidence arising out of the letter's context * * * is where it can be shown that the letter was sent in reply to a previous communication."); Purer & Co. v. Aktiebolaget Addo, 410 F.2d 871 (9th Cir.1969); Namerdy v. Generalcar, 217 A.2d 109 (D.C.App.

1966); Whelton v. Daly, 93 N.H. 150, 37 A.2d 1 (1944) (Page, J.: "It is a fair inference, considering the habitual accuracy of the mails, that the letter addressed to B reached the real B, and that an answer referring to the contents of A's letter and coming back in due course of mail, leaves only a negligible chance that any other than B has become acquainted with the contents of A's letter so as to forge a reply.").

7. Washington v. State, 539 So.2d 1089 (Ala.Crim.App.1988) (replies collected from defendant's truck referring to letters personally delivered to defendant by intermediaries held authenticated by analogy to reply letter doctrine); Milner Hotels, Inc. v. Mecklenburg Hotel, 42 N.C.App. 179, 256 S.E.2d 310 (1979) (mailgram referring in detail to contents of earlier authenticated phone conversation held authenticated).

8. Smith v. Easton, 54 Md. 138, 146, 39 Am.St.Rep. 355 (1880); Howley v. Whipple, 48 N.H. 487, 488 (1869).

9. House Grain Co. v. Finerman & Sons, 116 Cal.App.2d 485, 253 P.2d 1034 (1953) (reply telegram held "self-authenti-

When the reply letter purports to be signed by an agent or other representative of X, the addressee of the first letter, the authority of the signing representative is presumed.[10]

The first step in authentication of the reply letter is to prove that the first letter was dated and was duly mailed at a given time and place addressed to X.[11] Seemingly oral testimony to these facts should suffice as to the first letter if the reply letter refers to it by date.[12] If, however, the reply letter only refers to it by reciting or responding to its terms, then since the terms of the first letter become important,[13] probably it would be necessary to satisfy the Best Evidence Rule. If X, as usually would be the case, is the party-opponent, and has the first letter in his hands, it would be necessary to give him notice to produce it, before a copy could be used to prove its terms.[14]

§ 226. Authentication by Circumstantial Evidence: (e) Telephone Messages and Other Oral Communications [1]

Modern technology makes commonplace the receipt of oral communications from persons who are heard but not seen. The problems of authentication raised by these communications are substantively analogous to the problems of authenticating writings. Thus, if the witness has received, e.g., a telephone call out of the blue from one who identified himself as "X", this is not sufficient authentication of the call as in fact coming from X.[2] The requisite additional proof may take the form of testimony by the witness that he is familiar with X's voice and that the caller was X.[3] Or authentication may be accomplished by

cating"); Peterman v. Vermont Savings Bank, 181 La. 403, 159 So. 598 (1935); Annot. 5 A.L.R.3d 1018. The same principle, of course, should serve to authenticate telegrams in response to letters and vice versa. See Menefee v. Bering Manufacturing Co., 166 S.W. 365 (Tex.Civ.App.1914) (telegram received in response to letter admitted).

10. Reliance Life Insurance Co. v. Russell, 208 Ala. 559, 94 So. 748 (1922) (to rebut presumption of genuineness of reply letter not sufficient to show that purported sender did not sign it but must show that he did not authorize another to sign for him); Capitol City Supply Co. v. Beury, 69 W.Va. 612, 72 S.E. 657 (1911) (similar to last); Anstine v. McWilliams, 24 Wash.2d 230, 163 P.2d 816 (1945) (authority of purported agent, signing for principal presumed; full discussion and citations); Dec.Dig.Evidence ☜378(3).

11. Consolidated Grocery Co. v. Hammond, 99 C.C.A. 195, 175 Fed. 641 (5th Cir.1910) (statement in purported reply letter referring to previous letter does not suffice); Kvale v. Keane, 39 N.D. 560, 168 N.W. 74 (1918) (must make preliminary

proof that first letter was duly addressed, stamped and posted).

12. See § 233 infra.

13. See § 233 infra.

14. See § 239 supra.

§ 226

1. 7 Wigmore, Evidence § 2155 (Chadbourn rev. 1978); Annot., 79 A.L.R.3d 79; Dec.Dig.Evidence ☜148; 29 Am.Jur.2d Evidence §§ 380–386; C.J.S. Evidence § 188.

2. State v. Williams, 64 Ohio App.2d 271, 413 N.E.2d 1212 (1979) (self-identification by caller insufficient authentication in criminal case); Texas Candy & Nut Co. v. Horton, 235 S.W.2d 518, 521 (Tex.Civ.App. 1950) ("When the party called over a telephone depends entirely upon the word of the party calling as to his identity, the conversation is * * * inadmissible.").

3. People v. Patten, 105 Ill.App.3d 892, 61 Ill.Dec. 682, 435 N.E.2d 171 (1982); Ingle v. Allen, 69 N.C.App. 192, 317 S.E.2d 1 (1984). The familiarity with a voice necessary to authenticate by voice identification may be acquired subsequent to the call.

circumstantial evidence pointing to X's identity as the caller,[4] such as if the communication received reveals that the speaker had knowledge of facts that only X would be likely to know.[5] These same modes of authentication are also recognized where communications have been received [6] by radio.

Whatever the means of transmission, oral communications today will frequently be perpetuated in some type of recording.[7] Where such is the case the authentication of the communication is likely to be facilitated simply because otherwise unavailable proof of various kinds may be generated by use of the recording.[8] However, it must be constantly born in mind that authentication does not necessarily equate with admissibility, and that recordings will often raise evidentiary problems other than authentication.[9]

A somewhat easier problem is presented when the witness testifies that she placed a telephone call to a number listed to X, and that the person answering identified himself as X.[10] In such a situation the accuracy of the telephone system, the probable absence of motive to falsify and the lack of opportunity for premeditated fraud all tend to support the conclusion that the self-identification of the speaker is

United States v. Watson, 594 F.2d 1330 (10th Cir.1979); Ex parte Favors, 437 So.2d 1370 (Ala.1983). Authentication by voice identification is treated in Fed.R.Evid. 901(b)(5), supra § 218, note 1.

4. Jackson v. State, 12 Ark.App. 378, 677 S.W.2d 866 (1984) (received call held sufficiently authenticated by circumstantial evidence that purported caller arrived at time and place agreed on during call); State v. Gardner, 743 S.W.2d 472 (Mo.App. 1987) (purported caller stated that his lawyer would call, which call subsequently was received); Robinson v. Branch Brook Manor Apartments, 101 N.J.Super. 117, 243 A.2d 284 (1968) ("preferred rule" allows authentication by circumstantial evidence, including events occurring both before and after call).

5. Santora, McKay & Ranieri v. Franklin, 79 N.C.App. 585, 339 S.E.2d 799 (1986) (call authenticated by circumstances including caller's possession of information "known peculiarly" to defendant); People v. Lynes, 64 A.D.2d 543, 406 N.Y.S.2d 816 (1978) (detective called defendant and left message he wished defendant to call back; return call held sufficiently authenticated); State v. Nickles, 728 P.2d 123 (Utah 1986) (call indicated knowledge of subject matter only possessed by named party). But compare Smithers v. Light, 305 Pa. 141, 157 A. 489 (1931) (caller purporting to be customer X of brokerage house orders sale of designated stocks held by broker; authentication held insufficient without adverting to knowledge factor).

6. LeRoy v. Sabena Belgian World Airlines, 344 F.2d 266 (2d Cir.1965) (radio transmission from airliner prior to crash held authenticated by equivocal voice identification plus circumstantial evidence); United States v. Sansone, 231 F.2d 887 (2d Cir.1956) (incriminating comments of defendant transmitted over concealed transmitter held authenticated by voice identification plus long range visual identification).

7. See, e.g., State v. Robinson, 38 Wash. App. 871, 691 P.2d 213 (1984) (telephone answering device); Hunt v. State, 312 Md. 494, 540 A.2d 1125 (1988) (tapes of police radio transmissions); People v. Siler, 171 Mich.App. 246, 429 N.W.2d 865 (1988) (recording of 911 call). Cases are collected in Annot., 58 A.L.R.2d 1024.

8. United States v. Sliker, 751 F.2d 477 (2d Cir.1984) (authentication by judge's comparison of voice with defendant's spoken testimony at trial; opinion by Friendly, J., suggests the innovative analogy of authentication of handwriting by exemplars); State v. Rinck, 303 N.C. 551, 280 S.E.2d 912 (1981) (tape recording of call to sheriff authenticated by relatives of speaker). Use of spectrographic analysis for voice identification purposes is treated in § 207 supra.

9. See, e.g., § 214 supra, Ch. 23 infra.

10. See Johnson v. Chilcott, 658 F.Supp. 1213 (D.Colo.1987) (distinguishing incoming and outgoing calls from the standpoint of susceptibility to fraud).

reliable. Thus most courts today view proof of proper placing of a call plus self-identification of the speaker as sufficient proof of authenticity to admit the substance of the call.[11] Moreover, it is likewise held that where it is shown that the witness has called the listed number of a business establishment and spoken with someone purporting to speak for the concern, with respect to matters within its ordinary course of business, it is presumed that the speaker was authorized to speak for the employer.[12]

§ 227. Functions of Judge and Jury in Authentication [1]

If direct testimony of the authorship of a writing or of an oral statement is given, this is sufficient authentication and the judge has no problem on that score.[2] The writing or statement comes in,[3] if not otherwise objectionable. When the authenticating evidence is circumstantial, however, the question whether reasonable men could find its authorship as claimed by the proponent, may be a delicate and balanced one, as to which the judge must be accorded some latitude of judgment.[4] Accordingly, it is often said to be a matter of discretion.[5] It

---

11. United States v. Hines, 717 F.2d 1481 (4th Cir.1983) (phone call sufficiently authenticated where person answering identified himself as "Ronnie," phone was listed in defendant's parents' name, and defendant was at the house when visited by DEA investigator; court notes that provisions of Fed.R.Evid. 901(b)(6) are "by way of illustration only"); Palos v. United States, 416 F.2d 438 (5th Cir.1969) (government informer shown to have dialed listed number, asked for defendant and received answer, "This is he"; sufficient to authenticate); United States v. Benjamin, 328 F.2d 854 (2d Cir.1964) (applying rule that proper dialing plus self-identification of party call constitute prima facie authentication); United States v. Scully, 546 F.2d 255 (9th Cir.1976) (semble). See Fed. R.Evid. 901(b)(6), supra § 218, note 1.

12. Crist v. Pennsylvania Railroad Co., 96 F.Supp. 243, 245 (W.D.Pa.1951) (" * * * one who answers a telephone call from the place of business of the person called for, and undertakes to respond as his agent, is presumed to have authority to speak for him in respect to the general business there carried on and conducted."); Ratliff v. City of Great Falls, 132 Mont. 89, 314 P.2d 880 (1957) (presumption of authority in absence of affirmative proof of wrong connection or officious intermeddler); Fielding Home for Funerals v. Public Savings Life Insurance Co., 271 S.C. 117, 245 S.E.2d 238, 240 (1978) ("[A] business by installing a telephone and impliedly inviting its use for business communications, creates a prima facie presumption that the

person who answers and responds in regard to its ordinary business is authorized to speak in such matters"); Group Life and Health Ins. Co. v. Turner, 620 S.W.2d 670 (Tex.Civ.App.—Dallas 1981). The rule applies even lacking any indication of the identity of the answerer. Lynn v. Farm Bureau Mutual Auto Insurance Co., 264 F.2d 921 (4th Cir.1959). While the probabilities of the situation alone adequately support the rule, it is sometimes said to rest upon the agency principle of apparent authority. Sauber v. Northland Insurance Co., 251 Minn. 237, 87 N.W.2d 591 (1958). This latter justification, however, may possibly generate unfortunate limitations on the rule.

§ 227

1. Dec.Dig. Evidence ⟷382; C.J.S. Evidence §§ 624, 625.

2. See §§ 219–221 supra.

3. See Epperson v. State, 600 P.2d 1051 (Wyo.1979) (receipt for sale of property defendant charged with converting admitted authentic by complaining witness; error to exclude on ground witness claimed to have been drunk when he signed).

4. See §§ 222–226 supra.

5. United States v. Sutton, 426 F.2d 1202 (D.C.Cir.1969) (determination of admissibility by trial court held largely discretionary); United States v. Caldwell, 776 F.2d 989 (11th Cir.1985) (trial court decisions on authenticity within discretionary function under Fed.R.Evid.), Lundgren v.

must be noticed, however, that authenticity is not to be classed as one of those preliminary questions of fact conditioning admissibility under technical evidentiary rules of competency or privilege. As to these latter, the trial judge will permit the adversary to introduce controverting proof on the preliminary issue in support of his objection, and the judge will decide this issue, without submission to the jury, as a basis for his ruling on admissibility.[6] On the other hand, the authenticity of a writing or statement is not a question of the application of a technical rule of evidence. It goes to genuineness and conditional relevance, as the jury can readily understand. Thus, if a prima facie showing is made, the writing or statement comes in, and the ultimate question of authenticity is left to the jury.[7]

§ 228. Escapes From the Requirement of Producing Evidence of Authenticity: Modern Theory and Practice

As the foregoing sections clearly imply, the authentication of writings and other communications by formal proof may prove troublesome, time consuming, and expensive even in cases where no legitimate doubt concerning genuineness would appear to exist. The ultimate explanation for the continuing insistence upon the furnishing of such proof, justifiable only upon assumptions which accord very little with common sense, is of course obscure. It may be speculated, however that in part the explanation is to be found in various procedural devices which afford escape from authentication requirements. Use of these devices will avert some of the impatience which might otherwise be engendered by formal authentication requirements. The legislatures, too, have frequently nibbled at the problem by enacting statutes relieving the rigors of authentication in what would otherwise be particularly troublesome contexts. Among these "escapes from authentication," the following are particularly noteworthy.

Requests for Admission.[1] Under the practice in the Federal courts as provided by Rules 36 and 37(c) of the Federal Rules of Civil Procedure, and under analogous rules or statutes in many states, a party may serve upon an adversary a written request for admission of the genuine-

---

Union Indemnity Co., 171 Minn. 122, 213 N.W. 553 (1927) (exclusion of telegrams, where more convincing evidence of authenticity available, not abuse of discretion).

6. See § 53 supra.

7. Adv.Com.Notes, Fed.R.Evid. 104(a) and (b) and 901(a). Authentication under the Federal Rules of Evidence is exhaustively discussed by Friendly, J., in United States v. Sliker, 751 F.2d 477 (2d Cir.1984). See also United States v. Goichman, 547 F.2d 778 (3d Cir.1976) (only prima facie showing of authenticity necessary for admission); Inland USA, Inc. v. Reed Stenhouse, Inc., 660 S.W.2d 727 (Mo.App.1983) (by determining sufficiency of authentica-

tion, court does not decide ultimate issue of genuineness).

In a multi-party action, authentication as against one party renders the document admissible against all. In re Japanese Electronic Products Antitrust Litigation, 723 F.2d 238 (3d Cir.1983) (reversing trial court ruling that authentication was valid only as against particular parties), reversed on other grounds sub nom. Matsushita Elec. Ind. Co., Ltd. v. Zenith Radio Corp., 475 U.S. 574.

§ 228

1. Wright, The Law of Federal Courts § 89 (4th ed. 1983).

ness of any relevant document described in the request. If the adversary unreasonably fails within a specified time to serve an answer or objection, genuineness is admitted. If genuineness is denied and the requesting party thereafter proves the genuineness of the document at trial, the latter may apply for an order of court requiring the adversary to pay her the reasonable costs of making the authenticating proof.

Securing Admission at Pretrial Conference.[2] Under Rule 16 in the Federal courts and under analogous rules and statutes in many states, it is provided that a pretrial conference of the attorneys may be called by the court to consider among other things, "the possibility of obtaining admissions of fact and of documents which will avoid unnecessary proof." Of course, similar stipulations often are secured in informal negotiation between counsel, but a skilful judge may create at a pretrial conference an atmosphere of mutual concession unusually favorable for such admissions. This function of the pretrial practice has been considered one of its most successful features.

Statutes and Rules Requiring Special or Sworn Denial of Genuineness of Writing. A provision of practice acts and rules of procedure may require that when an action is brought upon a written instrument, such as a note or contract, copied in the complaint, the genuineness of the writing will be deemed admitted unless a sworn denial be included in the answer.[3]

Writings Which "Prove Themselves:" Acknowledged Documents, Certified Copies, and Law Books Which Purport to be Printed by Authority. There are certain kinds of writings which are said to "prove themselves" or to be "self-identifying." In consequence one of these may be tendered to the court and, even without the shepherding angel of an authenticating witness, will be accepted in evidence for what it purports to be. This convenient result is reached in two stages. First, by statutes which often provide that certain classes of writings, usually in some manner purporting to be vouched for by an official, shall be received in evidence "without further proof." This helpful attribute is most commonly given by these statutes to (1) deeds, conveyances or other instruments, which have been acknowledged by the signers before a notary public,[4] (2) certified copies of public records,[5] and (3) books of

---

2. Id. at § 91.

3. See, e.g., Ariz.R.Civ.Pro., Rule 9(i)6.

4. West's Ann.Cal.Evid.Code § 1451 ("A certificate of the acknowledgment of a writing other than a will, or a certificate of the proof of such a writing, is prima facie evidence of the facts recited in the certificate and the genuineness of the signature of each person by whom the writing purports to have been signed, if the certificate meets [designated statutory requirements]."; Ky.Rev.Stat. 422.100 (1988) ("All instruments of writing required by law to be notarized, that are notarized, shall be received as evidence without further authentication."). Statutes of this general variety are collected in 5 Wigmore, Evidence § 1676 (Chadbourn rev. 1974) and are discussed in Tracy, Introduction of Documentary Evidence, 24 Iowa L.Rev. 436, 439 (1939). See Fed.R.Evid. 902(8), supra § 218, note 1.

5. The doctrine and statutes are discussed in 5 Wigmore, Evidence § 1677 (Chadbourn rev. 1974). Dec.Dig.Evidence ⟐338–349 collects cases. See Fed.R.Evid. 902(4), supra § 218, note 1.

statutes which purport to be printed by public authority.[6]

But in the first two of these classes of writings, which can qualify only when the acknowledgment is certified by a notary or the copy certified by the official who has custody of the record, how is the court to know without proof that the signature or seal appearing on the writing is actually that of the official whose name and title are recited? This second step is supplied by the traditional doctrines which recognize the seal or signature of certain types of officers, including the keeper of the seal of state, judicial officers, and notaries public, as being of themselves sufficient evidence of the genuineness of the certificate.[7] Moreover in many state codes particular provisions supplement or clarify tradition by specifying that the seals or signatures of certain classes of officialdom shall have this self-authenticating effect.[8]

Federal Rules of Evidence. The concept of self-authentication, previously recognized by statute in the case of the certain relatively limited classes of writings noted above, is given an expanded ambit of operation by the Federal Rules of Evidence. Rule 902 accords prima facie authenticity not only to those types of writings such as acknowledged writings and public records which have commonly enjoyed such treatment by statute but also to various other types of writings not previously so favored. Among these new classes of self-authenticating writings are included books, pamphlets and other publications issued by public authority, newspapers and periodicals, and trade inscriptions and labels indicating ownership, control or origin.[9] Presumptive authenticity, as provided for by the rule, does not preclude evidentiary challenge of the genuineness of the offered writing, but simply serves to obviate the necessity of preliminary authentication by the proponent to secure admission. This commonsense approach was long overdue and might well be extended to apply to all writings purporting to have a connec-

---

6. Statutes are compiled in 5 Wigmore, Evidence § 1684 (Chadbourn rev. 1974). Their most frequent and useful employment is in the proof of statutes of sister states and of foreign countries, see § 335 infra.

7. The history and theory of the subject are reviewed and the decisions and statutes collected in 7 Wigmore, Evidence §§ 2161–2168 (Chadbourn rev. 1978).

8. See, e.g., the Uniform Acknowledgment Act, 14 U.L.A. 201 which attributes self-authenticating effect to acknowledgments taken by officers of the state in which the document is offered, and officers of the United States acting outside the country. Other statutes are collected in 7 Wigmore, Evidence §§ 2162, 2167 (Chadbourn rev. 1978).

9. Government publications: California Ass'n of Bioanalysts v. Rank, 577 F.Supp. 1342 (C.D.Cal.1983) (USDHHS report self-authenticating under Fed.R.Evid. 902(5) by virtue of facsimile seal on cover); Schneider v. Cessna Aircraft Co., 150 Ariz. 153, 722 P.2d 321 (App.1985) (FAA videotape self-authenticating due to official seal at start of tape). Newspapers and periodicals: Snyder v. Whittaker Corp., 839 F.2d 1085 (5th Cir.1988) (magazine article self-authenticating under Fed.R.Evid. 902(6); State v. Banta, 188 N.J.Super. 115, 456 A.2d 119 (1982) (noting absence of state counterpart to 902(6) but admitting newspaper based upon appearance and feel as a newspaper). Trade inscriptions: State v. Rines, 269 A.2d 9 (Me.1970) (relying upon proposed version of 902(7) in holding that the manufacturer's certificate made a sufficient prima facie case of the contents of swab and tubes in a kit designed for drawing and preservation of blood).

tion with the party against whom offered.[10]

The concept of self-authentication was subsequently extended dramatically in federal criminal proceedings by enactment of a statute which confers self-authenticating effect on foreign records of regularly conducted activity which are certified by the custodian in accordance with the statute.[11] This development in turn motivated the Conference of Commissioners on Uniform State Laws to amend Uniform Rule 902 to provide for self-authentication of "certified" business records, domestic as well as foreign.[12]

10. Broun, Authentication and Contents of Writings, 1969 Law & Soc. Order 611; Strong, Liberalizing the Authentication of Private Writings, 52 Cornell L.Q. 284 (1967).

11. 18 U.S.C.A. § 3506 provides:

(a)(1) In a criminal proceeding in a court of the United States, a foreign record of regularly conducted activity, or a copy of such record, shall not be excluded as evidence by the hearsay rule if a foreign certification attests that—

(A) such record was made, at or near the time of the occurrence of the matters set forth, by (or from information transmitted by) a person with knowledge of those matters;

(B) such record was kept in the course of a regularly conducted business activity;

(C) the business activity made such a record as a regular practice; and

(D) if such record is not the original, such record is a duplicate of the original; unless the source of information or the method or circumstances of preparation indicate lack of trustworthiness.

(2) A foreign certification under this section shall authenticate such record or duplicate.

(b) At the arraignment or as soon after the arraignment as practicable, a party intending to offer in evidence under this section shall provide written notice of that intention to each other party. A motion opposing admission in evidence of such record shall be made by the opposing party and determined by the court before trial. Failure by a party to file such motion before trial shall constitute a waiver of objection to such record or duplicate, but the court for cause shown may grant relief from the waiver.

(c) As used in this section, the term—

(1) "foreign record of regularly conducted activity" means a memorandum, report, record, or data compilation, in any form, of acts, events, conditions, opinions, or diagnoses, maintained in a foreign country;

(2) "foreign certification" means a written declaration made and signed in a foreign country by the custodian of a foreign record of regularly conducted activity or another qualified person that, if falsely made, would subject the maker to criminal penalty under the laws of that country; and

(3) "business" includes business, institution, association, profession, occupation, and calling of every kind, whether or not conducted for profit.

12. Uniform Rule of Evidence 902(11) reads:

Certified records of regularly conducted activity. The original or a duplicate of a record of regularly conducted activity, within the scope of Rule 803(6), which the custodian thereof or another qualified individual certifies (i) was made, at or near the time of the occurrence of the matters set forth, by (or from information transmitted by) a person with knowledge of those matters, (ii) is kept in the course of the regularly conducted activity, and (iii) was made by the regularly conducted activity as a regular practice, unless the sources of information or the method or circumstances of preparation indicate lack of trustworthiness; but a record so certified is not self-authenticating under this subsection unless the proponent makes his or her intention to offer it known to the adverse party and makes it available for inspection sufficiently in advance of its offer in evidence to provide the adverse party with a fair opportunity to challenge it. As used in this subsection "certifies" means with respect to a domestic record, a written declaration under oath subject to the penalty of perjury and, with respect to a foreign record, a written declaration signed in a foreign country which, if falsely made, would subject the maker to criminal penalty under the laws of that country. The certificate relating to a foreign record must be accompanied by a final certification as to the genuineness of the signature and official position (i) of the individual executing the certificate or (ii) of any foreign official who certifies the genuineness of signature and official position of the executing individual or is the last in a chain of certificates that collectively certify the genuineness of signature and official position of the executing person. A final certification may be made by a secretary of embassy or legation, consul general, consul, vice consul, or consular agent of the United States, or a diplomatic or consular official of the foreign country who is assigned or accredited to the United States.

Chapter 23

THE REQUIREMENT OF THE PRODUCTION OF THE ORIGINAL WRITING AS THE "BEST EVIDENCE"

Table of Sections

§ 229. The "Best Evidence" Rule

Thayer[1] tells us that the first appearance of the "best evidence" phrase, is a statement in 1700 by Holt, C.J. (in a case in which he admitted evidence questioned as secondary) to the effect that "the best proof that the nature of the thing will afford is only required."[2] This statement given as a reason for receiving evidence, that it is the best which can be had—a highly liberalizing principle—not surprisingly gives birth to a converse and narrowing doctrine that a man must produce the best evidence that is available—second-best will not do. And so before 1726 we find Baron Gilbert in one of the earliest treatises on Evidence saying, "the first and most signal rule in relation to evidence is this, that a man must have the utmost evidence the nature of the fact is capable of * * *."[3] Blackstone continues the same broad generalizing and combines both the positive and negative aspects of the "best evidence" idea when he says, " * * * the best evidence the nature of the case will admit of shall always be required, if possible to be had; but if not possible then the best evidence that can be had shall be allowed."[4] Greenleaf in this country in 1842 was still repeating these wide abstractions.[5]

Thayer, however, writing in 1898, points out that these broad principles, though they had some influence in shaping specific evidence rules in the 1700s, were never received as adequate or accurate statements of governing rules, and that actually "the chief illustration of the Best Evidence principle, the doctrine that if you would prove the contents of a writing, you must produce the writing itself" is an ancient rule far older than any notion about the "best" evidence.[6] While some modern opinions still refer to the "best evidence" notion as if it were today a general governing legal principle[7] most would adopt the view of mod-

§ 229

1. Thayer, Preliminary Treatise on Evidence at the Common Law 489 (1898).

2. Ford v. Hopkins, 1 Salk. 283, 91 Eng. Rep. 250 (1700).

3. Gilbert, Evidence (2d ed.) 4, 15–17, quoted Thayer, op. cit. 490.

4. Blackstone, Commentaries 368, quoted Thayer op. cit. 491.

5. 1 Greenleaf, Evidence Part 2, ch. 4, §§ 82–97 (1842), quoted and analyzed in Thayer, op. cit., 484–487.

6. Arnett v. Helvie, 148 Ind.App. 476, 267 N.E.2d 864 (1971) (principle relied upon to uphold exclusion of expert testimo-ny as to yield of farm; court states testimony of tenant farmers would have been best evidence); Matter of Fortney's Estate, 5 Kan.App.2d 14, 611 P.2d 599 (1980) (no abuse of discretion to exclude evidence on ground other more reliable evidence existed); Thayer, op. cit. 497–506.

7. Padgett v. Brezner, 359 S.W.2d 416, 422 (Mo.App.1962) (" * * * the best evidence of which the case in its nature is susceptible and which is in the power of the party to produce, or is capable of being produced must always be produced in proof of every disputed fact;" rule applied to writing but said also to control operation of hearsay rule).

ern textwriters[8] that there is no such general rule.[9] The only actual rule that the "best evidence" phrase denotes today is the rule requiring the production of the original writing.[10]

§ 230. Original Document Rule[1]

The specific context in which it is generally agreed that the best evidence principle is applicable today should be definitely stated and its limits clearly defined. The rule is this: in proving the terms of a writing, where the terms are material, the original writing must be produced unless it is shown to be unavailable for some reason other than the serious fault of the proponent. The discussion in the following sections is directed to adding content to this basic framework.

8. See 4 Wigmore, Evidence § 1174 (Chadbourn rev. 1972). See also Maguire, Evidence: Common Sense and Common Law 32 (1947); 2 Morgan, Basic Problems of Evidence 332 (1954); Comment, 14 Ark. L.Rev. 153 (1959) (pointing out a consistent broader application essentially impracticable).

9. See, e.g., People of Territory of Guam v. Ojeda, 758 F.2d 403 (9th Cir.1985); Chandler v. United States, 318 F.2d 356 (10th Cir.1963) (rule held not to require production of whiskey bottles alleged not to have carried federal revenue stamps); Meyer v. State, 218 Ark. 440, 236 S.W.2d 996 (1951) ("The best evidence rule deals with writings alone * * *;" rule held not to require production of piece of bologna); State v. Dow, 392 A.2d 532 (Me.1978) (rule did not apply to require production of lobsters alleged to be less than 3³⁄₁₆ inches); State ex rel. Alderson v. Holbert, 137 W.Va. 883, 74 S.E.2d 772 (1953) (semble).

10. Buffalo Insurance Co. v. United Parking Stations, Inc., 277 Minn. 134, 152 N.W.2d 81 (1967) (the rule applies only to writings and is not a broad general principle applicable throughout the law of evidence).

As a moral argument, however, which may be marshaled on many evidence questions, the idea still has appeal. "* * * The fact that any given way of proof is all that a man has must be a strong argument for receiving it if it be in a fair degree probative; and the fact that a man does not produce the best evidence in his power must always afford strong ground of suspicion." Thayer, op. cit. 507. The "best evidence" notion has sometimes been given as a reason for admitting hearsay evidence when it is the most reliable which can be procured. See, e.g., Edwards v. Swilley, 196 Ark. 633, 118 S.W.2d 584 (1938). Contra: Fordson Coal Co. v. Vanover, 291 Ky. 447, 164 S.W.2d 966 (1942).

The effect of failure to call witnesses or to produce evidence is discussed in § 272, infra.

§ 230

1. 4 Wigmore, Evidence §§ 1177–1282 (Chadbourn rev. 1972); Dec.Dig.Crim.Law ⚷398–403, Evidence ⚷157–187; 32A C.J.S. Evidence, §§ 776–850; 29 Am.Jur.2d Evidence §§ 448–492. See also Model Code of Evidence Rule 602, and the comments thereon in Rogers, The Best Evidence Rule, 1945 Wis.L.Rev. 278.

Fed.R.Evid. 1002 states the basic rule as follows:

> To prove the content of a writing, recording, or photograph, the original writing, recording, or photograph is required, except as otherwise provided in these rules or by Act of Congress.

Rule 1001(3) defines the term "original:"

> An "original" of a writing or recording is the writing or recording itself or any counterpart intended to have the same effect by a person executing or issuing it. An "original" of a photograph includes the negative or any print therefrom. If data are stored in a computer or similar device, any printout or other output readable by sight, shown to reflect the data accurately, is an "original".

The corresponding provisions of the Revised Uniform Rules (1974) are identical, except that Rule 1002 has changes appropriate for state use.

§ 231. The Reasons for the Rule

Since its inception in the early 18th century, various rationales have been asserted to underlie the "best evidence rule." Many older writers have asserted that the rule is essentially directed to the prevention of fraud.[1] Wigmore, however, vigorously attacked this thesis on the analytical ground that it does not square with certain recognized applications and non-applications of the rule.[2] Most modern commentators follow his lead in asserting that the basic premise justifying the rule is the central position which the written word occupies in the law.[3] Because of this centrality, presenting to a court the exact words of a writing is of more than average importance, particularly in the case of operative or dispositive instruments such as deeds, wills or contracts, where a slight variation of words may mean a great difference in rights. In addition, it is to be considered (1) that there has been substantial hazard of inaccuracy in some of the commonly utilized methods of making copies of writings, and (2) oral testimony purporting to give from memory the terms of a writing is probably subject to a greater risk of error than oral testimony concerning other situations generally. The danger of mistransmitting critical facts which accompanies the use of written copies or recollection, but which is largely avoided when an original writing is presented to prove its terms, justifies preference for original documents.[4]

At the same time, however, it would appear a mistake totally to disregard all other justifications for the rule. It has long been observed that the opportunity to inspect original writings may be of substantial importance in the detection of fraud.[5] At least a few modern courts

§ 231

1. 1 Greenleaf, Evidence 93 (1842); 1 Starkie, Evidence 387 (5th Am. ed. 1834); 1 Taylor, Evidence § 391 (1887).

2. 4 Wigmore, Evidence § 1180 (Chadbourn rev. 1972).

The inconsistencies noted by Wigmore are three: (1) that the rule is properly applicable even where the court may be satisfied that the proponent of secondary evidence is in utmost good faith; (2) that the rule is similarly applicable where possession by a third party should logically remove any suspicion of fraudulent suppression by the proponent, and (3) that were inference of fraud the foundation of the rule it should also apply to objects as well as writings, which it is at least generally agreed it does not.

3. See, e.g., Morgan, Basic Problems of Evidence 385 (1962).

4. Thompson v. State, 62 Md.App. 190, 488 A.2d 995 (1985), cert. denied 303 Md. 471, 494 A.2d 939 (quoting extensively from earlier edition of treatise and declining to apply rule where danger of mistransmission largely absent).

5. Thus Quintilian, writing circa A.D. 88, is quoted by Osborn as stating:

It is therefore necessary to examine all the writings related to a case; it is not sufficient to inspect them; they must be read through; for very frequently they are either not at all such as they were asserted to be, or they contain less than was stated, or they are mixed with matters that may injure the client's cause, or they say too much and lose all credit from appearing to be exaggerated. We may often, too, find a thread broken, or wax disturbed, or signatures without attestation * * *.

Osborn, Questioned Documents, XVI (2d ed. 1929).

The fact that the rule here involved possesses some value in preventing fraud does not imply that the "best evidence" is not subject to ordinary rules of authentication calculated to require some proof of genuineness. See Justus v. State, 438 So.2d

and commentators appear to regard the prevention of fraud as an ancillary justification of the rule.[6] Unless this view is accepted it is difficult to explain the rule's frequent application to copies produced by modern techniques which virtually eliminate the possibility of unintentional mistransmission.

Finally, one leading opinion [7] intimates that the rule should be viewed to protect not only against mistaken or fraudulent mistransmissions but also against intentional or unintentional misleading through introduction of selected portions of a comprehensive set of writings to which the opponent has no access. This seems to engraft upon the best evidence rule an aspect of completeness not heretofore observed.

Whatever rationale is viewed to support the rule, it will be observed that the advent of modern discovery and related procedures under which original documents may be examined before trial rather than at it, have substantially reduced the need for the rule. Nevertheless, it has been pointed out that at present limitations on the availability of these alternatives leaves the original documents rule a continuing and important sphere of operations.[8]

§ 232. What Are Writings? Application to Objects Inscribed and Uninscribed [1]

A rule which permitted the judge to insist that all evidence must pass the court's scrutiny as being the "best" or most reliable means of proving the fact would be a sore incumbrance upon the parties, who in our system have the responsibility of proof. In fact, as we have seen, no such general scrutiny is sanctioned, but only as to "writings" is a demand for the "best," the original, made.[2] This limitation on the ambit of the rule rests largely on the practical realization that writings exhibit a fineness of detail, lacking in chattels generally, which will often be of critical importance. Prevention of loss of this fine detail

358, 365 (Fla.1983), cert. denied 465 U.S. 1052 (assertion of "best evidence" objection held not to waive objection to lack of authentication; the rules "are not correlative as conceived by the trial court but are separate and independent rules of evidence, each with its own scope and purpose").

6. United States v. Manton, 107 F.2d 834 (2d Cir.1939), cert. denied 309 U.S. 664; Rogers, The Best Evidence Rule, 20 Wis. L.Rev. 278 (1945).

7. Toho Bussan Kaisha, Limited v. American President Lines, Limited, 265 F.2d 418, 76 A.L.R.2d 1344 (2d Cir.1959).

8. Cleary & Strong, The Best Evidence Rule: An Evaluation in Context, 51 Iowa L.Rev. 825 (1966).

Fed.R.Evid. and Rev.Unif.R.Evid. (1974) 1003 implicitly recognize these justifications of the original documents rule by allowing admission of "duplicates" produced by modern copying methods where only exactitude is at stake, but withholding admissibility if a genuine question of authenticity of the original is raised or it would be unfair to allow use of the duplicate rather than the original. For text of the Rule and further discussion, see § 236 infra.

§ 232

1. 4 Wigmore, Evidence § 1182 (Chadbourn rev. 1972); Dec.Dig. Evidence ⚎170, Criminal Law ⚎400(1).

2. See § 229 supra. But see Nance, The Best Evidence Principle, 73 Iowa L.Rev. 227 (1988) (contending the principle is much more extensive than here described).

through mistransmission is a basic objective of the rule requiring production of documentary originals.

But while writings may be generally distinguished from other chattels with respect to the amount and importance of the detail they exhibit, chattels bearing more or less detailed inscriptions are far from uncommon. Thus, when an object such as a policeman's badge, a flag, or a tombstone bears a number or legend the terms of which are relevant the problem is raised as to whether the object shall be treated as a chattel or a writing. It is here clearly unwise to adapt a purely semantic approach and to classify the object according to whether its written component predominates sufficiently to alter the label attached to it in common parlance.[3] At the same time, however, it would seem also unnecessary to classify as writings, as apparently do the Federal and Revised Uniform Rules (1974),[4] any object which carries an inscription of any sort whatsoever. In the final analysis, it is perhaps impossible to improve upon Wigmore's suggestion,[5] followed by a number of courts,[6] that the judge shall have discretion to apply the present rule to inscribed chattels or not in light of such factors as the need for

---

3. Comment, 21 Rut.L.Rev. 526, 538 (1967).

4. Fed.R.Evid. 1001(1) and (2) contain the following definitions:

"Writings" and "recordings" consist of letters, words, or numbers, or their equivalent, set down by handwriting, typewriting, printing, photostating, photographing, magnetic impulse, mechanical or electronic recording, or other form of data compilation.

"Photographs" include still photographs, X-ray films, video tapes, and motion pictures.

The Advisory Committee's Note to Federal Rule Evid. 1001(1), however, observes, "Traditionally the rule requiring the original centered upon accumulations of data and expressions affecting legal relations set forth in words and figures."

The corresponding provisions of the Revised Uniform Rules differ only in inserting "sounds" after "words" in paragraph (1).

Under Rule 1002, supra note 11, the original documents rule applies to writings, recordings, and photographs as thus defined.

Application of the rule has not, traditionally, been so broad. See, e.g., Streeter v. State, 60 Ga.App. 190, 3 S.E.2d 235 (1939) (witness allowed to testify that numbers of stolen automobile tires were on list found in defendant's possession); Quillen v. Commonwealth, 284 Ky. 792, 145 S.W.2d 1048 (1940) (testimony as to license number without production of plate).

Note, Article X: Contents of Writings, Recordings, and Photographs, 12 Land & W.L.Rev. 716 (1977) observes that "[b]ecause Rule 1002 by itself is susceptible to the possibility of an excessively technical application by the courts, the remainder of the Rules in Article X include built-in exceptions to prevent this possibility." None of the exceptions contained in Fed.R.Evid. 1003–1007, however, appears to speak directly to the problem here noted.

5. 4 Wigmore, Evidence § 1182 (Chadbourn rev. 1972).

6. United States v. Duffy, 454 F.2d 809 (5th Cir.1972) (testimony that shirt inscribed "D–U–F" was found in stolen car; admission did not violate rule where inscription was simple and evidence not critical); State v. Lewark, 106 Kan. 184, 186 P. 1002 (1920) (receiving stolen automobile; judge in discretion properly permitted testimony that engine number appeared to be altered, without requiring production of automobile); Quillen v. Commonwealth, 284 Ky. 792, 145 S.W.2d 1048 (1940) (theft of automobile, testimony as to license number properly allowed without producing plate, where number not disputed); Mattson v. Minnesota & North Wisconsin Railroad Co., 98 Minn. 296, 108 N.W. 517 (1906) (wrappers on dynamite, not shown to be detachable; proper exercise of discretion to allow description without production).

precise information as to the exact inscription, the ease or difficulty of production, and the simplicity or complexity of the inscription.

Within this general framework, certain types of chattels warrant specific mention. Thus, sound recordings, where their content is sought to be proved,[7] so clearly involve the identical considerations applicable to writings as to warrant inclusion within the present rule.[8] Somewhat more questionable are the provisions of the Federal and Revised Uniform Rules of Evidence (1974) which bring photographs within the rule in those relatively rare instances in which their contents are sought to be proved.[9] However, while it is difficult to accept that photographs of objects exhibit more intricacy of detail than do the objects photographed, concentrating attention upon content does provide a rationale for bringing photographs within it where their contents are sought to be proved. Certainly, the original of a photograph may afford indices of chicanery which secondary evidence of its contents would not betray,[10] and this is likely to be of unusual importance where photographic products are offered "to speak for themselves." Further, it should be noted that X rays were frequently held to be within the rule even before the advent of the recent codifications.[11]

§ 233. What Constitutes Proving the Terms

It is apparent that this danger of mistransmission of the contents of the writing, which is the principal reason for the rule, is only important

7. For a discussion of those instances in which content is sought to be proved, see § 233 infra.

8. See Forrester v. State, 224 Md. 337, 167 A.2d 878 (1961) (rule applied to exclude testimony concerning conversation which had been recorded, but which witness had not overheard; recording in such case treated like writing). But, under the currently prevailing theory described in § 233 infra, the rule does not apply to recordings the "contents" of which are not sought to be shown. See, e.g., People v. Swayze, 220 Cal.App.2d 476, 34 Cal.Rptr. 5 (1963) (rule not applicable to require recording of conversation actually overheard by officer offering to testify). The application of the rule to tapes is the subject of Annot., 58 A.L.R.3d 598.

9. The usual theory on which photographs and representations are admitted does not require proof of the "contents" of the picture. See § 214 supra. But contents will be seen to be involved in copyright and defamation cases where the picture is the allegedly offending article, or where a photograph is tendered as having evidentiary value apart from merely "illustrating" the testimony of a witness. See,

adopting this analysis under the Fed.R.Ev., Seiler v. Lucasfilm, Ltd., 797 F.2d 1504 (9th Cir.1986) (rule held applicable in copyright action to bar "reconstructions" of original drawings of science fiction creatures).

The common law view was apparently contra. See Lucas v. Williams [1892] 2 Q.B. 113 (C.A.) (original of painting not required in action for infringing copyright by selling photos of it).

10. See, e.g., United States v. Tranowski, 659 F.2d 750 (7th Cir.1981) (to support alibi, defendant introduced photo allegedly taken at time of alleged crime; government unsuccessfully sought to introduce testimony of astronomer to the effect that shadows in photo were inconsistent with position of sun on that date).

11. Cellamare v. Third Avenue Transit Corp., 273 App.Div. 260, 77 N.Y.S.2d 91 (1948) (rule applicable to X ray); Simon v. Hendricks, 330 P.2d 186 (Okl.1958) (expert not permitted to testify to contents of X ray).

Decisions considering the question of the application of the present rule to motion pictures are collected in Annot., 62 A.L.R.2d 658.

when evidence other than the writing itself is offered for the purpose of proving its terms. Consequently, evidence that a certain document is in existence [1] or as to its execution [2] or delivery [3] is not within the rule and may be given without producing the document.[4]

In what instances, then, can it be said that the terms of a writing are sought to be proved, rather than merely its identity, or existence? First, there are certain writings which the substantive law, e.g., the Statute of Frauds, the parol evidence rule, endow with a degree of either indispensability or primacy.[5] Transactions to which substantive rules of this character apply tend naturally to be viewed as written transactions, and writings embodying such transactions, e.g., deeds, contracts, judgments, etc., are universally considered to be within the present rule when actually involved in the litigation. Contrasted with the above described types of writings are those, essentially unlimited in variety, which the substantive law does not regard as essential or primary repositories of the facts recorded. Writings of this latter sort may be said merely to happen to record the facts of essentially nonwritten transactions.[6] Testimony descriptive of nonwritten transactions is not generally considered to be within the scope of the present rule and may be given without producing or explaining the absence of a writing recording the facts.[7] Thus, evidence of a payment may be given

---

§ 233

1. Fish v. Fleishman, 87 Idaho 126, 391 P.2d 344 (1964) (check stub to show existence of check); Mickle v. Blackmon, 252 S.C. 202, 166 S.E.2d 173 (1969) (existence of scientific writings properly established through testimony).

2. Redwine v. King, 366 P.2d 921 (Okl. 1961) (proof that lease had been executed not requiring production of lease); Villiers v. Republic Financial Services, Inc., 602 S.W.2d 566 (Tex.Civ.App.—Texarkana 1980) refused n.r.e. (oral testimony as to fact of assignment does not violate rule).

3. Higgins v. Arizona Savings & Loan Association, 90 Ariz. 55, 365 P.2d 476 (1961) (oral testimony receivable to show handwritten notes had been sent, rather than their contents).

4. See Dec.Dig. Evidence ⟨key⟩159, 161(1). This sort of evidence will usually entail a more or less general discription of a writing not considered to be proof of its terms. See, e.g., Hardy v. Hardy, 221 Ga. 176, 144 S.E.2d 172 (1965) (description of notes including testimony of dates and amounts held not proof of terms); Chambless v. State, 94 Okl.Cr. 140, 231 P.2d 711 (1951) (officers could testify that there was a federal liquor license on defendant's premises, but could not give "contents"). The problem will be seen to be very similar to that described above, § 232 supra.

5. See 4 Wigmore, Evidence § 1242 (Chadbourn rev. 1972). See also State v. Buffalo, 4 Hawaii App. 646, 674 P.2d 1014 (1983) (in prosecution for being felon in possession of firearm, judgment of conviction was required as "best evidence"); Marson Coal Co. v. Insurance Co., 158 W.Va. 146, 210 S.E.2d 747 (1974) (insurance policy covering only flights piloted by person with 1900 "logged" flying hours; held, "logged" hours not synonymous with actual flying hours, thus rule required production of logs).

6. Lund v. Starz, 355 Mich. 497, 94 N.W.2d 912 (1959) ("where the matter to be proved is a substantive fact which exists independently of any writing, although evidenced thereby, and which can be as fully and satisfactorily established by parol as by written evidence, then both classes of evidence are primary * * * ").

7. Sayen v. Rydzewski, 387 F.2d 815 (7th Cir.1967) (amount of income allowed to be proved without records); Allen v. W.H.O. Alfalfa Milling Co., 272 F.2d 98 (10th Cir.1959) (costs of production); Herzig v. Swift & Co., 146 F.2d 444 (2d Cir. 1945) (earnings provable without records); Lin Manufacturing Co. v. Courson, 246 Ark. 5, 436 S.W.2d 472 (1969) (company policy provable without production of written statement thereof); People v. Kulwin, 102 Cal.App.2d 104, 226 P.2d 672 (1951)

without production of the receipt,[8] or evidence of a marriage without production of the marriage certificate.[9]

While, however, many facts may be proved without resort to writings which record them, the party attempting to prove a fact may choose to show the contents of a writing for the purpose. Thus, for example, a writing may contain a recital of fact which is admissible under an exception to the hearsay rule. Here the recited fact might possibly be established without the writing, but if the contents are relied upon for the purpose, the present rule applies and oral testimony as to its contents will be rejected unless the original writing is shown to be unavailable.[10]

Distinguishable from the situation in which the witness undertakes to state the fact based upon what he has seen in a writing, is the situation in which the witness testifies that the fact did not occur because relevant records contain no mention of it. This negative type of testimony is usually held not to constitute proof of contents and thus not to require production of records.[11] But it will be seen that care in the application of this exception is required, since testimony as to what does not appear may easily involve a questionable description by the witness of the details which do appear. Perhaps a better approach would be to treat such "non-entry" testimony as a form of summary, which in fact it is, and to subject it to the safeguards employed in that context.[12]

It has long been held that records too voluminous to be conveniently produced and examined in court may be summarized and their import testified to by a witness, usually an expert, who has reviewed the

(policeman who overheard conversation between defendants can testify thereto without producing sound-recording); Aluminum Products Enterprises, Inc. v. Fuhrmann Tooling and Mfg. Co., 758 S.W.2d 119 (Mo.App.1988) (rule does not apply to bar testimony based on personal knowledge of fact; damages); Hedgecock Builders Supply Co. v. White, 92 N.C.App. 535, 375 S.E.2d 164 (1989); Mars v. Meadville Telephone Co., 344 Pa. 29, 23 A.2d 856 (1942) (earnings).

8. R & R Associates, Inc. v. Visual Scene, Inc., 726 F.2d 36, 38 (1st Cir.1984) (testimony as to cost of items admissible; "No evidentiary rule * * * prohibits a witness from testifying to a fact simply because the fact can be supported by written documentation"); Canady v. Canady, 285 Ark. 378, 687 S.W.2d 833 (1985) (bank deposit); Gonzalez v. Hoffman, 9 Mich.App. 522, 157 N.W.2d 475 (1968) (medical expenses); Gerrick v. State, 451 N.E.2d 327 (Ind.1983) (ballistics test results). But admission of such testimony does not deprive

a writing recording the fact of probative value, and the writing may also be admitted in the trial court's discretion. Getz Services, Inc. v. Perloe, 173 Ga.App. 532, 327 S.E.2d 761 (1985).

9. Lopez v. Missouri, Kansas & Texas Railway Co. of Texas, 222 S.W. 695 (Tex. Civ.App.1920) (foreign marriage).

10. Mitchell v. Emblade, 80 Ariz. 398, 298 P.2d 1034 (1956) (error to allow witness with no knowledge of independent fact to testify as to what records showed); People v. Poindexter, 18 Ill.App.3d 436, 305 N.E.2d 400 (1973) (semble); Mel–Mar Co. v. Chemical Products Co., 273 S.W.2d 126 (Tex.Ct.App.—Houston [1st Dist.] 1954), refused n.r.e. (semble).

11. State v. Nano, 273 Or. 366, 543 P.2d 660 (1975). See also Fed.R.Evid. and Rev. Unif.R.Evid. (1974) 803(7) and 803(10), discussed infra respectively in § 287 and § 300.

12. See text infra at note 16.

entirety.[13] The Federal and Revised Uniform Rules of Evidence (1974)
recognize and clarify this helpful practice, and also provide appropriate
safeguards by requiring that the originals be made available for examination and copying by other parties.[14] These requirements, of course,
tacitly assume that reasonable notice be given of the intent to offer
summaries.[15] And, since the summaries admitted under this rule are
being introduced substantively in place of the matters summarized, it
has reasonably been held that a foundation is required for such evidence which establishes both the admissibility of the underlying data
and the accuracy of the summary.[16]

Certain criticisms may be leveled at the commonly applied distinction
between facts the legal efficacy of which is affected by recordation, and
facts which are legally effective whether or not contained in a writing.
Thus it has been suggested that in modern law there are few if any
instances in which a writing is anything more than a recordation of
some nonwritten fact. For example, a written contract, it may be
contended, merely records the operative legal fact, which is the agreement of the parties.[17] Moreover, the distinction has proved a difficult

13. Harris v. United States, 356 F.2d 582 (5th Cir.1966) (summarization by expert of records available for inspection held proper); State v. Schrader, 64 N.M. 100, 324 P.2d 1025 (1958) (summary testimony admissible where records available for inspection but not introduced); Aldridge v. Burchfiel, 421 P.2d 655 (Okl.1966). But compare Bolling Co. v. Barrington Co., 398 S.W.2d 28 (Mo.App.1965) (summaries inadmissible where records not introduced and unavailable through absence from jurisdiction).

A distinction must be made between the situation treated here, in which the matters summarized are themselves being offered into evidence, and the situation discussed elsewhere, § 212 at notes 32–36, in which the summary is merely illustrative. In the latter situation, juries are commonly instructed that the summary or chart is not itself evidence but should be used only as an aid in understanding the evidence. See Holland v. United States, 348 U.S. 121 (1954); United States v. Conlin, 551 F.2d 534 (2d Cir.1977), cert. denied 434 U.S. 831.

14. Fed.R.Evid. and Rev.Unif.R.Evid. (1974) 1006 provide:

The contents of voluminious writings, recordings, or photographs which cannot conveniently be examined in court may be presented in the form of a chart, summary, or calculation. The originals, or duplicates, shall be made available for examination or copying, or both, by other parties at a reasonable time and place. The court may order that they be produced in court.

And see United States v. Kim, 595 F.2d 755 (D.C.Cir.1979) (summary of Korean bank records inadmissible where underlying records not made available at trial); International Technical Instruments, Inc. v. Engineering Measurements Co., 678 P.2d 558 (Colo.App.1983) (admission of summaries of documents not made available until trial in progress constituted reversible error). Compare State Office Systems, Inc. v. Olivetti Corp. of America, 762 F.2d 843 (10th Cir.1985) (holding summaries of expert's projections of lost profits, not based upon existing documents, admissible under Fed.R.Evid. 1006; query whether such summaries would better have been treated as pedagogic or illustrative exhibits).

See also United States v. Stephens, 779 F.2d 232 (5th Cir.1985) (rejecting novel contention that Fed.R.Evid. 1006 allows admission of summaries only where original writings are not introduced and upholding trial court's admission of summaries as evidence where underlying records had already been placed in evidence).

15. Annot., 80 A.L.R.3d 405.

16. United States v. Sorrentino, 726 F.2d 876 (1st Cir.1984) (summaries unsupported by documentation and incorporating figures based on speculation properly excluded); Needham v. White Laboratories, Inc., 639 F.2d 394 (7th Cir.1981), cert. denied 454 U.S. 927.

17. See the dissenting opinion of Prettyman, J., in Meyers v. United States, 171 F.2d 800 (D.C.Cir.1948), cert. denied 336 U.S. 912.

one to apply, and does not adequately serve to reconcile various common applications and nonapplications of the rule. Thus it is commonly held that oral evidence of a witness's prior testimony is receivable even though that testimony is embodied in a transcript.[18] But when a confession has been both orally made and reduced to writing, numerous courts require the writing.[19] Dying declarations both spoken and reduced to writing have produced a similar contrariety of opinion.[20]

Perhaps the most satisfactory solution to the problem would be to abandon the distinction between transactions essentially written and nonwritten and allow the application of the rule to turn upon the trial judge's determination of such factors as the centrality of the writing to the litigation, the importance of bringing the precise words of the writing before the trier, and the danger of mistransmission or imposition in the absence of the original. The result would simply be to merge the present confusing and confused doctrine with the collateral documents exception discussed below,[21] or at least to enlarge the scope of the latter.

§ 234. Writings Involved Only Collaterally [1]

At nearly every turn in human affairs some writing—a letter, a bill of sale, a newspaper, a deed—plays a part. Consequently any narration by a witness is likely to include many references to transactions consisting partly of written communications or other writings. A witness to a confession, for example, identifies the date as being the day after the crime because he read of the crime in the newspaper that day, or a witness may state that he was unable to procure a certain article because it was patented. It is apparent that it is impracticable to forbid such references except upon condition that the writings (e.g., the newspaper, and the patent) be produced in court. Recognition of an exception exempting "collateral writings" from the operation of the basic rule has followed as a necessary concession to expedition of trials and clearness of narration, interests which outweigh, in the case of merely incidental references to documents, the need for perfect exactitude in the presentation of these documents' contents.

---

18. See, e.g., Meyers v. United States, supra, note 17; State v. Bixby, 27 Wash.2d 144, 177 P.2d 689 (1947). But compare, Benge v. Commonwealth, 298 Ky. 562, 183 S.W.2d 631 (1944). Annot., 11 A.L.R.2d 30.

19. See 4 Wigmore, Evidence § 1332 (Chadbourn rev. 1972).

20. See Annot., 112 A.L.R. 43.

21. See § 234 infra. Such a merger has been previously suggested. Comment, 41 Or.L.Rev. 138 (1962). See also Comment, 14 Ark.L.Rev. 153 (1960) (noting that the two rules are inseparably commingled).

§ 234

1. 4 Wigmore, Evidence § 1254 (Chadbourn rev. 1972); Dec.Dig. Evidence ⟨=171, Criminal Law ⟨=401; C.J.S. Evidence § 781; Annot., 1 A.L.R. 1143. See also Note, 11 N.C.L.Rev. 342 (1933).

While writings are frequently held to be collateral within the meaning of the present exception,[2] the purposes for which references to documents may be made by witnesses are so variegated that the concept of collateralness defies precise definition. Three principal factors, however, should, and generally do, play a role in making the determination of collateralness. These are: the centrality of the writing to the principal issues of the litigation;[3] the complexity of the relevant features of the writing;[4] and the existence of genuine dispute as to the contents of the writing.[5] Evaluation and weighting of these factors in the particular instance may perhaps best be left to the discretion of the trial judge, and as elsewhere in the application of this essentially administrative rule, exercise of that discretion should be reviewed only for grave abuse.[6]

2. Lin Manufacturing Co. v. Courson, 246 Ark. 5, 436 S.W.2d 472 (1969) (evidence of local companies' policies against hiring persons with back trouble allowed on damage without production of written policy statements; result also justified on ground that policy not a written fact, see § 233 supra); Farr v. Zoning Board of Appeals, 139 Conn. 577, 95 A.2d 792 (1953) (parties allowed to establish standing as aggrieved property owners without producing documents of title); Wilkins v. Hester, 119 Ga.App. 389, 167 S.E.2d 167 (1969) (witness testifying to value of car allowed to establish status as used car dealer without production of license, even though license was "best evidence"); Wilson Transp. Co. v. Owens–Illinois Glass Co., 125 N.J.L. 686, 17 A.2d 581 (1941) (plaintiff seeking to show damages due to defendant's breach of contract by proving sale of trucks acquired to haul defendant's goods not required to produce documentary proof of ownership); State v. Vaughan, 243 Ind. 221, 184 N.E.2d 143 (1962) (testimonial reference to ownership of properties surrounding tract condemned permissible as collateral fact); Sundberg v. Hurley, 89 N.M. 511, 554 P.2d 673 (1976), cert. denied 90 N.M. 9, 558 P.2d 621 (in medical malpractice action, testimony as to how many patients with similar injury had been treated in hospitals in last five years did not require hospital records); Prudential Insurance Co. of America v. Black, 572 S.W.2d 379 (Tex.Civ. App.—Houston [14th Dist.] 1978) (in suit to recover unpaid rent, plaintiff's status as successor in interest to original lessor should have been allowed to be proved by parol).

See also, Annot., 1 A.L.R. 1143 (admissibility of parol evidence to prove title involved only collaterally).

3. A few courts have gone so far as to classify as collateral all writings which do not form the foundation of the cause of action or defense. Freeman v. Commercial Union Assurance Co., 317 S.W.2d 563 (Tex. Civ.App.1958); Doman v. Baltimore & Ohio Railroad Co., 125 W.Va. 8, 22 S.E.2d 703 (1942); C.J.S. Evidence § 781. This rule would appear unduly restrictive as excluding from the operation of the general rule all nonwritten facts and even many written facts which, though not the basis of the action, possess substantial evidentiary significance. See, e.g., State v. Anderson, 5 N.C.App. 614, 169 S.E.2d 38 (1969) (production of threatening note handed prosecuting witness during perpetration of alleged attempted rape held not excused as collateral fact).

Cf. Fed.R.Evid. and Rev.Unif.R.Evid. (1974) 1004 provide:

The original is not required, and other evidence of the contents of a writing, recording, or photograph is admissible if—

. . .

(4) Collateral Matters. The writing, recording, or photograph is not closely related to a controlling issue.

4. Testimony as to the nature of inscribed chattels is thus sometimes admitted as evidence of collateral facts. See § 232 supra.

5. Farr v. Zoning Board of Appeals, 139 Conn. 577, 95 A.2d 792 (1953) (citing absence of evidentiary challenge of status of plaintiffs as property owners as one basis for failing to require documentary evidence of title).

6. Compare 4 Wigmore, Evidence § 1253 (Chadbourn rev. 1972).

§ 235. Which Is the "Writing Itself" That Must Be Produced? [1] Telegrams, [2] Counterparts [3]

What should be the application of the basic rule where two documents, X and Y, exist, X having been created first and Y being some variety of reproduction of X? Copies, of course, are frequent and in most cases the document first prepared will be the one whose initial production is required by the rule. But the problem is not always so simple. For example, X may be a telegram written by the sender and handed to the company for transmission; or X may be a libelous handwritten letter given to a stenographer for copying and sending, and Y the letter actually received by the addressee; or X may be a ledger sheet in the creditor's books and Y the account rendered made up therefrom and sent to the debtor.

In any of the above cases, if a party in court offers document Y in evidence, what determines whether the document is "the writing itself" offered to prove its own terms, or merely a "copy" offered to establish the terms of X? The answer here clearly does not depend upon the chronology of creation or the ordinary semantic usage which would denominate Y as a "copy." [4] Instead it will depend upon the substantive law of contracts, defamation, property, and the like. The question to be asked, then, is whether, under the substantive law, the creation, publication, or other use of Y may be viewed as affecting the rights of the parties in a way material to the litigation. If the answer to this question is affirmative, the fact that Y happens to be a copy of another writing is completely immaterial. [5] Decisions illustrative of instances in which the terms of "copies" are the facts sought to be proved are cited below. [6]

§ 235

1. 4 Wigmore, Evidence § 1232 (Chadbourn rev. 1972).

2. 4 Wigmore, Evidence § 1236 (Chadbourn rev. 1972); Dec.Dig. Evidence ⟐168, 183(14); C.J.S. Evidence §§ 792, 814.

3. 4 Wigmore, Evidence § 1233 (Chadbourn rev. 1972); Dec.Dig. Evidence ⟐186(6); C.J.S. Evidence § 821.

4. 4 Wigmore, Evidence §§ 1232, 1235(2) and (3) (Chadbourn rev. 1972); Comment, 14 Ark.L.Rev. 153, 160 (1960).

5. McDonald v. Hanks, 52 Tex.Civ.App. 140, 113 S.W. 604, 607 (1908), where the court said: "If a writer desiring to preserve a copy of a letter, writes at the same time two copies exactly alike, one of which he proposes to send and the other to keep, it is a matter of indifference which copy he sends, but the one sent becomes the original and the other a copy, no matter by what force of evidence it is shown to be an absolutely accurate copy." See also Illinois Tuberculosis Association v. Springfield

Marine Bank, 282 Ill.App. 14 (1935) (bank mailed carbon of statement to customer; held, original).

6. United States v. Rangel, 585 F.2d 344 (8th Cir.1978) (altered photocopies of charge card receipts submitted in support of fraudulent claim for reimbursement were best evidence rather than "original" altered charge slips); United States v. Gerhart, 538 F.2d 807 (8th Cir.1976) (photocopies of original checks, submitted in support of loan application, were "originals" required by rule, but secondary evidence admissible under circumstances); Carpenter v. Dressler, 76 Ark. 400, 89 S.W. 89 (1905) (executed deed rather than public transcript of grant held the original under then existing state substantive law); Fuchs & Lang Manufacturing Co. v. R.J. Kittredge & Co., 242 Ill. 88, 89 N.E. 723 (1909) (blueprint from which machine had been assembled, rather than drawing of which blueprint was a copy, held original when offered to show operation of machine); Prussing v. Jackson, 208 Ill. 85, 69 N.E.

It will also frequently occur that a written transaction, such as a contract or deed, will be evidenced by several counterparts or identical copies, each of which is signed by the parties or, at any rate, intended to be equally effective as embodying the transaction.[7] Such multiple counterparts are frequently termed "duplicate (or triplicate, etc.) originals". Each of these counterparts is admissible as an "original" without producing or accounting for the others,[8] but before secondary evidence may be resorted to, all of the counterparts must be shown to be unavailable.[9]

§ 236. Reproductions: Carbons: Printed and Multigraph Copies: Photo and Xerographic Copies [1]

The treatment of copies under the rule requiring the production of the original document can only properly be understood when viewed in light of the technological history of copying itself. In its earliest stages, the rule appears to have developed against a background of copying performed by individuals of the Bob Cratchit sort, transcribing manually not always under the best of conditions. Errors under such circumstances were routinely to be expected. Only marginally greater relia-

---

771 (1904) (libel action against writer of letter printed in newspaper; letter rather than printed matter held original); State v. Calongne, 111 Kan. 332, 206 P. 1112 (1922) (prosecution for fraud defended on ground facts represented were believed by defendant to be true; telegrams received by defendant purporting to detail financial status of corporation held originals); In re Stringer's Estate, 80 Wyo. 389, 343 P.2d 508 (1959) (where testator actually executed only a "copy" of will, copy held the original dispositive instrument).

7. Courts have differed considerably with respect to what may constitute a duplicate original. Compare Tampa Shipbuilding & Eng. Co. v. General Const. Co., 43 F.2d 309 (5th Cir.1930) ("Duplicates exist only when the two instruments have both been recognized and established by the parties concerned as evidence of their act, as where the parties to the sale sign a memorandum with carbon copy and each keeps one") with Parr Construction Co. v. Pomer, 217 Md. 539, 144 A.2d 69 (1958) (holding an ordinary unsigned retained copy is a duplicate), commented upon in Note, 20 Md.L.Rev. 50 (1960). See also American Fire & Casualty Insurance Co., Inc. v. Bryan, 379 So.2d 605 (Ala.Civ.App. 1979) (critical fact to be shown is intent of parties to create two or more copies equal to one another). Compare Fed.R.Evid. 1001 which avoids the internally contradictory phrase "duplicate originals." See also § 236 infra.

8. Fistere, Inc. v. Helz, 226 A.2d 578, 579 (D.C.App.1967) ("When a document is executed in duplicate or multiplicate form, each of the parts is deemed an original and may be used without accounting for any other part"); Thompson v. State, 62 Md. App. 190, 488 A.2d 995 (1985), cert. denied 303 Md. 471, 494 A.2d 939 (multiple copies of search warrant all executed by magistrate constituted originals) (alternate holding); In re King's Estate, 572 S.W.2d 200 (Mo.App.1978) (duplicate deposit slip stamped and delivered to depositor held admissible as duplicate original); Cross v. Everybodys, 357 S.W.2d 156 (Tex.Civ.App. 1962) (production of one duplicate original satisfies best evidence rule).

9. Norris v. Billingsley, 48 Fla. 102, 37 So. 564 (1904); Raceland Stockyards, Inc. v. Giaise, 352 So.2d 392 (La.App.1977), writ denied 354 So.2d 206 (La.) (subsequent copy held inadmissible where offeror failed to account for multiple originals); American Empire Life Insurance Co. v. Long, 344 S.W.2d 513 (Tex.Civ.App.1961) (photostatic copy of newspaper admissible; showing that no original copy of newspaper available).

§ 236

1. 4 Wigmore, Evidence § 1234 (Chadbourn rev. 1972); Dec.Dig. Evidence ☞174(1), 186(6); C.J.S. Evidence §§ 815, 816, 821; Annot., 65 A.L.R.2d 342 (carbons), 76 A.L.R.2d 1356 (photographic copies).

bility was to be found in the so-called letter-press. Here the original was written or typed in copying ink or with copying pencil. Presumably influenced by the infirmities present in such modes of copying, the courts generally declined to accept subsequently created copies as equivalent to originals.[2]

The advent of carbon paper, however, made possible the creation of copies of substantially greater reliability and legibility. Here, since the copy is made by the same stroke as the original, there was an apparent factual distinction between these copies and copies produced subsequent to the original by the older methods.[3] It moreover became common, as it is today, to create multiple counterparts of a contract or transaction through the use of carbon paper, with each copy duly signed either through the same medium or individually. What makes such writings counterparts, of course, is the signing with intent to render each co-equal with the others, and the doctrine of counterparts can therefore hardly apply to a retained carbon copy which is not intended as a communication at all.[4] However, the fact that many true counterparts are made by the use of carbons coupled with the notion that writings generated simultaneously by the same stroke are in some way superior, has caused a great number of courts to treat all carbons as if they were duplicate originals, i.e., as admissible without accounting for the original.[5]

More comprehensibly, there is warrant for believing that the courts will accept as primary evidence of the contents of a given book or a given issue of a newspaper any other book or newspaper printed from the same sets of fixed type, or the same plates or mats. A like result should be reached as to all copies run off from the same mat by the multigraph, lithoprint or other duplicating process.[6]

2. See Philipson v. Chase, 2 Camp. 110, 170 Eng.Rep. 1097 (K.B.1809) (book entry on attorney's bill not admissible); Nodin v. Murray, 3 Camp. 228, 170 Eng.Rep. 1363 (1812) (deficiencies of letter-press copy noted by Lord Ellenborough); Federal Union Security Co. v. Indiana Lumber & Manufacturing Co., 176 Ind. 328, 95 N.E. 1104 (1911).

3. Many of the early cases dealing with carbons emphasize the simultaneous nature of the duplicate's creation. See, e.g., International Harvester Co. v. Elfstrom, 101 Minn. 263, 112 N.W. 252 (1907).

4. Lockwood v. L. & L. Freight Lines, 126 Fla. 474, 171 So. 236 (1936).

5. Carmichael Tile Co. v. McClelland, 213 Ga. 656, 100 S.E.2d 902 (1957) (retained carbon copy of letter admissible though unsigned); Eastover Co. v. All Metal Fabricators, Inc., 221 Md. 428, 158 A.2d 89 (1960) (fact that offered bills were carbons "of no importance"); State v. Stockton, 38 Tenn.App. 90, 270 S.W.2d 586

(1954) (carbon copies of records or reports created simultaneously admissible as duplicate originals, no indication of signing or other manifestation of intent). Contra: Lockwood v. L. & L. Freight Lines, 126 Fla. 474, 171 So. 236 (1936) (carbon is duplicate only when intended to stand equal); Shirer v. O.W.S. & Associates, 253 S.C. 232, 169 S.E.2d 621 (1969) (semble; general rule of carbons as duplicates distinguished and rejected). See also, Annot., 65 A.L.R.2d 342; Notes, 20 Md.L.Rev. 50 (1960), 19 Ohio St.L.J. 520 (1958), 3 Vill.L.Rev. 217 (1958).

6. See Rex v. Watson, 2 Stark. 116, 171 Eng.Rep. 591 (N.P.1817) (to prove contents of printed placard which had been posted, other placards from same printing admitted); Verble v. State, 172 Ga.App. 321, 323 S.E.2d 239 (1984) (copy of magazine); Redding v. Snyder, 352 Mich. 241, 89 N.W.2d 471 (1958) (copy of printed instruction pamphlet admitted).

In the present day, copying by various photographic and other processes has become commonplace, replacing the carbon for many purposes. Various types of photographic copying, of course, produce facsimiles of an extremely high degree of verisimilitude, and thus might have been expected, as have carbons, to win recognition as duplicate originals. In fact, an early judicial step in this direction was taken in a celebrated federal court of appeals decision [7] which held that "recordak" photographs of checks which had been paid, preserved by a bank as part of its regular records were admissible under the Federal Business Records Act. Subsequently, a uniform act was prepared under which photographic copies, regularly kept, of business and public records are admissible without accounting for the original.[8] This act has been widely adopted.[9] In the cases, however, in which photographs of writings have been offered to show the terms of the original, without the aid of specific statutes, they have been almost uniformly treated as secondary evidence, inadmissible unless the original is accounted for.[10]

The resulting state of authority, favorable to carbons but unfavorable to at least equally reliable photographic and xerographic reproductions, appears inexplicable on any basis other than that the courts, having fixed upon simultaneous creation as the characteristic distinguishing of carbons from copies produced by earlier methods have on the whole been insufficiently flexible to modify that concept in the face of newer technological methods which fortuitously do not exhibit that characteristic. Insofar as the primary purpose of the original documents requirement is directed at securing accurate information from the contents of material writings, free of the infirmities of memory and the mistakes of hand-copying, we may well conclude that each of these forms of mechanical copying is sufficient to fulfill the policy. Insistence upon the original, or accounting for it, places costs, burdens of planning, and hazards of mistake upon the litigants. These may be worth imposing where the alternative is accepting memory or hand-copies. They are probably not worth imposing when risks of inaccuracy are reduced to a minimum by the offer of a mechanically produced copy.

At the same time, however, if the original documents requirement is conceded to be supported by the ancillary purpose of fraud prevention, it will be seen that even copies produced by photographic or xerographic processes are not totally as desirable as the original writing. Many indicia of putative fraud such as watermarks, types of paper and inks, etc., will not be discernable on the copy. The most reasonable accom-

---

7. United States v. Manton, 107 F.2d 834 (2d Cir.1939).

8. Uniform Photographic Copies of Business and Public Records as Evidence Act, 9A U.L.A. 584.

9. 14 U.L.A. (1980). Following preparation of the uniform act, its substance was expressly incorporated into the Federal Business Records Act, now 28 U.S.C.A. § 1732.

10. Cox v. State, 93 Ga.App. 533, 92 S.E.2d 260 (1956) (photostatic copy secondary evidence); Benefield v. State, 355 P.2d 874 (Okl.Cr.1960) (photostat held admissible under the uniform act; court noting by way of dictum that common law rule was contrary). See also, Annot. 76 A.L.R.2d 1356, 142 A.L.R. 1270, and Note, 34 Iowa L.Rev. 83 (1948).

modation of the purposes of the basic rule to modern copying to date would appear to be that of the Federal Rules of Evidence.[11] Under Federal Rule 1001(4) copies produced by photography or chemical reproduction or equivalent techniques are classed as "duplicates," and, under Rule 1003 are declared admissible as originals unless a genuine question is raised as to the authenticity of the original or it appears under the circumstances that it would be unfair to admit the duplicate in lieu of the original.[12]

An even more recent challenge to the flexibility of the rule requiring documentary originals has appeared in the form of machine readable records stored on punch cards or magnetic tape. Obviously, where records are originally deposited in such media nothing akin to a conventional documentary original will be created. To the credit of the courts, records there stored have generally fared well in the face of objection predicated on the original document rule, and machine print-outs of such records have been admitted.[13]

---

11. Fed.R.Evid. and Rev.Unif.R.Evid. (1974) 1001(4) define "duplicate":

    A "duplicate" is a counterpart produced by the same impression as the original, or from the same matrix, or by means of photography, including enlargements and miniatures, or by mechanical or electronic re-recording, or by chemical reproduction, or by other equivalent techniques which accurately reproduces [sic] the original.

Fed.R.Evid. and Rev.Unif.R.Evid. (1974) 1003 provide:

    A duplicate is admissible to the same extent as an original unless (1) a genuine question is raised as to the authenticity of the original or (2) in the circumstances it would be unfair to admit the duplicate in lieu of the original.

See discussions in Weinstein & Berger, Evidence ¶ 1003 (1978); Broun, Authentication and Content of Writings, 1969 Law & Soc. Ord. 611, 613.

12. Under the Federal Rule, if there is neither a challenge to authenticity nor potential unfairness the duplicate will be admissible; there is no need to establish one of the excuses for non-production of original provided for by Fed.R.Evid. 1004. United States v. Benedict, 647 F.2d 928 (9th Cir.1981), cert. denied 454 U.S. 1087.

Decided cases suggest that the requisite challenge to genuineness must be relatively specific. See United States v. Georgalis, 631 F.2d 1199 (5th Cir.1980), rehearing denied 636 F.2d 315 (exclusive government possession of duplicates for five year period raised no issue of genuineness); CTS Corp. v. Piher International Corp., 527 F.2d 95 (7th Cir.1975), cert. denied 424 U.S. 978

(error to exclude duplicate where record reflected no basis for questioning genuineness); United States v. Garmany, 762 F.2d 929 (11th Cir.1985), cert. denied 474 U.S. 1062 (photocopy admissible as duplicate where opponent suggested no basis for claim of unfairness). The requirement that introduction of the duplicate entail no "unfairness" to other parties continues the doctrine that the duplicate must be a full rendition of the relevant material. See Toho Bussan Kaisha, Limited v. American President Lines, Inc., 265 F.2d 418 (2d Cir. 1959) (photostats of portions of records in Japan prepared for litigation excluded); Adv.Com.Notes, Fed.R.Evid. 1003.

13. United States v. De Georgia, 420 F.2d 889 (9th Cir.1969) (negative information obtained from computer of business corporation admitted on basis of foundation testimony establishing mode of recordation and company's reliance thereon); King v. State for Use and Benefit of Murdock Acceptance Corp., 222 So.2d 393 (Miss.1969) (computer printouts admissible as "shop books" in absence of modern business records statute); Transport Indemnity Co. v. Seib, 178 Neb. 253, 132 N.W.2d 871 (1965) (business entries made into computer in ordinary course of business held admissible in form of computer printout). See also, Note, 55 Cornell L.J. 1033 (1970); Annot., 11 A.L.R.3d 1377; § 314 infra.

    Fed.R.Evid. and Rev.Unif.R.Evid. (1974) 1001(3) provide in part:

    If data are stored in a computer or similar device, any printout or other output readable by sight, shown to reflect the data accurately, is an "original."

§ 237. Excuses for Nonproduction of the Original Writing: (a) Loss or Destruction [1]

The production-of-documents rule is principally aimed, not at securing a writing at all hazards and in every instance, but at securing the best *obtainable* evidence of its contents.[2] Thus, if as a practical matter the document cannot be produced because it has been lost or destroyed, the production of the original is excused and other evidence of its contents becomes admissible.[3] Failure to recognize this qualification of the basic rule would in many instances mean a return to the bygone and unlamented days in which to lose one's paper was to lose one's right. Recognition of the same qualification also squares with the ancillary purpose of the basic rule to protect against the perpetration of fraud, since proof that failure to produce the original is due to inability to do so tends logically to dispel the otherwise possible inference that the failure stems from design.

Loss or destruction may sometimes be provable by direct evidence but more often the only available evidence will be circumstantial, usually taking the form that appropriate search for the document has been made without discovering it. It would appear that where loss or destruction is sought to be proved by circumstantial evidence of unavailing search, the declarations of a former custodian as to loss or destruction may be admitted to show the nature and results of the search,[4] though if offered as direct evidence of loss or destruction itself

---

§ 237

1. 4 Wigmore, Evidence §§ 1193–1198 (Chadbourn rev. 1972); Dec.Dig. Evidence ⊕178; C.J.S. Evidence §§ 823, 824.

Fed.R.Evid. and Rev.Unif.R.Evid. (1974) 1004 provide:

> The original is not required, and other evidence of the contents of a writing, recording, or photograph is admissible if—
>
> > (1) *Originals Lost or Destroyed.* All originals are lost or have been destroyed, unless the proponent lost or destroyed them in bad faith * * *.

Since the original writing rule is classed as a technical rule of evidence, preliminary questions of fact arising in connection with its application are resolved by the judge in most instances. See § 53 supra. Fed. R.Evid. 1008 provides:

> When the admissibility of other evidence of contents of writings, recordings, or photographs under these rules depends upon the fulfillment of a condition of fact, the question whether the condition has been fulfilled is ordinarily for the court to determine in accordance with the provisions of rule 104. However, when an issue is raised (a) whether the asserted writing ever existed, or (b) whether another writing, recording, or photograph produced at the trial is the original, or (c) whether other evidence of contents correctly reflects the contents, the issue is for the trier of fact to determine as in the case of other issues of fact.

The Revised Uniform Rule (1974) is identical except for slight, and meaningless, changes in style.

2. Fauci v. Mulready, 337 Mass. 532, 150 N.E.2d 286 (1958) (common law "best evidence" rule preferential rather than exclusionary); Vreeland v. Essex Lock & Manufacturing Co., Inc., 135 Vt. 1, 370 A.2d 1294 (1976) (semble).

3. See Sellmayer Packing Co. v. Commissioner, 146 F.2d 707 (4th Cir.1944); Stipe v. First National Bank, 208 Or. 251, 301 P.2d 175 (1956); Hayes v. Bouligny, 420 S.W.2d 800 (Tex.Civ.App.1967).

4. Massie v. Hutcheson, 296 S.W. 939 (Tex.Civ.App.1927), error refused (testimony that deceased grantee said: "Ashes tell no story" when questioned concerning deed, held admissible over objection that it was hearsay). See Interstate Investment Co. v. Bailey, 93 S.W. 578, 580 (Ky.1906)

such declarations would be incompetent as hearsay.[5]

Where loss or destruction is sought to be shown circumstantially by proof of unsuccessful search, it is obvious that the adequacy of the showing will be largely dependent upon the thoroughness and appropriateness of the search. It was laid down in certain early decisions that when the writing is last known to have been in a particular place or in the hands of a particular person, then that place must be searched or the person produced,[6] and statements to the same effect are to be found in modern decisions.[7] It is believed, however, that these statements are best considered as general guides or cautions, rather than strict and unvarying rules. Virtually all jurisdictions view the trial judge as possessing some degree of discretion in determining the preliminary question as to whether it is feasible to produce the original document.[8] Such discretion is particularly appropriate since the character of the search required to show probability of loss or destruction will, as a practical matter, depend on the circumstances of each case. Factors such as the relative importance of the document and the lapse of time since it was last seen have been seen to bear upon the extent of search required before loss or destruction may be inferred.[9] The only general requirement, however, should be that all reasonable avenues of search should be explored to the extent that reasonable diligence under the circumstances would dictate.[10]

("What Elijah Davis learned that Stidham said about the loss of the paper may not have been evidence of its loss * * * yet it was evidence of his good faith in not prosecuting the inquiry further.") 4 Wigmore, Evidence § 1196(3) (Chadbourn Rev.1972).

5. Moore v. State, 179 Miss. 268, 175 So. 183 (1937) (testimony that addressee of letter said she had destroyed it properly excluded as hearsay, but error to admit secondary evidence of letter's contents).

6. Cook v. Hunt, 24 Ill. 535 (1860); Vandergriff v. Piercy, 59 Tex. 371 (1883).

7. Ragen v. Bennigsen, 10 Ill.App.2d 356, 135 N.E.2d 128 (1956).

8. See, e.g., American Fire & Casualty Insurance Co., Inc. v. Bryan, 379 So.2d 605 (Ala.Civ.App.1979) (sufficiency of foundation laid for introduction of secondary evidence largely discretionary with trial court; proof of destruction properly held sufficient); Pennsylvania National Mutual Casualty Insurance Co. v. Burns, 375 So.2d 302 (Fla.App.1979) (semble; proof of loss); Stipe v. First National Bank, 208 Or. 251, 301 P.2d 175 (1956) (no absolute rule governing sufficiency of search; matter absolutely within discretion of trial judge; Vaught v. Nationwide Mutual Insurance Co., 250 S.C. 65, 156 S.E.2d 627 (1967) (trial court has discretion, though not absolute, to determine sufficiency of search).

9. Gathercole v. Miall, 15 M. & W. 319, 153 Eng.Rep. 872 (Exch.1846); United States v. Ross, 321 F.2d 61 (2d Cir.1963) cert. denied 375 U.S. 894 (insignificant paper prepared three years before trial; much less search required where subject is a useless paper which may reasonably be supposed lost); Agee v. Messer–Moore Insurance & Real Estate Co., 165 Ala. 291, 51 So. 829 (1910) (search required varies with value and importance of document). Compare United States v. Marcantoni, 590 F.2d 1324 (5th Cir.1979), cert. denied 441 U.S. 937 (failure to discover stolen bills on execution of search warrant raised sufficient inference of destruction to allow testimony concerning serial numbers by detective who had seen bills earlier); Proffitt v. Ricci, 463 A.2d 514 (R.I.1983) (citing earlier edition of treatise and holding destruction might be inferred from lapse of time).

10. Rash v. Peoples Deposit Bank & Trust Co., 91 F.Supp. 825 (E.D.Ky.1950) (no fixed degree of diligence required in search, but rather such search as nature of the case suggests); Pendley v. Murphy, 112 Ga.App. 33, 143 S.E.2d 674 (1965) (proponent must exhaust those sources which are suggested by facts of case); Chagnon Lumber Co. v. Patenaude, 103 N.H. 448, 174 A.2d 415 (1961) (every case of loss must be determined on its own facts). Of course, testimony by the last custodian, or lack of

If the original document has been destroyed by the person who offers evidence of its contents, the evidence is not admissible unless, by showing that the destruction was accidental or was done in good faith, without intention to prevent its use as evidence, he rebuts to the satisfaction of the trial judge, any inference of fraud.[11]

§ 238. Excuses for Nonproduction of the Original Writing: (b) Possession by a Third Person [1]

When the writing is in the hands of a third person who is within the geographical limits of the trial court's subpoena power, the safest course is to have a writ of subpoena duces tecum served on the possessor summoning him to bring the writing to court at the trial,[2]

---

it, is properly viewed as a significant circumstance. Sylvania Electric Products, Inc. v. Flanagan, 352 F.2d 1005 (1st Cir. 1965) (each case of loss to be determined on its own circumstances; however, foundation insufficient where proponent never denied records were in existence and in fact testified he had some at home); Wray Williams Display Co. v. Finley, 391 So.2d 1253 (La.App.1980), writ refused 396 So.2d 930 (La.) (testimony that originals were in plaintiff's files insufficient, but error held harmless); In re 716 Third Avenue Holding Corp., 225 F.Supp. 268 (S.D.N.Y.1964) reversed on other grounds, 340 F.2d 42 (2d Cir.) (testimony by president of corporation that corporation records had disappeared held insufficient proof of loss without showing of search); Wiggins v. Stapleton Baptist Church, 282 Ala. 255, 210 So.2d 814 (1968).

11. Reynolds v. Denver & Rio Grande Western Railway Co., 174 F.2d 673 (10th Cir.1949) (secondary evidence admissible if no "fraud or bad faith" in destruction); McDonald v. United States, 89 F.2d 128 (8th Cir.1937) (government not precluded in kidnapping case from giving evidence of numbers on ransom bills by fact that subordinate official had improvidently had bills destroyed); Estate of Gryder v. Commissioner of Internal Revenue, 705 F.2d 336 (8th Cir.1983), cert. denied 464 U.S. 1008 (no error to admit secondary evidence where finding of negligent rather than bad faith destruction not clearly erroneous). In re Rasick's Will, 77 N.J.Super. 380, 186 A.2d 527 (1962) (secondary evidence allowed where proponent had voluntarily destroyed original in a fit of rage where trial court found destruction free from suspicion under circumstances); Schroedl v. McTague, 256 Iowa 772, 129 N.W.2d 19 (1964) (semble; discussion and criticism of strict prohibition against offer of secondary evidence by destroyer of original). For an

example of the stricter view, see Booher v. Brown, 173 Or. 464, 146 P.2d 71 (1944) (offering party must be "without neglect or fault").

Fed. and Rev.Unif.R.Evid. (1974) 1004 provide:

The original is not required, and other evidence of the contents of a writing, recording, or photograph is admissible if—

(1) *Originals lost or destroyed.* All originals are lost or have been destroyed, unless the proponent lost or destroyed them in bad faith; or

* * *

§ 238

1. 4 Wigmore, Evidence §§ 1211–1213 (Chadbourn rev.1972); Dec.Dig. Evidence ⊕179(3); C.J.S. Evidence §§ 830, 831.

Fed. and Rev.Unif.R.Evid. (1974) 1004 provide:

The original is not required, and other evidence of the contents of a writing, recording, or photograph is admissible if—

* * *

(2) *Original Not Obtainable.* No original can be obtained by any available judicial process or procedure; or

* * *

2. Many decisions require this. See, e.g., Security Trust Co. v. Robb, 142 Fed. 78 (3d Cir.1906); Pendley v. Murphy, 112 Ga. App. 33, 143 S.E.2d 674 (1965) (error to admit secondary evidence where no subpoena duces tecum issued to last known custodian); Schall v. Northland Motor Car Co., 123 Minn. 214, 143 N.W. 357 (1913) (in possession of trustee in bankruptcy; "he is subject to subpena the same as other citi-

though some decisions will excuse resort to subpoena if the possessor is privileged not to produce it,[3] and others suggest that proof of a hostile or unwilling attitude on his part will be a sufficient excuse.[4]

If the writing is in the possession of a third person out of the state or out of the reach of the court's process, a showing of this fact alone will suffice, in the view of many courts, to excuse production of the writing.[5] This practice has the merit of being an easy rule of thumb to apply, but the basic policy of the original document requirement would tend to support the view of a substantially equal number of courts that a further showing must be made. These latter courts require that, before secondary evidence is used, the proponent must show either that he has made reasonable but unavailing efforts to secure the original from its possessor,[6] or circumstances which persuade the court that such efforts, had they been made, would have been fruitless.[7]

zens"). If the possessor disobeys the summons, the party's production of the original should, of course, be excused.

3. See, e.g., People v. Powell, 71 Cal. App. 500, 236 P. 311 (1925) (letters tending to incriminate possessors).

4. Mahanay v. Lynde, 48 Cal.App.2d 79, 119 P.2d 430 (1941) (adversary's mother got possession of paper and refused to give it back); Ragley–McWilliams Lumber Co. v. Hare, 61 Tex.Civ.App. 509, 130 S.W. 864, 868 (1910) (family Bible of third person, which plaintiffs tried to and were unable to obtain).

5. United States v. Ratliff, 623 F.2d 1293 (8th Cir.1980), cert. denied 449 U.S. 876; Waters v. Mines, 260 Ala. 652, 72 So.2d 69 (1954); Moss v. State, 208 Ark. 137, 185 S.W.2d 92 (1945); Silvey v. Wynn, 102 Ga.App. 283, 115 S.E.2d 774 (1960); Flaharty v. Reed, 170 Kan. 215, 225 P.2d 98 (1950); Longobardi v. Chubb Ins. Co., 234 N.J.Super. 2, 560 A.2d 68 (1989); Thurman v. St. Louis Public Service Co., 308 S.W.2d 680 (Mo.1957); Haire v. State, 118 Tex.Cr.R. 16, 39 S.W.2d 70 (1931).

6. E.g., Londoner v. Stewart, 3 Colo. 47, 50 (1876); McDonald v. Erbes, 231 Ill. 295, 83 N.E. 162 (1907); Sherman v. Sherman, 290 Ky. 237, 160 S.W.2d 637 (1942); Summons v. State, 156 Md. 390, 144 A. 501 (1929); Gasser v. Great Northern Insurance Co., 145 Minn. 205, 176 N.W. 484 (1920) (sufficiency of efforts a matter for judge's discretion); Mahoney–Jones Co. v. Osborne, 189 N.C. 445, 127 S.E. 533 (1925); Pringey v. Guss, 16 Okl. 82, 83, 86 P. 292, 8 Ann.Cas. 412 (1906); Bruger v. Princeton & St. Marie Mut. Fire Ins. Co., 129 Wis. 281, 109 N.W. 95 (1906).

In McDonald, Sherman, Summons and Bruger, it is suggested that in some circumstances due diligence may require the pro-

ponent to take the deposition of the out-of-state possessor of the writing. Deposing the out-of-state holder, however, in addition to being inconvenient and expensive, will often be ineffective to obtain documents in the holder's possession. See Orton v. Poe, 19 Conn.Sup. 145, 110 A.2d 623 (Super.1954) (statute authorizing issuance of state subpenas to procure depositions needed in out-of-state litigation construed not to authorize subpenas duces tecum). The problems incident to obtaining documents held by third persons outside the jurisdiction are reviewed in Cleary & Strong, The Best Evidence Rule: An Evaluation in Context, 51 Iowa L.Rev. 825 (1966). The uncertainties of the available techniques are such that resort to them should seemingly not ordinarily be required.

7. Viereck v. United States, 139 F.2d 847, 850 (D.C.Cir.1944), cert. denied 321 U.S. 794 ("It is hard for even a fertile imagination to conjure up so futile a gesture under the circumstances, as a demand by the United States upon Germany for the production of these letters."); Missouri, Kansas & Texas Railway Co. v. Dilworth, 95 Tex. 327, 67 S.W. 88, 89 (1902) (waybill in hands of carrier outside the state, which they probably would not part with); Bruger v. Princeton & St. Marie Mut. Fire Ins. Co., 129 Wis. 281, 109 N.W. 95, 97 (1906) ("unless it is clear that they would have been fruitless").

On this ground, efforts to secure public records in another state or country, which are not allowed to be removed under their law or practice, would not be required to be shown before using a copy. Sansone v. Selvaggi, 121 N.J.L. 274, 2 A.2d 355 (1938) (postal savings passbook impounded by post-office in Italy); De la Garza v. Macma-

§ 239. Excuses for Nonproduction of the Original Writing: (c) Failure of Adversary Having Possession to Produce After Notice [1]

A frequently used method of showing that it is impracticable for the proponent to produce the original writing is to prove, first, that the original is in the hands of his adversary or under his control,[2] and second, that the proponent has notified him to produce it at the trial and he has failed to do so. Observe that the notice is without compulsive force,[3] and is designed merely to account for nonproduction of the writing by the proponent, and thus to enable him to use secondary evidence of the writing's terms. If the proponent actually needs the production of the original itself he will resort to subpoena duces tecum or under modern rules the motion for an order to produce. But when the notice is offered as an excuse for resorting to secondary evidence the adversary cannot fairly complain that he was only given opportunity, not compelled, to make the writing available.

An oral notice may be sufficient,[4] but the safest and almost universal practice is to give written notice beforehand to the party or his attorney, describing the particular documents, and then to call upon

---

nus, 44 S.W. 704 (Tex.Civ.App.1898) (deed in archives in Mexico, presumably not removable, provable by examined copy). As to domestic public records, see § 240 infra.

§ 239

1. 4 Wigmore, Evidence §§ 1202–1210 (Chadbourn rev.1972); Dec.Dig. Evidence ⬅179(2), 184, 185(1–12), Criminal Law ⬅402(2); C.J.S. Evidence §§ 832–834, 843–848; 29 Am.Jur.2d Evidence §§ 467–469.

Fed.R.Evid. and Rev.Unif.R.Evid. (1974) 1004 provide:

> The original is not required, and other evidence of the contents of a writing, recording, or photograph is admissible if—
>
> * * *
>
> (3) *Original in Possession of Opponent.* At a time when an original was under the control of the party against whom offered, he was put on notice, by the pleadings or otherwise, that the contents would be a subject of proof at the hearing, and he does not produce the original at the hearing * * *.

2. American Fire & Casualty Co. v. Kaplan, 183 A.2d 914 (D.C.Mun.App.1962); Jones v. Texas Department of Public Safety, 392 S.W.2d 176 (Tex.Civ.App.1965); Threatt v. Threatt, 212 Miss. 555, 54 So.2d 907 (1951) (notice to defendant provided sufficient foundation where original shown to be in possession of defendant's father).

Proof of possession by the opponent without proof of notice is generally insufficient. Padgett v. Brezner, 359 S.W.2d 416 (Mo. App.1962) (mere possession by adversary did not afford basis for admitting secondary evidence); In re Reuss' Estate, 422 Pa. 58, 220 A.2d 822 (1966) (copy of letter excluded where no demand made for original in hands of opponent). But compare Transamerica Insurance Co. v. Bloomfield, 401 F.2d 357 (6th Cir.1968) (not error to admit copies of corporate records, apparently without notice, where opponent "was familiar with * * * books and could produce them himself if he so desired"); Gardner v. Bernard, 401 S.W.2d 415 (Mo.1966) (semble). Compare Jones v. State, 473 So.2d 1197 (Ala.Crim.App.1985) (stating notice requirement does not apply to criminal cases).

3. Bova v. Roanoke Oil Co., 180 Va. 332, 23 S.E.2d 347, 144 A.L.R. 364 (1942). The failure to produce, however, might have another tactical consequence, namely, that of giving rise to an inference adverse to the party so failing. Missouri, K.T. Railroad Co. v. Elliott, 102 Fed. 96, 102 (8th Cir. 1900). See § 272 infra.

By contrast, production following notice may in some states lead to the tactical advantage of procuring admission of otherwise inadmissible material. See § 55 supra.

4. Especially when given in open court during the trial. Kerr v. McGuire, 28 N.Y. 446, 453 (1863). But see note 7 infra.

the adversary orally at the trial for the writings requested.[5] It is held
that the nature of the complaint or of the defense may constitute a
sufficient implied notice that the pleader is charging the adversary
with possession of the original and that he considers its production
essential.[6] As to the time of serving notice it is sufficient if it allows
the adversary a fair opportunity under the existing circumstances to
produce the writing at the trial.[7] Accordingly, if it appears at the trial
itself that the adversary has the original paper in the courtroom, an
immediate notice then and there is timely.[8]

Some exceptions, under which notice is unnecessary before using
secondary evidence of a writing in the adversary's possession, have been
recognized. The first is well sustained in reason. It dispenses with the
need for notice when the adversary has wrongfully obtained or fraudulently suppressed the writing.[9] The others seem more questionable.
There is a traditional exception that no notice is required to produce a
writing which is itself a notice.[10] This is understandable in respect to
giving notice to produce a notice to produce, which would lead to an
endless succession of notices, but there seems little justification for
extending the exception, as the cases do, to notices generally. Finally
an exception is made by the majority view for writings in the hands of
the accused in a criminal prosecution. Under this view, secondary
evidence may be received without notice to the accused to produce.[11]
The logic of deriving this position, as seems to have been done, from the

5. For details of the practice, see 4 Wigmore, Evidence § 1208 (Chadbourn rev.
1972).

6. How v. Hall, 14 East 274, 104 Eng.
Rep. 606 (K.B.1811) (trover for bond);
A.F.L. Falck, S.p.A. v. E.A. Karay Co., 722
F.Supp. 12 (S.D.N.Y.1989) (pleading may
satisfy notice requirement); 612 North Michigan Avenue Building Corp. v. Factsys-
tem, Inc., 54 Ill.App.3d 749, 12 Ill.Dec. 613,
370 N.E.2d 236 (1977); Stipe v. First National Bank, 208 Or. 251, 301 P.2d 175
(1956) (copy of document attached to pleading is sufficient notice to other party to
produce); Harris v. State, 150 Tex.Cr.R.
137, 199 S.W.2d 522 (1947) (notice held
afforded by content of indictment for forgery). Similarly, a defensive pleading
charging plaintiff with possession of a document necessary to the defense may serve
as notice. J.L. Owens v. Bemis, 22 N.D.
159, 133 N.W. 59 (1911).

7. Beard v. Southern Railway Co., 143
N.C. 136, 55 S.E. 505 (1906) (notice during
trial not timely when adversary would
have to go to his home in another town to
get the writing). See also Waddell v. Trow-
bridge, 94 W.Va. 482, 119 S.E. 290 (1923)
(notice to produce given at the trial timely
as to one document, not as to another).

8. Brownlee v. Hot Shoppes, Inc., 23
A.D.2d 848, 259 N.Y.S.2d 271 (1965) (held

error to refuse secondary evidence where
plaintiff during trial demanded the original which he asserted was in the courtroom in defendant's possession and defendant did not deny the allegation); Williams
v. Metropolitan Life Insurance Co., 202
S.C. 384, 25 S.E.2d 243 (1943) (no previous
notice required where paper called for is in
court).

9. Cheatham v. Riddle, 8 Tex. 162
(1852) (party's principal "had gotten possession of the instrument and fled the
country with it"); Meyer v. General American Corp., 569 P.2d 1094 (Utah 1977) (semble); 4 Wigmore, Evidence § 1207 (Chadbourn rev. 1972).

10. Colling v. Treweek, 6 B. & C. 394,
108 Eng.Rep. 497 (1827); Eisenhart v. Slay-
maker, 14 Serg. & R. 153 (Pa.1826) ("otherwise * * * a fresh necessity would be constantly arising, *ad infinitum,* to prove notice of the preceding notice; so that the
party would at every step be receding instead of advancing.")

11. Lisansky v. United States, 31 F.2d
846 (4th Cir.1929); Dean v. State, 240 Ala.
8, 197 So. 53 (1940); State v. Pascarelli, 2
Conn.Cir. 305, 198 A.2d 239 (1963); Annot.,
67 A.L.R. 77.

privilege against self-incrimination is dubious. For while a demand upon the accused to produce which is delivered before the jury clearly has a tendency to coerce the defendant and thus cheapen the privilege,[12] there is no logical necessity that the demand be so delivered.[13] Since the object of notice is to protect against imposition upon the opponent, and since this object may be achieved in the case of the criminal defendant by notice before trial, the minority view under which the prosecution must give notice as a necessary precondition to the use of secondary evidence [14] seems the fairer and more reasonable stand.[15]

§ 240. Excuses for Nonproduction of the Original Writing: (d) Public Records [1]

If the contents of the judgment of a court or of an executive proclamation are to be proved, shall the proponent be required to produce the original writing? The accepted view is that, in general, public and judicial records and public documents are required by law to be retained by the official custodian in the public office designated for their custody, and courts will not require them to be removed.[2] To require

---

12. Notice delivered before the jury has frequently been held a violation of the privilege. See, e.g., McKnight v. United States, 115 Fed. 972 (6th Cir.1902); Commonwealth v. Valeroso, 273 Pa. 213, 116 A. 828 (1922); Powell v. Commonwealth, 167 Va. 558, 189 S.E. 433 (1937); and cases collected in 110 A.L.R. 101.

As to compelling production generally by an accused, see § 128 supra.

13. Thus courts following the minority view discussed below commonly require that the notice be outside the jury's presence. State v. Hollingsworth, 191 N.C. 595, 132 S.E. 667 (1926) (accused should be given notice outside jury's presence). More questionable is the position that demand before the jury is improper but may be cured by jury instruction. State v. Haye, 72 Wash.2d 461, 433 P.2d 884 (1967).

14. "The object of the notice is not to compel the party to produce the paper, for no such power is assumed, either directly or indirectly, by placing him under a disadvantage if he does not produce it. Its object is to enable the prisoner to protect himself against the falsity of the secondary evidence." State v. Kimbrough, 13 N.C. (2 Dev.L.) 431 (1830).

15. Rex v. Ellicombe, 5 Car. & P. 522, 172 Eng.Rep. 1681 (1933); Kirk v. State, 227 So.2d 40 (Fla.App.1969); Annot., 67 A.L.R. 77.

§ 240

1. 4 Wigmore, Evidence §§ 1215–1222 (Chadbourn rev. 1972); Dec.Dig. Evidence ⟜177, Criminal Law ⟜444.

2. Doe v. Roberts, 13 M. & W. 520, 530, 153 Eng.Rep. 217 (Exch.1844) ("When directed to be kept in any particular custody, and so deposited they are provable by examined copies * * * on the ground of the great inconvenience of removing them"); State v. Black, 31 N.J.Super. 418, 422, 107 A.2d 33, 35 (1954) ("It is firmly established in this State that a public document may be proved by producing the original * * * and on grounds of public convenience a well-known rule of the common law allows proof of such document by duly authenticated copies whenever the original would be admissible, a public document being for this purpose, a document, either judicial or non-judicial, which is public in its nature and which the public had the right to inspect.").

If, however, the original record of which proof is to be made is a record of the very court which is trying the present case, then it seems, since the original writing can be produced without violating the rule and policy against removal, production should be required, if formal proof is to be made. Roby v. Title Guarantee & Trust Co., 166 Ill. 336, 46 N.E. 1110 (1896); 4 Wigmore, Evidence § 1215(b) (Chadbourn rev. 1972). But judicial notice would be simpler, see § 330 infra.

removal would be inconvenient for the public who might desire to consult the records and would entail a risk of loss of or damage to the official documents. Accordingly, statutes and rules have provided for the issuance of certified copies and for their admission in evidence in lieu of the original.[3] In addition, examined copies, authenticated by a witness who has compared it with the original record, are usually receivable.[4]

§ 241. Preferences Among Copies and Between Copies and Oral Testimony [1]

The basic policy of the original document requirement is that of specially safeguarding the accuracy of the presentation in court of the terms of a writing. If the original is unavailable does the same policy require a preference among the secondary methods of proving the terms? Some means of proof are clearly more reliable than others. In order of reliability the list might go something like this: (1) a mechanically produced copy, such as a photograph or xerograph, a carbon, a letter-press copy, etc.,[2] (2) a firsthand copy by one who was looking at the original while he copied (immediate copy, sworn copy), (3) a copy, however made, which has been compared by a witness with the original and found correct (examined copy), (4) a secondhand or mediate copy, i.e., a copy of a firsthand copy, (5) oral testimony as to the terms of the writing, with memory aided by a previously made memorandum, and (6) oral testimony from unaided memory. There are many additional variations.

There is one rule of preference that is reasonable and is generally agreed on by the courts, namely, that for judicial and other public

---

3. Fed.R.Evid. 1005 provides:

The contents of an official record, or of a document authorized to be recorded or filed and actually recorded or filed, including data compilations in any form, if otherwise admissible, may be proved by copy, certified as correct in accordance with rule 902 or testified to be correct by a witness who has compared it with the original. If a copy which complies with the foregoing cannot be obtained by the exercise of reasonable diligence, then other evidence of the contents may be given.

The Revised Uniform Rule is identical except for a slight, and meaningless, difference in style. As to computerized records, see Annot., 71 A.L.R.3d 232.

Compare State v. Griffin, 336 N.W.2d 519 (Minn.1983) (certified copy of conviction not absolute requirement; no error to accept other documentation constituting a fair preponderance of evidence of conviction).

4. See Doe v. Roberts, quoted supra note 2 and Fed.R.Evid. 1005 quoted supra note 3. Nor have certified copies traditionally been preferred to examined copies. See Smithers v. Lowrance, 100 Tex. 77, 93 S.W. 1064 (1906); 4 Wigmore, Evidence § 1273(1) (Chadbourn rev. 1972).

However, it should be noted that state statutes sometimes impose requirements beyond those of the "rule" itself. See, e.g., Dames v. Strong, 659 S.W.2d 127 (Tex.App. 1983) (notice requirement of intent to use certified copy of deed imposed by state statute).

§ 241

1. 4 Wigmore, Evidence §§ 1265–1280 (Chadbourn rev. 1972); Byrdseye, Degrees of Secondary Evidence, 6 Wash.L.Rev. 21 (1931); Notes, 30 So.Cal.L.Rev. 355 (1957), 38 Mich.L.Rev. 864 (1940); Dec.Dig. Evidence ⊙=186; C.J.S. Evidence § 784.

2. See § 236 supra.

records, a certified, sworn or examined copy is preferred,[3] and other evidence of the terms of the record cannot be resorted to unless the proponent has no such copy available, and the original record has been lost or destroyed so that a copy cannot now be made.[4]

As to writings other than public records, there are two general approaches to the problem. First there is the view, fathered by some of the English decisions and espoused by a minority of the American cases, that "there are no degrees of substantive evidence."[5] This position has the virtues of simplicity and easiness of application. In addition, it may be observed that failure to apply the basic rule as between varieties of secondary evidence leaves unimpaired a substantial practical motivation to produce more satisfactory secondary evidence where it appears to exist. This practical motivation, of course, stems from apprehension of the adverse inference which may be drawn from failure to produce more satisfactory secondary evidence indicated to exist and not shown to be unavailable. These considerations have led the draftsmen of most modern codes of evidence to adopt the so-called "English" view.[6]

The second view is followed by a majority of the courts which have passed on the question. Here a distinction is recognized between types of secondary evidence, with a written copy being preferred to oral

3. Jones v. Melindy, 62 Ark. 203, 36 S.W. 22 (1896) (proof of record of mortgage through testimony of custodian disallowed; use of examined or certified copy required); Whittier v. Leifert, 72 N.D. 528, 9 N.W.2d 402 (1943) (rule stated; dictum); 4 Wigmore, Evidence § 1269 (Chadbourn rev. 1972).

The requirement is relaxed in most jurisdictions, by statute or decision, to allow a witness to be asked upon cross-examination as to his conviction of crime. Bosarge v. State, 273 Ala. 329, 139 So.2d 302 (1961) (best evidence rule did not require certified copy of records where accused had already testified to convictions); Gaskill v. Gahman, 255 Iowa 891, 124 N.W.2d 533 (1963) (proof of witness' prior conviction may, under statute, be made by his own testimony or proof of record); Clemens v. Conrad, 19 Mich. 170, 175 (1869) ("The danger that he will falsely testify to a conviction that never took place or that he may be mistaken about it, is so slight, that it may almost be looked upon as imaginary"). But compare Rolland v. State, 235 Ga. 808, 221 S.E.2d 582 (1976) (witness cannot be discredited even by own testimony of conviction; record required); People v. Moses, 11 Ill.2d 84, 142 N.E.2d 1 (1957) (where witness is accused, conviction must be proved by introduction of record). See Dec.Dig. Witnesses ⟨=⟩350, 359. Impeachment by proof of conviction is treated generally in § 43 supra.

4. People v. Cotton, 250 Ill. 338, 95 N.E. 283 (1911).

5. Doe D. Gilbert v. Ross, 7 M. & W. 102, 151 Eng.Rep. 696 (Exch.1840) (shorthand notes of counsel's statement at former trial of contents of settlement allowed, although attested copy requiring but not bearing a stamp was in existence); W.C. Beaty & Co. v. Southern Railway Co., 80 S.C. 527, 61 S.E. 1006 (1908) ("there is no division of degrees of proof in case of the loss of an instrument"); Rick Furniture Co. v. Smith, 202 S.W. 99 (Tex.Civ.App. 1918). Cases subscribing to the English view are collected in Byrdseye, Degrees of Secondary Evidence, 6 Wash.L.Rev. 21 (1931); Note, 38 Mich.L.Rev. 864 (1940).

6. The Federal and Revised Uniform Rules contain no provision for "degrees" of secondary evidence. Fed.R.Evid. 1004, Advisory Committee's Note; United States v. Gerhart, 538 F.2d 807 (8th Cir.1976); White Ind., Inc. v. Cessna Aircraft Co., 611 F.Supp. 1049 (W.D.Mo.1985) (no degree of secondary evidence recognized under Fed. R.Evid.). But compare, Report of New Jersey Supreme Court Committee on Evidence 232 (1963); West's Ann.Cal.Evid.Code § 1505.

testimony,[7] and, under circumstances varying from state to state, and an immediate copy being preferred to a more remote one.[8] This view is justifiable chiefly on the ground that there is some incongruity in pursuing the policy of obtaining the terms of writings with fullest accuracy, by structuring a highly technical rule to that end, only to abandon it upon the unavailability of the original. In formulating this general approach of discrimination among types of secondary evidence, the courts following the American rule have sought to avoid a position which would require the proponent to produce or account for all possible copies that may have existed. A reasonable standard is suggested by an early New York judge, who said:

"I do not mean to contend that there are any arbitrary or inflexible degrees of secondary evidence, rendering it necessary for a party, who is driven to that description of proof, to show affirmatively, in every instance that there is no higher degree within his power, than the one he offers; but I think it may be safely said, that where it appears in the very offer, or from the nature of the case itself, or from the circumstances attending the offer, that the party has better and more reliable evidence at hand, and equally within his power, he shall not be permitted to resort to the inferior degree first".[9]

§ 242. Adversary's Admission as to the Terms of a Writing[1]

Many American courts have followed the lead of Baron Parke's decision in Slatterie v. Pooley[2] and have held admissions by a party opponent admissible to prove the terms of a writing.[3] Upon reflection,

---

7. Riggs v. Tayloe, 22 U.S. (9 Wheat.) 483, 486, 6 L.Ed. 140 (1824) (original contract destroyed, oral testimony permitted; "the party [after accounting for original] may read a counterpart or if there is no counterpart an examined copy, or if there should not be an examined copy, he may give parole evidence of its contents."); Murphy v. Nielsen, 132 Cal.App.2d 396, 282 P.2d 126 (1955) (held error to receive parol where copies shown to exist; holding now codified by West's Ann.Cal.Evid.Code § 1505); Cummins v. Pennsylvania Fire Insurance Co., 153 Iowa 579, 134 N.W. 79 (1912); Baroda State Bank v. Peck, 235 Mich. 542, 209 N.W. 827 (1926) (application of American rule affirmed by equally divided appellate court; full discussion). See also Note, 38 Mo.L.Rev. 475 (1973).

8. When the original is a public record and hence not producible, a certified or examined copy may be obtained at any time, and a copy of a copy would everywhere be excluded. Lasater v. Van Hook, 77 Tex. 650, 655, 14 S.W. 270 (1890) (deed record; examined copy of a certified copy excluded). When the original is unavailable and there is no copy of record, then under the majority view the proponent

would be required to produce an immediate copy, if available, before using a copy of a copy. Schley v. Lyon, 6 Ga. 530, 538 (1849); State v. Cohen, 108 Iowa 208, 78 N.W. 857 (1899). Contra, under the minority, "no degrees" doctrine: Goodrich v. Weston, 102 Mass. 362 (1869).

The various situations are distinguished and the decisions collected in 4 Wigmore, Evidence § 1275 (Chadbourn rev. 1972).

9. Slossen, J. in Healy v. Gilman, 1 Bosw. (14 N.Y.Super.) 235 at 242 (1857), quoted in note, 38 Mich.L.Rev. 864, 874 (1940).

§ 242

1. 4 Wigmore, Evidence §§ 1255–1257 (Chadbourn rev. 1972); Dec.Dig. Evidence ⊚=172; C.J.S. Evidence § 788; Notes, 20 Md.L.Rev. 50 (1960), 17 Tex.L.Rev. 371 (1939).

2. 6 M. & W. 665, 151 Eng.Rep. 579 (Exch.1840).

3. In the following cases testimony of a third person as to a party's oral admission was received: Dunbar v. United States, 156

however, it will be seen that Baron Parke's decision squares rather poorly with the primary modern day policy in favor of obtaining the contents of writings with accuracy.[4] The evidence determined admissible in Slatterie v. Pooley was actually at two removes from the writing itself, being witness' report of the defendant's comment. Perhaps the policy of holding admissible any admission which a party-opponent chooses to make will suffice to justify the first step, but the second frequently raises the possibility of erroneous transmission without corresponding justification. Accordingly, some American decisions have rejected testimony relating oral admissions concerning contents of writings.[5]

It will be observed, however, that the second possibility of mistransmission noted above is effectively eliminated where no testimonial report of the admission is required. Thus, the desirable solution, towards which it is believed the decisions may be drifting, is to receive admissions to evidence a document's terms (1) when the admission itself is in writing and is produced in evidence,[6] or (2) when the party himself, on the stand in this or some other trial or hearing, makes the admission about the contents of the writing or concedes that he made such an admission on a former occasion.[7] Oral testimony by a witness that he heard the party's admission as to the terms of the writing, despite the authority of Slatterie v. Pooley, should be excluded.[8]

§ 243. Review of Rulings Admitting Secondary Evidence

It will be seen from the earlier sections of this chapter that the requirement of the production of original writings, with the several

U.S. 185 (1895) (oral admission that telegram received was identical to one sent by party); Metropolitan Life Insurance Co. v. Hogan, 63 F.2d 654 (7th Cir.1933) (oral admission by agent of nature of paper received from beneficiary); Morey v. Hoyt, 62 Conn. 542, 26 A. 127 (1893) (reviewing older authorities and approving Slatterie v. Pooley).

4. See 1 Jones, Evidence § 261 (5th ed. 1958); Fed.R.Evid. 1007, Advisory Committee's Note.

5. Grimes v. Fall, 15 Cal. 63 (1860) (oral testimony that party admitted that he was assignee under what court assumed to be written assignment, held inadmissible); Prussing v. Jackson, 208 Ill. 85, 69 N.E. 771 (1904) (stating that verbal admissions as to content of writings would, if admitted, abrogate basic rule).

6. Written admissions were held receivable in Clarke v. Warwick Cycle Mfg. Co., 174 Mass. 434, 54 N.E. 887 (1899); Swing v. Cloquet Lumber Co., 121 Minn. 221, 141 N.W. 117 (1913) ("The rule is sound in principle, at least where the admissions

are in writing"); Taylor v. Peck, 21 Grat., (62 Va.) 11 (1871). Even more clearly should a written pleading containing the admission be sufficient. Coca–Cola Bottling Co. v. International Filter Co., 62 Ind.App. 421, 113 N.E. 17 (1916).

7. Admissions on the witness stand have frequently been viewed as sufficient though the distinction between in and out-of-court admissions is not generally made: Johnson v. U–Haul of Southern Alabama, 357 So.2d 665 (Ala.Civ.App.1978) (admission by party in open court); Parr Construction Co. v. Pomer, 217 Md. 539, 144 A.2d 69 (1958); Gardner v. City of Columbia Police Department, 216 S.C. 219, 57 S.E.2d 308 (1950). Contra, Prussing v. Jackson, supra, note 5.

8. Fed. and Rev.Unif.R.Evid. (1974) 1007 provide:

Contents of writings, recordings, or photographs may be proved by the testimony or deposition of the party against whom offered or by his written admission, without accounting for the nonproduction of the original.

excuses for nonproduction and the exceptions to the requirement itself, make up a fairly complex set of regulations for administration by the trial judge.   Mistakes in the application of these rules are, understandably, not infrequent.   The purpose of this system of rules, on the other hand, is simple and practical.   That purpose is to secure the most reliable information as to the contents of documents, when those terms are disputed.   A mystical ideal of seeking "the best evidence" or the "original document," as an end in itself is no longer the goal.   Consequently when an attack is made, on motion for new trial or on appeal, upon the judge's admission of secondary evidence, it seems that the reviewing tribunal, should ordinarily make inquiry of the complaining counsel, "Does the party whom you represent actually dispute the accuracy of the evidence received as to the material terms of the writing?"   If the counsel cannot assure the court that such a good faith dispute exists, it seems clear that any departure from the regulations in respect to secondary evidence must be classed as harmless error.[1]

§ 243

1.   Myrick v. United States, 332 F.2d 279 (5th Cir.1963), cert. denied 377 U.S. 952 (not error to admit photostatic copies of checks in absence of suggestion to trial judge that they were incorrect); Johns v. United States, 323 F.2d 421 (5th Cir.1963) (not error to admit admittedly accurate copy of wire recording); Sauget v. Johnston, 315 F.2d 816 (9th Cir.1963) (not error to admit copy when opponent had original agreement and on appeal made no claim of any discrepancy).

Compare, National Fire Insurance Co. v. Evertson, 153 Neb. 854, 46 N.W.2d 489 (1951) where the possibility of this approach was overlooked.   There a judgment was reversed, partly on the ground that a material written settlement was proved only by a carbon copy.   On the motion for new trial the winning plaintiff produced the original writing which corresponded with the carbon, but the court on appeal said that the judgment could not be "propped up" in that way.

As stated in the Advisory Committee's Note, the prevailing attitude toward harmless error in part furnishes the basis for Federal Rule 1003, dealing with admissibility of duplicates.   See § 236 supra.

*

Title 10

THE HEARSAY RULE AND
ITS EXCEPTIONS

Chapter 24

THE HEARSAY RULE

Table of Sections

§ 244. The History of the Rule Against Hearsay [1]

In an oft-quoted passage, Wigmore calls the rule against hearsay "that most characteristic rule of the Anglo–American Law of Evidence—a rule which may be esteemed, next to jury trial, the greatest contribution of that eminently practical legal system to the world's methods of procedure." [2] How did this rule come about?

§ 244

1. The brief discussion here is based upon 5 Wigmore, Evidence § 1364 (Chadbourn rev.1974). See also 9 Holdsworth's History of English Law 214–219 (3d ed. 1944). The story of the development of jury trial and of the emergence of the practice of producing witnesses in court to testify before the jury is recounted in Thayer, Preliminary Treatise on Evidence, chs. 2–4, esp. ch. 3 (1898). See also Plucknett, A Concise History of the Common Law 120–130 (5th ed. 1956).

2. 5 Wigmore, supra n. 1, at p. 28.

The development of the jury was, no doubt, an important factor.[3] It will be remembered that the jury in its earlier forms was in the nature of a committee or special commission of qualified persons in the neighborhood to report on facts or issues in dispute. So far as necessary its members conducted its investigations informally among those who had special knowledge of the facts. Attesting witnesses to writings were summoned with the jurors and apparently participated in their deliberations,[4] but the practice of calling witnesses to appear in court and testify publicly about the facts to the jury is a late development in jury trial. Though something like the jury existed at least as early as the 1100's,[5] this practice of hearing witnesses in court does not become frequent until the later 1400's. The change-over to the present conception that the normal source of proof is not the private knowledge or investigation of the jurors, but the testimony of witnesses in open court, is a matter of gradual evolution thereafter. Finally, in the 1500's it has become, though not yet the exclusive source of proof, the normal and principal one.[6]

It is not until this period of the gradual emergence of the witness testifying publicly in court that the consciousness of need for exclusionary rules of evidence begins to appear. It had indeed been required even of the early witnesses to writings that they could speak only of "what they saw and heard"[7] and this requirement would naturally be applied to the new class of testifying witnesses. But when the witness has heard at firsthand the statement of X out of court that she has seen and heard a blow with a sword, or witnessed a trespass on land, as evidence of the blow or the trespass, a new question is presented. Certainly it would seem that the earlier requirement of knowledge must have predisposed the judges to skepticism about the value of hearsay.[8]

Accordingly, it is the value of hearsay, its sufficiency as proof, that is the subject of discussion in this gestation period. And so through the reigns of the Tudors and the Stuarts there is a gradually increasing drumfire of criticism and objections by parties and counsel against evidence of oral hearsay declarations. While the evidence was constantly admitted, the confidence in its reliability was increasingly undermined.[9] It was derided as "a tale of a tale"[10] or "a story out of another man's mouth."[11] Parallel with this increasingly discredited

---

3. Professor Morgan chose rather to view the rule as a development of the adversary system. See note 19, infra.

4. Thayer, Preliminary Treatise on Evidence 97 (1898).

5. Thayer, supra note 1, at pp. 53–65.

6. 5 Wigmore, supra note 1, at p. 15.

7. Thayer, supra note 1, at pp. 101, 519; 9 Holdsworth, History of English Law 211 (3d ed. 1944).

8. See Thayer, supra note 1, at pp. 518, 519; 9 Holdsworth, History of English Law 215 (3d ed. 1944).

9. 5 Wigmore, supra note 1, at p. 18.

10. Colledge's Trial, 8 How.St.Tr. 549, 663 (1681) (counsel for prosecution warning his own witness), cited in 5 Wigmore, supra note 1, at n. 32.

11. Gascoigne's Trial, 7 How.St.Tr. 959, 1019 (1680) (warning by judge, but evidence finally admitted) cited in 5 Wigmore, supra note 1, at n. 32.

use of casual oral hearsay was a similar development in respect to transcribed statements made under oath before a judge or judicial officer, not subject to cross-examination by the party against whom it is offered.[12] In criminal cases in the 1500's and down to the middle 1600's the main reliance of the prosecution was the use of such "depositions" to make out its case.[13] As oral hearsay was becoming discredited, uneasiness about the use of "depositions" began to take shape, first in the form of a limitation that they could only be used when the witness could not be produced at the trial.[14] It will be noted that the want of oath and the unreliability of the report of the oral statement cannot be urged against such evidence but only the want of cross-examination and observation of demeanor.

It was in the first decade after the Restoration that the century or so of criticism of hearsay had its final effect in decisions rejecting its use, first as to oral hearsay and then as to depositions. Wigmore finds that the period between 1675 and 1690 is the time of crystallization of the rule against hearsay.[15] For a time the rule was qualified by the notion that hearsay, while not independently admissible, could come in as confirmatory of other evidence,[16] and this qualification survived down to the end of the 1700's in the limited form of admitting a witness's prior consistent statements out of court to corroborate his testimony.[17]

Whether the rule against hearsay was, with the rest of the English law of evidence, in fact "the child of the jury"[18] or the product of the adversary system[19] may be of no great contemporary significance. The important thing is that the rule against hearsay taking form at the end of the seventeenth century was neither a matter of "immemorial usage" nor an inheritance from Magna Charta but, in the long view of English legal history, was a late development of the common law.

Holdsworth thinks that the immediate influences leading to the crystallization of the rule against hearsay, at the particular time in the late 1600's when this occurred, were first, a strong dictum by Coke in his Third Institute denouncing "the strange conceit that one may be an accuser by hearsay,"[20] and second, the rejection of the attempt to naturalize in English law the canon and civil law requirement of "two witnesses"[21] and the consequent urge to provide some compensating

12. 5 Wigmore, Evidence supra note 1, at pp. 20–25.

13. 9 Holdsworth, History of English Law 218 (3d ed. 1944).

14. 5 Wigmore, supra note 1, at p. 23.

15. 5 Wigmore, supra note 1, at p. 18.

16. 5 Wigmore, supra note 1, at p. 19.

17. 5 Wigmore, supra note 1, at p. 20.

18. Thayer, Preliminary Treatise on Evidence 47, also 2–4, 180 (1898).

19. Morgan, The Jury and the Exclusionary Rules of Evidence, 4 U.Chi.L.Rev. 247, 258 (1937), Hearsay Dangers and the Application of the Hearsay Concept, 62 Harv.L.Rev. 177 (1948), also in Selected Writings on Evidence and Trial 764, 766–768 (Fryer ed. 1957).

20. Coke thus condemned the holding in Thomas's case, Dyer 99b (1553) to the effect that under a statute of Edward VI requiring two witnesses in treason if one accuser speaks from his own knowledge, "and he relate it to another, the other may well be an accuser." Coke Third Inst. 25 (1641).

21. An elaborate system attaching numerical values to various kinds of evidence.

safeguard.[22] As we have seen, a century of increasing protests against the use of hearsay had preceded the establishment of the rule. However, most of the specific weaknesses of hearsay, which were the underlying reasons for the adoption of the rule, and which have explained its survival, were not clearly pointed out until after the beginning of the 1700's when the newly established rule came to be rationalized by the judges and the text writers.[23]

§ 245. The Reasons for the Rule Against Hearsay:[1] Exceptions to the Rule

The factors upon which the credibility of testimony depends are the perception, memory, and narration of the witness. (1) *Perception.* Did the witness perceive what he describes, and did he perceive it accurately? (2) *Memory.* Has the witness retained an accurate impression of his perception? (3) *Narration.* Does his language convey that impression accurately?[2] Some writers subdivide inaccuracy of narration into ambiguity and insincerity, resulting in four rather than three factors.[3] However, it seems apparent that ambiguity and insincerity, as well as honest mistake, all manifest themselves as inaccuracy of narration.

In order to encourage witnesses to put forth their best efforts and to expose inaccuracies which might be present with respect to any of the foregoing factors, the Anglo–American tradition evolved three conditions under which witnesses ordinarily will be required to testify: oath, personal presence at the trial, and cross-examination.[4] The rule against hearsay is designed to insure compliance with these ideal conditions, and when one of them is absent the hearsay objection becomes pertinent.

In the hearsay situation, two "witnesses" are involved. The first complies with all three of the ideal conditions for the giving of testimony, but his testimony consists of reporting what the second "witness" said. The second "witness" is the out-of-court declarant; his statement

---

22. 9 Holdsworth, History of English Law 217, 218 (3d ed. 1944).

23. See Landsman, The Rise of the Contentious Spirit: Adversary Procedure in Eighteenth Century England, 75 Cornell L.Rev. 497 (1990) for a discussion of the rise of the adversary system and the corresponding solidification of the hearsay rule.

§ 245

1. See 5 Wigmore, Evidence § 1362 (Chadbourn rev. 1974); Weinstein & Berger, Evidence ¶ 800[01]; Maguire, The Hearsay System: Around and Through the Thicket, 14 Vand.L.Rev. 741, 743–749 (1961); Morgan, Hearsay Dangers and the Application of the Hearsay Concept, 62 Harv.L.Rev. 177 (1948); Introductory Note: The Hearsay Problem, Fed.R.Evid., 28 U.S.C.A. Art. VIII p. 130.

2. 2 Wigmore, Evidence § 478 (Chadbourn rev. 1979); Strahorn, A Reconsideration of the Hearsay Rule and Admissions, 85 U.Pa.L.Rev. 484 (1937). In United States v. Byrnes, 644 F.2d 107 (2d Cir. 1981), some considerable confusion resulted when both judge and court reporter understood that witness was describing unlawfully imported foreign parrots as "citizen" birds, when in fact "psittacine" was intended.

3. Morgan, supra note 1; Tribe, Triangulating Hearsay, 87 Harv.L.Rev. 957 (1974).

4. California v. Green, 399 U.S. 149, 155 (1970); Strahorn, supra note 2.

was not given in compliance with the ideal conditions, yet it contains the information that is of concern in the case.

Oath. Among the earliest of the criticisms of hearsay, and one often repeated in judicial opinions down to the present, is the objection that the out-of-court declarant who made the hearsay statement commonly speaks or writes without the solemnity of the oath administered to witnesses in a court of law.[5] The oath may be important in two aspects. As a ceremonial and religious symbol it may induce in the witness a feeling of special obligation to speak the truth, and also it may impress upon the witness the danger of criminal punishment for perjury, to which the judicial oath or an equivalent solemn affirmation would be a prerequisite condition. Wigmore considers that the objection for want of an oath is incidental and not essential, and suggests that this is demonstrated by the fact that a hearsay statement, even if under oath, is still rejected.[6] But the fact that the oath is not the only requirement of the rule against hearsay does not prove that it is not an important one. Nor does the fact that the oath may have diminished in significance with the passage of time mean that today it is without significance; no disposition to abolish it (other than to allow affirmation as a substitute) is apparent.[7]

Personal presence at trial. Another objection early asserted and repeated of late is the want of opportunity, in respect to the out-of-court declarant, for observation of his demeanor, with the light that this may shed on his credibility, that would be afforded if he were a witness on the stand.[8]

The solemnity of the occasion and possibility of public disgrace can scarcely fail to impress the witness,[9] and falsehood no doubt becomes more difficult if the person against whom directed is present.

Moreover, personal presence eliminates the danger that in the oral reporting of an out-of-court statement the witness reporting the statement may do so inaccurately. It seems probable that the reporting of words spoken is subject to special dangers of inaccuracy beyond the fallibility common to all reproduction from memory of matters of observation,[10] and this seems a substantial danger in the admission of hearsay. It is true as Wigmore points out [11] that not all hearsay is

---

5. Bridges v. Wixon, 326 U.S. 135, 153 (1945); Chapman v. Chapman, 2 Conn. 347, 7 Am.Dec. 277 (1817); State v. Saporen, 205 Minn. 358, 285 N.W. 898 (1939); Hawkins, Pleas of the Crown, b. II, c. 46, § 44 (1716), in 5 Wigmore, Evidence, p. 7 (Chadbourn rev. 1974); Gilbert, Evidence, p. 4 (1760 ed.).

6. 5 Wigmore, supra note 5, at p. 10.

7. See, e.g., Fed.R.Evid. 603:

Before testifying, every witness shall be required to declare that the witness will testify truthfully, by oath or affirmation administered in a form calculated to awaken the witness' conscience and impress the witness' mind with his duty to do so.

8. Mattox v. United States, 156 U.S. 237, 242 (1895), quoted with approval, Ohio v. Roberts, 448 U.S. 56 (1980); Sahm, Demeanor Evidence: Elusive and Intangible Imponderables, 47 A.B.A.J. 580 (1961).

9. Strahorn, supra note 2.

10. Stewart, Perception, Memory, and Hearsay, 1970 Utah L.Rev. 1, 13, 19.

11. 5 Wigmore, supra note 6, at § 1363(1).

subject to this danger. Written statements can be produced in court and can be tested with reasonable accuracy for genuineness and freedom from alteration. Moreover, as Morgan has suggested, the reporting in court of spoken words for nonhearsay purposes, as in proving the making of an oral contract or the utterance of a slander,[12] is subject to this same risk of misreporting. Neither argument seems conclusive. In any event, no distinction is in general made between written and spoken hearsay.[13]

Cross-examination. It would be generally agreed today that noncompliance with the third condition is the main justification for the exclusion of hearsay. This is the lack of any opportunity for the adversary to cross-examine the absent declarant whose out-of-court statement is reported by the witness. Thus as early as 1668 we find a court rejecting hearsay because "the other party could not cross-examine the party sworn."[14] Judicial expressions stress this as a principal reason for the hearsay rule.[15] Cross-examination, as Bentham pointed out,[16] was a distinctive feature of the English trial system, and the one which most contributed to the prestige of the institution of jury trial. He called it "a security for the correctness and completeness of testimony." The nature of this safeguard which hearsay lacks is indicated by Chancellor Kent: "Hearsay testimony is from the very nature of it attended with * * * doubts and difficulties and it cannot clear them up. 'A person who relates a hearsay is not obliged to enter into any particulars, to answer any questions, to solve any difficulties, to reconcile any contradictions, to explain any obscurities, to remove any ambiguities; he entrenches himself in the simple assertion that he was told so, and leaves the burden entirely on his dead or absent author.' * * * "[17] In perhaps his most famous remark, Wigmore described cross-examination as "beyond any doubt the greatest legal engine ever invented for the discovery of truth."[18]

Hearsay that is admitted. It is easy, however, to overplay the unreliability of hearsay. Eminent judges have spoken of its "intrinsic weakness."[19] If this were meant to imply that all hearsay of its very

---

12. Where the utterance of the words is an "operative fact," see Morgan, A Suggested Classification of Utterances Admissible as Res Gestae, 31 Yale L.J. 229 (1922). See § 249, infra.

13. The English Evidence Act 1938, 1 & 2 Geo. VI, c. 28, accorded a greater admissibility to hearsay evidence in documentary form. The distinction was virtually abandoned when the Civil Evidence Act 1968, c. 64, Pt. I, § 2, greatly broadened the admissibility of hearsay without regard to its form. Compare Stewart, Perception, Memory, and Hearsay, 1970 Utah L.Rev. 1.

14. 2 Rolle's Abr. 679, pl. 9 (1668), cited by Morgan, Jury Trials and the Exclusionary Rules of Evidence, 4 U.Chi.L.Rev. 247, 253 (1937).

15. Pointer v. Texas, 380 U.S. 400, 404 (1965); California v. Green, 399 U.S. 149, 158 (1970).

16. Rationale of Judicial Evidence, b. II, ch. IX, and b. III, ch. XX (1827) quoted 5 Wigmore, Evidence § 1367 (Chadbourn rev. 1974).

17. Coleman v. Southwick, 9 John. 50 (N.Y.1812), in 5 Wigmore, supra note 16, § 1362 at p. 6.

18. 5 Wigmore, supra note 16, at p. 32. Quoted with approval, California v. Green, 399 U.S. 149, 158 (1970).

19. Marshall, C.J. in Mima Queen v. Hepburn, 7 Cranch 290, 11 U.S. 290 (1813) and Story, J. in Ellicott v. Pearl, 35 U.S. 412, 436 (1836), both cited 5 Wigmore, supra note 16, § 1363 at p. 11.

nature is unworthy of reliance in a court of law, of course the implication is quite insupportable. The contrary is proved by the fact that courts are constantly receiving, as we shall see, hearsay evidence of various kinds under the numerous exceptions to the hearsay rule,[20] and by the doctrine established in most jurisdictions that when hearsay evidence, which would have been excluded if objected to, is let in without objection, it may be taken into consideration if it appears to be reliable in the particular case, as sufficient to sustain a verdict or finding of the fact thus proved.[21] The truth, of course, is that hearsay evidence, ranging as it does from mere thirdhand rumors to sworn affidavits of credible observers, has as wide a scale of reliability, from the highest to the lowest, as we find in testimonial or circumstantial evidence generally, depending as they all do upon the frailties of perception, memory, narration, and veracity of men and women. Notice may also be taken at this point that hearsay is widely used and usable in our judicial system in proving probable cause.[22] Much of our learning comes in the form of hearsay.[23] Indeed, it is the failure to adjust the rules of admissibility more flexibly and realistically to these variations in the reliability of hearsay that as we shall see has constituted one of the pressing needs for liberalization of evidence law.[24]

Few persons question the desirability of a general policy of requiring that testimony be given by witnesses in open court, under oath, and subject to cross-examination, which is the objective of the rule against hearsay.[25] The problem area is found in the operation of the rule in excluding evidence as a means of effectuating that policy.

20. Chs. 25–33 infra; Ladd, The Hearsay We Admit, 5 Okla.L.Rev. 271 (1952). Most of the cases dealing with hearsay involve the exceptions.

21. See Annot., 104 A.L.R. 1130, 79 A.L.R.2d 890, and § 54, supra, where the matter is developed.

22. Since the issue to be decided is whether sufficient evidence exists to justify taking the step in question, hearsay usually is not in fact involved. However, it is commonly said that hearsay may serve as the basis for a warrant. Jones v. United States, 362 U.S. 257, 271 (1960), cert. dismissed 448 U.S. 83. For this reason, and others, the Federal Rules of Evidence are in general not applicable to grand jury proceedings and to the issuance of various kinds of warrants. Fed.R.Evid. 1101(d)(2) and (3). For more extended discussion, see § 170 supra.

23. See Note, The Hearsay Rule and Epistemological Suicide, 74 Georgetown L.J. 1301 (1986), where the author notes that hearsay is the basis for all knowledge. The hearsay aspects of learning are seldom noted except with respect to the manner in which a witness obtained information. However, the manner in which an expert

witness became an expert is an exception. Jefferis v. Marzano, 298 Or. 782, 696 P.2d 1087 (1985). See also United States v. Rollins, 862 F.2d 1282 (7th Cir.1988), cert. denied 490 U.S. 1074 where the court permitted expert testimony with regard to the meaning of certain "code words" used in narcotics trade. The testimony was based upon the agent's training and experience, rather than on information supplied by a single informant. See generally § 13, supra.

24. See § 325 infra. Loevinger, Facts, Evidence and Legal Proof, 9 W.Res.L.Rev. 154, 165 (1958), suggests "that there can be little utility in a class which is so broad as to include the prattling of a child and the mouthings of a drunk, the encyclical of a pope, a learned treatise, an encyclopedia article, a newspaper report, an unverified rumor from anonymous sources, an affidavit by a responsible citizen, a street corner remark, the judgment of a court * * *."

25. One author, urging the abolition of the hearsay rule in civil cases, argues that the rule is not based solely on reliability considerations, but on considerations of unfair surprise, unbridled discretion for the

§ 246.   A Definition of Hearsay [1]

A definition cannot, in a sentence or two, furnish ready answers to all the complex problems of an extensive field, such as hearsay. It can, however, furnish a helpful general focus and point of beginning, as well as a memory aid in arranging some of the solutions.

The following definition is from the Federal Rules of Evidence, in effect in about half the states as well as in the federal courts.[2] It has, in addition, been quoted with approval or adopted outright on a case-by-case basis in states where the Federal Rules have not been adopted in their entirety,[3] and is generally consistent with the views now expressed in common law jurisdictions.[4] Federal Rule of Evidence 801 provides:

(a) **Statement.** A "statement" is (1) an oral or written assertion or (2) nonverbal conduct of a person, if it is intended by the person as an assertion.

(b) **Declarant.** A "declarant" is a person who makes a statement.

(c) **Hearsay.** "Hearsay" is a statement, other than one made by the declarant while testifying at the trial or hearing, offered in evidence to prove the truth of the matter asserted.

Before going into the sections of text that follow, dealing with various aspects of what is and is not hearsay, certain preliminary observations should be made.

The word "assert" appears prominently in the quoted rule but is nowhere defined. What does it mean? The contemporary dictionary meaning is to state positively or strongly, and accordingly a person may be described as being assertive. However, in the world of evidence, the word "assert" carries no connotation of being positive or strong. A

trial judge and trustworthiness of the in-court witness. See Park, A Subject Matter Approach to Hearsay Reform, 86 Mich. L.Rev. 51 (1987).

§ 246

1. For discussions, see 5 Wigmore, Evidence § 1361 (Chadbourn rev. 1974), 6 id. § 1766 (Chadbourn rev. 1976); Maguire, The Hearsay System: Around and Through the Thicket, 14 Vand.L.Rev. 741 (1961); Morgan, Hearsay Dangers and the Application of the Hearsay Concept, 62 Harv.L.Rev. 177 (1948); Strahorn, A Reconsideration of the Hearsay Rule and Admissions, 85 U.Pa.L.Rev. 484 (1937); Tribe, Triangulating Hearsay, 87 Harv.L.Rev. 957 (1974); Weinstein, Probative Force of Hearsay, 46 Iowa L.Rev. 331 (1961); Federal Rules of Evidence, Introductory Note: The Hearsay Problem, 28 U.S.C.A. Art. VIII, p. 130.

Formulating definitions of hearsay has proved to be a great challenge to the writers, less so to the courts.

2. For a review of the state provisions, see Joseph et al., Evidence in America, ch. 56, Rule 801. None varies significantly from the federal version.

3. State v. Miller, 204 N.W.2d 834 (Iowa 1973); Long v. Asphalt Paving Co., 47 N.C.App. 564, 268 S.E.2d 1 (1980).

4. Isaacson v. Obendorf, 99 Idaho 304, 581 P.2d 350 (1978); People v. Carpenter, 28 Ill.2d 116, 190 N.E.2d 738 (1963); McClain v. State, 274 Ind. 250, 410 N.E.2d 1297 (1980); People v. Edwards, 47 N.Y.2d 493, 419 N.Y.S.2d 45, 392 N.E.2d 1229 (1979); State v. Santos, 122 R.I. 799, 413 A.2d 58 (1980).

favorite of writers in the field for at least a century and a half, the word simply means *to say that something is so,* e.g. that an event happened or that a condition existed.[5]

The definition of hearsay contained in Federal Rule of Evidence 801(a)–(c), quoted above, is affirmative in form; it says that an out-of-court assertion, offered to prove the truth of the matter asserted, is hearsay. For example, witness W reports on the stand that declarant D has stated that X was driving a car at a given time and place. Proponent is trying with this evidence to prove that X did so act. The out-of-court assertion is being offered to prove the truth of the matter asserted, and by definition it is hearsay. Alternatively, if the out-of-court statement is measured against the policy underlying the hearsay rule, its evidentiary value depends upon the credibility of the declarant without the assurances of oath, presence, or cross-examination, and again the result is classification as hearsay.

The definition in the rule does not in terms say that everything not included within the definition is not hearsay. However, exclusion from the definition of everything not included within its terms was the intended effect of the rule, according to the Advisory Committee's Notes which accompanied the rules during their submission to the public, submission to the Supreme Court, transmission to the Congress, consideration by the Congress, and eventual adoption. No challenge to this reading of the rule was offered.[6] The rule's definition must, therefore, be taken as meaning that out-of-court conduct that is not an assertion, or that, even though assertive, is not offered to prove the truth of the matter asserted, is not hearsay. What is, or is not, an assertion thus becomes an important inquiry in some situations. Moreover, if the policy underlying the hearsay rule is stretched to include all situations where the evidentiary value of a statement depends on the credibility of an out-of-court declarant, in however slight a degree or without regard to offsetting factors, there exists the possibility of conflict between the rule's underlying policy and the definition. These matters will be considered in the sections which follow.

Not in presence of party against whom offered. A remarkably persistent bit of courthouse folklore is the practice of objecting to out-of-court statements because not made in the presence of the party against whom offered. From the foregoing discussion, the lack of relationship be-

5. This meaning appears in the Oxford Dictionary but is labeled obsolete. The meaning ascribed in the text is clear, however, from the context of the writers. Bentham, Rationale of Judicial Evidence, b. 6, c. 4 (1827); Wigmore, supra n. 1; American Law Institute Model Code of Evidence, Rule 501. The frequency of usage of the term makes the absence of definition more noteworthy; apparently the writers have all understood what was meant. Professor Morgan did attempt a definition, Hearsay Dangers and the Application of the Hearsay Concept, 62 Harv.L.Rev. 177, 216 (1948), but the result is less helpful than his other writings.

6. This construction finds obvious reinforcement in the provision of Rule 802 that "Hearsay is not admissible * * *." It could scarcely be contemplated that, with hearsay just having been defined in Rule 801, some different concept of hearsay is intended in Rule 802.

tween this objection and the concept of hearsay is apparent.[7] The presence or absence of the party against whom an out-of-court statement is offered has significance only in a few particular situations, e.g., when a statement spoken in her presence is relied upon to charge her with notice,[8] or when failure to deny a statement spoken in her presence is the basis for claiming that she acquiesced in or adopted the statement.[9]

§ 247. Distinction Between Hearsay Rule and Rule Requiring Firsthand Knowledge

There is a rule, more ancient than the hearsay rule, and having some kinship in policy, which is to be distinguished from it. This is the rule that a witness is qualified to testify to a fact susceptible of observation, only if it appears that he had a reasonable opportunity to observe the facts.[1] Thus, if a witness testifies that on a certain day flight 450 arrived at the airport at X on time, and from his other evidence it appears that he was not in X at the time in question, and hence could only have spoken from conjecture or report of other persons, the proper objection is not hearsay but want of personal knowledge. Conversely, if the witness testifies that his brother *told* him that he came in on the flight and it arrived on time, the objection for want of knowledge of when the plane arrived is inappropriate, because the witness purports to speak from his own knowledge only of what his brother said, and as to this he presumably had knowledge. If the testimony in this latter case was offered to show the time of the plane's arrival, the appropriate objection is hearsay.[2] The distinction is one of the form of the testimony, whether the witness purports to give the facts directly upon his own credit (though it may appear later that he was speaking only on the faith of reports from others) or whether he purports to give an account of what another has told him and this is offered to evidence the truth of the other's report. However, when it appears, either from the phrasing of his testimony or from other sources, that the witness is testifying on the basis of reports from others, though he does not in terms testify to their statements, the distinction loses much of its significance, and courts may simply apply the label "hearsay." [3]

---

7. Adkins v. Brett, 184 Cal. 252, 193 P. 251 (1920); People v. Carpenter, 28 Ill.2d 116, 190 N.E.2d 738 (1963); Mason & Hengen, The Hearsay Rule in Mississippi: "Out of the Presence of the Adverse Party—In the Presence of the Adverse Party," 47 Miss.L.J. 423 (1976).

8. See § 249, infra.

9. See § 250, infra.

§ 247

1. See § 10 supra.

2. For discussion of the distinction, see 2 Wigmore, Evidence § 657 (Chadbourn rev. 1979), 5 id. §§ 1361, 1363(3) (Chadbourn rev. 1974).

3. See, e.g., United States v. Brown, 548 F.2d 1194 (5th Cir.1977) (prosecution for preparing fraudulent income tax returns; IRS auditor testified, on basis of interviews with taxpayers, that high percentage of returns prepared by defendant overstated deductions); State v. Conway, 351 Mo. 126, 171 S.W.2d 677 (1943) (testimony of officer as to money in possession of accused when arrested, apparently based on reports of others); Capan v. Divine Providence Hospital, 270 Pa.Super. 127, 410 A.2d 1282 (1979), reversed on other grounds 287

§ 248. Instances of the Application of the Hearsay Rule

A few examples of the rejection of evidence under the general hearsay rule excluding extra-judicial assertions offered to prove the facts asserted will indicate the scope of its operation. Evidence of the following oral statements has been excluded: on the issue whether deceased had transferred his insurance to his new automobile, testimony that he said he had made the transfer;[1] to prove that veniremen had read newspaper articles, testimony of deputy sheriff that attorney said that one venireman said that other venireman had read the articles;[2] to prove that driver was driving with consent of insured owner, testimony that owner said after the accident that the driver had his permission;[3] in rebuttal of defense of entrapment, criminal reputation of defendant to show predisposition;[4] to show defendant's control of premises where marijuana was found, testimony of police officer that neighbors said person of same name occupied the premises;[5] statements of child to social workers describing sexual abuse.[6]

Instances of exclusion of written statements as hearsay when offered in court as evidence of their truth are likewise frequent. Thus, the following have been determined to be hearsay: written estimates of damages or cost of repairs, made by an estimator who does not appear as a witness;[7] written appraisal of stolen trailer by appraiser who did not testify;[8] invoices, bills, and receipts as independent evidence of the making of repairs, payment, and reasonableness of charges;[9] the written statement of an absent witness to an accident;[10] newspaper ac-

---

Pa.Super. 364, 430 A.2d 647 (wife, who was not present at the time, attempted to testify that hospital supplied physician for late husband); Robertson v. Coca Cola Bottling Co. of Walla Walla, Wash., 195 Or. 668, 247 P.2d 217 (1952) (testimony of bottling plant manager as to strength and thickness of glass in bottle based upon measurements made by third parties). When a hearsay statement is offered as coming within an exception to the hearsay rule, it is usually required that the declarant must meet the knowledge-qualification, see § 10 supra. This is sometimes confused with the hearsay objection.

§ 248

1. Carantzas v. Iowa Mutual Insurance Co., 235 F.2d 193 (5th Cir.1956).

2. Lowell v. Daly, 148 Conn. 266, 169 A.2d 888 (1961).

3. Coureas v. Allstate Insurance Co., 198 Va. 77, 92 S.E.2d 378 (1956). Distinguish the speaking of words of permitting as a verbal act under § 249 infra.

4. United States v. McClain, 531 F.2d 431 (9th Cir.1976), cert. denied 429 U.S. 835.

5. State v. Klutts, 204 Neb. 616, 284 N.W.2d 415 (1979).

6. Hall v. State, 539 So.2d 1338 (Miss. 1989).

7. Home Mutual Fire Insurance Co. v. Hagar, 242 Ark. 693, 415 S.W.2d 65 (1967); Alliance Mutual Casualty Co. v. Atkins, 316 S.W.2d 783 (Tex.Civ.App.1958); Miles v. New Orleans Public Service Co., 393 So.2d 877 (La.App.1981).

8. United States v. Williams, 661 F.2d 528 (5th Cir.1981).

9. Pacific Gas & Electric Co. v. G.W. Thomas Drayage & Rigging Co., 69 Cal.2d 33, 69 Cal.Rptr. 561, 442 P.2d 641 (1968). The courts have indicated, however, that the items would be admissible to corroborate testimony. And see People v. Davis, 269 Ill. 256, 110 N.E. 9 (1915); Byalos v. Matheson, 328 Ill. 269, 159 N.E. 242 (1927), as to receipted bills.

10. Izzo v. Crowley, 157 Conn. 561, 254 A.2d 904 (1969).

counts as proof of matters of fact reported therein; [11] statements in will that testator's second wife had agreed to devise property to his children, as proof of that agreement; [12] medical report, by a physician who did not testify, to prove that plaintiff had sustained injuries in a subsequent accident; [13] manufacturer's advertising claims as proof of reliability of "Intoximeter." [14]

§ 249. Some Out-of-Court Utterances Which Are Not Hearsay [1]

The hearsay rule forbids evidence of out-of-court assertions to prove the facts asserted in them. If the statement is not an assertion or is not offered to prove the facts asserted, it is not hearsay. A few of the more common types of nonhearsay utterances are discussed in the present section.

Verbal acts.[2] When a suit is brought for breach of a written contract, it would not occur to anyone, when a writing is offered as evidence of the contract sued on, to suggest that it is hearsay. Similarly proof of oral utterances by the parties in a contract suit constituting the offer and acceptance which brought the contract into being, are not evidence of assertions offered testimonially but rather of utterances—verbal conduct—to which the law attaches duties and liabilities.[3] Other obvious instances are evidence of the utterance by the defendant of words relied on as constituting a slander or deceit for which damages are sought. Additional cases illustrating the principle are described in the note.[4]

---

11. Hickock v. Hand, 190 Kan. 224, 373 P.2d 206 (1962); Marley v. Providence Journal Co., 86 R.I. 229, 134 A.2d 180 (1957); Deramus v. Thornton, 160 Tex. 494, 333 S.W.2d 824 (1960); Compare State v. Sharpe, 195 Conn. 651, 491 A.2d 345 (1985) (not hearsay for officer to testify on redirect that reading newspaper account triggered his memory so that he included in his testimony on direct matters not in his report). Annot., 55 A.L.R.3d 663.

12. Colgrove v. Goodyear, 325 Mich. 127, 37 N.W.2d 779, 10 A.L.R.2d 1029 (1949).

13. Potts v. Howser, 274 N.C. 49, 161 S.E.2d 737 (1968).

14. City of Sioux Falls v. Kohler, 80 S.D. 34, 118 N.W.2d 14 (1962).

§ 249

1. Martin, Basic Problems of Evidence, 299–303 (1988) Weinstein & Berger, Evidence ¶¶ 801(a)[01]–801(c)[01]; 6 Wigmore, Evidence § 1766 (Chadbourn rev. 1976).

2. A distinction must be drawn between objectively manifested intent or other state of mind and actual intent or other state of mind. Professor Morgan was severely critical of the terms "verbal act" and "verbal part of an act" when used to describe out-of-court statements offered as proof of the actual intent or other state of mind of the declarant. However, he conceded the propriety and convenience of the terms when "confined to utterances entirely without the scope of the [hearsay] rule, because not offered to prove the matter asserted in them." Morgan, A Suggested Classification of Utterances Admissible as Res Gestae, 31 Yale L.J. 229, 235 (1922). He described the verbal conduct here being considered as "Utterance[s which are] operative fact[s]." Id. at 231. Wigmore, Evidence § 1770 (Chadbourn rev. 1976) uses the phrase "utterances forming a part of the issue." Weinstein & Berger ¶ 801(c)[01] employ the terminology here used, describing it as generally used by courts and commentators.

3. NLRB v. H. Koch and Sons, 578 F.2d 1287 (9th Cir.1978); Gyro Brass Manufacturing Corp. v. United Auto, Aircraft and Agricultural Implement Workers, 147 Conn. 76, 157 A.2d 241 (1959).

4. Tennessee v. Street, 471 U.S. 409 (1985) (confession of accomplice to rebut claim that sheriff read confession to defen-

Verbal parts of acts.[5] The legal significance of acts taken alone and isolated from surrounding circumstances may be unclear. Thus the bare physical act of handing over money to another person is susceptible of many interpretations. The possibilities include loan, payment of a debt, bribe, bet, gift, and no doubt many other kinds of transactions. Explanatory words which accompany and give character to the transaction are not hearsay when under the substantive law the pertinent inquiry is directed only to objective manifestations rather than to the actual intent or other state of mind of the actor.[6] Similar considerations are commonly said to prevail when the character of an establishment is sought to be proved by evidence of statements made in connection with activities taking place on the premises.[7]

dant and made him say the same things); United States v. Bruner, 657 F.2d 1278 (D.C.Cir.1981) (properly authenticated prescriptions about 5,000 in number, issued by nontestifying physician in prosecution for controlled substance conspiracy); United States v. Jones, 663 F.2d 567 (5th Cir.1981) (in prosecution for threatening court officers, threatening words were "paradigmatic nonhearsay"); United States v. Gibson, 675 F.2d 825 (6th Cir.1982), cert. denied 459 U.S. 972 (a command); United States v. Feldman, 825 F.2d 124 (7th Cir.1987) (testimony of investors as to statements by salesmen admissible to show existence of fraudulent scheme); Digman v. Johnson, 18 Ill.2d 424, 164 N.E.2d 34 (1960) (agent's testimony as to principal's statement granting him authority to act as agent); Kindred v. State, 524 N.E.2d 279 (Ind.1988) (perjury prosecution; application for driver's license in false name admissible to show false statement was made); Hanson v. Johnson, 161 Minn. 229, 201 N.W. 322 (1924) (spoken words constituting a partition of corn crop between landlord and tenant); Patterson–Stocking, Inc. v. Dunn Brothers Storage Warehouses, 201 Minn. 308, 276 N.W. 737 (1937) (evidence of instructions given by owner to driver, to show whether driver was acting with consent of owner at time of accident).

5. Weinstein & Berger, Evidence ¶ 801(c)[01]; 6 Wigmore, Evidence §§ 1772–1786 (Chadbourn rev. 1976).

6. National Bank of Metropolis v. Kennedy, 84 U.S. (17 Wall.) 19 (1873) (conversation between parties on issue whether cashier made loan for bank or for himself); United States v. Giraldo, 822 F.2d 205 (2d Cir.1987), cert. denied 484 U.S. 969 (answering machine tape admissible to show that defendant possessed cocaine with intent to distribute); Rush v. Collins, 366 Ill. 307, 8 N.E.2d 659 (1937) (statements by party claiming prescriptive easement in alley, showing his use was adverse); In re

Cronholm's Estate, 38 Ill.App.2d 141, 186 N.E.2d 534 (1962) (statement of depositor indicating lack of donative intent in establishing joint bank account); Butler v. Butler, 253 Iowa 1084, 114 N.W.2d 595 (1962) (statements showing that conveyance was in trust). See also the discussion in connection with the nebulous concept *res gestae*, infra § 268.

7. Numerous cases involve prosecutions for conducting a gambling establishment, often those accepting bets on horse races. If a person, while handing over money, says, "Here's $100. on Thunderer to show in the fourth," the words would qualify as the verbal part of an act, i.e. the act of betting. In some of the cases, police who were on the premises during a raid, answered incoming telephone calls by persons saying they wished to place specified bets. These phone calls have been classed as verbal acts. State v. Tolisano, 136 Conn. 210, 70 A.2d 118, 13 A.L.R.2d 1405 (1949); State v. Romano, 165 Conn. 239, 332 A.2d 64 (1973); See also United States v. Gaines, 726 F.Supp. 1457 (E.D.Pa.1989), affirmed 902 F.2d 1562 (3d Cir.) (testimony of police as to telephone calls received at defendant's apartment admissible to show that apartment and its occupants were a known source of drugs) Annot., 13 A.L.R.2d 1409. Morgan suggested that the "dangers of misinterpretation of this non-narrative language seems frequently not to be perceived," it being "quite possible, though perhaps highly improbable" that the caller intended something other than a bet and was using a secret code. He admitted that "it would be an extremely rare case where either counsel or court would even notice, much less discuss, such a problem." Morgan, Hearsay Dangers and the Application of the Hearsay Concept, 62 Harv.L.Rev. 177, 198 (1948). In fact, the hearsay question has been raised rather often but apparently never with success. Annot., 13 A.L.R.2d 1409.

Utterances and writings offered to show effect on hearer or reader.[8]
When it is proved that D made a statement to X, with the purpose of
showing the probable state of mind thereby induced in X, such as being
put on notice or having knowledge,[9] or motive,[10] or to show the information which X had as bearing on the reasonableness [11] or good faith or
voluntariness [12] of the subsequent conduct of X, or anxiety,[13] the evidence is not subject to attack as hearsay. The same rationale applies to
proof by the defendant, in cases of assault or homicide, of communicated threats made to him by the person whom he is alleged to have killed
or assaulted. If offered to show his reasonable apprehension of danger
it is not offered for a hearsay purpose; [14] its value for this purpose does
not depend on the truth of the statement.

In the situations discussed above, as will appear from the illustrative
cases cited in the notes, the out-of-court statement will frequently have
an impermissible hearsay aspect as well as the permissible nonhearsay
aspect. For example, the inspector's statement that the tires were
defective is susceptible of being used improperly by the trier of fact as
proof that the tires were in fact defective, rather than only as notice of

For an alternative analytical route to
classification as nonhearsay in the gambling cases, see United States v. Zenni, 492
F.Supp. 464 (E.D.Ky.1980), infra § 250, n.
19.

8. Weinstein & Berger, Evidence
¶ 801(c)[01]; 6 Wigmore, Evidence § 1789
(Chadbourn rev. 1976).

9. Worsham v. A.H. Robins Co., 734
F.2d 676 (11th Cir.1984) (reports, complaints, other lawsuits admissible to show
notice of adverse reactions to Dalkon
Shield); Player v. Thompson, 259 S.C. 600,
193 S.E.2d 531 (1972) (testimony that inspector said in presence of defendants that
tires were defective, to prove notice of that
condition).

10. Emich Motors Corp. v. General Motors Corp., 181 F.2d 70 (7th Cir.1950), reversed on other grounds 340 U.S. 558 (complaining letters from customers offered to
show that cancellation of dealer's franchise
was not motivated by dealer's refusal to
finance car sales through defendant's finance affiliate); United States v. Cline, 570
F.2d 731 (8th Cir.1978) (threat by victim
that he would turn defendant in to the
U.S. marshal, to show motive for murder);
State v. Hull, 210 Conn. 481, 556 A.2d 154
(1989) (testimony that victim told defendant husband that she was involved with
another man and would not return to him,
admissible to show motive in murder prosecution).

11. McAfee v. Travis Gas Corp., 137
Tex. 314, 153 S.W.2d 442 (1941) (injuries
due to gas explosion which occurred when

man to whom plaintiff was pointing out
leaks in pipeline struck match; on issue of
contributory negligence, plaintiff's testimony that man said he was from pipeline
company); Johnson v. Misericordia Community Hospital, 97 Wis.2d 521, 294
N.W.2d 501 (App.1980) (negligent investigation of qualifications of physician granted surgical privileges; records and committee reports of other hospital not hearsay to
show information available to defendant
hospital). As to probable cause, see § 180
note 8 supra.

12. United States v. Rubin, 591 F.2d
278 (5th Cir.1979), cert. denied 444 U.S.
864 (prosecution of labor organizer for em-
bezzling union funds by taking unauthorized salary increases; error to exclude testimony of defendant that union presidents
told him union constitutions were flexible,
offered on issue of intent); United States v.
Eisenstein, 731 F.2d 1540 (11th Cir.1984)
(to show complete disclosure to attorney by
client defending on grounds of good faith
reliance on advice of counsel); Gray v.
Maxwell, 206 Neb. 385, 293 N.W.2d 90
(1980) (proper to admit evidence of telephone conversation as bearing on listener-
party's voluntariness in relinquishing
child).

13. Ferrara v. Galluchio, 5 N.Y.2d 16,
176 N.Y.S.2d 996, 152 N.E.2d 249 (1958)
(statement to plaintiff by dermatologist
that condition might become cancerous, in
medical malpractice action for causing X-
ray burns).

14. See § 275 infra.

defective condition, with other proof being required of the fact of defective condition. Or the evidence that the man who lit the match said he was from the gas company might improperly be taken as proof of agency, rather than as a circumstance bearing on the reasonableness of plaintiff's conduct. Generally the disposition has been to admit the evidence with a limiting instruction, unless the need for the evidence for the proper purpose is substantially outweighed by the danger of improper use.[15] However, one area of apparently widespread abuse should be noted. In criminal cases, an arresting or investigating officer should not be put in the false position of seeming just to have happened upon the scene; he should be allowed some explanation of his presence and conduct. His testimony that he acted "upon information received," or words to that effect, should be sufficient.[16] Nevertheless, cases abound in which the officer is allowed to relate historical aspects of the case, replete with hearsay statements in the form of complaints and reports, on the ground that he was entitled to give the information upon which he acted.[17] The need for the evidence is slight, the likelihood of misuse great.

Indirect versions of hearsay statements; group statements. If the purpose of offered testimony is to use an out-of-court statement to evidence the truth of facts stated therein, the hearsay objection cannot be obviated by eliciting the purport of the statement in indirect form.[18] Thus evidence as to the purport of "information received" by the

15. See § 59 supra.

16. United States v. Hilliard, 569 F.2d 143 (D.C.Cir.1977); State v. Turner, 392 So.2d 436 (La.1980); People v. Eady, 409 Mich. 356, 294 N.W.2d 202 (1980); State v. Braxter, 568 A.2d 311 (R.I.1990). See also United States v. Lamberty, 778 F.2d 59, 61 (1st Cir.1985) ("We do not find that the evidence introduced to show the government's motive in setting the trap is in any way relevant to proving the elements of the counts charged. While the jurors may have been curious as to why the inspectors began their operation, enlightenment on this matter had no probative value."); United States v. Taylor, 900 F.2d 779 (4th Cir.1990) (reason why suspect targeted not relevant to guilt); Comment, 36 Mercer L.Rev. 733 (1985).

17. Illustrative cases are United States v. Lazcano, 881 F.2d 402 (7th Cir.1989) (officer testified that Colombian man told him that defendant was part of a Mexican drug family; admissible to show context of investigation); United States v. Freeman, 816 F.2d 558 (10th Cir.1987) (officer testified that informant told him that defendant was passing counterfeit money; admissible to explain the government's investigation); Cobb v. State, 244 Ga. 344, 260 S.E.2d 60 (1979) (officer testified to "victim's statements as to the details of the crimes and partial identification of his as-

sailant and the getaway car"); Walters v. State, 271 Ind. 598, 394 N.E.2d 154 (1979) (murder; officer testified that victim's father said accused had a "vendetta" against the victim); State v. Thomas, 61 Ohio St.2d 223, 400 N.E.2d 401 (1980) (officer testified that he had information about a bookmaking operation).

Contra: United States v. Brown, 767 F.2d 1078 (4th Cir.1985) (testimony of investigator that defendant had stolen goods went beyond background information); United States v. Hernandez, 750 F.2d 1256 (5th Cir.1985) (referral by U.S. Customs of defendant as a drug smuggler inadmissible to explain motivation behind DEA's investigation, particularly in light of government's subsequent use of testimony); United States v. Escobar, 674 F.2d 469 (5th Cir.1982) (error to allow officer to testify that he ran name of one defendant through computer and obtained print-out that he was "a known narcotics smuggler"); State v. Doughty, 359 N.W.2d 439 (Iowa 1984) (testimony about statement of victim to police officer went beyond scope of simply explaining officer's actions culminating in defendant's arrest).

18. Falknor, "Indirect" Hearsay, 31 Tul.L.Rev. 3 (1956).

witness,[19] or testimony of the results of investigations made by other persons,[20] offered as proof of the facts asserted out of court, are properly classed as hearsay.

Whether this approach should be applied to collective or group decisions presented by the testimony of one of the group is a matter of some uncertainty. The situation most likely to arise is probably a decision reached after consultation by a group of doctors. Authority on the hearsay question is scattered.[21] In any event, the problem seems largely academic in view of the liberalization of the expert opinion rule to allow opinions to be based on reports of others [22] and of the regular entry rule to include opinions and diagnoses.[23]

Reputation. In the earlier stages of jury trial, when the jurors were expected to seek out the facts by neighborhood inquiries (instead of having the witnesses bring the facts through their testimony in court) community reputation was a frequent source of information for the jurors. When in the late 1600's the general doctrine excluding hearsay began to take form [24] the use of reputation either directly by the jurors or through the testimony of the witnesses, in certain areas of proof, was so well established that exceptions to the hearsay rule for reputation in these ancient uses soon came to be recognized.[25]

Reputation is a composite description of what the people in a community have said and are saying about a matter. A witness who testifies to reputation testifies to his generalized memory of a series of out-of-court statements. Whether reputation is hearsay depends on the same tests we have applied to evidence of other particular out-of-court statements.[26] Accordingly proof of reputation will often not be hearsay at all. Thus, in an action for defamation, where an element of damages is injury to the plaintiff's reputation, and the defendant offers on the issue of damages, evidence that the plaintiff's reputation was bad before

19. Hobart v. Hobart Estate Co., 26 Cal.2d 412, 159 P.2d 958 (1945) (dictum); Dougherty v. City of New York, 267 App. Div. 828, 45 N.Y.S.2d 808 (1944), affirmed 295 N.Y. 786, 66 N.E.2d 299.

20. Greenland Development Corp. v. Allied Heating Products Co., 184 Va. 588, 35 S.E.2d 801, 164 A.L.R. 1312 (1945) (trial court excluded on grounds of want of knowledge and of hearsay and ruling held correct; as to which rule was applicable, the form of the testimony, not clearly disclosed, would in principle determine, see § 247, supra); Schaffer v. State, 777 S.W.2d 111 (Tex.Cr.App.1989) (defendant claimed he was a police informant in Abilene; detective's testimony that, after checking with an officer in Abilene, he did not think state should drop the case, held inadmissible as an indirect assertion that the Abilene officer told him that defendant was not an informant).

21. Bauman v. People, 130 Colo. 248, 274 P.2d 591 (1954) (staff report inadmissible hearsay); Village of Ponca v. Crawford, 18 Neb. 551, 26 N.W. 365 (1886) (consultation among independent practitioners inadmissible hearsay; Clark v. Hudson, 265 Ala. 630, 93 So.2d 138 (1956) (inadmissible hearsay, whether consultation of independent practitioners or staff, resolving conflict in earlier decisions); Nail v. State, 231 Ark. 70, 328 S.W.2d 836 (1959), and Rodgers v. State, 261 Ark. 293, 547 S.W.2d 419 (1977) (staff report not hearsay or in violation of confrontation rights).

22. See § 15 supra.

23. See § 287 infra.

24. See § 244 supra.

25. 5 Wigmore, Evidence § 1580 (Chadbourn rev. 1974).

26. See § 246 supra.

the slander,[27] the evidence is not hearsay. Another example is proof of reputation in the community offered as evidence that some person in the community had knowledge of the reputed facts.[28]

Applying again the general definition we may conclude that evidence of reputation is hearsay only when offered to prove the truth of the fact reputed and hence depending for its value on the veracity of the collective asserters.[29] There are moreover, exceptions to the rule against hearsay, for reputation of particular facts, often restricted to certain uses and issues.[30]

Evidence of reputation, not falling within the established exceptions, when offered to prove the fact reputed, is constantly being excluded as hearsay,[31] as for example, when reputation is offered to prove ownership,[32] sanity,[33] the existence of a partnership,[34] or a predisposition to commit crime, to rebut a defense of entrapment.[35]

Prior statements of witnesses; admissions of party-opponents. The status of prior statements of witnesses [36] and of admissions by party-opponents [37] as hearsay is discussed in later sections.

§ 250. Conduct as Hearsay: "Implied Assertions"

Nonverbal conduct. Thus far our examination into what is and is not hearsay has been confined to out-of-court words, either spoken or written. Under the definition in § 246, if they constitute an assertion

---

27. As to the restrictions upon, and the allowability of the evidence under varying circumstances, see 1A Wigmore, Evidence §§ 70–76 (Tillers rev. 1983).

28. Lubbock Feed Lots, Inc. v. Iowa Beef Processors, Inc., 630 F.2d 250 (5th Cir.1980), rehearing denied 634 F.2d 1355 (apparent agency); Otis Elevator Co. v. McLaney, 406 P.2d 7 (Alaska 1965) (knowledge of condition of elevator door); Brennan v. Mayo, Sheriff, 105 Mont. 276, 72 P.2d 463 (1937) (sheriff's knowledge of plaintiff's ownership in action for conversion by him). In these cases, an inference is required from the existence of reputation to the fact of knowledge.

Other cases inject reputation as an element of negligent failure to inquire as to matters which inquiry would have disclosed. Western Stone Co. v. Whalen, 151 Ill. 472, 38 N.E. 241 (1894) (negligence in employing incompetent servant). The reputation of a third person may be a circumstance bearing upon the reasonableness of conduct in other ways. E.g. Lopez v. Heesen, 69 N.M. 206, 365 P.2d 448 (1961) (on issue whether defendant negligently sold firearm with improperly designed safety device, good reputation of manufacturer of device properly admitted).

In general, see 2 Wigmore, Evidence §§ 249, 251–259 (Chadbourn rev. 1979).

29. Brown v. Brown, 242 Ala. 630, 7 So.2d 557 (1942); Otis Elevator Co. v. McLaney, supra note 3; 5 Wigmore, Evidence §§ 1580, 1609 (Chadbourn rev. 1974); and see § 322 infra.

30. See § 322 infra.

31. See cases collected in Dec.Dig.Evidence ⊗322, 324.

32. Brown v. Brown, 242 Ala. 630, 7 So.2d 557 (1942); Louisville & Nashville Terminal Co. v. Jacobs, 109 Tenn. 727, 72 S.W. 954 (1903).

33. In re Nelson's Will, 210 N.C. 398, 186 S.E. 480, 105 A.L.R. 1441 (1936) with annotation on this point.

34. Greep v. Bruns, 160 Kan. 48, 159 P.2d 803, 811 (1945); 5 Wigmore, Evidence § 1624 (Chadbourn rev. 1974).

35. United States v. McClain, 531 F.2d 431 (9th Cir.1976), cert. denied 429 U.S. 835.

36. § 251 infra.

37. Chap. 25 infra.

and are offered as proof that the matter asserted happened or existed, they are hearsay.

Additional inquiry readily shows that non-verbal conduct may unmistakably be just as assertive in nature as though expressed in words. No one would contend, if, in response to a question "Who did it?," one of the auditors held up her hand, that this gesture could be treated as different from an oral or written statement. Other illustrations are the act of pointing to a particular person in a lineup as the equivalent of saying "That's the person," [1] or the sign language used by persons with impaired speech or hearing. These are clear instances of "non-verbal conduct of a person, if it is intended by him as an assertion," which under our hearsay definition receives the same treatment as oral or written assertions. The only difference is that an oral or written assertion is assumed, without further ado, to have been intended as such by virtue of being assertive in form, while in the case of the nonverbal conduct an intent to assert must be found by the judge as a precondition to classification as hearsay.

In contrast to the examples of clearly assertive nonverbal conduct given in the preceding paragraph, other situations may arise in which the conduct is just as clearly nonassertive. Thus an uncontrollable action or reaction by its very nature precludes any intent to make an assertion. Two cases will illustrate the difference. In the first, People v. Clark,[2] a murder suspect was described by witnesses as wearing a jacket with a fur-lined collar. The officer who arrested defendant at his home testified that he asked defendant if he had a jacket with a fur-lined collar, and that defendant turned to his wife and said, "I don't have one like that, do I dear?" The wife fainted. In the second case,

---

§ 250

1. United States v. Caro, 569 F.2d 411 (5th Cir.1978) (conspiracy to possess heroin; government agent testified that one defendant "pointed out" the house of his source; held hearsay); United States v. Katsougrakis, 715 F.2d 769 (2d Cir.1983), (to prove that burn victim participated in arson scheme, government offered testimony of a friend that victim, while wrapped in bandages from head to foot, nodded in the affirmative when asked whether he was paid to commit arson), cert. denied 464 U.S. 1040.

In the most frequently encountered instance, testimony as to the making of a prior out-of-court identification by pointing or similar act, the identifier usually also testifies as a witness, thus raising the question whether prior statements by witnesses are hearsay. See § 251 infra.

2. 6 Cal.App.3d 658, 86 Cal.Rptr. 106 (1970). It is, of course, possible that the wife feigned the fainting, or that it was genuine but caused by the general stress of the situation rather than by the reference to the jacket. These aspects are discussed at a later point in the text. Stronger instances of involuntary conduct may be Cole v. United States, 327 F.2d 360 (9th Cir. 1964) (to establish that robbery was by intimidation, testimony that bank teller was pale and shaking not hearsay); Bagwell & Stewart, Inc. v. Bennett, 214 Ga. 780, 107 S.E.2d 824 (1959) (testimony that members of family became sick and vomited because of odors of defendant's plant not hearsay).

See also People v. Gwinn, 111 Mich.App. 223, 314 N.W.2d 562 (1981) (rape victim cried upon viewing defendant's photograph).

Compare State v. Posten, 302 N.W.2d 638 (Minn.1981) (sexual assault; proper to admit evidence that 6-year old victim had nightmares and in her sleep exclaimed, "Stop it, Ray";) and Plummer v. Ricker, 71 Vt. 114, 41 A. 1045 (1898) (damages for dog bite of child; evidence that child in sleep said, "Take him off," not admissible, though offered only to show effect on victim's nerves).

Stevenson v. Commonwealth,[3] also a prosecution for murder, an officer testified he went to defendant's home and asked the wife for the shirt defendant was wearing when he arrived home after the time the murder was committed, and that she handed him a shirt. (Blood stains were found on the shirt.) In the first case, the conduct was held to have been nonassertive and hence not subject to the hearsay rule, while in the second it was held that the wife intended to assert that the shirt was the one in question, and her conduct was within the hearsay rule.

The disputed area lies between these extremes.

So-called "implied assertions." In the early part of the 19th century, the celebrated case of Wright v. Tatham [4] wound its way through the English courts. John Marsden, a country gentleman, had by will left his estate to one Wright, who had risen from a menial station to the position of steward and general man of business for Marsden. The legal heir, Admiral Tatham, brought proceedings to recover the manors of the estate, alleging that Marsden was not competent to make a will. Defendant Wright, supporting the will, offered in evidence several letters that had been written to the deceased by third persons no longer living.[5] The theory of the offer was that the letters indicated a belief on the part of the writers that Marsden was mentally competent, from which it might be inferred that he was in fact competent. The letters were admitted and the will sustained. However, upon retrial after reversal, the letters were excluded, and the verdict was against the will. The House of Lords ended eight years of litigation by upholding the ruling that the letters were inadmissible as being equivalent to hearsay evidence of the opinions of the writers. The holding was perhaps most pithily put by Baron Parke in these words:

> The conclusion at which I have arrived is, that proof of a particular fact which is not of itself a matter in issue, but which is relevant only as implying a statement or opinion of a third person on the matter in issue, is inadmissible in all cases where such a statement or opinion not on oath would be of itself inadmissible; and, therefore, in this case the letters which are offered only to prove the competence of the testator, that is the truth of the implied statements therein contained, were properly rejected, as the mere statement or opinion of the writer would certainly have

---

3. 218 Va. 462, 237 S.E.2d 779 (1977).

4. 7 Adolph. & E. 313, 112 Eng.Rep. 488 (Exch.Ch.1837), and 5 Cl. & F. 136 (H.L.1838). For further details of the litigation occasioned by "Silly" Marsden's will, see the entertaining and perceptive article, Maguire, The Hearsay System: Around and Through the Thicket, 14 Vand.L.Rev. 741 (1961).

5. The letters are set out in full in 112 Eng.Rep.Repr. 490–494 (1837). One of the letters, from the Vicar of the Parish, strongly urges the testator to have his attorney meet with the attorney of the Par-

ish, for the purpose of agreeing upon a statement of facts about some dispute between the testator and the Parish to be laid before counsel to whose opinions both sides should submit. Another is from a curate appointed by the testator, written on his resignation and expressing his gratitude and respect. Two others invite the testator to come, in company with the steward, to certain meetings to be held apparently for purposes connected with local public business or politics. A letter from a cousin describes conditions that he found on a voyage to America.

been inadmissible.[6]

To describe the evidence in Wright v. Tatham as "implied statements," i.e. implied assertions, as suggested by Baron Parke is, of course, to prejudge the issue, for it is to extrajudicial assertions that the hearsay rule applies.

During the progress of the case hundreds of pages of opinions were written by the judges and numerous examples posed, including these:

(1) proof that the underwriters have paid the amount of the policy, as evidence of the loss of a ship; (2) proof of payment of a wager, as evidence of the happening of the event which was the subject of the bet; (3) precautions of the family, to show the person involved was a lunatic; (4) as evidence of sanity, the election of the person in question to high office; (5) "the conduct of a physician who permitted a will to be executed by a sick testator;" (6) "the conduct of a deceased captain on a question of seaworthiness, who, after examining every part of the vessel embarked in it with his family."

Taking example (6) as an illustration, the line of reasoning suggested is (a) that the captain's conduct tends to prove that he believed the ship to be seaworthy, and (b) that from this belief the conclusion might be drawn that the ship was in fact seaworthy. This, the judges said, was the equivalent of an out-of-court statement by the captain that the ship was seaworthy and hence inadmissible hearsay. Functional equivalence can, however, be misleading. The vital element of intent to assert is missing from each of the examples.

In many of the cases after Wright v. Tatham the presence of an arguable hearsay issue went unrecognized.[7] The earlier cases tended to favor the objection,[8] but the current trend is much in the opposite direction. The Federal Rule,[9] for example, as well as numerous decisions,[10] requires that nonverbal conduct must be intended to be an assertion if it is to be classed as hearsay.

---

6. 7 Adolph. & E. at 388, 112 Eng.Rep. at 516.

7. Falknor, The "Hear–Say" Rule as a "See–Do" Rule: Evidence of Conduct, 33 Rocky Mt.L.Rev. 133, 135 (1961).

8. Hanson v. State, 160 Ark. 329, 254 S.W. 691 (1923) (to show failing condition of bank, evidence that other banks demanded payment of collections in cash); People v. Bush, 300 Ill. 532, 133 N.E. 201 (1921) (on issue whether prosecuting witness had venereal disease, evidence that institution in which she was placed did not segregate her, as was done with venereal cases); Powell v. State, 88 Tex.Cr.R. 367, 227 S.W. 188 (1921) (to rebut claim of accused that his grandmother had authorized him to sell her cow, evidence that on her return she demanded back the cow from the purchaser).

Similarly, flight of a third person has been held to be the equivalent of a confession by him and hence inadmissible as hearsay. People v. Mendez, 193 Cal. 39, 223 P. 65 (1924); State v. Menilla, 177 Iowa 283, 158 N.W. 645 (1916). However, note should be taken of the trend to admit third-person confessions under the hearsay exception for declarations against interest. See § 318, infra.

9. See § 246 supra.

10. State v. Izzo, 94 Ariz. 226, 383 P.2d 116 (1963) (evidence that wife did not return home night before her murder as proof of her fear of accused husband); Taylor v. Centennial Bowl, Inc., 65 Cal.2d 114, 52 Cal.Rptr. 561, 416 P.2d 793 (1966) (evidence of requests for police assistance as proof of prior disturbances on premises); Belvidere Land Co. v. Owen Park Plaza, Inc., 362 Mich. 107, 106 N.W.2d 380 (1960) (evidence of receipt of telephone calls and visitors asking for Owen Park Plaza to

Is this trend consistent with the policies that underlie the hearsay rule? A satisfactory resolution can be had only by making an evaluation in terms of the dangers which the hearsay rule is designed to guard against, i.e., imperfections of perception, memory, and narration. It is believed that such an analysis can result only in rejecting the view that evidence of conduct, from which may be inferred a belief, from which in turn may be inferred the happening of the event which produced the belief, is the equivalent of an assertion that the event happened and hence hearsay. People do not, prior to raising their umbrellas, say to themselves in soliloquy form, "It is raining," nor does the motorist go forward on the green light only after making an inward assertion, "The light is green." [11] The conduct offered in the one instance to prove it was raining and in the other that the light was green, involves no intent to communicate the fact sought to be proved, and it was recognized long ago that purposeful deception is less likely in the absence of intent to communicate.[12] True, the threshold question whether communication was in fact intended may on occasion present difficulty,[13] yet the probabilities against intent are so great as to justify imposing the burden of establishing it upon the party urging the hearsay objection.[14]

Even though the risks arising from purposeful deception may be slight or nonexistent in the absence of intent to communicate, the objection remains that the actor's perception and memory are untested by cross-examination for the possibility of honest mistake. However, in contrast to the risks from purposeful deception those arising from the chance of honest mistake seem more sensibly to be factors useful in evaluating weight and credibility rather than grounds for exclusion. Moreover, the kind of situation involved is ordinarily such as either to minimize the likelihood of flaws of perception and memory or to present circumstances lending themselves to their evaluation. While the suggestion has been advanced that conduct evidence ought to be

show confusion with Owen Park Apartments); Puget Sound Rendering, Inc. v. Puget Sound By–Products, 26 Wash.App. 724, 615 P.2d 504 (1980) (semble); Long v. Asphalt Paving Co., 47 N.C.App. 564, 268 S.E.2d 1 (1980) (issue whether North Carolina residents killed in plane crash on trip to Florida were in course of employment; evidence that they were seen walking around Florida job site); Matter of C.L., 397 N.W.2d 81 (S.D.1986) (child's play-acting with anatomically correct dolls was not an assertion of child abuse and therefore not hearsay).

See also the discussion of conduct as evidence of marriage, legitimacy, family history, etc., in 2 Wigmore, Evidence §§ 268–272 (Chadbourn rev. 1979).

11. The examples are from Falknor, The "Hear–Say" Rule as a "See–Do" Rule:

Evidence of Conduct, 33 Rocky Mt.L.Rev. 133 (1960).

12. Seligman, An Exception to the Hearsay Rule, 26 Harv.L.Rev. 146, 148 (1912): "only conduct apparently intended to convey thought can come under the ban of the hearsay rule."

13. Finman, Implied Assertions as Hearsay: Some Criticism of the Uniform Rules of Evidence, 14 Stan.L.Rev. 682, 695 (1962). See, e.g., Norris v. Detroit United Railway, 185 Mich. 264, 151 N.W. 747 (1915) (testimony of physician that plaintiff flinched when pressure was applied to allegedly injured ankle, held hearsay).

14. Falknor, supra note 11 at 136; Maguire, The Hearsay System: Around and Through the Thicket, 14 Vand.L.Rev. 741, 765 (1961); Advisory Committee Note, Fed. R.Evid. 801(a).

admitted only when the actor's behavior has an element of significant reliance as an assurance of trustworthiness,[15] a sufficient response here too is that the factor is one of evaluation, not a ground for exclusion.[16] Undue complication ought to be avoided in the interest of ease of application. The same can be said with respect to the possibility that the conduct may be ambiguous so that the trier of fact will draw a wrong inference.[17] Finally, a rule attaching the hearsay tag to the kind of conduct under consideration is bound to operate unevenly, since the possibility of a hearsay objection will more often than not simply be overlooked.[18]

Out-of-court assertions not offered to prove the truth of the matter asserted. The preceding discussion relates to hearsay aspects of nonassertive conduct. Wright v. Tatham, on which the discussion is largely based, did not, however, involve nonassertive conduct; it involved conduct that was, in a measure at least, assertive. The hearsay status of assertive conduct must now be considered. If one of the letters had said, "Marsden, you are competent to make a will," it would clearly fall within the definition of hearsay, an out-of-court assertion offered to prove the truth of the matter asserted. But that was not the case: the letters, though assertive in form, were not offered to prove the truth of what was asserted. The letter from the cousin describing conditions found on his voyage to America for example was not offered as evidence of conditions in America but as evidence that the writer believed Marsden to be of reasonable intelligence, from which belief competency might be inferred. Under these conditions, should the evidence be treated as hearsay?

The pattern of the current decisions [19] and the Federal Rules and

---

15. Varying versions are found in McCormick, The Borderland of Hearsay, 39 Yale L.J. 489, 504 (1930); Morgan, Hearsay and Non–Hearsay, 48 Harv.L.Rev. 1138, 1159 (1935); Falknor, Silence as Hearsay, 89 U.Pa.L.Rev. 192, 217 (1940). The position was essentially a transitional one, with the element of reliance being advanced as a justification for breaking away from the existing pattern of exclusion, rather than as a requirement. See note 24 infra.

16. Morgan, Hearsay, 25 Miss.L.J. 1, 8 (1953); Falknor, The "Hear–Say" Rule as a "See–Do" Rule: Evidence of Conduct, 33 Rocky Mt.L.Rev. 133, 137 (1961).

17. Maguire, The Hearsay System: Around and Through the Thicket, 14 Vand.L.Rev. 741, 760 (1961). Compare Finman, Implied Assertions as Hearsay: Some Criticism of the Uniform Rules of Evidence, 14 Stan.L.Rev. 682, 688 (1962). Or the conduct may be so "insolubly ambiguous", as the Court said of silence following a *Miranda* warning, in Doyle v. Ohio, 426 U.S. 610 (1976), that it permits no rational inference to be drawn. See

also, United States v. Carroll, 710 F.2d 164 (4th Cir.1983) (accused claimed he was tricked into making incriminating remarks by officer's smiling when he looked at the footprints of accused; held not the functional equivalent of interrogation under *Miranda*), cert. denied 464 U.S. 1008; United States v. Laughlin, 772 F.2d 1382 (7th Cir.1985) (shrug of shoulders not a statement for purposes of self-incrimination); United States v. Disbrow, 768 F.2d 976 (8th Cir.1985) (cellmate testified accused smiled when asked whether he supplied the cocaine, claimed to be an adoptive admission, but the objection was not considered in light of all the evidence), cert. denied 474 U.S. 1023.

18. Falknor supra note 16, at 137.

19. United States v. Mejias, 552 F.2d 435 (2d Cir.1977), cert. denied 434 U.S. 847 (receipted hotel bill found in defendant's possession not hearsay for purpose of establishing connection between him and hotel); United States v. Marino, 658 F.2d 1120 (6th Cir.1981) (semble); United States v. Mazyak, 650 F.2d 788 (5th Cir.1981),

their counterparts [20] is to answer the question in the negative: the out-of-court assertion is not hearsay if offered as proof of something other than the matter asserted. The supporting arguments, however, are somewhat less compelling than is so with respect to nonassertive conduct, since the presence of an assertion reintroduces intent as an element of risk to be considered. This risk is believed not to be of such dimension as to mandate treatment as hearsay: the intent does not embrace the inference suggested, and the likelihood of purposeful deception is accordingly lessened.[21]

At this point it is apparent from the treatment of what is and what is not hearsay that the definition of hearsay previously advanced is less inclusive than the logical and analytical possibilities would allow. At a fairly early stage of his career, Professor Morgan, whose bright mind contributed much to the law of evidence, suggested:

> A comprehensive definition of hearsay * * * would include (1) all conduct of a person, verbal or nonverbal, intended by him to operate as an assertion when offered either to prove the truth of the matter asserted or to prove that the asserter believed the matter asserted to be true, and (2) all conduct of a person, verbal or nonverbal, not intended by him to

cert. denied 455 U.S. 922 (letter found on vessel addressed to all four defendants and vessel, not hearsay for purpose of linking defendants with vessel and one another); United States v. Hensel, 699 F.2d 18 (1st Cir.1983), cert. denied 461 U.S. 958 (drinking glass bearing defendant's nickname not hearsay for purpose of connecting him with occupants of premises where found); United States v. Ashby, 864 F.2d 690 (10th Cir.1988), cert. denied 110 S.Ct. 1793 (work order for car repair admissible to tie defendant to car containing packages of marijuana). Wilkinson v. Service, 249 Ill. 146, 94 N.E. 50 (1911) (statements by testator that children lacked affection for him, not hearsay for purpose of showing his state of mind); Loetsch v. New York City Omnibus Corp., 291 N.Y. 308, 52 N.E.2d 448 (1943) (action by husband for wrongful death; on issue of damages, statements in wife's will castigating husband and bequeathing him one dollar, not hearsay for purpose of showing unlikelihood of contribution by wife to support of husband; error to exclude); Long v. Asphalt Paving Co., 47 N.C.App. 564, 268 S.E.2d 1 (1980) (evidence that one employee while driving past asphalt plant near job site in Florida said to other, "That is where you can get the asphalt," not hearsay to prove they were in course of employment on plane trip from North Carolina to Florida during which both were killed), But see United States v. Reynolds, 715 F.2d 99 (3d Cir.1983) (co-defendant's statement that he did not tell police anything about defendant, hearsay when offered to establish existence of con-

spiracy and joint participation in the offenses charged).

20. See § 246 supra. The history of the development is traced in 5 Wigmore § 1362 note 1 (Chadbourn rev. 1974).

21. Implied assertions should be distinguished, although perhaps only as a matter of degree, from some other kinds of indirect statements. For example, the statement "it will stop raining in an hour," is hearsay if offered to prove that it was raining at the time of the statement. The fact to be proved is a "necessary implication" of the statement made. See Seligman, supra note 12 at 150–151, n. 13; Wellborn, The Definition of Hearsay in the Federal Rules of Evidence, 61 Tex.L.Rev. 49, 75 (1982). Similarly, metaphorical speech such as a statement that the "sky is on fire" would be hearsay to prove that the sun was setting. Id. at 78. Intuitively, both types of statements fall within the Federal Rules definition of hearsay and no case has held to the contrary. The inclusion of such statements within the definition of hearsay can be distinguished from implied assertions on several bases including the more certain intent of the declarant, the inevitability of the implication from the statement or simply based upon the greater likelihood of deception. Compare the approaches in Salzburg & Redden, Federal Rules of Evidence Manual 717 (4th ed. 1986); Graham, Handbook of Federal Rules of Evidence § 801.7, at 714–717; Wellborn, supra at 73–83.

operate as an assertion, when offered either to prove both his state of mind and the external event or condition which caused him to have that state of mind, or to prove that his state of mind was truly reflected by that conduct.[22]

Further thought and observation, however, apparently convinced him that a definition of hearsay expanded to the outer limits suggested by logic and analysis was undesirable, with needless complication of the hearsay rule that outweighed any supposed advantage. He first advocated removing nonassertive conduct from the hearsay definition.[23] Then he took the final step of removing from the definition assertive conduct not offered to prove the matter asserted.

The adoption of Uniform Rule 62(1) and Rule 63 defining hearsay evidence would be a boon to lawyers and judges. Rule 62(1) reads " 'Statement' means not only an oral or written expression but also nonverbal conduct of a person intended by him as a substitute for words in expressing the matter stated." And Rule 63 states: "Evidence of a statement which is made other than by a witness while testifying at the hearing offered to prove the truth of the matter asserted is hearsay." These provisions would avoid all the conflicts in the decisions where the evidence describes conduct from which a relevant inference may be drawn and where very careful analysis is required to determine whether the process of reasoning requires the trier to treat the party exhibiting the conduct as if he were testifying.[24]

One further word should be added. The decision that a given item of evidence is not hearsay, or that it is hearsay but falls within an exception to the hearsay rule, may not in every case be conclusive when the evidence is attacked as contrary to the values sought to be protected by the hearsay rule. One class of litigants, namely accused persons in criminal cases, are the objects of special solicitude. Among the rights conferred upon them by the Sixth Amendment is the right of confrontation, and though evidence may not be classed as hearsay the possibility that it may violate the right of confrontation may require further examination.[25]

Knowledge. On an issue whether a given person was alive at a particular time, evidence that she said something at the time would be proof that she was alive. Whether she said, "I am alive," or "Hi, Joe,"

---

22. Morgan, Hearsay and Non–Hearsay, 48 Harv.L.Rev. 1138, 1144 (1935).

23. "It would be a boon to lawyers and litigants if hearsay were limited by the court to assertions, whether by words or substitutes for words, made otherwise than by a witness in the process of testifying in the instant trial or hearing. * * * It would exclude [from the definition of hearsay] evidence of a declarant's conduct offered to prove his state of mind and the facts creating that state of mind if the conduct did not consist of assertive words or symbols." Morgan, Hearsay, 25 Miss. L.J. 1, 8 (1953).

24. Morgan, Basic Problems of Evidence 253 (1962). Compare the transition apparent in Blakey, You Can Say That if You Want—The Redefinition of Hearsay in Rule 801 of the Proposed Federal Rules of Evidence, 35 Ohio St.L.J. 601 (1974), both "nonassertive acts and implied assertions" should be treated as hearsay, and Blakey, An Introduction to the Oklahoma Evidence Code: Hearsay, 14 Tulsa L.J. 635, 681 (1979), "implied assertions" based on assertive conduct should be classed and treated as hearsay.

25. See § 252 infra.

would be immaterial; the inference of life is drawn from the fact that she spoke, not from what was said. No problem of veracity is involved. In terms of the definition of hearsay, the first statement is not offered to prove what is asserted, since that is merely coincidence; the second statement is not even an assertion. Neither is hearsay.[26]

An extension of this analysis is applicable to declarations evincing knowledge, notice, or awareness of some fact. Proof that one talks about a matter demonstrates on its face that she was conscious or aware of it, and veracity does not enter into the situation. Caution is, however, indicated, since the self-proving aspect is limited strictly to what is said. Thus, the statement, "I know geometry," establishes no more than that the speaker is aware of the term "geometry", not that she has command of that subject. On the other hand, if the statement is itself a proposition of geometry, it is self-evident that the speaker does know geometry pro tanto; whether she prefaces her statement with "I know," is immaterial.[27]

When the existence of knowledge is sought to be used as the basis for a further inference, the possibility of infringing upon the hearsay rule is apparent. That possibility becomes a reality when the purpose of the evidence of knowledge is to prove the existence of the fact known. Statements of memory or belief are not generally allowed as proof of the happening of the event remembered or believed, since allowing the evidence would destroy the hearsay rule.[28] For this purpose, knowledge seems to be indistinguishable from memory and belief. There remains, however, the possibility of drawing from evidence of knowledge an inference other than the existence of the fact known.

Cases of establishing the identity of a person offer the possibility of an inference of this kind. Thus evidence that a person made statements indicating knowledge of matters likely to have been known only to X is receivable as tending to prove that she was in fact X.[29] In somewhat different vein, the often discussed case of Bridges v. State,[30] a

---

26. State v. Peeler, 126 Ariz. 254, 614 P.2d 335 (App.1980) (officer's testimony that elderly victim was mentally competent following sexual assault, based on what she said, not hearsay).

27. United States v. Parry, 649 F.2d 292 (5th Cir.1981) (defendant in narcotics prosecution claimed good faith belief that he was helping agents locate dealers; error to exclude mother's testimony that, when she asked defendant about incoming phone calls, he said they were from S., a narcotics agent with whom he was working; admissible to show knowledge of identity of caller); Borderland Coal Co. v. Kerns, 165 Ky. 487, 177 S.W. 266 (1915) (declarations by foreman before accident as to incompetence of fellow servant to show knowledge by foreman and company); Annot., 141 A.L.R. 704, 713; 2 Wigmore, Evidence §§ 265, 266 (Chadbourn rev. 1979).

28. See § 276 infra.

29. Nehring v. McMurrian, 94 Tex. 45, 57 S.W. 943 (1900); In re Moxley's Will, 103 Vt. 100, 152 A. 713 (1930). In the famous Tichborne heirship litigation a reverse application, i.e. lack of knowledge of things that would have been known to the missing son, was used to discredit the claimant to the estate. 2 Wigmore, Evidence § 270 (Chadbourn rev. 1979); Jaffee, Son and Heir—The Story of the Tichborne Case, 21 A.B.A.J. 107 (1935).

30. 247 Wis. 350, 19 N.W.2d 529 (1945), rehearing denied 247 Wis. 350, 19 N.W.2d 862. Compare State v. Galvan, 297 N.W.2d 344 (Iowa 1980) (defendant charged with aiding and abetting murder in which victim was bound, then stabbed and bludgeoned; evidence indicated defendant's two-year old daughter was in his company

prosecution for taking indecent liberties with a female child, involved the admissibility of evidence that the victim, in reporting the incident, gave a description of the house and its surroundings and of the room and its furnishings, where the alleged offense occurred. Other evidence showed that the description fitted the house and room where the defendant lived. While it has been suggested that the evidence depended for its value upon the observation, memory, and veracity of the child, and thus shared the hazards of hearsay,[31] the testimony nevertheless had value independently of these factors. Other witnesses had described the physical characteristics of the locale, and her testimony was not relied upon for that purpose. Once other possible sources of her knowledge were eliminated, which the court was satisfied was the case, the only remaining inference was that she had acquired that knowledge through a visit to the premises. The evidence was not within the ban of the hearsay rule.[32]

Silence as hearsay. One aspect of the conduct-as-hearsay problem is presented by cases where a failure to speak or act is offered to support an inference that conditions were such as would not evoke speech or action in a reasonable person.[33] The cases are likely to fall into two classes: (1) evidence of absence of complaints from other customers as disproof of claimed defects of goods or food or from other persons who would have been affected as disproof of a claimed injurious event or condition,[34] and (2) evidence from members of a family that a particular member never mentioned an event, or claim to or disposition of property, to prove nonoccurrence or nonexistence.[35] Often the presence of an arguable hearsay question is neither noted nor discussed.[36]

during the time when the murder was committed; the disputed evidence was that two days later the child bound her own hands with a belt from her mother's robe and made gestures as though beating herself on the chest; held hearsay but admissible as part of the *res gestae*). The end result is certainly defensible but scarcely on the grounds advanced. Comment, 66 Iowa L.Rev. 985 (1981). See § 268, infra.

31. Morgan, Evidence 1941–1945, 59 Harv.L.Rev. 481, 544 (1946).

32. See also United States v. Muscato, 534 F.Supp. 969 (E.D.N.Y.1982) (declarant's statements showing knowledge of a gun allegedly received from defendants admissible).

33. Falknor, Silence as Hearsay, 89 U.Pa.L.Rev. 192 (1940), The "Hear–Say" Rule as a "See–Do" Rule, 33 Rocky Mt. L.Rev. 133, 134 (1961).

34. Cases favoring a nonhearsay classification include Cain v. George, 411 F.2d 572 (5th Cir.1969); Silver v. New York Central Railroad Co., 329 Mass. 14, 105

N.E.2d 923 (1952); St. Louis Southwestern Railway Co. of Texas v. Arkansas & Texas Grain Co., 42 Tex.Civ.App. 125, 95 S.W. 656 (1906), error dismissed. Contrary, Payson v. Bombardier, Limited, 435 A.2d 411 (Me.1981) (hearsay but admissible under exception for absence of regular entry); Menard v. Cashman, 94 N.H. 428, 55 A.2d 156 (1947); Leech v. Hudson & Manhattan Railroad Co., 113 N.J.L. 366, 174 A. 537 (1934), affirmed 115 N.J.L. 114, 178 A. 754; George W. Saunders Live Stock Commission Co. v. Kincaid, 168 S.W. 977 (Tex.Civ. App.1914), error dismissed. Comment, 84 Dick.L.Rev. 605 (1980); Annot., 31 A.L.R.2d 190, 230.

35. Favoring nonhearsay are Latham v. Houston Land & Trust Co., 62 S.W.2d 519 (Tex.Civ.App.1933), error dismissed; State v. Childers, 196 La. 554, 199 So. 640 (1940). Contrary Sherling v. Continental Trust Co., 175 Ga. 672, 165 S.E. 560 (1932); Lake Drainage Commissioners v. Spencer, 174 N.C. 36, 93 S.E. 435 (1917).

36. E.g., Landfield v. Albiani Lunch Co., 268 Mass. 528, 168 N.E. 160 (1929).

While the cases at common law were divided as to the hearsay status of this kind of evidence, it appears under the definition of hearsay in Section 246 supra that the evidence, not being intended as an assertion, is not hearsay.[37]   It should be noted, however, that the support for admissibility, aside from any question of hearsay, may be stronger in the cases of absence of complaints than in other cases of silence.   The other cases present a variety of situations which in some instances suggest motivations for silence other than nonoccurrence of the disputed event, calling for evaluation in terms of whether the probative value of the evidence is outweighed by its prejudicial effect.[38]

Negative results of inquiries.   Somewhat related questions arise in respect to testimony by a witness that she has made inquiries among the residents of a given place where a certain person is claimed to live, and that she has been unable to find anyone who knows her or has any information about her.   When offered upon an issue as to whether due diligence has been exercised in attempting to locate a missing witness or other person, it is clear that testimony as to the results of the inquiries is not hearsay but is merely a narration of acts and efforts showing due diligence.[39]   However, the evidence of inquiries and inability to secure information may be offered as proof of the nonexistence of the person sought to be located, or of the fact that no such person lives at the place in question.   Then it may be argued that this is merely an indirect way of placing in evidence the statements of those of whom inquiry was made for the purpose of proving the truth of what they asserted.[40]   It is true that the residents of whom inquiry was made could be brought in to testify as to their want of knowledge but only at the price of substantial inconvenience and loss of time.[41]   However, application of the hearsay definition [42] yields a satisfactory avoidance of the hearsay argument.   The question asked would in essence have been, "Do you know, or have you ever heard of, a person named Mary Jones in this community?", with the answer, "No."   The assertion in the answer is that the declarant has not heard of the person, but the

---

37.   Federal Rule Evid. 803(7) treats the absence of a regular entry when one would ordinarily have been made, offered to prove the nonoccurrence of the event that would have been recorded, as an exception to the hearsay rule.   The Advisory Committee's Note, however, observes that it probably is not hearsay under the Federal Rules but is included as an exception to lay at rest any question raised by cases that have held not only that such evidence is hearsay but also that it does not fall within any exception to the hearsay rule.   See § 287 infra.

38.   Fed.R.Evid. 403.   See § 185 supra.

39.   Britton v. State, 2 Md.App. 285, 234 A.2d 274 (1967) (efforts to locate witness); Kraynick v. Nationwide Insurance Co., 72 N.J.Super. 34, 178 A.2d 50 (App.Div.1962),

on remand 80 N.J.Super. 296, 193 A.2d 419 (Law Div.) (efforts to locate insured under liability policy, in support of defense of failure to cooperate); 5 Wigmore, Evidence § 1414(2) (Chadbourn rev. 1974).

Absence of tidings and inability to locate a missing person are elements of the presumption of death after absence of a person for seven years.   See § 343 infra.

40.   The argument was upheld in State ex rel. Leonard v. Rosenthal, 123 Wis. 442, 102 N.W. 49 (1905).

41.   As was done in People v. Kosearas, 410 Ill. 456, 102 N.E.2d 534 (1951), and Dunn v. State, 15 Okl.Cr. 245, 176 P. 86 (1918).

42.   See § 246 supra.

inference suggested from the aggregate of the answers is not that the declarants had not heard of such a person, but rather that such a person does not exist. Almost all the cases have in any event ruled in favor of admitting the evidence, influenced no doubt by considerations of convenience, probable accuracy, and the difficulties that often attend the proving of a negative, often without reference to a possible hearsay problem[43] but classifying as nonhearsay when the question is raised.[44]

Silence as an admission by a party-opponent is treated elsewhere.[45]

§ 251. Prior Statements of Witnesses as Substantive Evidence [1]

As previously observed,[2] the traditional view had been that a prior statement of a witness is hearsay if offered to prove the happening of matters asserted therein. This categorization has not, of course, precluded using the prior statement for other purposes, e.g., to impeach the witness by showing a self-contradiction if the statement is inconsistent with his testimony[3] or to support his credibility under certain circumstances when the statement was consistent with his testimony.[4] But the prior statement has been admissible as proof of matter asserted therein, i.e. as "substantive" evidence, only when falling within one of the exceptions to the hearsay rule. This position has increasingly come under attack in recent years on both logical and practical grounds.

The logic of the orthodox view is that the previous statement of the witness is hearsay since its value rests on the credit of the declarant, who, when the statement was made, was not (1) under oath, (2) in the

---

43. E.g., People v. Sharp, 53 Mich. 523, 19 N.W. 168 (1884).

44. State v. Wentworth, 37 N.H. 196, 200, 217 (1858) (nonexistence of person in whose company accused claimed to have been at time of crime); Thomas v. State, 54 Okl.Cr. 97, 14 P.2d 953 (1932) (nonexistence of purported drawer of check); Annot., 49 A.L.R.2d 877. In Warrick v. Giron, 290 N.W.2d 166 (Minn.1980), a medical malpractice action, defense witnesses testified that a search of textbooks and recent articles showed no evidence that the surgical procedures employed were improper; held not hearsay, not offered to prove the truth of the matter asserted in the literature.

The analogy to public opinion polls and surveys will be apparent. See § 274, note 4 infra. Compare the discussion of reputation in § 249 supra.

45. See the general coverage in § 262 infra, and the discussion of the particular problems of treating the silence of a crimi-

nal defendant as an admission or confession in § 161 supra.

§ 251

1. 3A Wigmore, Evidence § 1018 (Chadbourn rev. 1970), 4 id. § 1132 (1972); Weinstein & Berger, Evidence ¶¶ 801(d)(1)[01]–801(d)(1)(C)[02]; Annot., 133 A.L.R. 1454; Dec.Dig. Witnesses ⊗397.

2. See § 34 supra with respect to prior inconsistent statements, and § 49 supra as to prior consistent statements.

3. The opposite party has, of course, been entitled to a jury instruction as to the limited use of the evidence. United States v. Tafollo–Cardenas, 897 F.2d 976 (9th Cir. 1990); Ritter v. People, 130 Ill. 255, 22 N.E. 605 (1889); Medlin v. County Board of Education, 167 N.C. 239, 83 S.E. 483 (1914). Failure to give the instruction, though not requested, has been held plain error. United States v. Lipscomb, 425 F.2d 226 (6th Cir.1970). Contra, State v. Ray, 259 La. 105, 249 So.2d 540 (1971).

4. See § 49 supra.

presence of the trier, or (3) subject to cross-examination.[5]

The counter-argument goes as follows: (1) The oath is no longer a principal safeguard of the trustworthiness of testimony.[6] Affidavits, though under oath, are not exempted from the hearsay rule. Moreover, of the numerous exceptions where evidence is admitted despite its being hearsay, in only one instance is the out-of-court statement required to have been under oath. And that instance, namely prior testimony, may arguably be regarded as a case of nonhearsay rather than as a hearsay exception.[7]

(2) With respect to affording the trier of fact the advantage of observing the demeanor of the witness while making the statement, Judge Learned Hand's classic statement puts it:

> If, from all that the jury see of the witness, they conclude that what he says now is not the truth, but what he said before, they are none the less deciding from what they see and hear of that person and in court.[8]

(3) The principal reliance for achieving credibility is no doubt cross-examination,[9] and this condition is thought to be satisfied. As Wigmore, who originally adhered to the traditional view, expressed it:

> Here, however, by hypothesis the witness is present and subject to cross-examination. There is ample opportunity to test him as to the basis for his former statement. The whole purpose of the hearsay rule has been already satisfied.[10]

The question remains whether cross-examination in order to be effective must take place at the time when the statement is made. The opinion where the orthodox view finds its most vigorous support urges:

> The chief merit of cross-examination is not that at some future time it gives the party opponent the right to dissect adverse testimony. Its principal virtue is the immediate application of the testing process. Its strokes fall while the iron is hot. False testimony is apt to harden and become unyielding to the blows of truth in proportion as the witness has

5. State v. Saporen, 205 Minn. 358, 285 N.W. 898 (1939); Ruhala v. Roby, 379 Mich. 102, 150 N.W.2d 146 (1967); Beaver and Biggs, Attending Witnesses' Prior Declarations as Evidence: Theory vs. Reality, 3 Ind.Leg.Forum 309 (1970). The Supreme Court of California used the same logic to conclude that a departure from traditional doctrine violated the Sixth Amendment right of confrontation. People v. Johnson, 68 Cal.2d 646, 68 Cal.Rptr. 599, 441 P.2d 111 (1968), cert. denied 393 U.S. 1051, and People v. Green, 70 Cal.2d 654, 75 Cal. Rptr. 782, 451 P.2d 422 (1969). This conclusion was rejected and *Green* reversed in California v. Green, 399 U.S. 149 (1970). See also on remand, People v. Green, 3 Cal.3d 981, 92 Cal.Rptr. 494, 479 P.2d 998 (1971).

6. Morgan, Hearsay Dangers and the Application of the Hearsay Concept, 62 Harv.L.Rev. 177 (1948). See 6 Wigmore, Evidence § 1827 (Chadbourn rev. 1976) for discussions of value of oath and id. § 1831 for similar references on the efficacy of penalties for perjury.

7. See § 301 infra.

8. Di Carlo v. United States, 6 F.2d 364 (2d Cir.1925).

9. Morgan, supra note 6; 5 Wigmore, Evidence § 1367 (Chadbourn rev. 1974).

10. 3A Wigmore, Evidence § 1018, p. 996 (Chadbourn rev. 1970). See also Model Code of Evidence, Comment to Rule 503(b), p. 234.

opportunity for reconsideration and influence by the suggestions of others * * *.[11]

Yet the fact in the case was that the witness did change his story very substantially; rather than hardening, his testimony yielded to something between the giving of the statement and the time of testifying.[12] This appears to be so in a very high proportion of the cases, and the circumstances most frequently suggest that the "something" which caused the change was an improper influence.

An additional persuasive factor against the orthodox rule is the superior trustworthiness of earlier statements, on the basis that memory hinges on recency. The prior statement is always nearer and usually very much nearer to the event than is the testimony. The fresher the memory, the fuller and more accurate it is.[13] The requirement of the hearsay exception for memoranda of past recollection, that the matter have been recorded while fresh in memory,[14] is based precisely on this principle.

These various considerations led to a substantial movement to abandon the orthodox view completely. Thus the Model Code of Evidence provided:

> Evidence of a hearsay declaration is admissible if the judge finds that the declarant * * * is present and subject to cross-examination.[15]

Substantial support for this position began to appear in the decisions.[16]

Under the Model Code Wigmore position, all prior statements of witnesses, regardless of their nature, were exempted from the ban of the hearsay rule. This complete rejection of the orthodox rule resulted in uneasiness that a practice might develop among lawyers whereby a carefully prepared statement would be offered in lieu of testimony,

---

11. State v. Saporen, 205 Minn. 358, 362, 285 N.W. 898, 901 (1939).

12. Both *Saporen,* supra note 11 and Ruhala v. Roby, 379 Mich. 102, 150 N.W.2d 146 (1967), a more recent vociferous defense of the orthodox view, reveal a searching disclosure of the inconsistencies between earlier statement and testimony and of the witness' explanation of his change of position. The orthodox position was effectively demolished in California v. Green, 399 U.S. 149 (1970).

13. Stewart, Perception, Memory, and Hearsay: A Criticism of Present Law and the Proposed Federal Rules of Evidence, 1970 Utah L.Rev. 1, 8–22, discussing the characteristics of memory, with citations of numerous psychological authorities. A counter-argument which carried considerable weight when the Federal Rules were under review in the Congress, particularly in the House of Representatives, was that law enforcement officials and claim adjust-

ers often improperly influence the making and content of statements.

14. See § 281 infra. Note also that the regularly kept records exception requires that the entry be made at or near the time of the transaction recorded. Infra § 286.

15. Model Code of Evidence Rule 503(b). To the same effect was the original Uniform Rule 63(1) (1953).

16. Hobbs v. State, 359 P.2d 956 (Alaska 1961), cert. denied 367 U.S. 909; Jett v. Commonwealth, 436 S.W.2d 788 (Ky.1969); Thomas v. State, 186 Md. 446, 47 A.2d 43 (1946); Letendre v. Hartford Accident & Indemnity Co., 21 N.Y.2d 518, 289 N.Y.S.2d 183, 236 N.E.2d 467 (1968); Vance v. State, 190 Tenn. 521, 230 S.W.2d 987 (1950), cert. denied 339 U.S. 988; Gelhaar v. State, 41 Wis.2d 230, 163 N.W.2d 609 (1969). See also the discussion in United States v. De Sisto, 329 F.2d 929 (2d Cir.1964), cert. denied 377 U.S. 979.

merely tendering the witness for cross-examination on the statement.[17] The practice seems not in fact to have materialized in the jurisdictions where the orthodox rule was rejected,[18] but the potential for abuse nevertheless remained. As a consequence, the Advisory Committee on Federal Rules of Evidence adopted an intermediate position, neither admitting nor rejecting prior statements of witnesses *in toto,* but exempting from classification as hearsay certain prior statements thought by circumstances to be free of the danger of abuse. The exempt statements are (A) inconsistent statements, (B) consistent statements when admissible to rebut certain attacks upon the credibility of the witness, and (C) statements of identification. Federal Rule of Evidence 801(d)(1) provides:

> **(d) Statements which are not hearsay.**—A statement is not hearsay if—

>> **(1) Prior statement by witness.**—The declarant testifies at the trial or hearing and is subject to cross-examination concerning the statement, and the statement is (A) inconsistent with the declarant's testimony, and was given under oath subject to the penalty of perjury at a trial, hearing, or other proceeding, or in a deposition, or (B) consistent with the declarant's testimony and is offered to rebut an express or implied charge against the declarant of recent fabrication or improper influence or motive, or (C) one of identification of a person made after perceiving the person; or

(A) Prior inconsistent statements. The witness who has told one story aforetime and another today has opened the gates to all the vistas of truth which the common law practice of cross-examination and re-examination was invented to explore. The reasons for the change of face, whether forgetfulness, carelessness, pity, terror, or greed, may be explored by the two questioners in the presence of the trier of fact, under oath, casting light on which is the true story and which the false. It is hard to escape the view that evidence of a prior inconsistent statement, when declarant is on the stand to explain it if he can, has in high degree the safeguards of examined testimony.[19] In addition, allowing it as substantive evidence pays a further dividend in avoiding a limiting instruction quite unlikely to be heeded by a jury.

17. E.g. Dow, KLM v. Tuller: A New Approach to Admissibility of Prior Statements of a Witness, 41 Neb.L.Rev. 598 (1962).

18. Probably for the commonsensical reason that testimony of a live witness in the vast majority of cases will carry greater conviction than his previously prepared statement. And see Maguire, Evidence: Common Sense and Common Law 63 (1947).

19. Almost all the cases cited in note 16 supra involved prior inconsistent statements, as did California v. Green, 399 U.S. 149 (1970), overruling the claim that admission of such evidence violated Sixth Amendment confrontation rights. For more recent decisions adopting the allowance of prior inconsistent statements as substantive evidence, see Gibbons v. State, 248 Ga. 858, 286 S.E.2d 717 (1982), and State v. Copeland, 278 S.C. 572, 300 S.E.2d

When is a prior statement inconsistent?[20] On the face of it, a prior statement describing an event would not be inconsistent with testimony by the witness that he no longer remembers the event.[21] Yet the tendency of unwilling or untruthful witnesses to seek refuge in forgetfulness is well recognized.[22] Hence the judge may be warranted in concluding under the circumstances the claimed lack of memory of the event is untrue and in effect an implied denial of the prior statement, thus qualifying it as inconsistent and nonhearsay.[23] In the absence of such a finding, the presence of inconsistency is difficult to maintain.

As originally drafted by the Advisory Committee and transmitted to the Congress by the Supreme Court, the Federal Rule contained no requirement as to the conditions under which the prior inconsistent statement must be made. The Congress, however, imposed strict limitations, adding the language "given under oath subject to the penalty of perjury [24] at a trial, hearing, or other proceeding, or in a deposition * * *."[25] The result of the limitation is to confine substantive use of prior inconsistent statements virtually to those made in the course of judicial proceedings, including grand jury testimony,[26] although allowing use for impeachment without regard to the Congressional limitation. Where both are present in the same case, the likelihood of jury confusion is evident.

(B) Prior consistent statements. While prior consistent statements are hearsay by the traditional view and inadmissible as substantive

63 (1982), cert. denied 460 U.S. 1103 rehearing denied 462 U.S. 1124.

20. See § 34 supra, as to the requirement of inconsistency in prior statements used for impeachment.

21. E.g., People v. Sam, 71 Cal.2d 194, 77 Cal.Rptr. 804, 454 P.2d 700 (1969) (two years between event and trial). See also United States v. Bonnett, 877 F.2d 1450 (10th Cir.1989) (witness's prior statement properly excluded as not inconsistent where witness's response to statement on cross-examination was: "It's possible.").

22. 3A Wigmore, Evidence § 1043 (Chadbourn rev. 1970).

23. United States v. Insana, 423 F.2d 1165 (2d Cir.1970), cert. denied 400 U.S. 841; California v. Green, 399 U.S. 149 (1970), on remand in People v. Green, 3 Cal.3d 981, 92 Cal.Rptr. 494, 479 P.2d 998, petition dismissed 404 U.S. 801; Vogel v. Percy, 691 F.2d 843 (7th Cir.1982); State v. Lenarchick, 74 Wis.2d 425, 247 N.W.2d 80, 99 A.L.R.3d 906 (1976); Annot., 99 A.L.R.3d 934.

24. The contention that a statement under oath was constitutionally mandated by Bridges v. Wixon, 326 U.S. 135 (1945) was laid at rest in California v. Green, 399 U.S. 149, 163 n. 15 (1970).

25. A proposal to include also a requirement that the prior statement have been subject to cross-examination was rejected. The effect was to allow use of grand jury testimony.

26. E.g., United States v. Mosley, 555 F.2d 191 (8th Cir.1977), cert. denied 434 U.S. 851, and United States v. Morgan, 555 F.2d 238 (9th Cir.1977), both allowing grand jury testimony. In United States v. Castro–Ayon, 537 F.2d 1055, 37 A.L.R.Fed. 848 (9th Cir.1976), cert. denied 429 U.S. 983, testimony given before an immigration officer during an interrogation authorized by statute was allowed as given in an "other proceeding," perhaps opening up a wide area of administrative proceedings. However, statements given to law enforcement officers generally, even under oath, do not qualify. United States v. Livingston, 661 F.2d 239 (D.C.Cir.1981); Martin v. United States, 528 F.2d 1157 (4th Cir. 1975); United States v. Micke, 859 F.2d 473 (7th Cir.1988). See also United States v. Perez, 870 F.2d 1222 (7th Cir.1989), cert. denied 493 U.S. 844 (because witness's pretrial interview with defendant's counsel, although given under oath, did not fulfill requirements of a deposition, prior inconsistent statements made in interview were not admissible under Rule 801(d)(1)(A)).

evidence,[27] they have nevertheless been allowed a limited admissibility for the purpose of supporting the credibility of a witness, particularly to show that a witness whose testimony has allegedly been influenced told the same story before the influence was brought to bear.[28] No sound reason is apparent for denying substantive effect when the statement is otherwise admissible. The witness can be cross-examined fully. No abuse of prepared statements is evident. The attack upon the witness has opened the door. The giving of a limiting instruction is needless and useless.

The Federal Rule's exemption of prior consistent statements from the hearsay rule has given rise to some controversy with regard to the admissibility of statements that do not come within the language of Rule 801(d)(1)(B). The rule exempts consistent statements "offered to rebut an express or implied charge against the declarant of recent fabrication or improper influence or motive" from the hearsay rule. Are other consistent statements admissible based on the traditional view that they support the witness's credibility? Some courts have said that consistent statements are either admissible under Rule 801 or inadmissible for any purpose.[29] Others have held that the rule applies only to the substantive use of such statements and that consistent statements not falling within the language may be admissible for purposes of supporting credibility.[30] Under the latter view, statements not within the language of Rule 801(d)(1)(B) would, of course, be subject to a relevancy analysis.[31] Such an analysis would preclude the admission of most such statements.

(C) Statements of identification. When A testifies that on a prior occasion B pointed to the accused and said, "That's the man who robbed me," the testimony is clearly hearsay. If, however, B is present in court, testifies on the subject of identity, and is available for cross-examination, a case within the present section is presented. Similarly if B has himself testified to the prior identification. Admissibility of the prior identification in all these situations has the support of substantial authority in the cases, often without recognition of the presence of a hearsay problem.[32] Justification is found in the unsatis-

27. United States v. Smith, 490 F.2d 789 (D.C.Cir.1974). See generally Travers, Prior Inconsistent Statements, 57 Neb. L.Rev. 974 (1978).

28. United States v. Shulman, 624 F.2d 384 (2d Cir.1980). Compare United States v. Hamilton, 689 F.2d 1262 (6th Cir.1982), cert. denied 459 U.S. 1117. See generally § 49 supra.

29. E.g., United States v. Quinto, 582 F.2d 224 (2d Cir.1978); United States v. Miller, 874 F.2d 1255 (9th Cir.1989).

30. United States v. Pierre, 781 F.2d 329 (2d Cir.1986); United States v. Harris, 761 F.2d 394 (7th Cir.1985). See also concurring opinion of Judge Friendly in United States v. Rubin, 609 F.2d 51, 66 (2d Cir.1979), affirmed 449 U.S. 424; Weinstein & Berger, Weinstein's Evidence 607[08] (1990).

31. See discussion in United States v. Miller, supra note 29 and United States v. Harris, supra note 30. See generally, Ohlbaum, The Hobgoblin of the Federal Rules of Evidence: An Analysis of Rule 801(d)(1)(B), Prior Consistent Statements and a New Proposal, 1987 B.Y.U.L.Rev. 231, 287. With regard to the question of when a consistent statement rebuts a charge of recent fabrication or improper influence or motive, see § 49, supra.

32. Annot., 71 A.L.R.2d 449.

factory nature of courtroom identification [33] and the safeguards which now surround staged out-of-court identifications. [34]

The requirement of cross-examination. With respect to each of the categories of prior statements discussed above, the Federal Rule requires that declarant testify at the trial or hearing and that he be "subject to cross-examination concerning the statement * * *." [35] The requirement that he testify appears to offer no problem, but the requirement that he be subject to cross-examination concerning the statement calls for exploration. [36] The problem area will usually be prior inconsistent statements. As has been observed, if the witness testifies that he does not remember the event and the judge finds the asserted lack of memory to be genuine, the prior statement is not inconsistent with the testimony and does not fall within the exemption, and the question of cross-examination upon the statement is not reached. [37] If the asserted lack of memory is found to be false under the circumstances, and the witness does not deny making the statement but offers explanation of his change of position, he may be cross-examined as to the circumstances and as to his explanation, and the cross-examination requirement is satisfied. [38] If he denies making the statement, [39] and also denies the event, it has been held that the result is more favorable to the cross-examiner than could be produced by elicit-

33. 4 Wigmore, Evidence § 1130 (Chadbourn rev. 1972).

34. United States v. Wade, 388 U.S. 218 (1967); Gilbert v. California, 388 U.S. 263 (1967); Stovall v. Denno, 388 U.S. 293 (1967); §§ 124, 176 supra. Although the California Court generally condemned prior statements of witnesses as violating the right of confrontation, n. 5 supra, admissibility of a prior statement of identification was upheld in People v. Gould, 54 Cal.2d 621, 7 Cal.Rptr. 273, 354 P.2d 865 (1960). See generally Mauet, Prior Identification in Criminal Cases: Hearsay and Confrontation Issues, 24 Ariz.L.Rev. 29 (1982).

35. Fed.R.Evid. 801(d)(1). Constitutional aspects of cross-examination generally are discussed in § 252 infra.

36. The requirements of the rule are satisfied if the witness is *available* for cross-examination, regardless of whether he is actually cross-examined. See, e.g., United States v. Piva, 870 F.2d 753 (1st Cir.1989).

37. Text supra at notes 20–23.

38. This was the situation in California v. Green, 399 U.S. 149 (1970), as developed on remand in People v. Green, 3 Cal.3d 981, 92 Cal.Rptr. 494, 479 P.2d 998, petition dismissed 404 U.S. 801.

See also United States v. DiCaro, 772 F.2d 1314 (7th Cir.1985), cert. denied 475 U.S. 1081, where the prior statement consisted of the testimony of the witness before the grand jury; although he disclaimed any memory of giving the testimony or of the events recounted therein, he was nevertheless found to be feigning the loss of memory, was cross-examined by both parties, and the matters developed were found to satisfy cross-examination and confrontation requirements.

39. An issue as to the making of the inconsistent statement is unlikely to arise under the limitations incorporated in the Federal Rule by the Congress, elimination of such issues being the purpose of the limitations. See text supra at n. 25. Issues of this nature can arise, however, in states which have adopted the Federal Rule without the Congressional limitations, e.g. State v. Cruz, 128 Ariz. 538, 627 P.2d 689 (1981), and may require decision under Rule 403, the so-called "prejudice" rule or in terms of the sufficiency of the evidence. It has been suggested that the objective of the Congressional limitations can be achieved with a less strictly drawn provision, extending to statements in writing, or admitted by declarant to have been made, or electronically recorded. Graham, Employing Inconsistent Statements for Impeachment and as Substantive Evidence: A Critical Review and Proposed Amendments of Federal Rules of Evidence 801(d)(1)(A), 613, and 607, 75 Mich.L.Rev. 1565 (1977).

ing an admission that the statement was made and an explanation of change of position, and that cross-examination requirements are satisfied.[40]

Statements of identification, introduced under Rule 801(d)(1)(C), present a somewhat different set of problems where the witness claims lack of memory of either the statement or the underlying events. Because identification statements do not depend upon their inconsistency with prior statements for their admissibility, they come within the meaning of the rule even if the witness genuinely says that he has no memory, provided the witness is considered to be "subject to cross-examination" concerning the statement. Despite a persuasive argument that effective cross-examination is precluded under such circumstances, the United States Supreme Court, in United States v. Owens,[41] held that neither Rule 801(d)(1) nor the Confrontation Clause is violated by the introduction of prior statements of identification where the witness claims a lack of memory. The court held that both the constitutional and hearsay exceptions were satisfied by the opportunity to cross-examine the witness about his bad memory.[42]

§ 252. Constitutional Problems of Hearsay: Confrontation and Due Process[1]

A discussion of the constitutional problems of hearsay must focus primarily on the Confrontation Clause of the Sixth Amendment. The

40. Nelson v. O'Neil, 402 U.S. 622 (1971). While the cross-examination question was presented as a claimed denial of confrontation rights, the result seems no less valid as a construction of the Federal Rule requirement.

For discussion of various possible situations raising the cross-examination requirement, see Weinstein & Berger, Evidence ¶ 801(d)(1)(A)[02]–[08]. Compare Bein, Prior Inconsistent Statements: The Hearsay Rule, 801(d)(1)(A) and 803(24), 26 UCLA L.Rev. 967 (1979).

41. 484 U.S. 554 (1988).

42. In *Owens,* the witness had no memory of the events contained in his prior statement of identification, but did remember making the statement itself. Id. at 556. Such facts would seem to make an even stronger case for the application of the Confrontation Clause and the inapplicability of Rule 801(d)(1)(C) than an instance where the witness remembers the events, but not the statement. Thus, it is safe to predict that cases where the witness has a loss of memory only with regard to the making of the statement will find admissibility on the same basis as did the Court in *Owens.*

§ 252

1. See generally 5 Wigmore, Evidence §§ 1365, 1395–1400 (Chadbourn rev. 1974); Weinstein & Berger, Evidence ¶ 800[04]; Epps, Passing the Confrontation Clause Stop Sign: Is All Hearsay Constitutionally Admissible? 77 Ky.L.J. 7 (1988); Goldman, Not So "Firmly Rooted": Exceptions to the Confrontation Clause, 66 N.C.L.Rev. 1 (1987); Graham, The Confrontation Clause, the Hearsay Rule, and Child Sexual Abuse Prosecutions: The State of the Relationship, 72 Minn.L.Rev. 523 (1988); Griswold, The Due Process Revolution and Confrontation, 119 U.Pa.L.Rev. 711 (1971); Jonakait, Restoring the Confrontation Clause to the Sixth Amendment, 35 UCLA L.Rev. 557 (1988); Mauet, Prior Identification in Criminal Cases: Hearsay and Confrontation Issues, 24 Ariz.L.Rev. 29 (1982); Natali, Green, Dutton and Chambers: Three Cases in Search of a Theory, 7 Rutgers Cam.L.J. 43 (1975); Read, The New Confrontation—Hearsay Dilemma, 45 So. Cal.L.Rev. 1 (1971); Seidelson, Hearsay Exceptions and the Sixth Amendment, 40 Geo.Wash.L.Rev. 76 (1971); Westen, The Future of Confrontation, 77 Mich.L.Rev. 1185 (1979); Dec.Dig.Criminal Law ⚖=662; C.J.S. Criminal Law §§ 999–1009; Annot., 23 L.Ed.2d 853.

clause requires "that in all criminal prosecutions, the accused shall enjoy the right * * * to be confronted with the witnesses against him." Nearly every state constitution has a like provision.[2] In 1965, the Supreme Court ruled that the Fourteenth Amendment made the federal Confrontation Clause obligatory upon the states.[3]

The Confrontation Clause is applicable only to criminal prosecutions [4] and may be invoked only by the accused. Thus it is unavailable to the prosecution in a criminal proceeding or to either party in civil litigation. So basic, however, are the values thought to be served by confrontation that confrontation requirements on occasion are found constitutionally extended to persons other than the accused in a criminal case as an aspect of due process.[5]

Certain facets of the right of confrontation and the right to due process, while relevant to the values sought to be protected by the hearsay rule, do not bear directly upon it. Of these facets, one is the right of an accused to be present at every stage of her trial as an aspect of confrontation.[6] Another is the defense right to disclosure by the prosecution of material exculpatory evidence as an element of due process.[7] In the same vein, though ostensibly not constitutionally based, is the disclosure of prior statements of government witnesses mandated by the *Jencks* decision and the statute that it sired.[8] The right to counsel is a thread running through much of this constitutional fabric.

Turning to examination of the relationship between the hearsay rule and constitutional right of confrontation, the similarity of their under-

2. They are collected and quoted in 5 Wigmore, Evidence § 1397 (Chadbourn rev. 1974).

3. Pointer v. Texas, 380 U.S. 400 (1965) This section focuses on the United States Supreme Court's interpretation of the Confrontation Clause of the federal constitution. A State's interpretation of its own confrontation requirements could result in exclusion even though the federal constitution would not dictate that result. See, e.g., State v. Storm, 127 Mont. 414, 265 P.2d 971 (1953).

4. An investigative proceeding may be so essentially criminal in nature as to make the clause applicable. Jenkins v. McKeithen, 395 U.S. 411 (1969) (Louisiana Labor–Management Commission charged with exposing violators of criminal laws).

5. Greene v. McElroy, 360 U.S. 474 (1959) (security clearance proceeding; alternative basis for holding); Willner v. Committee on Character and Fitness, 373 U.S. 96 (1963) (denial of admission to bar after passing examination); Rauh, Nonconfrontation in Security Cases: The Greene Decision, 45 Va.L.Rev. 1175 (1959).

6. See Maryland v. Craig, 110 S.Ct. 3157 (1990); Coy v. Iowa, 487 U.S. 1012 (1988). Both *Craig* and *Coy* involved the use of closed circuit television to permit a child to give testimony outside the presence of the accused in a sexual abuse case. See also Diaz v. United States, 223 U.S. 442 (1912) (accused may lose the right to be present by voluntarily absenting himself after the trial has begun); Illinois v. Allen, 397 U.S. 337 (1970) (disruptive conduct justified exclusion of accused from the courtroom).

7. Arguably at least, this right of disclosure might be based on the confrontation clause. The prototype case of Brady v. Maryland, 373 U.S. 83 (1963), was, however, decided before *Pointer,* supra note 3, ruled that the confrontation clause applies to the States. The scope of the right is delineated in United States v. Agurs, 427 U.S. 97 (1976).

8. See § 97 supra. Semerjian, The Right of Confrontation, 55 A.B.A.J. 152 (1969), maintains that the *Jencks* disclosure is constitutionally mandated.

pinnings is evident.[9] The hearsay rule operates to preserve the ability of a party to confront the witnesses against him in open court. The Confrontation Clause does the same for an accused in a criminal case. The hearsay rule has numerous exceptions and so does the Confrontation Clause. To what extent do these exceptions overlap?

In the late 1700's when confrontation provisions were first included in American bills of rights, the general rule against hearsay had been accepted in England for a hundred years,[10] but it was equally well established that hearsay under certain circumstances might be admitted.[11] One could certainly argue that the purpose of the American provision was to guarantee the maintenance in criminal cases of the hard-won principle of the hearsay rule, without abandoning the accepted exceptions which had not been questioned as to fairness, but forbidding especially the practice of using depositions taken in the absence of the accused. This latter practice was later abandoned by the English judges [12] and forbidden by statute.[13]

The debate that has raged in the courts and the law journals has boiled down to whether the Confrontation Clause merely constitutionalizes the hearsay rule for the accused in a criminal case or whether it operates to limit the introduction of evidence admissible under the rule and its exceptions.[14] The more recent decisions of the Supreme Court seem to point strongly in the direction of the former analysis. A secondary question, if the Clause constitutionalizes the hearsay rule, is at what point did it do so? In other words, to what extent may modern expansions of the rule run afoul of the constitutional limitation? Here the issue is still an open one.

The Supreme Court's progression toward its present view of the relationship of the hearsay rule and the Confrontation Clause effectively began with the case of California v. Green.[15] In *Green*, the Court

---

9. As to hearsay, see § 245 supra.

In Mattox v. United States, 156 U.S. 237, 242 (1895) the Court pointed out that the primary purpose of the Confrontation Clause "was to prevent depositions or *ex parte* affidavits * * * in lieu of a personal examination and cross-examination of the witness in which the accused has an opportunity, not only of testing the recollection and sifting the conscience of the witness, but of compelling him to stand face to face with the jury in order that they may look at him, and judge by his demeanor on the stand and the manner in which he gives his testimony whether he is worthy of belief."

10. See § 244, supra.

11. E.g., former testimony, Rex v. Vipont, 2 Burr. 1163, 97 Eng.Repr. 767 (1761); Rex v. Radbourne, 1 Leach C.L. 457 (1787); Rex v. Jolliffe, 4 Term R. 285, 100 Eng. Repr. 1022 (1791), all cited 15 A.L.R. 498, 500; and dying declarations, 5 Wigmore,

Evidence § 1430 (Chadbourn rev. 1974); § 281, supra.

"We are bound to interpret the Constitution in the light of the law as it existed at the time it was adopted. * * * Many of its provisions in the nature of a Bill of Rights are subject to exceptions, recognized long before its adoption, and not interfering at all with its spirit. Such exceptions were obviously intended to be respected." Mattox v. United States, 156 U.S. 237, 243 (1895).

12. 5 Wigmore, Evidence § 1364(8) (Chadbourn rev. 1974); 9 Holdsworth, Hist. Eng.Law 219 (3d ed. 1944).

13. 11 and 12 Vict. ch. 42 (1848), known as Sir John Jervis' Act; see 1 Stephen, Hist.Crim.Law of England 220 (1883).

14. See, for example, the many law review articles cited in note 1, supra.

15. 399 U.S. 149 (1970).

found that the clause did not limit the introduction of prior statements of witnesses actually produced at the trial. Ten years later, in Ohio v. Roberts,[16] the court laid down a two-part test for the application of the Confrontation Clause to hearsay evidence. First, "the prosecutor must either produce, or demonstrate the unavailability of, the declarant whose statements it wishes to use against the defendant." [17] Secondly, if the declarant is unavailable, the statement must have been made under circumstances providing sufficient "indicia of reliability." The Court in *Roberts* further noted that sufficient reliability to satisfy the demands of the confrontation clause "can be inferred without more in a case where the evidence falls within a firmly rooted hearsay exception. In other cases, the evidence must be excluded at least absent a showing of particularized guarantees of trustworthiness." [18]

In United States v. Inadi,[19] the Court backed away from the unavailability requirement pronounced in *Roberts*. In *Inadi*, the Court found no need to produce or demonstrate the unavailability of a conspirator whose statement was used against the accused.[20] The statements in *Roberts* were limited to instances involving the introduction of prior testimony, which has always required unavailability under the hearsay rule.[21] In the case of co-conspirator's statements, the Court found that such statements "provide evidence of the conspiracy's context that cannot be replicated, even if the declarant testifies to the same matters in court." [22] The Court also noted that the benefits of an unavailability rule for co-conspirator declarants would be slight and the burdens substantial, and concluded that "the Confrontation Clause does not embody such a rule." [23]

Both *Roberts* and *Inadi* leave open the impact of the Confrontation Clause in cases, such as those involving former testimony, where the hearsay exception itself requires unavailability. Earlier decisions, such as Barber v. Page,[24] seem to dictate a more rigorous test for unavailability for the prosecution in a criminal case than for the defense or for either party in a civil case.

Inadi did not expand on the other prong of the *Roberts* test, i.e., when are sufficient "indicia of reliability" present? The issue of whether co-conspirators statements were within a "firmly rooted" exception to hearsay rule was resolved in the affirmative in Bourjaily v. United States.[25] The co-conspirator exception was held to be firmly enough

---

16. 448 U.S. 56 (1980).

17. Id. at 65.

18. Ibid.

19. 475 U.S. 387 (1986).

20. In an earlier case, Dutton v. Evans, 400 U.S. 74 (1970), the Court had held that a defendant's right of confrontation was not violated by the admission of a statement of a nontestifying, but available, co-conspirator. However, the rationale of the *Evans* case was based more on the nature of the particular statement involved in

that case than on principles applicable to the co-conspirator's exception generally. See Graham, supra note 1 at 543–547.

21. See Fed.R.Evid. 804(b)(1).

22. United States v. Inadi, supra, at 395.

23. Id. at 400.

24. 390 U.S. 719 (1968). See discussion § 253, infra.

25. 483 U.S. 171 (1987).

rooted in our jurisprudence that a court need not independently inquire into the reliability of such statements.[26]

Most recently, some constitutional limitations on the creation of nontraditional exceptions to the hearsay rule were imposed. In Idaho v. Wright,[27] the Court dealt with statements of a child to a doctor, admitted pursuant to Idaho's residual hearsay exception.[28] The Court held that the introduction of the statements violated the Confrontation Clause, noting that the residual exception is not a "firmly rooted" exception for Confrontation Clause purposes [29] and that therefore statements admitted under it would be constitutionally admissible based only upon a finding "particularized guarantees of trustworthiness." [30] The Court directed the search for such guarantees to the totality of circumstances surrounding the making of the statement "that render the declarant particularly worthy of belief." [31] The Court expressly rejected the use of evidence corroborating the truth of a hearsay statement to support the guarantees of trustworthiness.[32]

In summary, hearsay falling within a traditional or "firmly rooted" exception to the rule will be admissible under the Confrontation Clause.[33] Where the exception does not require unavailability, it is unlikely that the Court will hold that the Constitution requires it.[34] Where the exception requires unavailability, the clause will also require such a finding and will likely require a more rigorous demonstration by the prosecution than by other parties. Where the hearsay is admissible under a residual exception on behalf of the prosecution in a criminal case, the courts will look for "particularized guarantees of trustworthiness," a test apparently more demanding than the "equivalent circumstantial guarantees of trustworthiness" required by the Federal Rules and their state counterparts. In addition, the prosecution will have to rely on the trustworthiness of the statement itself, rather than on its likely truth in light of corroborating circumstances. Newly created statutory hearsay exceptions arguably should be subject to the test set forth in Wright.[35]

Some questions still remain for adjudication, probably by the United States Supreme Court. What are the firmly rooted exceptions to the hearsay rule?[36] To what extent will the Confrontation Clause limit the

26. Id. at 183.

27. 110 S.Ct. 3139 (1990).

28. Idaho R.Evid. 803(24) (identical to Fed.R.Evid. 803(24)).

29. Idaho v. Wright, supra note 27 at 3147.

30. Id. at 3148.

31. Id. at 3149.

32. Id. at 3150–3152.

33. But see discussion in Goldman, supra note 1; Jonakait, supra note 1.

34. But see discussion in Epps, supra note 1; Graham, supra note 1.

35. The Court in Idaho v. Wright, supra note 27, at 3148, noted: " * * * were we to agree that the admission of hearsay statements under the residual exception automatically passed Confrontation Clause scrutiny, virtually every codified hearsay exception would assume constitutional stature, a step this Court has repeatedly declined to take."

36. Some lower court cases upholding traditional hearsay exceptions against constitutional challenge include: Reed v. Beto, 343 F.2d 723 (5th Cir.1965), affirmed sub nom., Spencer v. Texas, 385 U.S. 554 (public records); United States v. Kelly, 349

application of traditional hearsay exceptions to nontraditional circumstances. For example, is a state free to apply the traditional exception for public records to permit the introduction of police reports against the accused in a criminal case?[37] How far can a state go in admitting statements against penal interest of nondefendants which implicate the accused?[38] In such instances, will the Court look only to the existence of a traditional hearsay exception as in *Bourjaily*, regardless of how unorthodox the application, or will it require at least a specific finding of particularized guarantees of trustworthiness as in *Wright?* Furthermore, could a state dispense with a traditional requirement of unavailability, for example, for declarations against interest?[39] Logic and policy favor a limit on the state's ability to expand hearsay exceptions to assist the prosecution in instances such as those posed here, but in this area as in so many, the Court is capable of some surprising decisions.

In contrast to the right of confrontation, which results in exclusion when ruled to be applicable to an item of hearsay, the due process clause may require the admission of hearsay, though inadmissible under applicable hearsay rules, if of sufficient reliability and importance. In Chambers v. Mississippi,[40] the Supreme Court ruled that due process was denied by the exclusion of several confessions exculpating the accused given "under circumstances that provided considerable assurances of their reliability," coupled with the inability of the accused to cross-examine the confessing person, who testified as a witness, because of the local "voucher rule." The decision was carefully limited to the situation presented and is of uncertain constitutional dimension, though suggesting possibilities of further application.

§ 253. The Hearsay Exceptions: Unavailability of the Declarant [1]

In the concluding portion of the earlier section discussing the reasons for the rule against hearsay,[2] the point was made that the difficulty

---

F.2d 720 (2d Cir.1965), cert. denied 384 U.S. 947 (recorded past recollection); United States v. Lipscomb, 435 F.2d 795 (5th Cir.1970), cert. denied 401 U.S. 980 (entries in the regular course of business); United States v. Nick, 604 F.2d 1199 (9th Cir.1979) (excited utterances); Lenza v. Wyrick, 665 F.2d 804 (8th Cir.1981) (declarations of state of mind). In the original appeal in Mattox v. United States, 146 U.S. 140 (1892), exclusion of a dying declaration offered by defendant was held error. In the second appeal, supra note 9, dying declarations were used to demonstrate that both cross-examination and presence might be foregone without offending confrontation rights.

See generally Goldman, supra note 1, for a discussion of the problems of application of the "firmly rooted" hearsay exception principle.

37. Fed.R.Evid. 803(8) and similar state rules currently prohibit such a use. See § 296, infra.

38. See Fed.R.Evid. 804(b)(3); §§ 318, 319, infra.

39. See §§ 318–320, infra.

40. 410 U.S. 284 (1973). The decision is discussed within the context of third-party confessions in § 318 infra, especially note 9.

§ 253

1. 5 Wigmore, Evidence §§ 1401–1414, 1420–1422 (Chadbourn rev. 1974); Dec.Dig.Evidence ⚙284, 576, 577, Criminal Law ⚙542, 543.

2. § 245 supra.

with the rule lies in the procedure of excluding evidence as a means of effectuating the policy of requiring that testimony be given in open court, under oath, and subject to cross-examination. The problem arises from the wide variation in the reliability of evidence which by definition is classed as hearsay. The traditional solution has been found in recognition of numerous exceptions where it has been thought that "circumstantial guarantees of trustworthiness"[3] justified departure from the general rule excluding hearsay. These exceptions are the subjects of several of the chapters which follow.

The pattern of the exceptions as evolved by the decisional process of the common law and generally in effect today divides the hearsay exceptions into two groups.[4] In the first, the availability or unavailability of the declarant is not a relevant factor: the exception is applied without regard to it. In the second group, a showing of unavailability is a condition precedent to applying the exception. The theory of the first group is that the out-of-court statement is at least as reliable as would be his testimony in person, so that producing him would involve pointless delay and inconvenience. The theory of the second group is that, while it would be preferable to have live testimony, if the declarant is unavailable, the out-of-court statement will be accepted.[5] The pattern to a large extent is the product of history and experience, and, as might be expected of a body of law created by deciding cases as they arose in necessarily random fashion, it is not in all respects consistent. Nevertheless, it has stood the test of time and use, and offers a substantial measure of predictability. While the number of the exceptions may at first glance appear extraordinarily complex,[6] many are encountered only rarely; the actual working collection probably numbers no more than 10 or a dozen.

The importance accorded unavailability in the scheme of hearsay exceptions requires that it be considered in some detail.

Preliminarily it may be observed that while the rather general practice is to speak loosely of unavailability of the witness, the critical

---

3. 5 Wigmore, Evidence § 1422 (Chadbourn rev. 1974).

4. See, e.g. Fed.R.Evid. 803 and 804. The requirement that a declarant have firsthand knowledge, applicable to most but not all hearsay exceptions, is discussed in § 10 supra.

5. The usual exceptions requiring a showing of unavailability are former testimony, § 302 infra; dying declarations, § 310 infra; declarations against interest, § 320 infra; and statements of pedigree and family history, § 322. See Fed.R.Evid. 804. After an uneasy history, unavailability has virtually disappeared as a requirement for entries in the regular course of business.

While most of the earlier cases on what constitutes unavailability involved former testimony, the increased scope of the exception for declarations against interest has shifted the flow of decisions in that direction.

For advocacy of extending the unavailability requirement to additional hearsay exceptions where not now applicable, see Stewart, Perception, Memory, and Hearsay: A Criticism of Present Law and the Proposed Federal Rules of Evidence, 1970 Utah L.Rev. 1, 25–36.

6. For example, Federal Rules Evid. 803 and 804 together include 27 specifically defined exceptions and two "residual" exceptions.

factor is actually the unavailability of his testimony.[7] As will be seen, the witness may be physically present in court but his testimony nevertheless unavailable. Of course if the unavailability is by procurement of the party offering the hearsay statement, the requirement ought not to be regarded as satisfied.[8]

In principle, probably anything which constitutes unavailability in fact ought to be considered adequate. However, the rules have grown up around certain recurring fact situations, and the problem is therefore approached in that pattern. Depositions receive special treatment at the end of the section.

Federal Rule of Evidence 804(a) provides a convenient list of the generally recognized unavailability situations, as follows:[9]

(a) **Definition of Unavailability.** "Unavailability as a witness" includes situations in which the declarant—

(1) is exempted by ruling of the court on the ground of privilege from testifying concerning the subject matter of the declarant's statement; or

(2) persists in refusing to testify concerning the subject matter of the declarant's statement despite an order of the court to do so; or

(3) testifies to a lack of memory of the subject matter of the declarant's statement; or

(4) is unable to be present or to testify at the hearing because of death or then existing physical or mental illness or infirmity; or

(5) is absent from the hearing and the proponent of his statement has been unable to procure the declarant's attendance (or in the case of a hearsay exception under subdivision (b)(2), (3), or (4), his attendance or testimony) by process or other reasonable means.

A declarant is not unavailable as a witness if exemption, refusal, claim of lack of memory, inability, or absence is due to the procurement or

---

7. Phillips v. Wyrick, 558 F.2d 489, 494 (8th Cir.1977), cert. denied 434 U.S. 1088; Johnson v. People, 152 Colo. 586, 384 P.2d 454 (1963), cert. denied 376 U.S. 922; State v. Stewart, 85 Kan. 404, 116 P. 489 (1911).

8. Motes v. United States, 178 U.S. 458 (1900) (chief witness for government disappeared from custody because of extraordinary conduct of officer in charge of case, which Court charitably described as "negligent"). This is the effect of the final paragraph of Fed.R.Evid. 804(a), text infra at note 9. The provision was held inapplicable in United States v. Seijo, 595 F.2d 116 (2d Cir.1979) (depositions of illegal aliens who had been deported before trial used at trial), and United States v. Mathis, 550 F.2d 180 (4th Cir.1976), cert. denied 429 U.S. 1107 (witness mistakenly released from federal prison because of confusion with another prisoner of same name). But

see United States v. Guadian–Salazar, 824 F.2d 344 (5th Cir.1987) (prosecution for illegal transportation of aliens; government confessed error with regard to admission of deposition testimony of witnesses who were released to Mexico).

In United States v. Evans, 635 F.2d 1124 (4th Cir.1980), cert. denied 452 U.S. 943, defendant offered his own out-of-court admission of another crime, asserting his claim of the privilege against self-incrimination as grounds of unavailability. The court found that the statement under the circumstances did not qualify as a declaration against interest, noting but not deciding that the defendant by claiming the privilege might be procuring his own unavailability.

9. The corresponding Revised Uniform Rule (1986) is to the same effect.

wrongdoing of the proponent of a statement for the purpose of preventing the witness from attending or testifying.

(1) Exercise of privilege. The exercise of a privilege not to testify renders the witness unavailable to the extent of the scope of the privilege.[10]

(2) Refusal to testify. If a witness simply refuses to testify, despite the bringing to bear upon him of all appropriate judicial pressures, the conclusion that as a practical matter he is unavailable can scarcely be avoided, and that is the holding of the great weight of authority.[11]

(3) Claimed lack of memory. A claim of lack of memory made by the witness on the stand should satisfy the requirement of unavailability.[12] If the claim is genuine, the testimony is simply unavailable by any realistic standard. The earlier cases, however, indicated concern that the claimed lack might not be genuine, particularly in former testimony cases, where the witness who learns that the adversary has discovered new fuel for cross-examination or for other reasons seeks refuge in forgetfulness.[13] This concern appears not to be well grounded, especially when the parallel to the witness who simply refuses to testify, discussed above, is noted. The witness who falsely asserts loss of memory is simply refusing to testify in a way that he hopes will avoid a collision with the judge. He is present in court, by definition, and

10. United States v. Zurosky, 614 F.2d 779 (1st Cir.1979), cert. denied 446 U.S. 967; Phillips v. Wyrick, 558 F.2d 489 (8th Cir.1977), cert. denied 434 U.S. 1088; People v. Settles, 46 N.Y.2d 154, 412 N.Y.S.2d 874, 385 N.E.2d 612 (1978); Fed.R.Evid. 804(a)(1), text supra at note 9; Annot., 45 A.L.R.2d 1354. As the Advisory Committee's Note points out, the requirement of a ruling by the court clearly implies that an actual claim of privilege must be made. See United States v. Pelton, 578 F.2d 701 (8th Cir.1978), cert. denied 439 U.S. 964. Compare United States v. Thomas, 571 F.2d 285 (5th Cir.1978), where declarant was a codefendant being jointly tried, who elected not to take the stand. Though no formal claim of privilege was made, the court ruled that the existence of the privilege, his right to assert it, and his unavailability were "patent."

Most of the cases involve claims of self-incrimination.

11. E.g., United States v. Doerr, 886 F.2d 944 (7th Cir.1989) (witness held unavailable where he refused to testify, spending eighteen months in jail for criminal contempt); Britt v. State, 721 P.2d 812 (Okl.Cr.1986) (prior testimony admissible where witness refused to testify based on religious principles). Annot., 92 A.L.R.3d 1138; Fed.R.Evid. 804(a)(2), text supra at note 9. An actual order is required, United States v. Oliver, 626 F.2d 254 (2d Cir.

1980), pointing out that a recalcitrant witness bent on helping a defendant by not testifying may point to the court's order as forcing him to do so.

12. Fed.R.Evid. 804(a)(3), text supra at note 9, so provides. See McDonnell v. United States, 472 F.2d 1153 (8th Cir.1973), cert. denied 412 U.S. 942.

In United States v. Owens, 484 U.S. 554 (1988), the Court held that a witness who testified to a lack of memory was "subject to cross-examination" within the meaning of Federal Rule 801(d)(1). In so holding, the Court described the seeming inconsistency between its holding and the provisions of Rule 804(a)(3) as a "semantic oddity."

13. Annot., 129 A.L.R. 843.

The Report of the House Committee on the Judiciary said with respect to Federal Rule Evid. 804(a)(3) that "the Committee intends no change in existing federal law under which the court may choose to disbelieve the declarant's testimony as to his lack of memory." House Comm. on Judiciary, Fed.Rules of Evidence, H.R.Rep. 650, 93d Cong., 1st Sess., p. 15 (1973). The consequences of such belief are not explained. If the result was thought to be exclusion, it is simply contrary to the wording of the rule which operates whether the claim is true or false.

subject to cross-examination. If his claim is false, he is in principle at least liable to contempt proceedings, though perhaps less effectively than in cases of simple refusal. The trend is to recognize asserted loss of memory as sufficient.[14] If the forgetfulness is only partial, the appropriate solution would appear to be resort to present testimony to the extent of recollection, implementing with the hearsay testimony to the extent required.[15]

(4) Death; physical or mental illness. Death was the form which unavailability originally assumed with most of the relevant exceptions.[16] Physical disability to attend the trial or testify is a recognized ground.[17] Mental incapacity,[18] including failure of faculties due to disease, senility, or accident,[19] is also a good ground of unavailability. The relative scarcity of decisions passing upon the required degree of permanency of either physical and mental incapacity supports the conclusion that most of the cases are handled by continuance. Some authority accepts a relatively temporary disability as sufficient.[20] The matter would appear to be appropriate generally for the exercise of discretion by the judge, with due regard for the prospects for recovery, the importance of the testimony and the prompt administration of justice. In criminal cases where absence is relied upon to establish unavailability of a witness against the accused, a higher standard may

14. United States v. Garris, 616 F.2d 626 (2d Cir.1980), cert. denied 447 U.S. 926; United States v. Palumbo, 639 F.2d 123 (3d Cir.1981), cert. denied 454 U.S. 819; United States v. Amaya, 533 F.2d 188 (5th Cir.1976), cert. denied 429 U.S. 1101, all decided under the Federal Rule; Anderson v. Gaither, 120 Fla. 263, 162 So. 877 (1935); Commonwealth v. Graves, 484 Pa. 29, 398 A.2d 644 (1979).

15. Anderson v. Gaither, 120 Fla. 263, 162 So. 877 (1935); Commonwealth v. Graves, 484 Pa. 29, 398 A.2d 644 (1979).

16. Mattox v. United States, 156 U.S. 237 (1895). The grounds discussed in this subsection are all recognized in Fed.R.Evid. 804(a)(4), text supra at note 9.

17. United States v. Campbell, 845 F.2d 1374 (6th Cir.1988), cert. denied 488 U.S. 908 (elderly witnesses to Medicare fraud held to be unavailable because unable to travel). Vigoda v. Barton, 348 Mass. 478, 204 N.E.2d 441, 26 A.L.R.3d 482 (1965) (illness such as to render witness unable to travel); Norburn v. Mackie, 264 N.C. 479, 141 S.E.2d 877 (1965) (detrimental to health to appear as witness).

18. As to mental capacity of witnesses generally, see § 62 supra. Marler v. State, 67 Ala. 55 (1880); George v. Moorhead, 399 Ill. 497, 78 N.E.2d 216 (1948).

See text accompanying notes 43–48, this section, infra, for a discussion of special

problems involving children as witnesses, including the possibility that their testimony may result in emotional trauma to them.

19. Walden v. Sears, Roebuck and Co., 654 F.2d 443 (5th Cir.1981) (proper to admit earlier deposition of child victim who suffered memory impairment as result of bicycle accident). In United States v. Amaya, 533 F.2d 188, 191 (5th Cir.1976), cert. denied 429 U.S. 1101, the court said that impairment of memory from supervening accident need not be permanent but "only be in probability long enough so that, with proper regard to the importance of the testimony, the trial cannot be postponed."

20. Chase v. Springvale Mills Co., 75 Me. 156 (1883); People v. Droste, 160 Mich. 66, 125 N.W. 87 (1910); Harris v. Reeves, 421 S.W.2d 689 (Tex.Civ.App.1967). Compare United States v. Faison, 679 F.2d 292 (3d Cir.1982) (court admitted former testimony of witness in hospital following heart attack; remanded with directions to grant new trial if he would be available to testify). Contra, Peterson v. U.S., 344 F.2d 419 (5th Cir.1965) (pregnancy not sufficient). See also Sahagian v. Murphy, 871 F.2d 714 (7th Cir.1989) (prior testimony admissible where defendant refused to accept a continuance to allow witness to recover from open heart surgery).

be required with respect to disability.[21]

(5) Absence. Mere absence of the declarant from the hearing, standing alone, does not establish unavailability. Under the Federal Rule,[22] the proponent of the hearsay statement must in addition show that he is unable to procure declarant's attendance (1) by process or (2) by other reasonable means. State requirements vary, especially with respect to (2). Furthermore, the requirements of the confrontation clause must be observed. (1) The relevant process is subpoena, or, in appropriate situations, writ of habeas corpus ad testificandum. If a witness is beyond the reach of process, obviously process cannot procure his attendance. Substantial differences in the reach of process exist between civil and criminal cases. For example, service of a civil subpoena is relatively limited [23] while a criminal subpoena may be served anywhere in the country and under some circumstances even abroad.[24] And, while in State courts process in civil cases will usually not be effective beyond State boundaries, all States have enacted the Uniform Act To Secure the Attendance of Witnesses from Without a State in Criminal Proceedings,[25] which in effect permits extradition of witnesses from another State in criminal cases. If a witness against the accused in a criminal case is within the reach of process, the prosecution must resort to process in both State and federal cases.[26] If a witness cannot be found, it is evident that resort to process cannot be effective. The proponent of the hearsay statement must, however, show that the witness cannot be found. In criminal cases, the showing required of the prosecution with regard to witnesses against the accused is strict, described as a "good-faith effort," [27] applicable in both State and federal prosecutions. A lesser showing may be adequate as to defense witness-

21. See discussion of Barber v. Page, text infra at notes 26, 29. See also discussion in Burns v. Clusen, 798 F.2d 931 (7th Cir.1986) (finding of unavailability based on mental illness set aside as based on a "stale and confused record").

22. Fed.R.Evid. 804(a)(5), text supra at note 9.

23. See, e.g., Fed.R.Civ.P. 45(e)(1).

24. Fed.R.Crim.P. 17(e); 28 U.S.C.A. § 1783.

25. 11 U.L.A. 1.

26. Barber v. Page, 390 U.S. 719 (1968).

27. Ohio v. Roberts, 448 U.S. 56, 74 (1980). The witness, soon after testifying at the preliminary hearing, had left her Ohio apartment about a year before the trial. The prosecution issued five subpoenas to her at her parents' home, also in Ohio, without service. Her parents had talked by telephone with her through contact established via a social worker in San Francisco, about a year before trial. She called her parents by telephone and said she was traveling outside Ohio, but did not say where she was traveling or the place from which she was calling. No member of the family knew where she was. The prosecution did not attempt to telephone the social worker. On these facts, the Court held that the prosecution had satisfied the good-faith effort requirement, saying that "the great improbability" that attempting to locate the social worker would have resulted in locating the witness "neutralizes any intimation that a concept of reasonableness" required that it be done. 448 U.S. at 76. Compare United States v. Quinn, 901 F.2d 522 (6th Cir.1990) and People v. Louis, 42 Cal.3d 969, 232 Cal. Rptr. 110, 728 P.2d 180 (1986) where the efforts of the prosecution to secure attendance of witnesses were found to be inadequate to support a finding of unavailability with State v. Wells, 437 N.W.2d 575 (Iowa 1989) and Commonwealth v. Siegfriedt, 402 Mass. 424, 522 N.E.2d 970 (1988) where the efforts were found sufficient.

es in criminal cases and witnesses generally in civil cases, where confrontation requirements do not apply.[28] (2) In addition to inability to procure attendance by process, the confrontation clause requires the prosecution, before introducing a hearsay statement of the type where unavailability is required, also to show that declarant's attendance cannot be procured through good-faith efforts by other means. Here, too, the standard is strict. In Barber v. Page,[29] the confrontation clause was held to require a State prosecutor, before using at trial the preliminary hearing testimony of a witness presently incarcerated in a federal penitentiary in an adjoining State, to take appropriate steps to induce the federal authorities to produce him at the trial. When the witness is beyond the reach of process for reasons other than imprisonment, the least that would seem to satisfy confrontation requirements would be a request to appear, with reimbursement for travel and subsistence expenses.[30] When the confrontation clause does not apply, i.e. civil cases and defense witnesses in criminal cases, the authorities are divided as to whether attempts must be made to induce the witness to attend voluntarily. Some authorities, including the Federal Rule, require an effort through reasonable means.[31] Others require no more than a showing that the witness is beyond the reach of process.[32]

---

28. However, some effort at locating the witness is apparently necessary. See, e.g., Moore v. Mississippi Valley State University, 871 F.2d 545 (5th Cir.1989) (deposition inadmissible in civil trial where no evidence to establish unavailability offered); Rosario v. Kuhlman, 839 F.2d 918 (2d Cir.1988) (good faith effort to locate witness sufficient under facts to show unavailability). In Perricone v. Kansas City Southern Railway Co., 630 F.2d 317 (5th Cir.1980), appeal after remand 704 F.2d 1376, no subpoena was issued; a telephone call to the directory listing of the witness would have reached a recording with his new number; and after verdict, within two hours defendant's investigator found the witness working about a mile from the courthouse. Admission of the former testimony of the witness was held without sufficient predicate.

29. Supra note 26.

30. See, e.g., Gillie v. State, 512 N.E.2d 145 (Ind.1987) (witness not unavailable where he told prosecutor he could not afford to make trip from Texas to Indiana). But see Mancusi v. Stubbs, 408 U.S. 204 (1972), where the Court ruled that permanent residence in a foreign country was a sufficient showing that the witness was beyond the reach of process and that efforts to induce him to return voluntarily to testify in a State trial need not be shown. The result may well have been influenced by the fact that the disputed former testimony had been used in a Tennessee trial

resulting in a murder conviction which New York sought to use as the predicate for stiffer punishment for a New York conviction; it was not used in New York on the issue of guilt.

31. Ibanez v. Winston, 222 Mass. 129, 109 N.E. 814 (1915); Williams v. Collins Communications, Inc., 720 P.2d 880 (Wyo. 1986); Fed.R.Evid. 804(a)(5), text supra at note 9.

32. Wolski v. National Life & Acc. Ins. Co., 135 Neb. 643, 283 N.W. 381 (1939) (decided before local adoption of Federal Rules); Healy v. Rennert, 9 N.Y.2d 202, 213 N.Y.S.2d 44, 173 N.E.2d 777 (1961).

If the witness was legally competent at the time his former testimony was given, but becomes incompetent before trial, as by death of the adverse party under a Dead Man statute, the unavailability requirement has been held satisfied. Habig v. Bastian, 117 Fla. 864, 158 So. 508 (1935). See 5 Wigmore, Evidence § 1409 (Chadbourn rev. 1974). Since the Federal Rules as promulgated by the Supreme Court contained no provision on legal incompetency of this kind, no provision was made for supervening disqualification, nor is any now included. The question may arise in diversity cases under Rule 601 as revised by the Congress. Recognition of supervening disqualification as unavailability would be in accord with the spirit of the Federal Rules.

When absence is relied upon as grounds of unavailability, some jurisdictions impose a further requirement that inability to take the deposition of the missing witness also be shown.[33]

Depositions.[34] Unavailability may appear as a requirement at two different stages in connection with depositions: (1) the right to take a deposition at all may be subject to certain conditions, of which the most common is unavailability to testify at the trial,[35] or (2) the right to use a deposition at the trial in place of the personal appearance of the deponent is usually conditioned upon his unavailability.[36] The matter is largely governed by statute or rule, and those in force locally should be consulted.[37]

The use of depositions in criminal cases requires particular consideration in view of the higher standards of confrontation applicable to evidence presented against an accused. Legislation providing for depositions in criminal cases, sometimes by express constitutional sanction, is in effect in a number of jurisdictions.[38] No constitutional problems are apparent when the deposition is to be taken and used by the

---

33. Fed.R.Evid. 804(a)(5) imposes the requirement except as to former testimony. Despite the similarity of former testimony and depositions, some jurisdictions have imposed the deposition requirement without excepting former testimony. Brownlie v. Brownlie, 351 Ill. 72, 183 N.E. 613 (1932). The Federal Rules as promulgated by the Supreme Court had no deposition requirement. It was added at the insistence of the House of Representatives over the objection of the Senate Committee on the Judiciary that it was needless, impractical, highly restrictive, expensive, and time-consuming. Senate Comm. on Judiciary, Fed. Rules of Evidence, S.Rep. No. 1277, 93d Cong., 2d Sess., p. 20 (1974); H.R.Fed.Rules of Evidence, Conf.Rep. No. 1597, 93d Cong., 2d Sess., p. 12 (1974).

34. 5 Wigmore, Evidence §§ 1411, 1415, 1416 (Chadbourn rev. 1974); 23 Am.Jur.2d Depositions §§ 7, 11, 112–120, 311; C.J.S. Depositions §§ 9–16, 92(2).

35. For state statutes and rules containing such restrictions in both civil and criminal cases, see 5 Wigmore, Evidence § 1411 (Chadbourn rev. 1974).

Restrictions on the right to take a deposition lose their significance and tend to disappear as emphasis on depositions shifts away from use at trial as a substitute for testimony by the deponent in person to such other uses as discovery and obtaining statements with a view to impeachment or introduction as an admission of a party-opponent. Thus no general restrictions upon the right to take depositions are imposed by the Federal Rules of Civil Procedure and State rules patterned upon them,

although judicial restraints may be imposed in exceptional situations. See F.R.Civ.P. 26(c), 30(d).

36. E.g., F.R.Civ.P. 32(a)(3):

The deposition of a witness, whether or not a party, may be used by any party for any purpose if the court finds: (A) that the witness is dead; or (B) that the witness is at a greater distance than 100 miles from the place of trial or hearing, or is out of the United States, unless it appears that the absence of the witness was procured by the party offering the deposition; or (C) that the witness is unable to attend or testify because of age, sickness, infirmity, or imprisonment; or (D) that the party offering the deposition has been unable to procure the attendance of the witness by subpoena; or (E) upon application and notice, that such exceptional circumstances exist as to make it desirable, in the interest of justice and with due regard to the importance of presenting the testimony of witnesses orally in open court, to allow the deposition to be used.

The high degree of similarity between the foregoing specifications of what satisfies unavailability and those for hearsay discussed earlier in this section is of course, evident.

37. See statutes and rules collected in 5 Wigmore, Evidence § 1411 (Chadbourn rev. 1974).

38. See 5 Wigmore, Evidence §§ 1398, n. 6, 1411 (Chadbourn rev. 1974).

accused.[39] When, however, the deposition is to be used *against* the accused, it seems evident that the unavailability standards of Barber v. Page,[40] previously discussed in this section, are applicable.[41] If these standards are met, there must, of course, be meaningful opportunity to confront and cross-examine, with its concomitant right to counsel, when the deposition is taken.[42]

Children. Children, particularly in sexual abuse cases, often present difficult questions of unavailability for purposes of the application of both a hearsay exception and the Confrontation Clause. In at least some jurisdictions, a finding of incompetence will make a witness unavailable.[43] Other courts have found unavailability based upon the inability of the child to remember the events.[44] Often, a finding of unavailability is justified based upon a determination that testifying will cause emotional trauma to the child and that therefore the child is unavailable.[45] Courts finding the child unavailable within the meaning

---

39. Under Fed.R.Crim.P. 15(a) the taking of depositions by either side remains limited:

   (a) When taken. Whenever due to exceptional circumstances of the case it is in the interest of justice that the testimony of a prospective witness of a party be taken and preserved for use at trial * * *.

Their use at trial, under Fed.R.Crim.P. 15(e), is also more restricted than in civil cases:

   (e) Use. At the trial or upon any hearing, a part or all of a deposition, so far as otherwise admissible under the rules of evidence, may be used as substantive evidence if the witness is unavailable, as unavailability is defined in Rule 804(a) of the Federal Rules of Evidence, or the witness gives testimony at the trial or hearing inconsistent with that witness' deposition. Any deposition may also be used by any party for the purpose of contradicting or impeaching the testimony of the deponent as a witness. * * *

Compare n. 36 supra.

40. Supra notes 26, 29.

41. Fed.R.Crim.P. 15(c) provides:

   (c) Payment of expenses. Whenever a deposition is taken at the instance of the government, or whenever a deposition is taken at the instance of a defendant who is unable to bear the expenses of the taking of the deposition, the court may direct that the expense of travel and subsistence of the defendant and the defendant's attorney for attendance at the examination and the cost of the tran-

script of the deposition shall be paid by the government.

   In United States v. King, 552 F.2d 833, 41 A.L.R.Fed. 735 (9th Cir.1976), cert. denied 430 U.S. 966, the Government took the depositions of two witnesses who were incarcerated in a Japanese prison. Defendants, on bail, and their attorneys attended at government expense. In the course of the depositions, defendants and counsel withdrew, complaining of the strict security measures imposed by the Japanese government, and the taking proceeded without them. The court found no infringement of constitutional rights.

42. Courts have upheld the admissibility of depositions taken in foreign countries, despite a wide variance in procedure from that in use in the United States. See, e.g., United States v. Casamento, 887 F.2d 1141 (2d Cir.1989), cert. denied 110 S.Ct. 1138 (Switzerland; no oath or affirmation); United States v. Salim, 855 F.2d 944 (2d Cir.1988) (no oath; questioning done by French magistrate).

43. E.g., Kansas Stat.Ann. § 60–459(g)(2) (1989); State v. Kuone, 243 Kan. 218, 757 P.2d 289 (1988); State v. Myatt, 237 Kan. 17, 697 P.2d 836 (1985). The Federal Rules of Evidence do not make incompetency or disqualification a separate ground for unavailability. See Rule 804(a).

44. E.g., State v. Slider, 38 Wash.App. 689, 688 P.2d 538 (1984).

45. Such a finding is usually based upon rules similar to Federal Rule 804(a)(4), dealing with physical or mental illness or infirmity. E.g. State v. Robinson, 153 Ariz. 191, 203–204, 735 P.2d 801, 813–814 (1987); State v. Kuone, supra note 43;

of the hearsay rule have usually also found any Confrontation Clause requirement of unavailability also satisfied.[46] Some states have enacted statutes making a child unavailable, and permitting either the introduction of videotaped statements or closed-circuit testimony, based upon a finding that the child would suffer emotional or mental distress if required to testify in open court.[47] In Maryland v. Craig,[48] an individualized finding of potential serious emotional distress was held sufficient to permit a child to give testimony via closed circuit television outside the physical presence of the accused.

State v. Drusch, 139 Wis.2d 312, 407 N.W.2d 328 (App.1987), review denied 140 Wis.2d 874, 416 N.W.2d 66.

46. See cases cited notes 43–45. See generally Mosteller, Child Sexual Abuse and Statements for the Purpose of Medical Diagnosis or Treatment, 67 N.C.L.Rev. 257, 286 (1989).

In Idaho v. Wright, 110 S.Ct. 3139, 3147 (1990), where the Court found that the introduction of a child's statement under a residual exception to the hearsay rule violated the Confrontation Clause (see discussion, § 252, supra), both parties agreed that the child was "incapable of communicating with the jury." Based on that agreement, the Court assumed, "without

deciding," that the child was an unavailable witness within the meaning of the Confrontation Clause.

47. E.g.   West's   Ann.Cal.Evid.Code § 240 (West.Supp.1990); Me.Rev.Stat.Ann., Tit. 15 § 1205(1) (Supp.1990); N.M.Sup. Ct.R. 10–217 (1990). See Graham, The Confrontation Clause, the Hearsay Rule, and Child Sexual Abuse Prosecutions: The State of the Relationship, 72 Minn.L.Rev. 523, 559 (1988), where the author, writing before the decision in Maryland v. Craig, 110 S.Ct. 3157 (1990), finds it doubtful that the statutory standards of these three statutes are sufficient to constitute unavailability under the Confrontation Clause.

48. Supra, note 47.

Chapter 25

ADMISSIONS OF A PARTY-
OPPONENT

Table of Sections

§ 254. Nature and Effect [1]

"Anything that you say may be used against you," according to the familiar phrase. It offers a convenient point of beginning for the examination of the use of admissions in evidence.

§ 254

1. 4 Wigmore, Evidence §§ 1048–1087 (Chadbourn rev. 1972); Falknor, Vicarious Admissions and the Uniform Rules, 14 Vand.L.Rev. 855 (1961); Falknor, Hearsay, 1969 Law & Soc.Order 591, 600–605; Hetland, Admissions in the Uniform Rules: Are They Necessary? 46 Iowa L.Rev. 307

Admissions are the words or acts of a party-opponent or a representative that are offered as evidence against the party. They may be *express* admissions, which are statements of the opposing party or an agent whose words may fairly be used against the party, or admissions by *conduct*. Among the theories on which the probativity and admissibility of admissions have been explained and supported, the following seem most helpful.

Morgan's view was that admissions came in as an exception to the hearsay rule, assuming hearsay is given the usual definition of declarations made out of court, not subject to cross-examination, and received as evidence of the truth of the matter declared. Exceptions to the hearsay rule usually are justified on the ground that evidence meeting the requirements of the exception possesses special reliability, plus perhaps special need because of the unavailability of the declarant. Yet no objective guaranty of trustworthiness is furnished by the admissions rule. The party is not required to have firsthand knowledge of the matter declared; the declaration may be self-serving when made; and the declarant is probably sitting in the courtroom. As Morgan himself admitted, "The admissibility of an admission made by the party himself rests not upon any notion that the circumstances in which it was made furnish the trier means of evaluating it fairly, but upon the adversary theory of litigation. A party can hardly object that he had no opportunity to cross-examine himself or that he is unworthy of credence save when speaking under sanction of an oath." [2]

Wigmore, after pointing out that the party's declaration has generally the probative value of any other person's assertion, argued that it had a special value when offered *against* the party. In that circumstance, the admission discredits the party's statements inconsistent with the present claim asserted in pleadings and testimony, much like a witness impeached by contradictory statements. Moreover, he continued, admissions pass the gauntlet of the hearsay rule, which requires that extra-judicial assertions be excluded if there was no opportunity for the opponent to cross-examine because it is the opponent's own declaration, and "he does not need to cross-examine himself." Wigmore then added that "the Hearsay Rule is satisfied" since the party "now as opponent has the full opportunity to put himself on the stand and explain his former assertion." [3]

Strahorn suggested a further theory that classified all admissions when offered against a party, whether words or acts, as being *conduct* offered as circumstantial evidence rather than for its assertive, testimonial value. This circumstantial value is, as noted by Wigmore, the quality of inconsistency with the party's present claim:

(1961); Morgan, Admissions, 12 Wash. L.Rev. 181 (1937); Strahorn, A Reconsideration of the Hearsay Rule and Admissions, 85 U.Pa.L.Rev. 484 (1937); Dec.Dig.Evidence ∞200–265, Criminal Law ∞405–415; C.J.S.Evidence §§ 270–383; West's Ann.Cal.Evid.Code §§ 1220–1227.

2. Morgan, Basic Problems of Evidence 265–266 (1963).

3. 4 Wigmore, Evidence § 1048 (Chadbourn rev. 1972).

The hearsay rule applies to those statements for which the only justification is their narrative content. It is inapplicable to those which are conduct, i.e., for which the trustworthiness of the utterance is a matter of indifference. So it is with admissions. The writer feels that inasmuch as all admissions, express and otherwise, can be rationalized as the relevant conduct of the speaker, it is unnecessary to predicate their admissibility on the basis of a possible narrative effect not possessed by all of them.[4]

On balance, the most satisfactory justification of the admissibility of admissions is that they are the product of the adversary system, sharing on a lower level the characteristics of admissions in pleadings or stipulations.[5] Under this view, admissions need not satisfy the traditional requirement for hearsay exceptions that they possess circumstantial guarantees of trustworthiness. Rather admissions are simply classed as nonhearsay and outside the framework of exceptions to the hearsay rule.

Federal Rule 801(d)(2)[6] takes the view that admissions are not hearsay. It provides:[7]

A statement is not hearsay if—* * * The statement is offered against a party and is (A) the party's own statement, in either an individual or a representative capacity, or (B) a statement of which the party has manifested an adoption or belief in its truth, or (C) a statement by a person authorized by the party to make a statement concerning the subject, or (D) a statement by the party's agent or servant concerning a matter within the scope of the agency or employment, made during the existence of the relationship, or (E) a statement by a coconspirator of a party during the course and in furtherance of the conspiracy.

Regardless of the precise theory of admissibility, it is clear that admissions of a party are received as substantive evidence of the facts admitted and not merely to contradict the party.[8] As a result, no

---

4. Strahorn, supra note 1, at 576. See also Schloss v. Trounstine, 135 N.J.L. 11, 49 A.2d 677 (1946).

5. While this theory of adversary system supports introduction of this class of evidence, the presence in each case of adversary testing is not a prerequisite to admissibility. For example, the fact that the party making the statement, who was sued in a representative capacity, is dead at the time of trial and cannot counter it as an adversary does not result in exclusion of the admission. Savarese v. Agriss, 883 F.2d 1194, 1200–1201 (3d Cir.1989).

6. Except for minor stylistic difference, Revised Uniform Rule (1986) 801(d)(2) is the same.

7. The decision to classify admissions as nonhearsay in the Federal Rules, rather than as a hearsay exception, was not based on purely theoretical grounds. Believing that no catalog of hearsay exceptions could possibly include all trustworthy hearsay evidence that might evolve, the Advisory Committee included provisions in general terms for hearsay not within one of the enumerated exceptions but having comparable guarantees of trustworthiness. See infra § 324. The inclusion of admissions, which possess no objective guarantee of trustworthiness, as an exception would not have been consistent with this pattern.

As to treating admissions as nonhearsay, see also Cox v. Esso Shipping Co., 247 F.2d 629, 632 (5th Cir.1957); United States v. United Shoe Mach. Corp., 89 F.Supp. 349, 351 (D.Mass.1950).

8. United States v. Cline, 570 F.2d 731 (8th Cir.1978); Olson v. Hodges, 236 Iowa 612, 19 N.W.2d 676 (1945); Lambros v. Coolahan, 185 Md. 463, 45 A.2d 96 (1945) (witness' report of party's oral admission, though denied by party, sufficient to take the issue to the jury); Greenwood v. Harris, 362 P.2d 85 (Okl.1961) (admission sufficient to supply need for expert testimony

foundation by first examining the party, as required for impeaching a witness with a prior inconsistent statement,[9] is a prerequisite for proof of admissions.[10]

When the term admission is used without any qualifying adjective, the customary meaning is an evidentiary admission, that is, words in oral or written form or conduct of a party or a representative offered in evidence against the party. *Evidentiary* admissions are to be distinguished from *judicial* admissions. Judicial admissions are not evidence at all. Rather, they are formal concessions in the pleadings in the case or stipulations by a party or its counsel that have the effect of withdrawing a fact from issue and dispensing wholly with the need for proof of the fact.[11] Thus, the judicial admission, unless allowed by the court to be withdrawn, is conclusive in the case, whereas the evidentiary admission is not conclusive but is always subject to contradiction or explanation.[12]

Confessions of crime are a particular kind of admission, governed by special rules discussed in the chapter on Confessions.[13] Admissions do not need to have the dramatic effect or be the all-encompassing acknowledgement of responsibility that the word confession connotes. They are simply words or actions inconsistent with the party's position at trial, relevant to the substantive issues in the case, and offered against the party.[14] Moreover, while generally received in evidence because of their substantial probative value in most situations, admissions may be excluded if their probative value is substantially outweighed by the prejudicial impact.[15]

in medical malpractice action); Silvey & Co., Inc. v. Engel, 204 Neb. 633, 284 N.W.2d 560 (1979) (error to instruct jury that an admission could be considered merely as discrediting the party's testimony); Dec.Dig.Evidence ⊙➞200, 217, 222(1), 265(1); 4 Wigmore, Evidence §§ 1055, 1056 (Chadbourn rev. 1972). Additional circumstances, e.g., want of knowledge by person making the statement, may deprive the admission of substantial weight.

9. See supra § 37.

10. Cox v. Esso Shipping Co., 247 F.2d 629 (5th Cir.1957); Brown v. Calumet River Ry. Co., 125 Ill. 600, 18 N.E. 283 (1888); 4 Wigmore, Evidence § 1051(1) (Chadbourn rev. 1972).

11. See infra § 257. In the same category are admissions in response to a request to admit under Fed.R.Civ.P. 36. Finman, The Request for Admissions in Federal Civil Procedure, 71 Yale L.J. 371 (1962).

12. Aide v. Taylor, 214 Minn. 212, 7 N.W.2d 757 (1943); 4 Wigmore, Evidence §§ 1058, 1059 (Chadbourn rev. 1972). As to admissions in pleadings other than the

effective pleadings in the case, see infra § 257.

13. See supra Ch. 14.

Beyond the differences arising from constitutional principles that govern much of criminal procedure, some courts have special rules in dealing with confessions, as opposed to admissions, by a criminal defendant. State v. Sabers, 442 N.W.2d 259, 264–265 (S.D.1989).

14. See State v. Stuck, 434 N.W.2d 43, 54–55 (S.D.1988) (employing broad definition of admission and rejecting out-of-hand argument that defendant's denial of statement affected its admissibility).

15. See State v. Maurer, 770 P.2d 981 (Utah 1989) (highly inflammatory admission by defendant excluded on ground that its relatively slight value on the contested issue in the case was outweighed by its prejudicial effect on jury). But see United States v. Kehm, 799 F.2d 354, 357 (7th Cir.1986) (defendant's statements showing him to be a "big-talking, high-rolling, profane drug smuggler," while prejudicial, were admissible under Rule 801(d)(2)(A) because inseparable from other statements in

A type of evidence with which admissions may be confused is evidence of declarations against interest. The latter, treated under a separate exception to the hearsay rule,[16] must have been against the declarant's interest when made. No such requirement applies to admissions. For example, if a person states that a note is forged and then later acquires the note and sues upon it, the previous statement may be introduced as an admission although the party had no interest when he or she made the statement. Of course, most admissions are actually against interest when made, but there is no such requirement.[17] Hence the common phrase in judicial opinions, "admissions against interest,"[18] is an invitation to confuse two separate exceptions to the hearsay rule and erroneously to engraft upon admissions an against-interest requirement.

Other distinctions between admissions and declarations against interest are that admissions must be the statements of a party to the lawsuit.[19] Also, admissions must be offered against the party opponent. By contrast, declarations need not be made by a party but may be, and typically are, made by some third person, and they may be offered by either party.[20] Finally, the declaration against interest exception admits the statement only when the declarant has become unavailable as a witness, while unavailability is not required of admissions of a party.[21]

a taped conversation that was inconsistent with his defense).

16. See infra § 316.

17. One of the clearest expressions to this effect is in State v. Anderson, 10 Or. 448, 452 (1882). On a charge of murdering his brother, the state gave in evidence defendant's admissions that he had no means before his brother's death. In holding these admissible over the objection that they were not against interest, the court said:

> But the admissibility of a party's own previous statements or declarations in respect to the subject in controversy, as evidence against him, does not in any manner depend upon the question whether they were for or against his interest at the time they were made, or afterwards. The opposite party has a right to introduce them if relevant and voluntarily made, no matter how they may stand or have stood in relation to the interest of the party making them.

The court's statement retains its validity. See also United States v. Rios Ruiz, 579 F.2d 670, 676 (1st Cir.1978) (in prosecution of police officer charged with assault, statement in arrest report and in grand jury testimony constituted admission, although not necessarily "an admission against in-

terest"); O'Donnell v. Georgia Osteopathic Hosp., Inc., 748 F.2d 1543, 1548 n. 6 (11th Cir.1984) (admission may be received even though at the time statement made its damaging impact could not be detected). See generally 4 Wigmore, Evidence § 1048 (Chadbourn rev. 1972).

18. The phrase continues to appear with embarrassing frequency. See, e.g., Kassel v. Gannett Co., Inc., 875 F.2d 935, 951 (1st Cir.1989); Heydinger v. Adkins, 360 S.E.2d 240, 244–246 (W.Va.1987). See also Kekua v. Kaiser Found. Hosp., 61 Hawaii 208, 601 P.2d 364 (1979), and Hofer v. Bituminous Casualty Co., 260 Iowa 81, 148 N.W.2d 485 (1967), both characterizing the phrase as misleading and deploring the usage.

19. State v. Antillon, 229 Neb. 348, 354–355, 426 N.W.2d 533, 538 (1988) (victim in criminal case is not party and accordingly statements cannot be introduced by defendant as admission of opponent).

20. See infra § 316.

21. See 4 Wigmore, Evidence §§ 1048, 1049 (Chadbourn rev. 1972); Fed.R.Evid. 801(d)(2), 804(b)(4). In some cases, however, the party who made an admission may be unavailable. See, e.g., Savarese v.

§ 255. Testimonial Qualifications: Mental Competency; Personal Knowledge [1]

The nature of admissions as a general proposition denies any significance to the question whether the party making the admission must meet standards of competency established for witnesses.[2] Thus, disqualifications arising from the marital relationship or "dead man's" acts, for example, lack relevancy in the case of admissions. No reason exists to exclude an otherwise receivable admission because the party making it was married or is now dead.

The single exception calling for consideration is lack of mental capacity. Some cases involve statements by badly injured persons, possibly also under sedation.[3] While the older decisions tended to examine the capacity of the declarant and to exclude the evidence if capacity was found not to exist,[4] more recent opinions view the question as going to weight rather than admissibility.[5] The latter position represents a preferable allocation of the functions of judge and jury and is consistent with current treatment of mental competency as a qualification of witnesses.[6] The adversary roots of admissions by parties make caution appropriate in applying this reasoning to statements by children.[7] Substantive rules of liability for torts may suggest acceptable standards of responsibility for such admissions.[8] Hearsay exceptions such as that for excited utterances should be explored as possibly offering a more satisfactory avenue to admissibility in evidence in a particular case.[9]

The requirement that a witness speak from firsthand knowledge is

Agriss, 883 F.2d 1194, 1201 (3d Cir.1989) (citing additional cases).

§ 255

1. See 4 Wigmore, Evidence § 1053 (Chadbourn rev. 1972).

2. See supra Ch. 7.

3. In some states, legislation restricts the admissibility of statements obtained from injured persons within a specified time after the injury was sustained. Mass. Gen.Laws Ann. c. 233, § 23A; Wis.Stats. Ann. 904.12; Annot., 22 A.L.R.2d 1269.

4. Jacobson v. Carlson, 302 Mich. 448, 4 N.W.2d 721 (1942); Ammundson v. Tinholt, 228 Minn. 115, 36 N.W.2d 521 (1949). Oddly, both cases speak of utterances of a party incapable of narrating.

5. Currier v. Grossman's of New Hampshire, Inc., 107 N.H. 159, 219 A.2d 273 (1966); Finnerty v. Darby, 391 Pa. 300, 138 A.2d 117 (1958).

6. See supra § 62.

7. Occasional broad statements that an infant cannot make an admission, Knights Templar & Masons' Life Indem. Co. v. Crayton, 209 Ill. 550, 70 N.E. 1066 (1904), generally have not been followed.

8. See, e.g., Howard v. Hall, 112 Ga. App. 247, 145 S.E.2d 70 (1965); Reed v. Kabureck, 229 Ill.App. 36 (1923), suggesting substantive tort liability as a measure for admissions. See Keeton, Bobbs, Keeton & Owen, Prosser and Keaton on Torts 179–182, 1071–1072 (5th Lawyer's ed. 1984). Contract law, in view of its tenderness toward even very mature infants, is unhelpful.

An admission by a child under 9 years of age was upheld in Hardman v. Helen Curtis Industries, Inc., 48 Ill.App.2d 42, 198 N.E.2d 681 (1964); under 7 in Atchison, Topeka & Santa Fe Ry. Co. v. Potter, 60 Kan. 808, 58 P. 471 (1899); and 6 years old in Rolfe v. Olson, 87 N.J.Super. 242, 208 A.2d 817 (App.Div.1965). In Fontaine v. Devonis, 114 R.I. 541, 336 A.2d 847 (1975), exclusion of the statement of a 3½ year old child that he ran into the street and was hit by a car was upheld. Cases are collected in Annot., 12 A.L.R.3d 1051.

9. See infra § 272.

applicable to hearsay declarations generally,[10] and it has on some rare occasions been applied to admissions.[11] However, the traditional view espoused by the vast majority of courts [12] and adopted by the Federal Rules [13] is that such firsthand knowledge is not required of admissions.

The general theory supporting the elimination of firsthand knowledge as a requirement is supported by a number of arguments. First, when people speak against their own interest, it is generally to be supposed that they have made an adequate investigation.[14] While this disserving feature might attach to most admissions, we have seen that admissions are competent evidence though not against interest when made, and as to these, the argument does not apply. However, a sufficient basis for generally dispensing with the requirement of firsthand knowledge qualification rests on the argument that admissions that become relevant in litigation usually concern some matter of substantial importance to declarants upon which they would likely have informed themselves. As a result, such admissions possess greater reliability than the general run of hearsay, even when not based on firsthand observation. Moreover, the possibility is substantial that the declarant may have come into possession of significant information not known to the opponent.

The validity of dispensing with firsthand knowledge in the case of admissions by agents has been questioned vigorously by a leading text on the Federal Rules, advocating the insertion of such a requirement by

---

10. See, e.g., infra §§ 280, 290, 313.

11. Coca–Cola Bottling Co. v. Munn, 99 F.2d 190, 197 (4th Cir.1938) (previous admission by plaintiff, now suing for injury due to lye in bottled drink, that it would be impossible for a bottle to have any lye in it after going through defendant's plant, held properly excluded).

12. Mahlandt v. Wild Canid Survival & Research Center, Inc., 588 F.2d 626, 630 (8th Cir.1978) (agent's statement without firsthand knowledge admissible against both agent and principal); Janus v. Akstin, 91 N.H. 373, 20 A.2d 552 (1941) (action for attack by defendant's dog; defendant's statement that dog jumped on the decedent held admissible although defendant not present); Reed v. McCord, 160 N.Y. 330, 341, 54 N.E. 737 (1899) (statement by defendant-employer as to how injury happened although he was not present); Salvitti v. Throppe, 343 Pa. 642, 23 A.2d 445 (1942) (evidence admitted that owner of truck, who was not present, acknowledged that his driver was at fault in collision); Lockwood v. AC & S, Inc., 109 Wash.2d 235, 263, 744 P.2d 605, 621 (1987) (firsthand knowledge generally not required, although court notes possibility of exclusion of vicarious admissions where affirmative indication that they are based on rumor or

speculation). Additional cases are collected in Annot., 54 A.L.R.2d 1069. See 4 Wigmore, Evidence § 1053 (Chadbourn rev. 1972).

This question is often joined with the problem of whether repetition of another's statement is an adoptive admission. See Reed supra and infra § 261.

13. In approaching admissions generally, the Advisory Committee's Note to Federal Rule 801(d)(2) observed:

> The freedom which admissions have enjoyed from technical demands of searching for an assurance of trustworthiness in some against-interest circumstance, and from the restrictive influences of the opinion rule and the rule requiring firsthand knowledge, when taken with the apparently prevalent satisfaction with the results, calls for generous treatment of this avenue to admissibility.

56 F.R.D. 183, 297.

14. On occasion it may appear affirmatively that an investigation was in fact conducted. Pekelis v. Transcontinental & Western Air, Inc., 187 F.2d 122, 128–129 (2d Cir.1951), cert. denied 341 U.S. 951; Mahlandt v. Wild Canid Survival & Research Center, Inc., 588 F.2d 626, 628–629 (8th Cir.1978).

construction.[15] The proposal has not been accepted by the courts, however.[16]

§ 256. Admissions in Opinion Form; Conclusions of Law

If the lack of firsthand knowledge of the party does not exclude an admission, as indicated in the preceding section, it would seem clear that the opinion rule should not. As we have seen, the purpose of the latter rule is to regulate the in-court interrogation of a witness so as to elicit answers in a more concrete form rather than in terms of inference. In its modern form, it is a rule of preference for the more concrete answers, if the witness can give them, rather than a rule of exclusion.[1]

This rule, which is designed to promote the concreteness of answers on the stand, is grotesquely misapplied to out-of-court statements such as admissions where the declarant's statements are made without thought of the form of courtroom testimony. While counsel may reframe the question in the preferred form if an objection is sustained regarding in-court testimony, the rule can only be applied by excluding an out-of-court statement. Accordingly, the prevailing view is that admissions in the form of opinions are competent.[2]

---

15. 4 Weinstein & Berger, Weinstein's Evidence ¶ 801(d)(2)(C)[01], at 277–280 (1990) (arguing that the desired result could be reached by applying the rationale of Rule 805 or Rule 403). See also Bein, Parties' Admission, Agents' Admissions: Hearsay Wolves in Sheep's Clothing, 12 Hofstra L.Rev. 393 (1984) (proposing firsthand knowledge requirement for employee admissions); 2 Saltzburg & Martin, Federal Rules of Evidence Manual 147 (5th ed. 1990) (arguing that the structure of the rules suggests that agents' admission should be treated more restrictively than personal admissions where personal knowledge lacking but acknowledging that cases have not adopted this view). Cf. Lockwood v. AC & S, Inc., 109 Wash.2d 235, 263, 744 P.2d 605, 621 (1987) (although firsthand knowledge generally not required, court notes possibility of exclusion of vicarious admissions if opponent shows that they are based on rumor or speculation).

The fact that admissions are subject to explanation to avoid or lessen their force affords, in the typical case, adequate safeguards without sacrificing their evidentiary usefulness.

16. Mahlandt v. Wild Canid Survival & Research Center, Inc., 588 F.2d 626, 630 (8th Cir.1978) (report of alleged biting of child by wolf, made by employee of research center in whose backyard wolf was confined after investigation but without

personal knowledge, admissible against research center under Federal Rule 801(d)(2)(D)). See also Brookover v. Mary Hitchcock Memorial Hosp., 893 F.2d 411, 416–418 (1st Cir.1990) (under 801(d)(2)(D), personal knowledge by nurses of patient's fall and injury not required in malpractice action against hospital); MCI Communications Corp. v. American Tel. & Tel. Co., 708 F.2d 1081, 1143 (7th Cir.1983), cert. denied 464 U.S. 891; Russell v. United Parcel Service, Inc., 666 F.2d 1188, 1190–1191 (8th Cir.1981) (firsthand knowledge not required for admissions and accordingly statements in employment discrimination case not excluded even though stated as conclusions without indicating supporting facts).

§ 256

1. See supra § 18.

2. Pekelis v. Transcontinental & Western Air, Inc., 187 F.2d 122 (2d Cir.1951), cert. denied 341 U.S. 951 (report by airline investigating board as to cause of accident); Cox v. Esso Shipping Co., 247 F.2d 629 (5th Cir.1957) (master's report that seaman's injury was due in part to own neglect); Russell v. United Parcel Service, Inc., 666 F.2d 1188, 1190–1191 (8th Cir.1981) (in discrimination action by employee, proper to admit statements by supervisors, even though stated as conclusions, that plaintiff was being treated in manner complained of

Most often the question arises in connection with statements of a participant in an accident that the mishap was the speakers fault. Additionally, it is often argued that such statements should be excluded because they are conclusions of law. While conceivably a party might give an opinion on an abstract question of law, such are not the typical statements actually offered. These statements normally include an application of a standard to the facts; thus they reveal the facts as the declarant thinks them to be, to which the standard of "fault" or other legal or moral standard involved in the statement was applied. In these circumstances, the factual information conveyed should not be ignored merely because the statement may also indicate the party's assumptions about the law.[3] However, it is conceivable that the legal principle may be so technical as to deprive an admission of significance or the party may indeed give an opinion regarding solely an abstract issue of law. In those cases, exclusion is warranted. In addition, it should be generally remembered that evidentiary admissions are subject to explanation.

§ 257. Admissions in Pleadings;[1] Pleas of Guilty

The final pleadings upon which the case is tried state the contentions of each party as to the facts, and by admitting or denying the opponent's pleading, they define the factual issues that are to be tried by the process of proof. Thus, the court must look to the pleadings as part of the record in passing on the relevancy of evidence and to determine the issues to be submitted to the jury. For these purposes, it is not necessary to offer the pleadings in evidence.[2] They are used as judicial

because manager was out to cause her trouble for filing lawsuits and claims against the company); Strickland v. Davis, 221 Ala. 247, 128 So. 233 (1930) (defendant's statement after accident that it was his fault held admissible, rejecting the application of requirements for in-court testimony to admissions and the objection that the statement expressed a legal conclusion); Swain v. Oregon Motor Stages, 160 Or. 1, 82 P.2d 1084 (1938) (statement by plaintiff, bus passenger suing for injury in collision with automobile, in accident report that driver of automobile to blame ruled admissible); Wells v. Burton Lines, Inc., 228 N.C. 422, 45 S.E.2d 569 (1947) (plaintiff after collision said it was his fault); Southern Passenger Motor Lines v. Burks, 187 Va. 53, 46 S.E.2d 26 (1948) (plaintiff's statement that collision not due to fault or negligence of defendant's driver); Lockwood v. AC & S, Inc., 109 Wash.2d 235, 262–263, 744 P.2d 605, 618–619 (1987) (opinions by employees charged with studying asbestos dangers admissible, admissions rule making no distinction between statements in form of opinion or fact); 4

Wigmore, Evidence § 1053(3) (Chadbourn rev. 1972); Annot., 118 A.L.R. 1230. See Adv.Comm.Note, supra § 255 note 13.

3. Dreier v. Upjohn Co., 196 Conn. 242, 248–250, 492 A.2d 164, 168–169 (1985) (allegation of negligence in pleading against one defendant, later withdrawn, constituted admission despite claim that it was a legal conclusion and even the party may not be qualified as an expert to make such conclusion). See also decisions cited supra note 2.

§ 257

1. 4 Wigmore, Evidence §§ 1064–1067 (Chadbourn rev. 1972); Dec.Dig.Evidence ⇐208, 265(8)(11); C.J.S. Evidence §§ 300–306; Annot., 52 A.L.R.2d 516.

2. Wright v. Lincoln City Lines, Inc., 160 Neb. 714, 71 N.W.2d 182 (1955). The same principle applies to unequivocal oral statements made to define issues by attorney within the scope of his or her authority in judicial proceedings. See, e.g., First Pennsylvania Bank v. Harris (In re Eagson Corp.), 37 B.R. 471, 480–481 (Bkrtcy.

and not as evidentiary admissions, and for these purposes, they are conclusive until withdrawn or amended.[3]

A party may also seek to use an averment or admission in an adversary's final pleading as a basis for arguing the existence of some subordinate fact or as the foundation for an adverse inference. Some courts permit the party to do this by quoting or reading the pleading as part of the record,[4] while others require that the party, in order to make this use of the final pleading, introduce the relevant passage from the opponent's pleading as part of its own evidence during the course of the trial.[5] Such a requirement allows the pleader to give explanatory evidence, such as that the allegation was made through inadvertence or mistake,[6] and avoids the possibility of a surprise inference from the pleading in closing argument. These considerations may justify the departure from consistency.

Subject to the qualifications developed later in this section, pleadings are generally usable against the pleader. If they are the effective pleadings in the case, they have the standing of judicial admissions.[7] Amended, withdrawn, or superseded pleadings in the case are no longer judicial admissions,[8] but may be used as evidentiary admissions.[9] A party's pleading in one case may generally be used as an evidentiary admission in other litigation.[10] These same principles apply to the use in a subsequent trial of counsel's oral in-court statements representing the factual contentions of the party, even including assertions made during opening statement.[11]

E.D.Pa.1984). By contrast, binding effect is not to be given to statements by counsel during deposition of witness not intended to constitute substitute for evidence of facts. Surovcik v. D & K Optical, Inc., 702 F.Supp. 1171, 1179 (M.D.Pa.1988).

3. Roth v. Roth, 45 Ill.2d 19, 256 N.E.2d 838 (1970) (pleadings); Hake v. George Wiedemann Brewing Co., 23 Ohio St.2d 65, 262 N.E.2d 703 (1970) (admission in opening statement); Note, 64 Colum.L.Rev. 1121 (1964).

4. Grand Trunk Western R. Co. v. Lovejoy, 304 Mich. 35, 7 N.W.2d 212 (1942); Hork v. Minneapolis St. R. Co., 193 Minn. 366, 258 N.W. 576 (1935); Hildreth v. Hudloe, 282 S.W. 747 (Mo.App.1926).

5. Louisville & Nashville R. Co. v. Hull, 113 Ky. 561, 68 S.W. 433 (1902); Smith v. Nimocks, 94 N.C. 243 (1885); Mullen v. Union Cent. Life Ins. Co., 182 Pa. 150, 37 A. 988 (1897) (affidavit of defense).

6. This reason is found in Smith v. Nimocks, 94 N.C. 243 (1886).

7. See supra note 3.

8. Taliaferro v. Reirdon, 197 Okl. 55, 168 P.2d 292 (1946); Kirk v. Head, 137 Tex. 44, 152 S.W.2d 726 (1941).

9. See Dreier v. Upjohn Co., 196 Conn. 242, 244, 492 A.2d 164, 167 (1985); Annot., 52 A.L.R.2d 516. See also United States v. GAF Corp., 928 F.2d 1253 (2d Cir.1991) (original bill of particulars admissible against government in criminal case under these principles).

10. Williams v. Union Carbide Corp., 790 F.2d 552, 555–556 (6th Cir.1986), cert. denied 479 U.S. 992 (pleadings in prior case admissible as evidentiary admission in spite of claim that first lawsuit filed simply to prevent running of statute of limitations); Missouri Pac. R. Co. v. Zolliecoffer, 209 Ark. 559, 191 S.W.2d 587 (1946); Bartolatta v. Calvo, 112 Conn. 385, 152 A. 306 (1930); Korelski v. Needham, 77 Ill.App.2d 328, 222 N.E.2d 334 (1966); Himelson v. Galusz, 309 Mich. 512, 15 N.W.2d 727 (1944); Dec.Dig.Evidence ⊕208(2); C.J.S. Evidence § 303.

The use of pleading as admissions presents substantial potential for prejudice and mischief. As a result, individualized examination of the inconsistent pleading may be required before a determination regarding admissibility can be rendered. See infra text accompanying notes 17–26.

11. United States v. McKeon, 738 F.2d 26, 33 (2d Cir.1984) (opening statement in-

How closely is it necessary to connect the pleading with the party against whom it is to be introduced as an admission? Certainly if it be shown to have been sworn to,[12] or signed by, the party that would be sufficient.[13] More often, however, the pleading is prepared and signed by counsel, and the older view holds that it is not sufficient to show that the pleading was filed or signed by the party's attorney of record, and statements therein will be presumed to be merely "suggestions of counsel" unless other evidence is produced that they were actually sanctioned by the client.[14] The dominant current position, however, is that pleadings shown to have been prepared or filed by counsel employed by the party are prima facie regarded as authorized by the client and are entitled to be received as his admissions.[15] The party opposing admission may offer evidence that the pleading was filed upon incorrect information and without his or her actual knowledge, but, except in extraordinary circumstances, such a showing goes only to the weight and not to the admissibility of the pleading.[16]

An important exception to the use of the pleadings as admissions must be noted. A basic problem which attends the use of written pleadings is uncertainty whether the evidence as it actually unfolds at trial will prove the case described in the pleadings. Traditionally a

dicating factual position of client). Because of the stylized nature of an opening statement, the court in McKeon imposed further requirements. Before an opening statement can be used as an admission it must be clear that it is an assertion of fact rather than counsel's argument and some participatory role of the client must be evident indicating that in all probability the client would have confirmed counsel's statement.

Oral statements by an attorney as the client's agent made out of court may likewise be admissible. See, e.g., United States v. Arrington, 867 F.2d 122, 126–128 (2d Cir.1989), cert. denied 493 U.S. 817 (threats by attorney against witnesses); Harris v. Steelweld Equipment Co., Inc., 869 F.2d 396, 403 (8th Cir.1989), cert. denied 493 U.S. 817 (statements to expert); Hanson v. Waller, 888 F.2d 806, 813–814 (11th Cir.1989) (letter to opposing attorney). See generally infra § 259 regarding vicarious admissions by representatives of the party.

12. Hall v. Guthrie, 10 Mo. 621 (1847) (sworn bill in chancery); Johnson v. Butte & Superior Copper Co., 41 Mont. 158, 108 P. 1057 (1910) (admission in sworn answer); Dec.Dig.Evidence ☞208(4).

13. Kassel v. Gannett Co., Inc., 875 F.2d 935, 951 (1st Cir.1989) (statements from brief signed by party, which he filed pro se,

considered admission); Radclyffe v. Barton, 161 Mass. 327, 37 N.E. 373 (1894); Annot., 14 A.L.R. 22, 26.

14. Fidelity & Deposit Co. v. Redfield, 7 F.2d 800 (9th Cir.1925); Reichert v. Jerome H. Sheip, Inc., 206 Ala. 648, 91 So. 618 (1921). Cases pro and con are collected in Annots. 14 A.L.R. 22, 23, 90 A.L.R. 1393, 1394, 63 A.L.R.2d 412, 428, 444–445.

15. Williams v. Union Carbide Corp., 790 F.2d 552, 556 (6th Cir.1986), cert. denied 479 U.S. 992; Jelleff, Inc. v. Braden, 233 F.2d 671 (D.C.Cir.1956); Fibreboard Paper Products Corp. v. East Bay Union, 227 Cal.App.2d 675, 707, 39 Cal.Rptr. 64, 83 (1964); Collens v. New Canaan Water Co., 155 Conn. 477, 234 A.2d 825 (1967); Allen v. United States Fidelity & Guar. Co., 269 Ill. 234, 109 N.E. 1035 (1915); Carlson v. Fredsall, 228 Minn. 461, 37 N.W.2d 744 (1949).

16. Williams v. Union Carbide Corp., 790 F.2d 552, 556 (6th Cir.1986), cert. denied 479 U.S. 992 (statements that prior lawsuit filed solely for purpose of preserving legal rights may be quite persuasive but should have been made to jury); Kucza v. Stone, 155 Conn. 194, 230 A.2d 559 (1967) (error to exclude plaintiff's testimony as to whether he had discussed allegations with attorney in earlier case after opponent had introduced complaint from earlier case making allegations inconsistent with testimony). See also cases cited in supra note 15.

failure in this respect, i.e., a variance between pleading and proof, could bring disaster to the pleader's case. As a safeguard against developments of this kind, the common law permitted the use of counts, each a complete separate statement of a different version of the same basic claim, combined in the same declaration, to take care of variance possibilities.[17] The same was done with defenses. Inconsistency between counts or between defenses was not prohibited; in fact it was essential to the successful use of the system.[18] Also essential to the success of the system was a prohibition against using allegations in one count or defense as admissions to prove or disprove allegations in another.[19]

Under the influence of the Field Code of 1848, the view prevailed for a time that there could exist only one set of facts in a case and that inconsistent statements and defenses were therefore not allowable.[20] Nevertheless, uncertainty as to how a case will in fact develop at trial is now recognized as a reality, with a concomitant need for some procedure for dealing with problems of variance. The modern equivalent of the common law system is the use of alternative and hypothetical forms of statement of claims and defenses, regardless of consistency.[21] It can readily be appreciated that pleadings of this nature are directed primarily to giving notice and lack the essential character of an admission. To allow them to operate as admissions would frustrate their underlying purpose. Hence the decisions with seeming unanimity deny them status as judicial admissions,[22] and generally disallow them

---

17. Thus, in Hart v. Longfield, 7 Mod. 148, 87 Eng.Rep. 1156 (1703), where plaintiff wished to proceed in both indebitatus assumpsit and quantum meruit for nourishing Edward Longfield, Holt, C.J., observed that Edward Longfield should be stated as a different child in each count, multiplying him as many times as there were counts.

"Records containing from ten to fifteen special counts or pleas are by no means rare * * *. Of these, the greater proportion and frequently the whole relate to the same substantial cause of action or defence. They are merely different expositions of the same case, and expositions of it often inconsistent with each other." Report of Common Law Procedure Commission, Parliament Papers 1830, quoted in 9 Holdsworth, Hist.Eng.Law 305, 306 (3d ed. 1944).

The counterpart in equity practice was to allege in the alternative.

18. Gould v. Oliver, 2 Man. & G. 208 (C.P.1840); Note, 17 Tex.L.Rev. 191 (1939). See also Garman v. Griffin, 666 F.2d 1156, 1158–1159 (8th Cir.1981) (quoting treatise on this issue).

19. Harington v. Macmorris, 5 Taunt. 228, 128 Eng.Rep. 675 (1813); Herman v. Fine, 314 Mass. 67, 49 N.E.2d 597 (1943). See also supra note 18.

20. Clark, Code Pleading 460 (2d ed. 1947).

21. Fed.R.Civ.P. 8(e)(2); James & Hazard, Civil Procedure 156 (3d ed. 1985); Green, Basic Civil Procedure 114–118 (2d ed. 1979).

22. Schneider v. Lockheed Aircraft Corp., 658 F.2d 835, 844–847 (D.C.Cir.1981), cert. denied 455 U.S. 994 (error to allow use as evidentiary admission concession of correctness of allegations in pleading made only for purposes of arguing motion directed against sufficiency of pleading); McCormick v. Kopmann, 23 Ill.App.2d 189, 161 N.E.2d 720 (1959) (allegation of decedent's freedom from contributory negligence in count 1 not negated by allegation that his intoxication caused accident in count 4); Aetna Ins. Co. v. Klein, 318 S.W.2d 464 (Tex.Civ.App.1958), reversed on other grounds 160 Tex. 61, 325 S.W.2d 376 (general denial not negated by contrary statements in special pleas).

as evidentiary admissions.[23]

Some courts have exhibited sensitivity to the potential unfairness involved in admitting pleadings where a more skillful pleader would have avoided the pitfalls of creating an admission, particularly where the pleading at issue concerned the conduct of third parties.[24] Another approach is to recognize the potential of receiving an inconsistent pleading to unfairly prejudice a party and to be overvalued in relation to its true probative worth, excluding the pleading in appropriate cases after balancing the relevant factors.[25] A final possible exception, not widely recognized, is denial of status as an admission to amended, withdrawn, or superseded pleadings on the theory that to admit them into evidence contravenes the policy of liberality in amendment.[26]

A recurring question is whether a plea of guilty to a criminal charge should be allowed in evidence in a related civil action. Generally the evidence is admitted.[27] While a plea of guilty to a traffic offense is in theory no different from a plea of guilty to other offenses,[28] recognition

23. Macheca v. Fowler, 412 S.W.2d 462 (Mo.1967); Van Sickell v. Margolis, 109 N.J.Super. 14, 262 A.2d 209 (App.Div.1969), affirmed 55 N.J. 355, 262 A.2d 203; Furlong v. Donhals, Inc., 87 R.I. 46, 137 A.2d 734 (1958). Contra Tway v. Hartman, 181 Okl. 608, 75 P.2d 893 (1938).

24. Estate of Spinosa, 621 F.2d 1154, 1157 (1st Cir.1980) (in product liability action against truck manufacturer for death of driver and injury to passenger, proper to exclude complaint in earlier action against owner alleging that a cause of the accident was his negligent failure properly to maintain the vehicle on the basis that the pleadings were not inconsistent); Garman v. Griffin, 666 F.2d 1156, 1158–1159 (8th Cir. 1981) (in action against driver and erroneously identified bus manufacturer for death of child run over by school bus from which he had alighted, it was error to admit, after dismissal against bus manufacturer, plaintiffs' allegation that bus was defectively constructed so as to preclude complete view by driver); Meador v. City of Salem, 51 Ill.2d 572, 284 N.E.2d 266 (1972) (proper to exclude workman's compensation claim, offered in statutory action against city for same injury, on issue of employment); Schusler v. Fletcher, 74 Ill. App.2d 249, 219 N.E.2d 588 (1966) (separate actions by plaintiff, each alleging different cause for injuries; exclusion upheld). Several of the cases involve third-party complaints or cross-claims for indemnity with concessions in the original pleadings being offered to offset the indemnity claims. See Douglas Equipment, Inc. v. Mack Trucks, Inc., 471 F.2d 222 (7th Cir. 1972); Continental Ins. Co. v. Sherman, 439 F.2d 1294 (5th Cir.1971); Malauskas v.

Tishman Const. Corp., 81 Ill.App.3d 759, 36 Ill.Dec. 875, 401 N.E.2d 1013 (1980).

25. See Vincent v. Louis Marx & Co., 874 F.2d 36, 41 (1st Cir.1989) (court refusing to adopt "a flat rule admitting or excluding" inconsistent pleadings but requiring instead examination under Rule 403 regarding balance of prejudicial impact against probative value).

26. Fed.R.Civ.P. 15(a) provides "leave [to amend] shall be freely given when justice so requires." Cases on the use of withdrawn or superseded pleadings as evidentiary admissions are collected in Annot., 52 A.L.R.2d 516 and predominate in favor of admissibility. See, e.g., Dreier v. Upjohn Co, 196 Conn. 242, 248–250, 492 A.2d 164, 167–169 (1985) (allegations from abandoned complaint admissible as evidential admission against plaintiff, court concluding policy supporting liberal pleading rules and permitting inconsistent theories of liability requires no limitation on principle of admissibility).

27. Teitelbaum Furs, Inc. v. Dominion Ins. Co., 58 Cal.2d 601, 25 Cal.Rptr. 559, 375 P.2d 439 (1962), cert. denied 372 U.S. 966; Jacobs v. Goodspeed, 180 Conn. 415, 429 A.2d 915 (1980); Scogin v. Nugen, 204 Kan. 568, 464 P.2d 166 (1970); Brohawn v. Transamerica Ins. Co., 276 Md. 396, 347 A.2d 842 (1975); Annot., 18 A.L.R.2d 1287, 1307. The authorities agree that evidence is admissible to explain the guilty plea.

28. Ando v. Woodberry, 8 N.Y.2d 165, 203 N.Y.S.2d 74, 168 N.E.2d 520 (1960); Notes, 9 Buffalo L.Rev. 373 (1960), 74 Harv.L.Rev. 1452 (1961).

that people plead guilty to traffic charges for reasons of convenience and with little regard to guilt or collateral consequences has led to some tendency to exclude them from evidence.[29] Pleas of *nolo contendere* or *non vult,* in jurisdictions where allowed,[30] are generally regarded as inadmissible,[31] and in fact that attribute is a principal reason for use of such pleas.[32]

A related question involves whether a plea of guilty can be introduced as an admission in a criminal case where the accused is allowed to withdraw the guilty plea and is subsequently tried on the charge. The result depends on the resolution of competing considerations of policy. On the one hand, a plea of guilty if freely and understandingly made is so likely to be true that to withhold it from the jury seems to ask them to do justice without knowledge a very significant item of evidence. On this basis, some courts have received admissions in civil cases, leaving it to the adversary to rebut or explain.[33] The competing concern is that if the withdrawn plea is admitted the effectiveness of the withdrawal itself is substantially impaired.[34] In addition, admitting the guilty plea virtually compels the accused to explain why it was initially entered, with resultant encroachment upon the privilege against self-incrimination and intrusion into sensitive areas of the attorney-client relationship. The Federal Rules Advisory Committee accepted the policy arguments against receiving evidence of a withdrawn guilty plea, and Rule 410 excludes such evidence in both civil and criminal cases.[35]

29. Hannah v. Ike Topper Structural Steel Co., 120 Ohio App. 44, 201 N.E.2d 63 (1963). Statutory prohibitions against introducing traffic convictions have been construed as applying also to guilty pleas. Jones v. Talbot, 87 Idaho 498, 394 P.2d 316 (1964). See also Graham, Admissibility in Illinois of Convictions and Pleas of Guilty to Traffic Offenses in Related Civil Litigation, 1979 So.Ill.U.L.J. 209, 222 (arguing that Federal Rule 803(22), which excludes offenses punishable by imprisonment for less than one year, affords an analogy for also excluding pleas of guilty to minor offenses); 4 Weinstein & Berger, Weinstein's Evidence ¶ 803(22)[01], at 354–555 (1990) (same); infra § 298.

30. E.g., Fed.R.Crim.P. 11.

31. Federal Deposit Ins. Corp. v. Cloonan, 165 Kan. 68, 193 P.2d 656 (1948); State v. La Rose, 71 N.H. 435, 52 A. 943 (1902); Fed.R.Evid. 410, infra note 35. It may be assumed that this is a factor considered by the judge in exercising his discretion to allow or deny the plea.

32. For the use of the plea in antitrust actions, see City of Burbank v. General Elec. Co., 329 F.2d 825 (9th Cir.1964); Seamans et al., Use of Criminal Pleas in Aid of Private Antitrust Actions, 10 Antitrust Bull. 795 (1965); 10 A.L.R.Fed. 328.

33. Morrissey v. Powell, 304 Mass. 268, 23 N.E.2d 411 (1939) (upholding admissibility of plea of guilty although it was later withdrawn and defendant acquitted).

34. It would seem particularly inappropriate to penalize the withdrawal of the plea where leave to withdraw is granted because of denial of assistance of counsel, lack of ratification by the accused, involuntariness, or similar reason. See 1979 A.B.A. Standards for Criminal Justice § 14–2.1 (specifying such grounds as basis for withdrawal).

35. 56 F.R.D. 183, 229, citing Kercheval v. United States, 274 U.S. 220 (1927); People v. Spitaleri, 9 N.Y.2d 168, 212 N.Y.S.2d 53, 173 N.E.2d 35 (1961). See also 1979 ABA Standards for Criminal Justice § 14–2.2. Cases pro and con are collected in Annot., 86 A.L.R.2d 326.

Federal Rule of Evidence 410 generally excludes from civil or criminal proceedings evidence of a plea of guilty which was later withdrawn, a plea of nolo contendere, any statement made in the course of judicial proceedings entering the plea, and any statement made in the course of plea dis-

§ 258. Testimony by the Party as an Admission [1]

While testifying on pretrial examination or at trial, a party may admit some fact that is adverse, and sometimes fatal, to a cause of action or defense. If at the end of the trial the party's admission stands unimpeached and uncontradicted, then like unimpeached and uncontradicted testimony generally it is conclusive against the party. Frequently this situation is what the courts are referring to when they say somewhat misleadingly that a party is "bound" by his or her own testimony. The controversial question is whether the party is bound by such testimony in the sense that the party will not be allowed to contradict it with other testimony, or if contradictory testimony has been received, the judge or jury is required to disregard it and to accept as true the party's disserving testimony as a judicial admission.

Three main approaches are reflected in the decisions, which to some extent tend to merge and do not necessarily lead to different results in particular situations. First, some courts take the view that a party's testimony in this respect is like the testimony of any other witness called by the party, that is, the party is free (as far as any rule of law is concerned) to elicit contradictory testimony from the same witness or to call other witnesses to contradict the statement.[2] Obviously, however, the problem of persuasion may be a difficult one when the party seeks to explain or contradict his or her own words, and equally obviously, the trial judge would often be justified in ruling on motion for directed verdict that reasonable minds could only believe that the party's testimony against interest was true.

Second, others take the view that the party's testimony is not conclusive against contradiction except when testifying unequivocally to matters in his or her "peculiar knowledge." These matters may consist of subjective facts, such as the party's own knowledge or

cussions with an attorney for the prosecuting authority which do not result in a plea of guilty or which result in a plea of guilty later withdrawn. For full text of Rule 410, see infra § 266 text accompanying note 35. Federal Rule of Criminal Procedure 11(e)(6) is to the same effect. See also West's Ann.Cal.Evid.Code § 1153.

The admissibility of offers and statements made in the course of plea bargaining is discussed in infra § 266.

§ 258

1. See 9 Wigmore, Evidence § 2594a (Chadbourn rev. 1981); Annot., 169 A.L.R. 798; Note, 9 Vand.L.Rev. 879 (1956); Dec.Dig.Evidence ☞265(10); C.J.S. Evidence § 1040(3).

2. Alamo v. Del Rosario, 98 F.2d 328 (D.C.Cir.1938) (in case involving personal injury from automobile collision, court ruled that plaintiff was not estopped by his own testimony, which would have absolved the driver of the car from liability, and jury was entitled to believe other witnesses). See also Guenther v. Armstrong Rubber Co., 406 F.2d 1315 (3d Cir.1969) (variance in describing tire which caused injury); Kanopka v. Kanopka, 113 Conn. 30, 154 A. 144 (1931) (plaintiff, foreigner speaking through interpreter, excited at time of accident and trial, not bound by her testimony; general rule that party's testimony, unless intended as unequivocal concession, not conclusive); Wiley v. Rutland R. Co., 86 Vt. 504, 86 A. 808 (1913) (in case involving injury to pedestrian run over by backing train, plaintiff's testimony as to when she looked at track was not a judicial admission); Gale v. Kay, 390 P.2d 596 (Wyo.1964).

motivation,[3] or they may consist of objective facts observed by the party.[4]

Third, some courts adopt the doctrine that a party's disserving testimony is to be treated as a judicial admission, conclusive on the issue,[5] so that the party may not bring other witnesses to contradict the admission, and if the party or the adversary does elicit such conflicting testimony, it will be disregarded. Obviously, this third rule demands many qualifications and exceptions. Among these are the following: (1) The party is free to contradict, and thus correct, his or her own testimony; only when the party's own testimony taken as a whole unequivocally affirms the statement does the rule of conclusiveness apply.[6] The rule is inapplicable, moreover, when the party's testimony (2) may be attributable to inadvertence[7] or to a foreigner's mistake as to meaning,[8] (3) is merely negative in effect,[9] (4) is explicitly uncertain or is an estimate or opinion[10] rather than an assertion of concrete fact, or (5) relates to a matter as to which the party could easily have been mistaken, such as the swiftly moving events just preceding a collision in which the party was injured.[11]

Of these three approaches the first seems preferable in policy and most in accord with the tradition of jury trial. It rejects any restrictive rule and leaves the evaluation of the party's testimony and the conflict-

---

3. Monsanto Chem. Co. v. Payne, 354 F.2d 965 (5th Cir.1966); Findlay v. Rubin Glass & Mirror Co., 350 Mass. 169, 213 N.E.2d 858 (1966); Peterson v. American Family Mut. Ins. Co., 280 Minn. 482, 160 N.W.2d 541 (1968); Bockman v. Mitchell Bros. Truck Lines, Inc., 213 Or. 88, 320 P.2d 266 (1958).

4. Bell v. Harmon, 284 S.W.2d 812 (Ky. 1955) (plaintiff's version of automobile collision in which he was involved); Verry v. Murphy, 163 N.W.2d 721, 735 (N.D.1968) (plaintiff's version of business transaction).

5. Stearns v. Chicago, Rock Island & Pacific Ry. Co., 166 Iowa 566, 578, 148 N.W. 128, 133 (1914) (plaintiff's testimony that he did not stop his train as he should have, though contradicted, conclusive on contributory negligence); Taylor v. Williams, 190 So.2d 872 (Miss.1966) (plaintiff passenger's testimony that defendant was not driving, conclusive—"Swore herself out of court"—despite admission in his answer and testimony); Massie v. Firmstone, 134 Va. 450, 114 S.E. 652 (1922) (despite contradictory evidence, plaintiff bound by his testimony that commission was conditional on completion of sale, which had not occurred). Cf. Fox v. Taylor Diving & Salvage Co., 694 F.2d 1349, 1355–1356 (5th Cir.1983) (testimony of plaintiff's expert that was fundamentally at odds with one theory of recovery held to be a binding adoptive admission of plaintiff be-

cause of the great potential for jury prejudice likely from what the appellate court viewed as a manipulative trial strategy).

See also cases in supra note 4.

6. Chaplain v. Dugas, 323 Mass. 91, 80 N.E.2d 9 (1948); Virginia Elec. & Power Co. v. Mabin, 203 Va. 490, 125 S.E.2d 145 (1962).

7. Martin v. Kansas City, 340 S.W.2d 645 (Mo.1960) (statement immediately corrected); Security Nat. Bank v. Johnson, 195 Okl. 107, 155 P.2d 249, 169 A.L.R. 790 (1944) (where doubtful whether statement of party was a slip of the tongue and was inconsistent with other parts of his testimony, question is for jury).

8. Krikorian v. Dailey, 171 Va. 16, 197 S.E. 442 (1938).

9. Waller v. Waller, 187 Va. 25, 32, 46 S.E.2d 42, 45 (1948).

10. Taylor v. Williams, 190 So.2d 872 (Miss.1966); Van Buskirk v. Missouri–Kansas–Texas R. Co., 349 S.W.2d 68 (Mo.1961); Petit v. Klinke, 152 Tex. 142, 254 S.W.2d 769 (1953); Mendoza v. Fidelity & Guar. Ins. Underwriters, Inc., 606 S.W.2d 692 (Tex.1980).

11. Crew v. Nelson, 188 Va. 108, 49 S.E.2d 326 (1948). See generally McCormack v. Haan, 20 Ill.2d 75, 169 N.E.2d 239 (1960).

ing evidence to the judgment of the jury, the judge, and the appellate court, with only the standard of reason to guide them.

The second theory, binding as to facts within the party's "peculiar knowledge," is based on the assumption that as to such facts the possibility that the party may be mistaken largely disappears. If the facts are subjective ones (e.g., knowledge, motivation), the likelihood of successful contradiction is slight, but even then the assumption may be questioned. "Knowledge may be 'special' without being correct. Often we little note nor long remember our 'motives, purposes, or knowledge.' There are few if any subjects on which plaintiffs are infallible." [12]

The third theory is also of doubtful validity. In the first place the party's testimony, uttered by a layman in the stress of examination, cannot with justice be given the conclusiveness of the traditional judicial admission in a pleading or stipulation,[13] deliberately drafted by counsel for the express purpose of limiting and defining the facts in issue.[14] Again, a general rule of conclusiveness necessitates an elaboration of qualifications and exceptions, which represents a transfer to the appellate court of some of the traditional control of the jury by the trial judge, or in a nonjury case of the judge's factfinding function. These duties call for an exercise of judgment by the judge who has heard and seen the witnesses. Supervision by appellate judges of this process can best be exercised under a flexible standard, rather than a rule of conclusiveness.

Moreover, the third rule leads to mechanical solutions, unrelated to the needs of justice and calculated to proliferate appeals, in certain special situations. One is the situation where the opponent, by adroit cross-examination, has maneuvered the party into an improvident concession.[15] Another is the case of the defendant who is protected by liability insurance testifying to facts that will help the plaintiff to win.[16] Yet another is the situation where both parties testify against their

---

12. Alamo v. Del Rosario, 98 F.2d 328, 332 (D.C.Cir.1938).

13. As to judicial admissions, see supra § 254 text accompanying notes 11–12; 9 Wigmore, Evidence §§ 2588–2594 (Chadbourn rev. 1981).

14. Even under the liberal view that a party is not generally bound by his or her testimony, the trial court may grant a nonsuit or directed verdict if a party testifies deliberately to a fatal fact and if counsel, on inquiry, indicates no intention to elicit contradictory testimony. Under these circumstances, the party and counsel manifest an intention to be bound. See Oscanyan v. Arms Co., 103 U.S. 261, 263 (1880) (holding it proper to direct a verdict on counsel's opening statements, which disclosed that the purpose of the action was to collect a bribe); Kanopka v. Kanopka, 113

Conn. 30, 39–40, 154 A. 144, 147 (1931); Annot., 169 A.L.R. 801.

15. Driscoll v. Virginia Elec. & Power Co., 166 Va. 538, 181 S.E. 402 (1935).

16. Vondrashek v. Dignan, 200 Minn. 530, 274 N.W. 609 (1937) (on question of contributory negligence of plaintiff passenger, defense precluded by defendant's testimony that nobody could tell that he was under the influence). Preferable results are to deny conclusiveness to the testimony of defendant-insured, Christie v. Eager, 129 Conn. 62, 26 A.2d 352 (1942), or to allow the introduction of contradicting evidence by the defense, King v. Spencer, 115 Conn. 201, 161 A. 103 (1932); Horneman v. Brown, 286 Mass. 65, 190 N.E. 735 (1935) (defense was allowed to impeach the defendant-insured by a prior inconsistent statement).

respective interests.[17] Here the rule of conclusiveness may be thought to decide the issue against the party who has the burden of proof.[18]

Finally, the moral emphasis is wrong. Early cases where the rule of conclusiveness was first used may have been cases where judges were outraged by apparent attempts by parties to play fast and loose with the court. However, examination of numerous decisions demonstrates that this is far from being the typical situation of the party testifying to disserving facts. Instead of the unscrupulous party, it is either the one who can be pushed into an admission by the ingenuity or persistence of adverse counsel [19] or the unusually candid or conscientious party willing to speak the truth regardless of its consequences who is penalized by the rule of conclusiveness.[20] Courts should employ the more flexible practice, which is older and simpler.

§ 259. Representative Admissions; Coconspirator Statements [1]

When a party to the suit has expressly authorized another person to speak, it is an obvious and accepted extension of the admission rule to admit against the party the statements of such persons.[2] In the absence of express authority, how far will the statements of an agent be received as the principal's admission by virtue of the employment relationship? The early texts and cases used as analogies the doctrine of the master's substantive responsibility for the acts of the agent and the notion then prevalent in evidence law that words accompanying a relevant act were admissible as part of the *res gestae*. Together, these concepts produced the inadequate theory that the agent's statements could be received against the principal only when made at the time of,

---

17. Sutherland v. Davis, 286 Ky. 743, 151 S.W.2d 1021 (1941) (in suit by passenger, who had been given a ride by defendant, where plaintiff testified that she knew that defendant was too drunk to drive and could have left vehicle after she learned this while defendant testified he was sober, court held that plaintiff's admissions barred her from producing evidence to the contrary and precluded recovery).

18. See Chakales v. Djiovanides, 161 Va. 48, 170 S.E. 848 (1933); Annot., 169 A.L.R. at 815.

19. Gilbert v. Bostona Mines Co., 121 Mont. 397, 195 P.2d 376 (1948); Kipf v. Bitner, 150 Neb. 155, 33 N.W.2d 518 (1948) (admission extracted from plaintiff on taking of deposition ruled not conclusive).

20. "Since his testimony was adverse to his interests, he is more likely to have been mistaken than lying. The proposed rule actually punishes him for two things, his honesty and his error." Alamo v. Del Rosario, 98 F.2d 328, 331 (D.C.Cir.1938). See also Burruss v. Suddith, 187 Va. 473, 47 S.E.2d 546 (1948).

§ 259

1. Federal Rule 801(d)(2) includes in its definition of admissions of a party:

(C) a statement by a person authorized by the party to make a statement concerning the subject, or (D) a statement by the party's agent or servant concerning a matter within the scope of the agency or employment, made during the existence of the relationship, or (E) a statement by a coconspirator of a party during the course and in furtherance of the conspiracy.

The Revised Uniform Rule (1986) is to the same effect.

2. Nuttall v. Holman, 110 Utah 375, 173 P.2d 1015 (1946).

Under Federal Rule of Civil Procedure 30(b)(6) a party which is a corporation, partnership, association, or governmental agency may be required to designate a person who will testify on its behalf by deposition. Rule 32(a)(2) makes the deposition usable by an adverse party for any purpose against the party.

and in relation to, some act then being performed in the scope of the agent's duty.[3]

A later theory that gained currency in the writings [4] and opinions [5] was that the admissibility of the agent's statements as admissions of the principal was measured by precisely the same tests as the principal's substantive responsibility for the conduct of the agent, that is, the words of the agent would be received as the admissions of the principal if they were spoken within the scope of the authority of the agent to speak for the employer. This formula made plain that the statements of an agent employed to give information (a so-called "speaking agent") could be received as the employer's admissions, regardless of want of authority to act otherwise, and conversely that authority to act, e.g., the authority of a chauffeur to drive a car, would not carry with it automatically the authority to make statements to others describing the duties performed. Cases applying the test are given in the footnote.[6]

---

3. Fairlie v. Hastings, 10 Ves.Jr. 123, 127, 32 Eng.Rep. 791, 792 (Ch. 1804); Vicksburg & Meridian R. Co. v. O'Brien, 119 U.S. 99 (1886).

4. See 4 Wigmore, Evidence § 1078 (Chadbourn rev. 1972); Morgan, Admissions, 12 Wash.L.Rev. 181, 193 (1937); Restatement (Second) of Agency §§ 284–291, especially § 286:

> In an action between the principal and a third person, the statements of an agent to a third person are admissible against the principal to prove the truth of facts asserted in them as though made by the principal, if the agent was authorized to make the statement or was authorized to make, on the principal's behalf, any statements concerning the subject matter.

§ 288: * * *

> (2) Authority to do an act or to conduct a transaction does not of itself include authority to make statements concerning the act or transaction.

> (3) Authority to make statements of fact does not of itself include authority to make statements admitting liability because of such facts.

5. Griffiths v. Big Bear Stores, Inc., 55 Wash.2d 243, 247, 347 P.2d 532, 535 (1959) ("[D]eclarations and admissions against interest by an agent may not be shown except when they are within the scope of the agency, as established by the evidence in the case."); Rudzinski v. Warner Theatres, Inc., 16 Wis.2d 241, 245, 114 N.W.2d 466, 468 (1962) ("In order for an agent's statement to be admissible against his principal, it must have been spoken within the scope of the authority of the agent to speak

for the principal."). Compare Fed.R.Evid. 801(d)(2)(C) & (D), see infra text accompanying notes 10–11. For subsection (D), Washington substitutes "a statement by his agent or servant acting within the scope of his authority to make the statement for the party." Wash.R.Evid. 801(d)(2)(iv).

6. Statements of agent received against principal: Pan–American Petroleum & Transp. Co. v. United States, 273 U.S. 456 (1927) (statements by president of corporations before Senate Committee investigating Teapot Dome oil leases admissible in suit by government against corporations to cancel leases); Cox v. Esso Shipping Co., 247 F.2d 629 (5th Cir.1957) (shipmaster's report of accident); Partin v. Great Atlantic & Pac. Tea Co., 102 N.H. 62, 149 A.2d 860 (1959) (store manager's statement indicating plaintiff's fall due to negligence of employees); Spett v. President Monroe Bldg. & Mfg. Corp., 19 N.Y.2d 203, 278 N.Y.S.2d 826, 225 N.E.2d 527 (1967) (statement by manager of business indicating that skid causing plaintiff's injury was put in place by employees); McDonnell v. Montgomery Ward & Co., 121 Vt. 221, 154 A.2d 469 (1959) (statement by service representative as to condition of appliance).

Statements of agent excluded: Bristol Wholesale Grocery Co. v. Municipal Lighting Plant Com'n, 347 Mass. 668, 200 N.E.2d 260 (1964) (statement of plant manager that explosion was defendant's fault); Roush v. Alkire Truck Lines, Inc., 299 S.W.2d 518 (Mo.1957) (truck driver's statement that brakes were defective); Kovar v. Lakeside Hosp., 131 Ohio St. 333, 2 N.E.2d 857 (1936) (statement of managing director

Probably the most frequent use of these tests occurred in the exclusion of statements made by employees involved in an accident to someone at the scene regarding the accident, not made in furtherance of the employer's interest, but as a "mere narrative." [7] This result represents the logical application of these tests, but the assumption that the determinant of the master's responsibility for the agent's *acts* should be the test for using the agent's statements as *evidence* against the master is a shaky one.

The rejection of such post-accident statements coupled with the admission of the employee's testimony on the stand resulted in preferring the weaker to the stronger evidence. Typically the agent is well informed about acts in the course of the business, the statements are offered against the employer's interest, and while the employment continues, the employee is not likely to make the statements unless they are true. Moreover, if admissions are viewed as arising from the adversary system, responsibility for statements of one's employee is consistent with that theory. Accordingly, even before adoption of the Federal Rules, the predominant view was to admit a statement by an agent if it concerned a matter within the scope of the declarant's employment and was made before that relationship was terminated.[8] Of course, admissibility of the traditional authorized statement was continued as well.

Federal Rule 801(d)(2)(C) & (D) follow the expansive view described in the preceding paragraph.[9] They provide:

of hospital of circumstances of giving an injection of the wrong solution); Preston v. Lamb, 20 Utah 2d 260, 436 P.2d 1021 (1968) (statement of waitress that floor where plaintiff slipped had been waxed excessively); Rudzinski v. Warner Theatres, Inc., 16 Wis.2d 241, 114 N.W.2d 466 (1962) (usher's admonition of janitor for not having mopped wet spots). Some of these jurisdictions have since adopted rules that would change the result.

It is important to distinguish situations where the declaration of the agent is admitted on other theories. Thus, if the agent and the principal are both parties to the suit, the agent's statement is received against the agent, though it may not be admissible against the principal. Annot., 27 A.L.R.3d 966. Again, the agent's declaration often comes in against both as a spontaneous exclamation made under stress of excitement. See infra § 272.

7. See cases of exclusion in supra note 6.

8. See, e.g., Joseph T. Ryerson & Son, Inc. v. H.A. Crane & Bro., Inc., 417 F.2d 1263 (3d Cir.1969); Grayson v. Williams, 256 F.2d 61 (10th Cir.1958); Koninklijke Luchtvaart Maatschappij N.V. KLM Royal Dutch Airlines v. Tuller, 292 F.2d 775 (D.C.Cir.1961), cert. denied 368 U.S. 921; Martin v. Savage Truck Line, 121 F.Supp. 417 (D.D.C.1954); 4 Wigmore, Evidence § 1078 (Chadbourn rev. 1972) (collecting state cases).

Furthermore, the adoption of rules modeled on the Federal Rules has changed others which had previously adhered to the traditional view, see Tullgren v. Phil Lamoy Realty Corp., 125 N.H. 604, 608, 484 A.2d 1144, 1147 (1984) (agent's admission depends on authority to speak for party), to define the admissibility of an agent's statements in terms of the subject matter of the agency rather than a specific authorization to speak, Daigle v. City of Portsmouth, 129 N.H. 561, 585–86, 534 A.2d 689, 703 (1987). However a few jurisdictions still have not adopted this more liberal position. See Durkin v. Equine Clinics, Inc., 376 Pa.Super. 557, 572–575, 546 A.2d 665, 672–673 (1988), appeal denied 524 Pa. 608, 569 A.2d 1367 (Pennsylvania continues to require authority of the agent to speak for party); Passovoy v. Nordstrom, Inc., 52 Wash.App. 166, 171–172, 758 P.2d 524, 527 (1988) (even under rule modeled on Federal Rules, Washington requires speaking authority).

A statement is not hearsay if—

* * *

The statement is offered against a party and is * * * (C) a statement by a person authorized by the party to make a statement concerning the subject,[10] or (D) a statement by the party's agent or servant concerning a matter within the scope of the agency or employment, made during the existence of the relationship.[11]

The party offering evidence of the alleged agent's admission must first prove the fact and scope of the agency of the declarant for the

9. See, e.g., United States v. Portsmouth Paving Corp., 694 F.2d 312, 321 (4th Cir.1982) (orthodox rule requiring speaking authority broadened by 801(d)(2)(D)).

10. Illustrative of statements by persons authorized to speak on the subject are Baughman v. Cooper–Jarrett, Inc., 530 F.2d 529 (3d Cir.1976), cert. denied 429 U.S. 825 (in action for conspiring to prevent obtaining employment in trucking industry, statement of reason for denying plaintiff employment made by employee charged with duty to screen applications and to inform applicants of reason for rejection); Kinglsey v. Baker/Beech–Nut Corp., 546 F.2d 1136 (5th Cir.1977) (in action for severance pay, overheard telephone conversation in which plaintiff's superior said he would make plaintiff quit); Reid Bros. Logging Co. v. Ketchikan Pulp Co., 699 F.2d 1292 (9th Cir.1983), cert. denied 464 U.S. 916 (report prepared at request of chairman of the board of defendant's company on the basis of free access to all of company's books and records and circulated to officers and managers was authorized statement). As a general matter, an attorney is authorized to speak for the client when handling matters directly related to the management of litigation. Hanson v. Waller, 888 F.2d 806, 814 (11th Cir.1989).

11. As to statements relating to matters within scope of employment or agency, see Staheli v. University of Miss., 854 F.2d 121, 127 (5th Cir.1988) (in case challenging denial of tenure to professor, statement by another professor regarding reason that university chancellor was upset with plaintiff not admission because personnel matters not within scope of declarant's agency relationship); Scofi v. McKeon Const. Co., 666 F.2d 170, 173–174 (5th Cir.1982) (statement by subcontractor's superintendent indicating that he understood that his employer was responsible for safety precautions on the job within scope of employment); Nekolny v. Painter, 653 F.2d 1164,

1171–1172 (7th Cir.1981), cert. denied 455 U.S. 1021 (statements made by advisor or liaison to senior citizen's program concerning reasons for employment termination were admissions since they concerned matters within the scope of the declarant's duties); Miles v. M.N.C. Corp., 750 F.2d 867, 874–875 (11th Cir.1985) (racial slur by employee involved in hiring evaluations and decisions admissible against corporation as within scope of employee's duties).

The difficulty of drawing a clear line between authorized statements and those relating to matters within the scope of employment is apparent. United States v. Gregory, 871 F.2d 1239, 1242–1243 (4th Cir.1989), cert. denied 493 U.S. 1020 (statement of attorney regarding sheriff's policy not to hire women as deputies treated ambiguously under either 801(d)(2)(C) or (D)). Often a statement will fall into both categories, e.g., statements by agent authorized to investigate and report. Collins v. Wayne Corp., 621 F.2d 777, 782 (5th Cir. 1980) (motor vehicle collision expert); Rutherford v. State, 605 P.2d 16 (Alaska 1979) (state trooper's report of motor vehicle accident involving another trooper). The distinction may sometimes be important, however, since statements need only relate to a matter within the scope of the agency under subparagraph (D), while making the statement itself must be within the authority of the declarant under subparagraph (C). See Hoptowit v. Ray, 682 F.2d 1237, 1262 (9th Cir.1982) (report admissible under 801(d)(2)(D) because related to matter within scope of agency).

To be admissible, the statement must be made while the agent is still employed by the organization. See, e.g., Blanchard v. Peoples Bank, 844 F.2d 264, 265, 267 n. 7 (5th Cir.1988) (statement by former employee not admissible); Robinson v. Audi NSU Auto Union Aktiengesellschaft, 739 F.2d 1481, 1487 (10th Cir.1984) (statements made before agency relationship created not admissible).

adverse party.[12] This may, of course, be done directly by the testimony of the asserted agent, or by anyone who knows, or by circumstantial evidence. Traditionally, courts held that evidence of the purported agent's past declarations asserting the agency were inadmissible hearsay when offered to show the relation.[13] This analysis no longer appears correct under the Federal Rules, although it likely remains true that statements of the purported agent alone are not sufficient to establish agency.[14] If the preliminary fact of the declarant's agency is disputed, the question is one to be decided by the court under Rule 104(a).[15]

The question also arises whether a statement by an agent, in order to qualify as an admission, must be made to an outsider rather than to the principal or to another agent. Typical instances are the railway conductor's report of an accident or a letter to the home office from a

12. Labor Hall Ass'n v. Danielsen, 24 Wash.2d 75, 163 P.2d 167 (1945); 4 Wigmore, Evidence § 1078 (Chadbourn rev. 1972); Dec.Dig.Evidence ⊕258(1).

13. See, e.g., United States v. Portsmouth Paving Corp., 694 F.2d 312, 321 n. 12 (4th Cir.1982). Under this traditional view, neither the fact nor the extent of the agency could be so proved. 4 Wigmore, Evidence § 1078, at 176 (Chadbourn rev. 1972). However, even under a restrictive view, the purported agent's declarations would not be hearsay and would be admitted if offered to show that the other party dealt with him or her as an agent. Armstrong Bldg. Finish Co. v. Friend Lumber Co., 276 Mass. 361, 177 N.E. 794 (1931). Also, the asserted agent's declarations were admissible to show intention to act for the principal rather than the agent. See infra § 260. The possibility of using the spontaneous declaration of the agent should also be considered. See infra § 272.

14. There is not yet a direct statement by the United States Supreme Court on this issue and few lower courts have spoken to the question. However, in Bourjaily v. United States, 483 U.S. 171, 175–181 (1987), the Court concluded that the putative coconspirator statement itself could be used to determine whether the statement met the requirements of Rule 801(d)(2)(E). The Court there rejected the defendant's argument that "bootstrapping" was not to be permitted, concluding that the adoption of the Federal Rules significantly altered established principles. There appears little reason to assume that the Supreme Court, if faced with issue, would disallow any reliance upon the hearsay statement itself in deciding preliminary issues regarding agency under the instant provision. See In re Coordinated Pretrial Proceedings in Petroleum Products Antitrust

Litigation, 906 F.2d 432, 458 (9th Cir.1990) (accepting Bourjaily analysis as applying to Rule 801(d)(2)(D) so that statements of the purported agent can be used to determine employment duties). But see 4 Weinstein & Berger, Weinstein's Evidence ¶ 801(d)(2)(C)[01], at 271–72 (1990) (continuing to adhere to the traditional position).

At the same time, the Court reserved ruling in Bourjaily on whether the statement itself could constitute the entire proof of the conspiracy. 483 U.S. at 181. See Reuschlein & Gregory, The Law of Agency and Partnership 28 (1990) ("declarations of the agent alone are generally insufficient to establish the fact or extent of his authority").

15. Again the analysis rests principally on the Supreme Court's opinion in Bourjaily. In that case, with little discussion, the Court concluded that Rule 104(a) controlled the determination of whether a conspiracy existed. 483 U.S. at 175–178. There appears no reason to distinguish the decision on whether a conspiracy exists from the basic determination whether the statement qualifies as a vicarious admission. See United States v. Flores, 679 F.2d 173, 178 (9th Cir.1982), cert. denied 459 U.S. 1148 (concluding that Rule 104(a) governs preliminary question of whether agency exists and noting analogy to determination of admissibility of coconspirator statements); 2 Saltzburg & Martin, Federal Rules of Evidence Manual 154 (5th ed. 1990). At the same time, isolated issues may arise relating to the existence of an agency relationship that should properly be determined under principles of conditional relevancy of Rule 104(b), but the major preliminary factual questions are for the court exclusively.

manager of a branch office of a bank. Historically, though plainly made in the scope of authority, some courts refused to admit such statements [16] unless they were adopted by the principal.[17] Others admitted them in either situation.[18] Those courts which excluded such statements relied chiefly on the fact that the doctrine of *respondeat superior* does not apply to transactions between the agent and the principal,[19] determining the hearsay question by the rules of substantive liability of principals. However, other analogies could just as reasonably control, such as the fact that statements made by a party not intended for the outside world—entries in a secret diary, for example—are receivable as admissions.[20]

Reliability also favored admissibility of such in-house statements. While slightly less reliable as a class than the agent's authorized statements to outsiders, intra-organization reports are generally made as a basis for some action, and when this is so, they share the reliability of business records.[21] They will only be offered against the principal

---

16. Swan v. Miller, [1919] 1 Ir.R. 151 (C.A.) (reviewing English authorities); Lever Bros. Co. v. Atlas Assurance Co., 131 F.2d 770, 776 (7th Cir.1942) (report of investigating engineers on explosion); Standard Oil Co. v. Moore, 251 F.2d 188, 218 (9th Cir.1957), cert. denied 336 U.S. 975 (reports of employees); United States v. United Shoe Mach. Corp., 89 F.Supp. 349 (D.Mass.1950) (intra-corporate letters and reports); Carroll v. East Tenn., Va. & Ga. Ry., 82 Ga. 452, 10 S.E. 163 (1889) (written report of accident, made after investigation, by conductor to superintendent); Atchison, Topeka & Santa Fe Ry. Co. v. Burks, 78 Kan. 515, 96 P. 950 (1908) (reports of car inspectors as to defective coupler); Warner v. Maine Cent. R. Co., 111 Me. 149, 88 A. 403 (1913) (station agent's report to general manager about fire); Bell v. Milwaukee Elec. Ry. & Light Co., 169 Wis. 408, 172 N.W. 791 (1919) (written report of accident made by street-car conductor, at end of his run); Restatement (Second) of Agency § 287: "Statements by an agent to the principal or to another agent of the principal are not admissible against the principal as admissions; such statements may be admissible in evidence under other rules of evidence."

17. Pekelis v. Transcontinental and Western Air, Inc., 187 F.2d 122 (2d Cir. 1951), cert. denied 341 U.S. 951 (reports of investigating boards, appointed by airline, admitted as adoptive admissions); United States v. United Shoe Mach. Corp., 89 F.Supp. 349 (D.Mass.1950).

18. The Solway, 10 P.D. 137 (1885) (letter by master of ship to owners); Chicago, St. Paul, Minneapolis & Omaha Ry. Co. v. Kulp, 102 F.2d 352 (8th Cir.1939), cert.

denied 307 U.S. 636 (conductor's report to employer as to cause of injury to brakeman); Hilbert v. Spokane Intern. Ry. Co., 20 Idaho 54, 116 P. 1116 (1911) (section foreman's written report to company about a fire); Lemen v. Kansas City Southern Ry. Co., 151 Mo.App. 511, 515, 132 S.W. 13, 14 (1910) (oral report by conductor to station-agent, "Better send your section gang up the road. I think we set something on fire there."); Metropolitan Life Ins. Co. v. Moss, 109 S.W.2d 1035 (Tex.Civ.App.1937, error dismissed) (medical examiner's report to insurance company concerning state of health of applicant); Supreme Lodge, Knights of Honor v. Rampy, 45 S.W. 422 (Tex.Civ.App.1898, error refused) (report by officers of local lodge to supreme lodge concerning good standing of member).

19. Morgan, The Rationale of Vicarious Admissions, 42 Harv.L.Rev. 461, 463 (1929).

20. While it may be argued that the agent authorized to make statements to the principal does not speak for the principal, Morgan, Basic Problems of Evidence 273 (1962), communication to an outsider has not generally been thought to be an essential characteristic of an admission. Thus a party's books or records are usable against the party, without regard to any intent to disclose to third persons. 5 Wigmore, Evidence § 1557 (Chadbourn rev. 1974).

21. This special trustworthiness is noted by Professor Morgan, although he contends that this furnishes no reason for using the representation formula in this situation as a theory of admissibility. Morgan supra note 19, at 463 n. 4.

when they admit some fact damaging to the principal, and this kind of statement by an agent is likely to be trustworthy. No special danger of surprise, confusion, or prejudice from the use of the evidence is apparent.

The drafters of the Federal Rule found the arguments in favor of receiving such in-house admissions persuasive.[22] The expansion has been held to apply both to statements by agents authorized to speak and by those without "speaking authority" but only authorized to act for the principal.[23]

While the Federal Rule greatly expands the scope of statements within a corporation that will qualify as admissions, it leaves a number of difficult issues to be resolved by analysis of the individual facts of the situation. For example, even though statements made by corporate officers or employees are found to be admissions of the corporation, further inquiry is required before such statements can be used as vicarious admissions of other corporate employees.[24] Also, while first-hand knowledge is not required for vicarious admissions of corporate employees, uncertainty about the identity of the person who was the source of a statement may result in exclusion because of a failure to establish that the statement concerned a matter within the scope of the declarant's employment as opposed to mere "gossip." [25]

The general principles developed above are applied in the remainder of this section to special categories of agents and to types of vicarious admissions that are frequently encountered:

22. "The rule is phrased broadly so as to encompass both [statements to principals and to third persons]." Adv.Comm. Note, Fed.R.Evid. 801(d)(2)(C), 56 F.R.D. 183, 298. See Reid Bros. Logging Co. v. Ketchikan Pulp Co., 699 F.2d 1292, 1307 n. 25 (9th Cir.1983), cert. denied 464 U.S. 916 (recognizing that the common law requirement that statement must be made to third party was legislatively overruled).

23. Mahlandt v. Wild Canid Survival & Research Center, Inc., 588 F.2d 626, 630 (8th Cir.1978); United States v. Young, 736 F.2d 565, 567–568 (10th Cir.1983), reversed on other grounds 470 U.S. 1.

24. Mahlandt v. Wild Canid Survival & Research Center, Inc., 588 F.2d 626, 631 (8th Cir.1978) (statement by members of board of directors not admission of director of education for corporation); United States v. Young, 736 F.2d 565, 567–568 (10th Cir.1983), reversed on other grounds 470 U.S. 1 (statement made by corporate employee concerning matter within scope of employment, while admission of the corporation, constitutes admission of higher corporate officer individually only upon

showing of specific agency relationship); Durkin v. Equine Clinics, Inc., 376 Pa.Super. 557, 574–575, 546 A.2d 665, 673 (1988), appeal denied 524 Pa. 608, 569 A.2d 1367 (statement of co-employee not admission. But see United States v. Draiman, 784 F.2d 248, 256–257 (7th Cir.1986) (statement of accountant constituted admission of individual corporate employee where personal agency relationship shown from fact that two worked closely together on issue).

25. Litton Systems, Inc. v. American Tel. & Tel. Co., 700 F.2d 785, 816–817 (2d Cir.1983), cert. denied 464 U.S. 1073 (notes made by corporate attorney regarding statements of employees not admission because statements not shown to be within scope of employment of reporting employees). The limitation of *Litton Systems,* however, is a narrow one. It does not require a showing of knowledge from non-hearsay sources. Brookover v. Mary Hitchcock Memorial Hosp., 893 F.2d 411, 416–417 (1st Cir.1990); United States v. Southland Corp., 760 F.2d 1366, 1376 n. 4 (2d Cir.1985), cert. denied 474 U.S. 825.

Attorneys.[26] If an attorney is employed to manage a party's conduct of a lawsuit, the attorney has *prima facie* authority to make relevant judicial admissions by pleadings, by oral or written stipulations, or by formal opening statement, which unless allowed to be withdrawn are conclusive in the case.[27] Such formal and conclusive admissions should be, and are, framed with care and circumspection, and in a leading English case, these admissions are contrasted with an attorney's oral out-of-court statement. The latter were characterized as "merely a loose conversation," [28] and it is often said that the client is not "bound" by the "casual" statements of counsel made outside of court.[29] The use of the word "bound" is obviously misleading. The issue is not whether the client is "bound," as he or she is by a judicial admission, but whether the attorney's extrajudicial statement is admissible against the client as a mere evidentiary admission made by an agent.

A natural, if unconscious, tendency to protect the client and, perhaps the attorney, against the hazard of evidence of statements by counsel produced a tendency in the older cases to restrict introduction of such statements more than statements by other types of agents.[30] More recent cases generally measure the authority of the attorney to make out-of-court admissions by the same tests of express or implied authority as would be applied to other agents, and when they meet these tests, admit as evidentiary admissions the statements of attorneys.[31] These

26. 4 Wigmore, Evidence § 1063 (Chadbourn rev. 1972); Morgan, Admissions, 12 Wash.L.Rev. 181, 188 (1937); Dec.Dig.Evidence ⚓246.

27. See the discussion of judicial admissions supra § 257.

28. Petch v. Lyon, 9 Q.B. 147, 153, 115 Eng.Rep. 1231, 1233 (1846).

29. E.g., Jackson v. Schine Lexington Corp., 305 Ky. 823, 825, 205 S.W.2d 1013, 1014 (1947) (A copy of an intended pleading, although never filed, that was sent to the plaintiff's attorney by the defendant's lawyer containing an admission was held inadmissible with the following explanation: "The general rule is that an attorney has no power to prejudice his client by admissions of fact made out of court. Though he may be the agent of his client, such agency does not carry the implication of authority to make binding admissions other than in the actual management of the litigation."); Hogenson v. Service Armament Co., 77 Wash.2d 209, 214, 461 P.2d 311, 314 (1969) (Regarding a letter from plaintiff's attorney to defendant giving notice of breach of warranty and inaccurate version of circumstances of injury, the court stated: "The sentence * * * was gratuitous information * * * tentative and casual * * *. It is neither distinct nor formal nor intended to dispense with the formal proof of a fact at trial.").

30. Wagstaff v. Wilson, 4 Barn. & Ad. 339, 110 Eng.Rep. 483 (1832) (in action for improperly taking a horse, letter offered from defendant's attorney stating that defendant had distrained the horse written in reply to letter from plaintiff's attorney to defendant excluded for want of proof that it was written with defendant's sanction); Saunders v. McCarthy, 90 Mass. (8 Allen) 42, 45 (1864) (oral statements by attorney of relevant facts during conversation with adverse party before suit for the purpose of settling the controversy held "mere matters of conversation").

31. United States v. Gregory, 871 F.2d 1239, 1242–243 (4th Cir.1989), cert. denied 493 U.S. 1020 (statements in telephone conversation by county attorney who represented sheriff in employment discrimination case constituted admission of client where attorney had not exceeded scope of authority by, for example, exposing client to criminal responsibility); Hanson v. Waller, 888 F.2d 806, 814 (11th Cir.1989) (statements by attorney in "representational capacity" constitute admissions of agent authorized to speak); Brown v. Hebb, 167 Md. 535, 547, 175 A. 602, 607 (1934) ("If the admission is clearly within the scope of his agency, express or implied, he has the same authority to bind his client as any other agent."). Cf. United States v. Arrington, 867 F.2d 122, 126–128 (2d Cir.

admissions occur, for example, in letters or oral conversations made in the course of efforts for the collection or resistance of claims, or settlement negotiations, or the management of any other business in behalf of the client.[32]

Partners.[33] A partner is an agent of the partnership for the conduct of the firm's business.[34] Accordingly, when the existence and scope of the partnership have been proved,[35] the statement of a partner made in the conduct of the business of the firm is receivable as the admission of the partnership.[36] What of statements of a former partner made after dissolution? The cases are divided,[37] but since a continuing power is recognized in each former partner to do such acts as are reasonably necessary to wind up and settle the affairs of the firm,[38] one former partner should be regarded as having authority to speak for the others in making statements of fact as are reasonably incident to collecting

---

1989) (no special restrictions, except regarding the unusual form of arguments to the jury, on treating attorney's statements as admissions against criminal defendant).

32. Gerhart v. Henry Disston & Sons, Inc., 290 F.2d 778, 789 (3d Cir.1961) (statement by lawyer handling business negotiation); United States v. Gregory, 871 F.2d 1239, 1242–243 (4th Cir.1989), cert. denied 493 U.S. 1020 (statement in telephone conversation by county attorney representing sheriff to equal employment opportunity specialist investigating employment discrimination claim); Harris v. Steelweld Equip. Co., 869 F.2d 396, 403 (8th Cir.1989), cert. denied 493 U.S. 817 (out-of-court statement of attorney to expert); Suntken v. Suntken, 223 Iowa 347, 272 N.W. 132 (1937) (admissions of fact in attorney's letter written in course of negotiations for compromise); Graber v. Griffin, 210 Kan. 142, 500 P.2d 35 (1972) (tenant's attorney wrote landlord that tenant considered he had lease for stated term); Brown v. Hebb, 167 Md. 535, 175 A. 602 (1934) (where doctor sent bill for $1500 and patient's lawyer replied by letter offering $300 "for the services rendered," held admissible as an acknowledgment of a debt for services); Noel v. Roberts, 449 S.W.2d 572 (Mo.1970) (letter from plaintiff's attorney stating that employee rather than defendant assaulted plaintiff).

Possible application of the rule excluding offers of compromise should not be overlooked. See infra § 266.

33. 4 Wigmore, Evidence § 1078, at 180 (Chadbourn rev. 1972); Crane & Bromberg, Partnership 320, 459 (3d ed. 1968); Reuschlein & Gregory, Agency and Partnership § 199 (1990); 2 Rowley, Partnership § 51.9

(2d ed. 1960); Dec.Dig.Evidence ⊕249; Annot., 73 A.L.R. 447.

34. As to the scope of the partner's agency, see Crane & Bromberg, Partnership § 49, at 275 (3d ed. 1968).

35. Traditionally, this fact had to be established by evidence other than the out-of-court declarations of the purported partner. Humboldt Livestock Auction, Inc. v. B & H Cattle Co., 261 Iowa 419, 155 N.W.2d 478 (1967). However, as with proof of the existence of a conspiracy, see infra notes 56–59 and accompanying text, the current view under the Federal Rules should logically be that the statements of the purported partner can be considered in determining the existence and the scope of the partnership. See also supra note 14.

36. Uniform Partnership Act, § 11: "An admission made by any partner concerning partnership affairs within the scope of his authority as conferred by this act is evidence against the partnership." Wieder v. Lorenz, 164 Or. 10, 99 P.2d 38 (1940) (failure by one member of firm to answer letter to him on firm business admitted against partnership); King v. Wesner, 198 S.C. 49, 16 S.E.2d 289 (1941) (statement of partner about accident of employee, made to representative of Industrial Commission who was investigating accident was in course of firm business and admissible against firm).

The relevance of Federal Rule 801(d)(2)(C) & (D), see supra text accompanying notes 10–11, to partnerships seems apparent, and earlier cases to the contrary should be considered overruled.

37. They are collected in Annot., 73 A.L.R. 447, 459–473.

38. Crane & Bromberg, Partnership § 80, at 454 (3d ed. 1968).

the claims and paying the debts of the firm.[39] Beyond this, it seems that one partner's admissions should be competent only against that partner.

Coconspirator.[40] Conspiracies to commit a crime or an unlawful or tortious act are analogous to partnerships. If A and B are engaged in a conspiracy, the acts and declarations of B occurring while the conspiracy is actually in progress and in furtherance of the design are provable against A, because they are acts for which A is criminally or civilly responsible as a matter of substantive law.[41] But B's declarations may also be introduced against A as representative admissions to prove the truth of the matter declared. Only statements of the latter sort are at issue within this section on representative admissions. However, courts have seldom discriminated between declarations offered as conduct constituting part of the conspiracy and declarations offered as vicarious admissions of the facts declared.[42] Instead, even when offered as admissions, courts have generally imposed the same test applicable to statements that form part of the conduct of the crime, namely that the declaration must have been made while the conspiracy was continuing and must have constituted a step in furtherance of the venture.[43]

Federal Rule 801(d)(2)(E) is generally consistent with the foregoing analysis. When offered against a party, it treats as "not hearsay" "a statement by a coconspirator of a party during the course and in furtherance of the conspiracy."

Literally applied, the "in furtherance" requirement calls for exclusion of statements possessing evidentiary value solely as admissions,[44]

39. Crane & Bromberg, Partnership § 80, at 459 (3d ed. 1968); 2 Rowley, Partnership § 51.9, at 447 (2d ed. 1960).

40. 4 Wigmore, Evidence § 1079 (Chadbourn rev. 1972); Kirkpatrick, Confrontation and Hearsay: Exemptions from the Constitutional Unavailability Requirements, 70 Minn.L.Rev. 665 (1986); Mueller, The Federal Coconspirator Exception: Action, Assertion, and Hearsay, 12 Hofstra L.Rev. 323 (1984); Davenport, The Confrontation Clause and the Co-conspirator Exception in Criminal Cases: A Functional Analysis, 85 Harv.L.Rev. 1378 (1972); Klein, Conspiracy—The Prosecutor's Darling, 24 Brooklyn L.Rev. 1 (1957); Levie, Hearsay and Conspiracy, 52 Mich.L.Rev. 1159 (1954); Morgan, Admissions, 12 Wash.L.Rev. 181, 194 (1937); Morgan, Rationale of Vicarious Admissions, 42 Harv. L.Rev. 461, 464 (1929); Note, 1988 Wis. L.Rev. 577; Dec.Dig.Criminal Law ☜423–427, Evidence ☜253.

41. 4 Wigmore, Evidence § 1079 (Chadbourn rev. 1972).

Judge Learned Hand in Van Riper v. United States, 13 F.2d 961, 967 (2d Cir.

1926), cert. denied 273 U.S. 702 described the doctrine as follows:

Such declarations are admitted upon no doctrine of the law of evidence, but of the substantive law of crime. When men enter into an agreement for an unlawful end, they become ad hoc agents for one another, and have made "a partnership in crime." What one does pursuant to their common purpose, all do, and, as declarations may be such acts, they are competent against all.

42. Many, if not most, conspirator statements qualify as nonhearsay verbal acts, as is occasionally recognized. United States v. Hassell, 547 F.2d 1048 (8th Cir. 1977), cert. denied 430 U.S. 919. A conspiracy mounted and carried on without words is difficult to imagine.

43. Krulewitch v. United States, 336 U.S. 440 (1949); Wong Sun v. United States, 371 U.S. 471, 490 (1963); Marjason v. State, 225 Ind. 652, 75 N.E.2d 904 (1947); People v. Davis, 56 N.Y. 95, 102 (1874).

44. For examples of statements held not to have been "in furtherance," see United States v. Green, 600 F.2d 154 (8th

yet in fact more emphasis seems to be placed upon the "during the course" aspect and any statement so qualifying temporally may be admitted without much regard to whether it in fact furthered the conspiracy.[45] These latter decisions may represent a parallel to the cases allowing in evidence against the principal declarations of an agent which relate to the subject of the agency, even though the agent was not authorized to make a statement.[46]

Both the "in furtherance" and the "during the course" requirement call for exclusion of admissions and confessions made after the termination of the conspiracy.[47] Questions arise, of course, as to when termination occurs. Under some circumstances, extending the duration of the conspiracy beyond the commission of the principal crime to include concomitant and closely connected disposition of its fruits[48] or concealment of its traces appears justifiable, as in the case of police officers engaged in writing up a false report to conceal police partic-

Cir.1979) (in prosecution for conspiracy to possess checks stolen from the mail, statement by one conspirator to unindicted coconspirator that one of the other two had taken the checks from mailbox made while waiting in car for other two conspirators to cash check); United States v. Eubanks, 591 F.2d 513 (9th Cir.1979) (statement by member of conspiracy to nonmember that he was going to Tucson to obtain narcotics from another member); State v. Podor, 154 Iowa 686, 135 N.W. 421 (1912) (statement of one coconspirator to outsider that he and another were going to cause girls to become prostitutes not admissible against others). The line between pure history or description and statements "in furtherance" is obviously difficult to draw. See United States v. Haldeman, 559 F.2d 31, 110 (D.C.Cir.1976) (en banc) cert. denied 431 U.S. 933 (discussing the tangled skeins of past, present, and future in the Watergate cover-up).

When the Federal Rules were pending in the Congress, strenuous but unsuccessful efforts were made to delete the "in furtherance" requirement. United States v. Harris, 546 F.2d 234 (8th Cir.1976). Similar, and also unsuccessful, efforts had been made with the Advisory Committee. Model Code of Evidence Rule 508(b) (1942) had no "in furtherance" requirement. Kansas does not require that the statement be in furtherance of the conspiracy but only that it be relevant to the plan. State v. Bird, 238 Kan. 160, 177, 708 P.2d 946, 960 (1985).

45. See, e.g., United States v. Patton, 594 F.2d 444 (5th Cir.1979) (testimony by member of conspiracy that two other members each told him marijuana was being purchased for appellant held admissible); United States v. Piccolo, 696 F.2d 1162 (6th

Cir.1983) (statement as to source of cocaine intended to give confidence to those involved held admissible); United States v. Harris, 546 F.2d 234 (8th Cir.1976) (in conspiracy to defraud insurance companies by faking accidents, statements while in hospital made by conspirator who was acting as "victim" to another individual there under the same circumstances in an unrelated scheme held "a close case," but harmless if erroneous); United States v. Haldeman, 559 F.2d 31 (D.C.Cir.1976) (en banc), cert. denied 431 U.S. 933 (narratives of past events considered in furtherance of Watergate cover-up since discussion necessary for planning strategy). Cf. United States v. Fields, 871 F.2d 188, 193–194 (1st Cir.1989), cert. denied 493 U.S. 955 (statements and conduct involving commission of crimes not charged were admissible as akin to a "hazing" by which one conspirator proved his worth). But see United States v. Fielding, 645 F.2d 719, 727 (9th Cir.1981) (statements that are mere narrative declarations and do not further the objectives of the conspiracy, such as by helping to induce others to join, are not admissible because not in furtherance of the conspiracy).

46. See supra notes 8–11 and text accompanying note 8.

47. See the many cases in Annot., 4 A.L.R.3d 671. By contrast, conspiracy law principles dictate that statements of conspirators may be introduced against a new member even if made before the member joined the conspiracy. See United States v. Liefer, 778 F.2d 1236, 1249 (7th Cir. 1985).

48. United States v. Kahan, 572 F.2d 923 (2d Cir.1978), cert. denied 439 U.S. 832 (sale of hijacked property).

ipation in a burglary,[49] disposal of the body after a murder,[50] or continuation of a racketeering enterprise that involved on-going concealment to effectuate the scheme.[51] The Supreme Court's conclusion in Krulewitch v. United States [52] that it was error to admit evidence of a coconspirator's statement regarding concealment efforts after arrest of the participants established the position of the federal courts and was cited with approval in the Advisory Committee Note to the Federal Rule.[53] As a result, attempts to expand the so-called "concealment phase" to include all efforts to avoid detection have generally not been accepted by the courts.[54] While statements made after the termination of the conspiracy are inadmissible, subsequent acts which shed light upon the nature of the conspiratorial agreement have been held admissible.[55]

Preliminary questions of fact with regard to declarations of coconspirators are governed by Federal Rule 104(a) and must be established by a preponderance of the evidence.[56] Changing longstanding practice in

---

49. Reed v. People, 156 Colo. 450, 402 P.2d 68 (1965). See also United States v. Howard, 752 F.2d 220, 229–230 (6th Cir. 1985), cert. denied 472 U.S. 1029 (in scheme to burn house and defraud insurance company, statements involving concealment would have been admissible if made to avoid detection by insurance company as part of continuing effort to defraud but were not in furtherance of that objective when made to avoid detection by the police).

50. Dailey v. State, 233 Ala. 384, 171 So. 729 (1937).

51. United States v. Tille, 729 F.2d 615, 620–621 (9th Cir.1984), cert. denied 469 U.S. 845. See also United States v. Whitehorn, 710 F.Supp. 803, 823–824 (D.D.C.1989), reversed on other grounds 888 F.2d 1406 (D.C.Cir.) (conspiracy radically to transform the political structure of United States through violence contemplated concealment after arrest as part of an on-going conspiracy rather than attempt to hide completed one).

52. 336 U.S. 440 (1949).

53. Adv.Comm.Note,   Fed.R.Evid. 801(d)(2)(E), 56 F.R.D. 183, 299.

But see Evans v. State, 222 Ga. 392, 150 S.E.2d 240 (1966), cert. denied 385 U.S. 953 in which the "concealment phase" was extended to the extraordinary limit of allowing a coconspirator's statement implicating the accused, made more than a year after the commission of the crime, and wholly unrelated to any effort at concealment, immediate or otherwise. The conviction was sustained against constitutional attack in

Dutton v. Evans, 400 U.S. 74 (1970); see supra § 252.

54. See, e.g., United States v. Serrano, 870 F.2d 1, 8–9 (1st Cir.1989) (statements, which were part of concealment effort after central objectives had been attained, were outside rule); United States v. Floyd, 555 F.2d 45 (2d Cir.1977), cert. denied 434 U.S. 851 (burning the getaway car was ruled not a part of conspiracy to rob a bank); United States v. Vowiell, 869 F.2d 1264, 1268–1269 (9th Cir.1989) (in conspiracy to aid in escape from a federal prison, statements made after conspirators reached point of temporary safety were inadmissible). But see United States v. Medina, 761 F.2d 12, 18 (1st Cir.1985) (statements about burning the car used to pickup the ransom held admissible in kidnapping conspiracy, which the court concluded continued so long as the conspirators acted together to destroy incriminating evidence). See also Annot., 4 A.L.R.3d 671.

55. Lutwak v. United States, 344 U.S. 604 (1953) (subsequent acts of parties admissible to show phony nature of marriages in prosecution for conspiracy to evade immigration laws).

56. Bourjaily v. United States, 483 U.S. 171, 175–176 (1987). See generally supra § 53.

Prior to the decision in *Bourjaily,* whether Rule 104(a) or 104(b) should govern the determination of preliminary facts incident to admission of coconspirator statements was the subject of some debate. See United States v. Enright, 579 F.2d 980 (6th Cir.1978).

the federal courts, the Supreme Court held in Bourjaily v. United States [57] that the putative coconspirator statement itself can be considered by the trial court in determining whether a conspiracy exists and its scope.[58] However, the Court left undecided whether the trial court could have relied exclusively on the purported conspirator statement to make this determination.[59]

The existence of a conspiracy in fact is sufficient to support admissibility, and a conspiracy count in the indictment is not required and the declarant need not be charged.[60] The evidence is similarly admissible in civil cases, where the conspiracy rule applies to tortfeasors acting in concert.[61]

Statements of government agents in criminal cases. In a criminal prosecution, statements by the agent of an accused may be admitted against the accused, but statements by agents of the government have been held not admissible against the government.[62] "This apparent discrimination is explained by the peculiar posture of the parties in a criminal prosecution—the only party on the government side being the government itself whose many agents and actors are supposedly uninterested personally in the outcome of the trial and are historically unable to bind the sovereign." [63] A more plausible explanation is the desirability of affording the government a measure of protection

---

57. 483 U.S. 171 (1987).

58. Id. at 176–179.

In reaching this result, the Court concluded that enactment of the Federal Rules had altered the so-called "bootstrapping rule" that prohibited courts from considering the statement at issue in making the determination on admissibility. For statement of "bootstrapping rule", see United States v. Nixon, 418 U.S. 683, 701 & n. 14 (1974); Glasser v. United States, 315 U.S. 60, 74–75 (1942).

59. Id. at 181. Some courts have decided to retain the requirement of independent evidence. See People v. Montoya, 753 P.2d 729, 736 (Colo.1988) (must be some evidence independent of alleged coconspirator's statement); Harjo v. State, 797 P.2d 338, 345 n. 3 (Okl.Cr.App.1990) (same). But cf. United States v. DeJesus, 806 F.2d 31, 35 (2d Cir.1986), cert. denied 479 U.S. 1090 (no bootstrapping involved when alleged coconspirator statement is admissible under another hearsay exception).

60. United States v. Nixon, 418 U.S. 683, 701 (1974); United States v. Dawson, 576 F.2d 656 (5th Cir.1978), cert. denied 439 U.S. 1127; United States v. Kendricks, 623 F.2d 1165 (6th Cir.1980). Moreover, acquittal of the declarant on the conspiracy charge does not preclude use of his statement, in view of the different burdens

of proof for guilt and admissibility. United States v. Cravero, 545 F.2d 406 (5th Cir. 1976), cert. denied 430 U.S. 983; United States v. Gil, 604 F.2d 546 (7th Cir.1979).

61. Nathan v. St. Paul Mut. Ins. Co., 251 Minn. 74, 86 N.W.2d 503 (1957); Greer v. Skyway Broadcasting Co., 256 N.C. 382, 124 S.E.2d 98 (1962).

62. United States v. Santos, 372 F.2d 177 (2d Cir.1967); United States v. Pandilidis, 524 F.2d 644 (6th Cir.1975), cert denied 424 U.S. 933; United States v. Kampiles, 609 F.2d 1233 (7th Cir.1979), cert. denied 446 U.S. 954; United States v. Durrani, 659 F.Supp. 1183, 1185 (D.Conn.1987), judgment affirmed 835 F.2d 410; State v. Theriault, 485 A.2d 986, 992 (Me.1984). Sometimes a distinction is drawn between criminal and civil cases, admitting such statements in civil cases. United States v. D.K.G. Appaloosas, Inc., 630 F.Supp. 1540, 1564 (E.D.Tex.1986), affirmed 829 F.2d 532 (5th Cir.), cert. denied 485 U.S. 976.

63. *Santos,* supra note 62, at 180. See also *Kampiles,* supra note 62, at 1246. But see State v. Worthen, 765 P.2d 839, 848 (Utah 1988) (questioning validity of this rationale for government agents involved in law enforcement work); 2 Saltzburg & Redden, Federal Rules of Evidence Manual 147 (5th ed. 1990); 4 Louisell & Mueller, Federal Evidence § 426, at 328–29 (1980).

against errors and indiscretions on the part of at least some of its many agents.

The cases ruling against admissibility involve statements by agents at the investigative level,[64] with statements by government attorneys after the initiation of proceedings having been held admissible.[65] A dividing line in terms of the relative position of the agent in question may well serve to balance the conflicting interests involved.[66] While Federal Rule 801(d)(2) does not specifically address the question, it is very hard to find any support in its language or structure for a blanket exclusion of statements by government agents. However, a balancing approach of the type suggested above appears consistent with its basic approach and the various policy concerns involved.[67]

§ 260. Declarations by "Privies in Estate," Joint Tenants, Predecessors in Interest, Joint Obligors, and Principals Against Surety [1]

Historically, courts generally accepted the notion that "privity," or identity of interest between the declarant and a party justified introduction of the statement of the declarant as an admission of the party. Thus, the declaration of one joint tenant or joint owner against another could be received,[2] but not that of a tenant in common,[3] a co-legatee or

---

64. Cases cited supra note 62. Cf. 4 Louisell & Mueller, Federal Evidence § 426, at 330 (1980) (arguing against treating informants as agents under 801(d)(2)(D)).

65. United States v. Kattar, 840 F.2d 118, 130–131 (1st Cir.1988) (questioning exclusion of government agents from rule but avoiding clear ruling on basis that briefs filed by Justice Department demonstrated adoption by government under 801(d)(2)(B); United States v. Morgan, 581 F.2d 933 (D.C.Cir.1987) (error to excluded affidavit of detective offered by defendant that contained statement by informant, approved by Assistant United States Attorney, and presented to magistrate in support of application for search warrant, with the court emphasizing the authority of the attorney to represent the government and suggesting as alternative ground that government adopted the statement); United States v. American Tel. & Tel. Co., 498 F.Supp. 353, 356–58 (D.D.C.1980) (statements by officials of executive branch agencies before Federal Communications Commission constituted admissions of United States as plaintiff); State v. Worthen, 765 P.2d 839, 848 (Utah 1988) (following analysis of this treatise in finding statements of prosecuting attorney admissible).

66. See Note, 59 B.U.L.Rev. 400 (1979).

67. See Jonakait, The Supreme Court, Plain Meaning, and the Changed Rules of

Evidence, 68 Tex.L.Rev. 745, 774–78 (1990) (arguing that under the Supreme Court's recent approach to the Federal Rules under which the plain meaning of the rule is enforced in preference to evidentiary history, vicarious admissions of government employees in both criminal and civil cases will be treated similarly to those of other agents). See also cases cited in supra note 65.

§ 260

1. 4 Wigmore, Evidence §§ 1080–1087 (Chadbourn rev. 1972); Morgan, Admissions, 12 Wash.L.Rev. 181, 197 (1937); Morgan, Rationale of Vicarious Admissions, 42 Harv.L.Rev. 462, 470 (1929); Falknor, Hearsay, 1969 Law & Social Order 591, 603; Model Code of Evidence (1942); Comment on Rule 508; Dec.Dig. Evidence ☞226, 229–236; C.J.S. Evidence §§ 322–341.

2. 4 Wigmore, Evidence § 1081 (Chadbourn rev. 1972); LaFuria v. New Jersey Ins. Co., 131 Pa.Super. 413, 200 A. 167 (1938) (in suit against fire insurance company by husband and wife where property held by entireties, husband's admission receivable against wife).

3. Dan v. Brown, 4 Cow. 483, 492 (N.Y.1825); Johnson v. Hunnicutt, 86 N.C.App. 405, 408–409, 358 S.E.2d 74, 76 (1987).

co-devisee,[4] or a co-trustee [5]—so strictly is the distinction derived from the law of property applied in this context.

The more frequent and important application of this property analogy was the use of declarations of a predecessor in title to land, personalty, or choses in action against a successor. The successor was viewed as acquiring an interest burdened with the same liability of having declarations used against him or her as could have been used against the predecessor.[6] The declarations had to relate to the declarant's transactions, intent, or interest in the property, and they must have been made while the declarant was the owner of the interest now claimed by the successor.[7] Under this theory, courts have received the declarations of grantors, transferors, donors, and mortgagors of land and personalty against the transferees and mortgagees; [8] of decedents against their representatives, heirs and next of kin; [9] by a prior possessor against one who claims prescriptive title relying on such prior possession; [10] and of former holders of notes and other choses in action

---

4. Shailer v. Bumstead, 99 Mass. 112, 127 (1868). In will contests, most courts go to the extreme of saying that since the declaration is not admissible against the others, it is not even admissible against the co-legatee who made the declaration, since there can only be a judgment for or against the will as a whole. Belfield v. Coop, 8 Ill.2d 293, 134 N.E.2d 249 (1956).

5. Davies v. Ridge, 3 Esp. 101, 170 Eng. R.R. 553 (N.P.1800).

6. 4 Wigmore, Evidence § 1080 (Chadbourn rev. 1972).

7. Austin v. Austin, 237 Ark. 127, 372 S.W.2d 231 (1963) (grantor's statement made after delivery of deed not admissible against grantee); Charles R. Allen, Inc. v. Island Co-op. Services Co-op. Ass'n, Ltd., 234 S.C. 537, 109 S.E.2d 446 (1959) (assignor's statement made after assignment of draft not admissible against assignee); Dec.Dig. Evidence ⟨⇒230(3); C.J.S. Evidence § 323.

8. Kennedy v. Oleson, 251 Iowa 418, 100 N.W.2d 894 (1960) (admission of predecessor that building encroached upon plaintiff's land); Liberty Nat. Bank & Trust Co. v. Merchant's and Manufacturer's Paint Co., 307 Ky. 184, 209 S.W.2d 828 (1948) (statement of predecessor about party wall); 4 Wigmore, Evidence § 1082 (Chadbourn rev. 1972); Dec.Dig. Evidence ⟨⇒231–233.

9. Webb v. Martin, 364 F.2d 229 (3d Cir.1966) (testimony given by decedent in criminal case receivable as admission in action against his administrator); Fushanis' Estate v. Poulos, 85 Ill.App.2d 114, 229 N.E.2d 306 (1967) (writing in files of decedent admissible to establish trust against his estate); Mannix v. Baumgardner, 184

Md. 600, 42 A.2d 124 (1945) (statement in subsequently revoked will admissible on issue of existence of contract to devise); Dec.Dig. Evidence ⟨⇒236.

In wrongful death actions by administrators or other representatives, some courts by a hypertechnical concept of privity have said that, since the statute gives a new cause of action at death, the administrator's death claim is not derivative, and statements of the deceased are not receivable against the administrator as admissions. They may, of course, qualify under other hearsay exceptions but with stricter requirements for admissibility. In other aspects of the same case, however, privity undeniably exists, e.g., when liability is asserted against the estate or when the administrator joins a claim for conscious suffering, if it survives. The result is a hodgepodge of inconsistencies. See Shamgochian v. Drigotas, 343 Mass. 139, 177 N.E.2d 580 (1961) (decedent's statement of not blaming driver who struck him received as admission on count for conscious suffering, but barely admitted on wrongful death count under statute allowing statements of decedents made on personal knowledge); Carpenter v. Davis, 435 S.W.2d 382 (Mo.1968) (statement by decedent about defendant's lack of fault barred as admission in wrongful death case by lack of privity and not admissible as declaration against interest because in opinion form, although opinion aspect would not require exclusion of an admission). The results are indefensible.

10. Barnes v. Young, 238 Ark. 484, 382 S.W.2d 580 (1964); Atlantic Coast Line R. Co. v. Gunn, 185 Ga. 108, 194 S.E. 365 (1938).

against their assignees.[11] Of course, concepts such as bona fide purchaser and holder in due course may make the evidence irrelevant and therefore inadmissible.[12]

Similarly, it is asserted that when two parties are jointly liable as obligors, the declarations of one are receivable as an admission against the other.[13] However, the element of authorization to speak in furtherance of the common enterprise, as in the case of agency, partnership, or conspiracy can hardly be spelled out from the mere relationship of joint obligors, and admissibility of declarations on this basis has been criticized.[14] In fact, most of the cases found in support are cases involving the special situation of declarations of a principal offered as admissions against a surety, guarantor, indemnitor, or other person secondarily liable.[15] These declarations were usually held admissible.[16]

Morgan criticized importing into the law of evidence the property doctrines of identity of interest and privity of estate:

> The dogma of vicarious admissions, as soon as it passes beyond recognized principles of representation, baffles the understanding. Joint ownership,

---

11. Baptist v. Bankers Indem. Ins. Co., 377 F.2d 211 (2d Cir.1967) (statement by insured admissible against judgment creditor in latter's action against liability insurer on theory that judgment creditor was in effect assignee of insured); Taylor–Reed Corp. v. Mennen Food Products, Inc., 324 F.2d 108 (7th Cir.1963) (statement by assignor of patent admissible against assignee); Johnson v. Riecken, 185 Neb. 78, 173 N.W.2d 511 (1970) (statement by assignor of claim for medical expenses); Trudeau v. Lussier, 123 Vt. 358, 189 A.2d 529 (1963) (statement by assignor of past due note).

In a suit on a life insurance policy by the beneficiary, may the declarations of the insured in his or her lifetime be offered by the defendant insurance company against the beneficiary as the admissions of a predecessor in interest? The answer has depended in some cases upon the technical distinction between policies where the insured reserves the power to change the beneficiary and those where no such power is reserved. Bernard v. Metropolitan Life Ins. Co., 316 Ill.App. 655, 45 N.E.2d 518 (1942); Rosman v. Travelers' Ins. Co., 127 Md. 689, 96 A. 875 (1916); 4 Wigmore, Evidence § 1081 (Chadbourn rev. 1972); Annot., 86 A.L.R. 146, 161. The distinction is tenuous.

12. Bradstreet v. Bradstreet, 158 Me. 140, 147, 180 A.2d 459, 463 (1962); 4 Wigmore, Evidence § 1084 (Chadbourn rev. 1972).

13. 4 Wigmore, Evidence § 1077 (Chadbourn rev. 1972); Lowe v. Huckins, 356 Ill. 360, 190 N.E. 683 (1934) (joint makers of note).

14. Morgan, Admissions, 12 Wash. L.Rev. 181, 195 (1937).

15. See 4 Wigmore, Evidence § 1077 (Chadbourn rev. 1972).

16. See e.g., Scovill Mfg. Co. v. Cassidy, 275 Ill. 462, 469, 114 N.E. 181, 185 (1916) (statement of president of corporation, whose account was guaranteed by defendant, made to plaintiff, to whom guaranty was made, admissible since made as part of the operations of the business which was the subject of the guaranty); Linnell v. London & Lancashire Indem. Co., 74 N.D. 379, 22 N.W.2d 203 (1946) (suit on fidelity bond of manager of business; books kept by manager or under his supervision with respect to business covered by bond, admissible against surety); United Am. Fire Ins. Co. v. American Bonding Co., 146 Wis. 573, 131 N.W. 994 (1911) (suit on surety bond of agent of insurance company; agent's statement to secretary of insurance company as to amount collected, made after he had resigned but while he was under duty to account, admissible as "res gestae"); Annots., 60 A.L.R. 1500, 65 A.L.R.2d 631. But see Atlas Shoes Co. v. Bloom, 209 Mass. 563, 95 N.E. 952 (1911) (admissions of one, whose account was guaranteed by defendant, of receiving goods described in account inadmissible against defendant).

joint obligation, privity of title, each and all furnish no criterion of credibility, no aid in the evaluation of testimony.[17]

Following Morgan's view, the Model Code omitted any provision for admitting these declarations, and the Federal Rules followed the same pattern.[18] Most meritorious cases will qualify as a declaration against interest, vicarious admissions of agents, or some other hearsay exception more soundly grounded than an admission based on privity.

§ 261. Admissions by Conduct: (a) Adoptive Admissions [1]

One may expressly adopt another's statement. That is an explicit admission like any other and calls for no further discussion. In this treatise, the term adoptive admission is used somewhat restrictively to apply to evidence of other conduct of a party which manifests circumstantially the party's assent to the truth of a statement made by another.[2]

Adoptive admissions under the Federal Rules are governed by Rule 801(d)(2)(B).[3] In conformity with traditional practice, it provides that a statement is not hearsay if offered against a party and is "a statement of which the party has manifested an adoption or belief in its truth."

The fact that the party declares that he or she has heard that another person has made a given statement is not alone sufficient to justify finding that the party has adopted the third person's statement.[4]

---

17. Morgan, Admissions, 12 Wash. L.Rev. 181, 202 (1937). If the admissibility of admissions is regarded as the product of the adversary system, rather than as arising from circumstantial guarantees of trustworthiness justifying a hearsay exception, the conclusion is the same, since the privity concept goes beyond reasonable standards of party responsibility.

Wigmore disagreed, countering that "the Hearsay rule stands in dire need, not of stopping its violation, but of a vast deal of (let us say) elastic relaxation. And this is one of the places where that relaxation can best be granted, in view of the commonly useful service of this class of evidence. After the heat of a controversy has brought it into court, testimony on the stand is often much less trustworthy than the original statements of the same persons made before controversy." 4 Wigmore, Evidence § 1080a, at 144 (Chadbourn rev. 1972). The argument was actually one for expanding the admissibility of contemporaneous statements, with privity a more or less fortuitous aspect.

Professor Mueller, from a modern perspective, is not entirely sanguine about the elimination of the privity concept for admissions and questions the adequacy of other exceptions to fill the void. 4 Louisell & Mueller, Federal Evidence § 428, at 384–86 (1980).

18. Calhoun v. Baylor, 646 F.2d 1158, 1162–1163 (6th Cir.1981); Huff v. White Motor Corp., 609 F.2d 286, 290–291 (7th Cir.1979); Anaconda–Ericsson, Inc. v. Hessen (Matter of Teltronics Services, Inc.) 29 B.R. 139, 165 (Bkrtcy.E.D.N.Y.1983); 4 Weinstein & Berger, Weinstein's Evidence ¶ 801(d)(2)(D)[01], at 299–300 (1990).

§ 261

1. See generally 4 Wigmore, Evidence §§ 1069–1075 (Chadbourn rev. 1972); Annots. 87 A.L.R.3d 706, 48 A.L.R.Fed. 721.

2. In this text, admissions by silence are treated separately. See infra § 262.

3. Except for a minor grammatical variation, Revised Uniform Rule (1986) 801(d)(2)(ii) is identical.

4. Cedeck v. Hamiltonian Fed. Sav. & Loan Ass'n, 551 F.2d 1136 (8th Cir.1977) (in sex discrimination action, proper to exclude as not an adoptive admission statement by since-deceased branch manager to plaintiff concerning her request for promotion, "I was told [by unidentified person] that 'Yes, we know she's qualified but unless she's flat-chested and wears pants, there's no way.'"); Stephens v. Vroman, 16 N.Y. 381 (1857) (stresses the hearsay nature of the statements, without discussing whether repetition is adoption); Reed

The circumstances surrounding the party's declaration must be examined to determine whether they indicated an approval of the statement.[5]

The question of adoption often arises in life and accident insurance cases when the defendant insurance company offers statements which the plaintiff beneficiary attached to the proof of death or disability, such as the certificate of the attending physician or the coroner's report. The fact that the beneficiary has thus tendered it as an exhibit accompanying a formal statement of "proof" presented for the purpose of having the company act upon it by paying the claim would appear to be enough to secure the admission of the accompanying statements.[6] In actuality, however, the surrounding circumstances often show that an inference of adoption would be most unrealistic. This is clear when the beneficiary expressly disavows the accompanying statement,[7] and it

v. McCord, 160 N.Y. 330, 341, 54 N.E. 737, 740 (1899) (employer's statement as to facts of accident, though he was without personal knowledge, admissible, but distinguishing a statement that "he had heard" that such was the fact, which would be inadmissible); FCX, Inc. v. Caudill, 85 N.C.App. 272, 279, 354 S.E.2d 767, 772 (1987) (scientific test results requested by party not adopted by him where party received results but took no affirmative conduct based on statements).

5. Pekelis v. Transcontinental & Western Air, Inc., 187 F.2d 122 (2d Cir.1951), cert. denied 341 U.S. 951 (report of accident investigating board constituted adoptive admission when used by defendant as a basis for remedial measures and also filed with CAB); United States v. Marino, 658 F.2d 1120, 1124–1125 (6th Cir.1981) (defendant's possession of airline tickets, receipted hotel bills, and other documents offered by prosecution to prove interstate travel, characterized as adoption); Wagstaff v. Protective Apparel Corp., 760 F.2d 1074, 1078 (10th Cir.1985) (in fraud case, defendants' actions in reprinting newspaper articles and distributing them to persons with whom they were doing business indicated adoption of inflated statement in the articles); United States v. Morgan, 581 F.2d 933 (D.C.Cir.1978) (adoption of statement found where Assistant United States Attorney approved affidavit, which contained informant's statements, for presentation to magistrate for purpose of obtaining warrant and characterized informant as reliable); In re Gaines' Estate, 15 Cal.2d 255, 100 P.2d 1055 (1940) (statement by nephew to bank officers, as to what uncle said was his purpose in placing deposit box and bank account in joint tenancy with nephew); Oxley v. Linnton Plywood Ass'n, 205 Or. 78, 284 P.2d 766 (1955) (timber cruiser's report filed by defendant in support of SEC registration statement); State v. Howerton, 174 W.Va. 801, 329 S.E.2d 874, 879–880 (1985) (defendant's playing of tape made earlier by him while under the influence of sodium amytal constituted adoptive admission where the defendant produced and played it voluntarily at the home of an acquaintance, describing it as his conversation under truth serum). See also United States v. Felix–Jerez, 667 F.2d 1297 (9th Cir.1982) (typed statement of nonEnglish-speaking prisoner, through guard acting as interpreter, not adopted in that statement prepared in his absence and not read to him nor signed by him). See also cases cited in supra n. 4.

6. Cases admitting the statements on this theory are numerous, Russo v. Metropolitan Life Ins. Co., 125 Conn. 132, 3 A.2d 844 (1939) (but court stressed there was no contractual obligation here to furnish the doctor's certificate filed with the proof); Rudolph v. John Hancock Mut. Life Ins. Co., 251 N.Y. 208, 167 N.E. 223 (1929) (statement in doctor's certificate an adoptive admission, though contrary to beneficiary's own statement in the proof of death and though attending doctor's statement was required by policy); Thornell v. Missouri State Life Ins. Co., 249 S.W. 203 (Tex.Com.App.1923) (rule applied though proofs prepared by agents of company). Contra Liberty Nat. Life Ins. Co. v. Reid, 276 Ala. 25, 158 So.2d 667 (1963) (claimant not "bound" unless "made at his request or ratified by him"). Decisions are collected in 4 Wigmore, Evidence § 1073 n. 10 (Chadbourn rev. 1972); Dec.Dig.Evidence ⟜215(1); Annot., 1 A.L.R.2d 365.

7. Krantz v. John Hancock Mut. Life Ins. Co., 335 Mass. 703, 141 N.E.2d 719 (1957); Goldschmidt v. Mutual Life Ins.

seems that exclusion of the attached statement should likewise follow when the statements of the beneficiary in the proofs are clearly contrary to those in the exhibits.[8] Moreover, when the company's agent prepared the proof for signature and procured the accompanying documents, as is frequently done as a helpful service to the beneficiary, the inference of adoption of statements in the exhibits should not be drawn if the agent has failed to call the beneficiary's attention to inconsistencies between the proof and the exhibits.[9] By similar reasoning, furnishing a copy of an examining physician's report to the opponent under the requirement of a discovery rule should not be considered an adoption.[10] The argument for exclusion is particularly strong if accompanying statements, such as the certificate of the attending physician regarding particular facts, are required under the terms of the policy. In such cases, the statements are not attached at the choice of the beneficiary, and the sponsorship generally to be inferred from a voluntary tendering of another's statement cannot be made.[11]

Does the introduction of evidence by a party constitute an adoption of the statements therein, so that they may be used against the party as an admission in a subsequent lawsuit?[12] The answer ought to depend upon whether the particular circumstances warrant the conclusion that adoption in fact occurred and not upon the discredited notion that a party vouches for its own witnesses. When a party offers in evidence a deposition or an affidavit to prove the matters stated therein, the party knows or should know the contents of the writing so offered and presumably desires that all of the contents be considered on its behalf since only the portion desired could be offered. Accordingly, it is reasonable to conclude that the writing so introduced may be used against the party as an adoptive admission in another suit.[13]

With respect to oral testimony, however, the inference of sponsorship of the statements is not always so clear. However, here too circum-

---

Co., 102 N.Y. 486, 7 N.E. 408 (1886). In the absence of disavowal, it is arguable that the case is one of admission by failure to deny. See infra § 262.

8. See the dissenting opinion in Rudolph v. John Hancock Mut. Life Ins. Co., 251 N.Y. 208, 214–217, 167 N.E. 223, 225–226 (1929).

9. New York Life Ins. Co. v. Taylor, 147 F.2d 297 (D.C.Cir.1944).

10. Ortez v. Van Wagoner, 197 N.J.Super. 523, 528–529, 485 A.2d 341, 344 (Law Div.1984).

11. This view is supported by the decision in Bebbington v. California Western States Life Ins. Co., 30 Cal.2d 157, 180 P.2d 673 (1947); Carson v. Metropolitan Life Ins. Co., 156 Ohio St. 104, 100 N.E.2d 197 (1951). It is opposed by Rudolph v. John

Hancock Mut. Life Ins. Co., 251 N.Y. 208, 167 N.E. 223 (1929).

12. Thus escaping the requirements which would be imposed if it were offered under the hearsay exception for Former Testimony (see infra Ch. 31) such as identity of parties and issues, and unavailability of the witness.

Whether offering the testimony on direct satisfies the former testimony requirement of cross-examination is discussed in infra § 302 text accompanying note 14.

13. Richards v. Morgan, 122 Eng.Rep. 600 (Q.B.1864) (depositions); Hallett and Walker v. O'Brien, 1 Ala. 585, 589 (1840) (affidavit or deposition said to be adopted if used in evidence, but not where merely filed); 4 Wigmore, Evidence § 1075 n. 2 (Chadbourn rev. 1972).

stances may justify the conclusion that, when the proponent placed the witness on the stand to prove a particular fact and the witness so testified, the party has created an adoptive admission of the fact that may be admitted in a later suit.[14] But how is the party offering the testimony in the later suit to show that a given statement of the witness at the former trial was intended to be elicited by the party who called the witness or was contrary to or outside that intention? The form and context of the question would usually, but not always, give the clue. In view of the prevailing practice of interviewing one's witnesses before putting them on the stand, it would seem that a practical working rule would admit against the proponent the direct testimony of its own witness as presumptively elicited to prove the facts stated, in the absence of counter proof that the testimony came as a surprise to the interrogator or was repudiated in the course of argument.[15] By contrast, testimony elicited on cross-examination may be drawn out to reveal the witness' errors and dishonesty and should not be assumed to have been relied on by the examiner as evidence of the facts stated.[16] To constitute an adoptive admission, reliance must be affirmatively established.

In the main, preliminary factual issues arising with regard to whether a statement was adopted are to be decided as questions of conditional relevancy under Rule 104(b).[17]

Similar to adoptive admissions are the instances where the party has referred an inquirer to another person whose anticipated statements the party accepts in advance.[18] However, these admissions by reference to a third person are probably more properly classifiable as representative or vicarious admissions, rather than adoptive.[19]

14. See Fox v. Taylor Diving & Salvage Co, 694 F.2d 1349, 1355–1356 (5th Cir.1983) (expert testimony constituted adoptive admission of party calling him where expert gave detailed testimony as to which admission was central and explicit theme, without attempt by counsel to question those facts).

15. Bageard v. Consolidated Traction Co., 64 N.J.L. 316, 45 A. 620 (Err. & App. 1900) (testimony of witness at former trial which corroborated plaintiff's testimony which is now inconsistent with his present version); Keyser Canning Co. v. Klots Throwing Co., 98 W.Va. 487, 128 S.E. 280 (1925) (testimony as to cause of fire). But see British Thomson–Houston Co. v. British Insulated & Helsby Cables Ltd. [1924] 2 Ch. 160 (involving expert testimony, a most unlikely situation for finding nonadoption).

16. In O'Connor v. Bonney, 57 S.D. 134, 231 N.W. 521 (1930) (questions and answers on cross-examination by the present defendant of expert witnesses at a previous trial of the present malpractice action held inadmissible against the defendant).

17. See discussion of related issues in infra § 262 note 19. See also Graham, Handbook of Federal Evidence § 801.20, at 784 (3d ed. 1991). But see State v. Carlson, 311 Or. 201, 808 P.2d 1002 (1991) (preliminary issues regarding adoption to be decided under Rule 104(a)).

18. See, e.g., General Finance v. Stratford, 109 F.2d 843 (D.C.Cir.1940) (plaintiff in garnishment directed by garnishee's agent to go over records with bookkeeper; bookkeeper's statements admissible against garnishee); 4 Wigmore, Evidence § 1070 (Chadbourn rev. 1972).

19. See generally supra § 259.

§ 262. Admissions by Conduct: (b) Silence [1]

When a statement is made in the presence of a party containing assertions of facts which, if untrue, the party would under all the circumstances naturally be expected to deny, failure to speak has traditionally been received as an admission.[2] Whether the justification for receiving the evidence is the assumption that the party has intended to express its assent and thus has adopted the statement or that the probable state of belief can be inferred from the conduct is probably unimportant.[3] Since it is the failure to deny that is significant, an equivocal or evasive response may similarly be used against the party on either theory,[4] but if the total response adds up to a clear-cut denial, this theory of implied admission is not properly available.[5]

Despite the offhand appeal of this kind of evidence, courts have often suggested that it be received with caution, an admonition that is especially appropriate in criminal cases.[6] Several characteristics of the evidence should be noted. First, its nature and the circumstances under which it arises often amount to an open invitation to manufacture evidence.[7] Second, ambiguity of inference is often present. Silence may be motivated by many factors other than a sense of guilt or

§ 262

1. See generally 4 Wigmore, Evidence §§ 1071–1073 (Chadbourn rev. 1972); Heller, Admissions by Acquiescence, 15 U. of Miami L.Rev. 161 (1960); Morgan, Admissions, 12 Wash.L.Rev. 181, 187 (1937); Note, 112 U.Pa.L.Rev. 210 (1960); Annots. 70 A.L.R.2d 1099, 48 A.L.R.Fed. 741; Dec. Dig. Evidence ⟜220, Criminal Law ⟜407; C.J.S. Evidence §§ 294–298.

The general question whether silence is hearsay is treated in supra § 250 text accompanying notes 33–38, and particular aspects of silence as an admission in criminal cases are discussed in supra § 160.

2. 4 Wigmore, Evidence § 1071 (Chadbourn rev. 1972).

3. The language of the Federal Rule includes both "adoption" and "belief in its truth." See supra § 261 text accompany note 3.

4. Examples of responses held to be equivocal: People v. Tolbert, 70 Cal.2d 790, 76 Cal.Rptr. 445, 452 P.2d 661 (1969), cert. denied 406 U.S. 971 ("Forget about it," in reply to landlady's statement that police had found gun in bathroom and question whether he had put it there); Commonwealth v. Jefferson, 430 Pa. 532, 243 A.2d 412 (1968) ("Glad it was all over," when confronted with a statement implicating him). Not infrequently the equivocal response is the result of trying to outsmart a skilled interrogator who knows the ground rules. E.g., Commonwealth v. McGrath,

351 Mass. 534, 222 N.E.2d 774 (1967). Examples of responses held not to be equivocal: People v. Hanley, 317 Ill. 39, 147 N.E. 400 (1925) ("It will take twelve men to try me."); Boulton v. State, 214 Tenn. 94, 377 S.W.2d 936 (1964) ("Why did you do this to me?," in response to accusation in presence of alleged victim). The lack of a satisfactory dividing line deprives the "equivocal response" theory of much of its validity.

5. United States v. Lilley, 581 F.2d 182 (8th Cir.1978) (after hearing without comment husband's statement implicating her, defendant made contradictory statement; held, no adoption); Commonwealth v. Locke, 335 Mass. 106, 138 N.E.2d 359 (1956); Commonwealth of Pennsylvania ex rel. Smith v. Rundle, 423 Pa. 93, 223 A.2d 88 (1966).

6. People v. Aughinbaugh, 36 Ill.2d 320, 223 N.E.2d 117 (1967); Boulton v. State, 214 Tenn. 94, 377 S.W.2d 936 (1964); Gamble, The Tacit Admission Rule: Unreliable and Unconstitutional, 14 Ga.L.Rev. 27 (1979); Note, 112 U.Pa.L.Rev. 210, 213–14 (1963).

7. This is particularly true in criminal cases when the accused is conveniently at hand to be confronted with a detailed accusatory statement. People v. Bennett, 413 Ill. 601, 110 N.E.2d 175 (1953) (error to admit). Many of the cases cited would now, of course, be decided on constitutional grounds under Miranda v. Arizona, 384 U.S. 436 (1966).

lack of an exculpatory story.[8] For example, silence may be valued. As indicated at the beginning of this chapter, everyone knows that anything you say may be used against you. Third, the constitutional limitations of *Miranda* apply to the use of this type of evidence in criminal cases, but only where there is custodial interrogation.[9] Fourth, while in theory the statement is not offered as proof of its contents but rather to show what the party accepted,[10] the distinction is indeed a subtle one; the statement is ordinarily highly damaging and of a nature likely to draw attention away from the basic inquiry whether acquiescence did in fact occur.

Despite the array of circumstances raising doubts regarding the reliability of this kind of evidence, the Supreme Court has not found any absolute federal constitutional barriers against its use other than those imposed in some circumstances by *Miranda*.[11] Nevertheless, courts have evolved a variety of safeguards against misuse: (1) The statement must have been heard by the party claimed to have acquiesced.[12] (2) It must have been understood by the party.[13] (3) The subject matter must have been within the party's knowledge. At first glance, this requirement may appear inconsistent with the general dispensation with firsthand knowledge with respect to admissions, yet the unreasonableness of expecting a person to deny a matter of which he or she is not aware seems evident.[14] Otherwise the party simply does not have the incentive or the wherewithal to dispute the accusation. (4) Physical or emotional impediments to responding must not be present.[15] (5) The personal makeup of the speaker, e.g., young child, or

8. In Doyle v. Ohio, 426 U.S. 610 (1976), the Court spoke of silence following receipt of *Miranda* warnings as "insolubly ambiguous," id. at 617, and on that and other grounds overturned a state conviction in which it was admitted. The year before, the Court had overturned a federal conviction on nonconstitutional grounds, simply on account of the inadequacy of the inference from silence. United States v. Hale, 422 U.S. 171 (1975). However, in Jenkins v. Anderson, 447 U.S. 231 (1980), the Court held that impeaching the defendant with his silence before he was arrested and given *Miranda* warnings did not violate either the Fifth Amendment or the Due Process Clause. Finally, in Fletcher v. Weir, 455 U.S. 603, 607 (1982), the Court held that, where the defendant had been arrested but not advised of his rights, the absence of the "affirmative assurances" contained in *Miranda* warnings meant that using his silence to impeach did not violate Due Process. See supra § 160.

9. See supra § 160.

10. Greenberg v. Stanley, 30 N.J. 485, 153 A.2d 833 (1959).

11. See supra note 8.

12. United States v. McKinney, 707 F.2d 381, 384 (9th Cir.1983) (statement improperly admitted when, from the evidence, it was impossible to determine where defendant was when statement made); United States v. Sears, 663 F.2d 896, 904–905 (9th Cir.1981), cert. denied 455 U.S. 1027 (for jury to determine whether defendant, with impaired hearing, heard statement). For discussion of allocation of factfinding duties between court and jury, see infra note 19.

13. People v. Aughinbaugh, 36 Ill.2d 320, 223 N.E.2d 117 (1967) (error to admit evidence of defendant's failure to respond to identification in lineup in absence of showing that he knew the crime charged).

14. Dierks Lumber & Coal Co. v. Horne, 216 Ark. 155, 224 S.W.2d 540 (1949); People v. Aughinbaugh, supra note 13; Refrigeration Discount Corp. v. Catino, 330 Mass. 230, 112 N.E.2d 790 (1953). But see 4 Wigmore, Evidence § 1072 (Chadbourn rev. 1972). The general absence of a firsthand knowledge requirement for admissions is discussed in supra § 255.

15. Physical injury of the party or confusion attending an accident present exam-

the person's relationship to the party or the event, e.g., bystander,[16] may be such as to make it unreasonable to expect a denial. (6) Probably most important of all, the statement itself must be such as would, if untrue, call for a denial under the circumstances.[17] Beyond the constitutional issues that can be raised, the fact that the police are present when an accusatory statement is made may constitute a critical circumstance that eliminates the naturalness of a response.[18]

The above list is not an exclusive one, and other factors will suggest themselves. The essential inquiry in each case is whether a reasonable person under the circumstances would have denied the statement, with answers not lending themselves readily to mechanical formulations.

Most preliminary questions of admissibility in connection with admissions by acquiescence fall within the category of conditional relevancy. While some preliminary issues involved with admissions by silence are entrusted to final determination by the court, questions such as whether the statement was made in the person's hearing and whether there was an opportunity to reply should be submitted for jury determination if the court concludes sufficient evidence has been introduced so that a reasonable jury could find that those facts have been established.[19]

ples of potential impediments. Klever v. Elliott, 212 Or. 490, 320 P.2d 263 (1958); Beck v. Dye, 200 Wash. 1, 92 P.2d 1113 (1939). But see Doherty v. Edwards, 227 Iowa 1264, 290 N.W. 672 (1940) (proper to admit evidence of defendant driver's failure to deny fatally injured passenger's statement, "We were going too fast."); State v. Pacheco, 481 A.2d 1009, 1014–1015 (R.I.1984) (statement received in spite of defendant's claim that his highly intoxicated state rendered him unable to understand and respond).

16. Robinson v. State, 235 Miss. 100, 108 So.2d 583 (1959) (error to admit evidence of failure to deny statement of 2½-year–old child, "Daddy shot mother dear."); Beck v. Dye, 200 Wash. 1, 92 P.2d 1113 (1939).

17. United States v. Flecha, 539 F.2d 874, 876–877 (2d Cir.1976) (upon arrest, statement by one arrestee, "Why so much excitement? If we are caught, we are caught," was not such as to call for response from fellow arrestee against whom offered). Although not a requirement where adoption otherwise shown, the against interest nature of the statement or its incriminating content is generally to be considered in determining whether an ordinary person would deny it. United States v. Shulman, 624 F.2d 384, 390 (2d Cir. 1980). Similarly, the graphic nature of the crime described may render a denial even more expected. See State v. Neslund, 50 Wash.App. 531, 553, 749 P.2d 725, 738 (1988) (description of murder and dismem-

berment and disposal of body was such that in informal and noncustodial atmosphere innocent person would have denied).

18. See United States v. Williams, 577 F.2d 188, 193–194 (2d Cir.1978), cert. denied 439 U.S. 868. The court contrasted the situation in *Williams,* where the accusatory statement was made to the defendant far from police custody in a situation such that a denial would have been expected if the defendant were, as he contended, an innocent bystander to the crime with that in *Flecha,* supra note 17. In *Flecha,* the combination of custody and the vaguely phrased accusatory statement made it reasonable and understandable not to respond.

19. In a series of cases, the Ninth Circuit has ruled that some of the preliminary factual issues involved are to be determined under Rule 104(a) by the court, while most are to be determined as matters of conditional relevancy under Rule 104(b). The trial court under Rule 104(a) is to determine whether the statement was such that under the circumstances a innocent person would have responded. The questions of whether the party heard, understood, and acceded to the statement are, however, to be decided under Rule 104(b) by the jury, with the court determining only that sufficient evidence has been admitted so that the jury could reasonably find those facts. United States v. Giese, 597 F.2d 1170, 1195–1196 (9th Cir.1979),

Failure to Reply to Letter or other Written Communication.[20]   If a written statement is given to a party and read in the presence of others, the party's failure to deny its assertions may be received as an admission, when under the circumstances it would be natural for the person to deny them if he or she did not acquiesce. The principle in operation here is similar to the failure to deny an oral statement.[21] Moreover, if a party receives a letter containing several statements, which he or she would naturally deny if untrue, and states a position as to some of the statements but fails to comment on the others, this failure will usually be received as evidence of an admission to those omitted.[22]

More debatable is the question whether the failure to reply at all to a letter or other written communication should be received as an admission by silence.[23] Certainly such a failure to reply will often be less convincing than silence in the face of an oral charge.[24] Indeed, it is sometimes announced as a "general rule," subject to exceptions, that

---

cert. denied 444 U.S. 979; United States v. Moore, 522 F.2d 1068, 1075–76 (9th Cir. 1975), cert. denied 423 U.S. 1049; Graham, Handbook of Federal Evidence § 801.21, at 787–788 (3d ed. 1991). See also United States v. Barletta, 652 F.2d 218, 219–220 (1st Cir.1981) (reaching roughly the same result under different analysis and recognizing the role of the court to exclude in some cases under Rule 403). But see State v. Carlson, 311 Or. 201, 808 P.2d 1002 (1991) (preliminary issues regarding adoption to be decided under Rule 104(a)).

The above division of responsibility is a sensible one, entrusting to the judge the principally legal decision on whether under all the circumstances a failure to deny would have logical relevance. The jury is entrusted with the basic factual and credibility determinations of what occurred. Finally, the court has a responsibility, as with the admission of all evidence, to exclude where the prejudice from the evidence dictates that result. See the general treatment of preliminary questions in supra §§ 53, 58. See also 4 Louisell & Mueller, Federal Evidence § 424, at 291–292 (1980) (suggesting a variable approach).

20. See 4 Wigmore, Evidence § 1073 nn. 3–4 (Chadbourn rev. 1972); Note, 4 Vand.L.Rev. 364 (1951); Dec.Dig. Evidence ⟨key⟩220(8); C.J.S. Evidence § 297(b); Annots., 8 A.L.R. 1163, 34 A.L.R. 560, 55 A.L.R. 460.

21. See Grier v. Deputy, 15 Del. 19, 40 A. 716 (Err. & App.1894) (item in newspaper read to party); FCX, Inc. v. Caudill, 85 N.C.App. 272, 278–280, 354 S.E.2d 767, 772–773 (1987) (failure to respond to test results sent to customer not found to be adoptive admission, applying general doctrine).

22. Hellenic Lines Ltd. v. Gulf Oil Corp., 340 F.2d 398 (2d Cir.1965); Wieder v. Lorenz, 164 Or. 10, 99 P.2d 38 (1940).

23. The party seeking to introduce failure to respond as an adoptive admission has the burden of establishing that the recipient read the document and of proving his or her reaction from which acquiescence can be established. Ricciardi v. Children's Hosp. Medical Center, 811 F.2d 18, 24 (1st Cir.1987) (failure to respond excluded where proponent failed to establish foundation facts).

24.

Men use the tongue much more readily than the pen. Almost all men will reply to and deny or correct a false statement verbally made to them. It is done on the spot and from the first impulse. But when a letter is received making the same statement, the felling which readily prompts the verbal denial not unfrequently [sic] cools before the time and opportunity arrive for writing a letter. Other matters intervene. A want of facility in writing, or an aversion to correspondence, or habits of dilatoriness may be the real causes of the silence. As the omission to reply to letters may be explained by so many causes not applicable to silence when the parties are in personal conversation, we do not think the *same weight* should be attached to it as evidence.

Fenno v. Weston, 31 Vt. 345, 352 (1858). Certainly it is clear that mere possession of a document does not constitute an adoptive admission of its contents. See United States v. Ordonez, 737 F.2d 793, 800–801 (9th Cir.1983).

failure to answer a letter does not constitute an admission.[25] The negative form of the rule seems undesirable in that it tends toward over-strict rulings excluding evidence of material value.[26] The preferable view is that the failure to reply to a letter containing statements which it would be natural under all the circumstances for the addressee to deny if he or she believed them untrue is receivable as evidence of an admission by silence.[27] Two factors particularly tend to show that a denial would be naturally forthcoming: first, where the letter was written as part of a mutual correspondence between the parties,[28] and second, where the proof shows that the parties were engaged in some business, transaction, or relationship which would make it improbable that an untrue communication about the transaction or relationship would be ignored.[29]

25. See, e.g., Fidelity & Casualty Co. v. Beeland Bros. Mercantile Co., 242 Ala. 591, 594, 7 So.2d 265, 267 (1942); Levin v. Van Horn, 412 Pa. 322, 194 A.2d 419 (1963); Annot., 8 A.L.R. 1163.

26. See cases described in the second paragraph of infra note 29.

27. Megarry Bros., Inc. v. United States, 404 F.2d 479 (8th Cir.1968); Boerner v. United States, 117 F.2d 387, 390, 391 (2d Cir.1941), cert. denied 313 U.S. 587; Mahoney v. Kennedy, 188 Wis. 30, 40, 205 N.W. 407, 411 (1925).

As with oral statement, a number of factors will be involved in determining whether it would have been expected that the party would have denied an erroneous assertion in the written communication. Among those factors would be whether the statement contained facts that relative to the party's current position would have been considered "outrageous." See Boswell v. County of Sherburne, 717 F.Supp. 686, 689 (D.Minn.1989).

28. The significance of this is always conceded, see, e.g., Boerner v. United States, 117 F.2d 387, 391 (2d Cir.1941), cert. denied 313 U.S. 587; Wieder v. Lorenz, 164 Or. 10, 99 P.2d 38, 44, 45 (1940); Annot., 8 A.L.R. 1163.

29. Willard Helburn, Inc. v. Spiewak, 180 F.2d 480, 482 (2d Cir.1950) (letter stating terms of previous oral transaction held constituted circumstances making an answer natural); E.P. Hinkel & Co. v. Washington Carpet Corp., 212 A.2d 328 (D.C.App.1965) (correspondence arising from 6-year course of mutual dealings); Commonwealth Life Ins. Co. v. Elliott, 423 S.W.2d 898 (Ky.1968) (rule applied to retention of premium receipt book by beneficiary who could not read!); Ross v. Reynolds, 112 Me. 223, 91 A. 952 (1914) (failure of seller to reply to letter from buyer, complaining that automobile sold had been misrepresented by seller); Keeling–Easter Co. v. R.B. Dunning & Co., 113 Me. 34, 92 A. 929 (1915) (similar to last); Trainer v. Fort, 310 Pa. 570, 578, 165 A. 232, 235 (1933) (in action by real estate broker for commission under oral contract made in telephone conversation with defendant, failure to answer letter written by defendant to plaintiff immediately after conversation reciting different terms ruled admissible).

A letter from one with whom the addressee is engaged in business transactions is often inexplicably treated as if it no more called for a reply than would a letter from a stranger, "a bolt from the blue." See, e.g., A.B. Leach & Co. v. Peirson, 275 U.S. 120 (1927) (In a suit by one who had purchased bonds from defendant upon alleged oral agreement by its agent that defendant would repurchase bonds at same price on demand, the Court held that defendant's failure to answer plaintiff's letter asserting such contract was inadmissible: "A man cannot make evidence for himself by writing a letter containing the statements that he wishes to prove. He does not make the letter evidence by sending it to the party against whom he wishes to prove the facts. He no more can impose a duty to answer a charge then he can impose a duty to pay by selling goods." But is it not "natural" to answer such a letter from a customer who has bought bonds? The issue should not be one not of duty but of probability); Fidelity & Casualty Co. v. Beeland Bros. Mercantile Co., 242 Ala. 591, 7 So.2d 265 (1942) (in suit for attorney's fees against insurance company, failure to answer letter excluded where letter written by plaintiffs to defendants after original suit concluded, setting out their version of the arrangement for their services). See also Southern Stone Co., Inc. v. Singer, 665 F.2d 698, 702–703 (5th Cir.1982) (error

The most common instance of this latter situation is the transmission by one party to a business relationship to the other of a statement of account or a bill. Failure to question such a bill or statement is uniformly received as evidence of an admission of its correctness.[30] On the other hand, if the negotiations have been broken off by one party's taking a final stand, thus indicating a view that further communication would be fruitless [31] or if the letter was written after litigation was instituted, these circumstances tend to show that failure to answer should not be received as an admission.[32]

§ 263. Admissions by Conduct: (c) Flight and Similar Acts [1]

"The wicked flee when no one pursues." [2] Many acts of a defendant after the crime seeking to escape are uncritically received as admissions by conduct, constituting circumstantial evidence of consciousness of guilt and hence of the fact of guilt itself.[3] In this class are flight

to admit failure to answer letter from other party's lawyer regarding corporation that had ceased operation a year earlier, although apparently there had previously been an extensive course of dealings).

30. Megarry Bros., Inc. v. United States, 404 F.2d 479 (8th Cir.1968); Milliken v. Warwick, 306 Mass. 192, 28 N.E.2d 224 (1940); Bradley v. McDonald, 218 N.Y. 351, 113 N.E. 340 (1916).

31. Kitzke v. Turnidge, 209 Or. 563, 307 P.2d 522 (1957) (to defendant's letter suggesting settlement the "Bible way," plaintiff responded by filing suit). Cf. Southern Stone Co., Inc. v. Singer, 665 F.2d 698, 702–703 (5th Cir.1982) (letter from other party's lawyer regarding corporation that had ceased operation a year earlier held to call for no response where recipient consider corporation defunct).

32. Canadian Bank of Commerce v. Coumbe, 47 Mich. 358, 365–366, 11 N.W. 196, 199 (1882).

§ 263

1. See, for general statements, United States v. Jackson, 572 F.2d 636 (7th Cir. 1978); State v. Torphy, 217 Ind. 383, 386–387, 28 N.E.2d 70, 72 (1940); State v. Barry, 93 N.H. 10, 34 A.2d 661 (1943); State v. Henderson, 182 Or. 147, 195–196, 184 P.2d 392, 413 (1947). See also Hutchins & Slesinger, Consciousness of Guilt, 77 U.Pa. L.Rev. 725 (1929); 2 Wigmore, Evidence § 276 (Chadbourn rev. 1979); Note, 65 Va. L.Rev. 597 (1979); Dec.Dig.Criminal Law ⇌351.

2. Proverbs 28:1 (New Rev. Standard).

3. Often such conduct should not be classified as an admission since it is not hearsay at all because the actor exhibited no intent to assert anything. Fed.R.Evid. 801(c). It does no harm to consider the conduct as an admission, however, since under either theory it meets the hearsay objection.

from the scene,[4] from one's usual haunts,[5] or from the jurisdiction [6] after the crime; assuming a false name; [7] shaving off a beard; [8] resisting arrest; [9] attempting to bribe arresting officers; [10] forfeiture of bond by failure to appear [11] or departure from the trial while it is proceeding; [12] escapes or attempted escapes from confinement,[13] and suicide attempts by the accused.[14]

If the flight is from the scene of the crime, evidence of it seems to be wholly acceptable as a means of locating the accused at the critical time and place. However, in many situations, the inference of consciousness of guilt of the particular crime is so uncertain and ambiguous and the evidence so prejudicial [15] that one is forced to wonder whether the evidence is not directed to punishing the "wicked" generally rather than resolving the issue of guilt of the offense charged.[16] Particularly

4. State v. Little, 194 Conn. 665, 669–671, 674, 485 A.2d 913, 915–916, 918 (1984) (defendant found running from scene of burglary, leaving behind working automobile to which he had keys); State v. Townsend, 201 Kan. 122, 439 P.2d 70 (1968); Davis v. State, 171 Neb. 333, 106 N.W.2d 490 (1960), cert. denied 366 U.S. 973. If a "flight" instruction is given, it must be reasonable to infer flight. United States v. Myers, 550 F.2d 1036 (5th Cir.1977). Compare State v. Bruton, 66 Wash.2d 111, 401 P.2d 340 (1965) (error to instruct that flight might be considered as evidence of guilt when defendants merely walked away from scene of alleged shoplifting) with State v. Owen, 94 Ariz. 404, 385 P.2d 700 (1963), vacated on other grounds 378 U.S. 574 (flight instruction not erroneous when defendants left rape victim in desert and returned to town).

5. Pierce v. State, 253 Ind. 650, 256 N.E.2d 557 (1970). Testimony which merely describes a search of certain areas, without establishing them as customary resorts of the accused, does not qualify. Commonwealth v. Carita, 356 Mass. 132, 249 N.E.2d 5 (1969).

6. Lipscomb v. State, 700 P.2d 1298, 1301, 1308–1309 (Alaska App.1985) (defendant left state after indictment).

7. United States v. Boyle, 675 F.2d 430 (1st Cir.1982); United States v. Guerrero, 756 F.2d 1342, 1347 (9th Cir.1984), cert. denied 469 U.S. 934; Kidd v. State, 24 Ark.App. 55, 62, 748 S.W.2d 38, 41 (1988); People v. Waller, 14 Cal.2d 693, 96 P.2d 344 (1939).

8. People v. Slutts, 259 Cal.App.2d 886, 66 Cal.Rptr. 862 (1968). See also United States v. Jackson, 476 F.2d 249 (7th Cir. 1973) (prior to lineup accused cut his hair, shaved his mustache and sideburns, and grew a goatee).

9. People v. Sustak, 15 Ill.2d 115, 153 N.E.2d 849 (1958) (details admissible as going to weight; fact that resisting arrest is a separate offense does not require exclusion); State v. Rounds, 476 So.2d 965, 966–76 (La.App.1985). Nor is resistance essential in order to admit the circumstances of arrest. Lenzi v. State, 456 S.W.2d 99 (Tex.Cr.App.1970) (possession of pistol at time of arrest).

10. Cortes v. State, 135 Fla. 589, 597, 185 So. 323, 327 (1938); State v. Nelson, 65 N.M. 403, 338 P.2d 301 (1959), cert. denied 361 U.S. 877.

11. Affronti v. United States, 145 F.2d 3 (8th Cir.1944) (government could show defendant by failing to appear forfeited bonds in other cases pending against him, as well as this one); Williams v. State, 148 Tex.Cr. 427, 187 S.W.2d 667 (App.1945).

12. Sorrell v. State, 315 Md. 224, 228–229, 554 A.2d 352, 353–354 (1989).

13. State v. Ford, 259 Iowa 744, 145 N.W.2d 638 (1966); State v. Edison, 318 Md. 541, 548, 569 A.2d 657, 661 (1990); State v. Thomas, 63 Wash.2d 59, 385 P.2d 532 (1963).

14. People v. Duncan, 261 Ill. 339, 103 N.E. 1043 (1914); Commonwealth v. Goldenberg, 315 Mass. 26, 51 N.E.2d 762 (1943); State v. Painter, 329 Mo. 314, 44 S.W.2d 79 (1931); State v. Lawrence, 196 N.C. 562, 146 S.E. 395 (1929) (but see Brogden, J., dissenting); Commonwealth v. Giacobbe, 341 Pa. 187, 19 A.2d 71 (1941); Annot., 22 A.L.R.3d 840.

15. "Flight evidence tends to be highly prejudicial but only marginally probative * * *." Note, 65 Va.L.Rev. 597, 612 (1979).

16. See, e.g., Wong Sun v. United States, 371 U.S. 471, 483 n. 10 (1963): "[W]e have consistently doubted the proba-

troublesome are the cases where defendant flees when sought to be arrested for another crime,[17] is wanted for another crime,[18] or is not shown to know that he or she is suspected of the particular crime.[19] Some courts appear to accept a general sense of guilt as sufficient.[20] Perhaps the chief offenders are the cases of attempted suicide.[21]

A leading case suggests with respect to evidence of flight:

> Its probative value as circumstantial evidence of guilt depends upon the degree of confidence with which four inferences can be drawn: (1) from the defendant's behavior to flight; (2) from flight to consciousness of guilt; (3) from consciousness of guilt to consciousness of guilt concerning the crime charged; and (4) from consciousness of guilt concerning the crime charged to actual guilt of the crime charged.[22]

In recent years, a number of courts have begun to look with particular care at the timing of the flight relative to the offense and the strength of the inference that in fleeing the defendant was aware of, and motivated by fear of apprehension for, a particular offense.[23] The

tive value in criminal trials of evidence that the accused fled the scene of an actual or supposed crime." Earlier the Court had denied that the biblical quotation opening this section was "an accepted axiom of criminal law." Alberty v. United States, 162 U.S. 499, 511 (1896).

17. State v. Nelson, 65 N.M. 403, 338 P.2d 301 (1959), cert. denied 361 U.S. 877 (in murder prosecution, proper to admit evidence of attempt to bribe officer and flight when arrested for reckless driving).

18. People v. Yazum, 13 N.Y.2d 302, 246 N.Y.S.2d 626, 196 N.E.2d 263 (1963) (evidence of flight not excluded in New York trial because accused was also wanted in Ohio). United States v. Boyle, 675 F.2d 430 (1st Cir.1982), suggests that the defendant by using an alias may have been trying to evade detection for *all* his crimes.

19. Shorter v. United States, 412 F.2d 428 (9th Cir.1969), cert. denied 396 U.S. 970 (showing of knowledge is not required). Cf. Ex parte Jones, 541 So.2d 1052, 1057 (Ala.1989) (evidence of flight from police in robbery prosecution even though chase began in response to routine traffic offense 5 days after robbery at a time when defendant was not a suspect ruled admissible because of the extreme nature of chase and defendant's actions in discarding robbery proceeds during the chase). Many of the cases, particularly older ones, simply overlook the problem. However an occasional case specifies knowledge as a requirement. Embree v. United States, 320 F.2d 666 (9th Cir.1963); Hale v. Frazee (In re Frazee), 60 B.R. 109, 112–13 (Bkrtcy.W.D.Mo.1986); People v. Harris, 23 Ill.2d 270, 178 N.E.2d 291 (1961). Circumstantial proof of knowledge may, of course, suffice. Common-

wealth v. Osborne, 433 Pa. 297, 249 A.2d 330 (1969). Compare 2 Wigmore, Evidence § 276 (Chadbourn rev. 1979).

20. Martin v. State, 236 Ind. 524, 528, 141 N.E.2d 107, 109 (1957), cert. denied 354 U.S. 927 (resistance to arrest is evidence of guilt, "though not necessarily guilt of the crime charged.").

21. See supra note 14; Note, 7 N.C.L.Rev. 290 (1929).

22. United States v. Myers, 550 F.2d 1036, 1049 (5th Cir.1977). See also United States v. Dillon, 870 F.2d 1125, 1127 (6th Cir.1989) (adopting this four-part rationale, citing a list of cases that have adopted it, and recognizing these factors as permitting an orderly inquiry into admissibility of flight).

23. See United States v. Dillon, 870 F.2d 1125 (6th Cir.1989) (immediacy of flight important to show defendant's motivation except where other facts demonstrate that defendant was aware of imminent accusation); Ex parte Jones, 541 So.2d 1052, 1057 (Ala.1989) (where at time of flight defendant not shown to be aware that he or she was subject to criminal investigation, evidence generally inadmissible); State v. Burk, 234 Mont. 119, 761 P.2d 825, 827–828 (1988) (generally mere failure to appear at trial not sufficiently immediate to crime and therefore not probative enough to be admissible). Other courts continue to take the position that alternative explanations for flight or the lack of comtemporaneity with the crime go to the weight of the evidence under the jury's determination rather than to its admissibility. See Sorrell v. State, 315 Md.

potential for prejudice of flight evidence should also be weighed against its probative value.[24] Critical scrutiny of the balance between the often weak probative value of this type of evidence and its prejudicial impact is appropriate in each case.[25]

While the great bulk of the decisions involve criminal prosecutions, flight also finds recognition in civil actions.[26]

§ 264. Admissions by Conduct: (d) Failure to Call Witnesses or Produce Evidence;[1] Refusal to Submit to a Physical Examination[2]

When it would be natural under the circumstances for a party to call a particular witness,[3] or to take the stand as a witness in a civil case,[4] or voluntarily to produce documents or other objects in his or her possession as evidence[5] and the party fails to do so, tradition has allowed the adversary to use this failure as the basis for invoking an adverse inference. An analogous inference may be drawn if a party unreasonably declines to submit, upon request, to a physical examination[6] or refuses to furnish handwriting exemplars.[7]

224, 230, 554 A.2d 352, 353–354 (1989) (defendant's unauthorized absence from trial after proceedings began). Cf. State v. Givens, 356 N.W.2d 58, 63–64 (Minn.App.1984) (in robbery case, explanation that flight motivated by possession of drugs at time of arrest rather than consciousness of guilt of robbery went only to weight, not admissibility).

24. See Bedford v. State, 317 Md. 659, 666–668, 566 A.2d 111, 114–115 (1989) (possession of sharpened wire while in jail so equivocal that its admission to show escape effort ruled excessively prejudicial).

25. Particularly where the indication is weak that the defendant's flight was motivated by knowledge of the crime, prejudice may outweigh probativity. Ex parte Jones, 541 So.2d 1052, 1057 (Ala.1989). See generally Federal Rule 403 and supra § 185.

26. Gaul v. Noiva, 155 Conn. 218, 230 A.2d 591 (1967) (attempt to flee from scene of automobile accident); Jones v. Strelecki, 49 N.J. 513, 231 A.2d 558 (1967) (failure to stop after striking pedestrian in violation of state law).

§ 264

1. See 2 Wigmore, Evidence §§ 285–291 (Chadbourn rev. 1979); Livermore, Absent Evidence, 26 Ariz.L.Rev. 27 (1984); Stier, Revisiting the Missing Witness Inference— Quieting the Loud Voice from the Empty Chair, 44 Md.L.Rev. 135 (1985); Comment, 15 Mem.St.U.L.Rev. 105 (1984), 61 Calif.L.Rev. 1422 (1973); Dec.Dig.Evidence

⊕77, Criminal Law ⊕317; C.J.S. Evidence § 156.

Saltzburg, A Special Aspect of Relevance: Countering Negative Inferences Associated with the Absence of Evidence, 66 Calif.L.Rev. 1011 (1978), deals with the related but distinct problem where the absence of evidence is occasioned by judicial ruling.

2. 8 Wigmore, Evidence § 2220 n. 19 (McNaughton rev. 1961); Dec.Dig.Damages ⊕206(8).

3. Secondino v. New Haven Gas Co., 147 Conn. 672, 165 A.2d 598 (1960).

4. Kelsey v. Connecticut State Employees Ass'n, 179 Conn. 606, 427 A.2d 420 (1980); Williams v. Ricklemann, 292 S.W.2d 276 (Mo.1956).

See supra § 132 as to extent to which an accused waives privilege against self-incrimination by testifying. See infra note 27.

5. Gray v. Callahan, 143 Fla. 673, 679, 197 So. 396, 400 (1940); Martin v. T. L. James & Co., 237 La. 633, 112 So.2d 86 (1958); Welsh v. Gibbons, 211 S.C. 516, 46 S.E.2d 147 (1948).

6. Texas & New Orleans Ry. Co. v. Rooks, 292 S.W. 536 (Tex.Com.App.1927) (but request addressed to attorneys insufficient); 8 Wigmore, Evidence § 2220 n. 19 (McNaughton rev. 1961). The significance of the inference in respect to physical examination is greatly diminished by prevail-

7. See note 7 on page 185.

Most of the controversy arises with respect to failure to call a witness. The classic statement is:

[I]f a party has it peculiarly within his power to produce witnesses whose testimony would elucidate the transaction, the fact that he does not do it creates the presumption that the testimony, if produced, would be unfavorable.[8]

The cases fall into two groups.[9] In the first, an adverse inference may be drawn against a party for failure to produce a witness reasonably assumed to be favorably disposed to the party.[10] In the second, the inference may be drawn against a party who has exclusive control over a material witness but fails to produce him or her, without regard to any possible favorable disposition of the witness toward the party.[11] Cases in the second group are increasingly less frequent due to the growth of discovery and other disclosure requirements.[12] In either

ing rules providing for compulsory physical examination and penalties for noncompliance. Fed.R.Civ.P. 35, 37(b). See supra § 3. As to blood-alcohol tests, see Annot., 87 A.L.R.2d 370.

7. United States v. Nix, 465 F.2d 90 (5th Cir.1972), cert. denied 409 U.S. 1013; State v. Haze, 218 Kan. 60, 542 P.2d 720 (1975).

8. Graves v. United States, 150 U.S. 118, 121 (1893).

9. United States v. Ariza–Ibarra, 651 F.2d 2 (1st Cir.1981), cert. denied 454 U.S. 895.

10. United States v. Mahone, 537 F.2d 922 (7th Cir.1976), cert. denied 429 U.S. 1025 (government failed to call state police officer who was present at scene of arrest and might have testified on disputed matters); Secondino v. New Haven Gas Co., 147 Conn. 672, 165 A.2d 598 (1960) (personal injury plaintiff failed to call treating physician); Feldstein v. Harrington, 4 Wis.2d 380, 90 N.W.2d 566 (1958) (defendant failed to call physician who examined plaintiff at defendant's request). In the foregoing cases the inference was allowed. In the following cases the relationship and circumstances were held not to warrant the inference: United States v. Ariza–Ibarra, 651 F.2d 2 (1st Cir.1981), cert. denied 454 U.S. 895 (no effort by defense to produce informer on basis of information furnished by government; no showing that testimony would have benefitted defendant); Labit v. Santa Fe Marine, Inc., 526 F.2d 961 (5th Cir.1976), cert. denied 429 U.S. 827 (judge allowed argument but denied instruction; plaintiff in suit against employer did not call fellow employee, of relatively subordinate status, with deposi-

tion available); United States v. Bramble, 680 F.2d 590 (9th Cir.1982), cert. denied 459 U.S. 1072 (defense counsel interviewed informer and said she did not want him to stay around to testify). Cases dealing with the effect of particular relationships between party and witness are collected in Annot., 5 A.L.R.2d 893.

Separate from the general rules discussed in this section, some jurisdictions require the state to produce or account for all material witnesses in hearings on the issue whether a confession was voluntary. People v. Sims, 21 Ill.2d 425, 173 N.E.2d 494 (1961), cert. denied 369 U.S. 861.

11. Stuart v. Doyle, 95 Conn. 732, 112 A. 653 (1921) (defendant failed to produce two licensed drivers in his employ, identity unknown to plaintiff, to testify whether third employee driving defendant's car was in scope of employment); Haas v. Kasnot, 371 Pa. 580, 92 A.2d 171 (1952) (defendant failed to produce third motorist claimed by him to have been responsible for collision, whose identity was unknown to plaintiff).

12. Given the elimination of the antiquated voucher concept when rules modeled on the Federal Rules are enacted, one state has eliminated the missing witness inference entirely. State v. Brewer, 505 A.2d 774, 776–777 (Me.1985). A panel of the Fifth Circuit also reached the conclusion that no missing witness inference or argument should be permitted in cases tried under the Federal Rules of Evidence and Civil Procedure. Herbert v. Wal–Mart Stores, Inc., 911 F.2d 1044, 1048 (5th Cir. 1990). See also Jones v. Otis Elevator Co., 861 F.2d 655, 659 n. 4 (11th Cir.1988) (questioning whether instruction should survive changes produced by Federal Rules).

group, if the testimony of the witness would be merely cumulative, the inference is unavailable.[13]

Despite an abundance of cases recognizing the inference, refusal to allow comment or to instruct rarely results in a reversal, while erroneously instructing the jury on the inference or even an erroneous argument by counsel much more frequently requires retrial.[14] The appellate courts often counsel caution.[15] A number of factors support a conservative approach. Conjecture or ambiguity of inference is often present.[16] The possibility that the inference may be drawn invites waste of time in calling unnecessary witnesses[17] or in presenting evidence to explain why they were not called.[18] Failure to anticipate that the inference may be invoked entails substantial possibilities of surprise.[19] Finally, the availability of modern discovery and other

---

13. Gafford v. Trans–Texas Airways, 299 F.2d 60 (6th Cir.1962) (no inference from failure to call command pilot where co-pilot testified); State v. Brown, 169 Conn. 692, 364 A.2d 186 (1975) (where chief toxicologist testified, no inference from failure to call two subordinates who analyzed substance under his direction); Commonwealth v. Schatvet, 23 Mass.App.Ct. 130, 133–136, 499 N.E.2d 1208, 1210–1212 (1986) (reversible error committed in permitting the prosecutor to inquire about, and court to give instruction regarding, failure to call cumulative witnesses). Testimony that would aid in resolving a conflict in testimony is not regarded as cumulative. Geiger v. Schneyer, 398 Pa. 69, 157 A.2d 56 (1959).

Other courts have listed as a separate requirement that the party seeking the inference must show that the alleged missing witness is either available or competent. Shelnitz v. Greenberg, 200 Conn. 58, 73, 509 A.2d 1023, 1031–32 (1986) (must show ability to procure witness' physical presence); State v. Alfonso, 195 Conn. 624, 632, 490 A.2d 75, 80 (1985) (for physical evidence, its availability must be shown); State v. Francis, 669 S.W.2d 85, 90 (Tenn. 1984) (party seeking inference must affirmatively show competency of 6–year–old child).

14. Commonwealth v. Groce, 25 Mass. App.Ct. 327, 517 N.E.2d 1297 (1988) (reversal on basis of erroneous argument and instruction); State v. Francis, 669 S.W.2d 85, 89 (Tenn.1984) (reversal base on erroneous argument); McGlone v. Superior Trucking Co., 363 S.E.2d 736 (W.Va.1987) (reversal for erroneous instruction on "presumption" and supporting argument).

15. Commonwealth v. Groce, 25 Mass. App.Ct. 327, 329, 517 N.E.2d 1297, 1299 (1988); State v. Francis, 669 S.W.2d 85, 89 (Tenn.1984).

16. United States v. Busic, 587 F.2d 577 (3d Cir.1978), cert. dismissed 435 U.S. 964 (listing numerous reasons other than fear of unfavorable testimony for not calling a witness); Dent v. United States, 404 A.2d 165, 171 (D.C.App.1979) (danger of adding "fictitious weight" to one side of case and according missing witness "undeserved significance"); Oliphant v. Snyder, 206 Va. 932, 937, 147 S.E.2d 122, 126 (1966) ("Any presumption that he [10–year old passenger-son of defendant driver] would have testified adversely to his father is pure speculation.").

17. See, e.g., Ballard v. Lumbermens Mut. Casualty Co., 33 Wis.2d 601, 615, 148 N.W.2d 65, 73 (1967) ("A party to a lawsuit does not have the burden, at his peril, of calling every possible witness to a fact, lest his failure to do so will result in an inference against him.").

18. The party is, of course, entitled to explain the nonproduction. United States v. McCaskill, 481 F.2d 855 (8th Cir.1973); Case v. New York Cent. R. Co., 329 F.2d 936 (2d Cir.1964). Explanation must be based on what appears in the record. United States v. Latimer, 511 F.2d 498, 502–503 (10th Cir.1975) (government testimony in bank robbery prosecution showed surveillance camera was activated, but neither pictures nor explanation of absence was offered; defense argued that film was not produced because it did not identify defendant; error to allow government in reply argument to state that camera malfunctioned and in fact photographed FBI agent who arrived some time later).

19. State v. Clawans, 38 N.J. 162, 183 A.2d 77 (1962) (suggesting that proper practice is to require party proposing to invoke the inference give notice at the close of the opponent's case). See also cases cited in note 22 infra.

disclosure procedures serves to diminish both the justification [20] and the need [21] for the inference. In recognition of these factors, courts often require the party expecting to make a missing witness argument or intending to request such an instruction to give notice as early as possible.[22]

It is often said that if a witness is "equally available" to both parties, no inference springs from the failure of either to call the witness.[23] This can hardly be accurate, as the inference may be allowed when the witness could easily be called or subpoenaed by either party. What is in fact meant is that when so far as appears the witness would be as likely to be favorable to one party as the other, there will be no inference.[24] But even here, it seems that equality of favor is nearly always debatable and that although the judge thinks the witness would be as likely to favor one party as the other, either party should be permitted to argue the inference.[25]

A party may be at liberty to call a witness, but may have a privilege against the witness's being called by the adversary, as when in a criminal case the accused may call his or her spouse but the state may not. Similarly, it may be clear that all the information that a witness has is subject to a privilege which the party may exert, such as the doctor-patient privilege. In these situations probably the majority of courts would forbid an adverse inference from a failure to call.[26] Of

---

20. If discovery is available but not employed, the party ought not to be allowed to resort to the necessarily somewhat speculative inference when discovery would substitute certainty. Jenkins v. Bierschenk, 333 F.2d 421 (8th Cir.1964). The argument against allowing the inference is even stronger when a deposition has been taken. Labit v. Santa Fe Marine, Inc., 526 F.2d 961 (5th Cir.1976), cert. denied 429 U.S. 827; Atlantic Coast Line R. Co. v. Larisey, 269 Ala. 203, 112 So.2d 203 (1959); Critzer v. Shegogue, 236 Md. 411, 204 A.2d 180 (1964); Bean v. Riddle, 423 S.W.2d 709 (Mo.1968).

21. Discovery procedures offer a more direct means of compelling the production of evidence. A parallel to the diminished importance of the so-called best evidence rule is evident. Cleary & Strong, The Best Evidence Rule: An Evaluation in Context, 51 Iowa L.Rev. 825 (1966).

22. Thomas v. United States, 447 A.2d 52, 58 (D.C.App.1982) (because of dangers of creating evidence out of nonevidence, permission of court must be obtained before inference can be suggested to jury); People v. Boyajian, 148 A.D.2d 740, 741, 539 N.Y.S.2d 683, 685 (1989), appeal denied 74 N.Y.2d 661, 543 N.Y.S.2d 404, 541 N.E.2d 433 (defendant not entitled to instruction in part because request first made at end of trial when opponent could

not alter strategy); State v. Francis, 669 S.W.2d 85, 90 (Tenn.1984) (advance ruling saves time and possible expense of new trial).

23. Atlantic Coast Line R. Co. v. Larisey, 269 Ala. 203, 112 So.2d 203 (1959); Ellerman v. Skelly Oil Co., 227 Minn. 65, 34 N.W.2d 251 (1948); Bean v. Riddle, 423 S.W.2d 709 (Mo.1968).

24. United States v. Mahone, 537 F.2d 922 (7th Cir.1976), cert. denied 429 U.S. 1025. The unusual stretching of the meaning of "availability" apparently is the result of the need to fit the two previously mentioned groups of cases into the language of Graves v. United States, 150 U.S. 118 (1893).

25. Wilson v. Merrell Dow Pharmaceuticals, Inc., 893 F.2d 1149, 1152 (10th Cir. 1990); United States v. Erb, 543 F.2d 438 (2d Cir.1976), cert. denied 429 U.S. 981; Dawson v. Davis, 125 Conn. 330, 5 A.2d 703 (1939); Commonwealth v. Niziolek, 380 Mass. 513, 404 N.E.2d 643 (1980); Baker v. Salvation Army, Inc., 91 N.H. 1, 12 A.2d 514 (1940).

26. See supra § 80. But see United States v. Dowell (Matter of Dowell), 61 B.R. 75, 78–79 & n. 10 (Bkrtcy.W.D.Mo.1986), affirmed on remand 95 B.R. 690 (failure of debtor to call husband permitted adverse

course, an inference from the failure of the criminal defendant to take the stand is constitutionally forbidden.[27] The policy considerations with respect to comment upon the exercise of evidentiary privileges are discussed elsewhere.[28]

The specific procedural effect of the inference from failure to call a witness is seldom discussed. Some courts have said that the party's failure to call the witness or produce the evidence creates a "presumption" that the testimony would have been unfavorable.[29] It is usually phrased in terms, however, of "may" rather than "must" and seemingly could at most be only a "permissive," not a mandatory presumption, i.e. an inference described as a presumption in order to avoid local prohibitions against judges commenting on the evidence.[30] Moreover, unlike the usual presumption, it is not directed to any specific presumed fact or facts which are required or permitted to be found. The burden of producing evidence of a fact cannot be met by relying on this "presumption." [31] Rather, its effect is to impair the value of the opponent's evidence and to give greater credence to the positive evidence of the adversary upon any issue upon which it is shown that the missing witness might have knowledge.[32]

Instead, most courts speak of the party's failure to call the witness as creating an "inference." [33] Some of these courts consider that the party has a right to have such inference explained in the instructions on proper request while others consider that the instruction is proper but

inference in spite of existence of privilege); People v. Ford, 45 Cal.3d 431, 247 Cal.Rptr 121, 754 P.2d 168 (1988) (failure of defendant to call codefendants, who might assert privilege, permitted adverse inference); 76 A.L.R.4th 812.

27. See supra § 131. While the defendant is not subject to the inference with regard to the absence of his or her testimony as a result of exercising the constitutional right not to take the stand, an inference may be applied against the criminal defendant for refusal to disclose non-testimonial evidence. People v. Rumph, 128 Misc.2d 438, 442–443, 488 N.Y.S.2d 998, 1003–04 (1985), judgment affirmed 141 A.D.2d 576, 529 N.Y.S.2d 185, appeal denied 72 N.Y.2d 1049, 534 N.Y.S.2d 949, 531 N.E.2d 669 (defendant's refusal to reveal appearance of knee).

28. See supra § 80.

29. Tepper v. Compo, 398 Ill. 496, 76 N.E.2d 490 (1947); Stephenson v. Golden, 279 Mich. 710, 276 N.W. 849 (1938); Robinson v. Haydel, 177 Miss. 233, 171 So. 7 (1936). But see McGlone v. Superior Trucking Co., 363 S.E.2d 736, 743–745 (W.Va.1987) (use of the term "presumption" in combination with counsel's argument required reversal because they erroneously suggested the jury was required to

draw the inference that the witness would have testified unfavorably unless rebutted by evidence explaining nonproduction)

30. See discussion of these terms infra in Ch. 37.

31. Maszczenski v. Myers, 212 Md. 346, 129 A.2d 109 (1957); Stimpson v. Hunter, 234 Mass. 61, 125 N.E. 155 (1919); Pacific Finance Corp. v. Rucker, 392 S.W.2d 554 (Tex.Civ.App.1965); 2 Wigmore, Evidence § 290 (Chadbourn rev. 1979). Compare Morrow v. United States, 408 F.2d 1390 (8th Cir.1969) (in prosecution for placing life in jeopardy, jury could infer that gun was loaded in absence of introduction of contrary evidence by accused); City of Omaha v. American Theatre Corp., 189 Neb. 441, 203 N.W.2d 155 (1973) (defendant's failure to produce film in response to subpoena established violation of obscenity law).

32. Stocker v. Boston & Maine R.R., 84 N.H. 377, 382, 151 A. 457, 459 (1930). See Annot., 70 A.L.R. 1326.

33. See, e.g., Gross v. Williams, 149 F.2d 84 (8th Cir.1945); National Life Co. v. Brennecke, 195 Ark. 1088, 115 S.W.2d 855 (1938); Dawson v. Davis, 125 Conn. 330, 5 A.2d 703 (1939).

not required.[34] Still others would condemn an instruction as a comment on the evidence.[35] Of course, all courts permit counsel to argue the inference where the inference is an allowable one.

In jurisdictions where the judge retains the common law power to comment on the evidence, a fair comment on failure to produce witnesses or evidence is traditionally allowable. Furthermore, there is no harm in permitting judicial discretion to instruct on the inference. However, a practice that gives a party a right to such instruction is undesirable.[36] If made a matter of right, it is hard to escape the development of elaborate rules defining the circumstances when the right exists. To make instruction a matter of right has the advantage, it is true, of focusing past experience on the problem presented at the trial, but the cost here of complex rules far outweighs the gain.[37]

A web of rules also can develop by tightly controlling counsel's argument on the inference.[38] It is wiser to hold that if an argument on failure to produce proof is fallacious, the remedy is the answering argument and the jury's good sense.[39] Thus, the judge should be required to intervene only when the argument, under the general standard, can be said to be not merely weak or unfounded, but unfair and prejudicial.[40]

§ 265. Admissions by Conduct: (e) Misconduct Constituting Obstruction of Justice [1]

We have seen in the preceding section that a party's failure to produce evidence that he or she is free to produce or withhold may be

34. See Knott v. Hawley, 163 Minn. 239, 203 N.W. 785 (1925).

For illustrative instructions, see Cromling v. Pittsburgh & Lake Erie R. Co., 327 F.2d 142, 148 (3d Cir.1963); Schemenauer v. Travelers Indem. Co., 34 Wis.2d 299, 307 n. 1, 149 N.W.2d 644, 648 n. 1 (1967).

35. Hartman v. Hartman, 314 Mo. 305, 284 S.W. 488 (1926).

36. "If it commends itself to reason, born of common judgment and experience, the jury will apply it without hint or argument from the Court * * *. Those cases are sound which deny to the inference any quality other than mere argument. Here again a safe and logical test is: if counsel is free to argue it, the Court is not." Alexander, Presumptions: Their Use and Abuse, 17 Miss.L.J. 1, 14 (1945).

37. Bailey v. Maryland, 63 Md.App. 594, 611–612, 493 A.2d 396, 404–405 (1985), cert. denied 304 Md. 296, 498 A.2d 1183 (right of counsel to ask questions and argue regarding missing witnesses freely permitted, but in accord with suggestion in treatise, party not entitled to instruction).

38. For example, in the District of Columbia, rules have been developed for missing witness arguments, Lawson v. United States, 514 A.2d 787, 789 (D.C.App. 1986), "incomplete missing witness" arguments, Arnold v. United States, 511 A.2d 399, 416 (D.C.App.1986), and questioning of the witness to suggest the missing witness inference, Price v. United States, 531 A.2d 984, 993 (D.C.App.1987).

39. Wilson v. Merrell Dow Pharmaceuticals, Inc., 893 F.2d 1149, 1152 (10th Cir. 1990). See also United States v. Cotter, 60 F.2d 689, 692 (2d Cir.1932) (L. Hand, J.), cert. denied 287 U.S. 666 ("A judge is not required to intervene [to correct prosecution's argument on missing witness] any more than in any other issue of fact.").

40. In passing on this the trial judge has a substantial measure of discretion. Lebas v. Patriotic Assurance Co., 106 Conn. 119, 137 A. 241 (1927).

§ 265

1. 2 Wigmore, Evidence §§ 278, 291 (Chadbourn rev. 1979); Gorelick, Marzen &

treated as an admission. As might be expected, wrongdoing by the party in connection with its case amounting to an obstruction of justice is also commonly regarded as an admission by conduct. By resorting to wrongful devices, the party is said to provide a basis for believing that he or she thinks the case is weak and not to be won by fair means, or in criminal cases that the accused is conscious of guilt. Accordingly, the following are considered under this general category of admissions by conduct: [2] a party's false statement about the matter in litigation, whether before suit [3] or on the stand; [4] subornation of perjury; [5] fabrication of documents; [6] undue pressure by bribery,[7] intimidation,[8] or

Solum, Destruction of Evidence (1989); Solum & Marzen, Truth and Uncertainty: Legal Control of the Destruction of Evidence, 36 Emory L.J. 1085 (1987); Maguire & Vincent, Admissions Implied from Spoliation or Related Conduct, 45 Yale L.J. 226 (1935); Comment, 19 Mem.St.U.L.Rev. 229 (1989); Dec.Dig.Criminal Law ⊂⊃351(8), 351(10), Evidence ⊂⊃78, 79, 110, 219(2); C.J.S. Evidence §§ 151–155, 293.

2. Often such conduct should not be classified as an admission since it is not hearsay at all because either the actor exhibited no intent to assert anything or the statement is not being used to prove the matter asserted. Fed.R.Evid. 801(c). It does no harm, however, to consider the conduct as an admission, since under either theory it satisfies the objection to receiving hearsay.

3. Wilson v. United States, 162 U.S. 613 (1896) (false explanations of incriminating circumstances in murder case); United States v. Boekelman, 594 F.2d 1238 (9th Cir.1979) (false exculpatory statements); State v. Rea, 145 Ariz. 298, 299, 701 P.2d 6, 7 (App.1985) (false and conflicting statements regarding passing check constituted affirmative proof of involvement in check falsification scheme); People v. Showers, 68 Cal.2d 639, 68 Cal.Rptr. 459, 440 P.2d 939 (1968) (false explanation by accused as to why he was searching in patch of ivy where heroin was found); State v. DeMatteo, 186 Conn. 696, 443 A.2d 915 (1982) (false statement to police as to whereabouts at time of crime); McKinney v. State, 466 A.2d 356, 359 (Del.1983) (efforts to feign both a suicide attempt and mental illness); Commonwealth v. Lettrich, 346 Pa. 497, 31 A.2d 155 (1943) (in murder trial of child's custodian, false statements of child's whereabouts to avert inquiry and suspicion). Cf. McQueeney v. Wilmington Trust Co., 779 F.2d 916–921 (3d Cir.1985) (subornation of perjury by plaintiff involving witness' deposition testimony admissible as spoliation even though deposition never offered at trial).

4. Sheehan v. Goriansky, 317 Mass. 10, 56 N.E.2d 883 (1944) (defendant's testimony which from other evidence jury could find to be false); Hall v. Merrimack Mut. Fire Ins. Co., 91 N.H. 6, 13 A.2d 157 (1940) (deliberately false testimony at first trial acknowledged to be false at the second).

5. McQueeney v. Wilmington Trust Co., 779 F.2d 916–921 (3d Cir.1985) (plaintiff's subornation of perjury at deposition admissible as spoliation even though deposition was never offered at trial).

6. United States v. Wilkins, 385 F.2d 465 (4th Cir.1967), cert. denied 390 U.S. 951 (letter fabricated to explain failure to report income for tax purposes); Western States Grocery Co. v. Mirt, 190 Okl. 299, 123 P.2d 266 (1942) (falsified witness statement placed in evidence).

7. State v. Waterman, 7 Conn.App. 326, 349, 509 A.2d 518, 530–531 (1986), certification denied 200 Conn. 807, 512 A.2d 231 (statement by defendant that "if we get the stories straight you will be taken care of" admissible for consciousness of guilt); State v. Rolfe, 92 Idaho 467, 444 P.2d 428 (1968) (attempt to bribe witness); People v. Gambony, 402 Ill. 74, 83 N.E.2d 321 (1948) (attempts to "buy off" the prosecuting witnesses); Davis v. Commonwealth, 204 Ky. 601, 265 S.W. 10 (1924) (letter offering bribe for favorable testimony); Commonwealth v. Leo, 379 Mass. 34, 393 N.E.2d 410 (1979) (same as Gambony, supra).

8. State v. Adair, 106 Ariz. 4, 469 P.2d 823 (1970); State v. McEachern, 431 A.2d 39, 43–44 (Me.1981) (letter written from jail by defendant threatening witness admitted, court requiring also that prejudice be weighed against probativity); State v. Belkner, 117 N.H. 462, 374 A.2d 938 (1977) (plan to kill witness); State v. Hill, 47 N.J. 490, 221 A.2d 725 (1966); Price v. State, 37 Wis.2d 117, 154 N.W.2d 222 (1967), cert. denied 391 U.S. 908.

other means [9] to influence a witness to testify favorably or to avoid testifying; destruction or concealment of relevant documents or objects; [10] attempt to corrupt the jury; [11] and hiding [12] or transferring [13] property in anticipation of judgment.

Of course, it is not enough to show that a third person did the acts charged as obstructive. They must be connected to the party, or in the case of a corporation to one of its superior officers, by showing that an officer did the act or authorized it by words or other conduct.[14] Moreover, the circumstances of the act must manifest bad faith. Mere negligence is not enough, for it does not sustain the inference of consciousness of a weak cause.[15]

A question may well be raised whether the relatively modest probative value of such evidence is not often outweighed by its prejudicial effect.[16] The litigant who would not like to have a stronger case must

9. State v. Updike, 151 Ariz. 433, 433–434, 728 P.2d 303, 303–304 (App.1986) (telling codefendant not to talk constituted obstruction of justice and admissible to show consciousness of guilt, even though subject to varying interpretations).

10. Jones v. State, 223 Ga. 157, 154 S.E.2d 228 (1967), reversed on other grounds 389 U.S. 24 (accused buried body); Hubbard v. State, 187 So.2d 885 (Miss. 1966) (accused pushed his automobile into 40–foot deep lake after fatal accident); Welborn v. Rigdon, 231 S.W.2d 127 (Mo. 1950) (in suit by plaintiff for money advanced to improve defendant's property, defendant's conduct in wilfully destroying plaintiff's receipts held "an admission of plaintiff's claim").

11. People v. Marion, 29 Mich. 31, 39 (1874); McHugh v. McHugh, 186 Pa. 197, 40 A. 410 (1898).

12. State v. Bruce, 24 Me. 71 (1844) (procuring property by threats; evidence of concealment).

13. Burdett v. Hipp, 252 Ala. 37, 39 So.2d 389 (1949) (defendant's conveyance of property to kin after suit filed); Johnson v. O'Brien, 258 Minn. 502, 105 N.W.2d 244 (1960) (same); Annots., 88 A.L.R.2d 577, 80 A.L.R. 1139.

14. State v. Sorbo, 174 Conn. 253, 256, 386 A.2d 221, 223 (1978) (unconnected threats); Morgan v. Commonwealth, 283 Ky. 588, 142 S.W.2d 123 (1940) (error to admit attempted bribery of witness because no showing of defendant's connection with the act); Annot., 79 A.L.R.3d 1156. Family relationship is not a sufficient connection. Roby v. State, 587 P.2d 641 (Wyo. 1978).

As to corporations, see Maguire & Vincent, supra note 1, at 251. See also No-

wack v. Metropolitan St. Ry. Co., 166 N.Y. 433, 439, 60 N.E. 32, 34 (1901) (evidence of attempted bribery by defendant's claim agent was held receivable, not only as the representative admission of defendant corporation, but because it cast doubt upon the other witnesses secured by him); City of Austin v. Howard, 158 S.W.2d 556 (Tex. Civ.App.1941) (attempts by mayor and city manager to prevent witness from testifying in suit against city held admissible although assent of city council not shown).

15. Stanojev v. Ebasco Services, Inc., 643 F.2d 914, 923–924 (2d Cir.1981) (reasonable explanation for discarding records meant that no inference should be drawn against party); Berthold–Jennings Lumber Co. v. St. Louis, Iron Mountain & So. Ry. Co., 80 F.2d 32 (8th Cir.1935), cert. denied 297 U.S. 715 (in action for overcharge, doctrine of spoliation held inapplicable to destruction of waybills covering shipments because it only applies to conduct indicating fraud, whereas destruction here was routine); Gallup v. St. Louis, Iron Mountain & So. R. Co., 140 Ark. 347, 215 S.W. 586 (1919) (similar); State v. Ueding, 400 N.W.2d 550, 552 (Iowa 1987) (defendant not entitled to spoliation instruction because of failure to have stolen truck examined for fingerprints before its return since loss of fingerprint evidence not intentional). Cf. Empire Gas Corp. v. American Bakeries Co., 646 F.Supp. 269, 274–275 (N.D.Ill.1986) (delay in production of documents does not constitute destruction). But see case cited in note 24 infra.

16. Occasionally such evidence is excluded where the conduct is particularly macabre or inflammatory. United States v. Weir, 575 F.2d 668 (8th Cir.1978) (three assassination threats plus attempted kill-

indeed be a rarity. It may well be that the real underpinning of the rule of admissibility is a desire to impose swift punishment, with a certain poetic justice, rather than concern over niceties of proof.[17] In any event, the evidence is generally admitted, despite incidental disclosure of another crime.[18]

What is the probative reach of these various kinds of "spoliation" admissions, beyond their great tactical value in darkening the atmosphere of the party's case?[19] They should entitle the proponent at least to an instruction that the adversary's conduct may be considered generally as tending to corroborate the proponent's case and to discredit that of the adversary.[20] This result is worthwhile in itself, and it carries with it the corresponding right of the proponent's counsel to argue these inferences.

However, a crucial and perplexing question remains, namely, does the adverse inference from the party's obstructive conduct substitute for evidence of a fact essential to the adversary's case? Certainly the primitive impulse to answer "yes" is strong, and an analogy has been suggested to the practice under statutes and rules permitting the court to enter a default against a party who refuses to provide discovery.[21] Certainly, when the conduct points toward an inference about a particular specific fact, as in the case of bribing an attesting witness to be absent or destroying a particular document, there is likely to be a greater willingness to allow an inference of that fact although the only available information regarding it is the proponent's claim in the pleadings.[22] Where the conduct is not directed toward suppression of

---

ing); United States v. McManaman, 606 F.2d 919, 926 (10th Cir.1979) ("inflammatory talk of the plan of murders * * * predominated in impact over the discussion of drug dealing").

See generally supra § 185.

17. Few opinion writers have been as frank as in Pomeroy v. Benton, 77 Mo. 64, 86 (1882): "It is because of the very fact that the evidence of the plaintiff, the proofs of his claim or the muniments of his title, have been destroyed [by defendant], that the law, in hatred of the spoiler, baffles the destroyer, and thwarts his iniquitous purpose, by indulging a presumption which supplies the lost proof, and thus defeats the wrongdoer by the very means he had so confidently employed to perpetrate the wrong."

18. Sireci v. State, 399 So.2d 964 (Fla. 1981), cert. denied 456 U.S. 984 (attempt to have the prosecution witness killed); State v. Armstrong, 170 Mont. 256, 552 P.2d 616 (1976) (shoplifting to obtain coat to replace bloodstained similar coat worn during homicide).

19. For an illuminating discussion, see Maguire & Vincent, supra note 1, at 235–249.

20. See Maguire & Vincent, supra note 1, at 243–249; Prudential Ins. Co. v. Lawnsdail, 235 Iowa 125, 15 N.W.2d 880 (1944) (destruction of record "authorizes an inference which tends to corroborate the evidence" on the other side); Hay v. Peterson, 6 Wyo. 419, 434, 45 P. 1073, 1076–79 (1896) (destruction of records of deceased by plaintiff entitled defendant to properly qualified instruction on presumption).

21. Maguire & Vincent, supra note 1, at 235. Fed.R.Civ.P. 37(b)(2) authorizes default judgments and orders that facts be taken as established or the offender be precluded from introducing evidence. For extensive remedies, see, e.g., Fashion House, Inc. v. K Mart Corp., 892 F.2d 1076 (1st Cir.1989) (precluding admission of evidence on damages); Telectron, Inc. v. Overhead Door Corp., 116 F.R.D. 107 (S.D.Fla. 1987) (default judgment); Barker v. Bledsoe, 85 F.R.D. 545 (W.D.Okl.1979) (evidence excluded regarding autopsy, which was subject of discovery violations).

22. See 2 Wigmore, Evidence § 291 (Chadbourn rev. 1979), where the author contends that the failure or refusal to produce or the destruction of an adequately

any particular fact, as in attempts to "buy off" the prosecution, to suborn the jury, or to defeat recovery by conveyance of property, an inference as to the existence of a particular fact not proved is more strained. Without adverting to this distinction, many decisions have supported the general doctrine that the inference from obstructive conduct will not satisfy the need for proof of a particular fact essential to the proponent's case.[23]

Some recent cases have indicated a willingness to rethink these traditionally established principles. Several cases have found intentional actions that result in the destruction of evidence either to shift the burden of proof or to provide affirmative evidence on a critical issue.[24] Other cases have begun to develop a separate tort for spoliation of evidence.[25] This area of the law appears to be in the process of

identified document is sufficient that its contents can be inferred to be unfavorable to one chargeable with the obstructive conduct. For support of this view, see McCleery v. McCleery, 200 Ala. 4, 75 So. 316 (1917). Perhaps in a separate category are the false statements of a defendant regarding some element of the case. Courts rather routinely use such false statements as affirmative evidence of guilt. See, e.g., State v. Rea, 145 Ariz. 298, 299, 701 P.2d 6, 7 (App.1985) (false and conflicting statements regarding passing check constituted affirmative proof of involvement in check falsification scheme).

In the famous case of Armory v. Delamirie, 1 Str. 505, 93 Eng.Rep. 664 (K.B.1722), the chimney sweeper's boy found a mounted jewel and took it to a goldsmith's shop to be valued. But the goldsmith's apprentice kept the stone, and gave back only the socket. The boy sued the goldsmith for the conversion of the jewel. After evidence had been given of what a jewel of the finest water that would fit the socket would be worth, the Chief Justice instructed the jury, "that unless the defendant did produce the jewel, and shew it not to be of the finest water, they should presume the strongest against him, and make the value of the best jewels the measure of their damages." It should be noted that in this picturesque landmark case, the limits of the inference were established by evidence of the size of the socket and of the value of the finest jewel that would fit it.

23. In Gage v. Parmelee, 87 Ill. 329, 343 (1877), which concerned the legal effect of the defendant's destruction of records of the firm in response to a suit to set aside a partnership settlement agreement because of fraud, the court stated: "Proof must be made of the allegation of the bill. The destruction of the books does not make such proof. The presumption of law does

not go to that extent. In the weighing of conflicting testimony, there might be scope for the operation of this presumption against the appellee; or, in the denial to him of any benefit of secondary evidence." See also Stanojev v. Ebasco Services, Inc., 643 F.2d 914, 924 n. 7 (2d Cir.1981); Larsen v. Romeo, 254 Md. 220, 255 A.2d 387 (1969); Parsons v. Ryan, 340 Mass. 245, 163 N.E.2d 293 (1960); Login v. Waisman, 82 N.H. 500, 136 A. 134 (1927); F.R. Patch Mfg. Co. v. Protection Lodge, 77 Vt. 294, 329, 60 A. 74, 85 (1905); Walker v. Herke, 20 Wash.2d 239, 147 P.2d 255 (1944).

24. Nation–Wide Check Corp. v. Forest Hills Distributors, Inc., 692 F.2d 214, 217–19 (1st Cir.1982) (destruction of documents amounting to "knowing disregard" for plaintiff's claim, although not necessarily constituting "bad faith," gave rise to inference that satisfied plaintiff's burden of proof on issue); Welsh v. United States, 844 F.2d 1239, 1245–249 (6th Cir.1988) (opinion of Merritt, J.) (proper to create a rebuttable presumption sufficient to survive a directed verdict from the negligent loss or destruction of evidence by adverse party); Public Health Trust v. Valcin, 507 So.2d 596 (Fla.1987) (rebuttable presumption that shifts burden of proof as result of negligent destruction of evidence). But see Stanojev v. Ebasco Services, Inc., 643 F.2d 914, 924 n. 7 (2d Cir.1981) (inference from destruction of evidence cannot supply missing element of proof); Comment, 19 Mem. St.U.L.Rev. 229 (1989) (questioning result in *Welsh*).

25. Hazen v. Municipality of Anchorage, 718 P.2d 456, 463–464 (Alaska 1986); Smith v. Superior Court, 151 Cal.App.3d 491, 198 Cal.Rptr. 829 (1984); Rodgers v. St. Mary's Hosp. of Decatur, 198 Ill.App.3d 871, 145 Ill.Dec. 295, 556 N.E.2d 913 (1990). But see Wilson v. Beloit Corp., 725 F.Supp.

rather rapid change, although the patterns of the new order are not yet entirely clear.

§ 266. Admissions by Conduct: (f) Offers to Compromise Disputed Claim in Civil Suits and Plea Negotiations in Criminal Cases [1]

In general. Arguably an offer to accept a sum in compromise of a disputed claim might be used against the party as an admission of the weakness of the claim. Conversely, an offer by the adversary to pay a sum in compromise might be used against that party as an admission of the weakness of his or her position. In either situation, there is general agreement that the offer of compromise is not admissible on the issue of liability, although the reason for exclusion is not always clear.

Two grounds for the rule of inadmissibility are advanced: lack of relevancy and policy considerations.[2] First, the relevancy of the offer will vary according to circumstances, with a very small offer of payment to settle a very large claim being much more readily construed as a desire for peace rather than an admission of weakness of position. Relevancy would increase, however, as the amount of the offer approaches the amount claimed. Second, the policy aspect is to promote the settling of disputes, which would be discouraged if offers of compromise were admitted. Resting the rule on this basis has the advantage of avoiding difficult questions of relevancy. On this ground, the rule is available as an objection to one who made the offer and is a party to the suit in which the evidence is offered.

To invoke the exclusionary rule, there must be an actual dispute,[3] preferably some negotiations,[4] and at least an apparent difference of

1056 (W.D.Ark.1989), order affirmed 921 F.2d 765 (8th Cir.); Koplin v. Rosel Well Perforators, Inc., 241 Kan. 206, 734 P.2d 1177 (1987); Coley v. Arnot Ogden Memorial Hosp., 107 A.D.2d 67, 485 N.Y.S.2d 876 (1985). See generally Annot., 70 A.L.R.4th 984; Comment, 20 U.Rich.L.Rev. 191 (1986); Note, 43 Ark.L.Rev. 453 (1990).

§ 266

1. 4 Wigmore, Evidence §§ 1061, 1062 (Chadbourn rev. 1972); Dec.Dig.Evidence ⊜213, 214, 219(3), Criminal Law ⊜408; C.J.S.Evidence §§ 285–290.

2. See the discussion of theory in Morgan, Basic Problems of Evidence 209 (1963). The cases in general do not display much concern as to the basis of the rule.

3. Deere & Co. v. International Harvester Co., 710 F.2d 1551, 1557–558 (Fed. Cir.1983) (Rule 408 inapplicable to offer to license patent because no dispute or contest existed at time of offer); Ogden v. George F. Alger Co., 353 Mich. 402, 91 N.W.2d 288 (1958) (substantial offer to

plaintiff for surrender of his contract, made before controversy arose, not excludable under rule). See also Cassino v. Reichhold Chemicals, Inc., 817 F.2d 1338, 1342–342 (9th Cir.1987), cert. denied 484 U.S. 1047 (severance pay given contemporaneously with termination of employment and conditioned on release of potential claims not protected by rule since no dispute yet existed and since such arrangements are likely to be coercive rather than conciliatory).

4. Hanson v. Waller, 888 F.2d 806, 813–814 (11th Cir.1989) (early letter by lawyer not covered by rule because it made no mention of compromise, either directly or indirectly); S. Leo Harmonay, Inc. v. Binks Mfg. Co., 597 F.Supp. 1014, 1022–23 (S.D.N.Y.1984), judgment affirmed 762 F.2d 990 (2d Cir.) (court examines two letters, finding one admissible under the rule because no compromise negotiations and no actual dispute were then in existence and excluding one as part of compromise negotiations because such intent shown by ter-

view between the parties as to the validity or amount of the claim.[5] An offer to pay an admitted claim is not privileged [6] since there is no policy of encouraging compromises of undisputed claims. They should be paid in full. If the validity of the claim or the amount due are undisputed, an offer to pay a lesser sum in settlement [7] or to pay in installments [8] would accordingly be admissible.

What is excluded? The offer is excluded, of course,[9] as well as any suggestions or overtures of settlement.[10] How far do any accompanying statements of fact made by either party during oral negotiations or correspondence looking to settlement share the privilege? The historically accepted doctrine held that an admission of fact in the course of negotiations was not privileged [11] unless it was stated hypothetically [12] ("we admit for the sake of the discussion only"); expressly made "without prejudice"; [13] or inseparably connected with the offer [14] so that it could not be correctly understood without reading the two together.[15]

minology used in the letter). Given the policy interest in fostering negotiated settlements, it is probably appropriate to construe the rule liberally to include initial efforts that facilitate settlement. See 2 Weinstein & Berger, Weinstein's Evidence ¶ 408[01], at 14 (1990).

5. Tindal v. Mills, 265 N.C. 716, 144 S.E.2d 902 (1965). However, careful distinctions must be made. Statement " 'All right, I was negligent. Let's talk about damages' " should be held inadmissible because, while liability is not disputed, the amount due is in contest. On the other hand, statement " 'Of course, I owe the money, but unless you're willing to settle for less, you'll have to sue me for it,' " should be admissible since neither issue is contested. 2 Weinstein & Berger, Weinstein's Evidence ¶ 408[01], at 11 (1990).

6. Hunter v. Hyder, 236 S.C. 378, 387–388, 114 S.E.2d 493, 497–498 (1960) (defendant admitted cutting timber from plaintiff's land and said he wanted to "straighten it up").

7. Person v. Bowe, 79 Minn. 238, 82 N.W. 480 (1900) (in suit for wages due, evidence admissible that, when plaintiff demanded pay, defendant said he could not pay then but would give plaintiff part now and the rest later, and if plaintiff would reduce bill, defendant would pay at once).

8. Alaska Statebank v. Kirschbaum, 662 P.2d 939, 943–944 (Alaska 1983) (statement made by creditor regarding remedies not protected by rule because no dispute existed regarding amount of debt to be paid); Tindal v. Mills, 265 N.C. 716, 144 S.E.2d 902 (1965) (offer to give a series of notes for undisputed claim).

9. Outlook Hotel Co. v. St. John, 287 Fed. 115 (3d Cir.1923) (letter offering settlement privileged though not expressly without prejudice).

10. Armstrong v. Kline, 64 Cal.App.2d 704, 149 P.2d 445 (1944) ("she asked me what I thought about settling"); North River Ins. Co. v. Walker, 161 Ky. 368, 170 S.W. 983 (1914) ("if you will come to Paducah we will try to make a compromise settlement"); Coulter, Inc. v. Allen, 624 P.2d 1199 (Wyo.1981) (letter from party that it would like to "settle this out of court"). Contra Shaeffer v. Burton, 151 W.Va. 761, 155 S.E.2d 884 (1967) (statement, "I am sure that if we get together * * * we can settle this problem amicably," ruled admissible).

11. State v. Stevens, 248 Minn. 309, 80 N.W.2d 22 (1956) (admission of paternity in effort to compromise paternity claim); Cole v. Harvey, 200 Okl. 564, 198 P.2d 199 (1948) (in suit for work done, no error to receive evidence of statements of amount due made during negotiations for compromise); Dunning v. Northwestern Elec. Co., 186 Or. 379, 199 P.2d 648 (1948), reversed on other grounds 186 Or. 379, 206 P.2d 1177 (reference in letter to injuries sustained "when you ran into fallen pole"). Cases are collected in Annot., 15 A.L.R.3d 13.

12. Jones v. Jernigan, 29 N.M. 399, 223 P. 100 (1924).

13. White v. Old Dominion Steamship Co., 102 N.Y. 660, 6 N.E. 289 (1886) and cases cited, Annot., 15 A.L.R.3d 13, 33.

14. See cases on "independent" statements, Annot., 15 A.L.R.3d 13, 27.

15. Home Ins. Co. v. Baltimore Warehouse Co., 93 U.S. (3 Otto) 527 (1876); San-

This traditional doctrine of denying the protection of the exclusionary rule to statements of fact had serious drawbacks, however. It discouraged freedom of communication in attempting compromise and, taken with its exceptions, involved difficulties of application. As a result, the trend has been to extend the protection to all statements made in compromise negotiations.[16]

Federal Rule 408, set forth below, is consistent with the foregoing observations, including an extension of its protection to all statements made in compromise negotiations.

Evidence of (1) furnishing or offering or promising to furnish, or (2) accepting or offering or promising to accept, a valuable consideration in compromising or attempting to compromise a claim which was disputed as to either validity or amount, is not admissible to prove liability for or invalidity of the claim or its amount. Evidence of conduct or statements made in compromise negotiations is likewise not admissible. This rule does not require the exclusion of any evidence otherwise discoverable merely because it is presented in the course of compromise negotiations.[17] This rule also does not require exclusion when the evidence is offered for another purpose, such as proving bias or prejudice of a witness, negativing a contention of undue delay, or proving an effort to obstruct a criminal investigation or prosecution.[18]

The exclusionary rule is designed to exclude the offer of compromise only when it is tendered as an admission of the weakness of the offering party's claim or defense, not when the purpose is otherwise. Thus, for example, the rule does not call for exclusion when the compromise negotiations are offered to explain delay in taking action,[19] prior statements,[20] or failure to seek employment to mitigate damages[21] or to show the extent of legal services rendered in conducting them.[22] As in other situations where evidence is admissible for one purpose but not for another, an evaluation is required in terms of weighing probative

ford v. John Finnigan Co., 169 S.W. 624 (Tex.Civ.App.1914, error refused).

16. Hatfield v. Max Rouse & Sons Northwest, 100 Idaho 840, 606 P.2d 944 (1980) (adopting approach of Federal Rule 408 prior to general enactment of state rules of evidence).

17. Out of an overabundance of caution and to allay fears that the rule might be used as a device for immunizing all kinds of evidence simply by mentioning it during the course of negotiations, Congress added the third sentence to the rule as adopted by the Supreme Court. Senate Comm. on Judiciary, S.Rep. No. 1277, 93d Cong., 2d Sess. 10 (1974), reprinted in 1974 U.S.Code Cong. & Admin.News 7051, 7057.

18. Revised Uniform Rule (1986) 408 differs in two respects. First, it adds "or any other claim" at the end of the first sentence, and second, it does not include

the third sentence dealing with discovery. See supra note 17.

19. Federal Mut. Ins. Co. v. Lewis, 231 Md. 587, 191 A.2d. 437 (1963); Travelers Ins. Co. v. Barrett, 366 S.W.2d 692 (Tex. Civ.App.1963); Graham v. San Antonio Mach. & Supply Corp., 418 S.W.2d 303 (Tex.Civ.App.1967, error refused n.r.e.); Annot., 49 A.L.R.2d 87.

20. Central Soya Co. v. Epstein Fisheries, Inc., 676 F.2d 939 (7th Cir.1982); Fieve v. Emmeck, 248 Minn. 122, 78 N.W.2d 343 (1956); Malatt v. United Transit Co., 99 R.I. 263, 207 A.2d 39 (1965).

21. Kubista v. Romaine, 87 Wash.2d 62, 549 P.2d 491 (1976) (insurance adjuster told plaintiff he would be taken care of if he went to school to learn new trade).

22. Wolf v. Mutual Benefit Health & Accident Ass'n, 188 Kan. 694, 366 P.2d 219 (1961).

value and need against likelihood of prejudice, with due regard to the probable efficacy of a limiting instruction.[23]

Evidence of present party's compromise with third persons. In an action between plaintiff (P) and defendant (D), a compromise offer or a completed compromise by D with a third person having a claim similar to P's arising from the same transaction may be relevant as showing D's belief in the weakness of the defense in the present action. Nevertheless, the same consideration of policy which prompts exclusion of a compromise offer made by D to P, namely the danger of discouraging such compromises, also applies here. Accordingly, the prevailing view is that the compromise offer or payment made by the present defendant is privileged when offered as an implied admission of liability.[24]

Although inadmissible to show liability, the completed compromise agreement may be admissible for another purpose. A defendant in a personal injury case, for example, may call a witness who was injured in the same collision. If the witness has made a claim account against the defendant, inconsistent with the witness' present favorable testimony, this may be proved to impeach the witness. Furthermore, if the witness has been paid or promised money in compromise of his or her claim, this may likewise be shown as evidence of bias or used more generally to impeach.[25] The need to evaluate properly the credibility of the witness is, like the policy of encouraging compromise, an important interest. If, however, the witness sought to be impeached by showing

---

23. See supra § 59.

24. McInnis v. A.M.F., Inc., 765 F.2d 240, 247–251 (1st Cir.1985) (release of settlement with third party inadmissible under Rule 408 when used to show causation, an issue the court found integral to the finding of liability in a tort case and therefore barred under the rule); Masemer v. Delmarva Power & Light Co., 723 F.Supp. 1019, 1022–23 (D.Del.1989) (excluding payment of OSHA fine in suit for wrongful death as completed compromise under very broad reading of rule and its policy of encouraging compromise and settlement). The basic principle had been accepted prior to enactment of the Federal Rules. See, e.g., Hawthorne v. Eckerson Co., 77 F.2d 844 (2d Cir.1935); Lewis v. Dixie–Portland Flour Mills, Inc., 356 F.2d 54 (6th Cir. 1966); McCallum v. Harris, 379 S.W.2d 438 (Ky.1964); Tregellas v. American Oil Co., 231 Md. 95, 188 A.2d 691 (1963); Annot., 20 A.L.R.2d 304.

A settlement which is offered as proof of the liability of a third party, arising out of the transaction in suit, is not within the privilege since the evidence will not harm the parties to the compromise. But it may be attacked as conduct-as-hearsay. See, e.g., Daly v. Publix Cars, 128 Neb. 403, 259 N.W. 163 (1935) (suit by passenger against operator of taxicab for injury incurred when another automobile collided with taxicab; evidence offered by taxicab operator that driver of other automobile paid damages to taxicab excluded as hearsay as to passenger; decided before Nebraska adopted rules modeled on the Federal Rules). See supra § 250.

25. County of Hennepin v. AFG Indus., Inc., 726 F.2d 149, 152–153 (8th Cir.1984) (settlement admitted to impeach assertion of counsel at trial); Brocklesby v. United States, 767 F.2d 1288, 1292–293 (9th Cir. 1985), cert. denied 474 U.S. 1101 (indemnity agreement between two defendants admissible by plaintiff to attack credibility of their witnesses and to show nonadverse relationship between the defendants); Dornberg v. St. Paul City Ry. Co., 253 Minn. 52, 91 N.W.2d 178 (1958); Joice v. Missouri–Kansas–Texas Ry. Co., 354 Mo. 439, 189 S.W.2d 568 (1945); Rynar v. Lincoln Transit Co., 129 N.J.L. 525, 30 A.2d 406 (Err. & App.1945) (discusses balance of need for impeachment and danger of improper use; here admissible in judge's discretion). Of course, the opponent would be entitled to an instruction limiting the use of the evidence to the question of credibility. Contra Fenberg v. Rosenthal, 348 Ill. App. 510, 109 N.E.2d 402 (1952). See supra § 40.

the compromise with a third person, is one of the present parties, the question is more debatable. The danger that the evidence will be used substantively as an admission is greater, and, as the party's interest is apparent, the need for additional evidence on credibility is less. This impeachment of party-witnesses, however, has occasionally been sanctioned.[26]

Effect of acceptance of offer of compromise. If an offer of compromise is accepted and a contract is thus created, the party aggrieved may sue on the contract and obviously may prove the offer and acceptance.[27] Moreover, if after such a contract is made and the offering party repudiates it, the other may elect to sue on the original cause of action and here again the repudiating party may not claim privilege against proof of the compromise.[28] The shield of the privilege does not extend to the protection of those who repudiate the agreements, which the privilege is designed to encourage.

Compromise evidence in criminal cases.[29] The policy of protecting offers of compromise in civil cases does not extend to efforts to stifle criminal prosecution by "buying off" the prosecuting witness or victim.[30] Indeed, such efforts are classed as an implied admission and generally admissible.[31] The public policy against compounding crimes is said to prevail.[32] On the other hand, the legitimacy of settling criminal cases by negotiations between prosecuting attorney and accused, whereby the latter pleads guilty in return for some leniency, has been generally recognized.[33] Effective criminal law administration would be difficult if a large proportion of the charges were not disposed of by guilty pleas. Public policy accordingly encourages compromise, and as in civil cases, that policy is furthered by protecting from disclosure at trial not only the offer but also statements made during negotiations.[34]

26. Luis v. Cavin, 88 Cal.App.2d 107, 198 P.2d 563 (1948); Burke v. Commercial Standard Ins. Co., 38 So.2d 644 (La.App. 1948).

When a payment made by another tortfeasor is relied upon to reduce the liability of the defendant, the preferable practice is for the judge, rather than the jury, to perform the arithmetic. McHann v. Firestone Tire & Rubber Co., 713 F.2d 161, 166 n. 10 (5th Cir.1983); Brooks v. Daley, 242 Md. 185, 218 A.2d 184 (1966); Sheets v. Davenport, 181 Neb. 621, 150 N.W.2d 224 (1967).

27. Union Trust Co. v. Resisto Mfg. Co., 169 Md. 381, 181 A. 726 (1935); C.J.S. Evidence § 290.

28. Reese v. McVittie, 119 Colo. 29, 200 P.2d 390 (1948).

29. See Dec.Dig.Criminal Law ⊄408.

30. State v. Burt, 249 N.W.2d 651 (Iowa 1977) (in shoplifting prosecution, fact that two days later defendant returned to store

and offered to pay for coat, denying having stolen it, admissible in support of inference he stole coat); Carter v. State, 161 Tenn. 698, 34 S.W.2d 208 (1931) (offer by accused to settle with complaining witness admissible).

31. See supra § 265 note 7 and accompanying text.

32. State v. Burt, 249 N.W.2d 651 (Iowa 1977).

33. See, e.g., Santobello v. New York, 404 U.S. 257, 261 (1971).

34. As to offers, see Bennett v. Commonwealth, 234 Ky. 333, 28 S.W.2d 24 (1930); State v. Abel, 320 Mo. 445, 8 S.W.2d 55 (1928). As to statements, State v. Byrd, 203 Kan. 45, 453 P.2d 22 (1969); Shriver v. State, 632 P.2d 420 (Okl.Cr.App. 1980), cert. denied 449 U.S. 983 (no rule or statute needed).

Federal Rule 410 [35] provides:

Except as otherwise provided in this rule, evidence of the following is not, in any civil or criminal proceeding, admissible against the defendant who made the plea or was a participant in the plea discussions:

(1) a plea of guilty which was later withdrawn;

(2) a plea of nolo contendere;

(3) any statement made in the course of any proceedings under Rule 11 of the Federal Rules of Criminal Procedure or comparable state procedure regarding either of the foregoing pleas; or

(4) any statement made in the course of plea discussions with an attorney for the prosecuting authority which do not result in a plea of guilty or which result in a plea of guilty later withdrawn.

However, such a statement is admissible (i) in any proceeding wherein another statement made in the course of the same plea or plea discussions has been introduced and the statement ought in fairness be considered contemporaneously with it, or (ii) in a criminal proceeding for perjury or false statement if the statement was made by the defendant under oath, on the record and in the presence of counsel.[36]

The original version of the rule did not explicitly state that its protection extended only to offers and statements made in the course of negotiations between the accused and the United States Attorney or representative. As a consequence, some decisions held that efforts to make deals with a considerable variety of federal law enforcement officers were within the rule.[37] The rule accordingly was amended as stated above to make clear that only negotiations "with an attorney for the prosecuting authority" fall within its protection.[38]

While the rule permits use of statements made as part of plea negotiations for certain limited purposes, impeachment of the defendant's subsequent testimony is not one of those permissible purposes.[39]

35. Revised Uniform Rule (1986) 410 consists of only the first sentence of the original Federal Rule and reads as follows:

Evidence of a plea later withdrawn, of guilty, or admission of the charge, or nolo contendere, or of an offer so to plead to the crime charged or any other crime, or of statements made in connection with any of the foregoing withdrawn pleas or offers, is not admissible in any civil or criminal action, case, or proceeding against the person who made the plea or offer.

36. Fed.R.Crim.P. 11(e)(6) is to the same effect. See 1979 A.B.A. Standards for Criminal Justice § 14–2.2 (withdrawal of plea of guilty not admissible) & § 14–3.4 (discussion and agreement not admissible); Annot., 59 A.L.R.3d 441.

37. The cases are collected in United States v. Grant, 622 F.2d 308 (8th Cir. 1980).

38. United States v. Perez–Franco, 873 F.2d 455, 460–461 (1st Cir.1989) (statements made to probation officer for presentence report not barred under Rule 410 because not made to prosecuting attorney); United States v. Sebetich, 776 F.2d 412, 421–422 (3d Cir.1985), cert. denied 484 U.S. 1017 (statements by defendant to police chief not barred under rule since not made to attorney for government); United States v. Bernal, 719 F.2d 1475, 1478 (9th Cir. 1983) (statement to drug enforcement agent admissible under this rationale). See also United States v. Penta, 898 F.2d 815 (1st Cir.1990), cert. denied 111 S.Ct. 246 (analyzing what constitutes plea discussions and adopting extremely narrow view).

39. United States v. Lawson, 683 F.2d 688, 693 (2d Cir.1982) (citing legislative history); United States v. Wood, 879 F.2d 927, 936–937 (D.C.Cir.1989) (reaching same conclusion as to legislative history).

If the transaction on which the prosecution is based also gives rise to a civil cause of action, a compromise or offer of compromise of the civil claim should be privileged when offered at the criminal trial, assuming that no agreement to stifle the criminal prosecution is involved.[40]

§ 267. Admissions by Conduct: (g) Safety Measures After an Accident;[1] Payment of Medical Expenses

Remedial Measures. After an accident causing injury, the owner of the premises or the enterprise will often take remedial measures, such as repairing a defect or changing safety rules. Are these new safety measures, which might have prevented the injury, admissible to prove negligence as an implied acknowledgment by conduct that due care required that these measures should have been taken before the injury?[2] Particularly when the remedial measures follow the injury immediately, they may be very persuasive of the owner's belief as to the precautions required by due care before the accident. Nevertheless, courts occasionally broadly assert that the evidence is irrelevant for this purpose.[3] While such remedial changes permit varying explanations,[4] some of which are consistent with due care, the evidence would often meet the usual standards of relevancy if treated only as raising issues of the admissibility of circumstantial evidence and admission by conduct.[5]

The predominant reason for excluding such evidence, however, is not lack of probative significance, but rather a policy against discouraging the taking of safety measures.[6] At all events, courts do exclude

---

40. United States v. Hays, 872 F.2d 582, 588–589 (5th Cir.1989); Ecklund v. United States, 159 F.2d 81 (6th Cir.1947); Carter v. State, 161 Tenn. 698, 34 S.W.2d 208 (1931).

§ 267

1. 2 Wigmore, Evidence § 283 (Chadbourn rev. 1979); Fincham, Federal Rule of Evidence 407 and Its State Variations, 49 UMKC L.Rev. 338 (1981); Dec.Dig. Negligence ⊗131; Annots., 170 A.L.R. 7, 64 A.L.R.2d 1296, 50 A.L.R.Fed. 935.

2. Often such conduct should not be classified as hearsay because either the actor exhibited no intent to make an assertion or the statement is not offered to prove the truth of the matter asserted. Fed.R.Evid. 801(c). However, it does no harm to consider the conduct as an admission since the hearsay objection is satisfied regardless of whether the conduct is treated as nonhearsay or as an admission.

3. See, e.g., Columbia & Puget Sound R. Co. v. Hawthorne, 144 U.S. 202 (1892); Terre Haute & Indiana R. Co. v. Clem, 123 Ind. 15, 17, 23 N.E. 965, 966 (1890); Morse v. Minneapolis & St. Louis Ry. Co., 30 Minn. 465, 468–469, 16 N.W. 358, 359 (1883).

Also see Bramwell, B., in Hart v. Lancashire & Yorkshire Ry. Co., 21 L.T.R. 261, 263 (1869), denying that "because the world gets wiser it gets older, therefore it was foolish before."

4. See supra § 185.

5. See supra § 185.

6. See supra § 74. Compare the court's statement in Ashland Supply Co. v. Webb, 206 Ky. 184, 266 S.W. 1086 (1925): "There are two reasons why evidence of subsequent repair should not be admitted. One is that, while it may be necessary to subsequently repair the appliance, it does not follow from that the appliance was defective at the time of the accident. The other reason is that, if such evidence were admitted, it would have a tendency to cause employers to omit making needed repairs for fear that the precaution thus taken by them could be used as evidence against them."

The policy basis of the rule is attacked vigorously in Schwartz, The Exclusionary

evidence of remedial safety measures taken after an injury when offered as admissions of negligence or fault.[7] These include: repairs [8] and alterations in construction; [9] installation of new safety devices,[10] such as lights, gates, or guards; changes in rules and regulations [11] or the practice of the business; [12] or the discharge of an employee charged with causing the injury.[13] However, when the remedial measures are taken by a third person, the policy ground for exclusion is no longer present, and the tendency is to admit the evidence.[14]

The ingenuity of counsel in suggesting other purposes has made substantial inroads upon the general rule of exclusion.[15] Thus evidence of subsequent repairs or changes has been admitted as evidence of the defendant's ownership or control [16] of the premises or duty to repair [17]

Rule on Subsequent Repairs—A Rule in Need of Repair, 7 Forum 1 (1971); Comment, 31 Mercer L.Rev. 801 (1980). Maine Evidence Rule 407(a) explicitly allows such evidence to be admitted.

7. See Annot., 64 A.L.R.2d 896.

8. Kentucky & West Virginia Power Co. v. Stacy, 291 Ky. 325, 164 S.W.2d 537 (1942); Potter v. Dr. W.H. Groves Latter-Day Saints Hosp., 99 Utah 71, 103 P.2d 280 (1940).

9. Limbeck v. Interstate Power Co., 69 F.2d 249 (8th Cir.1934); Livingston v. Fuel, 245 Ark. 618, 433 S.W.2d 380 (1968).

10. Erickson's Dairy Products Co. v. Northwest Baker Ice Mach. Co., 165 Or. 553, 109 P.2d 53 (1941) (use of asbestos to protect wall against fire).

11. SEC v. Geon Industries, Inc., 531 F.2d 39, 52 (2d Cir.1976) (under Fed.R.Evid. 407); Ware v. Boston & Maine R.R., 92 N.H. 373, 31 A.2d 58 (1943). Distinguish rules in effect at the time of the occurrence, which are generally held admissible, though somewhat similar policy considerations are present. Young v. Illinois Cent. Gulf R. Co., 618 F.2d 332, 338–339 (5th Cir.1980); Winters, The Evidentiary Value of Defendant's Safety Rules in a Negligence Action, 38 Neb.L.Rev. 906 (1959); Annot., 50 A.L.R.2d 16.

12. Hatfield v. Levy Bros., 112 P.2d 277 (1941), reversed on other grounds 18 Cal.2d 798, 117 P.2d 841 (evidence that defendant company stopped waxing floor after accident).

13. Armour & Co. v. Skene, 153 Fed. 241 (1st Cir.1907) (discharge of driver one year after accident erroneously admitted but not prejudicial); Turner v. Hearst, 115 Cal. 394, 47 P. 129 (1896) (error to permit plaintiff to prove discharge of reporter in libel action since conduct "similar to proof of precaution taken after an accident"). See also Rynar v. Lincoln Transit Co., 129

N.J.L. 525, 30 A.2d 406 (Err. & App.1943); Engel v. United Traction Co., 203 N.Y. 321, 96 N.E. 731 (1911).

14. Farner v. Paccar, Inc., 562 F.2d 518 (8th Cir.1977) (under Fed.R.Evid. 407); Davis v. Fox River Tractor Co., 518 F.2d 481 (10th Cir.1975); Wallner v. Kitchens of Sara Lee, Inc., 419 F.2d 1028 (7th Cir.1969) (guards installed on machine by owner after accident, properly admitted against manufacturer); Brown v. Quick Mix Co., 75 Wash.2d 833, 454 P.2d 205 (1969) (same). The relevancy problem of course becomes more acute since the theory of an admission is not available. Moreover, since not a party admission, a serious hearsay problem arises if the conduct is regarded as hearsay. See supra § 250.

15. Norwood Clinic, Inc. v. Spann, 240 Ala. 427, 431, 199 So. 840, 843 (1941) ("if such evidence has a tendency to prove some other disputed issue," then evidence admissible); Annot., 64 A.L.R.2d 1296, 1305.

16. Powers v. J.B. Michael & Co., 329 F.2d 674 (6th Cir.1964), cert. denied 377 U.S. 980 (defendant-contractor's actions in subsequently putting out warning signs admissible to show control of that section of highway); Kuhn v. General Parking Corp., 98 Ill.App.3d 570, 54 Ill.Dec. 191, 424 N.E.2d 941 (1981) (defective floor); Dubonowski v. Howard Sav. Inst., 124 N.J.L. 368, 12 A.2d 384 (1941) (control by landlord of stairs); Scudero v. Campbell, 288 N.Y. 328, 43 N.E.2d 66 (1942) (similar).

17. Wallner v. Kitchens of Sara Lee, Inc., 419 F.2d 1028 (7th Cir.1969); Kuhn v. General Parking Corp., 98 Ill.App.3d 570, 54 Ill.Dec. 191, 424 N.E.2d 941 (1981) (repair of floor); Carleton v. Rockland, T. & C. Street Ry., 110 Me. 397, 86 A. 334 (1913) (repairs by street railway of steps leading from platform).

where these are disputed; as evidence of the possibility or feasibility of preventive measures, when properly in issue;[18] as evidence to explain that the situation at the time of accident was different where the jury has taken a view or where the opposing party has introduced a photograph of the scene;[19] as evidence of what was done later to show that the earlier condition as of the time of the accident was as plaintiff claims, if the defendant disputes this;[20] as evidence that the faulty condition later remedied was the cause of the injury by showing that after the change the injurious effect disappeared;[21] and as evidence contradicting facts testified to by the adversary's witness.[22]

18. Determining when feasibility is properly an issue has proved troublesome. If defendant claims the precaution was not feasible, the evidence is clearly admissible. See infra note 25. The nature of the accident as proven by plaintiff may raise a doubt whether preventive measures were practicable. Indianapolis & St. Louis R. Co. v. Horst, 93 U.S. 291, 295, 296 (1876); Boeing Airplane Co. v. Brown, 291 F.2d 310 (9th Cir.1961); Brown v. Quick Mix Co., 75 Wash.2d 833, 454 P.2d 205 (1969). Or the plaintiff may rely on a statute which is construed to make proof of feasibility a part of plaintiff's case. Rich v. Tite–Knot Pine Mill, 245 Or. 185, 421 P.2d 370 (1966). But even in these later cases the plaintiff might well be limited to other types of evidence, such as opinion or customary practices of such businesses, where these are available and sufficient. See Miniea v. St. Louis Cooperage Co., 175 Mo.App. 91, 110, 157 S.W. 1006, 1012 (1913); Blais v. Flanders Hardware Co., 93 N.H. 370, 374, 42 A.2d 332, 335 (1945) ("descriptive testimony could readily be given"). Unrestricted use of feasibility evidence would obviously eliminate the exclusionary rule in its entirety. See infra notes 24–29 and accompanying text.

19. Lunde v. National Citizens Bank, 213 Minn. 278, 6 N.W.2d 809 (1942) (view); Achey v. Marion, 126 Iowa 47, 101 N.W. 435 (1904) (to explain photograph introduced by defendant). But the plaintiff may not introduce a photograph of the altered scene merely for the purpose of showing the repairs in the guise of explanation. Gignoux v. St. Louis Public Service Co., 180 S.W.2d 784 (Mo.App.1944); Hadges v. New York Rapid Transit Corp., 259 App.Div. 154, 18 N.Y.S.2d 304 (1940).

20. Chicago v. Dalle, 115 Ill. 386, 5 N.E. 578 (1885) (injury due to alleged loose plank in sidewalk, evidence that sidewalk repaired at this place to show previous condition); Chicago Burlington & Quincy R. Co. v. Krayenbuhl, 65 Neb. 889, 911, 91 N.W. 880, 885 (1902) (agent's locking of turntable to show it was unlocked at time of injury to child); Eargle v. Sumpter Lighting Co., 110 S.C. 560, 96 S.E. 909 (1918) (defect in electrical appliances provable, where necessary, by evidence of later repairs). This doctrine, unless limited to cases where the condition is disputed and the proof by repairs is essential, can serve to rob the principal rule of practical effect. See e.g., City of Montgomery v. Quinn, 246 Ala. 154, 19 So.2d 529 (1944) (in action for death caused by falling of rotten limb of tree, act of city in immediately removing other dead limbs admitted to show condition).

21. Kentucky Utilities Co. v. White Star Coal Co., 244 Ky. 759, 52 S.W.2d 705 (1932) (proof that everything went well following a second fire, when a defective transformer was removed, admissible to show cause); Texas & New Orleans R. Co. v. Anderson, 61 S.W. 424 (Tex.Civ.App. 1901) (evidence of removal of obstruction in ditch and that thereafter flood water flowed away admitted to show obstruction cause of flooding).

22. American Airlines, Inc. v. United States, 418 F.2d 180 (5th Cir.1969) (evidence of change in instrument and in flight practices after accident to rebut claims of adequacy and nonfeasibility); Daggett v. Atchison, Topeka & Santa Fe Ry. Co., 48 Cal.2d 655, 313 P.2d 557 (1957) (evidence that flashing light was installed in place of wigwag signal after crossing accident to impeach testimony that wigwag was safest type); Runkle v. Burlington Northern, 188 Mont. 286, 613 P.2d 982 (1980) (error to exclude evidence of installation of flasher to impeach testimony that crossing was not extrahazardous).

Federal Rule 407,[23] which is in conformity with the foregoing discussion, provides as follows:

When, after an event, measures are taken which, if taken previously, would have made the event less likely to occur, evidence of the subsequent measures is not admissible to prove negligence or culpable conduct in connection with the event. This rule does not require the exclusion of evidence of subsequent measures when offered for another purpose, such as proving ownership, control or feasibility of precautionary measures, if controverted, or impeachment.

The encouragement of remedial measures, as has already been indicated, is the principal reason for the rule excluding evidence that such measures were taken. Liberal admission of remedial measure evidence for purposes other than as an admission of negligence seriously undercuts the basic policy of the rule. Hence Rule 407 specifically requires that, when the evidence is offered for another purpose, that purpose must be controverted.[24] Ownership, control, and feasibility of precautionary measures are mentioned as illustrations of other purposes. If the other purpose is not controverted, the evidence is inadmissible.[25] The fact that the other purpose is controverted should not be taken as a guarantee of admissibility; the possibility of misuse of the evidence as an admission of fault still requires a balancing of probative value and need against potential prejudice under Rule 403. The availability of other means of proof is an important factor in this balancing process.[26]

Of particular concern is the provision of the rule that permits evidence of remedial measures to be admitted for impeachment, an exception which, if applied expansively, could "swallow up" the rule.[27] At the same time, there will be situations where impeachment should be permitted. One example is when the statement of the witness constitutes, not simply a general denial of negligence,[28] but a statement that is directly contradicted by the remedial conduct.[29]

---

23. Revised Uniform Rule (1986) 407 is identical.

24. For an example of controverting feasibility, see Anderson v. Malloy, 700 F.2d 1208, 1214 (8th Cir.1983) (in action against motel owners for rape of guest, error to exclude evidence that defendants installed peepholes and chain locks on doors after event, when defendants testified that to have done so would have been "false security").

Nonrule cases have not insisted on a requirement that the other purpose be controverted. Boeing Airplane Co. v. Brown, 291 F.2d 310 (9th Cir.1961) (subsequent design change admissible though feasibility stipulated; nonjury case); doCanto v. Ametek, Inc., 367 Mass. 776, 328 N.E.2d 873 (1975) (general concession of practicability did not require exclusion of evidence of subsequent design changes to show feasibility).

25. Grenada Steel Industries v. Alabama Oxygen Co., 695 F.2d 883, 888–889 (5th Cir.1983) (evidence excluded where feasibility not disputed). See also Werner v. Upjohn Co., 628 F.2d 848, 854–855 (4th Cir.1980), cert. denied 449 U.S. 1080; Bauman v. Volkswagenwerk Aktiengesellschaft, 621 F.2d 230, 233 (6th Cir.1980).

26. See supra § 185.

27. Bickerstaff v. South Cent. Bell Telephone Co., 676 F.2d 163, 168 (5th Cir.1982).

28. Hardy v. Chemetron Corp., 870 F.2d 1007, 1011 (5th Cir.1989) (evidence of remedial measures "no more admissible to rebut a claim of non-negligence than it is to prove negligence directly").

29. Petree v. Victor Fluid Power, Inc., 887 F.2d 34, 40–42 (3d Cir.1989); Bickerstaff v. South Cent. Bell Telephone Co., 676 F.2d 163, 168–69 (5th Cir.1982); Dollar v. Long Mfg., N.C., Inc., 561 F.2d 613, 618–

In product liability cases, a trend away from the basic rule of exclusion of evidence of subsequent remedial measures was initiated by Ault v. International Harvester Co.[30] It has been suggested that the difference in result is warranted by the fact that negligence cases focus on the conduct of the defendant, while product liability cases focus on the nature of the product.[31] However, the true bases of the departure are probably a rejection of the assumption that admitting the evidence discourages remedial steps when the enterprise involved is a large manufacturer [32] and a general desire to spread the cost of injuries.[33] A number of courts have followed *Ault,* either as a matter of construing Rule 407 or as common law,[34] while others have rejected both its reasoning and its results.[35]

The admissibility of recall letters has been approached in somewhat similar vein, as the first step in the taking of remedial steps. The courts have divided on the question, those admitting the letters often taking the view that the action should not be protected since it is not likely to be deterred because undertaken under regulatory command and not voluntarily.[36]

Payment of medical expenses. Similar considerations of doubtful relevancy and of public policy underlie the generally accepted exclusion of evidence of payment or offers to pay medical and like expenses of an injured person. Federal Rule 409 [37] accordingly provides:

619 (5th Cir.1977), cert. denied 435 U.S. 996.

30. 13 Cal.3d 113, 117 Cal.Rptr. 812, 528 P.2d 1148 (1974).

31. Shaffer v. Honeywell, Inc., 249 N.W.2d 251, 257 n. 7 (S.D.1976).

32. Ault v. International Harvester Co., 13 Cal.3d 113, 120, 117 Cal.Rptr. 812, 815, 528 P.2d 1148, 1151 (1974).

33. Caprara v. Chrysler Corp., 52 N.Y.2d 114, 436 N.Y.S.2d 251, 417 N.E.2d 545 (1981).

34. Robbins v. Farmers Union Grain Terminal Ass'n, 552 F.2d 788 (8th Cir. 1977); Farner v. Paccar, Inc., 562 F.2d 518 (8th Cir.1977); Caterpillar Tractor Co. v. Beck, 624 P.2d 790 (Alaska 1981); Caprara v. Chrysler Corp., 52 N.Y.2d 114, 436 N.Y.S.2d 251, 417 N.E.2d 545 (1981); Shaffer v. Honeywell, Inc. 249 N.W.2d 251, 257 n. 7 (S.D.1976); Chart v. General Motors Corp., 80 Wis.2d 91, 258 N.W.2d 680 (1977); Annot., 50 A.L.R.Fed. 1001. See Krause v. American Aerolights, 307 Or. 52, 58–59 & n. 6, 762 P.2d 1011, 1015 & n. 6 (1988) (noting that most state courts addressing the issue have held the rule inapplicable but that the majority of federal circuits have reached the opposite conclusion).

35. See, e.g., Cann v. Ford Motor Co., 658 F.2d 54, 59–60 (2d Cir.1981), cert. de-

nied 456 U.S. 960; Knight v. Otis Elevator Co., 596 F.2d 84, 91 (3d Cir.1979); Werner v. Upjohn Co., 628 F.2d 848, 856 (4th Cir. 1980), cert. denied 449 U.S. 1080; Grenada Steel Industries, Inc. v. Alabama Oxygen Co., 695 F.2d 883, 886–888 (5th Cir.1983); Krause v. American Aerolights, Inc., 307 Or. 52, 762 P.2d 1011 (1988). See also DeLuryea v. Winthrop Laboratories, 697 F.2d 222, 228–231 (8th Cir.1983) (applying rule to products liability cases based on duty to warn).

36. Supporting admissibility: In re Aircrash in Bali, Indonesia, 871 F.2d 812, 816–817 (9th Cir.1989) (report did not constitute voluntary action), cert. denied 493 U.S. 917 (1989); Farner v. Paccar, Inc., 562 F.2d 518, 526–527 (8th Cir.1977) (recall compelled by law). See also Manieri v. Volkswagenwerk A.G., 151 N.J.Super. 422, 376 A.2d 1317 (App.Div.1977); Barry v. Manglass, 55 A.D.2d 1, 389 N.Y.S.2d 870 (1976); Fields v. Volkswagen of America, Inc., 555 P.2d 48 (Okl.1976). Excluding such measures: Vockie v. General Motors Corp., 66 F.R.D. 57 (E.D.Pa.1975), affirmed mem. 523 F.2d 1052 (3d Cir); Landry v. Adam, 282 So.2d 590 (La.App.1973). See Annot., 84 A.L.R.3d 1220.

37. Revised Uniform Rule (1986) 409 is identical.

Evidence of furnishing or offering or promising to pay medical, hospital, or similar expenses occasioned by an injury is not admissible to prove liability for the injury.

The rule is in general conformity with the run of common law decisions.[38]

Unlike compromise negotiations covered by Rule 408, where the discussion of issues is an essential part of the process and requires protection against disclosure, communications are incidental to the providing of care and hence are unprotected.[39]

38. Holguin v. Smith's Food King Properties, Inc., 105 N.M. 737, 741, 737 P.2d 96, 100 (App.1987); Hughes v. Anchor Enterprises, Inc., 245 N.C. 131, 136–138, 95 S.E.2d 577, 582–584 (1956); Annots., 20 A.L.R.2d 291, 65 A.L.R.3d 932.

39. Adv.Comm. Note, Fed.R.Evid. 409, 56 F.R.D. 183, 228. Compare Holguin v. Smith's Food King Properties, Inc., 105 N.M. 737, 741, 737 P.2d 96, 100 (App.1987) (statement on insurance form that company would "take full responsibility" was part of offer to pay medical bills and therefore inadmissible) with Port Neches Independent School Dist. v. Soignier, 702 S.W.2d 756, 757 (Tex.App.1986, error refused n.r.e.) (in addition to stating that all bills should be sent to employer's insurer, letter was admissible in going beyond rule's protection and acknowledging coverage of worker's compensation). See also Hughes v. Anchor Enterprises, Inc., 245 N.C. 131, 136–137, 95 S.E.2d 577, 582–583 (1956) (drawing general distinction between statements that are offers of assistance and those that go further to admit fault).

Evidence of payment may be used for purposes other than proving negligence, such as to show an employment relationship. Savoie v. Otto Candies, Inc., 692 F.2d 363, 370 n. 7 (5th Cir.1982).

Chapter 26

SPONTANEOUS STATEMENTS

Table of Sections

§ 268. Res Gestae and the Hearsay Rule [1]

The term *res gestae* seems to have come into common usage in discussions of admissibility of statements accompanying material acts or situations in the early 1800's.[2] At this time the theory of hearsay was not well developed, and the various exceptions to the hearsay rule were not clearly defined. In this context, the phrase *res gestae* served as a convenient vehicle for escape from the hearsay rule in two primary

§ 268

1. See generally 6 Wigmore, Evidence §§ 1745, 1767 (Chadbourn rev. 1976); Comment, 20 Baylor L.Rev. 229 (1968); 29 Am. Jur.2d Evidence §§ 708–737; C.J.S. Evidence §§ 403–421.

2. 6 Wigmore, Evidence § 1767 (Chadbourn rev. 1976).

situations. In the first, it was used to explain the admissibility of statements that were not hearsay at all.[3] In the second, it was used to justify the admissibility of statements which today come within the four exceptions discussed in this chapter: (1) statements of present sense impressions, (2) excited utterances, (3) statements of present bodily condition, and (4) statements of present mental states and emotions. Despite the increased sophistication of the hearsay rule and its exceptions today, however, courts still occasionally speak in terms of *res gestae*[4] rather than a more precise hearsay doctrine.

Initially the term *res gestae* was employed to denote words which accompanied the principal litigated fact, such as the murder, collision, or trespass, which was the subject of the legal action. However, usage developed to the point where the phrase seemed to embody the notion that evidence of any concededly relevant act or condition might also bring in the words which accompanied it. Two main policies or motives are discernible in this recognition of *res gestae* as a password for the admission of otherwise inadmissible evidence. One is a desire to permit each witness to tell his or her story in a natural way by telling all that happened at the time of the narrated incident, including those details that give life and color to the story. Events occur as a seamless web, and the naturalness with which the details fit together gives confirmation to the witness' entire account.[5] The other policy, emphasized by Wigmore and those following his leadership, is the recognition of spontaneity as the source of special trustworthiness. This quality of spontaneity characterizes to some degree nearly all the types of statements which have been labeled *res gestae*.

Commentators[6] and, with ever greater frequency, courts[7] have criticized use of the phrase *res gestae*. Its vagueness and imprecision are, of course, apparent. Moreover, traditional limitations on the doctrine, such as the requirement that it be used only in regard to the principal

---

3. See supra § 269.

4. See, e.g., Gross v. Greer, 773 F.2d 116, 119–120 (7th Cir.1985); State v. Galvan, 297 N.W.2d 344, 347 (Iowa 1980); Flanagin v. State, 473 So.2d 482, 486 (Miss. 1985).

5. "[T]he admissibility of the proofs as res gestae has as its justifying principle that truth, like the Master's robe, is of one piece, without seam, woven from the top throughout, that each fact has its inseparable attributes and its kindred facts materially affecting its character, and that the reproduction of a scene with its multiple incidents, each created naturally and without artificiality and not too distant in point of time, will by very quality and texture tend to disclose the truth." Robertson v. Hackensack Trust Co., 1 N.J. 304, 312, 63 A.2d 515, 519 (1949).

6. "The marvelous capacity of a Latin phrase to serve as a substitute for reasoning, and the confusion of thought inevita-

bly accompanying the use of inaccurate terminology, are nowhere better illustrated than in the decisions dealing with the admissibility of evidence as 'res gestae'." Morgan, A Suggested Classification of Utterances Admissible as Res Gestae, 31 Yale L.J. 229, 229 (1922). See also 6 Wigmore, Evidence § 1767 (Chadbourn rev. 1976).

7. See, e.g., Miller v. Keating, 754 F.2d 507, 509 & n. 1 (3d Cir.1985) ("old catchall, 'res gestae,' is no longer part of the law of evidence"); Hilyer v. Howat Concrete Co., 578 F.2d 422, 425–26 (D.C.Cir.1978); Cassidy v. State, 74 Md.App. 1, 15, 536 A.2d 666, 673 (1988), cert. denied 312 Md. 602, 541 A.2d 965 (term ambiguous and unmanageable in all its uses); State v. Williams, 673 S.W.2d 32, 34 (Mo.1984) (use of res gestae term discouraged since it lacks analytical precision).

litigated fact and the frequent insistence of concurrence (or at least a close relationship in time) between the words and the act or situation, have restricted its usefulness as a tool for avoiding unjustified application of the hearsay rule. Historically, however, the phrase served its purpose. Its very vagueness made it easier for courts to broaden its coverage and thus permit the admissibility of certain statements in new situations. However, the law has now reached a stage where expanding admissibility will be best accomplished by other means. The ancient phrase can well be jettisoned, with due acknowledgment that it served its era in the evolution of evidence law.

§ 269. Spontaneous Statements as Nonhearsay: Circumstantial Proof of a Fact in Issue [1]

The types of spontaneous statements discussed in this chapter are often treated by courts as hearsay, and thus to be admissible they must come within an exception to the general rule excluding hearsay. In many cases, however, this maneuver is unnecessary because the statements are not hearsay in the first place. As suggested in an earlier section,[2] hearsay is most appropriately defined as assertive statements or conduct offered to prove what is asserted. But many so-called spontaneous statements are in fact not assertive statements or, if assertive, are not offered to prove the truth of the assertions made. For example, it is clear that the statements, "I plan to spend the rest of my life here in New York" and "I have lost my affection for my husband" are hearsay, when offered to prove the plan to remain in New York or the loss of affection. On the other hand, statements such as "I have been happier in New York than in any other place," when offered to show the speaker's intent to remain in New York, and "My husband is a detestable wretch," offered to show lack of affection for the husband, will or will not be classed as hearsay, depending upon the position taken with respect to the long debated question whether "implied assertions" are to be classed as hearsay. That issue is discussed elsewhere.[3]

If the statement which is offered in evidence is not classed as hearsay, then no further consideration of the matters developed in this chapter is required.[4] If, however, it is classed as hearsay, then these matters may become pertinent to the question of admissibility. Nevertheless, the issue is often almost entirely academic, for statements offered to prove the declarant's state of mind, if relevant, are admissible either as an exception to the hearsay rule or as nonhearsay.[5]

§ 269

1. See generally 6 Wigmore, Evidence §§ 1715, 1766–1792 (Chadbourn rev. 1976).

2. See supra § 246.

3. See supra § 250.

4. Attention should then turn to the issue of relevance since the fact that a

statement is offered for a nonhearsay purpose does not automatically render it admissible. See, e.g., State v. Martin, 458 So.2d 454, 461 (La.1984).

5. See Santoni v. Moodie, 53 Md.App. 129, 149–151, 452 A.2d 1223, 1233–234 (1982) (only point that troubles legal scholars about the admissibility of declarations

§ 270. "Self–Serving" Aspects of Spontaneous Statements [1]

The notion that parties' out-of-court statements could not be evidence in their favor because of the "self-serving" nature of the statements seems to have originated with the now universally discarded rule forbidding parties to testify.[2] When this rule of disqualification for interest was abrogated by statute, any sweeping rule of inadmissibility regarding "self-serving" statements should have been regarded as abolished by implication. This, however, was often not the case.

The hearsay rule excludes all hearsay statements unless they fall within some exception to the rule. Thus, no specific rule is necessary to exclude self-serving out-of-court statements if not within a hearsay exception.[3] If a statement with a self-serving aspect falls within an exception to the hearsay rule, the judgment underlying the exception that the assurances of trustworthiness outweigh the dangers inherent in hearsay should be taken as controlling, and the declaration should be admitted despite its self-serving aspects.

Historically, most courts agreed that this was the proper approach when the self-serving statement fell within one of the well-established exceptions, such as the exclusion of business records, excited utterances, and spontaneous statements of present bodily sensations or symptoms. However, with regard to the somewhat more recently developed exceptions, such as statements of present state of mind or emotion, there was less agreement. Some courts applied a purported general rule of exclusion of self-serving statements in this area.[4] Others rejected any blanket rule of exclusion, although the self-serving aspects of the declaration were taken into account in applying a requirement that the statements must have been made under circumstances of apparent sincerity.[5]

The Federal Rules covering hearsay exceptions for spontaneous statements, discussed in the remaining sections of this chapter, make no

showing state of mind is whether they are classed as nonhearsay or hearsay that is admissible under the state of mind exception, a distinction often dependent on an accident of phrasing).

§ 270

1. See generally 6 Wigmore, Evidence § 1732 (Chadbourn rev. 1976); Comment, 61 Mich.L.Rev. 1306 (1963), 14 Ark.L.Rev. 105 (1959); 29 Am.Jur.2nd Evidence §§ 621–622; C.J.S. Evidence § 216; Dec. Dig. Evidence ⬤271, Criminal Law ⬤413.

2. See Phipson, Evidence ¶¶ 33–51 to – 52 (Buzzard 13th ed. 1982). The rule forbidding parties to testify is discussed in supra § 65.

3. State v. Price, 301 N.C. 437, 450, 272 S.E.2d 103, 112 (1980); Commonwealth v. Murphy, 493 Pa. 35, 42–43, 425 A.2d 352, 356 (1981). Some courts, however, contin-

ue to treat the matter in terms of a rule excluding self-serving statements. Dickey v. State, 240 Ga. 634, 641–642, 242 S.E.2d 55, 61 (1978); Marts v. State, 432 N.E.2d 18, 24 (Ind.1982).

4. People v. Smith, 15 Cal.2d 604, 104 P.2d 510 (1940) (letters of defendant to his wife not admissible to prove affection in prosecution for her murder); State v. Barnett, 156 Kan. 746, 137 P.2d 133 (1943) (statement of defendant tending to show fear not admissible).

5. E.g., United States v. Matot, 146 F.2d 197 (2d Cir.1944); Lee v. Mitcham, 98 F.2d 298 (D.C.Cir.1938); Kelly v. Bank of America, Nat. Trust Sav. Ass'n, 112 Cal.App.2d 388, 246 P.2d 92 (1952); Caplan v. Caplan, 83 N.H. 318, 142 A. 121 (1928).

special provision for self-serving statements.[6] What is clear, however, is that since spontaneity is the principal, and often the only, guarantee of trustworthiness for the exceptions in this chapter, its absence should result in exclusion of the statement. Circumstances indicating a lack of spontaneity, which may be related to the self-serving character of the statement, are accordingly extremely important to the determination of admissibility.[7]

While some issues can be determined by reference to spontaneity, a very difficult issue remains: may courts properly exclude statements because of judicial doubts about the sincerity of the declarant as evidenced by the self-serving nature of the statement? There is no theoretical impediment to judicial consideration of credibility in determining an issue of preliminary-fact-finding of the type involved in admitting or excluding hearsay. The chief problem with this approach under hearsay rules modeled on the Federal Rules is one of legislative intent. The rules give no authorization to such considerations,[8] and indeed their omission of a requirement found in the original Uniform Rule that the statement must not be made in "bad faith" strongly indicates a contrary legislative intent.[9] Moreover, in some other exceptions, the self-serving character of a statement, appearing in the form of motive to falsify, is specified as a ground for exclusion.[10]

A somewhat more comfortable place for the general exercise of such judicial judgment is under the balancing of probativity and prejudice authorized by Rule 403, although this home is hardly secure since neither the rule itself nor its history gives explicit authorization. Nevertheless, in exercising discretion to exclude evidence where the

---

6. The Revised Uniform Rules (1986) similarly have no special provision for excluding self-serving statements.

7. See 4 Weinstein & Berger, Weinstein's Evidence ¶ 803(3)[01], at 105 (1990) ("Since contemporaneity is the guarantee of trustworthiness, statements indicative of reflection rather than spontaneity are excluded."); United States v. Faust, 850 F.2d 575, 585–586 (9th Cir.1988) (draft of letter expressing state of mind regarding coercion at time of illegal acts excluded because contemporaneousness disputed and opportunity for reflection rendered letter unreliable).

8. For example, statements by a party of physical condition made after litigation has begun are, and should be, routinely admissible under Rule 803(3) in spite of the fact that self interest could hardly be clearer. The text of Rule 803(3) suggests no basis for distinguishing between contemporaneous statements of physical condition and those of state of mind, where courts have historically shown the greatest willingness to exclude statements based on questions about motivation.

9. 4 Weinstein & Berger, Weinstein's Evidence ¶ 803(3)[01], at 106 (1990) (noting

that the Federal Rules Advisory Committee, in recognition of the jury's decisive role in determining credibility, decided to eliminate this aspect of the Uniform Rule 63(12)(a) from Federal Rule 803(3)). See also United States v. Lawal, 736 F.2d 5, 8 (2d Cir.1984) ("relevant declarations which fall within the parameters of Rule 803(3) are *categorically* admissible, even if they are self-serving and made under circumstances which undermine their trustworthiness. The truth or falsity of such declarations is for the jury to determine, and their 'self-serving nature' goes only to their weight."); Advisory Committee Introductory Note: The Hearsay Problem, 56 F.R.D. 183, 290 ("For a judge to exclude evidence because he does not believe it has been described as 'altogether atypical, extraordinary,' " (quoting Chadbourn, Bentham and the Hearsay Rule—A Benthamic View of Rule 63(4)(c) of the Uniform Rules of Evidence, 75 Harv.L.Rev. 932, 947 (1962))). See also infra § 274, note 7.

10. E.g., accident reports, infra § 288, and police reports, infra § 296.

danger of prejudice, confusing the issues, misleading the jury, or wasting time outweighs its probative value, circumstantial or direct evidence revealing a self-serving motive should logically have a place.[11] Rarely, however, should statements of substantial importance to the case be excluded even under this rule based upon judicial doubts about the declarant's motivation. Under the structure of the Federal Rules, judgments about credibility should generally be left to the jury rather than preempted by a judicial determination of inadmissibility. This is particularly true when the credibility issue can be readily appreciated by the jury, as is generally the case when the reason to question credibility rests upon the declarant's self-serving motivation.

§ 271. Unexcited Statements of Present Sense Impressions [1]

Although Wigmore's creative work did much to clarify the murky concept of *res gestae*, his analysis of spontaneous declarations may have led to one unfortunate restricting development of this exception. Professor Thayer, reviewing the *res gestae* cases in 1881,[2] concluded that this was an exception based on the contemporaneousness of statements. He read the law as creating an exception for statements "made by those present when a thing took place, made about it and importing what is present at the very time." [3] Wigmore, however, saw as the basis for the spontaneous exclamation exception, not the contemporaneousness of the exclamation, but rather the nervous excitement produced by the exposure of the declarant to an exciting event.[4] As a result, the American law of spontaneous statements shifted in its emphasis from what Thayer had observed to an exception based on the requirement of an exciting event and the resulting stifling of the declarant's reflective faculties.[5] This, as Professor Morgan noted, was unfortunate.[6] Given the danger of unreliability caused by the very emotional impact required for excited utterances, it makes little sense to admit them while excluding other out-of-court statements that may have equal assurances of reliability and lack the inherent defects of excited utterances.[7]

11. 4 Weinstein & Berger, Weinstein's Evidence ¶ 803(3)[04], at 121 (1990); 4 Louisell & Mueller, Federal Evidence § 441, at 538–39; § 442, at 551–53 (1980). See generally supra § 185.

§ 271

1. See generally Waltz, The Present Sense Impression Exception to the Rule Against Hearsay: Origins and Attributes, 66 Iowa L.Rev. 869 (1981); Morgan, Res Gestae, 12 Wash.L.Rev. 91 (1937); Hutchins & Slesinger, Some Observations on the Law of Evidence, 28 Colum.L.Rev. 432, 439–40 (1928); Morgan, A Suggested Classification of Utterances Admissible as Res Gestae, 31 Yale L.J. 229, 236–38 (1922); Note, Spontaneous Exclamations in the Absence of a Startling Event, 46 Colum.L.Rev. 430 (1946); Annot., 60 A.L.R.Fed. 524, 140 A.L.R. 874.

2. Thayer, Bedingfield's Case—Declarations as a Part of the Res Gesta, 15 Am. L.Rev. 1 (1881).

3. Id. at 83.

4. 6 Wigmore, Evidence § 1747 (Chadbourn rev. 1976). Compare Morgan, Res Gestae, 12 Wash.L.Rev. 91, 98 (1937).

5. Morgan, supra, 12 Wash.L.Rev. at 96.

6. Id.

7. Morgan, A Suggested Classification of Utterances Admissible as Res Gestae, 31 Yale L.J. 229, 236 (1922).

Under Morgan's leadership, arguments were made for restoring Thayer's view of the law by recognizing another exception to the hearsay rule for statements concerning nonexciting events that the declarant was observing while making the declaration. Although these statements lack whatever assurance of reliability is produced by the effect of an exciting event, other factors offer safeguards. First, since the report concerns observations being made at the time of the statement, it is safe from any error caused by a defect of the declarant's memory. Second, a requirement that the statement be made contemporaneously with the observation means that there will be little or no time for calculated misstatement. Third, the statement will usually have been made to a third person (the witness who subsequently testifies to it), who was also present at the time and scene of the observation. Thus, the witness in most cases will have observed the situation and thus can provide a check on the accuracy of the declarant's statement and furnish corroboration.[8] Moreover, since the declarant will often be available for cross-examination, his or her credibility will be subject to substantial verification before the trier of fact.

The courts generally did not rush to the support of the proposed exception for unexcited statements of present sense impressions. A considerable number continued to admit contemporaneous statements under *res gestae* language without emphasis on the presence or absence of an exciting event.[9] In a large proportion of these decisions, an arguably exciting event was present. However, cases recognizing the exception for unexcited statements of present sense impressions began to emerge. The case most commonly cited to illustrate judicial recognition of the exception is Houston Oxygen Co. v. Davis.[10] Although an apparently exciting event transpired, the opinion disclaimed reliance

---

8. For discussion of corroboration as a suggested requirement for admission, see infra text accompanying notes 22–25.

9. Kelly v. Hanwick, 228 Ala. 336, 153 So. 269 (1934) (bystander's statement when he saw speeding automobile that it could not make the curve held admissible); Moreno v. Hawbaker, 157 Cal.App.2d 627, 321 P.2d 538 (1958) (testimony of witness that when he saw two motorcycles proceeding at a high rate of speed and without lights he said, "look at those fools go," admissible as a spontaneous utterance); Sellers v. Montana–Dakota Power Co., 99 Mont. 39, 41 P.2d 44 (1935) (statements by persons in burning building that the smell of the smoke indicated that the fire came from gas held admissible); Hornschuch v. Southern Pacific Co., 101 Or. 280, 203 P. 886 (1921) (testimony that bystander called to those in automobile to stop held admissible); Marks v. I.M. Pearlstine & Sons, 203 S.C. 318, 26 S.E.2d 835 (1943) (statement by one watching trucks racing that the "trucks are going to kill someone" held admissible). Contra: Wrage v. King, 114

Kan. 539, 220 P. 259 (1923); Ideal Cement Co. v. Killingsworth, 198 So.2d 248 (Miss. 1967); Barnett v. Bull, 141 Wash. 139, 250 P. 955 (1926). See generally Note, 46 Colum.L.Rev. 430 (1946).

10. 139 Tex. 1, 161 S.W.2d 474 (Com. App.1942). In that case, the Texas Supreme Court held admissible a statement that, when the plaintiff's car passed declarant about four miles before the accident, she had said that "they must have been drunk, that we would find them somewhere on the road wrecked if they kept that rate of speed up." Id. at 5–6, 161 S.W.2d at 476. The court concluded that it "is sufficiently spontaneous to save it from the suspicion of being manufactured evidence. There was no time for a calculated statement." Id. at 6, 161 S.W.2d at 476. See also Anderson v. State, 454 S.W.2d 740 (Tex.Cr.App.1970) (statement admissible where neighbor said, "Seems like there is a car being stripped down the street there"). It is, of course, arguable that an exciting event was in fact present in these cases.

upon it and instead expressly based its decision upon the exception for unexcited declarations of present sense impressions. A more compelling case on its facts, decided in the same year, is Tampa Electric Co. v. Getrost.[11] Judicial acceptance gradually gained momentum.[12] The relative infrequence of such cases results from the fact that unexciting events do not often give rise to statements that later become relevant in litigation.[13]

The principal impetus for recognition of the hearsay exception for unexcited statements of present sense impressions came through the rulemaking process. The Model Code of Evidence [14] and the original Uniform Rules [15] included such an exception. Federal Rule 803(1) provides a hearsay exception, without regard to the availability of the declarant, for "a statement describing or explaining an event or condition made while the declarant was perceiving the event or condition, or immediately thereafter." [16]

In addition to the absence of any requirement of an exciting event, the hearsay exception for statements of present sense impressions differs from the exception for excited utterances in two other significant respects. First, while excited utterances "relating to" [17] the startling event or condition are admissible, present sense impressions are limited to "describing or explaining" the event or condition perceived.[18]

11. 151 Fla. 558, 10 So.2d 83 (1942) (in action for wrongful death of lineman by electrocution, statement of fellow lineman that deceased had returned from nearby house and said he had telephoned central station to deactivate line that they were repairing).

12. State v. Flesher, 286 N.W.2d 215 (Iowa 1979) (husband of murder victim properly permitted to testify that he had a telephone conversation with her shortly before her death, that he heard a knock, that she left the phone, returned, and said, "It's Joan [the accused]"); State v. Cawthorne, 290 N.C. 639, 227 S.E.2d 528 (1976) (in prosecution for murder of cab driver, proper to admit testimony of dispatcher that victim radioed that he had two fares for particular address); Hall v. DeSaussure, 41 Tenn.App. 572, 297 S.W.2d 81 (1956), cert. denied 201 Tenn. 164, 297 S.W.2d 90 (in medical malpractice case, error to exclude testimony offered by plaintiff that another doctor on examining X-ray taken nine months after the operation said, "He certainly did take a big chunk out of your spine"). See also Commonwealth v. Coleman, 458 Pa. 112, 326 A.2d 387 (1974) (testimony of witness that prospective murder victim said over telephone that defendant would not let her leave apartment, that he would hang up phone, and that he was going to kill her, admissible as present sense impression; concurring judge believed better classed as excited utterance).

13. One class of cases where the statement has utility is those involving statements describing what appear to be ordinary events later shown to be of substantial significance. See, e.g., Booth v. State, 306 Md. 313, 316, 508 A.2d 976, 977 (1986) (in murder prosecution, apparently inconsequential statement in telephone call by individual subsequently murdered that girlfriend was then "talking to 'some guy' behind the door").

14. Model Code of Evidence Rule 512(a) (1942).

15. Unif.R.Evid. 64(4)(a), (b) (1953).

16. Revised Uniform Rule (1986) 803(1) is identical.

17. See infra § 272 text accompanying notes 32–34.

18. For interesting uses of the "describing" or "explaining" requirement, see United States v. Andrews, 765 F.2d 1491, 1501 (11th Cir.1985), cert. denied 474 U.S. 1064 (tape recording of events declarant was seeing as he looked through window of defendant's home); United States v. Obayagbona, 627 F.Supp. 329, 339–340 (E.D.N.Y.1985) (undercover agent's tape recording of events of drug transfer recorded 15 minutes after event and 2½ minutes after defendant's arrest); United States v. Abell, 586 F.Supp. 1414, 1425 (D.Me.1984) (translation of statement from Spanish to English).

This more restrictive limitation is consistent with the theory underlying the present sense impression exception. Although fabrication and forgetfulness are precluded by the absence of time lapse between perception and utterance, the absence of a startling event makes the assumption of spontaneity difficult to maintain unless the statements immediately pertain to that perception.[19] Second, while the time within which an excited utterance may be made is measured by the duration of the stress caused by the exciting event,[20] the present sense impression statement may be made only while the declarant was actually "perceiving" the event or "immediately thereafter." [21] This shortened period is also consistent with the theory of the present sense impression exception. While principle might seem to call for a limitation to exact contemporaneity, some allowance must be made for the time needed for translating observation into speech. Thus, the appropriate inquiry is whether sufficient time elapsed to have permitted reflective thought.

The suggestion has been made that corroboration by an "equally percipient" witness should be a further requirement for admitting statements of present sense impression into evidence.[22] The proposal represents a significant departure from the general pattern of exceptions to the hearsay rule. The only instance in which a requirement of corroboration is found is where a statement against penal interest by a third person—a third-party confession—is offered by way of exculpation of an accused person. There, the common law had a firmly established position against admission. In order to increase the acceptability of a

---

19. Adv.Comm. Note, Fed.R.Evid. 803(1) & (2), 56 F.R.D. 183, 305 (describing "subject matter").

20. See infra § 272 text accompanying notes 18–23.

21. For statement of rule, see supra text accompanying note 16.

In the following cases the time requirement for present sense impressions was held to have been satisfied: United States v. Peacock, 654 F.2d 339, 350 (5th Cir. 1981), vacated in part on another issue on rehearing 686 F.2d 356, cert. denied 464 U.S. 965 (comments made by deceased husband of witness as to contents of telephone conversation with defendant immediately following conversation); United States v. Blakey, 607 F.2d 779, 60 A.L.R.Fed. 509 (7th Cir.1979) (statement by decedent to witnesses indicating payment of bribe to police officer defendants in adjoining room, spoken between several and 23 minutes after officers departed); United States v. Earley, 657 F.2d 195 (8th Cir.1981) (statement by murder victim immediately after hanging up telephone, expressing concern and saying voice sounded like defendant). Some cases have appeared to stretch the allowable time limits too far, generally in

contexts that suggest an exciting event. See Fratzke v. Meyer, 398 N.W.2d 200, 205 (Iowa App.1986) (15 to 20 minutes); State v. Odom, 316 N.C. 306, 313, 341 S.E.2d 332, 335–336 (1986) (10 minutes after incident); Harris v. State, 736 S.W.2d 166, 167 (Tex. App.1987) (30 minutes to an hour).

In these cases, the period was found to be too long: United States v. Cain, 587 F.2d 678 (5th Cir.1979), cert. denied 440 U.S. 975 (CB transmission received by state trooper, reporting seeing men answering description of defendants leaving stolen truck, made when they were some 5 miles from the truck, apparently by foot travel); Hilyer v. Howat Concrete Co., 578 F.2d 422 (D.C.Cir.1978) (lapse of not less than 15 minutes between accidental death of co-worker and statement held to bar present sense impression, but statement admissible as excited utterance).

22. Waltz, The Present Sense Impression Exception to the Rule Against Hearsay: Origins and Attributes, 66 Iowa L.Rev. 869, 883 (1981); Foster, Present Sense Impressions: An Analysis and a Proposal, 10 Loy.U.Chi.L.J. 299 (1979). Compare Note, 56 Tex.L.Rev. 1053 (1978).

reversal of this position, the Advisory Committee incorporated into Federal Rule 804(b)(3) a requirement that the hearsay statement must be corroborated.[23] The present sense impression exception presents no such need. Its underlying rationale offers sufficient assurances of reliability without the additional requirement of corroboration, and neither the Federal Rule [24] nor the decisions have required it.[25]

It is true that the limitation of the exception in terms of time and subject matter usually insures that the witness who reports the making of the statement will have perceived the event or at least observed circumstances strongly suggesting it. This aspect has been mentioned by the writers as an added assurance of accuracy, but a justification for admission is not the same as a requirement for admission. The matter is better left for consideration by the judge or jury as an aspect of weight and sufficiency of the evidence, rather than becoming a needlessly complicating requirement for admissibility.

§ 272. Excited Utterances [1]

While historically often lumped together with the amalgam of concepts under the term *res gestae*,[2] an exception to the hearsay rule for statements made under the influence of a startling event is now universally recognized.[3] Formulations of the exception differ, but all

---

23. See infra § 318.

24. The rules by their terms impose no requirement regarding corroboration, and the Advisory Committee Note and legislative history are silent regarding any such requirement. It is difficult to interpret such silence to impose any such requirement since corroboration was not part of the pre-rules formulation of this exception. Moreover, with regard to statements against interest, when Congress wished to impose such a requirement, and with regard to habit evidence, when the Advisory Committee wanted to eliminate a common law requirement of corroboration, it made its intention clear. See Fed.R.Evid. 406 (evidence of habit relevant for certain purposes "whether corroborated or not").

25. Booth v. State, 306 Md. 313, 329, 508 A.2d 976, 983–984 (1986); People v. Luke, 136 Misc.2d 733, 736–738, 519 N.Y.S.2d 316, 318–319 (1987), order affirmed 147 A.D.2d 989, 538 N.Y.S.2d 886, appeal denied 74 N.Y.2d 663, 543 N.Y.S.2d 406, 541 N.E.2d 435; Waltz, supra, note 22, at 889. But see In re Japanese Electronic Products Antitrust Litigation, 723 F.2d 238, 303 (3d Cir.1983), reversed on other grounds sub nom. Matsushita Elec. Indus. Co., Ltd. v. Zenith Radio Corp., 475 U.S. 574 (1986).

Similarly, Revised Uniform Rule (1986) 803(1) does not impose such a requirement.

§ 272

1. See generally 6 Wigmore, Evidence §§ 1745–64 (Chadbourn rev. 1976); Stewart, Perception, Memory, and Hearsay: A Criticism of Present Law and the Proposed Federal Rules of Evidence, 1970 Utah L.Rev. 1; Slough, Spontaneous Statements and State of Mind, 46 Iowa L.Rev. 224 (1961); Hutchins & Slesinger, Spontaneous Exclamations, 28 Colum.L.Rev. 432 (1928); Notes, 15 Wayne L.Rev. 1077 (1969), 29 La.L.Rev. 661 (1969), 45 Cornell L.Q. 810 (1960), 54 Mich.L.Rev. 133 (1955); Annots., 13 A.L.R.3d 1114, 80 A.L.R.3d 369, 4 A.L.R.3d 149, 74 A.L.R.3d 963, 78 A.L.R.2d 300, 56 A.L.R.2d 372, 53 A.L.R.2d 1245, 163 A.L.R. 15, 48 A.L.R.Fed. 451; 29 Am.Jur.2d Evidence §§ 708–737; C.J.S. Evidence §§ 403–421; Dec.Dig. Evidence ⚖118–128½, Criminal Law ⚖363, 366, 368.

2. See supra § 268. 6 Wigmore, Evidence § 1745 (Chadbourn rev. 1976) (use of term, which also included verbal act concept, to apply to excited utterances produced much confusion).

3. Federal and Revised Uniform (1986) Rule 803(2) define an exception for an "excited utterance," which imposes no unavailability requirement, as follows:

A statement relating to a startling event or condition made while the de-

agree on two basic requirements. First, there must be an occurrence or event sufficiently startling to render inoperative the normal reflective thought processes of the observer. Second, the statement of the declarant must have been a spontaneous reaction to the occurrence or event and not the result of reflective thought. Although additional requirements will be discussed subsequently, these two elements constitute the essence of the exception.

The rationale for the exception lies in the special reliability that is furnished when excitement suspends the declarant's powers of reflection and fabrication.[4] This factor also serves to justify dispensing with any requirement that the declarant be unavailable because it suggests that testimony on the stand, given at a time when the powers of reflection and fabrication are operative, is no more (and perhaps less) reliable than the out-of-court statement.[5]

The entire basis for the exception is, of course, subject to question. While psychologists would probably concede that excitement minimizes the possibility of reflective self-interest influencing the declarant's statements, they have questioned whether this might be outweighed by the distorting effect of shock and excitement upon the declarant's observation and judgement.[6] Despite these questions concerning its justification, however, the exception is well established.

The sufficiency of the event or occurrence itself to qualify under this exception is seldom questioned. Physical violence, though often

clarant was under the stress of excitement caused by the event or condition.

4. See generally 6 Wigmore, Evidence § 1747 (Chadbourn rev. 1976). The hearsay exception entails no denial of confrontation rights as a "firmly rooted" hearsay exception, at least when the declarant is unavailable. See, e.g., Puleio v. Vose, 830 F.2d 1197, 1204–206 (1st Cir.1987), cert. denied 485 U.S. 990; Martinez v. Sullivan, 881 F.2d 921, 928 (10th Cir.1989), cert. denied 493 U.S. 1029.

5. See Gross v. Greer, 773 F.2d 116, 120 (7th Cir.1985) (emphasizing limited memory and probable confusion that would be caused by cross-examination of 4–year old child, making the out-of-court statement probably the most reliable and trustworthy account of the events); Mobile & Montgomery R. Co. v. Ashcraft, 48 Ala. 15, 31 (1872) ("We regard these declarations as * * * more convincing * * * than the testimony to that effect of the persons themselves some time after the occurrence.").

6. One need not be a psychologist to distrust an observation made under emotional stress; everybody accepts such statements with mental reservation * * *. Fiore tells of an emotionally upset man who testified that hundreds were killed in

an accident; that he had seen their heads rolling from their bodies. In reality only one man was killed, and five others injured. Another excited gentleman took a pipe for a pistol. Besides these stories from real life, there are psychological experiments which point to the same conclusion. After a battle in a classroom, prearranged by the experimenter but a surprise to the students, each one was asked to write an account of the incident. The testimony of the most upset students was practically worthless, while those who were only slightly stimulated emotionally scored better than those left cold by the accident.

Hutchins & Slesinger, Spontaneous Exclamations, 28 Colum.L.Rev. 432, 437 (1928). See also Stewart, Perception, Memory, and Hearsay: A Criticism of Present Law and the Proposed Federal Rules of Evidence, 1970 Utah L.Rev. 1, 27.

While viewed as of less importance than the reduction of conscious fabrication as a justification, the trustworthiness of statements under the exception is also enhanced because there is little danger of lapse of memory since the stimuli was recently perceived. 4 Louisell & Mueller, Federal Evidence § 439, at 492 (1980).

present, is not required. An automobile accident,[7] pain or an injury,[8] an attack by a dog,[9] a fight,[10] or even seeing a photograph in a newspaper[11] all may qualify. The courts look primarily to the effect upon the declarant, and, if satisfied that the event was such as to cause adequate excitement, the inquiry is ended.

A somewhat more serious issue is raised by the occasional requirement of proving the exciting event by some proof other than the statement itself. Under generally prevailing practice, the statement itself is taken as sufficient proof of the exciting event, and therefore the statement is admissible despite absence of other proof that an exciting event occurred.[12] Some courts, however, have taken the position that an excited utterance is admissible only if other proof is presented which supports a finding of fact that the exciting event did occur.[13] The issue has not yet been definitively resolved under the Federal Rules.[14] Fortunately, only a very few cases need actually confront this knotty theoretical problem if the courts view the independent evidence concept

7. McCurdy v. Greyhound Corp., 346 F.2d 224 (3d Cir.1965).

8. Arkansas Louisiana Gas Co. v. Evans, 397 P.2d 505 (Okl.1964) (pain in chest running into arms).

9. Johnston v. Ohls, 76 Wash.2d 398, 457 P.2d 194 (1969).

10. Martin v. Estrella, 107 R.I. 247, 266 A.2d 41 (1970).

11. United States v. Napier, 518 F.2d 316 (9th Cir.1975), cert. denied 423 U.S. 895 (exclamation by victim of kidnapping and severe assault with "great distress and horror" on seeing newspaper photograph of defendant, "He killed me"). See also United States v. Bailey, 834 F.2d 218, 228 (1st Cir.1987) (bribe offer to juror by neighbor); United States v. Moore, 791 F.2d 566, 570–571 (7th Cir.1986) (secretary finding bid sheet, which was evidence of bid rigging, in boss' waste basket); State v. Buschkopf, 373 N.W.2d 756, 771 (Minn.1985) ("unsettling" phone call).

12. See, e.g., Stewart v. Baltimore & Ohio R. Co., 137 F.2d 527 (2d Cir.1943); United States v. Moore, 791 F.2d 566, 571 (7th Cir.1986) (dicta); Industrial Com'n v. Diveley, 88 Colo. 190, 294 P. 532 (1930); Johnston v. W. S. Nott Co., 183 Minn. 309, 236 N.W. 466 (1931); State v. Smith, 358 S.E.2d 188, 194–95 (W.Va.1987) (dicta); Collins v. Equitable Life Ins. Co., 122 W.Va. 171, 8 S.E.2d 825 (1940). See also supra § 53 (pointing out that the rules of evidence do not generally apply to preliminary fact questions of admissibility); Bourjaily v. United States, 483 U.S. 171, 178 (1987) (in determining whether a conspiracy exists to permit admission of a co-

conspirator's statement, the putative hearsay statement itself may be considered, although the Court did not determine whether such statement alone could establish the existence of the conspiracy); 4 Weinstein & Berger, Weinstein's Evidence ¶ 803(2)[01], at 88 (1990).

13. People v. Burton, 433 Mich. 268, 445 N.W.2d 133 (1989) (questioning whether in fact generally prevailing practice is to admit statements without corroboration of exciting event and holding that absent some independent evidence of the startling event, either direct or circumstantial, the statement may not be admitted); Truck Ins. Exchange v. Michling, 364 S.W.2d 172 (Tex.1963) (excluding in workmen's compensation case statement to spouse that he had struck his head when the bulldozer he had been driving had slipped off a hill since there was no evidence of the exciting event other than the assertion in the statement itself). See also Hartford Accident and Indem. Co. v. Hale, 400 S.W.2d 310 (Tex.1966).

14. The Supreme Court in Bourjaily v. United States, 483 U.S. 171, 183 (1987) reserved consideration of whether alleged co-conspirator statements could alone establish the existence of the conspiracy and its membership. The Advisory Committee Note to this rule, which describes an increasing trend to treat the statement itself as sufficient and notes that hearsay may be considered in making a preliminary fact determination under Rule 104(a), would appear to provide implicit support for a liberal construction here. See 56 F.R.D. 183, 305.

broadly, as they should where the circumstances and content of the statement indicate trustworthiness.[15]

The question most frequently raised when a purported excited utterance is offered involves the second requirement. In all cases, the ultimate question is whether the statement was the result of reflective thought or whether it was rather a spontaneous reaction to the exciting event. Initially, it is necessary that the declarant be affected by the exciting event. The declarant need not actually be involved in the event; an excited utterance by a bystander is admissible.[16] However, if the identity of the bystander-declarant is undisclosed, the courts have been reluctant to admit such statements, principally because of uncertainty that a foundation requirement has been satisfied, such as the impact of the event on the declarant.[17]

Probably the most important of the many factors entering into this determination is the temporal element. If the statement occurs while the exciting event is still in progress, courts have little difficulty finding that the excitement prompted the statement.[18] But as the time between the event and the statement increases, courts become more reluctant to find the statement an excited utterance. However, passage of time viewed in isolation is not an entirely accurate indicator of admissibility. For example, while courts have held statements made twelve or more hours after a physical beating to be the product of the excitement caused by the beating,[19] other courts have held statements made within minutes of the event not admissible.[20]

A useful rule of thumb is that where the time interval between the event and the statement is long enough to permit reflective thought,

15. See 4 Louisell & Mueller, Federal Evidence § 439, at 509–10 (1980).

16. People v. Caviness, 38 N.Y.2d 227, 379 N.Y.S.2d 695, 342 N.E.2d 496 (1975); El Rancho Restaurants, Inc. v. Garfield, 440 S.W.2d 873 (Tex.Civ.App.1969, error refused n.r.e.); Annot., 53 A.L.R.2d 1253.

17. Miller v. Keating, 754 F.2d 507 (3d Cir.1985) (error to admit statement of unidentified individual, stressing lack of showing of personal knowledge or excitement of declarant); Cummiskey v. Chandris, S.A., 719 F.Supp. 1183, 1187 (S.D.N.Y.1989), judgment affirmed 895 F.2d 107 (2d Cir.) (statement of unidentified witness excluded because no evidence of personal observation); Schuller v. Hy–Vee Food Stores, Inc., 407 N.W.2d 347, 354 (Iowa App.1987) (unknown bystanders statements properly excluded under Rule 403); Garrett v. Howden, 73 N.M. 307, 387 P.2d 874 (1963); Potter v. Baker, 162 Ohio St. 488, 124 N.E.2d 140 (1955). But see State v. Rawlings, 402 N.W.2d 406, 408–410 (Iowa 1987) (statement of unknown bystander identifying defendant held admissible under theory that personal knowledge can be inferred from the statement).

The key concern here, it should be clear, is not the literal identity of the bystander, although such identity would be helpful to permit possible impeachment, but rather the position of the declarant with regard to the events and their impact upon him or her.

18. Schwam v. Reece, 213 Ark. 431, 210 S.W.2d 903 (1948) (bus driver's exclamation, "I have no brakes," just before collision admissible); New York, Chicago & St. Louis R. Co. v. Kovatch, 120 Ohio St. 532, 166 N.E. 682 (1929) (exclamation that train had run over child made while train was still passing crossing held admissible).

19. Gross v. Greer, 773 F.2d 116 (7th Cir.1985) (statement made 12–15 hours after murder admitted when made by four-year old petrified with fear and found under bed-clothes in apartment with victim's body); State v. Stafford, 237 Iowa 780, 23 N.W.2d 832 (1946).

20. Alabama Power Co. v. Ray, 249 Ala. 568, 32 So.2d 219 (1947) (5 minutes); Swearinger v. Klinger, 91 Ill.App.2d 251, 234 N.E.2d 60 (1968) (5 to 15 minutes).

the statement will be excluded in the absence of some proof that the declarant did not in fact engage in a reflective thought process.[21] Testimony that the declarant still appeared "nervous" or "distraught" and that there was a reasonable basis for continuing emotional upset will often suffice.[22] The nature of the exciting event and the declarant's concern with it are relevant, of course. Thus a statement made by the victim's wife one hour after a traffic accident was held admissible where the husband was still in the emergency room and the wife was obviously still concerned about his condition.[23]

Other factors may indicate the opposite conclusion. Evidence that the statement was self-serving [24] or made in response to an inquiry,[25]

21. Tait v. Western World Ins. Co., 220 So.2d 226 (La.App.1969) (error to admit statements concerning accident by another patient in nursing home made 30 minutes after patient had fallen); Fontenot v. Pan American Fire & Casualty Co., 209 So.2d 105 (La.App.1968), cert. denied 252 La. 460, 211 So.2d 328; (statement by driver made 40 minutes after accident inadmissible); Marshall v. Thomason, 241 S.C. 84, 127 S.E.2d 177 (1962) (statements to police officer 30 minutes after accident inadmissible).

22. United States v. Vazquez, 857 F.2d 857, 864 (1st Cir.1988) (witness testified that when making the statement the declarant "got mad at that moment"); McCurdy v. Greyhound Corp., 346 F.2d 224 (3d Cir.1965) (statement to police officer 15 minutes after accident admissible; testimony that declarant was still "nervous" and "shooken up" when police arrived); United States v. Golden, 671 F.2d 369 (10th Cir. 1982), cert. denied 456 U.S. 919 (statement 15 minutes after assault by officer, with 120 m.p.h. chase in interval); Hilyer v. Howat Concrete Co., 578 F.2d 422 (D.C.Cir. 1978) (statement made by worker 15–45 minutes after fellow worker was fatally run over by truck, with evidence indicating continuing excitement); May v. Wright, 62 Wash.2d 69, 381 P.2d 601 (1963) (statement by witness about accident involving an automobile running over a child made 20 minutes after accident admissible; officer testified declarant "seemed upset").

23. Gibbs v. Wilmeth, 261 Iowa 1015, 157 N.W.2d 93 (1968). See also Gross v. Greer, 773 F.2d 116, 119–120 (7th Cir.1985) (statement by four-year old found "petrified and cowering beneath the covers of a bed" in an apartment where police discovered murder victim admissible even though made 12 hours after killing).

24. United States v. Elem, 845 F.2d 170, 174 (8th Cir.1988) (exculpatory statements made by defendant after he was in custody excluded because he had "every motive to

fabricate a statement after some reflection in an attempt to extricate himself"); State v. Burton, 115 Idaho 1154, 1156, 772 P.2d 1248, 1250 (App.1989) (exculpatory quality of statement important factor leading court to exclude statement made by defendant five minutes after altercation); Micheli v. Toye Bros. Yellow Cab Co., 174 So.2d 168 (La.App.1965) (self-serving statement made to employer's investigator 15 minutes after automobile accident properly excluded); State v. Fullwood, 323 N.C. 371, 387, 373 S.E.2d 518, 528 (1988), vacated on other grounds 110 S.Ct. 1464 (exculpatory statement excluded where one hour interval gave opportunity to manufacture statement); Berry v. State, 759 S.W.2d 12, 13 (Tex.App.1988) (where defendant seeks to introduce exculpatory statement, he bears burden of demonstrating that it was not product of reflection or fabrication); State v. Cude, 784 P.2d 1197, 1200–201 (Utah 1989) ("real issues" considered whether defendant "smart enough" to "come up" with explanation for injury in short time).

25. Gibbs v. Wilmeth, 261 Iowa 1015, 157 N.W.2d 93 (1968) ("[A] statement in answer to a question does not necessarily violate the res gestae rule. The important consideration is the spontaneity of the statement, however elicited."); Bosin v. Oak Lodge Sanitary Dist. No. 1, 251 Or. 554, 447 P.2d 285 (1968) (fact that statement was made in response to question is "not conclusive against admissibility," but a factor for consideration). But see People v. Centers, 141 Mich.App. 364, 373, 367 N.W.2d 397, 401 (1985), reversed on other grounds 422 Mich. 951, 377 N.W.2d 4 (detailed statement produced by question and answer session between victim and police officer "exactly the opposite of spontaneous and unreflecting"); Bowman v. Barnes, 168 W.Va. 111, 282 S.E.2d 613 (1981) (error to admit statement by since-deceased railroad engineer 44 minutes after accident to investigating police officer, taken down in writing).

while not justification for automatic exclusion, is an indication that the statement was the result of reflective thought. Where the time interval permitted such thought, those factors might swing the balance in favor of exclusion. Proof that the declarant performed tasks requiring relatively careful thought between the event and the statement provides strong evidence that the effect of the exciting event had subsided.[26] Because of the wide variety of factual situations, appellate courts have recognized substantial discretion in trial courts to determine whether a declarant was still under the influence of an exciting event at the time of an offered statement.[27]

Whether the excited utterance should be required to concern the exciting event and the strictness of the necessary relationship between the exciting event and the content of the statement has been the subject of historical disagreement.[28] One of the major positions in this debate was set out by District of Columbia Circuit in Murphy Auto Parts Co. v. Ball.[29] There the court concluded that a requirement that the statement "explain or illuminate" the event was, if "mechanically and narrowly construed," a "spurious element," but that failure to describe the exciting event was a factor to consider in evaluating the spontaneity of the statement.[30] On the facts of the case, the court sustained admission of a driver's statement following an accident that he had to call on a customer and was in a hurry to get home, which statement helped to established agency.[31]

Federal Rule 803(2) takes a somewhat different position but reaches a similar result to that in *Murphy Auto Parts*. The rule *requires* a connection between the event and the content of the statement, but it defines that connection reasonably broadly as "relating to" the event.[32] This terminology is intended to extend beyond merely a description or an explanation of the event.[33] The courts have been quite liberal in applying this requirement.[34]

26. Compare Hamilton v. Missouri Petroleum Products Co., 438 S.W.2d 197 (Mo. 1969) (where evidence showed that after accident declarant put out flares to warn traffic, went to the aid of an injured party, and advised injured party not to move, statements made 25 minutes after accident inadmissible) with McCurdy v. Greyhound Corp., 346 F.2d 224 (3d Cir.1965) (where proof showed that after accident declarant first muttered incomprehensibly and then walked around aimlessly and was still nervous when police arrived, statement made 15 minutes after accident admissible).

27. Swearinger v. Klinger, 91 Ill.App.2d 251, 234 N.E.2d 60 (1968); Johnston v. Ohls, 76 Wash.2d 398, 457 P.2d 194 (1969).

28. Wigmore suggests that a requirement that the declaration elucidate the event seems to have been taken from the verbal act doctrine without adequate analysis. 6 Wigmore, Evidence § 1752 (Chadbourn rev. 1976). However, it seems undeniable that the probabilities are substantially greater that a statement related to an exciting event is a spontaneous reaction than a statement related to something else.

29. 249 F.2d 508 (D.C.Cir.1957), cert. denied 355 U.S. 932.

30. 249 F.2d at 511.

31. Id. at 512.

32. Revised Uniform Rule (1986) 803(2) is identical to the Federal Rule.

33. Fed.R.Evid. 803(1) & (2) Advisory Committee Note contrasts the subject matter of the two exceptions using these terms. 56 F.R.D. 183, 305.

34. David by Berkeley v. Pueblo Supermarket, 740 F.2d 230, 234–235 (3d Cir. 1984) (statement that declarant told "them

The formulation used by Rule 803(2) has the advantage of simplicity while at the same time preserving the trustworthiness gained by requiring a relationship between the exciting event or condition and the resulting statement. It also permits clarification of the difference in theory between excited utterances and statements of present sense impressions, discussed in the preceding section.

Another major issue frequently encountered with excited utterances is whether the declarant meet the tests of competency for a witness. In a modified manner the requirement that a witness have had an opportunity to observe that to which he or she testifies is applied.[35] Direct proof is not necessary; if the circumstances appear consistent with opportunity by the declarant, the requirement is met.[36] If there is doubt, the question is for the jury.[37] Especially in cases where the declaration is of low probative value, however, the statement is usually held inadmissible if there is no reasonable suggestion that the declarant had an opportunity to observe.[38]

---

to clean it up" concerned circumstances surrounding customer's fall on supermarket floor); People v. Ojeda, 745 P.2d 274 (Colo.App.1987) (statement by victim regarding a conversation with defendant 5 months before attack in which he learned when victim would be alone was admissible because it would likely have been evoked by the event and its significance was revealed by that event); State v. Clothier, 381 N.W.2d 253, 255–256 (S.D.1986) (statement by defendant to his wife to kill witnesses related to the act of shooting witnesses' companion); City of Dallas v. Donovan, 768 S.W.2d 905, 906–908 (Tex.App. 1989) (statement by declarant who witnessed accident that she had reported to the city the fact the stop sign was down at that intersection held admissible in that it related to events causative of the accident). See also 4 Weinstein & Berger, Weinstein's Evidence ¶ 803(2)[01], at 95 (1990) (while wholly unrelated event brought to mind by free association with event would not meet the "relating to" requirement, a statement should be admitted if its subject matter is such that it would likely be evoked by the event). But see State v. Murray, 375 S.E.2d 405, 410 (W.Va.1988) (statements by victim of child abuse about incident inadmissible because they related to two-week-old assault and not to the contemporary startling event, the pain and distress of venereal disease).

For cases applying the older, more rigid requirements, see, e.g., Cook v. Hall, 308 Ky. 500, 214 S.W.2d 1017 (1948) (statement by son of automobile's owners after accident that he had permission to drive the car inadmissible); Bagwell v. McLellan Stores Co., 216 S.C. 207, 57 S.E.2d 257 (1949) (bystander's statement, after observ-

ing fall, that the floor had just been oiled ruled inadmissible).

35. See supra § 10.

36. Compare McLaughlin v. Vinzant, 522 F.2d 448, 451 (1st Cir.1975), cert. denied 423 U.S. 1037 (content of statement plus fact that witness was somewhere in vicinity of the shooting sufficient even though no evidence precisely where witness was and what events she observed) with People v. Kent, 157 Mich.App. 780, 788, 404 N.W.2d 668, 671–672 (1987) (error to admit statement by defendant's spouse accusing him of burning trailer because proponent of evidence failed to show personal knowledge where witnesses testified that she did not arrive until after fire was well under way).

37. See supra §§ 53, 58.

38. Warfield v. Shell Oil Co., 106 Ariz. 181, 472 P.2d 50 (1970) (offer of statement of bystander failed to show that speaker had witnessed event); Ungefug v. D'Ambrosia, 250 Cal.App.2d 61, 58 Cal.Rptr. 223 (1967) (where ambulance driver merely reported that someone had said the victim had been hit by a car that had not stopped, there was insufficient proof of an opportunity to observe; although direct proof that declarant witnessed the event is not necessary, "the fact that the declarant was a percipient witness should not be purely a matter of speculation or conjecture"); Clements v. Peyton, 398 S.W.2d 477 (Ky. 1965) (testimony that "some guys sitting in the bar" said there had been another wreck at the corner inadmissible because there was no showing of their reasonable opportunity to observe facts on which to

On the theory that there is a countervailing assurance of reliability in the excitement of the event, the other aspects of competency are not applied. Thus, an excited utterance is admissible despite the fact that the declarant was a child and would have been incompetent as a witness for that reason,[39] or the declarant was incompetent by virtue of mental illness,[40] or the declarant was a spouse of the defendant in the criminal case in which the statement was offered.[41]

Some courts have argued that an excited utterance must not be an opinion.[42] Such a blanket limitation is unjustified, in view of the nature and present standing of the opinion rule.[43] Where the declarant is an in-court witness, it is probably appropriate to require testimony in concrete terms rather than conclusory generalizations. But in everyday life, people often talk in conclusory terms, and when these statements are later offered in court, there is no opportunity to require the declarant to testify in more specific language. Here, as elsewhere, the opinion rule should be applied sparingly, if at all, to out-of-court speech. Nevertheless, courts have sometimes excluded excited utterances on the grounds that they violate the opinion rule, especially in situations in which the declarants' statements place blame on themselves or others.[44] Despite possible danger that these opinions may be given exaggerated weight by a jury, the need for knowledge of the facts usually outweighs this danger, and the better view admits excited statements of opinion.[45]

base this conclusion). Compare Annot., 7 A.L.R.2d 1324 (inability of declarant to recollect and narrate facts as to which statement relates as affecting admissibility of excited utterance).

39. Morgan v. Foretich, 846 F.2d 941, 946 (4th Cir.1988); State v. Bingham, 116 Idaho 415, 422, 776 P.2d 424, 431 (1989). See also New York, Chicago & St. Louis R. Co. v. Kovatch, 120 Ohio St. 532, 166 N.E. 682 (1929) (5–year–old girl); Ortega v. State, 500 S.W.2d 816 (Tex.Cr.App.1973) (5–year–old child; state required to make no additional showing that child is of sufficient age and intelligence to render declaration reliable); Johnston v. Ohls, 76 Wash.2d 398, 457 P.2d 194 (1969) (4–year–old girl "presumably not competent to testify directly"); Marcum v. Bellomy, 157 W.Va. 636, 203 S.E.2d 367 (1974) (boy under 6). See Annot., 15 A.L.R.4th 1043, 83 A.L.R.2d 1368.

40. Wilson v. State, 49 Tex.Cr. 50, 90 S.W. 312 (App.1905). But cf. Gough v. General Box Co., 302 S.W.2d 884 (Mo.1957) (excited utterance inadmissible because declarant was unconscious at the time of the statement).

41. Robbins v. State, 73 Tex.Cr. 367, 166 S.W. 528 (App.1914) (declaration of murder defendant's wife, "Poor man! He lost his life trying to protect me," admissible).

42. Johnston v. Ohls, 76 Wash.2d 398, 457 P.2d 194 (1969).

43. See supra § 18.

44. Whitney v. Sioux City, 172 Iowa 336, 154 N.W. 497 (1915) (statement by passenger in automobile, "We were going too fast," inadmissible); Gray v. Boston Elevated Ry. Co., 215 Mass. 143, 102 N.E. 71 (1913) (statement by spectator about sudden start of train, "It was his own fault," inadmissible); Bowers v. Kugler, 140 Neb. 684, 1 N.W.2d 299 (1941) (statement by driver of one vehicle in accident, "Oh, my God! It might have been my fault," inadmissible); Neisner Bros. v. Schafer, 124 Ohio St. 311, 178 N.E. 269 (1931) (store clerk's declaration, "I am sorry I caused it; I should not have dropped the paper on the floor," inadmissible).

45. Cross Lake Logging Co. v. Joyce, 83 Fed. 989 (8th Cir.1897) (statement, "I wouldn't have lost my leg if you had done as you agreed to and put another man in his place," ruled admissible); Atlantic Coast Line R. Co. v. Crosby, 53 Fla. 400, 43 So. 318 (1907) (statement of mother of injured child, "It was all my fault," admissible); State v. Sloan, 47 Mo. 604 (1871) (statement of shooting victim held admissible to the effect that defendant had not been at fault because victim had drawn on the difficulty by attacking the defendant).

§ 272.1   Excited Utterances and Other Hearsay Exceptions in Sexual Abuse Cases

Rape cases and other sexual offenses, particularly those involving minors, raise a number of difficult hearsay issues. Several different exceptions may be involved, including statements for the purpose of medical diagnosis and the catchall exception, which are treated elsewhere.[1] The application of the excited utterance exception and several new specific exceptions developed to deal with issues involved with the prosecution of offenses against children are treated below.[2]

Before moving into modern developments, one historical artifact should be noted. In rape cases, out-of-court statements that the victim made a complaint were historically admissible to corroborate the assault.[3] The only time requirement is that the complaint must have been made without a delay that is either unexplained or inconsistent with the occurrence of the offense, which is generally less demanding in terms of the temporal element than would be the case under typical excited utterance analysis.[4] In its origin, the theory of admissibility was to rebut any inference that, because the victim did not immediately complain, no crime had in fact occurred.[5] Accordingly, if the victim did not testify, evidence of the complaint was not admissible,[6] and only the fact that a complaint was made could be admitted.[7]

§ 272.1

1. See supra §§ 277–78 & 324.

2. See generally Graham, The Confrontation Clause, the Hearsay Rule, and Child Sexual Abuse Prosecutions: The State of the Relationship, 72 Minn.L.Rev. 523 (1988); Graham, Indicia of Reliability and Face to Face Confrontation: Emerging Issues in Child Sexual Abuse Prosecutions, 40 U.Miami L.Rev. 19 (1985); Myers, Hearsay Statements by the Child Abuse Victim, 38 Baylor L.Rev. 775 (1986); Annot., 89 A.L.R.3d 102.

3. 4 Wigmore, Evidence §§ 1134–1140 (Chadbourn rev. 1972), 6 Wigmore, Evidence §§ 1760, 1761 (Chadbourn rev. 1976). For excellent discussions of the fresh complaint of rape doctrine in modern caselaw, see Cole v. State, 83 Md.App. 279, 574 A.2d 326 (1990), cert. denied 321 Md. 68, 580 A.2d 1077; State v. Hill, 121 N.J. 150, 578 A.2d 370 (1990); State v. Campbell, 299 Or. 633, 640–644, 705 P.2d 694, 699–702 (1985) (discussing history of report of rape doctrine). Some states expanded this traditional doctrine to sex crimes generally, see People v. Burton, 55 Cal.2d 328, 11 Cal. Rptr. 65, 359 P.2d 433 (1961) (indecent liberties with child).

4. See the careful explication of the distinctions between excited utterances and complaint of rape in People v. Damen, 28 Ill.2d 464, 193 N.E.2d 25 (1963). See also State v. Stevens, 289 N.W.2d 592 (Iowa 1980).

5. The New Jersey Supreme Court recently described the misguided history of this doctrine as "rooted in sexist notions of how the 'normal' woman responds to rape." State v. Hill, 121 N.J. 150, 170, 578 A.2d 370, 380 (1990). The court nevertheless saw merit in continuing the admissibility of such reports where made to neutralize the possible negative inference that some jurors might draw from silence. Id.

6. People v. Lewis, 252 Ill. 281, 96 N.E. 1005 (1911) (victim died before trial); 4 Wigmore, Evidence § 1136 (Chadbourn rev. 1972).

7. 6 Wigmore, Evidence § 1760 (Chadbourn rev. 1976). See, e.g., Cole v. State, 83 Md.App. 279, 294, 574 A.2d 326, 333 (1990), cert. denied 321 Md. 68, 580 A.2d 1077 (when complaint is offered under this theory, narrative details not admissible); State v. Murray, 375 S.E.2d 405, 410 (W.Va.1988).

There is some trend to allow details of the offense and the identity of the offender within this doctrine. See cases cited in 6 Wigmore, Evidence § 1761 n. 2 (Chadbourn rev. 1976). But cf. People v. Kreiner, 415 Mich. 372, 379, 329 N.W.2d 716, 719 (1982) (common law "tender years" exception

Moving to modern practice, particularly where children are the victims of sexual offenses, many courts have liberally interpreted the allowable period of time between the exciting event and the child's description of it.[8] The theory of these courts is that the general psychological characteristics of children typically extend the period that is free of the dangers of conscious fabrication.[9] In addition, a growing number of states have enacted specific hearsay exceptions to cover the situations where children are involved as witnesses or victims.[10] One of the advantages of this latter approach is that it reduces the pressure to distort the traditional time limitations of the excited utterance exception to deal with this difficult set of cases.[11]

The new exception is illustrated by the Washington statute,[12] which has become a model for many other states. It admits a child's extrajudicial statement if (1) the court finds after a hearing that the time, content, and circumstances of the statement provide sufficient indicia of reliability, and (2) the child either testifies at the proceeding or is unavailable as a witness and, if unavailable, corroborative evidence is produced to support trustworthiness.[13]

that permitted details of complaint by victim of child sexual abuse does not survive enactment of state rules of evidence).

8. United States v. Iron Shell, 633 F.2d 77, 86 (8th Cir.1980), cert. denied 450 U.S. 1001 (45 to 75 minutes); State v. Smith, 315 N.C. 76, 86–90, 337 S.E.2d 833, 841–843 (1985) (2 to 3 days); State v. Logue, 372 N.W.2d 151, 159 (S.D.1985) (1 to 2 days).

One particularly innovative, although theoretically largely unexplored, approach is to examine the period of time not from the incident to the declarant but from the child's "first real opportunity to report" the incident to the statement. Morgan v. Foretich, 846 F.2d 941, 947 (4th Cir.1988).

Some states have recently shown a counter-tendency and limited the time period for excited utterances in child sexual abuse cases. See In Interest of Doe, 70 Hawaii 32, 39, 761 P.2d 299, 303–304 (1988) (3 hours after first report to mother and half day after event too long); Cassidy v. State, 74 Md.App. 1, 20, 536 A.2d 666, 675–676 (1988), cert. denied 312 Md. 602, 541 A.2d 965 (recognizing that earlier case permitting statement 4½ hours after incident went to extreme outer limit and the exception did not extend to 3 days); People v. Straight, 430 Mich. 418, 425–426, 424 N.W.2d 257, 260 (1988) (1 month too long); State v. Murray, 375 S.E.2d 405, 410 (W.Va.1988) (2 weeks too long).

9. State v. Smith, 315 N.C. 76, 88, 337 S.E.2d 833, 842 (1985); State v. Logue, 372 N.W.2d 151, 159 (S.D.1985).

The psychological impact of rape, which may both leave the victim in an excited emotional state for hours and delay a statement until the victim believes she is secure, may similarly result in a lengthening of the time period. State v. Smith, 34 Ohio App.3d 180, 190, 517 N.E.2d 933, 945 (1986).

Cases on time lapse for excited utterances in sex cases are collected in Annot., 89 A.L.R.3d 102.

10. See State v. Myatt, 237 Kan. 17, 21, 697 P.2d 836, 841 (1985) (noting that it and four other states—Arizona, Colorado, Utah, and Washington—at that point had adopted specific hearsay exceptions to cover child-victims); People v. Straight, 430 Mich. 418, 432–433, 424 N.W.2d 257, 263 (1988) (proposing new rule to deal with evidentiary problems involved in child sexual abuse prosecutions).

11. State v. Myatt, 237 Kan. 17, 23–24, 697 P.2d 836, 842 (1985); People v. Straight, 430 Mich. 418, 430–431, 424 N.W.2d 257, 262 (1988); State v. J.C.E., 235 Mont. 264, 767 P.2d 309, 314 (1988).

12. West's Rev.Code Wash.Ann. 9A.44.-120.

13. The general constitutionality of the statute was upheld in State v. Ryan, 103 Wash.2d 165, 691 P.2d 197 (1984).

For a discussion of this and related statutes, see notes and comments in 40 Baylor L.Rev. 267 (1988); 98 Harv.L.Rev. 806 (1985); 34 Cath.U.L.Rev. 1021 (1985); 13 Pepperdine L.Rev. 157 (1985); 83 Colum.L.Rev. 1745 (1983).

States have also undertaken a major effort to ameliorate the trauma associated with the judicial process by changing the mechanics of the trial in child abuse and related cases. Part of this process has involved the development of new methods of receiving testimony, some of which include the development of new hearsay exceptions. Drawing on a broad base of statutory and other material, the drafters of the Uniform Rules added Rule 807 to help address this set of problems. The rule exempts from the ban of the hearsay rule the audio-visually recorded statement of a child victim or witness describing an act of sexual abuse or physical violence if the court finds that (1) the minor will suffer severe emotional or psychological stress if required to testify in open court; (2) the time, content, and circumstances of the statement provide sufficient circumstantial guarantees of trustworthiness; and (3) other enumerated requirements are followed regarding the conduct of the recording process. Presence of judge, accused, or counsel is not required or apparently contemplated; any person may conduct the interview. However, before the admission of a statement under the rule, the court, on defendant's request, shall provide for further questioning of the minor in a manner as the court may direct. Finally, the rule provides that admission of a statement under these provisions does not preclude the court from permitting any party to call the child as a witness if the interests of justice require it.[14]

Another provision of Uniform Rule 807 permits the taking of testimony by either deposition recorded by audio-visual means or by contemporaneous examination communicated to the courtroom by closed-circuit television if the court concludes the child will suffer severe emotional or psychological harm if required to testify in open court. In this proceeding, the court may order the testimony to be taken outside the presence of any party, including the defendant, if it finds such presence would contribute to the likelihood of harm to the child, and the court shall in that situation place the excluded party so that he or she may see and hear the testimony of the child and may consult with counsel but not be seen by the child.[15]

These provisions, and others like them, raise difficult constitutional issues involving the Confrontation Clause. Two of those issues have been treated extensively by the courts. First, the provisions similar to those of the Uniform Rules that permit the creation and introduction of a recording of the child's statement as part of the state's case, which is made without the opportunity for contemporaneous cross-examination by defense counsel, have been held by several state supreme courts to violate the Confrontation Clause.[16] Second, a procedure which shields

---

14. Rev.Unif.R.Evid. (1986) 807(a)–(c).

15. Rev.Unif.R.Evid. (1986) 807(d).

16. People v. Bastien, 129 Ill.2d 64, 133 Ill.Dec. 459, 541 N.E.2d 670 (1989); State v. Pilkey, 776 S.W.2d 943, 950–951 (Tenn. 1989), cert. denied 110 S.Ct. 1483; Long v. State, 742 S.W.2d 302 (Tex.Cr.App.1987),

cert. denied 485 U.S. 993. But see State v. Schaal, 806 S.W.2d 659 (Mo.1991).

These cases place primary reliance upon the Supreme Court's analysis in California v. Green, 399 U.S. 149, 159 (1970) regarding the virtues of contemporaneous cross-examination.

the child witness from facing the defendant while testifying is constitutionally valid only if resting upon an individualized finding that the child will suffer trauma otherwise.[17] Clearly, it will take some time for the courts and the legislatures to accommodate the special needs for preservation and presentation of the testimony of child victims or witnesses and the constitutional commands of Due Process and the Confrontation Clause.

§ 273. Statements of Physical or Mental Condition: (a) Statements of Bodily Feelings, Symptoms, and Condition [1]

Statements of the declarant's present bodily condition and symptoms, including pain and other feelings, offered to prove the truth of the statements have been generally recognized as an exception to the hearsay rule.[2] Special reliability is provided by the spontaneous quality of the declarations, assured by the requirement that the declaration purport to describe a condition presently existing at the time of the statement.[3] This assurance of reliability is almost certainly not always effective, however, since some of these statements describing present symptoms are probably not spontaneous but rather calculated misstatements. Nevertheless, a sufficiently large percentage are undoubtedly spontaneous to justify the exception.

Being spontaneous, the hearsay statements are considered of greater probative value than the present testimony of the declarant.[4] Moreover, the alternative of insisting upon the in-court testimony of the declarant, when he or she is available, promises little improvement since cross-examination and other methods of exposing deliberate misrepresentation are relatively ineffective.[5] Together, these factors of trustworthiness and necessity not only provide a basis for admitting statements of this type but also justify dispensing with any requirement of unavailability of the declarant.

Despite occasional indications to the contrary,[6] declarations of present bodily condition generally do not have to be made to a physi-

---

17. Maryland v. Craig, 110 S.Ct. 3157 (1990). See also Coy v. Iowa, 487 U.S. 1012 (1988).

§ 273

1. See generally 6 Wigmore, Evidence §§ 1718–1723 (Chadbourn rev. 1976); Annot., 64 A.L.R. 557; 29 Am.Jur.2nd Evidence §§ 655–656; C.J.S. Evidence §§ 242–246; Dec.Dig. Evidence ⊗127, 128, 268.

2. E.g., Fidelity Service Ins. Co. v. Jones, 280 Ala. 195, 191 So.2d 20 (1966) (declarant complained of sickness or blackouts); Shover v. Iowa Lutheran Hosp., 252 Iowa 706, 107 N.W.2d 85 (1961) (witness testified, concerning plaintiff, that "she said she hurt"); Caspermeyer v. Florsheim Shoe Store Co., 313 S.W.2d 198 (Mo.App.

1958) (wife complained to husband that she had a pain in her chest); Fagan v. City of Newark, 78 N.J.Super. 294, 188 A.2d 427 (App.Div.1963) (deceased said he felt dizzy and ill); Indian Oil Tool Co. v. Thompson, 405 P.2d 104 (Okl.1965) (deceased stated that he had a tight feeling in his chest).

3. See 6 Wigmore, Evidence § 1714 (Chadbourn rev. 1976).

4. See 6 Wigmore, Evidence § 1718 (Chadbourn rev. 1976).

5. 6 Wigmore, Evidence § 1714, at 90 (Chadbourn rev. 1976).

6. West Chicago St. Ry. Co. v. Kennelly, 170 Ill. 508, 48 N.E. 996 (1897); Kennedy v. Rochester City & Brighton R. Co., 130 N.Y. 654, 29 N.E. 141 (1891).

cian in order to qualify for the present exception. Any person hearing the statement may testify to it.[7] The exception is, however, limited to descriptions of present condition and therefore excludes description of past pain or symptoms,[8] as well as accounts of the events furnishing the cause of the condition.[9]

Federal Rule 803(3) defines a hearsay exception, without regard to the unavailability of the declarant, for "a statement of the declarant's then existing * * * physical condition (such as * * * pain and bodily health) * * *."[10] Not only does the rule mandate that the statement must be spontaneous by its requirement that the statement describe a "then existing" physical condition, but also it is clear from the Advisory Committee's Note to the Federal Rule that the rule is a specialized application of the broader rule recognizing a hearsay exception for statements describing a present sense impression,[11] the cornerstone of which is spontaneity. If circumstances demonstrate a lack of spontaneity, exclusion should follow.[12]

§ 274. Statements of Physical or Mental Condition: (b) Statements of Present Mental or Emotional State to Show a State of Mind or Emotion in Issue [1]

The substantive law often makes legal rights and liabilities hinge upon the existence of a particular state of mind or feeling. Thus, such matters as the intent to steal or kill, or the intent to have a certain paper take effect as a deed or will, or the maintenance or transfer of

---

7. Shover v. Iowa Lutheran Hosp., 252 Iowa 706, 107 N.W.2d 85 (1961) (hospital patient's roommate); Caspermeyer v. Florsheim Shoe Store Co., 313 S.W.2d 198 (Mo. App.1958) (wife); Fagan v. City of Newark, 78 N.J.Super. 294, 188 A.2d 427 (App.Div. 1963) (wife); Plank v. Heirigs, 83 S.D. 173, 156 N.W.2d 193 (1968) (nurse).

8. Lowery v. Jones, 219 Ala. 201, 121 So. 704 (1929); Martin v. P.H. Hanes Knitting Co., 189 N.C. 644, 127 S.E. 688 (1925). See generally, 6 Wigmore, Evidence § 1722(b) (Chadbourn rev. 1976). Particularly before a separate exception had been established that admitted historical statements made for purposes of medical diagnosis, courts were relatively lax in classifying symptoms as "present" symptoms. See Hartford Accident & Indem. Co. v. Baugh, 87 F.2d 240 (5th Cir.1936), cert. denied 300 U.S. 679 ("He came to the office and told me that his sputum was stained with blood" held admissible); Bloomberg v. Laventhal, 179 Cal. 616, 178 P. 496 (1919) (testimony that plaintiff complained that he had pains in the head and could not sleep admissible).

9. See 6 Wigmore, Evidence § 1722(a) (Chadbourn rev. 1976).

10. Revised Uniform Rule (1986) 803(3) is identical except for minor stylistic differences.

11. Adv.Comm.Note, Fed.R.Evid. 803(3), 56 F.R.D. 183, 305.

12. As discussed in supra § 270, while exclusion based upon judicial suspicion about the declarant's motivation appears improper under the rule, exclusion is warranted where an intention to manufacture evidence demonstrates that the statement lacked contemporaneousness. Also, the judge's discretion to exclude evidence under Rule 403 because it is misleading, etc., should be considered. See supra § 185.

§ 274

1. See generally 6 Wigmore, Evidence §§ 1714, 1725–1740 (Chadbourn rev. 1976); Morgan, Evidence 1941–1945, 59 Harv. L.Rev. 481 (1946); Hinton, States of Mind and the Hearsay Rule, 1 U.Chi.L.Rev. 394 (1934); 29 Am.Jur.2nd Evidence §§ 650– 652, 654; C.J.S. Evidence §§ 255–258; Dec. Dig. Evidence ☞268, 269, 271(6), Criminal Law ☞415(1), (5).

the affections of a spouse may come into issue in litigation. When this is so, the mental or emotional state of the person becomes an ultimate object of search. It is not introduced as evidence from which the person's earlier or later conduct may be inferred but as an operative fact upon which a cause of action or defense depends. While a state of mind may be proved by the person's actions, the statements of the person are often a primary source of evidence.[2]

In many instances, statements used for this purpose are not assertive of the declarant's present state of mind and are therefore not hearsay.[3] Courts, however, have tended to lump together statements asserting the declarant's state of mind, hence arguably hearsay, with those tending to prove the state of mind circumstantially, arguably nonhearsay, applying a general exception to the hearsay rule and ignoring the possibility that many of these statements could be treated simply as nonhearsay.[4]

---

2. The person in question may, of course, testify as to his or her own mental or emotional state. United States v. Dozier, 672 F.2d 531 (5th Cir.1982), cert. denied 459 U.S. 943.

3. See supra § 246.

In Loetsch v. New York City Omnibus Corp., 291 N.Y. 308, 52 N.E.2d 448 (1943), the issue was the damages suffered by a husband for the death of his wife, which would be measured by the pecuniary value to the husband of his wife's continuance of life. The defendant offered in evidence the will of the wife, containing this statement:

Whereas I have been a faithful, dutiful, and loving wife to my husband, Dan Yankovich, and whereas he reciprocated my tender affections for him with acts of cruelty and indifference, and whereas he has failed to support and maintain me in that station of life which would have been possible and proper for him, I hereby limit my bequest to him to one dollar.

On appeal, the exclusion of this statement was held erroneous, and the court stated:

No testimonial effect need be given to the statement, but the fact that such a statement was made by the decedent, whether true or false, is compelling evidence of her feelings toward, and relations to, her husband. As such it is not excluded under the hearsay rule but is admissible as a verbal act.

Id. at 311, 52 N.E.2d at 449.

4. United States v. Southland Corp., 760 F.2d 1366, 1376 (2d Cir.1985), cert. denied 474 U.S. 825 (generally does not matter whether statement admitted only to prove a relevant state of mind is treated as nonhearsay or under Fed.R.Ev. 803(3));

Santoni v. Moodie, 53 Md.App. 129, 149–150, 452 A.2d 1223, 1233 (1982) (whether statement indicating patient's unawareness of risk of taking medication was classified as nonhearsay or statement under hearsay exception irrelevant since statement admissible).

Courts often gloss over this issue, tending more often than not to treat the statement, which may be nonhearsay, under the instant exception. See, e.g., United States v. Taglione, 546 F.2d 194, 200–201 (5th Cir.1977) (in prosecution for extortion, defendant should have been permitted to show, as relevant to intent, that he asked his lawyer if it would be all right to negotiate for a reward; the court treated the evidence, which appears not to be hearsay, as falling within the hearsay exception for declarations of state of mind); United States v. Green, 680 F.2d 520 (7th Cir. 1982), cert. denied 459 U.S. 1072 (proper to admit under the state of mind exception contemporaneous derogatory statements of victim about defendant to prove lack of consent in kidnapping prosecution); Beliveau v. Goodrich, 185 Neb. 98, 173 N.W.2d 877 (1970) (agent's declaration after loss of suit that a new petition would be filed was admissible to prove the bona fides of the defense of the first suit); Doern v. Crawford, 36 Wis.2d 470, 153 N.W.2d 581 (1967) (statement of plaintiff that he did not like being away from his wife was admissible to prove his intent that his absence be only temporary where plaintiff's status as an insured under an insurance policy depended upon whether his absence was intended to be permanent).

Similar hearsay questions arise with respect to public opinion and other polls.

The special assurance of reliability for statements of present state of mind rests, as in the case of statements of bodily condition, upon their spontaneity and resulting probable sincerity.[5] This has been assured principally by the requirement that the statements must relate to a condition of mind or emotion existing at the time of the statement. In addition, some formulations of the exception require that the statement must have been made under circumstances indicating apparent sincerity,[6] although Federal Rule 803(3) imposes no such explicit condition.[7]

See Zippo Mfg. Co. v. Rogers Imports, Inc., 216 F.Supp. 670 (S.D.N.Y.1963). Since the question whether responses given by those polled are hearsay does not affect admissibility, the critical issues tend to hinge upon the acceptability of techniques employed, which lie in the realm of relevancy and the admissibility of expert testimony. See Adv.Comm. Note, Fed.R.Evid. 703, 56 F.R.D. 183, 283.

5. See 6 Wigmore, Evidence § 1714 (Chadbourn rev. 1976); see supra § 273.

6. West's Ann.Cal.Evid.Code § 1252 (excluding statements of mental or physical condition "under circumstances such as to indicate its lack of trustworthiness"); Vergie M. Lapelosa, Inc. v. Cruze, 44 Md.App. 202, 210, 407 A.2d 786, 791 (1979), cert. denied 287 Md. 754 ("apparent sincerity" required); N.J.Evid.R. 63(12) (statement is admissible "if it was made in good faith"). With regard to common law treatment of this difficult issue, see Elmer v. Fessenden, 151 Mass. 359, 362, 24 N.E. 208, 208 (1889) (must be "made with no apparent motive for misstatement"); Hall v. American Friends Service Committee, Inc., 74 Wash.2d 467, 473, 445 P.2d 616, 620 (1968) (must be "circumstantial probability" of trustworthiness); but see Smith v. Smith, 364 Pa. 1, 70 A.2d 630 (1950) (self-serving nature of declaration goes only to weight).

7. See generally supra § 270.

The federal courts are in some conflict over the issue of whether the court in admitting a statement under Rule 803(3) is authorized to exclude statements based on questionable motivation of the declarant or circumstances of making of the statement. The Second Circuit has taken the position that the self-serving nature of statements otherwise fitting within Rule 803(3) is not a grounds for exclusion but goes only to the weight to be given the statement by the jury. United States v. Lawal, 736 F.2d 5, 8 (2d Cir.1984); United States v. DiMaria, 727 F.2d 265, 271–272 (2d Cir.1984). See also United States v. Torres, 901 F.2d 205, 239 (2d Cir.1990), cert. denied 111 S.Ct. 273 (exclusion of testimony on the ground that its unlikely untrustworthiness and unreliability improper though harmless); United States v. Wright, 783 F.2d 1091, 1099 (D.C.Cir.1986) (trial court should not have excluded statement because self-serving).

The Ninth Circuit takes a different approach. It directs the court in determining admissibility to "evaluate three factors: contemporaneousness, chance for reflection, and relevance." United States v. Ponticelli, 622 F.2d 985, 991 (9th Cir.1980), cert. denied 449 U.S. 1016. Under this test, the court affirmed the trial court's exclusion of a statement made by the defendant to his lawyer after his arrest because the defendant "had a chance for reflection and misrepresentation in making the proffered statements." Id. at 992. See also United States v. Miller, 874 F.2d 1255, 1264 (9th Cir.1989) (two hour period between incriminating statement and defendant's explanatory statement that he was confused inadmissible because sufficient opportunity to fabricate); United States v. Faust, 850 F.2d 575, 585–586 (9th Cir.1988) (draft of letter expressing state of mind regarding coercion at time of illegal acts excluded under *Ponticelli* analysis because contemporaneousness disputed and opportunity for reflection rendered letter unreliable).

These positions share some common ground and several conclusions are possible, although uncertainty remains on some issues. First, there is no categorical exclusion of self-serving statements under the Federal Rule. 4 Weinstein & Berger, Weinstein's Evidence ¶ 803(3)[01], at 106 (1990) (noting that the Advisory Committee, in recognition of the jury's decisive role in determining credibility, decided to eliminate the Uniform Rule's requirement that the statement not be found by the court to have been made in bad faith). More generally, trial courts are not empowered, except as specifically authorized by the hearsay rules, to exclude statements because of judicial doubts about credibility. See Advisory Committee Introductory Note: The Hearsay Problem, 56 F.R.D.

Such statements are also admitted because of a form of the same necessity argument that underlies most hearsay exceptions. Often there is no better way to prove a relevant mental or physical condition than through the statements of the individual whose condition is at issue, and the alternative of using the declarant's testimony, even with cross-examination, is likely to be no better, and perhaps an inferior, manner of proof. As was said in a famous case, if the declarant were called to testify, "his own memory of his state of mind at a former time is no more likely to be clear and true than a bystander's recollection of what he then said." [8] As a result, unavailability of declarant is not required. [9]

Common examples of statements used to prove mental state at the time of the statement include: statements of intent to make a certain place the declarant's home offered to establish domicile, [10] statements expressive of mental suffering to prove that element of damages, [11] statements by customers regarding anger to prove loss of good will, [12] statements of patients regarding lack of knowledge of risk of taking

183, 290 ("For a judge to exclude evidence because he does not believe it has been described as 'altogether atypical, extraordinary,'" (quoting Chadbourn, Bentham and the Hearsay Rule—A Benthamic View of Rule 63(4)(c) of the Uniform Rules of Evidence, 75 Harv.L.Rev. 932, 947 (1962))). Second, Rule 403 grants authority to exclude statements of questionable probative value. It is through this rule that the self-serving nature of the statement, certainly in combination with other factors indicating questionable value, may provide a basis for exclusion. 4 Louisell & Mueller, Federal Evidence § 441, at 538–39 (1980). Third, exclusion in a case like *Ponticelli* should raise no major theoretical issues regarding trustworthiness analysis. To be admissible, the mental or physical condition described by the hearsay statement must be relevant to prove a fact at issue in the litigation. A change in circumstance, such as the defendant's arrest and his consultation with counsel as transpired in *Ponticelli,* occurring between the time the crime was allegedly committed, when state of mind mattered, and the time of the statement, may render the statement inadmissible. Exclusion under these circumstances results from relevancy rather than hearsay analysis. The normal assumption that states of mind continue, see text infra, at notes 18–23, simply does not obtain in this circumstance. See United States v. Jackson, 780 F.2d 1305, 1315 (7th Cir.1986) (statements by defendants two years after offense regarding criminal intent relevant only at time of offense held not admissible chiefly on relevancy grounds, the court noting also the absence of contemporane-

ousness and potential for deliberate misrepresentation).

8. Mutual Life Ins. Co. v. Hillmon, 145 U.S. 285, 295 (1892).

9. See United States v. Ouimette, 753 F.2d 188, 192 (1st Cir.1985) (trial court erred in excluding statements falling within Rule 803(3) on basis that defendant had alternative method of introducing evidence by calling as witnesses the police officers who allegedly made statements and who were available to testify). See generally supra § 253 as to unavailability.

10. In re Newcomb's Estate, 192 N.Y. 238, 84 N.E. 950 (1908) (evidence that declarant wrote to friends indicating her intention to make New Orleans her permanent home admissible); Smith v. Smith, 364 Pa. 1, 70 A.2d 630 (1950) (statement of intent to live in Florida admissible). See generally 6 Wigmore, Evidence §§ 1727, 1784 (Chadbourn rev. 1976); Restatement (Second) of Conflict of Laws 18 (1971).

11. Missouri, Kansas & Texas Ry. Co. v. Linton, 141 S.W. 129, 130 (Tex.Civ.App. 1911, error refused) (plaintiff's statement that "she felt like her heart would burst and that she could not live" admissible to prove damages for mental anguish).

12. Morris Jewelers, Inc. v. General Elec. Credit Corp., 714 F.2d 32, 34 (5th Cir.1983). Cf. Embrey v. Holly, 48 Md. App. 571, 599–600, 429 A.2d 251, 268 (1981), affirmed in part, reversed in part on other grounds 293 Md. 128, 442 A.2d 966 (statements made by telephone callers stating their reactions to defamatory comment made by radio broadcaster).

medication in malpractice suit,[13] statements of willingness to allow one to use the declarant's automobile offered to prove that the car was used with the owner's consent,[14] statements accompanying a transfer of property showing intent, or lack of intent, to defraud creditors,[15] statements of ill will to show malice or the required state of mind in criminal cases,[16] and statements showing fear.[17]

Although the statement must describe a state of mind or feeling existing at the time of the statement, the evidentiary effect of the statement is broadened by the notion of the continuity in time of states of mind. For example, if a declarant asserts on Tuesday a then-existing intention to go on a business trip the next day, this will be evidence not only of the intention at the time of the statement, but also of the same purpose the next day when the declarant is on the road.[18] Continuity may also look backwards.[19] Thus, when there is evidence that a will

13. Santoni v. Moodie, 53 Md.App. 129, 149–150, 452 A.2d 1223, 1233 (1982) (whether unawareness of risk of taking medication was classified as nonhearsay or statement under hearsay exception, it was admissible since it described relevant state of mind).

14. American Employers Ins. Co. v. Wentworth, 90 N.H. 112, 5 A.2d 265 (1939). Perhaps more properly classed as a verbal act. See supra § 249.

15. Sanger v. Colbert, 84 Tex. 668, 19 S.W. 863 (1892) (transferor's statement when receiving price that he intended to pay his debts admissible).

16. E.g., People v. Karis, 46 Cal.3d 612, 637, 250 Cal.Rptr. 659, 672, 758 P.2d 1189, 1202 (1988), cert. denied 490 U.S. 1012 (statement of intent to kill witnesses if defendant were to commit a crime admissible to prove deliberation and premeditation as to subsequent killing); Hall v. State, 31 Tex.Cr. 565, 21 S.W. 368 (App. 1893) (threats against victim admissible in murder case in which accused introduced evidence of intoxication to disprove malice). See generally 6 Wigmore, Evidence § 1732 (Chadbourn rev. 1976).

17. United States v. Adcock, 558 F.2d 397 (8th Cir.1977), cert. denied 434 U.S. 921 (statements by extortion victim); People v. Thompson, 45 Cal.3d 86, 103–104, 246 Cal.Rptr. 245, 254, 753 P.2d 37, 46–47 (1988), cert. denied 488 U.S. 960 (statement of fear of defendant by victim to prove lack of consent to intercourse); L.K.M. v. Department for Human Resources, 621 S.W.2d 38 (Ky.App.1981) (statements by children in proceeding to terminate parental rights).

18. Lewis v. Lowe & Campbell Athletic Goods Co., 247 S.W.2d 800 (Mo.1952). See also Ickes v. Ickes, 237 Pa. 582, 85 A. 885

(1912) (husband's statements on day before leaving wife admissible to prove his motive on that day and the next when he did leave); In re Goldsberry Estate, 95 Utah 379, 81 P.2d 1106 (1938) (statements of testator on day before will executed admissible to show undue influence on that day and on next when will was executed).

Some of the cases of statements of intent have insisted that the statement closely accompany in time some step in furtherance of the act. Common examples are purpose or destination of a journey, domicile, and suicide. Greenacre v. Filby, 276 Ill. 294, 114 N.E. 536 (1916) (in dram shop action for death of deceased killed by train while lying on track, proper to exclude statements showing preoccupation with suicide over two-year period since no such statement was made for previous two weeks); Viles v. Waltham, 157 Mass. 542, 32 N.E. 901 (1892) (proper to admit statement of intent to change residence since close in time to departure for new residence); Gassaway v. Gassaway & Owen, Inc., 220 N.C. 694, 18 S.E.2d 120 (1942) (error in compensation case to admit statement of decedent showing intent to be on job when killed in automobile collision since not connected with act of departure or preparation to depart).

No such requirement is found in Federal or Revised Uniform (1986) Rules 803(3), nor is one founded in reason. Any problem of remoteness in time should be approached from the point of view of relevancy. See supra § 185.

19. Cf. People v. Haymaker, 716 P.2d 110, 112 (Colo.1986) (statements of apparent victim of rape for several months after the incident that she was fearful and distraught constituted evidence of victim's

has been mutilated by the maker, the declarant's subsequent statements of a purpose inconsistent with the will are received to show his or her intent to revoke it at the time it was mutilated.[20] Similarly, whether payment of money or a conveyance was intended by the donor as a gift may be shown by statements made before, at the time of, or after the act of transfer.[21] Since, however, the duration of states of mind or emotion varies with the particular attitudes or feelings at issue and with the cause, it is reasonable to require that the statement mirror a state of mind, which in light of all the circumstances, including proximity in time, is reasonably likely to have been the same condition existing at the material time.[22] The decision on whether a state of mind continues is a decision left to the determination of the trial judge.[23]

Declarations such as those involved here frequently include assertions other than state of mind. For example, the victim may assert that the defendant's acts caused the state of mind. The truth of those assertions may coincide with other issues in the case, as where the defendant is charged with acts similar to those described. When this is so, the normal practice is to admit the statement and direct the jury to consider it only as proof of the state of mind and to disregard it as evidence of the other issues.[24] Compliance with these instructions is probably beyond the jury's ability and almost certainly beyond their

state of mind and was admissible because relevant to corroborate credibility of victim that she was raped).

20. Crampton v. Osborn, 356 Mo. 125, 201 S.W.2d 336 (1947).

21. Casey v. Casey, 97 Cal.App.2d 875, 218 P.2d 842 (1950) (statements of decedent after conveyance admissible to show whether it was intended as gift or in trust); O'Neal v. O'Neal, 9 N.J.Super. 36, 74 A.2d 614 (App.Div.1950), certification denied 5 N.J. 483, 76 A.2d 22 (oral statements of transferor of land admissible to rebut resulting trust). It has been held that if the donor's words at the time of transfer unequivocally indicate an intent to make a gift, subsequent statements to the contrary will not be received. Shaver v. Canfield, 21 Cal.App.2d 734, 70 P.2d 507 (1937); Wilbur v. Grover, 140 Mich. 187, 103 N.W. 583 (1905). But this has been held inapplicable where the issue is whether there was, at the time of the transfer, the intent required for delivery and thus for a gift. Williams v. Kidd, 170 Cal. 631, 151 P. 1 (1915). See generally Annot., 105 A.L.R. 398, 402, 410.

22. United States v. Hedgcorth, 873 F.2d 1307, 1313 (9th Cir.1989), cert. denied 493 U.S. 857 (trial court properly excluded writings of defendant showing his state of mind years before offense).

23. This is a matter of logical relevancy rather than conditional relevancy. See Fed.R.Evid. 104(a) & (b). See generally supra § 53.

24. Greater New York Live Poultry Chamber of Commerce v. United States, 47 F.2d 156 (2d Cir.1931), cert. denied 283 U.S. 837 (in prosecution for conspiracy to restrain interstate trade in poultry, statements of receivers as to why they refused to sell to recalcitrant market men admissible to show state of mind of declarants but not to show external facts asserted as the basis for this state of mind); Adkins v. Brett, 194 Cal. 252, 193 P. 251 (1920) (in alienation of affection case, wife's statements concerning relations with defendant admissible to show feelings of wife but not to prove acts and conduct of defendant described in the statements); Johnson v. Richards, 50 Idaho 150, 294 P. 507 (1930) (husband's statements concerning wife, when admissible in suit for alienation of affections, competent only to prove husband's state of mind); Elmer v. Fessenden, 151 Mass. 359, 24 N.E. 208 (1889); Scott v. Townsend, 106 Tex. 322, 166 S.W. 1138 (1914).

The legitimacy of inferring from state of mind the happening of the act claimed to have caused the state of mind is discussed in infra § 276.

willingness. Where there is adequate evidence on the other issues, this probably does little harm. But in a case where the mental state is provable by other available evidence and the danger of harm from improper use by the jury of the offered declarations is substantial, the judge's discretion to exclude the statements has been recognized.[25]

Federal Rule 803(3) provides a hearsay exception, without regard to unavailability of declarant, for a "statement of the declarant's then existing state of mind, emotion, sensation * * * (such as intent, plan, motive, design, mental feeling * * *)."[26] The rule is generally consistent with the hearsay exception as developed by the courts at common law.

Insanity. A main source of proof of mental competency or incompetency is the conduct of the person in question, showing normal and abnormal response to the circumstances of his or her environment. By this test, every act of the subject's life, within reasonable limits of time, would be relevant to the inquiry.[27] Whether the conduct is verbal or nonverbal is immaterial, and the same is true as to whether it is assertive or nonassertive in form. It is offered as a response to environment, not to prove anything that may be asserted, and is accordingly not hearsay.[28] Thus it makes no difference whether declarant says "I am King Henry the Eighth" or "I believe that I am King Henry the Eighth." Both are offered as evidence of irrationality, and niceties of form should not determine admissibility. If, nevertheless, it is argued that abnormal conduct can be simulated, thereby becoming assertive and therefore hearsay, a short answer is that in that event the evidence would be admissible under the hearsay exception that is the subject of this section.[29] Such inquiries are largely superfluous, and little effort should be spent by courts determining whether the statement should be treated as nonhearsay or as a hearsay evidence showing an abnormal state of mind.[30]

---

25. People v. Coleman, 38 Cal.3d 69, 92–93, 211 Cal.Rptr. 102, 116–117, 695 P.2d 189, 203–204 (1985); Adkins v. Brett, 184 Cal. 252, 259–260, 193 P. 251, 254 (1920); People v. Madson, 638 P.2d 18, 29–30 (Colo. 1981) (statements of victim's fear, including other factual reference, created danger of jury misuse and prejudice and required reversal). See also United States v. Cohen, 631 F.2d 1223, 1225 (5th Cir.1980) (court admitted statements of fear offered by defendant but properly excluded statements by same witnesses that defendant related he had been threatened because exception does not authorize receipt of statements as to why the declarant held particular state of mind); United States v. Emmert, 829 F.2d 805, 810 (9th Cir.1987) (court properly excluded defendant's statement of fear that also included statements of threats made that caused fear).

26. Revised Uniform Rule (1986) 803(3) is identical except for minor stylistic differences.

27. State v. Rodriguez, 126 Ariz. 28, 612 P.2d 484 (1980); Lock v. State, 273 Ind. 315, 403 N.E.2d 1360 (1980); 2 Wigmore, Evidence §§ 228, 229 (Chadbourn rev. 1979); Green, Proof of Mental Incompetency and the Unexpressed Major Premise, 53 Yale L.J. 272, 276 (1944); Dec.Dig. Criminal Law ⟜354, Mental Health ⟜8.

28. See supra §§ 246, 250.

29. People v. Wolff, 61 Cal.2d 795, 40 Cal.Rptr. 271, 394 P.2d 959 (1964); Ross v. State, 217 Ga. 569, 124 S.E.2d 280 (1962); McGarrh v. State, 249 Miss. 247, 277, 148 So.2d 494, 506 (1963), cert. denied 375 U.S. 816.

30. There seems little point in debating whether it is preferable to admit such

§ 275. Statements of Physical or Mental Condition: (c) Statements of Intention Offered to Show Subsequent Acts of Declarant [1]

As the previous sections made clear, statements of mental state are generally admissible to prove the declarant's state of mind when that state of mind is at issue. But the probative value of a state of mind obviously may go beyond the state of mind itself. Where a state of mind would tend to prove subsequent conduct, can the two inferential processes be linked together, with the declarations of state of mind being admitted as proof of the conduct? [2] For example, can the declarant's statements indicating an intent to kill another be admitted to prove not only intent but also that the declarant did in fact subsequently commit the murder? The answer involves both concerns of hearsay and relevancy.

These issues are somewhat more difficult than the matter of admissibility of statements to show only the state of mind. The special reliability of the statements is less in the present situation since it is significantly less likely that a declared intention will be carried out than it is that a declared state of mind is actually held. A statement of intention to kill another is much stronger proof of malice toward the victim at the time of the statement (or subsequently) than it is proof that the declarant committed the murder. Nevertheless, a person who expresses an intent to kill is undeniably more likely to have done so than a person not shown to have had that intent. The accepted standard of relevancy, i.e., more probable than without the evidence,[3] is easily met.

Despite the failure until fairly recently to recognize the potential value of statements of state of mind to prove subsequent conduct, it is now clear that out-of-court statements that tend to prove a plan, design, or intention of the declarant are admissible, subject to the usual limitations as to remoteness in time and perhaps apparent sincerity [4]

statements as an exception to the hearsay rule or under the somewhat simpler formulation of nonhearsay. Indeed, debating the issue may lead to a failure to focus on what are often the most important issues—the relative trustworthiness and probativity as compared with its potential to confuse, mislead, or create prejudice. See 4 Weinstein & Berger, Weinstein's Evidence ¶ 803(3)[02], at 108–109 (1990).

§ 275

1. See generally 6 Wigmore, Evidence §§ 1725–1726 (Chadbourn rev. 1976); McFarland, Dead Men Tell Tales: Thirty Times Three Years After Hillmon, 30 Vill. L.Rev. 1 (1985); Payne, The Hillmon Case—An Old Problem Revisited, 41 Va. L.Rev. 1011 (1955); Hinton, States of Mind

and the Hearsay Rule, 1 U.Chi.L.Rev. 394 (1934); Hutchins & Slesinger, Some Observations on the Law of Evidence—State of Mind to Prove an Act, 38 Yale L.J. 283 (1929); Maguire, The Hillmon Case—Thirty–Three Years After, 38 Harv.L.Rev. 709 (1925); Seligman, An Exception to the Hearsay Rule, 26 Harv.L.Rev. 146 (1912); Note, 35 Vand.L.Rev. 659 (1982); 29 Am. Jur.2nd Evidence § 653; C.J.S. Evidence § 256, at 675. For an historical account of Hillmon, see MacCracken, The Case of the Anonymous Corpse, 19 American Heritage 51 (No. 4, June, 1968).

2. See 1A Wigmore, Evidence § 102 (Tillers rev. 1983).

3. See supra § 185.

4. See supra § 274 note 7.

common to all statements of mental state, to prove that the plan, design, or intention of the declarant was carried out by the declarant.[5]

The leading case is Mutual Life Insurance Co. v. Hillmon,[6] which concerned a suit on life insurance policies by the wife of the insured, Hillmon. The principal issue was whether Hillmon had in fact died; a body had been found at Crooked Creek, Kansas, and the parties disputed whether the body was that of Hillmon. Plaintiff's theory was that Hillmon left Wichita, Kansas, about March 5, 1879, with a man named Brown and that on the night of March 18, 1879, while Hillmon and Brown were camped at Crooked Creek, Hillmon was killed by the accidental discharge of a gun. The defendants, on the other hand, maintained that another individual named Walters had accompanied Hillmon and that the body found at Crooked Creek was Walters'.

Defendants offered testimony that Walters had, on or about March 5, 1879, written to his sister that "I expect to leave Wichita on or about March 5, with a certain Mr. Hillmon." [7] An objection to this and similar evidence was sustained. The United States Supreme Court reversed on the ground that the evidence of the letters should have been admitted:

> The letters * * * were competent not as narratives of facts communicated to the writer by others, nor yet as proof that he actually went away from Wichita, but as evidence that, shortly before the time when other evidence tended to show that he went away, he had the intention of going, and of going with Hillmon, which made it more probable both that he did go and that he went with Hillmon than if there had been no proof of such intention.[8]

While Federal Rule 803(3) does not explicitly address the question of admitting intent for the purpose of proving the doing of the intended act, there can be no doubt that the *Hillmon* rule continues. In fact, the Federal Advisory Committee's Note states, "The rule of Mutual Life Ins. Co. v. Hillmon, 145 U.S. 285 (1892), allowing evidence of intention as tending to prove the doing of the act intended, is, of course, left

---

5. United States v. Annunziato, 293 F.2d 373 (2d Cir.1961), cert. denied 368 U.S. 919 (testimony that declarant had received a phone call from defendant requesting some money and that he had agreed to deliver it ruled admissible to prove delivery); Nuttall v. Reading Co., 235 F.2d 546, 551–552 (3d Cir.1956) (testimony that deceased asked his employer over the phone, "Why are you forcing me to come to work the way I feel?" and then said, "I guess I will have to come, then," admissible in suit under Federal Employers' Liability Act to show that he went to work under compulsion); United States v. Jenkins, 579 F.2d 840 (4th Cir.1978), cert. denied 439 U.S. 967 (statement of W that she was going to L's house admissible in perjury case to show falsity of D's testimo-

ny that she did not); Maryland Paper Products Co. v. Judson, 215 Md. 557, 139 A.2d 219 (1958) (wife's testimony that deceased told her that it would be necessary to go to work because he had to stop off on the way to pick up a gear wheel admissible to prove that deceased had in fact picked up the gear wheel); Johnson v. Skelly Oil Co., 288 N.W.2d 493, 493–494 (S.D.1980) (statement that secretary planned to mail company letters on next work day admissible to prove that at time of accident she was on company business).

6. 145 U.S. 285 (1892). The case is discussed in the sources cited in supra note 1.

7. 145 U.S. at 288.

8. Id. at 295–296.

undisturbed." [9]   A number of subsidiary problems remain to be considered, however, under the rule and the common law decisions.

The suggestion has been made that unavailability of the declarant should be a requirement.[10]   In fact, in virtually all the cases admitting the statements of intent as proof of the doing of the intended act, the declarant has been unavailable, and it may well be that the resulting need for the evidence influenced the courts in the direction of admissibility.   However, neither the decisions nor the Federal Rule require unavailability.

In somewhat similar vein, in virtually all the cases admitting the evidence the intent stated was quite concrete, e.g., to do a specific act at a specific time.   Again, this quality of specificity is not generally stated as a requirement, but undeniably probative value is enhanced by its presence.   Its absence not only detracts from probative value but, in its vague generality, may tend to stray into areas of character evidence that is inadmissible against a criminal defendant.[11]

The danger of unreliability is greatly increased when the action sought to be proved is not one that the declarant could have performed alone, but rather is one that required the cooperation of another person.   If completion of a plan or design requires not only the continued inclination and ability of the declarant to complete it, but also the inclination and ability of someone else, arguably the likelihood that the design or plan was completed is substantially less.   In *Hillmon* itself, Walters' successful completion of his plan to leave Wichita depended upon the continued willingness of Hillmon to have Walters as a companion and upon Hillmon's willingness and ability to leave at the time planned.   However, it was common ground to all parties that Hillmon did in fact go to Crooked Creek, and the Supreme Court had no occasion to consider this aspect of the case.[12]

The issue is made more difficult when the cooperative actions between the declarant and another are themselves at issue.   For example, in the homicide prosecution of Frank, a witness testifies that on the morning of the killing the victim said, "I am going out with Frank tonight."   While this tends to prove the victim's acts, it also tends to

9.   Adv.Comm.Note, Fed.R.Evid. 803(3), 56 F.R.D. 183, 305.

10.   Hunter v. State, 40 N.J. 495 (1878); Hutchins & Slesinger, Some Observations on the Law of Evidence—State of Mind to Prove an Act, 38 Yale L.J. 283, 289 (1929). Contra, Hinton, States of Mind and the Hearsay Rule, 1 U.Chi.L.Rev. 394, 416 (1934).

11.   E.g., United States v. Curtis, 568 F.2d 643, 645 (9th Cir.1978) (in rape and murder prosecution, not error to admit statement by defendant one month before event that "if he ever took a lady out and she didn't give him what he wanted, he'd kick their [expletive deleted] and take it").

12.   The Federal Advisory Committee's Note to Rule 803(3) is silent as to this aspect of the *Hillmon* rules.   The report of the House Judiciary Committee states, "[T]he Committee intends that the Rule be construed to limit the doctrine of [*Hillmon*], * * * so as to render statements of intent by a declarant admissible only to prove his future conduct, not the future conduct of another person."   House Comm. on Judiciary, H.R.Rep. No. 650, 93d Cong., 1st Sess. 13 (1973), reprinted in 1974 U.S.Code Cong. & Admin.News 7051, 7087. However, neither the Senate Committee nor the Conference Report responded to the House position.

prove that the defendant "went out" with the victim, a fact very much in issue. Despite some objection,[13] courts have admitted these statements.[14] The result is that the statement is used as proof of the other person's intent and as proof that this intent was achieved.[15] The additional dangers present here have, however, prompted some courts to impose additional limitations, restrictions, or requirements. These include: instructing the jury to consider the evidence only to prove the conduct of the declarant,[16] requiring independent evidence to establish the defendant's conduct, permitting the declaration to be used only to explain the declarant's intent,[17] and limiting use of such statements only to cases where the declarant is dead or unavailable and to situations where both the statement of intent is shown to be serious and the event realistically likely to be achieved.[18]

13. Johnson v. Chrans, 844 F.2d 482, 485 (7th Cir.1988), cert. denied 488 U.S. 835 (summarizing law in Illinois as excluding declaration of state of mind to prove subsequent conduct of another); People v. Alcalde, 24 Cal.2d 177, 189, 148 P.2d 627, 633 (1944) (Traynor, J., dissenting) ("A declaration as to what one person intended to do, however, cannot safely be accepted as evidence of what another probably did."); Clark v. United States, 412 A.2d 21, 30 (D.C.App.1980) (statement of intention only reliable as to declarant's intention).

14. See United States v. Pheaster, 544 F.2d 353 (9th Cir.1976), cert. denied 429 U.S. 1099 (pre-rules case admitting statement by alleged kidnap victim of intent to meet accused at specified time and place); State v. Santangelo, 205 Conn. 578, 592, 534 A.2d 1175, 1184 (1987) (statement of murder victim admissible that she was going to meet with a named individual at a certain location and accompany him to a job interview); People v. Malizia, 92 A.D.2d 154, 160, 460 N.Y.S.2d 23, 27 (1983), affirmed 62 N.Y.2d 755, 476 N.Y.S.2d 825, 465 N.E.2d 364, cert denied 469 U.S. 932 (statement that murder victim intended to meet another admissible where circumstances indicated the intent was a serious one and it was realistically likely the meeting would take place); State v. McElrath, 322 N.C. 1, 19, 366 S.E.2d 442, 452 (1988) (statement of decedent admissible to show that he was going with defendant); State v. Terrovona, 105 Wash.2d 632, 642, 716 P.2d 295, 300 (1986) (statement of decedent could be used to prove both that he acted on those intentions and that he acted with the person mentioned in the statement). See also People v. Alcalde, 24 Cal.2d 177, 185–188, 148 P.2d 627, 630–632 (1944) (admitting the statement of murder victim that she was going out with Frank, defendant's nickname, but limited to show intent of deceased).

15. State v. Terrovona, 105 Wash.2d 632, 642, 716 P.2d 295, 300 (1986) (statement of decedent could be used to prove both his actions and those of the person mentioned in the statement).

16. People v. Alcalde, 24 Cal.2d 177, 185–188, 148 P.2d 627, 630–632 (1944) (limiting instruction given directing the jury to consider the statement of murder victim that she was going out with Frank, defendant's nickname, only to show intent of deceased); but see id. at 189, 148 P.2d at 633 (Traynor, J. dissenting) (limiting instruction cannot reasonably be assumed to be effective). See also State v. Farnam, 82 Or. 211, 161 P. 417 (1916) (in homicide prosecution, admission of testimony affirmed that on the day of the killing the victim, when invited to a friend's house, replied that she could not come because she thought the accused was coming, although appellate court indicated that had defendant requested limiting instruction he would have been entitled to it).

17. In a series of cases, the Second Circuit has applied this compromise repeatedly in drug related cases where the key issue is the defendant's involvement in a drug transaction that occurred involving a number of actors. United States v. Badalamenti, 794 F.2d 821, 825–826 (2d Cir. 1986); United States v. Sperling, 726 F.2d 69, 73–74 (2d Cir.1984), cert. denied 467 U.S. 1243; United States v. Cicale, 691 F.2d 95, 103–104 (2d Cir.1982), cert. denied 460 U.S. 1082.

18. State v. Santangelo, 205 Conn. 578, 592, 534 A.2d 1175, 1184 (1987) (statement admissible where declarant unavailable, statement made in good faith and not self-serving, and it expressed intention to take action in immediate future); People v. Malizia, 92 A.D.2d 154, 160, 460 N.Y.S.2d 23, 27 (1983), affirmed 62 N.Y.2d 755, 476

Acceptance of the use of statements of state of mind to prove subsequent conduct and recognition of occasions for its application by the courts have differed among types of situations. In will cases, for example, it is now generally established that when the acts of the decedent are at issue, previous declarations of intention are received as evidence of his or her later conduct.[19] Such statements are admissible on issues of forgery,[20] alteration,[21] contents of a will,[22] and whether acts of revocation were done by the testator.[23] Despite early decisions to the contrary, or decisions greatly restricting their use,[24] statements of intent to commit suicide have been admitted when offered by the accused in homicide cases to prove that the victim took his or her own life and similarly in insurance cases to show suicide.[25] Historically, there has been some greater resistance, however, to admitting threats of a third person to commit the act with which the accused is charged as evidence that the act was committed by the third person and therefore not by the accused. Although some opinions suggest an absolute exclusionary rule,[26] others recognize a discretionary power in the trial judge to admit threats upon finding sufficient accompanying evidence of motive, overt acts, opportunity, or other circumstances giving substantial significance to them.[27] Greater liberality should

N.Y.S.2d 825, 465 N.E.2d 364, cert. denied 469 U.S. 932 (statement admissible where circumstances indicated the intent was a serious one and it was realistically likely the meeting would take place). See also People v. Alcalde, 24 Cal.2d 177, 185, 148 P.2d 627, 631 (1944) (court noted that declarant unavailable and statement possessed high degree of trustworthiness).

19. See 6 Wigmore, Evidence § 1735 (Chadbourn rev. 1976).

20. Atherton v. Gaslin, 194 Ky. 460, 239 S.W. 771 (1922); State v. Ready, 78 N.J.L. 599, 75 A. 564 (1909); Johnson v. Brown, 51 Tex. 65 (1879). Contra Throckmorton v. Holt, 180 U.S. 552 (1901). Such evidence, however, has little effect when contradicted by the testimony of expert document examiners. See generally Annot., 62 A.L.R.2d 855.

21. Doe d. Schallcross v. Palmer, 16 Q.B. 747, 117 Eng.Rep. 1067 (1851).

22. Sugden v. Lord St. Leonards, 1 Prob.Div. 154 (C.A.1876).

23. Stuart v. McWhorter, 238 Ky. 82, 36 S.W.2d 842 (1931). See generally Annot., 24 A.L.R.2d 514.

24. Commonwealth v. Felch, 132 Mass. 22 (1882); State v. Punshon, 124 Mo. 448, 27 S.W. 1111 (1894), both overruled by decisions cited in infra note 25. See generally 6 Wigmore, Evidence § 1726 n. 4 (Chadbourn rev. 1976).

25. Probably the leading homicide case is Commonwealth v. Trefethen, 157 Mass.

180, 31 N.E. 961 (1892), overruling previous case law. See also Bowie v. State, 185 Ark. 834, 49 S.W.2d 1049 (1932); People v. Salcido, 246 Cal.App.2d 450, 54 Cal.Rptr. 820 (1966); People v. Parriera, 237 Cal. App.2d 275, 46 Cal.Rptr. 835 (1965); State v. Ilgenfritz, 263 Mo. 615, 173 S.W. 1041 (1915); Commonwealth v. Santos, 275 Pa. 515, 119 A. 596 (1923). In regard to insurance cases, see Brawner v. Royal Indem. Co., 246 Fed. 637 (5th Cir.1917); Smith v. National Beneficial Soc., 123 N.Y. 85, 25 N.E. 197 (1890); Klein v. Knights and Ladies of Sec., 87 Wash. 179, 151 P. 241 (1915). See generally, Annot., 86 A.L.R. 146, 157; Dec.Dig. Homicide ⟲177. Compare Annot., 93 A.L.R. 413, 426.

26. People v. King, 276 Ill. 138, 114 N.E. 601 (1916); Buel v. State, 104 Wis. 132, 80 N.W. 78 (1899). See generally 1A Wigmore, Evidence § 140 (Tillers rev. 1983).

27. Alexander v. United States, 138 U.S. 353 (1891); Marrone v. State, 359 P.2d 969, 984–985 (Alaska 1961); People v. Perkins, 59 P.2d 1069, 1074–1075 (Cal.App. 1937), affirmed 8 Cal.2d 502, 66 P.2d 631; Du Bose v. State, 10 Tex.App. 230 (1881). The restricted admissibility of the evidence has been justified as follows:

[T]his rule * * * rests fundamentally upon the same consideration which led to the early adoption of the elementary rules that evidence to be admissible must be both relevant and material. It rests

follow under the Federal Rules since Rule 803(3) provides no basis to restrict admission of threats by others, and the Federal Rules' flexible approach to relevancy should provide fewer reasons to treat this as a special class of evidence.[28]

Homicide and assault cases present other special problems. If the accused asserts self-defense and knows of threats of the victim against the accused, these threats are admissible to prove the accused's apprehension of danger and its reasonableness.[29] When used for this purpose, of course, the statements of the victim are not hearsay. But uncommunicated threats pose a more serious problem. They are only admissible to show the victim's intention to attack the accused and further that the victim carried out this intention, thus committing the first act of aggression in the fatal altercation.[30] Fear that juries will abuse the evidence has led some courts to admit proof of uncommunicated threats only under qualification.[31] No qualification appears in

upon the necessity that trials of cases must be both orderly and expeditious * * *. To this end it is necessary that the scope of inquiry into collateral and unimportant issues must be severely limited. It is quite apparent that if evidence of motive alone upon the part of other person were admissible, that in a case involving the killing of a man who had led an active and aggressive life it might easily be possible for the defendant to produce evidence tending to show that hundreds of other persons had some motive or animus against the deceased; that a great many trial days might be consumed in the pursuit of inquiries which could not be expected to lead to any satisfactory conclusion.

People v. Mendez, 193 Cal. 39, 52, 223 P. 65, 70 (1924). Compare Fed.R.Evid. 403, supra § 185.

28. United States v. Sebetich, 776 F.2d 412, 428 (3d Cir.1985), cert. denied 484 U.S. 1017 (in bank robbery trial, court erred, albeit harmless, in refusing to admit statement by another indicating intention to rob bank, appellate court appearing to impose nothing beyond requirements typical to Rule 803(3)).

29. State v. Jackson, 94 Ariz. 117, 382 P.2d 229 (1963); Morrison v. Lowe, 267 Ark. 361, 590 S.W.2d 299 (1979); McBride v. United States, 441 A.2d 644, 650–651 (D.C.App.1982); State v. Mitchell, 144 Me. 320, 68 A.2d 387 (1949). See generally 2 Wigmore, Evidence § 247 (Chadbourn rev. 1979); Dec.Dig. Homicide ⬉190(8).

30. McBride v. United States, 441 A.2d 644, 651–654 (D.C.App.1982). Some courts have held the evidence admissible without

mention of qualification, Wilson v. Commonwealth, 551 S.W.2d 569, 570 (Ky.1977), or with an ambiguous statement suggesting the liberal influence of Federal Rule 803(3) and relevance rules, Dixon v. State, 256 Ga. 658, 660 & n. 2, 352 S.E.2d 572, 574 & n. 2 (1987). See also Commonwealth v. Rubin, 318 Mass. 587, 63 N.E.2d 344 (1945).

Communicated threats are also admissible for this purpose, of course, but this use is usually ignored because of their stronger significance as proof of reasonable apprehension by the accused. See generally 18 U.Chi.L.Rev. 337 (1951); Annot., 98 A.L.R.2d 9, 98 A.L.R.2d 195; Dec.Dig. Homicide ⬉190(7).

31. Some of them require only that there be some additional evidence that the victim was the aggressor, and testimony by the accused will ordinarily be sufficient. Harris v. State, 400 P.2d 64 (Okl.Crim.App. 1965) (some other evidence to support a plea of self-defense); State v. Griffin, 277 S.C. 193, 285 S.E.2d 631 (1981) (same).

Others require that there must be doubt as to who was the aggressor. Decker v. State, 234 Ark. 518, 353 S.W.2d 168 (1962); Bowyer v. State, 2 Md.App. 454, 235 A.2d 317 (1967) (must be some evidence of self-defense and some question as to who was aggressor); State v. Debo, 8 Ohio App.2d 325, 222 N.E.2d 656 (1966) (evidence must leave it doubtful who was aggressor).

Still others hold that the other evidence must itself be sufficient to present a jury question on the issue of which participant was the initial aggressor. State v. Hurdle, 5 N.C.App. 610, 613, 169 S.E.2d 17, 19 (1969) (requiring "testimony *ultra* sufficient to carry the case to the jury tending

the Federal Rule 803(3), and under its influence changes in the qualifications imposed can be anticipated. However, even under the Federal Rule, courts can certainly impose reasonable restrictions on admissibility of such statements to reduce dangers of confusion and misleading under relevancy concerns, which provide the principal focus for determining admissibility of these statements rather than the hearsay doctrine.

The matter of the admissibility of declarations of state of mind to prove subsequent conduct is a far different question from that of the sufficiency of these statements, standing alone, to support a finding that the conduct occurred.[32] In the typical case, it is reasonable to hold that the declarations are themselves insufficient to support the finding and therefore that statements of intention must be admitted in corroboration of other evidence to show the acts.[33]

§ 276. Statements of Physical or Mental Condition: (d) Statements of State of Mind to Show Memory or Belief as Proof of Previous Happenings [1]

As was seen in the preceding section, under the *Hillmon* [2] doctrine, statements of intent to perform an act are admissible as proof that the act was in fact done. By contrast, a statement by the declarant that he or she had in fact done that act would be excluded by the hearsay rule. Thus Walters' statement that he intended to go to Crooked Creek is admissible, but a later statement by him that he had been to Crooked Creek would be excluded. As a matter of common experience, this result seems wrong. It would appear that the first statement, which is admissible, is inferior as evidence to the second, which would be excluded. This is because while both statements involve the truthfulness of the declarant, the second statement involves the further risk that supervening events may prevent the stated intent from being accomplished. Minds are changed, tickets are lost; popular sayings, literature, and experience are filled with plans that went awry. Ac-

to show that the killing may have been done from a principle of self-preservation"). Some courts would apparently require that the proof amount to a showing of some specific overt act on the part of the victim. State v. Mitchell, 144 Me. 320, 68 A.2d 387 (1949) (must be evidence of some act on the part of the victim that might constitute an attack justifying self-defense).

32. See Atherton v. Gaslin, 194 Ky. 460, 239 S.W. 771 (1922).

33. E.g., United States v. Moore, 571 F.2d 76 (2d Cir.1978) (statements of intent insufficient under circumstances to prove interstate transportation in federal kidnap case); Pritchard v. Harvey, 272 Ky. 58, 113 S.W.2d 865 (1938) (declarations alone insuf-

ficient to rebut presumption of revocation of lost will).

§ 276

1. See generally Hinton, States of Mind and the Hearsay Rule, 1 U.Chi.L.Rev. 394, 403–423 (1934); Hutchins & Slesinger, Some Observations on the Law of Evidence—State of Mind to Prove an Act, 38 Yale L.J. 283, 289–298 (1929); Maguire, The Hillmon Case—Thirty-three Years After, 38 Harv.L.Rev. 709, 719–731 (1925); Seligman, An Exception to the Hearsay Rule, 26 Harv.L.Rev. 146 (1912).

2. Mutual Life Ins. Co. v. Hillmon, 145 U.S. 285 (1891). See supra § 275 text accompanying notes 6–8.

cordingly, the argument goes, if the inferior evidence of intent is admitted as proof that the act was done, the superior statement that the act was in fact done should certainly be admitted. In other words, hearsay statements of memory or belief should be admitted as proof that the matter remembered or believed did happen.[3]

Forty years after *Hillmon,* in Shepard v. United States,[4] the Supreme Court dealt with an aspect of this argument. In *Shepard,* the trial court had admitted in a murder prosecution testimony that the victim, the wife of the physician-defendant, had stated to a nurse, "Dr. Shepard has poisoned me." Reversing, the Supreme Court rejected the argument that the statement was admissible as a declaration of state of mind:

> [*Hillmon*] marks the high water line beyond which courts have been unwilling to go. It has developed a substantial body of criticism and commentary. Declarations of intention, casting light upon the future, have been sharply distinguished from declarations of memory, pointing backwards to the past. There would be an end, or nearly that, to the rule against hearsay if the distinction were ignored.
>
> The testimony now questioned faced backward and not forward. This at least it did in its most obvious implications. What is even more important, it spoke to a past act by someone not the speaker.[5]

In more formal hearsay terms, forward-looking statements of intention are admitted while backward-looking statements of memory or belief are excluded because the former do not present the classic hearsay dangers of memory and narration. The weakness inherent in forward-looking statements—the uncertainty that the intention will be carried out—may lead to exclusion, but this is under the relevancy doctrine rather than hearsay analysis.[6]

Nevertheless, after the decision in *Shepard,* the blanket exclusion of statements of memory or belief to prove past events was the subject of substantial re-examination.[7] From the blanket exclusion of statements of memory or belief to prove past events, the courts carved out an area of admissibility for statements by a testator made after the execution of an alleged will. Thus, the testator's statements that he or she has or has not made or revoked a will or made a will of a particular purport were excepted from the ban of the hearsay rule by a preponderance of the decisions.[8] Impetus to recognize such an exception is furnished by

---

3. Seligman, An Exception to the Hearsay Rule, 26 Harv.L.Rev. 146, 157 (1912).

4. 290 U.S. 96 (1933).

5. Id. at 105–106.

6. Lempert & Saltzburg, A Modern Approach to Evidence 428 (2d ed. 1982); 4 Louisell & Mueller, Federal Evidence § 442, at 570 (1980).

7. As some commentators have noted, the substantial differences suggested above between forward-looking and backward-looking statements with regard to memory and narration are not necessarily so impressive. See 4 Weinstein & Berger, Weinstein's Evidence ¶ 803(3)[05], at 124–126 (1990) (quoting Payne, The Hillmon Case—An Old Problem Revisited, 41 Va.L.Rev. 1011, 1023–1024 (1955)).

8. See, e.g., Burton v. Wylde, 261 Ill. 397, 103 N.E. 976 (1914) (later statements of testator admissible on issue of intent to revoke by mutilation); Loy v. Loy, 246 S.W.2d 578 (Ky.App.1952) (statements of testator competent to corroborate other ev-

the unavailability of the person who best knew the facts and often was the only person with that knowledge, *viz.*, the testator. Special reliability is suggested by the undeniable firsthand knowledge and lack of motive to deceive,[9] though the possibility may exist that the testator wished to deceive his or her relatives.[10] Federal Rule 803(3) admits statement that "relates to the execution, revocation, identification, or terms of declarant's will," exempting such statements from the general prohibition against receiving declarations of state of mind offered to prove the happening of the event causing the state of mind.[11]

More broadly, occasional statutes allowed receipt of statements by deceased persons made in good faith and upon personal knowledge before the commencement of the action.[12] The Model Code of Evidence went much further by allowing any hearsay statement by an unavailable declarant.[13] The original Uniform Rules represented a substantial retreat: they broadly excluded statements of "memory or belief to prove the fact remembered or believed," [14] but opened up a small area by allowing statements by an unavailable declarant describing an event or condition recently perceived while the declarant's recollection was clear and made in good faith prior to the commencement of the action.[15]

The Federal Rules, as presented to and adopted by the Supreme Court, incorporated this base, with the added limitation that the statement must not be in response to the instigation of a person engaged in investigating, litigating, or settling a claim.[16] The Rules as finally enacted prohibit the introduction of statements of memory or belief to prove the fact remembered or believed, except as to wills,[17]

idence of execution); Lewis v. Lewis, 241 Miss. 83, 93, 129 So.2d 353, 358 (1961) (testimony that deceased had said, "I have got [my will] right here in my pocket," admissible to show existence of will when authorship of offered holographic will in doubt); In re Roeder's Estate, 44 N.M. 429, 103 P.2d 631 (1940) (statements admissible to corroborate other evidence of changes in will); In re Karras' Estate, 109 Ohio App. 403, 166 N.E.2d 781 (1959) (statements of deceased in regard to execution of will admissible where execution was at issue). See generally 6 Wigmore, Evidence § 1736 (Chadbourn rev. 1976); Annots., 28 A.L.R.3d 994, 5 A.L.R.3d 360, 41 A.L.R.2d 393, 399–400, 148 A.L.R. 1225, 79 A.L.R. 1447; Dec.Dig. Wills ⟨=297.

9. See the argument of Jesell, M.R., in Sugden v. Lord St. Leonards, L.R. [1876] 1 Prob.Div. 154, 241 (C.A.).

10. Boylan v. Meeker, 28 N.J.L. 274, 283 (1860):

[A devisor] may, to secure his own peace and comfort during life, to relieve himself from unpleasant importunities of expectant heirs, conceal the nature of his testamentary dispositions, and make

statements calculated and intended to deceive those with whom he is conversing.

11. In Howard Hughes Medical Institute v. Gavin, 96 Nev. 905, 621 P.2d 489 (1980), the court held that the rule does not permit declarations of the testator to be used to supply one of the two credible witnesses required by statute to prove a lost will.

12. Mass.Gen.Laws Ann. c. 233, § 65; R.I.Gen.Laws 1956, § 9–19–11. The Massachusetts statute was enacted before *Shepard*, that of Rhode Island after. The Massachusetts statute in terms applied in civil cases only. The Rhode Island statute was not thus limited, but in practice appears to have been used only in civil cases.

13. Model Code of Evidence Rule 503(a) (1942).

14. Unif.R.Evid. 63(12) (1953).

15. Id. 63(4)(c).

16. Fed.R.Evid. 804(b)(2) (Rev.Draft 1971); 51 F.R.D. 315, 438.

17. Federal Rule 803(3), as pertinent, states:

omitting the liberalizing provision for statements of unavailable declarants. That latter provision is, however, included for civil cases in the Revised Uniform Rules (1986),[18] although courts generally have shown unwillingness to move to the liberal treatment of the Uniform Rules in the absence of legislative direction.[19]

A recurring problem arises in connection with the admissibility of accusatory statements made before the act by the victims of homicide.[20] If the statement is merely an expression of fear—i.e., "I am afraid of D"—no hearsay problem is involved, since the statement falls within the hearsay exception for statements of mental or emotional condition. This does not, however, resolve the question of admissibility. The

The following are not excluded by the hearsay rule, even though the declarant is available as a witness:

* * *

(3) Then existing mental, emotional, or physical condition. A statement of the declarant's then existing state of mind * * * but not including a statement of memory or belief to prove the fact remembered or believed unless it relates to the execution, revocation, identification, or terms of declarant's will.

See Marshall v. Commonwealth Aquarium, 611 F.2d 1 (1st Cir.1979) (proper to exclude party's earlier statement as to terms of contract, offered by him to prove terms); Prather v. Prather, 650 F.2d 88 (5th Cir. 1981) (error to admit similar testimony).

The effect of the rule is also to exclude in some cases statements of memory or belief accompanying statements of state of mind. See United States v. Cohen, 631 F.2d 1223, 1225 (5th Cir.1980) (court admitted statements of fear but properly excluded statements by same witnesses that defendant said he had been threatened under this limitation of the rule); United States v. Emmert, 829 F.2d 805 (9th Cir.1987) (court properly excluded defendant's statement of fear that also included recitation of threats causing fear). However, whether particular statements that are backward-looking and accompany statements of state of mind will be admitted is complicated. First, the decision often involves a question of balancing. See supra § 274 note 25 and accompanying text. Second, some courts, following the influential decision in United States v. Annunziato, 293 F.2d 373, 378 (2d Cir.1961), cert. denied 368 U.S. 919, have received statements of memory or belief that are "integrally included in" a forward-looking statement of intention. See also United States v. Margiotta, 688 F.2d 108, 136 (2d Cir.1982), cert. denied 461 U.S. 913 (*Annunziato* followed in part).

18. Rev.Unif.R.Evid. (1986) 804(b)(5):

(b) Hearsay exceptions. The following are not excluded by the hearsay rule if the declarant is unavailable as a witness:

* * *

(5) Statement of recent perception. In a civil action or proceeding, a statement, not in response to the instigation of a person engaged in investigating, litigating, or settling a claim, which narrates, describes, or explains an event or condition recently perceived by the declarant, made in good faith, not in contemplation of pending or anticipated litigation in which the declarant was interested, and while the declarant's recollection was clear.

Revised Uniform Rule (1986) 803(3) also includes the prohibition against memory or belief to prove the fact remembered or believed.

19. See Beech Aircraft Corp. v. Harvey, 558 P.2d 879 (Alaska 1976) (court rejects invitation to adopt hearsay exception for statement of recent perception); State v. Barela, 97 N.M. 723, 643 P.2d 287 (App. 1982) (while statement of recent perception adopted by rule in New Mexico, it operates only sparingly in criminal cases because of Confrontation Clause concerns); Kluever v. Evangelical Reformed Immanuels Congregation, 143 Wis.2d 806, 814, 422 N.W.2d 874, 877 (App.1988), review denied 144 Wis.2d 958, 428 N.W.2d 555 (statement of recent perception effective in Wisconsin under rule, although court recognizes that it has been rejected by most states). See generally Comment, 1985 Wis.L.Rev. 1525 (1985). Where, however, strong need exists and indications of reliability are present, some courts have admitted such statements, Quayle v. Mackert, 92 Idaho 563, 447 P.2d 679 (1968). Presumably many such statements might currently be treated instead under the catchall exception. See infra § 324.

20. Annot., 74 A.L.R.3d 963.

victim's emotional state must relate to some legitimate issue in the case. For example, the victim's emotional state may permit the inference of some fact of consequence, such as lack of consent where the prosecution charges that the killing occurred during the commission of either a kidnapping or rape.[21]

However, the most likely inference that jurors may draw from the existence of fear, and often the only logical inference that could be drawn, is that some conduct of the defendant, probably mistreatment or threats, occurred to cause the fear.[22] The possibility of overpersuasion, the prejudicial character of the evidence, and the relative weakness and speculative nature of the inference, all argue against admissibility as a matter of relevance.[23] Moreover, even if the judgment is made that evidence of fear standing alone should be admitted, statements of fear are rarely stated pristinely. Instead, that state of mind usually assumes the form either of a statement by the victim that the accused has made threats, from which fear may be inferred, or perhaps more likely a statement of fear because of the defendant's threats.[24] Not only does the evidence possess the weaknesses suggested above for expressions of fear standing alone, but in addition it seems unlikely that juries can resist using the evidence for forbidden purposes in the presence of specific disclosure of misconduct of the defendant.[25]

In either event, the cases have generally excluded the evidence.[26] While the same pressing need for the evidence may be present as that

21. People v. Thompson, 45 Cal.3d 86, 246 Cal.Rptr. 245, 753 P.2d 37 (1988), cert. denied 488 U.S. 960 (statement of victim's fear admissible in homicide case where state's theory was that murder occurred during commission of rape).

Statements akin to fear—statements of ill will by victim for defendant—may be admissible where they are probative of motive for the killing, although here there is an additional requirement that these feelings or statements must be communicated to the defendant. See United States v. Donley, 878 F.2d 735 (3d Cir.1989), cert. denied 110 S.Ct. 1528 (victim's intention to leave defendant provided motive for killing, evidence permitting the jury to infer that defendant was informed of that plan); State v. Greene, 324 N.C. 1, 376 S.E.2d 430 (1989), vacated on other grounds 110 S.Ct. 1465 (father's intention to disinherit defendant provided motive for murder, court ignoring issue of proof that intention communicated). But see State v. Doze, 384 So.2d 351, 354 (La.1980) (landlady's intention to evict defendant not admissible to prove motive without further showing that she converted intention into action and communicated that to defendant).

22. For an excellent summary of the issues involved see United States v. Brown, 490 F.2d 758 (D.C.Cir.1973).

23. See supra § 185.

24. United States v. Brown, 490 F.2d 758 (D.C.Cir.1973).

25. United States v. Day, 591 F.2d 861, 883 (D.C.Cir.1978).

26. See United States v. Day, 591 F.2d 861 (D.C.Cir.1978); United States v. Brown, 490 F.2d 758 (D.C.Cir.1973); People v. Ruiz, 44 Cal.3d 589, 244 Cal.Rptr. 200, 749 P.2d 854 (1988), cert. denied 488 U.S. 871; Kennedy v. State, 385 So.2d 1020 (Fla.App. 1980); Commonwealth v. DelValle, 351 Mass. 489, 221 N.E.2d 922 (1966); State v. Machado, 111 N.J. 480, 545 A.2d 174 (1988); State v. Wauneka, 560 P.2d 1377 (Utah 1977); Evans–Smith v. Commonwealth, 5 Va.App. 188, 197–201, 361 S.E.2d 436, 441–444 (1987). See generally Seidelson, The State of Mind Exception to the Hearsay Rule, 13 Duquesne L.Rev. 251 (1974); Rice, The State of Mind Exception to the Hearsay Rule: A Response to "Secondary Relevance," 14 Duquesne L.Rev. 219 (1976); Note, 1977 Utah L.Rev. 85. But see State v. Cummings, 326 N.C. 298, 389 S.E.2d 66 (1990) (victim's fear of defendant admissible as relevant to their relationship prior to her disappearance, court in this and other cases applying a broad view of admissibility of fear); Lamb v.

which led to the development of the hearsay exception for dying declarations, the case for trustworthiness is much weaker,[27] and need alone has never been thought sufficient to support a hearsay exception.[28] Exclusion is not universal, however, for in some circumstances statements may be admissible under other hearsay exceptions, such as that for startled utterances or dying declarations.[29] Moreover, the decedent's fear may be relevant for other legitimate purposes beyond proof of the defendant's act or state of mind. There is broad agreement that such statements are admissible where the defense claims self-defense, suicide, or accidental death, because in each of those situations the decedent's fear helps to rebut aspects of the asserted defense.[30]

State, 767 P.2d 887, 890 (Okl.Cr.App.1988) (ill feelings, threats, or similar conduct admissible in marital homicide cases).

27. The weaknesses identified by Shepard v. United States, supra with regard to backward-looking statements are present here. See supra notes 4–6 and accompanying text.

28. Note, 1977 Utah L.Rev. 85, 101 ("[A] person gains no credibility by dying").

29. See supra § 272 & infra Ch. 32. As a matter of application of the Federal Rules, equating fear with "memory or belief" under Rule 803(3) seems acceptable in the unexcited utterance situation, leaving the credible excited utterance situation to

be treated under Rule 803(2). Similar analysis operates under Rule 803(1) for present sense impressions.

30. See, e.g., State v. Langley, 354 N.W.2d 389 (Minn.1984) (defendant's claim of accidental death); State v. Magruder, 234 Mont. 492, 765 P.2d 716 (1988) (decedent's statements admissible where defendant raised self-defense). See also State v. Riley, 532 So.2d 1174 (La.App.1988) (statements of fear admissible where defendant's testimony that victim accompanied him voluntarily made her state of mind relevant).

Chapter 27

STATEMENTS FOR THE PURPOSE OF MEDICAL DIAGNOSIS OR TREATMENT

Table of Sections

§ 277. Statements of Bodily Feelings, Symptoms, and Condition: (a) Statements Made to Physicians Consulted for Treatment [1]

Statements of a presently existing bodily condition made by a patient to a doctor consulted for treatment [2] have almost universally been admitted as evidence of the facts stated,[3] and even courts that otherwise limited the admissibility of declarations of bodily condition have admitted statements made under these circumstances.[4] Since statements made to physicians are usually made in response to questions, they are not likely to be entirely spontaneous. However, their reliability is assured by the likelihood that the patient believes that the effectiveness of the treatment received will depend upon the accuracy of the informa-

---

§ 277

1. See generally 6 Wigmore, Evidence §§ 1719–1729 (Chadbourn rev. 1976); Mosteller, Child Sexual Abuse and Statements for the Purpose of Medical Diagnosis or Treatment, 67 N.C.L. Rev. 257 (1989); 29 Am.Jur.2d Evidence §§ 683–686; C.J.S. Evidence § 246(b); Annot., 37 A.L.R.3d 778, 783–816, 55 A.L.R.Fed. 689; Dec.Dig. Evidence ⚌128.

2. Statements made to nontreating physicians are discussed in infra § 278.

3. Kometani v. Heath, 50 Hawaii 89, 431 P.2d 931 (1967); 6 Wigmore, Evidence § 1719 (Chadbourn rev. 1976).

4. Greinke v. Chicago City Ry. Co., 234 Ill. 564, 85 N.E. 327 (1908).

tion provided to the physician.[5]

As this exception developed, many courts expanded it to include statements made by a patient to a physician concerning *past* symptoms because of the strong assurance of reliability.[6] This is generally sound, as patients are likely to recognize the importance to their treatment of accurate statements as to past, as well as present, symptoms.[7] Some courts continued, however, to admit the testimony only for the limited purpose of "explaining the basis for the physician's conclusion" rather than to prove the fact of the prior symptoms.[8]

A major issue involving the scope of the exception is the treatment of statements made to a physician concerning the cause or the external source of the condition to be treated. In some cases, the special assurance of reliability—the patient's belief that accuracy is essential to effective treatment—also applies to statements concerning the cause. Moreover, a physician who views cause as related to diagnosis and treatment might reasonably be expected to communicate this to the patient and perhaps take other steps to assure a reliable response.[9]

5. "All * * * declarations made by the patient to the examining physician as to his present or past symptoms are known by the patient who is seeking medical assistance to be required for proper diagnosis and treatment and by reason thereof, are viewed as highly reliable and apt to state true facts." Goldstein v. Sklar, 216 A.2d 298, 305 (Me.1966).

6. Meaney v. United States, 112 F.2d 538 (2d Cir.1940) (discussion by L. Hand, J.); Roosa v. Boston Loan Co., 132 Mass. 439 (1882); Peterson v. Richfield Plaza, 252 Minn. 215, 89 N.W.2d 712 (1958) (physician permitted to testify as to plaintiff's statements concerning symptoms experienced prior to examination); Kennedy v. Upshaw, 66 Tex. 442, 1 S.W. 308 (1886); Missouri, Kansas & Texas Ry. Co. v. Dalton, 56 Tex.Civ.App. 82, 120 S.W. 240 (1909, error refused).

7. See the discussions in Meaney v. United States, 112 F.2d 538 (2d Cir.1940) and Peterson v. Richfield Plaza, 252 Minn. 215, 89 N.W.2d 712 (1958).

8. Bases for expert opinions are discussed in supra § 15.

With regard to statements to psychiatrists, the reasoning that supports the hearsay exception for statements to physicians generally may be questioned, since the credibility of the statement may be skewed by the very condition under inquiry, as well as by the breadth of the psychiatric interview. The practice of admitting psychiatric interviews with instructions limiting their use to showing the basis of the psychiatrist's opinion has greater validity than a similar limitation

upon medical history generally. See State v. Griffin, 99 Ariz. 43, 406 P.2d 397 (1965); State v. Wade, 296 N.C. 454, 251 S.E.2d 407 (1979); State v. Myers, 159 W.Va. 353, 222 S.E.2d 300 (1976). The wide variation of possible situations suggests resort to the judge's discretion to exclude under Federal Rule 403 if appropriate. See supra § 185; Annot., 55 A.L.R.Fed. 689, 699.

9. The trend prior to adoption of the Federal Rules was to take an increasingly liberal view to admission of statements relating to causation. See Shell Oil Co. v. Industrial Com'n, 2 Ill.2d 590, 119 N.E.2d 224 (1954) (patient's statement that he slipped while pulling pipe and injured back); Cody v. S. K. F. Industries, Inc., 447 Pa. 558, 291 A.2d 772 (1972) (statement of employee that he was struck by overhead door held admissible). However, some courts, while admitting statements of cause, took a restrictive view of the relationship of such statements to diagnosis or treatment. State v. Contreras, 105 R.I. 523, 535, 253 A.2d 612, 619 (1969) (while statements relating to cause or circumstances of injury will usually be inadmissible, statement that officer said he was hit on back admissible because useful to pinpoint injury and prescribe cure). Others suggested a general exclusion of statements related to cause. Brewer v. Henson, 96 Ga.App. 501, 100 S.E.2d 661 (1957) (physician's testimony as to what plaintiff said concerning circumstances of automobile collision not admissible); Bauer v. Indep. Stave Co., 417 S.W.2d 693 (Mo.App.1967) (surgeon's testimony that plaintiff reported that he did considerable tugging and pull-

However, the result is different when statements as to causation enter the realm of establishing fault. It is generally unlikely that the patient or the physician regards them as related to diagnosis or treatment. In such cases, the statements lack any assurance of reliability based on the declarant's interest in proper treatment and should properly be excluded. "Thus a patient's statement that he was struck by an automobile would qualify, but not his statement that the car was driven through a red light." [10]

Federal Rule 803(4) [11] provides a hearsay exception, regardless of availability of declarant for

[s]tatements made for purpose of medical diagnosis or treatment and describing medical history, or past or present symptoms, pain, or sensation, or the inception or general character of the cause or external source thereof insofar as reasonably pertinent to diagnosis or treatment.

The statement need not have been made to a physician; one made to a hospital attendant, ambulance driver, or member of the family may qualify.[12] Nor does the rule require that the statement be made by the patient.[13] The rule is broadly drawn as to subject matter, including medical history and descriptions of past and present symptoms, pain, and sensations. The test for admissibility is whether the subject matter of the statements is reasonably pertinent to diagnosis or treatment—an apparently objective standard.[14] Descriptions of cause are

ing on a small cart properly disregarded in determining how injury occurred).

10. Adv.Comm. Note, Fed.R.Evid. 803(4), 56 F.R.D. 183, 306. See, e.g., State v. Lima, 546 A.2d 770, 774 (R.I.1988) (father's statement to physician that baby-sitter had submerged child in hot water inadmissible because fixing fault not pertinent to treatment).

11. Revised Uniform Rule (1986) 803(4) is identical.

12. Adv.Comm. Note, Fed.R.Evid. 803(4), 56 F.R.D. 183, 306.

See, e.g., State v. Maldonado, 13 Conn. App. 368, 536 A.2d 600 (1988), certification denied 207 Conn. 808, 541 A.2d 1239 (statement by child abuse victim, who could not speak English, to security guard, who was acting as translator, admissible where security guard told victim that he was questioning her to aid in her treatment); State v. Smith, 315 N.C. 76, 337 S.E.2d 833 (1985) (statements by child to grandmother admissible since children would be expected to rely on caretaker to obtain medical treatment); McKenna v. St. Joseph Hosp., 557 A.2d 854 (R.I.1989) (statements to emergency personnel attending call admissible under exception).

Psychologists and social workers have been included within the exception, Morgan v. Foretich, 846 F.2d 941 (4th Cir.1988)

(psychologist); United States v. DeNoyer, 811 F.2d 436 (8th Cir.1987) (social worker).

13. See Mendez v. United States, 732 F.Supp. 414 (S.D.N.Y.1990) (statement by grandmother concerning child's condition admissible under exception); Welter v. Bowman Dairy Co., 318 Ill.App. 305, 47 N.E.2d 739 (1943) (statement by mother of sick baby admitted); McKenna v. St. Joseph Hosp., 557 A.2d 854 (R.I.1989) (statements by bystanders to emergency personnel that man was driving erratically and then wandered into street admissible under exception as well as subsequent repetition of those statements to emergency room staff).

14. See Cook v. Hoppin, 783 F.2d 684, 690 (7th Cir.1986) ("much will depend on the treating physician's own analysis").

This objective standard, which presumably views pertinence from the perspective of the medical professional, has the benefit of being easily applied. Also, in most circumstances, the view of the patient should coincide with that of the medical expert, since typically the conversation will be guided by the latter. 4 Louisell & Mueller, Federal Evidence § 444, at 597–598 (1980). However, since the rationale for admissibility is the self-interest of the declarant, presumably the objective view should be abandoned, where indicated by the facts, in

similarly allowed if they are medically pertinent,[15] but statements of fault are unlikely to qualify.[16]

§ 278. Statements of Bodily Feelings, Symptoms, and Condition: (b) Statements Made to Physicians Consulted Only to Testify [1]

Historically, many courts drew a sharp line between statements made to physicians consulted for purposes of treatment and those made to physicians consulted solely with the anticipation that the physician would testify in court on the declarant's behalf. Courts were hesitant to admit statements made to doctors consulted only for diagnosis under the instant exception. This restriction was based on the conclusion that, where the declarant does not anticipate that the effectiveness of treatment depends upon the accuracy of his or her statement, the underlying rationale for the exception does not exist. Indeed, if the declarant anticipates that enhancement of symptoms will aid in the subsequent litigation, there is an affirmative motive to falsify or at least exaggerate.

The precise nature of the restrictions upon statements made to doctors not consulted for treatment differed among the jurisdictions, although a very common pattern permitted the doctor to recite the statements of the declarant for the limited purpose of providing a basis for the doctor's medical opinion.[2] The dubious propriety of these

favor of a subjective perspective to either admit or exclude statements that would otherwise be treated differently. Where the court is provided specific information indicating that the declarant believed information medically pertinent which the doctor would consider irrelevant, admission is indicated. Id. at 598. Similarly, where the patient does not appreciate the significance of facts the medical expert considers important, the rationale for admission is lacking under a theory of trustworthiness resting upon the declarant's self-interest. See Mosteller, supra note 1, at 265–257. Cf. Cassidy v. State, 74 Md. App. 1, 29–31, 536 A.2d 666, 680 (1988), cert. denied 312 Md. 602, 541 A.2d 965 (statements by two-year-old excluded because child not advanced enough to appreciate the purpose of interview by medical expert or to be concerned with physical self-interest).

15. United States v. Iron Shell, 633 F.2d 77 (8th Cir.1980), cert. denied 450 U.S. 1001 (child victim's description of rape to medical examiner admitted); State v. Red Feather, 205 Neb. 734, 289 N.W.2d 768 (1980) (same).

16. Roberts v. Hollocher, 664 F.2d 200 (8th Cir.1981) (proper to exclude physician's diagnosis, in suit claiming police

brutality, that plaintiff's condition was "consistent with excessive force" as probably based on plaintiff's account); Garcia v. Watkins, 604 F.2d 1297 (10th Cir.1979) (statement by one of plaintiffs to driver that defendant had forced their vehicle off the road).

As discussed in infra § 278, a number of courts have admitted statements closely related to fault—statements identifying the perpetrator of the offense—in cases involving child sexual abuse where such identity is found pertinent to treatment. See United States v. Renville, 779 F.2d 430 (8th Cir.1985).

§ 278

1. See generally 29 Am.Jur.2d Evidence § 684; C.J.S. Evidence § 246(b); Annot., 37 A.L.R.3d 778, 816–826.

2. These statements were not admissible as substantive evidence. See, e.g., Wolfson v. Rumble, 121 Ga.App. 549, 174 S.E.2d 469 (1970) (subjective complaints of pain made to "examining physician" not admissible to prove pain but admissible to explain diagnosis); Gentry v. Watkins–Carolina Trucking Co., 249 S.C. 316, 154 S.E.2d 112 (1967) (physician consulted as a prospective witness may testify to the plain-

restrictions was probably at least partially responsible for the restrictive view taken by the courts as to what constituted consultation solely for purposes of obtaining testimony. An inquiry was made to determine whether there was any significant treatment motive; if this existed, an additional motive to obtain testimony was to be ignored.[3]

These restrictions were abandoned by the drafters of the Federal Rule. The Advisory Committee concluded that permitting statements to be admitted as a basis for a medical expert's opinion but not for their truth was likely to be a distinction lost on juries, and rejected the limitation.[4] The Rule was enacted without congressional modification.[5] The general reliance upon "subjective" facts by the medical profession and the ability of its members to evaluate the accuracy of statements made to them is considered sufficient protection against contrived symptoms. Within the medical profession, the analysis of the rule appears to be that facts reliable enough to be relied on in reaching a

---

tiff's statements of present condition and past symptoms, not as proof of the facts stated, but as information relied upon to support opinion).

Historically, some courts took the position that physicians consulted solely for purposes of testimony could not recount what was told them even for the purpose of explaining their opinions or conclusions. Korleski v. Needham, 77 Ill.App.2d 328, 222 N.E.2d 334 (1966); Mary Helen Coal Corp. v. Bigelow, 265 S.W.2d 69 (Ky.1954); Cruce v. Gulf, Mobil, & Ohio R. Co., 361 Mo. 1138, 238 S.W.2d 674 (1951). Others, emphasizing the self-serving nature of representations made to physicians consulted for purposes of subsequent testimony, adopted the extreme position that those physicians were confined to giving opinions based solely upon objective facts personally observed by them or upon hypothetical questions. See Shaughnessy v. Holt, 236 Ill. 485, 86 N.E. 256 (1908) (error to admit testimony of physicians that plaintiff's responses when touched with test tubes of hot and cold water indicated nervous deterioration). These rigid limitations on reliance upon subjective symptoms have generally been abandoned as the concepts underlying Federal Rules 703 and 705 have been accepted. See Melecosky v. McCarthy Bros. Co., 115 Ill.2d 209, 214–216, 104 Ill.Dec. 798, 800–801, 503 N.E.2d 355, 357–358 (1986); but cf. People v. Britz, 123 Ill.2d 446, 460–464, 124 Ill.Dec. 15, 22–23, 528 N.E.2d 703, 710–711 (1988), cert. denied 489 U.S. 1044 (experts may not base opinion of criminal defendant's sanity solely on his self-serving statements).

3. Jensen v. Elgin, Joliet & Eastern Ry. Co., 24 Ill.2d 383, 182 N.E.2d 211 (1962);

Erdmann v. Frazin, 39 Wis.2d 1, 158 N.W.2d 281 (1968).

Some courts held that physicians' testimony should not be governed by these restrictions despite the fact that the doctors were consulted after the declarant retained counsel or even at the counsel's recommendation, providing a treatment motive existed. Fisher Body Div., General Motors Corp. v. Altson, 252 Md. 51, 249 A.2d 130 (1969); Yellow Cab Co. v. Hicks, 224 Md. 563, 168 A.2d 501 (1961); Plesko v. City of Milwaukee, 19 Wis.2d 210, 120 N.W.2d 130 (1963). The fact that no treatment was actually given was not considered controlling. Fisher Body Div., supra. However, subsequent reliance upon advice of a treatment nature given by the physician was found to be strong evidence of a treatment motive for the initial consultation. Padgett v. Southern Ry. Co., 396 F.2d 303, 308 (6th Cir.1968) (actual reliance by plaintiff upon physician's advice "is sufficient to eliminate the danger of self-serving declarations made to physician merely to qualify him as an expert for trial"); Conway v. Tamborini, 68 Ill.App.2d 190, 215 N.E.2d 303 (1966) (daily performance of exercises prescribed by physician relied upon in sustaining trial court's finding that consultation was not solely for purposes of obtaining testimony).

4. Adv.Comm. Note, Fed.R.Evid. 803(4), 56 F.R.D. 183, 306.

The bases of expert opinion are discussed in supra § 15. A quasi-hearsay exception for data relied upon by experts is discussed in infra § 324.3.

5. Revised Uniform Rule 803(4) is identical to the Federal Rule as enacted.

diagnosis have sufficient trustworthiness to satisfy hearsay concerns.[6]

The result also has its practical dimension. Under prior practice, contrived evidence was avoided at too great a cost and in substantial departure from the realities of medical practice. Rule 803(4) eliminates any differences in the admissibility of statements made to testifying, as contrasted with treating, physicians.[7] Here, as for statements made to receive treatment, the test for admissibility is whether the statement is medically pertinent to the diagnosis.[8]

The changes in the hearsay exception for statements made for medical diagnosis or treatment have had their biggest impact in cases pertaining to child sexual abuse. In this area, a number of courts have admitted a broad range of statements by children, including statements identifying a particular individual as the perpetrator of the offense. This evidence is admitted under the rationale that such information is pertinent to treatment of the abused child.[9] Statements have been received when made to a rather wide array of professionals and in a

---

6. 4 Weinstein & Berger, Weinstein's Evidence ¶ 803(4)[01], at 146 (1990). See also Mosteller, Child Sexual Abuse and Statements for the Purpose of Medical Diagnosis or Treatment, 67 N.C.L.Rev. 257, 261–264 (1989) (examining the rationale for admitting statements forming the basis for a medical expert's opinion for their truth, while statements relied upon by experts in other fields are generally received for the limited purpose of supporting the opinion).

7. Rule 803(4) provides a hearsay exception for statements "made for purposes of diagnosis *or* treatment." (Emphasis added.)

The elimination of the distinction between statements made for the purpose of obtaining treatment and those for the purpose of preparing expert testimony for trial has not been universally accepted. See Melecosky v. McCarthy Bros. Co., 115 Ill.2d 209, 214, 104 Ill.Dec. 798, 800, 503 N.E.2d 355, 357 (1986) (hearsay exception for subjective statements to physician does not apply to nontreating physician who is consulted solely for purposes of rendering opinion at trial); Cassidy v. State, 74 Md. App. 1, 536 A.2d 666 (1988), cert. denied 312 Md. 602, 541 A.2d 965 (arguing that Federal Rule definition of exception erred critically in admitting statements for purpose solely of diagnosis because that definition of exception focuses on the mind of the expert rather than on that of the declarant); People v. LaLone, 432 Mich. 103, 437 N.W.2d 611 (1989) (Michigan's hearsay rule requires that statement be made for the purpose of obtaining treatment).

Other courts, while apparently accepting the new theory of admissibility, purport also to require the statement to be consistent with both treatment and diagnosis purposes. Morgan v. Foretich, 846 F.2d 941, 949 (4th Cir.1988); United States v. Renville, 779 F.2d 430, 436 (8th Cir.1985); State v. Edward Charles L., 398 S.E.2d 123, 136 (W.Va.1990).

8. Here, an objective standard applied by the expert is theoretically appropriate. It limits statements to those that the medical expert would rely upon in rendering an opinion, which provides the theoretical basis for receiving the statements. 4 Louisell & Mueller, Federal Evidence § 444, at 598 (1980); Mosteller, supra n. 6, at 266.

9. United States v. Renville, 779 F.2d 430, 436–439 (8th Cir.1985); State v. Robinson, 153 Ariz. 191, 200, 735 P.2d 801, 810 (1987); State v. Maldonado, 13 Conn.App. 368, 371–374, 536 A.2d 600, 602–603 (1988), certification denied 207 Conn. 808, 541 A.2d 1239; State v. Altgilbers, 109 N.M. 453, 457–460, 786 P.2d 680, 684–687 (App. 1989); State v. Smith, 315 N.C. 76, 85, 337 S.E.2d 833, 840 (1985); State v. Nelson, 138 Wis.2d 418, 432, 406 N.W.2d 385, 391 (1987); Goldade v. State, 674 P.2d 721 (Wyo.1983), cert. denied 467 U.S. 1253.

The theory of pertinence here is that knowledge of the perpetrator is important to the treatment of psychological injuries that may relate to the identity of the perpetrator and to the removal of the child from the abuser's custody or control. See, e.g., United States v. Renville, supra, 779 F.2d at 437–438.

number of different situations.[10]   These uses of the expanded hearsay exception challenge the wisdom of its extension to cover statements made without any treatment purpose [11] and may raise constitutional problems regarding the right of confrontation in criminal cases.[12]

10. The statements may be made for the purpose of preparing testimony for defendant's criminal trial without a treatment purpose. United States v. Iron Thunder, 714 F.2d 765, 772–773 (8th Cir. 1983). Cf. Morgan v. Foretich, 846 F.2d 941, 949–950 (4th Cir.1988) (statement admissible when made to psychologist who was expert in child abuse for purpose of testifying in civil case).

They may also be made where the expert renders no opinion at trial. State v. Nelson, 138 Wis.2d 418, 434, 406 N.W.2d 385, 392 (1987) (statement to psychologist ruled admissible even though statement not used to form medical opinion).

11. Some courts have questioned the extension of the hearsay exception under Federal Rule 803(4) to admit statements because they are relied upon by medical experts. Cassidy v. State, 74 Md.App. 1, 536 A.2d 666 (1988), cert. denied 312 Md. 602, 541 A.2d 965 (refusing to admit statement of two-year-old child identifying defendant as assailant, arguing that Federal Rule definition of exception erred critically when it focused on the expert's mind rather than the declarant's and concluding that child was too young to appreciate any self-interested purpose in making state-

ment of identity); People v. LaLone, 432 Mich. 103, 437 N.W.2d 611 (1989) (court excludes statements to psychologist regarding identity of assailant on the basis that (1) state's hearsay exception requires treatment to be involved, (2) psychological statements are less reliable than those made to physicians, and (3) use of statement to take protective action not type of reliance anticipated by drafters of Federal Rule); Hall v. State, 539 So.2d 1338, 1342 & n. 8 (Miss. 1989) (statements to social workers about child abuse not admissible because mental health professions are not physicians and services rendered are not medical, court criticizing other courts' efforts to stretch exception to cover such statements). See also State v. Veluzat, 578 A.2d 93, 96–97 (R.I.1990) (statement identifying father as perpetrator of sexual assault does not assist physician in diagnosis and treatment of sexual assault and doctor's repetition of statement highly prejudicial).

12. See Mosteller, supra n. 6, at 285–90 (arguing that where statement is offered under the rationale that it was relied upon as the basis for diagnosis rather than treatment, hearsay exception is not "firmly rooted" and "particularized guarantees of trustworthiness" must be demonstrated).

Chapter 28

RECORDS OF PAST RECOLLECTION

Table of Sections

§ 279. History and Theory of the Exception [1]

By the middle 1600's it had become customary to permit a witness to refresh a failed memory by looking at a written memorandum and to testify from a then-revived memory.[2] Frequently, while examination of the writing did not revive memory, the witness recognized the writing as one that he or she had prepared and was willing to testify on the basis of the writing that the facts recited in it were true. By the 1700's this later procedure was also accepted as proper,[3] although the theoretical difficulty of justifying the new practice was often avoided by labeling it with the somewhat ambiguous term of "refreshing recollec-

§ 279

1. See generally 3 Wigmore, Evidence §§ 734–755 (Chadbourn rev. 1970). Blakely, Past Recollection Recorded: Restrictions on Use as Exhibit and Proposals for Change, 17 Hous.L.Rev. 411 (1980); Note, Past Recollection Recorded: The "Forward–Looking" Federal Rules of Evidence Lean Backward, 50 Notre Dame Law. 737 (1975); Morgan, The Relation between Hearsay and Preserved Memory, 40 Harv.

L.Rev. 712 (1927); Annot., 82 A.L.R.2d 473; 125 A.L.R. 19, 80–187, 35 A.L.R.Fed. 605; 29 Am.Jur.2d Evidence § 877; C.J.S. Evidence § 696; Dec.Dig. Evidence ⬥355, 356, 377, Criminal Law ⬥435, Witnesses ⬥253–260.

2. 3 Wigmore, Evidence § 735 (Chadbourn rev. 1970). See supra § 9.

3. 3 Wigmore, Evidence § 735 (Chadbourn rev. 1970).

tion," which clearly was not strictly accurate.[4] Beginning in the early 1800's, courts began to distinguish between the two situations and to recognize that the use of past recollection recorded was a far different matter from permitting the witness to testify from a memory refreshed by examining a writing.[5]

As the rule permitting the introduction of past recollection recorded developed, it required that four elements be met: (1) the witness must have had firsthand knowledge of the event, (2) the written statement must be an original memorandum made at or near the time of the event while the witness had a clear and accurate memory of it, (3) the witness must lack a present recollection of the event, and (4) the witness must vouch for the accuracy of the written memorandum.[6]

With the passage of time, these requirements have been the subject of modifications and refinements, discussed in the sections that follow. The exception appears as Rule 803(5) of the Federal Rules of Evidence [7] with no formal unavailability of the declarant specified. It reads as follows:

> A memorandum or record concerning a matter about which a witness once had knowledge but now has insufficient recollection to enable the witness to testify fully and accurately, shown to have been made or adopted by the witness when the matter was fresh in the witness' memory and to reflect that knowledge correctly. If admitted, the memorandum or record may be read into evidence but may not itself be received as an exhibit unless offered by an adverse party.

The usefulness of the hearsay exception is apparent from the variety of items the courts have admitted into evidence under its sponsorship: hospital records,[8] reporter's transcripts of testimony,[9] police reports,[10] statements of witnesses,[11] and safe deposit box inventories.[12]

Whether recorded recollection should be classed as a hearsay exception, or as not hearsay at all, is arguable since the reliability of the

4. Id.

5. Acklen's Ex'r v. Hickman, 63 Ala. 494 (1879); State v. Easter, 185 Iowa 476, 170 N.W. 748 (1919); State v. Legg, 59 W.Va. 315, 53 S.E. 545 (1906).

6. Vicksburg & Meridian R. Co. v. O'Brien, 119 U.S. 99 (1886); Kinsey v. State, 49 Ariz. 201, 65 P.2d 1141 (1937); Mathis v. Stricklind, 201 Kan. 655, 443 P.2d 673 (1968).

7. Revised Uniform Rule of Evidence 803(5) (1986) is identical in substance with only minor grammatical differences from the Federal Rule.

8. Minor v. City of Chicago, 101 Ill. App.3d 823, 57 Ill.Dec. 410, 428 N.E.2d 1090 (1981).

9. United States v. Ray, 768 F.2d 991, 994–995 (8th Cir.1985) (unsworn statement by counsel at arraignment); United States v. Patterson, 678 F.2d 774, 778–780 (9th

Cir.1982), cert. denied 459 U.S. 911 (grand jury testimony); United States v. Arias, 575 F.2d 253 (9th Cir.1978), cert. denied 439 U.S. 868.

10. United States v. Sawyer, 607 F.2d 1190 (7th Cir.1979), cert. denied 445 U.S. 943; Dennis v. Scarborough, 360 So.2d 278 (Ala.1978); State v. Bloss, 3 Hawaii App. 274, 278, 649 P.2d 1176, 1178–1179 (1982) (parking ticket); State v. Scally, 92 Or.App. 149, 151–152, 758 P.2d 365, 366 (1988). Compare United States v. Oates, 560 F.2d 45 (2d Cir.1977) and see infra § 296.

11. United States v. Williams, 571 F.2d 344 (6th Cir.1978), cert. denied 439 U.S. 841; United States v. Senak, 527 F.2d 129 (7th Cir.1975), cert. denied 425 U.S. 907.

12. Mathis v. Strickland, 201 Kan. 655, 443 P.2d 673 (1968).

assertions rests upon the veracity of a witness who is present and testifying.[13] Which way the argument is decided seems not to have affected the requirements for admissibility, however, and it is convenient to treat recorded recollection as a hearsay exception since at least some failure of memory is required.[14]

Should the writing be admitted into evidence and be allowed to be taken to the jury room? Some difference of opinion is apparent.[15] However, the testimonial character of the writing makes a strong argument against the practice, just as depositions are generally not given to the jury.[16] Federal Rule 803(5) solves the problem by resort to the ancient practice of reading the writing into evidence but not admitting it as an exhibit unless offered by the adverse party.[17]

§ 280.　Firsthand Knowledge

The usual requirement of firsthand knowledge [1] that applies to witnesses and hearsay declarants, since in reality they are witnesses, is also enforced in regard to past recollection recorded. Thus, where an inventory was offered and the witness produced to lay the necessary foundation testified that it had been made only partly from his own inspection and partly from information provided by his assistant, the inventory was inadmissible.[2]

13. See Kinsey v. State, 49 Ariz. 201, 65 P.2d 1141 (1937); Curtis v. Bradley, 65 Conn. 99, 110–112, 31 A. 591, 595 (1894); Morgan, The Relation between Hearsay and Preserved Memory, 40 Harv.L.Rev. 717, 719 (1927). Compare the treatment of prior inconsistent statements of a witness in supra § 251. As to possible constitutional problems of confrontation, see supra § 252.

While not explicitly stated in the Federal Rule or its legislative history, the declarant under most circumstances would be required to testify as indicated by the use of the term witness rather than declarant in the Rule. Sieber v. Wigdahl, 704 F.Supp. 1519, 1525 (N.D.Ill.1989).

14. Adv. Comm. Note, Fed.R.Evid. 803(5), 56 F.R.D. 183, 307.

15. Fisher v. Swartz, 333 Mass. 265, 130 N.E.2d 575 (1955), overruling Bendett v. Bendett, 315 Mass. 59, 52 N.E.2d 2 (1943).

16. See supra § 217. United States v. Judon, 567 F.2d 1289, 1294 (5th Cir.1978). For a contrary view, see Blakely, supra note 1.

17. United States v. Ray, 768 F.2d 991, 995 (8th Cir.1985) (conviction for failure to appear reversed where transcript constituting past recollection was submitted to the jury over objection and constituted the only evidence of defendant's notice to ap-

pear). But see United States v. Ramsey, 785 F.2d 184, 192–193 (7th Cir.1986), cert. denied 476 U.S. 1186 (difference between reading calendar into evidence and receiving it as an exhibit found too small for reversal in complex case); Del.Uniform R.Evid. 803(5) (1980) & Commentary (memorandum admissible under court discretion depending upon whether likely to unduly influence jury); Holcomb v. State, 307 Md. 457, 464, 515 A.2d 213, 216 (1986) (memorandum admissible as exhibit in Maryland).

§ 280

1. See supra § 10.

2. Town of Norwalk ex rel. Fawcett v. Ireland, 68 Conn. 1, 35 A. 804 (1896). See also Ricciardi v. Children's Hosp. Medical Center, 811 F.2d 18, 23 (1st Cir.1987) (statement in medical records not admissible under exception because recorder did not have personal knowledge of event); Eldridge v. United States, 492 A.2d 879, 883 (D.C.App.1985) (memorandum containing figures obtained by preparer from store department managers was properly excluded because not witness' past recollection); People v. Zalimas, 319 Ill. 186, 149 N.E. 759 (1925) (druggist's memorandum of sale of arsenic to a given person not admissible to prove sale to that person because druggist did not have firsthand knowledge of

§ 281. Written Statement Made While the Witness' Memory Was Clear

Despite some cases suggesting the contrary,[1] the exception as generally stated requires that there be a written formulation of the memory.[2] Federal Rule 803(5) uses the somewhat broader terms "memorandum or record,"[3] which a tape recording, for example, should satisfy. Moreover, the original memorandum must be produced or accounted for as is generally required when the contents of documents are sought to be proved.[4]

This writing need not, however, have been prepared by the witness personally if the witness read and adopted it. Multiple-participant situations are considered further in section 283, below.

The writing must have been prepared or recognized as correct at a time close enough to the event to ensure accuracy.[5] Some opinions use the older strict formulation that requires the writing to have been either made or recognized as correct "at or near the time" of the events recorded.[6] This finds some support in psychological research suggesting that a rapid rate of memory loss occurs within the first two or three days following the observation of an event.[7] But the trend is toward accepting the formulation favored by Wigmore,[8] which would require only that the writing be made or recognized at a time when the events were fairly fresh in the mind of the witness. The formula of Federal Rule 803(5) is "when the matter was fresh in the witness' memory."[9] The cases vary as to the length of time lapse allowable,[10] and while the

purchaser's identity); Mercurio v. Fascitelli, 116 R.I. 237, 354 A.2d 736 (1976) (proper to exclude officer's accident report based in part on what he observed and in part on what parties told him).

§ 281

1. Shear v. Van Dyke, 17 N.Y.S.Ct.Rep. 528, 10 Hung. 528 (1877) (to prove amount of hay loaded, plaintiff offered witness' testimony to the effect that he could not now recall, but that he had known and had told the plaintiff, who then testified that he had been told by witness that fourteen loads had been loaded); Hart v. Atlantic Coast Line R.R., 144 N.C. 91, 56 S.E. 559 (1907).

2. See Wigmore, Evidence § 744 (Chadbourn rev. 1970).

3. See supra § 279 text following note 7.

4. Dayan v. McDonald's Corp., 125 Ill. App.3d 972, 81 Ill.Dec. 156, 466 N.E.2d 958 (1984); Commonwealth v. Galvin, 27 Mass. App.Ct. 150, 535 N.E.2d 623 (1989) (police report containing car registration number admitted where officer's original notes discarded after preparation of report). See generally supra Ch. 23.

5. Maxwell's Ex'r v. Wilkinson, 113 U.S. 656 (1885); 3 Wigmore, Evidence § 745 (Chadbourn rev. 1970).

6. E.g., Gigliotti v. United Illuminating Co., 151 Conn. 114, 123–124, 193 A.2d 718, 723 (1963) (written statement must be excluded if it was not made "at or about the time of the events recorded in it").

7. Hutchins & Slesinger, Some Observations on the Law of Evidence—Memory, 41 Harv.L.Rev. 860 (1928); Gardner, The Perception and Memory of Witnesses, 18 Cornell L.Q. 391, 393 (1933); Stewart, Perception, Memory, and Hearsay: A Criticism of Present Law and the Proposed Federal Rules of Evidence, 1970 Utah L.Rev. 1.

8. 3 Wigmore, Evidence § 745 (Chadbourn rev. 1970).

9. See supra § 279 text following note 7.

10. Nonrules cases: Gigliotti v. United Illuminating Co., 151 Conn. 114, 193 A.2d 718 (1963) (six weeks, proper to exclude); Calandra v. Norwood, 81 A.D.2d 650, 438 N.Y.S.2d 381 (1981) (4½ months, error to admit). Rules cases: Cathey v. Johns–Manville Sales Corp., 776 F.2d 1565 (6th

period of time between the event and the making of the memorandum or record is a critically important factor,[11] a mechanical approach that looks only to the length of time that has passed, rather than focusing on indications that the memory remained fresh,[12] should not be employed.

§ 282. Impairment of Recollection [1]

The traditional formulation of the rule requires that, before a past recollection recorded statement can be received in evidence, the witness who made or recognized it as correct must testify that he or she lacks any present memory of the event and therefore is unable to testify concerning it.[2] A few courts have rejected this requirement in circumstances suggesting that, although the witness may have sufficient present recollection to cause the offer not to meet the traditional requirement, the prior recorded statement would appear to be more complete and more reliable than testimony based upon the witness' present memory.[3] An occasional case has supported complete abandonment of the requirement, arguing that failure of memory adds nothing

Cir.1985), cert. denied 478 U.S. 1021 (several years between event and making of memorandum too great particularly since document was prepared after litigation was begun); United States v. Williams, 571 F.2d 344 (6th Cir.1978), cert. denied 439 U.S. 841 (6 months, not error to admit); United States v. Senak, 527 F.2d 129 (7th Cir.1975), cert. denied 425 U.S. 907 (3 years, not error to admit).

11. Wininger v. State, 526 N.E.2d 1216, 1220 (Ind.App.1988) (transcript made 10 years after events was not contemporaneous enough to satisfy requirements of past recollection recorded).

12. In making the determination of whether the matter was fresh in the witness' mind, a court should examine factors such as those discussed in United States v. Senak, 527 F.2d 129 (7th Cir.1975), cert. denied 425 U.S. 907. They include whether the record suggests any omissions or lapses in memory, whether the record's detail is consistent with the witness' memory at the time of trial, and, most importantly, whether the matter is of a type that would likely have a significant impact on the witness' memory or would typically be rather quickly forgotten.

§ 282

1. See generally, 3 Wigmore, Evidence § 738 (Chadbourn rev. 1970).

2. Bennefield v. State, 281 Ala. 283, 202 So.2d 55 (1967); Chisum v. State, 273 Ark. 1, 616 S.W.2d 728 (1981) (Arkansas evidence rule, which tracks Federal Rule language, interpreted merely to recognize state's common law rule that memory must be totally lacking and efforts to revive it must be unsuccessful); Minor v. City of Chicago, 101 Ill.App.3d 823, 57 Ill. Dec. 410, 428 N.E.2d 1090 (1981); Wininger v. State, 526 N.E.2d 1216, 1219 (Ind.App. 1988) (citing cases adhering to traditional rule).

If it is apparent from the face of the statement that a reasonable person could not presently recall the facts, failure to establish lack of present knowledge by direct testimony will not render the statement inadmissible. Cohen v. Berry, 188 A.2d 302 (D.C.App.1963) (despite lack of record on present knowledge, admission of record of exact days and hours worked over an eight-month period not error because it is "inconceivable" that witness could have recalled figures).

3. State v. Bindhammer, 44 N.J. 372, 387, 209 A.2d 124, 132 (1965) ("Since the judicial search is for truth and accuracy it would indeed be self-defeating for a court to compel a reporter to testify from memory rather than from his notes or transcription; and this would be so regardless of the extent of the reporter's present recollection"); State v. Sutton, 253 Or. 24, 450 P.2d 748 (1969) (checklist used by police officer in administering breath analysis machine admissible despite officer's apparently refreshed recollection, because it was likely to be more trustworthy).

to the credibility of the statement.[4]

It is undoubtedly true that present recollection, clouded by the passage of time, is often less accurate than a statement made at a time when recollection was fresh and clear. However, complete abandonment of the requirement that the witness must have some memory impairment would likely encourage the use of statements prepared for purposes of the litigation under the supervision of claims adjusters or attorneys or under other circumstances casting significant doubt upon the reliability of the statement.[5]

Phrasing the requirement not in absolute terms but as a lack of sufficient present recollection to enable the witness to testify fully and accurately accommodates these competing concerns. This standard, which is used in the Federal Rule,[6] has gained increasing judicial adherents in preference to a total elimination of any requirement of impaired memory.[7]

Is the requirement of "insufficient recollection to enable the witness to testify fully and accurately" satisfied where an apparently reluctant witness seeks to avoid testifying to a particular fact by claiming no memory? Courts have answered this question affirmatively.[8] Perhaps that result does no great violence to the underlying hearsay concerns since the witness is still required to establish the accuracy of the statement and since he or she is available for at least some limited cross-examination.[9] However, it is far from clear that this pattern

---

4. Jordan v. People, 151 Colo. 133, 376 P.2d 699 (1962), cert. denied 373 U.S. 944; Colo.R.Evid. 803(5) (1980) (codifying result in *Jordan*). See also Wigmore, Evidence § 738 (Chadbourn rev. 1970).

5. See Adv.Comm.Note, Fed.R.Evid. 803(5), 56 F.R.D. 183, 307.

6. See supra § 279 text following note 7. See also United States v. Felix–Jerez, 667 F.2d 1297 (9th Cir.1982) (defendant's conviction reversed because a translation of his statement to investigators was admitted as past recollection recorded in the absence of any showing of absence of memory).

7. E.g., Commonwealth v. Shaw, 494 Pa. 364, 431 A.2d 897 (1981). In Elam v. Soares, 282 Or. 93, 577 P.2d 1336 (1978), under the reasoning of the Federal Advisory Committee, supra text accompanying note 5, the Oregon Supreme Court abandoned its advocacy that impaired memory not be required, *Sutton* supra note 3, in favor of the Federal Rule formulation.

8. United States v. Williams, 571 F.2d 344, 349 (6th Cir.1978), cert. denied 439 U.S. 841 (even if the claim of no memory in fact constitutes a willful refusal to testify, the rule's requirement is met if the claim results in incomplete testimony); Commonwealth v. Shaw, 494 Pa. 364, 368–369, 431 A.2d 897, 899–890 (1981) (phony claim of memory considered satisfactory where witness' conduct demonstrated refusal to testify).

9. This result can be supported reasonably well by analogy to practices permitted under Federal Rule 801(d)(1)(A). Under that rule, the admissibility of prior inconsistent statements is limited to testimony given under oath in a prior proceeding, assuring accuracy of the statement. See House Comm. on Judiciary, H.R.Rep. No. 650, 93d Cong., 1st Sess. 13 (1973) reprinted in 1974 U.S.Code Cong. & Admin.News 7075, 7087. Under Rule 801(d)(1) generally, cross-examination of the witness at trial is guaranteed, but the requirement may be satisfied even when the witness has no memory of the event. United States v. Owens, 484 U.S. 554 (1988).

With the instant exception, accuracy depends upon the witness' own testimony at the current trial, and cross-examination is available after the fashion sufficient under Rule 801(d)(1). For this analysis to work properly, however, the other requirements of the instant exception must be met, in particular the requirement that the witness acknowledge the accuracy of the prior statement. See infra § 283 text accompanying note 10.

meets the literal requirement of the rule that the witness "has insufficient recollection" as found by the court or that it is consistent with either the historical function of this exception or the legislative intention of its framers.[10]

§ 283. Proving the Accuracy of the Written Statement; Multi-Party Situations [1]

As a final assurance of reliability, it has traditionally been required that either the person who prepared the writing or one who read it at a time close to the event testify to its accuracy.[2] This may be accomplished by a statement that the person presently remembers recording the fact correctly or remembers recognizing the writing as accurate when he or she read it at an earlier time.[3] But if the present memory is less effective, it is sufficient if this person testifies that he or she knows it is correct because of a habit or practice to record such matters accurately or to check them for accuracy.[4] At the extreme, it is even sufficient if the individual testifies to recognizing his or her signature on the statement and believes the statement correct because the witness would not have signed it if he or she had not believed it true at the time.[5]

No particular method of proving the accuracy of the memorandum is prescribed by Federal 803(5), which merely requires that it be "shown * * * to reflect that knowledge correctly." [6] If an adequate foundation has been laid, it is not grounds for exclusion that the witness' testimony

10. But see 4 Louisell & Mueller, Federal Evidence §§ 623–624 (1980) (arguing that evidence should be admitted under this exception where there is no collusion between the witness and the proponent of the hearsay and where other requirements of the rule are met). Under such analysis, the court appeared to err in Phea v. State, 767 S.W.2d 263 (Tex.App.1989), where a prior statement of the witness was admitted even though she testified at trial that she gave the statement because she was promised that she would not have to testify at trial.

§ 283

1. 3 Wigmore, Evidence § 747 (Chadbourn rev. 1970).

2. Williams v. Stroh Plumbing & Elec., Inc., 250 Iowa 599, 94 N.W.2d 750 (1959).

3. Stanton v. Pennsylvania R. Co., 32 Ill.App.2d 406, 178 N.E.2d 121 (1961) (patient-slips from doctor's office admissible where nurse testified that she had made entries and that they were accurate when made); Mathis v. Stricklind, 201 Kan. 655, 443 P.2d 673 (1968) (inventory of safe deposit boxes admissible when those making

examination testified that notes were correct when taken). Compare Bennefield v. State, 281 Ala. 283, 202 So.2d 55 (1967) (only stenographer who took down confession could authenticate it; detective's affirmance of its correctness "merely confounded its hearsay character").

4. Hancock v. Kelly, 81 Ala. 368, 2 So. 281 (1887); Newton v. Higdon, 226 Ga. 649, 177 S.E.2d 57 (1970) (lawyer testifies to practice in witnessing wills); Minor v. City of Chicago, 101 Ill.App.3d 823, 57 Ill.Dec. 410, 428 N.E.2d 1090 (1981) (doctor gives his practice regarding patient's medical history).

5. Dennis v. Scarborough, 360 So.2d 278 (Ala.1978) (it is adequate if one with knowledge recognizes the signature as his and testifies that he would not have signed it without reading it and determining it to be accurate); Walker v. Larson, 284 Minn. 99, 169 N.W.2d 737 (1969) (same). But see Hodas v. Davis, 203 A.D. 297, 196 N.Y.S. 801 (1922); 4 Louisell & Mueller, Federal Evidence § 445, at 626–27 (1980).

6. See supra § 279 text following note 7.

as to the accuracy of the statement is contradicted by other testimony.[7] However, the witness must acknowledge at trial the accuracy of the statement. An assertion of its accuracy in the acknowledgment line of a written statement or such an acknowledgment made previously under oath will not be sufficient.[8]

The courts have been relatively liberal in finding that the witness has acknowledged the accuracy of a prior statement, particularly where the witness is apparently hostile or reluctant to testify.[9] A special danger of misuse of the exception occurs when this weak proof of the statement's accuracy operates in combination with the argument, discussed in the preceding section, that a refusal to testify satisfies the exception's requirement that a witness have insufficient memory of the event.[10]

The traditional past recollection recorded was a one-person affair with a single witness making the original observation, recording it, and verifying its accuracy. When the verifying witness did not prepare the report but merely examined it and found it accurate, the matter involved what might be called a cooperative report. But in this situation, the substantive requirements of the exception could be met by calling only the person who read and verified the report. A somewhat different type of cooperative report exists when a person reports orally facts to another person who writes them down. A store clerk or timekeeper, for example, may report sales or time to a bookkeeper. In this type of situation, courts have held the written statement admissible if the person reporting the facts testifies to the correctness of the oral report (although at the time of this testimony, the detailed facts may not still be remembered) and the recorder of that statement testifies that he or she faithfully transcribed that oral report.[11] While subject to some ambiguity because of inartful drafting

---

7. Asaro v. Parisi, 297 F.2d 859, 863 (1st Cir.1962), cert. denied 370 U.S. 904.

8. Commonwealth v. Bookman, 386 Mass. 657, 436 N.E.2d 1228 (1982) (excluding grand jury testimony); Superior Tile, Marble Terrazzo Corp. v. Rickey Office Equip., Inc., 70 N.C.App. 258, 319 S.E.2d 311 (1984), review denied 313 N.C. 336, 327 S.E.2d 899 (excluding deposition); State v. Vento, 533 A.2d 1161 (R.I.1987) (excluding prior testimony on this basis); 4 Louisell & Mueller, Federal Evidence § 445, at 628–29 (1980) (no intention to authorize trial by affidavits under this rule).

9. United States v. Riley, 657 F.2d 1377 (8th Cir.1981), cert. denied 459 U.S. 1111 (witness acknowledged only reading and signing statement and did not repudiate it); United States v. Patterson, 678 F.2d 774 (9th Cir.1982), cert. denied 459 U.S. 911 (witness acknowledged recalling events better at time of grand jury testimony and stated he did not believe he had lied to grand jury); State v. Paquette, 146 Vt. 1,

497 A.2d 358 (1985) (court found sufficient witness' testimony admitting that she made, read, and signed a statement containing an acknowledgment of its truth and accuracy). But see Commonwealth v. Bookman, 386 Mass. 657, 664 & n. 10, 436 N.E.2d 1228, 1233 & n. 10 (1982) (equivocal answer to whether witness told truth to grand jury does not constitute adequate verification of truthfulness).

10. Under these circumstances, the statement's guarantees of trustworthiness in general and its accuracy in specific are very weak. Moreover, use of this exception appears to constitute an end run around the restrictions on use of prior inconsistent statements under Federal Rule 801(d)(1). See supra § 282 note 9.

11. Rathbun v. Brancatella, 93 N.J.L. 222, 107 A. 279 (Err. & App.1919) (A saw the license number of the car that struck plaintiff and called it out; B wrote it on an envelope, since destroyed, and gave it to

by Congress, the Federal Rule continues to permit such multi-party statements to be admitted.[12]

the investigating officer, who copied it into his report, produced in court; each testified; held, admissible). See also United States v. Booz, 451 F.2d 719 (3d Cir.1971), cert. denied 414 U.S. 820; Curtis v. Bradley, 65 Conn. 99, 31 A. 591 (1894); State v. Kreuser, 91 Wis.2d 242, 280 N.W.2d 270 (1979). But see Ricciardi v. Children's Hosp. Medical Center, 811 F.2d 18 (1st Cir.1987) (two-party statement inadmissible where source of information unknown).

12. See Chaney v. Brown, 730 F.2d 1334, 1354 n. 26 (10th Cir.1984), cert. denied 469 U.S. 1090.

As prescribed by the Supreme Court, the rule simply stated "made when the matter was fresh in his memory," leaving unrestricted the persons who might contribute to making the memorandum. This was consistent with multi-party involvement in the process of observing and recording, as the Advisory Committee pointed out. Adv. Comm.Note, Fed.R.Evid. 803(5), 56 F.R.D. 183, 307. The Congress unfortunately amended the quoted phrase to read "made or adopted by the witness when the matter was fresh in his memory." If the phrase, "by the witness," is read as modifying "made," the result is to restrict the scope of the rule by raising doubt as to whether multiple party participation is allowed. However, the legislative history indicates that it was not the purpose of the Congress to narrow the scope of the rule or to preclude the various multi-party situations. Senate Comm. on Judiciary, S.Rep. No. 1277, 93d Cong., 2d Sess. 27 (1974), reprinted in 1974 U.S.Code Cong. & Admin.News 7051, 7073. Hence the words "by the witness" should be read as modifying only the word "adopted" and not as requiring that the memorandum be the product of a single witness.

Chapter 29

REGULARLY KEPT RECORDS

Table of Sections

§ 284. Admissibility of Regularly Kept Records

Regularly kept records may be offered in evidence in many different situations, although in almost all, the record is offered as evidence of the truth of its terms.[1] In such cases the evidence is clearly hearsay and some exception to the hearsay rule must be invoked if the record is to be admitted. Often no special exception is needed, however, as the record comes within the terms of another exception. For example, if the record was made by a party to the suit, it is admissible against that party as an admission.[2] If the entrant is produced as a witness, the

---

§ 284

1. See Brown v. J.C. Penney Co., 297 Or. 695, 688 P.2d 811 (1984) (even where purpose of introducing police reports was merely to show that complaints were made rather than that a crime occurred, reports were hearsay statements by officer that such report was made).

2. Stein v. Commissioner, 322 F.2d 78, 82 (5th Cir.1963) ("It was not error for the Tax Court to accept the entries in Stein's notebooks that showed daily net gambling winnings and fail to give credence to the

record may be used to refresh memory,[3] or it may be admissible as a record of past recollection.[4] Sometimes the record may be admissible as a declaration against interest.[5] The present chapter is concerned only with those situations in which none of these alternative theories of admissibility is available or, if available, is not utilized, and a specific exception to the hearsay rule for regularly kept records must be invoked.

§ 285. The Origin of the Regularly Kept Records Exception and the Shopbook Vestige [1]

By the 1600's in England, a custom emerged in the common law courts of receiving the "shop books" of tradesmen and craftsmen as evidence of debts for goods sold or services rendered on open accounts. Since most tradesmen were their own bookkeepers, the rule permitted a reasonable means of avoiding the harsh common law rule preventing a party from appearing as its own witness. Nevertheless, theoretical objections to the self-serving nature of this evidence, apparently coupled with abuse of it in practice, led to a statutory curb in 1609 that limited the use of a party's shopbooks to a period of one year after the debt was created unless a bill of debt was given or the transaction was between merchants and tradesmen.[2] The higher courts refused to recognize the books at all after the year had elapsed, although in practice such evidence was received in the lower courts with small claims jurisdiction.

During the 1700's a broader doctrine began to develop in the English common law courts. At first, this doctrine permitted only the use of regular entries in the books of a party by a deceased clerk, but it was expanded to cover books regularly kept by third persons who had since died. By 1832 the doctrine was firmly grounded, and its scope was held to include all entries made by a person, since deceased, in the ordinary course of the maker's business.

entries in said notebooks that showed daily net losses. The entries showing daily net gambling winnings were in the nature of declarations against interest, while the entries showing daily net losses were in the nature of self-serving declarations."); Vickers v. Ripley, 226 Ark. 802, 295 S.W.2d 309 (1956); Parker v. Priestley, 39 So.2d 210 (Fla.1949) (party's account books admitted against him as admission despite statute providing such books shall be admissible in his favor); Wentz v. Guaranteed Sand & Gravel Co., 205 Minn. 611, 287 N.W. 113 (1939); Utilities Ins. Co. v. Stuart, 134 Neb. 413, 278 N.W. 827 (1938). See generally supra § 254; Dec.Dig.Evidence ⟨key⟩354(18).

3. E.g., Cohen v. Berry, 188 A.2d 302 (D.C.App.1963). See generally supra § 9; Dec.Dig.Witnesses ⟨key⟩255(7)–(8).

McCormick, Evidence 4th Ed. Vol. 2 PT—10

4. Ettelson v. Metropolitan Life Ins. Co., 164 F.2d 660 (3d Cir.1947); Note, 9 U.C.Davis L.Rev. 147 (1976). See generally supra Ch. 28; Dec.Dig.Evidence ⟨key⟩355(5)–(6).

5. See generally infra Ch. 33; Dec.Dig.Evidence ⟨key⟩354(24).

§ 285

1. See generally 5 Wigmore, Evidence § 1518 (Chadbourn rev. 1974); Radtke v. Taylor, 105 Or. 559, 210 P. 863 (1922); 30 Am.Jur.2d Evidence §§ 918–926.

2. An Acte to avoide the double Payment of Debte, 7 Jac. 1, ch. 12 (1609).

The development of the doctrine in America was less satisfactory, however. In the colonies, limited exceptions for the books of a party based on the English statute of 1609 and Dutch practice were in force. In addition to requiring that the entries be regularly made at or about the time of the transaction and as a part of the routine of the business, other common restrictions were that (1) the party using the book not have had a clerk, (2) the party file a "supplemental oath" to the justness of the account, (3) the books bear an honest appearance, (4) each transaction not exceed a certain limited value, (5) witnesses testify from their experience in dealing with the party that the books are honest, (6) the books be used only to prove open accounts for goods and services furnished the defendant (thus making them unavailable for proof of loans and goods and services furnished under special contract or furnished to third persons on defendant's credit), and (7) other proof be made of the actual delivery of some of the goods.[3]

Not until the early 1800's did the American equivalent of the English general exception for regular business entries by deceased persons emerge. As the doctrine gained acceptance, however, often no provision was made for the "shop books" of a party, whose admissibility continued to be controlled by the restrictive statutes. This made little sense, especially in view of the fact that abolition of the party's disqualification as a witness[4] removed the justification for treating the books of a party as a special problem.

Most courts today take the reasonable position that shop book statutes, where they remain, are to be regarded as an alternative ground of admissibility. As a result, when a party offers its books in evidence, they may be admissible either if they meet the shop book act requirements or if they meet the tests for regularly kept records generally.

§ 286. The Regularly Kept Records Exception in General[1]

The hearsay exception for regularly kept records is justified on grounds analogous to those underlying other exceptions to the hearsay rule. Unusual reliability is furnished by the fact that regularly kept

3. See sources cited in supra note 1.

4. See supra § 65. The retention of a vestige of the old common law disqualification of a party in the "dead man's statutes" adopted by many jurisdictions created a special problem. These statutes prohibited a party from testifying in an action brought by or against a decedent's estate regarding transactions with the deceased. Id. It has generally been held, however, that use of the shop books (and the supplemental oath necessary for their use) was not "testimony" within the meaning of the dead man's statutes, Roth v. Headlee, 238 Iowa 1340, 29 N.W.2d 923 (1947), or that the use of shop books of a party was an exception to the dead man's statute, House v. Beak, 141 Ill. 290, 30 N.E.

1065 (1892). See generally 5 Wigmore, Evidence § 1554 (Chadbourn rev. 1974); Annot., 6 A.L.R. 756.

§ 286

1. See generally 5 Wigmore, Evidence §§ 1517–1561b (Chadbourn rev. 1974); Morgan, et al., The Law of Evidence: Some Proposals for Its Reform 65–68 (1927); Laughlin, Business Entries and the Like, 46 Iowa L.Rev. 276 (1961); Note, 48 Colum.L.Rev. 920 (1948); Annot., 13 A.L.R.3d 284, 77 A.L.R.3d 115, 31 A.L.R.Fed. 457; 30 Am.Jur.2d Evidence §§ 927–961; C.J.S. Evidence §§ 682–95; Dec.Dig.Evidence ⊗350, 354, 361, 376, 383(8), Criminal Law ⊗434.

records typically have a high degree of accuracy. The very regularity and continuity of the records are calculated to train the recordkeeper in habits of precision; if of a financial nature, the records are periodically checked by balance-striking and audits; and in actual experience, the entire business of the nation and many other activities function in reliance upon records of this kind. The impetus for resort to these hearsay statements at common law arose when the person or persons who made the entry, and upon whose knowledge it was based, were unavailable as witnesses because of death, insanity, disappearance, or other reason.

The common law exception had four elements: (1) the entries must be original entries made in the routine of a business, (2) the entries must have been made upon the personal knowledge of the recorder or of someone reporting the information, (3) the entries must have been made at or near the time of the transaction recorded, and (4) the recorder and the informant must be shown to be unavailable.[2] If these conditions were met, the business entry was admissible to prove the facts recited in it.

The regularly kept records exception had evolved within the context of simple business organizations, with the typical records of a double-entry system of journal and ledger. In this setting, the common law requirements were not unduly burdensome. Control and management of complex organizations require correspondingly complicated records, however, and the organizations of business, government, and institutions in general were becoming increasingly intricate. While the theory of the exception was sound, some of the common law requirements were incompatible with modern conditions. The limitation to records of a business was unduly restrictive. The requirement of an "original" record was inconsistent with modern developments in record keeping. The need to account for nonproduction of all participants in the process of assembling and recording information was a needless and disruptive burden in view of the unlikelihood that any of the persons involved would remember a particular transaction or its details. And there were uncertainties as to what witnesses were required to lay the necessary foundation for the records. Since the courts seemed unable to resolve these difficulties, relief was sought in legislation, and even before the enactment of the Federal Rules, the exception was governed by statute or rule virtually everywhere.

The Commonwealth Fund Act and the Uniform Business Records as Evidence Act[3] provided the principal models for the early legislative

---

2. Laughlin, supra note 1, at 282.

3. The Commonwealth Fund Act provided as follows:

Any writing or record, whether in the form of an entry in a book or otherwise, made as a memorandum or record of any act, transaction, occurrence or event shall be admissible in evidence in proof of said act, transaction, occurrence or event, if the trial judge shall find that it was made in the regular course of any business, and that it was the regular course of such business to make such memorandum or record at the time of such act, transaction, occurrence or event or within a reasonable time thereafter. All other circumstances of the

reforms. Their essential features are now incorporated in Federal Rule 803(6) [4], which provides a hearsay exception, without regard to unavailability of declarant, as follows:

> A memorandum, report, record, or data compilation, in any form, of acts, events, conditions, opinions, or diagnoses, made at or near the time by, or from information transmitted by, a person with knowledge, if kept in the course of a regularly conducted business activity, and if it was the regular practice of that business activity to make the memorandum, report, record, or data compilation, all as shown by the testimony of the custodian or other qualified witness, unless the source of information or the method or circumstances of preparation indicate lack of trustworthiness. The term "business" as used in this paragraph includes business, institution, association, profession, occupation, and calling of every kind, whether or not conducted for profit.[5]

§ 287. Types of Records; [1] Opinions; Absence of Entry

The usual statement of the "business records" exception to the hearsay rule suggests that oral reports are not within it, even if the other requirements for admissibility are met. The common law cases tended to speak in terms of entries in account books, the subject usually

making of such writing or record, including lack of personal knowledge by the entrant or maker, may be shown to affect its weight, but they shall not affect its admissibility. The term business shall include business, profession, occupation and calling of every kind.

Morgan, supra note 1, at 63.

Several states and the Congress adopted this act. For federal courts it has been superseded by Federal Rule 803(6).

The Uniform Act provided as follows:

§ 1. Definition. The term "business" shall include every kind of business, profession, occupation, calling or operation of institutions, whether carried on for profit or not.

§ 2. Business Record. A record of an act, condition or event, shall, in so far as relevant, be competent evidence if the custodian or other qualified witness testifies to its identity and the mode of its preparation, and if it was made in the regular course of business, at or near the time of the act, condition or event, and if, in the opinion of the court, the sources of information, method and time of preparation were such as to justify its admission.

9A U.L.A. 506 (1965).

After wide adoption, the Uniform Act was superseded by Original Uniform Rule 63(13), which in turn has been superseded by Revised Uniform Rule (1986) 803(6).

4. Revised Uniform Rule (1986) 803(6) is identical.

5. The language "if kept in the course of a regularly conducted business activity, and if it was the regular practice of that business activity to make the memorandum, report, record, or data compilation, all" was substituted by the Congress for the Supreme Court's provision, "all in the course of a regularly conducted activity." The Congress also added the definition of "business" in the second sentence and made a few other changes of no significance. House Comm. on Judiciary, H.R.Rep. No. 650, 93d Cong., 1st Sess. 14 (1973), reprinted in 1974 U.S.Code Cong. & Admin.News 7051, 7087–88; Senate Comm. on Judiciary, S.Rep. No. 1277, 93d Cong., 2d Sess. 16 (1974), reprinted in 1974 U.S. Code Cong. & Admin. News 7051, 7063–64; Conference Comm., Conf.Rep. No. 1597, 93d Cong., 2d Sess. 11 (1974), reprinted in 1974 U.S.Code Cong. & Admin.News 7098, 7104.

§ 287

1. See generally 5 Wigmore, Evidence § 1528 (Chadbourn rev. 1974). See also Annot., 83 A.L.R. 806.

under consideration.[2] The Commonwealth Fund Act used the terms "writing or record," [3] the Uniform Act spoke of "record," [4] and the Federal Rule includes a "memorandum, report, record, or data compilation." [5] Of these, only the term "report" in the Federal Rule is arguably broad enough to include an oral report, and there, the provision that the report be "kept" negates the idea that oral reports are within the rule.[6] Nevertheless, the English position is that oral reports may qualify under the exception,[7] and some American courts have admitted oral reports on the basis of a partial analogy to business records.[8]

Under the common law exception, the entries were required to be "original" entries and not mere transcribed records or copies.[9] This was based on the assumption that the original entries were more likely to be accurate than subsequent copies or transcriptions. In business practice, however, it is customary for daily transactions, such as sales or services rendered, to be noted upon slips, memorandum books, or the like by the person most directly concerned. Then someone else collects these memoranda and from them makes entries in a permanent book, such as a journal or ledger. In these cases, the entries in the permanent record sufficiently comply with the requirement of originality.[10]

2. See supra § 285. In Baltimore & Ohio Southwestern Ry. Co. v. Tripp, 175 Ill. 251, 51 N.E. 833 (1898), a record of engine inspections was held properly excluded because not a book of account.

3. See supra § 286 note 3.

4. Id.

5. See supra § 286 text following note 4.

6. Id.

7. 5 Wigmore, Evidence § 1528 (Chadbourn rev. 1974) (citing Sussex Peerage Case, 11 Cl. & F. 113, 8 Eng.Rep. 1034, 1035 (H.L.1844)). See also Cross & Tapper, Cross on Evidence 646 (7th ed. 1990). Wigmore suggests that the English requirement that the person making the report have a duty to do so (see infra § 288 n. 23 and accompanying text) provides a sufficient additional assurance of reliability to justify expanding the exception to include oral reports. 5 Wigmore, Evidence § 1528 (Chadbourn rev. 1974).

8. Williams v. Walton & Whann Co., 14 Del. (9 Houst.) 322, 32 A. 726 (1892) (oral reports admissible if made regularly); Geralds v. Champlin, 93 N.H. 157, 37 A.2d 155 (1944) (oral reports of deceased foreman to superintendent regarding employee's complaints of trouble with his leg made as part of checkup system admissible).

The possibility of achieving admissibility of otherwise conforming oral reports by resort to the "residual" hearsay exception should not be overlooked. See infra § 324.

9. See generally 5 Wigmore, Evidence §§ 1532, 1558 (Chadbourn rev. 1974); Annot., 17 A.L.R.2d 235; 30 Am.Jur.2d Evidence §§ 941–945. In a typical double-entry bookkeeping system, the journal or daybook in which transactions are entered in chronological order is the first permanent record. A strict literal interpretation of "book of original entry" under this system would be limited to the journal. The ledger, to which items are transferred according to classification and which furnishes the "controls" of the business, however, obviously maintains information in far more usable form, and its accuracy is equally assured by its being a part of the entire system. Accordingly, while insistence is sometimes found that the journal be used, the case has generally been otherwise. Statutes containing the expression "book of original entry" offer occasional difficulty.

10. Vickers v. Ripley, 226 Ark. 802, 295 S.W.2d 309 (1956) (ledger account made up from sales tickets or invoices); Tull v. Turek, 38 Del.Ch. 182, 147 A.2d 658 (1958) (ledger in which entries were made once each year from data supplied by plaintiffs); Cascade Lumber Terminal, Inc. v. Cvitanovich, 215 Or. 111, 332 P.2d 1061 (1958) (looseleaf subsidiary ledger in which bookkeeper made entries from log scalers' sheets on which number of logs delivered

They would certainly be admissible if the slips or memoranda disappeared and should be admissible as the original permanent entry without proof as to the unavailability of the tentative memoranda. This practice also serves the interest of convenience, since it is much easier to use a ledger or similar source than slips or temporary memoranda when the inquiry is into the whole state of an account. Of course, the slips or memoranda would also be admissible if they should be offered.[11] The Federal Rule does not require that the entry be original, but allows "any form." [12]

With regard to opinions in business records, two types of issues arise. The first concerns lay opinions or conclusions, which are largely conclusory forms of expression. The opinion rule should be restricted to governing the manner of presenting live testimony where a more specific and concrete answer can be secured if desired and should have little application to the admissibility of out-of-court statements, including business records.[13] The second and more difficult issue regards so-called expert opinions within business records. Federal Rule 803(6) specifically provides that an admissible regularly kept record may include opinions.[14] These will ordinarily be expert opinions, and they will be subject to requirements governing proper subjects for expert opinions and qualifications of experts.[15] For further discussion in connection with hospital records, see infra section 293.

Sometimes the absence of an entry relating to a particular transaction is offered as proof that no such transaction took place.[16] For example, a car rental agency's records showing no lease or rental activity for a certain vehicle may be offered to prove that the defen-

---

was initially entered); Grand Strand Const. Co. v. Graves, 269 S.C. 594, 239 S.E.2d 81 (1977) (secretary made entries in ledger from man-hours tabulated by job foreman sometimes transmitted by telephone, sometimes provided on scraps of paper, which were not retained, either handed to her or left under office door); Tri–Motor Sales, Inc. v. Travelers Indem. Co., 19 Wis.2d 99, 119 N.W.2d 327 (1963) (account books made from purchase invoices and hard copies of sales slips, and not the invoices and slips themselves, were "original entries").

11. Annot., 21 A.L.R.2d 773.

12. See supra § 286 text following note 4.

13. See § 18 supra.

14. See supra § 286 text following note 4.

15. Courts have reached different conclusions as to whether the proponent of the record must affirmatively establish the expert qualifications of the declarant in a business record. Compare United States v. Licavoli, 604 F.2d 613, 622–623 (9th Cir. 1979), cert. denied 446 U.S. 935 (no inflexible rule that qualifications must be affirmatively established but the court has discretion to exclude opinion where qualifications are seriously challenged) with Forward Communications Corp. v. United States, 608 F.2d 485, 510–11 (Ct.Cl.1979) (expert opinions which are not part of factual reports of contemporaneous events are inadmissible unless preparer testifies and establishes qualifications). The approach in *Licavoli* is more consistent with the structure of the Federal Rule, which explicitly admits opinions, and accordingly should allow their admission if they are made and recorded in the regular course of a business unless the opponent raises a challenge to their trustworthiness. With regard to hospital records, see infra § 293 note 16 and accompanying text.

16. See generally, 5 Wigmore, Evidence § 1531 (Chadbourn rev. 1974); 30 Am. Jur.2d Evidence § 959; C.J.S. Evidence § 687.

dant, found in possession of the car, had stolen it.[17] The majority of courts have admitted the evidence for this purpose,[18] and Federal Rule 803(7) [19] specifically so provides:

> Evidence that a matter is not included in the memoranda reports, records, or data compilations, in any form, kept in accordance with the provisions of paragraph (6), to prove the nonoccurrence or nonexistence of the matter, if the matter was of a kind of which a memorandum, report, record, or data compilation was regularly made and preserved, unless the sources of information or other circumstances indicate lack of trustworthiness.[20]

§ 288. Made in the Routine of a "Business"; [1] Accident Reports

The early cases construed the requirement of a "business" literally and excluded, for example, records kept in connection with loans made by an individual not in the business of loaning money to others on the basis that they were not concerned with "business".[2] The Commonwealth Fund Act defined "business" much more expansively to "include business, profession, occupation and calling of every kind." [3] The Uniform Act added "operation of institutions, whether carried on for profit or not." [4]

In Federal Rule 803(6), the term includes "business, institution, association, profession, occupation, and calling of every kind, whether or not conducted for profit." [5] This rule, applying to a "memorandum, report, record, or data compilation, in any form," of a "business" thus broadly defined, is of great scope. It has been held to encompass such diverse items as a diary of tips kept by a blackjack dealer,[6] notations on calendar of daily illegal drug sales,[7] a catalog,[8] attaching envelopes to bids upon opening,[9] a hospital's scrapbook of newspaper articles show-

17. United States v. De Georgia, 420 F.2d 889 (9th Cir.1969).

18. Id. at 891–94.

19. Revised Uniform Rule 803(7) is identical except for minor stylistic differences.

20. For paragraph (6), see supra § 286 text following note 4.

The Federal Advisory Committee's Note suggests such evidence is probably not hearsay under Rule 801, 56 F.R.D. at 311, presumably because the absence of a record typically is not intended to be an assertion.

§ 288

1. See generally 30 Am.Jur.2d Evidence §§ 937, 939; 32 C.J.S. Evidence § 685(1).

2. Ketcham v. Cummins, 226 Iowa 1207, 286 N.W. 409 (1939) (plaintiff's memorandum book of loans made by him inad-

missible because he was not in the loan business). See Annot., 68 A.L.R. 692 (check stubs).

3. See supra § 286 note 3.

4. Id.

5. See supra § 286 text following note 4. A definition of "business records" has two alternative ways to limit the class of records covered. Either it can limit the kind of entity that conducts the activity or the kind of activity that is conducted. The Federal Rule follows the latter approach.

6. Keogh v. Commissioner, 713 F.2d 496 (9th Cir.1983).

7. United States v. Lizotte, 856 F.2d 341, 344 (1st Cir.1988).

8. United States v. Grossman, 614 F.2d 295 (1st Cir.1980).

9. United States v. Patterson, 644 F.2d 890 (1st Cir.1981).

ing visiting hours,[10] prison counselor's report to staff psychiatrist of incident involving prisoner,[11] invoices from suppliers,[12] a bill of lading,[13] an automobile lease by dealer,[14] a logbook of malfunctions of a machine,[15] and an appraisal of a painting for purposes of insurance.[16] These examples are all in addition, of course, to account books and their counterparts, which might more readily fall within the usual concept of business records.[17]   Hospital records are specially treated below in section 283 and computer-stored records are the subject of section 284.

Records, such as diaries, if of a purely personal nature not involved in declarant's business activities, do not fall within the rule,[18] but if kept for business purposes are within the rule.[19]   Memoranda of telephone conversations are treated similarly.[20]   The breadth of the exception is also demonstrated by cases holding that the activity need not be legal for the record to qualify.[21]   Some church records are covered generally by the business records exception while those related to the family history of members are the subject of Federal Rule 803(11).[22]

Under the English rules, both the matter or event recorded and the recording of it must have been performed pursuant to a duty to a third person.[23]   This is not the case under the American law.[24]

---

10. United States v. Reese, 568 F.2d 1246 (6th Cir.1977).

11. Stone v. Morris, 546 F.2d 730 (7th Cir.1976).

12. Falcon Jet Corp. v. King Enterprises, Inc., 678 F.2d 73 (8th Cir.1982).

13. United States v. Henneberry, 719 F.2d 941 (8th Cir.1983), cert. denied 465 U.S. 1107.

14. United States v. Page, 544 F.2d 982 (8th Cir.1976).

15. Gulf South Mach., Inc. v. Kearney & Trecker Corp., 756 F.2d 377 (5th Cir. 1985), cert denied 474 U.S. 902.

16. United States v. Licavoli, 604 F.2d 613 (9th Cir.1979), cert. denied 446 U.S. 935.

17. Nonrule cases include: State v. Spray, 221 Kan. 67, 558 P.2d 129 (1976) (retail price tags on merchandise); Porter v. State, 623 S.W.2d 374 (Tex.Cr.App.1981), cert. denied 456 U.S. 965 (tape of police radio messages); Hill v. Joseph T. Ryerson & Son, Inc., 165 W.Va. 22, 268 S.E.2d 296 (1980) (paint stick markings on shipment of pipe).

18. Clark v. City of Los Angeles, 650 F.2d 1033 (9th Cir.1981), cert. denied 456 U.S. 927.

19. United States v. McPartlin, 595 F.2d 1321 (7th Cir.1979), cert. denied 444 U.S. 833; United States v. Hedman, 630 F.2d 1184 (7th Cir.1980), cert. denied 450

U.S. 965. See also United States v. Huber, 772 F.2d 585, 591 n. 4 (9th Cir.1985) (inventory of firearms kept by gun collector, who kept guns both for sport and for investment); Keogh v. Commissioner, 713 F.2d 496 (9th Cir.1983) (personal diary, not a record of the casino, were nevertheless records of blackjack dealer's own business activity).

20. Annot., 94 A.L.R.3d 975.

21. United States v. Hedman, 630 F.2d 1184, 1198 (7th Cir.1980), cert. denied 450 U.S. 965 (diary recording payoffs); United States v. McPartlin, 595 F.2d 1321 (7th Cir.1979), cert. denied 444 U.S. 833 (desk calendar recording events involved in extortion scheme); United States v. Foster, 711 F.2d 871, 882 n. 6 (9th Cir.1983), cert. denied 465 U.S. 1103 (record of illegal drug sales).

22. Federal Rule 803(11) includes:

Statements of births, marriages, divorces, deaths, legitimacy, ancestry, relationship by blood or marriage, or other similar facts of personal or family history, contained in a regularly kept record of a religious organization.

Uniform Rule (1986) 803(11) is identical.

23. Cross & Tapper, Tapper on Evidence 647 (7th ed. 1990).

24. LeBrun v. Boston & Maine R.R., 83 N.H. 293, 142 A. 128 (1928) (dictum); Hutchins v. Berry, 75 N.H. 416, 75 A. 650

How far the rule goes in requiring not only that the record must be made in the regular course of a business but that it "be the regular practice of that business to make the memorandum"[25] is disputed. What might be termed nonroutine records, which are nevertheless made in the course of regularly conducted activities, are the focus of concern here. Often such records, because not regularly made, will be outside the expertise of the organization and properly excluded.[26] Other records of this type will be properly excluded because of motivational concerns arising from the fact they were generated for litigation purposes, discussed immediately below. Where these specific threats to trustworthiness are absent but, nevertheless, the record is nonroutine, the authorities reach contrary decisions depending upon whether the focus is on the basic concern of trustworthiness[27] or the apparent intention of Congress as reflected in the literal requirement of the rule.[28]

An important set of concerns revolves around the purpose of the report and the circumstances of its preparation, particularly reports of accidents. The leading case is Palmer v. Hoffman,[29] a suit against railroad trustees arising out of an accident at a railroad crossing. The engineer of the train involved was interviewed two days after the accident by a representative of the railroad and a representative of the state public utilities commission. He signed a statement giving his version of the incident. The engineer died before trial, and the statement was offered by the defendants, who contended that the railroad obtained such statements in the regular course of its business. Affirming the trial court's exclusion of the report, the Supreme Court of the United States stated:

> [The report] is not a record made for the systematic conduct of the business as a business. An accident report may affect that business in the sense that it affords information on which the management may act. It is not, however, typical of entries made systematically or as a matter of

(1910). See generally, 5 Wigmore, Evidence, § 1524 (Chadbourn rev. 1974). No requirement in terms of duty is found in the Federal Rules, but the same result is produced by the requirement that all participants be in this course of the business. See infra § 290.

25. Federal 803(6), see supra § 286 text following note 4.

26. See 4 Louisell & Mueller, Federal Evidence § 446, at 654–55 (1980).

27. 4 Weinstein & Berger, Weinstein's Evidence ¶ 803(6)[03], at 182 (1990). The treatise argues that such nonroutine records should be admitted unless questions regarding trustworthiness are raised.

28. The language of the rule requiring that it be the "regular practice of the business to make the memorandum," was not part of the rule as submitted to Congress by the Supreme Court. This provision, which was part of the earlier federal statute, was added by the House Judiciary Committee. H.R.Rep. No. 650, 93d Cong., 1st Sess. 14 (1973), reprinted in 1974 U.S.Code Cong. & Admin.News 7075, 7087–88.

In United States v. Freidin, 849 F.2d 716, 723 (2d Cir.1988), the court excluded a nonroutine, albeit apparently trustworthy record, because it did not meet the requirements of the rule, the court giving deference to the apparent legislative intent in adding the requirement. Clearly, however, some nonroutineness or selectivity in recording particular events is permissible. Kassel v. Gannett Co., 875 F.2d 935, 945 (1st Cir.1989).

29. 318 U.S. 109 (1943).

routine to record events or occurrences, to reflect transactions with others, or to provide internal controls * * *. Unlike payrolls, accounts receivable, accounts payable, bills of lading and the like, these reports are calculated for use essentially in the court, not in the business. Their primary use is in litigating, not in railroading.[30]

Consequently, the report was held not to have been made "in the regular course" of the business within the meaning of the federal statute then providing for the admissibility of business records.[31]

While *Palmer* has been subject to various interpretations,[32] the most reasonable reading of it is that it did not create a blanket rule of exclusion for accident reports or similar records kept by businesses. Rather, it recognized a discretionary power in the trial court to exclude evidence which meets the letter of the business records exception, but which, under the circumstances, appears to lack the reliability business records are assumed ordinarily to have. The existence of a motive and opportunity to falsify the record, especially in the absence of any countervailing factors, is of principal concern.[33] The Federal Rule incorporates this reading of *Palmer* by permitting admission if the report otherwise complies with the requirements of the rule, "unless the source of information or the method or circumstances of preparation indicate lack of trustworthiness." [34]

Police reports and records can, of course, meet the requirements for the regularly kept records exception to the hearsay rule. They can also qualify under the hearsay exception for public records and reports.[35] Federal Rule 803(8) contains certain restrictions upon the use of police reports in criminal cases, and the question has arisen whether those restrictions can be avoided by offering police reports under the regularly kept records exception, which imposes no such limitations. The answer, while somewhat complicated, has generally been in the negative. This subject is discussed in greater detail in section 297 infra.

---

30. Id. at 113–114.

31. Id. at 114–115.

32. Compare Laughlin, Business Entries and the Like, 46 Iowa L.Rev. 276, 289 (1961) with Comment, 43 Colum.L.Rev. 392 (1943).

33. Thus where the only function that the report serves is to assist in litigation or its preparation, many of the normal checks upon the accuracy of business records are not operative. Reliance upon the report's accuracy in the day-to-day operation of the business is significant. Lewis v. Baker, 526 F.2d 470 (2d Cir.1975) (railroad accident report made pursuant to railroad and I.C.C. rules held admissible); Coates v. Johnson & Johnson, 756 F.2d 524 (7th Cir. 1985) (employee disciplinary records admissible in employment discrimination case because prepared, not primarily with view

toward subsequent adversarial proceeding, but as part of systematic conduct of running business).

34. See supra § 286 text following note 4.

For cases finding a lack of trustworthiness, see, e.g., United States v. Williams, 661 F.2d 528, 531 (5th Cir.1981) (memorandum estimating value of company's trailer stolen three years earlier made by head of maintenance department lacked trustworthiness because not prepared in course of regularly conducted business but rather for trial); Paddack v. Dave Christensen, Inc., 745 F.2d 1254 (9th Cir.1984) (audit reports ordered by trustees of trust account only upon suspicion of deficiency were prepared for litigation and lacked trustworthiness).

35. See generally infra Ch. 30.

§ 289. Made at or Near the Time of the Transaction Recorded [1]

A substantial factor in the reliability of any system of records is the promptness with which transactions are recorded.

The formula of Federal Rule 803(6) is "at or near the time." [2] Whether an entry made subsequent to the transaction has been made within a sufficient time to render it within the exception depends upon whether the time span between the transaction and the entry was so great as to suggest a danger of inaccuracy by lapse of memory.[3] In addition, the failure to make a timely record may suggest nonregularity in the making of the statement and may indicate motivational problems related to records prepared for litigation purposes.[4]

§ 290. Personal Knowledge; All Participants in Regular Course of Business [1]

The common law exception for regularly kept records required that the entries have been made by one with personal knowledge of the matter entered or upon reports to the maker by one with personal knowledge.[2] The entrant was required to be acting in the regular course of business, and if the information was supplied by another, that person also was required to be acting in the regular course of business.[3] If the information was transmitted through intermediaries, they were subject to the same requirement.[4] The application of the regular

§ 289

1. See generally 5 Wigmore, Evidence §§ 1526, 1550 (Chadbourn rev. 1974); 30 Am.Jur.2d Evidence § 938; C.J.S. Evidence § 690; Dec.Dig.Evidence ⟐354(12).

2. See supra § 286 text following note 4. Compare the hearsay exception for recorded past recollection where insurance against lapse of memory is phrased "when the matter was fresh in his memory." Supra § 281. This appearance of inconsistency is resolved by the fact that recorded recollection entails an inquiry into the actual recollection of the witness on the stand, while regularly kept records involve an objective standard for persons participating in the process but not called as witnesses.

3. The circumstances must be taken into consideration in each case. Missouri Pacific R. Co. v. Austin, 292 F.2d 415 (5th Cir.1961). Periods of varying length have been ruled too long under the facts: Hiram Ricker & Sons v. Students Intern. Meditation Soc., 501 F.2d 550 (1st Cir.1974) (one week); Missouri Pacific R. Co. v. Austin, supra (two months); United States v. Kim, 595 F.2d 755 (D.C.Cir.1979) (two years).

4. See Willco Kuwait (Trading) S.A.K. v. deSavary, 843 F.2d 618, 628 (1st Cir.

1988) (telex made three months after event is excluded as not satisfying timeliness requirement of rule, the court also noting it was a non-routine record that supported the party's forthcoming litigation position); United States v. Lemire, 720 F.2d 1327 (D.C.Cir.1983), cert. denied 467 U.S. 1226 (20 month interval between events and preparation of record did not meet timeliness requirement, the court also noting that the making of the record was not a regular business practice and appeared akin to an accident report).

§ 290

1. See generally 5 Wigmore, Evidence §§ 1530, 1555, 1561b (Chadbourn rev. 1974); 30 Am.Jur.2d Evidence §§ 951–953; C.J.S. Evidence §§ 692–693; Dec.Dig.Evidence ⟐354(11).

2. Lord v. Moore, 37 Me. 208, 220 (1854).

3. 5 Wigmore, Evidence § 1530 (Chadbourn rev. 1974).

4. Rathborne v. Hatch, 80 App.Div. 115, 80 N.Y.S. 347 (1903) (floor member of stock brokerage firm reported his sales to boys who telephoned the information to office).

course requirement to all participants in the process of acquiring, transmitting, and recording information was consistent with, indeed mandated by, the theory of the hearsay exception.[5]

Reform legislation in general has not dealt clearly with the question whether the information must initially be acquired by a person with firsthand knowledge and whether that person and all others involved in the process must be acting in the regular course of the business. The Commonwealth Fund Act required that the record be "made in the regular course of * * * business" and provided that "other circumstances * * *, including lack of personal knowledge by the entrant or maker, may be shown to affect its weight, but they shall not affect its admissibility."[6] The Uniform Act also required that the record be "made in the regular course of business," and in addition required that "in the opinion of the court, the sources of information, method and time of preparation were such as to justify its admission."[7] Federal Rule 803(6) requires that the record be "made * * * by, or from information transmitted by, a person with knowledge, if kept in the course of a regularly conducted business activity."[8]

Assuming, as is reasonable, that "knowledge" means firsthand knowledge, then Rule 803(6) answers the first part of the above question affirmatively, to the effect that the person who originally feeds the information into the process must have firsthand knowledge. As to whether the person making the record must be in the regular course of business, both the acts and Rule 803(6) answer in the affirmative, the first two using the term "made" and the latter "kept" to describe records produced in the regular course of business. However, stretching "made" and "kept" to include both the original acquisition of the information and its transmission to the recorder is troublesome.

These doubts have largely been resolved by referring to the underlying theory of the exception, namely, a practice and environment encouraging the making of accurate records. If any person in the process is not acting in the regular course of the business, then an essential link in the trustworthiness chain fails, just as it does when the person feeding the information does not have firsthand knowledge. The leading case is Johnson v. Lutz,[9] decided under the New York version of the Commonwealth Fund Act, holding inadmissible a police officer's report insofar as it was not based upon his personal knowledge but on information supplied by a bystander. Wigmore was bitterly critical of the decision,[10] but the courts generally have followed its lead in requir-

---

5. See supra § 286.

6. See supra § 286 note 3.

7. See supra § 286 note 3.

8. See supra § 306 text following note 4.

9. 253 N.Y. 124, 170 N.E. 517 (1930).

10. 5 Wigmore, Evidence § 1561a, at 490, § 1561b, at 507 (Chadbourn rev. 1974). But see id., § 1530, at 451:

(4) the conclusion is, then, that *where an entry is made by one person in the regular course of business, recording an oral or written report, made to him by other persons in the regular course of business, of a transaction lying in the personal knowledge of the latter persons, there is no objection to receiving that entry under the present exception, verified by the testimony of the former person only, or of a superior who*

ing all parts of the process to be conducted under a business duty.[11] The reasoning of *Johnson v. Lutz* has been applied to various formulations of the exception.[12]

When the matter recorded itself satisfies the conditions of some other hearsay exception, the requirement that the person initially acquiring the information must be in the regular course of the business is not enforced. For example, a police officer may include in a report of an automobile accident a damaging statement by one of the drivers, who later becomes a party to litigation. The statement qualifies as an admission, and the report may be used to prove it was made. That the officer has no firsthand knowledge of the correctness of the statement is immaterial. This matter is discussed further in connection with multiple hearsay.[13]

Direct proof that the maker of the statement had actual knowledge may be difficult, and it may even be impossible to prove specifically the identity of the informant with actual knowledge. Evidence that it was someone's business duty in the organization's routine to observe the matter will be prima facie sufficient to establish actual knowledge. This does not dispense with the need for personal knowledge, but permits it to be proved by evidence of practice and a reasonable assumption that general practice was followed with regard to a particular matter, or by other appropriate circumstances.[14]

testifies to the regular course of business, provided the practical inconvenience of producing on the stand the numerous other persons thus concerned would in the particular case outweigh the probable utility of doing so. (Italics in original.)

11. It should be noted that the requirement of firsthand knowledge by a person in the regular course of business may be satisfied even though someone outside the regular course of business prepared the report as long as that information was verified by someone acting under a business duty. United States v. Zapata, 871 F.2d 616 (7th Cir.1989) (hotel registration completed by guest admitted where hotel employee testified that it was standard practice to verify the information provided).

12. Under Federal Rule 803(6): United States v. Bortnovsky, 879 F.2d 30 (2d Cir. 1989) (statement contained within insurance adjuster's report not admissible because person giving information had no duty to report information); United States v. Lieberman, 637 F.2d 95 (2d Cir.1980) (hotel guest registration card filled out with name of defendant by person registering not admissible as business record to prove that defendant did register); United

States v. Baker, 693 F.2d 183 (D.C.Cir.1982) (prosecution for selling stolen government checks; error, though harmless, to admit Treasury form executed by payee to prove nonpayment and nonnegotiation, since payee not in regular course).

Under the various acts: United States v. Grayson, 166 F.2d 863 (2d Cir.1948); United States v. Smith, 521 F.2d 957 (D.C.Cir. 1975); Hutchinson v. Plante, 175 Conn. 1, 392 A.2d 488 (1978); Fagan v. City of Newark, 78 N.J.Super. 294, 188 A.2d 427 (App. Div.1963); Haas v. Kasnot, 371 Pa. 580, 92 A.2d 171 (1952).

13. See infra § 324.1. Record containing statements usable for a nonhearsay purpose are also admissible. United States v. Smith, 521 F.2d 957 (D.C.Cir.1975) (entry in police record of what complaining witness said not competent to prove truth of what was said, since he was not acting in the course of business, but usable for impeachment).

14. United States v. Lieberman, 637 F.2d 95 (2d Cir.1980); United States v. McGrath, 613 F.2d 361 (2d Cir.1979), cert. denied 446 U.S. 967; Senate Comm. on Judiciary, S.Rep. No. 1277, 93d Cong., 2d Sess. 17 (1974), reprinted in 1974 U.S.Code Cong. & Admin.News 7051, 7063.

§ 291. Unavailability [1]

Historically, if the person who made a business record was present as a witness, the record could be used to refresh recollection, or if that person could not then recall the facts, his or her testimony might be such as to qualify the record as past recollection recorded.[2] If, however, the witness for some reason could not be produced in court—i.e., was unavailable—then these alternative avenues to admissibility for the business record could not be used. A need for a special hearsay exception for business records in such cases was apparent. Unfortunately, as sometimes happens, the reason why the rule came into existence was incorporated into the rule as a requirement, in this instance a requirement of unavailability.

The process of calling a series of participants, only to have them testify that referring to the business record did not refresh their recollection, or at best to give rote testimony that it was their practice to be accurate, was a manifest waste of the court's time and disruptive to the business involved with no corresponding benefit. Yet no other response could reasonably be expected from participants in the keeping of records under modern conditions.[3] The reliability of the record could be shown by evidence other than the testimony of participants, as had been done when a participant was unavailable. Accordingly, unavailability virtually disappeared as a requirement.[4]

The Commonwealth Fund Act[5] and the Uniform Act[6] did not in terms address the unavailability requirement, but their silence was clearly meant to do away with that requirement.[7] Federal Rule 803(6) specifically eliminates the unavailability requirement by including the regularly kept records exception in a rule dealing with a group of

§ 291

1. See generally 5 Wigmore, Evidence § 1521 (Chadbourn rev. 1974); Dec.Dig.Evidence ☞354(22)–(22½).

2. 5 Wigmore, Evidence § 1521 (Chadbourn rev. 1974); supra § 286.

3. As Learned Hand stated in Massachusetts Bonding & Insurance Co. v. Norwich Pharmacal Co., 18 F.2d 934, 938 (2d Cir.1927), "[T]he missing entrants, if called, would in the nature of things have no recollection of the events recorded and could do no more than corroborate the existing testimony as to the course of business in which they had a part * * *."

4. Jennings v. United States, 73 F.2d 470, 473 (5th Cir.1934) (work record vouched for by employment manager in charge or records admissible—"It was not necessary to produce or account for the person or persons who had made the notations in the absence of some proof throwing suspicion upon the genuineness of the record itself."); Continental Nat. Bank v. First Nat. Bank, 108 Tenn. 374, 68 S.W. 497 (1902); Heid Bros., Inc. v. Commercial Nat. Bank, 240 S.W. 908 (Tex.Com.App. 1922); French v. Virginian Ry. Co., 121 Va. 383, 93 S.E. 585 (1917); Willett v. Davis, 30 Wash.2d 622, 193 P.2d 321 (1948); State v. Larue, 98 W.Va. 677, 128 S.E. 116 (1925).

5. See supra § 286 note 3.

6. See supra § 286 note 3.

7. See Rossomanno v. Laclede Cab Co., 328 S.W.2d 677 (Mo.1959), holding that a medical report was admissible under the Uniform Act although the doctor who made the report was in the city and apparently available. After suggesting that there was no requirement of unavailability, the court added, "Moreover, it is inconceivable that a busy medical practitioner would have an independent recollection of each entry made in his business records and be able to testify from personal recollection as to when and by whom all entries were made." Id. at 681–682.

exceptions where the hearsay rule does not operate to exclude the evidence "even though the declarant is available as a witness." The unavailability requirement has now almost entirely disappeared from American jurisdictions.[8]

§ 292. Proof; Who Must Be Called to Establish Admissibility [1]

The demise of the requirement of unavailability, discussed in the preceding section, had its impact upon the method of proving business records, as was intended. No longer was it necessary to call each available participant and exhaust the possibility of refreshing memory or establishing the record as past recollection recorded;[2] compliance with the requirements for regularly kept records could be proved by other means. Thus any witness with the necessary knowledge about the particular recordkeeping process could testify that it was the regular practice of the business to make such records, that the record was made in the regular course of business upon the personal knowledge of the recorder or of someone reporting to him or her in the regular course of business, and that the entries were made at or near the time of the transaction. The Commonwealth Fund Act did not deal with the matter of proof expressly, although a principal purpose of the act was to alleviate the burdensome requirements of proof imposed by the common law.[3] The Uniform Act, however, provided that the foundation might be laid by "the custodian or other qualified witness,"[4] and this language is incorporated in Federal Rule 803(6).

Perhaps the most commonly used foundation witness is a person in authority in the recordkeeping department of the business. Whether or not such a person falls within the term "custodian" may be questioned, but certainly he or she is "a qualified witness."[5] In fact, anyone with the necessary knowledge is qualified; there is no requirement that this witness must have firsthand knowledge of the matter reported or actually have prepared the report or observed its preparation.[6]

8. Louisiana appears to stand alone in retaining the unavailability requirement but imposes it only in criminal cases. See State v. Cade, 539 So.2d 650, 655 (La.App. 1989), writ denied 548 So.2d 1245 (La.) (use of business records against criminal defendant limited to situations where declarant is unavailable); La.Code of Evid., Art. 803(6) (eliminates unavailability requirement but only applicable to civil cases).

§ 292

1. See generally 5 Wigmore, Evidence § 1530 (Chadbourn rev. 1974); Green, The Model and Uniform Statutes Relating to Business Entries as Evidence, 31 Tul. L.Rev. 49, 55 (1956); Laughlin, Business Entries and the Like, 46 Iowa L.Rev. 276, 294–296 (1961); 30 Am.Jur.2d Evidence

§§ 947–953; C.J.S. Evidence §§ 682(3), 693; Annot., 21 A.L.R.2d 773.

2. See supra § 291 text following note 4.

3. See supra § 296 note 3.

4. Id.

5. Rosario v. Amalgamated Ladies' Garment Cutters' Union, 605 F.2d 1228 (2d Cir.1979), cert. denied 446 U.S. 919 (police report prepared under supervision of testifying officer and containing substance of complaint, offered against complaining witness in false arrest action).

6. United States v. Franco, 874 F.2d 1136, 1139–1141 (7th Cir.1989) (narcotics agent who talked with owner and employee of money exchange constituted a "quali-

Problems may arise when one business organization seeks to introduce records in its possession but actually prepared by another. It seems evident that mere possession or "custody" of records under these circumstances does not qualify employees of the possessing party to lay the requisite foundation,[7] and that the transmittal of information by the custodian regarding the contents of records in the custodian's possession does not qualify the recipient to lay the foundation.[8] However, when the business offering the records of another has made an independent check of the records,[9] or can establish accuracy by other means,[10] the necessary foundation may be established.

In order to facilitate the introduction of regularly kept records, Congress recently enacted a statute providing a certification procedure for foreign records in criminal cases.[11]

fied witness" within the meaning of the rule, which does not require personal participation but only an understanding of system used); United States v. Wables, 731 F.2d 440, 449 (7th Cir.1984) (witness need have only knowledge about the procedures used in producing records); Miller v. Fairchild Industries, Inc., 876 F.2d 718, 733 (9th Cir.1989), cert. denied 110 S.Ct. 1524 (stating general principles); Central Fidelity Bank v. Denslow (In re Denslow), 104 B.R. 761 (E.D.Va.1989) (custodian who assumed responsibilities after bankruptcy could lay foundation for records created before employment). But see United States v. Furst, 886 F.2d 558, 573 & n. 18 (3d Cir.1989), cert. denied 493 U.S. 1062 (foundation inadequate where witnesses had inadequate information regarding method of preparation of documents); Noble v. Alabama Dept. of Environmental Management, 872 F.2d 361, 366 (11th Cir. 1989) (summary statement that letter prepared in "ordinary course" of business inadequate).

7. NLRB v. First Termite Control Co., Inc., 646 F.2d 424 (9th Cir.1981) (to prove interstate transportation of lumber, bookkeeper of respondent testified she had received and paid freight bill showing origin outside state; she had no knowledge of circumstances or preparation; held, witness not qualified and freight bill inadmissible); Zundel v. Bommarito, 778 S.W.2d 954, 958 (Mo.App.1989) (records prepared elsewhere and merely received and held in bank's file did not render them business records of bank); People v. Pierre, 157 A.D.2d 750, 751, 550 N.Y.S.2d 44, 46 (1990), appeal denied 75 N.Y.2d 969, 556 N.Y.S.2d 253, 555 N.E.2d 625 (bank letter indicating balance of account not business record of court-appointed receiver to whom letter addressed ruled inadmissible under this principle).

8. United States v. Davis, 571 F.2d 1354 (5th Cir.1978).

9. United States v. Ullrich, 580 F.2d 765 (5th Cir.1978) (documents originating with Ford Motor Company retained by dealer and integrated into its records); United States v. Carranco, 551 F.2d 1197 (10th Cir.1977) (freight bill prepared by one carrier for transshipment by another carrier, whose representative testified to procedure of checking and use).

10. United States v. Veytia–Bravo, 603 F.2d 1187 (5th Cir.1979), cert. denied 444 U.S. 1024 (adequate foundation laid by government agent to admit records of former firearms dealer where records kept pursuant to ATF regulations and sent to ATF for permanent storage); Allen v. Safeco Ins. Co., 782 F.2d 1517 (11th Cir.1986) (state fire marshall could lay foundation for report of tests done by law enforcement department that regularly analyzed samples sent from his office); United States v. Parker, 749 F.2d 628, 633 (11th Cir.1984) (reliance upon customs certificate by distributor of imported spirits provided circumstantial evidence of trustworthiness); National Tea Co. v. Tyler Refrigeration Co., 339 N.W.2d 59, 60–61 (Minn.1983) (employee of another business, who was familiar with operations and procedures employed by testing lab, permitted to lay foundation for admission of lab's report).

11. 18 U.S.C.A. § 3506. The text is set forth in supra § 228 note 11. See United States v. Hing Shair Chan, 680 F.Supp. 521, 523 (E.D.N.Y.1988) (Hong Kong hotel registration admitted under this act, which the court notes should be interpreted in a similar manner to Rule 803(6)).

Similarly, Revised Uniform Rule 902 was amended adding a new paragraph providing certification procedures applicable in

§ 293. Special Situations: (a) Hospital Records [1]

In some jurisdictions, specific statutory authority for the admission of hospital records exists.[2] Although some courts hesitated to expand the business record exception by decision to noncommercial establishments such as hospitals, all would concede today that hospital records are admissible upon the same basis as other regularly kept records.[3] This result is appropriate, for the safeguards of trustworthiness of records of the modern hospital are at least as substantial as the guarantees of reliability of records of business establishments generally.[4] Progress in medical skills has been accompanied by improvements and standardization of the practice of recording facts concerning the patient, and these recorded facts are routinely used to make decisions upon which the health and life of the patient depend.

History. Under standard practice, a trained attendant at hospitals enters upon the record a "personal history,"[5] including an identification of the patient, an account of the present injury or illness, and the events and symptoms leading up to it. This information, which may be obtained from the patient directly or from a companion, is elicited to aid in the diagnosis and treatment of the patient's injury or disease. Is this history admissible to prove assertions of facts it may contain? Two layers of hearsay are involved here, with the first being the use of the hospital record to prove that the statement was made. The primary issue is whether the specific entry involved was an entry made in the regular course of the hospital's business. If the subject matter falls within those things which under hospital practice are regarded as relevant to diagnosis or treatment or other hospital business, it is within the regular course of business.[6] If, on the other hand, the subject matter does not relate to those concerns, the making of the entry is not within the regular course of the hospital's business, and

both civil and criminal cases and to both foreign and domestic records. Rev. Unif. R.Evid. (1986) 902(11). The text is set forth in supra § 228 note 12.

§ 293

1. See generally 6 Wigmore, Evidence § 1707 (Chadbourn rev. 1976); Hale, Hospital Records as Evidence, 14 So.Cal.L.Rev. 99 (1941); Braham, Case Records of Hospitals and Doctors under Business Records Act, 21 Temple L.Q. 113 (1948); Laughlin, Business Entries and the Like, 46 Iowa L.Rev. 276, 299–305 (1961); Annots., 75 A.L.R. 378, 120 A.L.R. 1124, 69 A.L.R.3d 22.

2. See 6 Wigmore, Evidence § 1707 n. 1 (Chadbourn rev. 1976).

Some statutes allow certified copies. Ohio Rev.Code Ann. § 2317.422 (Anderson Supp.1989).

3. United States v. Sackett, 598 F.2d 739 (2d Cir.1979) (under Federal Rule); Buckler v. Commonwealth, 541 S.W.2d 935 (Ky.1976) (under "shopbook" hearsay exception); Graham v. State, 547 S.W.2d 531 (Tenn.1977) (under Uniform Act).

4. See Globe Indem. Co. v. Reinhart, 152 Md. 439, 446, 137 A. 43, 46 (1927); Schmidt v. Riemenschneider, 196 Minn. 612, 265 N.W. 816, 817 (1936).

5. See Hale, Hospital Records as Evidence, 14 So.Cal.L.Rev. 90, 113–114 (1941).

6. See supra §§ 292–293.

Hospital business will cover some statements beyond those relevant to diagnosis or treatment, such as financial information regarding the patient, which is important to the collection of hospital charges.

thus it is not admissible even for the limited purpose of proving that the statement was made.[7]

Assuming that the hospital record is admissible to prove that the statement contained in the history was made, is this statement admissible to prove the truth of assertions made in it? In accordance with the general rule, the business record exception cannot support admission of the history because the declarant's action in relating the history was not part of a business routine of which he or she was a regular participant. Here as elsewhere, however, if the history comes within one of the other exceptions to the hearsay rule, it is admissible.[8] The statements may, for example, constitute admissions of a party opponent when the patient is a party,[9] dying declarations,[10] declarations against interest,[11] excited utterances,[12] and most frequently, statements for the purpose of diagnosis or treatment.[13]

Diagnostic statements. Professional standards for hospital records contemplate that entries will be made of diagnostic findings at various stages.[14] These entries are clearly in the regular course of the operations of the hospital. The problem which they pose is one of the admissibility of "opinions."[15] In the hospital records area, the opinion is usually one of an expert who would unquestionably be permitted to give it if personally testifying. While the requirement of qualification does not disappear, if the record is shown to be from a reputable institution, it may be inferred that regular entries were made by qualified personnel in the absence of any indication to the contrary.[16]

When an expert opinion is offered by a witness personally testifying, the expert is available for cross-examination on that opinion. If the

---

7. See Green v. Cleveland, 150 Ohio St. 441, 83 N.E.2d 63 (1948) (statement of patient that she fell off a street car and caught her heel not incident to treatment); Commonwealth v. Harris, 351 Pa. 325, 41 A.2d 688 (1945) (patient's statement that he had been shot by a white man not related to treatment since race of assailant was not material to treatment). See supra §§ 292–293.

8. See infra § 324.1.

9. Watts v. Delaware Coach Co., 44 Del. 283, 58 A.2d 689 (Super.1948).

10. See infra Ch. 32.

11. See infra Ch. 33.

12. See supra § 272.

13. See supra Ch. 27.

If no hearsay exception can be successfully invoked, the record is not admissible. Petrocelli v. Gallison, 679 F.2d 286 (1st Cir.1982) (in malpractice action, proper to exclude statement that nerve was severed during operation, in hospital record for later surgery, apparently on information from patient's wife); A. H. Angerstein, Inc.

v. Jankowski, 55 Del. 304, 187 A.2d 81 (Super.1962) (statement in medical record by unidentified person who called physician at hospital could not be used to prove that patient had received electrical shock); Bouchie v. Murray, 376 Mass. 524, 381 N.E.2d 1295 (1978) (error to admit evidence that wife, who was not a passenger, told plaintiff's psychiatrist that plaintiff was "enraged and out of control" just before and at time of automobile accident).

14. See Hale, Hospital Records as Evidence, 14 So.Cal.L.Rev. 90, 113–14 (1941).

15. See supra § 287.

16. Allen v. St. Louis Public Service Co., 365 Mo. 677, 285 S.W.2d 663 (1956) (qualifications of physician will be "presumed"); Webber v. McCormick, 63 N.J.Super. 409, 164 A.2d 813 (App.Div. 1960) (X-ray prepared by hospital technician and entered in hospital admissible without proof of technician's qualifications, since would be presumed from making of report in course of business). Contra: Martin v. Baldwin, 215 Ga. 293, 110 S.E.2d 344 (1959).

opinion is offered by means of a hospital record, no cross-examination is possible. Consequently, the courts have tended to limit the scope of opinions that can be introduced by this method. The admissibility of ordinary diagnostic findings customarily based on objective data and not presenting more than average difficulty of interpretation is usually conceded.[17] By contrast, diagnostic opinions which on their face are conjectural have generally been excluded.[18]

Given that Federal Rule 803(6) specifically includes opinions or diagnoses, this historical distinction based on whether the opinion is objective or conjectural does not appear to survive,[19] at least directly. However, admissibility of all such entries is not assured. First, where there are indications of lack of trustworthiness, which may result from a lack of expert qualifications or from a lack of factual support, exclusion is warranted under the rule.[20] Moreover, inclusion of opinions or diagnoses within the rule only removes the bar of hearsay. In the absence of the availability of the expert for explanation and cross-examination, the court may conclude that probative value of this evidence is outweighed by the danger that the jury will be misled or confused.[21] This is of particular concern if the opinion involves difficult matters of interpretation and a central dispute in the case, such as causation. Under these circumstances, a court operating under the Federal Rules, like earlier courts, is likely to be reluctant to permit a decision to be made upon the basis of an un-cross-examined opinion and may require that the witness be produced.[22]

Privilege. In most states, patients have been afforded a privilege against disclosure by physicians of information acquired in attending

---

17. See United States v. Bohle, 445 F.2d 54, 61 (7th Cir.1971) (drawing distinction between diagnosis of mental condition that was ruled inadmissible and statements about appearance, affect, and previous mental treatment that were admissible); New York Life Ins. Co. v. Taylor, 147 F.2d 297, 306 (D.C.Cir.1945) (entries recording readily observable condition or treatment are admissible).

18. Durant v. United States, 551 A.2d 1318 (D.C.App.1988) (diagnosis of PCP intoxication complicated by mental illness is the type of opinion involving conjecture that may not be admitted through business record); Boland v. Jando, 395 S.W.2d 206 (Mo.1965) (interpretation of X-ray as "could be a small chip fracture" could have been excluded as based upon speculation); LaMantia v. Bobmeyer, 382 S.W.2d 455 (Mo.App.1964) (statement in record by physician that "I have a hunch [the patient] will have further difficulty from time to time" not admissible because it was based on speculation and conjecture).

19. 4 Weinstein & Berger, Weinstein's Evidence ¶ 803(6)[06], at 200 (1990).

Of course, all states do not follow the model of the Federal Rule in admitting opinions and diagnoses. See, e.g., Spivey v. State, 184 Ga.App. 118, 361 S.E.2d 9 (1987) (expert must testify for opinions and diagnoses to be admissible); People v. Shipp, 175 Mich.App. 332, 437 N.W.2d 385 (1989) (Michigan's Rule 803(6) omits opinions and diagnoses from business record exception); Commonwealth v. Hemingway, 369 Pa.Super. 112, 534 A.2d 1104 (1987) (diagnoses, opinions, and conclusions not admissible unless expert testifies).

20. 4 Weinstein & Berger, Weinstein's Evidence ¶ 803(6)[06], at 200–201 (1990).

21. Exclusion here would be under Federal Rule 403 or its state law counterpart. See Nauni v. State, 670 P.2d 126, 131 (Okl. Cr.App.1983) (diagnoses of mental or psychiatric conditions are too complex and speculative to be admitted without cross-examination). See generally supra § 185.

22. Skogen v. Dow Chemical Co., 375 F.2d 692 (8th Cir.1967) (not error to exclude entry that plaintiff's condition was caused by inhalation of insecticide).

the patient and necessary for diagnosis and treatment.[23] It is possible to interpret the privilege broadly as including any information obtained by hospital personnel related to treatment. While hospital records are generally privileged to the extent that they incorporate statements made by the patient to the physician and the physician's diagnostic findings,[24] application of the privilege to information obtained by nurses or attendants presents a greater problem. On one hand, it is arguable that privilege statutes should be strictly construed, and most do not mention nurses or attendants.[25] On the other hand, information is usually gathered and recorded by them as agents for the physician and for the purpose of aiding the physician in treatment and diagnosis.[26] The problem is one of interpreting the underlying privilege. If it would bar the direct testimony of a nurse or attendant, it should also bar use of their hearsay statement under this exception; if it would not, such statements in hospital records should not be held privileged.

§ 294. Special Situations: (b) Computer Records [1]

Even though the scrivener's quill pens in original entry books have been replaced by computer printouts, magnetic tapes, and microfiche files, the theory behind the reliability of regularly kept business records

---

23. See supra Ch. 11.

24. The language in most cases suggests that hospital records are privileged only to the extent that they contain communications from physicians that would be privileged were the physician testifying in person. Ferguson v. Quaker City Life Ins. Co., 129 A.2d 189 (D.C.Mun.App.1957); Newman v. Blom, 249 Iowa 836, 89 N.W.2d 349 (1958); State ex rel. Benoit v. Randall, 431 S.W.2d 107 (Mo.1968); Unick v. Kessler Memorial Hosp., 107 N.J.Super. 121, 257 A.2d 134 (Law Div.1969); Sims v. Charlotte Liberty Mut. Ins. Co., 257 N.C. 32, 125 S.E.2d 326 (1962).

25. A few statutes do specifically mention nurses. See 8 Wigmore, Evidence § 2380 n. 5 (McNaughton rev. 1961).

26. The general approach seems to be that a nurse or other member of a hospital staff comes within the privilege only if acting under the direction of a specific physician. See Sims v. Charlotte Liberty Mut. Ins. Co., 257 N.C. 32, 125 S.E.2d 326 (1962) (dictum) (entries by nurses, technicians, or others in hospital records not privileged unless assisting or acting under the direction of a physician). See also Collins v. Howard, 156 F.Supp. 322 (S.D.Ga. 1957) (dictum) (nurse taking blood test was agent of hospital rather than physician and therefore privilege would not include

her); State v. Burchett, 302 S.W.2d 9 (Mo. 1957) (nurse who was on duty as hospital employee and helped patient into hospital before physician arrived was not acting as agent of physician and therefore not within privilege). The privilege has been held applicable to an intern. Franklin Life Ins. Co. v. William J. Champion & Co., 353 F.2d 919 (6th Cir.1965), cert. denied 384 U.S. 928.

§ 294

1. 2 Bender, Computer Law (1990); Fenwick, Admissibility of Computerized Business Records, 14 Am.Jur.2d Proof of Facts 173; Warton, Litigators Byte the Apple: Utilizing Computer Generated Evidence at Trial, 41 Baylor L.Rev. 731 (1989); Snyder, Assuring the Competency of Computer–Generated Evidence, 9 Computer L.J. 103 (1989); Peritz, Computer Data and Reliability: A Call for Authentication of Business Records Under the Federal Rules of Evidence, 80 Nw.U.L.Rev. 956 (1986); Johnston, A Guide for the Proponent and Opponent of Computer–Based Evidence, 1 Computer L.J. 667 (1979); Singer, Proposed Changes to the Federal Rules of Evidence as Applied to Computer–Generated Evidence, 7 Rut.J. Computers, Tech. & Law 157 (1979); Comments, 18 J. Marshall L.Rev. 115 (1984); 126 U.Pa.L.Rev. 423 (1977); Annots., 71 A.L.R.3d 232; 7 A.L.R.4th 8.

remains the same. Provided a proper foundation is laid, computer-generated evidence is no less reliable than original entry books and should be admitted under the exception.[2]

With the explosive development of electronic data processing, most business and business-type records are generated by computers. Courts have agreed that their admissibility is governed by the hearsay exception for regularly kept records, whether at common law or in the form of a statute or rule.[3] Federal Rule 803(6) specifically applies to a "data compilation, in any form," terminology intended to include records stored in computers.[4]

The usual conditions for the exception are applicable.[5] The differences between traditional record-keeping methods and sophisticated electronic equipment, however, require some further exploration of foundation requirements. While paper records can be inspected visually and the process of keeping the record can often be tracked in a step-by-step manner, electronically processed data is not a visual counterpart of the machine record and for the most part is not subject to visual inspection until it takes the final form of a printout.

The theory of trustworthiness supporting the regularly kept records exception assumes a reliable method for entering, processing, storing, and retrieving data. Moreover, the rule excludes statements when "the source of information or the method or circumstances of preparation indicate lack of trustworthiness."[6] Issues may arise at any of the stages of the handling of the data regarding (1) computer hardware, (2) software or programming, and (3) accuracy and/or security.

Serious problems are rarely presented regarding computer hardware because most computer equipment used to produce records otherwise

---

2. Brandon v. State, 272 Ind. 92, 98, 396 N.E.2d 365, 370 (1979).

As a prerequisite to admissibility, the collection of the data must satisfy the requirements of the exception before the data is entered into the computer.

3. Monarch Fed. Sav. & Loan Ass'n v. Genser, 156 N.J.Super. 107, 383 A.2d 475 (Ch. 1977) (citing many cases).

4. Adv. Comm. Note, Fed.R.Evid. 803(6), 56 F.R.D. 183, 311 ("[the term] includes, but is by no means limited to, electronic computer storage"). See also Senate Comm. on Judiciary, S.Rep. No. 1277, 93d Cong., 2d Sess. 16 (1974), reprinted in 1974 U.S.Code Cong. & Admin.News 7051, 7063.

The same or similar terminology also appears in varying contexts in Rules 803(7), (8), (9) & (10) and in Rule 1001(1) & (3).

5. See supra §§ 286–290.

6. The aspects of trustworthiness peculiar to computer-generated evidence are occasionally treated as problems of authenti-

cation. 5 Weinstein & Berger, Weinstein's Evidence ¶ 901(b)(9)[02] (1990); Singer, supra note 1, at 167. Federal Rule 901(b)(9), which covers authentication through "a process or system used to produce a result and showing that the process or system produces an accurate result," is applicable and aptly describes trustworthiness aspects peculiar to computers.

However, the emphasis of Rule 901 is upon showing that the offered item of evidence is what it is claimed to be—that it is genuine. The rule as applied to computer evidence may be viewed as covering the accuracy of the process in reproducing the data that was entered into the computer. In this regard, it merely reproduces the trustworthiness concerns of Rule 803(6), which also focuses on whether the data in the machine is accurate. The courts generally have found Rule 803(6) adequate to cover all aspects and seldom refer to an authentication approach. Johnston, supra note 1, at 669.

meeting the requirements of the exception is both standard [7] and highly reliable, with few data errors resulting from defects in equipment.[8] Hence testimony describing equipment should ordinarily be limited to the function that each unit performs in the process and that each is adequate for the purpose. Excursions into theory are not required or ordinarily appropriate.[9]

Much more realistic potential for errors is presented by human factors involved in the programming of the computer and the development of software. However, the trend here is not to require the proponent of the statement to call the programmer to lay the foundation for admission.[10]

With regard to questions of inaccuracy and data security, the courts have moved in the direction of not imposing rigid requirements. Thus, in the typical case, the proponent is not required initially to show periodic testing for programming errors or the elimination of all possibilities of data alteration or errors in data entry or programming.[11]

While a well-laid foundation will touch upon each of these three general areas noted above, the trend among courts has been to treat computer records like other business records and not to require the proponent of the evidence initially to show trustworthiness beyond meeting the general requirements of the rule.[12] The fact that the

7. Apparently drawing upon the practice of witnesses in describing equipment as "standard," some courts have mandated such testimony. See Brandon v. State, 272 Ind. 92, 396 N.E.2d 365 (1979); State v. Jones, 544 So.2d 1209 (La.App.1989); King v. State for Use and Benefit of Murdock Acceptance Corp., 222 So.2d 393 (Miss. 1969). As an approach to adequacy, the requirement is unduly restrictive and has been specifically rejected by some courts. See McAllen State Bank v. Linbeck Const. Corp., 695 S.W.2d 10 (Tex.App.1985, error refused n.r.e.); State v. Kane, 23 Wash. App. 107, 594 P.2d 1357 (1979). For a different general approach to foundational requirements, see discussion of United States v. Vela, 673 F.2d 86 (5th Cir.1982), infra text accompanying note 12.

8. "[C]omputer evidence is not intrinsically unreliable." United States v. Vela, 673 F.2d 86, 90 (5th Cir.1982). "[N]o court could fail to notice the extent to which businesses today depend on computers for a myriad of functions." United States v. Russo, 480 F.2d 1228, 1239 (6th Cir.1973), cert. denied 414 U.S. 1157. "[T]he scientific reliability of such machines can scarcely be questioned." People v. Gauer, 7 Ill.App.3d 512, 288 N.E.2d 24 (1972). As to accuracy of equipment, see also Singer, supra note 1, at 163.

9. Foundational proof occupied 141 pages of the record in the seminal case of

Transport Indem. Co. v. Seib, 178 Neb. 253, 132 N.W.2d 871 (1965). History shows, however, that as new technologies develop and win acceptance, courts move in the direction of taking judicial notice of the validity of the underlying scientific principle. Radar is a case in point, § 210 supra and § 330 infra. Similarly, the principles of electronic data processing are now a proper subject of judicial notice and should not require proof. In a somewhat different setting, the Advisory Committee's Note to Federal Rule 901(b)(9) suggests the taking of judicial notice of the accuracy of a process or system. Indeed, in jurisdictions requiring proof that computer equipment is standard, judicial notice may be taken. People v. Hendricks, 145 Ill.App.3d 71, 99 Ill.Dec. 20, 495 N.E.2d 85 (1986), reversed on other grounds 137 Ill.2d 31, 148 Ill.Dec. 213, 560 N.E.2d 611.

10. United States v. Young Bros., Inc., 728 F.2d 682 (5th Cir.1984), cert. denied 469 U.S. 881; United States v. Miller, 771 F.2d 1219 (9th Cir.1985).

11. United States v. Briscoe, 896 F.2d 1476 (7th Cir.1990), cert. denied 111 S.Ct. 173; United States v. Bonallo, 858 F.2d 1427 (9th Cir.1988); United States v. Catabran, 836 F.2d 453 (9th Cir.1988).

12. United States v. Vela, 673 F.2d 86 (5th Cir.1982) (no requirement that proponent treat computer records different from

organization relies upon the record in the regular course of its business may itself provide sufficient indication of reliability, absent realistic challenge, to warrant admission.[13]

While it was suggested initially that the Federal Rules should be amended by adding a rule specifically dealing with computer-generated evidence,[14] the courts have generally dealt competently with the admissibility of such evidence by applying Rule 803(6) or its common law or statutory counterparts. Any attempt at more specific treatment ought to be undertaken only with awareness of unfortunate English experience with efforts to enact specific statutes.[15]

As noted in an earlier section, in order to qualify under the hearsay exception for regularly kept records, a record must have been made in the regular course of business, and documents made for use in litigation do not meet that requirement. Because of the motivation factor, such records often lack the trustworthiness contemplated by the exception.[16] Also, the regularly kept records exception requires that entries must be made at or near the time of the event recorded.[17]

The application of these general principles to the creation of a computer printout raise several specific problems. These issues are presented by a computer printout that is made (1) long after the data were entered into the system and (2) after litigation has commenced.

The question as to the timeliness of the creation of the record is answered by observing that the time requirement refers to when the entry into the data bank was originally made, not the time the printout was produced.[18] With regard to documents prepared for use in litigation, the arrangement of the data in a form designed to aid the litigation should not result in exclusion if the data and the retrieval processes are themselves reliable. For example, when information is recorded in the computer in the sequence in which it was received

any other records or to establish the type of computer used or its operating condition). See also State for Use of Elec. Supply Co. v. Kitchens Const., Inc., 106 N.M. 753, 750 P.2d 114 (1988); Voss v. Southwestern Bell Telephone Co., 610 S.W.2d 537 (Tex.Civ.App.1980); State v. Ben–Neth, 34 Wash.App. 600, 663 P.2d 156 (1983).

13. See United States v. De Georgia, 420 F.2d 889, 893 n. 11 (9th Cir.1969); Commonwealth v. Reed, 23 Mass.App.Ct. 294, 502 N.E.2d 147 (1986), review denied 399 Mass. 1102, 504 N.E.2d 1066.

14. Singer, supra note 1, at 174.

15. The first effort to draft a specific statute in the Civil Evidence Act of 1968 was met with substantial criticism. "[T]he section is a morass of drafting. The problem with computer evidence is not the accuracy of the calculation but the reliability of the data fed in and the transcription and interpretation of the 'print-out' data produced." Newark & Samuels, Civil Evi-

dence Act 1968, 31 Mod.L.Rev. 668, 670 (1968). See generally Tapper, Cross on Evidence 558–60 (7th ed. 1990). Recent efforts at drafting under the Police and Criminal Evidence Act 1984 have been more successful. However, criticism continues of special provisions for documents produced by computer rather than treating them as any other document. Id. at 636.

16. See supra § 288. The documents may, however, come in under some other theory, such as a summary under supra § 233.

17. See supra § 289.

18. United States v. Russo, 480 F.2d 1228 (6th Cir.1973), cert. denied 414 U.S. 1157; Brown v. J.C. Penney Co., 297 Or. 695, 688 P.2d 811 (1984); Westinghouse Elec. Supply Co. v. B.L. Allen, Inc., 138 Vt. 84, 413 A.2d 122 (1980).

rather than organized by customers or transactions, reordering the data by computer should not present a barrier to its admission greater than a manual collation of related business records would. The evidence should not be rejected merely because it is not a visual counterpart of the machine record. However, the court must carefully consider whether the process producing the printout is reliable and whether the record may have been compromised in any way by that process.[19]

Another specific issue encountered with regard to computer records is whether such records when self-generated by the computer are hearsay at all. A frequently encountered example of a record of this type is the trace report produced by telephone company computers when tracking a call made to a specific number. Because records of this type are not the counterpart of a statement by a human declarant, which should ideally be tested by cross-examination of that declarant, they should not be treated as hearsay, but rather their admissibility should be determined on the basis of the reliability and accuracy of the process involved.[20]

19. In United States v. Sanders, 749 F.2d 195 (5th Cir.1984), the court drew a distinction between a printout produced by a program that only orders the data, which would be admissible, rather than one that sorts, compiles, or summarizes the information, that would be excluded. See also United States v. Miller, 771 F.2d 1219 (9th Cir.1985) (telephone records listing subscriber name, address, telephone number, and date service initiated ruled inadmissible because prepared in response to litigation). This approach is too restrictive. The question should be rather whether the basic process involved in producing the printout is part of the business routine so as to provide a basis for concluding that the retrieval process is reliable. See 4 Louisell & Mueller, Federal Evidence § 449, at 688 (1980). Under this analysis, the routine processes noted in *Sanders* and *Miller* would not raise serious admissibility problems. See also Westinghouse Elec. Supply Co. v. B. L. Allen, Inc., 138 Vt. 84, 413 A.2d 122 (1980); Johnson, supra note 1, at 674–75.

20. See People v. Holowko, 109 Ill.2d 187, 93 Ill.Dec. 344, 486 N.E.2d 877 (1985); State v. Armstead, 432 So.2d 837 (La.1983). See also Penny v. Commonwealth, 6 Va. App. 494, 370 S.E.2d 314 (1988). See generally Lempert & Saltzburg, A Modern Approach to Evidence (2d ed. 1982) (hearsay rule does not apply to statements by non-human sources which cannot be cross-examined); City of Webster Groves v. Quick, 323 S.W.2d 386 (Mo.App.1959) (analyzing issue as applied to speed detection devices).

Chapter 30

PUBLIC RECORDS, REPORTS, AND CERTIFICATES

Table of Sections

§ 295. The Exception for Public Records and Reports: (a) In General [1]

The common law developed an exception to the hearsay rule for written records and reports of public officials under a duty to make them,[2] made upon firsthand knowledge of the facts.[3] These statements are admissible as evidence of the facts recited in them. The common view has generally prevailed that the duty requirement is satisfied if the record is reasonably necessary for the efficient administration of the office. Annot., 80 A.L.R.3d 414. See United States v. Puente, 826 F.2d 1415 (5th Cir.1987) (directives of the agency itself promulgated in compliance with its authorized purposes satisfy rule's requirement).

§ 295

1. See generally 5 Wigmore, Evidence §§ 1630–1684 (Chadbourn rev. 1974); Dutton, The Official Records Exception to the Hearsay Rule in California, 6 Santa Clara Law. 1 (1965); Wallace, Official Written Statements, 46 Iowa L.Rev. 256 (1961); Note, 30 Mont.L.Rev. 227 (1969); Dec.Dig.Evidence ☞318(4), 333–349, 383(3), (4), Criminal Law ☞429, 430.

2. While there has been some insistence that the duty be imposed by statute, the

3. Firsthand knowledge by a subordinate is sufficient. See Olender v. United States, 210 F.2d 795 (9th Cir.1954).

287

law formulation of this hearsay exception has been relaxed and broadened by decisions, statutes, and rules, discussed in the sections that follow. The most important of these modern formulations of the exception is the Federal Rule.

Federal Rule 803(8) [4] provides, without regard to the unavailability of the declarant, a hearsay exception for the following:

> Records, reports, statements, or data compilations, in any form, of public offices or agencies, setting forth (A) the activities of the office or agency, or (B) matters observed pursuant to duty imposed by law as to which matters there was a duty to report, excluding, however, in criminal cases matters observed by police officers and other law enforcement personnel, or (C) in civil actions and proceedings and against the Government in criminal cases, factual findings resulting from an investigation made pursuant to authority granted by law, unless the sources of information or other circumstances indicate lack of trustworthiness.

The special trustworthiness of official written statements is found in the declarant's official duty and the high probability that the duty to make an accurate report has been performed.[5] The possibility that public inspection of some official records will reveal any inaccuracies and cause them to be corrected (or will deter the official from making them in the first place) has been emphasized by the English courts, which have imposed a corresponding requirement that the official statement be one kept for the use and information of the public.[6] This limitation has been criticized, and the American courts reasonably have

---

4. Revised Uniform Rule of Evidence (1986) 803(8) reads as follows:

Unless the sources of information or other circumstances indicate lack of trustworthiness, records, reports, statements, or data compilations in any form of a public office or agency setting forth its regularly conducted and regularly recorded activities, or matters observed pursuant to duty imposed by law and as to which there was a duty to report, or factual findings resulting from an investigation made pursuant to authority granted by law. The following are not within this exception to the hearsay rule: (i) investigative reports by police and other law enforcement personnel, except when offered by an accused in a criminal case; (ii) investigative reports prepared by or for a government, a public office, or an agency when offered by it in a case in which it is a party; (iii) factual findings offered by the government in criminal cases; and (iv) factual findings resulting from special investigation of a particular complaint, case, or incident, except when offered by an accused in a criminal case.

This formulation of the exception corrects an oversight in Federal Rule 803(8)(B), which if read literally would exclude statements made by law enforcement officials even when offered by the criminal defendant. See infra § 296 text accompanying note 19. Other differences between this rule and the Federal Rule are more problematic.

5. Chesapeake & Delaware Canal Co. v. United States, 250 U.S. 123 (1919).

Compare United States v. Lange, 466 F.2d 1021 (9th Cir.1972) (not error to admit householders' forms and letters informing post office that second mailings had been received after post office order to dealers in erotic literature to cease mailing). See also supra § 286 concerning regular entries.

6. See Lilley v. Pettit, 1 [1946] K.B. 401, [1946] 1 All.E.R. 593, holding the regimental records of a soldier inadmissible because they were not kept for the use and information of the public. See generally Cross & Tapper, Cross on Evidence 577–578 (7th ed. 1990).

not adopted it.[7] Although public inspection might provide a modest additional assurance of reliability, strictly limiting admissibility to records that are open to public inspection would be unwise because many documents with sufficiently reliability to justify admission would be excluded.[8]

The impetus for the development of this hearsay exception is found in the inconvenience of requiring public officials to appear in court and testify concerning the subject matter of their records and reports.[9] Not only would this disrupt the administration of public affairs, but it almost certainly would create a class of official witnesses. Moreover, given the volume of business in public offices, the official written statement will usually be more reliable than the official's present memory. For these same reasons, there is no requirement that the declarant be shown to be unavailable.

The convenience of proving by certified copy [10] and the simplicity of foundation requirements in most cases [11] make the official records exception an attractive choice over business records when an option is afforded.

§ 296. The Exception for Public Records and Reports: (b) Activities of the Office; Matters Observed; Investigative Reports; Restrictions on Prosecutorial Use [1]

Under Federal Rule 803(8) [2] matters falling within the hearsay exception for public records and reports are divided into three groups. This grouping offers a convenient approach also to the common law and statutory background.

(A) Activities of the office. The first group includes probably the oldest and most straightforward type of public records, records of the activities of the office itself. An example is the record of receipts and

---

7. Jones v. State, 267 Ind. 205, 369 N.E.2d 418 (1977); 5 Wigmore, Evidence § 1632 (Chadbourn rev. 1974).

8. 5 Wigmore, Evidence § 1632, at 620–621 (Chadbourn rev. 1974).

9. 5 Wigmore, Evidence § 1631 (Chadbourn rev. 1974).

10. See supra § 240.

11. See supra § 224.

§ 296

1. See generally Grossman & Shapiro, The Admission of Government Fact Findings Under Federal Rule of Evidence 803(8)(c): Limiting the Dangers of Unreliable Hearsay, 38 Kan.L.Rev. 767 (1990); Giannelli, The Admissibility of Laboratory Reports in Criminal Trials: The Reliability

of Scientific Proof, 49 Ohio St.L.J. 671 (1988); Grant, The Trustworthiness Standard for the Public Records and Reports Hearsay Exception, 12 Western St. U.L.Rev. 53 (1984); Alexander, The Hearsay Exception for Public Records in Federal Criminal Trials, 47 Alb.L.Rev. 699 (1983); Imwinkelried, The Constitutionality of Introducing Evaluative Laboratory Reports Against Criminal Defendants, 30 Hastings L.J. 621 (1979); Comment, 64 Wash.L.Rev. 975 (1989), 54 J.Air L. & Com. 1089 (1989), 63 Tul.L.Rev. 121 (1988); Note, 96 Harv.L.Rev. 492 (1982), 59 Tex.L.Rev. 155 (1980); Annots., 37 A.L.R.Fed. 831, 56 A.L.R.Fed. 168.

2. For text of rule, see supra § 295 text following note 4.

disbursements of the Treasury Department.[3] In addition to the assurances of reliability common to public records and reports generally, this group also has the assurances of accuracy that characterize business records. Accordingly, they are routinely admitted.

(B) Matters observed pursuant to duty. The second group consists of matters observed and reported, both pursuant to duty imposed by law.[4] Rainfall records of the National Weather Service are illustrative.[5] These records are also of a relatively noncontroversial nature,[6] except where the matter is observed by a police officer or other law enforcement personnel. This limitation is discussed in the concluding portion of (C) below.

(C) Investigative reports. Investigative reports have produced the greatest division among the courts due to their considerable range of potential content. In Beech Aircraft Corporation v. Rainey,[7] however, the Supreme Court resolved one of the issues that had previously divided lower federal courts. In that case, the Court rejected the narrow interpretation of "factual findings," holding that "factually based opinions and conclusions" may be included within the exception.[8] The Court noted that the primary protection against admission of unreliable evidence was the rule's escape provision that directs exclusion of all elements of the report—both factual and evaluative—if the court determines that they lack trustworthiness.[9] In making the

3. Chesapeake & Delaware Canal Co. v. United States, 250 U.S. 123 (1919).

The exact dimensions of this provision are somewhat unclear because the relationship between clause (A) and (B) is uncertain. However, a relatively narrow reading of part (A) seems appropriate such that "records focusing primarily upon the behavior of citizens, or events or conditions outside of the functioning of a public office or agency, should not be viewed as being within clause (A)." 4 Louisell & Mueller, Federal Evidence § 455, at 726 (1980). However, the courts have not necessarily agreed with this narrow construction. See United States v. Hardin, 710 F.2d 1231, 1237 (7th Cir.1983), cert. denied 464 U.S. 918 (record of average price and purity of illicit cocaine purchases by federal drug enforcement agents). See also United States v. Mena, 863 F.2d 1522, 1531–1532 (11th Cir.1989), cert. denied 493 U.S. 834, 110 (document showing registry of vessel considered under clause (A) under analysis that registration of vessels was regular activity of government).

4. See supra § 295 note 2.

5. United States v. Meyer, 113 F.2d 387 (7th Cir.1940), cert. denied 311 U.S. 706, 311 U.S. 707. See also United States v. Arias, 575 F.2d 253 (9th Cir.1978), cert. denied 439 U.S. 868 (official court reporter's transcript of trial).

6. As with business records, hearsay statements contained within these reports are not admissible simply because of their inclusion as matters observed within a public record or report. United States v. De Peri, 778 F.2d 963, 976–977 (3d Cir. 1985), cert. denied 475 U.S. 1110, 476 U.S. 1159.

7. 488 U.S. 153 (1988).

8. 488 U.S. at 163.

Legal conclusions are, however, not admissible under this exception. Hines v. Brandon Steel Decks, Inc., 886 F.2d 299, 303 (11th Cir.1989). Cf. Adv.Com. Note, Fed.R.Evid. 704, 56 F.R.D. 183, 284–85 (opinions excluded when "phrased in terms of inadequately explored legal criteria").

9. Rule 803(6) has a similar escape provision.

Under the rule's structure, factors such as skill of the investigator are assumed in the first instance, and the burden is on the opponent of the evidence to demonstrate untrustworthiness. Complaint of Paducah Towing Co., Inc., 692 F.2d 412, 421 (6th Cir.1982) (while court questioned trustworthiness of source of information, it sustained admission of report since opponent, who had the burden, failed to produce transcripts of administrative hearing to demonstrate the trial court's reliance upon

determination of trustworthiness, the four factors to be examined include: [10] the timeliness of the investigation, the skill or experience of the investigator,[11] whether a formal hearing was held,[12] and the bias of the investigator.[13]

As the name indicates, these reports embody the results of investigation and accordingly are often not the product of firsthand knowledge of the declarant, which is required under most hearsay exceptions.[14] Nevertheless, the nature and trustworthiness of the information relied upon, including its hearsay nature, is important in determining the admissibility of the report.[15]

In order to meet the requirements of the exception, the statement must constitute the conclusion of a governmental agency as opposed to mere accumulation of information,[16] and it must not be merely an interim or preliminary document.[17]

information of questionable trustworthiness); Masemer v. Delmarva Power & Light Co., 723 F.Supp. 1019, 1021 n. 3 (D.Del.1989) (rule presumes admissibility of report and burden is on opponent to produce evidence of inadequacy of investigator's skill and experience).

10. The Court noted that this non-exclusive list of factors was set out by the Advisory Committee. Beech Aircraft Corp. v. Rainey, 488 U.S. at 167 n. 11, citing Adv.Comm. Note, Fed.R.Evid. 803(8). The Court also recognized that evaluative reports might be excluded under concepts of relevance and prejudice embodied in other rules. Id. at 167.

11. Reports may be excluded because of lack of expertise of preparer. Matthews v. Ashland Chemical, Inc., 770 F.2d 1303, 1309–310 (5th Cir.1985) (report rejected where investigator had no special skill or experience); Jenkins v. Whittaker Corp., 785 F.2d 720, 725–727 (9th Cir.1986), cert. denied 479 U.S. 918 (would be anomalous to admit uncross-examined opinions through report which could not be admitted if the declarant testified because of lack of expertise).

12. Lloyd v. American Export Lines, Inc., 580 F.2d 1179 (3d Cir.1978), cert. denied 439 U.S. 969 (Coast Guard hearing officer's conclusion admitted where testimony taken under oath and subject to cross-examination). Compare Koonce v. Quaker Safety Products & Mfg. Co., 798 F.2d 700, 720 (5th Cir.1986) (report excluded where did not involve hearing or comprehensive investigation).

13. Baker v. Firestone Tire & Rubber Co., 793 F.2d 1196 (11th Cir.1986) (congressional subcommittee report was not admissible under exception because it contained heated conclusions of politically motivated debate).

14. Lack of firsthand knowledge does not necessarily require exclusion. See Robbins v. Whelan, 653 F.2d 47 (1st Cir. 1981), cert. denied 454 U.S. 1123 (government report on stopping distances admissible even though based on data supplied by automobile manufacturers of which agency had no firsthand knowledge); Kehm v. Procter & Gamble Mfg. Co., 724 F.2d 613, 618 (8th Cir.1983) (burden is on opponent to show lack of trustworthiness beyond reliance on hearsay).

15. Indeed, another factor to be considered in determining whether the statement is trustworthy, beyond the four noted above, is the unreliable nature of the data on which the report is based. While clearly evaluative reports may rely upon hearsay in reaching conclusions, the fact that the report is based upon hearsay, particularly of an unreliable sort, is a factor cutting against admission. Dallas & Mavis Forwarding Co. v. Stegall, 659 F.2d 721, 722 (6th Cir.1981) (report that relied on hearsay statement of potentially biased witness without physical evidence to corroborate conclusion inadmissible); Faries v. Atlas Truck Body Mfg. Co., 797 F.2d 619, 622–624 (8th Cir.1986) (report based upon incomplete investigation and relying on hearsay statement of potentially interested eyewitnesses lacked trustworthiness).

16. Marsee v. United States Tobacco Co., 866 F.2d 319, 325 (10th Cir.1989) (report did not qualify because not prepared by a public office or agency and did not represent findings of governmental agency).

17. City of New York v. Pullman Inc., 662 F.2d 910, 914 (2d Cir.1981), cert. denied

Restrictions on use by prosecution in criminal cases. As submitted by the Supreme Court and enacted by the Congress, clause (C) of the Federal Rule prohibits the use of investigative reports as evidence against the accused in a criminal case. The limitation was included because of "the almost certain collision with confrontation rights which would result" from using investigative reports against accused.[18]

As transmitted by the Supreme Court to the Congress, clause (B) simply provided for including in the pubic records and reports exception "matters observed pursuant to duty imposed by law." In the course of debate on the floor of the House, concern was expressed that the provision might allow the introduction against the accused of a police officer's report without producing the officer as a witness subject to cross-examination. Accordingly, the provision was amended by adding the italicized words to read "(B) matters observed pursuant to duty imposed by law *as to which matters there was a duty to report, excluding, however, in criminal cases matters observed by police officers and other law enforcement personnel.*" It was enacted as so amended.[19]

The amendment raises a number of questions of varying importance. (1) Can the accused in a criminal case use a report falling under (B)? Clearly the criminal defendant can use an investigative report which falls under (C). However, the language of (B) appears to prohibit the admission of all records of matters observed in criminal cases, which would exclude use by both prosecution or defense if read literally. This meaning is quite evidently not what the Congress had in mind, and the cases have construed the provision to permit the defendant to introduce police reports under clause (B).[20] (2) Who are "other law enforcement personnel"? In its broadest form, this term has been construed to include "any officer or employee of a governmental agency which has law enforcement responsibilities."[21] In specific, "law enforcement personnel" has been held to include a Customs Service chemist analyzing the seized substance in a narcotics case,[22] border inspectors,[23] and I.R.S.

454 U.S. 1164 (interim report subject to revision does not constitute agency finding); Brown v. Sierra Nevada Memorial Miners Hosp., 849 F.2d 1186, 1189–190 (9th Cir.1988) (tentative results of staff investigation do not constitute findings of agency admissible under exception; it is the administrative body's findings that are assumed trustworthy).

18. Adv.Comm.   Note,   Fed.R.Evid. 803(8)(C), 56 F.R.D. 183, 313.

19. 120 Cong.Rec., Pt. 2,2387 (1974).

20. United States v. Smith, 521 F.2d 957 (D.C.Cir.1975). See also United States v. Versaint, 849 F.2d 827, 830–832 (3d Cir. 1988) (police report admissible when of-

fered by defendant to show misidentification); State v. Therriault, 485 A.2d 986, 997 (Me.1984) (error to exclude police laboratory report by deceased preparer favorable to accused and offered by him). See generally 31 A.L.R.Fed. 437.

21. United States v. Oates, 560 F.2d 45, 68 (2d Cir.1977).

22. Id. Compare United States v. Coleman, 631 F.2d 908 (D.C.Cir.1980) (a "difficult question," not decided).

23. United States v. Puente, 826 F.2d 1415, 1417 (5th Cir.1987) (custom service officials); United States v. Orozco, 590 F.2d 789 (9th Cir.1979), cert. denied 442 U.S. 920 (same).

agents,[24] but not a city building inspector[25] or judge.[26] This second inquiry has, however, become somewhat less important as the courts have developed the exceptions examined below for routine or nonadversarial governmental records[27] and for circumstances where the declarant testifies at trial.[28] (3) Does the limitation of clause (B) apply to routine records? The courts have consistently answered that Congress did not intend to exclude observations characterized as "objective" and "nonadversarial" even though these observations are incorporated into law enforcement reports.[29]

(4) Can the limitation of (B) and also that of (C) be avoided by resorting to some other hearsay exception? This question arises when the statement satisfies the requirements of some other hearsay exception that does not prohibit the use of police records and reports or investigative reports against the accused. For example, police reports can often meet the exception for recorded past recollection, and laboratory tests of materials have often been admitted as business records. Neither of these hearsay exceptions contains any limitation like those of Rule 803(8)(B) & (C).

The case first considering this issue answered with an unequivocal and uncompromising "no." It concluded that Congress meant to ex-

24. United States v. Bohrer, 807 F.2d 159, 162 (10th Cir.1986); United States v. Ruffin, 575 F.2d 346 (2d Cir.1978).

25. United States v. Hansen, 583 F.2d 325, 333 (7th Cir.1978), cert. denied 439 U.S. 912.

26. United States v. Gotti, 641 F.Supp. 283, 290 (E.D.N.Y.1986).

27. United States v. Gilbert, 774 F.2d 962, 964–965 (9th Cir.1985) (record of law enforcement personnel indication of location of fingerprint admitted even though within literal terms of rules exclusion because matter recorded was termed "ministerial, objective, and nonevaluative").

28. See, e.g., United States v. Hayes, 861 F.2d 1225, 1229–230 (10th Cir.1988) (report of I.R.S. employee admitted despite performing what could be considered law enforcement duties because employee testified at trial).

29. United States v. Grady, 544 F.2d 598 (2d Cir.1976) (not error to admit records of Ulster constabulary of serial number and receipt of weapons in Northern Ireland to show unlawful export of firearms; congressional purpose was to prevent proof of government's case by police reports of observations of crime and consequently routine recording not within prohibition); United States v. Quezada, 754 F.2d 1190 (5th Cir.1985) (warrant of deportation showing defendant's thumb-print and date and location of deportation admissible since any motivational problems of

officer presented no real danger when recording unambiguous factual matter); United States v. Enterline, 894 F.2d 287, 289–291 (8th Cir.1990) (law enforcement computer records showing cars reported stolen admissible because records both objective and not adversarial in that not made at crime scene); United States v. Orozco, 590 F.2d 789 (9th Cir.1979), cert. denied 442 U.S. 920 (in narcotics case, not error to admit Customs Service computer cards with license numbers of cars crossing border since they involve no adversarial confrontation of nature that might cloud perception).

Numerous state court decisions have ruled in favor of routine laboratory or similar reports. Hing Wan Wong v. Liquor Control Com'n, 160 Conn. 1, 273 A.2d 709 (1970), cert. denied 401 U.S. 938 (analysis of contents of seized glass by state toxicologists); People v. Black, 84 Ill.App.3d 1050, 40 Ill.Dec. 322, 406 N.E.2d 23 (1980) (decal affixed to breathalyzer by department of public health certifying tested and found accurate); State v. Walker, 53 Ohio St.2d 192, 374 N.E.2d 132 (1978) (police log book showing calibration of breath testing device); Law v. Kemp, 276 Or. 581, 556 P.2d 109 (1976) (report of blood-alcohol test by technician in office of state medical examiner); Robertson v. Commonwealth, 211 Va. 62, 175 S.E.2d 260 (1970) (positive report of test for seminal fluid by state medical examiner in rape case).

clude law enforcement and investigative reports against defendants in criminal cases whatever route around the hearsay rule was chosen.[30] Further consideration by other courts, however, has led to a most substantial modification: the limitations of (B) and (C) will not be extended to other hearsay exceptions if the maker is produced in court as a witness and subject to cross-examination, since the essential purpose of Congress was to avoid admission of evidence not subject to cross-examination.[31] Similar analysis indicates that this limitation is inapplicable to proof of the absence of an entry in a governmental record.[32]

§ 297. The Exception for Public Records and Reports: (c) Vital Statistics

If the requirement that the out-of-court declarant must have an official duty to make the report were strictly enforced, such matters as a clergyman's return upon a marriage license indicating that the ceremony had been conducted and the report of an attending physician as to the fact and date of birth or death would not be admissible. Consequently this requirement has been relaxed with regard to matters involving various general statistics. Where the report was made to a public agency by one with a professional, although not necessarily an "official," duty to make the report, such as a minister or a physician, the courts have generally admitted the record to prove the truth of the reporter's statement. An alternative approach is to regard the maker of the report as acting as an official for purposes of making the report.[1] However, the mere fact that a report is required by law is not sufficient to convert it into a public report.[2] The person making the report—a

30. United States v. Oates, 560 F.2d 45, 78 (2d Cir.1977). Cf. United States v. Sims, 617 F.2d 1371, 1377 (9th Cir.1980) (Rule 803(8) covers reports of law enforcement personnel and Rule 803(6) is inapplicable).

31. When declarant testifies, the restriction not applicable under Rule 803(6). See United States v. King, 613 F.2d 670 (7th Cir.1980); United States v. Hayes, 861 F.2d 1225, 1230 (10th Cir.1988).

A similar result has been reached under Rule 803(5). See United States v. Picciandra, 788 F.2d 39, 44 (1st Cir.1986), cert. denied 479 U.S. 847; United States v. Sawyer, 607 F.2d 1190 (7th Cir.1979), cert. denied 445 U.S. 943.

32. United States v. Yakobov, 712 F.2d 20, 23–27 (2d Cir.1983) (statement under Rule 803(10) that record was not found differs from direct statement relating to guilt, which are often part of statements excluded under 803(8)); United States v. Metzger, 778 F.2d 1195, 1201–202 (6th Cir. 1985), cert. denied 477 U.S. 906 (had Congress intended the same restrictions in

Rule 803(8) to apply, it could have explicitly added them to Rule 803(10), an equally specific exception).

§ 297

1. See 5 Wigmore, Evidence § 1633a (Chadbourn rev. 1974).

2. See 4 Weinstein & Berger, Weinstein's Evidence ¶ 803(8)[02], at 243–244 (1990) (legislative history of Federal Rules shows that reports of such "ad hoc" officials not within Rule 803(8)); John McShain, Inc. v. Cessna Aircraft Co., 563 F.2d 632 (3d Cir.1977) (accident reports, including statements filed by pilots, not admissible because Rule 803(8) admits only reports by officials); Ezzo v. Geremiah, 107 Conn. 670, 142 A. 461 (1928) (driver's required report of how accident occurred not admissible).

Statutes requiring such reports commonly provide that they are not admissible in evidence. See, e.g., Leebove v. Rovin, 363 Mich. 569, 111 N.W.2d 104 (1961) (statement of witness in officer's required acci-

motorist, for example, completing a required accident report—can scarcely be regarded as acting in a temporary official capacity or under a professional duty.

The law concerning records of vital statistics is largely statutory, and states generally have legislation on the subject. Federal Rule 803(9)[3] provides a hearsay exception for the following:

> Records or data compilations, in any form, of births, fetal deaths, deaths, or marriages, if the report thereof was made to a public office pursuant to requirements of law.

While the rule looks largely to local law to determine the duty to make the report and for its content, it should not be regarded as borrowing and incorporating the local law as to admissibility. The federal rule governs on that issue.[4]

As to routine matters, such as place and date of birth or death and "immediate" cause of death, such as drowning or gunshot wound, admissibility is seldom questioned. However, entries in death certificates as to the "remote" cause of death, such as suicide, accident, or homicide, usually are made on the basis of information obtained from other persons and predictably involve the questions that have been raised with regard to investigative reports generally,[5] and courts have divided on admissibility.[6] When conclusions of this type are involved, the provisions of Rule 803(8), which is equally applicable and involves a much more careful treatment of the issues, should be applied. Thus, the restrictions on using police and investigative reports against accused persons contained in Federal Rule 803(8)(B) & (C) should be applied to this aspect of records of vital statistics.[7] Similar tests for the admissibility of investigative reports under Federal Rule 803(8)(C), such

---

dent report not admissible). See generally Annot., 46 A.L.R.4th 291; Note, 56 Nw. U.L.Rev. 283 (1961).

3. Revised Uniform Rule (1986) 803(9) is identical.

4. See discussions of these issues in 4 Louisell & Mueller, Federal Evidence § 457, at 786–788 (1980).

5. See supra § 296 notes 7–17 and accompanying text.

6. Annot., 21 A.L.R.3d 418. See also Morgan, The Law of Evidence 1941–1945, 59 Harv.L.Rev. 481, 560–561 (1946); Comment, 25 Rutgers L.Rev. 507 (1971), 15 Wayne L.Rev. 1077, 1162–1165 (1969).

Statutes commonly provide that a death certificate is prima facie evidence of the "facts" stated therein. Courts desiring to exclude the evidence often justify the result on the ground that investigative-type entries are opinions or conclusions rather than facts. Others determine admissibility based on source of information. See, e.g.,

Bowman v. Redding & Co., 449 F.2d 956 (D.C.Cir.1971) (cause of death admissible in death certificate when based on doctor's anatomical diagnosis but information such as how a fatal fall occurred inadmissible when based on hearsay reports); State v. Gould, 216 Mont. 455, 704 P.2d 20 (1985) (statement in death certificate that deceased was passenger in vehicle should have been omitted because based on hearsay). See generally Annot., 21 A.L.R.3d 418.

7. See supra § 296 text accompanying notes 18–32.

Compare California State Life Ins. Co. v. Fuqua, 40 Ariz. 148, 10 P.2d 958 (1932) (error in civil action to exclude death certificate describing cause of death as "gunshot wounds inflicted by officers * * * in the performance of their duties") with State v. Barker, 94 Ariz. 383, 385 P.2d 516 (1963) (proper in murder prosecution to exclude death certificate stating "justifiable homicide"; civil rule not applicable in criminal cases).

as the broad scope of investigative reports and analysis of the expertise of the preparer, should prevail.[8]

§ 298. The Exception for Public Records and Reports: (d) Judgments in Previous Cases, Especially Criminal Convictions Offered in Subsequent Civil Cases [1]

Insofar as reports of official investigations are admissible under the official written statement exception, it would seem that the judgment of a court, made after the full investigation of a trial, would also be admissible in subsequent litigation to prove the truth of those things necessarily determined in the first action. Guilty pleas and statements made in the course of litigation may constitute declarations against interest [2] or admissions of a party-opponent [3] and under those exceptions avoid the bar of the hearsay rule. Where the doctrines of res judicata, collateral estoppel, or claim or issue preclusion make the determinations in the first case binding in the second, not only is the judgment in the first case admissible in the second, but, as a matter of substantive law, it is conclusive against the party. If neither res judicata nor collateral estoppel applies, however, the courts have traditionally been unwilling to admit judgments in previous cases.[4] The judgments have been regarded as hearsay and not within any exception to the hearsay rule.

A variety of reasons have been advanced for this rule. Civil cases often involve numerous issues, and it may be difficult to determine what issues a judgment in fact determined. This, however, argues only for a requirement that one offering a judgment establish as a prerequisite for its admissibility that it did in fact determine an issue relevant to the instant litigation. It is also argued that the party against whom the judgment is offered may not have had an opportunity to be present and to participate in the first action. This misses the point, however, as the appropriate question in deciding whether the hearsay should be admitted in this context is not the party's opportunity to have been present at the official investigation, but rather whether that investigation provided adequate assurance of reliability. In many cases, the party will in fact have been present and have had not only an opportunity but a strong motive to defend.

8. See supra § 296 notes 7–17 and accompanying text.

§ 298

1. See generally 4 Wigmore, Evidence § 1346a (Chadbourn rev. 1972); 5 Wigmore, Evidence § 1671a (Chadbourn rev. 1974); Motomura, Using Judgments as Evidence, Minn.L.Rev. 979 (1986); Cowen, The Admissibility of Criminal Convictions in Subsequent Civil Proceedings, 40 Calif.L.Rev. 225 (1952); Hinton, Judgment of Conviction—Effect on a Civil Case as Res Judicata or as Evidence, 27 Ill.L.Rev. 195 (1932); Note, 39 Va.L.Rev. 995 (1953); Annots., 18 A.L.R.2d 1287, 31 A.L.R. 261; Dec.Dig.Judgments ⊙648.

2. See infra Ch. 33.

3. See supra Ch. 25. As to guilty pleas, see especially § 257.

4. 5 Wigmore, Evidence § 1671a (Chadbourn rev. 1974).

The argument against admissibility does have merit with regard to judgments offered against a criminal defendant when that judgment was rendered against another. Admitting such judgments violates the defendant's constitutional right of confrontation.[5] Admitting civil judgments rendered against the defendant directly raises constitutional issues as well. Other arguments against admissibility of prior judgments relate to the danger of undue prejudice and the need for orderly administration of trials. Also juries may have difficulty grasping the distinction between a prior judgment offered as evidence and one that is conclusive, giving the judgment binding effect even if this is contrary to substantive law. Finally, it is argued that, if prior judgments are admissible, parties offering them will tend to rely heavily upon them and not introduce significant amounts of other evidence. The result feared is that the evidence available in the second case will be inadequate for a reliable decision.

These arguments have caused many courts to exclude a prior civil judgment offered in a subsequent civil case. There is, however, a growing tendency to admit a prior conviction for a serious criminal offense in a subsequent civil action. In these situations, the party against whom the judgment is offered was generally the defendant in the criminal case and therefore had not only the opportunity but also the motive to defend fully. In addition, because of the heavy burden of proof in criminal cases, a judgment in such a situation represents significantly more reliable evidence than a judgment in a civil case. The tendency is most noticeable when the judgment is offered in a subsequent civil case in which the convicted defendant seeks affirmatively to benefit from his criminal offense—for example, a convicted arsonist sues to recover upon his fire insurance policy. The strong desire to prevent this result undoubtedly influenced courts to permit the introduction of the judgment of conviction,[6] and some courts also held that the judgment was conclusive proof that the party committed the relevant acts with the state of mind required for criminal liability.[7]

---

5. Kirby v. United States, 174 U.S. 47 (1899) (error to convict for possession of stolen postage stamps where only evidence that stamps were stolen was the record of thieves' conviction). However, where the conviction of another is an element of an offense, e.g., selling firearms to a convicted felon, this prohibition does not apply.

6. The leading case is Schindler v. Royal Ins. Co., 258 N.Y. 310, 179 N.E. 711 (1932) (in suit by plaintiff on insurance policy, defended by insurer on ground that plaintiff's fraudulent claim voided policy, insurer could introduce plaintiff's conviction for presenting false and fraudulent proof of loss, although this would only be prima facie proof of facts). For additional cases, see Annot., 18 A.L.R.2d 1287.

7. The leading case is Eagle, Star & British Dominions Ins. Co. v. Heller, 149

Va. 82, 140 S.E. 314 (1927) (in suit by plaintiff on insurance policy, defended by insurer on theory that loss was not accidental but rather fraudulently caused by insured, plaintiff's conviction for wilfully burning goods with intent to injure insurer was not only admissible, but also determinative, and could only be attacked upon grounds of fraud, perjury, collusion, or some similar theory). The Virginia court has denied any intention to repudiate the requirement of mutuality in preclusion situations generally and has confined the reach of the *Eagle* case to the convict seeking to profit from his own wrong. Norfolk & Western Ry. Co. v. Bailey Lumber Co., 221 Va. 638, 272 S.E.2d 217 (1980). For additional cases, see Annot., 18 A.L.R.2d 1287.

It was but a short step from this position to the general admissibility of a prior criminal conviction in a civil action against the party who was previously the criminal defendant.[8] A number of courts limited this rule to convictions for serious offenses, reasoning that convictions for misdemeanors do not represent sufficiently reliable determinations to justify dispensing with the hearsay objections.[9] Judgments of acquittal, however, are still inadmissible in large part because they may not present a determination of innocence, but rather only a decision that the prosecution has not met its burden of proof beyond a reasonable doubt.[10]

Federal Rule 803(22)[11] incorporates these general developments. It provides a hearsay exception for the following:

> Evidence of a final judgment, entered after a trial or upon a plea of guilty (but not upon a plea of nolo contendere), adjudging a person guilty of a crime punishable by death or imprisonment in excess of one year, to prove any fact essential to sustain the judgment, but not including, when offered by the Government in a criminal prosecution for purposes other than impeachment, judgments against persons other than the accused. The pendency of an appeal may be shown but does not affect admissibility.

8. See, e.g., Asato v. Furtado, 52 Hawaii 284, 290, 474 P.2d 288, 293 (1970):

While there is a divergence of authority on this point, we think the better reasoned rule is that * * * the prior judgment should be admissible as evidence where the following factors are present. (1) It must be shown that the issues on which the judgment is offered was necessarily decided in the prior trial. (2) A judgment on the merits must have been rendered. (3) It must appear that the party against whom the judgment is offered had a full and fair opportunity to litigate the claim and especially to contest the specific issue on which the judgment is offered. In other words, it must appear that the party against whom the judgment is offered had a full and complete "day in court" on that issue, with the opportunity to call and cross examine witnesses and to be presented by counsel.

See also Scott v. Robertson, 583 P.2d 188, 191–192 (Alaska 1978).

9. Haynes v. Rollins, 434 P.2d 234 (Okl. 1967); Kirkendall v. Korseberg, 247 Or. 75, 427 P.2d 418 (1967); Loughner v. Schmelzer, 421 Pa. 283, 218 A.2d 768 (1966) (evidence of defendant's conviction for failure to drive on the right side of the highway not admissible in personal injury action, although felony conviction would be); Graham, Admissibility in Illinois of Convictions and Pleas of Guilty to Traffic Of-

fenses in Related Civil Litigation, 1979 So. Ill.U.L.J. 209; Notes, 50 Colum.L.Rev. 529 (1950), 35 Cornell L.Q. 872 (1950); Annot., 18 A.L.R.2d 1287.

10. Mew Sun Leong v. Honolulu Rapid Transit Co., 52 Hawaii 138, 472 P.2d 505 (1970) (acquittal of driver on criminal charges arising out of accident not admissible in civil action, "nor should it be mentioned by counsel to the jury"); Massey v. Meurer, 25 A.D.2d 729, 268 N.Y.S.2d 735 (1966) (error to admit defendant's acquittal for driving while intoxicated in personal injury action).

11. Revised Uniform Rule (1986) 803(22) is identical, with two exceptions. It omits, without change of meaning, the somewhat redundant language in parentheses. It also places in brackets, as an optional deletion, "entered after a trial or upon a plea of guilty," thus making the rule applicable also to judgments rendered on pleas of nolo contendere. See infra n. 17.

The problem of ascertaining what facts are "essential to sustain the judgment" where a general verdict is rendered is considered in Columbia Plaza Corp. v. Security Nat. Bank, 676 F.2d 780, 789 (D.C.Cir.1982) (where defendant charged with conspiracy involving 85 overt acts, general verdict of guilty did not establish commission of specific act). See also Index Fund, Inc. v. Hagopian, 677 F.Supp. 710, 720 (S.D.N.Y.1987).

The following characteristics of the exception should be noted: (1) Only criminal judgments of conviction are included. Judgments in civil cases are not included, their effect being left to the law of res judicata or preclusion.[12] (2) Only crimes of felony grade, i.e., punishable by death or imprisonment for more than one year,[13] are included, thus eliminating problems associated with convictions of lesser crimes.[14] (3) The rule does not apply to judgments of acquittal.[15] (4) When offered by the government in criminal prosecutions, judgments of conviction of persons other than the accused are admissible only for purposes of impeachment.[16] When the judgment of conviction is offered in a civil case, however, it is treated as are investigative reports generally, and there is restriction as to the parties against whom the evidence is admissible. (5) Judgments entered on pleas of nolo contendere are not included within the exception.[17] (6) The provision merely excludes a qualifying judgment from the bar of the hearsay rule. It does not purport to dictate the use to be made of the judgment once it is admitted in evidence. Applicable rules of res judicata or preclusion will be given effect. Otherwise the evidence may be used "substantively" or for impeachment, as may be appropriate.[18]

§ 299. The Exception for Official Certificates: (a) In General

For purposes of the law of evidence, a certificate is a written statement issued to an applicant by an official that recites certain matters of

12. In Lloyd v. American Export Lines, Inc., 580 F.2d 1179, 1179–180 (3d Cir.1978), cert. denied 439 U.S. 969, a shipping line appealed from a judgment in favor of a crew member for failure to protect him from another crew member. The court ruled that it was error to exclude a Japanese criminal conviction of the claimant for the assault. The proceedings, said the court, met the standards of civilized jurisprudence.

13. See supra § 43 as to convictions under the law of another jurisdiction.

14. See supra note 9 and accompanying text. Banek v. Thomas, 733 P.2d 1171, 1176 (Colo.1986) (crime of resisting arrest, which carries maximum sentence of one year, not admissible).

15. United States v. Viserto, 596 F.2d 531 (2d Cir.1979), cert. denied 444 U.S. 841. See also McKinney v. Galvin, 701 F.2d 584, 586 & n. 5 (6th Cir.1983); United States v. Irvin, 787 F.2d 1506, 1516–517 (11th Cir. 1986). The effect of the omission is merely to leave the bar of the hearsay rule in place with respect to such judgments. The status of an acquittal in other settings is not affected by the rule.

16. United States v. Crispin, 757 F.2d 611, 613 (5th Cir.1985) (use of aliens' conviction to prove unlawful presence improper to establish element of conspiracy charge against defendant for allegedly transporting illegal aliens); United States v. Vandetti, 623 F.2d 1144 (6th Cir.1980) (in prosecution for conducting a gambling enterprise by five or more persons, error in defendant's separate trial to admit earlier convictions of codefendants). See also supra note 5 and accompanying text.

17. To admit the judgment would effectively nullify the most important characteristic of nolo pleas. See supra § 257 text accompanying notes 30–32. Whether the rule, with its exclusion of judgments based on nolo pleas, applies to convictions used for impeachment is discussed in supra § 84. However, the admissibility of the underlying facts is unaffected by the nolo plea. United States v. Wyatt, 762 F.2d 908, 911–912 (11th Cir.1985), cert. denied 475 U.S. 1047.

18. Eastern Renovating Corp. v. Roman Catholic Bishop of Springfield, 554 F.2d 4 (1st Cir.1977) (in action on construction contracts, not error to admit convictions of plaintiff based on fraudulent alterations of contracts sued upon; jury could use substantively rather than just for impeachment).

fact. It is not a part of the public records of the issuing office, although a common form of certificate is a statement that a document to which it is attached is a correct copy of such a record.[1] The common law was strict about admitting certificates as hearsay exceptions, for the most part requiring statutory authority.[2]

The relation between certification and a public record may be illustrated by proof of marriage. If the celebrant of a marriage issues a certificate that he or she has performed the marriage and gives it to the parties, this document is not a public record, and admission in evidence must be under some other hearsay exception. If, however, the celebrant makes a "return" of the license, i.e., a redelivery to the issuing official with an endorsement of the manner in which the authority was exercised, then the return becomes a part of the public record, admissible under that hearsay exception.

Federal Rule 803(12)[3] provides a certification procedure with respect to marriage and similar ceremonies:

> Statements of fact contained in a certificate that the maker performed a marriage or other ceremony or administered a sacrament, made by a clergyman, public official, or other person authorized by the rules or practices of a religious organization or by law to perform the act certified, and purporting to have been issued at the time of the act or within a reasonable time thereafter.[4]

Certification is also provided for a large variety of matters by statutes, with corresponding provisions for admissibility in evidence.[5] These statutes are continued in effect under Federal Rule 802.[6]

§ 300. The Exception for Official Certificates: (b) Certified Copies or Summaries of Official Records; Absence of Record

When a purported copy of a public record is presented in court accompanied by a certificate that the purported copy is correct, a two-layered hearsay problem is presented. First, is the public record within

§ 299

1. Certification of copies of public records receives further treatment in infra § 300.

2. 5 Wigmore, Evidence § 1674 (Chadbourn rev. 1974).

3. Revised Uniform Rule (1986) 803(12) is identical.

4. Compare the wider range of matters provable by records of religious organizations under Federal and Revised Uniform Rule (1986) 803(11):

> Statements of births, marriages, divorces, deaths, legitimacy, ancestry, relationship by blood or marriage, or other similar facts of personal or family history, contained in a regularly kept record of a religious organization.

However, this exception admits only records of such personal information. Hall v. Commissioner, 729 F.2d 632, 635 (9th Cir.1984) (statements of contribution to church does not come within exception).

5. 5 Wigmore, Evidence § 1674 n. 7 (Chadbourn rev. 1974) collects numerous federal and state statutes.

6. Federal Rule 802 states:

> Hearsay is not admissible except as provided by these rules or by other rules prescribed by the Supreme Court pursuant to statutory authority or by Act of Congress.

Revised Uniform Rule (1986) 802 is to the same effect.

the hearsay exception for that kind of record? Second, is the certificate within the hearsay exception for official certificates? The first question has been considered in the earlier sections of this chapter. The second question involves a specialized application of the certification procedure discussed generally in the immediately preceding section.

The early common law generally required a statutory duty to certify.[1] The Supreme Court of the United States, however, long ago rejected this position with respect to certification of copies of public records,[2] and the American common law rule remains that a custodian has, by virtue of the office, the implied duty and authority to certify the accuracy of a copy of a public record in the custodian's official possession.[3] Present-day usual practice is to prove public records by copy certified to be correct by the custodian, and many statutes so provide.[4] Federal Rule 1005 allows proof of public records by copy, without producing or accounting for the original,[5] and Rule 902(4)[6] provides for authentication by certificate as follows:

> A copy of an official record or report or entry therein, or of a document authorized by law to be recorded or filed and actually recorded or filed in a public office, including data compilations in any form, certified as correct by the custodian or other person authorized to make the certification, by certificate complying with paragraph (1), (2), or (3) of this rule or complying with any Act of Congress or rule prescribed by the Supreme Court pursuant to statutory authority.

In the absence of a statute to the contrary, the usual view has been that the authority to certify copies of public records is construed literally as requiring a copy and does not include paraphrases or summaries. Thus a certificate saying "our records show X" is not admissible to prove X.[7]

By analogy to the rule that nonoccurrence of an event may be proved by a business record containing no entry of the event where the

§ 300

1. 5 Wigmore, Evidence § 1677 (Chadbourn rev. 1974).

2. United States v. Percheman, 32 U.S. (7 Pet.) 51 (1833); Church v. Hubbart, 6 U.S. (2 Cranch) 187 (1804).

3. Stevison v. Earnest, 80 Ill. 513 (1875); Adv.Comm.Note, Fed.R.Evid. 902(4), 56 F.R.D. 183, 338.

4. 5 Wigmore, Evidence § 1680 (Chadbourn rev. 1974).

5. The corresponding Revised Uniform Rule (1986) differs only in minor detail. See supra § 230.

6. The corresponding Revised Uniform Rule (1986) differs only in minor detail.

7. State v. Williams, 144 Ariz. 433, 698 P.2d 678 (1985) (letter from correctional records supervisor reciting certain matters as contained in records of department held not self-authenticating under rule); Golder v. Bressler, 105 Ill. 419 (1883) (error to admit certificate of secretary of state that records showed appointment of named persons as trustees of Bank of Illinois, instead of actual copy of record); In re Kostohris' Estate, 96 Mont. 226, 29 P.2d 829 (1934) (custodian's certificate that records showed listed payments to veteran inadmissible to prove payments). Wigmore criticizes the requirement and collects statutes allowing certification of effect or substance of records. 5 Wigmore, Evidence § 1678(6) (Chadbourn rev. 1974). See Department of Public Aid v. Wall's Estate, 81 Ill.App.3d 394, 36 Ill.Dec. 798, 401 N.E.2d 639 (1980) (proper to admit list of payments made on behalf of decedent certified by director of department; need not be a literal copy of record).

practice was to record such events,[8] proof of nonoccurrence may be made by absence of an entry in a public record where such matters are recorded.[9] However, absence of the entry or record could at common law be proved only by testimony of the custodian.[10] This limitation has been modified by many statutes,[11] and Federal Rule 803(10) [12] provides the following:

> To prove the absence of a record, report, statement, or data compilation, in any form, or the nonoccurrence or nonexistence of a matter of which a record, report, statement, or data compilation, in any form, was regularly made and preserved by a public office or agency, evidence in the form of a certification in accordance with rule 902, or testimony, that diligent search failed to disclose the record, report, statement, or data compilation, or entry.

The rule is phrased to include not only proving nonoccurrence of an event of which a record would have been made,[13] but also the nonfiling of a document allowed or required by law to be filed.[14] The courts have insisted that the requirement of a "diligent search" must be satisfied [15] but have not required that a specific form of words be used to meet that requirement.[16]

8. See supra § 287.

9. 5 Wigmore, Evidence § 1633(6) (Chadbourn rev. 1974).

10. 5 Wigmore, Evidence § 1678(7) (Chadbourn rev. 1974).

11. Id. at note 4.

12. The Revised Uniform Rule (1986) is identical.

13. United States v. Lee, 589 F.2d 980 (9th Cir.1979), cert. denied 444 U.S. 969 (affidavit that records showed no employment of accused by CIA, contrary to his contention).

14. United States v. Neff, 615 F.2d 1235 (9th Cir.1980), cert. denied 447 U.S. 925 (in prosecution for willful failure to file income tax returns, proper to admit IRS certificate of nonfiling during years in question).

15. United States v. Yakobov, 712 F.2d 20, 24 (2d Cir.1983) ("diligent search" is an essential requirement of rule—a requirement of substance, not form—and not satisfied where search for records was conducted under misspelled name).

16. United States v. Harris, 551 F.2d 621, 622 (5th Cir.1977), cert. denied 434 U.S. 836 (failure of certificate to recite "diligent search" not fatal where substance of requirement has been satisfied and where inquiry is simple determination of whether license issued); United States v. Martinez, 700 F.2d 1358 (11th Cir.1983) ("magic words" not required, particularly involving translated document and substance of requirement was proved by indication of extensive search).

Chapter 31

TESTIMONY TAKEN AT A
FORMER HEARING OR
IN ANOTHER ACTION [1]

Table of Sections

§ 301. Introduction; Is It Hearsay? Scope of Statutes and Rules

Upon compliance with requirements designed to guarantee an adequate opportunity for cross-examination and after showing that the

1. See 5 Wigmore, Evidence §§ 1370, 1371, 1386–1389, 1402–1417, 1660–1669 (Chadbourn rev. 1974); Weissenberger, The Former Testimony Hearsay Exception: A Study in Rulemaking, Judicial Revisionism, and the Separation of Powers, 67 N.C.L.Rev. 295 (1989); Martin, The Former–Testimony Exception in the Proposed Federal Rules of Evidence, 57 Iowa L.Rev. 547 (1972); Falknor, Former Testimony and the Uniform Rules: A Comment, 38 N.Y.U.L.Rev. 651 (1963); Hinton, Changes in Hearsay Exceptions, 29 Ill.L.Rev. 422, 427 (1934); Note, 42 Miami L.Rev. 975 (1988).

See also Dec.Dig. Evidence ⊗=575–583, Criminal Law ⊗=540–548; C.J.S. Evidence §§ 384–402; Annots., 40 A.L.R.4th 514, 15 A.L.R. 495, 79 A.L.R. 1392, 122 A.L.R. 425, 159 A.L.R. 1240.

witness is unavailable, testimony given previously may be received in the pending case in the form of a written transcript or an oral report of that testimony. This testimony may have been given during a deposition or at a trial. It may have been received in a separate proceeding or in an earlier hearing of the present case.[2]

Depending upon the precise formulation of the rule against hearsay, this evidence, which is usually called "former testimony," may be classified as an exception to the hearsay prohibition, or it may be considered as nonhearsay under the theory that the requirements of the hearsay concept have been met. The former view is accepted generally today;[3] the latter was espoused by Wigmore.[4] In this treatise, former testimony is classified as a hearsay exception under the general definition of hearsay developed earlier which defines hearsay as including all prior testimony that is offered for its truth.[5]

Cross-examination, oath, the solemnity of the occasion, and, in the case of transcribed testimony, the accuracy of reproduction of the words spoken all combine to give former testimony a high degree of credibility. Accordingly, to allow its use only upon a showing of unavailability may seem to relegate "former testimony" to an undeserved second-class status. The result is, however, explained by the strong preference to have available witnesses testify in open court.[6]

Many of the exceptions to the hearsay rule have been developed almost solely through the judicial process while others have been widely regulated by statute. The present exception is of the latter class, which had important implications for interpreting the exception prior to the recent trend for most American jurisdictions to adopt

§ 301

2. For opinions stating the common law rule, see, e.g., Gaines v. Thomas, 241 S.C. 412, 128 S.E.2d 692 (1962); State v. Carr, 67 S.D. 481, 294 N.W. 174 (1940); State v. Ortego, 22 Wash.2d 552, 157 P.2d 320 (1945).

3. See, e.g., Cross & Tapper, Cross on Evidence 655–656 (7th ed. 1990); 1 Greenleaf, Evidence § 163 (3d ed. 1846); 2 Jones, Evidence § 308 (5th ed. 1958); Morgan, Basic Problems of Evidence 255 (1962); George v. Davie, 201 Ark. 470, 145 S.W.2d 729 (1940); Walker v. Walker, 14 Ga. 242, 249 (1853); Gaines v. Thomas, 241 S.C. 412, 128 S.E.2d 692 (1962); Lone Star Gas Co. v. State, 137 Tex. 279, 153 S.W.2d 681 (1941), motion denied 315 U.S. 8.

Federal Rule 804(b)(1) treats former testimony as a hearsay exception as does the Revised Uniform Rule. The Federal Rule is quoted infra in text following note 8.

4. 5 Wigmore, Evidence § 1370 (Chadbourn rev. 1974). This view has occasionally been approved by the courts and adopted by some textwriters. See, e.g., Habig v. Bastian, 117 Fla. 864, 158 So. 508 (1935); Garner v. Pennsylvania Public Utility Com'n, 177 Pa.Super. 439, 110 A.2d 907 (1955); Chamberlayne, Trial Evidence § 729 (2d ed. 1936).

5. See supra § 246.

6. See United States v. Inadi, 475 U.S. 387, 394 (1986):

> Unlike some other exceptions to the hearsay rules, or the exemption from the hearsay definition involved in this case [co-conspirator statements], former testimony often is only a weaker substitute for live testimony. It seldom has independent evidentiary significance of its own, but is intended to replace live testimony. If the declarant is available and the same information can be presented to the trier of fact in the form of live testimony, with full cross-examination and the opportunity to view the demeanor of the declarant, there is little justification for relying on the weaker version.

general evidence codes.[7]

In many instances the predecessor statutes have been replaced by rules that are identical to, or modeled upon, the Federal Rule 804(b)(1),[8] which provides:

(b) **Hearsay exceptions.** The following are not excluded by the hearsay rule if the declarant is unavailable as a witness:

(1) **Former testimony.** Testimony given as a witness at another hearing of the same or a different proceeding, or in a deposition taken in compliance with law in the course of the same or another proceeding, if the party against whom the testimony is now offered, or, in a civil action or proceeding, a predecessor in interest, had an opportunity and similar motive to develop the testimony by direct, cross, or redirect examination.

It is important to notice at the outset that former testimony may often be admitted without meeting the requirements discussed in this chapter, such as opportunity and motive to cross-examine and the unavailability of the witness. These requirements are applicable only when the evidence is offered under this particular exception. When the former testimony is offered for some nonhearsay purpose [9]—to show the commission of the act of perjury,[10] to show that testimony against the accused furnished the motive for the murder of the witness,[11] to refresh recollection,[12] or to impeach a witness at the present trial by proving that earlier testimony was inconsistent [13]—the restrictions of

---

7. It would be impossible in this brief work to give an adequate historical treatment of the variations in the statutes of the different states. The usual approach, however, was that these statutes were considered "declaratory" of the common law, so far as they went, and were not the exclusive test of admissibility. Accordingly, if the evidence met the common law requirements, it was generally admitted even though the permissive provisions of the statute did not mention the particular common law doctrine which the evidence satisfies. In re White's Will, 2 N.Y.2d 309, 160 N.Y.S.2d 841, 141 N.E.2d 416 (1957) (testimony given in lunacy proceeding held admissible in proceeding to contest lunatic's will, under statute declaring former testimony admissible if subject matter and parties are the same); State v. Ham, 224 N.C. 128, 29 S.E.2d 449 (1944) (statute making testimony on preliminary hearing admissible when subscribed and certified does not limit admission under common law practice where stenographer swears report accurate).

When the common law imposed a restriction not mentioned in the statute, the restriction controls unless the circumstances show a legislative intention to abrogate it. Illinois Steel Co. v. Muza, 164 Wis. 247, 159 N.W. 908 (1916) (statute providing for ad-

mission of former testimony conditioned on an opportunity to cross-examine considered declaratory of common law and hence qualified by common law condition that such opportunity must be on substantially the same issues).

8. Revised Uniform Rule (1986) (804)(b)(1) is identical.

9. See 5 Wigmore, Evidence § 1387 nn. 5–7 (Chadbourn rev. 1974).

10. See State v. Wykert, 198 Iowa 1219, 199 N.W. 331 (1924) (admissibility to show perjury assumed and former testimony of other witnesses also admitted to show the materiality of the perjured testimony).

11. Suggested by the facts in Nordan v. State, 143 Ala. 13, 39 So. 406 (1905) although the opinion does not quite reach this point.

12. See supra § 9.

13. People v. Ferraro, 293 N.Y. 51, 55 N.E.2d 861 (1944). See also People v. Hawley, 111 Cal. 78, 43 P. 404 (1896) (testimony of accused at preliminary hearing admissible to impeach; it seems that it would have been as readily receivable as an admission).

Use of depositions to impeach or contradict the deponent's testimony as a witness

the hearsay exception do not apply. Likewise, if offered for a hearsay purpose but under some other exception, e.g., as the admission of a party-opponent [14] or past recollection recorded,[15] only the requirements of that other exception, and not those of the former testimony exception, must be satisfied.

§ 302. The Requirement of Oath and Opportunity for Cross–Examination; Confrontation and Unavailability

To be admitted under this exception to the hearsay rule, former testimony must have been given under the sanction of an oath [1] or affirmation.[2] More important, and more often drawn into question, is the requirement that the party against whom the former testimony is now offered, or perhaps a party in like interest,[3] must have had a reasonable opportunity to cross-examine.[4]

Actual cross-examination is not required if the opportunity was afforded and waived.[5] Whether cross-examination was conducted or waived, admissibility under this exception is not judged by the use made of the opportunity to cross-examine but rather the availability of the opportunity. This point is amply demonstrated in cases holding that the opportunity to cross-examine at a preliminary hearing in a criminal case provides sufficient opportunity even though few litigants,

is provided under Fed.R.Civ.P. 32(a)(1) and Fed.R.Crim.P. 15(e).

14. Bogie v. Nolan, 96 Mo. 85, 9 S.W. 14 (1888); Tuttle v. Wyman, 146 Neb. 146, 18 N.W.2d 744 (1945). See 5 Wigmore, Evidence § 1416(1) (Chadbourn rev. 1974). As to depositions, see Fed.R.Civ.P. 32(a)(2).

15. State v. Hacker, 177 N.J.Super. 533, 427 A.2d 109 (App.Div.1981), certification denied 87 N.J. 364, 434 A.2d 1054.

§ 302

1. Some courts have required an affirmative showing that the witness was sworn before allowing admission of former testimony. Monahan v. Clemons, 212 Ky. 504, 279 S.W. 974 (1926); Jolly v. State, 269 So.2d 650 (Miss.1972). The preferable view is that evidence that the witness testified justifies an inference that he or she was sworn. Poe v. State, 95 Ark. 172, 129 S.W. 292 (1910); Meyers v. State, 112 Neb. 149, 198 N.W. 871 (1924); Keith v. State, 53 Ohio App. 58, 4 N.E.2d 220 (1936).

2. See Fed.R.Evid. 603 (defining flexible "oath or affirmation" standard).

3. See infra § 303 for discussion of "predecessor in interest" issue.

4. United States v. Jones, 402 F.2d 851 (2d Cir.1968), and Young v. United States,

406 F.2d 960 (D.C.Cir.1968) (testimony given by witnesses before grand jury not admissible against accused); Fender v. Ramsey & Phillips, 131 Ga. 440, 62 S.E. 527 (1908) (ex parte affidavit used in former trial inadmissible); Stearsman v. State, 237 Ind. 149, 143 N.E.2d 81 (1957) (when witness died of a heart attack during cross-examination, that part of his testimony as to which he had been cross-examined admitted); Edgerley v. Appleyard, 110 Me. 337, 86 A. 244 (testimony taken at coroner's inquest inadmissible for want of opportunity to cross-examine); Citizens Bank & Trust Co. v. Reid Motor Co., 216 N.C. 432, 5 S.E.2d 318 (1939) (direct examination taken before Workmen's Compensation Commissioner where witness refused to submit to cross-examination not receivable in evidence in judicial proceeding for compensation); and cases cited C.J.S. Evidence § 390; Dec.Dig. Evidence ⊙578, Criminal Law ⊙544.

For consideration of when a party is "in like interest," see infra § 303.

5. State v. Logan, 344 Mo. 351, 126 S.W.2d 256 (1939) (witness at former trial not cross-examined by counsel for accused); State v. Roebuck, 75 Wash.2d 67, 448 P.2d 934 (1968); 5 Wigmore, Evidence § 1371 (Chadbourn rev. 1974).

for a number of reasons, fully exercise that opportunity.[6] However, circumstances may differ sufficiently between the prior hearing and the present trial to bar admission under this requirement, as where questions on a particular subject would have been largely irrelevant at the earlier proceeding.[7] Moreover, as discussed in later sections, the opportunity to cross-examine must have been such as to render the cross-examination actually conducted or the decision not to cross-examine meaningful in the light of the circumstances prevailing when the former testimony was given.[8]

If a right to counsel exists when the former testimony is offered, a denial of counsel when the testimony was taken renders it inadmissible.[9] However, a general finding of ineffective representation at the prior hearing does not automatically require rejection of the testimony; the adequacy of the cross-examination under the facts must be determined.[10] Improper judicial interference may render the opportunity to cross-examine inadequate.[11] However, restrictions upon cross-examination do not have this consequence unless very substantial,[12] some courts

6. State v. Parker, 161 Conn. 500, 504, 289 A.2d 894, 896 (1971) (in admitting preliminary hearing testimony against state, court declared that "test is the opportunity for full and complete cross-examination rather than the use made of that opportunity"); Commonwealth v. Mustone, 353 Mass. 490, 233 N.E.2d 1 (1968) (risk of unavailability of witness at trial and consequent loss of cross-examination is assumed); State v. Crawley, 242 Or. 601, 410 P.2d 1012 (1966) (preliminary hearing testimony admissible where opportunity to cross-examine and confront afforded). Cf. Government of Virgin Islands v. Aquino, 378 F.2d 540 (3d Cir.1967) (rule of admissibility followed although court notes practical differences between the proceedings).

In California v. Green, 399 U.S. 149 (1970) and Ohio v. Roberts, 448 U.S. 56, 72 (1980), the argument against admitting preliminary hearing testimony was rejected as a ground of constitutional attack.

7. Cf. United States v. Wingate, 520 F.2d 309, 315–316 (2d Cir.1975), cert. denied 423 U.S. 1074 (testimony at another defendant's motion to suppress statements on ground of involuntariness not admissible to show innocence of defendant where issues were so different as to render opportunity to cross-examine not meaningful); United States v. Atkins, 618 F.2d 366 (5th Cir.1980) (proper to exclude testimony on preliminary matter, now offered to exculpate defendant, in which he did not participate and the government had no motive to cross-examine regarding his role).

United States v. Zurosky, 614 F.2d 779, 792–793 (1st Cir.1979), cert. denied 466 U.S. 967, presents an interesting reversal

of the situation in *Wingate*. In *Zurosky*, testimony at a prior hearing, which was equally irrelevant to the defendant's innocence, was admitted because the trial court invited cross-examination, correctly anticipating that the witness would be unavailable at trial because of his asserting the Fifth Amendment right not to testify.

8. These issues are generally treated with regard to the motive to cross-examine rather than the naked opportunity to do so. See infra § 304.

9. Pointer v. Texas, 380 U.S. 400 (1965) (error to admit at trial testimony given at preliminary hearing where defendant was not represented by counsel; Sixth Amendment right of confrontation includes opportunity to cross-examine by counsel in this situation and applies to proceedings in state as well as federal courts).

10. Mancusi v. Stubbs, 408 U.S. 204 (1972); State v. West, 363 So.2d 513 (La. 1978).

11. State v. Halsey, 34 N.M. 223, 279 P. 945 (1929); Gill v. State, 148 Tex.Cr. 513, 188 S.W.2d 584 (App.1945), and see the original opinion in the same case, 147 Tex. Cr. 392, 181 S.W.2d 276 (1944).

12. See Complaint of Paducah Towing Co., 692 F.2d 412, 418–419 (6th Cir.1982) (court concluded that the examination did not provide even minimal assurance of reliability because the Coast Guard, which was not represented by an attorney, was prohibited by the administrative law judge from challenging the credibility of its witness' testimony). But see United States v. King, 713 F.2d 627, 630 (11th Cir.1983),

holding that they must render the testimony inherently unreliable.[13]

Is the opportunity for direct and redirect examination the equivalent of the opportunity for cross-examination? If a party calls and examines a witness and this testimony is offered against that same party in a subsequent trial, may the direct testimony be admitted over the objection that there was no opportunity to cross-examine? The decisions sensibly hold that it may.[14]

If evidence is offered under the former testimony exception to the hearsay rule, it is offered as a substitute for testimony given in person in open court, and the strong policy favoring personal presence requires that unavailability of the witness be shown before the substitute is acceptable.[15] If the witness is present in court and is available for cross-examination, his or her former testimony may be admitted under some circumstances as a prior statement of a witness.[16] Thus, exclusion of prior testimony for reasons relating to availability will generally occur only when the witness is absent from court but does not meet the unavailability definition used under either the Federal Rules or the Confrontation Clause.[17] The definition of unavailability under the hearsay rule and problems of confrontation, which are common to a number of hearsay exceptions, are discussed elsewhere.[18] By contrast, if the former testimony is used as a prior inconsistent statement for impeachment or as an admission of a party-opponent, unavailability is not required.[19]

cert. denied 466 U.S. 942 (limitations in both scope and breadth of cross-examination held not to require exclusion of testimony from prior trial, the court concluding that the curtailment was not significant and still permitted "adequate" or "meaningful," although not "unbounded," cross-examination).

13. United States ex rel. Haywood v. Wolff, 658 F.2d 455 (7th Cir.1981), cert. denied 454 U.S. 1088 (denial of inquiry as to address and prior statements did not render testimony inherently unreliable); Commonwealth v. Scarborough, 491 Pa. 300, 421 A.2d 147 (1980) (not unfair to limit cross to scope of direct).

14. Louisville & Nashville R. Co. v. Scott, 232 Ala. 284, 167 So. 572 (1936); People v. Bird, 132 Cal. 261, 64 P. 259 (1901); Dwyer v. State, 154 Me. 179, 145 A.2d 100 (1958). See also Fed.R.Evid. 804(b)(1). However, if motivation to explore a particular aspect was absent, the effect is the same as with cross-examination. Commonwealth v. Meech, 380 Mass. 490, 403 N.E.2d 1174 (1980). See infra § 304.

Federal Rule 804(b)(1) treats opportunity for direct and redirect as equivalent to

cross-examination. See supra § 301 text following note 8.

In view of the close parallel between depositions and former testimony, it is noteworthy that Fed.R.Civ.P. 32(a) makes depositions admissible against any party present or represented at the deposition or with due notice of its taking. See also 5 Wigmore, Evidence § 1389 (Chadbourn rev. 1974).

For examination of whether testimony previously offered by a party may be treated as an adoptive admission, see infra § 261.

15. See United States v. Inadi, 475 U.S. 387, 394 (1986), supra § 301 note 6.

16. See supra § 251.

17. See California v. Green, 399 U.S. 149 (1970) (with respect to constitutional requirements of confrontation, former testimony may be admitted if the witness is unavailable to the requisite degree or if the witness is actually produced).

18. See supra §§ 252, 253.

19. See supra § 37 (prior inconsistent statements) and § 254 (admissions).

§ 303. Identity of Parties; "Predecessor in Interest" [1]

The haste and pressure of trials cause lawyers and judges to speak in catchwords or shorthand phrases to describe evidence rules. Thus "identity of parties" is often spoken of as a requirement for the admission of former testimony.[2] It is a convenient phrase to indicate a situation where the underlying requirement of adequacy of the present opponent's opportunity for cross-examination would usually be satisfied. But as a *requirement,* identity of parties (or, for that matter, identity of issues[3]) is hardly a useful generalization. It both obscures the true purpose of the requirement and must be hedged with too many qualifications to be helpful.

Historically, courts recognized a number of situations where identity of parties has not been required. It is clear, for example, that if the two present adversary parties, both the proponent and opponent of the evidence, were parties in the former proceedings where the testimony was taken, the presence of additional parties in either or both proceedings is immaterial.[4] A second more important inroad upon strict identity of parties results from the recognition, developed under Wigmore's guidance,[5] that it is only the party *against* whom the former testimony is now offered whose presence as a party in the previous suit is significant.[6] Older decisions that insisted on "reciprocity" or "mutu-

§ 303

1. See generally 5 Wigmore, Evidence § 1386 (Chadbourn rev. 1974); Weissenberger, The Former Testimony Hearsay Exception: A Study in Rulemaking, Judicial Revisionism, and the Separation of Powers, 67 N.C.L.Rev. 295 (1989); Falknor, Former Testimony and the Uniform Rules: A Comment, 38 N.Y.U.L.Rev. 651, 652–655 (1963); Note, 42 Miami L.Rev. 975 (1988); 20 Am. Jur.2d Evidence §§ 744–745; C.J.S. Evidence §§ 387, 388; Dec.Dig. Evidence ⬅580, Criminal Law ⬅546; Annot. 142 A.L.R. 673.

2. Unfortunately, some statutes and rules are phrased in this way. See, e.g., N.Y.Civ.Prac.L. & R. 4517 (McKinney Supp.1990). But see Fleury v. Edwards, 14 N.Y.2d 334, 251 N.Y.S.2d 647, 200 N.E.2d 550 (1964).

3. See infra § 304.

4. Philadelphia, Wilmington & Baltimore R. Co. v. Howard, 54 U.S. (13 How.) 307 (1851) (additional co-plaintiff in former suit); Allen v. Chouteau, 102 Mo. 309, 14 S.W. 869, 871 (1890) (additional parties in former suit); Annot., 142 A.L.R. 689.

The result is the same if parties have been dropped. Freeby v. Incorporated Town of Sibley, 195 Iowa 200, 186 N.W. 685 (1922), modified 195 Iowa 200, 191 N.W. 867.

5. 5 Wigmore, Evidence § 1388, at 111 (Chadbourn rev. 1974).

6. Insul–Wool Insulation Corp. v. Home Insulation, 176 F.2d 502 (10th Cir.1949) (depositions taken in prior action for infringement admissible against plaintiff in subsequent action against other defendants for infringement of same patent); North River Ins. Co. v. Walker, 161 Ky. 368, 170 S.W. 983 (1914) (in suit on fire insurance policy defended on grounds that plaintiff and her deceased husband were guilty of arson, testimony of deceased witness taken at examining trial of plaintiff and husband ruled admissible against plaintiff); School Dist. v. Sachse, 274 Mich. 345, 264 N.W. 396 (1936) (evidence taken in criminal trial for fraud admitted against same defendant when sued civilly for restitution); Harrell v. Quincy, Omaha & Kansas City R. Co., 186 S.W. 677 (Mo.1916) (deposition taken in widow's action for wrongful death admissible against same defendant in similar action by children); Gaines v. Thomas, 241 S.C. 412, 128 S.E.2d 692 (1962) (testimony of deceased witness given at instance of defendant in action by administrator of driver of other car against owner of truck involved in collision properly admitted in action by injured bystander against administrator).

Federal Rule 804(b)(1) is to the same effect. See supra § 301 text following note

ality," requiring that the party *offering* the former testimony in the present suit must also have been a party in the prior proceeding,[7] are without any supporting basis and are now historical relics.[8]

Furthermore, if the party against whom the former testimony is now offered, though not a party to the former suit, actually cross-examined the witness (personally or by counsel) about the relevant matters or was accorded a fair opportunity for such cross-examination and had a like motive for such examination, then the former testimony may be received.[9] Finally, identity of parties is not required as to a party against whom prior testimony is offered when that party is a successor in interest to the corresponding party in the former suit. This notion, to which the label "privity" is attached, is considered to offer adequate protection to the party-opponent.[10]

8. Bailey v. Southern Pacific Transp. Co., 613 F.2d 1385 (5th Cir.1980), cert. denied 449 U.S. 836.

7. See, e.g., Morgan v. Nicholl, L.R., 2 C.P. 117 (1866) (in ejectment action by father where plaintiff sought to use testimony of deceased witness taken in former action instituted by son for the same land who supposed that his father was dead, testimony excluded on ground that it could not have been used by defendants against present plaintiff for want of privity or identity of parties); Metropolitan Street Ry. Co. v. Gumby, 99 Fed. 192, 198 (2d Cir.1900) (in suit by infant's mother claiming damages for loss of services due to injury, held that testimony of deceased witness taken in suit brought in infant's behalf against the same defendant for the same injury could not be used by plaintiff because no privity or reciprocity).

8. Referring to some of these cases, the North Carolina court said, "These authorities, in our opinion, sacrifice substance to form, and exclude material evidence which has been subjected to the tests of truth, and in favor of a party who has had an opportunity to cross-examine." Hartis v. Charlotte Elec. Ry. Co. 162 N.C. 236, 237, 78 S.E. 165, 165 (1913).

9. Tug Raven v. Trexler, 419 F.2d 536 (4th Cir.1969), cert. denied 398 U.S. 938 (testimony given at Coast Guard inquiry into cause of disaster admissible in wrongful death proceeding against respondent who was represented and allowed to cross-examine); In re Durant, 80 Conn. 140, 67 A. 497 (1907) (in disbarment proceedings charging that defendant conspired to procure perjured testimony in a divorce suit, testimony from that divorce suit offered against defendant, who had cross-examined as attorney for the wife, held admissible: "The requirement of an identity of parties is only a means to an end. This end was

attained when the defendant availed himself of the unrestricted opportunity to cross-examine * * *"); Brownlee v. Bunnell, 31 Ky.L.Rptr. 669, 103 S.W. 284 (1907) (former testimony received against defendants in present suit on ground that though not parties to former suit they employed lawyers who defended the action at their instance); Fleury v. Edwards, 14 N.Y.2d 334, 251 N.Y.S.2d 647, 200 N.E.2d 550 (1964) (testimony of one driver, given at license revocation hearing of both drivers, held admissible in death action by his administrator against other driver, who was present and cross-examined); Charlesworth v. Tinker, 18 Wis. 633, 635 (1864) (in civil action for assault, testimony given at prior criminal assault prosecution ruled admissible, court relying on statute giving power to complainant to control prosecution for assault: "the true test * * * is, did the party who is to be affected by it have the power of cross-examining the witness, or at least have an opportunity of doing so?"). Compare Rumford Chemical Works v. Hygienic Chemical Co., 215 U.S. 156 (1909) (testimony in a former suit inadmissible against one who contributed to expense of defending former suit but had no "right to intermeddle").

Cases disclosing relaxation of strict requirements in disbarment proceedings are collected in Annot., 161 A.L.R. 898.

10. See Bryan v. Malloy, 90 N.C. 508, 511 (1883), where the court said, "Privity in the sense here used is a privity to the former action. To make one a privy to an action, he must be one who has acquired an interest in the subject-matter of the action, either by inheritance, succession, or purchase from a party to the action subsequent to its institution."

Illustrations of privity in the strict sense are grantor-grantee, Stephens v. Hoffman,

The next step in this progression away from the formalistic requirement of identity of parties would be to treat neither identity of parties
nor privity as requirements, but merely as means to an end. Under
this view, if a party in the former suit who had a motive similar to the
present party to cross-examine about the subject of the testimony and
was accorded an adequate opportunity for such examination, the testimony could be received against the present party. Identity of interest
in the sense of motive, rather than technical identity of cause of action
or title, would satisfy the test. Under this perspective, the argument
that it is unfair to force upon a party another's cross-examination or
decision not to cross-examine loses its validity with the realization that
other hearsay exceptions involve no cross-examination whatsoever and
that the choice is not between perfect and imperfect conditions for the
giving of testimony but between imperfect conditions and no testimony
at all.[11]

The impact of the enactment of Federal Rule 804(b)(1) in this area
remains uncertain.[12] As sent to Congress by the Supreme Court, the
prior testimony exception would clearly have taken that next step
described above. It would have admitted prior testimony if the party
against whom that testimony is now offered, or a party "with similar
motive and interest," had an opportunity to examine the witness.[13]
The House Judiciary Committee, however, objected to this formulation

263 Ill. 197, 104 N.E. 1090 (1914), and in
ordinary litigation a now deceased party
and his or her administrator, Gibson v.
Gagnon, 82 Colo. 108, 257 P. 348 (1927). In
wrongful death cases the decisions are divided, some ruling in favor of privity between deceased and his administrator,
Kentucky Traction & Terminal Co. v.
Downing's Adm'r, 159 Ky. 502, 167 S.W.
683 (1914), and others holding to the contrary on the dubious ground that the
wrongful death cause of action is a new
one created by statute rather than one
which survives, Arsnow v. Red Top Cab
Co., 159 Wash. 137, 292 P. 436 (1930).
Privity between the state, which prosecuted the defendant for assault, and the
police officer who sued him civilly for the
same conduct has been denied, Bolden v.
Carter, 269 Ark. 391, 602 S.W.2d 640
(1980), and held not to exist between wife
and husband, Lord v. Boschert, 47 Ohio
App. 54, 189 N.E. 863 (1934), or between
passenger and driver, Osburn v. Stickel,
187 So.2d 89 (Fla.App.1966).

For more recent cases using the "predecessor in interest" language and exhibiting
a formal relationship between the parties,
see Azalea Fleet, Inc. v. Dreyfus Supply &
Mach. Corp., 782 F.2d 1455, 1461 (8th Cir.
1986) (indemnity relationship between parties establishes predecessor in interest);
Creamer v. General Teamsters Local Un-

ion 326, 560 F.Supp. 495 (D.Del.1983) (testimony received in criminal trial of company's president admissible against it as he is
company's predecessor in interest).

It is important to recognize that the existence of a privity relationship does not
mean that the prior testimony is automatically admitted. The requirements of a
similar opportunity and motive to cross-
examine the testimony must still be met.
A privity relationship alone would not be
enough to satisfy the reliability concerns of
the hearsay rule. See Note, 42 Miami
L.Rev. 975, 991 & n. 111 (1988); 4 Louisell
& Mueller, Federal Evidence § 487, at
1105 (1980).

11. Morgan, The Law of Evidence,
1941–1945, 59 Harv.L.Rev. 481, 551 (1946).
See also Falknor, Former Testimony and
the Uniform Rules: A Comment, 38
N.Y.U.L.Rev. 651, 655 (1963).

12. The interpretation of the Federal
Rules on this point is significant both with
regard to the direct impact on the federal
courts but also its impact on state interpretations, since many states adopted the federal rule verbatim and look explicitly to
the federal courts for interpretation. See,
e.g., Temple v. Raymark Industries, Inc.,
551 A.2d 67 (Del.Super.1988).

13. 46 F.R.D. 377.

on the ground that "it is generally unfair to impose upon the party against whom the hearsay evidence is being offered responsibility for the manner in which the witness was previously handled by another party." [14]   Accordingly, it substituted a requirement that "the party against whom the testimony is now offered, or in a civil action or proceeding a *predecessor in interest,* had an opportunity and similar motive" to examine the witness,[15] and this version of the rule was enacted.[16]

While the impact of this congressional modification is cloudy in civil litigation, at least one point is clear when the testimony is offered against a criminal defendant: the defendant must have been a party to the former proceeding.[17]   The rule as enacted eliminates doubts under the Confrontation Clause raised by the Court's version, which would have allowed examination by a substitute.   However, by its literal terms the rule insists on identity of prosecution also, which would appear to bar a defendant in a federal prosecution from introducing exculpatory testimony from a related state case given by an unavailable witness.   Exclusion of such evidence implicates due process considerations,[18] and quite likely was not intended by Congress.[19]

For civil cases this unfortunately oblique legislative history is more troubling, providing no definitive meaning for the term "predecessor in interest."   As enacted, the rule requires that there have been opportunity to examine the witness by the party against whom now offered or by a "predecessor in interest" with similar motive.   The explanation offered by the report of the House Committee is only modestly helpful. After asserting the general unfairness of requiring a party to accept another's examination of a witness, quoted above,[20] the report stated, "The sole exception to this, in the Committee's view, is when a party's predecessor in interest in a civil action or proceeding had an opportunity and similar motive to examine the witness.   The committee amended the Rule to reflect these policy determinations." [21]   Presumably in adding the language regarding a predecessor in interest, the House

---

14. House Comm. on Judiciary, H.R.Rep. No. 650, 93d Cong., 1st Sess. 15 (1973) reprinted in 1974 U.S.Code Cong. & Admin.News 7075, 7088.

15. Id. (emphasis added).

16. See supra § 301 text following note 8.

17. See United States v. McDonald, 837 F.2d 1287 (5th Cir.1988); Government of the Canal Zone v. P. (Pinto), 590 F.2d 1344, 1354 (5th Cir.1979); 4 Weinstein & Berger, Weinstein's Evidence ¶ 804(b)(1)[05], at 97–98 (1990); 4 Louisell & Mueller, Federal Evidence § 487, at 1101 (1980). But see Comment, 19 Mem.St.U.L.Rev. 534 (1989) (arguing that, while laudable result, using rule to admit prior testimony against government under predecessor in interest provision is erroneous).

18. Chambers v. Mississippi, 410 U.S. 284 (1973). See discussions in supra § 19 and infra § 318 note 9.

19. See United States v. McDonald, 837 F.2d 1287 (5th Cir.1988) (admitting such evidence and noting that authorities, including this treatise, support construing "predecessor in interest" to include other sovereigns when evidence is offered by the criminal defendant).

20. See supra text accompanying note 14.

21. House Comm. on Judiciary, H.R.Rep. No. 650, 93d Cong., 1st Sess. 15 (1973), reprinted in 1974 U.S.Code Cong. & Admin.News 7075, 7088.

Committee meant to make some change. The Senate Committee, however, characterized the difference between the version transmitted by the Supreme Court and that developed by the House Committee as "not great," [22] and the Conference Committee remained silent on this point.

This state of legislative history has left little concrete guidance in determining congressional intent.[23] Having taken the view in the 1978 Pocket Part that privity was required between the parties to satisfy the "predecessor in interest" requirement and the view in the 1984 Third Edition that the intention was to leave the Supreme Court version intact in civil cases,[24] it is perhaps appropriate that this treatise now take an intermediate position. That, indeed, appears to be the proper course of action.

Recent scholarship has shed some new light on this issue, revealing that the House Subcommittee that drafted this modification intended it to require a "formal relationship" between the parties.[25] How much weight to give such obscure indications of legislative intent is itself uncertain,[26] particularly since even the Senate Judiciary Committee did not appear to understand the significance of the modification, which suggests no figurative Congressional meeting of the minds. Nevertheless, it is difficult to ignore entirely the addition of the predecessor in interest language by the House Committee and to construe the provision to mean precisely what it did prior to that change. Thus, those courts that have read the language to mean no more than the general requirement that the prior party have a similar interest [27] appear to have misconstrued the provision. On the other hand, construing the actions of Congress to require a strict privity approach, while not

---

22. Senate Comm. on Judiciary, S.Rep. No. 1277, 93d Cong., 2d Sess. 28 (1974), reprinted in 1974 U.S.Code Cong. & Admin.News 7051, 7074.

23. 4 Louisell & Mueller, Federal Evidence § 487, at 1103 (1980) ("not a shred of legislative history to indicate what this apparent term of art was designed to embrace"); Note, 42 Miami L.Rev. 975, 977 (1988) (legislative history does not define the term, and it "had little, if any, meaning at common law").

24. The 1978 Pocket Part to the Second edition had stated that Congress "did reinstate the earlier traditional requirement of identity or privity with the party against whom offered." § 256, at 77 (2d ed. pocket part 1978). The Third Edition of this work took the contrary view that "a sensible reading virtually compels the conclusion that the intent was to leave the Court's rule intact in civil cases." § 256, at 766 (3d ed. 1984). For the position of other commentators, see Weissenberger, supra note 1, at 315–16 & nn. 105–06.

25. Weissenberger, supra note 1, at 313.

26. See Green v. Bock Laundry Mach. Co., 490 U.S. 504 (1989) (Scalia, J., concurring) (arguing that statutory meaning should be chiefly determined by context and ordinary usage of language and by the surrounding body of law as opposed to legislative reports and statements known to but a handful of members of Congress).

27. In Murphy v. Owens–Illinois, Inc., 779 F.2d 340, 343 (6th Cir.1985), the court stated that while the rule requires (1) that the prior party be a predecessor in interest and (2) that the prior party had an opportunity and similar motive to develop the testimony, the Sixth Circuit had "in effect * * * collapsed the two criteria into one test" under which a party that satisfied the second requirement constituted a predecessor in interest. See also Clay v. Johns–Manville Sales Corp., 722 F.2d 1289 (6th Cir.1983), cert. denied 467 U.S. 1253.

unreasonable,[28] appears too rigid.

Courts construing the "predecessor in interest" language have taken several discrete approaches, which appear consistent with the murky intent of Congress. One interesting approach is the so-called community of interest analysis.[29] This approach requires some connection—some shared interest, albeit far less than a formal relationship—that helps to insure adequacy of cross-examination. A second approach appears consistent with congressional concerns about fairness and is even more broadly applicable than the community of interest analysis. This approach requires the courts to insure fairness directly by seriously considering whether the prior cross-examination can be fairly held against the later party. The testimony can be excluded if the objecting party shows that the cross-examination was inadequate by, for example, setting out the additional questions or lines of inquiry that he or she would have pursued.[30] The opportunity to challenge the adequacy of the prior cross-examination directly, while ostensibly available in all situations, is not applied with rigor where there is no change in the identity of the party between the different proceedings.[31] The suggested interpretation accomplishes all that we know for certain was intended by the published legislative history—an interpretation of the term predecessor in interest that makes it fair to hold the present party responsible for the actions of another.

§ 304. Identity of Issues; Motive to Cross–Examine [1]

Questions of identity of the issues involved in the former and present proceedings often arise in association with questions about identity of parties. This is to be expected because any supposed requirement of

28. Indeed, Professor Weissenberger argues that based on the legislative history, requiring a privity relationship is appropriate. Weissenberger, supra note 1, at 316.

29. The "community of interest" analysis appears to have its origins in a special relationship between the government and a private party whose interests it was protecting. In In re Master Key Antitrust Litigation, 72 F.R.D. 108 (D.Conn.1976), this special relationship existed between the government in enforcing antitrust laws and the injured competitors. The concept was expanded somewhat in Lloyd v. American Export Lines, Inc., 580 F.2d 1179 (3d Cir.1978), cert. denied 439 U.S. 969, where the court found a community of interest between the alleged victim of an assault and the public interest as represented by the Coast Guard in a license revocation hearing based on that alleged assault. See also Carpenter v. Dizio, 506 F.Supp. 1117 (E.D.Pa.1981), affirmed 673 F.2d 1298 (3d Cir.) (community of interest between prosecutor in criminal case and city solicitor in civil rights action arising from same facts).

30. Dykes v. Raymark Industries, Inc., 801 F.2d 810 (6th Cir.1986), cert. denied 481 U.S. 1038 (court suggests that litigants particularize both why the motive and opportunity of previous party was inadequate to develop testimony and the particular lines of questions the later party would have pursued); cf. United States v. McDonald, 837 F.2d 1287 (5th Cir.1988) (focusing on strategies and incentives of private institution as predecessor to the government). See also suggested analysis in Note, 42 Miami L.Rev. 975, 1005 (1988).

31. See infra § 304 text accompanying note 10 regarding, for instance, preliminary hearings.

§ 304

1. See 5 Wigmore, Evidence §§ 1386–1387 (Chadbourn rev. 1974); C.J.S. Evidence § 389; Dec.Dig. Evidence ⊕579, Criminal Law ⊕545; Annot., 70 A.L.R.2d 494.

identity of issues is, like the rule about parties,[2] merely a means of fulfilling the policy of securing an adequate opportunity and sufficient motive for cross-examination.

While occasionally stated as a requirement that the issue in the two suits must be the same,[3] the policy underlying this exception does not require that all the issues (any more than all the parties) in the two proceedings must be the same. At most, the issue on which the testimony was offered in the first suit must be the same as the issue upon which it is offered in the second. Additional issues or differences with regard to issues upon which the former testimony is not offered are of no consequence.[4] Moreover, insistence upon precise identity of issues, which might have some appropriateness if the question were one of res judicata or estoppel by judgment, is out of place with respect to former testimony where the question is not of binding anyone, but merely of salvaging, for what it may be worth, the testimony of an unavailable witness. Accordingly, even before the enactment of the Federal Rules, the trend was to demand only "substantial" identity of issues.[5]

It follows that neither the form of the proceeding, the theory of the case, nor the nature of the relief sought needs be the same between the proceedings. Though scattered cases have in the past imposed requirements of this sort,[6] such formalism is not warranted by a policy of insuring adequacy of opportunity and motive for cross-examination, and

2. See supra § 303.

3. Statutes occasionally so provide, e.g., 42 Pa.Cons.Stat.Ann. § 5917 (Purdon 1982).

4. Bartlett v. Kansas City Public Service Co., 349 Mo. 13, 160 S.W.2d 740 (1942) (immaterial that husband's prior action involved issue of loss of wife's services not present in wife's later personal injury action since witnesses did not testify on issue of damages); Hartis v. Charlotte Elec. Ry. Co., 162 N.C. 236, 78 S.E. 164 (1913) (similarly as to different measures of damages between personal injury action and later wrongful death action).

5. State v. Brinkley, 354 Mo. 337, 189 S.W.2d 314 (1945) (testimony for defendants in prosecution against police officers for fatally assaulting M admissible for accused in prosecution for perjured testimony before grand jury that police had beaten him and M); In re White's Will, 2 N.Y.2d 309, 160 N.Y.S.2d 841, 141 N.E.2d 416 (1957) (testimony given in lunacy proceeding where issue was capacity to manage affairs admissible in will contest on issue of competency to make a will). Many cases state the rule in terms of "substantial" identity of issues, e.g., School Dist. v. Sachse, 274 Mich. 345, 264 N.W.

396 (1936); Proulx v. Parrow, 115 Vt. 232, 56 A.2d 623 (1948). Some statutes likewise specify "substantial" identity of issues as the test. Official Code Ga.Ann. § 24–3–10.

For examples of failure to meet the test of substantial identity of issues, see State v. Augustine, 252 La. 983, 215 So.2d 634 (1968) (testimony given at hearing on competency to stand trial not admissible on issue of insanity at time of offense); Monahan v. Monahan, 29 A.D.2d 1046, 289 N.Y.S.2d 812 (1968) (impeachment testimony by female witness for prosecution in unrelated felony trial of D that she had stayed at hotels with D, not admissible to prove adultery in divorce action against D).

6. Tom Reed Gold Mines Co. v. Moore, 40 Ariz. 174, 11 P.2d 347 (1932) (under superseded statute limiting use to "the same action" testimony taken in personal injury action cannot be used in later death action); Hooper v. Southern Ry. Co., 112 Ga. 96, 37 S.E. 165 (1900) (testimony taken in suit for personal injuries to minor brought by father as next friend not admissible in suit by father for his own loss of the child's services, there being different defenses available in the two suits—not substantially the same issue).

such a wooden approach has been rejected by the body of caselaw.[7] Thus, in criminal cases where the first indictment charges one offense (robbery), and the second another distinct offense (murder of the person robbed), it is usually considered sufficient that the two indictments arise from the same transaction.[8]

The requirement has become, not a mechanical one of identity or even of substantial identity of issues, but rather that the issues in the first proceeding, and hence the purpose for which the testimony was offered, must have been such that the present opponent (or some person in like interest) had an adequate motive for testing on cross-examination the credibility of the testimony.[9] How this requirement has been worked out in practice gives definition to the general rule.

One important pattern involves introducing at the trial of a criminal case testimony given at the preliminary hearing,[10] or analogously, in a civil case introducing testimony given at a discovery deposition.[11] In

7. See cases cited in supra notes 4–5.

8. United States v. Licavoli, 725 F.2d 1040, 1048 (6th Cir.1984), cert. denied 467 U.S. 1252 (issues in state criminal prosecution that formed predicate acts for federal RICO prosecution provided similar motive for cross-examination); Fox v. State, 102 Ark. 393, 144 S.W. 516 (1912) (first trial of defendant for being accessory to murder, second, for being accessory to robbery, on same occasion); State v. Boyd, 140 Kan. 623, 38 P.2d 665 (1934) (embezzlement, misappropriation by custodian of public funds); State v. Brinkley, 354 Mo. 337, 189 S.W.2d 314 (1945) (first trial manslaughter prosecution against officers who arrested present defendant and his companion, who died after the arrest; second trial, prosecution of defendant for perjury in testifying before grand jury that he and his companion were beaten by officers at time of first arrest); State v. Swiden, 62 S.D. 208, 252 N.W. 628 (1934) (robbery, murder); State v. Dawson, 129 W.Va. 279, 40 S.E.2d 306 (1946) (robbery, murder); cases are collected in Annot., 122 A.L.R. 430.

9. See Fed.R.Evid. 804(b)(1), quoted in supra § 301 text following note 8.

Bailey v. Southern Pacific Transp. Co., 613 F.2d 1385 (5th Cir.1980), cert. denied 449 U.S. 836 (proper to admit testimony given for plaintiff in another case at same crossing also based on claim that lights were not working); State v. Von Klein, 71 Or. 159, 142 P. 549 (1914) (testimony as to polygamous marriage given on trial for larceny of jewels of supposed wife, as evidence of scheme, admissible on later trial for polygamy).

10. See supra § 302 note 6.

Admissibility of testimony given at the preliminary hearing is provided by statutes in fair number. 5 Wigmore, Evidence § 1375 (Chadbourn rev. 1974). Ample support also exists in the cases. Id.; Ohio v. Roberts, 448 U.S. 56 (1980); California v. Green, 399 U.S. 149 (1970); Annots., 15 A.L.R. 495, 79 A.L.R. 1392, 122 A.L.R. 425, 159 A.L.R. 1240. But see State v. Elisondo, 114 Idaho 412, 757 P.2d 675 (1988) (deciding not to admit preliminary hearing testimony as a matter of state public policy, citing, inter alia, the fact that defense counsel has little reason to cross-examine prosecution witnesses).

11. See DeLuryea v. Winthrop Laboratories, 697 F.2d 222 (8th Cir.1983) (neither fact that party represented by different counsel at deposition in worker's compensation case nor prior counsel's decision to limit cross-examination warranted exclusion since opportunity and motivation to cross-examine rather than actual extent is issue); Hendrix v. Raybestos–Manhattan, Inc., 776 F.2d 1492, 1506 (11th Cir.1985) ("a party's decision to limit cross-examination in a discovery deposition is a strategic choice and does not preclude his adversary's use of the deposition in a subsequent proceeding"). Similarly, Fed.R.Civ.P. 32(a) attaches no significance to the fact that many depositions are taken for discovery with little incentive to cross-examine when the witness becomes unavailable and the deposition is offered instead. Wright Root Beer Co. v. Dr. Pepper Co., 414 F.2d 887 (5th Cir.1969). Compare Ill.Sup.Ct.R. 202, 212.

The rules of evidence should be applicable to a deposition used in a separate civil or criminal action. Deposition rules themselves should govern admissibility in the

another frequently encountered situation, testimony given against the accused in an earlier criminal trial is offered against the same accused in a civil case to which the criminal defendant is a party.[12] Prior testimony is generally ruled admissible in all of these situations.

Courts do not require that the party at the earlier proceeding actually have conducted a full cross-examination of the witness.[13] The cases emphatically hold that judgments to limit or waive cross-examination at the earlier proceeding based on tactics or strategy, even though these judgments were apparently appropriate when made, do not undermine admissibility.[14] Instead, the courts look to the operative issue in the earlier proceeding, and if basically similar and if the opportunity to cross-examine was available, the prior testimony is admitted.[15] However, at some extreme point, differences in the nature of the proceeding, the stakes involved, and even factual details with regard to the same core issue will result in exclusion of the prior testimony.[16]

same proceeding. 4 Louisell & Mueller, Federal Evidence § 487, at 1081 (1980).

12. The modern decisions likewise support admissibility in the criminal-civil situation. Creamer v. General Teamsters Local Union 326, 560 F.Supp. 495 (D.Del. 1983); North River Ins. Co. v. Walker, 161 Ky. 368, 170 S.W. 983 (1914) (arson); School Dist. v. Sachse, 274 Mich. 345, 264 N.W. 396 (1936) (embezzlement); Bryant v. Trinity Universal Ins. Co., 411 S.W.2d 945 (Tex.Civ.App.1967, error refused n.r.e.) (arson).

13. See generally supra § 302 note 6.

A typical treatment of the issue is provided by the court in United States v. McClellan, 868 F.2d 210, 215 (7th Cir.1989), where the court stated:

McClellan argues that * * * the cross-examination at the bankruptcy proceeding was not "vigorous" enough to challenge the witness' credibility. This argument is somewhat misconceived; the emphasis in this inquiry is upon the motive underlying the cross-examination rather than the actual exchange that took place.

14. See United States v. Zurosky, 614 F.2d 779 (1st Cir.1979), cert. denied 446 U.S. 967; United States v. Pizarro, 717 F.2d 336 (7th Cir.1983), cert. denied 471 U.S. 1139; Hendrix v. Raybestos–Manhattan, Inc., 776 F.2d 1492 (11th Cir.1985). But see United States v. Serna, 799 F.2d 842 (2d Cir.1986), cert. denied 481 U.S. 1013 (while accepting that prosecutor arguably had a motive to cross examine witness at that witness' criminal prosecution, court concluded that because of "wise" choice not to challenge details of earlier state-

ment the prosecutor had no real motive to explore testimony).

The courts here appear to be employing a type of fairness analysis, perhaps more appropriately termed rough justice. When the choice is between excluding the testimony to the detriment of an innocent party or receiving it at the expense of the other party, who was personally present at the earlier proceeding and had an opportunity to cross-examine, the feeling is that it is not unfair to hold the party who had the chance to cross-examine responsible for his or her strategic judgments. Adv.Comm. Note, Fed.R.Evid. 804(b)(1), 56 F.R.D. 183, 323–24; United States v. Pizarro, 717 F.2d 336, 349 (7th Cir.1983), cert. denied 471 U.S. 1139.

15. United States v. Poland, 659 F.2d 884 (9th Cir.1981), cert. denied 454 U.S. 1059 (testimony at pretrial identification suppression motion was admissible at trial as prior testimony since under constitutional principles reliability is an issue at stake in the suppression hearing that would provide motive to challenge witness similar to that which would have existed at trial).

16. See United States v. Feldman, 761 F.2d 380 (7th Cir.1985) where the court held that testimony given in a civil deposition was not admissible in a subsequent criminal prosecution because the requirement of similarity of motive was not satisfied. While the criminal defendants were parties in the civil case, the court concluded that there were substantial differences between trial strategies between the civil and criminal actions and also that the potential penalties or financial stakes be-

§ 305. The Character of the Tribunal and of the Proceedings in Which the Former Testimony Was Taken

If the accepted requirements of the administration of the oath, adequate opportunity to cross-examine on substantially the same issue, and present unavailability of the witness, are satisfied, then character of the tribunal and the form of the proceedings are immaterial, and the former testimony should be received.[1] Accordingly, when these conditions are met, testimony taken before arbitrators,[2] or before a committing magistrate at a preliminary hearing,[3] or in a sworn examination before the comptroller by the corporation counsel of a person asserting a claim against a city,[4] or at a driver's license revocation hearing,[5] or at a broker's license revocation hearing,[6] or at a Coast Guard hearing,[7] or a hearing on motion to suppress,[8] or a bankruptcy proceeding [9] has been held admissible. For lack in the particular proceeding of some of these requisites, testimony given in the course of a coroner's inquest [10] or a

tween the two actions differed markedly. These differences meant that the required similarity of motive was not present. With *Feldman,* compare United States v. McClellan, 868 F.2d 210 (7th Cir.1989) (testimony of wife admissible at subsequent criminal trial since defendant had sufficient motive to impeach her when she testified for creditors in contested bankruptcy proceeding involving several million dollars). See also United States v. Wingate, 520 F.2d 309 (2d Cir.1975), cert. denied 423 U.S. 1074 (testimony at another defendant's motion to suppress statements on ground of involuntariness not admissible to show innocence of defendant where issues were so different as to render opportunity to cross-examine not meaningful); United States v. Atkins, 618 F.2d 366 (5th Cir. 1980) (proper to exclude testimony on preliminary matter, now offered to exculpate defendant in which he did not participate and the government had no motive to cross-examine); Hannah v. City of Overland, 795 F.2d 1385 (8th Cir.1986) (testimony received at deposition in criminal case not admissible in civil rights action for false arrest because, in court's judgment, witnesses' testimony posed little danger to prosecutor's case).

§ 305

1. See 5 Wigmore, Evidence §§ 1373–1376 (Chadbourn rev. 1974); C.J.S. Evidence §§ 385–386; Dec.Dig.Evidence ⊕557½, Criminal Law ⊕539(1).

2. Bailey v. Woods, 17 N.H. 365, 372 (1845) ("It does not seem to be an objection to the competency of the evidence of the deceased witness, that it was given at a hearing before arbitrators. We do not understand that the admissibility of such evi-

dence depends so much upon the particular character of the tribunal, as upon other matters. If the testimony be given under oath in a judicial proceeding, in which the adverse litigant was a party, and where he had the power to cross-examine, and was legally called upon to do so, the great and ordinary tests of truth being no longer wanting, the testimony so given is admitted in any subsequent suit between the parties.").

3. See supra § 302 note 6 & § 304 note 10; Dec.Dig., Criminal Law ⊕539–545.

4. Rothman v. City of New York, 273 App.Div. 780, 75 N.Y.S.2d 151 (1947); Boschi v. City of New York, 187 Misc. 875, 65 N.Y.S.2d 425 (1946).

5. Fleury v. Edwards, 14 N.Y.2d 334, 251 N.Y.S.2d 647, 200 N.E.2d 550 (1964).

6. Wellden v. Roberts, 37 Ala.App. 1, 67 So.2d 69 (1951), affirmed 259 Ala. 517, 67 So.2d 75.

7. Lloyd v. American Export Lines, Inc., 580 F.2d 1179 (3d Cir.1978), cert. denied 439 U.S. 969.

8. United States v. Zurosky, 614 F.2d 779 (1st Cir.1979), cert. denied 446 U.S. 967; United States v. Poland, 659 F.2d 884 (9th Cir.1981), cert. denied 454 U.S. 1059.

9. United States v. McClellan, 868 F.2d 210 (7th Cir.1989).

10. Wilson v. Marshall Enterprises, 361 F.2d 887 (4th Cir.1966); Edgerley v. Appleyard, 110 Me. 337, 86 A. 244 (1913) (for want of opportunity of cross-examination); 5 Wigmore, Evidence § 1374 (Chadbourn rev. 1976). Occasionally it is made competent by statute. Los Angeles County v.

legislative committee hearing [11] has been excluded. Also, exclusion in particular situations may be mandated by statute.[12]

Some courts have held that, if the court in the former proceeding lacked jurisdiction of the subject matter, the former testimony is inadmissible,[13] but others have concluded that the fact that it may ultimately be held that the court is without power to grant the relief sought does not deprive the court of power to compel attendance of witnesses and to administer oaths, and accordingly the former testimony was held admissible.[14] The question should not be one of regularity but of reliability. A glaring usurpation of judicial power would call for a different ruling, but where the first court has substantial grounds for believing that it has authority to entertain the proceeding, and the party called upon to cross-examine should consider that the existence of jurisdiction is reasonably arguable, it seems that the guaranties of reliability are present. The question should be viewed, not as one of limits of jurisdiction, but whether the sworn statement of a presently unavailable witness was made under such circumstances of opportunity and motive for cross-examination as to make it sufficiently trustworthy to be received in evidence. In like vein, no significance attaches to the circumstance that the earlier trial resulted in a mistrial [15] or a hung jury.[16]

§ 306. Objections and Their Determination [1]

May objections to the former testimony, or parts thereof, which could have been asserted when it was first given, be made for the first time when offered at the present trial? There are sweeping statements in some opinions that this may always be done [2] and in others that it is never allowable.[3] The more widely approved view, however, is that objections which go merely to the form of the testimony—as on the ground of leading questions, unresponsiveness, or opinion—must be

Industrial Accident Com'n, 123 Cal.App. 12, 11 P.2d 434 (1932) (in worker's compensation proceedings).

11. United States v. North, 910 F.2d 843, 905–908 (D.C.Cir.1990), opinion vacated on another issue on rehearing 920 F.2d 940, cert. denied 111 S.Ct. 2235; State ex rel. Blankenship v. Freeman, 440 P.2d 744 (Okl.1968).

12. State Road Dept. v. Levato, 199 So.2d 714 (Fla.1967) (provision requiring exclusion at trial of testimony of appraisers at pretrial hearing under "quick take" eminent domain statute).

13. In re Colbert's Estate, 51 Mont. 455, 153 P. 1022 (1915); Deering v. Schreyer, 88 App.Div. 457, 85 N.Y.S. 275 (1903); McAdams' Executors v. Stilwell, 13 Pa. 90 (1850) (court assumes that jurisdiction is essential).

14. Jerome v. Bohm, 21 Colo. 322, 40 P. 570 (1895). The result is consistent with United States v. United Mine Workers, 330 U.S. 258 (1947).

15. People v. Schwarz, 78 Cal.App. 561, 248 P. 990 (1926).

16. People v. Hines, 284 N.Y. 93, 29 N.E.2d 483 (1940).

§ 306

1. C.J.S. Criminal Law § 892; C.J.S. Evidence § 384, at 948; Annot., 40 A.L.R.4th 514.

2. Wellden v. Roberts, 37 Ala.App. 1, 67 So.2d 69 (1951), affirmed 259 Ala. 517, 67 So.2d 75; Calley v. Boston & Maine R.R., 93 N.H. 359, 42 A.2d 329 (1945).

3. Leach v. Nelson, 50 N.D. 538, 196 N.W. 755 (1924). But see Note, 8 Minn. L.Rev. 629 (1924).

made at the original hearing when they can be corrected.[4]   On the other hand, objections that go to the relevancy or the competency of the evidence may be asserted for the first time when the former testimony is offered at the present trial.[5]

Whether the former testimony meets the requirements of the present exception to the hearsay rule may depend on a question of fact.   For example, is the witness unavailable?   This and other preliminary questions of fact are treated elsewhere.[6]   Likewise, impeachment of witnesses whose former testimony is introduced is considered under the topic of impeaching hearsay declarants generally.[7]

§ 307. Methods and Scope of Proof [1]

When only a portion of the former testimony of a witness is introduced by the proponent, the result may be a distorted and inaccurate impression.   Hence the adversary is entitled to the introduction of such other parts as fairness requires and to have them introduced at that time rather than waiting until the presentation of his or her own case.[2] The adversary is permitted, however, to choose to wait.[3]

In proving the former testimony at least four theories of admissibility may be employed.

1.   Any firsthand observer of the giving of the former testimony may testify to its purport from *unaided memory*.[4]   This and the next method

4. Kemp v. Government of Canal Zone, 167 F.2d 938 (5th Cir.1948); People v. Britt, 62 Cal.App. 674, 217 P. 767 (1923); Sherman Gas & Elec. Co. v. Belden 103 Tex. 59, 123 S.W. 119 (1909); Note, 8 Minn. L.Rev. 629 (1924); Annot., 40 A.L.R. 4th 514.

5. Aetna Ins. Co. v. Koonce, 233 Ala. 265, 171 So. 269 (1936) (dictum).

A similar rule with respect to depositions is found in Fed.R.Civ.P. 32(d)(3). The similarities between depositions and former testimony are persuasive.

With respect to objections to the competency of the witness, compare State v. Pierson, 337 Mo. 475, 85 S.W.2d 48 (1935) (error to refuse to allow accused to go into possible incompetency at time of giving original testimony by witness whose insanity supervened) with Habig v. Bastian, 117 Fla. 864, 158 So. 508 (1935) (testimony given by party at former trial not rendered inadmissible by supervening death of opposite party which rendered witness incompetent).

6. See supra § 53.

7. See supra § 37.

§ 307

1. See 4 Wigmore, Evidence § 1330 (Chadbourn rev. 1972); 5 Wigmore, Evi-

dence §§ 1666–1669 (Chadbourn rev. 1974); 7 Wigmore, Evidence §§ 2098–2099, 2103 (Chadbourn rev. 1978); Dec.Dig. Criminal Law ☞547, Evidence ☞582; C.J.S. Criminal Law § 898; C.J.S. Evidence §§ 397–401; Annot., 11 A.L.R.2d 30.

2. The additional portions will usually, though not necessarily, consist of the original cross-examination. City of Boulder v. Stewardson, 67 Colo. 582, 189 P. 1 (1920); Waller v. State, 102 Ga. 684, 28 S.E. 284 (1897); Randall v. Peerless Motor Car Co., 212 Mass. 352, 99 N.E. 221, 231 (1912).

3. Federal Rule 106 provides:

When a writing or recorded statement or part thereof is introduced by a party, an adverse party may require him at that time to introduce any other part or any other writing or recorded statement which ought in fairness to be considered contemporaneously with it.

The Revised Uniform Rule is identical. This language virtually restates Fed. R.Civ.P. 32(a)(4).

4. Phillips v. Wyrick, 558 F.2d 489 (8th Cir.1977), cert. denied 434 U.S. 1088; Meyers v. United States, 171 F.2d 800 (D.C.Cir. 1948), cert. denied 336 U.S. 912; Vander Veen v. Yellow Cab Co., 89 Ill.App.2d 91,

were used much more frequently before court stenographers became commonplace. To qualify, the reporting witness need not profess to be able to give the exact words of the former witness [5] but must satisfy the court that he or she is able to give the substance of all that the former witness has said, both on direct and cross-examination,[6] about the subject matter relevant to the present suit.[7] By the more convenient practice, the proponent need not prove all of the former testimony relevant to the present case but only such as desired, leaving to the adversary to call for such of the remaining part as desired.[8]

2. A firsthand observer may testify to the purport of the former testimony by using a memorandum, such as the judge's, counsel's, or stenographer's notes, or the stenographer's transcript, to *refresh the present memory* of the witness.[9]

3. In most states the magistrate's report of the testimony at a preliminary criminal hearing [10] and the official stenographer's transcribed notes of the testimony [11] at the trial of a case, civil or criminal, are admitted, when properly authenticated, as evidence of the fact and purport of the former testimony, either by statute or under the hearsay

233 N.E.2d 68 (1967); State ex rel. Blankenship v. Freeman, 440 P.2d 744, 760 (Okl. 1968); State v. Crawley, 242 Or. 601, 410 P.2d 1012 (1966); State v. Roebuck, 75 Wash.2d 67, 448 P.2d 934 (1968).

5. Ruch v. Rock Island, 97 U.S. (7 Otto) 693, 694 (1878) (precise language not necessary; "if a witness from mere memory, professes to give the exact language, it is a reason for doubting his good faith and veracity"); Vander Veen v. Yellow Cab Co., 89 Ill.App.2d 91, 233 N.E.2d 68 (1967); 7 Wigmore, Evidence § 2098 n. 4 (Chadbourn rev. 1978).

6. Monahan v. Clemons, 212 Ky. 504, 279 S.W. 974 (1926); Tibbetts v. Flanders, 18 N.H. 284, 292 (1846).

7. Bennett v. State, 32 Tex.Cr. 216, 218, 22 S.W. 684, 684 (App.1893) ("If a witness can testify to the substance of all that is said on direct and cross examination upon one subject, it will be admissible, though there may be other portions of said testimony, as to other matters, not remembered by the witness."); Foley v. State, 11 Wyo. 464, 466, 72 P. 627, 630 (1903) (must state "the whole of what was said on the particular subject which he is called to prove"); 7 Wigmore, Evidence §§ 2098 n. 4, 2099(4) (Chadbourn rev. 1978). But the sensible qualification that it suffices if the proponent is able to fill the gaps by the testimony of other witnesses has been made in a case where the former testimony was proved, not under the present exception, but to support a charge of perjury. Commonwealth v. Shooshanian, 210 Mass. 123, 96 N.E. 70 (1911).

8. City of Boulder v. Stewardson, 67 Colo. 582, 189 P. 1 (1920); Waller v. State, 102 Ga. 684, 28 S.E. 284 (1897); Randall v. Peerless Motor Car Co., 212 Mass. 352, 99 N.E. 221 (1912).

9. Ruch v. Rock Island, 97 U.S. (7 Otto) 693 (1878); Armstrong Furniture Co. v. Nickle, 110 Ga.App. 686, 140 S.E.2d 72 (1964); Commonwealth v. Mustone, 353 Mass. 490, 233 N.E.2d 1 (1968); Travelers Fire Ins. Co. v. Wright, 322 P.2d 417 (Okl. 1958). As to refreshing recollection generally, see supra § 9.

10. Haines v. State, 109 Ga. 526, 35 S.E. 141 (1900); 5 Wigmore, Evidence § 1667 (Chadbourn rev. 1974) (citing cases pro and con).

11. See, e.g., Snyder v. Cearfoss, 190 Md. 151, 57 A.2d 786 (1948); Blalock v. Whisnant, 216 N.C. 417, 5 S.E.2d 130 (1939) (transcript contained in case on appeal); Proulx v. Parrow, 115 Vt. 232, 56 A.2d 623 (1948) (certified copy of transcript). Statutes to this effect and Fed. R.Civ.P. 80 are cited in 5 Wigmore, Evidence § 1669 n. 2 (Chadbourn rev. 1974). See also cases (and statutes cited therein) in Dec.Dig. Evidence ⊕582(3).

Objections to the use of the common law bill of exceptions based on the manner of its preparation are no longer pertinent in view of modern methods of reporting testimony. See Roth v. Smith, 54 Ill. 431 (1870); 5 Wigmore, Evidence § 1668 (Chadbourn rev. 1974).

exception for *official written statements.* [12]   There is generally no rule of preference for these reports, however, and any observer, including the stenographer, may be called to prove the former testimony without producing the official report or transcript.[13]

4.   A witness who has made written notes or memoranda of the testimony at the time of the former trial, or while the facts were fresh in his or her recollection, and who will testify that he or she knows that they are correct, may use the notes as memoranda of *past recollection recorded.* [14]

§ 308.   Possibilities of Improving Existing Practice

This treatise has long argued that hearsay admitted under the former testimony exception should be admitted regardless of the availability or unavailability of the declarant because few exceptions measure up in terms of the reliability of statements under former testimony.[1]   However, given the Supreme Court's recent analysis of the Confrontation Clause that treats former testimony as perhaps uniquely inferior hearsay and requires for that reason a showing of unavailability,[2] this proposed change has no real prospects of being accepted when the prior testimony is offered against the criminal defendant.

In spite of the Supreme Court's characterization of prior testimony as weaker form of live testimony, it remains incongruous to accord second-class status to former testimony.   The anomaly is apparent when prior

---

12.   For the requirements of this exception, see supra Ch. 30.

13.   Napier v. Commonwealth, 306 Ky. 75, 206 S.W.2d 53 (1947) (county attorney's evidence as to testimony before grand jury); Terry v. State, 132 Tex.Cr. 283, 103 S.W.2d 766 (App.1937) (stenographer can testify from recollection); 4 Wigmore, Evidence § 1330(2) (Chadbourn rev. 1972).

Since the matter sought to be proved is the former testimony and not the contents of the transcript, the so-called Best Evidence Rule does not apply.   See supra § 233.   However, the importance of accuracy and the superiority of the transcript in this respect make a powerful argument for the opposite result.   Meyers v. United States, 171 F.2d 800, 814 (D.C.Cir.1948), cert. denied 336 U.S. 912 (Prettyman, J., dissenting); Cowart v. State, 44 Ala.App. 201, 205 So.2d 250 (1967); Walker v. Walker, 14 Ga. 242 (1853); State v. Luttrell, 366 S.W.2d 453 (Mo.1963).   See also Note, 23 So.Cal.L.Rev. 113 (1949).

14.   Commonwealth v. Mustone, 353 Mass. 490, 233 N.E.2d 1 (1968) (any witness may qualify his or her notes as a reliable record of past recollection); State v. Maynard, 184 N.C. 653, 113 S.E. 682 (1922)

(proper for stenographer to read own notes of preliminary examination, where stenographer testifies to the correctness of the notes, though not subscribed or certified as required for official record); Newton v. State, 150 Tex.Cr. 500, 202 S.W.2d 921 (App.1947) (stenographer may read from notes, if he or she swears they are correct); 3 Wigmore, Evidence § 737(1) (Chadbourn rev. 1970).

For the requirements of this theory of admissibility, see supra §§ 279–283.

Whether the witness testifies on the basis of present recollection refreshed or past recollection recorded seems to be of little practical importance in proving former testimony, and the cases usually make no point of the matter.

§ 308

1.   See § 261 of the Third Edition for earlier argument to remove unavailability requirement.   See supra § 301 text accompanying note 6 for discussion of reliability of these statements.

2.   United States v. Inadi, 475 U.S. 387, 394 (1986) (unlike other hearsay exceptions, former testimony is only a weaker substitute for live testimony).

testimony is compared to hearsay exceptions that possess generally inferior guarantees of trustworthiness, such as declarations of present bodily or mental state, or excited or spontaneous utterances, where no showing of unavailability is required. The fears that the proponent of prior testimony would routinely resort to the use of such testimony when witnesses are available appears overblown, and when the witness is available, the opponent is able to conduct meaningful cross-examination under Rule 806 even if the declarant is not called on direct examination.[3]

Improvement would be gained from a procedure under which prior testimony is admitted in civil cases after giving the opposing party notice of intent to offer the testimony, thus affording an opportunity to produce the witness in person if desired and if the witness is available. In fact, in civil cases the matter might well be left to the ordinary processes of discovery, with no formal notice procedure at all.

A second area where reform regarding the admissibility of prior testimony should be considered concerns the application the predecessor in interest concept. Under Federal Rule 804(b)(1), prior testimony is admissible in civil cases "if the party against whom the testimony is now offered or * * * a predecessor in interest, had an opportunity and similar motive to develop the testimony." A very substantial issue is raised by the meaning of predecessor in interest and in particular whether the concept applies to situations where there is absolutely no economic or legal relationship between the parties.[4]

This problem in defining a predecessor in interest might be avoided if the courts recognized explicitly that the dimensions of the opportunity and motive to cross-examine may differ between the situation where the party itself was involved in the previous litigation and one where an unrelated party conducted the cross-examination. In the former situation, as exemplified by the use of preliminary hearing testimony against criminal defendants at trial,[5] parties have been, and should be, held responsible for previous strategic or tactical judgments and just plain poor lawyering. By contrast, in the situation where the parties are unconnected, the quality of the cross-examination should be scrutinized much more carefully. Even if opportunity and motive for cross-examination are fully adequate, the costs of poor lawyering should not be imposed on a separate party. Once courts become willing to examine directly and meaningfully the adequacy of the testing of the prior testimony, then issues about what constitutes a predecessor in interest will become much less important.[6]

---

3. See infra § 324.2.

4. See supra § 303 text accompanying notes 12–31.

5. See supra § 302 note 6 & § 304 note 10.

6. Under this new mode of analysis, it is not clear how to treat privity relationships. Rough justice may indicate a conclusion either way as indicated by the fact that there is no privity concept employed under the Federal Rules with regard to admissions. See supra § 260.

Chapter 32

DYING DECLARATIONS

Table of Sections

§ 309. Introduction [1]

Of the doctrines that authorize the admission of special classes of out-of-court statements as exceptions to the hearsay rule, the doctrine relating to dying declarations is the most mystical in its theory and traditionally the most arbitrary in its limitations. The notion of the special likelihood of truthfulness of deathbed statements was, of course, widespread long before the recognition of a general rule against hearsay in the early seventeen hundreds. It is natural enough, then, that about as soon as we find a hearsay rule we also find a recognized exception for dying declarations.[2]

§ 309

1. See 5 Wigmore, Evidence §§ 1430–1452 (Chadbourn rev. 1974); Dec.Dig. Homicide ⬤200–221, Evidence ⬤275½; C.J.S. Homicide §§ 286–306; 40 Am.Jur.2d Homicide §§ 347–394; Jaffee, The Constitution and Proof by Dead or Unavailable Declarants, 33 Ark.L.Rev. 227 (1979); Quick, Some Reflections on Dying Declarations, 6 How.L.J. 109 (1960); Note, 46 Iowa L.Rev. 375 (1961).

2. See the early cases listed in 5 Wigmore, Evidence § 1430 n. 1 (Chadbourn rev. 1974).

§ 310. Requirements That Declarant Must Have Been Conscious of Impending Death and That Declarant Must Be Dead or Otherwise Unavailable

The central notions of the popular reverence for deathbed statements are embodied in two important limitations upon the dying declaration exception as evolved at common law. Unlike several other limitations, which will be discussed in the next section, these two were arguably rational, although they drew the lines of restriction too sharply.

The first of these two limitations was that the declarant must have been conscious that death was near and certain when making the statement.[1] The declarant must have lost all hope of recovery.[2] A belief in the mere probability of impending death would arguably make most people strongly disposed to tell the truth and hence guarantee the

The classic statement of the basis of the rule is that of Chief Baron Eyre in Rex v. Woodcock, 1 Leach 500, 168 Eng.Rep. 352 (K.B.1789):

Now the general principle on which this species of evidence is admitted is, that they are declarations made in extremity, when the party is at the point of death, and when every hope of this world is gone; when every motive to falsehood is silenced, and the mind is induced by the most powerful considerations to speak the truth; a situation so solemn, and so awful, is considered by the law as creating an obligation equal to that which is imposed by a positive oath administered in a Court of Justice.

The current state of religious belief might appear to undercut the foundations of the exception. However, the modern formulation of the exception relies on "powerful psychological pressures" to replace, where necessary, religious belief as the guarantor of trustworthiness. See Adv.Comm.Note, Fed.R.Evid. 804(b)(3), 56 F.R.D. 183, 326.

Nevertheless, religious belief would appear relevant to the trustworthiness of some dying declarations, and whether the strength or weakness of such belief is a subject of permissible impeachment presents an interesting issue. There is some precedent that the declarant's lack of religious belief is the appropriate subject of impeachment. Carver v. United States, 164 U.S. 694, 697 (1897); State v. Quintana, 98 N.M. 17, 644 P.2d 531 (1982). However, under the Federal Rules, impeachment regarding religious belief would appear to be improper. Fed.R.Evid. 610, 806; 4 Louisell & Mueller, Federal Evidence § 488, at 1116 n. 31 (1980). See supra § 48 pertaining to religious beliefs. Most courts appear not to have permitted such exploration of declarant's religious views. Annot., 16 A.L.R. 411.

§ 310

1. For statements of the formula, see People v. Tilley, 406 Ill. 398, 94 N.E.2d 328 (1950); State v. Dunlap, 268 N.C. 301, 150 S.E.2d 436 (1966) ("full apprehension of danger of death" is necessary); Thomas v. Commonwealth, 183 Va. 501, 32 S.E.2d 711 (1945).

2. Shepard v. United States, 290 U.S. 96 (1933) (leading opinion by Cardozo, J.); Tillman v. State, 44 So.2d 644 (Fla.1950); People v. Allen, 300 N.Y. 222, 90 N.E.2d 48 (1949). If made under consciousness of doom, a later revival of hope will not be grounds for exclusion. State v. Reed, 53 Kan. 767, 37 P. 174 (1894); Goff v. Commonwealth, 433 S.W.2d 350 (Ky.1968). A request for an ambulance, United States v. Etheridge, 424 F.2d 951 (6th Cir.1970), cert. denied 400 U.S. 993, or for a physician, State v. Evans, 124 Mo. 397, 28 S.W. 8 (1894), does not necessarily negate loss of hope.

However, where future plans are announced that indicate an expectation of continued life, the exception is not met. Bratton v. Bond, 408 N.W.2d 39 (Iowa 1987) (decedent's belief in impending death negated by his action in contacting attorney regarding lawsuit against doctor alleged to have negligently treated him); State v. Elias, 205 Minn. 156, 285 N.W. 475 (1939) (decedent told defendant wife who had shot him that he was going to divorce her).

needed special reliability.[3] But belief in the certainty of impending death, not its mere likelihood or probability, is the formula that was rigorously required. Perhaps this limitation reflected some lack of confidence in the reliability of "deathbed" statements generally.[4]

The description of the declarant's mental state in the Federal Rules is less emphatic than in the common law cases, merely saying "while believing that declarant's death was imminent." [5] Evidence that would satisfy the common law would clearly satisfy the rule, and a growing number of courts are recognizing that a lesser showing will suffice.[6]

Often this belief in the imminence of death is proved by evidence of the declarant's own statements of belief at the time—an expression of a "settled hopeless expectation." [7] That the deceased should have made

3. Other theories for trustworthiness include the reduced likelihood of fabrication because the statement concerns an immediate happening, 4 Weinstein & Berger, Weinstein's Evidence ¶ 804(b)(2)[01], at 115 (1990), and reduced problems of memory derived from the same subject matter limitation, 4 Louisell & Mueller, Federal Evidence § 488, at 1116 (1980). Nevertheless, it may be that, rather than depending on any actual theory of trustworthiness, the dying declarant exception is in fact admitted because of a compelling need for the statement. United States v. Thevis, 84 F.R.D. 57, 63 (N.D.Ga.1979), affirmed 665 F.2d 616 (5th Cir.1982).

4. See People v. Nieves, 67 N.Y.2d 125, 501 N.Y.S.2d 1, 492 N.E.2d 109 (1986) (rejecting argument that traditional requirement that declarant believe death is near and certain should be loosened because court regards dying declarations with a "degree of skepticism").

5. The complete text of Fed.R.Evid. 804(b)(2) is:

The following are not excluded by the hearsay rule if the declarant is unavailable as a witness: * * * (2) In a prosecution for homicide or in a civil action or proceeding, a statement made by a declarant while believing that the declarant's death was imminent, concerning the cause or circumstances of what the declarant believed to be his impending death.

The Revised Uniform Rule (1986) differs substantively from the Federal Rule in omitting the language "In a prosecution for homicide or in a civil action or proceeding," which has the impact of admitting dying declaration in all types of litigation.

6. Johnson v. State, 579 P.2d 20 (Alaska 1978) (abandonment of all hope standard found too demanding, particularly given

advancements of modern medicine, and new standard adopted that requires awareness of probability of impending death sufficient to create solemnity and to remove ordinary worldly motives for misstatement); Ellis v. State 558 So.2d 826, 829–30 (Miss.1990) (accepting this treatise's suggestion that lesser showing required under rule's formulation); State v. Quintana, 98 N.M. 17, 20, 644 P.2d 531, 534 (1982) (no longer requirement of abandonment of all hope of recovery; only requirement is that the statement be made by a declarant while believing death imminent); State v. Young, 166 W.Va. 309, 273 S.E.2d 592, 603 (1980) (no requirement that all hope be abandoned "in fatalistic resignation" but rather that one believe "he is moving across the inevitable threshold into eternity"). But see People v. Nieves, 67 N.Y.2d 125, 501 N.Y.S.2d 1, 492 N.E.2d 109 (1986) (rejecting argument to loosen traditional requirement because of skepticism of reliability of exception). But cf. State v. Bergeron, 452 N.W.2d 918, 923 (Minn.1990) (dying declaration construed strictly by court).

Moreover, the modern elimination of the historical requirement that the declarant die has the impact of relaxing this element of the foundation.

7. State v. Garcia, 99 N.M. 771, 664 P.2d 969 (1983), cert. denied 462 U.S. 1112 (statement by victim that chances of recovery were "nil"); State v. Penley, 318 N.C. 30, 347 S.E.2d 783 (1986) (statement to nurse that he knew he was dying and repeated statements to another individual many times that declarant knew he would not return home). See also Long v. Commonwealth, 262 Ky. 619, 90 S.W.2d 1007 (1936); State v. Eubanks, 277 Minn. 257, 152 N.W.2d 453 (1967), cert. denied 390 U.S. 964; Hawkins v. State, 220 Tenn. 383, 417 S.W.2d 774 (1967). As to the sufficien-

such a statement is not required, however.[8] Such belief may be shown circumstantially by the apparent fatal quality of the wound,[9] by the statements made to the declarant by the doctor or by others that his or her condition is hopeless,[10] and by other circumstances.[11] These preliminary questions of fact are to be determined by the court.[12]

The second historical limitation related to the popular reverence for deathbed statements was that the declarant must be dead when the evidence is offered.[13] However, the Federal Rules do not generally

cy of such statements, see Annot., 53 A.L.R.3d 785.

8. Shepard v. United States, 290 U.S. 96, 100 (1933) ("There is no unyielding ritual of words to be spoken by the dying"); Ellis v. State, 558 So.2d 826, 830 (Miss. 1990) ("the dying will often not declare the end they know so imminent and so eminent"). See also State v. Mitchell, 209 N.C. 1, 182 S.E. 695 (1935); Commonwealth v. Knable, 369 Pa. 171, 85 A.2d 114 (1952).

9. Boone v. State, 282 Ark. 274, 668 S.W.2d 17 (1984) (knowledge of imminent, inevitable death need not be shown by the declarant's express words alone but can be supplied by inferences fairly drawn from condition); Bland v. State, 210 Ga. 100, 78 S.E.2d 51 (1953); State v. Foote, 379 So.2d 1058 (La.1980) (knowledge of declarant, who was veterinarian, of physiology indicated to him that six gunshot wounds were indeed fatal); Ellis v. State, 558 So.2d 826 (Miss.1990) (conclusion of court that declarant should have known his injury, a bullet wound to the side of the heart, was fatal); Commonwealth v. Smith, 424 Pa. 9, 225 A.2d 691 (1967). But the mere fact that the wound was mortal will not alone show consciousness of doom unless its nature were such as to reveal to the declarant its fatal character. Fulton v. State, 209 Miss. 565, 47 So.2d 883 (1950); State v. McDaniel, 272 N.C. 556, 158 S.E.2d 874 (1968), vacated on other grounds 392 U.S. 665 (showing that declarant was actually at the point of death and in great agony held insufficient). Moreover, where the nature of the wound is so serious that standing alone it would allow the inference of consciousness of imminent death, declarant's statement that he is unaware or uncertain of the seriousness will negate the inference. Jones v. State, 38 Md.App. 288, 380 A.2d 659, reversed on other grounds sub nom. State v. Frye, 283 Md. 709, 393 A.2d 1372 (1978).

10. Sisk v. State, 182 Ga. 448, 185 S.E. 777 (1936) (doctor); Chandler v. State, 7 Md.App. 646, 256 A.2d 695 (1969) (police officer); State v. Peters, 90 N.H. 438, 10 A.2d 242 (1939) (nurse).

11. Teffeteller v. State, 439 So.2d 840 (Fla.1983), cert. denied 465 U.S. 1074 (combination of declarant's earlier statement that he was "going," nature of wound and declarant's lucidity, and doctor's opinion that patients on "final glidepath" are aware of impending death); Commonwealth v. Key, 381 Mass. 19, 407 N.E.2d 327 (1980) (opinion evidence from witnesses regarding declarant's condition and attitude admissible to establish this requirement; combination of circumstances, including declarant's condition and statement of others to him that he was dying, overcame some statements by declarant that he expected to live); Thomas v. State, 699 S.W.2d 845 (Tex.Cr.App.1985) (combination of declarant's repeated questions about whether he was going to live, doctor's less than reassuring answers, and nature of injury—bullet wound to heart—was sufficient). See generally cases collected in 5 Wigmore, Evidence § 1442 (Chadbourn rev. 1974); Dec.Dig.Homicide ⊕203–205; Annot., 53 A.L.R.3d 1196.

12. State v. Gazerro, 420 A.2d 816 (R.I.1980); Kelly v. State, 694 P.2d 126 (Wyo.1985).

In some jurisdictions, either the court makes only a prima facie judgment on this issue with the ultimate determination being made by the jury, Holcomb v. State, 249 Ga. 658, 292 S.E.2d 839 (1982), or first the judge and then the jury each decides these preliminary facts, Commonwealth v. Key, 381 Mass. 19, 407 N.E.2d 327 (1980). However, in general, preliminary fact determinations that establish whether a hearsay exception has been established are made exclusively by the court. See Fed. R.Evid. 104(a). Despite this, counsel is still permitted to use, where relevant, the same preliminary facts, such as the weakness of the evidence that the declarant believed death was imminent, to affect the credibility of the statement. See Fed.R.Evid. 104(e). See generally supra § 53.

13. See, e.g., State v. Carden, 209 N.C. 404, 183 S.E. 898 (1935), cert. denied 298 U.S. 682. See generally 5 Wigmore, Evidence § 1431 (Chadbourn rev. 1974).

contain any requirement that the declarant must be dead.[14] Rather, they require that the declarant must be unavailable, which of course includes death as well as other situations.[15] Since the declarant need not die from his or her wounds or injuries, it is clear that the length of time between a statement and death is not dispositive of the statement's admissibility under the exception, and even under the earlier formulations it was not required that the death must have followed at any very short interval after the declaration.[16] The critical issue throughout is the declarant's belief in the nearness of death at the time the statement is made, not the actual swiftness with which death ensues after the statement or the immediacy of the statement after the injury.[17]

§ 311. Limitation to the Use in Criminal Homicide Cases, and Other Arbitrary Limitations

If the courts in their creation of rules about dying declarations had stopped with the limitations discussed above, the result would have had a narrow, but rational and understandable, exception. The requirement of consciousness of impending death arguably tends to guarantee a sufficient degree of special reliability, and the requirement that the declarant must have died and thus be unavailable as a witness provides an ample showing of the necessity for the use of hearsay. This simple rationale of dying declarations sufficed until the beginning of the 1800's, and these declarations were admitted in civil and criminal cases without distinction[1] and seemingly without untoward results. The subsequent history of the rule is an object lesson in the use of precedents to preserve and fossilize the judicial mistakes of an earlier generation.

The first error occurred in limiting admissibility to homicide prosecutions. Sergeant East, in his widely used treatise of 1803, Pleas of the Crown, wrote:

> Besides the usual evidence of guilt in general cases of felony, there is one kind of evidence more peculiar to the case of homicide, which is the declaration of the deceased, after the mortal blow, as to the fact itself, and the party by whom it is committed. Evidence of this sort is admissible in this case on the fullest necessity; for it often happens that

---

14. For text of applicable rules, see supra note 5.

15. Unavailability is discussed in supra § 253.

16. Periods even extending into months have been held not too long. See, e.g., Emmett v. State, 195 Ga. 517, 25 S.E.2d 9 (1943), cert. denied 320 U.S. 774 (survived 3½ months, admitted); People v. Denton, 312 Mich. 32, 19 N.W.2d 476 (1945) (survived 11 days); 5 Wigmore, Evidence § 1441 (Chadbourn rev.1974); Dec.Dig. Homicide ⊕204.

17. Kelly v. State, 694 P.2d 126, 133 (Wyo.1985) (passage of time between incident and statement and between incident and death relevant to question of whether declarant believed death imminent).

§ 311

1. See Wright v. Littler, 3 Burr. 1244, 1247, 1255, 97 Eng.Rep. 812, 814, 818 (K.B.1761) (in ejectment action, deathbed statement that declarant had forged a will received), and other cases cited 5 Wigmore, Evidence § 1431 n. 1 (Chadbourn rev. 1974).

there is no third person present to be an eye-witness to the fact; and the usual witness on occasion of other felonies, namely, the party injured himself, is gotten rid of.[2]

This statement was seized upon for a purpose obviously not intended, namely, an announcement that the sole justification of the admission of dying declarations is the necessity of punishing murderers who might otherwise escape for lack of the testimony of the victim. This need may exist, but the proposition that the use of dying declarations should be limited to instances where it exists surely does not follow. Nevertheless, this proposition was further developed into a series of largely arbitrary limiting rules.

The first of these was the rule that the use of dying declarations was limited to cases of criminal homicide.[3] Although the English courts in the 1700's had not done so,[4] nearly all courts, building upon the theory of necessity, refused to admit dying declarations in civil cases,[5] whether death actions or other civil cases, or in criminal cases other than those charging homicide as an essential part of the offense. Thus, in prosecutions for rape,[6] for example, the declarations were held inadmissible even though death of the victim may have ensued. Probably this restriction proceeded from a feeling on the part of judges that dying declarations both rest on a somewhat questionable guarantee of trustworthiness and constitute a dangerous kind of testimony, which a jury is likely to handle too emotionally. However, these dangers are not likely to be less serious in a murder prosecution, where the statements are admitted, than they are in a civil action for wrongful death or in a prosecution for rape, where they are excluded.

As promulgated by the Supreme Court, the Federal Rule contained no limitation as to type of case in which dying declarations were admissible.[7] However, led by the House Judiciary Committee, Congress amended the exception. As enacted, the exception is limited to prosecutions for homicide and civil actions or proceedings.[8] Thus under the

---

2. East, 1 Pleas of the Crown 353 (1803). See also 5 Wigmore, Evidence § 1431 (Chadbourn rev. 1974).

3. United States v. Sacasas, 381 F.2d 451 (2d Cir.1967) (bank robbery, etc. excluded); People v. Stison, 140 Mich. 216, 103 N.W. 542 (1905) (incest excluded); Taylor v. Commonwealth, 122 Va. 886, 894, 94 S.E. 795, 797 (1918) (assault excluded); Dec.Dig.Homicide ⟗211.

4. See supra note 1.

5. Prudential Ins. Co. v. Keeling's Adm'x, 271 Ky. 558, 112 S.W.2d 994 (1938) (claim for double indemnity for fatal accident, in suit on life policy); Ross v. Cooper, 38 N.D. 173, 164 N.W. 679 (1917) (death injury); Blair v. Rogers, 185 Okl. 63, 89 P.2d 928 (1939) (death injury); Dec.Dig.Evidence ⟗275½.

6. Frogge v. Commonwealth, 296 Ky. 726, 178 S.W.2d 405 (1944).

7. Revised Uniform Rule (1986) 804(b)(2), like the proposed Federal Rule, is applicable in civil cases. See supra § 310 note 5.

8. The Committee justified the restriction as follows:

The Committee did not consider dying declarations as among the most reliable forms of hearsay. Consequently, it amended the provision to limit their admissibility in criminal cases to homicide prosecutions, where exceptional need for the evidence is present.

House Comm. on Judiciary, H.R.Rep. No. 650, 93d Cong., 1st Sess. 15 (1973), reprinted in 1974 U.S.Code Cong. & Admin.News 7075, 7089.

Federal Rule, dying declarations are admissible in all cases except nonhomicide criminal cases.

The concept of necessity, limited to protection of the state against the slayer who might go free because of the death of his victim, produced another consequence. This was the further limitation that not only must the charge be homicide, but the defendant in the present trial must have been charged with the death of the declarant.[9] In a case in which a marauder shot a man and his wife at the same time and the defendant was put on trial for the murder of the husband only, the dying declaration of the wife identifying the defendant as the assailant was offered by the state. It was excluded under this doctrine.[10] Wigmore's comment is: "Could one's imagination devise a more senseless rule of exclusion, if he had not found it in our law?"[11] No such limitation appears in the Federal Rule.[12]

Less arbitrary, but a source of controversy, is the third of these corollary limitations, i.e., that the declarations are admissible only insofar as they relate to the circumstances of the killing and to the events more or less nearly preceding it in time and leading up to it.[13] Under this version, declarations about previous quarrels between the accused and the victim would be excluded, while transactions between them leading up to and shortly before the present attack would be received.[14] Some limitation as to time and circumstances is appropriate,[15] but proper phrasing of the limitation is difficult. Federal Rule 804(b)(2) requires only that the statement be one "concerning the cause or circumstances of what he believed to be his impending death."[16] Within this more liberal framework, decisions may be made in terms of remoteness and prejudice under Rule 403.[17]

Finally, in some jurisdictions, dying declarations are limited with

9. People v. Cox, 340 Ill. 111, 172 N.E. 64 (1930); State v. Puett, 210 N.C. 633, 188 S.E. 75 (1936); Dec.Dig. Homicide ⊕211.

10. Westberry v. State, 175 Ga. 115, 164 S.E. 905 (1932); see also People v. Cox, 340 Ill. 111, 172 N.E. 64 (1930).

11. 5 Wigmore, Evidence § 1433, n. 1 (Chadbourn rev. 1974).

12. See also Commonwealth v. Key, 381 Mass. 19, 26, 407 N.E.2d 327, 333 (1980) (reaching same conclusion under modern judicial analysis).

13. Lucas v. Commonwealth, 153 Ky. 424, 155 S.W. 721 (1913); Connor v. State, 225 Md. 543, 171 A.2d 699 (1961), cert. denied 368 U.S. 906 (proper for court to exclude reference to residence of defendant, etc., when remaining statement of deceased was complete); Walthall v. State, 144 Tex.Cr. 585, 165 S.W.2d 184 (App. 1942); 5 Wigmore, Evidence § 1344 (Chadbourn rev. 1974); Dec.Dig. Homicide ⊕214(2).

14. Smith v. Commonwealth, 236 Ky. 736, 33 S.W.2d 688 (1930) (that defendant had fired on deceased at previous times); Jones v. State, 94 Okl.Cr.App. 359, 236 P.2d 102 (1951) (that defendant had threatened to kill deceased the day before the killing); Webb v. State, 133 Tex.Cr. 32, 106 S.W.2d 683 (App.1937) (excluding description of previous quarrel, on same afternoon, which had subsided).

15. 4 Weinstein & Berger, Weinstein's Evidence ¶ 804(b)(2)[01], at 115 (1990) (since statement concerns immediate happening, danger of conscious or unconscious fabrication reduced); 4 Louisell & Mueller, Federal Evidence § 488, at 1116 (1980) (given subject matter restrictions, flawed or failed memory unlikely).

16. For text of rule, see supra § 310 note 5.

17. See supra § 185.

regard to statements elicited by questions of a leading sort.[18] However, no blanket limitation against statements in response to questions is generally recognized [19] or appropriate.

§ 312. Admissible on Behalf of Accused as Well as for Prosecution

One might have anticipated that the historical limitation on admissibility of dying declarations to homicide cases, based on the extreme necessity in those cases of admitting the statements of the decedent *and* the sense of rough justice that admitting such statements against the murderer was only fair,[1] might have led the courts to restrict the use of dying declarations to introduction by the prosecution. However, the unfairness of such a result was too apparent, and it has long been established that they will be received on behalf of the defendant as well.[2]

§ 313. Application of Other Evidentiary Rules: Personal Knowledge; Opinion; Rules About Writings

Other principles of evidence law present recurrent problems in their application to dying declarations. If it appears that the declarant did not have adequate opportunity to observe the facts recounted, the declaration will be rejected for lack of firsthand knowledge.[1] This knowledge requirement has sometimes been confused with the opinion rule, and in some instances this confusion may have led courts to make the statement that opinions in dying declarations will be excluded.[2] Of

18. See Herrera v. State, 682 S.W.2d 313, 319 (Tex.Cr.App.1984), cert. denied 471 U.S. 1131.

19. State v. Verrett, 419 So.2d 455, 456–457 (La.1982); Kelly v. State, 694 P.2d 126, 132 (Wyo.1985) (inquiry by daughter as to what had happened to declarant did not preclude admissibility); 4 Louisell & Mueller, Federal Evidence § 488, at 1123–24 (1980).

§ 312

1. See supra § 311 text accompanying notes 3–12.

2. Mattox v. United States, 146 U.S. 140 (1892); State v. Puett, 210 N.C. 633, 188 S.E. 75 (1936). Indeed, some decisions indicate that when statements are exculpatory to the defendant, the court should use greater leniency in admitting the declaration. Watts v. State, 492 So.2d 1281 (Miss. 1986).

Neither the Federal nor Revised Uniform (1986) Rule limits use to the prosecution.

§ 313

1. State v. Adamson, 136 Ariz. 250, 665 P.2d 972 (1983), cert. denied 464 U.S. 865 (statements by victim of bombing that mafia was responsible excluded because not within declarant's personal knowledge but were mere suspicions); Jones v. State, 52 Ark. 345, 12 S.W. 704 (1889) (where declarant could not see who shot him, statement identifying the shooter properly excluded); Strickland v. State, 167 Ga. 452, 457, 145 S.E. 879, 881 (1928) (requirement satisfied); 5 Wigmore, Evidence § 1445(2) (Chadbourn rev. 1974). See generally Fed.R.Evid. 602. However, when there is room for doubt as to whether the statement is based on knowledge, the question is for the jury. Bland v. State, 210 Ga. 100, 78 S.E.2d 51 (1953). See generally Fed.R.Evid. 104(b). Expressions of suspicion or conjecture are to be excluded, however. Shepard v. United States, 290 U.S. 96, 101 (1933).

2. Roberts v. Commonwealth, 301 Ky. 294, 191 S.W.2d 242 (1945) (but declarations here held admissible); State v. Wilks, 278 Mo. 481, 213 S.W. 118 (1919); Holly-

course the traditional opinion rule, designed as a regulation of the manner of questioning of witnesses in court, is entirely inappropriate as a restriction upon out-of-court declarations.[3] Accordingly, most courts, including some that have professed to apply the opinion rule here, have admitted declarations such as: "He shot me down like a dog,"[4] "He shot me without cause,"[5] "He done it a-purpose,"[6] and the like,[7] which at one time would have been excluded as opinions if spoken by a witness on the stand.

Another problem is the application of the so-called best evidence rule.[8] Often the dying victim will make one or more oral statements about the facts of the crime and, in addition, may make a written statement or the person hearing the statement may write it down and have the declarant sign it. When must the writing be produced or its absence be explained? As to any separate oral statement, it is clear that this is provable without producing a later writing.[9] It is equally clear that the terms of a written dying statement cannot be proved as such without producing or accounting for the writing.[10] What if the witness who heard the oral statement, which was taken down and signed, offers to testify to what he or she heard? Wigmore argued that the execution of the writing does not call into play the parol evidence rule since that rule is limited to contracts and other "legal acts."[11] To a limited extent the courts have held otherwise. They have not excluded evidence of other oral statements made on the same occasion although not embraced in the writing.[12] However, oral declarations embodied in a writing signed or adopted by the deceased have been held not to be provable by one who heard them, but only by producing the written statement itself where available.[13] Even though it represents a

wood v. State, 19 Wyo. 493, 120 P. 471 (1912). See also Miller v. Goodwin, 246 Ark. 552, 439 S.W.2d 308 (1969) (if both matter of fact and of opinion are involved, the judge has discretion to admit subject to request for instruction that matter of opinion not be considered).

3. See Commonwealth v. Plubell, 367 Pa. 452, 80 A.2d 825 (1951) and Pendleton v. Commonwealth, 131 Va. 676, 696–97, 109 S.E. 201, 208–209 (1921), following 5 Wigmore, Evidence § 1447 (Chadbourn rev. 1974). See supra § 18.

The Advisory Committee's note to Fed. R.Evid. 804(b)(2) indicates that statements may be in the form of an opinion, as permitted for testimony under Rule 701. 56 F.R.D. 183, 326. Federal Rules 701 and 704 should resolve most doubts in favor of admissibility.

4. State v. Saunders, 14 Or. 300, 12 P. 441 (1886). See Finley v. State, 92 Tex.Cr. 543, 244 S.W. 526 (App.1922) ("He shot me in cold blood.").

5. State v. Williams, 168 N.C. 191, 83 S.E. 714 (1914).

6. Pippin v. Commonwealth, 117 Va. 919, 86 S.E. 152 (1915).

7. Powell v. State, 238 Miss. 283, 118 So.2d 304 (1960). Decisions are collected in 5 Wigmore, Evidence § 1447 (Chadbourn rev. 1974); Annots., 25 A.L.R. 1370, 63 A.L.R. 567, 86 A.L.R.2d 905; C.J.S. Homicide § 299; Dec.Dig. Homicide ⊕215(4).

8. See supra Ch. 23.

9. Gray v. State, 185 Ark. 515, 48 S.W.2d 224 (1932); Dunn v. People, 172 Ill. 582, 50 N.E. 137 (1898); State v. Sweeney, 203 Iowa 1305, 214 N.W. 735 (1927).

10. See supra § 233.

11. 5 Wigmore, Evidence § 1450(b) (Chadbourn rev. 1974).

12. Commonwealth v. Haney, 127 Mass. 455 (1879) (oral declarations of consciousness of impending death on same occasion as the written statement admitted).

13. Rex v. Gay, 7 C. & P. 230, 173 Eng.Rep. 101 (N.P.1835); Williams v. State, 26 Ala.App. 531, 163 So. 663 (1935), cert. denied 231 Ala. 127, 163 So. 667 (rule

departure from the usual practice of freedom in proving oral statements and an extension of the doctrine of integration into a new field, the result may be justified by the need here for accuracy in transmitting to the tribunal the exact terms of the declarant's statement.

§ 314. Instructions Regarding the Weight to Be Given to Dying Declarations [1]

There has been much theorizing in texts and opinions as to the weight to be given to dying declarations, abstractly or in comparison with the testimony of a witness. In consequence, the practice has grown up in some states of requiring [2] or permitting [3] the judge to instruct the jury that these declarations are to be received with caution or that they are not to be regarded as having the same value and weight as sworn testimony.[4] In other jurisdictions, such instructions have been held to be improper.[5] Others have considered it proper to direct the jury that they should give the dying declaration the same weight as the testimony of a witness.[6]

While there may be merit in a standardized practice of giving cautionary instructions, the direction to give the declaration a predetermined fixed weight seems of questionable wisdom. The weight of particular dying declarations depends upon so many factors varying from case to case that no standardized instruction will fit all situations. Certainly in jurisdictions where the judge retains common law power to comment on the weight of the evidence, the dying declaration is an appropriate subject for individualized comment. But where the judge lacks this power, as in most states, it seems wiser to leave the weight of

stated but here not shown to be signed); People v. Glenn, 10 Cal. 32, 37 (1858) (prosecution bound to produce writing, but having done so, can prove similar oral declarations made at other times); Couch v. State, 93 Tex.Cr. 27, 245 S.W. 692 (App.1922) (similar to Williams v. State, above). Contra: State v. Whitson, 111 N.C. 695, 16 S.E. 332 (1892) (dictum).

§ 314

1. Cases are collected in Notes, 46 Iowa L.Rev. 375 (1961), 32 Neb.L.Rev. 461 (1953); Annot., 167 A.L.R. 147; C.J.S. Homicide § 304.

2. Humphreys v. State, 166 Tenn. 523, 64 S.W.2d 5 (1933); State v. Mayo, 42 Wash. 540, 85 P. 251 (1906).

3. Dowdell v. State, 194 Ga. 578, 22 S.E.2d 310 (1942); Commonwealth v. Meleskie, 278 Pa. 383, 123 A. 310 (1924).

4. Watts v. State, 492 So.2d 1281, 1288 (Miss.1986) (jury, upon request, must be instructed that dying declarations are not of equal weight to in-court testimony); People v. Nieves, 67 N.Y.2d 125, 133, 501 N.Y.S.2d 1, 6, 492 N.E.2d 109, 114 (1986)

(same); Mitchell v. Commonwealth, 178 Va. 407, 17 S.E.2d 370 (1941) (approving such a charge).

5. Young v. United States, 391 A.2d 248 (D.C.App.1978) (instruction on dangers of such testimony or weight to be accorded to it constitutes unwarranted comment on evidence); Shenkenberger v. State, 154 Ind. 630, 57 N.E. 519 (1900).

6. State v. Johns, 152 Iowa 383, 132 N.W. 832 (1911). See also Hubbard v. State, 208 Ga. 472, 67 S.E.2d 562 (1951) (holding it not erroneous to instruct that dying declarations "stand upon the same plane of solemnity as statements made under oath"); Commonwealth v. Brown, 388 Pa. 613, 131 A.2d 367 (1957) (court approved instruction that declaration can be given "the same effect as though it were made under oath," but added it would be advisable for judge to omit any comparison); State v. Gazerro, 420 A.2d 816, 824 & n. 10 (R.I.1980) (weight to be given to dying declaration is for jury to decide, weighing the declaration along with the credibility of the declarant).

the declaration to the arguments of counsel, the judgment of the jury, and the consideration of the judge on motion for new trial.[7]

§ 315. Decisional and Statutory Extensions of Common Law Admissibility

In a landmark decision,[1] the Kansas court had before it an action by the executor of the seller to recover on a land sale contract. Should the dying statement of the seller of "the truth about the sale" be admitted? An affirmative answer required departure from traditional common law limitations in two respects: (1) the case was civil, not a criminal homicide prosecution, and (2) the statement was unrelated to the cause or circumstances of death. "We are confronted," the court said, "with a restrictive rule of evidence commendable only for its age, its respectability resting solely upon a habit of judicial recognition, formed without reason, and continued without justification," and ruled in favor of admissibility.

As observed in earlier sections of this chapter, there has been some willingness to expand admissibility with respect to the type of case, as witnessed by the Revised Uniform Rules (1986), which would admit dying declarations in all cases.[2] The exclusion of such hearsay under the Federal Rules from criminal cases other than prosecutions for homicide because of Congressional concern about the reliability of this form of hearsay [3] seems to strike the wrong balance. Only a sense of very rough justice will admit statements in the most serious types of cases because the murder of the witness threatens to rob the court of valuable testimony but exclude them because of questionable trustworthiness in less serious criminal prosecutions. Under the terms of the Federal Rule, the need for the testimony is frequently just as great in nonhomicide cases because the declarant, while not the victim of murder, must be unavailable to testify. As a result, extension of the exception beyond its current limited scope would appear appropriate.

While the limitation on statements admissible under the exception to the circumstances of the declarant's death was not in the original Uniform Rules,[4] it is a requirement of the Federal Rule,[5] and departure from this limitation is found only in occasional rules and statutes. The restriction is generally sound because the connection between these circumstances and the statement helps to enhance its trustworthiness by reducing the dangers of poor memory and insincerity.

---

7. Young v. United States, 391 A.2d 248 (D.C.App.1978) (adopting the position advocated by this treatise).

§ 315

1. Thurston v. Fritz, 91 Kan. 468, 138 P. 625 (1914).

2. A substantial number of states have chosen not to follow the Federal Rule in limiting use of dying declarations in criminal cases to homicide prosecutions. See generally 4 Weinstein & Berger, Weinstein's Evidence ¶ 804(b)(2)[02] (1990).

3. House Comm. on Judiciary, H.R.Rep. No. 650, 93d Cong., 1st Sess., 15 (1973), reprinted in 1974 U.S.Code Cong. & Admin.News 7075, 7089.

4. Original Uniform Rule 63(5) (1953).

5. For text of rule, see supra § 310 note 5.

Chapter 33

DECLARATIONS AGAINST INTEREST

Table of Sections

§ 316. General Requirements; Distinction Between Declarations Against Interest and Admissions [1]

To satisfy the instant exception to the hearsay rule in its traditional form, two main requirements have been imposed: first, either the declaration must state facts that are against the pecuniary or proprietary interest of the declarant or the making of the declaration itself must create evidence that would harm such interests; [2] second, the declarant must be unavailable at the time of trial. [3] Under the theory

---

§ 316

1. See generally 5 Wigmore, Evidence §§ 1455–1477 (Chadbourn rev.1974); Haddad & Agin, A Potential Revolution in Bruton Doctrine: Is Bruton Applicable Where Domestic Evidence Rules Prohibit Use of A Codefendant's Confession as Evidence against a Defendant although the Confrontation Clause Would Allow such Use? 81 J.Crim.L. & Criminology 235 (1990); Jefferson, Declarations against Interest: An Exception to the Hearsay Rule, 58 Harv. L.Rev. 1 (1944); Morgan, Declarations against Interest, 5 Vand.L.Rev. 451 (1952); Note, 64 B.U.L.Rev. 148 (1976); Annots., 105 A.L.R. 398, 114 A.L.R. 921, 65 A.L.R.2d 631, 73 A.L.R.2d 1180, 34 A.L.R.Fed. 412; Dec.Dig.Evidence ☞272–284, Criminal Law ☞417(15); C.J.S. Evidence §§ 217–224.

2. See infra §§ 317–319.

3. See infra § 320.

that people generally do not lightly make statements that are damaging to their interests, the first requirement provides the safeguard of special trustworthiness justifying most of the exceptions to the hearsay rule. The second is largely an historical development but operates usefully as a limiting factor. Minor qualifications may be added. The interest involved must not be too indirect or remote.[4] The declarant, as in the case of hearsay exceptions generally,[5] must have had the opportunity to observe the facts.[6]

While sometimes erroneously called an admission against interest, the instant exception and the admission exclusion[7] are distinct. The traditional distinctions developed by Wigmore,[8] are generally followed. Thus, the admissions of a party-opponent may be introduced without satisfying any of the requirements for declarations against interest. First, while frequently admissions are against interest when made, they need not be and may, in fact, have been self-serving.[9] Second, the party making the admission need not be, and seldom is, unavailable.[10] Third, the party making the admission need not have had personal knowledge of the fact admitted.[11] Accordingly, when the opponent offers a statement of a party, it should be submitted as, and tested by, the requirements for parties' admissions and not those for declarations against interest. On the other hand, statements of nonparties, which may not

---

4. Smith v. Blakey, [1867] 2 L.R.–Q.B. 326, 332 (letter of clerk advising employer of arrival of "three huge cases" in his charge and stating terms of contract with consignor, held not admissible; "the possibility that this statement might make him liable in case of their being lost is an interest of too remote a nature"). See also United States v. Woolbright, 831 F.2d 1390, 1395 (8th Cir.1987) (statement that declarant was on a "honeymoon trip" not against interest since its impact in establishing constructive possession of drugs carried by companion unclear); Giberson v. Wilson, 322 S.W.2d 466, 468 (Ky.1959) ("The act of an insured in changing the beneficiary of an insurance policy is not against his pecuniary or proprietary interest," although he gives up the right to have proceeds paid to his estate); In re Simms' Estate, 442 S.W.2d 426 (Tex.Civ.App.1969, error refused n.r.e.) (statement of declarant that she had destroyed will and codicil of another, at a time when declarant had no interest in the estate of the maker of the will, was not a declaration against interest). But see infra § 317 notes 2–3 and accompanying text.

5. See, e.g., supra §§ 280, 290, 313.

6. The requirement is sometimes more stringently stated by demanding that the facts must have been "within the declarant's peculiar knowledge." See, e.g., Gleadow v. Atkins, 1 C. & M. 410, 149 Eng.Rep. 459 (Ex. 1833); Price v. Humble Oil & Ref.

Co., 152 S.W.2d 804, 813 (Tex.Civ.App.1941, error refused w.m.). But doubtless nothing more than the usual knowledge qualification is intended to, or can reasonably, be required. See Windorski v. Doyle, 219 Minn. 402, 409, 18 N.W.2d 142, 146 (1945) ("a matter of which he was personally cognizant"); 5 Wigmore, Evidence § 1471(a) (Chadbourn rev. 1974); C.J.S. Evidence § 220.

While neither the Federal nor the Revised Uniform Rules specifically mentions this requirement, Rule 602 requires firsthand knowledge of witnesses generally, and in hearsay situations the declarant is in reality the witness. See Adv.Comm. Note, Fed.R.Evid. 803, 56 F.R.D. 183, 303; United States v. Lang, 589 F.2d 92 (2d Cir.1978) (statements inadmissible under exception where declarant not present and lacked firsthand knowledge of event); United States v. Lanci, 669 F.2d 391 (6th Cir.1982), cert. denied 457 U.S. 1134 (statement against interest excluded where declarant did not know facts stated but rather imagined or guessed them).

7. See supra Ch. 25.

8. 5 Wigmore, Evidence § 1475 (Chadbourn rev. 1974); C.J.S. Evidence § 217(b).

9. See supra § 254; infra § 317.

10. See supra § 254.

11. See supra § 255.

be introduced as admissions, may be admitted if they are against interest and if the declarant is unavailable. Moreover, since the Federal Rules appear not to recognize admissions by persons in "privity" with parties,[12] the instant exception provides one of the principal alternative methods for introducing damaging statements made by a party's predecessor.[13]

The Federal Rules preserve the hearsay exception as broadly developed at common law with respect to statements against pecuniary or proprietary interest and, in addition, expand the definition to include statements against penal interest. Rule 804(b)(3) [14] admits statements of unavailable declarants as follows:

> A statement which was at the time of its making so far contrary to the declarant's pecuniary or proprietary interest, or so far tended to subject the declarant to civil or criminal liability, or to render invalid a claim by the declarant against another, that a reasonable person in the declarant's position would not have made the statement unless believing it to be true. A statement tending to expose the declarant to criminal liability and offered to exculpate the accused is not admissible unless corroborating circumstances clearly indicate the trustworthiness of the statement.

§ 317. Declarations Against Pecuniary or Proprietary Interest; Declarations Affecting Claim or Liability for Damages

The traditional field for this exception has been that of declarations against proprietary or pecuniary interest. Common instances of the former are acknowledgments that the declarant does not own certain land or personal property, or has conveyed or transferred it.[1] Moreover, a statement by one in possession that he or she holds an interest less than complete ownership has traditionally been regarded as a declaration against interest,[2] though it is obviously ambiguous, and in

---

12. See supra § 260.

13. Kwiatowski v. John Lowry, Inc., 276 N.Y. 126, 11 N.E.2d 563 (1937) (in death action, statements against interest by decedent admitted as declarations against interest); Aetna Life Ins. Co. v. Strauch, 179 Okl. 617, 67 P.2d 452 (1937) (suit by administrator of wife against insurance company on policy on her life; confession of husband, since executed, of plot to secure policy and kill her, admitted as declaration against interest). See generally C.J.S. Evidence § 219(d).

14. Revised Uniform Rule (1986) 804(b)(3) differs from the Federal Rule in two principal ways: first, it includes statements incurring social disapproval, and second, it excludes statements implicating both declarant and the accused. The differences between the Federal and the Revised Uniform Rule are discussed further under various topics below.

§ 317

1. Dean v. Wilkerson, 126 Ind. 338, 26 N.E. 55 (1890) (declarations of father, offered by the son after father's death, that he had given notes to son); Smith v. Moore, 142 N.C. 277, 55 S.E. 275 (1906) (declaration by deceased life tenant that she had made a deed to her son-in-law and the reason for making the deed); Mehus v. Thompson, 266 N.W.2d 920 (N.D.1978) (grantor's statements after delivery in support of deed); First Nat. Bank v. Holland, 99 Va. 495, 501, 39 S.E. 126, 128 (1901) (husband's declaration of gift to wife).

2. Lamar v. Pearre, 90 Ga. 377, 17 S.E. 92 (1892) (possessor's declarations that land had been bought with trust funds); McLeod v. Swain, 87 Ga. 156, 13 S.E. 315 (1891) (plaintiff in ejectment offers her former tenants' declarations that they held land as her tenants); Dooley v. Baynes, 86 Va. 644, 10 S.E. 974 (1890) (possessor's declarations that he held only a life estate).

England has even been received when offered to establish the existence of the interest claimed by the declarant.[3]

The clearest example of a declaration against pecuniary interest is an acknowledgment that the declarant is indebted.[4] Here the declaration, standing alone, is against interest on the theory that to owe a debt is against one's financial interest. This theory is routinely followed even though it may not be applicable in particular circumstances. Less obviously an acknowledgment of receipt of money in payment of a debt owing to the declarant is also traditionally classed as against interest.[5] Here the fact of payment itself is probably advantageous to the receiver, but the acknowledgment of it is regarded as against interest because it is evidence of the reduction or extinguishment of the debt.[6] Of course, a receipt for money which the receiver is to hold for another is an acknowledgment of a debt.[7] Similarly, a statement that one holds money in trust is against interest.[8]

The development of the exception by English courts narrowly focused it in the areas of debt and property, but the American cases extended

3. In Regina v. Overseers of Birmingham, 1 B. & S. 763, 121 Eng.Rep. 897 (K.B.1861), and in Regina v. Governors and Guardians of Exeter, [1869] 4 L.R.–Q.B. 341, declarant's assertions of tenancy were admitted, not to prove that he did not have a fee simple, but that he had a tenancy at the stated rental. This use is disapproved in 5 Wigmore, Evidence § 1458 (Chadbourn rev. 1974).

4. German Ins. Co. v. Bartlett, 188 Ill. 165, 58 N.E. 1075 (1900) (in suit of deceased husband's creditors against wife to whom he had conveyed property, she was allowed to prove his declarations that he was indebted to her); Truelsch v. Northwestern Mut. Life Ins. Co., 186 Wis. 239, 202 N.W. 352 (1925) (suit by wife on life policy on husband; husband's employer claims lien on policy for money embezzled and used to pay premiums; husband's letter to wife before his suicide acknowledging defalcations admitted as declaration against interest).

5. Palter Cap Co. v. Great Western Life Assurance Co. [1936] 2 D.L.R. 304 (physician's entry in cash book of money received from patient, to show date of consultation); Mentzer v. Burlingame, 85 Kan. 641, 118 P. 698 (1911) (declaration of holder that notes were paid). See suggestion that these examples of "astounding tortuous reasoning" may have only been result oriented efforts by early courts to admit statements that are now routinely admissible under other exceptions, such as business records. 4 Weinstein & Berger, Weinstein's Evidence ¶ 804(b)(3)[01], at 126 (1990).

6. Coffin v. Bucknam, 12 Me. 471, 473 (1835) (entry of part payment on note by deceased former holder admitted for administrator suing on note, to avoid statute of limitations; "the indorsement was then clearly against his interest, furnishing proof that he had received part of the contents of the note"); Chenango Bridge Co. v. Paige, 83 N.Y. 178, 192 (1880) (treasurer's books showing amount of tolls received admitted "as they charged him with the amount of such tolls"). Cases supporting this theory are cited and analyzed in Morgan, Declarations Against Interest, 5 Vand.L.Rev. 451, 454–456 (1952) and Jefferson, Declarations Against Interest: An Exception to the Hearsay Rule, 58 Harv. L.Rev. 1, 8–17 (1944).

7. Barry v. Bebbington, 4 Term R. 514, 100 Eng.Rep. 1149 (1792) (steward's receipts); Manning v. Lechmere, 1 Atk. 453, 26 Eng.Rep. 288 (Ch. 1737) (L.Ch.Hardwicke: "Where there are old rentals, and bailiffs have admitted money received by them, these rentals are evidence of the payment because no other can be had"); Keesling v. Powell, 149 Ind. 372, 49 N.E. 265 (1898) (statement by tax officer that taxes had been paid).

8. Gleadow v. Atkin, 1 C. & M. 410, 149 Eng.Rep. 459 (Ex.1833). See also Wilkins v. Enterprise TV, Inc., 231 Ark. 958, 333 S.W.2d 718 (1960) (declarant, ostensibly the president and principal stockholder of the corporation, stated he was only a salaried employee).

the field of declarations against interest to include acknowledgment of facts which would give rise to a liability for unliquidated damages for tort [9] or seemingly for breach of contract.[10] A corresponding extension to embrace statements of facts that would constitute a defense to a claim for damages otherwise available to the declarant has been recognized in this country.[11]

Federal Rule 804(b)(3) is broadly drawn to include statements against pecuniary or proprietary interest in general, and more specifically those tending to subject declarant to civil liability, without being limited to tort or contract, and those tending to invalidate a claim by the declarant against another.[12] This aspect of the rule thus occupies the entire area developed by the common law except for some of the more fanciful English decisions in tenancy cases.[13]

9. Weber v. Chicago, Rock Island & Pacific Ry. Co., 175 Iowa 358, 394, 151 N.W. 852, 864 (1915) (in action by passenger for injury in derailment, statement that declarant had unbolted the rails admitted as against interest because it provided a "basis of an action against him for damages"); Windorski v. Doyle, 219 Minn. 402, 18 N.W.2d 142 (1945) (where patron killed by blow from another patron, declarations of bartender that assault was unprovoked and that he had warned offending patron against threats admissible as declaration against interest; the facts "may reasonably furnish a basis of a pecuniary claim against him as he was in sole charge of the bar-room"); Halvorsen v. Moon & Kerr Lumber Co., 87 Minn. 18, 91 N.W. 28 (1902) (statement of employee that fire due to boiling over of lard kettle, of which he was in charge while out of the room, admissible since the facts furnish the basis of a "pecuniary claim" for negligence); Duncan v. Smith, 393 S.W.2d 798 (Tex.1965) (statement of a driver that he passed illegally on the right side of a vehicle and ran into a bridge).

In determining whether the statement sufficiently exposed the declarant to tort liability to be against interest, the courts have generally applied a liberal standard. See, e.g., Gichner v. Antonio Troiano Tile & Marble Co., 410 F.2d 238 (D.C.Cir.1969) (it is enough if the statement could reasonably provide an important link in a chain of evidence that is the basis for civil liability; statement that declarant smoked in a building later found burned held sufficiently against interest). But see Merritt v. Chonowski, 58 Ill.App.3d 192, 15 Ill.Dec. 588, 373 N.E.2d 1060 (1978) (in dram shop action, proper to exclude statement by customer on leaving bar that he had six

drinks; not against interest because before accident).

10. Jefferson, supra note 6, at 30 n. 62. However, receipt of the statements in the cases cited was also explainable under the theory that they were admissions of a party's predecessor.

11. Home Ins. v. Allied Telephone Co., 246 Ark. 1095, 442 S.W.2d 211 (1969) (statement of nonparty driver of automobile that "it looks like something that could not be helped" held against interest since declarant was potentially liable and statement absolved another driver in accident of fault); Walker v. Brantner, 59 Kan. 117, 52 P. 80 (1898) (in action for death of engineer, his declarations after the collision that he had not kept a lookout received as against interest); Kwiatowski v. John Lowry, Inc., 276 N.Y. 126, 11 N.E.2d 563 (1937) (statements by deceased showing no liability admissible both as admissions and as declarations against interest); Jewell v. El Paso Elec. Co., 47 S.W.2d 328 (Tex.Civ.App.1932) (statement of deceased that it was his own fault, admitted as against interest); Annot., 114 A.L.R. 921. But see Tucker v. Oldbury Urban Dist. Council, [1921] 2 K.B. 317 (C.A.) (in death action for alleged injury causing blood poisoning, declarations of deceased after the alleged injury that he left work because of an inflammation of finger were inadmissible because he then had made no claim and was not conscious that the statement was against interest).

12. For rule, see supra § 316 text following note 14.

13. See cases cited supra note 3.

§ 318. Penal Interest;[1] Interest of Prestige or Self–Esteem

In 1844, in the Sussex Peerage Case,[2] the House of Lords, ignoring precedents, determined that a declaration confessing a crime committed by declarant was not receivable as a declaration against interest. This decision was influential in confining the development of this exception to the hearsay rule within narrow materialistic limits. It was generally followed in this country in criminal cases for many years.[3] Courts, while not repudiating the limitation, have sometimes justified admission of a third person's confession of crime in the civil context on the basis that the particular crime was also a tort and thus the statement was against material interest by exposing the declarant to liability for damages.[4]

Was the practice of excluding third-person confessions in criminal cases justified? It certainly could not be justified on the ground that an acknowledgment of facts rendering one liable to criminal punishment is less trustworthy than an acknowledgment of a debt. The motivation for the exclusion was no doubt a different one, namely, the fear of opening the door to a flood of witnesses testifying falsely to confessions that were never made or testifying truthfully to confessions that were false. This fear was based on the likely criminal character of witness and declarant, reinforced by the requirement that declarant must be unavailable, which made perjury easier to accomplish and more difficult to punish.

Wigmore rejected the argument of the danger of perjury, since that danger is one that attends all human testimony, and concluded that "any rule which hampers an honest man in exonerating himself is a bad rule, even it if also hampers a villain in falsely passing for an innocent."[5] Under this argument, accepted by Justice Holmes in a famous dissent,[6] courts began to relax the rule of exclusion of declara-

---

§ 318

1. 5 Wigmore, Evidence §§ 1476–1477 (Chadbourn rev. 1974); Goodman & Waltuch, Declarations Against Penal Interest: The Majority Has Emerged, 28 N.Y.L.Sch. L.Rev. 51 (1983); Tague, Perils of the Rulemaking Process: The Development, Application, and Unconstitutionality of Rule 804(b)(3)'s Penal Interest Exception, 69 Geo.L.J. 851 (1981); Comment, 131 U.Pa. L.Rev. 999 (1983); Note, 56 B.U.L.Rev. 148 (1976); Annots., 90 A.L.R.3d 1173, 92 A.L.R.3d 1164, 34 A.L.R.Fed. 412; C.J.S.Criminal Law § 960; Dec.Dig.Criminal Law ☞417(15).

2. 11 Cl. & F. 85, 8 Eng.Rep. 1034 (1844).

3. See, e.g., State v. Stallings, 154 Conn. 272, 224 A.2d 718 (1966) (confession of declarant other than defendant, but the court

judicially noticed that the declarant had been tried and acquitted on the same charge); Bryant v. State, 197 Ga. 641, 30 S.E.2d 259 (1944); Rushing v. State, 88 Okl.Cr.App. 82, 199 P.2d 614 (1948); Commonwealth v. Antonini, 165 Pa.Super. 501, 69 A.2d 436 (1949) (offered against the accused).

4. Weber v. Chicago, Rock Island & Pacific Ry. Co., 175 Iowa 358, 392, 151 N.W. 852, 864 (1915) (confession that declarant had unbolted rail causing derailment of train).

5. 5 Wigmore, Evidence § 1477, at 359 (Chadbourn rev. 1974).

6.

The confession of Joe Dick, since deceased, that he committed the murder for which the plaintiff in error was tried,

tions against penal interest in particular situations [7] or generally.[8] The inclusion of declarations against penal interest in the Federal Rule 804(b)(3) has given great impetus to the use of this exception, and most of the recent case law and literature dealing with declarations against interest has centered on this aspect and its concomitant problems.[9]

During the course of the expansion of the hearsay exception to include declarations against penal interest, the situation principally examined was whether a confession or other statement by a third person offered by the defense to *exculpate* the accused should be admissible. The traditional distrust of declarations against penal interest had evolved in that setting, and, as a result, the Federal Rule included a prohibition against admitting an exculpatory statement in evidence "unless corroborating circumstances clearly indicate the trust-

coupled with circumstances pointing to its truth, would have a very strong tendency to make anyone outside of a court of justice believe that Donnelly did not commit the crime. I say this, of course, on the supposition that it should be proved that the confession really was made, and that there was no ground for connecting Donnelly with Dick. The rules of evidence in the main are based on experience, logic, and common sense, less hampered by history than some parts of the substantive law. There is no decision by this court against the admissibility of such a confession; the English cases since the separation of the two countries do not bind us; the exception to the hearsay rule in the case of declarations against interest is well known; no other statement is so much against interests as a confession of murder; it is far more calculated to convince than dying declarations, which would be let in to hang a man (Mattox v. United States, 146 U.S. 140); and when we surround the accused with so many safeguards, some of which seem to me excessive, I think we ought to give him the benefit of a fact that, if proved, commonly would have such weight. The history of the law and the arguments against the English doctrine are so well and fully stated by Mr. Wigmore that there is no need to set them forth at greater length. 2 Wigmore, Ev. §§ 1476, 1477.

Donnelly v. United States, 228 U.S. 243, 277–278 (1913) (Holmes, J., dissenting).

7. People v. Lettrich, 413 Ill. 172, 108 N.E.2d 488 (1952); Brady v. State, 226 Md. 422, 174 A.2d 167 (1961), affirmed 373 U.S. 83 (discussion of previous Maryland cases); Newberry v. Commonwealth, 191 Va. 445, 61 S.E.2d 318 (1950) (in case where circumstances indicated that defendant's brother, who refused to testify on ground of immunity as joint indictee, was possible killer, defendant entitled to introduce brother's confession); Hines v. Commonwealth, 136 Va. 728, 117 S.E. 843 (1923) (in prosecution where circumstantial evidence pointed both to accused and to third person, accused entitled to prove person's confession). See also 35 A.L.R. 441.

8. People v. Spriggs, 60 Cal.2d 868, 36 Cal.Rptr. 841, 389 P.2d 377 (1964); People v. Brown, 26 N.Y.2d 88, 308 N.Y.S.2d 825, 257 N.E.2d 16 (1970).

9. See criminal cases discussed throughout remainder of the chapter.

The effect was evident not only through adoption of the rules as a whole but also piecemeal by decision. See, e.g., State v. DeFreitas, 179 Conn. 431, 426 A.2d 799 (1980). Another source of encouragement for these developments was likely the Supreme Court's decision in Chambers v. Mississippi, 410 U.S. 284 (1973). In *Chambers,* the Court held that exclusion of several confessions of a third party exculpating the accused denied the defendant due process where the statements were given "under circumstances that provided considerable assurances of their reliability" and the accused was prevented from cross-examining the confessing party, who testified as a witness, because of the local "voucher rule." The Court emphasized the against-interest aspect of the statements as an assurance that they were trustworthy. Because the decision was carefully limited to the situation presented, the dimensions of the constitutional right it establishes are uncertain. Moreover, since the thrust of the opinion is to establish criteria where admission of evidence is *required,* it should not be read as establishing limitations on admissibility.

worthiness of the statement." [10] While the possibility was recognized that statements against penal interest by third parties inculpating both the declarant and the defendant might also be offered by the prosecution to *inculpate* the accused, prior to the adoption of the Federal Rules the possibility of their admissibility was raised infrequently in cases or the literature.[11] Under Rule 804(b)(3), admission of such statements

10. The federal courts have disagreed on whether the corroboration requirement applies to the veracity of the in-court witness testifying that the statement was made as well as to the clearly required showing that the statement itself is trustworthy. The majority has taken the position that the credibility of the in-court declarant is not subject to the corroboration requirement. United States v. Seeley, 892 F.2d 1 (1st Cir.1989) (credibility of in-court witness to be judged by jury and not an appropriate issue for corroboration); United States v. Katsougrakis, 715 F.2d 769 (2d Cir.1983), cert. denied 464 U.S. 1040 (preliminary determination of credibility would usurp jury function); United States v. Atkins, 558 F.2d 133, 135 (3d Cir.1977), cert. denied 434 U.S. 929, 972 & 1071. See also 4 Louisell & Mueller, Federal Evidence § 489, at 1163–65 (1980); 4 Weinstein & Berger, Weinstein's Evidence ¶ 804(b)(3)[03], at 147 (1990); Tague, supra note 1, at 974. However, in United States v. Bagley, 537 F.2d 162, 167–168 (5th Cir. 1976), cert. denied 429 U.S. 1075, the court argued that whether the exculpatory statement was actually made was a major concern of the drafters of the rule and is an important aspect of the corroboration requirement. Cf. United States v. Satterfield, 572 F.2d 687, 691–692 (9th Cir.1978), cert. denied 439 U.S. 840 (noting that while strong argument can be made that credibility of in-court witness is irrelevant to hearsay determination, some factors suggest that the courts are authorized under the rule to exclude statements based on credibility of witness).

As a matter of standard hearsay analysis, it is clear that the credibility of the in-court witness regarding the fact that the statement was made is not an appropriate inquiry. See infra § 324 note 15. However, given the strong legislative concern over the possibility of perjured testimony exculpating the defendant under this exception, it is not so obvious that the *Bagley* court erred in considering this factor. Nevertheless, absent more explicit direction from the drafters, the witness' credibility should be excluded from the corroboration requirement. Tague, supra note 1,

at 974 (concluding that legislative history does not support including this factor). A similar inquiry, however, may be made under Rule 403 in assessing the probative force of the evidence. Satterfield, supra, 572 F.2d at 692; 4 Weinstein & Berger, supra ¶ 804(b)(3)[03], at 147.

11. Douglas v. Alabama, 380 U.S. 415 (1965) and Bruton v. United States, 391 U.S. 123 (1968) involved confessions by a codefendant inculpating the accused. *Douglas* did not consider or discuss the possibility of admissibility as a declaration against interest, merely remarking that no recognized exception to the hearsay rule was involved. *Bruton* assumed inadmissibility and focused on the ineffectiveness of instructing the jury to apply the confession only to the confessing codefendant, although a dissenting opinion pointed to the Court's traditional distrust of codefendant confessions.

Against this uncertain background, the Federal Advisory Committee first proposed a rule excluding all inculpatory statements, Preliminary Draft, Rule 8–04(b)(4) (March 1969), 46 F.R.D. 161, 378. Eventually, however, the committee deleted the provision. It concluded that, although statements made while in custody would often be motivated by a desire to curry favor with the authorities and hence fail to qualify as against interest, other circumstances might lead to the opposite conclusion, and the matter should be decided on a case-by-case basis. 56 F.R.D. 183, 328. In that form, the Federal Rule was approved by the Supreme Court and enacted by the Congress. See Senate Comm. on Judiciary, S.Rep. No. 1277, 93d Cong., 2d Sess. 21, reprinted in 1974 U.S.Code Cong. & Admin.News 7051, 7067.

The deleted provision was reinstated in the Revised Uniform Rules (1986), which would exclude all such statements. A handful of states have taken this position either by decision, State v. Boyd, 214 Conn. 132, 139, 570 A.2d 1125, 1128 (1990) or rule, see State v. Parris, 98 Wash.2d 140, 160 & n. 5, 654 P.2d 77, 87 & n. 4 (1982) (Williams, J., dissenting) (listing, inter alia, Arkansas, Florida, Nevada, New Jersey,

has been far more common.[12] As will be seen in the section that follows, exculpatory and inculpatory statement raise some different as well as some similar questions.

Whether the hearsay exception for declarations against interest should be enlarged to include declarations against "social" interests has been the occasion of differences of opinion. Traditionally, interests of this nature were not regarded as sufficiently substantial to ensure reliability. Following the pattern of the original Uniform Rule, the Federal Rule, as promulgated by the Supreme Court, included statements tending to make the declarant "an object of hatred, ridicule, or disgrace," but it was deleted from the rule as enacted by Congress. The provision was reinstated in the Revised Uniform Rule (1986) and has been adopted in a handful of states.[13]

§ 319. Determining What Is Against Interest; Confrontation Problems

(a) The time aspect. As observed at the beginning of this chapter, the theory underlying the hearsay exception for declarations against interest is that people do not make statements that are harmful to their interests without substantial reason to believe that the statements are true.[1] Reason indicates that the harm must exist at the time the statement is made; otherwise it can exert no influence on declarant to speak accurately and truthfully. That the statement may at another time prove to be damaging—or, for that matter, beneficial—is without significance. This characteristic of contemporaneity is implicit in the cases, although it is only rarely discussed.[2] Occasionally it is suggested that this requirement is ignored to some extent when the admissibility of contextual statements, discussed below, is involved.

and North Dakota as excluding inculpating statements).

12. It appears that the general liberality of the standard for determining when the entire statement or a portion of it is against interest explains much of the reason that the federal courts after enactment of Rule 804(b)(3) have been far more inclined to admit against the defendant inculpatory statements of a third party implicating both the declarant and the accused. The phrasing of the requirement in terms "tending" to subject the declarant to criminal liability has been interpreted not to require a direct confession of guilt. As a result, portions of a statement by a third party involving the accused have been construed to satisfy the against interest requirement if either those portions of the statement are integral to the larger whole or if they, in context, support the declarant's involvement by strengthening the impression of personal knowledge. See, e.g., United States v. Garris, 616 F.2d 626, 630 (2d Cir.1980), cert. denied 447 U.S. 926;

United States v. Alvarez, 584 F.2d 694, 699–700 (5th Cir.1978).

13. See Timber Access Industries Co. v. United States Plywood–Champion Papers, Inc., 263 Or. 509, 503 P.2d 482 (1972) (statement by defendant's former plant manager that he had made an improvident contract); Heddings v. Steele, 514 Pa. 569, 575–576 & n. 3, 526 A.2d 349, 352–353 & n. 3 (1987) (while ultimately reversing decision of lower court to recognize statements against social interest under state's hearsay exception, court notes that rejected view has been adopted by a number of states by decision or rule).

§ 319

1. See also Adv.Comm.Note, Fed. R.Evid. 804(b)[3], 56 F.R.D. 183, 327.

2. Roberts v. City of Troy, 773 F.2d 720, 725–726 (6th Cir.1985) (statement by plaintiff's mother improperly admitted where it was only after she made the statement that she learned about state regulations making the facts damaging to her claim).

(b) The nature of the statement. The statement must be such "that a reasonable person in the declarant's position would not have made the statement unless believing it to be true,"[3] in view of the statement's adversity to declarant's interest. As indicated earlier,[4] the traditional declaration against interest was a statement that could be used in evidence in a manner adverse to declarant's pecuniary or proprietary interest. A declaration against penal interest is one that would be admissible against declarant in a criminal prosecution; it need not be a confession,[5] but must involve substantial exposure to criminal liability.[6]

A controversial area has been the so-called "contextual" or related statements. In the seminal case of Higham v. Ridgway,[7] in order to prove the date of birth of an individual, an entry in the record book of a midwife was introduced, showing a charge for attendance upon the mother for birth of a child, together with an entry six months later showing payment of the charge. The entry of payment, said the court, "was in prejudice of the party making it." But, though the entry of payment may have been against interest, the issue in the case was not payment, but the birth six months earlier. To this objection, the court replied, "By the reference to the ledger, the entry there [of the birth] is virtually incorporated in the other entry [of payment], of which it is explanatory." In civil cases, as in *Higham v. Ridgway,* to admit the critical related statement or part of the statement is acceptable, even though not itself against interest, if it is closely enough connected and neutral as to interest.[8]

Judicial scrutiny in criminal cases may be somewhat more exacting. When a statement both incriminates the declarant and exculpates the accused, complete rejection of related or contextual statements is not required,[9] although a rather tight integration between its two aspects is

---

3. For text of rule, see supra § 316 text following note 14.

4. Cases cited in supra § 317.

5. United States v. Barrett, 539 F.2d 244 (1st Cir.1976); United States v. Thomas, 571 F.2d 285 (5th Cir.1978); United States v. Bagley, 537 F.2d 162 (5th Cir. 1976), cert. denied 429 U.S. 1075.

6. United States v. Hoyos, 573 F.2d 1111 (9th Cir.1978).

7. 10 East 109, 103 Eng.Rep. 717 (K.B.1808). One senses that this feat of judicial imagination might not have been achieved if the hearsay exception for entries in the regular course of business had then been sufficiently developed to cover the situation.

8. Taylor v. Witham, 3 Ch.D. 605, 607 (1875) (Taylor paid Witham £2000; after Taylor's death his executor contended this was a loan, Witham that it was a gift; entry in Taylor's book of three months' interest, £20, paid by Witham admitted for the executor to show a loan "since the natural meaning of the entry standing alone" was against interest); Palter Cap. Co. v. Great Western Life Assurance Co., [1936] 2 D.L.R. 304; Knapp v. St. Louis Trust Co., 199 Mo. 640, 98 S.W. 70 (1906). For additional cases, see 5 Wigmore, Evidence § 1465 (Chadbourn rev. 1974). Model Code of Evidence Rule 509(2) (1942) allowed "a declaration against interest and such additional parts thereof, including matter incorporated by reference, as the judge finds to be so closely connected with the declaration against interest as to be equally trustworthy."

9. United States v. Barrett, 539 F.2d 244 (1st Cir.1976); United States v. Thomas, 571 F.2d 285 (5th Cir.1978). In both opinions the court buttressed its finding of sufficient integration by pointing out that the statement in any event disclosed guilty knowledge by the declarant. See also United States v. Brainard, 690 F.2d 1117 (4th Cir.1982).

occasionally suggested.[10] When the statement incriminates both the declarant and the accused and is offered by the prosecution against the accused, some commentators and decisions adopt an even stricter approach under the requirements of the confrontation clause, rejecting any part or related statement not in itself against interest.[11] In general, however, the trend in the federal cases is to admit the entire statement if the two parts are reasonably closely connected.[12]

(c) The factual setting. Whether a statement was against interest will often require a delicate examination of the circumstances under which it was made.[13] That determination may depend on outside facts that existed at the time the statement was made but were not disclosed in the statement. For example, whether a statement that declarant is a member of a certain partnership is against his or her pecuniary interest depends upon whether the firm is clearly solvent or is on an uncertain economic footing.[14] Likewise, a statement that one has a contract to purchase a commodity, such as wheat, at a certain price is against or for interest depending upon the price in the market at the time the statement was made.

If the factual setting suggests that declarant anticipated no damaging disclosure, is the circumstantial guarantee of trustworthiness present? A relation of trust and confidence between speaker and listener arguably militates against awareness that the making of the statement might be against declarant's interest. The question was raised in the Sussex Peerage case,[15] where the statement was to declarant's son, and was answered in the negative. The case has not, however, been followed, and the fact that the statement was made to declarant's

10. United States v. Hoyos, 573 F.2d 1111 (9th Cir.1978) (absent concurrent presence of solidly inculpatory statement against interest, statement exculpating accused not admissible); United States v. Porter, 881 F.2d 878 (10th Cir.1989), cert. denied 493 U.S. 944 (because exculpatory statement not necessary to admission of personal involvement, exculpatory statement severable and analyzed separately). See also United States v. Green, 694 F.Supp. 107 (E.D.Pa.1988), affirmed 875 F.2d 312 (3d Cir.) (recognizing that most courts find the exculpatory portion of the statement sufficiently related and integral, but excluding statement under trustworthiness analysis that questioned whether exculpatory statement was actually against interest).

11. People v. Leach, 15 Cal.3d 419, 124 Cal.Rptr. 752, 541 P.2d 296 (1975), cert. denied 424 U.S. 926. Cf. Comment, 66 Calif.L.Rev. 1189, 1213–16 (1978) (courts should require strict scrutiny of whether collateral element of statement is against

interest and impose stringent corroboration requirement).

12. United States v. Casamento, 887 F.2d 1141 (2d Cir.1989), cert. denied 493 U.S. 1081; United States v. Garris, 616 F.2d 626, 630 (2d Cir.1980), cert. denied 447 U.S. 926.

13. See, e.g., Donovan v. Crisostomo, 689 F.2d 869 (9th Cir.1982) (statement by alien workers to labor department investigator that they did not work overtime not against their interest since they may have felt it was in their interest to avoid the wrath of their employer, which could result in immediate deportation).

14. See Humes v. O'Bryan & Washington, 74 Ala. 64 (1883) (in suit on partnership debt, declaration made when business was insolvent that another individual was not a partner was a declaration against interest, although otherwise if business had been solvent).

15. 11 Cl. & F. 85, 8 Eng.Rep. 1034 (1844).

daughter,[16] or to a friend and cellmate,[17] or "in the course of a conversation with friends over cards," [18] has not ruled out admissibility.[19] The always-existent possibility of disclosure appears to be enough. In fact, the existence of a friendly relationship is on occasion mentioned as a factor supporting admissibility.[20]

The factual setting in which the statement is made is given particular importance in cases of statements against penal interest inculpating the accused, since admissibility must be measured against standards fixed by the Confrontation Clause of the Sixth Amendment, as well as by the rule of evidence. Particular significance is attached to the fact that the declarant was at the time in the custody of law enforcement authorities, if such was the case. While courts generally do not accord conclusive effect to the fact of custody, great weight is attributed to it.[21] Most courts have imposed an additional factual safeguard upon the use of statements inculpating an accused person under the Confrontation

16. United States v. Goins, 593 F.2d 88 (8th Cir.1979), cert. denied 444 U.S. 827.

17. United States v. Bagley, 537 F.2d 162 (5th Cir.1976), cert. denied 429 U.S. 1075.

18. United States v. Barrett, 539 F.2d 244 (1st Cir.1976).

19. United States v. Lang, 589 F.2d 92 (2d Cir.1978) (court finds no motive to lie to apparent confederate in crime and no requirement under rule that statement would subject him to immediate criminal prosecution); United States v. Harrell, 788 F.2d 1524 (11th Cir.1986) (secret tape recording of conversation admissible since no requirement that declarants must know they are speaking with persons who could cause their prosecution).

20. United States v. Katsougrakis, 715 F.2d 769 (2d Cir.1983), cert. denied 464 U.S. 1040 (statements made as declarant approaching death to friend confirmed reliability); United States v. Brainard, 690 F.2d 1117 (4th Cir.1982) (fact that statement made to secretary, which declarant had no reason to believe would reveal, added to trustworthiness); United States v. Badalamenti, 626 F.Supp. 658 (S.D.N.Y.1986) (fact that statements were made to organized crime figures with code of silence makes statements more trustworthy).

21. United States v. Garris, 616 F.2d 626 (2d Cir.1980), cert. denied 447 U.S. 926; United States v. Boyce, 849 F.2d 833 (3d Cir.1988); United States v. Riley, 657 F.2d 1377 (8th Cir.1981), cert. denied 459 U.S. 1111.

While unpredictability remains, some factual patterns emerge regarding the circumstances under which statements that are otherwise against interest will be admissible against third parties implicated by those statements. Where the defendant is in custody when making the statement and reaches a plea agreement, the statement is excluded. *Boyce*, supra; United States v. Sarmiento–Perez, 633 F.2d 1092 (5th Cir. 1981), cert. denied 459 U.S. 834. Cf. United States v. Riley, supra, 657 F.2d at 1384 (statement excluded where declarant, although not formally charged or explicitly engaging in plea bargaining was told that charge against her could jeopardize custody of her child).

Where, on the other hand, the declarant is not in custody and is not speaking to a person known to be a law enforcement agent, statements are generally admitted. United States v. Fields, 871 F.2d 188 (1st Cir.1989), cert. denied 493 U.S. 955; United States v. Briscoe, 742 F.2d 842 (5th Cir.1984); United States v. Holland, 880 F.2d 1091 (9th Cir.1989); United States v. Harrell, 788 F.2d 1524 (11th Cir.1986).

Likewise, even though the declarant is in custody, statements may be admitted where no plea occurs and where other factors suggest the statement was not made out of self-interest. United States v. Garcia, 897 F.2d 1413 (7th Cir.1990) (no indication of any effort to curry favor, no plea agreement entered, and statements made after waiver of *Miranda* rights); *Garris*, supra, 616 F.2d at 631–632 (statements inculpating brother as well as declarant, no indication of effort to curry favor, and no plea agreement).

Clause by requiring that they be corroborated.[22] The effect is to read into Federal Evidence Rule 804(b)(3) with regard to inculpatory statements a similar requirement of corroboration that is expressly stated with regard to exculpatory statements.[23]

(d) Motive: Actual state of mind of declarant. In strictest logic, attention in cases of declarations against interest, as with other hearsay exceptions, should focus on the actual state of mind produced in the declarant by the supposed truth-inducing circumstances, and a "reasonable-person" standard would be irrelevant. That, of course, is not the case: the usual standard is that found in Federal Evidence Rule 804(b)(3), "that a reasonable person in the declarant's position would not have made the statement unless believing it to be true." Difficulties of proof, probabilities, and the unavailability of the declarant all favor the accepted standard. It can scarcely be doubted, however, that statements of declarant disclosing his or her ostensible actual mental

---

22. See, e.g., United States v. Katsougrakis, 715 F.2d 769 (2d Cir.1983), cert. denied 464 U.S. 1040; United States v. Boyce, 849 F.2d 833 (3d Cir.1988); United States v. Garcia, 897 F.2d 1413 (7th Cir.1990). See generally Comment, 83 Colum.L.Rev. 159 (1983).

In United States v. Candoli, 870 F.2d 496 (9th Cir.1989), while not determining whether it agrees that corroboration is required for inculpatory statements, the Ninth Circuit noted that those circuits which had imposed the requirement had done so in order to satisfy the Confrontation Clause.

23. It is under this corroboration requirement that a number of courts have imposed more exacting requirements for third party statements used to inculpate the accused. United States v. Alvarez, 584 F.2d 694 (5th Cir.1978) (while statement is sufficiently incriminating to declarant's interest to pass liberal standard of rule, its weakness on this traditional guarantee of reliability helps exclude it under trustworthiness analysis of Confrontation Clause). See also United States v. Boyce, 849 F.2d 833 (3d Cir.1988) (statement excluded under trustworthiness analysis principally because made in police custody); United States v. Sarmiento–Perez, 633 F.2d 1092 (5th Cir.1981), cert. denied 459 U.S. 834 (expansive reading of against interest standard when applied to exculpatory statements may not be well suited to statement incriminating defendant because of requirements of Confrontation Clause).

What corroboration means has been somewhat uncertain. See United States v. Salvador, 820 F.2d 558 (2d Cir.1987), cert. denied 484 U.S. 966 (expressing uncertainty whether corroboration requirement properly focuses on declarant's reliability when the statement was made or corroborating the truth of the statement by other evidence). However, whether corroboration that the declaration was made is required for exculpatory statements, see supra § 318 note 10, the courts have not suggested such a requirement for corroboration under the commands of the Confrontation Clause for inculpatory statements. See, e.g., United States v. Casamento, 887 F.2d 1141, 1170 (2d Cir.1989), cert. denied 493 U.S. 1081. Some courts have looked to other evidence of guilt in the case to supply corroboration. See, e.g., United States v. Harrell, 788 F.2d 1524, 1527 (11th Cir. 1986). However, such evidence would appear no longer to constitute proper corroboration. In Idaho v. Wright, 110 S.Ct. 3139, 3148–3150 (1990), the Supreme Court held that in providing the particularized guarantees of trustworthiness required for admission of statements under the state's catchall exception, other evidence in the case supporting guilt could not be considered. Instead only the surrounding circumstances of the statement could be examined. Similarly here, corroboration is required because statements offered to inculpate the defendant do not constitute a firmly rooted hearsay exception. See State v. Parris, 98 Wash.2d 140, 654 P.2d 77 (1982) (statements inculpating both declarant and accused not firmly rooted but must be supported by particularized guarantees of trustworthiness to be admissible under Confrontation Clause). Accordingly, only the circumstances under which the statement was made, such as its degree of adversity to the declarant's interest and whether made in police custody, should be considered.

state would be received and would control in an appropriate case.[24]

The exception has often been stated as requiring that there have been no motive to falsify.[25] This is too sweeping, and the limitation can probably best be understood merely as a qualification that even though a statement must be against interest in one respect, if it appears that declarant had some motive, whether of self-interest or otherwise, which was likely to lead to misrepresentation of the facts, the statement should be excluded.[26]

§ 320. Unavailability of the Declarant

The Federal Rule and the vast majority of the states require unavailability.[1] While the requirement of unavailability followed its own course of development at common law with respect to declarations against interest, as was the case with other hearsay exceptions requiring unavailability of the declarant, the pattern is now largely standardized. See supra section 253 for discussion in detail of what satisfies the requirement.

24. State v. Woodman, 125 N.H. 381, 480 A.2d 169 (1984) (the inclusion of an objective test does not preclude courts from considering knowledge of the declarant's state of mind, and accordingly statement excluded where declarant stated that because incarcerated in a federal prison he was unafraid of state prosecution); 4 Weinstein & Berger, Weinstein's Evidence ¶ 804(b)(3)[02], at 130–32 (1990).

25. German Ins. Co. v. Bartlett, 188 Ill. 165, 58 N.E. 1075 (1900); Halvorsen v. Moon & Kerr Lumber Co., 87 Minn. 18, 91 N.W. 28 (1902); Hill v. Robinson, 592 S.W.2d 376 (Tex.Civ.App.1979, error refused n.r.e.).

26. United States v. Tovar, 687 F.2d 1210 (8th Cir.1982) (statement excluded where made to defendant's attorney after declarant plead guilty, court concluding that declarant knew that he was going to prison and may have wanted to help friend for whom he felt responsible); United States v. Atkins, 618 F.2d 366 (5th Cir. 1980) (statements made after sentencing and in aid of friend excluded because not necessarily against penal interest and may have been motivated by friendship); Demasi v. Whitney Trust & Sav. Bank, 176 So. 703 (La.App.1937) (affidavit of depositor that previous withdrawals had been with her consent excluded because it appeared that affidavit was presented by bank for her signature as prerequisite for withdrawing balance of account).

§ 320

1. Texas, however, has placed this exception under its Rule 803 where unavailability is not required. See Tex.R.Civ.Evid. 803(24) & Tex.R.Crim.Evid. 803(24). This position was advocated by a number of commentators and early formulations of model rules of evidence. 20 Hous.L.Rev. 1, 531 n. 248 (1983).

Chapter 34

VARIOUS OTHER EXCEPTIONS AND THE FUTURE OF THE RULES ABOUT HEARSAY

Table of Sections

§ 321 Learned Writings, Industry Standards, and Commercial Publications [1]

When offered to prove the truth of matters asserted in them, learned writings, such as treatises, books, and articles regarding specialized areas of knowledge, are clearly hearsay. Nevertheless, Wigmore ar-

---

§ 321

1. See generally 6 Wigmore, Evidence §§ 1690–1708 (Chadbourn rev. 1976); Hoffman & Hoffman, Use of Standards in Products Liability Litigation, 30 Drake L.Rev. 283 (1980–81); Goldman, The Use of Learned Treatises in Canadian and United States Litigation, 24 U.Toronto L.J. 423 (1974); Notes, 71 Nw.U.L.Rev. 678 (1976), 27 S.C.L.Rev. 766 (1976); 29 Am.Jur.2d Evidence §§ 888–893; C.J.S. Evidence §§ 717–722; Annot., 17 A.L.R.3d 993, 84 A.L.R.2d 1338, 58 A.L.R.3d 148; 64 A.L.R.Fed. 971; Dec.Dig. Evidence ⟨key⟩360–365, 381.

gued strongly for an exception for such material.[2] According to his view, permitting such sources to be proved directly would not be as great a change as might at first be supposed because much of the testimony of experts consists of information they have obtained from such sources. Also, admitting the sources would greatly improve the quality of information presented to trial courts in litigated cases. Wigmore concluded that there were sufficient assurances of trustworthiness to justify equating a learned treatise with the live testimony of an expert. First, authors of treatises have no bias in any particular case. Second, they are acutely aware that their material will be read and evaluated by others in their field, and accordingly there is strong pressure to be accurate.[3]

Virtually all courts permit some use of learned materials in the cross-examination of an expert witness.[4] Historically, several patterns developed. Most courts permitted use where the expert relied upon the specific material in forming the opinion to which he or she testified during direct examination.[5] Some of these courts extended the rule to situations in which the witness admitted to having relied upon some general authorities although not the particular impeaching material.[6] Other courts required only that the witness acknowledge that the material offered for impeachment was a recognized authority in the field and, on that basis, permitted use of the material in spite of the fact that the witness may not have personally relied upon it.[7] Finally, some courts permitted use of such material to impeach without regard to whether the witness relied upon or acknowledged the authority of the source if either the cross-examiner established, or the court judicially noticed, the general authority of the material.[8]

Traditionally, the material used to impeach was not admissible as substantive evidence received for its truth. Instead, its only impact was upon the witness' competency or the accuracy of the opinions rendered. Under the common law development of the practice, most courts were unwilling to adopt a broad exception to the hearsay rule for treatises and other professional literature.[9] Wigmore suggested a num-

---

2. 6 Wigmore, Evidence §§ 1690–1692 (Chadbourn rev. 1976).

3. Id.

Of course, the normal assumptions may not apply, such as the existence of bias by the author. See O'Brien v. Angley, 63 Ohio St.2d 159, 407 N.E.2d 490 (1980) (editorial in medical journal attacking practice of "defensive medicine" by following manufacturer's recommendations erroneously admitted in medical malpractice action claiming negligence in failing to follow recommendations of manufacturer of drug). Cf. Schneider v. Revici, 817 F.2d 987 (2d Cir.1987) (proper to exclude book written by defendant in medical malpractice case as learned treatise on basis of balance of prejudice versus probativity).

4. Annot., 60 A.L.R.2d 77.

5. Id. at 81–87.

6. Id. at 87–93.

7. Id. at 94–98.

8. Darling v. Charleston Community Memorial Hosp., 33 Ill.2d 326, 211 N.E.2d 253 (1965), cert. denied 383 U.S. 946; Thornton v. CAMC, Etc., 172 W.Va. 360, 305 S.E.2d 316, 321–322 (1983); Annot., 60 A.L.R.2d 77, 98–104.

9. Annot., 17 A.L.R.3d 993, 84 A.L.R.2d 1338.

There were some notable exceptions, however. See City of Dothan v. Hardy, 237 Ala. 603, 188 So. 264 (1939); Lewandowski v. Preferred Risk Mut. Ins. Co., 33 Wis.2d

ber of arguments in support of this position, although he concluded that none of them justified the refusal to recognize the exception: (a) professional skill and knowledge shift rapidly, so printed material is likely to be out of date; (b) a trier of fact is likely to be confused by being exposed to material designed for the professionally-trained reader; (c) the opportunity to take sections of material out of context creates a danger of unfair use; (d) most matters of expertise are really matters of skill rather than academic knowledge of the sort put in writing and therefore personally-appearing witnesses are likely to be better sources of evidence than written material. The only arguably meritorious objection according to Wigmore is the basic hearsay objection that the author is not available for cross-examination, but he concluded that this concern is outweighed by the need for the evidence and the other assurances of its accuracy.[10]

The Federal Rules addressed these various issues by creating a hearsay exception for "learned treatises."[11] Federal Rule 803(18)[12] provides:

> To the extent called to the attention of an expert witness upon cross-examination or relied upon by the expert witness in direct examination, statements contained in published treatises, periodicals, or pamphlets on a subject of history, medicine, or other science or art, established as a reliable authority by the testimony or admission of the witness or by other expert testimony or by judicial notice. If admitted, the statements may be read into evidence but may not be received as exhibits.

The rule is broadly worded as to subjects—"history, medicine, or other science or art"—and is sufficient to include standards and manuals published by government agencies and industry or professional organizations.[13] The reliability of the publication must be established as provided in the rule, which has the purpose of demonstrating that it

---

69, 146 N.W.2d 505 (1966). Also, statutes in a number of jurisdictions permitted some use of the material. 6 Wigmore, Evidence § 1693, n. 2 (Chadbourn rev. 1976) (listing statutes). Other courts made inroads upon the traditional position by allowing the use of published government agency, professional, and industry standards and manuals in tort cases as tending to prove the standard of care. Mississippi Power & Light Co. v. Johnson, 374 So.2d 772 (Miss.1979) (National Elec. Safety Code in electric shock case); Nordstrom v. White Metal Rolling & Stamping Corp., 75 Wash.2d 629, 453 P.2d 619 (1969) (American Standard Safety Code for Portable Metal Ladders); Annot., 58 A.L.R.3d 148.

10. 6 Wigmore, Evidence § 1690 (Chadbourn rev. 1976). See supra text accompanying note 3 for discussion of basis of trustworthiness.

11. Some jurisdictions continue not to recognize a hearsay exception for such documents. See Jackson v. Rodriquez, 173 Ga.App. 211, 216, 325 S.E.2d 857, 863 (1984) (Deen, concurring); Majdic v. Cincinnati Mach. Co., 370 Pa.Super. 611, 537 A.2d 334 (1988), appeal denied 520 Pa. 594, 552 A.2d 249.

12. Revised Uniform Rule (1986) 803(18) differs only grammatically.

13. McKinnon v. Skil Corp., 638 F.2d 270 (1st Cir.1981) (Underwriters Laboratory standards admissible in case involving injury from circular power saw); Dawson v. Chrysler Corp., 630 F.2d 950 (3d Cir.1980), cert. denied 450 U.S. 959 (automobile crashworthiness report prepared for federal Department of Transportation); Johnson v. William C. Ellis & Sons Iron Works, Inc., 609 F.2d 820 (5th Cir.1980) (American Standard Safety Code for Power Presses).

is viewed as trustworthy by professionals in the field.[14] A significant limitation is that the publication must be called to the attention of an expert on cross-examination or relied upon by the expert in direct examination. This provision is designed to ensure that the materials are used only under the sponsorship of an expert who can assist the fact finder and explain how to apply the materials.[15] This policy is furthered by the prohibition against admission as exhibits, which prevents sending the materials to the jury room.[16]

While Rule 803(18) defines a hearsay exception, its requirements have an impact beyond hearsay concepts, in effect setting the general limits on the use of such documents to impeach.[17] At the same time the rule has this impact beyond the hearsay area, satisfying its requirements does not automatically guarantee admissibility. Documents that meet the terms of the rule are still excluded if their probative value is outweighed by their prejudicial impact or potential to confuse or mislead.[18]

Courts have developed a somewhat related hearsay exception that

14. Schneider v. Revici, 817 F.2d 987, 991 (2d Cir.1987) (failure to lay foundation regarding authoritativeness requires exclusion because court given no basis for viewing it as trustworthy); Tart v. McGann, 697 F.2d 75, 78 (2d Cir.1982) (article must be shown to be authoritative).

The material must be published in a form that subjects it to widespread collegial scrutiny. United States v. Jones, 712 F.2d 115 (5th Cir.1983) (prior inconsistent testimony by expert witness did not qualify because absence of publication eliminated this element of trustworthiness). The foundation must demonstrate that the specific document is authoritative as opposed to a broadscale qualification of a periodical as highly regarded. Meschino v. North Am. Drager, Inc., 841 F.2d 429, 434 (1st Cir.1988). However, the method for establishing the foundation is flexible. Burgess v. Premier Corp., 727 F.2d 826 (9th Cir. 1984) (author preeminent industry expert and books required reading for salesmen and recommended reading for investors in cattle investment business). This appears particularly true when established on cross-examination of the adversary's expert. Allen v. Safeco Ins. Co. of America, 782 F.2d 1517, 1519 (11th Cir.1986) (foundation sufficient where adversary's expert acknowledged that periodical was used by him in remaining current and author of the article was member academic department enjoying a good reputation).

15. Dartez v. Fibreboard Corp., 765 F.2d 456 (5th Cir.1985) (purpose of rule's restriction is to avoid the possibility that the jury will misunderstand and misapply the technical language of the article if allowed to use it directly).

This restriction also helps ensure that the jurors will not be unduly impressed by the material. 4 Weinstein & Berger, Weinstein's Evidence ¶ 803(18)[02], at 330 (1990).

16. Adv.Comm.Note,   Fed.R.Evid. 803(18), 56 F.R.D. 183, 315; Dartez v. Fibreboard Corp., 765 F.2d 456 (5th Cir.1985) (court erred in sending articles to jury); Rossell v. Volkswagen of America, 147 Ariz. 160, 709 P.2d 517 (1985), cert. denied 476 U.S. 1108 (rule's purpose not violated where material sent to jury was summary of expert's position and not subject to misuse).

17. See Dawsey v. Olin Corp., 782 F.2d 1254 (5th Cir.1986) (since documents not established as reliable authority, court correctly prohibited cross-examination with them); Davies v. State, 286 Ark. 9, 688 S.W.2d 738 (1985) (court erred in permitting counsel to read from treatise on cross-examination where not established as reliable).

18. See Schneider v. Revici, 817 F.2d 987 (2d Cir.1987) (proper to exclude book written by defendant in medical malpractice case on basis of balance of prejudice versus probativity); Ellis v. International Playtex, Inc., 745 F.2d 292 (4th Cir.1984) (proper for trial court to exclude treatise because of its potential to confuse or invite unwarranted speculation where insufficient correspondence between facts of case and those discussed in treatise).

includes publications such as reports of market prices,[19] professional directories,[20] city and telephone directories,[21] and mortality and annuity tables used by life insurance companies.[22] The justification for this exception is that the motivation for accuracy is high, and public acceptance depends upon reliability.

Federal Rule 803(17)[23] defines a hearsay exception for such publications, covering "market quotations, tabulations, lists, directories, or other published compilations, generally used and relied upon by the public or by persons in particular occupations." While the precise definition of this exception is somewhat difficult, other than by example,[24] some of its basic characteristics are clear. The list must be published in written form and circulated for use by others; it must be relied upon by the general public or by persons in a particular occupation; and it must pertain to relatively straightforward objective facts.[25]

§ 322. Statements and Reputation as to Pedigree and Family History, Land Boundaries, and General History

A. Statements and Reputation Concerning Pedigree and Family History[1]

One of the oldest exceptions to the hearsay rule encompasses statements concerning family history, such as the date and place of birth and death of members of the family and facts about marriage, descent, and relationship.[2] Under the traditional rule, declarations of the

---

19. Virginia v. West Virginia, 238 U.S. 202 (1915); U.C.C. § 2–724 (1987); 6 Wigmore, Evidence § 1704 (Chadbourn rev. 1976).

20. Louisville & Nashville R. Co. v. Kice, 109 Ky. 786, 60 S.W. 705 (1901); Annot., 7 A.L.R.4th 639.

21. People v. Cowper, 145 Ill.App.3d 1074, 99 Ill.Dec. 868, 496 N.E.2d 729 (1986), appeal denied 113 Ill.2d 578, 106 Ill.Dec. 50, 505 N.E.2d 356; State ex rel. Keefe v. McInerney, 63 Wyo. 280, 182 P.2d 28 (1947).

22. Levar v. Elkins, 604 P.2d 602 (Alaska 1980) (lack of normal health does not require exclusion); Henderson v. Harness, 184 Ill. 520, 56 N.E. 786 (1900) (to show expectancy in valuing life estate).

23. Revised Uniform Rule (1986) 803(17) is identical.

24. For examples of items falling within this exception, see United States v. Mount, 896 F.2d 612 (1st Cir.1990) (book used by manuscript dealers to locate original historical documents admissible under this exception); United States v. Grossman, 614 F.2d 295 (1st Cir.1980) (company catalog admissible under this exception to prove value of stolen property and identity of items).

25. See White Industries, Inc. v. Cessna Aircraft Co., 611 F.Supp. 1049 (W.D.Mo. 1985) ("10–K" forms filed with SEC not within the exception applying these factors); 4 Weinstein & Berger, Weinstein's Evidence ¶ 803(17)[01], at 316–17 (1990); 6 Wigmore, Evidence § 1704, at 38 (Chadbourn rev. 1976). For somewhat conflicting analysis of whether credit reports, safety codes, and opinion polls should be included within this exception, compare 4 Louisell & Mueller, Federal Evidence § 465, at 832–38 (1980) with 4 Weinstein & Berger, supra ¶ 803(17)[01], at 317–21.

§ 322

1. See generally 5 Wigmore, Evidence §§ 1480–1503, 1602–1606 (Chadbourn rev. 1974); Hale, Proof of Facts of Family History, 2 Hastings L.J. 1 (1950); Notes, 5 Ark.L.Rev. 58 (1950–51), 32 Iowa L.Rev. 779 (1947); 29 Am.Jur.2d Evidence §§ 508–522; C.J.S. Evidence §§ 226–231; Annots., 15 A.L.R.2d 1412, 29 A.L.R. 372; Dec.Dig.Evidence ⟨key⟩285–297.

2. "Family history" is narrowly construed to include only such matters as are enumerated in the text. Sargent v. Coolidge, 399 A.2d 1333, 1345 (Me.1979) (what property mother intended to convey by

person whose family situation is at issue are admissible,[3] as are declarations by other members of the family.[4] Under a liberal view adopted by some courts, declarations by nonfamily members with a close relationship to the family are also admitted.[5] These statements were admissible, however, only upon a showing that the declarant is unavailable,[6] that the statement was made before the origin of the controversy giving rise to the litigation in which the statement is offered (i.e., *ante litem motam*),[7] and that there was no apparent motive for the declarant to misrepresent the facts.[8]

Under the strict traditional view, the relationship of declarant to the family had to be proved by independent evidence, but this requirement did not apply where declarant's own family relationships were the subject of the hearsay statement.[9] Firsthand knowledge by declarant of the facts of birth, death, kinship, or the like was not required.[10] The general difficulty of obtaining other evidence of family matters, reflected in the unavailability requirement, furnished impetus for the hearsay exception. Reliability was assured by the probability that, in the absence of any motive for lying, discussions with relatives (and others intimately associated) regarding family members would be accu-

deed not family history). In Strickland v. Humble Oil & Refining Co., 140 F.2d 83 (5th Cir.1944), cert. denied 323 U.S. 712, the court admitted statements relating to travels, but they were received for the narrow purpose of identifying the traveler and establishing kinship.

3. Balazinski v. Lebid, 65 N.J.Super. 483, 168 A.2d 209 (App.Div.1961); In re McClain's Estate, 481 Pa. 435, 392 A.2d 1371 (1978).

4. E.g., In re Paternity of Tompkins, 542 N.E.2d 1009 (Ind.App.1989) (statements of child's mother concerning child's true parentage admissible under pedigree exception since mother deceased); Minor Child v. Michigan State Health Com'r, 16 Mich.App. 128, 167 N.W.2d 880 (1969) (mother's statement as to identity of son's father); Brown v. Conway, 598 S.W.2d 549 (Mo.App.1980) (same).

5. For the "liberal" view, see Minor Child v. Michigan State Health Com'r, 16 Mich.App. 128, 167 N.W.2d 880 (1969) (statements of "family and close acquaintances" regarding child's paternity admissible); In re Lewis' Estate, 121 Utah 385, 242 P.2d 565 (1952) (declaration of paternity made by woman who had made arrangements for, and was present at, birth admissible because "the likelihood of her declarations being true are very great" even though she was not related to family whose pedigree was questioned).

See 5 Wigmore, Evidence § 1487 (Chadbourn rev. 1974) (criticizing the require-

ment of family membership); Annot., 15 A.L.R.2d 1412. Because a nonfamily member often offers to testify not simply as to the conclusory fact but rather to the community or neighborhood reputation regarding that fact, the issue may be intertwined with the admissibility of reputation.

6. In re Stone's Estate, 78 Idaho 632, 308 P.2d 597 (1957); Lopez v. Texas Dept. of Human Resources, 631 S.W.2d 251 (Tex. App.1982).

7. This requirement means that the statement must have been made not only prior to the litigation, but also prior to the development of the controversy that subsequently ended in litigation. Hartford Nat. Bank & Trust Co. v. Prince, 28 Conn.Sup. 348, 261 A.2d 287 (1968); In re Cunha's Estate, 49 Hawaii 273, 414 P.2d 925 (1966); 5 Wigmore, Evidence § 1483 (Chadbourn rev. 1974).

8. Hartford Nat. Bank & Trust v. Prince, 28 Conn.Sup. 348, 261 A.2d 287 (1968) (denials of paternity inadmissible because they were made at a time when the declarant was interested in another woman and therefore had motive to misrepresent his relationship to his estranged wife by denying sexual relations with her).

9. In re McClain's Estate, 481 Pa. 435, 392 A.2d 1371 (1978) (as the court observes, declarant is certainly a member of his own family).

10. See generally 5 Wigmore, Evidence § 1486 (Chadbourn rev. 1974).

rate.[11]

Federal Rule of Evidence 804(b)(4), continuing the requirement of unavailability of the declarant,[12] provides a hearsay exception for statements of personal or family history:

> (A) A statement concerning the declarant's own birth, adoption, marriage, divorce, legitimacy, relationship by blood, adoption, or marriage, ancestry, or other similar fact of personal or family history, even though declarant had no means of acquiring personal knowledge of the matter stated; or (B) a statement concerning the foregoing matters, and death also, of another person, if the declarant was related to the other by blood, adoption, or marriage or was so intimately associated with the other's family as to be likely to have accurate information concerning the matter declared.[13]

The rule follows the liberal view in allowing statements by intimate associates of the family. It eliminates the traditional requirements that the statement have been made *ante litem motam*[14] and without motive to misrepresent, leaving these aspects to be treated as questions of weight,[15] or possibly excluded under Rule 403 in extreme cases.[16] The narrow view of what is included in family history is continued.[17]

The traditional hearsay exception went beyond the statements described above and allowed the use of contemporary records of family history, such as entries in a family Bible[18] or on a tombstone,[19] even though the author may not be identifiable. Federal Rule 803(13)[20] follows this pattern in providing a hearsay exception, without regard to availability of the declarant, for the following:

> Statements of fact concerning personal or family history contained in family Bibles, genealogies, charts, engravings on rings, inscriptions on family portraits, engravings on urns, crypts, or tombstones, or the like.

Matters of family history traditionally have also been provable by

---

11. 5 Wigmore, Evidence § 1482 (Chadbourn rev. 1974).

12. Moore v. Goode, 375 S.E.2d 549, 564 (W.Va.1988) (statements ruled inadmissible under state rule similar to federal rule on basis that witnesses were available). As to unavailability, see generally supra § 253.

13. Revised Uniform Rule (1986) 804(b)(4) differs insignificantly.

14. See Adv.Comm.Note, Fed.Rule Evid. 804(b)(5), 56 F.R.D. 183, 328. See also supra note 7.

15. See Adv.Comm.Note, Fed.Rule Evid. 804(b)(5), 56 F.R.D. 183, 328.

16. See supra § 185. Cf. United States v. Medina–Gasca, 739 F.2d 1451 (9th Cir. 1984) (in criminal prosecution for transportation of aliens, court concludes that trial court should not have admitted under this exception statement that went to the heart

of the case as to which the declarant would necessarily have no personal knowledge).

17. See supra text accompanying note 2. Cf. United States v. Carvalho, 742 F.2d 146 (4th Cir.1984) (statement regarding declarant's motive for marrying defendant inadmissible because circumstances of trustworthiness is diminished regarding such controversial matter as compared with other statements within rule).

18. Annot., 29 A.L.R. 372. For use of family Bibles, as well as other methods, to prove family or personal history in Social Security matters, see 20 C.F.R. §§ 404.715–404.728 (1990).

19. Conn v. Boylan, 224 N.Y.S.2d 823 (Sup.1962).

20. Revised Uniform Rule (1986) 803(13) is identical.

reputation in the family,[21] or, under some decisions, in the community.[22] The tradition is continued in Federal Rule 803(19),[23] by a hearsay exception for the following:

> Reputation among members of a person's family by blood, adoption, or marriage, or among a person's associates, or in the community, concerning a person's birth, adoption, marriage, divorce, death, legitimacy, relationship by blood, adoption, or marriage, ancestry, or other similar fact of his personal or family history.

Also continuing a traditional exception is the admissibility of judgments as proof of family history under Federal Rule 803(23): [24]

> Judgments as proof of matters of personal family or general history, or boundaries, essential to the judgment, if the same would be provable by evidence of reputation.[25]

B. Reputation Regarding Land Boundaries and General History [26]

When the location of boundaries of land is at issue, reputation is admitted to prove that location.[27] Traditionally, the reputation not only had to antedate the beginning of the present controversy, but also it had to be "ancient," i.e., to extend beyond a generation.[28] Some recent cases suggest that the requirement is only that the monuments or markers of the original survey must have disappeared.[29] Federal

---

21. Kelly's Heirs v. McGuire, 15 Ark. 555 (1855); Geisler v. Geisler, 160 Minn. 463, 200 N.W. 742 (1924).

22. In re Estate of Wulf, 242 Iowa 1012, 48 N.W.2d 890 (1951) ("common talk or general report" that X was Y's father, admissible). Wigmore states that community reputation is always admissible to prove that persons living together were married. 5 Wigmore, Evidence § 1602 (Chadbourn rev. 1974). See also Daniels v. Johnson, 216 Ark. 374, 226 S.W.2d 571 (1950).

23. Revised Uniform Rule (1986) 803(19) is the same except for stylistic differences.

24. Revised Uniform Rule (1986) 803(23) differs minutely in wording.

25. See Adv.Comm.Note, Fed.R.Evid. 803(23), 56 F.R.D. 183, 315 for background.

26. See generally 5 Wigmore, Evidence §§ 1580–1626 (Chadbourn rev. 1974); 29 Am.Jur.2d Evidence §§ 503–507; C.J.S. Evidence §§ 422–453; Dec.Dig.Evidence ⟜322–324.

27. Eagan v. Colwell, 86 Idaho 525, 388 P.2d 999 (1964); Burrow v. Brown, 190 So.2d 855 (Miss.1966); Kardell v. Crouch, 326 S.W.2d 869 (Tex.Civ.App.1959, writ refused n.r.e.). See generally 5 Wigmore, Evidence §§ 1582–1595 (Chadbourn rev. 1974); 12 Am.Jur.2d Boundaries §§ 106–

110; C.J.S. Evidence § 234(b); Dec.Dig.Boundaries ⟜35(2).

In England the use of the evidence is limited to public boundaries or other public rights. Nicholls v. Parker, 104 Eng. Rep. 629 (K.B.1805). But in this country, except in a few states, it extends also to private boundaries. Hail v. Haynes, 312 Ky. 357, 227 S.W.2d 918 (1950); Hemphill v. Hemphill, 138 N.C. 504, 51 S.E. 42 (1905). See 5 Wigmore, Evidence § 1587 (Chadbourn rev. 1974). The exception has been expanded on occasion beyond evidence of reputation and admitted hearsay statements of specific individuals. Kay Corp. v. Anderson, 72 Wash.2d 879, 436 P.2d 459 (1967) (statement of out-of-court declarant as to location of boundary admitted under exception).

28. 5 Wigmore, Evidence § 1582 (Chadbourn rev. 1974).

29. Johnstone v. Nause, 233 Miss. 584, 102 So.2d 889 (1958) (where monuments of a survey have disappeared, evidence of common reputation is admissible as to location of boundaries and corners); Kardell v. Crouch, 326 S.W.2d 869 (Tex.Civ.App. 1959, writ refused n.r.e.) (admissible after destruction of markers and a "long lapse of time"); Blain v. Woods, 145 W.Va. 297, 115 S.E.2d 88 (1960) (where monuments of survey not lost, proper to exclude testimony of grantor's children as to boundary).

Rule 803(20), set forth below, dispenses completely with a requirement that the reputation be ancient or that the passage of time have rendered other evidence of the boundaries unavailable.

Reputation is also admissible to prove a variety of facts which can best be described as matters of general history.[30] Wigmore suggested that the matter must be ancient "or one as to which it would be unlikely that living witnesses could be obtained."[31] Federal Rule 803(20) does not impose that requirement, although by use of the term "history" some requirement of substantial age is imposed. In addition, the matter must be one of general interest, so that it can accurately be said that there is a high probability that the matter underwent general scrutiny as the community reputation was formed.[32] Thus when the navigable nature of a certain river was at issue, newspaper accounts and histories describing the use made of it during the nineteenth century were admissible to prove its general reputation for navigability at that time.[33]

Federal Rule 803(20)[34] provides a hearsay exception consistent with the foregoing observations for proof by reputation evidence of boundaries and matters of general history:

> Reputation in a community, arising before the controversy, as to boundaries of or customs affecting lands in the community, and reputation as to events of general history important to the community or State or nation in which located.

In addition to these well-developed exceptions, reputation evidence is sometimes admitted under statute or local law to prove a variety of other miscellaneous matters,[35] such as ownership of property,[36] finan-

---

30. See generally 5 Wigmore, Evidence §§ 1597–1599 (Chadbourn rev. 1974); 29 Am.Jur.2d Evidence §§ 506–507, 887; C.J.S. Evidence §§ 233–237; Annot., 58 A.L.R.2d 615. See also Morris v. Harmer's Heirs' Lessee, 32 U.S. (7 Pet.) 554, 558 (1833) ("Historical facts of general and public notoriety may indeed be proved by reputation, and that reputation may be established by historical works of known character and accuracy.").

The kinship to judicial notice is apparent. See infra § 330.

31. 5 Wigmore, Evidence § 1597 (Chadbourn rev. 1974).

32. Wigmore, Evidence § 1598, at 564 (Chadbourn rev. 1974). See Ute Indian Tribe v. State of Utah, 521 F.Supp. 1072 (D.Utah 1981), affirmed in part, reversed in part on other grounds 716 F.2d 1298 (10th Cir.) (reputation of reservation's jurisdictional boundary among non-Indian population before controversy arose did not fall within this exception because not likely to have undergone community scrutiny);

Kent County Rd. Com'n v. Hunting, 170 Mich.App. 222, 428 N.W.2d 353 (1988) (statements by two individuals to witness that trees had been planted to celebrate American centennial did not meet the requirement of general community interest); Annot., 58 A.L.R.2d 615, 619–626.

33. Montana Power Co. v. Federal Power Com'n, 185 F.2d 491 (D.C.Cir.1950), cert. denied 340 U.S. 947; Darlington County v. Perkins, 269 S.C. 572, 239 S.E.2d 69 (1977) (in action to establish existence of public right of way, old diaries and newspapers to show reputation for use admissible).

34. Revised Uniform Rule (1986) 803(20) is identical in substance.

35. See 5 Wigmore, Evidence §§ 1620–1626 (Chadbourn rev. 1974).

36. Chicago & Eastern Illinois R. Co. v. Schmitz, 211 Ill. 446, 71 N.E. 1050 (1904) (reputation that particular railway owned tracks sufficient evidence of ownership in personal injury action). See 5 Wigmore, Evidence § 1626(4) (Chadbourn rev. 1974).

cial standing,[37] and maintenance of a house as an establishment for liquor-selling or prostitution.[38]

§ 323. Recitals in Ancient Writings and Documents Affecting an Interest in Property [1]

As observed in a preceding section,[2] a writing has usually been regarded as sufficiently authenticated if the offering party proves that it is at least thirty years old,[3] the trial judge finds that it is unsuspicious in appearance, and the party proves that it was produced from a place of custody natural for such a writing. This "ancient documents" rule, however, traditionally has related only to authentication.[4] Nevertheless, American courts sometimes recognized a hearsay exception for statements in a writing which met these requirements.[5] Thus, what originated as an aspect of authentication also became, in some jurisdictions, an exception to the hearsay rule.

The primary stimulus for such a hearsay exception is found in the same reasons which gave rise to the special authentication rule: necessity. After passage of a long period of time, witnesses are unlikely to be available or, if available, to recall reliably the events at issue.[6] As to assurances of trustworthiness, the mere age of the writing, it may be contended, offers little assurance of truth; it is unlikely that lying was less common twenty or thirty years ago.

37. See Lucas v. Swan, 67 F.2d 106 (4th Cir.1933) (reputation of endorsers for insolvency); but see Coleman v. Lewis, 183 Mass. 485, 67 N.E. 603 (1903). See generally 5 Wigmore, Evidence § 1623 (Chadbourn rev. 1974).

38. Elder v. Stark, 200 Ga. 452, 37 S.E.2d 598 (1946) (reputation as illegal "road house"); State v. Mauch, 236 Iowa 217, 17 N.W.2d 536 (1945) (reputation of premises and defendant as to keeping house of ill fame); Commonwealth v. United Food Corp., 374 Mass. 765, 374 N.E.2d 1331 (1978). See 5 Wigmore, Evidence § 1620 (Chadbourn rev. 1974); Dec.Dig.Disorderly House ⊜16.

§ 323

1. See generally Wickes, Ancient Documents and Hearsay, 8 Tex.L.Rev. 451 (1930); Notes, 46 Iowa L.Rev. 448 (1961), 83 U.Pa.L.Rev. 247 (1934), 33 Yale L.J. 412 (1924), 26 Harv.L.Rev. 544 (1913); 29 Am. Jur.2d Evidence §§ 856, 861–865; C.J.S. Evidence §§ 743–752; Annots., 46 A.L.R.2d 1318, 6 A.L.R. 1437, 29 A.L.R. 630; Dec.Dig.Evidence ⊜372.

2. See supra § 223.

3. Federal and Revised Uniform (1986) Rule 901(b)(8) reduce the period to twenty years.

4. See, e.g., Town of Ninety Six v. Southern Ry. Co., 267 F.2d 579, 583 (4th Cir.1959) (ancient documents doctrine pertains to authentication not admissibility).

5. Kirkpatrick v. Tapo Oil Co., 144 Cal. App.2d 404, 301 P.2d 274 (1956); State Department of Roads v. Parks, 185 Neb. 794, 178 N.W.2d 788 (1970); Tillman v. Lincoln Warehouse Corp., 72 A.D.2d 40, 423 N.Y.S.2d 151 (1979); Muehrcke v. Behrens, 43 Wis.2d 1, 169 N.W.2d 86 (1969); Wickes, Ancient Documents and Hearsay, 8 Tex.L.Rev. 451 (1930).

6. Compton v. Davis Oil Co., 607 F.Supp. 1221, 1228–1229 (D.Wyo.1985) (such statements admissible due to necessity as well as comparative reliability of that evidence to other available forms); 4 Louisell & Mueller, Federal Evidence § 464, at 822 (1980).

Advocates of the exception [7] argue, however, that sufficient assurances of reliability exist. First, the dangers of mistransmission are minimized since the rule applies only to written statements. Second, the age requirement virtually assures that the assertion will have been made long before the beginning of the present controversy. Consequently, it is unlikely that the declarant had a motive to falsify, and, in any case, the statements are almost certainly uninfluenced by partisanship.[8] Finally, some additional assurance of reliability is provided by insistence, insofar as practicable, that the usual qualifications for witnesses and out-of-court declarants be met. As a result, the writing is inadmissible if the declarant lacked the opportunity for firsthand observation of the facts asserted.[9]

Well before the drafting of the Federal Rules, a number of courts accepted a hearsay exception for recitals in an ancient deed. Thus, recitals of the contents and execution of an earlier instrument, of heirship, and of consideration are nearly everywhere received to prove those facts.[10] Arguably these cases involve unusual assurances of reliability, especially where possession has been taken under the deed, and the rule should be limited to them.[11] However, a number of courts applied the exception to other types of documents.[12]

---

7. Wickes, Ancient Documents and Hearsay, 8 Tex.L.Rev. 451 (1930).

8. It is generally safe to assume that the motivational difficulties pertaining to the present law suit would not have affected the statement when made, but it cannot be assumed that there was not a motivational issue when the document was first made. See Moore v. Goode, 375 S.E.2d 549, 557–558 (W.Va.1988) (forty-two-year-old unsigned document purporting to represent a compromise of ancient paternity suit ruled inadmissible because of concern that it was not accurate when made during earlier litigation).

9. See supra §§ 10, 247.

Russell v. Emerson, 108 N.H. 518, 240 A.2d 52 (1968) (map dated 1888 not admissible under ancient documents rule because there was no evidence as to who prepared it); Budlong v. Budlong, 48 R.I. 144, 136 A. 308 (1927) (book found in desk of office of poor farm not admissible to prove truth of entry suggesting birth of child to specific individual because there was no proof of the qualifications of the writer to testify to such fact and indeed, no indication of writer's identity at all).

Also, the writing must not be suspicious on its face. See Muehrcke v. Behrens, 43 Wis.2d 1, 169 N.W.2d 86 (1969).

10. See 5 Wigmore, Evidence §§ 1573–1574 (Chadbourn rev. 1974); Annot., 6

A.L.R. 630. The age requirement is typically enforced. Caranta v. Pioneer Home Improvements, Inc., 81 N.M. 393, 467 P.2d 719 (1970) (recital in deed that grantor was sole heir not admissible because deed was only 12 years old).

11. See Town of Ninety Six v. Southern Ry. Co., 267 F.2d 579 (4th Cir.1959). See also Robinson v. Peterson, 200 Va. 186, 104 S.E.2d 788 (1958).

12. State Common Schools v. Taylor, 135 Ark. 232, 205 S.W. 104 (1918) (recital of sale of land in "plat book" of state land office); Kirkpatrick v. Tapo Oil Co., 144 Cal.App.2d 404, 301 P.2d 274 (1956) (account book); Whitman v. Shaw, 166 Mass. 451, 44 N.E. 333 (1896) (map to show boundaries); State Department of Roads v. Parks, 185 Neb. 794, 178 N.W.2d 788 (1970) (consent petition, filed to make land a public road); Tillman v. Lincoln Warehouse Corp., 72 A.D.2d 40, 423 N.Y.S.2d 151 (1979) (in action for failure to redeliver china, error to exclude ancient inventory certified by professional appraiser reciting that inspection took place at warehouse, offered to prove original delivery there). Wiener v. Zweib, 128 S.W. 699 (Tex.Civ. App.1910), affirmed 105 Tex. 262, 141 S.W. 771 (entries in minutes of lodge to show fact and time of member's death); Muehrcke v. Behrens, 43 Wis.2d 1, 169 N.W.2d 86 (1969) (town record book).

Federal Rule 803(16)[13] contains a broadly worded hearsay exception for statements in ancient documents: "Statements in a document in existence twenty years or more the authenticity of which is established." While the rule itself contains no limitation as to the kind of document that may qualify, as long as it is at least twenty years old and properly authenticated,[14] several limitations are imposed that provide additional assurance of trustworthiness. The declarant under this rule is subject to the general requirement of firsthand knowledge,[15] and the document must not be suspicious with regard to its genuineness and reliability.[16]

A related hearsay exception is recognized by Federal Rule 803(15):[17]

A statement contained in a document purporting to establish or affect an interest in property if the matter stated was relevant to the purpose of the document, unless dealings with the property since the document was made have been inconsistent with the truth of the statement or the purport of the document.

13. Revised Uniform Rule (1986) 803(16) is identical.

14. Authentication requirements are set forth in Federal and Revised Uniform Rule (1986) 901(b)(8). See supra § 223. Dartez v. Fibreboard Corp., 765 F.2d 456 (5th Cir.1985) (documents apparently otherwise qualifying under hearsay exception excluded because of failure of party properly to authenticate); United States v. Koziy, 728 F.2d 1314 (11th Cir.1984), cert. denied 469 U.S. 835 (documents purporting to link defendant to Ukrainian police organizations that were authenticated and were more than 20 years old were admissible in spite of claims of forgery).

15. Firsthand knowledge may appear from the statement or be inferable from circumstances. Adv.Comm.Note, Fed. R.Evid. 803, 56 F.R.D. 183, 303. Given the passage of time, it will often be difficult to ascertain much more than the apparent capacity to have gained firsthand knowledge. 4 Weinstein & Berger, Weinstein's Evidence ¶ 803(16)[02], at 313 (1990).

In Dallas County v. Commercial Union Assurance Co., 286 F.2d 388 (5th Cir.1961), the court admitted a 58–year–old newspaper story of a fire at the courthouse, then under construction, pointing out that the general public interest in such an occurrence and that the probability that a reporter would have written the story without a visit to the scene was indeed slight. See also Ammons v. Dade City, Florida, 594 F.Supp. 1274, 1280 n. 8 (M.D.Fla.1984), affirmed 783 F.2d 982 (11th Cir.) (newspaper article concerning large street paving project undertaken by city admissible).

However, firsthand knowledge by news reporters will generally be the exception rather than the rule. See Sherrill v. Plumley's Estate, 514 S.W.2d 286 (Tex.Civ.App. 1974 error refused n.r.e.) (obituary notice in ancient newspaper not admissible to prove heirship because no showing of identity of reporter or source of information).

16. See Hill v. Merrimac Cattle Co., 211 Mont. 479, 687 P.2d 59 (1984) (statement in pleading is not admissible to support the position of the party filing the document in spite of its substantial age since its self-serving character did not change with age); Moore v. Goode, 375 S.E.2d 549 (W.Va. 1988) (unsigned document purporting to recite facts about paternity inadmissible because it was not a recital of facts that could safely be assumed to have been true at the time made).

Such limitation is imposed by a two step process. While Rule 803(16) contains no direct provision on this point, it requires that authenticity must be established, and Rule 901(b)(8) specifies that to satisfy authentication requirements the condition of the document and the place it was found must raise no questions.

Documents may also be excluded under Rule 403 after balancing probativity against "prejudice," see supra § 185, although more commonly concerns about trustworthiness can be dealt with more directly through the ability to exclude documents that are questionable in appearance or content.

17. Revised Uniform Rule (1986) 803(15) is identical.

This exception has no requirement of age of the document, but it is limited to title documents, such as deeds, and to statements relevant to the purpose of the document. The circumstances under which documents of this nature are executed, the character of the statements that will qualify, and the inapplicability of this exception if subsequent dealings have been inconsistent with the truth of the statement or the purport of the document, are considered sufficient guarantees of trustworthiness.[18] A companion rule deals with the evidentiary status of recording such documents.[19]

§ 324. The Residual Hearsay Exceptions [1]

Despite the extensive array of specific hearsay exceptions in the Federal Rules, the Advisory Committee felt that "[i]t would * * * be presumptuous to assume that all possible desirable exceptions to the hearsay rule have been catalogued and to pass the hearsay rule to oncoming generations as a closed system." [2] Therefore the Committee proposed for both available and unavailable declarants admission of "statement[s] not specifically covered by any of the forgoing exceptions but having comparable circumstantial guarantees of trustworthiness." [3] As a precaution against excessive resort to these provisions as a means of effectively destroying the hearsay rule, the Advisory Committee observed, "They do not contemplate an unfettered exercise of judicial discretion, but they do provide for treating new and presently unanticipated situations which demonstrate a trustworthiness within the spirit of the specifically stated exceptions." [4]

While the rules were under consideration in the Congress, the House Judiciary Committee deleted the provisions in their entirety: too much uncertainty was injected into the law of evidence; any additional

---

18. Adv.Comm.Note, Fed.R.Evid. 803(15), 56 F.R.D. 183, 315.

19. Federal and Revised Uniform (1986) Rule 803(14) provide a hearsay exception for the following:

> The record of a document purporting to establish or affect an interest in property, as proof of the content of the original recorded document and its execution and delivery by each person by whom it purports to have been executed, if the record is a record of a public office and an applicable statute authorizes the recording of documents of that kind in that office.

§ 324

1. Black, Federal Rules of Evidence 803(24) & 804(b)(5)—The Residual Exceptions—An Overview, 25 Hous.L.Rev. 13 (1988); Lewis, The Residual Exceptions to the Federal Hearsay Rule: Shuffling the Wild Cards, 15 Rut.–Cam.L.J. 101 (1983);

Weissenberger, The Admissibility of Grand Jury Transcripts: Avoiding the Constitutional Issue, 59 Tul.L.Rev. 335 (1984); Sonenshein, The Residual Exceptions to the Federal Hearsay Rule: Two Exceptions in Search of a Rule, 57 N.Y.U.L.Rev. 867 (1982); Imwinkelried, The Scope of the Residual Hearsay Exceptions in the Federal Rules of Evidence, 15 San Diego L.Rev. 239 (1978); Comment, 1985 Wis.L.Rev. 1525; Notes, 61 Neb.L.Rev. 187 (1982), 31 Rutgers L.Rev. 687 (1978); Annot., 36 A.L.R.Fed. 742, 51 A.L.R.4th 999.

2. Adv.Comm.Note, Fed.R.Evid. 803(24), 56 F.R.D. 183, 320.

3. Fed.R.Evid. 803(24) & 804(b)[5], as adopted by the Supreme Court, 56 F.R.D. at 303, 321–22.

4. Adv.Comm.Note, Fed.R.Evid. 803(24), 56 F.R.D. 183, 320.

hearsay exceptions should be created by amending the rules.[5] The Senate Committee did not agree with this extreme position but suggested further restrictions to be incorporated.[6] The differences were compromised, and, as enacted, Federal Rule 803(24)[7] provides a hearsay exception for the following:

> A statement not specifically covered by any of the foregoing exceptions but having equivalent circumstantial guarantees of trustworthiness, if the court determines that (A) the statement is offered as evidence of a material fact; (B) the statement is more probative on the point for which it is offered than any other evidence which the proponent can procure through reasonable efforts; and (C) the general purposes of these rules and the interests of justice will best be served by admission of the statement into evidence. However, a statement may not be admitted under this exception unless the proponent of it makes known to the adverse party sufficiently in advance of the trial or hearing to provide the adverse party with a fair opportunity to prepare to meet it, the proponent's intention to offer the statement and the particulars of it, including the name and address of the declarant.

Rule 804(b)(5) differs only in requiring the unavailability of the declarant.

The rules contain five requirements, three of which impose substantial limitations on the admission of hearsay. They are considered below.

Equivalent circumstantial guarantees of trustworthiness In applying the residual exceptions, the most important issue is whether the statement before the court offers "equivalent circumstantial guarantees of trustworthiness" to those offered by the various other specific hearsay exceptions. In making the admissibility determination, courts frequently employ the technique of comparing the circumstances surrounding the statement at issue to the closest hearsay exception.[8]

---

5. House Comm. on Judiciary, H.R.Rep. No. 650, 93d Cong., 1st Sess. 5–6 (1973), reprinted in 1974 U.S.Code Cong. & Admin.News 7075, 7079.

Some states in enacting rules generally similar to the Federal Rules have declined to adopt a residual exception for reasons similar to those stated by the House Committee. See State v. Doucette, 544 A.2d 1290, 1294 & n. 3 (Me.1988); Commonwealth v. Pope, 397 Mass. 275, 282, 491 N.E.2d 240, 244 & n. 9 (1986); Shields v. Reddo, 432 Mich. 761, 783, 443 N.W.2d 145, 154 (1989).

6. Senate Comm. on Judiciary, S.Rep. No. 1277, 93d Cong., 2d Sess. 18 (1974), reprinted in 1974 U.S.Code Cong. & Admin.News 7051, 7065–66. The Senate Committee expressed the concern that without a separate residual provision, the specific exceptions "could become tortured beyond any reasonable circumstances

which they were intended to include." Id. at 7065.

7. The corresponding Uniform Rules are identical except for minor stylistic differences.

8. See United States v. Fernandez, 892 F.2d 976, 981 (11th Cir.1989), cert. dismissed 110 S.Ct. 2201 (court compared grand jury testimony to other four exceptions for unavailable witnesses).

When the circumstances of the statement as a whole are reasonably similar to those under a specific exception, this mode of analysis provides a very useful device to determine whether, as the rule requires, the statement possesses "equivalent circumstantial guarantees of trustworthiness." The fact that a statement is a "near miss" should accordingly strongly support admission. Graham, Handbook of Federal Evidence § 803.24, at 948–949 (3d ed. 1991).

Courts also focus on particular factors suggesting trustworthiness of those statements. However, since the specific exceptions themselves vary widely in the degree of trustworthiness possessed by each, a rather substantial variation in the types of statements admitted under the residual exceptions could properly be anticipated and has eventuated. Indeed, because the factors supporting and undermining trustworthiness are so varied and can occur in so many combinations, providing useful categorization is difficult. However, as the volume of decided cases increases, certain recurring factors are acquiring recognition as significant to the determination of admissibility under the residual exception.

Among these factors are: whether the declarant had a motivation to speak truthfully or otherwise,[9] whether the statement was under oath,[10]

Some courts have applied a "near miss" analysis to exclude statements. They argue that when a statement fails to satisfy the requirements of an exception, the result should be exclusion. Creamer v. General Teamsters Local Union 326, 560 F.Supp. 495, 498 (D.Del.1983). See also United States v. Vigoa, 656 F.Supp. 1499, 1505–1506 (D.N.J.1987), affirmed mem. 857 F.2d 1467 (3d Cir.) (implicitly using this theory to exclude grand jury testimony). Most courts have, however, rejected this interpretation. See In re Japanese Electronic Products Antitrust Litigation, 723 F.2d 238, 302 (3d Cir.1983), reversed on other grounds sub nom. Matsushita Elec. Indus. Co., Ltd. v. Zenith Radio Corp., 475 U.S. 574 (interpretation would create straitjacket contrary to purpose of residual rule); United States v. Popenas, 780 F.2d 545, 547 (6th Cir.1985) (while limitations in rule indicate its restrictive nature, adopting this "near miss" approach would render the rule a nullity which was not intent of Congress); United States v. Fernandez, 892 F.2d 976, 981 (11th Cir.1989), cert. dismissed 110 S.Ct. 220 (accepting such interpretation would create an arbitrary distinction between statements that "narrowly but conclusively" fail to meet requirements of exception and those that do not even arguably fit).

When the precise failure of the statement to meet an exception corresponds with an affirmative indication that Congress determined trustworthiness to be lacking, the failure of the statement to meet an exception may appropriately be used to exclude it from evidence. Such determinations are unfortunately hard to make, however. Compare United States v. Bailey, 581 F.2d 341, 349 n. 12 (3d Cir. 1978) (congressional rejection of exception for recent perception gives guidance that similar statement lacks trustworthiness) with Robinson v. Shapiro, 646 F.2d 734,

742 n. 6 (2d Cir.1981) (rejection of recent perception exception indicated only congressional unwillingness to admit all statements of that type, not an intention to exclude all similar statements if circumstances supported trustworthiness).

9. Robinson v. Shapiro, 646 F.2d 734 (2d Cir.1981); United States v. Bailey, 581 F.2d 341 (3d Cir.1978); United States v. White, 611 F.2d 531 (5th Cir.1980), cert. denied 446 U.S. 992; United States v. Barlow, 693 F.2d 954 (6th Cir.1982), cert. denied 461 U.S. 945; United States v. Vretta, 790 F.2d 651, 659 (7th Cir.1986), cert. denied 479 U.S. 851 (while declarant may have had motive to fabricate statements of threats to investigative officers, his making those statements to private citizens for whom there was no improper motivation supported admissibility); United States v. Boulahanis, 677 F.2d 586, 588 (7th Cir.1982), cert. denied 459 U.S. 1016 (witness before grand jury was "mere bystander, with no axe to grind"); Huff v. White Motor Corp., 609 F.2d 286, 292 (7th Cir.1979) (statement to friend by victim of fire contrary to pecuniary interest); United States v. Yonkers Contracting Co., 701 F.Supp. 431, 437 (S.D.N.Y.1988) (no suggestion of motive of declarant to lie to grand jury given fact that testimony incriminated many of declarant's friends and business associates and exposed him to substantial disgrace); United States v. Sheets, 125 F.R.D. 172, 177 (D.Utah 1989) (diary entries admissible since no apparent reason for declarant to lie to herself).

10. United States v. Bailey, 581 F.2d 341 (3d Cir.1978); United States v. White, 611 F.2d 531 (5th Cir.1980), cert. denied 446 U.S. 992; United States v. Barlow, 693 F.2d 954 (6th Cir.1982), cert. denied 461 U.S. 945; United States v. Hooks, 848 F.2d 785, 796–797 (7th Cir.1988) (factor in ex-

the duration of the time lapse between event and statement,[11] whether the declarant had firsthand knowledge [12], and other factors going to the declarant's credibility.[13] These are factors that bear upon the declarant at the time of making the statement, as is characteristic of the specific hearsay exceptions generally, and fairly fall within the description "equivalent circumstantial guarantees of trustworthiness."

In addition, the courts have recognized further facts which did not bear upon declarant at the time he or she was speaking, but which, viewed in retrospect, tend to support the truthfulness of the statement. The most important of these has been corroboration. Courts utilizing this factor have examined whether the other evidence in the case supports the truth of the declaration.[14] The recent opinion of the United States Supreme Court in Idaho v. Wright appears, however, to restrict the analysis of trustworthiness to the circumstances surrounding the making of the statement and to exclude any consideration of corroboration by external facts establishing the accuracy of the statement.[15] Another important factor is whether the declarant is available

cluding statement to prosecutor that it was not made under oath); United States v. Boulahanis, 677 F.2d 586, 588 (7th Cir. 1982), cert. denied 459 U.S. 1016 (statement to grand jury made under oath and subject to prosecution for perjury); United States v. Carlson, 547 F.2d 1346 (8th Cir. 1976), cert. denied 431 U.S. 914. But see United States v. Fernandez, 892 F.2d 976, 981 (11th Cir.1989), cert. dismissed 110 S.Ct. 220 (oath alone is an inadequate safeguard of trustworthiness).

11. Robinson v. Shapiro, 646 F.2d 734 (2d Cir.1981) (account of conversation with building superintendent by repair crew foreman upon immediately returning to work site); United States v. Medico, 557 F.2d 309 (2d Cir.1977), cert. denied 434 U.S. 986 (lapse of 5 minutes); United States v. White, 611 F.2d 531 (5th Cir. 1980), cert. denied 446 U.S. 992 (3 months); United States v. Vretta, 790 F.2d 651, 659 (7th Cir.1986), cert. denied 479 U.S. 851 (close proximity between threat and statements concerning them supports credibility); United States v. Iaconetti, 406 F.Supp. 554 (E.D.N.Y.1976), affirmed 540 F.2d 574 (2d Cir.), cert. denied 429 U.S. 1041 (same day); United States v. Sheets, 125 F.R.D. 172, 177 (D.Utah 1989) (diary entries made in close proximity to conversations).

12. United States v. Barlow, 693 F.2d 954 (6th Cir.1982), cert. denied 461 U.S. 945; Huff v. White Motor Corp., 609 F.2d 286, 292 (7th Cir.1979) (declarant relating in concrete terms circumstances of fire he had witnessed two to three days earlier); United States v. Carlson, 547 F.2d 1346 (8th Cir.1976), cert. denied 431 U.S. 914.

13. United States v. Fernandez, 892 F.2d 976, 983 (11th Cir.1989), cert. dismissed 110 S.Ct. 2201 (declarant's "almost comically reliable character" demonstrated by claims of employment with the CIA and three foreign intelligence services, acquaintance with several heads of state, admitted lies under oath in other case, and apparent lies under oath in present action).

14. In addition to the use of corroboration to support admissibility of statements in child sexual abuse cases, the factor is frequently employed to support the admission of grand jury testimony. See, e.g., United States v. Barlow, 693 F.2d 954, 962 (6th Cir.1982), cert. denied 461 U.S. 945; United States v. Guinan, 836 F.2d 350, 356–357 (7th Cir.1988), cert. denied 487 U.S. 1218. Frequently, the circumstances surrounding the making of statements before the grand jury would not be strong enough to support admissibility by themselves.

15. 110 S.Ct. 3139, 3149 (1990) (quoting 5 Wigmore, Evidence § 1420, at 251 (Chadbourn rev. 1974)).

The Court in Wright was addressing only the issue of whether "particularized guarantees of trustworthiness" were present for purposes of the confrontation clause. However, its analysis was based on the conclusion that the "rationale for permitting exceptions to the general rule against hearsay" considered only the surrounding circumstances and eliminated any consideration of corroboration by other facts in the case. 110 S.Ct. at 3148–3149. See also Huff v. White Motor Corp., 609 F.2d 286, 292 (7th Cir.1979).

for cross-examination. A number of courts have used the availability of the declarant as a basis to admit testimony that would not otherwise be admissible.[16] Other courts have ascribed precisely the opposite effect to this factor, ruling that the presence of the declarant renders the hearsay statement inadmissible because superior alternative evidence exists through the live testimony of the declarant.[17]

Other miscellaneous factors have also been employed from time to time by the courts pertaining to both the circumstances of making the statement and to subsequent events. These include whether the statement was spontaneous and/or produced in response to leading questions,[18] whether the declarant was subject to cross-examination at the time the statement was made,[19] and whether the declarant has recanted or reaffirmed the statement.[20]

Relative "Necessity" A second factor given varying significance by the opinions is the requirement that the statement must be "more probative on the point for which it is offered than any other evidence the proponent can procure through reasonable efforts."[21] Many courts interpret this as a general necessity requirement.[22] However, it does

Similarly, the credibility of the person reporting the statement should have no impact upon admissibility. Huff, supra 609 F.2d at 293. See also supra § 318 n. 10.

16. United States v. Leslie, 542 F.2d 285, 290 (5th Cir.1976); United States v. Iaconetti, 406 F.Supp. 554, 559 (E.D.N.Y.1976), affirmed 540 F.2d 574 (2d Cir.), cert. denied 429 U.S. 1041; State v. Edward Charles L., 398 S.E.2d 123, 138 (W.Va.1990).

17. United States v. Mathis, 559 F.2d 294, 299 (5th Cir.1977) (given availability of declarant to testify, hearsay evidence did not satisfy requirement of being more probative than other available evidence); State v. Smith, 315 N.C. 76, 95–96, 337 S.E.2d 833, 846 (1985) (same).

This argument should have no weight, however, where the hearsay has characteristics like many of the explicit exceptions under Rule 803, such as excited utterances, that make the hearsay statement superior to in-court testimony. Cleary, et al., Evidence: Cases and Materials 889 (4th ed. 1988); 4 Weinstein & Berger, Weinstein's Evidence ¶ 803(24)[01], at 374–75 (1990).

18. United States v. Hooks, 848 F.2d 785, 796–797 (7th Cir.1988) (statements properly excluded because, inter alia, they were made to prosecutor and were not spontaneous but were hesitant responses to questions frequently interrupted by witness' attorney); Huff v. White Motor Corp., 609 F.2d 286, 292 (7th Cir.1979) (statement

of fire victim not made in response to interrogation, making explanation of accident entirely voluntary); United States v. Fernandez, 892 F.2d 976, 982 (11th Cir. 1989), cert. dismissed 110 S.Ct. 2201 (fact that statements were given in response to leading questions factor against admissibility).

19. United States v. Fernandez, 892 F.2d 976, 982 (11th Cir.1989), cert. dismissed 110 S.Ct. 2201 (declarant not subject to cross-examination when giving statement to grand jury).

20. United States v. Leslie, 542 F.2d 285 (5th Cir.1976) (prosecution witnesses admitted making statements against accused, but testified in his favor, asserting forgetfulness of untruth of statements); United States v. Barlow, 693 F.2d 954 (6th Cir.1982), cert. denied 461 U.S. 945; United States v. Carlson, 547 F.2d 1346 (8th Cir.1976), cert. denied 431 U.S. 914 (witness reaffirmed truth of grand jury testimony but refused to testify for prosecution at trial).

21. See United States v. Kim, 595 F.2d 755, 766 (D.C.Cir.1979) (requirement not met where proponent of evidence failed to demonstrate that other more probative evidence of defendant's income could not be reasonably obtained).

22. United States v. Mathis, 559 F.2d 294, 299 (5th Cir.1977) (characterizing this requirement as "built-in requirement of necessity").

not mean that the hearsay evidence must be essential.[23] Indeed, some courts view the requirement as proving a basis for a trial court to evaluate the need for the statement in the case as compared to the costs of obtaining alternative evidence.[24] Others view it as imposing a requirement of diligence.[25]

Notice Another substantial requirement of the rule is that notice be given sufficiently in advance of trial to enable the adverse party to prepare to meet the hearsay evidence.[26] While occasionally strict compliance with this requirement is enforced,[27] courts generally have been willing to dispense with notice if the need for the hearsay arises on the eve of, or during, trial when possible injustice is avoided by the offer of a continuance or other circumstances.[28]

Other requirements The remaining requirements lettered (A) and (C) in the rules, have had no appreciable impact upon the application of the residual exception. Provision (A), requiring that the statement be offered as evidence of a material fact, is a restatement of the general requirement that evidence must be relevant.[29] Requirement (C), that the general purposes of the rules and the interests of justice will be

---

23. United States v. Boulahanis, 677 F.2d 586, 588 (7th Cir.1982), cert. denied 459 U.S. 1016 (no requirement that hearsay evidence must be essential but only that it be the most probative evidence reasonably available on a material issue); United States v. Shaw, 824 F.2d 601, 610 (8th Cir.1987), cert. denied 484 U.S. 1068 (fact that evidence somewhat cumulative should not result in exclusion if important in evaluating other evidence; first statements concerning sexual incident should be received). See also United States v. Vretta, 790 F.2d 651, 658–659 (7th Cir. 1986), cert. denied 479 U.S. 851 (evidence most probative because it completes a pattern of criminal conduct otherwise not clearly established); United States v. Marchini, 797 F.2d 759, 764 (9th Cir.1986), cert. denied 479 U.S. 1085 (testimony met this requirement even though largely cumulative to other evidence in linking pieces of evidence).

24. United States v. Simmons, 773 F.2d 1455, 1459 (4th Cir.1985) (government firearms trace form more probative than any other evidence that could be reasonably procured where alternative was to require the government to bring record custodians from across the country to prove simple fact that weapon moved in interstate commerce between place of manufacture and sale).

25. Noble v. Alabama Dept. of Environmental Management, 872 F.2d 361, 366 (11th Cir.1989) (admission of letters improper where proponent of evidence made no showing that reasonable efforts could not have produced the writers).

26. Schmunk v. State, 714 P.2d 724, 737–738 (Wyo.1986) (where witness interviewed nine months before trial failure to give timely notice was error). See generally Grant, The Pre–Trial Notice Requirement of Federal Rule of Evidence 803(24), 36 Drake L.Rev. 91 (1986–87).

27. United States v. Ruffin, 575 F.2d 346, 358 (2d Cir.1978) (Congress intended notice requirement to be applied rigidly).

28. Furtado v. Bishop, 604 F.2d 80, 91–93 (1st Cir.1979), cert. denied 444 U.S. 1035 (notice requirement should be construed liberally in civil litigation, court concluding no substantial violation where hearsay document of obvious importance was in possession of opponent for substantial period of time and where it was unclear what benefit further notice would have provided); United States v. Iaconetti, 540 F.2d 574, 578 (2d Cir.1976), cert. denied 429 U.S. 1041 (notice sufficient when given at beginning of weekend recess and opponent made no request for continuance). See also Distefano v. State, 526 So.2d 110, 114–115 (Fla.App.1988) (failure to comply with notice results in remedy only if harmful).

29. Fed.R.Evid. 401, 402. See Huff v. White Motor Corp., 609 F.2d 286, 294 (7th Cir.1979) (treating inquiry as examination of relevance under Rule 401).

served by admitting the evidence, in effect restates Rule 102.[30]

In restoring the residual exception after the House deleted it, the Senate Judiciary Committee stated that it intended that the residual exceptions should be used "very rarely,"[31] and only in exceptional circumstances."[32] Nevertheless, use of the exceptions has been substantial. Courts have employed the exceptions most extensively in admitting statements made by child witnesses, particularly in sexual abuse cases.[33] The courts admitting such statements under these exceptions have emphasized factors such as the spontaneity and consistency of the statement,[34] the general proposition that young children do not invent allegations of the type involved,[35] and the unusualness of explicit sexual knowledge by a young child.[36] Statements tend to be excluded in cases where a court finds that they are not spontaneous or that the child has a source for sexual knowledge outside of the offense,[37] or it disagrees with the premise that young children are generally more trustworthy than adult declarants.[38]

30. Robinson v. Shapiro, 646 F.2d 734, 743 (2d Cir.1981) (this requirement is essentially restatement of Rule 102); 4 Weinstein & Berger, Weinstein's Evidence ¶ 803(24)[01], at 379 (1990).

Some courts have given some content to this provision by according weight in the admissibility calculus to the role of the opponent of the evidence in securing the declarant's unavailability. See, e.g., United States v. Barlow, 693 F.2d 954, 962 (6th Cir.1982), cert. denied 461 U.S. 945 (court may consider role of defendant in making the witness unavailable in determining admissibility); United States v. Marchini, 797 F.2d 759, 763–764 (9th Cir.1986), cert. denied 479 U.S. 1085 (criminal defendant married declarant and created privilege).

The above position of the courts, which seems entirely unwarranted, is to be distinguished from the situation where the defendant waives his or her confrontation and hearsay objections by intimidating or killing the witness. United States v. Thevis, 665 F.2d 616, 629–633 (5th Cir.1982); United States v. Balano, 618 F.2d 624, 628–629 (10th Cir.1979), cert. denied 449 U.S. 840.

31. Occasionally in refusing to admit statements, courts will note that the exception should be used rarely. See, e.g., United States v. Thevis, 665 F.2d 616, 629 (5th Cir.1982) (legislative intent clear that residual exceptions would be used rarely and only in exceptional circumstance, and since corroborated grand jury testimony is neither rare nor exceptional, courts should be hesitant in admitting it); United States v. Kim, 595 F.2d 755, 765–766 (D.C.Cir.1979) (in light of narrow construction of residual exception, court found abuse of discretion in admitting evidence of some questionable reliability and importance); United States v. Vigoa, 656 F.Supp. 1499, 1505–1506 (D.N.J.1987), affirmed mem. 857 F.2d 1467 (3d Cir.) (grand jury testimony excluded because admitting such testimony would violate the principle that residual exception is to be used only in unanticipated situations).

32. Senate Comm. on Judiciary, S.Rep. No. 1277, 93d Cong., 2d Sess. 18–20 (1974), reprinted in 1974 U.S.Code Cong. & Admin.News 7051, 7065–66.

33. Indeed, the court in United States v. Shaw, 824 F.2d 601, 609 (8th Cir.1987), cert. denied 484 U.S. 1068, stated that an "exceptional circumstance generally exists when a child abuse victim relates to an adult the details of the abusive event."

34. State v. Robinson, 153 Ariz. 191, 201, 735 P.2d 801, 811 (1987).

35. Oldsen v. People, 732 P.2d 1132, 1136 (Colo.1986).

36. United States v. Dorian, 803 F.2d 1439, 1445 (8th Cir.1986); State v. Robinson, 153 Ariz. 191, 201–202, 735 P.2d 801, 811–812 (1987); State v. Sorenson, 143 Wis.2d 226, 246, 421 N.W.2d 77, 85 (1988).

37. State v. Allen, 157 Ariz. 165, 175, 755 P.2d 1153, 1162–1163 (1988).

38. Commonwealth v. Haber, 351 Pa.Super. 79, 83, 505 A.2d 273, 276 (1986).

§ 324.1. Hearsay Within Hearsay; Multiple Hearsay

"On principle it scarcely seems open to doubt that the hearsay rule should not call for exclusion of a hearsay statement which includes a further hearsay statement when both conform to the requirements of a hearsay exception." [1] The common law followed this reasoning,[2] and it is incorporated into Federal Rule 805: [3]

> Hearsay included within hearsay is not excluded under the hearsay rule if each part of the combined statements confirms with an exception to the hearsay rule provided in these rules.

In the usual situation, two stages of inquiry are involved.[4] First, does the primary statement qualify under a hearsay exception? If so, the hearsay rule allows its use to prove that the included statement was made, which may end the inquiry.[5] Ordinarily, however, the included statement will be offered to prove the truth of the facts that it asserts. In that event, the second stage of inquiry is required: Does the included statement also qualify under a hearsay exception? If the answer again is in the affirmative, the requirements of Rule 805 are met. However, if the included statement is inadmissible, the rule is not satisfied, and the statements are excluded.[6]

Police reports of accident investigations frequently provide examples of multiple hearsay, with admissibility depending upon the nature of the secondary statement. The primary statement—the written report of the officer—is admissible as a business or public record.[7] Statements of individuals made to the officer either qualify under various exceptions, such as excited utterances or dying declarations, or they fail to meet any additional exception and must be excluded as violating the

§ 324.1

1. Adv.Comm.Note, Fed.R.Evid. 805, 56 F.R.D. 183, 329.

2. United States v. Maddox, 444 F.2d 148 (2d Cir.1971); Minor v. City of Chicago, 101 Ill.App.3d 823, 57 Ill.Dec. 410, 428 N.E.2d 1090 (1981).

3. Revised Uniform Rule (1986) 805 is identical.

4. But see United States v. Portsmouth Paving Corp., 694 F.2d 312 (4th Cir.1982) (three levels); United States v. Abell, 586 F.Supp. 1414 (D.Me.1984) (three levels).

The number of layers of hearsay that may be involved in a multiple hearsay statement is not conceptually limited at common law or under the rules. However, attenuation of probative value may occur as the layers increase. Comment, 15 Wayne L.Rev. 1077, 1231 (1969). Exclusion under Federal Rule 403 may be the proper result where layers of unreliability undercut the probative value of the hearsay. Boren v. Sable, 887 F.2d 1032, 1037 (10th Cir.1989). See also 4 Weinstein &

Berger, Weinstein's Evidence ¶ 804[01], at 7–8 (1990).

5. Out-of-court utterances that are not hearsay are discussed in supra § 249.

6. See, e.g., Carden v. Westinghouse Elec. Corp., 850 F.2d 996 (3d Cir.1988) (statement regarding what "they" wanted excluded under Rule 805 since "they" not identified and consequently unclear that statements were within scope of declarant's duties required for statement to qualify as admission); United States v. De Peri, 778 F.2d 963 (3d Cir.1985), cert. denied 475 U.S. 1110 (trial court properly refused admission of F.B.I. report where report itself admissible under Rule 803(8) but statements contained within it met no hearsay exception).

7. For purposes of examples within this section, police reports will be treated as if they were a species of business record. Except when statements in police records are offered against the criminal defendant, see supra § 296, such treatment causes no conceptual difficulty.

rule.[8] The rule is not satisfied, for example, when a police officer testifies that A stated that B confessed to the crime. Although B's confession to A—the included statement—is against penal interest, A's statement to the police officer—the primary statement—meets no hearsay exception.[9]

An oft-recurring version of multiple hearsay involves a primary hearsay exception in the form of a regularly kept business record which includes a further hearsay statement. If both the primary and the included statements are by persons acting in the routine of the business, then both are admitted under the regularly kept records exception, and no further exception need be invoked. However, if the person whose statement is included is not acting in the routine of the business, resort must be had to a further exception.

It might be argued that, even if the included statement met some other hearsay exception, the primary statement could not qualify under a hearsay exception because the regularly kept records exception requires that the informant must be produced in the routine of the business. The courts, however, have not so held.[10] They have imposed, however, the requirement that the recorder must have a business duty to record the information provided by the outsider.[11]

Such a requirement will lead to a different result depending upon the nature of the business involved. For instance, a hospital intake worker has a business-related interest in a narrower and different type of information when talking to an assault victim about the circumstances surrounding the injury than a police officer.[12] The statement that the victim was shot by a person of a particular race would not be material to treatment and not admissible through the business records exception when made to a hospital employee even if the included statement met another hearsay exception.[13] By contrast, the same statement would be highly relevant to the "business" of the police officer in locating the assailant, and accordingly the primary statement would be admissible as a public or business record.

At common law, one of the hearsay statements might consist of an admission, which was regarded as a hearsay exception.[14] Since admis-

---

8. United States v. Smith, 521 F.2d 957 (D.C.Cir.1975). The basic principle is set out in numerous cases. See, e.g., Yates v. Bair Transport, Inc., 249 F.Supp. 681 (S.D.N.Y.1965).

9. People v. Hawkins, 114 Mich.App. 714, 319 N.W.2d 644 (1982); Boyer v. State, 91 Wis.2d 647, 284 N.W.2d 30 (1979).

10. United States v. Baker, 693 F.2d 183 (D.C.Cir.1982); Fleet v. United States Consumer Council, Inc. (In re Fleet), 95 B.R. 319 (E.D.Pa.1989).

11. See United States v. Maddox, 444 F.2d 148 (2d Cir.1971) (while statement regarding narcotics usage not relevant to any treatment to be received at detention center, maker of medical record was under business duty to accurately record responses of incoming prisoners).

12. Statements to hospital worker must be pertinent to diagnosis or treatment or some other hospital business. Otherwise they will not be the type of records that are regularly kept within the meaning of the rule. See supra § 293 text accompanying notes 6–7.

13. Commonwealth v. Harris, 351 Pa. 325, 41 A.2d 688 (1945).

14. United States v. Maddox, 444 F.2d 148, 151 (2d Cir.1971).

sions are not classed as hearsay under the Federal Rules, the question arises whether an admission may qualify as a hearsay exception for purposes of the multiple hearsay rule. One answer has been that admissions are within the spirit and purpose of the rule.[15] An easier answer may be that only one level of hearsay exists since an admission is not hearsay under the Federal Rules, and if the other statement satisfies an exception, no further hearsay difficulty remains.[16]

§ 324.2 Impeachment of Hearsay Declarant

When a hearsay statement is introduced, often the declarant does not testify. It is, however, ultimately the declarant's credibility that determines the value that should be accorded to the statement. How should that credibility be attacked or, where appropriate, supported?

Federal Rule 806[1] provides:

When a hearsay statement, or a statement defined in Rule 801(d)(2), (C), (D), or (E), has been admitted in evidence, the credibility of the declarant may be attacked, and if attacked may be supported, by any evidence which would be admissible for those purposes if declarant had testified as a witness. Evidence of a statement or conduct by the declarant at any time, inconsistent with the declarant's hearsay statement, is not subject to any requirement that the declarant may have been afforded an opportunity to deny or explain. If the party against whom a hearsay statement has been admitted calls the declarant as a witness, the party is entitled to examine the declarant on the statement as if under cross-examination.

The rule treats the hearsay declarant as effectively a witness for impeachment purposes.

The rule covers both statements admitted under hearsay exceptions and admissions,[2] but it does not apply to statements that are nonhearsay and not admitted for their truth.[3]

---

15. United States v. Lang, 589 F.2d 92, 99 n. 2 (2d Cir.1978).

16. United States v. Basey, 613 F.2d 198, 201 n. 1 (9th Cir.1979), cert. denied 446 U.S. 919. 4 Louisell & Mueller, Federal Evidence § 496, at 1223–24 (1980).

Similar arguments may be made concerning other out-of-court statements treated as not constituting hearsay by Federal Rule 801(d)(1). See generally supra § 251.

§ 324.2

1. Revised Uniform Rule (1986) 806 is identical except for minor stylistic differences.

2. Literally the rule appears to cover only representative admissions under subparagraphs (C) and (D) of Rule 801(d)(2) and co-conspirator statements under subparagraph (E). However, the legislative history makes clear that there was no intention to prohibit impeachment of declarants making admissions under subparagraphs (A) and (B). The Senate Judiciary Committee believed that it was "unnecessary to included statements contained in rule 801(d)(2)(A) and (B)—the statement by the party-opponent himself or the statement of which he has manifested his adoption—because the credibility of the party opponent is always subject to attack on his credibility." Senate Comm. on Judiciary, S.Rep. No. 1277, 93d Cong., 2d Sess. 22 n. 1 (1974), reprinted in 1974 U.S.Code Cong. & Admin.News 7051, 7068 n. 1.

3. United States v. Price, 792 F.2d 994 (11th Cir.1986) (statements made by confidential informant in recorded conversation with defendant were not admitted for truth but only to give context to defendant's statements and therefore informant

The declarant may be impeached by any of the standard methods of attacking credibility, including prior convictions,[4] inconsistent statements, bias or interest, and character for untruthfulness.[5] With regard to impeachment by prior inconsistent statements, the rule eliminates the requirement otherwise applicable to statements made by witnesses who testify in person [6] that an opportunity be afforded for them to explain or deny the inconsistency.[7]

The rule also provides that, if the hearsay declarant takes the stand to testify, the party seeking to impeach the declarant is entitled to examine on the statement "as if under cross-examination." This provision clearly permits the use of leading questions.[8] Moreover, when the statement is admitted against a criminal defendant, the accused can invoke the compulsory process clause to require assistance in securing the declarant's presence.[9]

not subject to impeachment under Rule 806).

4. United States v. Serna, 799 F.2d 842 (2d Cir.1986), cert. denied 481 U.S. 1013 (court properly conditioned admission of prior testimony of defendant upon informing jury of his conviction in the case where that testimony was given); United States v. Noble, 754 F.2d 1324 (7th Cir.1985), cert. denied 474 U.S. 818 (counterfeiting conviction admissible when defendant introduced his exculpatory hearsay statement).

Impeachment of one codefendant by another when the government introduces statements under the co-conspirator provision presents a special problem of balancing prejudice and probativity. Compare United States v. Robinson, 783 F.2d 64 (7th Cir.1986) (proper for trial court to exercise discretion to prohibit such impeachment because of feared prejudice) with United States v. Bovain, 708 F.2d 606 (11th Cir.1983), cert. denied 464 U.S. 898 (trial court's allowance of impeachment affirmed where based on judgment that probativity outweighed prejudice).

5. See generally 4 Louisell & Mueller, Federal Evidence § 501, at 1240–49 (1980); 4 Weinstein & Berger, Weinstein's Evidence ¶ 806[01], at 10–11 (1990).

6. Fed.R.Evid. 613(b). See generally supra § 37.

7. See United States v. Wali, 860 F.2d 588 (3d Cir.1988) (error to exclude exculpatory inconsistent statements of declarant in spite of fact that defendant had opportunity prior to trial to depose declarant since

no requirement in rule that declarant must be afforded opportunity to explain inconsistency); Smith v. Fairman, 862 F.2d 630 (7th Cir.1988), cert. denied 490 U.S. 1008 (foundational requirement particularly inappropriate for statement by now deceased declarant whom defendant never had opportunity to cross-examine).

Prior to enactment of the Federal Rules, many courts dispensed with the requirement of affording an opportunity to explain for certain hearsay statements, such as dying declarations. Carver v. United States, 164 U.S. 694 (1897). However, the requirement was often enforced for hearsay statements admitted under the former testimony exception because there was arguably an opportunity to solicit an explanation at the time of the prior testimony. Mattox v. United States, 156 U.S. 237 (1895). The Federal Rule eliminates this troubling distinction.

8. See Fed.R.Evid. 611(c).

9. United States v. Inadi, 475 U.S. 387 (1986).

The inability to attack credibility because the declarant is unavailable and unidentified has been found to support exclusion of a statement of questionable admissibility under the excited utterance exception. Miller v. Keating, 754 F.2d 507 (3d Cir.1985). However, the inability to secure the presence of the declarant is not grounds for exclusion of the statement. United States v. Paris, 827 F.2d 395 (9th Cir.1987).

§ 324.3 Basis for Expert Opinion as a Quasi–Hearsay Exception

Under Federal Rule 703, an expert may base an opinion on facts or data that are not "admissible in evidence" if of a type reasonably relied upon by experts in the field. The expert should as a general matter be allowed to disclose to the trier of fact the basis for his or her opinion, because otherwise the opinion is left unsupported with little way for the jury to evaluate its correctness.[1] The result is often that the expert may testify to evidence even though it is inadmissible under the hearsay rule.[2] However, this does not mean that the expert becomes the sole judge of the admissibility of the basis facts. The facts must still be of a type reasonably relied upon by experts in the field,[3] and they are subject to such general evidentiary principles as exclusion for prejudice or irrelevancy.[4]

Subject to these restrictions, the expert may testify to the basis of his or her opinion, and accordingly that supporting information is to some degree in evidence. What, however, is the status of the evidence thus admitted? The Third Edition of this treatise took the position that such evidence should be received for its truth because the trustworthiness of the evidence was assured by the requirements of Rule 703 that the evidence must be of a type reasonably relied upon by the expert.[5]

That position is now believed to be in error. Such statements are admissible for the limited purpose of informing the jury of the basis of the expert's opinion.[6] In most situations, the difference between limit-

§ 324.3

1. Blakey, An Introduction to the Oklahoma Evidence Code: The Thirty–Fourth Hearsay Exception, 16 Tulsa L.J. 1, 14 (1980); 2 Saltzburg & Martin, Federal Rules of Evidence Manual 74 (5th ed. 1990); Bryan v. John Bean Div. of FMC Corp., 566 F.2d 541, 545 (5th Cir.1978).

2. Adv.Comm.Note, Fed.R.Evid. 705, 56 F.R.D. 183, 285 ("[T]he rule allows counsel to make disclosure of the underlying facts or data as a preliminary to the giving of an expert opinion, if he chooses * * * ").

3. Fed.R.Evid. 703. See also Adv. Comm.Note, Fed.R.Evid. 703, 56 F.R.D. 183, 284.

4. Nachtsheim v. Beech Aircraft Corp., 847 F.2d 1261, 1270–1271 (7th Cir.1988) (judge has discretion to control or limit introduction of inadmissible facts in support of expert opinion and the opinion itself based on Rule 403); Marsee v. United States Tobacco Co., 866 F.2d 319 (10th Cir. 1989) (noting that whether expert must be permitted to testify on direct examination about otherwise inadmissible evidence supporting an opinion is open issue); Reed v.

United States, 584 A.2d 585, 587, 591 (D.C.App.1990) (appellate court approved judgment of trial court under Rule 403 to permit the hearsay basis for the expert's opinion to be presented only if basis put into issue on cross-examination). See generally supra § 185.

5. McCormick, Evidence § 324.2, at 910–11 (E. Cleary 3d ed. 1984).

6. American Universal Ins. Co. v. Falzone, 644 F.2d 65, 66 n. 1 (1st Cir.1981); Fox v. Taylor Diving & Salvage Co., 694 F.2d 1349 (5th Cir.1983); Paddack v. Dave Christensen, Inc., 745 F.2d 1254 (9th Cir. 1984); Wilson v. Merrell Dow Pharmaceuticals Inc., 893 F.2d 1149 (10th Cir.1990); United States v. Affleck, 776 F.2d 1451 (10th Cir.1985). See also 2 Saltzburg & Martin, Federal Rules of Evidence Manual 76 (5th ed. 1990); Graham, Federal Rules of Evidence Handbook § 703.1, at 643 (3d ed. 1991); Graham, Expert Witness Testimony and the Federal Rules of Evidence: Insuring Adequate Assurance of Trustworthiness, 1986 U.Ill.L.Rev. 43, 65; Carlson, Policing the Bases of Modern Expert Testimony, 39 Vand.L.Rev. 577 (1986); Rice, Inadmissible Evidence as a Basis for Ex-

ed admissibility and admission for the truth of the statement will make no difference; indeed, it is probably unrealistic to believe that the jurors will be able or willing to follow limiting instructions. However, limiting instructions are appropriate when requested,[7] and where such evidence is the only substantial evidence on a critical issue—such as the identity of the assailant in a child sexual abuse case—this theoretical distinction will prove decisive.[8]

§ 325. Evaluation of the Present Rules

In his treatise on evidence in 1842, Professor Greenleaf wrote:

> The student will not fail to observe the symmetry and beauty of this branch of the law * * * and will rise from the study of its principles convinced, with Lord Erskine, that "they are founded in the charities of religion,—in the philosophy of nature,—in the truths of history,—and in the experience of common life.[1]

Few today would apply this evaluation to the rule against hearsay developed in the common law tradition, and probably more would agree with the description of Professors Morgan and Maguire approximately a century later that the exceptions appear like "an old-fashioned crazy quilt made of patches cut from a group of paintings by cubists, futurists and surrealists."[2]

It is hard to quarrel with the common law's insistence upon a high quality of evidence for judicial fact-finding. However, the hearsay rules appear not to have yielded a quality fully commensurate with the high price they have exacted. As the above quotation by Morgan and Maguire suggests, the chief criticisms are that the rules are too complex and that in reality they fail to achieve their purpose of screening good evidence from bad.

First, with respect to the complexity of the rule against hearsay and its exceptions, the number of exceptions naturally depends upon the minuteness of the classification. The Federal Rules contain thirty-one exceptions and exclusions.[3] Wigmore requires over a thousand pages to

---

pert Opinion Testimony: A Response to Professor Carlson, 40 Vand.L.Rev. 583 (1987); Comment, 63 Temp.L.Rev. 543 (1990).

7. Paddack v. Dave Christensen, Inc., 745 F.2d 1254, 1262 & n. 12 (9th Cir.1984); United States v. Sims, 514 F.2d 147 (9th Cir.1975), cert. denied 423 U.S. 845.

8. See Mosteller, Child Sexual Abuse and Statements for the Purpose of Medical Diagnosis or Treatment, 67 N.C.L.Rev. 257, 262 (1989); Graham, Expert Witness Testimony and the Federal Rules, supra note 6, at 66 (evidence admitted solely to form the basis of expert's opinion under Rule 703 will not support a prima facie case); Smith

v. United States, 353 F.2d 838 (D.C.Cir. 1965), cert. denied 384 U.S. 974 (report relied upon by psychiatrist in reaching conclusion did not itself constitute affirmative evidence of mental disorder sufficient to submit insanity issue to jury).

§ 325

1. Greenleaf, Evidence § 584 (1st ed. 1842).

2. Morgan & Maguire, Looking Backward and Forward at Evidence, 50 Harv. L.Rev. 909, 921 (1937).

3. Included in the count are the two residual exceptions and two exclusions by definition.

cover hearsay, and its treatment occupies one quarter of the original edition of the present work.

Most of the complication, of course, arises in connection with the exceptions, leading readily to the conclusion that a general rule so riddled with exceptions is "farcical." [4] The conclusion may be too facile. Probably less than ten, and possibly no more than a half-dozen, of the exceptions are encountered with any frequency in the trial of cases. To require mastery of these, plus an awareness of the others and a working knowledge of what is and is not hearsay, should not unduly tax the intellectual resources of the legal profession.

The second complaint—that the rule against hearsay and its exceptions fail to screen reliable from unreliable hearsay on a realistic basis—is of more serious proportion. The trustworthiness of hearsay statements ranges from the highest reliability to almost utter worthlessness. It includes: history books, newspapers, business records, official records and certificates, affidavits, letters and other written statements, simple oral hearsay, multiple hearsay, reputation, and gossip or rumors.[5]

Whether these almost infinitely varying, plastic situations can ever be completely and satisfactorily treated by a set of rules may well be doubted. Yet similar doubts pervade most other areas of the law and are not generally regarded as cause for despair. If the heart of the problem is that the exceptions are unacceptable in detail, a perusal of the preceding chapters dealing with hearsay indicates that much has been done in recent years to rationalize the rules and to improve their practical workability, albeit more along evolutionary than revolutionary lines. But if the basic difficulty is simply that no hearsay system based on classes of exceptions can truly succeed, a totally different approach would be required.

§ 326. Basic Shifts in the Contemporary Pattern [1]

Wholesale efforts to reformulate the traditional common law hearsay pattern have been for the most part legislative in nature rather than judicial, and some of the more notable legislative efforts are discussed below.

Pursuant to a suggestion from Thayer, the Massachusetts Hearsay Statute of 1898 was enacted as follows: "A declaration of a deceased person shall not be inadmissible in evidence as hearsay if the Court finds that it was made in good faith before the commencement of the

---

4. Nokes, The English Jury and the Law of Evidence, 31 Tul.L.Rev. 153, 167 (1956). Professor Tapper describes the list of exceptions as "most unwieldy." Tapper, Cross on Evidence 569 (7th ed. 1990).

5. Morgan, Foreword, Model Code of Evidence 46 (1942); McCormick, Tomorrow's Law of Evidence, 24 A.B.A.J. 507, 512 (1938). See supra § 245 text accompanying note 24.

§ 326

1. For a comprehensive review of evidence law reform in the English-speaking world, see Brooks, The Law Reform Commission of Canada's Evidence Code, 16 Osgoode Hall L.J. 241 (1978).

action and upon the personal knowledge of the declarant." [2] After a quarter century of experience under the act, a questionnaire was addressed to the lawyers and judges of the state regarding its merits. The vast majority of those responding thought that its effects were positive.[3] The American Bar Association in 1938 recommended a liberalized version of the act for adoption by the states.[4]

The English Evidence Act of 1938[5] allowed the introduction of written statements, made on the personal knowledge of the maker or in the regular course of business, if the maker was called as a witness or was unavailable. Even though the maker was neither called nor unavailable, the judge might admit the statement if satisfied that undue delay or expense would otherwise be involved. Statements made by interested persons when proceedings were pending or instituted were excluded from the act. It applied only in civil cases.

These limitations were relaxed and new ones added in 1968.[6] Under the act, hearsay statements, whether written or oral, are admissible to the extent that testimony of the declarant would be admissible, regardless of whether he or she is called as a witness,[7] though prior statements are not ordinarily admissible at the request of the proponent if the declarant is called.[8] Notice is required of intent to offer a hearsay statement under the act, and the opposite party has the right to require production of declarant as a witness, if available.[9] The act is far more complex than the foregoing summary would indicate. Like its predecessor of 1938 and the Massachusetts statute, it applies only in civil cases. Efforts to reform in any substantial way the English law of evidence in criminal cases have not succeeded.[10]

2. Mass. Acts 1898, c. 535.

The present version of the act says, "In any action or other civil judicial proceeding, a declaration of a deceased person shall not be inadmissible in evidence as hearsay or as private conversation between husband and wife, as the case may be, if the court finds that it was made in good faith and upon the personal knowledge of the declarant." Mass.Gen.Laws.Ann. c. 233, § 65.

3. Morgan, et al. (constituting the Commonwealth Fund Committee), The Law of Evidence: Some Proposals for Its Reform 39–49 (1927).

4. "That declarations of a deceased or insane person should be received in evidence if the trial judge shall find (1) that the person is dead or insane, (2) that the declaration was made, (3) that it was made in good faith before the commencement of the action and upon the personal knowledge of the declarant." Vanderbilt, Minimum Standards of Judicial Administration 321, 338 (1949).

5. St.1938, c. 28, Evidence. See Cowen & Carter, The Interpretation of the Evidence Act, 1938, 12 Mod.L.Rev. 145 (1949); Maugham, Observations on the Law of Evidence, 17 Canadian B.Rev. 469 (1939); Comment, 34 U.Ill.L.Rev. 974 (1940).

6. St.1968, c. 64, Civil Evidence. Newark & Samuels, 31 Mod.L.Rev. 668 (1968).

7. St.1968, c. 64, Civil Evidence, Part I, § 2(1).

8. Id., Part II, § 2(2).

9. Id., Part I, § 8(2).

10. Broad ranging modification was proposed by the Criminal Law Revision Committee in its report in 1972. However, those recommendations attracted heavy criticism and were not enacted. A much more modest set of changes was enacted as part of the Police and Criminal Evidence Act 1984, pertaining chiefly to documentary evidence, and the Criminal Justice Act 1988. Tapper, Cross on Evidence 538–39 (7th ed. 1990). Nothing comparable to the liberal admissibility provisions of the 1968 act for civil cases exists for criminal cases. Elliott & Phipson, Manual of the Law of Evidence 292 (12th ed. 1987).

The drafters of the Model Code of Evidence of the American Law Institute took a bold course about hearsay. They drafted a sweeping new exception to the hearsay rule as follows:

Evidence of a hearsay declaration is admissible if the judge finds that the declarant

(a) is unavailable as a witness, or

(b) is present and subject to cross-examination.[11]

This rule, however, was qualified and safeguarded by other rules which (1) limited its application to declarations by persons with personal knowledge and excluded hearsay upon hearsay,[12] and (2) empowered the trial judge to exclude such hearsay whenever its probative value was outweighed by the likelihood of waste of time, prejudice, confusion, or unfair surprise.[13] The traditional exceptions, in addition to the new sweeping one, were generally retained.[14] The liberalizing of the use of hearsay was a chief ground of opposition to the Model Code in professional discussion and no doubt substantially accounted for the failure of the code to be adopted in any jurisdiction.[15]

Nevertheless, the controversy over the Model Code awakened a new interest in the improvement of evidence law. Accordingly, the Commissioners on Uniform State Laws, in cooperation with the American Law Institute and building on the foundation of the Model Code, drafted and adopted a more modestly reformative code, the Uniform Rules of Evidence.[16] The American Bar Association approved this action.[17]

Instead of admitting virtually all firsthand hearsay of an unavailable declarant, the original Uniform Rules, like the Model Code rule quoted above, substituted a hearsay exception for statements by unavailable declarants describing a matter recently perceived and made in good faith prior to the commencement of the action.[18] A similar provision is found in Rule 804(b)(5) of the Revised Uniform Rules, but its counterpart was dropped from the Federal Rules by the Congress. As to prior statements by witnesses present at the hearing, the original Uniform Rules adopted substantially the broad provisions of the Model Code rule quoted above, but the Revised Uniform Rules (1986) follow the much narrower congressional version of the Federal Rule of Evidence 801(d)(1).[19] The original Uniform Rules, like the Model Code, retained and liberalized the other traditional exceptions.

The Advisory Committee on the Federal Rules of Evidence approached its task with awareness of the criticisms that had been leveled against the common law system of class exceptions to the hearsay rule. It also was aware that the Model Code's lack of acceptance was largely

---

11. Model Code of Evidence Rule 503 (1942).

12. Id., Rule 501(3).

13. Id., Rule 303.

14. Id., Rules 504–529.

15. Despite its failure to achieve adoption, the influence of the code upon decisions and writings in the field of evidence has been enormous.

16. Unif.R.Evid. (1953).

17. 39 A.B.A. J. 1029 (1953).

18. Unif.R.Evid. 59(4)(c) (1953).

19. See supra § 251.

the result of having exceeded the profession's willingness to accept a fundamentally altered approach to hearsay that permitted broad admissibility of prior statements of unavailable declarants.[20]

In its first draft circulated for comment,[21] the committee endeavored to rationalize the hearsay exceptions in general terms, while at the same time maintaining continuity with the past. For these ends, two rules were included, one covering situations where it made no difference whether the declarant was available [22] and the other applying only when the declarant was unavailable.[23] The first of these rules opened with the following general provision:

> A statement is not excluded by the hearsay rule if its nature and the special circumstances under which it was made offer assurances of accuracy not likely to be enhanced by calling the declarant as a witness, even though he is available.

This general provision was followed by twenty-three illustrative applications derived from common law exceptions, which were not to be considered an exclusive listing. The second of the rules again opened with a general provision:

> A statement is not excluded by the hearsay rule if its nature and the special circumstances under which it was made offer strong assurances of accuracy and the declarant is unavailable as a witness.

It was also followed by a list, albeit a shorter one, of illustrative applications derived from the common law with again a caution that the enumeration not be considered exclusive.

While the response indicated a willingness to accept a substantial revision in the area of hearsay, the legal community opted for a larger measure of predictability than the proposal was thought to offer. As a result, the two general provisions quoted above were withdrawn, and the two rules were revised by converting the illustrations into exceptions in the common law tradition, with the addition of two residual exceptions to take care of unforeseen situations that might arise. Many of the exceptions were clarified and revised to take advantage of the common law experience and to conform with present-day thinking. In this form, the rules, with some alterations, were enacted into law by the Congress as Rules 803 and 804. In addition, rules modeled on the Federal Rules are now in effect in over thirty states, with local changes

---

20. Sections 28 and 29 of the proposed Evidence Code of the Law Reform Commission of Canada contain provisions similar to those of Model Code Rule 503, supra note 11. Report on Evidence, Law Reform Commission of Canada (1975). The proposal encountered similar resistance and was not adopted. Indeed, subsequent efforts to effect reform of evidence rules at the federal level have proved unsuccessful. 1 Schiff, Evidence in the Litigation Process 2 (3d ed. 1988).

21. Preliminary Draft of Proposed Rules of Evidence for the United States District Courts and Magistrates, Committee on Rules of Practice and Procedure of the Judicial Conference of the United States, 46 F.R.D. 161 (1969).

22. Id., Rule 8–03, 46 F.R.D. at 345.

23. Id., Rule 8–04, 46 F.R.D. at 377.

of varying significance. The pattern of a general rule excluding hearsay, subject to numerous exceptions, has shown substantial resilience.[24]

§ 327. The Future of Hearsay

This book and scores of others on the law of evidence are testimony that this area of the law of evidence can and does change. For example, in the general field of protecting triers of fact against false testimony, there has been a virtually complete shift from treating interest as a ground for exclusion to regarding it as bearing on weight and credibility.[1] Is a similarly dramatic shift in store for hearsay?

Regardless of whether the hearsay rule was as a matter of history the child of the jury system,[2] clearly the concern for controlling the use of hearsay is more pronounced in jury cases than in nonjury cases. In part, this attitude may be a product of the close association between the right to a jury and the right of confrontation in criminal cases. The English developments in the direction of relaxing limitations on hearsay in civil cases[3] were apparently inspired by the virtual disappearance there of jury trials in such cases. Corresponding changes have not transpired with respect to criminal cases where the jury remains.

In the United States, the constitutional rights of confrontation and jury trial combine to make unlikely any wholesale opening of the gates to hearsay in criminal cases or, for that matter, radical changes in the traditional hearsay exceptions.[4] One may, however, reasonably assume that the civil jury will continue to decline somewhat in importance.[5]

24. Even the civil English Act of 1968 specifically preserved some of the old landmark exceptions (admissions, public documents, records, and reputation) as proof of various matters and exempted them from the notice provisions of the act. St. 1968, c. 64, Part I, § 9. The English have not yet succeeded in updating the law of criminal evidence. A 1972 proposal raised "such a storm of protest, informed and ill informed, as to prevent the enactment of any of its recommendations, controversial or uncontroversial." Cross, Comment, 56 Canadian B.Rev. 306, 307 (1978).

§ 327

1. See supra § 65.

2. See supra § 244.

3. See supra § 326 text accompanying notes 5–9.

4. The Supreme Court's current analysis of the confrontation clause places additional emphasis on maintaining the historically accepted hearsay exceptions. The Court requires that statements must bear adequate "indicia of reliability," but such reliability can be inferred automatically where the evidence falls within a "firmly rooted" hearsay exception. Ohio v. Roberts, 448 U.S. 56, 66 (1980). The Court has made clear recently that it is long historical experience that satisfies the "firmly rooted" requirement. Idaho v. Wright, 110 S.Ct. 3139, 3147 (1990) (longstanding judicial and legislative experience in assessing trustworthiness provides justification for automatically treating firmly rooted exceptions as satisfying constitutional requirement of reliability); Coy v. Iowa, 487 U.S. 1012, 1021 (1988) (recently enacted statute covering statements by young children held not firmly rooted because of its recent origin).

5. The United States Supreme Court has been expanding somewhat the boundaries within which jury trials are required as a matter of right. See Chauffeurs, Teamsters & Helpers, Local No. 391 v. Terry, 494 U.S. 558 (1990) (jury trial constitutionally required in action for back pay against union for violation of duty of fair representation); Granfinanciera, S.A. v. Nordberg, 492 U.S. 33 (1989) (jury trial constitutionally required in certain bankruptcy proceedings); Tull v. United States, 481 U.S. 412 (1987) (jury trial constitutionally required in action by government for civil penalties and injunction under Clean

As noted in an earlier section,[6] courts exhibit a somewhat more relaxed attitude in administering the exclusionary rules of evidence in nonjury cases, including the rule against hearsay.[7] An even more relaxed attitude prevails in administrative proceedings.[8] Perhaps no more than an acceleration of this process is involved in the vigorous advocacy by some reformers to eliminate the hearsay rule entirely in nonjury civil cases.[9]

In a somewhat different vein is the suggestion that admissibility of hearsay in civil cases, jury or nonjury, be based upon the judge's ad hoc evaluation of its probative force, with certain procedural safeguards.[10] Obviously a substantially greater measure of discretion by the judge is contemplated, with a corresponding decrease in the impact of precedent and predictability.[11] Moreover, the judge is thrust squarely into the area of credibility, which has traditionally been reserved to juries. Suggested procedural safeguards are: notice to the opponent of the intention to use hearsay, expanding the judge's ability to comment on the weight of such evidence, greater control by judges over juries, and greater control by appellate courts over trial courts.[12] However, a notice requirement has the disadvantage of adding a further complication to an already overcrowded array of pretrial procedures and is contrary to modern theories of general pleading implemented by discovery.[13] Also, as with admissibility in the first instance, the controls envisioned find their roots in discretionary judicial evaluation of the

Water Act). Nevertheless, the importance of the jury in civil cases is likely to continue to decline if for no other reason than because of substantial and growing backlogs in the court dockets. See, e.g., Alschuler, Mediation with a Mugger: The Shortage of Adjudicative Services and the Need for a Two–Tier Trial System in Civil Cases, 99 Harv.L.Rev. 1808, 1858–59 (1986). Whether the civil jury should be eliminated because of its inability to handle competently its role in our complex world remains the subject of much debate. Compare Hans & Vidmar, Judging the Jury 113–29 (1986) (concluding that juries generally are competent to handle their tasks) with Alschuler, supra, 99 Harv.L.Rev. at 1825–28 (blaming part of litigation backlog on "lawlessness" of juries).

6. See supra § 60.

7. Cf. See United States v. Matlock, 415 U.S. 164 (1974) (reliable hearsay should be admissible in motions to suppress evidence, which are heard by trial judge).

8. See infra §§ 352–353.

9. See, e.g., Davis, Hearsay in Nonjury Cases, 83 Harv.L.Rev. 1362 (1970) (hearsay should be admitted in nonjury civil cases without ruling on its admissibility). But see Broadcast Music, Inc. v. Xanthas, Inc., 855 F.2d 233 (5th Cir.1988) (district court

erred when it admitted evidence on the ground that hearsay is admissible in bench trials).

10. See Weinstein, Probative Force of Hearsay, 46 Iowa L.Rev. 331 (1961) (collecting the literature and making an impressive case in its own right).

11. "It is tempting to meet such variability by giving trial judges some range of discretion as to admissibility. But it is uncomfortable to go to trial without knowing whether important evidence will be let in or excluded." Maguire, The Hearsay System: Around and Through the Thicket, 14 Vand.L.Rev. 741, 776 (1961).

"The suitor must feel that success is dependent upon the truth of his contentions and not upon the personality of the judge * * * who determines what evidence he will receive or submit to the consideration of the jury." Lehman, Technical Rules of Evidence, 26 Colum.L.Rev. 509, 512 (1926).

12. Weinstein, supra note 10, at 338–42.

13. The emphasis on notice in the English statute probably derives at least in part from the virtual nonexistence of discovery in the English practice. See supra § 326 note 9 and accompanying text.

evidence. These objections are by no means conclusive and might prove less objectionable than the deficiencies of the existing system.

More than fifty years ago, Professor McCormick wrote, much in the Benthamic tradition:

> Eventually, perhaps, Anglo–American court procedure may find itself gradually but increasingly freed from emphasis on jury trial with its contentious theory of proof. With responsibility for the ascertainment of facts vested in professional judges, the stress will be shifted from the crude technique of admitting or rejecting evidence to the more realistic problem of appraising its credibility. Psychologists meantime will have built upon their knowledge of the statistical reliability of witnesses in groups a technique of testing the veracity of individual witnesses and assessing the reliability of particular items of testimony. Judges and advocates will then become students and practitioners of an applied science of judicial proof.[14]

It becomes increasingly evident that this optimistic statement represents a long-term view indeed.[15]

Some take a completely opposed view, advocating instead a sort of hyperextension of Professor Morgan's finetuned analysis and definition of hearsay, with the result of increasing the complexity of the management of hearsay rather than simplifying it.[16] Somewhere in between are those who, though not maintaining that traditional hearsay principles are carved in granite, point to certain reasons to be cautious about radical change. These reasons include: the likelihood that oral statements may be misreported, the potential effect of relaxing hearsay rules on the advantage that the prosecution and wealthy organizations enjoy in litigation due to superior facilities for generating evidence, a distrust of the ability and impartiality of trial judges, and the fact that the hearsay rules presently are applied more liberally than they are written.[17]

The divergence of these points of view offers assurances that the law of hearsay will in the future be no more static than in the past, that it will continue to challenge its observers, and that proposals for its change will receive the most searching scrutiny. Other than to say that changes will generally move in the direction of liberalizing admission of hearsay, prediction is hazardous.

---

14. McCormick, Evidence, 3 Encyclopedia of the Social Sciences 637, 645 (1931, reissue of 1937).

15. See Mosteller, Legal Doctrines Governing the Admissibility of Expert Testimony Concerning Social Framework Evidence, 52 Law & Contemp.Probs., Autumn 1989, at 85, 128–32 (concluding that courts and social scientists are still relatively far from being able to determine and regulate the impact of various types of social science evidence on juries).

16. E.g., Park, McCormick on Evidence and the Concept of Hearsay, 65 Minn. L.Rev. 423 (1981). See supra § 250 notes 22–24 and accompanying text.

17. Lempert & Saltzburg, A Modern Approach to Evidence 519 (2d ed. 1982).

Title 11

JUDICIAL NOTICE

Chapter 35

JUDICIAL NOTICE

Table of Sections

§ 328. The Need for and the Effect of Judicial Notice [1]

The traditional notion that trials are bifurcated proceedings involving both a judge and a panel of twelve jurors has obviously had a profound impact on the overall development of common law doctrine pertaining to evidence. The very existence of the jury, after all, helped create the demand for the rigorous guarantees of accuracy which typify

§ 328

1. See generally, 9 Wigmore, Evidence §§ 2565–2583 (Chadbourn rev. 1981); Thayer, Preliminary Treatise on the Law of Evidence, c. 7 (1898); J. Maguire, Evidence—Common Sense and Common Law 166–175 (1947); Davis, Official Notice, 62 Harv.L.Rev. 537 (1949), Judicial Notice, 55 Colum.L.Rev. 945 (1955); R. Keeton, Legislative Facts and Similar Things: Deciding Disputed Premise Facts, 73 Minn.L.Rev. 1 (1988); Keeffe, Landis & Shaad, Sense and Nonsense about Judicial Notice, 2 Stan. L.Rev. 664 (1950); McNaughton, Judicial Notice—Excerpts Relating to the Morgan–Wigmore Controversy, 14 Vand.L.Rev. 779 (1961); Monahan & Walker, Social Authority: Obtaining, Evaluating, and Establishing Social Authority in the Law, 134 U.Pa. L.Rev. 477 (1986); Morgan, Judicial Notice, 57 Harv.L.Rev. 269 (1944); Roberts, Preliminary Notes Toward a Study of Judicial Notice, 52 Cornell L.Q. 210 (1967); Comment, 13 Vill.L.Rev. 528 (1968); Dec.Dig.Evidence ☞1–52; C.J.S. Evidence §§ 6–102; 29 Am.Jur.2d Evidence §§ 14–122.

the law of evidence, witness the insistence upon proof by witnesses having first-hand knowledge, the mistrust of hearsay, and the insistence upon original documents and their authentication by witnesses. Thus it is that the facts in dispute are commonly established by the jury after the carefully controlled introduction of formal evidence, which ordinarily consists of the testimony of witnesses. In light of the role of the jury, therefore, it is easy enough to conclude that, whereas questions concerning the tenor of the law to be applied to a case fall within the province of the judge, the determination of questions pertaining to propositions of fact is uniquely the function of the jury. The life of the law has never been quite so elementary, however, because judges on numerous occasions take charge of questions of fact and excuse the party having the burden of establishing a fact from the necessity of producing formal proof. These hybrid questions of fact, dealt with by judges as if they were questions pertaining to law, are the raw materials out of which the doctrine of judicial notice has been constructed.

A moment's reflection on the law-fact distinction is in order. The statement that it is necessary in a certain jurisdiction to have a testator's subscription attested by three witnesses if the document is going to be admitted to probate is an assertion that a certain state of affairs obtains. A speaker might actually preface the assertion with the words, "As a matter of fact * * *" Whether the statement is true or false presents, in the everyday vernacular, a question of fact. Persons engaged in social conversation might not agree on the accuracy of the statement, but agree to settle their difference by a straw poll of the other persons present. All of which would be of no moment, provided always no one present actually planned his or her estate on the basis of the result of the poll.

If this same conversation took the form of an argument between lawyers in a courtroom during an official proceeding wherein the answer was germane to the disposition of the matter at hand, very different considerations would come into play. The answer could not be seen to vary between cases in the same courtroom and between courtrooms across the jurisdiction. There must exist a standardized answer if the law *qua* system of dispute resolution is to maintain the necessary appearance of fairness and rationality. It is the apparatus of appellate review and one ultimately highest court in the jurisdiction which guarantees uniformity. Thus it is the case that, within the vernacular of the law, a question which can have only one right answer must be answered in a courtroom by a judge and is, therefore, a question of law.

The question who did what to whom when, where and in what state of mind implicates another set of considerations. The concrete human actions or inactions which precipitate lawsuits are water over the dam, history as it were. Reflection may suggest that history is actually a current event, because history is our present best judgment as to what happened in the past. Past events cannot be reconstituted; only a facsimile of them can be constructed in the mind's eye on the basis of the evidence presently available. In a courtroom the evidence available is a factor of the rules of evidence and the cleverness as well as industry of the opposing counsel.

If there is produced at trial enough evidence upon which seriously to deliberate about what actually happened in the past, and provided that in a civil case the evidence is not so overwhelming as to make deliberation unnecessary, there is no scientific litmus by which to assay the accuracy of the opposing versions of the affair. A verdict either way is possible. In the law's vernacular, we are met with a question of fact, which in Anglo–American tradition is meet for a jury to decide. But this compels the conclusion that a question of fact is one to which there are two right answers.[2]

This model finds its roots in Lord Coke.[3] Ad questionem facti non respondent judices: ad questionem juris non respondent juratores. To questions of fact judges do not answer: to questions of law the jury do not answer. Implicit in this model, however, is the notion inherent in the adversarial system that a judge presides over a trial after the fashion of an umpire who governs the play according to known rules but who does not participate in it. Implied, too, are the notions that trials involve straightforward contract or tort disputes, that complaints are abruptly dismissed if they do not state a familiar cause of action and that the concise elements of a well pleaded common law cause of action make the issues of fact at trial, if it comes to that, few and simple. Finally, the model presupposes that the law itself is composed primarily of private law rules which by and large remain immutable over the life of any one generation.

If during a trial a proposition of fact were to be implicated, the truth of which brooked no dispute among reasonable persons, this proposition would not fit comfortably within the principle that either of two answers is appropriate to a question of fact. The application of common sense to the principles thus far rehearsed leads inexorably to the conclusion that the existence of one right answer signals a question of law. Thus, at least if requested to do so, a judge would have to treat this question of fact as one of law and instruct the jury that the proposition could simply be taken as established in its own right.[4]

---

2. Cheetham v. Piggly Wiggly Madison Co., 24 Wis.2d 286, 290, 128 N.W.2d 400, 402 (1964) ("When a jury verdict is attacked we inquire only whether there is any credible evidence that, under any reasonable view, supports the verdict.").

3. I Co.Litt. 155b (1832 ed.).

4. Harper v. Killion, 345 S.W.2d 309, 311 (Tex.Civ.App.1961) ("The doctrine of judicial notice is one of common sense. The theory is that, where a fact is well-known by all reasonably intelligent people in the community, or its existence is so easily determinable with certainty from unimpeachable sources, it would not be good sense to require formal proof."); Holloway v. State, 666 S.W.2d 104 (Tex.Cr. App.1984). See also Porter v. Sunshine Packing Corp., 81 F.Supp. 566, 575 (W.D.Pa.1948), reversed in part 181 F.2d 348 (3d Cir.); Williams v. Commonwealth, 190 Va. 280, 291–292, 56 S.E.2d 537, 542–543 (1949).

With what manner of questions pertaining to facts do judges concern themselves?[5] Whether a well known street was in fact within a local business district as alleged by a litigant, in which case a certain speed limit obtained, may be dealt with by the judge during the trial of a negligence case.[6] That is to say, the judge may instruct the jury that the street in question was within a business district, dispensing thereby with the need to introduce evidence to this effect.[7] Then again, questions of fact arise about which reasonably intelligent people might not have in mind the information in question, but where they would agree that the facts are verifiable with certainty by consulting authoritative reference sources. At a time when Sunday contracts were taboo, for example, the question arose during the trial of a warranty action whether the relevant sales instrument, dated June 3, 1906, had been executed on a Sunday. In this instance the trial judge was reversed for leaving the question to the jury to deliberate upon as a question of fact.[8] Experience reveals, therefore, that two categories of facts clearly fall within the perimeters of judicial notice, these being facts generally known with certainty by all the reasonably intelligent people in the community and facts capable of accurate and ready determination by resort to sources of indisputable accuracy.

In both of the examples enumerated thus far it should be carefully noted that the facts of which judicial notice was taken were "adjudicative" facts. They were facts about the particular event which gave rise to the lawsuit and, like all adjudicative facts, they helped explain who did what, when, where, how, and with what motive and intent.[9] Fur-

---

5. Compare with the classification in the text:

Fed.R.Evid. 201:

(a) **Scope of Rule.** This rule governs only judicial notice of adjudicative facts.

(b) **Kinds of Facts.** A judicially noticed fact must be one not subject to reasonable dispute in that it is either (1) generally known within the territorial jurisdiction of the trial court or (2) capable of accurate and ready determination by resort to sources whose accuracy cannot reasonably be questioned.

(c) **When Discretionary.** A court may take judicial notice, whether requested or not.

(d) **When Mandatory.** A court shall take judicial notice if requested by a party and supplied with the necessary information.

(e) **Opportunity to Be Heard.** A party is entitled upon timely request to an opportunity to be heard as to the propriety of taking judicial notice and the tenor of the matter noticed. In the absence of prior notification, the request may be made after judicial notice has been taken.

(f) **Time of Taking Notice.** Judicial notice may be taken at any stage of the proceeding.

(g) **Instructing Jury.** In a civil action or proceeding, the court shall instruct the jury to accept as conclusive any fact judicially noticed. In a criminal case, the court shall instruct the jury that it may, but is not required to, accept as conclusive any fact judicially noticed.

Uniform Rule of Evidence 201 (1974) is identical except for the last subsection which reads:

(g) **Instructing Jury.** The court shall instruct the jury to accept as conclusive any fact judicially noticed.

6. Varcoe v. Lee, 180 Cal. 338, 181 P. 223 (1919).

7. Id. at 344, 181 P. at 226 ("Judicial notice is a judicial short cut, a doing away * * * with the formal necessity of evidence because there is no real necessity for it.").

8. Beardsley v. Irving, 81 Conn. 489, 71 A. 580 (1909).

9. United States v. Gould, 536 F.2d 216, 219–220 (8th Cir.1976), n. 12 infra; Main-

ther, either because they were facts so commonly known in the jurisdiction or so manifestly capable of accurate verification, they were facts reasonably informed people in the community would regard as propositions not reasonably subject to dispute.

Another species of facts figures prominently in discussions of judicial notice which, to employ the terminology coined by Professor K.C. Davis,[10] are denominated "legislative" facts. Judicial notice of these facts occurs when a judge is faced with the task of creating law, by deciding upon the constitutional validity of a statute,[11] or the interpretation of a statute,[12] or the extension or restriction of a common law rule,[13] upon grounds of policy, and the policy is thought to hinge upon social, economic, political or scientific facts. Illustrative of this phenomenon was Hawkins v. United States [14] in which the Court refused to discard the common law rule that one spouse could not testify against the other, saying, "Adverse testimony given in criminal proceedings would, we think, be likely to destroy almost any marriage." This conclusion rests upon a certain view of the facts about marriage but, needless to say, the facts taken to be true in this instance were hardly indisputable. Observe, moreover, that these facts were not part and parcel of the disputed event being litigated but bore instead upon the court's own thinking about the tenor of the law to be invoked in deciding that dispute.

The generic caption "legislative facts" fails to highlight any distinction between the use of extra-record data by judges when they craft a rule of law, whether of the constitutional [15] or private law [16] variety, and when they resort to extra-record data to assay whether there exist circumstances which constitutionally either legitimate the exercise of

line Investment Corp. v. Gaines, 407 F.Supp. 423 (N.D.Tex.1976) (in contract case where issue was one of impossibility, the economic events surrounding the oil embargo were adjudicative facts subject to judicial notice under Rule 201(b) both because they were generally known locally and capable of ready verification); Gilbertson v. State, 69 Wis.2d 587, 230 N.W.2d 874 (1975) (judicial notice cannot be taken of the potential damage which might be caused by placing a shovel in a generator because this was neither a matter of common knowledge nor one capable of ready verification from sources of indisputable accuracy); Davis, Judicial Notice, 55 Colum.L.Rev. 945, 952 (1955).

10. Davis, An Approach to Problems of Evidence in the Administrative Process, 55 Harv.L.Rev. 364 (1942).

11. Perez v. Lippold, 32 Cal.2d 711, 198 P.2d 17 (1948).

12. United States v. Gould, 536 F.2d 216 (8th Cir.1976) (proper for judge to in-

struct jury as a matter of statutory interpretation that cocaine hydrochloride is a derivative of the coca leaf and hence a controlled substance; Fed.R.Evid. 201(g) not applicable, since not an adjudicative fact).

13. Southern Cotton Oil Co. v. Anderson, 80 Fla. 441, 86 So. 629 (1920). Although the term judicial notice is not actually invoked, an excellent illustration of this phenomenon is inherent in Gillespie v. Dew, 1 Stew. 229, 230 (Ala.1827).

14. 358 U.S. 74, 78 (1958). See § 331 note 15 infra.

15. Roe v. Wade, 410 U.S. 113 (1973) (canvass of historical, social and medical data in opinion articulating constitutional norms governing abortions).

16. Schipper v. Levitt & Sons, Inc., 44 N.J. 70, 207 A.2d 314 (1965) (home building acquiring characteristics of manufacturing and so subjected to same style implied warranty doctrine).

legislative power [17] or substantiate the rationality of the legislative product.[18] Resort to a new subdivision like "law-making facts" might not, in its turn, bring home the reality that judges regularly resort to extra-record data not only when enunciating new substantive doctrine, but employ them in deciding questions which pertain to everything from the alpha of civil jurisdiction [19] to the omega of criminal sentencing.[20]

Concern for legislative facts does signal the recognition both that judges do not "find" the law but rather make it, and that questions of public law have become a staple of the case law menu. A judge may no longer be quite the disinterested umpire in the steady state system suggested by the common law model, but more an active participant making work what has come to be seen as process of adapting law to a volatile socio-political environment. In a very real sense it may be that a judge used to a steady diet of private law cases and a judge dealing with disputes arising out of a multiplicity of administrative agency actions may actually live in different worlds. At the same time modern procedure and trial practice have served to create a complexity that would confound the serjeants of yesteryear.

The picture is further complicated by a tendency of any brite-line distinction between adjudicative and legislative facts to dissolve in practice. Posit, for example, a statute making it a crime to possess coca leaves or any salt, compound or derivative thereof. If believed the testimony of witnesses, lay and expert, establishes that defendant possessed a quantity of cocaine hydrochloride and that the item is indeed a salt, compound or derivative of coca leaves. The last proposition is indisputable and subject to judicial notice. If this is an adjudicative fact, a federal judge would not feel free to instruct the jury that, if they were to find the defendant possessed this item, they must find the item was a proscribed one.[21] No such compunction would obtain if it were a legislative fact. Yet one judge might visualize the question in terms of, "What is it that defendant possessed?", which is part of the who, what, when and where litany signalling an adjudicative fact, while another judge might inquire, "What was it that the legislature intended

---

17. NLRB v. Jones & Laughlin Steel Corp., 301 U.S. 1, 42 (1937) (Need to create system of collective bargaining "such an outstanding fact in the history of labor disturbances that it is a proper subject of judicial notice and requires no citation of authority.").

18. Maryland v. Craig, 110 S.Ct. 3157 (1990) (Given state interest in protecting children and growing body of medical literature, court "will not second-guess the considered judgment of the Maryland Legislature regarding the importance of its interest in protecting child abuse victims from the emotional trauma of testifying."

19. Bulova Watch Co., Inc. v. K. Hattori & Co., Limited, 508 F.Supp. 1322 (E.D.N.Y.1981) (inquiry into Japanese management practices in determining whether control exercised over American subsidiary).

20. Williams v. New York, 337 U.S. 241 (1949) (longstanding practice to permit judges wide discretion as to sources and types of information used in determining sentences).

21. Fed.R.Evid. 201(g). See n. 5 § 328 supra.

to criminalize?'", access door to the realm of legislative facts.[22]   All of
which may warn the reader that the judicial notice of fact phenomemon
has many of the characteristics of an universal solvent: it cannot be
totally contained in any known vessel.

It is axiomatic, of course, that the judge decides whether a given set
of facts constitutes an actionable wrong or a certain line of cross-
examination is relevant.   A judge, unless he is to be reversed on appeal,
is bound to know the common and statutory law of his own jurisdiction.
Commonly enough even this truism has been incorporated into the law
of evidence by saying that judges must judicially notice the law of their
own forum.[23]   This manner of speaking has served to interpolate into
the field of judicial notice the procedural mechanisms by which the
applicable law is fed into the judicial process.[24]   Foreign law, of course,
was once more germane to the topic of judicial notice because that body
of law was (for convenience) treated as fact, so much so that the law of
a jurisdiction other than the forum had to be pleaded and proved just
like any other question of fact, but a peculiar one which only the judge
came to decide, and hence its inclusion within the topic of judicial
notice.[25]   Indeed, lumped along with foreign law as a proper subject for
treatment under the caption of judicial notice has been the forum's own
administrative law and local municipal ordinances, together with a
hotchpot of internal judicial administrative details concerning the
courts themselves, such as their own personnel, records, organization
and jurisdictional boundaries.[26]   The recognition appears to be growing,
however, that the manner in which the law is insinuated into the
judicial process is not so much a problem of evidence as it is a concern
better handled within the context of the rules pertaining to procedure.[27]

§ 329.   Matters of Common Knowledge

The oldest and plainest ground for judicial notice is that the fact is so
commonly known in the community as to make it unprofitable to
require proof, and so certainly known as to make it indisputable among
reasonable men.[1]   Though this basis for notice is sometimes loosely

---

22.   Compare United States v. Gould,
536 F.2d 216 (8th Cir.1976) with United
States v. Jones, 580 F.2d 219 (6th Cir.1978).

23.   Hoyt v. Russell, 117 U.S. 401 (1886).

24.   Cross, Evidence 155 (5th ed. 1979)
("It is sometimes said that the judges take
judicial notice of the Common Law, but
there is no need to deal separately with
this aspect of the subject.").

25.   Keeffe, Landis & Shaad, Sense and
Nonsense About Judicial Notice, 2 Stan.
L.Rev. 664, 673–675 (1950).

26.   See § 335 infra.

27.   Compare, e.g., Fed.R.Evid. 201, supra n. 5, Fed.R.Civ.P. 44.1, 28 U.S.C.A.

(determination of foreign law).   See § 335
infra.

§ 329

1.   Varcoe v. Lee, 180 Cal. 338, 346–347,
181 P. 223, 227 (1919).   ("The test, therefore in any particular case where it is
sought to avoid or excuse the production of
evidence because the fact to be proven is
one of general knowledge and notoriety, is:
(1) Is the fact one of common, everyday
knowledge in that jurisdiction, which
everyone of average intelligence and
knowledge of things about him can be presumed to know?   and (2) is it certain and
indisputable?   If it is, it is a proper case for
dispensing with evidence, for its production

described as universal knowledge, manifestly this could not be taken literally[2] and the more reflective opinions speak in terms of the knowledge of "most men,"[3] or of "what well-informed persons generally know,"[4] or "the knowledge that every intelligent person has."[5] Observe that these phrases tend progressively to widen the circle of facts within "common knowledge." Moreover, though usually facts of "common knowledge" will be generally known throughout the country, it is sufficient as a basis for judicial notice that they be known in the local community where the trial court sits.[6]

What a judge knows and what facts a judge may judicially notice are not identical data banks. A famous colloquy in the Year Books shows that a clear difference has long been taken between what judges may notice judicially and the facts that the particular judge happens personally to know.[7] It is not a distinction easy for a judge to follow in

cannot add or aid."); Indoor Recreation Enterprises, Inc. v. Douglas, 194 Neb. 715, 719, 235 N.W.2d 398, 401–402 (1975) ("For a fact to be judicially noticed [under Rule 201], it is not enough that it rests upon conjecture or suspicion, on gossip or rumor, or that it be commonly asserted, if that be true. The general rule is that in order that a fact may properly be the subject of judicial notice, if must be '*known*'—that is, well *established* and *authoritatively settled,* without qualification or contention.")

2. The late Dean F. McDermott of Suffolk Law School aptly exposed the absurdity of this approach by succinctly translating it into the rule that "Judicial notice may only be taken of those facts every damn fool knows." See, however, Layne v. Tribune Co., 108 Fla. 177, 183, 146 So. 234, 237 (1933) ("What everybody knows the courts are assumed to know, and of such matters may take judicial cognizance."); In re Buszta's Estate, 18 Misc.2d 716, 717, 186 N.Y.S.2d 192, 193 (Surr.1959) ("Generally speaking, a court may take judicial notice of facts which are universally known and recognized.").

3. Rives v. Atlanta Newspapers, Inc., 110 Ga.App. 184, 190, 138 S.E.2d 100, 104 (1964), reversed on other grounds 220 Ga. 485, 139 S.E.2d 395 ("Consequently, courts will take judicial notice of that which is within the knowledge of most men").

4. Brandon v. Lozier–Broderick & Gordon, 160 Kan. 506, 511, 163 P.2d 384, 387 (1945).

5. Strain v. Isaacs, 59 Ohio App. 495, 514, 18 N.E.2d 816, 825 (1938).

6. Varcoe v. Lee, 180 Cal. 338, 346, 181 P. 223, 226 (1919) ("It would be wholly unreasonable to require proof, if the fact became material, as to the general location in the city of San Francisco of its city hall

before a judge and jury made up of residents of that city and actually sitting in the building. But before a judge and jury in another county, proof should be made. The difference lies in the fact being one of common knowledge in one jurisdiction and not in the other."); Morgan, Judicial Notice, 57 Harv.L.Rev. 269, 277 (1944) ("Even in the federal court sitting in San Francisco the trial judge and jury might be ignorant of the fact and the judge might well without a further showing * * * let the jury determine the fact according to the weight of the evidence.").

But "night club gossip and stories appearing in newspapers" * * * while their content may be common knowledge, are not a source indisputable facts pertaining to "wealth or * * * any other necessary fact." Berry v. Chaplin, 74 Cal.App.2d 669, 675–676, 169 P.2d 453, 458 (1946) (Los Angeles trial court could not take judicial notice of extent of wealth of Charles Chaplin based upon his public image as presented in the press).

There are intimations that local customs may not be noticed. See, e.g., First National Bank v. Commercial Bank & Trust Co., 137 Wash. 335, 242 P. 356 (1926). But, under the present principle, if generally and certainly known in the community, they should be.

7. Anon., Y.B. 7 Hen. IV, f. 41, pl. 5 (1406), from which the following is an excerpt: "Tirwhit: Sir, let us put the case that a man kills another in your presence and sight, and another who is not guilty is indicted before you and is found guilty of the same death, you ought to respite the judgment against him, for you know the contrary, and report the matter to the King to pardon him. No more ought you

application, but the doctrine is accepted that actual private knowledge by the judge is no sufficient ground for taking judicial notice of a fact as a basis for a finding or a final judgment,[8] though it may still be a ground, it is believed, for exercising certain discretionary powers, such as granting a motion for new trial to avoid an injustice,[9] or in sentencing.[10]

Similarly, what a jury member knows in common with every other human being and what facts are appropriately circumscribed by the doctrine of judicial notice are not the same thing. Traditionally those facts so generally known within the community as not to be reasonably subject to dispute have been included within the perimeters of judicial notice under the caption of common knowledge. At the same time, however, it is often loosely said that the jury may consider, as if proven, facts within the common knowledge of the community.

When considering the award to make in a condemnation case, a jury were properly concerned whether the value of the remaining fee was diminished by the installation of a natural gas pipeline in the easement which was the discrete subject of the taking. The jurors factored in an amount to compensate for the contingency that, the fee being a farm,

to give judgment in this case * * * Gascoigne, C.J. One time the King himself asked me about this very case which you have put, and asked me what was the law, and I told him just as you say, and he was well pleased that the law was so." See Wilson v. State, 677 S.W.2d 518 (Tex.Cr. App.1984) (judge may personally know a fact of which he cannot take judicial notice, but he may be required to take judicial notice of a fact he does not know).

8. Gibson v. Von Glahn Hotel Co., 185 N.Y.S. 154, 155 (1920) (where the issue of absolute liability as an innkeeper turned on the question whether defendant's establishment was a hotel, the trial judge volunteered: "I know the Von Glahn Hotel as well as the witness does himself; I will give you a ruling now it is a hotel." Held, reversed). Accord: Darnell v. Barker, 179 Va. 86, 18 S.E.2d 271 (1942); Shafer v. Eau Claire, 105 Wis. 239, 81 N.W. 409 (1900).

It is believed that only rarely today would one encounter a trial judge who felt free to use his personal knowledge of facts. Morgan, Judicial Notice, 57 Harv.L.Rev. 269, 274 n. 7 (1944). But see: Beychok v. St. Paul Mercury Indemnity Co., 119 F.Supp. 52 (W.D.La.1954) (trial judge took judicial notice that the luncheonette stool from which plaintiff fell "had been in the same condition for at least fifteen years before plaintiff's unfortunate accident occurred, without any incidents having taken place, so far as we know, to have indicated that it was a source of danger." The judge,

however, treated this datum as a matter of "common knowledge.").

But see United States v. Alvarado, 519 F.2d 1133 (5th Cir.1975), cert. denied 424 U.S. 911 (trial judge could judicially notice location of border checkpoint because he had previously tried another case involving the facility and the same facts appeared in a previous appellate report).

9. It is clear that trial judges have a great deal of discretion in ruling upon motions for new trials. Osborne v. United States, 351 F.2d 111 (8th Cir.1965); Commonwealth v. Brown, 192 Pa.Super. 498, 162 A.2d 13 (1960). Given this wide discretion it has been suggested that not only can courts use judicial notice quite freely, but that "perhaps" they should. Comment, The Presently Expanding Concept of Judicial Notice, 13 Vill.L.Rev. 528, 540 (1968).

But see Government of Virgin Islands v. Gereau, 523 F.2d 140 (3d Cir.1975), cert. denied 424 U.S. 917 (in passing on motion for new trial, judge erred in determining credibility as between juror and jury matron on the basis of his own knowledge about the matron's need for extra income; in basing his fact finding on personal knowledge he was taking judicial notice of an adjudicative fact which did not possess the necessary cachet of either Fed.R.Evid. 201(b)(1) or (2)).

10. Williams v. New York, 337 U.S. 241 (1949).

deep chisel-style plowing might rupture the pipe and cause an explosion, the very notoriety of which would put off future purchasers of the farm. This possibility was taken seriously by the jurors, themselves residents of a farming community and familiar with local practices. Even though there had not been introduced into evidence any matter pertaining to deep chisel plowing, a court was willing to sustain the award precisely because, given the fund of common knowledge shared by this rural jury, there was no need for formal evidence to establish the point.[11]

Had the same case been transferred for trial to an urban venue, deep chisel plowing would not likely have ever been considered by a jury absent the introduction of evidence alerting them to the practice. It would be manifestly improper were a juror to investigate farming practices and to introduce the subject for the first time in the privacy of the jury room.[12] This juror should testify as a witness.[13] This leaves open the possibility that a former rural resident might introduce the subject into an urban jury room, pooling with his compatriots his distinct share of the fund of common knowledge. If the fund the jurors can draw upon is knowledge common to the community as a whole, this datum would appear to be illicit specie in an urban venue.

A similar problem would arise were evidence introduced pro and con the existence of a real threat posed by deep chisel plowing and one or more of the jurors shared their unique experience with the practice with the rest of the panel. Jurors do not think evidence; jurors think about the evidence, and to think at all requires a person to draw upon his or her experience.[14] Still, it has been held improper to invite jurors with personal experience on farms to share it with their fellows in a case which turned on the question whether an insured horse had indeed been killed by a lightning bolt.[15] It has been held appropriate, however, to invite jurors with personal experience in and about saw mills to share their insights in a personal injury case arising out of an accident at a saw mill.[16]

The parameters of the jury fund of common data may be vague precisely because trial lawyers find themselves embarrassed to insist upon brite-line rules when they themselves regularly employ summations to expose jurors to non-evidenced facts cross-dressed as rhetorical hypotheses.[17] What with voir dire examinations and challenges being

---

11. Tennessee Gas Transmission Co. v. Hall, 277 S.W.2d 733 (Tex.Civ.App.1955).

12. Thomas v. Kansas Power & Light Co., 185 Kan. 6, 340 P.2d 379 (1959).

13. But Fed.R.Evid. 606 makes a juror incompetent to be witness in the immediate trial. Compare Edelstein v. Roskin, 356 So.2d 38 (Fla.App.1978).

14. Marshall v. State, 54 Fla. 66, 44 So. 742, 743 (1907) (Instruction, "You will bring to bear in consideration of the evidence * * * in addition, all that common

knowledge of men and affairs, which you as reasonable men have and exercise in the everyday affairs of life," approved).

15. Downing v. Farmers' Mutual Fire Insurance Co., 158 Iowa 1, 138 N.W. 917 (1912).

16. Solberg v. Robbins Lumber Co., 147 Wis. 259, 133 N.W. 28 (1911).

17. Levin & Levy, Persuading the Jury with Facts not in Evidence: the Fiction–Science Spectrum, 105 U.Pa.L.Rev. 139 (1969).

available to exclude from juries anyone privy to information in excess of the local common denominator, any eccentric scenarios which do occur may simply be chalked up to self-inflicted hardship upon the part of counsel. Even so, all of this assumes that by and large each venue's jurors share relatively homogenous cultural roots so that, in fact, there does exist a rough hewn common fund of knowledge in which they all share.

In an increasingly multi-racial, multi-lingual, tri-gendered, ethnicity-fixated and highly mobile society, further fractured by class divisions, there may no longer exist a common fund of knowledge shared by the jurors resident in any venue. Out of academe there has come the suggestion that a common fund can be guaranteed by imposing a definition of that fund's parameters community to community.[18] This judge imposed construct would not only be the basis for an instruction confining deliberating jurors to this fund, but would serve as a benchmark during voir dire examinations and in determining relevancy. The efficacy of any instruction purporting to limit the data jurors use in their thinking about the outcome of a case may be questionable at best. Whether the very notion of imposing a chatechistical homogeneity on the ideational materials upon which jurors may draw is compatible with the evolving ethos of a heterogeneous polis promises, if it is taken seriously, to catalyze vigorous debate.[19]

Thus it is very easy to confound into one common denominator facts to which the evidentiary discipline of judicial notice applies and the residual data the jury members bring along with them as rational human beings. Whereas in the typical vehicular accident case the well-known character of a street can be dealt with informally as background information which helps everyone visualize the scene, the question becomes a formal one to be dealt with as part of the doctrine of judicial notice if the precise character of the street becomes an adjudicative fact in the case being tried.[20] Again, while the meaning of words is normally left to the informal common sense of the jury, the precise meaning of a word in a contract case which may be outcome determinative should be dealt with formally as a problem of judicial notice.[21]

The cases in which judicial notice is taken of indisputable facts commonly known in the community where the facts noticed are actually adjudicative ones appear to be relatively rare. In most instances, notwithstanding the invocation of the language of judicial notice, the facts either involve background information helpful in assaying the

18. Mansfield, Jury Notice, 74 Geo.L.J. 395 (1985).

19. Fraher, Adjudicative Facts, Non-Evidence Facts, and Permissible Jury Background Information, 62 Ind.L.J. 333 (1987).

20. Davis, A System of Judicial Notice Based on Fairness and Convenience, in Perspectives on Law 69, 73–74 (Pound ed. 1964).

21. Palestroni v. Jacobs, 8 N.J.Super. 438, 73 A.2d 89 (1950), reversed 10 N.J.Super. 266, 77 A.2d 183.

evidence relevant to the adjudicative facts [22] or involve facts relevant to the process of formulating the tenor of the law to be applied to the resolution of the controversy.[23] Indeed, there is a growing recognition that the common knowledge variety of fact plays only a very minor role on the judicial notice scene.[24]

§ 330. Facts Capable of Certain Verification

The earlier and probably still the most familiar basis for judicial notice is "common knowledge," but a second and distinct principle has come to be recognized as an even more significant ground for the invocation of the doctrine. This extension of judicial notice was first disguised by a polite fiction so that when asked to notice a fact not generally known, but which obviously could easily be ascertained by consulting materials in common use, such as the day of the week on which January 1 fell ten years ago, the judges resorted to calendars but purported to be "refreshing memory" as to a matter of common knowledge.[1] Eventually it was recognized that involved here was an important extension of judicial notice to the new field of facts "capable of accurate and ready demonstration,"[2] "capable of such instant and unquestionable demonstration, if desired, that no party would think of imposing a falsity on the tribunal in the face of an intelligent adversary,"[3] or "capable of immediate and accurate demonstration by resort to easily accessible sources of indisputable accuracy."[4] It is under this caption, for example, that courts have taken judicial notice of the scientific principles which, while verifiable but not likely commonly known, justify the evidentiary use of radar,[5] blood tests for intoxication[6] and nonpaternity,[7] handwriting[8] and typewriter identification,[9]

22. Pacific Gas & Electric Co. v. W. H. Hunt Estate Co., 49 Cal.2d 565, 319 P.2d 1044 (1957) (water pipes sometimes break from accidental causes); Portee v. Kronzek, 194 Pa.Super. 193, 166 A.2d 328 (1960) (people visit taverns to meet friends). Compare: Hughes v. Vestal, 264 N.C. 500, 142 S.E.2d 361 (1965); Ennis v. Dupree, 262 N.C. 224, 136 S.E.2d 702 (1964).

23. Hawkins v. United States, 358 U.S. 74 (1958); Perez v. Lippold, 32 Cal.2d 711, 198 P.2d 17 (1948).

24. Comment, 13 Vill.L.Rev. 528, 532 (1968) ("[T]he traditional test [is] whether the fact to be noticed is within the common knowledge of the community. However, there has been a modern trend away from this test and towards one which provides that a fact may be noticed if it is verifiably certain by reference to competent, authoritative sources.").

§ 330

1. Friend v. Burnham & Morrill Co., 55 F.2d 150, 151 (1st Cir.1932) ("The District Court in this case was warranted, therefore, in taking judicial notice of any common or general knowledge relating to canning cooked foods, and to refresh his recollection by reference to standard publications.").

2. Note, 47 Colum.L.Rev. 151 (1947).

3. 9 Wigmore, Evidence § 2571, p. 732 (Chadbourn rev. 1981).

4. See Fed.R.Evid. 201(b)(2) supra § 328, n. 5.

5. State v. Graham, 322 S.W.2d 188 (Mo.App.1959); State v. Dantonio, 18 N.J. 570, 115 A.2d 35 (1955).

6. State v. Miller, 64 N.J.Super. 262, 165 A.2d 829 (App.Div.1960). There has recently developed a tendency to make scientific evidence admissible by legislative enactment, e.g., N.Y.—McKinney's Vehicle and Traffic Law §§ 1194–1195.

7. Jordan v. Mace, 144 Me. 351, 69 A.2d 670 (1949); Houghton v. Houghton, 179 Neb. 275, 137 N.W.2d 861 (1965). See also, Uniform Act on Paternity, 9A U.L.A. 626.

8, 9. See notes 8, 9 on page 394.

and ballistics.[10] Whether the person employing any of this hardware was qualified to do so, whether the hardware was properly maintained and whether it was used correctly remain questions of fact.[11]

Attempts to formulate inventories of verifiable facts of which courts will take judicial notice have begun to fall into disrepute because the principle involved can better be illustrated by way of example.[12] Thus in State v. Damm [13] defendant was on trial for rape after one of his stepdaughters gave birth to a child. The defense sought a court order authorizing blood tests by which it was hoped to prove his innocence by way of negative results. Even if the tests produced a negative result, however, the testimony recounting the tests would be relevant to the question of guilt or innocence only if it was true that properly administered blood tests evidencing a negative result excluded the possibility of paternity. To leave this preliminary question pertaining to the then present state of scientific knowledge to the jury to decide as best they could on the basis of possibly conflicting testimony would appear absurd.[14] There being only one right answer to the question whether the principle was accepted in the appropriate scientific circles, the question fell within the province of judicial notice. Even so, the trial judge in this particular case was held not to have erred in refusing the request because, given the time and place, the defense was not able to produce the data necessary to illustrate to him that the principle was an accepted one within the scientific community. Presumably, of course, an opposite result would obtain today.[15]

Thus it is that while the various propositions of science are a suitable topic of judicial notice, the content of what will actually be noticed is subject to change as the tenets of science evolve.[16] It is manifest,

8. Adams v. Ristine, 138 Va. 273, 122 S.E. 126 (1924); Fenelon v. State, 195 Wis. 416, 217 N.W. 711 (1928). See generally, Note, 13 N.Y.L.F. 677 (1968).

9. United States v. Hiss, 107 F.Supp. 128 (S.D.N.Y.1952); People v. Risley, 214 N.Y. 75, 108 N.E. 200 (1915).

10. People v. Fisher, 340 Ill. 216, 172 N.E. 743 (1930).

11. People v. Flaxman. 74 Cal.App.3d Supp. 16, 141 Cal.Rptr. 799 (1977) (radar); State v. Finkle, 128 N.J.Super. 199, 319 A.2d 733 (App.Div.1974), affirmed 66 N.J. 139, 329 A.2d 65, cert. denied 423 U.S. 836 (speed gun). Thus far the results of lie detector tests have not been judicially noticed as reliable precisely because the results of the tests depend more upon the expertise of the operator than upon the reliability of the mechanism itself. See, e.g., Brown v. Darcy, 783 F.2d 1389 (9th Cir.1986); Commonwealth v. Vitello, 376 Mass. 426, 381 N.E.2d 582 (1978). Lie detection techniques are discussed in § 206 supra.

12. See, e.g., Keeffe, Landis & Shaad, Sense and Nonsense About Judicial Notice, 2 Stan.L.Rev. 664, 667 (1950) ("General rules describing particular facts that can be judicially noticed are worthless.").

13. 64 S.D. 309, 266 N.W. 667 (1936).

14. Keeffe, Landis & Shaad, op. cit. n. 11 supra, at 670. ("It brings discredit upon the legal profession and it makes a mockery of a court of justice to permit a jury to accept or reject in accordance with their prejudices a fact capable of exact scientific determination.").

15. See n. 7, supra.

16. State v. Damm, 64 S.D. 309, 266 N.W. 667 (1936) was decided five years after the trial, by which time the principle behind blood tests to determine paternity had become well established. While conceding as much, the appellate court did not reverse the trial judge's earlier decision to exclude the test results because when made, that decision had not been an erroneous one.

moreover, that the principle involved need not be commonly known in order to be judicially noticed; it suffices if the principle is accepted as a valid one in the appropriate scientific community. In determining the intellectual viability of the proposition, of course, the judge is free to consult any sources that he thinks are reliable,[17] but the extent to which judges are willing to take the initiative in looking up the authoritative sources will usually be limited. By and large, therefore, it is the task of counsel to find and to present in argument and briefs such references, excerpts and explanations as will convince the judge that the fact is certain and demonstrable. Puzzling enough in this regard, it has been noted that "nowhere can there be found a definition of what constitutes competent or authoritative sources for purposes of verifying judicially noticed facts." [18] And, it should be noted, after a number of courts take judicial notice of a principle, subsequent courts begin to dispense with the production of these materials and to take judicial notice of the principle as a matter of law established by precedent.[19]

Illustrative as they are, scientific principles hardly exhaust the verifiable facts of which courts take judicial notice. Historical facts fall within the doctrine, such as the dates upon which wars began and terminated.[20] Geographical facts [21] are involved, particularly with reference to the boundaries of the state in which the court is sitting [22] and of the counties,[23] districts [24] and townships [25] thereof, as well as the location of the capital of the state and the location and identity of the county seats.[26] Whether common knowledge or not, courts notice the identity of the principal officers of the national government [27] and the

17. Brown v. Piper, 91 U.S. (1 Otto) 37, 42 (1875) ("any means * * * which he may deem safe and proper"); People v. Mayes, 113 Cal. 618, 626, 45 P. 860, 862 (1896) ("any source of information which he may deem authentic, either by inquiry of others, or by the examination of books, or by receiving the testimony of witnesses"); Fringer v. Venema, 26 Wis.2d 366, 372–373, 132 N.W.2d 565, 569 (1965) ("can be verified to a certainty by reference to competent authoritative sources"); 9 Wigmore, Evidence § 2568a, at 720 (Chadbourn rev. 1981).

18. Comment, The Presently Expanding Concept of Judicial Notice, 13 Vill. L.Rev. 528, 545 (1968).

19. United States v. Bell, 335 F.Supp. 797 (E.D.N.Y.1971), affirmed 464 F.2d 667 (2d Cir.), cert. denied 409 U.S. 991; People v. Flaxman, 74 Cal.App.3d Supp. 16, 141 Cal.Rptr. 799 (1977).

20. Unity Co. v. Gulf Oil Corp., 141 Me. 148, 40 A.2d 4, 156 A.L.R. 297 (1944) (dates of declaration of World War II and beginning of rationing); Miller v. Fowler, 200 Miss. 776, 28 So.2d 837 (1947) (that acts of warfare between Japan and the United

States had not entirely ceased on Aug. 14, 1945; 29 Am.Jur.2d Evidence §§ 73–76.

21. See, e.g., Swarzwald v. Cooley, 39 Cal.App.2d 306, 103 P.2d 580 (1940) (meaning of phrase, "ordinary hightide," in the vicinity of Laguna Beach).

22. Watson v. Western Union Telegraph Co., 178 N.C. 471, 101 S.E. 81 (1919); 29 Am.Jur.2d Evidence § 63.

23. State ex inf. Gentry v. Armstrong, 315 Mo. 298, 286 S.W. 705 (1926) (location of city and county of St. Louis); Elmore County v. Tallapoosa County, 221 Ala. 182, 128 So. 158 (1930) (area and boundaries); 29 Am.Jur.2d Evidence § 64.

24. Board of Education v. State, 222 Ala. 70, 131 So. 239 (1930) (school district).

25. Nelson v. Thomas, 103 Cal.App. 108, 283 P. 982 (1930).

26. Bunten v. Rock Springs Grazing Association, 29 Wyo. 461, 215 P. 244 (1923).

27. United States ex rel. Petach v. Phelps, 40 F.2d 500 (2d Cir.1930) (assistants to the Secretary of Labor); Lyman Flood Prevention Association v. City of

incumbents of principal state offices.[28] Similarly, while obviously not necessarily a matter of common knowledge, judges take notice of the identity of the officers of their courts, such as the other judges,[29] the sheriffs,[30] clerks,[31] and attorneys;[32] of the duration of terms and sessions,[33] and of the rules of court.[34]

It would seem obvious that the judge of a court would take notice of all of the records of the institution over which he presides, but the courts have been slow to give the principle of judicial notice its full reach of logic and expediency. It is settled, of course, that the courts, trial and appellate, take notice of their own respective records in the present litigation, both as to matters occurring in the immediate trial,[35] and in previous trials or hearings.[36] The principle seemingly is equally applicable to matters of record in the proceedings in other cases in the same court, and some decisions have recognized this,[37] but many courts still adhere to the needless requirement of formal proof, rather than informal presentation, of recorded proceedings in other suits in the same court.[38] Matters of record in other courts are usually denied notice even though it would appear manifest that these public documents are logically subject to judicial notice as readily verifiable

Topeka, 152 Kan. 484, 106 P.2d 117 (1940) (time of retirement of Woodring as Secretary of War).

28. Picking v. Pennsylvania Railroad Co., 151 F.2d 240 (3d Cir.1945) (that named defendants were officials of Pennsylvania and New York); Patten v. Miller, 190 Ga. 123, 8 S.E.2d 757 (1940) (chairman, State Highway Board).

29. Payne v. Williams, 47 Ariz. 396, 56 P.2d 186 (1936) (Supreme Court notices names of superior court judges, their counties and terms); Alexander v. Gladden, 205 Or. 375, 288 P.2d 219 (1955) (Supreme Court notices the organization of its own court and lower courts under its supervision).

30. Sowers–Taylor Co. v. Collins, 14 S.W.2d 692 (Mo.App.1929) (names of officers authorized to serve process).

31. Favre v. Louisville & Nashville Railroad Co., 180 Miss. 843, 178 So. 327 (1938).

32. Squire v. Bates, 132 Ohio St. 161, 5 N.E.2d 690 (1936) (persons who have been admitted and dates of their admission).

33. Vance v. Harkey, 186 Ark. 730, 55 S.W.2d 785 (1932) (Supreme Court knows that term at which decree entered has elapsed).

34. A trial court, of course, knows its own rules without formal proof. Wallace v. Martin, 166 So. 874 (La.App.1936). And on general principles an appellate court knows judicially what the trial court judi-

cially knew. See § 333 n. 12 infra. In the absence of a statute, however, some courts may not take judicial notice of the rules of an equal or inferior court. C.J.S. Evidence § 49.

35. Nichols v. Nichols, 126 Conn. 614, 13 A.2d 591 (1940) (superseded pleading, claimed to constitute admission, will be noticed but must be called to trial court's attention); 29 Am.Jur.2d Evidence § 57.

36. Collins v. Leahy, 347 Mo. 133, 146 S.W.2d 609 (1940) (where city map was part of record of prior appeal to Supreme Court, court would take notice of it on subsequent appeal though not introduced in evidence at later trial); 29 Am.Jur.2d Evidence § 57.

37. Green v. Warden, United States Penitentiary, 699 F.2d 364 (7th Cir.1983), cert. denied 461 U.S. 960 (plaintiff's extensive record of litigation in both federal and other courts); Willson v. Security–First National Bank, 21 Cal.2d 705, 134 P.2d 800 (1943); South Shore Land Co. v. Petersen, 226 Cal.App.2d 725, 38 Cal.Rptr. 392 (1964); Johnson v. Marsh, 146 Neb. 257, 19 N.W.2d 366 (1945); Meck v. Allen Properties, Inc., 206 Misc. 251, 132 N.Y.S.2d 674 (1954).

38. Guam Investment Co. v. Central Building, Inc., 288 F.2d 19 (9th Cir.1961); Murphy v. Citizens' Bank, 82 Ark. 131, 100 S.W. 894 (1907); Fleming v. Anderson, 187 Va. 788, 48 S.E.2d 269 (1948); 29 Am. Jur.2d Evidence § 58.

facts.[39]

In the increasingly important practice of judicial notice of scientific and technological facts, some of the possibilities of error are, first, that the courts may fail to employ the doctrine of judicial notice in this field to the full measure of its usefulness; second, that they may mistakenly accept as authoritative scientific theories that are outmoded or are not yet received by the specialists as completely verified; and third, that in taking judicial notice of accepted scientific facts, the courts, in particular cases may misconceive the conclusions or applications which are supposed to flow from them. Of these, it seems that the first has thus far been the most frequent shortcoming.

In determining relevancy an informal system of judicial notice has always obtained, as for example, when it is decided that burglar tools are admissible evidence on the premise that only burglars likely possess such items. Whether the results of negative blood tests were admissible was again a question of relevancy, but the results were not admitted until it was established as incontrovertible fact that the principle behind the test itself was valid.[40] It seemed at the time quite self evident that juries could not pass upon the validity of the test principle because, a rule of science being implicated, there had to be only one right answer. Concomitantly, there might have been worry that juries might be overawed by scientific evidence and that the risk of prejudice ought not be run unless the principle met the stringent test of absolute truth. Whether the classic model ought still to be followed, however, is a question which has to be faced. In a technological era scientific truths are more readily recognized as theorems themselves subject to modification rather rapidly and juries are likely aware of the frailties inherent in technological equipment and analysis, the meanest juror being owner of electronic gear soon obsolete and always in need of fine tuning during its short life. This suggests that judicial notice, with its premise that facts must be indisputably true, be abandoned as the avenue by which scientific tests be admitted into evidence. Instead, the usual test of relevancy would obtain in which the question would be whether the test was supported by enough expert opinion to suggest that its results ought to be considered by the jury for whatever it was worth. The dogmatic theology of judicial notice would be replaced by pragmatism.

---

39. In re Bach's Estate, 81 Misc.2d 479, 365 N.Y.S.2d 454 (1975), affirmed 53 A.D.2d 612, 383 N.Y.S.2d 653 (while a court takes judicial notice of its own records, it is preferable that formal proof of proceedings in other actions in other courts be introduced into evidence). But see Zahn v. Transamerica Corp., 162 F.2d 36, 48 n. 20 (3d Cir.1947). See also Funk v. Commissioner, 163 F.2d 796 (3d Cir.1947). It has been suggested, moreover, that in practice trial judges do look at related court files. Weinstein, Mansfield, Abrams & Berger, Cases and Materials on Evidence 1284 (8th ed. 1988).

40. See text infra at n. 12.

§ 331. Social and Economic Data Used in Judicial Law–Making: "Legislative" Facts [1]

It is conventional wisdom today to observe that judges not only are charged to find what the law is, but must regularly make new law when deciding upon the constitutional validity of a statute,[2] interpreting a statute,[3] or extending or restricting a common law rule.[4] The very nature of the judicial process necessitates that judges be guided, as legislators are, by considerations of expediency and public policy.[5] They must, in the nature of things, act either upon knowledge already possessed or upon assumptions,[6] or upon investigation of the pertinent general facts, social,[7] economic,[8] political,[9] or scientific.[10] An older tradition once prescribed that judges should rationalize their result solely in terms of analogy to old doctrines leaving the considerations of expediency unstated. Contemporary practice indicates that judges in

§ 331

1. See Davis, Administrative Law Treatise, Ch. 15 (1958, supp. 1965), an unusually original and enlightening discussion; Davis, An Approach to Problems of Evidence in the Administrative Process, 55 Harv.L.Rev. 364, 402 (1942); Davis, Judicial Notice, 55 Colum.L.Rev. 945, 952 (1955); Note, 61 Harv.L.Rev. 692 (1948); Monahan & Walker, Social Authority: Obtaining, Evaluating, and Establishing Social Science in Law, 134 U.Pa.L.Rev. 477 (1986).

2. Perez v. Lippold, 32 Cal.2d 711, 198 P.2d 17 (1948) (statute outlawing interracial marriage); Stanton v. Stanton, 421 U.S. 7, 15 (1975) ("The presence of women in business, in the professions, in government and, indeed, in all walks of life where education is a desirable, if not always a necessary, antecedent is apparent and a proper subject of judicial notice." This data bore on the question whether it was any longer permissible constitutionally to vary the duty of child support between males and females on the basis of a different age of attaining adulthood).

3. Roe v. Wade, 410 U.S. 113 (1973) (history of abortion statutes).

4. Scurti v. City of New York, 40 N.Y.2d 433, 387 N.Y.S.2d 55, 354 N.E.2d 794 (1976) (ancient distinctions between licensees, trespassers and invitees seen not to reflect modern day needs).

5. Cardozo, The Nature of the Judicial Process, 113–125 (1921); Frank, Law and the Modern Mind, ch. 4 (1930).

6. Village of Euclid v. Ambler Realty Co., 272 U.S. 365 (1926) (proper exercise of police power to exclude apartment houses from residential districts because they tend to be mere parasites and come near to being nuisances); Potts v. Coe, 78 U.S.App. D.C. 297, 140 F.2d 470 (1944) (incentive to invent supplied by patent law will not work in organized research because it destroys teamwork).

7. Brown v. Board of Education, 347 U.S. 483 (1954) (racially segregated schools can never be equal notwithstanding their equality of teachers or equipment because the very act of segregation brands the segregated minority with a feeling of inferiority); Roe v. Wade, 410 U.S. 113 (1973), rehearing denied 410 U.S. 959 (canvass of historical, social and medical data in opinion articulating constitutional norms governing regulation of abortions).

8. SEC v. Capital Gains Research Bureau, Inc., 300 F.2d 745 (2d Cir.1961), reversed 375 U.S. 180 (judicial notice taken that advice tendered by small advisory service could not influence stock market generally); same case, 375 U.S. 180 (1963) (judicial notice taken that the advice tendered could influence the market price).

9. Baker v. Carr, 369 U.S. 186 (1962) (contemporary notions of justice require that equal apportionment of voting districts be made a legal and perforce largely mathematical question rather than a purely political one).

10. Durham v. United States, 94 U.S.App.D.C. 228, 214 F.2d 862 (1954) (psychiatric learning pertinent to the scientific soundness of the right-and-wrong test of criminal insanity).

See particularly Ballew v. Georgia, 435 U.S. 223 (1978) (critical evaluation of studies themselves to determine whether empirical data suggested that progressively

their opinions should render explicit their policy-judgments and the factual grounds therefor. These latter have been helpfully classed as "legislative facts," as contrasted with the "adjudicative facts" which are historical facts pertaining to the incidents which give rise to lawsuits.[11]

Constitutional cases argued in terms of due process typically involve reliance upon legislative facts for their proper resolution. Whether a statute enacted pursuant to the police power is valid, after all, involves a twofold analysis. First, it must be determined that the enactment is designed to achieve an appropriate objective of the police power; that is, it must be designed to protect the public health, morals, safety, or general welfare.[12] The second question is whether, in light of the data on hand, a legislature still beholden to reason could have adopted the means they did to achieve the aim of their exercise of the police power.[13] In Jay Burns Baking Co. v. Bryan,[14] for example, the question was whether, concerned about consumers being misled by confusing sizes of bread, the Nebraska legislature could decree not only that the bakers bake bread according to distinctively different weights but that they wrap their product in wax paper lest any post-oven expansion of some loaves undo these distinctions. A majority of the court held the enactment unconstitutional because, in their opinion, the wrapping requirement was unreasonable. Mr. Justice Brandeis, correctly anticipating the decline of substantive due process, dissented, pointing out that the only question was whether the measure was a reasonable legislative response in light of the facts available to the legislators themselves.[15] Then, in a marvelous illustration of the Brandeis-brief technique, he recited page after page of data illustrating how widespread was the problem of shortweight and how, in light of nationwide experience, the statute appeared to be a reasonable response to the environmental situation.[16]

Given the bent to test due process according to the information available to the legislature, the truth-content of these data are not

smaller juries were less likely to engage in group deliberation).

11. Davis, Administrative Law Treatise § 15.03 (1958).

12. Bilbar Construction Co. v. Board of Adjustment, 393 Pa. 62, 141 A.2d 851 (1958).

13. See the discussion running throughout the several opinions in Griswold v. Connecticut, 381 U.S. 479 (1965). See also Johnson v. Opelousas, 488 F.Supp. 433 (W.D.La.1980), reversed 658 F.2d 1065 (5th Cir.) (curfew reasonable in light of judicially noticed increasing after-dark crime rates).

14. 264 U.S. 504 (1924).

15. Accord: West Coast Hotel Co. v. Parrish, 300 U.S. 379 (1937); Olsen v. Nebraska ex rel. Western Reference & Bond Association, 313 U.S. 236, 133 A.L.R. 1500 (1941). See also Lochner v. New York, 198 U.S. 45 (1905) (Holmes, J., dissenting.)

16. The opponents of a statute can resort to extra-record legislative facts to support their argument that it is invalid. In Jay Burns Baking Co. v. Bryan, 264 U.S. 504 (1924), the statute regulating bread sizes was struck down because it was "contrary to common experience and unreasonable to assume there could be any danger of * * * deception." See also Defiance Milk Products Co. v. Du Mond, 309 N.Y. 537, 132 N.E.2d 829 (1956) (statute requiring inordinately large size cans for retail sale of evaporated skimmed milk held invalid because judicial notice was taken that it would be incredible to believe consumers needed protection against deception practiced with regard to the nature of this product).

directly relevant. The question is whether sufficient data exist which could influence a reasonable legislature to act, not whether ultimately these data are true.[17] This is not the same case as when a court proceeds to interpret a constitutional norm and, while they still rely upon data, the judges *qua* legislators themselves proceed to act as if the data were true. In Brown v. Board of Education,[18] for example, the Court faced the issue whether segregated schools, equal facility and teacher-wise, could any longer be tolerated under the equal protection clause. The question was not any longer whether a reasonable legislator could believe these schools could never be equal, but whether the *judges* believed that the very act of segregating branded certain children with a feeling of inferiority so deleterious that it would be impossible for them to obtain an equal education no matter how equal the facilities and teachers. Thus the intellectual legitimacy of this kind of decision turns upon the actual truth-content of the legislative facts taken into account by the judges who propound the decision. While not necessarily indisputably true, it would appear that these legislative facts must at least appear to be more likely than not true if the opinion is going to have the requisite intellectual legitimacy upon which the authority of judge-made rules is ultimately founded.[19]

When it comes to the utilization of these law making facts, three problems can beset constitutional law decisions. The first is that the forest can sometimes be lost sight of for the trees. That is to say, so much historical and sociological data are rehearsed that an opinion appears to be bottomed upon purely pragmatic considerations and not upon any compelling constitutional norm.[20] The second is that an outpouring of learning appears to be almost an exercise in the narcissus that afflicts academics, the problem at hand not demanding an expenditure of wit and learning on any such scale.[21] The third is that data can appear to be fired off as an exercise in fustian excess, often in a losing

---

17. Note that Fed.R.Evid. 201 deals only with adjudicative facts. See n. 5 § 328 supra.

18. 347 U.S. 483 (1954), supplemented 349 U.S. 294.

19. See, e.g., the reaction to Durham v. United States, 94 U.S.App.D.C. 228, 214 F.2d 862 (1954), wherein on the basis of psychiatric data the court formulated a new test for criminal insanity. Some psychiatrists accepted the result: Roche, Criminality and Mental Illness—Two Faces of the Same Coin, 22 U.Chi.L.Rev. 320 (1955). The American Law Institute rejected it. Model Penal Code, Tentative Draft No. 4, 159–60 (1955). See also Brown v. Board of Education, 347 U.S. 483 (1954), supplemented 349 U.S. 294, wherein for the psychological impact of segregation the court relied upon, inter alia, the work of Dr. Kenneth B. Clark. Dr. Clark felt com-pelled thereafter publicly to respond to critics of his work. Clark, The Desegregation Cases: Criticism of the Social Scientists Role, 5 Vill.L.Rev. 224, 236–40 (1960). But see Van den Haag, Social Science Testimony in the Desegregation Cases—A Reply to Professor Kenneth Clark, 6 Vill. L.Rev. 69 (1960).

20. See particularly Chief Justice Burger's concurring opinion in Roe v. Wade, 410 U.S. 113, 207 (1973), rehearing denied 410 U.S. 959 ("I am somewhat troubled that the Court has taken notice of various scientific and medical data in reaching its conclusion; however, I do not believe that the Court has exceeded the scope of judicial notice accepted in other contexts.").

21. See, e.g., Justice Blackmun's opinion in Flood v. Kuhn, 407 U.S. 258, 260–264 (1972) (mythopoetic romp through nostalgia of baseball).

cause.[22] The first would appear to be a problem of draftsmanship, hard cases perhaps making bad law, but the latter two tend to give lie to the notion that judges lack for time.

When making new common law, judges must, like legislators, do the best they can assaying the data available to them and make the best decision they can of which course wisdom dictates they follow. Should they, for example, continue to invoke the common law rule of *caveat emptor* in the field of real property, or should they invoke a notion of implied warranty in the instance of the sale of new houses? [23] Should they require landlords of residential units to warrant their habitability and fitness for the use intended? While sociological, economic, political and moral doctrine may abound about questions like this, none of these data are likely indisputable.[24]

Thus it is that, in practice, the legislative facts upon which judges rely when performing their lawmaking function are not indisputable. At the same time, cognizant of the fact that his decision as lawmaker can affect the public at large, in contradistinction to most rulings at trials which affect only the parties themselves, a judge is not likely to rely for his data only upon what opposing counsel tender him. Obviously enough, therefore, legislative facts tend to be the most elusive facts when it comes to propounding a codified system of judicial notice.[25] This seems to be confirmed by the fact that the Federal Rules of Evidence are a confession of intellectual bankruptcy in this regard.[26]

22. See particularly Chief Justice Rehnquist's dissent in Texas v. Johnson, 491 U.S. 397 (1989) (patriotic gore from Emerson, Francis Scott Key and Whittier massed in favor of respect for the flag) and Justice Brennan's dissent to the denial of certiorari in Glass v. Louisiana, 471 U.S. 1080 (1985), rehearing denied 472 U.S. 1033 (vivid descriptions of bodily reactions to lethal doses of electricity injected by official executioners).

23. Schipper v. Levitt & Sons, Inc., 44 N.J. 70, 207 A.2d 314 (1965) (mass developer of homes who assembled final product out of component parts treated as a manufacturer and implied warranty imposed).

24. Lemle v. Breeden, 51 Hawaii 426, 462 P.2d 470 (1969) (application of implied warranty recognizes changes in history of leasing transactions and takes into account contemporary housing realities).

25. Recall the notion in Hawkins v. United States, 358 U.S. 74 (1958), discussed supra at § 328, n. 12, that admitting the testimony of one spouse against another would destroy their marriage. Justice Stewart suggested at the time that the proposition might well be nothing more than an unsound assumption in cases where the spouse's testimony was actually voluntary. Id. at 81–82 (concurring opin-

ion). In 1980, the rule was modified to allow voluntary testimony. Trammel v. United States, 445 U.S. 40 (1980). Justice Stewart insisted that nothing had changed since 1958 except the Court's willingness to adhere to assumptions rooted in hoary sentiments. Id. at 53–54 (concurring opinion). For further discussion of *Trammel*, see § 66 supra.

See particularly Davis, A System of Judicial Notice Based on Fairness and Convenience, in Perspectives of Law, 69, 82 (Pound ed. 1964) ("judge-made law would stop growing if judges, in thinking about questions of law and policy, were forbidden to take into account the facts they believe, as distinguished from facts which are 'clearly * * * within the domain of the indisputable.' ") If the data available on appeal are conflicting, however, a court can remand the case to trial so these data can be more effectively explored by introducing them there in the form of evidence subject to cross-examination. See, e.g., Borden's Farm Products Co. v. Baldwin, 293 U.S. 194 (1934).

26. Fed.R.Evid. 201, reproduced at § 328 n. 5 supra, does not purport to regulate the notice of adjudicative facts. The advisory committee note on Rule 201(a) nonetheless takes for granted the existence

There are, however, efforts being made to rationalize this subject-matter. If one were to examine social science materials looking for help in enunciating a rule of law, one would be searching for authority much in the same fashion as one would be if one were looking to unearth decisional precedential authority. This has suggested to Professors John Monahan and Laurens Walker that a foray into social science materials is more akin to an effort to answer a question of law than one of fact.[27] Thus judges should not see themselves taking judicial notice of legislative facts but promulgating law. Social science materials would not be introduced into the system by expert testimony but by way of written briefs, and judges would have no hesitation at all carrying on their own independent researches. The very recognition that a question of law was involved would catalyze a more critical attitude toward these materials, because they would carry more *gravitas,* being law, than do the only arguably true episodic facts of the current approach. Soon enough a canon of precedential authority would come into being based upon a calculus of the precise court which relied on particular data and the peer review each decision received in the law reviews and other opinions. Thus these materials could be quickly accessed *in puisne* courts by simple reference and citation.[28]

§ 332. The Uses of Judicial Notice [1]

Judges have been prone to emphasize the need for caution in applying the doctrine of judicial notice.[2] The great writers of evidence, on the other hand, having perhaps a wider view of the needs of judicial administration, advocate a more extensive use of the doctrine. Thus Thayer suggests: "Courts may judicially notice much that they cannot be required to notice. That is well worth emphasizing; for it points to a great possible usefulness in this doctrine, in helping to shorten and simplify trials. * * * The failure to exercise it tends daily to smother trials with technicality and monstrously lengthens them out." [3] And Wigmore says, "The principle is an instrument of usefulness hitherto

---

of legislative facts, observing simply that "no rule deals with judicial notice of legislative facts."

27. Monahan & Walker, Social Authority: Obtaining, Evaluating, and Establishing Social Science in Law, 134 U.Pa.L.Rev. 477 (1986).

28. See text of § 330 at n. 19 supra and at § 334 n. 14 infra.

§ 332

1. Thayer, Preliminary Treatise on the Law of Evidence 308–309 (1898); 9 Wigmore, Evidence § 2567 (Chadbourn rev. 1981); Davis, A System of Judicial Notice Based on Fairness and Convenience, in

Perspectives of Law 69 (Pound ed. 1964); Morgan, Judicial Notice, 57 Harv.L.Rev. 269 (1941); McNaughton, Judicial Notice—Excerpts Relating to the Morgan–Wigmore Controversy, 14 Vand.L.Rev. 779 (1961); Roberts, Preliminary Notes Toward a Study of Judicial Notice, 52 Cornell L.Q. 210 (1967).

2. See, e.g., Varcoe v. Lee, 180 Cal. 338, 345, 181 P. 223, 226 (1919); State ex rel. Remick v. Clousing, 205 Minn. 296, 285 N.W. 711, 123 A.L.R. 465, 470 (1939); National Recruiters, Inc. v. Toro Co., 343 N.W.2d 704 (Minn.App.1984).

3. Thayer, Preliminary Treatise on Evidence 309 (1898).

unimagined by judges." [4]

The simple litany that judicial notice encapsulates facts commonly known and facts readily verifiable is useful as a rule-of-thumb but not as a precise litmus test. The courts' willingness to resort to judicial notice is apparently influenced by a number of less specifically definable circumstances. A court is more willing to notice a general than a specific fact, as for example, the approximate time of the normal period of human gestation, but not the precise maximum and minimum limits.[5] A court may be more willing to notice a fact if it is not an ultimate fact, that is, a fact which would be determinative of a case.[6] Suppose, for example, that a plaintiff in a vehicular negligence action specifically alleged that the defendant was driving too fast in a business district and the testimony, if believed, would indicate that the automobile in question caused a long skid mark on the highway surface. The trial judge might be less willing to notice that the street in question was within the business district than he would to notice that any properly equipped automobile travelling at the maximum speed appropriate in such a district could be stopped within x feet of the braking point. In the first example, the trial judge would appear to be invading the province of the jury to determine the facts pertinent to what had happened, whereas in the second he would be merely establishing rather quickly a piece of data which would aid the jury during their deliberations on the ultimate issue of negligence.[7]

Agreement is not to be had whether the perimeters of the doctrine of judicial notice enclose only facts which are indisputably true or encompass also facts more than likely true.[8] If, on the one hand, the function of the jury is to resolve disputed questions of fact, an argument can be made that judges should not purport to make decisions about facts unless they are indisputable facts. If this argument is accepted, it follows that once a fact has been judicially noticed, evidence contradicting the truth of the fact is inadmissible because by its very nature, a fact capable of being judicially noticed is an indisputable fact which the jury must be instructed to accept as true.[9] If, on the other hand, the

4. 9 Wigmore, Evidence § 2583, p. 819 (Chadbourn rev. 1981).

5. Compare Equitable Trust Co. v. McComb, 19 Del. Ch. 387, 168 A. 203 (1933), with Commonwealth v. Kitchen, 299 Mass. 7, 11 N.E.2d 482 (1937).

6. This idea was suggested in Thayer, Preliminary Treatise on the Law of Evidence 306 (1898) and was repeated in McCormick, Evidence § 323 (1954), and Comment, 13 Vill.L.Rev. 528, 533–534 (1968). Illustrative of a case involving the judicial notice of an ultimate fact is State v. Lawrence, 120 Utah 323, 234 P.2d 600 (1951), where the lower court took judicial notice of the fact that the value of the car allegedly stolen by the defendant was worth in excess of $50.00, the amount required for a larceny conviction, but on appeal was reversed.

7. However, in Varcoe v. Lee, supra § 328 n. 4, judicial notice was taken that the street was in a business district, and in Hughes v. Vestal, 264 N.C. 500, 142 S.E.2d 361 (1965) the trial judge was reversed for instructing the jury from a table of stopping distances. See n. 21 infra.

8. See e.g. McNaughton, Judicial Notice—Excerpts Relating to the Morgan–Wigmore Controversy, 14 Vand.L.Rev. 779 (1961).

9. Most convincingly expounded by Morgan, Judicial Notice, 57 Harv.L.Rev. 269 (1944), and by the same author in The Law of Evidence 1941–1945, 59 Harv.

function of judicial notice is to expedite the trial of cases, an argument can be made that judges should dispense with the need for time-consuming formal evidence when the fact in question is likely true. If this argument is accepted, it follows that evidence contradicting the judicially noticed fact is admissible and that the jury are ultimately free to accept or reject the truth of the fact posited by judicial notice.[10]

A facile resolution of this conflict suggests itself readily enough. That is, the controversy might be exposed as a misunderstanding caused by a failure to take into account the distinction between "adjudicative" and "legislative" facts.[11] This would be true if the instances where judicial notice was restricted to indisputable facts involved only adjudicative facts whereas potentially disputable facts were only noticed within a legislative context. Whether the decided cases sustain this symmetry is itself a matter of dispute because authority exists which illustrates that some courts are not loathe judicially to notice a

---

L.Rev. 481, 482–487 (1946). In agreement are Maguire, Evidence—Common Sense and Common Law, 174 (1947) ("the judge's decision to take judicial notice should be final"); Keeffe, Landis & Shaad, Sense and Nonsense About Judicial Notice, 2 Stan. L.Rev. 664, 668 (1950) ("The better view would seem to be that a fact, once judicially noticed, is not open to evidence disputing it"); McCormick, Judicial Notice, 5 Vand.L.Rev. 296, 321–322 (1952) ("the weight of reason and the prevailing authority support the view that a ruling that a fact will be judicially noticed precludes contradictory evidence and requires that the judge instruct the jury that they must accept the fact as true"); McNaughton, Judicial Notice—Excerpts Relating to the Morgan–Wigmore Controversy, 14 Vand. L.Rev. 779, 780 (1961) ("the impregnability of Morgan's position"). In accord also is Fed.R.Evid. 201 supra § 328 n. 5.

Judicial authority includes Phelps Dodge Corp. v. Ford, 68 Ariz. 190, 196, 203 P.2d 633, 638 (1949) ("A fact of which a court may take judicial notice must be indisputable. This being true it follows that evidence may not be received to dispute it"); Nicketta v. National Tea Co., 338 Ill.App. 159, 87 N.E.2d 30 (1949) (trial court properly took notice on pleadings that trichinosis cannot be contracted from eating properly cooked pork, and dismissed complaint; evidence thereon unnecessary); Commonwealth v. Marzynski, 149 Mass. 68, 21 N.E. 228 (1889) (court will take notice that tobacco and cigars are not medicine and exclude testimony to the contrary); Soyland v. Farmers Mutual Fire Insurance Co., 71 S.D. 522, 528, 26 N.W.2d 696, 699 (1947) ("it is not permissible for a court to take judicial knowledge of a fact that may be disputed by competent evidence.").

10. Most convincingly expounded by Wigmore in 9 Wigmore, Evidence § 2567a (Chadbourn rev. 1981) ("That a matter is judicially noticed means merely that it is taken as true without the offering of evidence by the party who should ordinarily have done so. This is because the Court assumes that the matter is so notorious that it will not be disputed. But the opponent is not prevented from disputing the matter by evidence if he believes it disputable"). In agreement are Thayer, A Preliminary Treatise on Evidence at the Common Law 308 (1898) ("taking judicial notice does not import that the matter is indisputable"); Davis, A System of Judicial Notice Based on Fairness and Convenience, in Perspectives of Law 69, 94 (Pound ed. 1964) ("the ultimate principle is that extra-record facts should be assumed whenever it is convenient to assume them"); Davis, Judicial Notice, 1969 L. & Soc. Order 513, 515–516 ("the practical course is to take notice and allow challenge later whenever the court believes that challenge is unlikely").

Makos v. Prince, 64 So.2d 670, 673 (Fla. 1953) (judicial notice "does not prevent an opponent's disputing the matter"); Macht v. Hecht Co., 191 Md. 98, 102, 59 A.2d 754, 756 (1948) ("judicial notice * * * does not * * * prevent the presentation of contrary evidence"); Timson v. Manufacturers' Coal & Coke Co., 220 Mo. 580, 598, 119 S.W. 565, 569 (1909) ("Judicial notice * * * does not preclude the opposite party from rebutting such prima facie case"). See also, State v. Duranleau, 99 N.H. 30, 104 A.2d 519 (1954); State v. Kincaid, 133 Or. 95, 285 P. 1105 (1930).

11. See §§ 328, 330, supra.

potentially disputable fact within what is at least arguably an adjudicative context.[12]

The most recent efforts to deal with judicial notice have exhibited a trend away from extrapolating an all-inclusive definition of a doctrine in favor of promulgating modest guidelines which would regularize what are perceived to be the essential applications of judicial notice. One approach would restrict formalized judicial notice regulation to those situations in which only adjudicative facts are involved.[13] Limiting judicial notice to adjudicative facts and then only to indisputable ones leaves unresolved the question whether a jury in a criminal case should be instructed that they must accept the inexorable truth of the noticed fact. In terms of logic and pure reason it would appear that a jury as a rational deliberative body must accept proper judicially noticed facts.[14] Viewed through the lens of democratic tradition as a protection against an overbearing sovereign, a criminal trial jury may be a body which ought to be free to return a result which as an exercise in logic flies in the face of reason.[15]

Another approach would narrow the range of judicial notice by de-escalating the significance of the conflict between questions peculiarly the province of juries and questions of fact handled by judges.[16] Judges have, for example, always dealt with preliminary questions of fact even in jury trials.[17] Thus, while the admissibility of the results of blood tests raises a question of fact pertaining to the reliability of such tests, the judges deal with this question as a preliminary step in ruling on relevancy, a function that is itself peculiarly a judicial one.[18] Indeed, if

12. See, e.g., Securities and Exchange Commission v. Capital Gains Research Bureau, Inc., 375 U.S. 180 (1963); Daniel v. Paul, 395 U.S. 298 (1969). Compare Davis, Judicial Notice, 1969 L. & Soc. Order 515, 521–523, and Cleary, Foreword to Symposium on Federal Rules of Evidence, 1969 L. & Soc. Order 509, 510.

13. Fed.R.Evid. 201, Advisory Committee's Note, Subdivision (a). "This is the only evidence rule on the subject of judicial notice. It deals only with judicial notice of 'adjudicative' facts."

14. Compare Rev.Uniform Rule of Evidence (1974) 201(g) with Fed.R.Evid. 201(g). See § 328 n. 3 supra.

15. United States v. Jones, 580 F.2d 219 (6th Cir.1978). See Fed.R.Evid. 201(g), supra § 328 n. 3; United States v. Anderson, 528 F.2d 590, 592 (5th Cir.1976), cert. denied 429 U.S. 837 (judicial notice taken that the Federal Correctional Institution at Tallahassee, Florida, was within federal jurisdiction. "The trial judge instructed the jury '* * * you may and are allowed to accept that as fact proven before you just as though there had been evidence to that effect before you.' The court did not tell the jury in the words of the rule that the jury 'may, but is not required to accept as conclusive any fact judicially noticed.' Such variance from the rule is not reversible error.")

Thus it is crucial to know whether a judicially noticed fact is actually an adjudicative or a legislative one. See, e.g., United States v. Gould, 536 F.2d 216 (8th Cir. 1976) (proper for judge to instruct jury that cocaine hydrochloride is a derivative of the coca leaf and hence a controlled substance legislators intend to include within a broad prohibition); National Organization for Reform of Marijuana Laws v. Bell, 488 F.Supp. 123 (D.D.C.1980).

16. See particularly Comment, 13 Vill. L.Rev. 528 (1968).

17. Maguire & Epstein, Preliminary Questions of Fact in Determining the Admissibility of Evidence, 40 Harv.L.Rev. 392 (1927). See § 53 supra.

18. Gorton v. Hadsell, 63 Mass. (9 Cush.) 508, 511 (1852) ("But it is the province of the judge, who presides at trial, to decide all questions on the admissibility of evidence.").

trials are examined functionally, it can be demonstrated that judges have always had to decide questions pertaining to facts without any apparent infringement of the jury's domain, whether this be in ruling on demurrers,[19] during pretrial hearings,[20] on motions for nonsuit or to set aside verdicts,[21] or at sentencing.[22] This may indicate, after all, that the scope of judicial notice varies according to the function the judge is performing when judicial notice is taken.

It may be the case that there is no easy rule-of-thumb technique adequate unto the day to serve as an easy capsulation of the judicial notice phenomenon. Protagonists of the indisputable-only definition of judicial notice concede that in criminal cases the jury must be left free in the ultimate analysis to determine the truth or falsity of any adjudicative fact.[23] Protagonists of the disputability thesis might be expected to resolve the controversy by suggesting that, whereas in jury cases there is some merit in the notion that judicial notice should be restricted to indisputable facts in order not to infringe on the role of the jury,[24] the disputable theory works quite efficiently within the context of the jury-waived cases, which probably means that it applies in most cases which come to trial.[25] The fact of the matter is that this solution has not received as much notoriety as might be expected.[26]

The very fact that the trend of these recent investigations has been calculated to resolve the problems associated with judicial notice by narrowing the dimensions of that concept has, however, raised a new

---

19. Nicketta v. National Tea Co., 338 Ill.App. 159, 87 N.E.2d 30 (1949).

20. Stafford v. Ware, 187 Cal.App.2d 227, 9 Cal.Rptr. 706 (1960).

21. Clayton v. Rimmer, 262 N.C. 302, 136 S.E.2d 562 (1964) (reviewing court took judicial notice of table of stopping distances of automobiles in reversing denial of motion for nonsuit). Compare Hughes v. Vestal, 264 N.C. 500, 142 S.E.2d 361 (1965) (error to instruct jury as to stopping distance at given speed, taken from same table).

22. Williams v. New York, 337 U.S. 241 (1949).

23. State v. Main, 94 R.I. 338, 180 A.2d 814 (1962); State v. Lawrence, 120 Utah 323, 234 P.2d 600 (1951).

24. In large measure the Morgan rationale limiting judicial notice to indisputable facts assumes a jury trial context, see particularly Morgan, Judicial Notice, 57 Harv. L.Rev. 269, particularly 269 (1944). Nonjury tried cases may be more analogous to administrative practice in which case it is suggested that judges "should assume facts freely, stating them whenever a party may possibly want to challenge them." Davis, A System of Judicial Notice Based on Fairness and Convenience, in Perspectives of Law 69, 80 (Pound ed. 1964).

25. See particularly, Davis, A System of Judicial Notice Based on Fairness and Convenience, in Perspectives of Law 69, 69–73 (Pound ed. 1964).

Note should be taken that the indisputable theory does not foreclose consideration of countervailing data but merely fixes the time of consideration at the preliminary determination whether judicial notice should be taken. In nonjury cases the difference may be without practical significance. See § 333 infra.

26. A possible explanation may be found in the close, if not complete, coincidence between a disputable judicially noticed fact and a rebuttable presumption. This relationship has largely passed undetected and without comment. One of the few cases sensing the relationship is Fringer v. Venema, 26 Wis.2d 366, 132 N.W.2d 565 (1965), rehearing denied 26 Wis.2d 366, 133 N.W.2d 809 (action under statute imposing absolute liability on owner of bull over six months old; absent proof of age of defendant's bull which escaped and serviced plaintiff's heifers, court refused to take judicial notice that bull with such capacity was six months old but raised a rebuttable presumption to that effect). See § 334 n. 5 infra; § 343, infra.

problem which must be dealt with in the future. If judicial notice is restricted to instances where judges deal with facts in an adjudicative context, the instances where judges deal with legislative facts is left unregulated insofar as procedural guide-lines are concerned. The significance of this problem can be best illustrated within the context of the next section.

§ 333. Procedural Incidents

An elementary sense of fairness might indicate that a judge before making a final ruling that judicial notice will be taken should notify the parties of his intention to do so and afford them an opportunity to present information which might bear upon the propriety of noticing the fact, or upon the truth of the matter to be noticed.[1] Although the original version of the Uniform Rules of Evidence required it,[2] only a rare case insists that a judge must notify the parties before taking judicial notice of a fact on his own motion,[3] and some authorities suggest that such a requirement is needless.[4] It may very well be the case that a trial judge need only consider notifying the parties if on his own motion he intends to take judicial notice of a less than obviously true fact.[5] In every other instance, after all, the request by one party asking the judge to take judicial notice will serve to apprise the opposing party of the question at hand. While there may, nevertheless, exist in practice a rough consensus with regard to procedural niceties when trial judges take judicial notice of adjudicative facts, this is not the end of the matter. The cases universally assume the nonexistence of any need for a structured adversary-style ancillary hearing with

§ 333

1. Model Code of Evidence Rule 804 (1942).

2. Original Uniform Rule 10(1) (1953) provided: "The judge shall afford each party reasonable opportunity to present to him information relevant to the propriety of taking judicial notice of a matter or the tenor of the matter to be noticed." Compare Fed.R.Evid. and Unif.R.Evid. 201(e), quoted at § 328 n. 5 supra, providing for a hearing on request.

3. Compare Fringer v. Venema, 26 Wis.2d 366, 373, 132 N.W.2d 565, 570 (1965), rehearing denied 26 Wis.2d 366, 133 N.W.2d 809 ("However, before judicial notice of such fact can be taken, adequate notice must be given to the parties to enable them to be heard on the question of verifiable certainty.") with Varcoe v. Lee, 180 Cal. 338, 343, 181 P. 223 (1919) ("It would have been much better if counsel for the plaintiff or the trial judge himself had inquired of defendants' counsel * * * whether there was any dispute").

4. Davis, A System of Judicial Notice Based on Fairness and Convenience, in Perspectives of Law 69, 75 (Pound ed. 1964) ("In ninety-nine instances of judicial notice out of a hundred, a notification of the parties of intent to take judicial notice is inconvenient and serves no good purpose.") The fact probably is that most instances of judicial notice pass without detection, and that most of those which are detected are not questioned. Hence an inclusive requirement of advance notice would result only in confusion and controversy where none existed before. See § 334 n. 10 infra.

5. Comment, 13 Vill.L.Rev. 528, 543–44 (1968) (suggesting that it would be a waste of time to notify the parties when the fact to be noticed is "a truly indisputable" one but warning that, should a trial judge notice a debatable adjudicative fact without notice to the parties, there might occur a denial of the right to trial by jury). See also Bulova Watch Co., Inc. v. K. Hattori & Co., Limited, 508 F.Supp. 1322 (E.D.N.Y.1981), at n. 11 infra.

regard to legislative facts.[6] Indeed, even with regard to adjudicative facts, the practices of appellate courts tend to support the argument that there exists no real felt need to formalize the practice of taking judicial notice.[7]

Legislative facts, of course, have not fitted easily into any effort to propound a formalized set of rules applicable to judicial notice. These facts, after all, tend to be less than indisputable ones and hence beyond the pale of judicial notice. What then of the requirement that, before judicial notice is taken, the parties be afforded a reasonable opportunity to present information relative to the propriety of taking judicial notice and the tenor of the matter to be noticed? By and large the parties have this opportunity during arguments over motions as to the appropriate law to be applied to the controversy, by exchanging briefs, and by employing the technique exemplified by the Brandeis brief. It appears, therefore, that there exists no felt need to formalize the procedures pertaining to the opportunity to be heard with reference to legislative facts.[8] Even so, there are cases where the legislative facts which form the basis of an appellate opinion first appear in the decision itself and counsel never have the opportunity to respond to them.[9] Presumably current practice relies upon the sound discretion of judges to maintain discipline in this regard by presupposing a peer-group style general insistence among the judges on a fundamental notion of elementary fairness.[10] However ill-defined because rooted in a sense of due process rather than bottomed on a precise calculus of rules, this notion of fairness may prove to be the common denominator which will continue to link together judicial notice of legislative and adjudicative facts.[11]

6. See, e.g., Judge Jerome Frank's concurring opinion in United States v. Roth, 237 F.2d 796, 814 (2d Cir.1956) (in case involving allegedly obscene publications, appellate judge relied in part upon letter written to him by a sociologist in response to his own inquiry); G. Currie, Appellate Courts Use of Facts Outside the Record by Resort to Judicial Notice and Independent Investigation, 1960 Wis.L.Rev. 39.

7. See, e.g., Mills v. Denver Tramway Corp., 155 F.2d 808 (10th Cir.1946).

8. See, e.g., Fed.R.Evid. 201 Advisory Committee Note (denying need for "any formal requirements of notice other than those already inherent in affording opportunity to hear and be heard and exchanging briefs.") But see Davis, Judicial Notice, 1969 Law & Soc. Order 513, 526 (suggesting that procedural rules are needed to assure adequate opportunity to be heard when legislative facts are noticed).

9. United States v. Roth, 237 F.2d 796, 814 (2d Cir.1956) (see note 6 above). When the same case was on appeal to the Supreme Court, the Solicitor General sent that court a carton of "hard-core pornography" for their perusal. Lockhart &

McClure, Censorship of Obscenity: The Developing Constitutional Standards, 45 Minn.L.Rev. 5, 26 (1960).

10. See also Durham v. United States, 94 U.S.App.D.C. 228, 214 F.2d 862 (1954) (court relied upon the articles by many medico-legal writers in establishing a new test for criminal responsibility, all of which may not have been debated by counsel as to their respective merits); People v. Finkelstein, 11 N.Y.2d 300, 229 N.Y.S.2d 367, 183 N.E.2d 661 (1962), cert. denied 371 U.S. 863.

11. Bulova Watch Co., Inc. v. K. Hattori & Co., Limited, 508 F.Supp. 1322 (E.D.N.Y.1981) (parties invited to respond to propriety of taking judicial notice and to tenor of what was noticed with regard to facts about operations of foreign multinational corporations bearing on jurisdiction in the forum, the purpose being both to avoid egregious errors and to reinforce confidence in the court's fairness); Davis, Facts in Lawmaking, 80 Col.L.Rev. 931 (1980) (need to create system of notice and comment when Supreme Court makes major policy decisions bottomed on judicially noticed legislative facts).

With regard to the treatment of adjudicative facts by appellate courts, the common starting point is the axiom that these tribunals can take judicial notice to the same extent as can trial courts.[12] At the very least, this rule suggests the obvious fact that appellate courts can review the propriety of the judicial notice taken by the court below [13] and can even take judicial notice on their own initiative of facts not noticed below.[14] Nonetheless the recitation of these principles fails to portray the full flavor of the actual practice of appellate courts in taking judicial notice on their own initiative of what would appear to be adjudicative facts.

In this regard the case of Mills v. Denver Tramway Corp.,[15] may be instructive. Plaintiff had alighted from a trolley car, walked behind it and crossed the parallel set of tracks, where he was struck by a car going in the opposite direction. Plaintiff appeared to be manifestly guilty of contributory negligence, a sound enough conclusion plaintiff next attempted to overcome by invoking the doctrine of the last-clear-chance. That is, at the penultimate moment of the trial, plaintiff requested a jury instruction to the effect that, if the motorman had had a chance to sound the trolley bell, the harm might still have been avoided, in which case plaintiff was entitled to prevail. The trial judge refused the instruction because no evidence was ever introduced to indicate that the trolley had a bell.[16] The appellate tribunal reversed, giving plaintiff a new trial, reciting the fact that "streetcars have bells." If all trolley cars had bells, a fact the trial court could have taken judicial notice of had it ever been requested to do so, it would be quite appropriate for the appellate court to take notice of the very same fact. But was it an indisputable fact that *all* streetcars had bells? Arguably most did, in which case the appellate court was taking judicial notice, not of an indisputable fact, but only of a more-than-likely-true fact. More plausibly, the court reasoned that, in all likelihood, the trolley had a bell, in which instance plaintiff should have, as part of his case, proceeded to introduce evidence to substantiate a plausible claim on the last-clear-chance theory. Alternatively, had no bell existed, plaintiff should have made that omission the basis of his claim. In either event, a sense of justice cried out for a trial of the case

12. Varcoe v. Lee, 180 Cal. 338, 181 P. 223 (1919). Note, 42 Mich.L.Rev. 509 (1943) (collection of cases.)

13. In re Bowling Green Milling Co., 132 F.2d 279 (6th Cir.1942); Verner v. Redman, 77 Ariz. 310, 271 P.2d 468 (1954); Fringer v. Venema, 26 Wis.2d 366, 132 N.W.2d 565 (1965).

14. Hunter v. New York, Ontario & Western Railway Co., 116 N.Y. 615, 23 N.E. 9 (1889) (took judicial notice of height of typical man to reverse judgment based upon notion that claimant was seated when box car entered railway tunnel). Fed.R.Evid. 201(f) allows judicial notice to be taken at any stage of the proceeding. § 328 n. 5 supra.

15. 155 F.2d 808 (10th Cir.1946).

16. Interestingly enough, Professor Davis might suggest in this instance that the trial judge would have been right not to take judicial notice. Davis, A System of Judicial Notice Based on Fairness and Convenience in Perspectives of Law 94 (Pound ed. 1964), ("Nothing short of bringing facts into the record, so that an opportunity is allowed for cross-examination and for presentation of rebuttal evidence and argument, will suffice for disputed adjudicative facts at the center of the controversy.")

with all the facts fully developed. If, however, this was the sense of justice which moved the appellate tribunal, their invocation of the statement that "all streetcars have bells," a disputable proposition, sheds no real light either on the question whether judicial notice extends to disputable adjudicative facts or whether the parties must be afforded a hearing before judicial notice is taken. Given the need for appellate courts on occasion to reverse results below on a factual basis, judicial notice serves as a convenient device by which to give the practice the appearance of legal propriety. This being true, it would appear that the chances of adequately formalizing judicial notice even of adjudicative facts at the appellate level may be a slim one indeed.[17]

§ 334. Trends in the Development of Judicial Notice of Facts

It appears that, by and large, agreement has been reached on a rough outline of the perimeters of judicial notice as applied to adjudicative facts at the trial level.[1] A workable procedural schemata which would appear to guarantee fairness already exists in the event that judicial notice is restricted to indisputable facts.[2] The only question remaining is whether, in order to expedite the trial of cases, judges should be allowed to excuse the proponent of a fact likely true of the necessity of producing formal evidence thereof, leaving it to the jury to accept or reject the judicially noticed fact, and of course, allowing the opponent to introduce evidence contradicting it.[3] Indeed, the present controversy might be put in a new light by limiting judicial notice to indisputable facts[4] and then raising the question, whether, as part of the law associated with the burden of proof and presumptions, a judge can properly expedite trials by himself ruling that very likely true facts are presumptively true unless the jury care to find otherwise.[5]

---

17. See *seriatim* the decisions in Securities and Exchange Commission v. Capital Gains Research Bureau, Inc., 191 F.Supp. 897 (S.D.N.Y.1961), affirmed 300 F.2d 745 (2d Cir.), reversed 375 U.S. 180.

§ 334

1. See Fed.R.Evid. and Unif.R.Evid. 201, quoted at § 328 n. 5 supra.

2. See § 333 supra.

3. See § 332 supra.

4. See e.g., Fed.R.Evid. 201, reproduced at § 328 n. 5 supra.

5. This obviously is a compromise. Some authorities limit judicial notice to indisputable facts in every instance, whether the facts be either adjudicative or legislative ones. Morgan, Judicial Notice, 57 Harv.L.Rev. 269 (1944). Others seem to suggest that all judicially noticed facts are assumptions capable of being rebutted by proof. Thayer, A Preliminary Treatise on Evidence at the Common Law 309 (1898); 9

Wigmore, Evidence § 2567 (Chadbourn rev. 1981). It has been the peculiar genius of Professor K.C. Davis to perceive the difference between adjudicative and legislative facts. Davis, Official Notice, 62 Harv. L.Rev. 537 (1949). Even so, recent efforts to codify judicial notice have insisted upon the indisputability concept with respect to adjudicative facts only. Fed.R.Evid. 201. Professor Davis remains adamant that adjudicative facts can be disputable ones. Davis, Judicial Notice, 1969 Law & Soc. Order 513. The Thayer–Wigmore–Davis argument is that efficiency cries out for a mechanism by which formal evidence can be dispensed with when a fact appears to be fairly incontestable. Thayer appears to have perceived that this kind of fact was a variant of the law of procedure. See, e.g., Morgan, Judicial Notice, 57 Harv.L.Rev. 269, 285–286 (1944) ("Both [Wigmore's] and Mr. Thayer's statements of the proper effect of taking judicial notice are startlingly like their statements of the effect of pre-

Whatever the ultimate doctrinal synthesis of judicial notice of adjudicative facts comes to be, a viable formulation of rules laying down a similarly rigid procedural etiquette with regard to legislative facts has not proved feasible.[6] Given the current recognition that nonadjudicative facts are inextricably part and parcel of the law formulation process in a policy-oriented jurisprudence, there may be no need to formulate a distinctly judicial notice-captioned procedure with regard to nonadjudicative facts. These data are fed into the judicial process now whenever rules of law are brought to the attention of judges in motions, memoranda and briefs. Thus, whatever rules govern the submission of law in the litigation process have already preempted the nonadjudicative field and made unnecessary separate treatment thereof within the context of judicial notice.[7]

There has been an increasing awareness, moreover, that quite apart from judicial notice, the trial process assumes that the participants therein bring with them a vast amount of everyday knowledge of facts in general.[8] To think, after all, presupposes some data about which to think. In an automobile accident case, for example, both the judge and the jury constantly draw on their own experiences as drivers, as observers of traffic, and as live human beings, and these experiences are reduced in their minds to propositions of fact which, since they have survived themselves, are probably fairly accurate. This substratum of data the participants bring into the courthouse has, however, tended to confuse the judicial notice scene. On the one hand, this subliminal-like data is sometimes confused with the "common knowledge"-style of adjudicative facts with which formal judicial notice is concerned. On the other hand, judges constantly invoke references to these same everyday facts when they write opinions because, when formally articulated, it is impossible "to think" without reference to them.[9] It may very well be the case that judges have tended, when extrapolating the obvious, to invoke the words, "I take judicial notice of" to explain the presence of these facts in their minds, thereby unnecessarily glutting the encyclopedias with trivia which are, when

sumptions.") See also Fringer v. Venema, 26 Wis.2d 366, 132 N.W.2d 565 (1965); § 332 n. 6 supra; § 343, infra.

It will be observed that the Federal Rules of Evidence make no effort to set forth a catalog of presumptions. Fed. R.Evid. 301. Compare West's Ann.Cal. Evid.Code §§ 630–668.

6. See § 333 supra.

7. See, e.g., Fed.R.Evid. 201, reproduced at § 328 n. 5 supra.

8. See § 329 supra.

9. See, e.g., Wygant v. Jackson Bd. of Educ., 476 U.S. 267, 314 (1986), rehearing denied 478 U.S. 1014 (in dissent calculated to show that race is not always irrelevant to governmental decisionmaking, Justice Stevens noted that "in a city with a recent history of racial unrest, the superintendent of police might reasonably conclude that an integrated police force could develop a better relationship with the community * * * "); People v. Enders, 38 Misc.2d 746, 237 N.Y.S.2d 879 (N.Y.C.Crim.Ct.1963) (in deciding which, if either, between an absentee store proprietor and his butcher to whom he gave orders, was liable under a statute making it a crime to doctor meat, judge concluded they both were because "the hamburger has become one of the most popular menu items in the United States.")

formally collected, highly misleading indices of the true scope of judicial notice as such.[10]

Federal Rule of Evidence 201 only applies to adjudicative facts, which might suggest that legislative facts simply cannot be fitted into the concept of judicial notice.[11] If they cannot, legislative facts would have to come into the judicial process in the form of "evidence." A problem would then arise if a trial court had to decide the question of law whether it was constitutional totally to exclude from a bifurcated jury in a capital case persons opposed to the death penalty. After hearing testimony and accepting documentary material, the court might conclude on the basis of available social science materials that either death disqualification produced conviction prone juries or it did not.[12] The court might bottom its decision of the constitutional issue on this "finding of fact." If the social science materials were not clearly inclined to sustain only one conclusion, and the ruling were treated as a factual ruling, the ruling whichever way it came out could not be reversed because it would not be clearly erroneous. Law would come to turn on fact and be susceptible to two right answers. This is not going to happen. Legislative facts are not "evidence" in the normal sense of the word, and judicial notice doctrine still obtains as to them.[13] The problem is one of refining that doctrine, and not confusing it with evidentiary proof of adjudicatory facts.

Arguably legislative facts might better be handled by treating them as one would a search for law amidst a canon of conflicting cases, ruling on the tenor of the applicable economic or social rule as if it were a question of law.[14] But as we have seen, judges are constantly asserting facts to be true in many contexts and at many stages of the judicial process, "facts" which while they appeal to common sense and prudence as work-a-day truths, lack the dignity and permanence of something

10. Often enough these propositions of generalized knowledge are not picked up as illustrations of judicial notice, which after all proves the point. See, e.g., Village of Euclid v. Ambler Realty Co., 272 U.S. 365 (1926) (apartment houses come near to being nuisances in single-family residential areas); Escola v. Coca Cola Bottling Co., 24 Cal.2d 453, 150 P.2d 436 (1944) (concurring opinion) (manufacturers are best situated to underwrite losses attributable to defective products); Webster v. Blue Ship Tea Room, Inc., 347 Mass. 421, 198 N.E.2d 309 (1964) (in considering whether restaurant impliedly warranted fish chowder to be free of all miniscule bones court reflected that "Chowder is an ancient dish preexisting even 'the appetites of our seamen and fishermen'").

11. Reproduced at § 328 n. 5 supra.

12. Compare Grigsby v. Mabry, 758 F.2d 226 (8th Cir.1985), reversed sub nom. Lockhart v. McCree, 476 U.S. 162, with

Keeten v. Garrison, 742 F.2d 129 (4th Cir. 1984), cert. denied 476 U.S. 1145.

13. Lockhart v. McCree, 476 U.S. 162, 168 n. 3 (1986) (question whether death qualified juries more conviction prone: "We are far from persuaded * * * that the 'clearly erroneous' standard of Rule 52(a) applies to the kind of legislative facts at issue here."); Dunagin v. Oxford, Mississippi, 718 F.2d 738, 748 n. 8 (5th Cir.1983), cert. denied 467 U.S. 1259 (question whether advertising stimulated consumption of alcohol so as to give state an interest in regulating commercial speech: "It is not a question related to this case or controversy. It is a question of social factors and happenings which may submit to some partial empirical solution but which is likely to remain subject to opinion, and reasoning. See Fed.R.Evid. 201, advisory committee note.").

14. See text at § 331 n. 27 supra.

that could be called "law." Law requires more than cracker-barrel folk wisdom behind it to command respect and obedience. What is needed is a new concept, perhaps oriented around the study of thinking-about-facts techniques involved throughout the judicial process. Judge Robert E. Keeton has spearheaded just such an endeavor in the most appropriate context of a William B. Lockhart Lecture, taking as his cue the notion that facts are the premise of innumerable rulings.[15] Oddly enough, this trend if continued would represent a return to Thayer.[16]

§ 335. The Judge's Task as Law–Finder: Judicial Notice of Law

It would appear to be self-evident that it is peculiarly the function of the judge to find and interpret the law applicable to the issues in a trial, and in a jury case, to announce his findings of law to the jury for their guidance. The heavy-footed common law system of proof by witnesses and authenticated documents is too slow and cumbrous for the judge's task of finding what the applicable law is. Usually this law is familiar lore and if not he relies on the respective counsel to bring before him the statutes, reports, and source books, and these everyday companions of judge and counsel are read from informally in discussion or cited and quoted in trial and appellate briefs. Occasionally the judge will go beyond the cited authorities to make his own investigation. In the ordinary process of finding the applicable law, the normal method then is by informal investigation of any sources satisfactory to the judge. Thus this process has been traditionally described in terms of the judge taking judicial notice of the law applicable to the case at hand. Indeed, when the source-material was not easily accessible to the judge, as in the case of "foreign law" or city ordinances, law has been treated as a peculiar species of fact, requiring formal proof. We shall see, however, that as these materials become more accessible, the tendency is toward permitting the judges to do what perhaps they should have done in the beginning, that is, to rely on the diligence of counsel to provide the necessary materials, and accordingly to take judicial notice of *all* law. This seems to be the goal toward which the practice is marching.

Domestic law. As to domestic law generally, the judge is not merely permitted to take judicial notice but required to do so,[1] at least if

---

15. Keeton, Legislative Facts and Similar Things: Deciding Disputed Premise Facts, 73 Minn.L.Rev. 1 (1988).

16. This would, in fact, represent a return to Thayer. See, Preliminary Treatise on Evidence at the Common Law 278–279 (1898) ("Whereabout in the law does the doctrine of judicial notice belong? Wherever the process of reasoning has a place, and that is everywhere. Not peculiarly in the law of evidence. * * * The subject of

judicial notice, then, belongs to the general topic of legal or judicial reasoning.")

§ 335

1. Strain v. Isaacs, 59 Ohio App. 495, 514, 18 N.E.2d 816, 825 (1938) (dictum); Randall v. Commonwealth, 183 Va. 182, 186, 31 S.E.2d 571, 572 (1944) (dictum); 29 Am.Jur.2d Evidence § 27. Some states provide by statute for judicial notice of local public statutes; e.g., West's Ann.Cal.

requested, although in a particular case a party may be precluded on appeal from complaining of the judge's failure to notice a statute where his counsel has failed to call it to the judge's attention.[2] This general rule that judicial notice will be taken of domestic law means that state trial courts will notice Federal law,[3] which is controlling in every state, and has been held to mean that in a Federal trial court the laws of the states, not merely of the state where it is sitting, are domestic and will be noticed.[4] Similarly all statewide or nationwide executive orders and proclamations, which are legally effective, will be noticed.[5] Under this same principle, even the laws of antecedent governments will be noticed.[6]

State and national administrative regulations having the force of law will also be noticed, at least if they are published so as to be readily available.[7] When such documents are published in the Federal Reg-

Evid.Code § 451; N.Y.—McKinney's CPLR 4511(a).

See also note 61 infra.

2. Great American Insurance Co. v. Glenwood Irrigation Co., 265 Fed. 594 (8th Cir.1920) (in action for damage from fire trial court's failure to charge that, under Colorado statute, leaving fire unextinguished would impose liability regardless of negligence, could not be complained of because plaintiff failed to call statute to judge's attention). See, however, an illuminating comment, Overlooking Statutes, 30 Yale L.J. 855 (1921), which suggests that errors arising from ignorance of a statute should be corrected on appeal except in cases where the public interest is not involved and counsel's failure to cite the statute can be construed as a waiver.

A judge, of course, may undertake an independent investigation of the applicable law, but ordinarily judges rely on opposing counsel to bring to their attention the appropriate sources of law. Matthews v. McVay, 241 Mo.App. 998, 1006, 234 S.W.2d 983, 988–989 (1950).

3. Peters v. Double Cola Bottling Co., 224 S.C. 437, 79 S.E.2d 710 (1954). Some states by statute provide for judicial notice of the Federal Constitution and statutes, e.g., West's Ann.Cal.Evid.Code § 451; N.Y.—McKinney's CPLR 4511(a).

See also note 61 infra.

4. In a federal court exercising original jurisdiction, its local law is the law of all the states. Hanley v. Donoghue, 116 U.S. 1 (1885); Lane v. Sargent, 217 Fed. 237 (1st Cir.1914); Gediman v. Anheuser Busch, 299 F.2d 537 (2d Cir.1962); Gallup v. Caldwell, 120 F.2d 90 (3d Cir.1941). This rule of judicial notice being a matter of procedure rather than substantive law, it seems that the controlling force of state substan-

tive law, under Erie Railroad Co. v. Tompkins, 304 U.S. 64 (1938), is inapplicable. But see Keeffe, Landis & Shaad, Sense and Nonsense about Judicial Notice, 2 Stan. L.Rev. 664, 686 (1950).

On appeal, however, from a state court, the federal Supreme Court will not notice the law of another state unless the state court below would have done so. Hanley v. Donoghue, 116 U.S. 1 (1885).

5. Dennis v. United States, 339 U.S. 162 (1950) (executive order of the President providing standards for discharge of government employees on loyalty grounds); Heyward v. Long, 178 S.C. 351, 183 S.E. 145, 114 A.L.R. 1130 (1935) (Governor's proclamation declaring highway department in state of insurrection); 29 Am. Jur.2d Evidence § 40; Dec.Dig. Evidence ⚖46.

6. Municipality Ponce v. Roman Catholic Apostolic Church, 210 U.S. 296 (1908) (Spanish laws in Puerto Rico); South Shore Land Co. v. Petersen, 226 Cal.App.2d 725, 38 Cal.Rptr. 392 (1964) (Mexican laws in California).

7. Case authority illustrates that some courts will take judicial notice of administrative regulations. Southwestern Bell Telephone Co. v. Bateman, 223 Ark. 432, 266 S.W.2d 289 (1954); Groendyke Transport v. State, 208 Okl. 602, 258 P.2d 670 (1953); Smith v. Highway Board, 117 Vt. 343, 91 A.2d 805 (1952). Contra: Atlanta Gas Light Co. v. Newman, 88 Ga.App. 252, 76 S.E.2d 536 (1953); Finlay v. Eastern Racing Association, 308 Mass. 20, 30 N.E.2d 859 (1941). Several states provide by statute for judicial notice of administrative regulations, e.g., West's Ann.Cal.Evid. Code § 451; N.Y.—McKinney's CPLR 4511. Other states provide by statute for

ister it is provided that their contents shall be judicially noticed.[8] Private laws [9] and municipal ordinances,[10] however, are not commonly included within the doctrine of judicial notice and these must be pleaded and proved. To the extent that these items become readily available in compilations, it may be expected that they will become subject to judicial notice; [11] whereas, in the meantime, it would appear appropriate for judges to take judicial notice of both private laws and municipal ordinances if counsel furnish a certified copy thereof.

The law of sister states. It is easy to see how the difference of languages and inaccessibility of source books should have led the English courts to develop the common law rule that the laws of foreign nations would not be noticed but must be pleaded and proved as facts.[12] The assumption in the earlier cases in this country [13] that the courts of one state must treat the laws of another state as foreign for this purpose is less understandable and to the afterview seems a deplorable instance of mechanical jurisprudence. Yet it remains today, in nearly every one of the increasingly few states which have not yet adopted a reformatory statute, the common law rule that notice will not be given to the laws of sister states.[14] This is probably the most inconvenient of all the limitations upon the practice of judicial notice. Notice here could certainly be justified on the principle of certainty and verifiability,[15] and the burden on the judge could be minimized by casting the responsibility upon counsel either to agree upon a stipulation as to the law or to produce on each side for the benefit of the court all materials necessary for ascertaining the law in question.

judicial notice of published compilations of administrative regulations, e.g., Wis.Stats. 1975, § 902.03.

See also note 61 infra.

8. 44 U.S.C.A. § 1507. While some state courts take judicial notice of federal administrative regulations, Hough v. Rapidair, Inc., 298 S.W.2d 378 (Mo.1957); Dallas General Drivers v. Jax Beer Co., 276 S.W.2d 384 (Tex.Civ.App.—Dallas 1955), others will not. Gladieux v. Parney, 93 Ohio App. 117, 106 N.E.2d 317 (1951); Buice v. Scruggs Equipment Co., 37 Tenn. App. 556, 267 S.W.2d 119 (1953). It would appear that the Federal Register Act should bind state courts. But see Mastrullo v. Ryan, 328 Mass. 621, 622, 105 N.E.2d 469, 470 (1952).

9. Chambers v. Atchison, Topeka & Santa Fe Railway Co., 32 Ariz. 102, 255 P. 1092 (1927); Bolick v. City of Charlotte, 191 N.C. 677, 132 S.E. 660 (1926).

10. Ramacciotti v. Zinn, 550 S.W.2d 217 (Mo.App.1977); Kamarath v. Bennett, 549 S.W.2d 784 (Tex.Civ.App.—Waco 1977), reversed on other grounds 568 S.W.2d 658. A municipal court may be required to take

judicial notice of the local municipal ordinances. Tipp v. District of Columbia, 69 App.D.C. 400, 102 F.2d 264 (1939); Wis. Stats.Ann. § 902.03.

11. Judicial notice of municipal ordinances is sometimes provided for by statute, e.g., Ill.—S.H.A. ch. 57, § 48a; N.Y.— McKinney's CPLR 4511.

See also note 61 infra.

12. See, e.g., Fremoult v. Dedire, 1 P.Wms. 429, 24 Eng.Rep. 458 (1718); Mostyn v. Fabrigas, 1 Cowp. 161, 98 Eng.Rep. 1021 (1774). For the history of this rule see Sass, Foreign Law in Civil Litigation: A Comparative Survey, 16 Am.J.Comp.L. 332, 335–339 (1968).

13. See, e.g., Brackett v. Norton, 4 Conn. 517, 520 (1823).

14. Southern Express Co. v. Owens, 146 Ala. 412, 41 So. 752 (1906); Gapsch v. Gapsch, 76 Idaho 44, 277 P.2d 278, 54 A.L.R.2d 416 (1954); Brown v. Perry, 104 Vt. 66, 156 A. 910 (1931). But see Prudential Insurance Co. of America v. O'Grady, 97 Ariz. 9, 12–13, 396 P.2d 246, 248 (1964).

15. See § 330 supra.

Under this hoary practice when a required pleading and proof of the foreign law has been overlooked, or has been unsuccessfully attempted, the resulting danger of injustice is somewhat mitigated by the presumption that the law of the sister state is the same as that of the forum,[16] or more simply the practice of applying local law if the law of the other state is not invoked and proven.[17] But this presumption-tool is too rough for the job in hand, particularly when the materials for ascertaining the laws of sister states are today almost as readily accessible as those for local law, and in any event counsel as officers of the court are available to find and present those materials to the judge in just the same informal and convenient fashion as if they were arguing a question of local law.[18]

In 1936 the Conference of Commissioners on Uniform Laws drafted the Uniform Judicial Notice of Foreign Law Act [19] which was adopted in substance by more than half the states.[20] This legislation provides that every court within the adopting state shall take judicial notice of the common law and statutes of every other state. While the Act removes the necessity to prove the law of another state, most courts do not feel obliged by it to notice the law of another state on their own initiative.[21] Indeed, in order to invoke the benefits of the Foreign Law Act a litigant must give reasonable notice in the pleadings or otherwise

---

16. Scott v. Scott, 153 Neb. 906, 46 N.W.2d 627, 23 A.L.R.2d 1431 (1951).

17. Haggard v. First National Bank, 72 N.D. 434, 8 N.W.2d 5 (1942).

18. Prudential Insurance Co. of America v. O'Grady, 97 Ariz. 9, 12, 396 P.2d 246, 248 (1964) ("In this modern day with easy access to many law libraries with copies of the state statutes and the state and national reporter systems, and the obvious fact that the states are not 'foreign' to each other, the reason for the common law rule no longer exists.").

19. Its substantive provisions follow:

"Section 1. (Judicial Notice.) Every court of this state shall take judicial notice of the common law and statutes of every state, territory and other jurisdiction of the United States. Section 2. (Information of the Court.) The court may inform itself of such laws in such manner as it may deem proper, and the court may call upon counsel to aid it in obtaining such information. Section 3. (Ruling Reviewable.) The determination of such laws shall be made by the court and not by the jury, and shall be reviewable. Section 4. (Evidence as to Laws of other Jurisdiction.) Any party may also present to the trial court any admissible evidence of such laws, but, to enable a party to offer evidence of the law in

another jurisdiction or to ask that judicial notice be taken thereof, reasonable notice shall be given to the adverse parties either in the pleadings or otherwise. Section 5. (Foreign Country.) The law of a jurisdiction other than those referred to in Section 1 shall be an issue for the court, but shall not be subject to the foregoing provisions concerning judicial notice." 1936 Handbook Nat'l. Conference of Commissioners on Unif. State Laws 355–359; 1945 id. 124; 9A Uniform Laws Ann. 553 (1965).

20. 9A Uniform Laws Ann. 550 (1965). Listed as having adopted this legislation are about half the states. See 13 U.L.A. § 403 Comment (1986).

Some states have enacted their own legislation providing for judicial notice of law of sister states, e.g. Ark.Stat. § 28–109; West's Ann.Cal.Evid.Code § 452; Mass. Gen.Laws Ann. c. 233, § 70; N.Y.—McKinney's CPLR 4511.

See also n. 61 infra.

21. Kingston v. Quimby, 80 So.2d 455 (Fla.1955) ("a party invoking * * * the Act is required to have the record reveal that fact and to have the record show the authorities which will be relied upon with reference to the foreign law."); Strout v. Burgess, 144 Me. 263, 68 A.2d 241, 12 A.L.R.2d 939 (1949).

to the adverse party of his intention to do so,[22] failing which the courts are apt to refuse to take judicial notice or admit evidence as to the sister-state law relied on, invoking once again the presumption that it is the same as the law of the forum.[23]

The Uniform Judicial Notice of Foreign Law Act pertained to the law of sister states and did not address the issue of the law of other nations.[24] It was supplanted in 1962 when the National Conference of Commissioners on Uniform Laws approved Article IV of the Uniform Interstate and International Procedure Act.[25] Calculated to address judicial notice of true foreign law, the new Act implicates the law of sister states as well because it imposes the same discipline when the law of *any* extraforum jurisdiction is invoked.[26] Thus a party who intends to raise an issue of the law of a sister state should give notice of an intention to do so, either in the pleadings or by any other reasonable method of written notice.[27] It is the court which determines the tenor of what actually will be noticed about the law of a sister state,[28] and the court may go beyond the materials furnished it by the parties in arriving at its own determination.[29] Article IV, however, has yet to win widespread adoption.[30]

The law of foreign countries. At common law, foreign law was treated as a matter of fact: pleading and proof were required, and the

---

22. Boswell v. Rio De Oro Uranium Mines, Inc., 68 N.M. 457, 362 P.2d 991 (1961) (cases construing Act generally hold that the judicial notice requirement merely relieves party of formal proof but was not designed to remove necessity of at least informing court of the content of foreign law to be noticed).

23. Scott v. Scott, 153 Neb. 906, 46 N.W.2d 627, 23 A.L.R.2d 1431 (1951).

24. See the text of that act produced at note 19, supra.

25. 13 U.L.A. 355 (1986).

Determination of Foreign Law

§ 4.01. [Notice]

A party who intends to raise an issue concerning the law of any jurisdiction or governmental unit thereof outside this state shall give notice in his pleadings or other reasonable written notice.

§ 4.02. [Materials to be Considered]

In determining the law of any jurisdiction or governmental unit thereof outside this state, the court may consider any relevant material or source, including testimony, whether or not submitted by a party or admissible under the rules of evidence.

§ 4.03. [Court Decision and Review]

The court, not jury, shall determine the law of any governmental unit outside this state. Its determination is subject

to review on appeal as a ruling on a question of law.

§ 4.04. [Other Provisions of Law Unaffected]

This Article does not repeal or modify any other law of this state permitting another procedure for the determination of foreign law.

26. See § 4.01 reproduced above at n. 25.

27. Id.

28. See § 4.03 reproduced above at n. 25.

29. See § 4.02 reproduced above at n. 25.

30. The Uniform Interstate and International Procedure Act has been adopted in Arkansas, Massachusetts, Michigan and Pennsylvania. 13 U.L.A. 355 (1986). One has, however, always to see whether Article IV thereof has been altered or deleted. Massachusetts omits Article IV entirely. See: 13 U.L.A. at 395. Massachusetts has a statute regulating the judicial notice of the law of sister states and another governing the judicial notice of both true foreign nations and sister states. Mass.Gen.Laws Ann. c. 233, § 70; Mass.R.Civ.Proc. Rule 44.1.

Delete Oklahoma; add at end, but see n. 61 infra.

jury decided what the foreign law was.[31] As early as 1936 the Uniform Judicial Notice of Foreign Law Act reflected the idea that the tenor of the law of a foreign country was a question for the court and not for the jury.[32] What is significant is the fact that this selfsame 1936 Act, adverted to in the preceding section, contained no provision for the judicial notice of the law of other nations.[33] The parties were left not only to pleading but proving, albeit to a judge and not a jury, the law of other nations.[34]

The longevity of the ancient notion that a party had "to prove" the law of another nation was likely rooted in the fact that the sources of extranational law were not easily accessible even in urban centers.[35] A healthy pragmatism seems to have ameliorated the harshness of any rule demanding strict proof. Sworn to or certified copies of extranational statutes or decisions gave way to the use of copies thereof in a book printed by the authority of the foreign state or proved to be commonly recognized in its courts.[36]

Even so, the very idea that a party was engaged in "proving" a point of extranational law fairly invited complications. The written text of any law suggests that its "black letter" be interpreted in light of any germane decisions, treatises or commentaries. This under common law proof must be accomplished by taking the testimony in person or by deposition of an expert in the foreign law.[37] The adversary of course is free to take the testimony of other experts if he can find them on his side, and the cross-examination of conflicting experts is likely to accentuate the disagreements.[38] This method of proof seems to maximize expense and delay[39] and hardly seems best calculated to ensure a correct decision by our judges on questions of foreign law. It could be vastly improved by pre-trial conferences in which agreements as to

---

31. See generally, 9 Wigmore, Evidence § 2573 (Chadbourn rev. 1981).

32. See § 5, reproduced at n. 19 supra.

33. See the text of that act reproduced at n. 19 supra.

34. That this can still be a problem, witness Schlesinger, A Recurrent Problem in Transnational Litigation: The Effect of Failure to Invoke or Prove the Applicable Foreign Law, 59 Cornell L.Rev. 1 (1973).

35. See, e.g., Report of the Committee on Foreign and Comparative Law of the Assoc. of the Bar of the City of New York, 22 The Record (Supplement—Committee Reports 1966–67) 31 (1967).

36. See, e.g., Uniform Interstate and International Procedure Act, § 5.03, 13 U.L.A. 401 (1986).

37. A case illustrating this practice is In re Nielsen's Estate, 118 Mont. 304, 165 P.2d 792 (1946) (deposition of legal counselor of Danish Legation discussing legal treatises and giving opinion as to inheritance rights of aliens under Danish law). See also, Application of Chase Manhattan Bank, 191 F.Supp. 206 (S.D.N.Y.1961) (a mere translation of foreign statute without the background, context, or area of internal application is insufficient to establish the precise tenor of what foreign law is).

38. "It is the writer's impression that under the present practice of the courts, skillful advocates may succeed in developing confusing divergencies between experts on purely verbal matters in situations where coherent and well-substantiated written opinions would eliminate all difficulties." Nussbaum, The Problem of Proving Foreign Law, 50 Yale L.J. 1018, 1029 (1941).

39. Professor Nussbaum cites an example where a court would not be satisfied unless plaintiffs brought an Argentine lawyer to New York City. Nussbaum, Proving the Law of Foreign Countries, 3 Am. J.Comp.L. 60, 63–64 (1954).

undisputed aspects of the foreign law could be secured, and by the appointment by the court of one or more experts on foreign law as referees or as court-chosen experts to report their findings to the court.[40]

Following the lead of several states which by statute have provided that the court must take judicial notice [41] or permit the court to do so in its discretion,[42] the practice obtaining in the federal courts has been codified to make the tenor of foreign law a question of law for the court.[43] Thus it is that a party who intends to raise an issue of foreign-nation law must give notice of his intention to do so, either in his pleadings or by any other reasonable method of written notice.[44] Once the issue of foreign law is raised, the court need not, in its effort to determine the tenor of that law, rely upon the testimony and other materials proffered by the litigant, but may engage in its own research and consider any relevant material thus found.

In turn the new Uniform Interstate and International Procedure Act's Article IV will, if generally enacted, unify state practice along the lines of the federal model.[45] Thus again the invocation of extranational law would necessitate written notice, by way of the pleadings or any reasonable alternative, and the court, licensed to engage in its own researches, would ultimately fix the actual tenor of whatever was noticed.[46] Concomitantly, recourse to the law of a sister state is included within the same process so that a single procedure will obtain whenever the law of a jurisdiction outside the forum becomes an issue.[47]

The unwillingness of the courts to notice the laws of other countries creates difficulties where the party whose case or defense depends, under conflicts rules, upon foreign law and he fails to prove that law as a fact. There are several solutions. First, the court may decide the

---

40. The parties can stipulate the tenor of the foreign law. Harris v. American International Fuel & Petroleum Co., 124 F.Supp. 878 (W.D.Pa.1954). Absent some manifest injustice, the parties can simply agree that the forum law applies. Watts v. Swiss Bank Corp., 27 N.Y.2d 270, 317 N.Y.S.2d 315, 265 N.E.2d 739 (1970).

41. See, e.g., Mass.Gen.Laws Ann. c. 233, § 70 ("The court shall take judicial notice of the law * * * of any state * * * or of a foreign country whenever the same shall be material.") The attention of the court must be drawn to the foreign law before this statute becomes mandatory. Commercial Credit Corp. v. Stan Cross Buick, Inc., 343 Mass. 622, 180 N.E.2d 88 (1962).

42. See, e.g., N.Y.—McKinney's CPLR 4511(b).

43. Fed.R.Civ.P. 44.1:

A party who intends to raise an issue concerning the law of a foreign country shall give notice in his pleadings or other reasonable written notice. The court, in determining foreign law, may consider any relevant material or source, including testimony, whether or not submitted by a party or admissible under the Federal Rules of Evidence. The court's determination shall be treated as a ruling on a question of law.

Rule 26.1 of the Federal Rules of Criminal Procedure is substantially the same.

44. Ruff v. St. Paul Mercury Insurance Co., 393 F.2d 500 (2d Cir.1968) (court would not take judicial notice of Liberian law when plaintiff never gave written notice of intent to rely upon foreign law).

45. 13 U.L.A. 355 (1986). See the text of this act reproduced at note 25 supra.

46. See §§ 4.01–4.03, reproduced at note 25 supra.

47. See particularly § 4.01, reproduced at note 25 supra.

issue against him for failure of proof.[48] This is often a harsh and
arbitrary result. Second, the court may simply apply the law of the
forum on the ground that no other law is before it,[49] especially if the
parties have tried the case as if local law were applicable.[50] Third, the
court may presume that the law of the other country is the same as
that of the forum,[51] thus reaching the same result as under the second
theory but raising intellectual difficulties because the presumption is so
frequently contrary to fact. When the doctrine involved is one of
common law, but the other nation is not a common law country, some
courts will decline to apply the presumption.[52] On the other hand,
when the common law rule invoked is a part of the common fund of all
civilized systems, such as the binding force of ordinary commercial
agreements, the presumption is applied though the foreign country is
not a common law country.[53] Moreover, by what is probably the
prevailing and more convenient view, if the question would be governed
locally by a statute, a like statute in the foreign country may be
presumed.[54]

International and Maritime Law. The rules, principles and traditions of "international law," or "the law of nations," will be noticed in
Federal and state courts.[55] Maritime law is similarly subject to judicial

48. Walton v. Arabian American Oil Co., 233 F.2d 541 (2d Cir.1956), cert. denied 352 U.S. 872 (Arkansas plaintiff sued Delaware corporation in federal court in New York for injuries sustained in Saudi Arabia, did not allege or offer to prove foreign law; case dismissed because plaintiff failed to introduce evidence of foreign law upon which issue burden of proof was his). See also Cuba Railroad Co. v. Crosby, 222 U.S. 473 (1912).

49. Leary v. Gledhill, 8 N.J. 260, 84 A.2d 725 (1951) (in suit arising out of transaction executed in France wherein plaintiff did not prove foreign law, court applied domestic law); Note, 37 Cornell L.Q. 748 (1952).

50. Watford v. Alabama & Florida Lumber Co., 152 Ala. 178, 44 So. 567 (1907).

Absent some manifest injustice, forum law obtains when the parties by default in pleading or proof of foreign law have agreed or acquiesced to its application. Watts v. Swiss Bank Corp., 27 N.Y.2d 270, 317 N.Y.S.2d 315, 265 N.E.2d 739 (1970).

51. See generally, the illuminating discussion in Nussbaum, op. cit. supra at n. 26, 50 Yale L.J. 1018, 1035 et seq. (1941); Medina Fernandez v. Hartman, 260 F.2d 569 (9th Cir.1958) (absent a showing to the contrary it is a familiar principle that foreign law is presumed same as domestic); Leary v. Gledhill, 8 N.J. 260, 84 A.2d 725 (1951).

52. Cuba Railroad Co. v. Crosby, 222 U.S. 473 (1912) (law of Cuba as to responsibility of employer for injury to employee); Philp v. Macri, 261 F.2d 945 (9th Cir.1958) (law of defamation of Peru cannot be presumed same as that of State of Washington). But see Louknitsky v. Louknitsky, 123 Cal.App.2d 406, 266 P.2d 910 (1954) (law of China presumed to be identical with community property law of California).

53. Cuba Railroad Co. v. Crosby, 222 U.S. 473 (1912) (dictum); Parrot v. Mexican Central Railway Co., Limited, 207 Mass. 184, 93 N.E. 590 (1911) (presumption that defendant would be liable in Mexico on agreement made there by its general passenger agent, under "universally recognized fundamental principles of right and wrong").

54. Wickersham v. Johnson, 104 Cal. 407, 38 P. 89 (1894) (sale of note by English executors, powers of executors presumed to be limited as under California statute); Murphy v. Murphy, 145 Cal. 482, 78 P. 1053 (1904) (California statutory rate of interest presumed to prevail as to amount due on English judgment). Contra: Parrot v. Mexican Central Railway Co., 207 Mass. 184, 93 N.E. 590 (1911) (dictum).

55. The Paquete Habana, 175 U.S. 677, 700 (1900) ("International law is part of our law and must be ascertained and administered by the courts of justice. * * * "); Skiriotes v. Florida, 313 U.S. 69,

notice but only insofar as these rules have become part of the general maritime law.[56] Less widely recognized maritime rules of foreign countries are treated like foreign law generally and are required to be proved,[57] unless they have been published here by government authority as the authentic foreign law,[58] or they have been embodied in a widely adopted international convention.[59] Peculiarly enough, the presumption of identity of foreign law with the local law, which would seem to be unusually convenient and realistic in the maritime field, has been narrowly restricted.[60]

The future of judicial notice of law. When a judge presiding in the presence of a jury decides a question of fact, a sufficiently unique event occurs to merit special treatment because the jury is thought to perform the factfinding role in common law countries. This appears to explain why judicial notice of facts has been a topic of evidence law ever since Thayer authored his pioneering treatise. There is nothing very remarkable about a judge ruling on the tenor of the law to be applied to the resolution of the controversy, however, because by definition this is the very function judges are supposed to perform. When the sources of law were dubious at best, the job of sorting out the applicable law was shifted to the jury, witness how foreign law and municipal ordinances were treated as questions of fact. When next judges began to rule on the tenor of this law, even though it was still "fact" to be developed by the parties, there may have been some justification for describing this process as judicial notice. As all law has become increasingly accessible and judges have tended to assume the duty to rule on the tenor of all law, the notion that this process is part of judicial notice has become increasingly an anachronism. Evidence, after all, involves the proof of facts. How the law is fed into the judicial machine is more appropriately an aspect of the law pertaining to procedure.[61] Thus it is that the electronic bleeps sounded by today's

73 (1941) (international law is "a part of our law and as such is the law of all States of the Union").

56. The New York, 175 U.S. 187 (1899); Boyd v. Conklin, 54 Mich. 583, 20 N.W. 595 (1884).

57. Black Diamond Steamship Corp. v. Robert Stewart & Sons, Limited, 336 U.S. 386 (1949).

58. The New York, 175 U.S. 187 (1899).

59. Black Diamond Steamship Corp. v. Robert Stewart & Sons, Limited, 336 U.S. 386 (1949).

60. Ozanic v. United States, 165 F.2d 738 (2d Cir.1948) (in libel for damage to Yugoslavian vessel on high seas libellant has burden to prove Yugoslav law as fact. "However it might be in respect to British maritime law, we cannot assume that the law of Yugoslavia, a civil law country and not even a great maritime power, is the

same in respect to the measure of damages as that of the United States."); Sonnesen v. Panama Transport Co., 298 N.Y. 262, 82 N.E.2d 569 (1948) (court would not notice Panamanian law as to seaman's right of maintenance and cure, nor would it assume Panamanian maritime law same as ours).

61. Note on Judicial Notice of Law, Adv.Com. Note, Fed.R.Evid. 201. Old habits are hard to break. "In the narrow sense of the word 'evidence' the Committee and Congress are probably right, but if 'evidence' is viewed as encompassing various means by which a tribunal informs itself then it is at least arguable that judicial notice of law is as much a part of 'evidence' as the judicial notice of facts." Evidence Subcommittee Note, Okla.R.Evid. 2201. Thus it is that some jurisdictions add a Rule 202 governing the judicial notice of statutes, ordinances and administra-

data processing equipment are actually tolling the intellectual death knell of this discrete subject-matter hitherto dealt with as a subdivision of the law of evidence.

tive regulations both of the forum and sister states. See, e.g., Alaska, Delaware, Hawaii, Michigan, Montana, Oregon, West Virginia as well as Nevada (R.S. 47.140), Oklahoma (rule 2201) and Puerto Rico (rule 12). There are echoes here of the Uniform Rules of Evidence (1953) and the Model Code of Evidence (1943), themselves reminders of the Indian Evidence Act of 1872.

Title 12

BURDEN OF PROOF AND PRESUMPTIONS

Chapter 36

THE BURDENS OF PROOF AND PRESUMPTIONS [1]

Table of Sections

1. See 9 Wigmore, Evidence §§ 2483–2498 (Chadbourn rev.1981) (general theory), id. 2499–2550 (burdens and presumptions in specific instances); Martin, Basic Problems of Evidence, chs. 2, 3 (6th ed. 1988); Morgan, Some Problems of Proof under the Anglo–American System of Litigation 70–86 (1956); James & Hazard, Civil Procedure §§ 7.5–7.11 (3d ed. 1985); Weinstein & Berger, Evidence, ¶¶ 300[01]–303[08]; 21 Wright & Graham, Federal Practice and Procedure §§ 5121–5148; Allen, Presumptions, Inferences and Burden of Proof in Federal Civil Actions—An Anatomy of Unnecessary Ambiguity and a Proposal for Reform, 76 Nw.U.L.Rev. 892 (1982); Allen, Structuring Jury Decisionmaking in Criminal Cases: A Unified Constitutional Approach to Evidentiary Devices, 94 Harv.L.Rev. 321 (1980); Allen, More on Constitutional Process-of-Proof Problems in Criminal Cases, 94 Harv. L.Rev. 1795 (1981); Ball, The Moment of Truth: Probability Theory and Standards of Proof, 14 Vand.L.Rev. 807 (1961);

§ 336. The Burdens of Proof: The Burden of Producing Evidence and the Burden of Persuasion

"Proof" is an ambiguous word. We sometimes use it to mean evidence, such as testimony or documents. Sometimes, when we say a thing is "proved" we mean that we are convinced by the data submitted that the alleged fact is true. Thus, "proof" is the end result of conviction or persuasion produced by the evidence. Naturally, the term "burden of proof" shares this ambivalence. The term encompasses two separate burdens of proof.[2] One burden is that of producing evidence, satisfactory to the judge, of a particular fact in issue.[3] The second is the burden of persuading the trier of fact that the alleged fact is true.[4]

The burden of producing evidence on an issue means the liability to an adverse ruling (generally a finding or directed verdict) if evidence on the issue has not been produced. It is usually cast first upon the party who has pleaded the existence of the fact, but as we shall see, the burden may shift to the adversary when the pleader has discharged its initial duty.[5] The burden of producing evidence is a critical mechanism

Cleary, Presuming and Pleading: An Essay on Juristic Immaturity, 12 Stan.L.Rev. 5 (1959); Gausewitz, Presumptions in a One–Rule World, 5 Vand.L.Rev. 324 (1952); Jeffries & Stephan, Defenses, Presumptions and Burden of Proof in the Criminal Law, 88 Yale L.J. 1325 (1979); Ladd, Presumptions in Civil Actions, 1977 Ariz.St. L.J. 275; Laughlin, In Support of the Thayer Theory of Presumptions, 52 Mich.L.Rev. 195 (1953); McCormick, Charges on Presumptions, 5 N.C.L.Rev. 291 (1927); McCormick, What Shall the Trial Judge Tell the Jury About Presumptions? 13 Wash.L.Rev. 185 (1938); McNaughton, Burden of Production of Evidence: A Function of a Burden of Persuasion, 68 Harv. L.Rev. 1382 (1955). Nesson, Rationality, Presumption and Judicial Comment: A Response to Professor Allen, 94 Harv.L.Rev. 1574 (1981); Nesson, Reasonable Doubt and Permissive Inferences: The Value of Complexity, 92 Harv.L.Rev. 1187 (1979); Sundby, The Reasonable Doubt Rule and the Meaning of Innocence, 40 Hastings L.Rev. 161 (1989); Underwood, The Thumb on the Scales of Justice: Burdens of Persuasion in Criminal Cases, 86 Yale L.J. 1299 (1977); Fed.R.Evid. 301, 302; C.J.S. Evidence §§ 103–157; 29 Am.Jur.2d Evidence §§ 159–248, 1163–1178; Dec.Dig. Evidence ⟆53–98, Trial ⟆205, 234(7), 237, Criminal Law ⟆305–336, 778, 789.

§ 336

2. The two meanings of "burden of proof" were pointed out by certain nineteenth century judges, e.g., Shaw, C.J., in Powers v. Russell, 30 Mass. (13 Pick.) 69, 76 (1832), and Brett, M.R., in Abrath v. N.E. Ry. Co., 11 Q.B.D. 440, 452 (1883), but the distinction and its consequences were first emphasized and elaborated by James Bradley Thayer in his Preliminary Treatise on Evidence ch. 9 (1898). Modern cases making the distinction are collected in Dec.Dig. Evidence ⟆90.

3. The burden of producing evidence is sometimes termed the "burden of evidence" (C.J.S. Evidence § 103) or "the duty of going forward." Thayer, supra note 2, at 355.

4. Wigmore terms this "the risk of nonpersuasion." 9 Evidence § 2485 (Chadbourn rev. 1981). Thayer, supra, note 2 at 353, noting one meaning of "burden of proof," said: " * * * It marks * * * [t]he peculiar duty of him who has the risk of any given proposition on which parties are at issue,—who will lose the case if he does not make this proposition out, when all has been said and done." Se–Ling Hosiery, Inc. v. Margulies, 364 Pa. 45, 70 A.2d 854, 856 (1950).

The discussion of burdens of proof in this chapter is directed to the burdens as they are applicable to an entire proceeding. Questions of burden of proof also occur in connection with rulings on the admissibility of individual items of evidence. See § 53 supra.

5. See § 338 infra.

in a jury trial, as it empowers the judge to decide the case without jury consideration when a party fails to sustain the burden.

The burden of persuasion becomes a crucial factor only if the parties have sustained their burdens of producing evidence and only when all of the evidence has been introduced. It does not shift from party to party during the course of the trial simply because it need not be allocated until it is time for a decision. When the time for a decision comes, the jury, if there is one, must be instructed how to decide the issue if their minds are left in doubt. The jury must be told that if the party having the burden of persuasion has failed to satisfy that burden, the issue is to be decided against that party. If there is no jury and the judge is in doubt, the issue must be decided against the party having the burden of persuasion.

What is the significance of the burden of persuasion? Clearly, the principal significance of the burden of persuasion is limited to those cases in which the trier of fact is actually in doubt. Possibly, even in those cases, juries disregard their instructions on this question and judges, trying cases without juries, pay only lip service to it, trusting that the appellate courts will not disturb their findings of fact.[6] Yet, even if an empirical study were conclusively to demonstrate both a regular disregard for jury instructions and a propensity on the part of judges to decide issues of fact without regard to their express statements concerning the allocation of the burden of persuasion, rules allocating and describing that burden could not be discarded by a rational legal system. A risk of nonpersuasion naturally exists any time one person attempts to persuade another to act or not to act. If the other does not change her course of action or nonaction, the person desiring change has, of course, failed.[7] If no burden of persuasion were acknowledged by the law, one possible result would be that the trier of fact would purport to reach no decision at all. The impact of nondecision would then fall by its own weight upon the party, usually the plaintiff, who sought a change in the status quo. Although this is generally where the law would place the burden anyhow, important policy considerations may dictate that the risk should fall on the opposing party.[8]

Another possibility would be that the trier of fact would itself assign a burden of persuasion, describing that burden as it saw fit by substituting its own notions of policy for those now made available to it as a matter of law. Such a result would be most undesirable. Considerations of policy that are sufficient to suggest that in some instances the

---

6. In the first edition of this text, Dean McCormick stated:

"In the writer's view [the burden of producing evidence] has far more influence upon the final outcome of cases than does the burden of persuasion, which has become very largely a matter of the technique of the wording of instructions to juries. This wording may be chosen in the particular case as a handle for reversal, but will seldom have been a factor in the jury's decision." § 307, at 634 note 2.

7. For a comparison of the burden of persuasion in litigated and in nonlitigated situations see 9 Wigmore, Evidence § 2485 (Chadbourn rev. 1981).

8. See § 337 infra.

burden of persuasion be assigned to the party desiring a maintenance of the status quo are strong enough to dictate the need for a consistent rather than a case by case determination of the question. Other policy considerations, such as those that have led the law to require that the prosecution in a criminal case prove the defendant guilty beyond a reasonable doubt,[9] are sufficient to require that the jury be explicitly and clearly instructed as to the measure of the burden as well as its allocation. Although judges and juries may act contrary to the law despite the best attempts to persuade them to do otherwise, we can at least give them the benefit of thoughtful guidance on the questions of who should bear the burden of persuasion and what the nature of that burden should be. In jury trials, perhaps the problem has not been in the concept of a burden of persuasion, but rather in the confusing jury instructions that abound on this point of law. In nonjury trials, if judges are not in fact following rules of law allocating the burden, the fault may lie not in the concept but with thoughtless judicial and legislative allocations and descriptions of the burden.

§ 337. Allocating the Burdens of Proof [1]

In most cases, the party who has the burden of pleading a fact will have the burdens of producing evidence and of persuading the jury of its existence as well.[2] The pleadings therefore provide the common guide for apportioning the burdens of proof. For example, in a typical negligence case the plaintiff will have the burdens of (1) pleading the defendant's negligence (2) producing evidence of that negligence and (3) persuading the trier of fact of its existence. The defendant will usually have the same three burdens with regard to the contributory negligence of the plaintiff.[3]

---

9. See § 341 infra.

§ 337

1. James & Hazard, Civil Procedure § 7.8 (3d ed. 1985); 9 Wigmore, Evidence § 2486 (Chadbourn rev. 1981); Cleary, Presuming and Pleading: An Essay on Juristic Immaturity, 12 Stan.L.Rev. 5 (1959); Epstein, Pleading and Presumptions, 40 U.Chi.L.Rev. 556 (1973); C.J.S. Evidence §§ 103–110, 112–113; Dec.Dig.Evidence ⚲90–97.

2. Reliance Life Insurance Co. v. Burgess, 112 F.2d 234 (8th Cir.1940), cert. denied 311 U.S. 699; Buda v. Fulton, 261 Iowa 981, 157 N.W.2d 336 (1968); In re Estate of Ewing, 234 Iowa 950, 14 N.W.2d 633 (1944); Dec.Dig.Evidence ⚲91.

3. The relationship of the burden of pleading to the burdens of proof raises the question of the consequences of a party mistakenly pleading a fact upon an issue which its adversary had the burden of raising by an affirmative pleading. In the relatively few cases dealing with the question, the prevailing view is that a mistake in pleading will not generally affect the allocation of the burdens of proof. For example, the courts have held that plaintiff's unnecessary allegation that he was in the exercise of due care, does not affect the defendant's burdens with regard to contributory negligence. Fitchburg Railway Co. v. Nichols, 85 Fed. 945 (1st Cir.1898); Bevis v. Vanceburg Telephone Co., 132 Ky. 385, 113 S.W. 811 (1908); Wintrobe v. Hart, 178 Md. 289, 13 A.2d 365 (1940). However, if a trial judge erroneously assigns the burdens of proof to a party who has mistakenly pleaded an issue, a few courts have held that this party has invited the error and has no ground of complaint. Vycas v. St. George Guard Society, 97 Conn. 509, 117 A. 692, 693 (1922) ("A defendant who unnecessarily elaborates a general denial by alleging facts inconsistent with the allegations denied is in no position to complain, in case

However, looking for the burden of pleading is not a foolproof guide to the allocation of the burdens of proof. The latter burdens do not invariably follow the pleadings. In a federal court, for example, a defendant may be required to plead contributory negligence as an affirmative defense and yet, where jurisdiction is based upon diversity of citizenship, the applicable substantive law may place the burdens of producing evidence and persuasion with regard to that issue on the plaintiff.[4] More significantly, reference to which party has pleaded a fact is no help at all when the rationale behind the allocation is questioned or in a case of first impression where there are no established pleading rules.

The burdens of pleading and proof with regard to most facts have been and should be assigned to the plaintiff who generally seeks to change the present state of affairs and who therefore naturally should be expected to bear the risk of failure of proof or persuasion. The rules which assign certain facts material to the enforcibility of a claim to the defendant owe their development partly to traditional happen-so and partly to considerations of policy.[5]

The determination of appropriate guidelines for the allocation of the burdens has been somewhat hindered by the judicial repetition of two doctrines, one erroneous and the other meaningless. Statements are found primarily in older cases to the effect that even though a party is required to plead a fact, it is not required to prove that fact if its averment is negative rather than affirmative in form.[6] Such a rule would place an entirely undue emphasis on what is ordinarily purely a matter of choice of forms.[7] Moreover, these statements were probably to be understood as properly applying only to the denial by a party of an opponent's previous pleading, and now one who has the burden of pleading a negative fact as part of its cause of action generally has the accompanying burdens of producing evidence and persuasion.[8] The

the court takes him at his word and erroneously instructs the jury as to the burden of proof."); Hatch v. Merigold, 119 Conn. 339, 176 A. 266, 96 A.L.R. 1114, 1116 (1935) (plaintiff by pleading lack of contributory negligence waived benefit of statute placing burden of persuasion on defendant on this issue); Boswell v. Pannell, 107 Tex. 433, 180 S.W. 593, 596 (1915) (defendant by pleading affirmatively voluntarily assumed burden of persuasion and cannot complain when assigned to him). Probably the greater number of cases would reject this qualification. See e.g., Schmitz v. Mathews, 133 Wash. 335, 336, 233 P. 660, 661 (1925) ("not an invitation * * * to commit error * * * merely an opportunity"). See Comment, 39 Yale L.J. 117 (1929).

4. See Palmer v. Hoffman, 318 U.S. 109 (1943); Sampson v. Channell, 110 F.2d 754 (1st Cir.1940), cert. denied 310 U.S. 650; James & Hazard, supra note 1, § 3.16 at

166–7; 2A Moore, Federal Practice ¶ 8.27[2] at 8–177 (2d Ed.1982).

5. Although the following discussion generally relates to all cases, civil and criminal, there are additional problems in criminal cases, particularly with regard to the allocation of the burden of persuasion. See §§ 341, 347, infra.

6. Walker v. Carpenter, 144 N.C. 674, 676, 57 S.E. 461 (1907) ("The first rule laid down in the books on evidence is to the effect that the issue must be proved by the party who states an affirmative, not by the party who states a negative.") Similar statements can be found in more recent cases. Levine v. Pascal, 94 Ill.App.2d 43, 236 N.E.2d 425 (1968).

7. But see Epstein, Pleading and Presumptions, supra note 1 at 571–582.

8. Chase Manhattan Bank v. O'Connor, 82 N.J.Super. 382, 197 A.2d 706, 709 (1964) (party alleging nondelivery of stock certifi-

second misleading doctrine is that the party to whose case the element is essential has the burdens of proof. Such a rule simply restates the question.[9]

The actual reasons for the allocation of the burdens may be no more complex than the misleading statements just discussed. The policy of handicapping a disfavored contention [10] probably accounts for the requirement that the defendant generally has all three burdens with regard to such matters as contributory negligence, statute of limitations, and truth in defamation. Convenience in following the natural order of storytelling may account for calling on the defendant to plead and prove those matters which arise after a cause of action has matured, such as payment, release, and accord and satisfaction.

A doctrine often repeated by the courts is that where the facts with regard to an issue lie peculiarly in the knowledge of a party, that party has the burden of proving the issue. Examples are the burdens commonly placed upon the defendant to prove payment, discharge in bankruptcy, and license.[11] This consideration should not be overemphasized. Very often one must plead and prove matters as to which his adversary has superior access to the proof. Nearly all required allega-

cates had the burden of proving that issue); Saari v. George C. Dates & Associates, 311 Mich. 624, 19 N.W.2d 121 (1945) (wrongful discharge: defendant pleaded plaintiff's failure to perform, burden on defendant); Johnson v. Johnson, 229 N.C. 541, 50 S.E.2d 569 (1948) (plaintiff alleging in reply that deed was forged had burden of establishing nonexecution by purported grantor). It is sometimes said that the party pleading a negative need not prove it when the facts are peculiarly within the knowledge of the other party. Allstate Finance Corp. v. Zimmerman, 330 F.2d 740, 744 (5th Cir.1964). Or more mildly that as to the party pleading a negative the law will be satisfied with a lesser quantum of proof, particularly when the facts are within the knowledge of the adverse party. In re Chicago Railways Co., 175 F.2d 282, 290 (7th Cir.1949), cert. denied 338 U.S. 850. The important consideration in these cases, however, is not which party has the negative, but which party has the knowledge of the facts. Fitzgerald v. Wright, 155 N.J.Super. 494, 382 A.2d 1162 (1978) (decision to allocate to plaintiff burden of proving extent of injury so as to reach no-fault threshold based on superior knowledge of injured party, not statutory terminology). See also Wiles v. Mullinax, 275 N.C. 473, 168 S.E.2d 366 (1969) (plaintiff had the burden of proving the defendant's failure to procure insurance coverage, notwithstanding negative form of the issue; Sharp, J. arguing in dissent that the burden should be placed upon the defendant, not

only because of its negative form but also because the defendant had "peculiar knowledge of the fact in issue and therefore the better means of proving it."); Pace v. Hymas, 111 Idaho 581, 726 P.2d 693 (1986) (defendant university had the burden of proving a financial exigency justifying its firing of plaintiff; court mentions that defendant had the affirmative of this issue, but relies principally on defendant's superior access to the facts). See text accompanying note 11 infra. See also C.J.S. Evidence §§ 105, 112; Dec.Dig. Evidence ⊜92, 93.

9. See Cleary, supra note 1, at 11.

10. The phrase is borrowed from Clark, Code Pleading § 96 at 610 (2d ed. 1947) where these considerations and the relation of the pleading rules to the burden of proof are lucidly discussed.

For a discussion of a disfavored contention, see In re Regional Rail Reorganization Proceedings, 421 F.Supp. 1061, 1073 (Special Court 1976) (railroad's position with regard to pension plan).

11. See, e.g., Fed.R.Civ.P. 8(c); Cleary, supra note 1 at 12; cases cited, n. 8, supra. Expanded pretrial discovery would seem to have diminished greatly whatever importance this factor had in allocating the burdens. However, there has been no rush by the courts to reassess allocations between the parties in the light of expanded discovery, perhaps attesting to the fact that exclusive knowledge in one party has sel-

tions of the plaintiff in actions for tort or breach of contract relating to the defendant's acts or omissions describe matters peculiarly in the defendant's knowledge. Correspondingly, when the defendant is required to plead contributory negligence, it pleads facts specially known to the plaintiff.

Perhaps a more frequently significant consideration in the fixing of the burdens of proof is the judicial estimate of the probabilities of the situation. The risk of failure of proof may be placed upon the party who contends that the more unusual event has occurred.[12] For example, where a business relationship exists, it is unlikely that services will be performed gratuitously. The burden of proving a gift is therefore placed upon the one who claims it. Where services are performed for a member of the family, a gift is much more likely and the burden of proof is placed on the party claiming the right to be paid.[13]

In allocating the burdens, courts consistently attempt to distinguish between the constituent elements of a promise or of a statutory command, which must be proved by the party who relies on the contract or statute, and matters of exception, which must be proved by its adversary.[14] Often the result of this approach is an arbitrary allocation of the burdens, as the statutory language may be due to a mere casual

dom been the controlling reason for assigning the burdens of proof.

12. See Cleary, supra n. 1 at 12–13, observing that in assigning the burdens the courts will occasionally consider the probabilities of the situation generally and sometimes will consider the probabilities with reference to litigated cases. "No reason for the shift is apparent, and it may be unconscious. The litigated cases would seem to furnish the more appropriate basis for estimating probabilities."

In Ball, The Moment of Truth: Probability Theory and Standards of Proof, 14 Vand.L.Rev. 807, 817–818 (1961) the author questions the use of probabilities to allocate the burden of persuasion. He suggests that if the burden is assigned to the party whose case depends upon the happening of the least likely event the probabilities are really counted against it twice—once in the jury's own initial assessment of the probabilities which is likely to be similar to that made by the courts and once in the assignment of the burden of persuasion. A similar point is made with regard to the use of presumptions having their basis in probability in Laughlin, In Support of the Thayer Theory of Presumptions, 52 Mich.L.Rev. 195, 212 (1953).

See also General Motors Corp. v. Toyota Motor Co., 467 F.Supp. 1142, 1173 (S.D.Ohio 1979), reversed in part on other grounds 667 F.2d 504 (6th Cir.), cert. denied 456 U.S. 937.

13. See James & Hazard, supra note 1 at 324.

14. With regard to contracts, see Corbin, Contracts § 751 (1960); 5 Williston, Contracts § 674 (1961). With regard to statutes, see Annot. 130 A.L.R. 440 and discussion in State v. Big John, 146 Wis.2d 741, 755–756, 432 N.W.2d 576, 583 (1988). On the question generally see, Cleary, supra note 1 at 8–10; Stone, Burden of Proof and the Judicial Process, 60 L.Q.Rev. 262 (1944).

The operation of the distinction in insurance contracts may be illustrated as follows: In an action on a life insurance policy with an exception for death by suicide the defendant has all of the burdens on the issue of suicide. But in a suit on an accident policy, or on the double indemnity provision of a life policy, since suicide is not an accident, the plaintiff must plead accident and, at least tentatively, will have both burdens of proof on the issue.

Schleunes v. American Casualty Co., 528 F.2d 634 (5th Cir.1976) (accidental death benefits); Blythe v. Kanawha Insurance Co., 279 F.Supp. 8 (W.D.N.C.1968) (double indemnity provision). See also, Note, 46 Colum.L.Rev. 802, 810 (1946). The allocation of the burdens of proof to the plaintiff in an accident policy or double indemnity provision case may be only tentative due to the operation of a presumption against suicide. See §§ 343, 344, infra.

choice of form by the draftsman. However, the distinction may be a valid one in some instances, particularly when the exceptions to a statute or promise are numerous. If that is the case, fairness usually requires that the adversary give notice of the particular exception upon which it relies and therefore that it bear the burden of pleading. The burdens of proof will not always follow the burden of pleading in these cases.[15] However, exceptions generally point to exceptional situations. If proof of the facts is inaccessible or not persuasive, it is usually fairer to act as if the exceptional situation did not exist and therefore to place the burden of proof and persuasion on the party claiming its existence.[16]

As has been stated, the burdens of producing evidence and of persuasion with regard to any given issue are both generally allocated to the same party. Usually each is assigned but once in the course of the litigation and a safe prediction of that assignment can be made at the pleading stage. However, the initial allocation of the burden of producing evidence may not always be final. The shifting nature of that burden may cause both parties to have the burden with regard to the same issue at different points in the trial.[17] Similarly, although the burden of persuasion is assigned only once—when it is time for a decision—a prediction of the allocation of that burden, based upon the pleadings, may have to be revised when evidence is introduced at trial.[18] Policy considerations similar to those that govern the initial allocation of the burden of producing evidence and tentatively fix the burden of persuasion govern the ultimate assignment of those burdens as well.[19]

15. An illustration of a divergence between the burdens of pleading and proof in an analogous situation is the treatment of conditions precedent in contracts, particularly in insurance contracts, by most courts. For example, in a federal court the defendant will be required to plead the nonoccurrence of a particular condition precedent [Fed.R.Civ.P. 9(c)] but it may not have the burdens of proof with regard to that issue. See 2A Moore, Federal Practice ¶ 9.04 at 9–62–63 (2d ed. 1987); 5 Williston, Contracts, § 674 at 181 (1961).

16. This consideration, of course, is simply a specific application of the use of an estimate of the probabilities to fix the burdens. In Stone, supra note 14 the learned writer examines the opinions in Joseph Constantine Steamship Ltd. v. Imperial Smelting Corp., Ltd., [1942] A.C. 154 (H.L.) which determined the novel question whether upon the plea of frustration in an action on a contract, the defendant or the plaintiff has the burdens of producing evidence and of persuasion on the issue whether the frustration was contributed to by the fault of the defendant. The opinions in placing the burdens upon the plaintiff stress the formal distinction between an essential element of the defense and an

exception to its operation, and purport to reach their conclusions mainly upon definitions, logic, and analogy. The author urges that as to this new question, the judges might more fruitfully have grounded their decision upon considerations of justice and policy, such as the following: "Let it be assumed then that in the great majority of frustration cases no fault of the parties was operative; and let it be assumed that in these cases the impossibility of proof mentioned by the lords is present. A rule requiring the defendant pleading frustration to negative fault will then *ex hypothesi* do injustice to the great majority of defendants. While on the other hand, a rule requiring the plaintiff to prove fault will *ex hypothesi* do injustice to only a small minority of plaintiffs." (p. 278).

See Northwestern Mutual Life Insurance Co. v. Linard, 498 F.2d 556 (2d Cir.1974), for discussion of allocation of burdens in actions on insurance policies and, in particular, exploration of difference between arson under fire policy and scuttling of ship under marine policy.

17. See § 338 infra.

18. See § 344 infra.

19. See § 343 infra.

In summary, there is no key principle governing the apportionment of the burdens of proof. Their allocation, either initially or ultimately, will depend upon the weight that is given to any one or more of several factors, including: (1) the natural tendency to place the burdens on the party desiring change, (2) special policy considerations such as those disfavoring certain defenses, (3) convenience, (4) fairness, and (5) the judicial estimate of the probabilities.[20]

§ 338. Satisfying the Burden of Producing Evidence

Let us suppose that the plaintiff, claiming an estate in land for John Smith's life, had the burden of pleading, and has pleaded, that John Smith was alive at the time the action was brought. She seeks to fulfill the burden of producing evidence of this fact.

---

20. Declaratory judgment actions provide an excellent example of the problems of allocating the burdens of proof. Where the plaintiff seeks a declaratory judgment as a basis for some further affirmative claim against the defendant, there is no special problem; the burdens will be allocated as usual, with the major share going to the plaintiff. Jerry Vogel Music Co. v. Forster Music Publisher, 147 F.2d 614 (2d Cir.1945), cert. denied 325 U.S. 880 (suit for declaration that plaintiff was owner of copyrighted song; plaintiff had burden to establish ownership and defendant to establish defense of joint ownership); McNally v. Moser, 210 Md. 127, 122 A.2d 555, 60 A.L.R.2d 388 (App.1956) (defendant landlord claiming illegal use of leased premises had both the burden of producing evidence and the burden of persuasion on the question). But when the traditional positions of plaintiff and defendant are transposed, the courts have had considerable difficulty in determining the allocation of the burdens. In these cases, the competing policies discussed in this section clearly emerge. For example, some courts have held that when an insurance company sues for a declaration of nonliability the defendant insured should have the burden on the issues on which it would bear the burden had it sued to establish his rights under the policy. The leading case is Travelers Insurance Co. v. Greenough, 88 N.H. 391, 190 A. 129 (1937), where the court stated that a contrary conclusion "would place the plaintiff in a position of undue disadvantage." See also Preferred Accident Insurance Co. v. Grasso, 186 F.2d 987 (2d Cir.1951) (opinion by Clark, J.) Accord, Utah Farm Bureau Insurance Co. v. Dairyland Insurance Co., 634 F.2d 1326 (10th Cir.1980); Fireman's Fund Insurance Co. v.

Videfreeze Corp., 540 F.2d 1171 (3d Cir. 1976), cert. denied 429 U.S. 1053; Barker v. Goldberg, 705 F.Supp. 102 (E.D.N.Y.1989). See also Fireman's Fund Ins. Companies v. Ex–Cell–O Corp., 702 F.Supp. 1317 (E.D.Mich.1988) (estimate of the probabilities, fairness and special policy considerations worked to place burdens on defendant in declaratory judgment action). Other courts have seen no such disadvantage and hold that the burdens should rest on the party bringing the suit. Reliance Life Insurance Co. v. Burgess, 112 F.2d 234 (8th Cir.1940), cert. denied 311 U.S. 699 (Sanborn, J. dissenting on this question); First National Bank of Or. v. Malady, 242 Or. 353, 408 P.2d 724 (1965) (strong dissent on this question by Perry, J.). The competing policies are also reflected in Professor Moore's discussion of this problem, 6A Moore, Federal Practice ¶ 57.31[2] at 57–286 (2d ed. 1982). He argues that the doctrine of the *Greenough* case is "unwise in its own context," in that it is "reasonable and fair" for the plaintiff insurer to bear the burdens in such a case. He takes a different view, however, of the burdens in an action by an alleged infringer for a declaration of noninfringement or invalidity of defendant's patent, copyright, or trademark. Professor Moore bases his argument on the relevant considerations that it may be difficult for the accused infringer to prove that its activities have in no way infringed the defendant's rights and that in the vast majority of such cases, the basis for the declaratory action is an extrajudicial charge of infringement "which the defendant has made and nobody knows better than he what lies behind his charge." Id. at 57–288. See generally on these questions, Annot., 23

To do this she may offer *direct* evidence, e.g., of witness Jones, who saw Smith alive in the clerk's office when the complaint in the action was filed. From this the inference of the truth of the fact to be proved depends only upon the truthfulness of Jones. Or, she may offer *circumstantial* evidence, which requires a weighing of probabilities as to matters other than merely the truthfulness of the witness. For example, she may secure the testimony of Jones that Jones received a letter in the mail which was signed "John Smith" one month before the action was brought and that she recognized the signature as Smith's. Patently in this latter case, the tribunal may be satisfied that Jones is speaking the truth, and yet the tribunal may decline to infer the fact of Smith's being alive when the action began.

How strongly persuasive must the offered evidence be to satisfy the burden? A "scintilla" of evidence will not suffice.[1] The evidence must be such that a reasonable person could draw from it the inference of the existence of the particular fact to be proved or, as put conversely by one federal court, "if there is substantial evidence opposed to the [motion for directed verdict], that is evidence of such quality and weight that reasonable and fair-minded men in the exercise of impartial judgment might reach different conclusions, the [motion] should be denied."[2]

One problem that has troubled the courts is whether the test for the granting of a directed verdict should vary, depending upon the required measure of persuasion if the case goes to the jury. For example in a criminal case where the prosecution must persuade the jury beyond a reasonable doubt,[3] should the test for a directed verdict be whether the evidence could satisfy reasonable people beyond a reasonable doubt? Some courts have said no, perhaps believing with Judge Learned Hand that, although the gravity of the consequences often makes judges more exacting in criminal cases, the line between proof that should satisfy reasonable men and the evidence that should satisfy reasonable men

---

A.L.R.2d 1243; Dic.Dig. Declaratory Judgment ☜341–343.

§ 338

1. See James & Hazard, Civil Procedure § 7.11 at 340 (3d ed. 1985) where the authors refer to the "judicial legend" that there once was a "scintilla rule" under which an adverse verdict could be directed only when there was literally no evidence and state that "if there ever was such a notion all that remains of it today is its well nigh universal repudiation." See also 9 Wigmore, Evidence § 2494 (Chadbourn rev. 1981); Friedenthal, et al, Civil Procedure (1985) § 12.3 at 544; Dec.Dig. Trial ☜139(1).

2. Boeing Co. v. Shipman, 411 F.2d 365, 374 (5th Cir.1969). The above quoted statement refers also to motions for judgment notwithstanding the verdict. The tests are usually the same. See 5A Moore, Federal Practice ¶ 50.07(2) (2d ed. 1985).

Because the ruling that a party has not satisfied its burden of producing evidence precludes a jury determination of the merits of the case, some courts, particularly federal courts, have been plagued by constitutional worries in formulating tests for the granting of directed verdicts. For an excellent discussion of the directed verdict in the federal courts, see Cooper, Directions for Directed Verdicts: A Compass for Federal Courts, 55 Minn.L.Rev. 903 (1971).

3. See § 341 infra.

beyond a reasonable doubt is, in the long run, "too thin for day to day use." [4]

However, most courts applied the stricter test.[5] A clear trend toward universal adoption of the stricter test [6] was effectively solidified into a constitutional dictate in Jackson v. Virginia,[7] where the Court held that a federal court reviewing a state court conviction on a *habeas corpus* petition must determine whether a rational factfinder could have found the petitioners guilty beyond a reasonable doubt. Arguably no trial judge should apply a lesser standard on a motion for a directed verdict.[8]

Generally no difficulty occurs where the evidence is direct. Except in rare cases,[9] it is sufficient, though given by one witness only, however negligible a human being she may be. But if the evidence is circumstantial, forensic disputes often arise as to its sufficiency to warrant a jury to draw the desired inference. In fact, in few areas of the law have so many words been spoken by the courts with so little conviction. One test frequently expounded in criminal cases is that where the prosecution relies upon circumstantial evidence, the evidence must be so conclusive as to exclude any other reasonable inference inconsistent therewith.[10] The test is accurate enough in criminal cases, but adds

---

4. United States v. Feinberg, 140 F.2d 592, 594 (2d Cir.1944), cert. denied 322 U.S. 726. See also Hays v. United States, 231 Fed. 106 (8th Cir.1916), affirmed sub nom. Caminetti v. United States, 242 U.S. 470; State v. Nutley, 24 Wis.2d 527, 129 N.W.2d 155, 163 (1964), cert. denied 380 U.S. 918. This approach, of course, leaves the beyond-a-reasonable-doubt standard as a test to be applied by the jury.

5. Riggs v. United States, 280 F.2d 949 (5th Cir.1960); Curley v. United States, 160 F.2d 229 (D.C.Cir.1947), cert. denied 331 U.S. 837; State v. Rocker, 52 Hawaii 336, 475 P.2d 684 (1970).

6. Even in Judge Hand's own circuit, his "single test" rule was replaced by a test requiring that the evidence be such as could satisfy reasonable people beyond a reasonable doubt. United States v. Taylor, 464 F.2d 240 (2d Cir.1972). See also State v. Stevens, 26 Wis.2d 451, 132 N.W.2d 502 (1965).

7. 443 U.S. 307 (1979), rehearing denied 444 U.S. 890. See also Anderson v. Liberty Lobby, Inc., 477 U.S. 242 (1986) (standard for summary judgment or directed verdict on the issue of actual malice in libel cases is whether the record could support a reasonable jury finding that plaintiff has shown actual malice by clear and convincing evidence).

8. For examples of state courts reaching this conclusion, see People v. Hampton, 407 Mich. 354, 285 N.W.2d 284 (1979), cert. denied 449 U.S. 885; State v. Hudson, 277

S.C. 200, 284 S.E.2d 773 (1981). But see Norris v. State, 275 Ind. 608, 419 N.E.2d 129 (1981) (court rejects "rational trier of fact" standard enunciated in *Jackson*). See also discussion in Brandis, North Carolina Evidence (3d Ed.1988) § 210 at 166.

9. In extreme circumstances, such as where a witness's testimony is flatly contradicted by indisputable physical facts or laws of nature, the testimony may be disregarded. Scott v. Hansen, 228 Iowa 37, 289 N.W. 710 (1940). In a few other instances, such as where a defendant is charged with perjury, the law imposes an artificial requirement of corroboration. See James & Hazard, supra note 1 at 341–342.

10. State v. Love, 106 Ariz. 215, 474 P.2d 806 (1970); People v. Branion, 47 Ill.2d 70, 265 N.E.2d 1 (1970), cert. denied 403 U.S. 907; Dec.Dig. Criminal Law ⟨⟩552(3). In Holland v. United States, 348 U.S. 121 (1954), the Court held that the trial court did not err in refusing to instruct the jury in these terms. Although this holding would not seem to compel the rejection of this language as a directed verdict test, most federal circuits have so held. E.g., United States v. Thomas, 303 F.2d 561 (6th Cir.1962); United States v. Hamrick, 293 F.2d 468 (4th Cir.1961). Contra: Battles v. United States, 388 F.2d 799 (5th Cir.1968).

At least one circuit has held that the federal standard enunciated in the *Jackson*

little at least to the stricter test for criminal cases discussed above. A similar formula is sometimes expounded in civil cases [11] but seems misplaced in civil litigation. It leaves little for the jury and far exceeds what is needed to prevent verdicts based upon speculation and conjecture. Courts rejecting the formula in civil cases have stated that the burden of producing evidence is satisfied, even by circumstantial evidence, if "there be sufficient facts for the jury to say reasonably that the preponderance favors liability." [12]

Other tests and other phrasings of the tests discussed here are myriad,[13] but irrespective of the test articulated, in the last analysis the judge's ruling must necessarily rest on her individual opinion, formed in the light of her own common sense and experience, as to the limits of reasonable inference from the facts proven. However, certain situations recur and give rise repeatedly to litigation, and a given judge, in a desire for consistency and the consequent saving of time and mental travail, will rule alike whenever the same situation is proved and its sufficiency to warrant a certain inference is questioned. Other judges follow suit and a standardized practice ripening into a rule of law results. Most of these rules are positive rather than negative. They announce that certain types of fact-groups are sufficient to enable the person who has the first duty to go forward with evidence to fulfill that burden, i.e., they enable the party to rest after proving them without being subject to the penalty of an adverse ruling.

Suppose the one who had the initial burden of offering evidence in support of the alleged fact, on pain of an adverse ruling, does produce evidence barely sufficient to satisfy that burden, so that the judge can just say, "A reasonable jury *could* infer that the fact is as alleged, from the circumstances proved." If the proponent then rests, what is the situation? Has the duty of going forward shifted to the adversary? Not if we define that duty as the liability to a peremptory adverse ruling on failing to give evidence, for if at this juncture the original proponent rests and the adversary offers no proof, the proponent will

---

case should apply in habeas corpus proceedings rather than a state law test couched in terms of excluding any other inconsistent reasonable inference. York v. Tate, 858 F.2d 322 (6th Cir.1988), cert. denied 490 U.S. 1049. See also Laird v. Lack, 884 F.2d 912 (6th Cir.1989), cert. denied 493 U.S. 1086.

11. Bowers v. Maire, 179 Neb. 239, 137 N.W.2d 796 (1965); Schmidt v. Pioneer United Dairies, 60 Wash.2d 271, 373 P.2d 764 (1962). See also Burns, Weighing Circumstantial Evidence, 2 S.Dak.L.Rev. 36 (1957).

12. Smith v. Bell Telephone Co., 397 Pa. 134, 153 A.2d 477 (1959). See also Rumsey v. Great Atlantic & Pacific Tea Co., 408 F.2d 89 (3d Cir.1969); Comment, 12 Vill.L.Rev. 326 (1967).

13. A frequently stated corollary to the rules concerning the sufficiency of circumstantial evidence is that one circumstantial inference may not be based upon another. See cases collected in Annot., 5 A.L.R.3d 100. Despite its frequent repetition by some courts, such a rule can actually amount to nothing more than a makeweight argument to be used when a court believes that the inferences sought to be drawn are too remote or speculative. See Shutt v. State, 233 Ind. 169, 117 N.E.2d 892 (1954). Any other interpretation of the rule would severely impede the ordinary and valid uses of circumstantial evidence. See generally 1A Wigmore, Evidence § 41 (Tillers rev. 1983).

not be entitled to the direction of a verdict in her favor on the issue, but rather the court will leave the issue to the decision of the jury. But it is frequently said that in this situation the duty of going forward has shifted to the adversary,[14] and this is unobjectionable [15] if we bear in mind that the penalty for silence is very different here from that which was applied to the original proponent. If she had remained silent at the outset she would irrevocably have lost the case on this issue, but the only penalty now applied to her adversary is the risk, if she remains silent, of the jury's finding against her, though it may find for her. Theoretically she may have this risk still, even after she has offered evidence in rebuttal. It is simpler to limit "duty of going forward" to the liability, on resting, to an adverse ruling, and to regard the stage just discussed (where the situation is that if both parties rest, the issue will be left to the jury) as one in which neither party has any duty of going forward.[16]

In the situation just discussed, the party who first had the duty, i.e., the necessity, of giving proof, has produced evidence which requires the judge to permit the jury to infer, as it chooses, that the fact alleged is or is not true. It is a permitted, but not a compulsory, inference. Is it possible for the original proponent of evidence to carry her proof to the stage where if she rests, she will be entitled to a directed verdict, or its equivalent, on the issue? Undoubtedly, with a qualification to be noted, this is possible, and when it occurs there is a shifting to the adversary of the duty of going forward with the evidence, in the strictest sense. Such a ruling means that in the judge's view the proponent has not merely offered evidence from which reasonable people could draw the inference of the truth of the fact alleged, but evidence from which (in the absence of evidence from the adversary) reasonable people could not help but draw this inference. Thus, as long ago as 1770, Lord Mansfield told the jury that upon the issue of whether defendant had published a libel, proof of a sale of the book in defendant's shop was, being unrebutted, "conclusive." [17]

In the case first supposed at the beginning of this section, if the plaintiff brought forward the *direct* evidence of Jones that Smith was alive when the complaint was filed, and there is no contrary evidence at all, or if she brings forward circumstantial evidence (that is, evidence that Smith was seen alive in perfect health 10 minutes before the complaint was filed) which is, in the absence of contrary circumstances, irresistibly convincing, the jury should not be left to refuse to draw the only rational inference.

14. Speas v. Merchants' Bank & Trust Co., 188 N.C. 524, 530, 125 S.E. 398, 401 (1924); C.J.S. Evidence § 110 at 187.

15. But see Stansbury, North Carolina Evidence § 203 (1963) at 526 note 27 where the author refers to such a characterization as "misleading at least." See also Brandis, supra note 8, § 203 at 149 note 27.

16. For a judicial discussion of the example given in this paragraph, see Pennsylvania v. United States, 361 F.Supp. 208 (M.D.Pa.1973), affirmed 414 U.S. 1017.

17. Rex v. Almon, 5 Burr. 2686, 98 Eng. Rep. 411 (K.B.1770).

If we do not permit the jury to draw an inference from insufficient data, as where the proponent has failed to sustain her initial duty of producing evidence, we should not permit the jury to act irrationally by rejecting compelling evidence. Here again the ruling, from repeated occurrence of similar facts, may become a standardized one. However, the statement that one who has the duty of going forward can go forward far enough not merely to escape an adverse peremptory ruling herself, but to subject her opponent to one if the latter declines to take up the gage by producing evidence, has the following qualification. Obviously if the testimony were conflicting as to the truth of the facts from which the inference of the fact in issue is desired to be drawn, and the judge believes the inference (conceding the truth of the premise) is irresistible to rational minds, he can only make a conditional peremptory ruling. He directs the jury, if you believe the evidence that fact A is so then you must find fact B, the fact in issue. In some jurisdictions, if the party seeking the ruling has the burden of persuasion on the issue, as assigned on the basis of the pleadings, she can only get a conditional ruling, though her witnesses are undisputed and unimpeached.[18] But, in either event, if the inference is overwhelming, the jury is instructed not to cogitate over that, but only over the truthfulness of those who testify to the basic data.

We have seen something of the mechanics of the process of "proceeding" or "going forward" with evidence, viewed from the point of view of the *first* party who is stimulated to produce proof under threat of a ruling foreclosing a finding in her favor. She may in respect to a particular issue pass through three states of judicial hospitality: (a) where if she stops she will be thrown out of court; (b) where if she stops and her adversary does nothing, her reception will be left to the jury; and (c) where if she stops and her adversary does nothing, her victory (so far as it depends on having the inference she desires drawn) is at once proclaimed. Whenever the first producer has presented evidence sufficient to get her to the third stage and the burden of producing evidence can truly be said to have shifted, her adversary may in turn pass through the same three stages. Her evidence again may be (a) insufficient to warrant a finding in her favor, (b) sufficient to warrant a finding, or (c) irresistible, if unrebutted.

§ 339. Satisfying the Burden of Persuasion: (a) The Measure of Persuasion in Civil Cases Generally [1]

According to the customary formulas a party who has the burden of persuasion of a fact must prove it in criminal prosecutions "beyond a

---

18. E.g., Alexander v. Tingle, 181 Md. 464, 30 A.2d 737 (1943); Hoerath v. Sloan's Moving & Storage Co., 305 S.W.2d 418 (Mo. 1957). Contra: Colthurst v. Lake View State Bank of Chicago, 18 F.2d 875 (8th Cir.1927). See generally cases cited in Annot., 62 A.L.R.2d 1191.

§ 339

1. 9 Wigmore, Evidence § 2498 (Chadbourn rev. 1981); Martin, Basic Problems of Evidence § 2.04 (6th ed. 1988); Morgan, Some Problems of Proof 81–86 (1956); Ball, The Moment of Truth: Probability Theory and Standards of Proof, 14 Vand.L.Rev.

reasonable doubt," [2] in certain exceptional controversies in civil cases, "by clear, strong and convincing evidence," [3] but on the general run of issues in civil cases "by a preponderance of evidence." [4] The "reasonable doubt" formula points to what we are really concerned with, the state of the jury's mind, whereas the other two divert attention to the evidence, which is a step removed, being the instrument by which the jury's mind is influenced.[5] These latter phrases, consequently, are awkward vehicles for expressing the degree of the jury's belief.[6]

What is the most acceptable meaning of the phrase, proof by a preponderance, or greater weight, of the evidence? Certainly the phrase does not mean simple volume of evidence or number of witnesses.[7] One definition is that evidence preponderates when it is more convincing to the trier than the opposing evidence. This is a simple commonsense explanation which will be understood by jurors and could hardly be misleading in the ordinary case. It may be objected, however, that it is misleading in a situation where, though one side's evidence is more convincing than the other's, the jury is still left in doubt as to the truth of the matter.[8] Compelling a decision in favor of a party who has introduced evidence that is simply better than that of his adversary would not be objectionable if we hypothesize jurors who bring none of their own experience to the trial and who thus view the evidence in a vacuum. Of course, no such case could exist.[9] We expect and encourage jurors to use their own experience to help them reach a

807 (1961); McBaine, Burden of Proof: Degrees of Belief, 32 Calif.L.Rev. 242 (1944); Winter, The Jury and the Risk of Nonpersuasion, 5 Law & Society Rev. 335 (1971); Annot., 93 A.L.R. 155; C.J.S. Evidence §§ 1020–1022; Dec.Dig. Evidence ⬤598, Trial ⬤237.

2. See § 341 infra.

3. See § 340 infra.

4. In McBaine, supra note 1 at 246, Prof. McBaine cogently suggests that these formulas are equivalent to statements that the trier must find that the fact is (a) almost certainly true, (b) highly probably true, and (c) probably true.

5. See Martin, Basic Problems of Evidence, supra note 1 at 32.

6. This may be evidenced by a study which showed that the jurors responding to a questionnaire asking them to express their beliefs in terms of numerical probabilities had a significantly different understanding of the phrase "by a preponderance of evidence" than did judges responding to the same questionnaire. The jurors thought the requirement called for a far greater showing of probability than did the judges. Simon, Quantifying Burdens of Proof, 5 Law & Society Rev. 319, 325 (1971). Similarly, in 1937, 843 jurors re-

sponded to a questionnaire asking the question, "What propositions of law were most difficult to understand?" Highest on the list was "preponderance of the evidence," named by 232 jurors. "Proximate cause" was second with 203. Trial by Jury (report of a conference), 11 U.Cin.L.Rev. 119, 192 n. 18 (1937).

7. Courts often specifically inform the jury that the number of witnesses is not conclusive. Illinois Pattern Jury Instruction (Civil) 2.07 (3d ed. 1988); South Dakota Pattern Jury Instruction (Civil) 2.07 (1968); Livingston v. Schreckengost, 255 Iowa 1102, 125 N.W.2d 126, 131 (1963).

8. See discussion by Wolfe, J., in McDonald v. Union Pacific Railroad Co., 109 Utah 493, 167 P.2d 685, 689 (1946) (" * * * I can conceive of a case where the jury might be more convinced that the evidence of one side is nearer the truth than that of the other side and yet not feel that the evidence satisfied them as to the right to recover.") See also McBaine, supra note 1 at 248; Trickett, Preponderance of Evidence and Reasonable Doubt, 10 The Forum, Dickinson School of Law 75, 77 (1906) quoted 9 Wigmore, Evidence § 2498 at 326.

9. See Winter, supra note 1 at 339.

decision, particularly in judging the credibility of witnesses.[10] That experience may tell them, for example, that although the plaintiff has introduced evidence and the defendant has offered nothing in opposition, it is still unlikely that the events occurred as contended by the plaintiff. Thus, it is entirely consistent for a court to hold that a party's evidence is sufficient to withstand a motion for directed verdict and yet to uphold a verdict for its adversary.[11]

The most acceptable meaning to be given to the expression, proof by a preponderance, seems to be proof which leads the jury to find that the existence of the contested fact is more probable than its nonexistence.[12] Thus the preponderance of evidence becomes the trier's belief in the preponderance of probability. Some courts have boldly accepted this view.[13]

Other courts have been shocked at the suggestion that a verdict, a truth-finding, should be based on nothing stronger than an estimate of probabilities. They require that the trier must have an "actual belief" in, or be "convinced of" the truth of the fact by this "preponderance of

---

10. See, e.g., Illinois Pattern Jury Instructions (Civil) §§ 1.04, 2.01 (3d ed. 1988). See also Ball, supra note 1 at 829, where the author suggests that "instructions which tell the jury that they shall use what they know in common as men, should be juxtaposed with the direction to find 'from the evidence.' "

11. See Martin, Basic Problems of Evidence, supra note 1 at 30–31.

12. See Model Code of Evidence Rule 1(3): " 'Burden of persuasion of a fact' means the burden which is discharged when the tribunal which is to determine the existence or non-existence of the fact is persuaded by sufficient evidence to find that the fact exists;" 1(5): " 'Finding a fact' means determining that its existence is more probable than its non-existence * * *." See also Morgan, Some Problems of Proof, supra note 1 at 84–85.

13. E.g., Murphy v. Waterhouse, 113 Cal. 467, 45 P. 866 (1896) (error to charge that jury must be "convinced"; "preponderance of probability" is sufficient); Norton v. Futrell, 149 Cal.App.2d 586, 308 P.2d 887, 891 (1957) ("The term 'probability' denotes an element of doubt or uncertainty and recognizes that where there are two choices, it is not necessary that the jury be absolutely certain or doubtless, but that it is sufficient if the choice selected is more probable than the choice rejected."); Beckwith v. Town of Stratford, 129 Conn. 506, 29 A.2d 775 (1942) (standard in civil cases is proof which produces a reasonable belief of probability of the existence of the mate-

rial facts); Moffie v. Slawsby, 77 N.H. 555, 94 A. 193 (1915) (a finding that the transferee probably knew that the note was usurious is a finding that the party having the burden had satisfied the trier of fact); Livanovitch v. Livanovitch, 99 Vt. 327, 328, 131 A. 799 (1926) ("If * * * you are more inclined to believe from the evidence that he did so deliver the bonds * * * even though your belief is only the slightest degree greater than that he did not, your verdict should be for the plaintiff," approved; "a bare preponderance is sufficient though the scales drop but a feather's weight"); Washington Pattern Jury Instructions (Civil) 21.01 (1967) ("When it is said that a party has the burden of proof on any proposition * * * it means that you must be persuaded, considering all the evidence in the case, that the proposition on which he has the burden of proof is more probably true than not true.") See also discussion by Judge Maris in Burch v. Reading Co., 240 F.2d 574 (3d Cir.1957), cert. denied 353 U.S. 965; C.J.S. Evidence § 1021 at 652, n. 99.

Despite the mathematical tone of the words used to describe this standard, any attempt to translate the standard into mathematical terminology (such as through the use of percentages) presents special problems which seem beyond the ken of most lawyers and the needs of the courts. See the interesting discussion in Kaye, The Paradox of the Gatecrasher and Other Stories, 1979 Ariz.St.L.J. 101.

evidence." [14] Does this mean that they must believe that it is certainly true? Hardly, since it is apparent that an investigation by fallible people based upon the testimony of other people, with all their defects of veracity, memory, and communication, cannot yield certainty. Does it mean a kind of mystical "hunch" that the fact must be true? This would hardly be a rational requirement. What it would most naturally be understood to mean by the jury (in the unlikely event that it should carry analysis so far) is that it must be persuaded that the truth of the fact is not merely more probable than not, but highly probable. This is more stringent than our tradition or the needs of justice warrant, and seems equivalent to the standard of "clear, strong and convincing proof," hitherto thought to be appropriate only in exceptional cases. [15]

Much of the time spent in the appellate courts over the metaphysics of "preponderance" has been wasted because of the courts' insistence upon the cabalistic word. This bemusement with word-magic is particularly apparent in the decisions dealing with the use of the word "satisfaction" or its derivatives in referring to the effect of the evidence on the jury's mind. [16] Some courts, with more logic than realism, have condemned its use as equivalent to proof beyond a reasonable doubt unless qualified by the word "reasonable." [17] Other courts have pragmatically, although perhaps reluctantly permitted its use, even without

---

14. Lummus, J. in Sargent v. Massachusetts Accident Co., 307 Mass. 246, 29 N.E.2d 825, 827 (1940) ("It has been held not enough that mathematically the chances somewhat favor a proposition to be proved; for example, the fact that colored automobiles made in the current year outnumbered black ones would not warrant a finding that an undescribed automobile of the current year is colored and not black, nor would the fact that only a minority of men die of cancer warrant a finding that a particular man did not die of cancer. * * * After the evidence has been weighed, that proposition is proved by a preponderance of the evidence if it is made to appear more likely or probable in the sense that actual belief in its truth, derived from the evidence, exists in the mind or minds of the tribunal notwithstanding any doubts that may still linger there.") See also Lampe v. Franklin American Trust Co., 339 Mo. 361, 96 S.W.2d 710, 723, 107 A.L.R. 465 (1936) (no error to refuse charge, "If you find and believe that it is more probable," etc., since a verdict must be based on "what the jury finds to be facts rather than what they find to be 'more probable'"); Anderson v. Chicago Brass Co., 127 Wis. 273, 106 N.W. 1077, 1079 (1906) (not only must charge require that party with burden produce evidence of greater convincing power but that "it must

be such as to satisfy or convince * * * the jury of the truth of his contention.")

See also Bazemore v. Davis, 394 A.2d 1377 (D.C.App.1978), where the court perceived a need for more certainty in child custody cases than would result in a correct determination "more often than not." However, the court referred to the value of evidence available in the case as opposed to the applicability of presumptions or standardized inferences.

15. See § 340 infra.

16. See the enormous number of decisions on this question in Annot., 147 A.L.R. 380. The volume of cases dealing with the issue has, however, decreased considerably in more recent years. See Dec.Dig. Trial ⟐237(6).

17. Torrey v. Burney, 113 Ala. 496, 21 So. 348, 351 (1897) ("Before it can be said that the mind is 'satisfied' of the truth of a proposition, it must be relieved of all doubt or uncertainty, and this degree of conviction is not required even in criminal cases."); Nelson v. Belcher Lumber Co., 232 Ala. 116, 166 So. 808 (1936) (usual statement, "reasonably satisfies the jury by the evidence"); Rasp v. Baumbach, 223 S.W.2d 472 (Mo.1949) (the word "reasonable" essential).

the qualification.[18] Although certainly juries should be clearly and accurately instructed with regard to the question of the measure of persuasion in civil cases, it is hard to believe that variations in language such as those involved in the courts' difficulties with the use of the word "satisfaction" lead to any differences in jurors' attitudes.[19] Thoughtfully drafted pattern jury instructions should prove helpful in reducing unnecessarily spent appellate court time on these questions.[20] Where no pattern instruction is available, however, trial judges would be wise to search for the locally accepted phraseology and to adhere to it religiously.

§ 340. Satisfying the Burden of Persuasion: (b) Requirement of Clear and Convincing Proof [1]

While we have seen that the traditional measure of persuasion in civil cases is by a preponderance of evidence,[2] there is a limited range of claims and contentions which the party is required to establish by a more exacting measure of persuasion. The formula varies from state to state, but among the phrases used are the following: "by clear and convincing evidence," [3] "clear, convincing and satisfactory," [4] "clear, cogent and convincing," [5] and "clear, unequivocal, satisfactory and convincing." [6] Some courts have used all of these phrases and then some to describe the applicable standard.[7] The phrasing within most jurisdictions has not become as standardized as is the "preponderance" formula, but even here the courts sometimes are surprisingly intolerant

18. Netzer v. Northern Pacific Railway Co., 238 Minn. 416, 57 N.W.2d 247 (1953), cert. denied 346 U.S. 831 (not misleading when use is in conjunction with a detailed and correct instruction of fair preponderance of the evidence); McDonald v. Union Pacific Railroad Co., 109 Utah 493, 167 P.2d 685 (1946) (use permitted); Burks v. Webb, 199 Va. 296, 99 S.E.2d 629, 639 (1957) (use was harmless error but phrase "preponderance of the evidence" preferable).

19. Difficulties of language have led some courts to hold that the phrase "preponderance of evidence" is one of common knowledge and that it is not necessary to define it. Brunton v. Stapleton, 65 Colo. 576, 179 P. 815 (1919); Hardee v. York, 262 N.C. 237, 136 S.E.2d 582 (1964) (in the absence of a prayer for special instructions); Annot., 93 A.L.R. 155, 156.

20. See, e.g., Illinois Pattern Jury Instruction (Civil) 21.01 (3d ed. 1988); North Carolina Pattern Instruction 101.10 (1980); Washington Pattern Jury Instruction (Civil) 21.01 (1967). Not all pattern jury instructions on this question are helpful to the jury even though they may withstand appeal. See, e.g., Florida Standard Jury Instruction 3.9 (1967): " 'Greater weight of the evidence' means the more persuasive and convincing force and effect of the entire evidence in the case."

§ 340

1. 9 Wigmore, Evidence § 2498, pp. 329–334 (Chadbourn rev. 1981); C.J.S. Evidence § 1023; 30 Am.Jur.2d Evidence §§ 1166, 1167; Dec.Dig. Trial ☞237(3).

2. See § 339 supra.

3. Murillo v. Hernandez, 79 Ariz. 1, 281 P.2d 786, 791 (1955) (oral trust).

4. In re Will of Williams, 256 Wis. 338, 41 N.W.2d 191 (1950) (mental incapacity and undue influence).

5. Frazier v. Loftin, 200 Ark. 4, 137 S.W.2d 750, 752 (1940) (claim of fraud inducing signing of contract, leases and deed).

6. Capps v. Capps, 110 Utah 468, 175 P.2d 470, 473 (1946) (oral trust).

7. See Rentenbach Engineering Co. v. General Realty Ltd., 707 S.W.2d 524 (Tenn. App.1985) (court notes, apparently approvingly, six different expressions used to describe the proof necessary in action for reformation of a contract).

of slight variations from the approved expression.[8] No high degree of precision can be attained by these groups of adjectives. It has been persuasively suggested that they could be more simply and intelligibly translated to the jury if they were instructed that they must be persuaded that the truth of the contention is "highly probable." [9] But as former Chief Justice Burger stated:

> We probably can assume no more than that the difference between a preponderance of the evidence and proof beyond a reasonable doubt probably is better understood than either of them in relation to the intermediate standard of clear and convincing evidence. Nonetheless, even if the particular standard-of-proof catchwords do not always make a great difference in a particular case, adopting a "standard of proof is more than an empty semantic exercise." * * * In cases involving individual rights, whether criminal or civil, "[t]he standard of proof [at a minimum] reflects the value society places on individual liberty." [10]

To this end, the United States Supreme Court has held that proof by a clear and convincing or similar standard is required, either by the United States Constitution or by the applicable federal statute, in a variety of cases involving deprivations of individual rights not rising to the level of criminal prosecution, including commitment to a mental hospital[11], termination of parental rights,[12] denaturalization[13] and deportation.[14]

Not all instances of requirements of proof more than usually convincing concern cases involving individual liberty. Indeed, the requirement of proof of this magnitude for certain types of contentions seems to have had its origins in the standards prescribed for themselves by the chancellors in determining questions of fact in equity cases.[15] However,

8. Molyneux v. Twin Falls Canal Co., 54 Idaho 619, 35 P.2d 651, 94 A.L.R. 1264 (1934) ("clear, positive, and unequivocal" imposes too heavy a burden as opposed to "clear and satisfactory" or "clear and convincing"). See also Williams v. Blue Ridge Building & Loan Association, 207 N.C. 362, 177 S.E. 176 (1934), where the court, with perhaps more justification, held that the trial judge had erred in telling the jury that the words "clear, strong and convincing" proof meant that the plaintiffs "must * * * satisfy you to a moral certainty."

9. McBaine, Burden of Proof: Degrees of Belief, 32 Calif.L.Rev. 242, 246, 253–254 (1944). See also State v. King, 158 Ariz. 419, 763 P.2d 239 (1988) and State v. Renforth, 155 Ariz. 385, 746 P.2d 1315 (App. 1987), review denied 158 Ariz. 487, 763 P.2d 983, where the courts held that an instruction describing the clear and convincing evidence needed by the accused to prove his or her insanity as "certain" and "unambiguous" required too much. Rather the jury should be instructed that the defendant must persuade the jury that his or her claim is "highly probable."

10. Addington v. Texas, 441 U.S. 418, 425 (1979).

11. Ibid.

12. Santosky v. Kramer, 455 U.S. 745 (1982). But see Rivera v. Minnich, 483 U.S. 574 (1987), where the Court held that paternity may be established by a preponderance of the evidence.

13. Schneiderman v. United States, 320 U.S. 118 (1943).

14. Woodby v. INS, 385 U.S. 276 (1966).

15. See Henkle v. Royal Exchange Assurance Co., 1 Ves.Sen. 317, 319, 27 Eng. Rep. 1055, 1056 (Ch.1749) (suit to reform insurance policy: relief denied for insufficiency of proofs; Lord Ch. Hardwicke: "There ought to be the strongest proof possible"); Marquis Townshend v. Stangroom, 6 Ves.Jun. 328, 333, 31 Eng.Rep. 1076 (Ch.1801) (similar); Carpenter v. Providence Washington Insurance Co., 45 U.S. (4 How.) 185, 224 (1846) (suit in equity to require the defendant insurance company to endorse an acknowledgment of notice

it has now been extended to certain types of actions tried before juries, and the chancellors' cautionary maxims are now conveyed to the jury in the form of instructions on the burden of persuasion.[16]

Among the classes of cases to which this special standard of persuasion commonly has been applied are: (1) charges of fraud [17] and undue influence,[18] (2) suits on oral contracts to make a will,[19] and suits to establish the terms of a lost will,[20] (3) suits for the specific performance of an oral contract,[21] (4) proceedings to set aside, reform or modify written transactions,[22] or official acts [23] on grounds of fraud, mistake or

on the policy; held, claim of fraud fails because such a charge should be strengthened "by very satisfactory auxiliaries though not perhaps by so strong evidence as is necessary in reforming contracts"). American equity cases on the degree of proof necessary in reforming contracts are collected in 3 Pomeroy Equity Jurisprudence § 859a (5th ed., Symons, 1941). In Iowa the requirement of "clear, satisfactory and convincing" proof is limited to cases in equity. Davis v. Davis, 261 Iowa 992, 156 N.W.2d 870 (1968); Jamison v. Jamison, 113 Iowa 720, 84 N.W. 705 (1900).

16. Minton v. Farmville–Woodward Lumber Co., 210 N.C. 422, 187 S.E. 568 (1936) (suit to establish oral trust; facts tried to jury in North Carolina); Kisting v. Westchester Fire Insurance Co., 290 F.Supp. 141 (W.D.Wis.1968), affirmed 416 F.2d 967 (7th Cir.) (defense of arson in action on fire insurance policy). Washington Pattern Jury Instructions (Civil) 160.-02, 160.03 (1967); Dec.Dig. Trial ⚖237(3).

17. Holley Coal Co. v. Globe Indemnity Co., 186 F.2d 291 (4th Cir.1950) (suit on employees' fidelity bond, defense that plaintiff's officers colluded with embezzlers); Buzard v. Griffin, 89 Ariz. 42, 358 P.2d 155 (1960) (election fraud); Dec.Dig. Fraud ⚖58(1). In some instances the policy of placing such a special burden on one who claims to be the victim of fraud is debatable. See Rice–Stix Dry Goods Co. v. Montgomery, 164 Ark. 161, 261 S.W. 325, 329 (1924), where the court said: "While fraud at law, as well as in equity, is never to be presumed and must be proved, yet in actions at law one who has the burden of proof to establish fraud meets the requirements of the rule when he proves the fraud only by a preponderance of the evidence. The same rule likewise prevails in equity, except in those cases where the rescission, cancellation, or reformation of a writing for fraud of one party and mistake of the other, or mutual mistake, is the relief sought, in which latter case, as we have stated, the proof of fraud or mistake must be clear, unequivocal, and decisive." See also Household Finance Corp. v. Altenberg,

5 Ohio St.2d 190, 214 N.E.2d 667 (1966) (no special standard in action to recover money, even where fraud is alleged).

18. In re Mazanec's Estate, 204 Minn. 406, 283 N.W. 745, 748 (1939).

19. Lindley v. Lindley, 67 N.M. 439, 356 P.2d 455 (1960). And so of an oral gift asserted after the donor's death. Wyatt v. Moran, 81 R.I. 399, 103 A.2d 801 (1954). Apparently even stronger proof is needed of such claims in Missouri. See St. Louis Union Trust Co. v. Busch, 346 Mo. 1237, 145 S.W.2d 426 (1940) (claim of oral gift; forceful, clear and conclusive testimony which convinces the court beyond a reasonable doubt of its truthfulness).

20. In re Ainscow's Will, 42 Del. 3, 27 A.2d 363, 365 (1942). See also 7 Wigmore, Evidence § 2106 (Chadbourn rev. 1978).

21. Hyder v. Newcomb, 236 Ark. 231, 365 S.W.2d 271, 274 (1963) (evidence of parol contract to convey land must be clear, satisfactory and convincing); Steketee v. Steketee, 317 Mich. 100, 26 N.W.2d 724, 726 (1947) (terms of agreement must be established by convincing proof).

22. Philippine Sugar Estates Development Co. v. Government of Philippine Islands, 247 U.S. 385 (1918) (reformation of written contract for mutual mistake); Newmister v. Carmichael, 29 Wis.2d 573, 139 N.W.2d 572 (1966) (same); Carlisle v. Carlisle, 225 N.C. 462, 35 S.E.2d 418, 421 (1945) (to establish an oral trust in land taken by deed absolute); Gillock v. Holdaway, 379 Ill. 467, 41 N.E.2d 504 (1942) (to show that deed was intended as mortgage); Dec.Dig. Mortgages ⚖38(2). But see, Ward v. Lyman, 108 Vt. 464, 188 A. 892, 893 (1937) ("The jurisdiction of a court of equity to reform a written instrument will be exercised only when the mistake is established by evidence so strong and conclusive as to place it beyond reasonable doubt.")

23. Bernstein v. Bernstein, 398 Ill. 52, 74 N.E.2d 785 (1947) (proof to impeach the

incompleteness, and (5) miscellaneous types of claims and defenses,[24] varying from state to state, where there is thought to be special danger of deception, or where the court considers that the particular type of claim should be disfavored on policy grounds.[25]

The appellate court, under the classical equity practice, tried the facts *de novo,* upon the deposition testimony in the record, and thus it was called on to apply anew the standard of clear and convincing proof in its study of the evidence. But in the modern system there are usually restrictions upon appellate review of a judge's findings of fact, even in equity issues. Thus, in the federal courts under Rule 52(a) the trial court's findings will be reversed only when "clearly erroneous." And in jury-tried cases the verdict will be reviewed only to the extent of determining whether there was evidence from which reasonable people could have found the verdict. Will the appellate court, then, today, if there was substantial evidence from which the judge or jury could have made the findings it did, consider the questions whether the evidence met the "clear and convincing" standard, in a case where it applies? The United States Supreme Court, in reviewing a summary judgment in a libel case where the plaintiff's burden was to prove actual malice by clear and convincing evidence, stated that the test on appeal should be "whether the evidence in the record could support a reasonable jury finding either that the plaintiff has shown actual malice by clear and convincing evidence or that the plaintiff has not."[26] However, in some

correctness of a notary's certificate of acknowledgment of a deed); Nichols v. Sauls' Estate, 250 Miss. 307, 165 So.2d 352 (1964) (same as to acknowledgment of power of attorney).

24. Krisher v. Duff, 331 Mich. 699, 50 N.W.2d 332 (1951) (statutory presumption that member of owner's family was driving it with his consent can be overcome only by testimony that is clear, positive and credible and plaintiff entitled to have jury instructed to that effect: see discussion § 344 n. 39 infra); In re Estate of Berge, 234 Minn. 31, 47 N.W.2d 428 (1951) (to establish oral contract to adopt); Vaux v. Hamilton, 103 N.W.2d 291 (N.D.1960) (negligence action; where agency is denied must be proved by clear, convincing and satisfactory evidence); Marcum v. Zaring, 406 P.2d 970 (Okl.1965) (invalidity of marriage); Stevenson v. Stein, 412 Pa. 478, 195 A.2d 268 (1963) (to prove adverse possession; "credible, clear and definitive proof"); Wilson v. Wilson, 145 Tex. 607, 201 S.W.2d 226 (1947) (presumption that property acquired during marriage is community property can only be overcome by clear and satisfactory evidence); King v. Prudential Insurance Co., 13 Wash.2d 414, 125 P.2d 282 (1942) (services by daughter in father's shop presumed gratuitous and

presumption could not be overcome except by clear and convincing evidence).

25. A few courts have stated that the requirement of a burden of proof greater than a preponderance of the evidence may depend upon the probability of proving the claim and, therefore, if it is unlikely that an allegation can be supported, clear and convincing evidence will be required to prove it. General Motors Corp. v. Toyota Motor Co., 467 F.Supp. 1142, 1173 (S.D.Ohio 1979), reversed in part on other grounds 667 F.2d 504 (6th Cir.), cert. denied 456 U.S. 937. See also Ziegler v. Hustisford Farmers Mutual Insurance Co., 238 Wis. 238, 298 N.W. 610 (1941) (citing Jones, Commentaries on Evidence (2d Ed.) Vol. 2, p. 1036 § 563). Such a rationale, if carried very far logically, would make it virtually impossible to prove a difficult claim. See also Ball, supra § 339, note 1.

26. Anderson v. Liberty Lobby, Inc., 477 U.S. 242, 255–256 (1986). See also dissenting opinion of Judge Traynor in Beeler v. American Trust Co., 24 Cal.2d 1, 29, 147 P.2d 583, 598 (1944). Examples of other cases where the appellate courts have imposed their own measure of "clear and convincing proof" to reverse the finding below include: Equitable Life Assurance Society v. Aaron, 108 F.2d 777 (6th Cir.

jurisdictions it is for the trial court, not the appellate court, to draw a distinction between evidence which is clear and convincing and evidence which merely preponderates.[27]

§ 341. Satisfying the Burden of Persuasion: (c) Proof Beyond a Reasonable Doubt [1]

As we have seen with reference to civil cases, a lawsuit is essentially a search for probabilities. A margin of error must be anticipated in any such search. Mistakes will be made and in a civil case a mistaken judgment for the plaintiff is no worse than a mistaken judgment for the defendant. However, this is not the case in a criminal action. Society has judged that it is significantly worse for an innocent person to be found guilty of a crime than for a guilty person to go free. The consequences to the life, liberty, and good name of the accused from an erroneous conviction of a crime are usually more serious than the effects of an erroneous judgment in a civil case. Therefore, as stated by the Supreme Court in recognizing the inevitability of error even in criminal cases, "[w]here one party has at stake an interest of transcending value—as a criminal defendant his liberty—this margin of error is reduced as to him by the process of placing on the other party the burden * * * of persuading the factfinder at the conclusion of the trial of his guilt beyond a reasonable doubt." [2] In so doing, the courts may have increased the total number of mistaken decisions in criminal cases, but with the worthy goal of decreasing the number of one kind of mistake—conviction of the innocent.[3]

1940) (reformation of policy); Langford v. Sigmon, 292 Ky. 650, 167 S.W.2d 820 (1943) (oral trust in land conveyed); Hurst v. Stowers, 399 P.2d 477 (Okl.1965) (adverse possession). See also discussion in In re L.R.M. and J.J.M., 763 S.W.2d 64 (Tex. App.—Fort Worth 1989), including a review of cases on both sides of the issue. The problem is quite similar to the question of the relationship of the measure of proof to the burden of producing evidence, discussed above, § 338, text accompanying notes 3–8. See also, Martin, Basic Problems of Evidence 33–34 (1988).

27. Beeler v. American Trust Co., supra n. 26 (review of judge's findings); Davis v. Pursel, 55 Colo. 287, 134 P. 107 (1913) (review of findings of judge and jury). In both these cases the lower court found that deeds were intended as mortgages and on appeal it was held that, there being substantial evidence, it was for the trial court alone to decide whether the evidence was clear and convincing. More recent examples are Webber v. Smith, 129 Ariz. 495, 632 P.2d 998 (App.1981); Buck v. Jewett, 170 Cal.App.2d 115, 338 P.2d 507 (1959);

Gem–Valley Ranches, Inc. v. Small, 90 Idaho 354, 411 P.2d 943 (1966). See also Dec. Dig. Appeal and Error ⟐1009(1)–(4).

§ 341

1. 9 Wigmore, Evidence § 2497 (Chadbourn rev. 1981); Morgan, Some Problems of Proof 85 (1956); McBaine, Burden of Proof: Degrees of Belief, 32 Calif.L.Rev. 242, 255 (1944); Nesson, Reasonable Doubt and Permissive Inferences: The Value of Complexity, 92 Harv.L.Rev. 1187 (1979); C.J.S. Criminal Law §§ 566–578, 1267–1284; Dec.Dig. Criminal Law ⟐326–336, 789.

2. Speiser v. Randall, 357 U.S. 513, 525–526 (1958). See also In re Winship, 397 U.S. 358, 369–372 (1970) (concurring opinion by Harlan, J.).

3. Ball, The Moment of Truth: Probability Theory and Standards of Proof, 14 Vand.L.Rev. 807, 816 (1961). See also Kaplan, Decision Theory and the Factfinding Process, 20 Stan.L.Rev. 1065, 1073–1077 (1968); Winter, The Jury and the Risk of Nonpersuasion, 5 Law & Society Rev. 335, 339–343 (1971).

The demand for a higher degree of persuasion in criminal cases was recurrently expressed from ancient times,[4] but its crystallization into the formula "beyond a reasonable doubt" seems to have occurred as late as 1798.[5] It is now accepted in common law jurisdictions as the measure of persuasion by which the prosecution must convince the trier of all the essential elements of guilt. In 1970, the Supreme Court explicitly held that the due process clause "protects the accused against conviction except upon proof beyond a reasonable doubt of every fact necessary to constitute the crime with which he is charged."[6]

A simple instruction that the jury will acquit if they have a reasonable doubt of the defendant's guilt of the crime charged in the indictment is ordinarily sufficient.[7] Courts, however, frequently paint the lily by giving the jury a definition of "reasonable doubt." A famous early instance was the oft-echoed statement of Chief Justice Shaw in the trial of Prof. Webster for the murder of Dr. Parkman: "It is that

4. Thayer, Preliminary Treatise on Evidence 558, 559 (1898) quotes passages in Corpus Juris, dating from the fourth century, and from Coke's 3d Institute, to this effect.

5. "Its first appearance, so far as we have been able to determine, was in the high-treason cases tried in Dublin in 1798, as reported by MacNally [Rules of Evidence on Pleas of the Crown; Dublin, 1802], who was himself counsel for the defense. 'It may also,' he says, 'at this day, be considered a rule of law, that, if the jury entertain a reasonable doubt upon the truth of the testimony of witnesses given upon the issue they are sworn well and truly to try, they are bound' to acquit." May, Reasonable Doubt in Civil and Criminal Cases, 10 Am.L.Rev. 642, 656 (1876) quoted in Note, 69 U.S.L.Rev. 169, 172 (1935).

6. In re Winship, supra note 2 at 364. In that case, the Court held that proof beyond a reasonable doubt is among the essentials of due process and fair treatment required during the adjudicatory stage when a juvenile is charged with an act which would constitute a crime if committed by an adult.

The jury is not required to believe each fact in an aggregate of circumstantial evidence beyond a reasonable doubt. People v. Klinkenberg, 90 Cal.App.2d 608, 204 P.2d 47, 62 (1949); State v. Raine, 93 Idaho 862, 477 P.2d 104 (1970); State v. Barry, 93 N.H. 10, 34 A.2d 661, 663 (1943) (not essential that each fact bearing on identity be established beyond reasonable doubt). However, an instruction that told the jury in a criminal case that individual facts could be proved by a preponderance of the evidence has been held to be misleading.

State v. McDonough, 205 Conn. 352, 533 A.2d 857 (1987), cert. denied 485 U.S. 906.

Facts unrelated to guilt, such as venue, need not be proved beyond a reasonable doubt. See Barragan v. State, 141 Tex. Cr.R. 12, 147 S.W.2d 254, 256 (1941).

A state may provide for sentencing considerations, such as whether an individual "visibly possessed a firearm," which are not elements of the offense, but which affect the sentence to be imposed, to be proved by a preponderance of the evidence rather than beyond a reasonable doubt. McMillan v. Pennsylvania, 477 U.S. 79 (1986). See also United States v. McGhee, 882 F.2d 1095 (6th Cir.1989) (defendant may be assigned the burden of proving that it was "clearly improbable" that weapons were connected with the offense).

The *Winship* case has also had an impact on instructions concerning the jury's consideration of the testimony of certain witnesses. In Cool v. United States, 409 U.S. 100 (1972), the Court held that an instruction, that the jury must believe an accomplice's testimony on behalf of the defendant beyond a reasonable doubt before giving it the same effect as other testimony, violated *Winship*. But see Cupp v. Naughten, 414 U.S. 141 (1973), where the Court held that an instruction stating that every witness is presumed to speak the truth did not violate *Winship,* despite the fact that the defendant had neither taken the witness stand nor presented any witnesses on his behalf.

7. See, e.g., United States v. Olmstead, 832 F.2d 642, 646 (1st Cir.1987), cert. denied 486 U.S. 1009; State v. Lafferty, 416 S.W.2d 157 (Mo.1967); Illinois Pattern Jury Instructions (Criminal) 2.03 (1981).

state of the case, which, after the entire comparison and consideration of all the evidence, leaves the minds of jurors in that condition that they cannot say they feel an abiding conviction, to a moral certainty, of the truth of the charge." [8] It is an ancient maxim that all definitions are dangerous and this one has been caustically criticized as raising more questions than it answers.[9] Other definitions, often more carefully balanced to warn against the overstressing of merely possible or imaginary doubts, have become customary in some jurisdictions.[10] Reasonable doubt is a term in common use almost as familiar to jurors as to lawyers. As one judge has said it needs a skillful definer to make it plainer by multiplication of words,[11] and as another has expressed it, the explanations themselves often need more explanation than the term explained.[12] A definition in terms locally approved is proper, but if not requested by accused is not required.[13] Whether if so requested it

8. Commonwealth v. Webster, 59 Mass. (5 Cush.) 295, 320 (1850). Where a charge based on *Webster* is given, significant deviations from it may result in error of constitutional proportions. See Lanigan v. Maloney, 853 F.2d 40 (1st Cir.1988), cert. denied 488 U.S. 1007 (error to instruct jury that it must find guilt "to a degree of moral certainty").

9. Trickett, Preponderance and Reasonable Doubt, 10 The Forum, Dickinson School of Law, 76 (1906) quoted 9 Wigmore, Evidence § 2497 at 322 (Chadbourn rev. 1981). The "moral certainty" language of *Webster* has been emphatically condemned by the United States Court of Appeals dealing with federal attacks on Massachusetts decisions. See, e.g., United States v. Drake, 673 F.2d 15, 21 (1st Cir.1982). Yet, the language has had amazing staying power in that state. As stated by one federal district court judge, the "moral certainty" language of *Webster* "seems to have something approaching a talismanic effect in the Massachusetts state courts, saving otherwise problematic jury instructions from causing reversals of criminal convictions." Smith v. Butler, 696 F.Supp. 748, 754 (D.Mass.1988) citing, among other cases, Commonwealth v. Morse, 402 Mass. 735, 737, 525 N.E.2d 364, 366 (1988).

10. They are set out by the hundreds in Dec.Dig. Criminal Law ⟜789 and in 36 Words and Phrases 483–544 (Perm.Ed. 1962).

11. Newman, J. in Hoffman v. State, 97 Wis. 571, 73 N.W. 51, 52 (1897).

12. Mitchell, J. in State v. Sauer, 38 Minn. 438, 38 N.W. 355 (1888), referring to the definition, "a doubt for which you can give a reason," said, "Like many other definitions of the term which have been given, it does not define, but itself requires definition. The most serious objection to it

is that it is liable to be understood as meaning a doubt for which a juror could express or state a reason in words. A juror may, after a consideration and comparison of all the evidence, feel a reasonable doubt as to the guilt of a defendant, and yet find it difficult to state the reason for the doubt. The term 'reasonable doubt' is almost incapable of any definition which will add much to what the words themselves imply. In fact it is easier to state what it is not than what it is; and it may be doubted whether any attempt to define it will not be more likely to confuse than to enlighten a jury. A man is the best judge of his own feelings, and he knows for himself whether he doubts better than any one else can tell him. Where any explanation of what is meant by a reasonable doubt is required, it is safer to adopt some definition which has already received the general approval of the authorities, especially those in our own state."

See also Bartels, Punishment and the Burden of Proof in Criminal Cases: A Modest Proposal, 66 Iowa L.Rev. 869 (1981) and the discussion in Nesson, supra note 1 at 1196, where the author argues that reasonable doubt is a concept intended to be complex. "As long as the concept is left ambiguous, members of the observing public may assume that they share with jury members common notions of the kinds and degrees of doubt that are unacceptable."

13. State v. Hall, 267 N.C. 90, 147 S.E.2d 548 (1966), and cases cited C.J.S. Criminal Law § 1268 at 658, n. 63. See also People v. Cagle, 41 Ill.2d 528, 244 N.E.2d 200, 204 (1969) ("This court has repeatedly held that the legal concept of 'reasonable doubt' needs no definition, and that where an involved instruction on that concept is given it may be deemed prejudicial error [citing cases].").

is the judge's duty to define the term, is a matter of dispute,[14] but the wiser view seems to be that it lies in the court's discretion,[15] which should ordinarily be exercised by declining to define, unless the jury itself asks for a fuller explanation.[16]

There are certain excuses or justifications allowed to the defendant, which although provable for the most part under the plea of not guilty, are spoken of for some purposes as "affirmative defenses." [17] Among these are self-defense,[18] duress,[19] insanity,[20] intoxication [21] and claims that the accused is within an exception or proviso in the statute defining the crime.[22] Sometimes only the burden of producing evidence will be assigned to the defendant.[23] Under certain circumstances the burden of persuasion with regard to some of these defenses may be allocated to the defendant and correspondingly, the prosecution may be relieved of proving the absence of the defense. The allocation and operation of the burdens of proof with regard to these defenses present difficult policy, as well as constitutional, problems. These problems will be discussed together with the special problems related to presumptions in criminal cases.[24]

Despite occasional statements to the contrary,[25] the reasonable doubt standard generally has been held inapplicable in civil cases, regardless of the nature of the issue involved.[26] For example, when a charge of

14. Recognizing a duty are Mundy v. United States, 176 F.2d 32 (D.C.Cir.1949) (here waived by failure to request); Blatt v. United States, 60 F.2d 481 (3d Cir.1932) (reversal for refusal to define); Friedman v. United States, 381 F.2d 155 (8th Cir. 1967) (duty recognized; given charge approved).

No duty: United States v. Lawson, 507 F.2d 433 (7th Cir.1974), cert. denied 420 U.S. 1004. Jackson v. State, 225 Ga. 553, 170 S.E.2d 281 (1969); State v. Velsir, 61 Wyo. 476, 159 P.2d 371 (1945). For cases pro and con, see Dec.Dig. Criminal Law ⚖789(3).

15. State v. Broome, 268 N.C. 298, 150 S.E.2d 416 (1966).

16. Pattern jury instructions defining reasonable doubt include California Jury Instruction (Criminal) 2.90 (5th Ed.1988) North Carolina Pattern Instructions (Criminal) 101.10 (1974).

17. 9 Wigmore, Evidence §§ 2501, 2512, 2514 (Chadbourn rev. 1981); 22A C.J.S. Criminal Law §§ 572–577; Dec.Dig. Criminal Law ⚖329–333.

18. Brown v. State, 48 Del. 427, 105 A.2d 646 (1954); see also cases collected C.J.S. Homicide § 195.

19. State v. Sappienza, 84 Ohio St. 63, 95 N.E. 381 (1911).

20. State v. Finn, 257 Minn. 138, 100 N.W.2d 508 (1960).

21. State v. Church, 169 N.W.2d 889 (Iowa 1969).

22. State v. Tonnisen, 92 N.J.Super. 452, 224 A.2d 21 (1966), cert. denied 48 N.J. 443, 226 A.2d 431 (separate proviso clause).

23. See, e.g., United States v. Bailey, 444 U.S. 394 (1980), on remand 675 F.2d 1292 (D.C.Cir.) (defenses of duress and necessity).

24. §§ 346–348 infra.

25. St. Louis Union Trust Co. v. Busch, 346 Mo. 1237, 145 S.W.2d 426, 430 (1940) ("It is a general rule that a gift, inter vivos, sought to be established after the alleged donor's death, must be proven by forceful, clear and conclusive testimony which convinces the court beyond a reasonable doubt of its truthfulness.")

26. See 9 Wigmore, Evidence § 2498 (Chadbourn rev. 1981).

However, note that, particularly in light of *Winship*, proceedings which are nominally civil but which may result in "the drastic impairment of the liberty and reputation of an individual" may be governed by the reasonable doubt standard. People v. Pembrock, 62 Ill.2d 317, 342 N.E.2d 28, 29 (1976) ("sexually dangerous person"). Accord: United States ex rel. Stachulak v. Coughlin, 520 F.2d 931 (7th Cir.1975), cert. denied 424 U.S. 947 (Illinois "sexually dan-

crime is at issue in a civil action, the threatened consequences of sustaining the accusation, though often uncommonly harmful to purse or prestige, are not generally as serious as in a prosecution for the crime. Accordingly the modern American cases have come around to the view that in the interest of justice and simplicity a reasonable doubt measure of persuasion will not be imposed.[27] Most courts have said that a preponderance of the evidence is sufficient,[28] although some have increased the standard to "clear and convincing." [29]

§ 342. Presumptions: In General [1]

One ventures the assertion that "presumption" is the slipperiest member of the family of legal terms, except its first cousin, "burden of proof." One author has listed no less than eight senses in which the term has been used by the courts.[2] Agreement can probably be secured to this extent, however: a presumption is a standardized practice, under which certain facts are held to call for uniform treatment with respect to their effect as proof of other facts.

Returning for a moment to the discussion of satisfying the burden of producing evidence,[3] assume that a party having the burden of producing evidence of fact A, introduces proof of fact B. The judge, using ordinary reasoning, may determine that fact A might reasonably be

gerous person" proceeding); People v. Burnick, 14 Cal.3d 306, 121 Cal.Rptr. 488, 535 P.2d 352 (1975) ("mentally disturbed sex offender").

27. Sundquist v. Hardware Mutual Fire Insurance Co., 371 Ill. 360, 21 N.E.2d 297, 124 A.L.R. 1375 (1939) (suit on fire policy, defense of false statement by assured; abandons earlier rule in Illinois, and reviews similar shift of decisions elsewhere); Phipps v. Barbera, 23 Mass.App.Ct. 1, 498 N.E.2d 411 (1986) (latent ambiguity in will); Sivley v. American National Insurance Co., 454 S.W.2d 799 (Tex.Civ.App. 1970) (drunk driving). See also cases cited in Annot., 124 A.L.R. 1378; Dec.Dig. Evidence ⊜596(2).

28. See cases cited note 27 supra.

29. Ziegler v. Hustisford Farmers Mutual Insurance Co., 238 Wis. 238, 298 N.W. 610 (1941) (suit on fire policy, defense, arson by insured; trial court correctly placed burden on defendant by "clear and satisfactory evidence.")

There are varying views on the necessary measure of persuasion in civil actions with criminal overtones, such as disbarment proceedings. In disbarment proceedings, most courts seem to reject the reasonable doubt standard as the measure of proof, but are divided upon whether "preponderance" or "clear and convincing" is the measure. Compare, In re Trask, 46

Hawaii 404, 380 P.2d 751 (1963) (preponderance) with In re Farris, 229 Or. 209, 367 P.2d 387 (1961) (clear and convincing). See also cases cited at C.J.S. Attorney and Client § 103.

§ 342

1. 9 Wigmore, Evidence §§ 2490–2492 (Chadbourn rev. 1981); Martin, Basic Problems of Evidence § 3.01 at 41–58 (6th Ed. 1988); Thayer, Preliminary Treatise on Evidence, ch. 8 (1898); Allen, Presumptions in Civil Actions Reconsidered, 66 Iowa L.Rev. 843 (1981); Gausewitz, Presumptions in a One–Rule World, 5 Vand.L.Rev. 324 (1952); Ladd, Presumptions in Civil Actions, 1977 Arizona St.L.J. 275; C.J.S. Evidence §§ 114–118; Dec.Dig. Evidence ⊜53–89.

2. Laughlin, In Support of the Thayer Theory of Presumptions, 52 Mich.L.Rev. 195, 196–207 (1953). The term may be used in a sense totally unrelated to this discussion. Thus, when the Illinois court said, "Courts are presumed to be no more ignorant than the public generally * * *," it was not dealing with any concern of procedure but was positing a point of beginning for thinking about the scope of judicial notice. Chicago v. Murphy, 313 Ill. 98, 104, 144 N.E. 802, 803 (1924).

3. See § 338 supra.

inferred from fact B, and therefore that the party has satisfied its burden, or as sometimes put by the courts, has made out a "prima facie" case.[4] The judge has not used a presumption in the sense of a standardized practice, but rather has simply relied upon a rational inference. However, in ruling on a motion for directed verdict the judge may go beyond her own mental processes and experience and find that prior decisions or existing statutes have established that proof of fact B is sufficient to permit the jury to infer the existence of fact A. The judge has thus used a standardized practice but has the court necessarily used a presumption? Although some courts have described such a standardized inference as a presumption,[5] most legal scholars have disagreed.[6] They have saved the term to describe a significantly different sort of a rule, one that dictates not only that the establishment of fact B is sufficient to satisfy a party's burden of producing evidence with regard to fact A, but also at least compels the shifting of the burden of producing evidence on the question to the party's adversary. Under this view, if proof of fact B is introduced and a presumption exists to the effect that fact A can be inferred from fact B, the party denying the existence of fact A must then introduce proof of its nonexistence or risk having a verdict directed or a finding made against it. Further some authorities state that a true presumption should not only shift the burden of producing evidence, but also require that the party denying the existence of the presumed fact assume the burden of persuasion on the issue as well.[7]

Certainly the description of a presumption as a rule that, at a minimum, shifts the burden of producing evidence is to be preferred, at least in civil cases.[8] Inferences that a trial judge decides may reasonably be drawn from the evidence need no other description, even though the judge relies upon precedent or a statute rather than personal experience in reaching a decision. In most instances, the application of any other label to an inference will only cause confusion.[9]

---

4. The term "prima facie case" is often used in two senses and is therefore an ambiguous and often misleading term. It may mean evidence that is simply sufficient to get to the jury, or it may mean evidence that is sufficient to shift the burden of producing evidence. See 9 Wigmore, Evidence § 2494. The term is used here in its former sense—evidence that is simply sufficient to withstand a motion for directed verdict.

5. Hunt v. Eure, 189 N.C. 482, 127 S.E. 593, 597 (1925): "A presumption of negligence, when establishing a prima facie case, is still only evidence of negligence for the consideration of the jury, and the burden of the issue remains on the plaintiff."

6. Thayer, supra note 1, at 317, 321, 326; 9 Wigmore, Evidence § 2490 (Chadbourn rev. 1981). See also Martin, supra note 1, at 42.

7. See § 344 infra.

8. See, e.g., Original Uniform Rule 13 (1953): "A presumption is an assumption of fact resulting from a rule of law which requires such fact to be assumed from another fact or group of facts found or otherwise established in the action." See, also Fed.R.Evid. 301; West's Ann.Cal.Evid.Code § 600(a).

9. In the first edition of this text, Dean McCormick used the term "permissive presumption" to describe a rule of law that held that a fact was sufficient to warrant, but not require, a desired inference. Some cases use the term "presumption of fact" to describe the same sort of rule. Bradley v. S.L. Savidge, Inc., 13 Wash.2d 28, 123 P.2d 780 (1942). For the reasons set forth in the text, both of these labels are here rejected. Certainly, standardized inferences are valuable to the law and there are times

In criminal cases, however, there are rules that traditionally have been labeled presumptions, even though they do not operate to shift even the burden of producing evidence. The jury is permitted but not required to accept the existence of the presumed fact even in the absence of contrary evidence.[10] Recently, the Supreme Court resurrected the term "permissive presumption" to describe these rules.[11] The term presumption will be used in this text in the preferred sense discussed above in referring to civil cases, but with the qualification suggested in referring to criminal cases.

There are rules of law that are often incorrectly called presumptions that should be specifically distinguished from presumptions at this point:

Conclusive presumptions. The term presumption as used above always denotes a rebuttable presumption, i.e., the party against whom the presumption operates can always introduce proof in contradiction. In the case of what is commonly called a conclusive or irrebuttable presumption, when fact B is proven, fact A must be taken as true, and the adversary is not allowed to dispute this at all. For example, if it is proven that a child is under seven years of age, the courts have stated that it is conclusively presumed that she could not have committed a felony. In so doing, the courts are not stating a presumption at all, but simply expressing the rule of law that someone under seven years old cannot legally be convicted of a felony.[12]

Res ipsa loquitur. Briefly and perhaps oversimply stated, res ipsa loquitur is a rule that provides that a plaintiff may satisfy his burden of producing evidence of a defendant's negligence by proving that the plaintiff has been injured by a casualty of a sort that normally would not have occurred in the absence of the defendant's negligence.[13] Although a few jurisdictions have given the doctrine the effect of a true presumption even to the extent of using it to assign the burden of persuasion,[14] most courts agree that it simply describes an inference of

when courts will specifically want to bring their existence to the attention of the jury. However, their value will remain intact and the jury may still be informed of their existence when it is beneficial to do so, without the need to refer to them by a label that implies that they have a greater procedural effect than the one with which they are naturally endowed. See discussion with regard to res ipsa loquitur, this section, below.

10. See § 346 infra.

11. County Court of Ulster County v. Allen, 442 U.S. 140 (1979).

12. See Martin, supra note 1, at 41–42; 9 Wigmore, Evidence § 2492 (Chadbourne rev. 1981). See also Michael H. v. Gerald D., 491 U.S. 110 (1989) where Justice Scalia, in a plurality opinion, refers to a presumption that a child born to a mother living with her husband is the child of the marriage, rebuttable only by the husband or the wife, as the "implementation of a substantive rule of law" rather than a true presumption. For a discussion of the constitutional implications of the *Michael H.* case, see § 345, note infra.

13. See Prosser & Keeton, Torts §§ 39, 40 (5th ed. 1984); 2 Harper, James & Gray, Law of Torts §§ 19.5–19.12 (2d Ed.1986); James, Proof of the Breach in Negligence Cases, 37 Va.L.Rev. 179, 194–228 (1951); Prosser, Res Ipsa Loquitur in California, 37 Calif.L.Rev. 183 (1949); 9 Wigmore, Evidence § 2509 (Chadbourn rev. 1981).

14. Weiss v. Axler, 137 Colo. 544, 328 P.2d 88 (1958); Prosser & Keeton, Torts, supra note 13, at 259. The authors state that the burden of persuasion may properly be shifted to the defendant for reasons of

negligence.[15] Prosser called it a "simple matter of circumstantial evidence." [16] Most frequently, the inference called for by the doctrine is one that a court would properly have held to be reasonable even in the absence of a special rule. Where this is so, res ipsa loquitur certainly need be viewed no differently from any other inference.[17] Moreover, even where the doctrine is artificial—where it is imposed for reasons of policy rather than logic [18]—it nevertheless remains only an inference, permitting but not requiring, the jury to find negligence. The only difference is that where res ipsa loquitur is artificially imposed, there is better reason for informing the jury of the permissibility of the inference than there is in the case where the doctrine simply describes a rational inference. Although theoretically a jury instruction of this kind might be viewed as violating a state rule prohibiting comment on the evidence, the courts have had little difficulty with the problem and have consistently approved and required, where requested, instructions that tell the jury that a finding of negligence is permissible.[19] Obviously these instructions can and should be given without the use of the misnomer "presumption."

The presumption of innocence. Assignments of the burdens of proof prior to trial are not based on presumptions. Before trial no evidence has been introduced from which other facts are to be inferred. The assignment is made on the basis of a rule of substantive law providing

policy in certain res ipsa loquitur cases such as those in which the defendant (e.g., a carrier) owed a special responsibility to plaintiff. They add, however, that for these same policy reasons, the burden of persuasion "should rest upon [the defendant] even when the plaintiff offers the direct testimony of eyewitnesses; and such a policy does not seem properly to be connected with res ipsa loquitur at all."

15. Sweeney v. Erving, 228 U.S. 233, 240 (1913) (injury to patient from X-ray machine; held, no error to refuse charge that placed burden of persuasion on defendant; "res ipsa loquitur means that the facts of the occurrence warrant the inference, not that they compel such an inference.") See also Gardner v. Coca Cola Bottling Co., 267 Minn. 505, 127 N.W.2d 557 (1964). Mobil Chemical Co. v. Bell, 517 S.W.2d 245 (Tex.1974).

16. Prosser, Torts, § 40 at 231 (4th Ed. 1971). The most recent edition of the Prosser text does not use this phrase but does state that the "great majority of the American Courts regard res ipsa loquitur as no more than one form of circumstantial evidence." Prosser & Keeton, supra note 13 at 257.

17. As in the case of any inference, on occasion res ipsa loquitur may have such rational force as to compel a shifting of the burden of producing evidence and a direct-

ed verdict for the plaintiff if defendant does not satisfy the shifted burden. See, e.g., Alabama & Vicksburg Railway Co. v. Groome, 97 Miss. 201, 52 So. 703 (1910); Whitley v. Hix, 207 Tenn. 683, 343 S.W.2d 851 (1961). Such a shift is not artificial in the sense that it is imposed for policy reasons. It occurs simply as a result of the logical strength of plaintiff's case. See discussion § 338, supra.

18. See, e.g., Ybarra v. Spangard, 25 Cal.2d 486, 154 P.2d 687 (1944) (unconscious patient permitted to have benefit of res ipsa loquitur against all the doctors and hospital employees involved despite fact that not all could reasonably have been held responsible). Accord: Kolakowski v. Voris, 83 Ill.2d 388, 47 Ill.Dec. 392, 415 N.E.2d 397 (1980).

19. Powell v. Moore, 228 Or. 255, 364 P.2d 1094 (1961) (instruction on res ipsa loquitur permissible). See also Centennial Mills, Inc. v. Benson, 234 Or. 512, 383 P.2d 103 (1963), where the court recognized the rule of the *Powell* case as an exception to the general rule prohibiting instructions on inferences. For other cases permitting or requiring an instruction that an inference of negligence is warranted in a res ipsa loquitur case see Annot., 173 A.L.R. 880. For an example of the form of such an instruction see Illinois Pattern Jury Instructions (Civil) 22.01 and B22.01 (1989).

that one party or the other ought to have one or both of the burdens with regard to an issue.[20] In some instances, however, these substantive rules are incorrectly referred to as presumptions. The most glaring example of this mislabeling is the "presumption of innocence" as the phrase is used in criminal cases.[21] The phrase is probably better called the "assumption of innocence" in that it describes our assumption that, in the absence of contrary facts, it is to be assumed that any person's conduct upon a given occasion was lawful.[22] In criminal cases, the "presumption of innocence" has been adopted by judges as a convenient introduction to the statement of the burdens upon the prosecution, first of producing evidence of the guilt of the accused and, second, of finally persuading the jury or judge of his guilt beyond a reasonable doubt. Most courts insist on the inclusion of the phrase in the charge to the jury,[23] despite the fact that at that point it consists of nothing more than an amplification of the prosecution's burden of persuasion. Although the phrase is technically inaccurate and perhaps even misleading in the sense that it suggests that there is some inherent probability that the defendant is innocent, it is a basic component of a fair trial.[24] Like the requirement of proof beyond a reasonable doubt, it at least indicates to the jury that if a mistake is to be made it should be made in favor of the accused, or as Wigmore

20. See § 337 supra.

21. The above discussion refers only to the common use of the term in reference to the accused in criminal cases. Although there may be a true presumption of innocence with regard to charges of misconduct or crime in civil cases or in criminal cases with regard to alleged crimes collaterally involved, most courts using the phrase in these cases are probably only talking about an inference of innocence. The language is usually ambiguous; e.g., TRW, Inc. v. N.L.R.B., 393 F.2d 771, 774 (6th Cir.1968) ("* * * it must be presumed in the absence of evidence, that one who chooses to exercise a right conferred by law intends to exercise that right in a legal manner."); Moroni v. Brawders, 317 Mass. 48, 57 N.E.2d 14, 18 (1944) ("[The presumption of innocence] is not only a technical presumption, one 'of law,' but is also * * * a presumption 'of fact,' which means that an inference that conduct is of that sort is warranted even when not required."); Immerman v. Ostertag, 83 N.J.Super. 364, 199 A.2d 869, 874 (1964) ("Ordinarily there is a reasonable presumption that individuals would not commit a crime as serious as perjury or false swearing. However, that presumption loses its force where, as here, the evidence shows that the persons in question lack respect for the truth.")

22. "In the first place, the so-called presumption of innocence is not, strictly speaking, a presumption in the sense of an inference deduced from a given premise. It is more accurately an assumption which has for its purpose the placing of the burden of proof upon anyone who asserts any deviation from the socially desirable ideal of good moral conduct." Alexander, J., in Carr v. State, 192 Miss. 152, 4 So.2d 887, 888 (1941). See also Ashford & Risinger, Presumptions, Assumptions and Due Process in Criminal Cases, A Theoretical Overview, 79 Yale L.J. 165, 173 (1969).

23. A leading case is Commonwealth v. Madeiros, 255 Mass. 304, 151 N.E. 297 (1926) (refusal to instruct on presumption reversible error though judge instructed that indictment and custody were not to be taken against him and that they should not decide on suspicion). See also McDonald v. United States, 109 U.S.App.D.C. 98, 284 F.2d 232 (1960), and cases collected in C.J.S. Criminal Law § 1221; Dec.Dig. Criminal Law ⇐778(3).

24. In Taylor v. Kentucky, 436 U.S. 478 (1978), the Court stated that, although the presumption of innocence is not articulated in the Constitution, it is a basic component of a fair trial under our system. Therefore, under the circumstances of the case, the trial court's refusal to give a requested instruction on the presumption resulted in a violation of the defendant's right to a fair trial as guaranteed by the Fourteenth Amendment.

stated, "the term does convey a special and perhaps useful hint * * * in that it cautions the jury to put away from their minds all the suspicion that arises from the arrest, the indictment, and the arraignment, and to reach their conclusion solely from the legal evidence adduced." [25]

§ 343. Reasons for the Creation of Presumptions: Illustrative Presumptions [1]

A presumption shifts the burden of producing evidence, and may assign the burden of persuasion as well. Therefore naturally the reasons for creating particular presumptions are similar to the considerations which have already been discussed,[2] that bear upon the initial or tentative assignment of those burdens.[3] Thus, just as the burdens of proof are sometimes allocated for reasons of fairness, some presumptions are created to correct an imbalance resulting from one party's superior access to the proof. An example of such a presumption is the rule that as between connecting carriers, the damage occurred on the line of the last carrier.[4] Similarly, notions, usually implicit rather than expressed, of social and economic policy incline the courts to favor one contention by giving it the benefit of a presumption, and correspondingly to handicap the disfavored adversary. A classic instance is the presumption of ownership from possession, which tends to favor the prior possessor and to make for the stability of estates.[5] A presumption may also be created to avoid an impasse, to reach some result, even though it is an arbitrary one. For example, presumptions dealing with the survivorship of persons who died in a common disaster are necessary in order that other rules of law may operate, even though there is actually no factual basis upon which to believe that one party or the other was likely to have died first.[6] Generally, however, the most important consideration in the creation of presumptions is probability. Most presumptions have come into existence primarily because the judges have believed that proof of fact B renders the inference of the

25. 9 Wigmore, Evidence § 2511 at 407 (Chadbourn rev. 1981).

§ 343

1. Particular presumptions are listed in 9 Wigmore, Evidence §§ 2499–2540 (Chadbourn rev. 1981); C.J.S. Evidence §§ 120–157; Dec.Dig. Evidence ⟨≈⟩55–83.

2. See § 337 supra.

3. For other discussions of the bases of presumptions see Watkins v. Prudential Insurance Co., 315 Pa. 497, 173 A. 644, 648 (1934); Martin, Basic Problems of Evidence § 302 at 42–44 (6th Ed.1988); Cleary, Presuming and Pleading: An Essay on Juristic Immaturity, 12 Stan.L.Rev. 5 (1959); Ladd, Presumptions in Civil Actions, 1977 Ariz.St.L.J. 275.

4. When the shipper proves that it delivered the goods to the first carrier in good condition and received them from the last in bad condition, the damage is presumed to have occurred on the line of the last carrier. Chicago & North Western Railway Co. v. C.C. Whitnack Produce Co., 258 U.S. 369 (1922) (the rule is not changed by the Carmack Amendment making initial carrier liable); C.J.S. Carriers § 440 n. 35.

5. Oklahoma Railway Co. v. Guthrie, 175 Okl. 40, 52 P.2d 18, 23 (1935) (railway premises); Guyer v. Snyder, 133 Md. 19, 104 A. 116 (1918) (personal property); 9 Wigmore, Evidence § 2515 (Chadbourn rev. 1981).

6. See Martin, supra note 3 at 43.

existence of fact A so probable that it is sensible and timesaving to assume the truth of fact A until the adversary disproves it.[7]

Obviously, most presumptions are based not on any one of these grounds alone, but have been created for a combination of reasons. Usually, for example, a presumption is based not only upon the judicial estimate of the probabilities but also upon the difficulties inherent in proving that the more probable event in fact occurred.[8] Moreover, as is the case with initial allocations of the burdens, the reasons for creation of presumptions are often tied closely to the pertinent substantive law. This is particularly true with regard to those presumptions which are created, at least in part, to further some social policy.[9]

Although it would be inappropriate to attempt to list the hundreds of recognized presumptions,[10] following is a brief discussion of a few illustrative presumptions and the reasons for their creation:

Official actions by public officers, including judicial proceedings, are presumed to have been regularly and legally performed.[11] Reason: probability and the difficulty of proving that the officer conducted himself in a manner that was in all ways regular and legal.

A letter properly addressed, stamped and mailed is presumed to have been duly delivered to the addressee.[12] Reason: probability and the difficulty of proving delivery in any other way.

7. In the first edition of this text, Dean McCormick stated that another ground for the creation of presumptions is "procedural convenience" and cited the example of the presumption of sanity as it operates in criminal cases to save "the state the fruitless trouble of proving sanity in the great number of cases where the question will not be raised." Undoubtedly, procedural convenience is a reason for this rule. However, the so-called presumption of sanity is simply a description of the initial assignment of the burden of producing evidence to the defendant and is not actually a presumption. See § 346 infra.

8. See § 337.

9. The presumptions in employment discrimination cases are a good example. See, e.g., Wards Cove Packing Co. v. Atonio, 490 U.S. 642 (1989); Price Waterhouse v. Hopkins, 490 U.S. 228 (1989); Texas Department of Community Affairs v. Burdine, 450 U.S. 248 (1981).

A court may also consider the bases for creation of a presumption suggested in this text and find the creation of a presumption inappropriate under the circumstances. See, e.g., Moreno v. People, 775 P.2d 1184 (Colo.1989) (failure to give notice "forthwith" of forfeiture of bail bond does not create presumption of prejudice to surety).

10. For a list of some traditional common law presumptions, see West's Ann.

Cal.Evid.Code § 600 et seq. No corresponding catalog appears in the Federal or Revised Uniform Rules (1974).

11. Thompson v. Consolidated Gas Utilities Corp., 300 U.S. 55 (1937) (regulations of administrative board, purporting to be made under delegated authority, presumed to be supported by justifying facts); Wilson v. Hodel, 758 F.2d 1369 (10th Cir.1985) (procedure for oil and gas leasing on public lands); S.S. Kresge Co. v. Davis, 277 N.C. 654, 178 S.E.2d 382 (1971) (good faith administration of the law by law enforcement officers and city officials is presumed); State ex rel. Lawrence v. Burke, 253 Wis. 240, 33 N.W.2d 242 (1948) (habeas corpus after judgment of conviction; judge presumed to have informed accused of right to counsel); West's Ann.Cal.Evid.Code § 664; 9 Wigmore, Evidence § 2534 (Chadbourn rev. 1981); Dec.Dig. Evidence ⟺82, 83. See also Hammond v. Brown, 323 F.Supp. 326, 355 (N.D.Ohio 1971), affirmed 450 F.2d 480 (6th Cir.) where, in an action to enjoin criminal prosecutions arising out of the Kent State rioting, the court presumed that the petit jurors who would hear the case would act impartially.

12. Franklin Life Insurance Co. v. Brantley, 231 Ala. 554, 165 So. 834 (1936); Employers' National Life Insurance Co. v. Willits, 436 S.W.2d 918 (Tex.Civ.App.1968); 9 Wigmore, Evidence § 2519 (Chadbourn rev. 1981); Dec.Dig. Evidence ⟺71.

When the plaintiff has been injured by the negligent operation of a vehicle, then upon proof of further facts he may have the benefit of presumptions in moving against the nondriving defendant. The plaintiff seeking to prove agency may secure the advantage of the presumption that the person driving the vehicle was doing so in the scope of his employment and in the course of the business of the defendant, merely by proving that the defendant was the owner.[13] In a number of states the plaintiff must not only prove ownership to gain the benefit of the presumption of agency, but also that the driver is regularly employed by the defendant.[14] If the plaintiff seeks to prove liability in a state having a statute making the owner liable for acts of one driving with the owner's consent, the plaintiff may secure the advantage of the presumption that the person driving was doing so with the owner's consent merely by showing ownership.[15] In some states the plaintiff must not only prove ownership to gain the benefit of the presumption but also that a special relationship existed between the driver and the defendant.[16] Reasons behind these presumptions: probability, fairness in the light of defendant's superior access to the evidence, and the social policy of promoting safety by widening the responsibility in borderline cases of owners for injuries caused by their vehicles.

When a bailor proves delivery of property to a bailee in good condition and return in a damaged state, or a failure to return after due demand, a presumption arises that the damage or loss was due to

---

13. 9 Wigmore, Evidence § 2510a (Chadbourn rev. 1981). Malone v. Hanna, 275 Ala. 534, 156 So.2d 626 (1963); Van Court v. Lodge Cab Co., 198 Wash. 530, 89 P.2d 206, 211 (1939); Hollen v. Reynolds, 123 W.Va. 360, 15 S.E.2d 163 (1941); and see decisions collected Dec.Dig. Automobiles ⏚242(5), 242(6); Annots., 42 A.L.R. 898, 900, 74 A.L.R. 951, 96 A.L.R. 634; Note, 1953 U.Ill.L.F. 121. Proof, in turn, that a business vehicle bore defendant's name raises a "presumption" of ownership, and hence of agency and scope of employment, under this view. Brill v. Davajon, 51 Ill.App.2d 445, 201 N.E.2d 253 (1964); Cappello's Adm'r v. Aero Mayflower Transit Co., 116 Vt. 64, 68 A.2d 913 (1949). So also as to proof that the car bore a license number issued to defendant.

Compare Frew v. Barto, 345 Pa. 217, 26 A.2d 905 (1942), with Lanteigne v. Smith, 365 Pa. 132, 74 A.2d 116 (1950).

In some states, there is an inference of agency from ownership rather than a presumption. Chappell v. Dean, 258 N.C. 412, 128 S.E.2d 830 (1963) (interpreting North Carolina statute); Breeding v. Johnson, 208 Va. 652, 159 S.E.2d 836 (1968). See also Walker v. Johnston, 236 S.W.2d 534 (Tex.Civ.App.1951) ("inference" of ownership from identification on vehicle); Rodgers v. Jackson Brewing Co., 289 S.W.2d 307 (Tex.Civ.App.1956) ("rebuttable presumption" of ownership from identification on vehicle); Kimbell Milling Co. v. Marcet, 449 S.W.2d 100 (Tex.Civ.App.1969) (citing both the *Walker* and the *Rodgers* case but finding it unnecessary to determine whether the rule describes an inference or a presumption).

14. Manion v. Waybright, 59 Idaho 643, 86 P.2d 181 (1938) ("operated by one in the general employ of defendant"); Galloway Motor Co. v. Huffman's Administrator, 281 Ky. 841, 137 S.W.2d 379 (1939); Collins v. Leahy, 347 Mo. 133, 146 S.W.2d 609 (1940); Howell v. Olson, 452 P.2d 768 (Okl.1969); Dec.Dig. Automobiles ⏚242(6); Annot., 42 A.L.R. 915, 74 A.L.R. 962, 96 A.L.R. 641.

15. Young v. Masci, 289 U.S. 253 (1933); McKirchy v. Ness, 256 Iowa 744, 128 N.W.2d 910 (1964); West's Ann.Cal.Vehicle Code § 17150; Iowa Code Ann. § 321.493; N.Y.—McKinney's Vehicle and Traffic Law § 388(1).

16. O'Dea v. Amodeo, 118 Conn. 58, 170 A. 486 (1934); Christiansen v. Hilber, 282 Mich. 403, 276 N.W. 495 (1937); Conn.Gen. St.Ann. § 52–182 (making presumption of consent applicable to the family car or boat); Mich.Comp.Laws Ann. § 9.2101. See also § 344, infra, notes 18–23 and accompanying text.

the negligence or fault of the bailee.[17]   Reason: fairness in the light of the superior access of the bailee to the evidence of the facts surrounding the loss; probability.

Proof that a person has disappeared from home and has been absent for at least seven years and that during this time those who would be expected to hear from the person have received no tidings and after diligent inquiry have been unable to find the person's whereabouts, raises a presumption that the person died at some time during the seven year period.[18]   The rule, though not very ancient,[19] is already

17. See, e.g., Compton v. Daniels, 98 Idaho 915, 575 P.2d 1303 (1978); Bowman v. Vandiver, 243 Ky. 139, 47 S.W.2d 947, 948 (1932); Gray v. E.J. Longyear Co., 78 N.M. 161, 429 P.2d 359 (1967); Trammell v. Whitlock, 150 Tex. 500, 242 S.W.2d 157 (1951); 9 Wigmore, Evidence § 2508 (Chadbourn rev. 1981); Comment, 4 Baylor L.Rev. 327 (1952); C.J.S. Bailments § 50; Dec.Dig. Bailments ⊕=31(1). The presumption casts the burden on the bailee of proceeding with evidence of the cause of the loss, e.g., fire, theft, damage from collision. Some cases hold that, if the facts thus disclosed are consistent with due care, e.g., a fire of unknown origin, the bailee has satisfied the burden. Exporters' & Traders' Compress & Warehouse Co. v. Schulze, 265 S.W. 133 (Tex.Com.App.1924) (fire); Chaloupka v. Cyr, 63 Wash.2d 463, 387 P.2d 740 (1963) (fire). But other cases, more soundly it seems, require the bailee to go further and give evidence of facts from which the jury could reasonably find that the loss was not caused by the bailee's negligence. Downey v. Martin Aircraft Service, Inc., 96 Cal.App.2d 94, 214 P.2d 581 (1950) (fire); General Exchange Insurance Corp. v. Service Parking Grounds, Inc., 254 Mich. 1, 235 N.W. 898 (1931) (damage to car while stolen).

The considerations giving rise to a presumption of negligence may or may not support a presumption of conversion where the goods are not returned. See discussion in International Nickel Co., Inc. v. Trammel Crow Distribution Corp., 803 F.2d 150, 153–154 (5th Cir.1986).

Section 7–403(1)(b) of the Uniform Commercial Code provides that a bailee may excuse failure to deliver goods to the party holding a document of title by establishing "damage to or delay, loss or destruction of the goods for which the bailee is not liable[, but the burden of establishing negligence in such cases is on the person entitled under the document]." The bracketed language is optional. Most jurisdictions have omitted it (37 out of 51 adopting the code). See Uniform Commercial Code Reporting Service, State Correlation Tables (1990).

In most jurisdictions in which the section has been adopted without the optional language the question is still open as to whether the bailee has the burden of persuasion as well as the burden of producing evidence on the question of negligence. See Bigham, Presumptions, Burden of Proof and the Uniform Commercial Code, 21 Vand.L.Rev. 177, 191 (1968).

See also Reserve Insurance Co. v. Gulf Florida Terminal Co., 386 So.2d 550 (Fla. 1980), upholding as constitutional an amendment to § 7–403(1) placing burden of proving negligence on bailor only in the event of losses exceeding $10,000.

18. Green v. Royal Neighbors of America, 146 Kan. 571, 73 P.2d 1 (1937); Magers v. Western & Southern Life Insurance Co., 335 S.W.2d 355 (Mo.App.1960); Donea v. Massachusetts Mutual Life Insurance Co., 220 Minn. 204, 19 N.W.2d 377 (1945). See the exhaustive treatment of this presumption in Jalet, Mysterious Disappearance: The Presumption of Death and the Administration of the Estates of Missing Persons or Absentees, 54 Iowa L.Rev. 177 (1968). See also 9 Wigmore, Evidence § 2531a (Chadbourn rev. 1981); C.J.S. Death § 6; Dec.Dig. Death ⊕=2. The presumption has been enacted into statute in somewhat more than half the states. See Jalet, supra at 198.

A few jurisdictions dispense with the requirement of search and inquiry. See, e.g., Banks v. Metropolitan Life Insurance Co., 142 Neb. 823, 8 N.W.2d 185 (1943). See also cases collected in Annot., 99 A.L.R.2d 307.

It is often stated that it is one of the required facts of the presumption that the absence be "unexplained." Butler v. Mutual Life Insurance Co., 225 N.Y. 197, 121 N.E. 758 (1919). See cases collected at C.J.S. Death § 6 n. 39. It is believed, however, that this is misleading. The more reasonable view, it seems, is not that the proponent of the presumption must show that the absence is "unexplained," but

19. See note 19 on page 458.

antiquated in that the seven year period is undoubtedly too long considering modern communications and transportation.[20] Reasons: probability and the social policy of enforcing family security provisions such as life insurance, and of settling estates.[21]

In the tracing of titles to land there is a useful presumption of identity of person from identity of name. Thus, when the same name appears in the chain of title first as grantee or heir and then as grantor, it will be presumed that it was the same person in each case.[22] Reasons: the convenience of enabling the court and the parties to rely upon the regularity of the apparent chain of title, until this is challenged by evidence contesting identity; the social policy of quieting claims based on the face of the record; and probability.

Proof that a child was born to a woman during the time when she was married creates the presumption that the offspring is the legit-

explanatory circumstances (e.g., that the person was a fugitive from justice), whether brought out by the proponent or the opponent, are to be considered by the jury in rebuttal of the presumption. Shaw v. Prudential Insurance Co. of America, 158 Wash. 43, 290 P. 694 (1930); see also Ewing v. Metropolitan Life Insurance Co., 191 Wis. 299, 210 N.W. 819 (1926).

Under the majority view, there is no presumption as to the time of death within the seven years. Peak v. United States, 353 U.S. 43 (1957) (construing federal statute); Ferril v. Kansas City Life Insurance Co., 345 Mo. 777, 137 S.W.2d 577 (1939). But a minority, in aid of the settlement of controversies over succession, recognize a presumption that the death occurred at the end of the seven years. In re Chicago & North Western Railway Co., 138 F.2d 753 (7th Cir.1943), cert. denied 321 U.S. 789 (Illinois law) (presumption of continuance of life controls for period up to the end of seven years, when person is first accounted dead); Edwards v. Equitable Life Assurance Society of United States, 296 Ky. 448, 177 S.W.2d 574 (1944). But under either view the circumstances of the disappearance may be sufficient evidence that the death occurred at or about the time of disappearance. See Edwards v. Equitable Life Assurance Society, supra; Ferril v. Kansas City Life Insurance Co., supra. See also Hefford v. Metropolitan Life Insurance Co., 173 Or. 353, 363, 144 P.2d 695 (1944).

19. Thayer traces it to an English case of 1804. Doe d. George v. Jesson, 6 East 80, 102 Eng.Rep. 1217. But the period of seven years seems to derive from the Bigamy Act of 1604 and from a statute of 1667 which provided "in the case of estates and leases depending upon the life of a person

who should go beyond the seas, or otherwise absent himself within the kingdom for seven years, that where the lessor or reversioner should bring an action to recover the estate, the person thus absenting himself should 'be accounted as naturally dead,' if there should be no 'sufficient and evident proof of the life,' and that the judge should 'direct the jury to give their verdict as if the person * * * were dead.' " Preliminary Treatise on Evidence 319–324 (1898).

20. See 9 Wigmore, Evidence § 2531b (Chadbourn rev. 1981). Wigmore advocated the adoption of the Uniform Absence as Evidence of Death and Absentees' Property Act which provides no set period for a presumption of death but left the matter of death to be determined in each case as a question of fact. 8 U.L.A. § 1 (1972). The act was adopted in three states, Maryland, Tennessee and Wisconsin in 1941, but has not been adopted since. Maryland repealed its act in 1973. 1st Sp.Sess. ch. 2 § 1.

Several states provide for a length of absence less than seven years. See, e.g., New Jersey Stat.Ann. 3A:40–1 (5 years); N.Y.—McKinney's EPTL 2–1.7 (5 years); Ark.Stat. § 62–1601 (5 years).

21. See Robb v. Horsey, 169 Md. 227, 181 A. 348, 351 (1935). See also Jalet, supra, note 18 at 181–182.

22. E.g., Edelstein v. Pon, 183 Cal. App.2d 795, 7 Cal.Rptr. 65 (1960); Huston v. Graves, 213 S.W. 77 (Mo.1919). See also Breznik v. Braun, 11 Ill.2d 564, 144 N.E.2d 586 (1957). See general discussion of inferences or presumptions from identical names in 9 Wigmore, Evidence § 2529 (Chadbourn rev. 1981) and cases collected in Dec.Dig. Evidence ⟩=55, Names ⟩=14.

imate child of the husband.[23] Despite the controversy over whether presumptions generally shift the burden of persuasion upon the opponent,[24] it is universally agreed that in the case of this presumption, the adversary contending for illegitimacy does have the burden.[25] This burden, moreover, is usually measured not by the normal standard for civil cases of preponderance of the evidence, but rather by the requirement of clear, convincing, and satisfactory proof, as most courts say,[26] or even by the criminal formula, beyond a reasonable doubt.[27] In addition, as pointed out elsewhere in this work, the contender for illegitimacy is further handicapped by a rule rendering incompetent the testimony or declarations of the spouses offered to show nonaccess, when the purpose is to bastardize the child.[28] Reasons: social policy, to avoid the visitation upon the child of the sins of the parents caused by the social stigma of bastardy and the common law rules (now generally alleviated by statutes) as to the incapacities of the *filius nullius,* the child of no one; probability.

23. In re Findlay, 253 N.Y. 1, 170 N.E. 471, 473 (1930) (opinion by Cardozo, C.J., tracing the history and limits of the presumption); Bernheimer v. First National Bank, 359 Mo. 1119, 225 S.W.2d 745 (1949) ("presumption of legitimacy is the strongest known to law"); 9 Wigmore, Evidence § 2527 (Chadbourn rev. 1981); Notes, 33 Harv.L.Rev. 306 (1920), 35 Mo.L.Rev. 449 (1970); C.J.S. Bastards § 3; 10 Am.Jur.2d Bastards §§ 10–44; Dec.Dig. Illegitimate Children ⊙2–4. The presumption applies even when the child was conceived before, and born after, marriage. State v. E.A.H., 246 Minn. 299, 75 N.W.2d 195 (1956). See cases collected Annot., 57 A.L.R.2d 729. Interesting problems of presumptions arise when a child is conceived while the wife is married to husband number one and is born after she married number two. See cases collected in Annot., 57 A.L.R.2d 729, 778 and 46 A.L.R.3d 158. Presumptions have often developed into rules of substantive law. Here, however, the course of evolution has been from a rule of substantive law into a rebuttable presumption. But the strictness of an older day when if the husband was not beyond the four seas, the child was conclusively assumed to be his, lingers in modified form. Thus, for example, West's Ann.Cal.Evid.Code § 621 provides that "the issue of a wife cohabiting with her husband, who is not impotent, is conclusively presumed to be legitimate." A recent amendment permits the presumption to be rebutted based upon evidence presented by the husband or wife, but no other person. See discussion in Michael H. v. Gerald D., 491 U.S. 110 (1989). Somewhat more moderately, the court in Haugen v. Swanson, 219 Minn. 123, 16 N.W.2d

900, 902 (1944), held that a husband's paternity could be excluded "by proof of miscegenation, or of his impotency, or of the negative results of reliable blood tests by impartial physicians."

The Minnesota Supreme Court subsequently softened its approach to the nature of the rebuttal proof required. Golden v. Golden, 282 N.W.2d 887, 889 (Minn.1979) (facts which would, if accepted, tend to exclude all reasonable probability of his parenthood of the child upon the ground of nonaccessibility). For blood tests to prove or disprove paternity, see § 211 supra.

24. See § 344, infra.

25. See the opinion of Sturdevant, J., in In re Jones' Estate, 110 Vt. 438, 8 A.2d 631, 128 A.L.R. 704 (1939) recognizing this allocation of the burden of persuasion, but characterizing this apportionment of the burden as a "rule of substantive law"—an analysis that may be questioned, see § 344 infra. Cases are collected in Annot., 128 A.L.R. 713.

26. The variations in phraseology are wide. In re Davis' Estate, 169 Okl. 133, 36 P.2d 471 (1934) ("strong, satisfactory and conclusive"); State ex rel. Walker v. Clark, 144 Ohio St. 305, 58 N.E.2d 773 (1944) ("clear and convincing"); In re Estate of Thorn, 353 Pa. 603, 606, 46 A.2d 258, 260 (1946) ("clear, direct, satisfactory and irrefragable"); Annot., 128 A.L.R. supra note 25 at 718–722.

27. In re Jones' Estate, 110 Vt. 438, 8 A.2d 631, 128 A.L.R. 704 (1939).

28. See § 67 supra.

When violent death is shown to have occurred and the evidence is not controlling as to whether it was due to suicide or accident, there is a presumption against suicide.[29] Reasons: the general probability in case of a death unexplained, which flows from the human revulsion against suicide, and, probably, a social policy which inclines in case of doubt toward the fruition rather than the frustration of plans for family protection through insurance.

§ 344. The Effect of Presumptions in Civil Cases [1]

The trial judge must consider the effect of a presumption in a civil jury trial at two stages: (1) when one party or the other moves for a directed verdict and (2) when the time comes to instruct the jury.[2]

Sometimes the effect of a presumption, at either stage, is easy to discern; it follows naturally from the definition of the term. Thus, where a party proves the basic facts giving rise to a presumption,[3] it

29. Dick v. New York Life Insurance Co., 359 U.S. 437 (1959) (North Dakota law); Life & Casualty Insurance Co. v. Daniel, 209 Va. 332, 163 S.E.2d 577 (1968); C.J.S. Evidence § 135(b); Dec.Dig. Evidence ⊕59. See also cases collected Annot., 85 A.L.R.2d 722. In some states an inference rather than a presumption against suicide is recognized. Watkins v. Prudential Insurance Co. of America, 315 Pa. 497, 173 A. 644 (1934); C.J.S. § 135(b) notes 29, 30.

§ 344

1. Martin, Basic Problems of Evidence §§ 3.04, 3.07–3.10 (6th ed. 1988); Morgan, Some Problems of Proof 74–81 (1956); 9 Wigmore, Evidence §§ 2490–2493 (Chadbourn rev.1981); James & Hazard, Civil Procedure § 7.9 (3d ed. 1985); Allen, Presumptions in Civil Actions Reconsidered, 66 Iowa L.Rev. 843 (1981); Allen, Presumptions, Inferences and Burden of Proof in Federal Civil Actions—An Anatomy of Unnecessary Ambiguity and a Proposal for Reform, 76 Nw.U.L.Rev. 892 (1982); Bohlen, The Effect of Rebuttable Presumptions of Law upon the Burden of Proof, 68 U.Pa. L.Rev. 307 (1920); Broun, The Unfulfillable Promise of One Rule for All Presumptions, 62 N.C.L.Rev. 697 (1984). Cleary, Presuming and Pleading: An Essay on Juristic Immaturity, 12 Stan.L.Rev. 5 (1959); Gausewitz, Presumptions in a One–Rule World, 5 Vand.L.Rev. 324 (1952); Hecht & Pinzler, Rebutting Presumptions: Order Out of Chaos, 58 B.U.L.Rev. 527 (1978); Ladd, Presumptions in Civil Actions, 1977 Ariz.St.L.J. 275; Laughlin, In Support of the Thayer Theory of Presumptions, 52 Mich.L.Rev. 195 (1953); Louisell,

Construing Rule 301: Instructing the Jury on Presumptions in Civil Actions and Proceedings, 63 Va.L.Rev. 281 (1977); Mueller, Instructing the Jury Upon Presumptions in Civil Cases: Comparing Federal Rule Evid. 301 with Uniform Rule 301, 12 Land & Water L.Rev. 219 (1977); Annot., 5 A.L.R.3d 19; C.J.S. Evidence §§ 116, 117, 119; Dec.Dig. Evidence ⊕85–89, Trial ⊕205.

2. A presumption may be similarly significant in a case tried without a jury. In such a case, the judge must consider what effect, if any, the presumption has, both when she decides whether a party having the burden of producing evidence has satisfied that burden and when she decides the case based upon all of the evidence. However, many of the problems concerning the effect to be given presumptions have centered around the question of what, if anything, a jury is to be told about them. This section is therefore primarily directed to the jury trial. Nevertheless, it should be remembered throughout the discussion that many of the problems raised, particularly with regard to the effect of a presumption upon the burden of persuasion, exist whether or not the case is tried to a jury.

3. The test for whether evidence is sufficient to support a finding of the existence of the basic facts of a presumption should be the same as that used to assess the sufficiency of any proof introduced for the purpose of satisfying a party's burden of producing evidence. The problem in general is discussed in § 338, supra. Theoretically, there is no reason why the basic facts of a presumption cannot be proved by

will have satisfied its burden of producing evidence with regard to the presumed fact and therefore its adversary's motion for directed verdict will be denied. If its adversary fails to offer any evidence or offers evidence going only to the existence of the basic facts giving rise to the presumption and not to the presumed fact, the jury will be instructed that if they find the existence of the basic facts, they must also find the presumed fact.[4] To illustrate, suppose plaintiff proves that a letter was mailed, that it was properly addressed, that it bore a return address, and that it was never returned. Such evidence is generally held to raise a presumption that the addressee received the letter.[5] Defendant's motion for a directed verdict, based upon nonreceipt of the letter, will be denied. Furthermore, if the defendant offers no proof on this question (or if she attempts only to show that the letter was not mailed and offers no proof that the letter was not in fact received) the jury will be instructed that if they find the existence of the facts as contended by plaintiff, they must find that the letter was received.

But the problem is far more difficult where the defendant does not rest and does not confine her proof to contradiction of the basic facts, but instead introduces proof tending to show the nonexistence of the presumed fact itself. For example, what is the effect of the presumption in the illustration given above, if the defendant takes the stand and testifies that she did not in fact receive the letter? If the plaintiff offers no additional proof, is the defendant now entitled to the directed verdict she was denied at the close of the plaintiff's case? If not, what effect, if any should the presumption have upon the judge's charge to the jury? The problem of the effect of a presumption when met by proof rebutting the presumed fact has literally plagued the courts and legal scholars. The balance of this section is devoted to that problem.

circumstantial rather than direct evidence, or even by the use of another presumption, the basic facts of which are established by sufficient evidence. See, e.g., Savarese v. State Farm Mutual Automobile Insurance Co., 150 Cal.App.2d 518, 310 P.2d 142 (1957) (proof of a regular business practice of mailing of a cancellation notice held to be sufficient to give rise to a presumption of receipt of that notice). A problem may arise, however, from the fact that a presumption is, by definition, a standardized inference. Therefore, a party seeking to establish the basic facts of a presumption through the use of circumstantial evidence may run head-on into the dogma that an inference may not be based upon another inference. See cases collected at 5 A.L.R.3d 100 (1966). The answer to the dilemma is that the "rule" against basing an inference on an inference or a presumption on a presumption should not be viewed as a rule at all but rather only as a

warning against the use of inferences that are too remote or speculative. See § 338, note 13. Such a warning ought to be heeded in the case of the basic facts of presumptions but should not be elevated to the status of an inflexible rule.

4. Whether a party who has relied on a presumption and who has introduced undisputed and unimpeached evidence with regard to the basic facts of that presumption may have a verdict directed in its favor on the issue, instead of the conditional peremptory ruling suggested in the text, will depend upon whether there is a prohibition in the jurisdiction against directing a verdict in favor of the party to whom the burden of persuasion is tentatively assigned on the basis of the pleadings. See § 338, note 18 and accompanying text, supra.

5. See § 343 note 12 and accompanying text supra.

(A) The "Bursting Bubble" Theory and Deviations from It

The theory. The most widely followed theory of presumptions in American law has been that they are "like bats of the law flitting in the twilight, but disappearing in the sunshine of actual facts." [6] Put less poetically, under what has become known as the Thayer or "bursting bubble" theory, the only effect of a presumption is to shift the burden of producing evidence with regard to the presumed fact. If that evidence is produced by the adversary, the presumption is spent and disappears. In practical terms, the theory means that, although a presumption is available to permit the party relying upon it to survive a motion for directed verdict at the close of its own case, it has no other value in the trial. The view is derived from Thayer,[7] sanctioned by Wigmore,[8] adopted in the Model Code of Evidence,[9] and seemingly been made a part of the Federal Rules of Evidence.[10] It has been adopted, at least verbally, in countless modern decisions.[11]

The theory is simple to state, and if religiously followed, not at all difficult to apply. The trial judge need only determine that the evidence introduced in rebuttal is sufficient to support a finding contrary to the presumed fact.[12] If that determination is made, certainly there is no need to instruct the jury with regard to the presumption.[13] The opponent of the presumption may still not be entitled to a directed verdict, but if its motion is denied, the ruling will have nothing to do with the existence of a presumption. As has been discussed, presumptions are frequently created in instances in which the basic facts raise a natural inference of the presumed fact. This natural inference may be sufficient to take the case to the jury, despite the existence of contrary

6. Lamm J. in Mackowik v. Kansas City, St. Josephs & Council Bluffs Railroad Co., 196 Mo. 550, 571, 94 S.W. 256, 262 (1906), quoted in 9 Wigmore, Evidence § 2491 (Chadbourn rev. 1981). See also Bohlen, supra note 1 at 314, where presumptions are described: "Like Maeterlinck's male bee, having functioned they disappear."

7. Thayer, Preliminary Treatise on Evidence, ch. 8, *passim,* and especially at 314, 336 (1898). Thayer, however, seems not to have had in mind a rule of law as inflexible as the doctrine that bears his name. He at least recognized the possibility of different rules for different presumptions. See Gausewitz, Presumptions, 40 Minn. L.Rev. 391, 406–408 (1956) where the "Thayer" doctrine, but not Thayer's scholarship, is criticized.

8. 9 Wigmore, Evidence § 2491(2) (Chadbourn rev. 1981). See, however, the apparent modification of his views as expressed later in the same volume, § 2498a, subsec. 21.

9. Model Code of Evidence Rule 704(2) (1942): "* * * when the basic fact * * * has been established * * * and evidence has been introduced which would support a finding of the nonexistence of the presumed fact * * * the existence or nonexistence of the presumed fact is to be determined exactly as if no presumption had ever been applicable * * *.," and Comment, "A presumption, to be an efficient legal tool must * * * (2) be so administered that the jury never hear the word presumption used since it carries unpredictable connotations to different minds * * *."

10. Fed.R.Evid. 301.

11. See cases collected at Annot., 5 A.L.R.3d 19; Dec.Dig. Evidence ⇐85–86, 89.

12. The evidence must be "credible." See Hildebrand v. Chicago, Burlington & Quincy Railroad Co., 45 Wyo. 175, 17 P.2d 651 (1933); Cleary, supra note 1 at 18. See also Gausewitz, supra note 1 at 327–328.

13. See, e.g., Orient Insurance Co. v. Cox, 218 Ark. 804, 238 S.W.2d 757 (1951); Ammundson v. Tinholt, 228 Minn. 115, 36 N.W.2d 521 (1949).

evidence and despite the resultant destruction of the presumption. For example, in the case of the presumption of receipt of a letter, referred to above, the defendant may destroy the presumption by denying receipt. Nevertheless, a jury question is presented, not because of the presumption, but because of the natural inference flowing from the plaintiff's showing that she had mailed a properly addressed letter that was not returned.[14] On the other hand, the basic facts may not present a natural inference of sufficient strength or breadth to take the case to the jury. In such an instance, the court may grant a directed verdict against the party who originally had the benefit of the presumption.[15]

Deviations from the theory—in general. The "bursting bubble" theory has been criticized as giving to presumptions an effect that is too "slight and evanescent" when viewed in the light of the reasons for the creation of the rules.[16] Presumptions, as we have seen, have been created for policy reasons that are similar to and may be just as strong as those that govern the allocation of the burdens of proof prior to the introduction of evidence.[17] These policy considerations may persist despite the existence of proof rebutting the presumed fact. They may be completely frustrated by the Thayer rule when the basic facts of the presumption do not give rise to an inference that is naturally sufficient to take the case to the jury. Similarly, even if the natural inference is sufficient to present a jury question, it may be so weak that the jury is unlikely to consider it in its decision unless specifically told to do so. If the policy behind certain presumptions is not to be thwarted, some instruction to the jury may be needed despite any theoretical prohibition against a charge of this kind.

14. Rosenthal v. Walker, 111 U.S. 185 (1884); American Surety Co. v. Blake, 54 Idaho 1, 27 P.2d 972, 91 A.L.R. 153 (1933); Winkfield v. American Continental Insurance Co., 110 Ill.App.2d 156, 249 N.E.2d 174, 176 (1969) ("If the addressee denies the receipt of the letter then the presumption is rebutted and receipt becomes a question to be resolved by the trier of fact."); Stacey v. Sankovich, 19 Mich.App. 688, 173 N.W.2d 225 (1969) ("[The] presumption may be rebutted by evidence, but whether it was is a question for the trier of fact."); Southland Life Insurance Co. v. Greenwade, 138 Tex. 450, 159 S.W.2d 854, 857 (1942) ("We agree * * * that a presumption as such is not evidence and that it vanished as such in view of the opposing evidence; but we do not agree that the evidentiary facts upon which it was established, could no longer be considered by the trier of facts."). But see Cliff v. Huggins, 724 S.W.2d 778 (Tex.1987) (presumption of receipt of notice of trial from mailing vanished in face of testimony of nonreceipt; no question of fact presented upon which trial judge could base refusal to set aside default judgment).

15. E.g., Lovelace v. Sherwin–Williams Co., 681 F.2d 230 (4th Cir.1982) (presumption in employment discrimination case rebutted; judgment notwithstanding the verdict entered against plaintiff); O'Brien v. Equitable Life Assurance Society, 212 F.2d 383 (8th Cir.1954), cert. denied 348 U.S. 835 (presumption of accidental death, rebutted by opponent).

16. Morgan & Maguire, Looking Backward and Forward at Evidence, 50 Harv. L.Rev. 909, 913 (1937). See also, Morgan, Some Problems of Proof 74–81 (1956). Other writers are in accord, see, e.g., Cleary, supra note 1 at 18; Gausewitz, supra note 1 at 342. Contra: Laughlin, supra note 1.

The strict operation of the bursting bubble theory may give a presumption less force than an inference such as res ipsa loquitur, which may not disappear with the introduction of evidence by the defendant explaining the situation. See, e.g., Mitchell v. Saunders, 219 N.C. 178, 13 S.E.2d 242 (1941), and discussion in Brandis, North Carolina Evidence, § 227 at 236–237 (3d ed. 1988).

17. See § 343 supra.

These considerations have not gone unrecognized by the courts. Thus, courts, even though unwilling to reject the dogma entirely, often find ways to deviate from it in their treatment of at least some presumptions, generally those which are based upon particularly strong and visible policies. Perhaps the best example is the presumption of legitimacy arising from proof that a child was born during the course of a marriage. The strong policies behind the presumption are so apparent that the courts have universally agreed that the party contending that the child is illegitimate not only has the burden of producing evidence in support of the contention, but also has a heavy burden of persuasion on the issue as well.[18]

Another example of special treatment for certain presumptions is the effect given by some courts to the presumption of agency or of consent arising from ownership of an automobile.[19] The classic theory would dictate that the presumption is destroyed once the defendant or the driver testifies to facts sufficient to support a finding of nonagency or an absence of consent. Some courts have so held.[20] However, other courts have recognized that the policies behind the presumption, i.e., the defendant's superior access to the evidence and the social policy of widening the responsibility for owners of motor vehicles, may persist despite the introduction of evidence on the question from the defendant, particularly when the evidence comes in the form of the party's own or her servant's testimony. These courts have been unwilling to rely solely upon the natural inferences that might arise from plaintiff's proof,[21] and instead require more from the defendant, such as, that the rebuttal evidence be "uncontradicted, clear, convincing and unimpeached."[22] Moreover, many courts also hold that the special policies behind the presumption require that the jury be informed of its existence.[23]

18. See § 343 notes 23–28 and accompanying text supra.

19. See § 343 notes 13–16 and accompanying text supra.

20. Peoples v. Seamon, 249 Ala. 284, 31 So.2d 88 (1947); McIver v. Schwartz, 50 R.I. 68, 145 A. 101 (1929). See additional cases collected at Annot., 5 A.L.R.3d 19, 66–69.

21. Where the presumption is held to be destroyed, the natural inference arising from plaintiff's proof of ownership may or may not be sufficient to send the case to the jury, depending both upon the court's view of the inference and the nature of the rebutting proof. Compare Peoples v. Seamon, supra note 20 (question for the jury), with Kavanaugh v. Wheeling, 175 Va. 105, 7 S.E.2d 125 (1940) (inference insufficient to prove car used in owner's business; verdict for plaintiff set aside).

22. Bradley v. S.L. Savidge, Inc., 13 Wash.2d 28, 123 P.2d 780, 791 (1942) (de-

fendant's evidence held to meet test). See also Standard Coffee Co. v. Trippet, 108 F.2d 161 (5th Cir.1939) (Texas law); Krisher v. Duff, 331 Mich. 699, 50 N.W.2d 332, 337 (1951) ("Generally speaking, the evidence to make this presumption disappear should be positive, unequivocal, strong and credible. The presumption is given more weight because of the dangerous instrumentality involved and the danger of permitting incompetent driving on the highway; and because the proof or disproof of consent or permission usually rests almost entirely with the defendants.").

23. Grier v. Rosenberg, 213 Md. 248, 131 A.2d 737 (1957); Kirsher v. Duff, supra note 22 (no need to mention statute, but jury should be told that defendant must come forward with evidence of a clear, positive and credible nature to refute the presumptions of knowledge or consent).

Deviations from the theory—conflicting presumptions. Frequent deviations from the rigid dictates of the "bursting bubble" theory occur in the treatment of conflicting presumptions. A conflict between presumptions may arise as follows: W, asserting that she is the widow of H, claims her share of his property, and proves that on a certain day she and H were married. The adversary then proves that three or four years before W's marriage to H, W married another man. W's proof gives her the benefit of the presumption of the validity of a marriage. The adversary's proof gives rise to the general presumption of the continuance of a status or condition once proved to exist, and a specific presumption of the continuance of a marriage relationship. The presumed facts of the claimant's presumption and those of the adversary's are contradictory.[24] How resolve the conflict? Thayer's solution would be to consider that the presumptions in this situation have disappeared and the facts upon which the respective presumptions were based shall simply be weighed as circumstances with all the other facts that may be relevant, giving no effect to the presumptions.[25] Perhaps when the conflicting presumptions involved are based upon probability or upon procedural convenience, the solution is a fairly practical one.[26]

The particular presumptions involved in the case given as an example, however, were not of that description. On the one hand, the presumption of the validity of a marriage is founded not only in probability, but in the strongest social policy favoring legitimacy and the stability of family inheritances and expectations.[27] On the other

---

24. For an exhaustive collection of cases discussing these presumptions and the conflict between them see Annot., 14 A.L.R.2d 7. See Yarbrough v. United States, 169 Ct.Cl. 589, 341 F.2d 621 (1965); Ventura v. Ventura, 53 Misc.2d 881, 280 N.Y.S.2d 5 (1967); DeRyder v. Metropolitan Life Insurance Co., 206 Va. 602, 145 S.E.2d 177 (1965).

25. See Thayer, Preliminary Treatise on Evidence 346 (1898) followed in 9 Wigmore, Evidence § 2493 (Chadbourn rev. 1981); Model Code of Evidence Rules 701(3), 704(2). For a convincing exposition of the contrary view that as between conflicting presumptions the one founded on the stronger policy should prevail, see Morgan, Some Observations Concerning Presumptions, 44 Harv.L.Rev. 906, 932 note 41 (1931).

26. City of Montpelier v. Town of Calais, 114 Vt. 5, 39 A.2d 350 (1944) (each side invoked the presumption of official regularity in respect to the acts of its own officers, and the court held that the case would be determined without regard to the presumptions).

See also Legille v. Dann, 544 F.2d 1 (D.C.Cir.1976) (presumption of regularity of the mails rebutted by evidence of the regu-

larity of Patent Office practice); McFetters v. McFetters, 98 N.C.App. 187, 390 S.E.2d 348 (1990), review denied 327 N.C. 140, 394 S.E.2d 177 (where presumption of control of student driver by person in right front seat conflicted with presumption of control by owner of vehicle, person who actually exercised control should bear responsibility).

27. State v. Rocker, 130 Iowa 239, 106 N.W. 645, 649 (1906) ("where necessary to sustain the legitimacy of children or in making disposition of property interests * * *."). See Nixon v. Wichita Land & Cattle Co., 84 Tex. 408, 19 S.W. 560, 561 (1892), where Gaines, J. quotes the following from 1 Bishop, Marriage and Divorce § 457 (6th Ed.1881): "It being for the highest good of the parties, of the children, and of the community that all intercourse between the sexes in form matrimonial should be such in fact, the law, when administered by enlightened judges, seizes upon all probabilities, and presses into its service all things else, which can help it in each particular case to sustain the marriage, and repel the conclusion of unlawful commerce."

hand, the presumptions of continuance of lives and marriage relationships are based chiefly on probability and trial convenience, and the probability, of course, varies in accordance with the length of time for which the continuance is to be presumed in the particular case. This special situation of the questioned validity of a second marriage has been the principal area in which the problem of conflicting presumptions has arisen. Here, courts have not been willing to follow Thayer's suggestion of disregarding both rival presumptions and leaving the issue to the indifferent arbitrament of a weighing of circumstantial inferences. They have often preferred to formulate the issue in terms of a conflict of presumptions and to hold that the presumption of the validity of marriage is "stronger" and should prevail.[28] The doctrine that the weightier presumption prevails should probably be available in any situation which involves conflicting presumptions, and where one of the presumptions is grounded in a predominant social policy.[29]

Another and perhaps even better approach to the problem is to sidestep the conflict entirely and create a new presumption. Such a presumption has evolved in cases involving conflicting marriages. Under this rule, where a person has been shown to have been married successively to different spouses, there is a presumption that the earlier marriage was dissolved by death or divorce before the later one was contracted.[30] While of course the presumption is rebuttable, as in the case of the presumption of legitimacy, many courts place a special burden of persuasion upon the party attacking the validity of the second marriage by declaring that the presumption can only be overcome by clear, cogent, and convincing evidence.[31]

---

28. Smiley v. Smiley, 247 Ark. 933, 448 S.W.2d 642 (1970); Apelbaum v. Apelbaum, 7 A.D.2d 911, 183 N.Y.S.2d 54 (1959); Meade v. State Compensation Commissioner, 147 W.Va. 72, 125 S.E.2d 771 (1962); Greensborough v. Underhill, 12 Vt. 604, 607 (1839); cases collected in Annot., 14 A.L.R.2d, supra, note 24, at 37–44; Dec. Dig. Marriage ⬅40(9). See also Rev. Uniform Rule Evid. (1974) 301(b) "If presumptions are inconsistent, the presumption applies that is founded upon weightier considerations of policy. If considerations of policy are of equal weight neither presumption applies."

29. A conflict may also arise in a situation where state law provides for an instruction that the law does not presume something, such as negligence from the mere happening of an accident. The facts may also give rise to a presumption of negligence arising, for example, from the violation of a statute. At least one court has held that, under the facts presented, it was error to instruct the jury as to the non-presumption. Ristaino v. Flannery, 317 Md. 452, 564 A.2d 790 (1989).

30. Clark v. Clark, 19 Ark.App. 280, 719 S.W.2d 712 (1986); J.J. Cater Furniture Co. v. Banks, 152 Fla. 377, 11 So.2d 776 (1943); Nicholas v. Idaho Power Co., 63 Idaho 675, 125 P.2d 321 (1942); Brown v. Brown, 51 Misc.2d 839, 274 N.Y.S.2d 484 (1966); cases collected in 9 Wigmore, Evidence § 2506 (Chadbourn rev. 1981); Annot., 14 A.L.R.2d at 20–29, 55 C.J.S. Marriage § 43(3) (1948); Dec.Dig. Marriage ⬅40(5, 6). Since the policy reasons are absent, the presumption is held inapplicable in prosecutions for bigamy. Fletcher v. State, 169 Ind. 77, 81 N.E. 1083 (1907); Wright v. State, 198 Md. 163, 81 A.2d 602 (1951).

31. Kolombatovich v. Magma Copper Co., 43 Ariz. 314, 30 P.2d 832 (1934); Marcum v. Zaring, 406 P.2d 970 (Okl.1965); Annot., 14 A.L.R.2d at 45–47; Dec.Dig. Marriage ⬅40(10, 11).

See also Panzer v. Panzer, 87 N.M. 29, 528 P.2d 888 (1974) (presumption of validity of latest marriage can be overcome by "clear and convincing" evidence).

Deviations from the theory—instructions to the jury. Because of the strength of the natural inferences that generally arise from the basic facts of a presumption, judges are seldom faced with the prospect of directing a verdict against the party relying upon a presumption. Similarly, conflicting presumptions are relatively rare. However, far more frequently courts have justifiably held that the policies behind presumptions necessitate an instruction that in some way calls the existence of the rule to the attention of the jury despite the Thayerian proscription against the practice. The digests give abundant evidence of the widespread and unquestioning acceptance of the practice of informing the jury of the rule despite the fact that countervailing evidence has been adduced upon the disputed inference.[32]

Given the frequency of the deviation, however, the manner in which the jury is to be informed has been a matter of considerable dispute and confusion. The baffling nature of the presumption as a tool for the art of thinking bewilders one who searches for a form of phrasing with which to present the notion to a jury. Most of the forms have been predictably bewildering. For example, judges have occasionally contented themselves with a statement in the instructions of the terms of the presumption, without more. This leaves the jury in the air, or implies too much.[33] The jury, unless a further explanation is made, may suppose that the presumption is a conclusive one, especially if the judge uses the expression, "the law presumes."

Another solution, formerly more popular than now, is to instruct the jury that the presumption is "evidence," to be weighed and considered with the testimony in the case.[34] This avoids the danger that the jury

32. Dec.Dig. Trial ⏞205, 234(7). Nevada Pattern Civil Jury Instructions 2.41; Washington Pattern Jury Instructions (Civil) 24.00 (1967).

33. See the criticism of such a charge in Garrettson v. Pegg, 64 Ill. 111 (1872). See also Kettlewell v. Prudential Insurance Co. of America, 6 Ill.App.2d 434, 128 N.E.2d 652 (1955). But an instruction merely directing the jury to consider the presumption against suicide without explaining its effect was thought sufficient in Radius v. Travelers Insurance Co., 87 F.2d 412 (9th Cir.1937).

34. For example, prior to 1965, the California courts held that a presumption is evidence to be weighed along with all other evidence in the case and that the jury should be so instructed. Smellie v. Southern Pacific Co., 212 Cal. 540, 299 P. 529 (1931) (setting forth the doctrine); Gigliotti v. Nunes, 45 Cal.2d 85, 286 P.2d 809, 815 (1955) (setting forth a typical instruction). In 1965, however, the state adopted a new evidence code which classified the procedural effect of presumptions according to the policies behind their creation and which specifically rejected the notion that a presumption is evidence. West's Ann. Cal.Evid.Code § 600. See thorough discussion of this shift in Note, 53 Calif.L.Rev. 1439, 1480–87 (1965). See also notes 56–58 and accompanying text infra.

During congressional consideration of the Federal Rules, the Senate and Conference Committees rejected as "ill-advised" a House of Representatives version of Rule 301 which in effect treated presumption as evidence. See Senate Comm. on Judiciary, Fed. Rules of Evidence, S.Rep. No. 1277, 93d Cong., 2d Sess., p. 9 (1974); H.R. Fed. Rules of Evidence, Conf.Rep. No. 1597, 93d Cong., 2d Sess., p. 5 (1974). With this legislative history, it seems highly unlikely that an instruction to the jury referring to a presumption as evidence would be proper under the Federal Rule. See Mueller, supra n. 1 at 285.

For cases holding that a presumption is evidence see Annot., 5 A.L.R.3d 19, 35–39. For criticisms of the "presumption is evidence" rule see McBaine, Presumptions; Are They Evidence? 26 Calif.L.Rev. 519 (1938); Gausewitz, Presumptions in a One-Rule World, 5 Vand.L.Rev. 324, 333–34 (1952).

may infer that the presumption is conclusive, but it probably means little to the jury, and certainly runs counter to accepted theories of the nature of evidence.

More attractive theoretically, is the suggestion that the judge instruct the jury that the presumption is to stand accepted, unless they find that the facts upon which the presumed inference rests are met by evidence of equal weight, or in other words, unless the contrary evidence leaves their minds in equipoise, in which event they should decide against the party having the burden of persuasion upon the issue.[35] It is hard to phrase such an instruction without conveying the impression that the presumption itself is "evidence" which must be "met" or "balanced." The overriding objection, however, is the impression of futility that it conveys. It prescribes a difficult metaphysical task for the jury, and, in actual use, may mystify rather than help the average juror.[36]

One possible solution, perhaps better than those already mentioned, would be for the trial judge simply to mention the basic facts of the presumption and to point out the general probability of the circumstantial inference as one of the factors to be considered by the jury.[37] By this technique, however, a true presumption would be converted into nothing more than a permissible inference. Moreover, the solution is simply not a feasible one in many jurisdictions without at least a new interpretation of another aspect of the law. The trial judge in most states must tread warily to avoid an expression of opinion on the facts. Although instructions on certain standardized inferences such as *res ipsa loquitur* are permitted,[38] the practice, wisely or not, may frown on any explanation of the allowable circumstantial inferences from partic-

---

35. See, e.g., Klunk v. Hocking Valley Railroad Co., 74 Ohio St. 125, 77 N.E. 752 (1906); Tresise v. Ashdown, 118 Ohio St. 307, 160 N.E. 898 (1928). Although the general rule in Ohio now seems to be that a presumption disappears when met by contrary proof, see, e.g., Ayers v. Woodard, 166 Ohio St. 138, 140 N.E.2d 401 (1957), 1 Ohio Jury Instructions § 5.13 (1968), a standard instruction has been issued in that state in substantially the form suggested in the text with regard to an inference of contributory negligence arising from the plaintiff's own proof, 1 Ohio Jury Instructions § 9.11 (1968) and in somewhat similar form with regard to the presumption of agency arising from the owner's presence in an automobile. 1 Id. § 15.31 (1968).

Two authors have recently argued in favor of instructing the jury, at least with regard to certain presumptions, that it should find the presumed fact "unless it finds on the basis of all the evidence in the case that the nonexistence of that fact is at least as probable as its existence." Louisell, supra note 1 at 305 et seq.; Mueller, supra note 1 at 285 et seq.

36. Similar problems exist with regard to instructions that inform the jury that they should find for the proponent of the instruction unless they believe evidence which reasonably tends to rebut the presumed fact in which case the presumption should be disregarded and the case decided from all of the evidence. See, e.g., Washington Pattern Jury Instructions 24.03 (1967).

37. A suggestion of the propriety of such a charge was made in Jefferson Standard Life Insurance Co. v. Clemmer, 79 F.2d 724 (4th Cir.1935). See also Evans v. National Life and Accident Insurance Co., 22 Ohio St.3d 87, 488 N.E.2d 1247 (1986). In federal court the trial judge retains the common law powers to explain allowable inferences from circumstantial evidence.

38. See § 342 note 19 and accompanying text supra.

ular facts as "invading the province of the jury." [39]

Where the "bursting bubble" rule is discarded in favor of a rule which operates to fix the burden of persuasion,[40] the problem of alerting the jury to the presumption should not exist. Under this theory, a presumption may ordinarily be given a significant effect without the necessity of mentioning the word "presumption" to the jury at all. There is no more need to tell the jury why one party or the other has the burden of persuasion where that burden is fixed by a presumption than there is where the burden is fixed on the basis of policies apparent from the pleadings. The jury may be told simply that, if it finds the existence of the basic facts, the opponent must prove the non-existence of the presumed fact by a preponderance of evidence, or, in some instances, by a greater standard. Even in those instances in which the presumption places the burden of persuasion on the same party who initially had the burden, there would seem to be no reason to mention the term.[41] If the courts feel that the operation of the presumption warrants a higher standard of proof, the measure of persuasion can be increased as is now done in the case of the presumption of legitimacy. However, unless we are willing to increase the measure of persuasion,[42] nothing can be gained by informing the jury of the coincidence. The word "presumption" would only tend to confuse the issue.[43]

39. See, e.g., Pridmore v. Chicago, Rock Island & Pacific Railway Co., 275 Ill. 386, 114 N.E. 176 (1916); Kennedy v. Phillips, 319 Mo. 573, 5 S.W.2d 33 (1928); Lappin v. Lucurell, 13 Wash.App. 277, 534 P.2d 1038, 1043 (1975).

40. Examples of such a rule or variations on it include Dick v. New York Life Insurance Co., 359 U.S. 437 (1959) (North Dakota rule re presumption of accidental death); Lewis v. New York Life Insurance Co., 113 Mont. 151, 124 P.2d 579 (1942) (presumption of accidental death); In re Swan's Estate, 4 Utah 2d 277, 293 P.2d 682 (1956) (presumption of fraud and undue influence in will contest). See also O'Dea v. Amodeo, 118 Conn. 58, 170 A. 486, 488 (1934) (statutory presumption that car driven by member of owner's family was being operated as a family car; " * * * the presumption shall avail the plaintiff until such time as the trier finds proven the circumstances of the situation with reference to the use made of the car and the authority of the person operating it to drive it, leaving the burden then upon the plaintiff to establish, in view of the facts so found, that the car was being operated at the time as a family car."); Krisher v. Duff, 331 Mich. 699, 50 N.W.2d 332, 339 (1951) (under statutory presumption that member of family using car is doing so with owner's consent, error to refuse to charge the jury that the adversary must come forward with evidence of a "clear,

positive and credible nature" to refute the presumption). See also Rev. Uniform Rule Evid. (1986) 301.

41. See discussion in Levin, Pennsylvania and the Uniform Rules of Evidence: Presumptions and Dead Man Statutes, 103 U.Pa.L.Rev. 1, 27 (1954). The problem of instructing the jury with regard to a presumption operating against the party having the burden of persuasion is most likely to occur in the case of the presumption of due care. See State of Maryland for the Use of Geils v. Baltimore Transit Co., 329 F.2d 738 (4th Cir.1964), cert. denied 379 U.S. 842, rehearing denied 379 U.S. 917, on remand 37 F.R.D. 34 (D.Md.), particularly the thoughtful dissent by Haynsworth, J., 329 F.2d at 742–748.

42. Rev. Uniform Rule Evid. (1986) 301, which adopts this rule for all presumptions, contains no provision for an increased measure of persuasion.

43. See also, James & Hazard, Civil Procedure 332–333 (3d ed. 1985). Dean McCormick in the first edition of this text disagreed with this position, stating (p. 672): "As I have indicated earlier in this paper, I am inclined to think that it is a more natural practice, especially under the American tied-judge system, to mention the presumption, so that the jury may appreciate the legal recognition of a slant of policy or probability as the reason for plac-

(B) Attempts to Provide a Single Rule Governing the Effect of Presumptions

Perhaps, the greatest difficulty with the "bursting bubble" approach is that, in spite of its apparent simplicity, the conflicting desires of the courts to adopt it in theory and yet to avoid its overly-rigid dictates have turned it into a judicial nightmare of confusion and inconsistency.[44] This state of affairs has caused legal scholars not only to search for a better rule, but for a single rule that would cover all presumptions.

Many writers came to the view that the better rule for all presumptions would provide that anything worthy of the name "presumption" has the effect of fixing the burden of persuasion on the party contesting the existence of the presumed fact.[45] A principal technical objection to such a rule has been that it requires a "shift" in the burden of persuasion something that is, by definition of the burden, impossible.[46] The argument seems misplaced, in that it assumes that the burden of persuasion is fixed at the commencement of the action. However, as we have seen,[47] the burden of persuasion need not finally be assigned until the case is ready to go to the jury. Thus, using a presumption to fix that burden would not cause it to shift, but merely cause it to be assigned on the basis of policy considerations arising from the evidence introduced at the trial rather than those thought to exist on the basis of the pleadings.[48] Certainly there is no reason why policy factors thought to be controlling at the pleading stage should outweigh factors bearing upon the same policies that arise from the evidence. Just the reverse should be true.

Certainly, some presumptions have been interpreted consistently as affecting the burden of persuasion without a great deal of discussion of

---

ing on the party this particular burden. If this is true when the presumption operates (as it usually would) in favor of the plaintiff, who has the general burden of proof, so that the presumption would result in an issue being singled out and the burden thereon placed on the defendant, much more is it true when the presumption operates in favor of the defendant. In such case under the orthodox view the presumption would be swallowed up in the larger instruction that the plaintiff has the burden on everything that he has pleaded. This smothers any hint of the recognized policy or probabilities behind the particular presumption."

44. The confused situation in two states is described in Graham, Presumptions in Civil Cases in Illinois: Do They Exist? 1977 S.Ill.L.J. 1 (1977), and Comment, Presumptions in Texas: A Study in Irrational Jury Control, 52 Tex.L.Rev. 1329 (1974).

45. See Morgan, Some Problems of Proof 74–81 (1956); Cleary, supra note 1 at 20; Gausewitz, supra note 1 at 342; Supreme Court Draft of the Federal Rules of Evidence, 56 F.R.D. 183, 208 (1972). The rule that a presumption operates to fix the burden of persuasion has been called the Pennsylvania rule. However, if the rule ever had general application in that state, it certainly no longer does. See, e.g., Allison v. Snelling & Snelling, Inc., 425 Pa. 519, 229 A.2d 861 (1967); Waters v. New Amsterdam Casualty Co., 393 Pa. 247, 144 A.2d 354 (1958).

46. Laughlin, supra note 1 at 211.

47. See § 336 supra.

48. The policies behind the allocation of the burden of persuasion are discussed generally in § 337 supra. The policies behind the creation of presumptions are discussed in § 343 supra.

a "shifting" burden of proof.[49] The real question is more fundamental: should this rule which is applicable to some presumptions be applicable universally? The answer to that query depends, not on theoretical distinctions between shifting as opposed to reassigning the burden of persuasion, but upon whether the policy behind the creation of all presumptions is always strong enough to affect the allocation of the burden of persuasion as well as the burden of producing evidence.

One of the leading proponents of the rule allocating the burden of persuasion as a universal rule was Professor Morgan.[50] Although Professor Morgan served as a reporter for the Model Code of Evidence, he was unable to persuade the draftsmen of that code to incorporate into it a provision embracing this view of the effect of presumptions.[51] The Model Code instead takes a rigid Thayerian position.[52] However, Morgan also was active in the drafting of the original Uniform Rules of Evidence where he had considerably more success in inducing an adoption of his theory. The original Uniform Rules provided that where the facts upon which the presumption is based have "probative value" the burden of persuasion is assigned to the adversary; where there is no such probative value, the presumption has only a Thayerian effect and dies when met by contrary proof.[53]

The Uniform Rules, although having much to commend them, presented problems.[54] Obviously, they did not provide for a single rule. Different courts could give different answers to the question whether a particular presumption has probative value. The possibilities of inconsistency and confusion, although reduced by the rules, were still present. Further, the distinction made was a thin one that disregarded the existence of strong social policies behind some presumptions that lack probative value. Certainly if a presumption is not based on probability but rather is based solely upon social policy, there may be more, and not less, reason to preserve it in the face of contrary proof. A presumption based on a natural inference can stand on its own weight either when met by a motion for a directed verdict or in the jury's deliberations. A presumption based on social policy may need an extra boost in order to insure that the policy is not overlooked. Morgan apparently recognized the weakness of the distinction made by the rule and seemed to have agreed to it only to allay fears that a provision

49. See § 343, text accompanying notes 23–27, supra, concerning the presumption of legitimacy. See also cases cited n. 40 supra and Brandis, North Carolina Evidence, § 235 at 259–261 (3d ed. 1988) for a discussion of the effect of a presumption of regularity.

50. Morgan, Some Problems of Proof, supra note 45 at 81.

"Just as the courts have come to recognize that there is no a priori formula for fixing the burden of persuasion, so they should recognize that if there is a good reason for putting on one party or the other the burden of going forward with evidence—if it might not as well have been determined by chance—it ought to be good enough to control a finding when the mind of the trier is in equilibrium."

51. See Morgan, Foreword to Model Code of Evidence at 54–65 (1942).

52. Model Code of Evidence Rule 704. For text see note 9 supra.

53. Original Unif.R.Evid. 14 (1953).

54. See the criticism in Cleary, supra note 1 at 28; Gausewitz, Presumptions, 40 Minn.L.Rev. 391, 401–410 (1956).

giving to all presumptions the effect of fixing the burden of persuasion might be unconstitutional.[55]

An approach almost directly opposite to the one taken in the Uniform Rules is taken in California's Code of Evidence, adopted in 1965. Under the California Code, presumptions based upon "public policy" operate to fix the burden of persuasion;[56] presumptions that are established "to implement no public policy other than to facilitate the determination of a particular action" are given a Thayerian effect.[57] The California approach is an improvement over the Uniform Rules but is still not completely satisfactory. The line between presumptions based on public policy and those which are not may not be easy to draw.[58] Furthermore, although the California distinction is sounder than that made in the Uniform Rules, it is not completely convincing. The fact that the policy giving rise to a presumption is one that is concerned with the resolution of a particular dispute rather than the implementation of broader social goals, does not necessarily mean that the policy is satisfied by the shifting of the burden of producing evidence and that it should disappear when contrary proof is introduced. California asks the wrong question about the policies behind presumptions. The inquiry should not be directed to the breadth of the policy but rather to the question whether the policy considerations behind a certain presumption are sufficient to override the policies that tentatively fix the burdens of proof at the pleading stage.

The Federal Rules of Evidence, as adopted by the Supreme Court and submitted to the Congress, took the approach advocated by Morgan. The proposed Rule 301 provided that "a presumption imposes on the party against whom it is directed, the burden of proving that the non-existence of the presumed fact is more probable than its existence."[59] However, the draft did not survive congressional scrutiny and Rule 301, as enacted, has a distinct Thayerian flavor:

In all civil actions and proceedings not otherwise provided for by Act of Congress or by these rules, a presumption imposes on the party against whom it is directed, the burden of going forward with evidence to rebut or meet the presumption but does not shift to such party the burden of proof in the sense of the risk of non-persuasion, which remains throughout the trial upon the party of whom it was originally cast.[60]

Some legal scholars have argued that Federal Rule 301 does not preclude instructions which at least alert the jury to the strength of logic and policy underlying a presumption, even though evidence contrary to the existence of the presumed fact has been introduced.[61]

55. Morgan, Presumptions, 10 Rutgers L.Rev. 512, 513 (1956).

56. West's Ann.Cal.Evid.Code §§ 605–606.

57. Id. §§ 603–604.

58. See note, 53 Calif.L.Rev. 1439, 1445–1450 (1965).

59. 56 F.R.D. 183, 208.

60. Fed.R.Evid. 301.

61. Louisell, Construing Rule 301: Instructing the Jury on Presumptions in Civ-

Furthermore, there has been willingness on the part of the federal courts to find that certain acts of Congress create presumptions of greater vitality than that provided by Rule 301 [62] or even that certain presumptions in existence at the time of the adoption of Rule 301 are not subject to the procedure set forth in that rule.[63] On the other hand, the rule has also served as a guideline for courts wishing to give a "bursting bubble" effect to a presumption, even where the court may not necessarily believe itself bound by the dictates of Rule 301.[64]

il Actions and Proceedings, 63 Va.L.Rev. 281 (1977); Mueller, Instructing the Jury Upon Presumptions in Civil Cases: Comparing Federal Rule 301 and Uniform Rule 301, 12 Land and Water L.Rev. 219 (1977). Certainly, given the federal judge's authority to comment on the evidence, the jury may be instructed that it may infer the existence of the presumed fact from the basic facts. Louisell and Mueller go further and argue that, depending upon the nature of the presumption, the jury may be instructed either (1) that upon finding of the basic facts it should also find the presumed fact unless upon all the evidence in the case it finds that the nonexistence of the presumed fact is at least as probable as its existence; or (2) that the basic facts are strong evidence of the presumed fact. Louisell, id. at 314; Mueller, id. at 285–286. See also Widmayer v. Leonard, 422 Mich. 280, 373 N.W.2d 538, 542 (1985), for a discussion of instructions under Michigan Rule 301 which is based on Federal Rule 301. The court stated that "instructions should be phrased entirely in terms of underlying facts and burden of proof." Although no probative effect was to be given to a presumption which had been rebutted by contrary evidence, the basic facts which created the presumption might also establish a permissible inference.

See also North Carolina Rule of Evidence 301 which provides that when the burden of producing evidence to meet a presumption is satisfied, the court must instruct the jury that it may, but is not required to, infer the existence of the presumed fact from the proved fact. Alas. R.Evid. 301 is to the same effect.

See also In re Yoder Co., 758 F.2d 1114 (6th Cir.1985) where the court held that a presumption in a bankruptcy proceeding had no probative effect once rebutted.

62. E.g., Fazio v. Heckler, 760 F.2d 187 (8th Cir.1985) (Social Security Act): ACS Hospital Systems, Inc. v. Montefiore Hospital, 732 F.2d 1572 (Fed.Cir.1984) (validity of a patent); WSM, Inc. v. Hilton, 724 F.2d 1320 (8th Cir.1984); American Coal Co. v. Benefits Review Board, 738 F.2d 387 (10th Cir.1984) (Black Lung Act). See also Mul-

lins Coal Co., Inc. v. Director, Office of Workers' Compensation Programs, 484 U.S. 135 (1987) (discussing proof necessary to invoke a presumption under the Black Lung Act).

A "middle-ground" presumption has apparently been created by the Bail Reform Act of 1984. The presumption shifts not only the burden of production but also, once contrary evidence is introduced, remains as a "factor" to be considered by the magistrate or judge in determining whether an accused poses a special risk of flight before trial. E.g., United States v. Jessup, 757 F.2d 378 (1st Cir.1985); United States v. Cook, 880 F.2d 1158 (10th Cir.1989).

63. James v. River Parishes Co., Inc., 686 F.2d 1129 (5th Cir.1982). (Custodian of drifting vessel bears burden of disproving fault by a preponderance of the evidence).

64. Lovelace v. Sherwin–Williams Co., 681 F.2d 230 (4th Cir.1982) (age discrimination case; presumption sufficient to shift burden of producing evidence, but not persuasion); Reeves v. General Foods Corp., 682 F.2d 515 (5th Cir.1982) (same); Pennzoil Co. v. Federal Energy Regulatory Commission, 789 F.2d 1128 (5th Cir.1986) (Natural Gas Policy Act). See also Texas Department of Community Affairs v. Burdine, 450 U.S. 248 (1981) (Title VII; analysis of a presumption in a manner consistent with Rule 301, but without reference to that rule) and Patterson v. McLean Credit Union, 491 U.S. 164 (1989) (§ 1981 action).

The effect of presumptions in Title VII employment discrimination cases remains the subject of considerable controversy in all three branches of government. Compare Price Waterhouse v. Hopkins, 490 U.S. 228 (1989) (plaintiff proved that her gender played a motivating part in employment decision; employer bore the burden of persuasion on issue of non-discrimination) with Wards Cove Packing Co. v. Atonio, 490 U.S. 642 (1989) (where statistical evidence shows disparate impact, burden of producing evidence shifts to employer but not burden of persuasion; Court relied, in part on Fed.R.Evid. 301). Congress re-

The matter is further complicated by the fact that many of the states thus far adopting new evidence rules based upon the federal rules, have taken the approach of original Rule 301 and allocate the burden of persuasion based upon the presumption.[65] Likewise, the Revised Uniform Rules of Evidence (1974), reject the "bursting bubble" and contain a Rule 301 almost identical to the rule submitted by the Supreme Court to the Congress.[66]

(C) The Search for the Grail

Despite the best efforts of legal scholars, instead of having one rule to govern all presumptions in all proceedings, we are left in some ways in a more confusing state than that which existed prior to the adoption of the Federal Rules.[67] Neither Morgan's view that all presumptions operate to assign the burden of persuasion nor the Thayerian concept of a disappearing presumption has yet to win the day.

The problem may be inherent in the nature of the concept of a "presumption." At least one author has argued that the concept is an artificial one, an attempt to do through a legal fiction what courts should be doing directly;[68] that the term "presumption" should be eliminated from legal usage and the functions which it serves replaced by direct allocations of the burdens of proof and by judicial comment accurately describing the logical implication of certain facts.[69] In one

sponded to the *Wards Cove* case by enacting a bill intended to alter the way in which the burden of persuasion was allocated in that case. S. Bill 2104, 101st Cong (1990). The bill was vetoed by President Bush. See Weekly Compilation of Presidential Documents, October 29, 1990 at 1631. An attempted override of the veto failed in the Senate. CCH, Congressional Index, 101st Congress, at 20, 106 (1990). See also Beard, Title VII and Rule 301: An Analysis of the *Watson* and *Atonio* Decisions, 23 Akron L.Rev. 105 (1989); Belton, Causation and Burden–Shifting Doctrines in Employment Discrimination Law Revisited; Some Thoughts on *Hopkins* and *Wards Cove*, 64 Tul.L.Rev. 1359 (1990); Player, Is *Griggs* Dead? Reflecting (Fearfully) on Wards Cove Packing Co. v. Atonio, 17 Fla.St.L.Rev. 2 (1989).

65. See compilation of state adaptations of Federal Rule 301 in Weinstein & Berger, Evidence at 301–50 (1982).

66. Rev. Uniform Rule Evid. (1986) 301(a) provides:

In all actions and proceedings not otherwise provided for by statute or by these rules, a presumption imposes on the party against whom it is directed the burden of proving that the nonexistence of the presumed fact is more probable than its existence.

Several of the states adopting the Federal Rules have taken the Uniform Rule approach, see, e.g., Ark.Evid.Rule 301; Maine Evid.Rule 301; Wyoming Evid.Rule 301.

67. The problem is made even more complex by Fed.R.Evid. 302 which provides:

In civil actions and proceedings, the effect of a presumption respecting a fact which is an element of a claim or defense as to which state law supplies the rule of decision is determined in accordance with state law. See also discussion in Broun, The Unfulfillable Promise of One Rule for All Presumptions, 62 N.C.L.Rev. 697 (1984) which closely follows the points made in this section.

68. Allen, Presumptions, Inferences and Burden of Proof in Federal Civil Actions—An Anatomy of Unnecessary Ambiguities and a Proposal for Reform, 76 Nw.U.L.Rev. 892 (1982); Allen, Presumptions in Civil Actions Reconsidered, 66 Iowa L.Rev. 843 (1981). Allen proposes a revision of Rule 301 which would reflect his analysis. 72 Nw.U.L.Rev. at 907–08.

69. The late editor of this book also suggested the elimination of the concept of a presumption, at least with regard to presumptions which transfer one of the burdens of proof with regard to an element of a case. Cleary, Presuming and Pleading:

sense, the suggestion is attractive. The courts should indeed be discussing the propriety of allocating the burdens of proof, rather than the conceptual technical application of a presumption. Yet, both the term and concept of a presumption, however misunderstood, are so engrained in the law that it is difficult to imagine their early demise. Furthermore, as the author recognizes, there are instances in which the evidence introduced at the trial may be such as to give rise to a rule of law which shifts or reassigns the burdens of proof. He calls this a "conditional imperative" [70] and recognizes that in such a case the allocation of the burdens of proof cannot be made prior to trial. While the term "conditional imperative" may be just as good as "presumption," it is no better and the same set of problems which exist with regard to presumptions are just as likely to occur regardless of the label employed.

The answer may be that there is no single solution to the problem. The resistance of the courts and legislatures to a universal rule of presumptions is reflective of the fact that there are policies of varying strength behind different presumptions and therefore a hierarchy of desired results. In one instance, the policy may be such as only to give rise to a standardized inference, a rule of law which gets the plaintiff to the jury but does not compel a directed verdict in its favor. In another instance, the policy may be strong enough to compel a directed verdict in its favor, thus shifting the burden of producing evidence to the opposing party, but not strong enough to reassign the burden of persuasion. [71] In still another instance, the policy may be strong enough to reassign the burden of persuasion. [72]

Attempts to categorize presumptions according to policy considerations have been thoughtful and well-meaning. [73] Unfortunately, they have fallen short of the mark, largely because of the inherent difficulty of the task. Each presumption is created for its own reasons—reasons

An Essay on Juristic Immaturity, 12 Stan. L.Rev. 5 (1959).

70. See Allen, supra note 68, 66 Iowa L.Rev. at 850–51. Allen, however, would attempt to solve the problem of the conditional imperative by having the trial judge decide all questions of fact upon which the allocation of a burden of production or persuasion is conditioned. See Allen's proposed Rule 301, supra, note 68, 72 Nw. U.L.Rev. at 907.

71. There are, various problems which remain even when a presumption clearly falls into this category. For example: If sufficient evidence contrary to the presumed facts is introduced, should the proponent of the presumption survive a renewed motion for directed verdict? What, if anything, should the jury be told about either the existence of the presumption or the strength of the basic facts? The answers to these questions may also vary

among various presumptions and with regard to evidence introduced in each case.

72. See, for example, Green v. District of Columbia Department of Employment Services, 499 A.2d 870 (D.C.App.1985) (presumption that claimant's separation from work was involuntary); Davis v. Altmann, 492 A.2d 884 (D.C.App.1985) (presumption that bank account opened for party and another person, without consideration, is opened for convenience). The procedural effect of presumptions may even be held to depend upon the strength of the particular facts giving rise to the presumption. See, e.g., Succession of Talbot, 530 So.2d 1132 (La.1988) (facts of destruction of will in presence of another person created presumption rebuttable only by clear proof).

73. See the discussion of the original Uniform Rules of Evidence and the California Evidence Code, text accompanying nn. 53–58, supra.

which are inextricably intertwined with the pertinent substantive law. These substantive considerations have a considerable impact on the procedural effect desirable for a particular presumption. The diversity of the considerations simply defies usable categorization. The law and lawyers are accustomed to considering the dictates of the substantive law in determining the initial allocation of the burdens of proof. The task should not be thought too onerous in connection with the operation of presumptions which, after all, simply operate to reallocate those burdens during the course of the trial.

Rather than attempting to provide a single rule for all presumptions, a task which has thus far proved futile, the draftsmen of evidence codes might instead provide guidelines for the appropriate but various effects which a presumption may have on the burdens of proof.[74] The courts and legislatures would then have the opportunity to select the appropriate effect to be given to a particular presumption. The term presumption seems likely to be with us forever; it also seems likely that different presumptions will continue to be viewed as having different procedural effects; we can only hope to insure that the concept which the term "presumption" represents is applied constructively and rationally.

§ 345. Constitutional Questions in Civil Cases

Serious questions under the United States Constitution are raised by the creation and use of presumptions in criminal cases. Those questions are discussed in subsequent sections.[1] Although there are constitutional considerations involved in the use of presumptions in civil cases, the problems are simply not of the same magnitude. In a criminal case, the scales are deliberately overbalanced in favor of the defendant through the requirement that the prosecution prove each element of the offense beyond a reasonable doubt.[2] Any rule that has even the appearance of lightening that burden is viewed with the most extreme caution. However, there is no need for this special protection for any one party to a civil action. The burdens of proof are fixed at the pleading stage, not for constitutional reasons, but for reasons of probability, social policy, and convenience.[3] There is no reason why the same policy considerations, as reflected in the operation of a presumption, should not be permitted further to effect an allocation of the burdens of proof during the course of the trial.

Nevertheless, the courts articulate a "rational connection" test in civil cases, which requires that such a connection exist between the basic facts and the presumed facts in order for the presumption to pass

74. In Broun, supra note 67, the author suggests a statute that would meet this description.

§ 345

1. Sections 347–348 infra.

2. See § 341 supra with regard to the nature of the prosecution's burden; see § 347 infra with regard to the constitutional limits on the effect that a presumption may have upon that burden.

3. See § 337 supra.

constitutional muster. Recent cases have applied the test, but upheld the presumption.[4] Perhaps under certain circumstances a presumption could operate in such an arbitrary manner as to violate fundamental due process considerations, even in a civil case.[5] But to impose a strictly applied "rational connection" limitation upon the creation of presumptions in civil cases would mean that only presumptions based on probability would be permissible. Such a limitation would ignore other, equally valid, reasons for the creation of the rules. Considerations which have been either explicitly rejected or severely limited in criminal cases, such as the comparative knowledge of the parties with regard to the facts [6] and the power of the legislature to do away with a claim or a defense entirely,[7] should remain significant in determining the validity of a civil presumption.[8]

Perhaps the most difficult question with regard to civil presumptions is whether a presumption may operate to assign the burden of persuasion. The question arises from the contrast between two Supreme Court cases considering the validity of presumptions of negligence operating against railroads. In the first, Mobile, J. & K.C.R.R. v. Turnipseed,[9] decided in 1910, the Court considered a Mississippi statu-

---

4. Usery v. Turner Elkhorn Mining Co., 428 U.S. 1, 28 (1976), where the Court stated that presumptions arising under the civil statute involving "matters of economic regulation" were to be tested by a rational connection test. See also United States Steel Corp. v. Oravetz, 686 F.2d 197 (3d Cir.1982); North American Coal Corp. v. Campbell, 748 F.2d 1124 (6th Cir.1984); Alabama By–Products Corp. v. Killingsworth, 733 F.2d 1511 (11th Cir.1984) (presumptions of total disability due to pneumoconiosis).

See also United States v. Jessup, 757 F.2d 378 (1st Cir.1985), where the court upheld as constitutional a presumption under the Bail Reform Act of 1984 that a person charged with a serious drug offense will likely flee before trial. In view of the nature of the proceeding, the court saw the need for the application of a more rigorous test than that applied in *Usery*. Instead, it found that the presumption was "a reasonable congressional response to a problem of legitimate legislative concern" and that there was a "substantial basis of information underlying 'drug offender/flight conclusions.'" The Bail Reform Act in its entirety was upheld against an attack of facial invalidity in United States v. Salerno, 481 U.S. 739 (1987).

5. See the discussion in Benham v. Ledbetter, 785 F.2d 1480 (11th Cir.1986) (presumption of continuing insanity upheld against both due process and equal protection arguments; earlier opinions in the same case had found that the presumption

violated equal protection. See Benham v. Edwards, 678 F.2d 511 (5th Cir.1982), vacated and remanded 463 U.S. 1222.

6. See Morrison v. California, 291 U.S. 82, 91 (1934), discussed in § 347 note 27 infra.

7. See Ferry v. Ramsey, 277 U.S. 88 (1928), a civil action in which the Court, through Holmes, J., upheld a Kansas statute imposing liability upon bank directors who, knowing of their bank's insolvency, assented to the reception of deposits, and further providing that proof of the bank's insolvency should be prima facie evidence of the directors' knowledge and assent. Mr. Justice Holmes noted: "It is said that the liability is founded by the statute upon the directors' assent to the deposit and that when this is the ground the assent cannot be proved by artificial presumptions that have no warrant from experience. But the short answer is that the statute might have made the directors personally liable to depositors in every case, if it had been so minded, and that if it had purported to do so, whoever accepted the office would assume the risk. The statute in short imposed a liability that was less than might have been imposed, and that being so, the thing to be considered is the result reached, not the possibly inartificial [i.e. inartistic] or clumsy way of reaching it."

8. See Weinstein & Berger, Evidence ¶ 301[01]; Note, 55 Colum.L.Rev. 527, 538–39 (1955).

9. 219 U.S. 35 (1910).

tory presumption of negligence operating against a railroad in an action for death of an employee in a derailment. The statute provided that proof of injury inflicted by the running of railroad cars would be "prima facie evidence of the want of reasonable skill and care" on the part of the railroad. Noting that the only effect of the statute was to impose on the railroad the duty of producing some evidence to the contrary, the court held that the rational connection between the fact proved and the fact presumed was sufficient to sustain the presumption.

However, in 1929, in Western & Atlantic R.R. v. Henderson,[10] the Court struck down a Georgia statute making railroads liable for damage done by trains, unless the railroad made it appear that reasonable care had been used, "the presumption in all cases being against the company." In *Henderson* the plaintiff alleged that her husband had been killed in a grade crossing collision. The jury was instructed that negligence was presumed from the fact of injury and that the burden was therefore on the railroad to show that it exercised ordinary care. The Court held that the mere fact of a collision between a train and a vehicle at a crossing furnished no basis for any inference as to negligence and that therefore the presumption was invalid. *Turnipseed* was distinguished on the ground that the Mississippi presumption raised "merely a temporary inference of fact" while the Georgia statute created "an inference that is given effect of evidence to be weighed against opposing testimony and is to prevail unless such testimony is found by the jury to preponderate." [11]

Although perhaps a grade crossing collision differs from a derailment and therefore *Turnipseed* and *Henderson* can be distinguished on their facts, it is nevertheless fair to read *Henderson* as imposing constitutional limitations on the effect of at least some presumptions. However, as has been cogently pointed out,[12] *Henderson* may simply no longer be valid law. The case assumed the necessity of a showing of negligence. But the concept of negligence has lost most of its sanctity since 1929.[13] Although there is considerable doubt as to what the Court would have done in that year, there is little doubt today that a legislature would be permitted at least to relegate lack of negligence to the status of an affirmative defense. If negligence could be so reduced, a presumption which assigned the burden of persuasion could logically be treated no differently.

Since *Henderson,* the Court has, on at least one occasion, approved a state presumption that operated to fix the burden of persuasion on the party controverting the presumed fact. In that case, Dick v. New York Life Insurance Co.[14] the Court approved a North Dakota common law

10.   279 U.S. 639 (1929).

11.   Id. at 643–644.

12. See Advisory Committee's Note to Federal Rule 301 as adopted by the Supreme Court, 56 F.R.D. 208; Fornoff, Presumptions—The Proposed Federal Rules of Evidence, 24 Ark.L.Rev. 401, 412–413 (1971).

13. See Prosser & Keeton, Torts 536–538 (5th ed. 1984).

14.   359 U.S. 437 (1959).

rule that imposed on the defendant insurance company, defending against the operation of an accidental death clause, the burden of persuading the jury that the death of the insured was due to suicide.[15]

The questionable status of *Henderson* in light of recent developments in tort law, the holding of the Court in *Dick,* and the illogic of treating presumptions differently from other rules of law allocating the burden of persuasion, all make it extremely unlikely that there are now serious constitutional limits on the effect that may be given to presumptions in civil cases.[16]

§ 346. Affirmative Defenses and Presumptions in Criminal Cases: (a) Terminology

As has been earlier pointed out, the courts and legislatures do not always use the term presumption in the sense either that the term is used in this text or by the same courts and legislatures on other occasions.[1] The use of loose terminology is perhaps even more preva-

---

15. See Lavine v. Milne, 424 U.S. 577 (1976), where the Court upheld a New York statutory "rebuttable presumption" which provided that a person applying for a certain type of welfare assistance within 75 days after voluntary cessation of employment would be deemed to have quit his employment for purposes of affecting his welfare rights. The Court noted that the applicant bore the burden of persuasion with regard to all issues under the application and that therefore the "presumption" did no more than make that burden absolutely clear with regard to this issue. In the course of its decision the Court states: " * * * it is not for us to resolve the question of where the burden ought to lie on this issue. Outside the criminal law area, where special concerns attend, the locus of the burden of persuasion is normally not an issue of federal constitutional moment." Id. at 585. See also Hicks on Behalf of Feiock v. Feiock, 485 U.S. 624 (1988) (if contempt proceeding criminal, presumption shifting burden of persuasion is unconstitutional; if civil, presumption constitutionally valid).

16. The possibility of constitutional limitations on the effect of presumptions in civil cases caused the draftsman of the original Uniform Rules of Evidence (1953) to distinguish between presumptions having probative value, as to which the burden of persuasion is upon the party against whom the presumption operates, and presumptions without probative value, which disappear where contrary proof is introduced. Unif.R.Evid. (1953) 14. See Morgan, Presumptions, 10 Rutgers L.Rev. 512, 513 (1956). This distinction now seems

completely unnecessary. See the excellent discussion of this question in Note, 53 Calif.L.Rev. 1439, 1967–71 (1965).

See also the discussion in § 344, text accompanying notes 50–54, supra. The Revised Uniform Rules (1974) provide that all presumptions operate to assign the burden of persuasion. Uniform Rule 301. See § 344, text accompanying n. 65, supra.

This discussion applies only to rebuttable presumptions. Conclusive presumptions are really statements of substantive law (see § 342 supra) and, if not necessarily or universally true in part, may be fundamentally unfair and therefore unconstitutional. E.g., Cleveland Board of Education v. La-Fleur, 414 U.S. 632 (1974) (conclusive presumption that teacher who is 4 or 5 months pregnant is physically incapable of continuing her duties held unconstitutional); Michael H. v. Gerald D., 491 U.S. 110 (1989) (justices split on whether California conclusive presumption of legitimacy of child born during cohabitation of husband and wife could constitutionally preclude natural father from asserting paternal rights).

§ 346

1. See § 342, text accompanying note 2. The converse of the proposition stated in the text is also true: rules that are treated as presumptions are not always called by that name. For an illustration of the use and misuse of terminology in this area of the law see the list of statutes "that provide that proof of specified facts has a procedural effect" contained in the Work-

lent in dealing with presumptions operating in criminal cases than in civil cases. The best example is one that has already been given. The "presumption of innocence" is not a presumption at all, but simply another way of stating the rule that the prosecution has the burden of proving the guilt of the accused beyond a reasonable doubt.[2]

Similarly, the courts and writers have struggled to define and distinguish presumptions and affirmative defenses.[3] Certainly, these procedural devices have factors in common. Yet, as the devices are traditionally defined, there are some significant variations between them that have caused the courts to treat them differently.

1. Affirmative defenses. The term affirmative defense is traditionally used to describe the allocation of a burden, either of production or of persuasion, or both, to the defendant in a criminal case.[4] The burden is fixed by statute or case law at the beginning of the case and does not depend upon the introduction of any evidence by the prosecution. For example, a crime may be statutorily defined as consisting of elements A and B. However, the accused may be exonerated or the offense reduced in degree upon proof of C. C is an affirmative defense. In some instances, the defendant may simply have the burden of production of evidence with regard to C; in the event that burden is satisfied, the prosecution will then have the burden of persuading the jury of elements A, B, *and* C beyond a reasonable doubt. In other instances, the defendant will have both the burden of production and the burden of persuasion.[5] Thus, the prosecution will have no burden with regard to C; the defendant must both introduce proof of C and persuade the jury of its existence. Usually, the measure of persuasion imposed on the defendant with regard to an affirmative defense is a preponderance of the evidence.[6]

2. Presumptions. Presumptions have already been defined as a standardized practice under which certain facts are held to call for uniform treatment with respect to their effect as proof of other facts.[7] In civil cases, the term presumption is properly reserved for a rule that

---

ing Papers of the National Commission on Reform of Federal Criminal Laws, Volume 1, at 27–31 (1970).

2. See § 342 supra.

3. See Allen, Structuring Jury Decision–Making in Criminal Cases: A Unified Constitutional Approach to Evidentiary Devices, 94 Harv.L.Rev. 321 (1980); Ashford & Rissinger, Presumptions, Assumptions, and Due Process in Criminal Cases: A Theoretical Overview, 79 Yale L.J. 165 (1969); Jeffries & Stephan, Defenses, Presumptions and Burden of Proof in the Criminal Law, 88 Yale L.J. 1325 (1979).

4. 9 Wigmore, Evidence §§ 2501, 2512, 2514 (Chadbourn rev. 1981); 22A C.J.S. Criminal Law §§ 572–577; Dec.Dig. Criminal Law ⊕329–333.

5. A New Federal Criminal Code, proposed in 1971 but not enacted by the Congress, divided what have been referred to generally as affirmative defenses into (1) defenses, which need not be negated by the prosecution unless "the issue is in the case as a result of evidence sufficient to raise a reasonable doubt on the issue," and (2) affirmative defenses, which must be proved by the defendant by a preponderance of the evidence. Proposed Federal Criminal Code § 103. Final Report of the National Commission on Reform of Federal Criminal Cases 3 (1971).

6. Patterson v. New York, 432 U.S. 197 (1977); State v. McCauley, 130 W.Va. 401, 43 S.E.2d 454 (1947).

7. Section 342 supra.

provides that upon proof of certain basic facts, at least the burden of producing evidence with regard to certain presumed facts shifts. As has been discussed, a presumption may in some instances operate to allocate the burden of persuasion as well.[8]

A somewhat different terminology has been used more or less consistently in criminal cases. The tendency in criminal cases has been to describe any standardized rule which permits the inference of one fact from another as a presumption, regardless of whether the rule operates to shift the burden of production. Thus, assume a crime with three elements, A, B and C. A rule of law provides that fact C may be inferred from proof of A and B. Such a rule is usually described as a presumption, whether or not any burden is actually shifted to the defendant. In most instances, no burden shifts; the presumption operates only to permit the prosecution to make out a prima facie case by proof of A and B alone. The jury will be instructed that it may, but is not required to, infer the existence of fact C from proof of facts A and B.

The United States Supreme Court has resurrected terminology used in the first edition of this text[9] to describe the different effects of presumptions in criminal cases. In County Court of Ulster County v. Allen,[10] the court distinguished between mandatory and permissive presumptions. A mandatory presumption is one which operates to shift at least the burden of production. It tells the trier of fact that it must find the presumed fact upon proof of the basic fact, "at least unless the defendant has come forward with some evidence to rebut the presumed connection between the two facts."[11] The Court further subdivided mandatory presumptions into two parts: presumptions that merely shift the burden of production to the defendant and presumptions that shift the burden of persuasion. A permissive presumption is one which allows, but does not require, the trier of fact to infer the presumed fact from proof of the basic facts. Under the *Allen* decision, these various kinds of presumptions differ not only procedurally, but also with regard to the tests for their constitutional permissibility as well.

§ 347. Affirmative Defenses and Presumptions in Criminal Cases: (b) Constitutionality

Recent years have brought some noteable developments with regard to the constitutionality of both affirmative defenses and presumptions.

1. Affirmative defenses. Historically, many states placed both the burden of production and the burden of persuasion on the accused with regard to several classical affirmative defenses, including insanity[1] and

8. Section 344 supra.
9. Section 308.
10. 442 U.S. 140 (1979).
11. Id. at 157.

§ 347

1. Leland v. Oregon, 343 U.S. 790 (1952), rehearing denied 344 U.S. 848; State v. Finn, 257 Minn. 138, 100 N.W.2d

self-defense.[2] The allocation to the defendant of the burdens of proof with regard to insanity survived constitutional challenge in 1952. In Leland v. Oregon,[3] the Supreme Court held that the defendant could be required to prove his insanity at the time of the alleged crime beyond a reasonable doubt. On the other hand, some limitations were imposed on the creation or effect of affirmative defenses. For example, one United States Court of Appeals held unconstitutional a state's allocation of the burden of persuasion to the accused with regard to alibi.[4] The court reasoned that an alibi was a mere form of denial of participation in the criminal act, not a true affirmative defense.

Although perhaps foreshadowed by the treatment given the defense of alibi, the real revolution in thought with regard to affirmative defenses occurred in the mid–1970's with two pivotal Supreme Court decisions.

In Mullaney v. Wilbur,[5] the Court reversed a Maine murder conviction where the jury had been instructed, in accordance with longstanding state practice, that if the prosecution proved "that the homicide was both intentional and unlawful, malice aforethought was to be conclusively implied unless the defendant proved by a fair preponderance of the evidence that he acted in the heat of passion on sudden provocation," in which event the defendant would be guilty only of manslaughter. The placing of this burden on the defendant was said to violate the dictates of In re Winship[6] that the due process clause requires the prosecution to prove beyond a reasonable doubt every fact necessary to constitute the crime charged. Although recognizing that under Maine law murder and manslaughter were but degrees of the same crime, the Court noted that *Winship* applied to instances in which the issue is degree of criminal culpability as well as to cases of guilt or innocence.[7]

The *Mullaney* case was surprising in view of the long history in some jurisdictions of placing the burden of reducing the degree of a homicide on the defendant.[8] However, given the holding and rationale of *Winship*, it was not totally unexpected. It was certainly possible, and

508 (1960). See also, cases in C.J.S. Homicide § 194.

2. Brown v. State, 48 Del. (9 Terry) 427, 105 A.2d 646 (1954); see also C.J.S. Homicide § 195.

3. Supra note 1.

4. Stump v. Bennett, 398 F.2d 111 (8th Cir.1968), cert. denied 393 U.S. 1001, striking down an Iowa practice, which Iowa discontinued. State v. Galloway, 167 N.W.2d 89 (Iowa 1969), appeal after remand 187 N.W.2d 725. See also, Commonwealth v. McLeod, 367 Mass. 500, 326 N.E.2d 905 (1975).

5. 421 U.S. 684, 686 (1975).

6. 397 U.S. 358 (1970), conformed to 27 N.Y.2d 728, 314 N.Y.S.2d 536, 262 N.E.2d

675. See discussion in text accompanying note 6, § 341 *supra.*

7. In *Winship,* the Court referred to the immensely important interests of the accused in a criminal case arising from both the possibility of loss of personal liberty and the stigma attached to conviction. In re Winship supra note 6, at 363–64. In *Mullaney,* the Court noted that the consequences of a verdict of murder differed significantly from that of manslaughter, both in terms of loss of liberty and in the stigma attached to the conviction. Mullaney v. Wilbur, supra note 5 at 697–98.

8. See, e.g., State v. Boyd, 278 N.C. 682, 180 S.E.2d 794 (1971). See also, LaFave & Scott, Handbook of Criminal Law 612–616 (2d ed. 1986).

perhaps fair, to read the *Mullaney* case broadly so as to require the imposition of the burden of persuasion on the prosecution with regard to many, if not all, of the traditional affirmative defenses.[9] Indeed, the opinion was read by several state courts as constitutionally compelling the prosecution to bear the burden of persuasion with regard to various affirmative defenses.[10] Only the existence of the *Leland*[11] opinion, not expressly overruled in *Mullaney*, prevented one federal court from applying *Mullaney* to impose upon a state the burden of persuasion with regard to an insanity defense.[12]

The first real indication that the holding in *Mullaney* had far more narrow limits came when the Court, in Rivera v. Delaware,[13] dismissed, as not presenting a substantial federal question, an appeal from a conviction in which the defendant had borne the burden of proving his insanity. The indication became a certainty when the Court decided Patterson v. New York.[14] In *Patterson*, the Court upheld a New York procedure under which an accused is guilty of murder in the second degree if he is found, beyond a reasonable doubt, to have intentionally killed another person. The crime may be reduced to manslaughter if the defendant proves by a preponderance of the evidence that he had acted under the influence of "extreme emotional disturbance." The Court held that the New York procedure did not violate due process noting, in the language of *Winship*, " 'every fact necessary to constitute the crime with which [Patterson was] charged had to be proved beyond a reasonable doubt.' "[15] *Mullaney* was distinguished as dealing with a situation in which the defendant was asked to disprove an essential element of the prosecution's case—malice aforethought.[16] New York, unlike Maine, did not include malice aforethought in its definition of murder. By this omission, New York had avoided the defect found fatal in *Mullaney*, even though the defense involved in the *Patterson* case was but an expanded version of the "heat of passion on sudden provocation" involved in *Mullaney*.

The Court in *Patterson* decided the constitutionality of the allocation of the burden of proof by a formalistic analysis of state law: due process was not violated because the defendant did not have the burden of proof on any fact that state law had identified as an element of the offense.

9. Comments, 36 Ohio St.L.J. 828 (1975), 11 Harv.C.R.–C.L.L.Rev. 390 (1976).

10. Commonwealth v. Rodriguez, 370 Mass. 684, 352 N.E.2d 203 (1976) (self-defense); State v. Matheson, 363 A.2d 716 (Me.1976) (entrapment). The broadest interpretation of *Mullaney* was in Evans v. State, 28 Md.App. 640, 349 A.2d 300, 307 (1975), affirmed 278 Md. 197, 362 A.2d 629, where the court stated that *Mullaney* applied to prohibit the placing of the burden of persuasion on the defendant with regard to "a. Any theory of justification * * * b. Any theory of excuse * * * c. Any theory

of mitigation * * * d. Intoxication, e. Entrapment, f. Duress or Coercion, g. Necessity."

11. Supra, notes 1 and 3.

12. Buzynski v. Oliver, 538 F.2d 6 (1st Cir.1976), cert. denied 429 U.S. 984.

13. 429 U.S. 877 (1976).

14. 432 U.S. 197 (1977). In *Patterson*, the Court indicated that, in dismissing *Rivera* it meant to confirm the continuing validity of *Leland*. Id. at 204.

15. Id. at 206.

16. Id. at 215.

Despite significant and persistent criticism,[17] the durability of this approach was confirmed ten years later in Martin v. Ohio[18]. In *Martin*, Ohio had defined the crime of murder as purposely causing the death of another with prior calculation or design and placed the burden of proving self-defense on the defendant. The Court upheld the conviction because the defendant did not have the burden of proving any of the elements included by the state in its definition of the crime. The dictates of *Winship* were not violated so long as the instructions to the jury made it clear that State had the burden of proving all of the elements—including prior calculation and design—beyond a reasonable doubt, and that the self-defense evidence could also be considered in determining whether there was reasonable doubt about any element of the State's case.[19]

The lower courts have, of course, followed the pattern of *Patterson* and *Martin*, holding invalid allocations of the burden of persuasion thought to involve nothing more than the rebuttal of an element of the offense[20] and sanctioning allocations where the jury has been instructed that the affirmative defense is held to come into play only after the state has proven the elements of the crime beyond a reasonable doubt.[21]

The analysis in *Patterson* and *Martin* deals only with the allocation of the burden of persuasion. As suggested by dicta in *Patterson*[22], the courts have had no trouble with an affirmative defense which simply requires the defendant to bear a burden of production.[23] For example, even though a state includes absence of self-defense as an element of a

17. Allen, Structuring Jury Decision–Making in Criminal Cases: A Unified Constitutional Approach to Evidentiary Devices, 94 Harv.L.Rev. 321 (1980); Jeffries & Stephan, Defenses, Presumptions and Burden of Proof in the Criminal Law, 88 Yale L.J. 1325 (1979); See also Cole v. Stevenson, 620 F.2d 1055, 1063–1066 (4th Cir. 1980), cert. denied 449 U.S. 1004 (dissent by Murnaghan, J.) For more recent criticism see Sundby, The Reasonable Doubt Rule and the Meaning of Innocence, 40 Hastings L.J. 457 (1989).

18. 480 U.S. 228 (1987). See also McMillan v. Pennsylvania, 477 U.S. 79 (1986) (state may provide that sentencing enhancing considerations, such as whether an individual "visibly possessed a firearm," which are not elements of the offense, to be proved by a preponderance of the evidence rather than beyond a reasonable doubt.)

19. 480 U.S. at 234. See Humanik v. Beyer, 871 F.2d 432 (3d Cir.1989), cert. denied 493 U.S. 812 for a thorough discussion of this aspect of *Martin*.

20. See, e.g., Humanik v. Beyer, supra n. 19 (New Jersey diminished capacity law); United States v. Lesina, 833 F.2d 156 (9th Cir.1987) (federal murder law; heat of

passion defense); United States v. Lofton, 776 F.2d 918 (10th Cir.1985) (same).

21. Rodriguez v. Scully, 788 F.2d 62 (2d Cir.1986) (duress); Farrell v. Czarnetzky, 566 F.2d 381 (2d Cir.1977), cert. denied 434 U.S. 1077 (weapon not loaded); Smart v. Leeke, 873 F.2d 1558 (4th Cir. en banc, 1989), cert. denied 493 U.S. 867 (self-defense); United States ex rel. Goddard v. Vaughn, 614 F.2d 929 (3d Cir.1980), cert. denied 449 U.S. 844 (voluntary intoxication); People v. Drew, 22 Cal.3d 333, 149 Cal.Rptr. 275, 583 P.2d 1318 (en banc 1978) (insanity); State v. James, 393 N.W.2d 465 (Iowa 1986), appeal dismissed 481 U.S. 1009 (insanity; valid under both federal and state constitutions).

22. Supra n. 14 at 230.

23. See discussion in Jeffries & Stephan, supra n. 16 at 1334. The placing of a burden of production on the defendant with regard to duress and necessity was approved by the Supreme Court in United States v. Bailey, 444 U.S. 394 (1980). See also Rook v. Rice, 783 F.2d 401 (4th Cir. 1986), cert. denied 478 U.S. 1022 and Davis v. Allsbrooks, 778 F.2d 168 (4th Cir.1985) (shift of burden of production with regard to heat of passion or self-defense).

crime so as to prohibit the allocation of the burden of persuasion to the accused, the accused may be required to introduce at least some evidence of self-defense in order for the issue to go the jury.[24]

2. *Presumptions.*

Like affirmative defenses, the Supreme Court's analysis of the constitutionality of presumptions has evolved significantly in recent years. The 1979 decisions in County Court of Ulster County v. Allen [25] and Sandstrom v. Montana [26], constitute the watershed in the Court's analysis of the issue.

Prior to *Allen* and *Sandstrom,* the Court had set limitations on the creation and application of presumptions in criminal cases in a series of cases beginning with Tot v. United States.[27] In *Tot,* the Court invalidated a presumption contained in a federal firearms statute stating that possession of a firearm was presumptive evidence that the weapon was received in interstate commerce. The Court stated that "a statutory presumption cannot be sustained if there be no rational connection between the fact proved and the ultimate fact presumed, if the inference of the one from proof of the other is arbitrary because of lack of connection between the two in common experience." [28]

Tot was followed by two 1965 cases dealing with presumptions enacted to aid the government in prosecuting liquor cases. In United States v. Gainey,[29] the Court applied the rational connection test of *Tot* to uphold the validity of a statute which provided that presence at the site is sufficient to convict a defendant of the offense of carrying on the business of distilling without giving bond, "unless the defendant explains such presence to the satisfaction of the jury." However, in United States v. Romano,[30] the Court struck down as violative of *Tot* an identical presumption with regard to the companion offense of possession of an illegal still. The Court distinguished *Gainey,* noting that the crime of *carrying on* an illegal distilling business, involved in *Gainey,* was an extremely broad one. A person's unexplained presence at the still made it highly likely that he had something to do with its operation. However, no such natural inference existed with regard to the presumption of *possession* from unexplained presence involved in *Romano.*[31]

Tot, Gainey and *Romano* left several questions unanswered. Most significantly, the "rational connection" test was vague. Was it a test of relevancy or a test of probative sufficiency? If it was a test of sufficiency, the existence of the presumed fact would have to be shown to be more likely than not to exist or perhaps even have to be shown to exist beyond a reasonable doubt.

24. State v. Patterson, 297 N.C. 247, 254 S.E.2d 604 (1979).

25. 442 U.S. 140 (1979).

26. 442 U.S. 510 (1979).

27. 319 U.S. 463 (1943).

28. Id. at 467.

29. 380 U.S. 63 (1965).

30. 382 U.S. 136 (1965).

31. Id. at 141.

The question was partially answered in 1969 and 1970 by two cases involving presumptions in narcotics prosecutions. In Leary v. United States,[32] the Court considered a presumption providing that possession of marihuana was sufficient evidence to authorize conviction of transporting and concealing the drug *with knowledge of its illegal importation* unless the defendant explained his possession to the satisfaction of the jury. The Court held that the presumption of knowledge was unconstitutional, stating:

"The upshot of *Tot, Gainey* and *Romano* is, we think, that a criminal statutory presumption must be regarded as 'irrational' or 'arbitrary,'" and hence unconstitutional, unless it can be said with substantial assurance that the presumed fact is more likely than not to flow from the proved fact on which it is made to depend * * *."[33]

In a footnote to this statement, the Court added that because of its finding that the presumption was unconstitutional under this standard, it would not reach the question "whether a criminal presumption which passes muster when so judged must also satisfy the criminal 'reasonable doubt' standard if proof of the crime charged or an essential element thereof depends upon its use."[34]

The next year, the Court dealt with two presumptions in Turner v. United States.[35] One was identical with the presumption struck down in *Leary,* except that the drugs involved in *Turner* were heroin and cocaine rather than marihuana. The other provided that the absence of appropriate tax paid stamps from narcotic drugs found in the defendant's possession would be "prima facie evidence" that he purchased or distributed the drugs from other than the original stamped package. The Court extensively reviewed the legislative records with regard to the statutes and surveyed the records of other narcotics cases for evidence to support or rebut the inferences called for by the statutes. It concluded that the "overwhelming evidence" was that the heroin consumed in the United States is illegally imported and that Turner therefore must have known this fact.[36] Based upon this conclusion, the Court upheld the presumptions of illegal importation and "stamped package" as to heroin. In contrast, the Court struck down the same presumptions with regard to cocaine, finding that it could not be "sufficiently sure either that the cocaine that Turner possessed came from abroad or that Turner must have known that it did," and that there was "a reasonable possibility" that Turner had in fact obtained the cocaine from a legally stamped package.

In *Turner,* the Court again found it unnecessary specifically to adopt a test that would require that the presumed fact be shown to exist beyond a reasonable doubt. However, the Court's frequent reference to

32. 395 U.S. 6 (1969) (opinion by Harlan, J.).

33. Id. at 36.

34. Id. at 36 n. 64.

35. 396 U.S. 398 (1970). For a relatively contemporaneous discussion of *Turner,*

see Christie & Pye, Presumptions and Assumptions in the Criminal Law: Another View, 1970 Duke L.J. 919.

36. Id. at 415–416.

that standard in *Turner*, [37] coupled with its decision in In re Winship [38] recognizing that such a measure of proof is constitutionally required in criminal cases, seemed to make it likely that the reasonable doubt standard would be applied to test the validity of presumptions.[39]

Not long after *Turner*, the Court applied the rationale of the cases involving statutory presumptions to a common law presumption. In Barnes v. United States,[40] the Court upheld a conviction for possession of stolen treasury checks in which the jury had been instructed in accordance with the traditional common law inference that the knowledge necessary for conviction may be drawn from the unexplained possession of recently stolen goods. The Court still refrained from adopting either a more-likely-than-not or a reasonable doubt standard in its review of the presumption, but held rather that the presumption in question satisfied both. The only question that seem to remain after *Barnes* whether the Court ultimately would require that all presumptions be tested by a reasonable doubt standard. Surprisingly, a whole new set of considerations arrived in 1979.

The New York prosecution in County Court of Ulster County v. Allen [41] was for illegal possession of, inter alia, handguns.[42] Four persons, three adult males and a 16–year–old girl, were tried jointly. The evidence showed that two large-caliber handguns were seen in the front of the car in an open handbag belonging to the 16–year–old. A New York statute provided that, with certain exceptions, the presence of a firearm in an automobile was presumptive evidence of its illegal possession by all persons then occupying the vehicle. The jury was instructed with regard to the presumption but told that the presumption "need not be rebutted by affirmative proof or affirmative evidence but may be rebutted by any evidence or lack of evidence in the case." [43]

The federal Court of Appeals affirmed the District Court's grant of habeas corpus, holding that the New York statute was unconstitutional

---

37. For example, the Court stated:

"* * * To possess heroin is to possess imported heroin. Whether judged by the more-likely-than-not standard applied in Leary v. United States, supra, or by the more exacting reasonable-doubt standard normally applicable in criminal cases, § 174 is valid insofar as it permits a jury to infer that heroin possessed in this country is a smuggled drug * * *." Id. at 416.

38. 397 U.S. 358 (1970). See § 341 supra at n. 6.

39. See Christie & Pye, supra note 35 at 923 n. 24. In its apparent adoption of the reasonable doubt standard, the Court did not recognize the argument put forth by some writers that in order for a presumption to be valid, not only must there be a high probability of correlation between the fact proved and the fact presumed, but

there must also be a high probability that the accused can rebut the presumption. See Ashford & Risinger, Presumptions, Assumptions and Due Process in Criminal Cases: A Theoretical Overview, 79 Yale L.J. 165 (1969); Note, 53 Va.L.Rev. 702, 735 (1967). For a criticism of this approach see Christie & Pye, supra, at 926–933. See also Abrams, Statutory Presumptions and the Federal Criminal Law: A Suggested Analysis, 22 Vand.L.Rev. 1135, 1145–46 (1969).

40. 412 U.S. 837 (1973).

41. 442 U.S. 140 (1979).

42. The defendants were also charged with the possession of a machinegun and heroin found in the trunk of the car. The jury acquitted all four defendants on these charges. Id. at 144.

43. Id. at 161 n. 20.

on its face because it swept within its compass many individuals who would in fact have no connection with a weapon even though they were present in a vehicle in which the weapon was found.[44]

The Supreme Court reversed, stating that the Court of Appeals had improperly viewed the statute on its face. The Court stated that the ultimate test of any device's constitutional validity is that it not undermine the factfinder's responsibility at trial, based on evidence adduced by the state, to find the ultimate facts beyond a reasonable doubt. Therefore, mandatory and permissive presumptions must be analyzed differently.[45] It is appropriate to analyze mandatory presumptions on their face. Where a mandatory presumption is used, the defendant may be convicted based upon the presumption alone as the result of the failure of the accused to introduce proof to the contrary. The Court reasoned that in such an instance the presumption would be unconstitutional unless the basic facts, standing alone, are sufficient to support the inference of guilt beyond a reasonable doubt.[46] In the case of a permissive presumption the jury is told only that it may, but need not, find the defendant guilty based upon the basic facts. Thus, the validity of the presumption must be tested, not in the abstract, but rather in connection with all of the evidence in the case. The Court stated:

> "Because this permissive presumption leaves the trier of fact free to credit or reject the inference and does not shift the burden of proof, it affects the application of the 'beyond a reasonable doubt' standard only if, under the facts of the case, there is no rational way the trier could make the connection permitted by the inference. For only in that situation is there any risk that an explanation of the permissible inference to a jury, or its use by a jury, has caused the presumptively rational factfinder to make an erroneous factual determination."[47]

The Court found that the instruction in *Allen* created a permissive, not a mandatory, presumption. The Court considered all of the evidence in the case and found a rational basis for a finding of guilty beyond a reasonable doubt, noting that the jury could have reasonably rejected the suggestion advanced on appeal by the adult defendants that the handguns were solely in the possession of the 16–year–old.[48]

In Sandstrom v. Montana,[49] the defendant was charged with deliberate homicide, which under Montana law would consist of purposely and

44. Allen v. County Court, 568 F.2d 998 (2d Cir.1977).

45. The Court in *Allen* revisited the jury instructions given in earlier Supreme Court cases concerning presumptions. Although the earlier decisions had spent no time whatsoever making such distinctions, the Court in *Allen* analyzed the presumptions upheld in earlier cases as permissive, while noting that the presumptions struck down had been mandatory. County Court of Ulster County v. Allen, supra note 41 at 157–159, nn. 16–17.

46. Id. at 167.

47. Id. at 157. The dissenting opinion in *Allen*, written by Justice Powell and joined by Justices Brennan, Marshall and Stewart rejected the majority's heavy reliance on the distinction between mandatory and permissive presumptions, noting that presumptions, even if permissive, pose dangers. " * * * [T]o be constitutional a presumption must be at least more likely than not true." 442 U.S. at 172.

48. Id. at 164.

49. 442 U.S. 510 (1979).

knowingly causing the death of another. Defendant claimed that the degree of the offense should be reduced in that he suffered from a personality disorder aggravated by alcohol consumption. The jury was instructed in accordance with Montana law that the "law presumes that a person intends the ordinary consequences of his voluntary acts." [50] Defendant was convicted and his conviction was upheld by the Montana Supreme Court. The United States Supreme Court reversed, holding that the jury could have interpreted the instruction with regard to the presumption of intention of the ordinary consequences of voluntary acts as creating either a conclusive presumption or shifting the burden of persuasion with regard to the question of intent to the defendant. Citing *Mullaney* and *Patterson* as well as *Ulster,* the Court found that such a shift of the burden would be constitutionally impermissible. The fact that the jury could have interpreted the instruction either as permissive or as shifting only the burden of production did not matter so long as the instruction could also have been interpreted as imposing heavier burdens on the defendant.

Several years later, in Francis v. Franklin,[51] the Court held that an instruction in a Georgia homicide prosecution, stating that the "acts of a person of sound mind and discretion are presumed to be the product of a person's will, but the presumption may be rebutted," violated *Sandstrom.* The Court held that the instructions had created the kind of mandatory presumption prohibited by *Sandstrom,* even though Georgia had interpreted such language as amounting to no more than a permissive inference. The fact that the presumption was expressly made rebuttable was not controlling so long as the jury could have interpreted the instruction as shifting the burden of persuasion to the accused.[52]

The upshot of all of these cases seems to be as follows: Presumptions in criminal cases will be divided into mandatory and permissive presumptions. A permissive presumption is one that will permit the jury to find the presumed facts, but neither compels the acceptance of such facts nor allocates a burden of persuasion to the defendant with regard to those facts. Regardless of how the state characterizes the presumption, the courts will analyze the jury instructions to determine their possible effect on the jury. A permissive presumption will be constitutionally acceptable if, considering all of the evidence in the case, there is a rational connection between the basic facts proved by the prosecu-

---

50. Id. at 513.

51. 471 U.S. 307 (1985).

52. Later Supreme Court cases set additional parameters for the application of *Sandstrom* and *Allen.* In Rose v. Clark, 478 U.S. 570 (1986), the Court held that, even though an instruction unconstitutionally allocates a burden of persuasion under *Sandstrom* or *Franklin,* a conviction should not be set aside if the reviewing court may confidently say, on the whole record, that the constitutional error was harmless beyond a reasonable doubt. In Yates v. Aiken, 484 U.S. 211 (1988), the Court applied the rule in the *Francis* case to reverse a South Carolina conviction that had occurred prior to *Francis.* The Court reasoned that *Francis* was merely an application of the principle of *Sandstrom,* which had been decided before the defendant's conviction. In Carella v. California, 491 U.S. 263 (1989), the Court voided California presumptions of intent from the failure to return rented property.

tion and the ultimate fact presumed, and the latter is more likely than not to flow from the former. A mandatory presumption is one that shifts the burden of production or persuasion to the defendant. Although the Supreme Court has not specifically so held, dictum in *Allen* [53] and the holdings of lower court decisions [54] seem to make it clear that a presumption that clearly shifts nothing other than the burden of production will be scrutinized in the same way as a permissive presumption and pass constitutional muster if it meets a rational connection test. Could a presumption that shifts the burden of persuasion be created? The Court in *Allen* suggests the possibility that such a presumption could be constitutional if a rational juror could find the presumed fact beyond a reasonable doubt from the basic facts. Some authors have suggested that such a presumption may not constitutionally exist after *Allen* and *Sandstrom*. [55] The courts have not had occasion to rule on the question. Certainly, the test suggested in *Allen* is a stiff one.

§ 348. Affirmative Defenses and Presumptions in Criminal Cases: (c) Special Problems

Not surprisingly, several questions remain from the active constitutional development in this area of the law.

1. The creation of affirmative defenses. The *Patterson* case tied the question of the constitutionality of affirmative defenses directly to the formalistic notion that a true affirmative defense is one that does not simply go to negative an element of the offense. The question remains as to when something is an element of an offense. Many cases have looked only to the language of the statute [1] although some have considered how the statute has been interpreted by the state courts. [2]

Can the state create an affirmative defense simply by carefully excluding it from the elements of the offense? The answer to this question seems to be a qualified yes. In *Patterson*, the Court suggested

53. County Court of Ulster County v. Allen, supra n. 41 at 158, n. 16. The Court in Francis v. Franklin, supra n. 51, noted that it was not expressing an opinion of the constitutionality of presumptions that shifted only the burden of production to the defendant. 471 U.S. at 314, n. 3.

54. See, e.g., McCandless v. Beyer, 835 F.2d 58 (3d Cir.1987); Rook v. Rice, 783 F.2d 401 (4th Cir.1986), cert. denied 478 U.S. 1022; Davis v. Allsbrooks, 778 F.2d 168 (4th Cir.1985). But see Burke, The Tension Between *In Re Winship* and the Use of Presumptions in Jury Instructions After *Sandstrom, Allen* and *Clark*, 17 N.Mex.L.Rev. 55, 68–71 (1987).

55. See Allen & DeGrazia, The Constitutional Requirement of Proof Beyond Reasonable Doubt in Criminal Cases: A Comment Upon Incipient Chaos in the Lower

Courts, 20 Amer.Crim.L.Rev. 1, 12 (1982); Graham, Presumptions—More Than You Wanted to Know and Yet Were Too Disinterested to Ask, 17 Crim.L.Bull. 431, n. 439 (1981).

§ 348

1. Farrell v. Czarnetzky, 566 F.2d 381 (2d Cir.1977). cert. denied 434 U.S. 1077.

2. Berrier v. Egeler, 583 F.2d 515 (6th Cir.1978), cert. denied 439 U.S. 955; Holloway v. McElroy, 632 F.2d 605 (5th Cir. 1980), cert. denied 451 U.S. 1028. In dissent from the denial of certiorari in *Holloway*, Justice Rehnquist stated that, in his view, the state should be permitted to label as an affirmative defense that which could otherwise be considered an element of a crime. 451 U.S. at 1028.

that there were constitutional limitations on the creation of affirmative defenses.[3] Those limits may depend upon whether the state may, under the U.S. Constitution, punish the activity without reference to the affirmative defense. For example, assume an offense which has consisted of the elements A, B, C, all of which had to be proved by the prosecution beyond a reasonable doubt. The legislature carefully amends the statute covering the offense so as to make the elements of the offense A and B only, but provides that the accused may be exonerated if the defense proves C by a preponderance of the evidence. Such a new statute would be constitutional if the state may, consistent with the Eighth Amendment and substantive due process, punish the individual to the extent provided by the statute based upon proof of A and B only.

Such an analysis has suggested another, less formalistic, approach to the treatment of affirmative defenses to some legal scholars. Under this approach, if the state can constitutionally exclude an element from an offense, it can require the defendant to bear the burden of persuasion with regard to that element. In other words, in the above example, if the state could exclude C from the definition of the crime, it could make the accused prove C, whether or not C is formally removed as an element of the offense.[4] Other scholars have rejected an Eighth Amendment approach entirely and have proposed tests that would more severely limit the state's options in the creation of affirmative defenses.[5]

As yet, no court has struck down an affirmative defense because the Eighth Amendment prohibited punishment based only upon the elements assigned to the definition of the offense. Indeed, the Eighth Amendment and related concepts of substantive due process have not proved to be an effective check on legislative decisions with regard to punishment.[6] Moreover, no court has used an alternative approach suggested in the law journals to limit the creation of affirmative defenses. Instead, the courts have relied upon the safer, formalistic notions of *Patterson*.

3. Patterson v. New York, 432 U.S. 197, 210 (1977).

4. See the excellent articulations of essentially this theory in Allen, Structuring Jury Decisionmaking in Criminal Cases: A Unified Constitutional Approach to Evidentiary Devices, 94 Harv.L.Rev. 321 (1980); Allen, More on Constitutional Process-of-Proof Problems in Criminal Cases, 94 Harv.L.Rev. 1795 (1981); Jeffries & Stephan, Defenses, Presumptions and Burden of Proof in the Criminal Law, 88 Yale L.J. 1325 (1979). Others have dissented from the analysis. Nesson, Rationality, Presumptions and Judicial Comment: A Response to Professor Allen, 94 Harv.L.Rev. 1574 (1981). See also, Underwood, The Thumb on the Scales of Justice: Burdens of Persuasion in Criminal Cases, 86 Yale L.J. 1299 (1977) where the author takes issue with similar approaches advocated by Professor Allen in earlier articles.

5. See Sundby, The Reasonable Doubt Rule and the Meaning of Innocence, 40 Hastings L.Rev. 457 (1989); Schwartz, "Innocence"—A Dialogue with Professor Sundby, 41 Hastings L.J. 153 (1989); Sundby, The Virtues of a Procedural View of Innocence—A Response to Professor Schwartz, 41 Hastings L.Rev. 161 (1989).

6. See Rummel v. Estelle, 445 U.S. 263 (1980), and discussion in Nesson, supra, note 4 at 1580–1581.

One possible approach to assessing the validity of affirmative defenses that is neither inconsistent with case law nor directly tied to the Eighth Amendment was suggested by Justice Powell in his dissent in *Patterson.* Powell suggested that the prosecution be required to prove beyond a reasonable doubt at least those factors which "in the Anglo-American legal tradition" had made a difference in punishment or stigma.[7] Although troublesome if taken to its logical extent,[8] the notion that we should consider historical factors has merit. At the very least, it would be appropriate for a court in assessing the validity of the creation of an affirmative defense to take into account not only the statutory language and judicial statements of the elements of the offense, but also the nature of the burden traditionally borne by the state with regard to the same or analogous factors.

2. Affirmative defenses or presumptions? Despite the differences between affirmative defenses and presumptions as the terms are used by the courts and legal scholars, the impact of these procedural devices on the accused can be identical. Thus, in one state, the accused may have the burden of producing evidence that she acted in self-defense—an affirmative defense. In another jurisdiction, the law may provide that, once the state has proved that the defendant intentionally killed the deceased, there is a presumption of unlawfulness that requires the defendant to introduce evidence with regard to self-defense, although the ultimate burden of persuasion remains with the state. The defendant must introduce some evidence of self-defense in order for the jury to be instructed on the issue. The effect of this presumption is identical to that of the affirmative defense. Both devices used in this way have been held to be constitutional.[9]

An affirmative defense that places the burden of persuasion on the defendant with regard to a factor that is not an element of the offense may be constitutional.[10] Could the state accomplish the same allocation of the burden of persuasion in the form of a presumption, i.e., a rule that states that once the state has proven the elements of the offense, the defendant is presumed guilty unless he proves some other factor? Such a rule simply delays the allocation of the burden of persuasion until after the state has proved its case. It places no different burden on the accused than would an affirmative defense.[11] However, as framed, the presumption would seem to run directly afoul of *Sandstrom.* The matter may simply be one of legislative drafting. The prudent legislature will choose the affirmative defense route rather

---

7. Patterson v. New York, Supra note 3 at 226–227 (1977).

8. See Jeffries & Stephan, supra note 4 at 1362–1363; Sundby, The Reasonable Doubt Rule and the Meaning of Innocence, supra note 5 at 507–509.

9. Compare Berrier v. Egeler, 583 F.2d 515 (6th Cir.1978), cert. denied 439 U.S. 955 (affirmative defense; Michigan procedure) and State v. Patterson, 297 N.C. 247,

254 S.E.2d 604 (1979). See also discussion in Brandis, North Carolina Evidence, § 218 (3d ed. 1988).

10. See Patterson v. New York, supra note 3 (1977) and the discussion in § 347, supra.

11. See Allen, supra note 4, 94 Harv. L.Rev. at 357; Weinstein & Berger, Evidence ¶ 303–41.

than the presumption language. It is yet to be seen whether the courts will look to the designation of a procedural device as a presumption or as an affirmative defense or whether they will more realistically decide the constitutionality of the procedural device based upon its actual effect on the defendant.

3. *When is it Proper to Submit an Issue Involving A Presumed Fact to the Jury?* In deciding the question whether a case involving a presumed fact should be submitted to the jury, the trial judge must necessarily be guided by the dictates of Jackson v. Virginia: [12] a jury verdict will be upheld, even against collateral attack, only if the evidence was sufficient for a reasonable person to find the defendant guilty beyond a reasonable doubt. In the rare instance in which a mandatory presumption is involved, the problem is not difficult. *Allen* suggests that the presumption will be tested by the constitutional test of whether the presumed fact flows beyond a reasonable doubt from the basic facts. If the presumption meets that test, it is by definition sufficient to get to the jury, provided the other elements of the crime are supported by sufficient evidence. However, because of the rigid requirements for the validity of mandatory presumptions, virtually all presumptions will be permissive. Therefore, under the *Allen* case, the trial judge must look to the rational effect of the presumption in connection with all of the other evidence in the case. Perhaps the best statement of a test for the sufficiency of the evidence under these circumstances is contained in Revised Uniform Rule (1974) 303(b):

> *(b) Submission to the jury.* The court is not authorized to direct the jury to find a presumed fact against the accused. If a presumed fact establishes guilt or is an element of the offense or negatives a defense, the court may submit the question of guilt or of the existence of the presumed fact to the jury, but only if a reasonable juror on the evidence as a whole, including the evidence of the basic facts, could find guilt or the presumed fact beyond a reasonable doubt. If the presumed fact has a lesser effect, the question of its existence may be submitted to the jury provided the basic facts are supported by substantial evidence or are otherwise established, unless the court determines that a reasonable juror on the evidence as a whole could not find the existence of the presumed fact.[13]

Given the dictates of Jackson v. Virginia and County Court of Ulster County v. Allen, no other proposed formulation of the rule seems acceptable.[14]

4. *Instructing the Jury on Presumptions.* The distinction made in the *Allen* case between permissive and mandatory presumptions, makes the exact language of instructions on presumptions critical. Unless a

---

12. 443 U.S. 307 (1979), rehearing denied 444 U.S. 890; see § 338 supra, text accompanying notes 6–7.

13. The Revised Uniform Rule (1986) is almost identical to Proposed Federal Rule 303(b) sent by the Supreme Court to Congress but not enacted.

14. See Model Penal Code § 112(5)(a); Proposed Federal Rule of Criminal Procedure 25.1, S. 1437, 95th Cong., 1st Session (1977) (not adopted).

presumption is strong enough to meet the stringent test for mandatory presumptions, the trial judge must use caution in charging the jury so as to place no burden whatsoever on the defendant.

Again, the Revised Uniform Rules provide a suggested pattern for such an instruction. Uniform Rule 303(c) provides:

> *Instructing the Jury.* Whenever the existence of a presumed fact is submitted to the jury, the court shall instruct the jury that it may regard the basic facts as sufficient evidence of the presumed fact but is not required to do so. In addition, if the presumed fact establishes guilt or is an element of the offense or negatives a defense, the court shall instruct the jury that its existence, on all the evidence, must be proved beyond a reasonable doubt.[15]

This instruction seems to meet most of the problems raised in the *Allen* case, as well as those suggested by Sandstrom v. Montana. One additional problem has been suggested.[16] In *Allen*, the court stated that the prosecution could not rest its case entirely on a presumption unless the facts proved were sufficient to support the inference of guilt beyond a reasonable doubt.[17] Therefore, where the prosecution relies solely upon a presumption and not any other evidence, as in *Allen*, not only must the presumed fact flow beyond a reasonable doubt from the basic facts, but the jury must be able to find the basic facts beyond a reasonable doubt. At least two states have adopted the essence of the Revised Uniform Rule, but, in order to cover this situation, have added language which requires that the basic facts be proved beyond a reasonable doubt.[18]

§ 349. Choice of Law [1]

The significance of the burdens of proof and of the effect of presumptions upon those burdens has already been discussed. Certainly the outcome of litigation may be altered depending upon which party has the burden of persuasion.[2] Where there is little evidence available on an issue, the burden of producing evidence may also control the outcome.[3] Recognizing the impact of these rules upon outcome, the federal courts, applying the doctrine of Erie Railroad Co. v. Tompkins,[4]

15. Again, the Revised Uniform Rule (1974) is almost identical to Proposed Federal Rule 303(c) sent by the Supreme Court to Congress but not enacted.

16. Weinstein & Berger, supra note 11 at 303–37.

17. County Court of Ulster County v. Allen, 442 U.S. 140, 167 (1979).

18. Hawaii Evidence Rule 306; Oregon Evidence Rule 309.

§ 349
1. Morgan, Choice of Law Governing Proof, 58 Harv.L.Rev. 153, 180–194 (1944); Sedler, The Erie Outcome Test as a Guide to Substance and Procedure in the Conflicts of Laws, 37 N.Y.U.L.Rev. 813, 855–865 (1962); Restatement, Second, Conflict of Laws §§ 133, 134 (1971); Annot., 35 A.L.R.3d 289; C.J.S. Conflict of Laws § 22(9); Dec.Dig. Actions ⚞66.

2. See § 336 supra.

3. See § 338 supra. See also §§ 342 and 344 supra as to the operation of presumptions with regard to both the burden of producing evidence and the burden of persuasion.

4. 304 U.S. 64 (1938).

have consistently held that where an issue is to be decided under state law, that law controls both the burdens of proof and presumptions with regard to that issue.[5]　Federal Rule of Evidence 302 limits the operation of this rule with respect to presumptions to cases in which the presumption operates "respecting a fact which is an element of a claim or defense as to which state law supplies the rule of decision."[6] "Tactical presumptions," those that operate as to a lesser aspect of the case, will be governed by the federal rule.[7]　While no court has specifically made the distinction contemplated in the rule, the reasoning is sound.　Although tactical presumptions may in some instances influence the outcome of a case, their effect is no greater than that of a rule governing the admission or exclusion of a single item of evidence. As in the case of those rules, the desirability of providing a uniform procedure for federal trials through a fixed rule governing tactical presumptions outweighs any preference for increased certainty of identity of result in state and federal courts.

Of course *Erie* problems are not the only choice of law problems.　The question remains, even for federal courts having resolved to apply state rather than federal law:[8] what state's law is applicable?　Unlike the federal courts applying the *Erie* rule, the state courts generally have not considered the impact of the burdens of proof and presumptions on the outcome of the lawsuit to be controlling.　The general rule expressed is that both the burdens of proof and presumptions are "procedural" in the sense that the law of the forum governs rather than the law of the state whose substantive rules are otherwise applicable.[9]

5. Dick v. New York Life Insurance Co., 359 U.S. 437 (1959); Palmer v. Hoffman, 318 U.S. 109 (1943); Cities Service Oil Co. v. Dunlap, 308 U.S. 208 (1939); Federal Insurance Co. v. Areias, 680 F.2d 962 (3d Cir.1982); Monger v. Cessna Aircraft Co., 812 F.2d 402 (8th Cir.1987).　See also, 10 Moore Federal Practice ¶ 3.02 (2d ed. 1982).

6. See Hewitt v. Firestone Tire and Rubber Co., 490 F.Supp. 1358 (E.D.Va.1980) and Ritter v. Prudential Insurance Co., 538 F.Supp. 398 (N.D.Ga.1982), for applications of this rule.　Conversely, Revised Uniform Rule of Evidence 802 provides:

> In civil actions and proceedings, the effect of a presumption respecting a fact which is an element of a claim or defense as to which federal law supplies the rule of decision is determined in accordance with federal law.

7. Fed.R.Evid. 302, Advisory Committee's Note.　The following example of a tactical presumption is taken from Cleary, Presuming and Pleading: An Essay on Juristic Immaturity, 12 Stan.L.Rev. 5, 26 (1959): "In an action upon an account, plaintiff, desiring to prove defendant's failure to deny as an admission of liability, may prove the mailing of a statement of

account to defendant and rely upon the presumption that it was received by him in due course of the mails.　The presumed fact of delivery is much smaller than an element in the case * * *."

8. In determining which state law to apply, the federal courts are bound by the conflict of laws rule of the state in which they are sitting.　Klaxon Co. v. Stentor Electric Manufacturing Co., 313 U.S. 487 (1941).　See generally cases collected in Annot., 21 A.L.R.2d 247, 257.　For examples of the approach taken by a federal court in a situation where a choice between the laws of two states with regard to presumptions had to be made, see Maryland Casualty Co. v. Williams, 377 F.2d 389 (5th Cir.1967); Melville v. American Home Assurance Co., 584 F.2d 1306 (3d Cir.1978).

9. Broderick v. McGuire, 119 Conn. 83, 174 A. 314 (1934) (New York presumption arising from certificate of superintendent of banks not applicable); Davis Cabs v. Evans, 42 Ohio App. 493, 182 N.E. 327 (1932) (Kentucky presumption of negligence where speed limit exceeded not applicable).　See cases in Annot., 35 A.L.R.3d 289, 299.

However, as in the case of most general rules with regard to the subject matter of this chapter, instances in which an exception to this general rule has been held applicable are perhaps as numerous as instances in which the rule has been applied. The principal exception to the basic dogma has been variously phrased but its gist is that the forum will apply the rule of a foreign jurisdiction with respect to the burdens of proof or presumptions where that rule is inseparably connected to the substantive right created by the foreign state.[10]

The general rule and its principal exception [11] have proved difficult to apply. The plethora of conflicting decisions under the test amply illustrates the problems inherent in attempting to distinguish between rules that are inseparably connected with substantive law and those that are not.[12] The distinction is indeed a hollow one. Regardless of the nature of the claim or defense, rules with respect to the burdens of proof always have the same potential effect upon the decision in the case. If insufficient evidence is available, the party having the burden of producing evidence will lose the decision. If the jury is in doubt, the party having the burden of persuasion will lose. As has been observed, cases in which the burden of proof is so closely interwoven with the substantive right as to make a separation of the two impossible constitute either all or none of the litigated cases.[13]

A somewhat better approach to the problem is taken by the Second Restatement of Conflict of Laws which states that the forum will apply its own local law in determining which party has the burdens of proof "unless the primary purpose of the relevant rule of the otherwise applicable law is to affect decision of the issue rather than to regulate the conduct of the trial." [14] The rule sounds very much like the test

---

10. Pilot Life Insurance Co. v. Boone, 236 F.2d 457, 462 (5th Cir.1956) ("The effect of this presumption against suicide is so inseparably connected with the substantive right to defend under the applicable policy exception, that we think that the law of South Carolina [which was held to govern the substantive issues] should be given effect in preference to the contrary rule prevailing in Alabama [the state in which the district court was sitting]."); Buhler v. Maddison, 109 Utah 267, 176 P.2d 118, 123 (1947); Precourt v. Driscoll, 85 N.H. 280, 157 A. 525, 527 (1931). For a more recent application of these same principles see Melville v. American Home Assurance Co., supra n. 8.

11. Another frequently stated exception is that the law of the foreign jurisdiction governs "conclusive presumptions." See, e.g., Maryland Casualty Co. v. Williams, supra n. 8 at 394–95. However, as discussed earlier in this chapter, § 342, n. 12 and accompanying text, these "presumptions" are better viewed as rules of substantive law and are therefore clearly not within the purview of the general rule.

12. See generally cases collected in Annot., supra n. 9, at 303 et seq. The courts are perhaps most divided on this issue where the forum's rule with regard to the burden of proving contributory negligence differs from that of the foreign state whose law is otherwise applicable. Compare Foley v. Pittsburgh–Des Moines Co., 363 Pa. 1, 68 A.2d 517 (1949), and Weir v. New York, New Haven & Hartford Railroad Co., 340 Mass. 66, 162 N.E.2d 793 (1959) (law of the forum controls) with Gordon's Transports, Inc. v. Bailey, 41 Tenn.App. 365, 294 S.W.2d 313 (1956); Valleroy v. Southern Railway Co., 403 S.W.2d 553 (Mo.1966) (foreign law controls.) See Restatement, Second, Conflict of Laws § 133, Reporter's Note at 369 (1971). See also cases collected at Annot., supra note 9 at 318–327.

13. Morgan, supra note 1, at 185.

14. §§ 133, 134 (1971). Section 595 of the first Restatement stated that the law of the forum governs both "proof" and "presumptions." The comment to that section (p. 710) noted that the foreign law might be applied if "the remedial and substantive

applied in *Erie* cases. However, the comments and illustrations to the applicable sections of the Restatement indicate that the Restatement is to be interpreted in much the same way as the more traditional statements just discussed; the assumption is that the rule is one concerned with "trial administration," not the decision of the issue.[15] The assumption seems wrong. The burdens of proof are almost always allocated for the primary purpose of affecting the decision in the case where there is no evidence or where the jury is in doubt. To say that these rules merely govern the conduct of the trial, as in the case of rules concerning the admission and exclusion of evidence, gives far too much emphasis to form over substance.[16]

A better approach to the choice of law problem would be to adopt the federal rule used in *Erie* cases as a rule of general application. Such a rule would provide that the law of the state or states supplying the substantive rules of law should govern questions concerning the burdens of proof as well as presumptions operating with regard to a fact constituting an element of a claim or defense.[17]

portions of the foreign law are so bound together that the application of the usual procedural rule of the forum would seriously alter the effect of the operative facts under the law of the appropriate foreign state."

15. Id., § 133, Comment at 366–68, § 134, Comment at 370–72.

16. Where the evidence is plentiful, of course, the allocation of the burden of producing evidence cannot have a significant effect upon the decision in the case. In such a case, the rule assigning the burden is simply a rule affecting the order of proof—a matter that logically should be governed by the law of the forum. However, providing different rules to be applied where there is sufficient evidence to satisfy the burden of producing evidence and where there is not, would require a full review of the evidence before a decision as to choice of law could be made, a procedure at best wasteful of precious judicial time.

As long as the allocation of the burden of producing evidence has a potentially signif-icant impact on the decision in the case, as it must have in every situation, a single rule, calling for the allocation of the burden of producing evidence as part of the substantive law to be applied in the case, should be followed. For a discussion suggesting the possibility of a different rule where there is plentiful evidence see Sedler, supra note 1, at 865.

17. For a similar view, see Sedler, supra note 1.

In the first edition of this text, Dean McCormick took the position that the burden of persuasion has a relatively insignificant effect upon the outcome of the litigation (see discussion of this question in § 336 supra) and that the allocation of that burden should therefore be viewed as a matter of "procedure." (p. 686). Professor Morgan took an opposite approach, recognizing the impact of the burden of persuasion upon the outcome, but relegating the burden of producing evidence to the status of procedure. Morgan, supra note 1, at 191–194.

*

Title 13

ADMINISTRATIVE EVIDENCE

Chapter 37

ADMINISTRATIVE EVIDENCE

Table of Sections

§ 350. Introduction to Administrative Adjudication [1]

As the problems facing federal and state governments have multiplied in number and complexity, these governments have created administrative agencies to devise and enforce new policies. This growth has been uneven and with few exceptions relatively slow. Even as late as 1960 the federal government exercised major regulatory responsibility in only five fields: antitrust, communications, financial markets and institutions, food and drugs, and transportation. Beginning in the mid–1960's, however, the number of federal regulatory agencies and the scope of regulatory activity greatly expanded. For example, between 1960 and 1990 the number of federal agencies substantially regulating some aspect of private activity grew from 34 to

§ 350

1. See generally 1 Davis, Administrative Law Treatise, ch. 1 (2d ed. 1978, 1989 Supp.) (hereinafter "Davis").

over 100; whereas in 1930 there were but 18 federal regulatory bodies.[2] This expansion is also reflected in other measures of agency activity. In 1970, federal regulatory agencies spent $800 million and employed 28,000 people. By 1980 these agencies employed 90,000 people and spent $6 billion. During the 1970's the pages of federal regulations in the Federal Register tripled, federal regulatory budgets increased six-fold, agency personnel grew from under 30,000 to over 80,000, and the amount of the gross national product produced by industries regulated by state or federal governments jumped from under 10 to around 25 percent.[3]

Much, perhaps most, of this growth has focused on the use of agency rulemaking to write new regulations. At the same time administrative trials—denominated "adjudications" by the federal Administrative Procedure Act (APA)[4]—have continued to grow and the federal government now employs approximately 1050 administrative law judges.[5] (By contrast, there are approximately 500 federal district judges hearing all federal civil and criminal cases.[6]) The number of administrative trials annually dwarfs the number of cases heard each year in federal court. Yet the range of administrative trials is as great as those heard by federal judges. That is, administrative adjudications extend from relatively insubstantial workers' compensation claims to precedent-setting antitrust merger rulings involving millions of dollars and affecting thousands of employees.

At first glance many, and perhaps most, administrative rulemaking hearings and hearings constituting formal adversarial adjudications appear to be merely carbon copies of judicial trials. Such an administrative hearing is usually public, and in most cases the hearing is conducted in an orderly and dignified manner, although not necessarily with the formality of a judicial trial. Evidence is admissible only if reliable and material; cross-examination is frequently relied upon to challenge witness credibility; and the administrative judge's decision must be supported by substantial evidence.[7]

Closer analysis, however, reveals several differences.[8] Agency hearings, especially those dealing with rulemaking, often tend to produce evidence of general conditions as distinguished from facts relating solely to the respondent. Administrative agencies in rulemaking and occasionally in formal adversarial adjudications more consciously formulate policy than do courts. Consequently, administrative adjudications may require that the administrative law judge consider more

2. See Schultze, The Public Use of Private Interest 7–8 (1977).

3. See Breyer, Regulation and Its Reform 1 (1982); United States Office of Personnel Management, Federal Civilian Work Force Statistics; Employment & Trends (January 1990).

4. 5 U.S.C.A. §§ 551(7), 554.

5. See Administrative Conference of the United States, Annual Report (1989).

6. See Administrative Conference of the United States, Annual Report (1981).

7. See Gellhorn, Rules of Evidence and Official Notice in Formal Administrative Hearings, 1971 Duke L.J. 1, 12–26; Deese, Relevancy of Evidence in Administrative Law Proceedings, 7 J.National Association of Administrative Law Judges 38 (1987).

8. See 3 Davis ch. 16 (1980).

consciously the impact of his decision upon the public interest as well as upon the particular respondent.[9] In addition, testimonial evidence and cross-examination often play less important roles in administrative hearings, especially when rulemaking is involved.[10]

An administrative hearing is tried to an *administrative law judge* and never to a *jury*. Since many of the rules governing the admission of proof in judicial trials are designed to protect the jury from unreliable and possibly confusing evidence,[11] it has long been asserted that such rules need not be applied at all or with the same vigor in proceedings solely before an administrative law judge.[12] The administrative judge decides both the facts and the law to be applied. Usually a lawyer, he is generally experienced on the very question he must decide. Consequently, the technical common law rules governing the *admissibility* of evidence have generally been abandoned by administrative agencies.[13]

Courts accept whatever cases the parties present; their familiarity with the subject matter is accidental. Agencies, on the other hand, have only limited jurisdictions and handle selected cases; administrative law judges and agency members who review the adjudicative decisions of administrative law judges are often either experts or have at least a substantial familiarity with the subject matter. The administrative agency may therefore be allowed greater leeway and deference (on appellate review) in deciding questions of fact and law. In addition, an agency usually is staffed by experts whose reports, commonly relating to matters adjudicated before the agency, are made available to administrative judges and commissioners alike.

While this development of agency experience and expertness is commonly offered as a justification for administrative agencies,[14] it also

9. See generally Chayes, The Role of the Judge in Public Law Litigation, 89 Harv.L.Rev. 1281 (1976); Skoler, Time to Shift Gears: The Changing Role of Administrative Law Judges, 22 Judges Journal 24 (1983); Ladenson, The Administrative Law Judge and an Ethical Ideal of the Judicial Role, 8 Journal of the National Association of Administrative Law Judges 39 (1988).

10. For particularly penetrating insights on whether such evidence can be dispensed with in deciding questions of policy, see Robinson, The Making of Administrative Policy: Another Look at Rulemaking and Adjudication and Administrative Procedure Reform, 118 U.Pa.L.Rev. 485, 521–522 (1970). See also Pierce, The Choice Between Adjudicating and Rulemaking for Formulating and Implementing Energy Policy, 31 Hast.L.J. 1 (1979); Baldwin, Circular Arguments: The Status and Legitimacy of Administrative Rules, 1986 Public Law 239; Stein, EPA Administrative Rulemaking: A View From the Outside, 1 Natural Resources and Environment 33 (1985).

11. "[The law of evidence is] a piece of illogical, but by no means irrational, patchwork; not at all to be admired, nor easily to be found intelligible, except as a product of the jury system. * * * where ordinary untrained citizens are acting as judges of fact." Thayer, Preliminary Treatise on Evidence at the Common Law 509 (1898).

12. See § 60 and Ch. 34 supra. Compare § 351 infra.

13. See generally Richardson v. Perales, 402 U.S. 389 (1971); TRW–United Greenfield Div. v. N.L.R.B., 716 F.2d 1391 (11th Cir.1983); Cunanan v. I.N.S., 856 F.2d 1373 (9th Cir.1988). See also §§ 352 and 353 infra.

14. The significance of this experience and expertness has, however, been authoritatively questioned. See Jaffe, Judicial Control of Administrative Action 25 (1965); Schwartz, Legal Restriction of Competition

creates a basic conflict between assuring fairness to the private respondent on the one hand and promoting efficient use of reliable information on the other. The respondent, for example, wants an opportunity to rebut or explain all the "evidence" which the administrative judge or agency relies upon in making its decision. Yet the agency, especially in rulemaking, wishes to avoid the burden of having to prove once again previously established "facts." This conflict has led to the development of the concept of official notice, specifically recognized in the APA (Administrative Procedure Act), which regularizes the procedure for agency reliance on proven facts.[15]

§ 351. Law Governing Administrative Evidence

The legal framework governing the conduct of formal administrative adjudication is not complex and can be best understood by first examining the law which determines the kind of proof an agency can receive into evidence.

(a) *Federal Law.* Until the passage of the Administrative Procedure Act of 1946,[1] the receipt of evidence in federal administrative proceedings was limited only by general constitutional requirements of fairness and privilege together with the vague directions implicit in the standard for judicial review developed by appellate courts or written into agency enabling acts.

The requirement of fairness generally means only that the respondent

> shall have an opportunity to be heard and cross-examine the witnesses against him and shall have time and opportunity at a convenient place, after the evidence against him is produced and known to him, to produce evidence and witnesses to refute the charges * * *[2]

The test for judicial review typically provides that "[t]he finding of the Commission as to the facts, if supported by substantial evidence, shall be conclusive."[3]

---

in the Regulated Industries: An Abdication of Judicial Responsibility, 67 Harv. L.Rev. 436, 471–75 (1954). For other theories on the justification for administrative agencies, see Stigler, The Theory of Economic Regulation, 2 Bell J. of Econ. & Mgmt.Sci. 3 (1971); Posner, Theories of Economic Regulation, 5 Bell J. of Econ. & Mgmt.Sci. 335 (1974); Breyer, Analyzing Regulatory Failure: Mismatches, Less Restrictive Alternatives, and Reform, 92 Harv.L.Rev. 547 (1979); Thompson, The Necessary Qualities of an Administrative Law Judge, 4 Journal of the National Association of Administrative Law Judges 12 (1984); Palmer, The Evolving Rule of Administrative Law Judges, 19 N.E.L.R. 755 (1984).

15. 5 U.S.C.A. § 556(e). See § 359 infra.

§ 351

1. 5 U.S.C.A. §§ 551–59, 701–06, 3105, 3344, 5362, 7521.

2. N.L.R.B. v. Prettyman, 117 F.2d 786, 790 (6th Cir.1941). See also Morgan v. United States, 304 U.S. 1 (1938); Hornsby v. Allen, 326 F.2d 605 (5th Cir.1964); Gates & Fox Co., Inc. v. Occupational Safety and Health Review Commission, 790 F.2d 154 (D.C.Cir.1986); Texas Eastern Products Pipeline Co. v. Occupational Safety and Health Review Commission, 827 F.2d 46 (7th Cir.1987).

3. 15 U.S.C.A. § 45(c) (Federal Trade Commission Act). See also Developments

Either standard could be read as a command that administrative agencies must rely upon common law rules of evidence barring hearsay and other secondary evidence, since the private respondent could neither confront nor cross-examine upon the evidence, or since the evidence was not competent and therefore not substantial. Neither the agencies nor the courts have accepted these contentions.[4] The exclusionary rules of evidence were designed in part to assure that evidence admitted would be relevant and reliable. But the opportunity for confrontation is not the sole measure of reliability.

As early as the turn of this century, the Supreme Court ruled that the Interstate Commerce Commission—the first regulatory agency to conduct formal adjudicatory hearings—was not bound by the exclusionary rules:

> The [ICC's] inquiry should not be too narrowly constrained by technical rules as to the admissibility of proof. Its function is largely one of investigation, and it should not be hampered in making inquiry pertaining to interstate commerce by those narrow rules which prevail in trials at common law * * * [5]

Occasionally federal authority has held that the admission of legally incompetent evidence is reversible error. But these decisions are exceptional and erroneous unless other grounds can be established for rejecting the evidence.[6] Indeed, by 1941 the Supreme Court had confidently noted that "it has long been settled that the technical rules for the exclusion of evidence applicable in jury trials do not apply to proceedings before federal administrative agencies in the absence of a statutory requirement that such rules are to be observed." [7]

With the adoption of the federal Administrative Procedure Act in 1946, Congress appeared to be codifying this case law by providing that "[a]ny oral or documentary evidence may be received" in an administrative adjudication.[8] Specific statutes may, however, override the application of the APA to agency hearings. In a few instances over the immediately ensuing years, Congress either exempted an agency's hearings from the APA or specified that the rules of evidence governing

in the Law—Remedies Against the United States and its Officials, 70 Harv.L.Rev. 827 (1957); Catreicher & Revasz, Nonacquiesence by Federal Administrative Agencies, 98 Yale L.J. 679 (1989); Anderson, The Availability of Judicial Review, 51 The Alabama Lawyer 28 (1990).

4. See 3 Davis § 16:4.

5. I.C.C. v. Baird, 194 U.S. 25, 44 (1904). In response to a challenge to an ICC order based partly on hearsay, the Court observed that "[e]ven in a court of law, if evidence of this kind is admitted without objection, it is to be considered, and accorded its natural probative effect * * *." Spiller v. Atchison, Topeka & Santa Fe Railway, 253 U.S. 117, 130 (1920).

6. Compare Tri–State Broadcasting Co. v. F.C.C., 96 F.2d 564 (D.C.Cir.1938), with FTC v. Cement Institute, 333 U.S. 683, 705–06 (1948), rehearing denied 334 U.S. 839. In response to the *Tri–State* ruling that the admission of all hearsay is improper since it deprives the respondent of its right to cross-examine, Dean Wigmore commented acidly: "No wonder the administrative agencies chafe under such unpractical control." 1 Wigmore, Evidence § 4b, p. 34 (3d ed. 1940).

7. Opp Cotton Mills, Inc. v. Administrator, Department of Labor, 312 U.S. 126, 155 (1941).

8. 5 U.S.C.A. § 556(d).

civil nonjury cases should be applied "so far as practicable." [9] Moreover, Congress' adoption of the "substantial evidence" standard for judicial review of formal adjudications [10]—partly in response to a perceived lack of rigor in the proof required in agency trials [11]—fostered the notion that the rule against hearsay or other restrictions might still be mandated in particular circumstances (e.g., where specific facts were in issue and witness credibility was key). This view seemed at least plausible where the congressional objective was not made clear.

In 1971, in Richardson v. Perales,[12] the Supreme Court gave strong evidence that narrow interpretation of agency authority to admit and rely on reliable hearsay and other evidence was not favored. There the Court sustained the Social Security Administration's denial of a claim for disability benefits even though the only testimony presented at the administrative hearing was by Perales, his doctor, and a fellow employee—and all supported Perales' claim. The agency, in denying the claim, relied on hospital records and the written reports of four examining physicians. Its decision had been overturned by the Court of Appeals which had ruled that hearsay uncorroborated by oral testimony could not constitute substantial evidence when the hearsay was directly contradicted by the testimony of live medical witnesses and by the claimant in person. The Supreme Court, however, upheld the

---

9. See S.Doc. 248, 79th Cong.2d Sess. 216 (1946); cf. 8 U.S.C.A. § 1252(b) applied in Marcello v. Bonds, 349 U.S. 302 (1955), rehearing denied 350 U.S. 856.

For example, the Taft–Hartley Act amended the National Labor Relations Act to provide that the Board's adjudications, "shall, so far as practicable, be conducted in accordance with the rules of evidence applicable in the district courts of the United States under the rules of civil procedure for the district courts of the United States * * *." Labor–Management Relations Act § 10(b), 61 Stat. 146 (1947), 29 U.S.C.A. § 160(b). Section 10(b) of the 1935 Act, which Taft–Hartley modified, provided that "rules of evidence prevailing in courts of law or equity shall not be controlling." 49 Stat. 454 (1935). Although it seems doubtful that this amendment was intended to impose jury trial rules on Board hearings, at least one court has held that "hearsay evidence must [now] be excluded from consideration by the Board and by [the reviewing court]." N.L.R.B. v. Amalgamated Meat Cutters, 202 F.2d 671, 673 (9th Cir.1953); accord, 1 Cooper, State Administrative Law 384 (1965) (hereinafter cited "Cooper"). But see N.L.R.B. v. International Union of Operating Engineers, Local 12, 413 F.2d 705, 707 (9th Cir.1969). In general, however, reviewing courts have concluded that the mere admission of hearsay is not within

the purview of the Taft–Hartley amendment. E.g., N.L.R.B. v. Philadelphia Iron Works, 211 F.2d 937, 942–43 (3d Cir.1954); N.L.R.B. v. Carpet, Linoleum and Resilient Tile Layers Local Union No. 419, 213 F.2d 49, 53 (10th Cir.1954); N.L.R.B. v. A. Duie Pyle, Inc., 606 F.2d 379 (3d Cir.1979). See generally Archer, Query: Should Administrative Agencies Tailor Exclusionary Evidence Rules Specifically for Their Own Proceedings? An Illustrative Study of the NLRB, 3 Ind.Leg.F. 339 (1970); Note, Administrative Procedure Act, 97 Harv. L.Rev. 230 (1983); Curran, The National Labor Relations Board's Proposed Rules on Health Care Bargaining Units, 76 Virg. L.R. 115 (1990).

10. 5 U.S.C.A. § 706(2)(E) (Administrative Procedure Act).

11. See Universal Camera Corp. v. N.L.R.B., 340 U.S. 474 (1951); Jaffe, Judicial Review: Substantial Evidence on the Whole Record, 64 Harv.L.Rev. 1233 (1951); Utton, The Use of the Substantial Evidence Rule to Review Administrative Findings of Fact in New Mexico, 10 New Mexico L.Rev. 103 (1980).

12. 402 U.S. 389 (1971). The particular ruling was that physicians' reports adduced by the agency were admissible and satisfied the requirement of "substantial evidence," though opposed by live expert testimony on behalf of claimant.

Social Security Administration. It emphasized that the reports were impartial, consistent, and based on personal examinations by competent physicians. Moreover, Perales had not exercised his right to subpoena the examining physicians in order to cross-examine them. It argued that the "sheer magnitude" of the administrative burden and desirability of informal procedures supported this approach. In the circumstances, the procedure satisfied both the congressional design as well as requirements of "fundamental fairness." [13]

(b) *State Law.* The constitutional limitations applied to federal agencies also impose restraints upon state hearings. The states in turn have freed their administrative agencies from the "rules of evidence," but not always for the same reasons. Most state agencies were created as political-administrative bodies rather than as quasi-judicial commissions. Thus, writing in 1965, Professor Cooper observed

> Fifty years ago, the typical state agencies would include, perhaps, rural township supervisors who as members of local boards of assessors would estimate the value of their neighbors' farms, and statehouse politicians who as a railroad commission would bargain with railroad attorneys concerning the granting of franchises and the fixing of rates, and insurance commissioners who would watch with a wary eye the premiums charged by fire insurance companies * * *, and—in the more progressive states—"committees of arbitration" who would informally arbitrate compensation claims of workers injured in industrial accidents under the newfangled workmen's compensation laws.[14]

Neither these state agencies nor the parties appearing before them could have followed judicial rules of evidence. As the agencies became more sophisticated, and their hearings more formal, the presentation of evidence was formalized. Now, as with federal agencies, their hearings are often indistinguishable from nonjury civil trials. Nevertheless, the original approach that state agencies are not restricted by common law rules in the admission of evidence has continued.[15] Professor Cooper

---

13. It should also be noted that three Justices dissented. They would have reversed the agency decision on the grounds that evidence which had not been tested by cross-examination "is of no value," that uncorroborated hearsay does not constitute "substantial evidence" under the APA, and that the agency's reliance on written reports was therefore an impermissible "cutting of corners."

It should also be noted that the hospital records and the written reports of the four examining physicians, upon the laying of a proper foundation through a records custodian, would be admissible under the business records or public records hearsay exception, Fed.R.Evid. 803(6) or 803(8).

14. 1 Cooper 379 (footnotes omitted). See generally, Cox, The Feasibility and Practicability of Establishing a Center of State Administrative Law, 39 Administrative Law Review 205 (1987).

15. Many state statutes explicitly provide that the common law rules of evidence applicable to jury trials shall not govern agency hearings. E.g., Mass.Gen. Laws Ann. c. 30A, § 11(2); West's Ann.Cal. Labor Code §§ 5708, 5709. Several practical reasons have been offered for not following rigid common law rules of evidence in state hearings; agency hearings are often held at one or a few central locations distant from the scene of events, making it difficult for eyewitness participants to testify; hearings may be held shortly after the complaint is filed, making the advance preparation and the marshalling of the best witnesses and documentary evidence difficult; and the heavy caseload volume, much of which is routine and involves only matters of small consequence, renders formal requirements of proof inappropriate. See Benjamin, Administrative Adjudica-

contended that this liberal approach had long ago outrun its reasons.[16] Attributing its continuance to legislative lethargy, to arbitrary agency desire to operate with a free hand, and to the judicial trend toward relaxation of exclusionary rules in court cases, he decried this laxity concerning the application of common law rules and suggested that state agencies be "required to follow the rules of evidence to about the same extent and in about the same way as judges do when trying cases without juries." [17] Whatever the then merits of Professor Cooper's position,[18] the 1961 Model State Administrative Procedure Act's provision,[19] that the rules of evidence applicable in nonjury civil cases be followed in state agency adjudications was adopted in only six states. The Model Act was revised once again in 1981, this time adhering more closely to the federal model. Section 4–212 provides that the hearing officer shall exclude evidence on proper objection only if it is "irrelevant, immaterial, unduly repetitious" or because it is privileged.[20] It further specifically provides that "[e]vidence may not be excluded solely because it is hearsay."

Enactment of the Federal Evidence Rules in 1975 brought about a perceptible change in attitude in Congress and in several of the administrative agencies themselves. No longer was it simply assumed that the rules of evidence would not apply in any given administrative agency hearing. As of the mid 1980's, either through congressional action or voluntarily by the federal administrative agencies themselves, of the 280 evidentiary regulations 37 made reference to the Federal Rules of Evidence, most requiring their use "as far as practical." [21]

tion in the State of New York 175–76 (1942) (hereinafter "Benjamin").

16. 1 Cooper 380–81.

17. Id.

18. In opposition to the application of the rules of evidence, it was asserted that the "nonjury evidence" standard was more indefinite than might be thought. 3 Davis §§ 16.3–16.4. Whatever the merits of such a contention in the early sixties, ascertainment of the rules of evidence was greatly facilitated by adoption of the Federal Rules of Evidence in 1975.

See § 60 supra for discussion of the application of the rules of evidence in civil nonjury cases.

19. Revised Model State Administrative Procedure Act § 10(1) (1961).

20. Revised Model State Administrative Procedure Act § 4–212 (1981):

(a) Upon proper objection, the presiding officer shall exclude evidence that is irrelevant, immaterial, unduly repetitious, or excludable on constitutional or statutory grounds or on the basis of evidentiary privilege recognized in the courts of this state. In the absence of proper objection, the presiding officer

may exclude objectionable evidence. Evidence may not be excluded solely because it is hearsay.

21. Pierce, Use of the Federal Rules of Evidence in Federal Agency Adjudications, 39 Ad.L.Rev. 1, 6 (1987) ("Of the agency evidentiary regulations that include a reference to the FRE, most require use of the FRE 'so far as practicable.' In the case of the NLRB, [29 U.S.C. § 160(B)] Congress required the agency to adopt such an evidentiary regulation. In other cases, such as the Occupational Safety and Health Review Commission (OSHRC), [29 C.F.R. § 2200.72] the U.S. Department of Interior (DOI), [43 C.F.R. § 4.122] Interstate Commerce Commission (ICC), [49 C.F.R. § 1114.1] and Federal Communications Commission (FCC), [47 C.F.R. § 1.351] the agency apparently adopted the 'so far as practicable' standard voluntarily. In a few cases, an agency's evidentiary regulation refers to the FRE, but only as a source of potentially useful guidance to Administrative Law Judges. The U.S. Department of Labor's (DOL) evidentiary regulation illustrates this approach. [29 C.F.R. § 18.44] The DOL's unusually long regulation begins with a general provision that de-

Alarmed by this trend the Administrative Conference of the United States on June 20, 1986 adopted Resolution 86–2(1) which states as follows:

> Congress should not require agencies to apply the FRE, with or without the qualification, "so far as practicable," to limit the discretion of presiding officers to admit evidence in formal adjudications.[22]

For years Professor Davis has opposed the introduction of formal rules of evidence in administrative agency hearings.[23] His letter to the Administrative Conference was undoubtedly influential.[24]

scribes the role of the FRE in DOL adjudications: '(a) Applicability of Federal Rules of Evidence. Unless otherwise provided by statute or these rules, and where appropriate, the Federal Rules of Evidence may be applied to all proceedings held pursuant to these rules.' The contrast between the permissive reference to the FRE in the DOL regulation and the mandatory reference in the 'so far as practicable' standard is evident. The DOL regulation goes on to paraphrase several Federal Rules, including Rule 103 (objections and offers of proof), Rule 402 (relevant evidence generally admissible), Rule 403 (exclusion of relevant evidence on grounds of prejudice, confusion, waste of time, or undue delay), and Rule 1006 (summaries admissible). The DOL regulation also expressly authorizes ALJs to limit the number of witnesses who testify on an issue and to limit the amount of cross-examination of witnesses in order to avoid prolonging the hearing or burdening the record—a power implicitly accorded federal judges by FRE 403."). With respect to current position of the DOL, see notes 25–28 infra and accompanying text.

22. Id. at 2.

23. Id. at 3 ("During the period from 1940 through 1971, scholars and appellate judges engaged in a lively debate concerning the appropriate role of formal evidentiary rules in agency adjudications. Professor Davis devoted much of his scholarship during this period to developing and supporting his thesis that formal rules of evidence have no place in agency proceedings because of the many differences between agencies and courts. Dean Gellhorn later joined him in this effort by writing what remains today the most complete statement of the case against the application of evidentiary rules designed to govern jury trials in agency adjudicatory proceedings.").

See, e.g., Davis, Hearsay in Administrative Hearings, 32 Geo.Wash.L.Rev. 689 (1964); Davis, The Residuum Rule in Administrative Law, 28 Rocky Mtn.L.Rev. 1 (1955); Davis, Evidence Reform: The Ad-

ministrative Process Leads the Way, 31 Minn.L.Rev. 584 (1950); Davis, An Approach to Problems of Evidence in the Administrative Process, 55 Harv.L.Rev. 364 (1942); Gellhorn, Rules of Evidence and Official Notice in Formal Administrative Hearings, 1971 Duke L.J. 1.

References to the dominance of the position asserted by Professor Davis on the admissibility of hearsay can be found throughout §§ 352 and 353 infra.

24. The letter reads as follows:

June 18, 1986

To: The Administrative Conference

From: Kenneth Culp Davis

Re: Agenda Item B on Evidence

The proposed recommendation says that agencies' presiding officers should use the Federal Rules of Evidence (FRE) as a source of general guidance. I believe that would be a step backward, and I oppose it.

The FRE were designed for juries, not for agencies, and I think they should not guide admission or exclusion of evidence in administrative proceedings.

Of all federal trials, 86% are in agencies, 8% are in courts without juries, and 6% are in courts with juries. What are still called "the" rules of evidence were originally designed for juries, and even the FRE are designed primarily for juries.

The committee apparently believes that the FRE should have greater influence on administrative proceedings than they now have. I think they should not. The FRE are designed for juries, not for agencies. I think that under the FRE much evidence is excluded that should be admitted in an administrative proceeding.

The agencies themselves are in apparent disagreement with the idea that ALJs should be guided by the FRE. Of

Not everyone agrees. In 1987, the United States Department of Labor undertook examination of the Federal Rules Evidence with a view towards adopting a modified version for application solely in formal adversarial adjudications,[25] not rulemaking. Modifications were

the 280 sets of agency rules about evidence, 243 do not refer to the FRE.

Not only do the agencies generally disagree with what the committee proposes, but so do nearly all federal judges who have addressed the question.

Judge Weinstein was a member of the advisory committee on the FRE, and he said in his 1976 evidence book that "the Rules themselves generally make no distinction between ... jury and nonjury trials: Nevertheless, the traditional approach of the courts, which make the rules applied in bench trials much more liberal than in jury trials, will continue to be followed."

In other words, the courts themselves, according to Judge Weinstein, depart from the FRE in nonjury cases. I agree with them in doing so, and I think the agencies should do likewise, because, as Judge Weinstein says, the FRE are designed for jury cases. They are not designed for judges or for administrators.

Instead of being guided by the FRE, I think agencies' presiding officers should be guided by the practices of nearly all judges in nonjury cases. The judges do not follow the FRE but freely depart from them in nonjury cases.

McCormick, building on the leadership of Thayer, Wigmore, and Morgan, asserted flatly that the exclusionary rules are "absurdly inappropriate when the factfinder is not a jury."

To the extent that the present proposal, if adopted and followed, would result in exclusion of evidence that is now admitted, the result would be, I think, "absurdly inappropriate."

The committee's recommendation specifically asks presiding officers to use Federal Rule 403 "as a source of general guidance." The committee failed to note that Rule 403 on its face, by its words, speaks of "the danger of misleading the jury." Rule 403 thus explicitly asserts that it is based on jury needs. A rule explicitly designed for a jury obviously is not an appropriate guide for an administrative law judge.

The dominant attitude of today's federal judges is contrary to what is proposed. Cases asserting that the spirit behind the FRE should not be used in administrative proceedings are numerous. In

§ 16:5 of my Treatise I have quoted at length from a typical good opinion. Multi-Medical Convalescent Center v. NLRB, 550 F.2d 974, 977–78 (4th Cir.), cert. denied 434 U.S. 835 (1977). I shall refrain from quoting at length now, but here are key excerpts: "[T]o exclude that which is competent and relevant by mechanistic application of an exclusionary rule is exceedingly dangerous to the administrative or trial process * * * Thus, we strongly advise administrative law judges: if in doubt, let it in."

In my Treatise, I say that the court's statement is thoroughly sound and in agreement with almost all judicial pronouncements: "The view of this court and other courts will in the long run prevail; application of the Federal Rules to nonjury trials will give way."

In nonjury cases, the Fourth Circuit and other federal courts are moving in one direction—toward excluding less evidence. The proposal before us is to move in the opposite direction—toward excluding more evidence.

Because I strongly agree with the courts, I oppose the committee's proposal.

For a responsible opposing view, see notes 25–28 infra and accompanying text. For a different perspective as to the application of rules of evidence in nonjury trials, see § 60 supra.

25. 29 C.F.R. § 18.1101 provides as follows:

Applicability of rules

(a) General provision. These rules govern formal adversarial adjudications conducted by the United States Department of Labor before a presiding officer (1) which are required by Act of Congress to be determined on the record after opportunity for an administrative agency hearing in accordance with the Administrative Procedure Act, 5 U.S.C. 554, 556 and 557, or (2) which by United States Department of Labor regulation are conducted in conformance with the foregoing provisions. "Presiding officer", referred to in these rules as "the judge", means an Administrative Law Judge, an agency head, or other officer who pre-

drafted in recognition of the civil nonjury nature of such hearings and in appreciation of the broad underlying values and goals of the administrative process. The United States Department of Labor Rules of Evidence were promulgated on April 9, 1990.[26] Additional hearsay exceptions and self-authentication provisions were added to the Federal Rules of Evidence to reflect the practical realities of formal adversarial administrative adjudication while maintaining the overall integrity of the rule against hearsay.[27] Whether the approach of the Department

sides at the reception of evidence at a hearing in such an adjudication.

(b) Rules inapplicable. The rules (other than with respect to privileges) do not apply in the following situations:

(1) Preliminary questions of fact. The determination of questions of fact preliminary to admissibility of evidence when the issue is to be determined by the judge under § 18.104.

(2) Longshore, black lung, and related acts. Other than with respect to §§ 18.-403, 18.611(a), 18.614 and without prejudice to current practice, hearings held pursuant to the Longshore and Harbor Workers' Compensation Act, 33 U.S.C. 901: the Federal Mine Safety and Health Act (formerly the Federal Coal Mine Health and Safety Act) as amended by the Black Lung Benefits Act, 30 U.S.C. 901; and acts such as the Defense Base Act, 42 U.S.C. 1651; the District of Columbia Workmen's Compensation Act, 36 D.C.Code 501; the Outer Continental Shelf Lands Act, 43 U.S.C. 1331; and the Nonappropriated Fund Instrumentalities Act, 5 U.S.C. 8171, which incorporate section 23(a) of the Longshore and Harbor Workers' Compensation Act by reference.

(c) Rules inapplicable in part. These rules do not apply to the extent inconsistent with, in conflict with, or to the extent a matter is otherwise specifically provided by an Act of Congress, or by a rule or regulation of specific application prescribed by the United States Department of Labor pursuant to statutory authority, or pursuant to executive order.

26. 55 Federal Register 13219, April 9, 1990.

27. See, e.g., 29 C.F.R. § 18.803(a)(26)–(30):

§ 18.803 Hearsay exceptions; availability of declarant immaterial

(a) The following are not excluded by the hearsay rule, even though the declarant is available as a witness:

* * *

(26) *Bills, estimates and reports.* In actions involving injury, illness, disease, death, disability, or physical or mental impairment, or damage to property, the following bills, estimates, and reports as relevant to prove the value and reasonableness of the charges for services, labor and materials stated therein and, where applicable, the necessity for furnishing the same, unless the sources of information or other circumstances indicate lack of trustworthiness, provided that a copy of said bill, estimate, or report has been served upon the adverse party sufficiently in advance of the hearing to provide the adverse party with a fair opportunity to prepare to object or meet it:

(i) Hospital bills on the official letterhead or billhead of the hospital, when dated and itemized.

(ii) Bills of doctors and dentists, when dated and containing a statement showing the date of each visit and the charge therefor.

(iii) Bills of registered nurses, licensed practical nurses and physical therapists, or other licensed health care providers when dated and containing an itemized statement of the days and hours of service and charges therefor.

(iv) Bills for medicine, eyeglasses, prosthetic device, medical belts or similar items, when dated and itemized.

(v) Property repair bills or estimates, when dated and itemized, setting forth the charges for labor and material. In the case of an estimate, the party intending to offer the estimate shall forward with his notice to the adverse party, together with a copy of the estimate, a statement indicating whether or not the property was repaired, and, if so, whether the estimated repairs were made in full or in part and by whom, the cost thereof, together with a copy of the bill therefore.

(vi) Reports of past earnings, or of the rate of earnings and time lost from work or lost compensation, prepared by an employer on official letterhead, when dated and itemized. The adverse party may not dispute the authenticity, the value or reasonableness of such charges, the necessity therefore or the accuracy of the report, unless the adverse party files and serves written objection thereto sufficiently in advance of the hearing stating the objections, and the grounds thereof, that the adverse party will make if the bill, estimate, or reports is offered at the time of the hearing. An adverse party may call the author of the bill, estimate, or report as a witness and examine the witness as if under cross-examination.

(27) *Medical reports.* In actions involving injury, illness, disease, death, disability, or physical or mental impairment, doctor, hospital, laboratory and other medical reports, made for purposes of medical treatment, unless the sources of information or other circumstances indicate lack of trustworthiness, provided that a copy of the report has been filed and served upon the adverse party sufficiently in advance of the hearing to provide the adverse party with a fair opportunity to prepare to object or meet it. The adverse party may not object to the admissibility of the report unless the adverse party files and serves written objection thereto sufficiently in advance of the hearing stating the objections, and the grounds therefor, that the adverse party will make if the report is offered at the time of the hearing. An adverse party may call the author of the medical report as a witness and examine the witness as if under cross-examination.

(28) *Written reports of expert witnesses.* Written reports of an expert witness prepared with a view toward litigation, including but not limited to a diagnostic report of a physician, including inferences and opinions, when on official letterhead, when dated, when including a statement of the expert's qualifications, when including a summary of experience as an expert witness in litigation, when including the basic facts, data, and opinions forming the basis of the inferences or opinions, and when including the reasons for or explanation of the inferences or opinions, so far as admissible under rules of evidence applied as though the witness was then present and testifying, unless the sources of information or the method or circumstances of preparation indicate lack of trustworthiness, provided that a copy of the report has been

filed and served upon the adverse party sufficiently in advance of the hearing to provide the adverse party with a fair opportunity to prepare to object or meet it. The adverse party may not object to the admissibility of the report unless the adverse party files and serves written objection thereto sufficiently in advance of the hearing stating the objections, and the grounds therefor, that the adverse party will make if the report is offered at the time of the hearing. An adverse party may call the expert as a witness and examine the witness as if under cross-examination.

(29) *Written statements of lay witnesses.* Written statements of a lay witness made under oath or affirmation and subject to the penalty of perjury, so far as admissible under the rules of evidence applied as though the witness was then present and testifying, unless the sources of information or the method or circumstances of preparation indicate lack of trustworthiness provided that (i) a copy of the written statement has been filed and served upon the adverse party sufficiently in advance of the hearing to provide the adverse party with a fair opportunity to prepare to object or meet it, and (ii) if the declarant is reasonably available as a witness, as determined by the judge, no adverse party has sufficiently in advance of the hearing filed and served upon the noticing party a written demand that the declarant be produced in person to testify at the hearing. An adverse party may call the declarant as a witness and examine the witness as if under cross-examination.

(30) *Deposition testimony.* Testimony given as a witness in a deposition taken in compliance with law in the course of the same proceeding, so far as admissible under the rules of evidence applied as though the witness was then present and testifying, if the party against whom the testimony is now offered had an opportunity and similar motive to develop the testimony by direct, cross, or redirect examination, provided that a notice of intention to offer the deposition in evidence, together with a copy thereof if not otherwise previously provided, has been served upon the adverse party sufficiently in advance of the hearing to provide the adverse party with a fair opportunity to prepare to object or meet it. An adverse party may call the deponent as a witness and examine the witness as if under cross-examination.

of Labor will have broad implications remains to be seen.[28]

§ 352. Admissibility of Evidence

Administrative agencies generally are not restricted in the kind of evidence they can admit. The mere admission of proof that would be excluded as irrelevant, immaterial, incompetent, or redundant under the rules of evidence adopted in a jury trial will not restrict enforcement of an agency's decision.[1] The APA confirms this practice in section 556(d) by providing that "[a]ny oral documentary evidence may be received, but the agency as a matter of policy shall provide for the exclusion of irrelevant, immaterial, or unduly repetitious evidence."[2]

---

28. Following enactment of the Federal Rules of Evidence in 1975, arguments as to the applicability of the rules of evidence to formal adversarial adjudications, stripped of all excessive rhetoric, focus almost exclusively upon the rule against hearsay. Can it seriously be asserted that, for example, a subsequent remedial measure, banned by Rule 407, should be admitted in a formal adversarial administrative adjudication? As to hearsay, the liberal approach of the Department of Labor Rules of Evidence permits extremely broad introduction of written reports of expert witnesses, even those prepared for the purpose of litigation. 29 C.F.R. § 18.803(a)(28), note 27 supra. The same is true of written statements of lay witnesses given under oath or affirmation subject to the penalty of perjury. 29 C.F.R. § 18.803(a)(29), note 27 supra. What is excluded are lay witness oral statements and written statements not under oath or affirmation subject to the penalty of perjury. Even if it is ultimately concluded that only nonapplicability of the rule against hearsay is liberal enough a rule to govern formal adversarial adjudications, strong consideration should be given to adaption of a modified version of the Federal Rules of Evidence, *sans* hearsay. See notes 23 and 24 supra and §§ 352 and 353 infra for the traditional arguments relating to the inappropriateness of the rule against hearsay in *all* administrative agency hearings.

§ 352

1. Opp Cotton Mills, Inc. v. Administrator, Department of Labor, 312 U.S. 126 (1941); Veg–Mix, Inc. v. United States Department of Agriculture, 832 F.2d 601 (D.C.Cir.1987); Williams v. United States Department of Transportation, 781 F.2d 1573 (11th Cir.1986). On the other hand, several states have followed the lead of the Revised Model Act that "[i]rrelevant, immaterial, or unduly repetitious evidence *shall* be excluded." Alaska Stat. § 44.62.-460(d) (1980); West's Ann.Cal.Gov.Code § 11513; Ga.Code § 3A–116(a); Vernon's Ann.Mo.Stat. § 536.070(8); R.I.Gen.Laws § 42–35–10(a); W.Va.Code, 29A–5–2(a); Wis.Stat.Ann. 227.08. There is, however, a paucity of case authority interpreting and applying these statutes, although courts have occasionally expressed their disproval of the admission of such evidence. See Bunting Bristol Transfer, Inc. v. Pennsylvania Public Utility Commission, 418 Pa. 286, 292, 210 A.2d 281, 284 (1965); D.F. Bast, Inc. v. Pennsylvania Public Utility Commission, 397 Pa. 246, 251, 154 A.2d 505, 508 (1959). Several cases suggest that state courts have been critical of agency receipt of hearsay evidence, essentially on grounds that the particular evidence lacked probative force. E.g., Gomez v. Industrial Commission, 72 Ariz. 265, 233 P.2d 827 (1951); Zawisza v. Quality Name Plate, Inc., 149 Conn. 115, 176 A.2d 578 (1961). But only occasional—and usually earlier—state decisions have reversed agency rulings merely on the grounds of the receipt of hearsay evidence. See, e.g., In re Trustees of Village of Westminster, 108 Vt. 352, 187 A. 519 (1936).

2. 5 U.S.C.A. § 556(d). Not only the Act's words but also the legislative history make clear that the exclusionary rules do not govern the admissibility of evidence in administrative hearings and that the provision for exclusion applied only to "irrelevant, immaterial, or unduly repetitious evidence" and not to legally incompetent evidence. United States ex rel. Dong Wing Ott v. Shaughnessy, 116 F.Supp. 745, 750 (S.D.N.Y.1953), affirmed on other grounds 220 F.2d 537 (2d Cir.), cert. denied 350 U.S. 847; see 2 Davis § 16:4. See also Richardson v. Perales, 402 U.S. 389 (1971); Steadman v. Securities and Exchange Commis-

Note that the APA opens the door to *any* evidence which the administrative law judge admits and only *suggests* that insignificant and redundant evidence should be rejected, giving the agencies broad discretion. Moreover, the APA pointedly omits hearsay or other "incompetent" evidence from the list of evidence which should not be received.[3] Thus, the exclusion of otherwise legally inadmissible evidence from an administrative hearing may be error.[4] Furthermore, it is clear that the exclusion of relevant, material, and competent evidence by the administrative law judge will be grounds for reversal if that refusal is prejudicial.[5]

The courts have pressed the agencies to abide by the spirit of these rules. The leading example of such pressure—which in fact antedates the APA—is found in Samuel H. Moss, Inc. v. FTC,[6] where a distinguished panel of the Second Circuit admonished a hearing examiner for rigidly following the rules of evidence:

> [I]f the case was to be tried with strictness, the examiner was right * * *. Why either he or the [Federal Trade] Commission's attorney should have thought it desirable to be so formal about the admission of evidence, we cannot understand. Even in criminal trials to a jury it is better, nine times out of ten, to admit, than to exclude, evidence and in such proceedings as these the only conceivable interest that can suffer by admitting any evidence is the time lost, which is seldom as much as that inevitably lost by idle bickering about irrelevancy or incompetence. In the case at bar it chances that no injustice was done, but we take this occasion to point out the danger always involved in conducting such a proceeding in such a spirit, and the absence of any advantage in depriving either the Commission or ourselves of *all evidence which can conceivably throw any light upon the controversy.*[7]

More recent cases have repeated their admonition.[8]

Many reasons support the open admission of hearsay and other

sion, 450 U.S. 91 (1981); Klinestiver v. Drug Enforcement Administration, 606 F.2d 1128 (D.C.Cir.1979) ("competent" evidence standard of DEA act is coextensive with APA § 556(d)).

3. See the authorities cited in note 2 supra. In this context, the definition of hearsay is secondhand information which would not come within any of the exceptions to the hearsay rule.

4. See e.g., Catholic Medical Center of Brooklyn and Queens, Inc. v. N.L.R.B., 589 F.2d 1166 (2d Cir.1978), appeal after remand 620 F.2d 20 (error under APA § 556(d) for NLRB to exclude evidence of alleged union misconduct that was relevant and not protected by privilege or countervailing policy); Bender v. Clark, 744 F.2d 1424 (10th Cir.1984).

5. N.L.R.B. v. Burns, 207 F.2d 434 (8th Cir.1953); Prince v. Industrial Commission, 89 Ariz. 314, 361 P.2d 929 (1961); People ex rel. Hirschberg v. Board of Supervisors, 251 N.Y. 156, 167 N.E. 204 (1929); see 1 Cooper 367–71 (collecting authorities). But see note 4, § 351 supra.

6. 148 F.2d 378 (2d Cir.1945), cert. denied 326 U.S. 734, rehearing denied 326 U.S. 809, motion denied 155 F.2d 1016 (2d Cir.) (per curiam, decision by Clark, A. Hand and L. Hand, JJ.).

7. Id. at 380 (emphasis added).

8. Multi–Medical Convalescent and Nursing Center v. N.L.R.B., 550 F.2d 974 (4th Cir.1977), cert. denied 434 U.S. 835; Resort Car Rental System, Inc. v. FTC, 518 F.2d 962 (9th Cir.1975), cert. denied 423 U.S. 827.

legally incompetent evidence in administrative hearings.[9] Foremost among them is the fact that the exclusionary rules do not determine the probative value of the proffered evidence. Professor Davis, the leading proponent that hearing officers should make no distinction between hearsay and nonhearsay evidence, makes the point this way:

> [T]he reliability of hearsay ranges from the least to the most reliable. The reliability of non-hearsay also ranges from the least to the most reliable. Therefore the guide should be a judgment about the reliability of particular evidence in a particular record in particular circumstances, not the technical hearsay rule with all its complex exceptions.[10]

Most hearsay in administrative hearings is documentary. The standard of admissibility thus applied by both reviewing courts and administrative law judges is that "an administrative tribunal is not required to exclude hearsay evidence in the form of a document if its authenticity is sufficiently convincing to a reasonable mind and if it carries sufficient assurance as to its truthfulness." [11]

To require that an administrative law judge refuse to admit hearsay makes no sense where there is no jury to protect and the trier of fact is equally exposed to the evidence whether he admits or excludes it.[12] Admission without a ruling—as long as the evidence has some element of reliability—does no harm and can prove more efficient than requiring a ruling which may later be held erroneous. Discarding the exclusionary rules of admission eliminates the need for the parties to interpose protective objections—the objections being preserved by their briefs to the law judge or agency—and relieves the law judge of making difficult rulings before all the evidence is available. It assures a complete, yet not necessarily unduly long, record and might well avoid the need to reopen the record. Hearsay, of course, is not subject to current, in-court cross-examination, but that limitation affects the weight the evidence carries, not its admissibility.[13]

9. Patterson, Hearsay and the Substantial Evidence Rule in the Federal Administrative Process, 13 Mercer L.Rev. 294, 304–06 (1962); cf. Builders Steel Co. v. Commissioner, 179 F.2d 377, 379 (8th Cir.1950); Davis, Hearsay in Nonjury Cases, 83 Harv. L.Rev. 1362, 1366 (1970).

10. Davis, Hearsay in Administrative Hearings, 2 Geo.Wash.L.Rev. 689 (1964). One commentator has asserted that nine-tenths of the problems involved in applying the exclusionary rules in administrative hearings—or, at least, those that come to reviewing courts—involve hearsay. Note, 46 Ill.L.Rev. 915, 919 n. 23 (1952).

For a contrasting view see United States Department of Labor Rules of Evidence, 29 C.F.R. 18.101 et seq. (1990), discussed in § 351 at notes 25–28 supra.

11. Fairfield Scientific Corp. v. United States, 222 Ct.Cl. 167, 611 F.2d 854, 859 (1979), appeal after remand 655 F.2d 1062.

12. Donnelly Garment Co. v. N.L.R.B., 123 F.2d 215 (8th Cir.1941); Evosevich v. Consolidated Coal Co., 789 F.2d 1021 (3d Cir.1986); see 3 Davis § 16:11. But see Note, Improper Evidence in Nonjury Trials: Basis for Reversal? 79 Harv.L.Rev. 407, 409–11 (1965).

13. See National Association of Recycling Industries, Inc. v. Federal Maritime Commission, 658 F.2d 816 (D.C.Cir.1980); Calhoun v. Bailar, 626 F.2d 145 (9th Cir. 1980), cert. denied 452 U.S. 906; Reil v. United States, 197 Ct.Cl. 542, 456 F.2d 777 (1972); Peters v. United States, 187 Ct.Cl. 63, 408 F.2d 719, 724 (1969); W. Gellhorn & Byse, Administrative Law 713–14, 772 (5th ed. 1970).

The fact that administrative hearings need not follow the exclusionary rules and the fact that the admission of remote or repetitious evidence is not reversible error does not suggest that "anything goes" or that all proffered evidence, whatever is relevance or trustworthiness, should be admitted. Wholesale admission would only add to delay and further expand records which are already often very long. Nor can an efficient adjudicatory system decide anew each time the question is presented whether some particular evidence should be admitted. However, most agencies have not fully developed regulations governing the extent to which the exclusionary rules should not be applied.[14] Nonetheless, the admissibility of evidence in administrative hearings depends more upon the *importance* of the evidence in relation to the ultimate issues rather than upon the legal standards of relevance and materiality.[15]

Several significant and useful deviations from the judicial pattern appear in administrative hearings. The first, already noted, involves the relatively free receipt of hearsay evidence. Equally important is the manner in which oral testimony is received. Witnesses in agency hearings are frequently permitted freedom to testify in a simple, natural and direct fashion, without unnecessary interruptions from either the attorney who is directing the questioning or his adversary.[16] Only when the witness strays far afield, or the question is remote will an objection be sustained. A third departure permitted from judicial practice occurs when the administrative law judge is uncertain whether to exclude the evidence on the grounds of incompetency, irrelevancy, or immateriality. In administrative hearings the tendency is to admit the evidence. Other techniques, principally the use of written presentations and shortened hearings, are discussed below.[17]

Since the administrative hearings differ so widely in scope and significance, it is impossible to suggest a single standard to govern the

14. 3 Davis § 16:5.

15. The basic point made earlier should not be ignored—namely, that administrative hearings generally follow the time-tested judicial pattern of receiving evidence. Cf. W. Gellhorn, Federal Administrative Proceedings 75–82 (1941). It is also clear that agencies have not adequately explored methods to streamline the process of obtaining reliable evidence. See Selected Reports of the Administrative Conference of the United States 1961–1962, S.Doc. No. 24, 88th Cong., 1st Sess. 90–91 (1963).

Concern that too much of the "anything goes" attitude permeates administrative agency hearings, lead the Administrative Conference of the United States, on June 20, 1986, to approve recommendation 86–2(2) urging adoption of Fed.R.Evid. 403:

2. Agencies should adopt evidentiary regulations applicable to formal adversarial adjudications that clearly confer on presiding officers discretion to exclude unreliable evidence and to use the weighted balancing test in Rule 403 of the FRE, which allows exclusion of evidence the probative value of which is substantially outweighed by other factors, including its potential for undue consumption of time.

Pierce, Use of the Federal Rules of Evidence in Federal Agency Adjudications, 39 Ad.L.Rev. 1, 2 (1987).

16. See W. Gellhorn & Lauer, Administration of the New York Workmen's Compensation Law II, 37 N.Y.U.L.Rev. 204, 209 (1962); Campbell, Agency Discretion to Accept Comment in Informal Rulemaking: What Constitutes "Good Cause" under the Administrative Procedure Act?, 1980 B.Y.U.L.Rev. 93.

17. See § 358 infra.

admission of all evidence. It is probably still true, however, as one keen observer noted over 40 years ago, that the more closely administrative proceedings approach judicial proceedings in formality and in the nature of the issues to be tried, the greater the degree to which the exclusionary rules will be applied.[18] Nor has improvement been made to the standard suggested by the Attorney General's Committee on Administrative Procedure in 1941: "The ultimate test of admissibility must be whether the proffered evidence is reliable, probative and relevant. The question in each case must be whether the probability of error justifies the burden of stricter methods of proof." [19]

§ 353. Evaluation of Evidence

In contrast to the effect of a trial court's decision to receive hearsay evidence in a jury trial, an administrative law judge's decision to receive hearsay in an administrative adjudication is only the first step in determining its impact upon the tribunal's decision. The admission of evidence in a jury trial is often considered the last effective legal control over the use (or abuse) of such evidence because of the assumption that the jury will rely upon or be swayed by it regardless of whether its reliability has been established. In an administrative hearing, on the other hand, as in the case of nonjury trials, it is generally assumed that the law judge will not rely upon untrustworthy evidence in reaching his decision. Thus if there is "competent" or trustworthy evidence to support the decision, the reviewing court usually presumes that the administrative law or trial judge relied on that evidence in reaching his decision.[1]

Nevertheless, the more difficult—and often crucial—question for the hearing officer is the determination of whether he should rely upon hearsay evidence in reaching his decision. The administrative law judge's concern is with the reliability or probative worth of the evidence.[2] Jury trial rules of evidence exclude hearsay on the theory that it is untrustworthy unless within an exception.[3] More specifically, the risk that hearsay evidence is untrustworthy and that it might be relied upon by the decision maker is, in general, so great that it must be excluded unless some other reason justifies its admission. The party

18. Benjamin 178; see Davis, An Approach to Problems of Evidence in the Administrative Process, 55 Harv.L.Rev. 364, 386–90 (1942).

19. Final Report of Attorney General's Committee on Administrative Procedure, S.Doc. No. 8, 77th Cong., 1st Sess. 71 (1941).

§ 353

1. See Fishing Fleet, Inc. v. Trident Insurance Co., 598 F.2d 925, 929 (5th Cir. 1979); Northwestern National Casualty Co. v. Global Moving & Storage, Inc., 533 F.2d 320, 324 (6th Cir.1976); Goodman v. Highlands Insurance Co., 607 F.2d 665, 668 (5th Cir.1979). See generally Note, 79 Harv.L.Rev. 407 (1965); § 60 supra.

2. The same weighing process is often involved in the examiner's decision whether to receive the evidence. If it is unlikely to be probative, he will not receive it regardless of the inapplicability of the hearsay rule. See § 352 supra.

3. See § 245 supra.

against whom the evidence is admitted can neither confront nor cross-examine the out-of-court declarant to test its probative worth.

But on the other side of the ledger is the fact that each of us constantly relies upon hearsay evidence in making important decisions. Without hearsay, commerce would stop, government would cease to function, and education would be reduced to each teacher's personal experience (and even the latter would often be based upon hearsay). It is not surprising, then, that no legal system outside the Anglo–American realm has adopted so restrictive a rule of evidence. Scholars have argued against its across-the-board application and the courts and Legislatures are increasingly liberalizing its application, even in jury cases.[4]

Nonetheless, the fact that some hearsay may prove reliable is no guarantee that all hearsay is reliable. Nor is it responsive to observe that the rules of evidence already admit much that is worthless. Why, it could be asked, should more that is worthless be admitted in order to find some that is trustworthy, particularly when there is no assurance that the factfinder will rely on the latter and disregard the former? It could also be contended that unless probative evidence could be distilled or some alternative protection devised, the admission of hearsay would not promote justice. The administrative regulations governing the receipt and evaluation of evidence indicate that the agencies themselves have not adequately wrestled with this issue.[5]

The courts have provided only scant guidance in upholding administrative reliance on some hearsay evidence. Judge Learned Hand has offered the classic formulation:

> [The examiner] did indeed admit much that would have been excluded at common law, but the act specifically so provides * * * [N]o doubt, that does not mean mere rumor will serve to "support" a finding, but hearsay may do so, at least if more is not conveniently available, and if in the end the finding is supported by *the kind of evidence on which responsible persons are accustomed to rely in serious affairs.*[6]

Administrative law judges and agencies have adhered to this common-sense standard instinctively.[7] At the same time, several criteria ap-

---

4. See, e.g., Weinstein, Probative Force of Hearsay, 46 Iowa L.Rev. 331 (1961). See also Fed.R.Evid. 803(24), 804(b)(5); § 324.1 supra.

5. See 3 Davis § 16:5. See also § 351 at note 27 supra.

6. N.L.R.B. v. Remington Rand, 94 F.2d 862, 873 (2d Cir.1938), cert. denied 304 U.S. 576 (emphasis added), reversed on other grounds 110 F.2d 148 (2d Cir.). See also International Association of Machinists, etc. v. N.L.R.B., 110 F.2d 29, 35 (D.C.Cir. 1939), affirmed 311 U.S. 72; Bene & Sons, Inc. v. FTC, 299 Fed. 468, 471 (2d Cir.1924). Several states—both by judicial decree and by statute—have adopted this test to per-

mit agency departures from the exclusionary rules where compliance is impracticable and where the evidence is "of a type commonly relied upon by reasonably prudent men in the conduct of their affairs." See, e.g., Ring v. Smith, 5 Cal.App.3d 197, 204, 85 Cal.Rptr. 227, 232 (1970); Official Code Ga.Ann. § 3A–116(a); Mich.Comp. Laws Ann. § 3.560(175); R.I.Gen.Laws 1956, § 42–35–10; W.Va.Code 29A–5–2(a).

7. See Multi–Medical Convalescent and Nursing Center of Towson v. N.L.R.B., 550 F.2d 974, 976–78 (4th Cir.1977), cert. denied 434 U.S. 835; Mobile Consortium of CETA, Alabama v. United States Department of Labor, 745 F.2d 1416 (11th Cir.

plied in evaluating the reliability of hearsay can be discerned.[8]

The following are the most significant:

(a) What is the "nature" of the hearsay evidence? If the hearsay is likely to be reliable, it usually becomes an exception to the hearsay rule. Moreover, if the evidence is intrinsically trustworthy, agencies have taken the next logical step and relied, if necessary, upon this evidence in deciding cases, even though it technically constitutes hearsay and does not fall within any of the recognized exceptions. One example of intrinsically reliable hearsay, intra- and inter-corporate documents not shown to be within the business records exception, was the subject of a celebrated opinion by Judge Wyzanski in a nonjury trial not dissimilar from an administrative hearing.[9] An even clearer example of the reliability criteria is newspaper reports.[10] Stories of significant news events are likely to be reliable. Newspapers normally do not report accidents which did not occur. On the other hand, newspaper summaries of public comments are commonly inaccurate— at least if one may believe those who claim to be misquoted—because of the difficulty of hearing and then summarizing another's views. Even so-called verbatim transcripts commonly suffer from significant errors as a result of the pressure of time deadlines. Note that the hearsay quality of each report is identical. Yet the accident report will be treated as solid support for an administrative decision and the speech summary, unless corroborated, will not.[11]

(b) Is better evidence available? The necessary substantiation for the reliability of hearsay evidence may arise from the failure of respondent to controvert the hearsay when the necessary proof is readily available to him, even though there is no testimonial or documentary exhibit of such available "support." A leading example of this position is United States ex rel. Vajtauer v. Commissioner,[12] where the Supreme Court upheld a deportation order based on a finding that the alien had advocated the overthrow of the government by force. The alien gave his name as Emanuel Vajtauer, a "Doctor of Psychology" and editor of the "Spravedlvost." In making his finding the director relied upon two items of hearsay: a pamphlet bearing the name of Dr. E.M. Vajtauer as author; and a newspaper report of a speech by a Dr.

1984); Sigmon, Rules of Evidence Before the I.C.C., 31 Geo.Wash.L.Rev. 258 (1962); Note, 55 Harv.L.Rev. 820, 827–33 (1942).

8. 3 Davis § 16:6, pp. 243–45.

9. United States v. United Shoe Machinery Corp., 89 F.Supp. 349, 355, 356 (D.Mass.1950), 60 Yale L.J. 363 (1951). More recently such questions have focused on computers and reliance on "computer evidence" in contested hearings. See Note, 126 U.Pa.L.Rev. 425 (1977). In general see Fed.R.Evid. 803(24), 804(b)(5); § 324.1 supra.

10. See Davis, An Approach to Problems of Evidence in the Administrative Process, 55 Harv.L.Rev. 364, 390 (1942); cf.

Dallas County v. Commercial Union Assurance Co., 286 F.2d 388 (5th Cir.1961); Wathen v. United States, 208 Ct.Cl. 342, 527 F.2d 1191, 1199 (1975), cert. denied 429 U.S. 821.

11. See Mikels v. Director, Office of Workers' Compensation Programs, 870 F.2d 1407 (8th Cir.1989); Montana Power Co. v. FPC, 185 F.2d 491, 498 (D.C.Cir. 1950), cert. denied 340 U.S. 947, rehearing denied 341 U.S. 912; United States ex rel. Vajtauer v. Commissioner, 273 U.S. 103 (1927).

12. Id. Note 11 supra.

Vajtauer, editor of the "Spravedlvost," supporting revolution. Both items became convincing evidence when "the appellant, confronted by this record, stood mute. * * * His silence without explanation other than that he would not testify until the entire evidence was presented, was in itself evidence that he was the author." [13]

(c) How important or unimportant is the subject matter in relation to the cost of acquiring "better" evidence? Many examples are available. If the out-of-hearing declarant is readily available and the question involves the respondent's livelihood or security—as is often the case in security and deportation matters—hearsay by itself carries little weight.[14] If, however, the matter is but one of thousands of compensation claims—as in social security and workers' compensation cases— and the declarant's appearance would be relatively costly or time-consuming, hearsay alternatives such as letters or other written evidence might prove decisive.[15] It has likewise been held that in the granting of a license an agency may rely upon evidence which would not be adequate in revoking the same license.[16]

(d) How precise does the agency's factfinding need to be? The Interstate Commerce Commission's reliance on "typical evidence" and the Federal Trade Commission's use of survey evidence are examples of agency dependence on statistical averages to determine facts in particu-

13. Id. at 111. But see Griffin v. California, 380 U.S. 609 (1965), rehearing denied 381 U.S. 957; §§ 131, 270 supra. Workers' compensation cases furnish a further illustration. In one typical case, the testimony revealed that the workman went home, told his wife that he was hurt while at work, repeated the same story to a doctor, and then died. No one saw the accident. No better evidence was available. Placing special reliance on the statute's remedial purpose, the agency relied upon this hearsay evidence even though it fell outside the spontaneous exclamation exception. Greenfarb v. Arre, 62 N.J.Super. 420, 163 A.2d 173 (1960), see John W. McGrath Corp. v. Hughes, 264 F.2d 314 (2d Cir.1959), cert. denied 360 U.S. 931; Associated General Contractors of America v. Cardillo, 106 F.2d 327, 329 (D.C.Cir.1939); cf. G. & C. Merriam Co. v. Syndicate Publishing Co., 207 Fed. 515, 518 (2d Cir.1913) (quoting trial court opinion by L. Hand, J.). See generally, Larson, The Law of Workmen's Compensation § 79 (1952) and 2 id. (Supp.1970). On the other hand, if credible firsthand witnesses were to have told another story—for example, that the accident happened elsewhere—the hearing officer would likely have rejected the hearsay testimony, especially if the eyewitness testimony is corroborated by convincing circumstantial evidence. Jacobowitz v. United States, 191 Ct.Cl. 444, 424 F.2d 555

(1970); In re Rath Packing Co., 14 N.L.R.B. 805, 817 (1939); see Glaros v. Immigration and Naturalization Service, 416 F.2d 441 (5th Cir.1969) (hearsay corroborated by other evidence); N.L.R.B. v. Operating Engineers, Local 12, 25 Ad.L.2d 832 (9th Cir. 1969) (no objection raised to admission of hearsay). See § 297 supra.

14. E.g., Young v. Board of Pharmacy, 81 N.M. 5, 462 P.2d 139 (1969); Outagamie County v. Town of Brooklyn, 18 Wis.2d 303, 118 N.W.2d 201 (1962); see Reilly v. Pinkus, 338 U.S. 269 (1949). Contra: Peters v. United States, 187 Ct.Cl. 63, 408 F.2d 719 (1969), criticized in Note, Hearsay and Confrontation in Administrative Hearings, 48 N.C.L.Rev. 608 (1970).

15. Richardson v. Perales, 402 U.S. 389 (1971), supra § 351, Note 6; Pacific Gas & Electric Co. v. F.E.R.C., 746 F.2d 1383 (9th Cir.1984); Marmon v. Railroad Retirement Board, 218 F.2d 716 (3d Cir.1955); Ellers v. Railroad Retirement Board, 132 F.2d 636 (2d Cir.1943). For a reverse application of this principle, see Staskel v. Gardner, 274 F.Supp. 861, 863 (E.D.Pa.1967) (hearsay not sufficient evidence to deny claim); Rios v. Hackney, 294 F.Supp. 885 (N.D.Tex.1967).

16. Davis, Hearsay in Administrative Hearings, 32 Geo.Wash.L.Rev. 689, 699 (1964); see FTC v. Cement Institute, 333 U.S. 683, 705–06 (1948), rehearing denied 334 U.S. 839.

lar cases where legal or policy decisions are not dependent upon exact determinations. For instance, survey evidence of consumer understanding indicating that a substantial proportion of the public were misled by respondent's advertising will support a finding that it constitutes an unfair or deceptive act.[17] Still another example is the fixing of a rate for commodities transported by one carrier on the basis of costs incurred by similarly situated carriers.[18]

(e) What is the administrative policy behind the statute being enforced? The range of necessary reliability is affected by the type of policy which the administrative hearing is designed to promote. For example, the social security and workers' compensation programs are intended to provide benefits quickly at low cost. The refusal to rely upon reports in such hearings would run counter to the purposes for which the statutes are designed.[19]

When focusing on these criteria, it is essential to consider the central point that evaluation of hearsay and other technically incompetent evidence cannot be accomplished in the abstract; the evidence must be examined in the light of the particular record. This includes, at a minimum, an examination of the quality and quantity of the evidence on each side, as well as the circumstantial setting of the case.[20]

§ 354. The Substantial Evidence Rule

Once the agency has determined that legally incompetent evidence can be admitted and relied upon in making an administrative decision, it might appear that the subject of hearsay evidence in administrative hearings has been exhausted. While the agency's admission and use of legally incompetent evidence is subject to judicial review, this review of administrative determinations of fact should be confined to determining whether the decision is supported by the evidence in the record. Judicial review of administrative evidence has not been so limited, however. As a substitute for rules of admissibility, courts apply the so-

---

17. E.g., Williams v. United States Department of Transportation, 781 F.2d 1573 (11th Cir.1986); Arrow Metal Products Corp., 53 F.T.C. 721, 727, 733–34 (1957), affirmed per curiam, 249 F.2d 83 (3d Cir.); Rhodes Pharmacal Co., 49 F.T.C. 263 (1952), affirmed 208 F.2d 382, 386–87 (7th Cir.), reversed on other grounds 348 U.S. 940. See generally Bernacchi, Trademark Meaning and Non–Partisan Survey Research, 30 Ad.L.Rev. 447 (1978).

18. Atchison, Topeka & Santa Fe Railway v. United States, 225 F.Supp. 584 (D.Colo.1964); New England Division Case, 261 U.S. 184, 197–198 (1923); see 2 Sharfman, The Interstate Commerce Com'n 376–80 (1931). See also Skelly Oil Co. v. FPC, 375 F.2d 6 (10th Cir.1967), modified sub nom. Permian Basin Area Rate Cases, 390

U.S. 747 (1968), rehearing denied 392 U.S. 917.

19. Richardson v. Perales, 402 U.S. 389 (1971), supra § 351, note 6. Several states have also adopted specific statutes governing the use of copies of documentary evidence. See Official Code Ga.Ann. § 3A–116(b); Hawaii Rev.Stat. § 91–10(2); Md. Code 1957, Art. 41, § 252(b); Mass.Gen. Laws Ann. c. 30A, § 11(4); Mich.Comp. Laws Ann. § 3.560(176); Minn.Stat.Ann. § 14.60; Neb.Rev.Stat. § 84–914(3); 75 Okl.Stat.Ann. § 310(2); Or.Rev.Stat. 183.-450(2); R.I.Gen.Laws 1956, § 42–35–10(b); West's RCWA 34.04.100(2). See also Fed. R.Evid. 1003.

20. For a review of the cases, see Jacobowitz v. United States, 191 Ct.Cl. 444, 424 F.2d 555 (1970).

called "substantial evidence" rule to judicial review of agency action in seeking to assure fairness to the parties.

As applied to administrative findings, the substantial evidence rule possesses two branches, one of which is sound, and the other unsound. The first consists of an overall standard of review of the findings of fact. Except for the distinctive features of judicial review of administrative action, it does not differ conceptually from the "sufficiency" standard applied in judicial review of jury verdicts.[1] In this sense, substantial evidence is evidence

> affording a substantial basis of fact from which the fact in issue can be reasonably inferred. * * * [I]t must be enough to justify, if the trial were to a jury, a refusal to direct a verdict when the conclusion sought to be drawn from it is one of fact for the jury.[2]

This standard measures both the quantitative and qualitative sufficiency of the evidence.[3] Its proper application takes into account the rationale of the exclusionary rules of evidence, the reliability of the hearsay evidence—including the opportunity for cross-examination, the availability of better evidence, and the appearance of corroborating evidence—and the needs of administrative economy. According to the still leading opinion of Universal Camera Corp. v. NLRB,[4] this judicially evolved standard of review of administrative factfinding is incorporated into the Administrative Procedure Act, except that the Act broadens judicial review to assure that the reviewing court takes "into account whatever in the record fairly detracts from its weight."[5] In other words, the reviewing court should review the whole record to determine whether there is a rational basis in it for the findings of fact supporting the agency's decision.[6]

In reviewing administrative decisions, some appellate courts—primarily state—added a second branch to the substantial evidence test, warping the test into a rigid rule for denying credibility to uncorroborated hearsay evidence. Known as the "legal residuum rule" because it required that an administrative finding be supported by some evi-

§ 354

1. E.g. Wilkerson v. McCarthy, 336 U.S. 53, 57 (1949), rehearing denied 336 U.S. 940; § 339 supra.

2. N.L.R.B. v. Columbian Enameling & Stamping Co., 306 U.S. 292, 299–300 (1939). See also Consolo v. FMC, 383 U.S. 607, 618–21 (1966), on remand 373 F.2d 674 (D.C.Cir.); Richardson v. Perales, 402 U.S. 389 (1971), supra § 351 note 12. The substantial evidence test applied to jury verdicts and administrative findings is in contrast to appellate review of a court's fact determinations in a nonjury case where findings are measured by the "clearly erroneous" test. See United States v. United States Gypsum Co., 333 U.S. 364, 395 (1948), rehearing denied 333 U.S. 869; Amadeo v. Zant, 486 U.S. 214 (1988);

Wright, Law of Federal Courts 647–50 (4th ed. 1983).

3. See Benjamin 192; 1 Cooper 404–05.

4. 340 U.S. 474 (1951).

5. Id. at 488.

6. The intricacies and problems which arise in applying this standard are not within our concern here. See generally Greater Boston Television Corp. v. FCC, 444 F.2d 841, 850–52 (D.C.Cir.1970), cert. denied 403 U.S. 923; Bates v. Sullivan, 894 F.2d 1059 (9th Cir.1990); Robinson, Gellhorn & Bruff, The Administrative Process 132–41 (2d ed. 1980). For a review of state authority, see Cooper 722–55, which is extremely critical of the substantial evidence standard.

dence admissible in a jury trial—that is, by a residuum of "legal" evidence—it has been severely criticized by scholars, and its application has strained judicial reasoning.[7]

The residuum rule is both logically unsound and administratively impractical. In a trial before a lay jury hearsay evidence admitted without objection is given its natural, probative effect and may be the sole support for a verdict. But under the residuum rule hearsay cannot support a decision by an experienced or expert administrator. The rule ignores the reliability of technically incompetent evidence, rendering all such evidence ineffective unless corroborated. However, if corroborated, regardless of how slight the legal evidence, the same hearsay evidence will provide the substantial evidence needed to support the administrative finding.

This rule may also become a trap for the unwary, particularly where the administrative law judge is not expert in the rules of evidence or where the parties are not represented by counsel. In fact it encourages administrative law judges to apply the hearsay rule and exclude probative evidence in order to avoid possible error. In its instinctive protection of fairness in administrative hearings, through assuring that the decision is supported by evidence subject to confrontation and cross-examination, the residuum rule seems unassailable. What it fails to consider, however, is that much "legal" evidence within the hearsay exceptions is equally untested. Yet the latter is accepted even in jury trials because of its probable reliability. Consequently the residuum rule's mechanical prohibition against uncorroborated hearsay is unsound. Its sound objectives can be secured through the sensitivity of the hearing officers and the wise application of the substantial evidence

---

7. 3 Davis § 16:6; Benjamin 189–92; 1 Wigmore, Evidence § 4B, p. 39 (3d ed. 1940). But see 1 Cooper 410–12.

The earliest case applying this rule illustrates its weakness. In Carroll v. Knickerbocker Ice Co., 218 N.Y. 435, 113 N.E. 507 (1916), the New York Court of Appeals reversed a worker's compensation award in a death case where the commission's finding of accidental injury was based wholly on hearsay testimony of statements by the deceased workman. The workman, who developed delirium tremens and died within six days, had told his wife, a neighbor, and his family and hospital physician that a 300–pound cake of ice had fallen upon his abdomen. Each party related this story to the commission. However, the case record also contained substantial contradictory evidence. The workman's helper on the ice truck, along with two cooks working in the saloon where the ice was delivered also testified that they were present at the same time and place where the accident presumably occurred but they neither saw nor heard the incident. In addition, the hospital physicians found no bruises, discolorations, or abrasions on the workman's body. In light of the lack of testimonial or physical corroboration of the workman's story which probably would have been available if the hearsay statement had been trustworthy, the obvious self-interest in the deceased's statement, and the possibility of the workman's being inebriated when he made his statement, the court reasonably could have ruled that credence could not be placed in the supporting hearsay evidence and that it did not, therefore, constitute substantial evidence. Instead, after noting that the commission could "accept any evidence that is offered" under the New York Workman's Compensation Act, the court laid down the rule that "still in the end there must be a residuum of legal evidence to support the claim before an award can be made." Id. at 441, 113 N.E. at 509. It therefore held that when substantial evidence is required, "hearsay testimony is no evidence." Id.

test which measures the quantity and quality of the supporting evidence regardless of its category or label.

As others have recounted at substantial length, the residuum rule generally lacks acceptance in federal courts.[8] Increasingly the states refuse to apply it.[9]

§ 355. Opinion Evidence and Expert Testimony [1]

The presentation of expert and nonexpert opinions is increasingly common in administrative hearings. Medical issues arising in workers' compensation claims are often complex, technical and beyond the knowledge of either the hearing officer or the agency. An administrative decision to license a hydroelectric plant, to locate a public housing project, to discontinue a bus line, or to grant a liquor license invariably evokes strong community concern.[2] The public views advanced are likely to be expressed in terms of opinions and to include reference to the views of others. To deny the public an opportunity to testify is to invite public rejection of the agency decision or judicial reversal because public participation is required under the agency's enabling legislation.

The general admissibility of expert and nonexpert testimony in administrative hearings is no longer open to question, but doubt still exists regarding the weight an expert's views should be given.[3] For a time agencies and reviewing courts followed early judicial reasoning and refused to hear expert testimony on the very question that the agency was created to decide.[4] Other courts took the position that it

8. 3 Davis § 16:6, and see Richardson v. Perales, 402 U.S. 389 (1971), supra § 351 note 12; Johnson v. United States, 628 F.2d 187 (D.C.Cir.1980).

9. See Tauber v. County Board of Appeals, 257 Md. 202, 262 A.2d 513, 518 (1970); Neuman v. City of Baltimore, 251 Md. 92, 246 A.2d 583 (1968); 1 Cooper 406–10. The 1981 Revised Model State Administrative Procedure Act provides in part:

4–215(d) * * * Findings must be based upon the kind of evidence on which reasonably prudent persons are accustomed to rely in the conduct of their serious affairs and may be based upon such evidence even if it would be inadmissible in a civil trial.

The Commissioners' Comment further dispels any doubts when it states: "this Act rejects the 'residuum rule,' under which findings can be made only if supported, in the record, by at least a 'residuum' of legally admissible evidence."

§ 355

1. See generally Gellhorn, Proof of Consumer Deception Before the Federal Trade Commission, 17 U.Kan.L.Rev. 559 (1969).

2. Cf. Vermont Yankee Nuclear Power Corp. v. Natural Resources Defense Council, Inc., 435 U.S. 519 (1978); Sierra Club v. Costle, 657 F.2d 298 (D.C.Cir.1981); Scenic Hudson Preservation Conference v. FPC, 354 F.2d 608 (2d Cir.1965), cert. denied 384 U.S. 941, appeal after remand 453 F.2d 463 (2d Cir.), cert. denied 407 U.S. 926; Citizens for Allegan County, Inc. v. FPC, 414 F.2d 1125 (D.C.Cir.1969); Office of Communication of United Church of Christ v. FCC, 359 F.2d 994 (D.C.Cir.1966); Norwalk CORE v. Norwalk Redevelopment Agency, 395 F.2d 920 (2d Cir.1968).

3. Duvall v. United States, 647 F.2d 131 (Ct.Cl.1981); Office of Communication of United Church of Christ v. FCC, supra note 2; see Gellhorn, Public Participation in Administrative Proceedings, 81 Yale L.J. 359 (1972).

4. Cf. § 12 supra; Corn v. State Bar, 68 Cal.2d 461, 67 Cal.Rptr. 401, 439 P.2d 313 (1968). The courts have generally discarded the earlier view that agency opinions need supporting expert testimony, and agencies are now free to use their own judgment. Compare Boggs & Buhl v. Com-

would be unfair for an agency to rely on its own expertness or the expert testimony of its staff when their opinions were contradicted by outside experts.[5] In rejecting these contradictory appeals to ignorance, courts now recognize legislative intention to establish expert agencies. Therefore, agency decisions which rely on the agency's own expertness are upheld when the respondent offers no contrary expert testimony or when expert testimony offered by staff members and outside experts conflicts.[6] Some courts have gone even further and given excessive deference to the knowledge of the administrative agency by upholding its decision in the face of uncontradicted expert testimony to the contrary.[7] However, the demands of fairness are now generally accepted, and an agency seeking to rely on its expertise must present expert testimony subject to cross-examination on the record or give the respondent fair notification that official notice will be taken of such "facts."[8]

§ 356. Privilege in Administrative Proceedings

Witnesses in administrative hearings have the same general duty incumbent on all citizens in judicial trials to give testimony; "the

missioner, 34 F.2d 859 (3d Cir.1929), with Kline v. Commissioner, 130 F.2d 742 (3d Cir.1942), cert. denied 317 U.S. 697.

5. Brennan v. State Board of Medical Examiners, 101 Cal.App.2d 193, 225 P.2d 11 (1950). See § 12 supra.

6. E.g., Penn Allegheny Coal Co. v. Mercatell, 878 F.2d 106 (3d Cir.1989); Pagel, Inc. v. S.E.C., 803 F.2d 942 (8th Cir. 1986); Pacific Power & Light Co. v. FPC, 141 F.2d 602 (9th Cir.1944); Contractors v. Pillsbury, 150 F.2d 310, 313 (9th Cir.1945); see McCarthy v. Industrial Commission, 194 Wis. 198, 215 N.W. 824 (1927).

This is an exceedingly brief summary of what can be a complex issue. For an excellent analysis and attempt to balance the right of respondent to a decision based on "record" evidence with the administrative need to avoid unproductive hearings, see Davis & Randall, Inc. v. United States, 219 F.Supp. 673 (W.D.N.Y.1963), where Judge Friendly applied the following test:

> Without wishing to be held to the letter, we suggest that a rejection of unopposed testimony by a qualified and disinterested expert on a matter susceptible of reasonably precise measurement, without the agency's developing its objections at a hearing, ought to be upheld only when the agency's uncommunicated criticisms appear to the reviewing court to be both so compelling and so deeply held that the court can be fairly sure the

agency would not have been affected by anything the witness could have said had he known of them, *and* the court would have been bound to affirm, despite the expert's hypothetical rebuttal out of deference for the agency's judgment on so technical a matter.

Id. at 679.

7. See, e.g., Arcadia Realty Co. v. Commissioner, 295 F.2d 98, 103 (8th Cir.1961); Gaddy v. State Board of Registration for Healing Arts, 397 S.W.2d 347, 355 (Mo. 1965); Abel Converting Inc. v. United States, 679 F.Supp. 1133 (D.D.C.1988). But see Jaffe, Judicial Control of Administrative Action 607–10 (1965). Judicial approval of agency reliance upon its own expertise is inappropriate, of course, where the expert opinion is patently fallacious or "intrinsically nonpersuasive." See Davis & Randall, Inc. v. United States, supra note 6 at 678; Sternberger v. United States, 185 Ct.Cl. 528, 401 F.2d 1012, 1016 (1968). Approval is equally inappropriate where the opinion is based on inferences from facts in the record. Interstate Power Co. v. Federal Power Commission, 236 F.2d 372, 385 (8th Cir.1956), cert. denied 352 U.S. 967; see Market St. Railway Co. v. Railroad Commission, 324 U.S. 548, 559–560 (1945).

8. McLeod v. I.N.S., 802 F.2d 89 (3d Cir.1986); Moschogianis v. Concrete Material & Manufacturing Co., 179 Minn. 177, 228 N.W. 607 (1930); see § 359 infra.

public has a right to every man's testimony."[1] Because the demand comes from the community as a whole, rather than from the parties, and because the obligation is essential to any search for justice, "all privileges of exemption from this duty are exceptional."[2] Read literally, the APA's provision in section 556(d) that "[a]ny oral or documentary evidence may be received,"[3] authorizes the receipt of privileged evidence in administrative hearings.[4]

Nevertheless, administrative hearings have generally followed the judicial lead in recognizing numerous exceptions to the obligation to testify. The exceptions are of two kinds. A few, such as the exclusion of illegally obtained evidence and the assertion of the right against self-incrimination, are constitutional commands. Others, such as the privileges protecting attorney-client and the attorney's work product, are founded upon the need to protect interests without constitutional dimension yet having sufficient social importance to warrant the sacrifice of full factual disclosure.[5]

Even though administrative agencies do not as a rule impose criminal penalties, their adjudicative procedures are not exempt from constitutional limitations, and the chapters of this text which deal with the various constitutional privileges should be consulted. In Camara v. Municipal Court,[6] and See v. Seattle,[7] the Supreme Court applied the Fourth Amendment's strictures against unreasonable searches and seizure of property to administrative health and fire inspections,[8] albeit in somewhat qualified form. These decisions left open the possibility that warrants would not be required for administrative searches where a license was required to conduct the business in question and the grant of a license was effectively conditioned on the applicant's consent to warrantless searches. Later cases confirmed that warrantless searches were permissible in industries subject to a licensing system which involved intensive regulation, i.e., "closely regulated."[9] Compare Mar-

§ 356

1. 12 Cobbett's Parliamentary History 675, 693 (1812), quoted in 4 Wigmore, Evidence 2965–66 (1st ed. 1905).

2. 8 Wigmore, Evidence § 2192, p. 73 (McNaughton rev. 1961).

3. 5 U.S.C.A. § 556(d).

4. Professor Davis once made the provocative suggestion that § 7(c) authorizes agency rejection of unsound or questionable privileges. 3 Davis § 16:12 at 266 (1980). It seems doubtful, however, that this provision can reasonably be interpreted as addressing itself to the question of testimonial privilege; rather, the legislative history suggests that its purpose is to avoid binding administrative agencies to technical rules of evidence. 92 Cong.Rec. 2157, 5653 (1946); see Attorney General's Manual on Administrative Procedure Act 76 (1947). In any case, it is now clear that the agencies generally "respect rules of

privilege" and thus litigation seldom results. See 3 Davis § 16:10.

Privileges under state law are generally governed by statutes sufficiently broad in terms to apply to administrative proceedings. The same generalization cannot be made in the federal area. See § 76 supra.

5. See Chapter 8 supra.

6. 387 U.S. 523 (1967).

7. 387 U.S. 541 (1967).

8. See generally Notes, 78 Harv.L.Rev. 801 (1965), 77 Yale L.J. 521 (1968); Williams, Liberty and Property: The Problem of Government Benefits, 12 J.Legal Studies 3 (1983); Pierce, The Role of Constitutional and Political Theory in Administrative Law, 64 Texas L.Rev. 469 (1985).

9. New York v. Burger, 482 U.S. 691, 701 (1987) (warrantless search of junkyard for stolen parts approved: "Because the

shall v. Barlow's, Inc.,[10] where the Supreme Court ruled that businesses subject to oversight by the Occupational Safety and Health Administration were not "pervasively regulated" and thus could assert the Fourth Amendment privilege against surprise inspections of the workplace. The privilege against unreasonable search is also limited to that which is truly private. Thus a warrant is not necessary if the evidence gathered by the inspector is in "plain view." [11]

While these cases involved direct challenges to administrative inspections, it is also clear that the constitutional objection is available at the hearing even though no objection is asserted at the time the inspection is made.[12] And, in Knoll Associates, Inc. v. FTC,[13] the Court of Appeals of the Seventh Circuit set aside an FTC order on the ground that the Commission's acceptance and use of corporate documents, known to be stolen on behalf of the government, violated the Fourth Amendment.

Many cases uphold the Fifth Amendment privilege against self-incrimination in administrative proceedings.[14] For the Fifth Amend-

owner or operator of commercial premises in a 'closely regulated' industry has a reduced expectation of privacy, the warrant and probable-cause requirements, which fulfill the traditional Fourth Amendment standard of reasonableness for a government search * * * have lessened application in this context. Rather, we conclude that, as in other situations of 'special need,' * * * where the privacy interests of the owner are weakened and the government interests in regulating particular businesses are concomitantly heightened, a warrantless inspection of commercial premises may well be reasonable within the meaning of the Fourth Amendment."). Accord Colonnade Catering Corp. v. United States, 397 U.S. 72 (1970) (licensed retail liquor establishment); United States v. Biswell, 406 U.S. 311 (1972) (firearms dealer); Donovan v. Dewey, 452 U.S. 594 (1981) (pervasive regulatory exception applicable to mining industry where statute required inspection of all mines and specified the frequency of inspection). See generally McManis & McManis, Structuring Administrative Inspections: Is There Any Warrant for a Search Warrant? 26 Am. U.L.Rev. 942 (1977); § 170, text at Notes 10–12 supra.

10. 436 U.S. 307 (1978). See discussion of administrative searches in § 170, text at Notes 10–16 supra.

11. Id. See also Air Pollution Variance Board of Colorado v. Western Alfalfa Corp., 416 U.S. 861 (1974) (emission from smokestack visible from public areas of factory grounds); Michigan v. Tyler, 436 U.S. 499 (1978); New York v. Burger, 482 U.S. 691 (1987).

12. See Finn's Liquor Shop, Inc. v. State Liquor Authority, 24 N.Y.2d 647, 301 N.Y.S.2d 584, 249 N.E.2d 440 (1969), cert. denied 396 U.S. 840; Leogrande v. State Liquor Authority, 25 A.D.2d 225, 268 N.Y.S.2d 433 (1966), reversed on other grounds 19 N.Y.2d 418, 280 N.Y.S.2d 381, 227 N.E.2d 302 (1967); Pennsylvania Liquor Control Board v. Leonardziak, 210 Pa.Super. 511, 233 A.2d 606 (1967); cf. Parrish v. Civil Service Commission, 66 Cal.2d 260, 57 Cal.Rptr. 623, 425 P.2d 223 (1967). Compare Elder v. Board of Medical Examiners, 241 Cal.App.2d 246, 50 Cal. Rptr. 304 (1966) (dictum), with Pierce v. Board of Nursing Education & Nurse Registration, 255 Cal.App.2d 463, 63 Cal.Rptr. 107 (1967) (dictum). Contra, National Labor Relations Board v. South Bay Daily Breeze, 415 F.2d 360, 364 (9th Cir.1969) (alternative holding), cert. denied 397 U.S. 915; Solomon v. Liquor Control Commission, 4 Ohio St.2d 31, 212 N.E.2d 595 (1966), cert. denied 384 U.S. 928.

13. 397 F.2d 530 (7th Cir.1968). Where the documents are obtained independently of any purpose to help the government, they have been held to be admissible. O'Conner v. Ortega, 480 U.S. 709 (1987); United States v. Marzano, 537 F.2d 257 (7th Cir.1976), cert. denied 429 U.S. 1038; United States v. Newton, 510 F.2d 1149 (7th Cir.1975).

14. E.g., United States Department of Labor v. Triplett, 494 U.S. 715 (1990); Murphy v. Waterfront Commission, 378 U.S. 52 (1964); Smith v. United States, 337 U.S. 137 (1949). In this situation, the respondent fears the potential administrative order less than the subsequent use of his testimony in a criminal proceeding.

ment privilege to apply certain conditions must be met. First, the threatened penalty must be criminal rather than civil in nature.[15] In many regulatory areas, the sanction which the witness fears may be labeled a "civil penalty," a "forfeiture" or a similar term rather than a crime. When this occurs, the court must determine whether the statutory penalty is sufficiently punitive in purpose or effect to be considered criminal. Second, the privilege is available only to natural persons and therefore does not protect corporations and other legal entities.[16] The purpose of the self-incrimination provision is to protect individuals from the government's use of the "third degree" and similar coercive tactics to extract confessions of personal wrong-doing. Thus it does not exempt the officers of corporations and other business associations from testifying about the records of their organizations.[17] Because the privilege is personal to the witness, an individual cannot refuse to testify on the ground that his testimony might incriminate some other person.[18] Third, the privilege attaches only to compelled testimonial utterances and not to other communications.[19] Numerous cases have dealt with the question of whether a particular statement has been coerced or whether it is testimonial in nature. Recent cases have, in general, taken a restrictive view of the privilege.[20] Thus, even if the documents being sought are personal records, are in his possession, and contain handwritten notations, the agency may still be able to obtain them through use of a search warrant.[21] On the other hand, the Fifth Amendment analysis may be different if the agency seeks to compel an individual to report information rather than trying to get access to existing documents.[22] That is, where the government requires an individual or business to keep business records and make them available to government on demand, such "required records" are not immune from disclosure so long as the underlying regulatory program was a proper exercise of governmental power and the recordkeeping requirement was not designed to make otherwise lawful conduct illegal.[23] Finally, the privilege can be defeated by the grant of immunity from criminal prosecution.[24] Federal agencies commonly have been authorized to grant immunity and compel a witness to testify even if the evidence implicates him.[25] The agency must find that the testimo-

---

See generally Ch. 13 supra.

15. United States v. Ward, 448 U.S. 242 (1980) (requirement that persons responsible for oil spills in navigable waters must report the spills to appropriate government agencies not a violation of Fifth Amendment despite civil penalties of $5,000 for each spill); Kennedy v. Mendoza–Martinez, 372 U.S. 144, 168–169 (1963). See generally Flemming v. Nestor, 363 U.S. 603, 613–21 (1960); § 121 supra.

16. See § 128 supra.

17. See Bellis v. United States, 417 U.S. 85 (1974); § 129 supra.

18. Couch v. United States, 409 U.S. 322 (1973); § 120 supra.

19. Couch v. United States, supra note 18; Fisher v. United States, 425 U.S. 391 (1976). See §§ 124, 125 supra.

20. Id. See 1 Davis § 4:24.

21. Andresen v. Maryland, 427 U.S. 463 (1976). See § 127 supra.

22. See Shapiro v. United States, 335 U.S. 1, 6 (1948), rehearing denied 335 U.S. 836.

23. See discussion of required reports in § 142 supra.

24. See § 143 supra.

25. 18 U.S.C.A. §§ 6001–6005.

ny is "necessary to the public interest," and it must obtain the approval of the Attorney General before immunizing the witness.[26]

On the federal level, neither the Congress nor the agencies have focused on whether administrative agencies must recognize testimonial privileges not constitutionally required. In a leading case concerning the enforcement of an SEC subpoena, Judge Learned Hand expressly assumed that agency proceedings are "subject to the same testimonial privileges as judicial proceedings." [27] Other federal courts have either made the same assumption or considered the matter a question of federal law.[28] Applying the law of privilege applicable in judicial proceedings has considerable merit. Accordingly federal agencies have accorded privileged treatment to communications between attorney and client and husband and wife.[29] But they have not been anxious to extend such privileges. For example, the accountant-client privileges recognized by a few states has not been accepted by federal agencies.[30] Business secrets have been protected grudgingly, although agencies have become more sophisticated in recent years in protecting both the witness and the adjudicative process by *in camera* receipt of sensitive data.[31]

Claims of privilege for government secrets are particularly important in administrative hearings. Any attempt to probe the government's case by discovery, subpoena of agency witnesses, or cross-examination is quickly met by claims that the information sought is privileged. Actually, government secrets privilege is asserted as an umbrella for three types of information: state secrets involving military or diplomatic information; requests that executive officers testify; and official government information which may range from the identity of informers and internal management materials to staff studies unrelated to any litigation.[32] Only the third, omnibus exception has special signifi-

---

26. 18 U.S.C.A. § 6004.

27. McMann v. Securities & Exchange Commission, 87 F.2d 377, 378 (2d Cir.1937), cert. denied 301 U.S. 684.

28. E.g. Colton v. United States, 306 F.2d 633 (2d Cir.1962), cert. denied 371 U.S. 951; Falsone v. United States, 205 F.2d 734 (5th Cir.1953), cert. denied 346 U.S. 864; United States v. Threlkeld, 241 F.Supp. 324 (W.D.Tenn.1965); In re Kearney, 227 F.Supp. 174 (S.D.N.Y.1964). Contra: Baird v. Koerner, 279 F.2d 623 (9th Cir.1960); In re Bretto, 231 F.Supp. 529 (D.Minn.1964) (*Baird* applied pursuant to stipulation of the parties). For a perceptive student comment questioning accuracy of this assessment of the choice of law problem, see Comment, Privileged Communications Before Federal Administrative Agencies: The Law Applied in the District Courts, 31 U.Chi.L.Rev. 395 (1964). For more about Baird v. Koerner, supra, see § 90 supra.

29. In re Federal Trade Commission Line of Business Report Litigation, 595 F.2d 685 (D.C.Cir.1978), cert. denied 439 U.S. 958; S.E.C. v. Forma, 117 F.R.D. 516 (S.D.N.Y.1987). See generally Chapters 9 and 10 supra.

30. See, e.g., Federal Trade Commission v. St. Regis Paper Co., 304 F.2d 731 (7th Cir.1962); Falsone v. United States, note 28 supra.

31. Federal Trade Commission v. Lonning, 539 F.2d 202 (D.C.Cir.1976); Federal Trade Commission v. Texaco, Inc., 517 F.2d 137 (D.C.Cir.1975), cert. denied 431 U.S. 974; Wearly v. Federal Trade Commission, 462 F.Supp. 589 (D.N.J.1978), vacated 616 F.2d 662, cert. denied 449 U.S. 822, 16 C.F.R. § 3.45; Occidental Petroleum Corp. v. S.E.C., 873 F.2d 325 (D.C.Cir.1989).

32. See Ch. 12 supra.

cance for administrative adjudications; the judicial rules applicable to state secrets and executive officer testimony are followed in agency hearings. An exploration of all the twists and turns given agency applications of the omnibus exception is beyond the scope of this chapter.[33] In any event, exculpatory information in an agency's possession or file data which may aid respondent's preparation or presentation of his case must be disclosed by the agency.[34] The alternative is to drop the prosecution against the respondent.[35] Anything less would violate the commands of procedural due process which every adjudication must observe.[36]

Almost half the states provide that rules of privilege applicable in court proceedings must apply in administrative hearings.[37] Courts and agencies in other states have reached the same position as a matter of policy.[38] The scope of the statutory recognition of privileged communications in the states tends to exceed the testimonial exception recognized by federal courts.[39] On the other hand, where agency proceedings are excepted or where no statutory mandate exists, state agencies have on occasion relaxed or avoided testimonial privileges where the rationale for the privilege is weak or not particularly appropriate. For example, several states have held that the physician-patient privilege cannot bar a worker's compensation commission's search for the truth.[40]

§ 357. Presentation of Case: Burden of Proof and Presumptions

The customary common law rule that the moving party has the burden of proof—including not only the burden of going forward but

33. For an explanation of one agency's approach, see Gellhorn, The Treatment of Confidential Information by the Federal Trade Commission: The Hearing, 116 U.Pa.L.Rev. 401, 423–27 (1968); Gellhorn, The Treatment of Confidential Information by the Federal Trade Commission: Pretrial Practices, 36 U.Chi.L.Rev. 113, 157–77 (1968); cf. Moore–McCormack Lines, Inc. v. United States, 188 Ct.Cl. 644, 413 F.2d 568 (1969). The Freedom of Information Act, 5 U.S.C.A. § 552 has eased access to some agency files for the public, but it has had little effect on agency application. Exxon Corp. v. FTC, 589 F.2d 582 (D.C.Cir.1978), cert. denied 441 U.S. 943; Federal Trade Commission v. Anderson, 442 F.Supp. 1118 (D.D.C.1977); see § 108 supra.

34. E.g., United States v. Atisha, 804 F.2d 920 (6th Cir.1986), cert. denied 479 U.S. 1067; Sperandeo v. Dairy Employees Local 537, 334 F.2d 381 (10th Cir.1964); National Labor Relations Board v. Capitol Fish Co., 294 F.2d 868 (5th Cir.1961); cf. Miller v. Pate, 386 U.S. 1 (1967); Giles v. Maryland, 386 U.S. 66 (1967); Brady v. Maryland, 373 U.S. 83, 87–88 (1963); United States v. Bryant, 439 F.2d 642 (D.C.Cir. 1971).

35. See Sperandeo v. Dairy Employees Local 537, note 34 supra; cf. United States v. Andolschek, 142 F.2d 503 (2d Cir.1944); Berger & Krash, Government Immunity from Discovery, 59 Yale L.J. 1451, 1453 (1950).

36. E.g., FCC v. Pottsville Broadcasting Co., 309 U.S. 134, 143–144 (1940); Bureau of Alcohol, Tobacco and Firearms v. Federal Labor Relations Authority, 464 U.S. 89 (1983).

37. 1 Cooper 396–97 (collecting authorities).

38. E.g., New York City Council v. Goldwater, 284 N.Y. 296, 31 N.E.2d 31 (1940); Benjamin 171.

39. E.g., Okl.Stat.Ann. § 75–310(1).

40. See, e.g., Cooper's, Inc. v. Long, 224 So.2d 866 (Miss.1969); Danussi v. Easy Wash, Inc., 270 Minn. 465, 134 N.W.2d 138 (1965).

also the burden of persuasion—is generally observed in administrative hearings. Section 556(d) of the APA, for example, provides: "Except as otherwise provided by statute, the proponent of a rule or order has the burden of proof." [1] State courts have reached the same result in connection with state administrative proceedings. [2]

In most hearings the burden of persuasion is met by the usual civil case standard of "a preponderance of evidence." The rule applicable to federal administrative adjudications was not settled, however, until 1981. In Steadman v. SEC, [3] a broker-dealer being prosecuted by the commission for fraudulent activities had challenged the proceeding, arguing that violation of the antifraud provisions of the securities laws must be proved by the equity standard of clear and convincing evidence. He contended that the potentially severe sanctions (revocation of his license) as well as the circumstantial and inferential nature of the evidence used to prove intent to defraud, required the higher standard of proof. A divided Court rejected his argument. The Court held that the language of Section 556(d) of the APA and the legislative history both show Congress intended that administrative adjudications be measured by the usual standard.

On the other hand, where Congress has not spoken and grave issues of personal security are at stake in an administrative hearing, as in a deportation proceeding, the courts are free to exercise their traditional oversight powers and fashion appropriate standards. Thus in Woodby v. INS, [4] the Supreme Court ruled that in deportation proceedings where liberty is at stake, the government must establish its allegations by "clear, unequivocal, and convincing evidence."

It is also not uncommon for courts to employ the substantial evidence standard to impose a special burden of proof on administrative agencies. This is particularly true in compensation benefits cases where the legislative design is read as favoring awards despite inadequate evidentiary support. A series of cases involving social security and other compensation proceedings has required that the agency accept the claimant's uncontroverted evidence even though the claimant has the burden of proof. [5] Nor can these cases be explained away on the

---

§ 357

1. 5 U.S.C.A. § 556(d).

2. E.g., State ex rel. Utilities Commission v. Carolina Power & Light Co., 250 N.C. 421, 109 S.E.2d 253 (1959); Pennsylvania Labor Relations Board v. Sansom House Enterprises, Inc., 378 Pa. 385, 106 A.2d 404 (1954); Crossroads Recreation, Inc. v. Broz, 4 N.Y.2d 39, 172 N.Y.S.2d 129, 149 N.E.2d 65 (1958); International Minerals & Chemical Corp. v. New Mexico Public Service Commission, 81 N.M. 280, 466 P.2d 557 (1970); National Retail Transportation, Inc. v. Pennsylvania Public Utility Commission, 109 Pa.Cmwlth. 72, 530 A.2d 987 (1987).

3. 450 U.S. 91 (1981).

4. 385 U.S. 276 (1966); Jaffe, Administrative Law: Burden of Proof and Scope of Review, 79 Harv.L.Rev. 914 (1966). A fact cannot be proved by less than a preponderance of the evidence. Charlton v. Federal Trade Commission, 543 F.2d 903, 907 (D.C.Cir.1976) ("in American law a preponderance of the evidence is rock bottom at the factfinding level of civil litigation.")

5. Kerner v. Flemming, 283 F.2d 916 (2d Cir.1960); Young & Co. v. Shea, 397 F.2d 185 (5th Cir.1968), rehearing en banc denied 404 F.2d 1059, cert. denied 395 U.S. 920; Stark v. Weinberger, 497 F.2d 1092 (7th Cir.1974); Newport News Shipbuilding

grounds of judicial acceptance of uncontradicted medical testimony in support of the claim, since the agencies are also dealing with malingering and false claims. On the other hand, reviewing courts are more concerned with the remedial, risk-spreading purposes of the statutes and the comparative inability of the claimant to present additional proof.[6] Similar tendencies occasionally appear in such diverse areas as police suspension matters[7] and draft exemption cases[8] where the courts have given increasing scrutiny to the overall fairness of administrative adjudications.

These cases can also be viewed as establishing a presumption in certain administrative adjudications since they affect the burden of proof. The history of workers' compensation illustrates this alternative analysis. Although many state acts have created a presumption in favor of the claimant, several state courts formerly gave these provisions no effect.[9] In interpreting a federal compensation act in Del Vecchio v. Bowers,[10] the Supreme Court held that this "benefit" presumption was sufficient to carry claimant's burden of persuasion in the absence of opposing evidence. However, once rebuttal evidence is introduced, the statutory presumption is overcome and the agency must decide the case solely on the evidence in the record.[11] Similar analysis supports the presumption of the correctness of official administrative action.[12]

On the other hand, the opposite approach is often taken in administrative adjudications where the activities of business respondents are tested. For example, an advertiser may have the burden of establishing any advertising claim, and if it is the type of claim whose truth can be determined only by scientific tests—for example, a claim that respondent's tires will stop a car 25 percent more quickly than other tires—the advertiser's fully-documented proof must *antedate* the representation; the prosecuting agency need only show that the claim was

---

Co. v. Director, 592 F.2d 762 (4th Cir.1979); Dawkins v. Bowen, 848 F.2d 1211 (11th Cir.1988). See generally, Jaffe, Judicial Control of Administrative Action 608 (1965).

6. However, where the evidence is likely to be available only to respondent, the burden of persuasion or of going forward may be imposed on him. See, e.g., Day v. National Transportation Safety Board, 414 F.2d 950 (5th Cir.1969); Roach v. National Transportation Safety Board, 804 F.2d 1147 (10th Cir.1986), cert. denied 486 U.S. 1006; Smyth v. United States Civil Service Commission, 291 F.Supp. 568, 573 (E.D.Wis.1968).

7. Kelly v. Murphy, 20 N.Y.2d 205, 282 N.Y.S.2d 254, 229 N.E.2d 40 (1967).

8. Dickinson v. United States, 346 U.S. 389, 396 (1953); cf. Mulloy v. United States, 398 U.S. 410 (1970). But see Dic-

kinson v. United States, supra, at 399 (dissenting opinion).

9. E.g., Joseph v. United Kimono Co., 194 App.Div. 568, 185 N.Y.S. 700 (1921).

10. 296 U.S. 280 (1935).

11. Id. at 286. This view now prevails in some state courts. E.g., In re Cellurale's Case, 333 Mass. 37, 127 N.E.2d 787 (1955); 2 Larson, The Law of Workmen's Compensation Sec. 80.33 (1952). This also illustrates that problems of burden of proof are, in essence, often questions of substantive law. See Republic Aviation Corp. v. National Labor Relations Board, 324 U.S. 793 (1945).

12. E.g., Committee of 100 on Federal City v. Hodel, 777 F.2d 711 (D.C.Cir.1985); Cupples Hesse Corp. v. State Tax Commission, 329 S.W.2d 696 (Mo.1959); Goldfarb v. Department of Revenue, 411 Ill. 573, 104 N.E.2d 606 (1952).

made.[13] That is to say, substantive law interpretations can affect the burden of proof as much as procedural requirements.

§ 358. Presentation of Case: Written Evidence and Cross-Examination

Perhaps the most distinctive feature of many administrative hearings, particularly in contrast to nonjury trials, is the substitution of written evidence for oral testimony. This written evidence takes several forms. In its simplest and least productive aspect, some witnesses appear, if at all, simply for cross-examination, with the written questions and answers read into the record in lieu of the usual oral question-answer format. This "canned dialogue" has been criticized as leading to the withholding of the true facts from the administrative law judge and assuring that the case will be decided on grounds other than the evidence in the record.[1] But if applied more sensitively, written evidence can expedite and simplify formal administrative proceedings through reducing the controversy to verified written statements which are then exchanged by the parties for the purpose of rebuttal.[2] Federal administrative agencies have frequently relied upon this technique, the Interstate Commerce Commission for almost half a century.[3] With the cooperation of the parties, this procedure can result in greater precision than where the facts are presented orally.

The ICC's written procedures are probably the most sophisticated of all agencies. In time, the Commission's "modified" procedure has been

---

13. Firestone Tire & Rubber Co., 81 F.T.C. 398 (1972), 481 F.2d 246 (6th Cir.), cert. denied 414 U.S. 1112: Pfizer, Inc., 81 F.T.C. 23 (1972); cf. 16 C.F.R. § 3.40.

§ 358

1. As one leading administrative practitioner describes the impact of canned testimony:

I don't believe that I am wholly unique in being put immediately to sleep when it is read. That tedium is eliminated when the written testimony is used, without reading, as direct examination subject to oral cross. I have not, however, yet seen an examiner who has really mastered the unspoken direct testimony. The 25% that is really strong won't be touched in cross-examination and cannot easily be brought out in redirect, so in most cases the examiner proceeds until briefing time, at the best, and forever at the worst, in amiable ignorance of the heart of the testimony. The few hours of direct examination that are saved by written direct testimony come at too high a price.

Gardner, Shrinking the Big Case, 16 Ad. L.Rev. 5, 12–13 (1963).

2. See W. Gellhorn, Federal Administrative Proceedings 100–15 (1941); Selected Reports of the Administrative Conference of the United States 1961–1962, S.Doc. No. 24, 88th Cong. 1st Sess. 92 (1963); Woll, Administrative Law 37–48 (1963); Final Report of Attorney General's Committee on Administrative Procedure, S.Doc. No. 8, 77th Cong., 1st Sess. 69–70 (1941); Brown, Public Service Commission Procedure—A Problem and a Suggestion, 87 U.Pa.L.Rev. 139 (1938). See also Deese, Relevancy of Evidence in Administrative Law Proceedings, 7 J. National Association of Administrative Law Judges 38 (1987); Postal, Litigating Cases Before Administrative Law Judges, 13 Litigation 47 (1987); Rodgers, The Natural Law of Administrative Law, 48 Missouri L.Rev. 101 (1983).

3. See American Public Gas Association v. Federal Power Commission, 498 F.2d 718 (D.C.Cir.1974) (example of effective use of written material in lieu of oral presentations). State agencies have also made extensive use of written evidence. See letter from member of State Corporation Commission of Virginia, 38 J.Am.Jud.Soc. 61 (1954).

streamlined into an administrative version of summary judgment.[4] Under the ICC's rules of procedure, any party may request use of the modified procedure by filing a verified statement setting forth the facts, argument, and exhibits on which he relies.[5] The opposing party must either admit or deny each material allegation, explaining each exception he takes to the facts and argument of his adversary. Unless there are material facts in dispute or the objecting party explains why he cannot properly present his case by affidavits, a decision will then be rendered on the written case. This rule exceeds the concept of summary judgment currently applied under the Federal Rules of Civil Procedure by placing the burden on the parties to prove that an oral hearing is necessary.[6] An oral hearing is not presumed to be the proper method for hearing a case.

Written evidence has been relied upon most successfully in rate or price control proceedings, where economic and expert analysis rather than sensorily-perceived phenomena provide the bulk of the evidence.[7] Credibility based upon conflicting stories relating what each witness observed is seldom involved. Often the advance preparation of written evidence is limited to the contentions of the party having the burden of proof; in others the opposing party's evidence is included. The elimination of surprise cannot be objected to since surprise has no proper place in the hearing when credibility is not in issue. Cross-examination is not used to establish a party's case. Its major purpose here is "not to reduce * * * [the expert] witness to a shattered hulk by the admission of error, but to explore all of the considerations entering into what must remain a matter of judgment." [8]

As explained by the Second Interim Administrative Conference, the benefits of written evidence are manifold:

---

4. Early in the 1920's, the ICC abbreviated the usual oral hearing before a commissioner or examiner through the use of a "shortened" procedure. Upon consent of the parties, oral testimony was dispensed with, and a decision was rendered upon stipulated, sworn statements of fact. Despite encomiums from administrative law experts, this procedure did not prove particularly successful, since the parties could avoid the shortened procedure at any time by requesting a formal hearing. Consequently, in 1942 the ICC substituted what it called a "modified" procedure whereby each party submitted his case in writing for the purpose of obtaining agreement on as many facts as possible. The parties then confined their oral testimony to the remaining points in dispute. While more successful than the "shortened" procedure, this modified procedure did not eliminate a formal hearing when the parties could not agree on the facts. See Woll, The Development of Shortened Procedure in American Administrative Law, 45 Cornell L.Q. 56, 62–66 (1959); Hosmer, Some Notes on a Perennial Procedural Problem, 5 I.C.C.Prac.J. 275 (1938); Mohundro, Improvements in Procedure Before the Commission, 20 I.C.C.Prac.J. 75, 79–81 (1952); Three Letters on Procedure Before the I.C.C., id. 196; Brown, Early Administrative Law Development (The Interstate Commerce Commission: The First One Hundred Years 1887–1987), 16 Transportation Law Journal 85 (1987).

5. 49 C.F.R. § 1100.45; see id. §§ 1100.-49, 1100.50, 1100.53.

6. See E. Gellhorn & Robinson, Summary Judgment in Administrative Adjudication, 84 Harv.L.Rev. 612 (1970); Fed. R.Civ.P. 56. The ICC's procedure has withstood attacks upon due process grounds. E.g., Allied Van Lines Co. v. United States, 303 F.Supp. 742 (C.D.Cal.1969).

7. See Selected Reports of the Administrative Conference of the United States 1961–1962, S.Doc. No. 24, 88th Cong., 1st Sess. 92 (1963).

8. Id.

(1) [The] exchange of written evidence facilitates settlement techniques in situations in which there is staff participation; (2) the hearing examiner, after studying the direct evidence of the parties prior to hearing, can participate in the case in an intelligent fashion, leading to more effective use of conference techniques and more informed rulings at the hearing; (3) in a substantial number of cases, particularly those of less moment, the parties may be satisfied with their written presentations, and an oral hearing becomes unnecessary; and (4) the efforts of the parties at the oral hearing, if one is necessary, are confined to clarifying the major issues through informed cross-examination. Properly handled, written procedures should result in a more adequate record being produced in a shorter space of time.[9]

Section 556(d) of the APA recognizes the propriety of written presentations with only limited cross-examination: "In rule making or determining claims for money or benefits or applications for initial licenses any agency may, when a party will not be prejudiced thereby, adopt procedures for the submission of all or part of the evidence in written form."[10] Existing case law supports the use of written presentations by any agency in a type of proceeding where the interest of any party is not prejudiced.[11]

Where cross-examination is necessary for protection against untrustworthy evidence, it cannot be avoided. Section 556(d) of the APA specifically preserves the right of cross-examination in agency adjudications: "A party is entitled * * * to conduct such cross-examination as may be required for a full and true disclosure of the facts."[12] State law is identical.[13] Through this provision the APA recognizes one of the fundamentals of a fair hearing—namely a reasonable opportunity to test and controvert adverse evidence whether or not such evidence is a statement of opinion, observation, or consideration of the witness. Cross-examination has several potential uses: to bring out matters left untouched by direct examination; to test the accuracy of a witness' perception as well as his ability to observe; to probe his truthfulness; to question his memory and narration; and to expose the basis of any opinions he has expressed. In other words, "cross-examination is a means of getting at the truth; it is not truth itself."[14] Yet unless credibility is directly in issue—and then only on occasion—cross-examination usually does no more than demonstrate forensic talent or score trial points irrelevant to the final decision.[15] As an experienced agency practitioner, who later became an eminent federal judge, observed:

9. Id. at 93.

10. 5 U.S.C.A. § 556(d).

11. See Yakus v. United States, 321 U.S. 414 (1944). The 1981 Revised Model State Administrative Act tracks this case law by providing in § 4–212(d) that "Any part of the evidence may be received in written form if doing so will expedite the hearing without substantial prejudice to the interests of any party."

12. 5 U.S.C.A. § 556(d).

13. See Hyson v. Montgomery County Council, 242 Md. 55, 67–68 n. 1, 217 A.2d 578, 585–86 n. 1 (1966); 1 Cooper 371–79 (collecting cases). The 1981 model state act makes similar provision for cross-examination. Revised Model State Administrative Procedure Act § 4–211(2) (1981).

14. W. Gellhorn & Byse, Administrative Law 713 (5th ed. 1970).

15. See § 30 supra.

"Only rarely * * * can you accomplish something devastating on cross-examining an expert * * *. [M]ore often it is love's labor lost." [16]

Perception of this point is the key to a reconciliation of the right of cross-examination with the seemingly inconsistent administrative practice of relying on hearsay testimony and written evidence whether or not the declarant is unavailable. The legislative history of the APA makes clear that Congress was seeking to draw a line between an unlimited right of unnecessary cross-examination and a reasonable opportunity to test opposing evidence.[17] The test, stated abstractly, is that cross-examination must be allowed when it is required for determining the truth. If witness veracity and demeanor are not critical, there is no requirement for cross-examination so long as sufficient opportunity for rebuttal exists; if credibility is a key factor, and the objecting party can show that the absence of cross-examination of the witness may have prejudiced his case, the denial of cross-examination could be fatal to an agency decision.[18] Statistical compilations and surveys are admissible only if the person responsible for—and having full knowledge of the preparation of—the exhibit is available. In addition, the raw data upon which the exhibit is based should be available to the opposing party.[19] It has been proposed that the right to cross-examine in at least some administrative proceedings be reduced to a privilege "to be granted only in the virtually unlimited discretion of the hearing officer." This proposal is only part of a recommended restructuring of the administrative hearing into a conference proceeding where almost all the evidence would be submitted in written form.[20]

Finally, administrative agencies are required to apply the "*Jencks* rule"—namely, that after a government witness has testified, the prosecution must disclose prior statements by the witness relating to his testimony.[21] Application of this rule in agency hearings has been

---

16. Leventhal, Cues and Compasses for Administrative Lawyers, 20 Ad.L.Rev. 237, 246 (1968); accord, Prettyman, Trying an Administrative Dispute, 45 Va.L.Rev. 179, 190–191 (1959); Postel, Litigating Cases Before Administrative Law Judges, 13 Litigation 47 (1987).

17. Sen.Doc. No. 248, 79th Cong., 2d Sess. 208–09, 271 (1946); Attorney General's Manual on the Administrative Procedure Act 77–78 (1947).

18. E.g., In re Chapman Radio & Television Co., 6 F.C.C.2d 768 (1967); see Peters v. United States, 187 Ct.Cl. 63, 408 F.2d 719 (1969); Brown v. Macy, 222 F.Supp. 639 (E.D.La.1963), affirmed 340 F.2d 115 (5th Cir.).

19. Wirtz v. Baldor Electric Co., 119 U.S.App.D.C. 122, 337 F.2d 518 (1963); see Carter–Wallace, Inc. v. Gardner, 417 F.2d 1086, 1095–1096 (4th Cir.1969), cert. denied 398 U.S. 938 (party not entitled to cross-examination if alternative method of inves-

tigating accuracy available); Zeisel, The Uniqueness of Survey Evidence, 45 Cornell L.Q. 322, 345–46 (1960). See generally § 251 supra.

20. Westwood, Administrative Proceedings; Techniques of Presiding, 50 A.B.A.J. 659, 660 (1964). See also Recommendation No. 19, Selected Reports of the Administrative Conference of the United States 1961–61, S.Doc. No. 24, 88th Cong. 1st Sess. 51, 96–97 (1963); Cramton, Some Modest Suggestions for Improving Public Utility Rate Proceedings, 51 Iowa L.Rev. 267, 276–78 (1966).

21. Jencks v. United States, 353 U.S. 657 (1957). The "*Jencks* Rule" was initially applied to administrative agencies in Communist Party of the United States v. Subversive Activities Control Board, 102 U.S.App.D.C. 395, 254 F.2d 314 (1958) and National Labor Relations Board v. Adhesive Products Corp., 258 F.2d 403 (2d Cir.1958); see Selected Reports of the Ad-

the subject of controversy.[22] The Administrative Conference has suggested that prior statements be made available to the respondent at the prehearing conference.[23] If this view were adopted the question would no longer be one of evidence but rather one of discovery.

§ 359. Official Notice [1]

Official notice, like its judicial notice counterpart, involves reliance by the presiding officer—in this case the administrative law judge—on extra-record information. That is, the law judge in making a decision bypasses the normal process of proof and relies upon facts and opinions not supported by evidence "on the record." Several characteristics of official notice should be observed. First, a specific procedure similar to that for judicial notice has been established to receive extra-record facts, with the parties receiving notice and an opportunity to rebut the "noticed" facts.[2] Second, extra-record facts usually have first been developed by the agency's expert staff or accumulated from previous agency decisions. But official notice is not limited to information in agency files. In fact, it may be taken at the initiation of one of the parties. Third, agency recognition of extra-record facts is clearly not limited to "indisputable" facts. Rather, official notice may extend to almost any information useful in deciding the adjudication as long as

ministrative Conference of the United States 1961–1962, S.Doc. No. 24, 88th Cong., 1st Sess. 132 (1963). See generally § 97 supra for discussion of the rule in its present form.

22. FTC: Papercraft Corp., 25 Ad.L.2d 1122 (FTC 1969); Star Office Supply Co., 24 Ad.L.2d 472 (FTC 1968); enforced by order [1967–1970 Transfer Binder] Trade Reg.Rep. Para. 19,228 (FTC 1970); Inter-State Builders, Inc., 19 Ad.L.2d 7 (FTC 1966), 21 Ad.L.2d 1078 (FTC 1967); L.G. Balfour Co., 19 Ad.L.2d 35 (FTC 1966); Viviano Macaroni Co., 19 Ad.L.2d 69 (FTC 1966); see E. Gellhorn, The Treatment of Confidential Information by the Federal Trade Commission: The Hearing, 116 U.Pa.L.Rev. 401, 428–33 (1968). NLRB: National Labor Relations Board v. Borden Co., 392 F.2d 412 (5th Cir.1968); see Alleyne, The "*Jencks* Rule" in NLRB Proceedings, 9 B.C. Ind. & Comm.L.Rev. 891 (1968). Department of Labor: Wirtz v. Rosenthal, 388 F.2d 290 (9th Cir.1967); Wirtz v. B.A.C. Steel Products, Inc., 312 F.2d 14 (4th Cir.1962); Mitchell v. Roma, 265 F.2d 633 (3d Cir.1959). Selective Service: Rogers v. United States, 263 F.2d 283 (9th Cir.1959), cert. denied 359 U.S. 967; Bouziden v. United States, 251 F.2d 728 (10th Cir.1958), cert. denied 356 U.S. 927.

23. ACUS Recommendation No. 70–4, 1 C.F.R. § 305.70–4; see Tomlinson, Discovery in Agency Adjudication, 1971 Duke L.J. 89; Benkin, The Inconstant Lady: Discovery in Administrative Adjudications and the Evidentiary Use of its Fruits, 4 Energy Law Journal 201 (1983).

§ 359

1. See generally 3 Davis, ch. 15; 1 Cooper 412–20; Final Report of the Attorney General's Committee on Administrative Procedure, S.Doc. No. 8, 77th Cong., 1st Sess. 71–73 (1941); Benjamin 206–21; W. Gellhorn, Federal Administrative Proceedings 82–99 (1941); W. Gellhorn, Official Notice in Administrative Adjudication, 20 Tex.L.Rev. 131 (1941); Jaffe, Administrative Procedure Re–Examined: The Benjamin Report, 56 Harv.L.Rev. 704, 717–719 (1943).

The term "official notice" is probably unfortunate in suggesting too much of a parallel to judicial notice. Much that is done and advocated to be done in the name of official notice might with less violence to the language be catalogued under presumptions. The latter affinity is noted elsewhere. See § 333 supra.

2. 5 U.S.C.A. § 556(d). See Fed.R.Evid. 201(e) and § 333 supra.

elemental fairness is observed.[3]

On the other hand, in administrative adjudication, official notice is frequently confused with the process of decisionmaking. In reaching a conclusion, the administrative law judge or agency may rely on its special skills, whether they include particular expertness in engineering, economics, medicine, or electricity, just as a federal or state judge may freely use his legal skills in reading statutes and applying decided cases in the preparation of his opinion. But such evaluations are not within the concept of official notice. Official notice is concerned with the *process of proof,* not with the *evaluation of evidence.* The difference between an administrative tribunal's use of non-record information included in its expert knowledge, as a substitute for evidence or notice, and its application of its background in evaluating and drawing conclusions from the evidence that is in the record, is, however, primarily a difference of degree rather than of kind. In principle, reliance upon the administrative law judge's knowledge in the process of proof is permissible only within the confines of official notice, whereas the administrative judge's use of his experience in the evaluating "*proof* is not only unavoidable but, indeed, desirable."[4]

The troublesome problem, as with most questions of law, is that a fine line cannot be drawn with precision. Benjamin illustrates the point:

> When the State Liquor Authority concludes, from evidence in the record as to the size of food bills and gas bills paid (in relation to the volume of liquor business), that the holder of a restaurant liquor license is not conducting a *bona fide* restaurant, is the Authority using its experience and knowledge to evaluate and draw conclusions from the evidence, or is it using its experience and knowledge as a substitute for further evidence as to the normal relation of the size of food and gas bills to the volume of food business? * * * My own view is that * * * the procedure described is permissible [evaluation]; but until the courts have decided specific questions of this character, it is impossible to anticipate with any certainty what their decision would be.[5]

Beyond this or other examples, little guidance can be offered.

The primary thrust behind official notice is to simplify or ease the process of proof. Where facts are known or can be safely assumed, the process of proving what is already known is both time-consuming and

---

3. At least one observer has suggested that agencies should apply the doctrine of judicial notice to broad, general facts of common knowledge which are of an undisputed nature, thus avoiding the notice and rebuttal requirements of official notice, and limit official notice—with its procedural requirements—to disputable facts. Muir, The Utilization of Both Judicial and Official Notice by Administrative Agencies, 16 Ad.L.Rev. 333 (1964).

The kinds of facts noticeable in judicial proceedings are discussed in Chapter 35 supra.

4. See, e.g., Interstate Commerce Commission v. Louisville & Nashville Railroad, 227 U.S. 88, 98 (1913); Feinstein v. New York Central Railroad, 159 F.Supp. 460, 464 (S.D.N.Y.1958) (L. Hand, J.); Gencom Inc. v. F.C.C., 832 F.2d 171 (D.C.Cir.1987). See the discussion of "legislative" facts in § 331 supra.

5. Benjamin 212.

unduly formal. When facts have been proven before, further proof becomes tiresome, redundant, and lacking in common sense. At times even the obvious could be difficult or time-consuming to prove, without affecting the final result, which was never in doubt. Moreover, administrative agencies were often created to become repositories of knowledge and experience. It would defeat their existence to require adherence to traditional methods of proof when alternative and equally fair methods are readily available. On the other hand, in developing an alternative method, it is necessary to safeguard the elements of a fair trial preserved by the traditional forms of proof. The 1941 Attorney General's Committee accurately summarized the need:

> The parties, then, are entitled to be apprised of the data upon which the agency is acting. They are entitled not only to refute but, what in this situation is usually more important, to supplement, explain, and give different perspective to the facts upon which the agency relies. In addition, upon judicial review, the court must be informed of what facts the agency has utilized in order that the existence of supporting evidence may be ascertained.[6]

The Congress sought to recognize and reconcile these concerns by a single sentence in section 556(e) of the APA: "When an agency decision rests on official notice of a material fact not appearing in the evidence in the record, a party is entitled, on timely request, to an opportunity to show the contrary."[7] The procedure is simple. Official notice is a means by which an agency can avoid hearing further evidence on a material fact in the case if it notifies the parties that unless they prove to the contrary the agency's findings will include that particular fact and allows the parties an opportunity to present contrary evidence.

Federal Trade Commission cases illustrate the practice. After hearing dozens of cases indicating that consumers preferred American to foreign-made goods—and holding, therefore, that a failure to disclose the foreign origin of these goods was a false and deceptive act[8]—the commission advised respondents in Manco Watch Strap Co.[9] that it would not hear evidence on this issue in the future. Then, in subsequent cases where the FTC took official notice and the respondents could not prove that American consumers preferred their foreign goods or that the consumers had no particular preference, the Commission

---

6. Final Report of the Attorney General's Committee on Administrative Procedure, supra note 8, at 72; see Ohio Bell Telephone Co. v. Public Utilities Commission, 301 U.S. 292, 303–04 (1937).

7. 5 U.S.C.A. § 556(e).

8. American Merchandise Co., 28 F.T.C. 1465 (1939) (gloves and thumbtacks); Vulcan Lamp Works, Inc., 32 F.T.C. 7 (1940) (flashlight bulbs); The Bolta Co., 44 F.T.C. 17 (1947) (sunglass lenses); L. Heller & Son, Inc., 47 F.T.C. 34 (1950), affirmed 191 F.2d 954 (7th Cir.1951) (imitation pearls);

Atomic Prods., Inc., 48 F.T.C. 289 (1951) (mechanical pencils); Rene D. Lyon Co., 48 F.T.C. 313, 787 (1951) (watch bands); Royal Sewing Mach. Corp., 49 F.T.C. 1351 (1953) (sewing machine parts); William Adams, Inc., 53 F.T.C. 1164 (1957) (cutlery handles); Utica Cutlery Co., 56 F.T.C. 1186 (1960) (stainless steel hardware); Oxwall Tool Co., 59 F.T.C. 1408 (1961) (hand tools). This listing is also further testimony to the FTC's historic concentration on trivia.

9. 60 F.T.C. 495 (1962).

upheld orders barring sales of goods not bearing the requisite disclosures.[10] On the other hand, if respondents could show that consumers preferred French over American perfumes, for example, the "noticed finding" would not apply.[11]

Practically, then, the primary effect of taking official notice is to transfer the burden of proof on that material fact—usually from the agency to the respondent. The significance of this tactic varies in proportion to the difficulty of the proponent in establishing that fact originally, and of the cost and effort of the opponent in disproving it. In most instances where agencies have taken official notice, the costs have been slight since the result has seemed obvious. Where the fact is less obvious, however, that cost could prove substantial.[12]

The academic controversy over official notice has centered upon the limitation of judicial notice to undisputed facts and attempts to categorize the types of facts which can be officially noticed. The former is examined elsewhere in this text.[13] On the other hand, the APA's guidance of what facts can be noticed is essentially nonexistent; it merely sets forth the procedure which must be followed for taking notice of "material facts." By omission it appears to suggest that facts which are not material can be noticed in the manner of a judge at a judicial trial, but it does not tell how to determine which facts are material and can therefore be noticed. In any event, the term "material" seems not to be used in its classic sense.

The Attorney General's Committee on Administrative Procedure suggested a distinction between "litigation" and "non-litigation" facts:

> If information has come to an agency's attention in the course of investigation of the pending case, it should be adduced only by the ordinary process. * * * But if the information has been developed in the usual course of business of the agency, if it has emerged from numerous cases, if it has become part of the factual equipment of the administrators, it seems undesirable for the agencies to remain oblivious of their

---

10. Savoy Watch Co., 63 F.T.C. 473 (1963) (watch cases); Baldwin Bracelet Corp., 61 F.T.C. 1345 (1962), affirmed 325 F.2d 1012 (1963) (watch cases); Brite Manufacturing Co., 65 F.T.C. 1067 (1964), affirmed 347 F.2d 477 (1965) (watch bands).

11. In its pursuit of the Grail, the FTC has in fact held that consumers prefer French perfumes and that it therefore is deceptive not to disclose the domestic origin of perfume. See, e.g., Fioret Sales Co., 26 F.T.C. 806, affirmed 100 F.2d 358 (2d Cir.1938); Etablissements Rigaud, Inc., 29 F.T.C. 1032 (1939), modified 125 F.2d 590 (2d Cir.1942); Harsam Distributors, Inc., 54 F.T.C. 1212 (1958), affirmed 263 F.2d 396 (2d Cir.1959).

12. In the unusual event that the evidence is split with the moving party having the burden of establishing that material fact by a preponderance of the evidence, official notice may be the difference between winning and losing the case. In assessing the place of official notice, one should also take into account (a) the cost of establishing a general negative—which is, in part, the reason for assigning the burden of proof to the moving party, see § 337 notes 6–8 supra; (b) the desirability of cross-examination; and (c) the impact of denying confrontation—all of which are intimately connected with the decision as to whether official notice is appropriate. The relevance of presumption theory is evident. See §§ 342, 343, supra.

13. Ch. 35 supra. See also note 24 infra.

own experience [and, they should take notice of such facts].[14]

Professor Davis, on the other hand, rejects the notion that significance could be attached to the time when the factual data was collected. His criticism of the Committee's distinction stems from his conclusion that it would "encourage guesswork" and "discourage extra-record research of the kind that is especially needed for creation of law or policy. It would mean [for example, that] an agency could notice only those statutes that it has previously encountered!"[15] This criticism seems somewhat unfair since the Committee's basic point defining reliable facts—those previously established by the agency—is sound. Davis is right, however, when he points out that the Committee rule is too narrow. As an alternative, he offers a different standard for deciding whether an administrator may use extra-record facts:

> When a court or an agency finds facts concerning the immediate parties—who did what, where, when, how, and with what motive or intent—[it] is performing an adjudicative function, and the facts are conveniently called adjudicative facts. When a court or an agency develops law or policy, it is acting legislatively; the courts have created the common law through judicial legislation, and the facts which inform the tribunal's legislative judgment are called legislative facts. * * * Legislative facts are ordinarily general and do not concern the immediate parties.[16]

On this basis, Davis asserts that legislative facts usually need not be brought into the record by official notice; where critical, a party should be able to challenge them by brief and argument. He contends that adjudicative facts, on the other hand, must be brought into the record—unless they are indisputable—either through direct proof or by official notice. Nothing less will meet the cardinal principles of a fair hearing—notice and an opportunity to test and rebut opposing evidence. Whether adjudicative facts can be officially noticed or must be established by direct proof depends, he says, on three variables: how close the facts are to the center of the controversy; the extent to which the facts are adjudicative or legislative; and the degree to which the facts are certain. As the adjudicative facts move closer to the basic issues of the hearing, relate to the parties, and are disputed, the usual methods of proof must be observed; as they move in the opposite direction, official notice is permissible.[17]

Professor Jaffe has suggested an attractive alternative approach:

> [W]here the facts bear closely and crucially on the issue, and are prima facie debatable, they should be developed in evidentiary fashion—by which is meant simply that they should be referred to in such a manner as to enable the opponent to offer rebuttal. Such facts will not necessarily be "adjudicative" * * *.[18]

---

14. Final Report of the Attorney General's Committee on Administrative Procedure, supra note 1 at 72.

15. 2 Davis § 15.03, at 363–64 note 43 (1958).

16. Id. § 15.03, at 353.

17. Id. § 15.10.

18. Jaffe, Administrative Procedure Re-Examined: The Benjamin Report, 56 Harv.L.Rev. 704, 719 (1943); cf. Wyzanski, A Trial Judge's Freedom and Responsibility, 65 Harv.L.Rev. 1281, 1295–1296 (1952).

Thus, as Davis himself concedes, the categories he defines do not in themselves resolve which facts can be noticed in particular cases. He is certainly correct when he points out that the central problem is to reconcile procedural fairness with convenience and the use of agency knowledge. The difficulty with his analysis lies not in his categories which are original and helpful, but rather that many cases fall outside his definitions. A sampling of cases illustrates this point. The existence of the Great Depression is a "legislative" fact which an agency can include in its findings without notice to the parties, but a specific price trend, also a general legislative fact, cannot be used to update the figures in the record without notice to the parties.[19] Since a specific price trend can be readily verified, taking notice is appropriate; the burden of proving any substantial error is not likely to be significant. Similarly, the courts have upheld agencies' official notice of scientific data, technical facts, and articles in academic journals,[20] although many courts contend that this places too great a burden on the opponent to refute the "noticed evidence."[21]

Of greater consequence is the fact that reliance upon Davis' categories distracts from the central question of fairness—that is, is it fair in the particular hearing to take official notice and *transfer the burden of proof* to the opposing party? Two cases involving the use of the record of a related hearing, each of which reaches an opposite result, are perhaps the clearest examples of this suggested "fairness of the transfer of the burden of proof" analysis. In United States v. Pierce Auto Freight Lines, Inc.,[22] the ICC held two separate hearings on competing applications for truck service between San Francisco and Portland. Each applicant intervened in the other hearing, but the cases were not consolidated. In reaching its decision, the Commission relied on evidence appearing in only one record. The procedure was upheld because both applicants were parties to both proceedings and both had ample opportunity to present evidence, to cross-examine witnesses, and otherwise to protect their interests.

The Davis labels of "adjudicative" and "legislative" facts are commonly recited by agencies and courts to justify official notice decisions.

19. Ohio Bell Telephone Co. v. Public Utilities Commission, 301 U.S. 292 (1937); West Ohio Gas Co. v. Public Utilities Commission, 294 U.S. 63, 68 (1935); cf. United States v. Baltimore & Ohio South Western Railroad, 226 U.S. 14, 20 (1912).

20. E.g., McDaniel v. Celebrezze, 331 F.2d 426 (4th Cir.1964); Alabama–Tennessee Natural Gas Co. v. Federal Power Commission, 359 F.2d 318 (5th Cir.1966), cert. denied 385 U.S. 847; Pagel, Inc. v. S.E.C., 803 F.2d 942 (8th Cir.1986); see 46 C.F.R. § 502.226 (FMC 1970). The CAB's rules note 43 separate reports and other resource materials of which it automatically takes official notice in economic proceedings. 14 C.F.R. § 302.24(m)(1).

21. See, e.g., McLeod v. I.N.S., 802 F.2d 89 (3d Cir.1986); Sayers v. Gardner, 380 F.2d 940 (6th Cir.1967); Sosna v. Celebrezze, 234 F.Supp. 289 (E.D.Pa.1964); Cook v. Celebrezze, 217 F.Supp. 366 (W.D.Mo.1963).

22. 327 U.S. 515 (1946); see Safeway Stores, Inc. v. Federal Trade Commission, 366 F.2d 795, 803 (9th Cir.1966), cert. denied 386 U.S. 932. Cf. Zimmerman v. Board of Regents, 31 A.D.2d 560, 294 N.Y.S.2d 435 (1968).

In the second case, Dayco Corp. v. FTC,[23] the FTC sought to take official notice of the distribution system and practices used by the respondent, a manufacturer of auto replacement parts, since the system had been the subject of a prior proceeding. That prior proceeding, in which respondent was only a witness, was brought against his customers. The court ruled that the FTC's attempt to take official notice of these "adjudicative facts" from the first proceeding was improper because the manufacturer was not a party, but only a witness to the prior proceeding. To allow official notice in this circumstance, the court reasoned, would have eliminated the commission's entire burden of proof. The agency had asserted that its reliance on prior knowledge merely shifted the burden of going forward to respondent and this burden (of correcting any FTC errors in describing respondent's distribution system) was minimal when compared with the cost of proving these same facts again. The FTC's argument is not persuasive. If the agency merely sought to shift the burden of going forward, it could have introduced the prior record as reliable hearsay evidence subject to rebuttal or as written evidence with an offer to make the witnesses available for cross-examination. If handled in this manner—rather than under the official notice rubric—the fact-trier would still have to determine whether the prior record accurately portrayed respondent's distribution system. The court may also have perceived that there was no compelling need to approve the commission's proposal since the FTC could (and should) have avoided the burden of re-proof by joining the respondent as a party in the first proceeding. Official notice, in other words, is not properly a procedural device to avoid the requirement of section 556(e) of the APA that the moving party has the burden of proof. If that burden is to be placed on respondent as a condition of doing business, it should be accomplished openly through a shift in substantive policy rather than covertly by manipulation of procedural devices.

When the issue of official notice is viewed in this manner, the Davis criteria and the Attorney General's Committee's distinctions are helpful, but not dispositive. On the other hand, judging from the small number of reported cases, the doctrine of official notice has apparently not been used extensively or creatively by many agencies. This reluctance may be partly the result of uncertainties in the applicable legal standards. Without clear tests indicating when official notice is proper, agencies may be unwilling to risk reversal by taking notice of nonrecord facts.[24] Nonetheless, it remains a potentially useful device for simplifying and expediting hearings.

23. 362 F.2d 180 (6th Cir.1966). The judicial reception is more hospitable where the fact being noticed is of a less personal (i.e. adjudicative) nature. See, e.g., Dombrovskis v. Esperdy, 321 F.2d 463, 467 (2d Cir.1963).

24. The United States Department of Labor Rules of Evidence, see § 351 at note 26 supra, treats official notice of adjudicative facts in § 18.201:

Official notice of adjudicative facts

(a) *Scope of rule.* This rule governs only official notice of adjudicative facts.

(b) *Kinds of facts.* An officially noticed fact must be one not subject to reasonable dispute in that it is either:

(1) Generally known within the local area.

(2) Capable of accurate and ready determination by resort to sources whose accuracy cannot reasonably be questioned, or

(3) Derived from a not reasonably questioned scientific, medical or other technical process, technique, principle, or explanatory theory within the administrative agency's specialized field of knowledge.

(c) *When discretionary.* A judge may take official notice, whether requested or not.

(d) *When mandatory.* A judge shall take official notice if requested by a party and supplied with the necessary information.

(e) *Opportunity to be heard.* A party is entitled, upon timely request, to an opportunity to be heard as to the propriety of taking official notice and the tenor of the matter noticed. In the absence of prior notification, the request may be made after official notice has been taken.

(f) *Time of taking notice.* Official notice may be taken at any stage of the proceeding.

(g) *Effect of official notice.* An officially noticed fact is accepted as conclusive.

Reporter's Note to § 18.201

A.P.A. section 556(e) provides that "when an agency decision rests on official notice of a material fact not appearing in the evidence in the record, a party is entitled, on timely request, to an opportunity to show the contrary." No definition of "official notice" is provided. An administrative agency may take official notice of any adjudicative fact that could be judicially noticed by a court. In addition "the rule is now clearly emerging that an administrative agency may take official notice of any generally recognized technical or scientific facts within the agency's specialized knowledge, subject always to the proviso that the parties must be given adequate advance notice of the facts which the agency proposes to note, and given adequate opportunity to show the inaccuracy of the facts or the fallacy of the conclusions which the agency proposes tentatively to

accept without proof. To satisfy this requirement, it is necessary that a statement of the facts noticed must be incorporated into the record. The source material on which the agency relies should, on request, be made available to the parties for their examination." 1 Cooper, State Administrative Law 412–13 (1965). Accord, Uniform Law Commissioners' Model State Administrative Procedure Act section 10[4] (1961) ("Notice may be taken of judicially cognizable facts. In addition, notice may be taken of generally recognized technical or scientific facts within the agency's specialized knowledge. Parties shall be notified either before or during the hearing, or by reference in preliminary reports or otherwise, of the material noticed, including any staff memoranda or data, and they shall be afforded an opportunity to contest the material so noticed. The agency's experience, technical competence, and specialized knowledge may be utilized in the evaluation of the evidence."); Schwartz, Administrative Law § 7.16 at 375 (2d ed. 1984) ("Clearly an agency may take notice of the same kinds of fact of which a court takes judicial notice. It has, however, been recognized that the differences between agencies and courts * * * may justify a broader approach. Under it, an agency may be permitted to take 'official notice' not only of facts that are obvious and notorious to the average man but also of those that are obvious and notorious to an expert in the given field. A commission that regulates gas companies may take notice of the fact that a well-managed gas company loses not more than 7 percent of its gas through leakage, condensation, expansion, or contraction, where its regulation of gas companies, over the years has made the amount of 'unaccounted for gas' without negligence obvious and notorious to it as the expert in gas regulation. A workers' compensation commission may similarly reject a claim that an inguinal hernia was traumatic in origin where the employee gave no indication of pain and continued work for a month after the alleged accident. The agency had dealt with numerous hernia cases and was expert in diagnosing them as any doctor would be. Its experience taught it that where a hernia was traumatic in origin, there was immediate discomfort, outward evidences of pain observable to fellow employees, and at least temporary suspension from work. The agency could notice this fact based upon its knowledge as an expert and reject uncontradicted opinion testimony that its own expertise renders unpersuasive."). Compare Uniform Law Commissioners' Model State Administrative Procedure Act section 4–212(1) (1981) ("Official notice may be taken of (i) any fact that could be judicially noticed in the courts of this State, (ii) the record of other proceedings before the agency, (iii) technical or scientific matters within the agency's specialized knowledge, and (iv) codes or standards that have been adopted by an agency of the United States, of this State or of another state, or by a nationally recognized organization or association. Parties must be notified before or during the hearing, or before the issuance of any initial or final order that is based in whole or in part on facts or materials noticed, of the specific facts or material noticed and the source thereof, including any staff memoranda and data, and be afforded an opportunity to contest and rebut the facts or materials so noticed."). Contra Davis, Official Notice, 62 Harv.L.Rev. 537, 539 (1949) ("To limit official notice to facts which are beyond the realm of dispute would virtually emasculate the administrative process. The problem of official notice should not be one of drawing lines between disputable and indisputable facts. Nor should it even be one of weighing the importance of basing decisions upon all available information against the importance of providing full and fair hearings in the sense of permitting parties to meet all materials that influence decision. The problem is the intensely practical one of devising a procedure which will provide both informed decisions and fair hearings without undue inconvenience or expense.").

Section 18.201 adopts the philosophy of Federal Rule of Evidence 201. The Advisory Committee's Note to Fed.R.Evid. 201(b) states:

> With respect to judicial notice of adjudicative facts, the tradition has been one of caution in requiring that the matter be beyond reasonable controversy. This tradition of circumspection appears to be soundly based, and no reason to depart from it is apparent. As professor Davis says:

> "The reason we use trial-type procedure, I think, is that we make the practical judgment, on the basis of experience, that taking evidence, subject to cross-examination and rebuttal, is the best way to resolve controversies involving reason we require a determination on the record is that we think fair procedure in resolving disputes of adjudicative facts calls for giving each party a chance to meet in the appropriate fashion the facts that come to the tribunal's attention, and the appropriate fashion for meeting disputed adjudicative facts includes rebuttal evidence, cross-examination, usually con-

frontation, and argument (either written or oral or both). The key to a fair trial is opportunity to use the appropriate weapons (rebuttal evidence, cross-examination, and argument) to meet adverse materials that come to the tribunal's attention." A system of Judicial Notice Based on Fairness and Convenience, in Perspective of Law 69, 93 (1964).

The rule proceeds upon the theory that these considerations call for dispensing with traditional methods of proof only in clear cases. Compare Professor Davis' conclusion that judicial notice should be a matter of convenience, subject to requirements of procedural fairness. Id., 94. Section 18.201 of the Federal Rules of Evidence incorporated the Morgan position on judicial notice. The contrary position, expressed by Wigmore and Thayer, and advocated by Davis, was rejected. See McNaughton, Judicial Notice–Excerpts Relating to the Morgan–Wigmore Controversy, 14 Vand.L.Rev. 779 (1961) ("They do not differ with respect to the application of the doctrine to 'law'. Nor do they reveal a difference with respect to so-called 'jury notice.' Their difference relates to judicial notice of 'facts.' Here Wigmore, following Thayer, insists that judicial notice is solely to save time where dispute is unlikely and that a matter judicially noticed is therefore only 'prima facie,' or rebuttable, if the opponent elects to dispute it. It is expressed in Thayer and implicit in Wigmore that (perhaps because the matter is rebuttable) judicial notice may be applied not only to indisputable matters but also to matters of lesser certainty. Morgan on the other hand defines judicial notice more narrowly, and his consequences follow from his definition. He limits judicial notice of fact to matters patently indisputable. And his position is that matters judicially noticed are not rebuttable. He asserts that it is wasteful to permit patently indisputable matters to be litigated by way of formal proof and furthermore that it would be absurd to permit a party to woo a jury to an obviously erroneous finding contrary to the noticed fact. Also, he objects to the Wigmorean conception on the ground that it is really a 'presumption' of sorts attempting to pass under a misleading name. It is, according to Morgan, a presumption with no recognized rules as to how the presmption works, what activates it, and who has the burden of doing how much to rebut it.").

Accordingly, notice that items (ii) and (iv) of the Uniform Law Commissioners' Model State Administrative Procedure Act quoted above are not included as separate items in § 18.201. However codes and standards, (iv), to the extent not subject to reasonable question fall within § 18.-201(b)(2). To the extent such codes and standards do not so fall, proof should be required. Official notice of records of other proceedings before the agency would "permit an agency to notice facts contained in its files, such as the revenue statistics contained in the reports submitted to it by a regulated company." Schwartz, supra at 377. Once again, to the extent such information is not capable of accurate and ready determination by resort to sources whose accuracy cannot reasonably be questioned, § 18.201(b)(2), proof should be required.

*

Appendix A

FEDERAL RULES OF EVIDENCE

Introduction [1]

This Appendix consists of the Federal Rules of Evidence and materials designed to aid in understanding, construing, and applying them.

Chief Justice Warren in 1965 appointed an advisory committee to draft rules of evidence for the federal courts. The committee's Preliminary Draft was published and circulated for comment in 1969. 46 F.R.D. 161. A Revised Draft was circulated in 1971. 51 F.R.D. 315. In 1972, the Supreme Court prescribed Federal Rules of Evidence, to be effective July 1, 1973. 56 F.R.D. 183. Justice Douglas dissented. Pursuant to the various enabling acts, Chief Justice Burger transmitted the rules to the Congress, which suspended the rules pending further study by the Congress. P.L. 93–12. After extensive study, the Congress enacted the rules into law with various amendments, to become effective July 1, 1975. P.L. 93–595, approved January 2, 1975, 88 Stat. 1926. The occasional amendments and additions that have since been made are reflected in the rules as here presented.

Thus the Federal Rules of Evidence are the product of both the rulemaking process established by the Supreme Court and the legislative process of the Congress. Of at least equal importance is the vast collection of common law precedents, with occasional statutes, that constituted the background against which the rules were evolved. It can be seen that each of these sources must be taken into consideration in reaching understanding of the rules.

The rules are in final analysis legislative in nature, and problems of their effect are problems of statutory interpretation. Questions whether interpretive inquiry should be directed to ascertaining the intent of the legislature or the meaning to its audience tend to be minimal, since the rules are directed to a skilled professional audience in the main, in contrast to, say, a criminal statute directed to the public generally. With the rules, intent and meaning tend to come together, with the same interpretive materials relevant to both. The basic relevant interpretive materials are the common law background and the legislative history, with the most significant aspects of the latter

1. This introductory material was prepared by the late Professor Edward W. Cleary, a former editor of this treatise and Reporter to the Advisory Committee for the Federal Rules of Evidence. For a more detailed discussion, see Cleary, Preliminary Notes on Reading the Rules of Evidence, 57 Neb.L.Rev. 908 (1978).

consisting of the Advisory Committee's Notes and various congressional reports and debates, briefly described below.

References to McCormick Text. The first item after each federal rule in the Appendix is a heading "Section References, McCormick 4th ed." [It should be noted that these references will differ somewhat from those to McCormick 1st Edition utilized in the Advisory Committee Notes following each rule.] Under it are the numbers of the text sections where the rule is mentioned or discussed, with the discussions more in depth shown in italics. Judicial decisions and other authorities construing the rule will be found in the listed sections. Any differences between the federal rule and the revised Uniform rule are pointed out in the text. Sections where the background and current posture of the common law are set forth and evaluated will be found near, usually preceding, sections discussing the rule.

Rules Prescribed by the Supreme Court. These rules were transmitted by the Court to the Congress, carried the prestige of the Court, and were the Court's exercise of the rulemaking powers granted by the various enabling acts. They constitute the framework and to a large extent also the particulars of the rules enacted by the Congress. Whether and how a Court's rule was amended by the Congress is described in the *Note by Federal Judicial Center* following each rule in the Appendix.

Advisory Committee's Notes. The Notes supported and explained the rules, were circulated with them, and were transmitted to the Congress with the rules. The involved congressional committees and subcommittees were thoroughly familiar with the Notes, and except where changes were made in the rules the Notes should be taken as the equivalent of a congressional committee report as representing the thinking of the Congress. The pertinent Note, or portion thereof, is set forth in the Appendix for each rule. Where the Congress returned to an earlier version of the rule, the Note is the one that corresponds to that version. Portions no longer relevant because of congressional changes in the rule are omitted.

Congressional Materials. The House took the lead in congressional consideration of the rules. Accordingly, in the Appendix any pertinent portion of the *Report of the House Committee on the Judiciary* is the first of the congressional materials under each rule. Senate consideration of the rules chronologically followed that of the House, and as a result any pertinent portion of the *Report of the Senate Committee on the Judiciary* is located under each rule in the Appendix after that of the House committee. Where House and Senate passed differing versions of a rule, the difference was resolved by conference, and the *Conference Report* generally concludes the congressional materials. In some instances other congressional materials which are authoritative and helpful are, however, also included.

Some General Observations

Questions as to what a rule really means present probably the most basic problem of interpretation. The language of the rule itself should be taken as the prime source of meaning, read in the light of such context as may be relevant. The most relevant context will often be legislative history, which on occasion may even override an apparently plain and unmistakeable meaning of the words of the rule.[2] The result may be startling, as when the Court of Appeals for the District of Columbia Circuit concluded that a conviction for attempted burglary used for impeachment under Rule 609(a) did not involve dishonesty as the language was used in the rule.[3] Yet the opposite conclusion would have been most difficult to reach in view of the legislative history of the rule.[4]

No common law of evidence in principle remains under the rules. "All relevant evidence is admissible except as otherwise provided. . . ."[5] In reality, of course, the common law remains as a source of guidance in identifying problems and suggesting solutions, within the confines of the rules.

A recurring question is that of the extent to which the application of the rules may be extended beyond their express provisions. Some explicit authorizations to courts to invent and create are found, as for example the provision of Rule 501 that privileges "shall be governed by the principles of the common law as they may be interpreted by the courts of the United States in the light of reason and experience," and the provisions of Rules 803(24) and 804(b)(5) for the restricted admission of hearsay statements not falling within an enumerated exception. A somewhat tighter rein is kept on the judiciary by the rules that obviously contemplate a measure of invention but only within the confines of a stated principle, as in Rule 404(b) where illustrations are given of purposes for which evidence of other crimes may be admitted.

With regard to the more particularized rules, how should parallel situations be treated? Should the rule be regarded as occupying the field exclusively, or should it be extended by analogy to related situations? The answer lies in the purpose of the rule: if the additional situation presents the same problem as that with which the rule was designed to deal, application of the rule is appropriate. For example, under Rule 801(d)(1)(C) an out-of-court identification statement made after viewing a photograph has been held to be governed by the nonhearsay rule specifically applicable to statements made after view-

---

2. The manner of exercise of its legislative powers by the Congress as spelled out in the Constitution is the passing of bills and obtaining the President's approval or overriding his veto. U.S. Const. art. 1 § 7. While this may suggest the irrelevance of legislative history, in the British tradition, the American commitment is contrary, and it can scarcely be denied that the reasoning of those involved is a helpful source of illumination, without having the authority of law.

3. United States v. Smith, 551 F.2d 348 (D.C.Cir.1976).

4. Id. at 362.

5. Fed.R.Evid. 402.

ing the accused in person.[6] Or again, the prohibition against testimony by the judge in the trial over which he is presiding, in Rule 605, was extended to preclude testimony by his clerk.[7]

Not to be confused with the foregoing is the judicial engrafting onto a rule of a requirement not set forth in the rule and not supported by legislative history or other relevant context. An example is the engrafting of a requirement that other crimes as proof of intent under Rule 404(b) be proved by clear and convincing evidence, although no such provision is found in the rule.[8]

Rule 102 provides:

> These rules shall be construed to secure fairness in administration, elimination of unjustifiable expense and delay, and promotion of growth and development of the law of evidence to the end that the truth may be ascertained and proceedings justly determined.

Entitled "Purpose and Construction," the rule sets a high standard for approaching problems of application and meaning but furnishes small guidance to solving particular questions. The most important aspect of the rule may well be its implicit recognition that the rules do not, and cannot, resolve in specific terms a very large proportion of evidentiary uncertainties that may arise, and that solutions must be reached through application of accepted principles of statutory construction.

6. United States v. Lewis, 565 F.2d 1248 (2d Cir.1977), cert. denied 435 U.S. 973.

7. Kennedy v. Great Atlantic & Pacific Tea Co., 551 F.2d 593 (5th Cir.1977), rehearing denied 554 F.2d 475.

8. United States v. Beechum, 555 F.2d 487 (5th Cir.1977). The panel decision was overturned in banc. 582 F.2d 898, cert. denied 440 U.S. 920.

FEDERAL RULES OF EVIDENCE FOR UNITED STATES COURTS AND MAGISTRATES *

PUBLIC LAW 93–595; 88 STAT. 1926

Approved Jan. 2, 1975

[H.R. 5463]

An Act to establish rules of evidence for certain courts and proceedings.

Be it enacted by the Senate and House of Representatives of the United States of America in Congress assembled, That:

The following rules shall take effect on the one hundred and eightieth day beginning after the date of the enactment of this Act. These rules apply to actions, cases, and proceedings brought after the rules take effect. These rules also apply to further procedure in actions, cases, and proceedings then pending, except to the extent that application of the rules would not be feasible, or would work injustice, in which event former evidentiary principles apply.

ORDER OF APRIL 30, 1979

1. That Rule 410 of the Federal Rules of Evidence be, and it hereby is, amended to read as follows:

[See amendment made thereby following Rule 410, post.]

2. That the foregoing amendment to the Federal Rules of Evidence shall take effect on November 1, 1979, and shall be applicable to all proceedings then pending except to the extent that in the opinion of the court the application of the amended rule in a particular proceeding would not be feasible or would work injustice.

3. That THE CHIEF JUSTICE be, and he hereby is, authorized to transmit to the Congress the foregoing amendment to the Federal Rules of Evidence in accordance with the provisions of 28 U.S.C. § 2076.

CONGRESSIONAL ACTION ON AMENDMENT PROPOSED APRIL 30, 1979

Pub.L. 96–42, July 31, 1979, 93 Stat. 326, provided that the amendment proposed and transmitted to the Federal Rules of Evidence affecting rule 410, shall not take effect until Dec. 1, 1980, or until and

---

* References to sections of *McCormick on Evidence*, 4th ed. follow the text of each   Rule. The more important section references are printed in italic.

then only to the extent approved by Act of Congress, whichever is earlier.

ORDER OF MARCH 2, 1987

1. That the Federal Rules of Evidence be, and they hereby are, amended by including therein amendments to Rules 101, 104, 106, 404, 405, 411, 602, 603, 604, 606, 607, 608, 609, 610, 611, 612, 613, 615, 701, 703, 705, 706, 801, 803, 804, 806, 902, 1004, 1007 and 1101, as hereinafter set forth:

[See amendments made thereby under respective rules, post.]

2. That the foregoing changes in the Federal Rules of Evidence shall take effect on October 1, 1987.

3. That THE CHIEF JUSTICE be, and he hereby is, authorized to transmit to the Congress the foregoing changes in the rules of evidence in accordance with the provisions of Section 2076 of Title 28, United States Code.

ORDER OF APRIL 25, 1988

1. That the Federal Rules of Evidence be, and they hereby are, amended by including therein amendments to Rules 101, 602, 608, 613, 615, 902, and 1101, as hereinafter set forth:

[See amendments made thereby under respective rules, post.]

2. That the foregoing changes in the Federal Rules of Evidence shall take effect on November 1, 1988.

3. That THE CHIEF JUSTICE be, and he hereby is, authorized to transmit to the Congress the foregoing changes in the rules of evidence in accordance with the provisions of Section 2076 of Title 28, United States Code.

ORDER OF JANUARY 26, 1990

1. That the Federal Rules of Evidence be, and they hereby are, amended by including therein amendments to Rule 609(a)(1) and (2), as hereinafter set forth:

[See amendment made thereby, post].

2. That the foregoing changes in the Federal Rules of Evidence shall take effect on December 1, 1990.

3. That THE CHIEF JUSTICE be, and he hereby is, authorized to transmit to the Congress the foregoing changes in the rules of evidence in accordance with the provisions of Section 2074 of Title 28, United States Code.

ORDER OF APRIL 30, 1991

1. That the Federal Rules of Evidence for the United States District Courts be, and they hereby are, amended by including therein amendments to Evidence Rules 404(b) and 1102.

[See amendments made thereby under respective rules, post.]

2. That the foregoing amendments to the Federal Rules of Evidence shall take effect on December 1, 1991, and shall govern in all proceedings thereafter commenced and, insofar as just and practicable, all proceedings then pending.

3. That THE CHIEF JUSTICE be, and he hereby is, authorized to transmit to the Congress the foregoing amendments to the Federal Rules of Evidence in accordance with the provisions of Section 2072 of Title 28, United States Code.

ARTICLE I.   GENERAL PROVISIONS

Rule 101.   Scope

These rules govern proceedings in the courts of the United States and before United States bankruptcy judges and United States magistrates, to the extent and with the exceptions stated in rule 1101.

(As amended Mar. 2, 1987, eff. Oct. 1, 1987; Apr. 25, 1988, eff. Nov. 1, 1988.)

Note by Federal Judicial Center

The rule enacted by the Congress is the rule prescribed by the Supreme Court without change.

Advisory Committee's Note

56 F.R.D. 183, 194

Rule 1101 specifies in detail the courts, proceedings, questions, and stages of proceedings to which the rules apply in whole or in part.

1987 Amendment. United States bankruptcy judges are added to conform this rule with Rule 1101(b) and Bankruptcy Rule 9017.

1988 Amendment. The amendment is technical. No substantive change is intended.

Rule 102. Purpose and Construction

These rules shall be construed to secure fairness in administration, elimination of unjustifiable expense and delay, and promotion of growth and development of the law of evidence to the end that the truth may be ascertained and proceedings justly determined.

Section references, McCormick 4th ed.

§ 60

Note by Federal Judicial Center

The rule enacted by the Congress is the rule prescribed by the Supreme Court without change.

Advisory Committee's Note

56 F.R.D. 183, 194

For similar provisions see Rule 2 of the Federal Rules of Criminal Procedure, Rule 1 of the Federal Rules of Civil Procedure, California Evidence Code § 2, and New Jersey Evidence Rule 5.

Rule 103. Rulings on Evidence

(a) **Effect of erroneous ruling.** Error may not be predicated upon a ruling which admits or excludes evidence unless a substantial right of the party is affected, and

(1) **Objection.** In case the ruling is one admitting evidence, a timely objection or motion to strike appears of record, stating the specific ground of objection, if the specific ground was not apparent from the context; or

(2) **Offer of proof.** In case the ruling is one excluding evidence, the substance of the evidence was made known to the court by offer or was apparent from the context within which questions were asked.

(b) **Record of offer and ruling.** The court may add any other or further statement which shows the character of the evidence, the form in which it was offered, the objection made, and the ruling thereon. It may direct the making of an offer in question and answer form.

(c) Hearing of jury. In jury cases, proceedings shall be conducted, to the extent practicable, so as to prevent inadmissible evidence from being suggested to the jury by any means, such as making statements or offers of proof or asking questions in the hearing of the jury.

(d) Plain error. Nothing in this rule precludes taking notice of plain errors affecting substantial rights although they were not brought to the attention of the court.

Section references, McCormick 4th ed.

Generally § *51*, § *52*, § 58.

  (a). § 183

    (1). § *52*, § 55, § 73

    (2). § *51*, § *52*

  (b). § *51*, § *58*

  (c). § *51*, § *52*, § 190

  (d). § *52*, § 55

Note by Federal Judicial Center

The rule enacted by the Congress is the rule prescribed by the Supreme Court, amended by substituting "court" in place of "judge," with appropriate pronominal change.

Advisory Committee's Note

56 F.R.D. 183, 195

Subdivision (a) states the law as generally accepted today. Rulings on evidence cannot be assigned as error unless (1) a substantial right is affected, and (2) the nature of the error was called to the attention of the judge, so as to alert him to the proper course of action and enable opposing counsel to take proper corrective measures. The objection and the offer of proof are the techniques for accomplishing these objectives. For similar provisions see Uniform Rules 4 and 5; California Evidence Code §§ 353 and 354; Kansas Code of Civil Procedure §§ 60–404 and 60–405. The rule does not purport to change the law with respect to harmless error. See 28 USC § 2111, F.R.Civ.P. 61, F.R. Crim.P. 52, and decisions construing them. The status of constitutional error as harmless or not is treated in Chapman v. California, 386 U.S. 18, 87 S.Ct. 824, 17 L.Ed.2d 705 (1967), reh. denied id. 987, 87 S.Ct. 1283, 18 L.Ed.2d 241.

Subdivision (b). The first sentence is the third sentence of Rule 43(c) of the Federal Rules of Civil Procedure [1] virtually verbatim. Its purpose is to reproduce for an appellate court, insofar as possible, a true reflection of what occurred in the trial court. The second sentence is in part derived from the final sentence of Rule 43(c).[1] It is designed to resolve doubts as to what testimony the witness would have in fact given, and, in nonjury cases, to

---

1. Rule 43(c) of the Federal Rules of Civil Procedure was deleted by order of the Supreme Court entered on November 20, 1972, 93 S.Ct. 3073, 3075, 3076, 3077, 34 L.Ed.2d lxv, ccv, ccviii, which action was affirmed by the Congress in P.L. 93–595 § 3 (January 2, 1975).—Federal Judicial Center.

provide the appellate court with material for a possible final disposition of the case in the event of reversal of a ruling which excluded evidence. See 5 Moore's Federal Practice § 43.11 (2d ed. 1968). Application is made discretionary in view of the practical impossibility of formulating a satisfactory rule in mandatory terms.

Subdivision (c). This subdivision proceeds on the supposition that a ruling which excludes evidence in a jury case is likely to be a pointless procedure if the excluded evidence nevertheless comes to the attention of the jury. Bruton v. United States, 389 U.S. 818, 88 S.Ct. 126, 19 L.Ed.2d 70 (1968). Rule 43(c) of the Federal Rules of Civil Procedure[1] provides: "The court may require the offer to be made out of the hearing of the jury." In re McConnell, 370 U.S. 230, 82 S.Ct. 1288, 8 L.Ed.2d 434 (1962), left some doubt whether questions on which an offer is based must first be asked in the presence of the jury. The subdivision answers in the negative. The judge can foreclose a particular line of testimony and counsel can protect his record without a series of questions before the jury, designed at best to waste time and at worst "to waft into the jury box" the very matter sought to be excluded.

Subdivision (d). This wording of the plain error principle is from Rule 52(b) of the Federal Rules of Criminal Procedure. While judicial unwillingness to be constricted by mechanical breakdowns of the adversary system has been more pronounced in criminal cases, there is no scarcity of decisions to the same effect in civil cases. In general, see Campbell, Extent to Which Courts of Review Will Consider Questions Not Properly Raised and Preserved, 7 Wis.L.Rev. 91, 160 (1932); Vestal, Sua Sponte Consideration in Appellate Review, 27 Fordham L.Rev. 477 (1958–59); 64 Harv.L.Rev. 652 (1951). In the nature of things the application of the plain error rule will be more likely with respect to the admission of evidence than to exclusion, since failure to comply with normal requirements of offers of proof is likely to produce a record which simply does not disclose the error.

Rule 104. Preliminary Questions

(a) **Questions of admissibility generally.** Preliminary questions concerning the qualification of a person to be a witness, the existence of a privilege, or the admissibility of evidence shall be determined by the court, subject to the provisions of subdivision (b). In making its determination it is not bound by the rules of evidence except those with respect to privileges.

(b) **Relevancy conditioned on fact.** When the relevancy of evidence depends upon the fulfillment of a condition of fact, the court shall admit it upon, or subject to, the introduction of evidence sufficient to support a finding of the fulfillment of the condition.

(c) **Hearing of jury.** Hearings on the admissibility of confessions shall in all cases be conducted out of the hearing of the jury. Hearings on other preliminary matters shall be so conducted when the interests of justice require, or when an accused is a witness and so requests.

(d) **Testimony by accused.** The accused does not, by testifying upon a preliminary matter, become subject to cross-examination as to other issues in the case.

(e) **Weight and credibility.** This rule does not limit the right of a party to introduce before the jury evidence relevant to weight or credibility.

(As amended Mar. 2, 1987, eff. Oct. 1, 1987.)

Section references, McCormick 4th ed.

Generally § 15, § 53

(a). § 53, § 68, § 70, § 227

(b). § 10, § 53, § 54, § 58, § 227

(c). § 52, § 53, § 162

(d). § 53

(e). § 53

Note by Federal Judicial Center

The rule enacted by the Congress is the rule prescribed by the Supreme Court, amended by substituting "court" in place of "judge," with appropriate pronominal change, and by adding to subdivision (c) the concluding phrase, "or when an accused is a witness, if he so requests."[1]

Advisory Committee's Note

56 F.R.D. 183, 196

Subdivision (a). The applicability of a particular rule of evidence often depends upon the existence of a condition. Is the alleged expert a qualified physician? Is a witness whose former testimony is offered unavailable? Was a stranger present during a conversation between attorney and client? In each instance the admissibility of evidence will turn upon the answer to the question of the existence of the condition. Accepted practice, incorporated in the rule, places on the judge the responsibility for these determinations. McCormick § 53; Morgan, Basic Problems of Evidence 45–50 (1962).

To the extent that these inquiries are factual, the judge acts as a trier of fact. Often, however, rulings on evidence call for an evaluation in terms of a legally set standard. Thus when a hearsay statement is offered as a declaration against interest, a decision must be made whether it possesses the required against-interest characteristics. These decisions, too, are made by the judge.

In view of these considerations, this subdivision refers to preliminary requirements generally by the broad term "questions," without attempt at specification.

This subdivision is of general application. It must, however, be read as subject to the special provisions for "conditional relevancy" in subdivision (b) and those for confessions in subdivision (c).

If the question is factual in nature, the judge will of necessity receive evidence pro and con on the issue. The rule provides that the rules of evidence

1. The effect of the amendment was to restore language included in the 1971 Revised Draft of the Proposed Rules but deleted before the rules were presented to and prescribed by the Supreme Court.— Federal Judicial Center.

in general do not apply to this process. McCormick § 53, p. 123, n. 8, points out that the authorities are "scattered and inconclusive," and observes:

> "Should the exclusionary law of evidence, 'the child of the jury system' in Thayer's phrase, be applied to this hearing before the judge? Sound sense backs the view that it should not, and that the judge should be empowered to hear any relevant evidence, such as affidavits or other reliable hearsay."

This view is reinforced by practical necessity in certain situations. An item, offered and objected to, may itself be considered in ruling on admissibility, though not yet admitted in evidence. Thus the content of an asserted declaration against interest must be considered in ruling whether it is against interest. Again, common practice calls for considering the testimony of a witness, particularly a child, in determining competency. Another example is the requirement of Rule 602 dealing with personal knowledge. In the case of hearsay, it is enough, if the declarant "so far as appears [has] had an opportunity to observe the fact declared." McCormick, § 10, p. 19.

If concern is felt over the use of affidavits by the judge in preliminary hearings on admissibility, attention is directed to the many important judicial determinations made on the basis of affidavits. Rule 47 of the Federal Rules of Criminal Procedure provides:

> "An application to the court for an order shall be by motion. . . . It may be supported by affidavit."

The Rules of Civil Procedure are more detailed. Rule 43(e), dealing with motions generally, provides:

> "When a motion is based on facts not appearing of record the court may hear the matter on affidavits presented by the respective parties, but the court may direct that the matter be heard wholly or partly on oral testimony or depositions."

Rule 4(g) provides for proof of service by affidavit. Rule 56 provides in detail for the entry of summary judgment based on affidavits. Affidavits may supply the foundation for temporary restraining orders under Rule 65(b).

The study made for the California Law Revision Commission recommended an amendment to Uniform Rule 2 as follows:

> "In the determination of the issue aforesaid [preliminary determination], exclusionary rules shall not apply, subject, however, to Rule 45 and any valid claim of privilege." Tentative Recommendation and a Study Relating to the Uniform Rules of Evidence (Article VIII, Hearsay), Cal.Law Revision Comm'n, Rep., Rec. & Studies, 470 (1962). The proposal was not adopted in the California Evidence Code. The Uniform Rules are likewise silent on the subject. However, New Jersey Evidence Rule 8(1), dealing with preliminary inquiry by the judge, provides:

> "In his determination the rules of evidence shall not apply except for Rule 4 [exclusion on grounds of confusion, etc.] or a valid claim of privilege."

Subdivision (b). In some situations, the relevancy of an item of evidence, in the large sense, depends upon the existence of a particular preliminary fact. Thus when a spoken statement is relied upon to prove notice to X, it is without probative value unless X heard it. Or if a letter purporting to be from Y is relied upon to establish an admission by him, it has no probative value unless Y wrote or authorized it. Relevance in this sense has been labelled "conditional relevancy." Morgan, Basic Problems of Evidence 45–46 (1962). Problems arising in connection with it are to be distinguished from problems of logical relevancy, e.g. evidence in a murder case that accused on the day before purchased a weapon of the kind used in the killing, treated in Rule 401.

If preliminary questions of conditional relevancy were determined solely by the judge, as provided in subdivision (a), the functioning of the jury as a trier of fact would be greatly restricted and in some cases virtually destroyed. These are appropriate questions for juries. Accepted treatment, as provided in the rule, is consistent with that given fact questions generally. The judge makes a preliminary determination whether the foundation evidence is sufficient to support a finding of fulfillment of the condition. If so, the item is admitted. If after all the evidence on the issue is in, pro and con, the jury could reasonably conclude that fulfillment of the condition is not established, the issue is for them. If the evidence is not such as to allow a finding, the judge withdraws the matter from their consideration. Morgan, supra; California Evidence Code § 403; New Jersey Rule 8(2). See also Uniform Rules 19 and 67.

The order of proof here, as generally, is subject to the control of the judge.

Subdivision (c). Preliminary hearings on the admissibility of confessions must be conducted outside the hearing of the jury. See Jackson v. Denno, 378 U.S. 368, 84 S.Ct. 1774, 12 L.Ed.2d 908 (1964).[2] Otherwise, detailed treatment of when preliminary matters should be heard outside the hearing of the jury is not feasible. The procedure is time consuming. Not infrequently the same evidence which is relevant to the issue of establishment of fulfillment of a condition precedent to admissibility is also relevant to weight or credibility, and time is saved by taking foundation proof in the presence of the jury. Much evidence on preliminary questions, though not relevant to jury issues, may be heard by the jury with no adverse effect. A great deal must be left to the discretion of the judge who will act as the interests of justice require.

Report of the House Committee on the Judiciary

House Comm. on Judiciary, Fed. Rules of Evidence, H.R.Rep. No. 650, 93d Cong., 1st Sess., p. 15 (1973); 1974 U.S.Code Cong. & Ad. News 7075, 7080

Rule 104(c) as submitted to the Congress provided that hearings on the admissibility of confessions shall be conducted outside the presence of the jury and hearings on all other preliminary matters should be so conducted when the interests of justice require. The Committee amended the Rule to provide that where an accused is a witness as to a preliminary matter, he has the right, upon his request, to be heard outside the jury's presence. Although recognizing that in some cases duplication of evidence would occur and that the procedure could be subject to abuse, the Committee believed that a proper regard for the right of an accused not to testify generally in the case dictates that he be given an option to testify out of the presence of the jury on preliminary matters.

2. At this point the Advisory Committee's Note to the 1971 Revised Draft contained the sentence, "Also, due regard for the right of an accused not to testify generally in the case requires that he be given an option to testify out of the presence of the jury upon preliminary matters." The statement was deleted in view of the deletion from the rule, mentioned in the preceding footnote.—Federal Judicial Center.

The Committee construes the second sentence of subdivision (c) as applying to civil actions and proceedings as well as to criminal cases, and on this assumption has left the sentence unamended.

Advisory Committee's Note

56 F.R.D. 183, 199

Subdivision (d). The limitation upon cross-examination is designed to encourage participation by the accused in the determination of preliminary matters. He may testify concerning them without exposing himself to cross-examination generally. The provision is necessary because of the breadth of cross-examination [possible] under Rule 611(b).

The rule does not address itself to questions of the subsequent use of testimony given by an accused at a hearing on a preliminary matter. See Walder v. United States, 347 U.S. 62 (1954); Simmons v. United States, 390 U.S. 377 (1968); Harris v. New York, 401 U.S. 222 (1971).

Report of Senate Committee on the Judiciary

Senate Comm. on Judiciary, Fed. Rules of Evidence, S.Rep. No. 1277, 93d Cong., 2d Sess., p. 24 (1974); 1974 U.S.Code Cong. & Ad. News 7051, 7070

Under Rule 104(c) the hearing on a preliminary matter may at times be conducted in front of the jury. Should an accused testify in such a hearing, waiving his privilege against self-incrimination as to the preliminary issue, Rule 104(d) provides that he will not generally be subject to cross-examination as to any other issue. This rule is not, however, intended to immunize the accused from cross-examination where, in testifying about a preliminary issue, he injects other issues into the hearing. If he could not be cross-examined about any issues gratuitously raised by him beyond the scope of the preliminary matters, injustice might result. Accordingly, in order to prevent any such unjust result, the committee intends the rule to be construed to provide that the accused may subject himself to cross-examination as to issues raised by his own testimony upon a preliminary matter before a jury.

Advisory Committee's Note

56 F.R.D. 183, 199

Subdivision (e). For similar provisions see Uniform Rule 8; California Evidence Code § 406; Kansas Code of Civil Procedure § 60–408; New Jersey Evidence Rule 8(1).

1987 Amendment. The amendments are technical. No substantive change is intended.

Rule 105. Limited Admissibility

When evidence which is admissible as to one party or for one purpose but not admissible as to another party or for another purpose is admitted, the court, upon request, shall restrict the evidence to its proper scope and instruct the jury accordingly.

Section references, McCormick 4th ed.

§ 59

Note by Federal Judicial Center

The rule enacted by the Congress is the rule prescribed by the Supreme Court as Rule 106, amended by substituting "court" in place of "judge." Rule 105 as prescribed by the Court, which was deleted from the rules enacted by the Congress, is set forth in the Appendix hereto, together with a statement of the reasons for the deletion.

Advisory Committee's Note

56 F.R.D. 183, 200

A close relationship exists between this rule and Rule 403 which . . . [provides for] exclusion when "probative value is substantially outweighed by the danger of unfair prejudice, confusion of the issues, or misleading the jury." The present rule recognizes the practice of admitting evidence for a limited purpose and instructing the jury accordingly. The availability and effectiveness of this practice must be taken into consideration in reaching a decision whether to exclude for unfair prejudice under Rule 403. In Bruton v. United States, 389 U.S. 818, 88 S.Ct. 126, 19 L.Ed.2d 70 (1968), the Court ruled that a limiting instruction did not effectively protect the accused against the prejudicial effect of admitting in evidence the confession of a codefendant which implicated him. The decision does not, however, bar the use of limited admissibility with an instruction where the risk of prejudice is less serious.

Similar provisions are found in Uniform Rule 6; California Evidence Code § 355; Kansas Code of Civil Procedure § 60–406; New Jersey Evidence Rule 6. The wording of the present rule differs, however, in repelling any implication that limiting or curative instructions are sufficient in all situations.

Report of House Committee on the Judiciary

House Comm. on Judiciary, Fed. Rules of Evidence, H.R.Rep. No. 650, 93d Cong., 1st Sess., p. 6 (1973); 1974 U.S.Code Cong. & Ad. News 7075, 7080

Rule 106 as submitted by the Supreme Court (now Rule 105 in the bill) dealt with the subject of evidence which is admissible as to one party or for one purpose but is not admissible against another party or for another purpose. The Committee adopted this Rule without change on the understanding that it does not affect the authority of a court to order a severance in a multi-defendant case.

Rule 106. Remainder of or Related Writings or Recorded Statements

When a writing or recorded statement or part thereof is introduced by a party, an adverse party may require the introduction at that time of any other part or any other writing or recorded statement which ought in fairness to be considered contemporaneously with it.

(As amended Mar. 2, 1987, eff. Oct. 1, 1987.)

Section references, McCormick 4th ed.

§ 21, § 32, § 47, § 56, § 57, § 59, § 307

Note by Federal Judicial Center

The rule enacted by the Congress is the rule prescribed by the Supreme Court as Rule 107 without change.

Advisory Committee's Note

56 F.R.D. 183, 201

The rule is an expression of the rule of completeness. McCormick § 56. It is manifested as to depositions in Rule 32(a)(4) of the Federal Rules of Civil Procedure, of which the proposed rule is substantially a restatement.

The rule is based on two considerations. The first is the misleading impression created by taking matters out of context. The second is the inadequacy of repair work when delayed to a point later in the trial. See McCormick § 56; California Evidence Code § 356. The rule does not in any way circumscribe the right of the adversary to develop the matter on cross-examination or as part of his own case.

For practical reasons, the rule is limited to writings and recorded statements and does not apply to conversations.

1987 Amendment. The amendments are technical. No substantive change is intended.

ARTICLE II. JUDICIAL NOTICE

Rule

201. Judicial Notice of Adjudicative Facts.
    (a) Scope of Rule.
    (b) Kinds of Facts.
    (c) When Discretionary.
    (d) When Mandatory.
    (e) Opportunity to be Heard.
    (f) Time of Taking Notice.
    (g) Instructing Jury.

Rule 201. Judicial Notice of Adjudicative Facts

(a) Scope of rule. This rule governs only judicial notice of adjudicative facts.

(b) Kinds of facts. A judicially noticed fact must be one not subject to reasonable dispute in that it is either (1) generally known within the territorial jurisdiction of the trial court or (2) capable of accurate and ready determination by resort to sources whose accuracy cannot reasonably be questioned.

(c) When discretionary. A court may take judicial notice, whether requested or not.

(d) When mandatory. A court shall take judicial notice if requested by a party and supplied with the necessary information.

(e) Opportunity to be heard. A party is entitled upon timely request to an opportunity to be heard as to the propriety of taking judicial notice and the tenor of the matter noticed. In the absence of prior notification, the request may be made after judicial notice has been taken.

(f) Time of taking notice. Judicial notice may be taken at any stage of the proceeding.

(g) Instructing jury. In a civil action or proceeding, the court shall instruct the jury to accept as conclusive any fact judicially noticed. In a criminal case, the court shall instruct the jury that it may, but is not required to, accept as conclusive any fact judicially noticed.

Section references, McCormick 4th ed.

Generally § *328*, § *332*, § *333*

(a). § 331, § *332*, § *334*

(b)(1). § *328*, § 329

(2). § 329, § *330*

(c). § *333*

(d). § *333*

(e). § *334*

(f). § *333*

(g). § *332*

Note by Federal Judicial Center

The rule enacted by the Congress is the rule prescribed by the Supreme Court with the following changes:

In subdivisions (c) and (d) the words "judge or" before "court" were deleted.

Subdivision (g) as it is shown was substituted in place of, "The judge shall instruct the jury to accept as established any facts judicially noticed." The substituted language is from the 1969 Preliminary Draft. 46 F.R.D. 161, 195.

Advisory Committee's Note

56 F.R.D. 183, 201

Subdivision (a). This is the only evidence rule on the subject of judicial notice. It deals only with judicial notice of "adjudicative" facts. No rule deals with judicial notice of "legislative" facts. Judicial notice of matters of foreign law is treated in Rule 44.1 of the Federal Rules of Civil Procedure and Rule 26.1 of the Federal Rules of Criminal Procedure.

The omission of any treatment of legislative facts results from fundamental differences between adjudicative facts and legislative facts. Adjudicative facts are simply the facts of the particular case. Legislative facts, on the other hand, are those which have relevance to legal reasoning and the lawmaking process, whether in the formulation of a legal principle or ruling by a judge or court or in the enactment of a legislative body. The terminology was coined by Professor Kenneth Davis in his article An Approach to Problems of Evidence in the Administrative Process, 55 Harv.L.Rev. 364, 404–407 (1942). The following discussion draws extensively upon his writings. In addition, see the same author's Judicial Notice, 55 Colum.L.Rev. 945 (1955); Administrative Law Treatise, ch. 15 (1958); A System of Judicial Notice Based on Fairness and Convenience, in Perspectives of Law 69 (1964).

The usual method of establishing adjudicative facts is through the introduction of evidence, ordinarily consisting of the testimony of witnesses. If particular facts are outside the area of reasonable controversy, this process is dispensed with as unnecessary. A high degree of indisputability is the essential prerequisite.

Legislative facts are quite different. As Professor Davis says:

"My opinion is that judge-made law would stop growing if judges, in thinking about questions of law and policy, were forbidden to take into account the facts they believe, as distinguished from facts which are 'clearly . . . within the domain of the indisputable.' Facts most needed in thinking about difficult problems of law and policy have a way of being outside the domain of the clearly indisputable." A System of Judicial Notice Based on Fairness and Convenience, supra, at 82.

An illustration is Hawkins v. United States, 358 U.S. 74, 79 S.Ct. 136, 3 L.Ed.2d 125 (1958), in which the Court refused to discard the common law rule that one spouse could not testify against the other, saying, "Adverse testimony given in criminal proceedings would, we think, be likely to destroy almost any marriage." This conclusion has a large intermixture of fact, but the factual aspect is scarcely "indisputable." See Hutchins and Slesinger, Some Observations on the Law of Evidence—Family Relations, 13 Minn.L.Rev. 675 (1929). If the destructive effect of the giving of adverse testimony by a spouse is not indisputable, should the Court have refrained from considering it in the absence of supporting evidence?

"If the Model Code or the Uniform Rules had been applicable, the Court would have been barred from thinking about the essential factual ingredient of the problems before it, and such a result would be obviously intolerable. What the law needs at its growing points is more, not less, judicial thinking about the factual ingredients of problems of what the law ought to be, and the needed facts are seldom 'clearly' indisputable." Davis, supra, at 83.

Professor Morgan gave the following description of the methodology of determining domestic law:

"In determining the content or applicability of a rule of domestic law, the judge is unrestricted in his investigation and conclusion. He may reject the propositions of either party or of both parties. He may consult the sources of pertinent data to which they refer, or he may refuse to do so. He may make an independent search for persuasive data or rest content with what he has or what the parties present. . . . [T]he parties do no more than to assist; they control no part of the process." Morgan, Judicial Notice, 57 Harv.L.Rev. 269, 270–271 (1944).

This is the view which should govern judicial access to legislative facts. It renders inappropriate any limitation in the form of indisputability, any formal requirements of notice other than those already inherent in affording opportunity to hear and be heard and exchanging briefs, and any requirement of formal findings at any level. It should, however, leave open the possibility of introducing evidence through regular channels in appropriate situations. See Borden's Farm Products Co. v. Baldwin, 293 U.S. 194, 55 S.Ct. 187, 79 L.Ed. 281 (1934), where the cause was remanded for the taking of evidence as to the economic conditions and trade practices underlying the New York Milk Control Law.

Similar considerations govern the judicial use of non-adjudicative facts in ways other than formulating laws and rules. Thayer described them as a part of the judicial reasoning process.

> "In conducting a process of judicial reasoning, as of other reasoning, not a step can be taken without assuming something which has not been proved; and the capacity to do this with competent judgment and efficiency, is imputed to judges and juries as part of their necessary mental outfit."
> Thayer, Preliminary Treatise on Evidence 279–280 (1898).

As Professor Davis points out, A System of Judicial Notice Based on Fairness and Convenience, in Perspectives of Law 69, 73 (1964), every case involves the use of hundreds or thousands of non-evidence facts. When a witness in an automobile accident case says "car," everyone, judge and jury included, furnishes, from non-evidence sources within himself, the supplementing information that the "car" is an automobile, not a railroad car, that it is self-propelled, probably by an internal combustion engine, that it may be assumed to have four wheels with pneumatic rubber tires, and so on. The judicial process cannot construct every case from scratch, like Descartes creating a world based on the postulate *Cogito, ergo sum.* These items could not possibly be introduced into evidence, and no one suggests that they be. Nor are they appropriate subjects for any formalized treatment of judicial notice of facts. See Levin and Levy, Persuading the Jury with Facts Not in Evidence: The Fiction-Science Spectrum, 105 U.Pa.L.Rev. 139 (1956).

Another aspect of what Thayer had in mind is the use of non-evidence facts to appraise or assess the adjudicative facts of the case. Pairs of cases from two jurisdictions illustrate this use and also the difference between non-evidence facts thus used and adjudicative facts. In People v. Strook, 347 Ill. 460, 179 N.E. 821 (1932), venue in Cook County had been held not established by testimony that the crime was committed at 7956 South Chicago Avenue, since judicial notice would not be taken that the address was in Chicago. However, the same court subsequently ruled that venue in Cook County was established by testimony that a crime occurred at 8900 South Anthony Avenue, since notice would be taken of the common practice of omitting the name of the city when speaking of local addresses, and the witness was testifying in Chicago. People v. Pride, 16 Ill.2d 82, 156 N.E.2d 551 (1951). And in Hughes v. Vestal, 264 N.C. 500, 142 S.E.2d 361 (1965), the Supreme Court of North Carolina disapproved the trial judge's admission in evidence of a state-published table of automobile stopping distances on the basis of judicial notice, though the court itself had referred to the same table in an earlier case in a "rhetorical and illustrative" way in determining that the defendant could not have stopped her car in time to avoid striking a child who suddenly appeared in the highway and that a nonsuit was properly granted. Ennis v. Dupree, 262 N.C. 224, 136 S.E.2d 702 (1964). See also Brown v. Hale, 263 N.C. 176, 139 S.E.2d 210 (1964); Clayton v. Rimmer, 262 N.C. 302, 136 S.E.2d 562 (1964). It is apparent that this use of non-evidence facts in evaluating the adjudicative facts of the case is not an appropriate subject for a formalized judicial notice treatment.

In view of these considerations, the regulation of judicial notice of facts by the present rule extends only to adjudicative facts.

What, then, are "adjudicative" facts? Davis refers to them as those "which relate to the parties," or more fully:

> "When a court or an agency finds facts concerning the immediate parties—who did what, where, when, how, and with what motive or intent—the court or agency is performing an adjudicative function, and the facts are conveniently called adjudicative facts. . . .

> "Stated in other terms, the adjudicative facts are those to which the law is applied in the process of adjudication. They are the facts that normally go to the jury in a jury case. They relate to the parties, their activities, their properties, their businesses." 2 Administrative Law Treatise 353.

Subdivision (b). With respect to judicial notice of adjudicative facts, the tradition has been one of caution in requiring that the matter be beyond reasonable controversy. This tradition of circumspection appears to be soundly based, and no reason to depart from it is apparent. As Professor Davis says:

> "The reason we use trial-type procedure, I think, is that we make the practical judgment, on the basis of experience, that taking evidence, subject to cross-examination and rebuttal, is the best way to resolve controversies involving disputes of adjudicative facts, that is, facts pertaining to the parties. The reason we require a determination on the record is that we think fair procedure in resolving disputes of adjudicative facts calls for giving each party a chance to meet in the appropriate fashion the facts that come to the tribunal's attention, and the appropriate fashion for meeting disputed adjudicative facts includes rebuttal evidence, cross-examination, usually confrontation, and argument (either written or oral or both). The key to a fair trial is opportunity to use the appropriate weapons (rebuttal evidence, cross-examination, and argument) to meet adverse materials that come to the tribunal's attention." A System of Judicial Notice Based on Fairness and Convenience, in Perspectives of Law 69, 93 (1964).

The rule proceeds upon the theory that these considerations call for dispensing with traditional methods of proof only in clear cases. Compare Professor Davis' conclusion that judicial notice should be a matter of convenience, subject to requirements of procedural fairness. Id., 94.

This rule is consistent with Uniform Rule 9(1) and (2) which limit judicial notice of facts to those "so universally known that they cannot reasonably be the subject of dispute," those "so generally known or of such common notoriety within the territorial jurisdiction of the court that they cannot reasonably be the subject of dispute," and those "capable of immediate and accurate determination by resort to easily accessible sources of indisputable accuracy." The traditional textbook treatment has included these general categories (matters of common knowledge, facts capable of verification), McCormick §§ 324, 325, and then has passed on into detailed treatment of such specific topics as facts relating to the personnel and records of the court, id. § 327, and other governmental facts, id. § 328. The California draftsmen, with a background of detailed statutory regulation of judicial notice, followed a somewhat similar pattern. California Evidence Code §§ 451, 452. The Uniform Rules, however,

were drafted on the theory that these particular matters are included within the general categories and need no specific mention. This approach is followed in the present rule.

The phrase "propositions of generalized knowledge," found in Uniform Rule 9(1) and (2) is not included in the present rule. It was, it is believed, originally included in Model Code Rules 801 and 802 primarily in order to afford some minimum recognition to the right of the judge in his "legislative" capacity (not acting as the trier of fact) to take judicial notice of very limited categories of generalized knowledge. The limitations thus imposed have been discarded herein as undesirable, unworkable, and contrary to existing practice. What is left, then, to be considered, is the status of a "proposition of generalized knowledge" as an "adjudicative" fact to be noticed judicially and communicated by the judge to the jury. Thus viewed, it is considered to be lacking practical significance. While judges used judicial notice of "propositions of generalized knowledge" in a variety of situations: determining the validity and meaning of statutes, formulating common law rules, deciding whether evidence should be admitted, assessing the sufficiency and effect of evidence, all are essentially nonadjudicative in nature. When judicial notice is seen as a significant vehicle for progress in the law, these are the areas involved, particularly in developing fields of scientific knowledge. See McCormick 712. It is not believed that judges now instruct juries as to "propositions of generalized knowledge" derived from encyclopedias or other sources, or that they are likely to do so, or, indeed, that it is desirable that they do so. There is a vast difference between ruling on the basis of judicial notice that radar evidence of speed is admissible and explaining to the jury its principles and degree of accuracy, or between using a table of stopping distances of automobiles at various speeds in a judicial evaluation of testimony and telling the jury its precise application in the case. For cases raising doubt as to the propriety of the use of medical texts by lay triers of fact in passing on disability claims in administrative proceedings, see Sayers v. Gardner, 380 F.2d 940 (6th Cir.1967); Ross v. Gardner, 365 F.2d 554 (6th Cir.1966); Sosna v. Celebrezze, 234 F.Supp. 289 (E.D.Pa.1964); Glendenning v. Ribicoff, 213 F.Supp. 301 (W.D.Mo.1962).

Subdivisions (c) and (d). Under subdivision (c) the judge has a discretionary authority to take judicial notice, regardless of whether he is so requested by a party. The taking of judicial notice is mandatory, under subdivision (d), only when a party requests it and the necessary information is supplied. This scheme is believed to reflect existing practice. It is simple and workable. It avoids troublesome distinctions in the many situations in which the process of taking judicial notice is not recognized as such.

Compare Uniform Rule 9 making judicial notice of facts universally known mandatory without request, and making judicial notice of facts generally known in the jurisdiction or capable of determination by resort to accurate sources discretionary in the absence of request but mandatory if request is made and the information furnished. But see Uniform Rule 10(3), which directs the judge to decline to take judicial notice if available information fails to convince him that the matter falls clearly within Uniform Rule 9 or is insufficient to enable him to notice it judicially. Substantially the same approach is found in California Evidence Code §§ 451–453 and in New Jersey Evidence Rule 9. In contrast, the present rule treats alike all adjudicative facts which are subject to judicial notice.

Subdivision (e). Basic considerations of procedural fairness demand an opportunity to be heard on the propriety of taking judicial notice and the tenor of the matter noticed. The rule requires the granting of that opportunity upon request. No formal scheme of giving notice is provided. An adversely affected party may learn in advance that judicial notice is in contemplation, either by virtue of being served with a copy of a request by another party under subdivision (d) that judicial notice be taken, or through an advance indication by the judge. Or he may have no advance notice at all. The likelihood of the latter is enhanced by the frequent failure to recognize judicial notice as such. And in the absence of advance notice, a request made after the fact could not in fairness be considered untimely. See the provision for hearing on timely request in the Administrative Procedure Act, 5 U.S.C. § 556(e). See also Revised Model State Administrative Procedure Act (1961), 9C U.L.A. § 10(4) (Supp.1967).

Subdivision (f). In accord with the usual view, judicial notice may be taken at any stage of the proceedings, whether in the trial court or on appeal. Uniform Rule 12; California Evidence Code § 459; Kansas Rules of Evidence § 60–412; New Jersey Evidence Rule 12; McCormick § 330, p. 712.

Subdivision (g). Much of the controversy about judicial notice has centered upon the question whether evidence should be admitted in disproof of facts of which judicial notice is taken.

The writers have been divided. Favoring admissibility are Thayer, Preliminary Treatise on Evidence 308 (1898); 9 Wigmore § 2567; Davis, A System of Judicial Notice Based on Fairness and Convenience, in Perspectives of Law, 69, 76–77 (1964). Opposing admissibility are Keeffe, Landis and Shaad, Sense and Nonsense about Judicial Notice, 2 Stan.L.Rev. 664, 668 (1950); McNaughton, Judicial Notice—Excerpts Relating to the Morgan-Whitmore Controversy, 14 Vand.L.Rev. 779 (1961); Morgan, Judicial Notice, 57 Harv.L.Rev. 269, 279 (1944); McCormick 710–711. The Model Code and the Uniform Rules are predicated upon indisputability of judicially noticed facts.

The proponents of admitting evidence in disproof have concentrated largely upon legislative facts. Since the present rule deals only with judicial notice of adjudicative facts, arguments directed to legislative facts lose their relevancy.

Report of House Committee on the Judiciary

House Comm. on Judiciary, Fed. Rules of Evidence, H.R.Rep. No. 650, 93d Cong., 1st Sess., p. 6 (1973); 1974 U.S.Code Cong. & Ad.News 7075, 7080

Rule 201(g) as received from the Supreme Court provided that when judicial notice of a fact is taken, the court shall instruct the jury to accept that fact as established. Being of the view that mandatory instruction to a jury in a criminal case to accept as conclusive any fact judicially noticed is inappropriate because contrary to the spirit of the Sixth Amendment right to a jury trial, the Committee adopted the 1969 Advisory Committee draft of this subsection, allowing a mandatory instruction in civil actions and proceedings and a discretionary instruction in criminal cases.

Advisory Committee's Note (Continued)

[The following portion of the Advisory Committee's Note is from the 1969 Preliminary Draft. 46 F.R.D. 161, 204.]

Within its relatively narrow area of adjudicative facts, the rule contemplates there is to be no evidence before the jury in disproof in civil cases. The judge instructs the jury to take judicially noticed facts as conclusive. This position is justified by the undesirable effects of the opposite rule in limiting the rebutting party, though not his opponent, to admissible evidence, in defeating the reasons for judicial notice, and in affecting the substantive law to an extent and in ways largely unforeseeable. Ample protection and flexibility are afforded by the broad provision for opportunity to be heard on request, set forth in subdivision (e).

Criminal cases are treated somewhat differently in the rule. While matters falling within the common fund of information supposed to be possessed by jurors need not be proved, State v. Dunn, 221 Mo. 530, 120 S.W. 1179 (1909), these are not, properly speaking, adjudicative facts but an aspect of legal reasoning. The considerations which underlie the general rule that a verdict cannot be directed against the accused in a criminal case seem to foreclose the judge's directing the jury on the basis of judicial notice to accept as conclusive any adjudicative facts in the case. State v. Main, 91 R.I. 338, 180 A.2d 814 (1962); State v. Lawrence, 120 Utah 323, 234 P.2d 600 (1951). Cf. People v. Mayes, 113 Cal. 618, 45 P. 860 (1896); Ross v. United States, 374 F.2d 97 (8th Cir.1967). However, this view presents no obstacle to the judge's advising the jury as to a matter judicially noticed, if he instructs them that it need not be taken as conclusive.

Note on Judicial Notice of Law (by the Advisory Committee)

56 F.R.D. 183, 207

By rules effective July 1, 1966, the method of invoking the law of a foreign country is covered elsewhere. Rule 44.1 of the Federal Rules of Civil Procedure; Rule 26.1 of the Federal Rules of Criminal Procedure. These two new admirably designed rules are founded upon the assumption that the manner in which law is fed into the judicial process is never a proper concern of the rules of evidence but rather of the rules of procedure. The Advisory Committee on Evidence, believing that this assumption is entirely correct, proposes no evidence rule with respect to judicial notice of law, and suggests that those matters of law which, in addition to foreign-country law, have traditionally been treated as requiring pleading and proof and more recently as the subject of judicial notice be left to the Rules of Civil and Criminal Procedure.

ARTICLE III. PRESUMPTIONS IN CIVIL ACTIONS AND PROCEEDINGS

Rule
301. Presumptions in General in Civil Actions and Proceedings.
302. Applicability of State Law in Civil Actions and Proceedings.

Rule 301. Presumptions in General in Civil Actions and Proceedings

In all civil actions and proceedings not otherwise provided for by Act of Congress or by these rules, a presumption imposes on the party against whom it is directed the burden of going forward with evidence to rebut or meet the presumption, but does not shift to such party the burden of proof in the sense of the risk of nonpersuasion, which remains throughout the trial upon the party on whom it was originally cast.

Section references, McCormick 4th ed.

§ 336, § 342, § 344

Note by Federal Judicial Center

The bill passed by the House substituted a substantially different rule in place of that prescribed by the Supreme Court. The Senate bill substituted yet a further version, which was accepted by the House, was enacted by the Congress, and is the rule shown above. . . .

Report of Senate Committee on the Judiciary

Senate Comm. on Judiciary, Fed. Rules of Evidence, S.Rep. No. 1277, 93d Cong., 2d Sess., p. 9 (1974); 1974 U.S. Code Cong. & Ad. News 7051, 7055

This rule governs presumptions in civil cases generally. Rule 302 provides for presumptions in cases controlled by State law.

As submitted by the Supreme Court, presumptions governed by this rule were given the effect of placing upon the opposing party the burden of establishing the nonexistence of the presumed fact, once the party invoking the presumption established the basic facts giving rise to it.

Instead of imposing a burden of persuasion on the party against whom the presumption is directed, the House adopted a provision which shifted the burden of going forward with the evidence. They further provided that "even though met with contradicting evidence, a presumption is sufficient evidence of the fact presumed, to be considered by the trier of fact." The effect of the amendment is that presumptions are to be treated as evidence.

The committee feels the House amendment is ill-advised. As the joint committees (the Standing Committee on Practice and Procedure of the Judicial Conference and the Advisory Committee on the Rules of Evidence) stated: "Presumptions are not evidence, but ways of dealing with evidence."[1] This treatment requires juries to perform the task of considering "as evidence" facts upon which they have no direct evidence and which may confuse them in performance of their duties. California had a rule much like that contained in the House amendment. It was sharply criticized by Justice Traynor in Speck v. Sarver[2] and was repealed after 93 troublesome years.[3]

Professor McCormick gives a concise and compelling critique of the presumption as evidence rule:

* * *

"Another solution, formerly more popular than now, is to instruct the jury that the presumption is 'evidence', to be weighed and considered with the

1. Hearings Before the Committee on the Judiciary, United States Senate, H.R. 5463, p. 56.

2. 20 Cal.2d 585, 594, 128 P.2d 16, 21 (1942).

3. Cal.Ev.Code 1965, § 600.

testimony in the case. This avoids the danger that the jury may infer that the presumption is conclusive, but it probably means little to the jury, and certainly runs counter to accepted theories of the nature of evidence.[4]"

For these reasons the committee has deleted that provision of the House-passed rule that treats presumptions as evidence. The effect of the rule as adopted by the committee is to make clear that while evidence of facts giving rise to a presumption shifts the burden of coming forward with evidence to rebut or meet the presumption, it does not shift the burden of persuasion on the existence of the presumed facts. The burden of persuasion remains on the party to whom it is allocated under the rules governing the allocation in the first instance.

The court may instruct the jury that they may infer the existence of the presumed fact from proof of the basic facts giving rise to the presumption. However, it would be inappropriate under this rule to instruct the jury that the inference they are to draw is conclusive.

Conference Report

H.R., Fed. Rules of Evidence, Conf.Rep. No. 1597, 93d Cong., 2d Sess., p. 5 (1974); 1974 U.S. Code Cong. & Ad. News 7098, 7099

The House bill provides that a presumption in civil actions and proceedings shifts to the party against whom it is directed the burden of going forward with evidence to meet or rebut it. Even though evidence contradicting the presumption is offered, a presumption is considered sufficient evidence of the presumed fact to be considered by the jury. The Senate amendment provides that a presumption shifts to the party against whom it is directed the burden of going forward with evidence to meet or rebut the presumption, but it does not shift to that party the burden of persuasion on the existence of the presumed fact.

Under the Senate amendment, a presumption is sufficient to get a party past an adverse party's motion to dismiss made at the end of his case-in-chief. If the adverse party offers no evidence contradicting the presumed fact, the court will instruct the jury that if it finds the basic facts, it may presume the existence of the presumed fact. If the adverse party does offer evidence contradicting the presumed fact, the court cannot instruct the jury that it may *presume* the existence of the presumed fact from proof of the basic facts. The court may, however, instruct the jury that it may infer the existence of the presumed fact from proof of the basic facts.

The Conference adopts the Senate amendment.

Rule 302. Applicability of State Law in Civil Actions and Proceedings

In civil actions and proceedings, the effect of a presumption respecting a fact which is an element of a claim or defense as to which State law supplies the rule of decision is determined in accordance with State law.

4. McCormick, Evidence, 669 (1954); id. 825 (2d ed. 1972).

Section references, McCormick 4th ed.

§ 336, § 344, § 349

Note by Federal Judicial Center

The rule enacted by the Congress is the rule prescribed by the Supreme Court, amended by adding "and proceedings" after "actions."

Advisory Committee's Note

56 F.R.D. 183, 211

A series of Supreme Court decisions in diversity cases leaves no doubt of the relevance of Erie Railroad Co. v. Tompkins, 304 U.S. 64, 58 S.Ct. 817, 82 L.Ed. 1188 (1938), to questions of burden of proof. These decisions are Cities Service Oil Co. v. Dunlap, 308 U.S. 208, 60 S.Ct. 201, 84 L.Ed. 196 (1939), Palmer v. Hoffman, 318 U.S. 109, 63 S.Ct. 477, 87 L.Ed. 645 (1943), and Dick v. New York Life Ins. Co., 359 U.S. 437, 79 S.Ct. 921, 3 L.Ed.2d 935 (1959). They involved burden of proof, respectively, as to status as bona fide purchaser, contributory negligence, and nonaccidental death (suicide) of an insured. In each instance the state rule was held to be applicable. It does not follow, however, that all presumptions in diversity cases are governed by state law. In each case cited, the burden of proof question had to do with a substantive element of the claim or defense. Application of the state law is called for only when the presumption operates upon such an element. Accordingly the rule does not apply state law when the presumption operates upon a lesser aspect of the case, i.e. "tactical" presumptions.

The situations in which the state law is applied have been tagged for convenience in the preceding discussion as "diversity cases." The designation is not a completely accurate one since *Erie* applies to any claim or issue having its source in state law, regardless of the basis of federal jurisdiction, and does not apply to a federal claim or issue, even though jurisdiction is based on diversity. Vestal, Erie R.R. v. Tompkins: A Projection, 48 Iowa L.Rev. 248, 257 (1963); Hart and Wechsler, The Federal Courts and the Federal System, 697 (1953); 1A Moore, Federal Practice ¶ 0.305[3] (2d ed. 1965); Wright, Federal Courts, 217–218 (1963). Hence the rule employs, as appropriately descriptive, the phrase "as to which state law supplies the rule of decision." See A.L.I. Study of the Division of Jurisdiction Between State and Federal Courts, § 2344(c), p. 40, P.F.D. No. 1 (1965).

Presumptions in Criminal Cases

Note by Federal Judicial Center

The rules prescribed by the Supreme Court included Rule 303, Presumptions in Criminal Cases. The rule was not included in the rules enacted by the Congress. . . .

ARTICLE IV.   RELEVANCY AND ITS LIMITS

Rule
401.   Definition of "Relevant Evidence."
402.   Relevant Evidence Generally Admissible; Irrelevant Evidence Inadmissible.

Rule 401. Definition of "Relevant Evidence"

"Relevant evidence" means evidence having any tendency to make the existence of any fact that is of consequence to the determination of the action more probable or less probable than it would be without the evidence.

Section references, McCormick 4th ed.

§ 39, § 44, § 45, § 47, § 52, § 185, § 196, § 197, § 199, § 200, § 202

Note by Federal Judicial Center

The rule enacted by the Congress is the rule prescribed by the Supreme Court without change.

Advisory Committee's Note

56 F.R.D. 183, 215

Problems of relevancy call for an answer to the question whether an item of evidence, when tested by the processes of legal reasoning, possesses sufficient probative value to justify receiving it in evidence. Thus, assessment of the probative value of evidence that a person purchased a revolver shortly prior to a fatal shooting with which he is charged is a matter of analysis and reasoning.

The variety of relevancy problems is coextensive with the ingenuity of counsel in using circumstantial evidence as a means of proof. An enormous number of cases fall in no set pattern, and this rule is designed as a guide for handling them. On the other hand, some situations recur with sufficient frequency to create patterns susceptible of treatment by specific rules. Rule 404 and those following it are of that variety; they also serve as illustrations of the application of the present rule as limited by the exclusionary principles of Rule 403.

Passing mention should be made of so-called "conditional" relevancy. Morgan, Basic Problems of Evidence 45–46 (1962). In this situation, probative value depends not only upon satisfying the basic requirement of relevancy as described above but also upon the existence of some matter of fact. For example, if evidence of a spoken statement is relied upon to prove notice, probative value is lacking unless the person sought to be charged heard the statement. The problem is one of fact, and the only rules needed are for the purpose of determining the respective functions of judge and jury. See Rules 104(b) and 901. The discussion which follows in the present note is concerned with relevancy generally, not with any particular problem of conditional relevancy.

Relevancy is not an inherent characteristic of any item of evidence but exists only as a relation between an item of evidence and a matter properly provable in the case. Does the item of evidence tend to prove the matter sought to be proved? Whether the relationship exists depends upon principles evolved by experience or science, applied logically to the situation at hand. James, Relevancy, Probability and the Law, 29 Calif.L.Rev. 689, 696, n. 15 (1941), in Selected Writings on Evidence and Trial 610, 615, n. 15 (Fryer ed. 1957). The rule summarizes this relationship as a "tendency to make the existence" of the fact to be proved "more probable or less probable." Compare Uniform Rule 1(2) which states the crux of relevancy as "a tendency in reason," thus perhaps emphasizing unduly the logical process and ignoring the need to draw upon experience or science to validate the general principle upon which relevancy in a particular situation depends.

The standard of probability under the rule is "more . . . probable than it would be without the evidence." Any more stringent requirement is unworkable and unrealistic. As McCormick § 152, p. 317, says, "A brick is not a wall," or, as Falknor, Extrinsic Policies Affecting Admissibility, 10 Rutgers L.Rev. 574, 576 (1956), quotes Professor McBaine, ". . . [I]t is not to be supposed that every witness can make a home run." Dealing with probability in the language of the rule has the added virtue of avoiding confusion between questions of admissibility and questions of the sufficiency of the evidence.

The rule uses the phrase "fact that is of consequence to the determination of the action" to describe the kind of fact to which proof may properly be directed. The language is that of California Evidence Code § 210; it has the advantage of avoiding the loosely used and ambiguous word "material." Tentative Recommendation and a Study Relating to the Uniform Rules of Evidence (Art. I. General Provisions), Cal. Law Revision Comm'n, Rep., Rec. & Studies, 10–11 (1964). The fact to be proved may be ultimate, intermediate, or evidentiary; it matters not, so long as it is of consequence in the determination of the action. Cf. Uniform Rule 1(2) which requires that the evidence relate to a "material" fact.

The fact to which the evidence is directed need not be in dispute. While situations will arise which call for the exclusion of evidence offered to prove a point conceded by the opponent, the ruling should be made on the basis of such considerations as waste of time and undue prejudice (see Rule 403), rather than under any general requirement that evidence is admissible only if directed to matters in dispute. Evidence which is essentially background in nature can scarcely be said to involve disputed matter, yet it is universally offered and admitted as an aid to understanding. Charts, photographs, views of real estate, murder weapons, and many other items of evidence fall in this category. A rule limiting admissibility to evidence directed to a controversial point would invite the exclusion of this helpful evidence, or at least the raising of endless questions over its admission. Cf. California Evidence Code § 210, defining relevant evidence in terms of tendency to prove a disputed fact.

Rule 402. Relevant Evidence Generally Admissible; Irrelevant Evidence Inadmissible

All relevant evidence is admissible, except as otherwise provided by the Constitution of the United States, by Act of Congress, by these rules, or by other rules prescribed by the Supreme Court pursuant to statutory authority. Evidence which is not relevant is not admissible.

Section references, McCormick 4th ed.

§ 44, § 45, § 47, § *184*, § 196, § 197, § 199, § 200, § 202, § *212*

Note by Federal Judicial Center

The rule enacted by the Congress is the rule prescribed by the Supreme Court, with the first sentence amended by substituting "prescribed" in place of "adopted", and by adding at the end thereof the phrase "pursuant to statutory authority."

Advisory Committee's Note

56 F.R.D. 183, 216

The provisions that all relevant evidence is admissible, with certain exceptions, and that evidence which is not relevant is not admissible are "a presupposition involved in the very conception of a rational system of evidence." Thayer, Preliminary Treatise on Evidence 264 (1898). They constitute the foundation upon which the structure of admission and exclusion rests. For similar provisions see California Evidence Code §§ 350, 351. Provisions that all relevant evidence is admissible are found in Uniform Rule 7(f); Kansas Code of Civil Procedure § 60–407(f); and New Jersey Evidence Rule 7(f); but the exclusion of evidence which is not relevant is left to implication.

Not all relevant evidence is admissible. The exclusion of relevant evidence occurs in a variety of situations and may be called for by these rules, by the Rules of Civil and Criminal Procedure, by Bankruptcy Rules, by Act of Congress, or by constitutional considerations.

Succeeding rules in the present article, in response to the demands of particular policies, require the exclusion of evidence despite its relevancy. In addition, Article V recognizes a number of privileges; Article VI imposes limitations upon witnesses and the manner of dealing with them; Article VII specifies requirements with respect to opinions and expert testimony; Article VIII excludes hearsay not falling within an exception; Article IX spells out the handling of authentication and identification; and Article X restricts the manner of proving the contents of writings and recordings.

The Rules of Civil and Criminal Procedure in some instances require the exclusion of relevant evidence. For example, Rules 30(b) and 32(a) (3) of the Rules of Civil Procedure, by imposing requirements of notice and unavailability of the deponent, place limits on the use of relevant depositions. Similarly, Rule 15 of the Rules of Criminal Procedure restricts the use of depositions in criminal cases, even though relevant. And the effective enforcement of the command, originally statutory and now found in Rule 5(a) of the Rules of Criminal Procedure, that an arrested person be taken without unnecessary delay before a commissioner or other similar officer is held to require the exclusion of statements elicited during detention in violation thereof. Mallory v. United States, 354 U.S. 449, 77 S.Ct. 1356, 1 L.Ed.2d 1479 (1957); 18 U.S.C. § 3501(c).

While congressional enactments in the field of evidence have generally tended to expand admissibility beyond the scope of the common law rules, in some particular situations they have restricted the admissibility of relevant evidence. Most of this legislation has consisted of the formulation of a privilege or of a prohibition against disclosure. 8 U.S.C. § 1202(f), records of refusal of visas or permits to enter United States confidential, subject to discretion of Secretary of State to make available to court upon certification of need; 10 U.S.C. § 3693, replacement certificate of honorable discharge from Army not admissible in evidence; 10 U.S.C. § 8693, same as to Air Force; 11 U.S.C. § 25(a)(10), testimony given by bankrupt on his examination not admissible in criminal proceedings against him, except that given in hearing upon objection to discharge; 11 U.S.C. § 205(a), railroad reorganization petition, if dismissed, not admissible in evidence; 11 U.S.C. § 403(a), list of creditors filed with municipal composition plan not an admission; 13 U.S.C. § 9(a), census information confidential, retained copies of reports privileged; 47 U.S.C. § 605, interception and divulgence of wire or radio communications prohibited unless authorized by sender. These statutory provisions would remain undisturbed by the rules.

The rule recognizes but makes no attempt to spell out the constitutional considerations which impose basic limitations upon the admissibility of relevant evidence. Examples are evidence obtained by unlawful search and seizure, Weeks v. United States, 232 U.S. 383, 34 S.Ct. 341, 58 L.Ed. 652 (1914); Katz v. United States, 389 U.S. 347, 88 S.Ct. 507, 19 L.Ed.2d 576 (1967); incriminating statement elicited from an accused in violation of right to counsel, Massiah v. United States, 377 U.S. 201, 84 S.Ct. 1199, 12 L.Ed.2d 246 (1964).

Report of House Committee on the Judiciary

House Comm. on Judiciary, Fed Rules of Evidence, H.R. Rep. No. 650, 93d Cong., 1st Sess., p. 7 (1973); 1974 U.S. Code Cong. & Ad. News 7075, 7081

Rule 402 as submitted to the Congress contained the phrase "or by other rules adopted by the Supreme Court". To accommodate the view that the Congress should not appear to acquiesce in the Court's judgment that it has authority under the existing Rules Enabling Acts to promulgate Rules of Evidence, the Committee amended the above phrase to read "or by other rules prescribed by the Supreme Court pursuant to statutory authority" in this and other Rules where the reference appears.

Rule 403. Exclusion of Relevant Evidence on Grounds of Prejudice, Confusion, or Waste of Time

Although relevant, evidence may be excluded if its probative value is substantially outweighed by the danger of unfair prejudice, confusion of the issues, or misleading the jury, or by considerations of undue delay, waste of time, or needless presentation of cumulative evidence.

Section references, McCormick 4th ed.

§ 7, § 11, § 12, § 13, § 16, § 19, § 26, § 30, § 35, § 36, § 39, § 41, § 42, § 44, § 45, § 47, § 52, § 56, § 57, § 58, § 59, § 185, § 193, § 196, § 197, § 199, § 200, § 202, § 212, § 250, § 255, § 293, § 322

Note by Federal Judicial Center

The rule enacted by the Congress is the rule prescribed by the Supreme Court without change.

Advisory Committee's Note

56 F.R.D. 183, 218

The case law recognizes that certain circumstances call for the exclusion of evidence which is of unquestioned relevance. These circumstances entail risks which range all the way from inducing decision on a purely emotional basis, at one extreme, to nothing more harmful than merely wasting time, at the other extreme. Situations in this area call for balancing the probative value of and need for the evidence against the harm likely to result from its admission. Slough, Relevancy Unraveled, 5 Kan.L.Rev. 1, 12–15 (1956); Trautman, Logical or Legal Relevancy—A Conflict in Theory, 5 Van. L.Rev. 385, 392 (1952); McCormick § 152, pp. 319–321. The rules which follow in this Article are concrete applications evolved for particular situations. However, they reflect the policies underlying the present rule, which is designed as a guide for the handling of situations for which no specific rules have been formulated.

Exclusion for risk of unfair prejudice, confusion of issues, misleading the jury, or waste of time, all find ample support in the authorities. "Unfair prejudice" within its context means an undue tendency to suggest decision on an improper basis, commonly, though not necessarily, an emotional one.

The rule does not enumerate surprise as a ground for exclusion, in this respect following Wigmore's view of the common law. 6 Wigmore § 1849. Cf. McCormick § 152, p. 320, n. 29, listing unfair surprise as a ground for exclusion but stating that it is usually "coupled with the danger of prejudice and confusion of issues." While Uniform Rule 45 incorporates surprise as a ground and is followed in Kansas Code of Civil Procedure § 60–445, surprise is not included in California Evidence Code § 352 or New Jersey Rule 4, though both the latter otherwise substantially embody Uniform Rule 45. While it can scarcely be doubted that claims of unfair surprise may still be justified despite procedural requirements of notice and instrumentalities of discovery, the granting of a continuance is a more appropriate remedy than exclusion of the evidence. Tentative Recommendation and a Study Relating to the Uniform Rules of Evidence (Art. VI. Extrinsic Policies Affecting Admissibility), Cal. Law Revision Comm'n, Rep., Rec. & Studies, 612 (1964). Moreover, the impact of a rule excluding evidence on the ground of surprise would be difficult to estimate.

In reaching a decision whether to exclude on grounds of unfair prejudice, consideration should be given to the probable effectiveness or lack of effectiveness of a limiting instruction. See Rule 106 [105] and Advisory Committee's Note thereunder. The availability of other means of proof may also be an appropriate factor.

Rule 404.   Character Evidence Not Admissible to Prove Conduct; Exceptions; Other Crimes

(a) **Character evidence generally.** Evidence of a person's character or a trait of character is not admissible for the purpose of proving action in conformity therewith on a particular occasion, except:

(1) **Character of accused.** Evidence of a pertinent trait of character offered by an accused, or by the prosecution to rebut the same;

(2) **Character of victim.** Evidence of a pertinent trait of character of the victim of the crime offered by an accused,[1] or by the prosecution to rebut the same, or evidence of a character trait of peacefulness of the victim offered by the prosecution in a homicide case to rebut evidence that the victim was the first aggressor;

(3) **Character of witness.** Evidence of the character of a witness, as provided in rules 607, 608, and 609.

(b) **Other crimes, wrongs, or acts.** Evidence of other crimes, wrongs, or acts is not admissible to prove the character of a person in order to show action in conformity therewith. It may, however, be admissible for other purposes, such as proof of motive, opportunity, intent, preparation, plan, knowledge, identity, or absence of mistake or accident, provided that upon request by the accused, the prosecution in a criminal case shall provide reasonable notice in advance of trial, or during trial if the court excuses pretrial notice on good cause shown, of the general nature of any such evidence it intends to introduce at trial.

(As amended Mar. 2, 1987, eff. Oct. 1, 1987; Apr. 30, 1991, eff. Dec. 1, 1991.)

Section references, McCormick 4th ed.

Generally, § 189, § 192, § 196, § 197, § 200

1. The applicability of this provision in cases of rape or assault with intent to commit rape is greatly circumscribed by Rule 412, infra, added by Act of Congress in 1978.—Ed.

(a). § 186, § 187, § 192

    (1). § 186, § 187, § 191

    (2). § 186, § 193

    (3). § 186, § 191

(b). § 59, § 186, § 187, § 190, § 193

Note by Federal Judicial Center

The rule enacted by the Congress is the rule prescribed by the Supreme Court, with the second sentence of subdivision (b) amended by substituting "It may, however, be admissible" in place of "This subdivision does not exclude the evidence when offered."

Advisory Committee's Note

56 F.R.D. 183, 219

Subdivision (a). This subdivision deals with the basic question whether character evidence should be admitted. Once the admissibility of character evidence in some form is established under this rule, reference must then be made to Rule 405, which follows, in order to determine the appropriate method of proof. If the character is that of a witness, see Rules 608 and 609 for methods of proof.

Character questions arise in two fundamentally different ways. (1) Character may itself be an element of a crime, claim, or defense. A situation of this kind is commonly referred to as "character in issue." Illustrations are: the chastity of the victim under a statute specifying her chastity as an element of the crime of seduction, or the competency of the driver in an action for negligently entrusting a motor vehicle to an incompetent driver. No problem of the general relevancy of character evidence is involved, and the present rule therefore has no provision on the subject. The only question relates to allowable methods of proof, as to which see Rule 405, immediately following. (2) Character evidence is susceptible of being used for the purpose of suggesting an inference that the person acted on the occasion in question consistently with his character. This use of character is often described as "circumstantial." Illustrations are: evidence of a violent disposition to prove that person was the aggressor in an affray, or evidence of honesty in disproof of a charge of theft. This circumstantial use of character evidence raises questions of relevancy as well as questions of allowable methods of proof.

In most jurisdictions today, the circumstantial use of character is rejected but with important exceptions: (1) an accused may introduce pertinent evidence of good character (often misleadingly described as "putting his character in issue"), in which event the prosecution may rebut with evidence of bad character; (2) an accused may introduce pertinent evidence of the character of the victim, as in support of a claim of self-defense to a charge of homicide or consent in a case of rape,[2] and the prosecution may introduce similar evidence in rebuttal of the character evidence, or, in a homicide case, to rebut a claim that deceased was the first aggressor, however proved; and (3) the character of a witness may be gone into as bearing on his credibility. McCormick §§ 155–161. This pattern is incorporated in the rule. While its basis lies more in

2. But see Rule 412, infra, added by Act of Congress in 1978.—Ed.

history and experience than in logic an underlying justification can fairly be found in terms of the relative presence and absence of prejudice in the various situations. Falknor, Extrinsic Policies Affecting Admissibility, 10 Rutgers L.Rev. 574, 584 (1956); McCormick § 157. In any event, the criminal rule is so deeply imbedded in our jurisprudence as to assume almost constitutional proportions and to override doubts of the basic relevancy of the evidence.

The limitation to pertinent traits of character, rather than character generally, in paragraphs (1) and (2) is in accordance with the prevailing view. McCormick § 158, p. 334. A similar provision in Rule 608, to which reference is made in paragraph (3), limits character evidence respecting witnesses to the trait of truthfulness or untruthfulness.

The argument is made that circumstantial use of character ought to be allowed in civil cases to the same extent as in criminal cases, i.e. evidence of good (nonprejudicial) character would be admissible in the first instance, subject to rebuttal by evidence of bad character. Falknor, Extrinsic Policies Affecting Admissibility, 10 Rutgers L.Rev. 574, 581–583 (1956); Tentative Recommendation and a Study Relating to the Uniform Rules of Evidence (Art. VI. Extrinsic Policies Affecting Admissibility), Cal. Law Revision Comm'n, Rep., Rec. & Studies, 657–658 (1964). Uniform Rule 47 goes farther, in that it assumes that character evidence in general satisfies the conditions of relevancy, except as provided in Uniform Rule 48. The difficulty with expanding the use of character evidence in civil cases is set forth by the California Law Revision Commission in its ultimate rejection of Uniform Rule 47, id., 615:

> "Character evidence is of slight probative value and may be very prejudicial. It tends to distract the trier of fact from the main question of what actually happened on the particular occasion. It subtly permits the trier of fact to reward the good man and to punish the bad man because of their respective characters despite what the evidence in the case shows actually happened."

Much of the force of the position of those favoring greater use of character evidence in civil cases is dissipated by their support of Uniform Rule 48 which excludes the evidence in negligence cases, where it could be expected to achieve its maximum usefulness. Moreover, expanding concepts of "character," which seem of necessity to extend into such areas as psychiatric evaluation and psychological testing, coupled with expanded admissibility, would open up such vistas of mental examinations as caused the Court concern in Schlagenhauf v. Holder, 379 U.S. 104, 85 S.Ct. 234, 13 L.Ed.2d 152 (1964). It is believed that those espousing change have not met the burden of persuasion.

Subdivision (b) deals with a specialized but important application of the general rule excluding circumstantial use of character evidence. Consistently with that rule, evidence of other crimes, wrongs, or acts is not admissible to prove character as a basis for suggesting the inference that conduct on a particular occasion was in conformity with it. However, the evidence may be offered for another purpose, such as proof of motive, opportunity, and so on, which does not fall within the prohibition. In this situation the rule does not require that the evidence be excluded. No mechanical solution is offered. The determination must be made whether the danger of undue prejudice outweighs the probative value of the evidence in view of the availability of other means of proof and other factors appropriate for making decisions of this kind under Rule 403. Slough and Knightly, Other Vices, Other Crimes, 41 Iowa L.Rev. 325 (1956).

Report of House Committee on the Judiciary

House Comm. on Judiciary, Fed. Rules of Evidence, H.R. Rep. No. 650, 93d Cong., 1st Sess., p. 7 (1973); 1974 U.S.Code Cong. & Ad. News 7075, 7081

The second sentence of Rule 404(b) as submitted to the Congress began with the words "This subdivision does not exclude the evidence when offered". The Committee amended this language to read "It may, however, be admissible", the words used in the 1971 Advisory Committee draft, on the ground that this formulation properly placed greater emphasis on admissibility than did the final Court version.

Report of Senate Committee on the Judiciary

Senate Comm. on Judiciary, Fed. Rules of Evidence, S. Rep. No. 1277, 93d Cong., 2d Sess., p. 24 (1974); 1974 U.S.Code Cong. & Ad. News 7051, 7071

This rule provides that evidence of other crimes, wrongs, or acts is not admissible to prove character but may be admissible for other specified purposes such as proof of motive.

Although your committee sees no necessity in amending the rule itself, it anticipates that the use of the discretionary word "may" with respect to the admissibility of evidence of crimes, wrongs, or acts is not intended to confer any arbitrary discretion on the trial judge. Rather, it is anticipated that with respect to permissible uses for such evidence, the trial judge may exclude it only on the basis of those considerations set forth in Rule 403, i.e. prejudice, confusion or waste of time.

1987 Amendment. The amendments are technical. No substantive change is intended.

1991 Amendment. Rule 404(b) has emerged as one of the most cited Rules in the Rules of Evidence. And in many criminal cases evidence of an accused's extrinsic acts is viewed as an important asset in the prosecution's case against an accused. Although there are a few reported decisions on use of such evidence by the defense, *see, e.g., United States v. McClure,* 546 F.2d 670 (5th Cir.1990) (acts of informant offered in entrapment defense), the overwhelming number of cases involve introduction of that evidence by the prosecution.

The amendment to Rule 404(b) adds a pretrial notice requirement in criminal cases and is intended to reduce surprise and promote early resolution on the issue of admissibility. The notice requirement thus places Rule 404(b) in the mainstream with notice and disclosure provisions in other rules of evidence. *See, e.g.,* Rule 412 (written motion of intent to offer evidence under rule), Rule 609 (written notice of intent to offer conviction older than 10 years), Rule 803(24) and 804(b)(5) (notice of intent to use residual hearsay exceptions).

The Rule expects that counsel for both the defense and the prosecution will submit the necessary request and information in a reasonable and timely fashion. Other than requiring pretrial notice, no specific time limits are stated in recognition that what constitutes a reasonable request or disclosure will depend largely on the circumstances of each case. *Compare* Fla.Stat.Ann. § 90.404(2)(b) (notice must be given at least 10 days before trial) *with* Tex.R. Evid. 404(b) (no time limit).

Likewise, no specific form of notice is required. The Committee considered and rejected a requirement that the notice satisfy the particularity requirements normally required of language used in a charging instrument. *Cf.* Fla. Stat.Ann. § 90.404(2)(b) (written disclosure must describe uncharged misconduct with particularity required of an indictment or information). Instead, the Committee opted for a generalized notice provision which requires the prosecution to apprise the defense of the general nature of the evidence of extrinsic acts. The Committee does not intend that the amendment will supercede other rules of admissibility or disclosure, such as the Jencks Act, 18 U.S.C. § 3500, et seq. nor require the prosecution to disclose directly or indirectly the names and addresses of its witnesses, something it is currently not required to do under Federal Rule of Criminal Procedure 16.

The amendment requires the prosecution to provide notice, regardless of how it intends to use the extrinsic act evidence at trial, i.e., during its case-in-chief, for impeachment, or for possible rebuttal. The court in its discretion may, under the facts, decide that the particular request or notice was not reasonable, either because of the lack of timeliness or completeness. Because the notice requirement serves as condition precedent to admissibility of 404(b) evidence, the offered evidence is inadmissible if the court decides that the notice requirement has not been met.

Nothing in the amendment precludes the court from requiring the government to provide it with an opportunity to rule *in limine* on 404(b) evidence before it is offered or even mentioned during trial. When ruling *in limine,* the court may require the government to disclose to it the specifics of such evidence which the court must consider in determining admissibility.

The amendment does not extend to evidence of acts which are "intrinsic" to the charged offense, *see United States v. Williams,* 900 F.2d 823 (5th Cir. 1990) (noting distinction between 404(b) evidence and intrinsic offense evidence). Nor is the amendment intended to redefine what evidence would otherwise be admissible under Rule 404(b). Finally, the Committee does not intend through the amendment to affect the role of the court and the jury in considering such evidence. *See United States v. Huddleston,* ___ U.S. ___, 108 S.Ct. 1496 (1988).

Rule 405. Methods of Proving Character

(a) **Reputation or opinion.** In all cases in which evidence of character or a trait of character of a person is admissible, proof may be made by testimony as to reputation or by testimony in the form of an opinion. On cross-examination, inquiry is allowable into relevant specific instances of conduct.

(b) **Specific instances of conduct.** In cases in which character or a trait of character of a person is an essential element of a charge, claim, or defense, proof may also be made of specific instances of that person's conduct.

(As amended Mar. 2, 1987, eff. Oct. 1, 1987.)

Section references, McCormick 4th ed.

Generally § 186, § 189, § 191, § 196, § 197, § 206

(a). § 191

(b). § 187

Note by Federal Judicial Center

The rule enacted by the Congress is the rule prescribed by the Supreme Court without change. The bill reported by the House Committee on the Judiciary deleted the provision in subdivision (a) for making proof by testimony in the form of an opinion, but the provision was reinstated on the floor of the House. [120 Cong.Rec. 2370–73 (1974)].

Advisory Committee's Note

56 F.R.D. 183, 222

The rule deals only with allowable methods of proving character, not with the admissibility of character evidence, which is covered in Rule 404.

Of the three methods of proving character provided by the rule, evidence of specific instances of conduct is the most convincing. At the same time it possesses the greatest capacity to arouse prejudice, to confuse, to surprise, and to consume time. Consequently the rule confines the use of evidence of this kind to cases in which character is, in the strict sense, in issue and hence deserving of a searching inquiry. When character is used circumstantially and hence occupies a lesser status in the case, proof may be only by reputation and opinion. These latter methods are also available when character is in issue. This treatment is, with respect to specific instances of conduct and reputation, conventional contemporary common law doctrine. McCormick § 153.

In recognizing opinion as a means of proving character, the rule departs from usual contemporary practice in favor of that of an earlier day. See 7 Wigmore § 1986, pointing out that the earlier practice permitted opinion and arguing strongly for evidence based on personal knowledge and belief as contrasted with "the secondhand, irresponsible product of multiplied guesses and gossip which we term 'reputation'." It seems likely that the persistence of reputation evidence is due to its largely being opinion in disguise. Traditionally character has been regarded primarily in moral overtones of good and bad: chaste, peaceable, truthful, honest. Nevertheless, on occasion nonmoral considerations crop up, as in the case of the incompetent driver, and this seems bound to happen increasingly. If character is defined as the kind of person one is, then account must be taken of varying ways of arriving at the estimate. These may range from the opinion of the employer who has found the man honest to the opinion of the psychiatrist based upon examination and testing. No effective dividing line exists between character and mental capacity, and the latter traditionally has been provable by opinion.

According to the great majority of cases, on cross-examination inquiry is allowable as to whether the reputation witness has heard of particular instances of conduct pertinent to the trait in question. Michelson v. United States, 335 U.S. 469, 69 S.Ct. 213, 93 L.Ed. 168 (1948); Annot., 47 A.L.R.2d 1258. The theory is that, since the reputation witness relates what he has heard, the inquiry tends to shed light on the accuracy of his hearing and reporting.

Accordingly, the opinion witness would be asked whether he knew, as well as whether he had heard. The fact is, of course, that these distinctions are of slight if any practical significance, and the second sentence of subdivision (a) eliminates them as a factor in formulating questions. This recognition of the propriety of inquiring into specific instances of conduct does not circumscribe inquiry otherwise into the bases of opinion and reputation testimony.

The express allowance of inquiry into specific instances of conduct on cross-examination in subdivision (a) and the express allowance of it as part of a case in chief when character is actually in issue in subdivision (b) contemplate that testimony of specific instances is not generally permissible on the direct examination of an ordinary opinion witness to character. Similarly as to witnesses to the character of witnesses under Rule 608(b). Opinion testimony on direct in these situations ought in general to correspond to reputation testimony as now given, i.e., be confined to the nature and extent of observation and acquaintance upon which the opinion is based. See Rule 701.

1987 Amendment. The amendment is technical. No substantive change is intended.

Rule 406. Habit; Routine Practice

Evidence of the habit of a person or of the routine practice of an organization, whether corroborated or not and regardless of the presence of eyewitnesses, is relevant to prove that the conduct of the person or organization on a particular occasion was in conformity with the habit or routine practice.

Section references, McCormick 4th ed.

§ 195, § 271

Note by Federal Judicial Center

The rule enacted by the Congress is subdivision (a) of the rule prescribed by the Supreme Court. Subdivision (b) of the Court's rule was deleted for reasons stated in the Report of the House Committee on the Judiciary set forth below.

* * *

Advisory Committee's Note

56 F.R.D. 183, 223

An oft-quoted paragraph, McCormick, § 162, p. 340, describes habit in terms effectively contrasting it with character:

"Character and habit are close akin. Character is a generalized description of one's disposition, or of one's disposition in respect to a general trait, such as honesty, temperance, or peacefulness. 'Habit,' in modern usage, both lay and psychological, is more specific. It describes one's regular response to a repeated specific situation. If we speak of character for care, we think of the person's tendency to act prudently in all the varying situations of life, in business, family life, in handling automobiles and in walking across the street. A habit, on the other hand, is the person's regular practice of meeting a particular kind of situation with a specific type of conduct, such as the habit of going down a particular stairway two stairs at a time, or of giving the hand-signal for a left turn, or of alighting from railway cars while they are moving. The doing of the habitual acts may become semi-automatic."

Equivalent behavior on the part of a group is designated "routine practice of an organization" in the rule.

Agreement is general that habit evidence is highly persuasive as proof of conduct on a particular occasion. Again quoting McCormick § 162, p. 341:

> "Character may be thought of as the sum of one's habits though doubtless it is more than this. But unquestionably the uniformity of one's response to habit is far greater than the consistency with which one's conduct conforms to character or disposition. Even though character comes in only exceptionally as evidence of an act, surely any sensible man in investigating whether X did a particular act would be greatly helped in his inquiry by evidence as to whether he was in the habit of doing it."

When disagreement has appeared, its focus has been upon the question what constitutes habit, and the reason for this is readily apparent. The extent to which instances must be multiplied and consistency of behavior maintained in order to rise to the status of habit inevitably gives rise to differences of opinion. Lewan, Rationale of Habit Evidence, 16 Syracuse L.Rev. 39, 49 (1964). While adequacy of sampling and uniformity of response are key factors, precise standards for measuring their sufficiency for evidence purposes cannot be formulated.

The rule is consistent with prevailing views. Much evidence is excluded simply because of failure to achieve the status of habit. Thus, evidence of intemperate "habits" is generally excluded when offered as proof of drunkenness in accident cases, Annot., 46 A.L.R.2d 103, and evidence of other assaults is inadmissible to prove the instant one in a civil assault action, Annot., 66 A.L.R.2d 806. In Levin v. United States, 119 U.S.App.D.C. 156, 338 F.2d 265 (1964), testimony as to the religious "habits" of the accused, offered as tending to prove that he was at home observing the Sabbath rather than out obtaining money through larceny by trick, was held properly excluded:

> "It seems apparent to us that an individual's religious practices would not be the type of activities which would lend themselves to the characterization of 'invariable regularity.' [1 Wigmore 520.] Certainly the very volitional basis of the activity raises serious questions as to its invariable nature, and hence its probative value." Id. at 272.

These rulings are not inconsistent with the trend towards admitting evidence of business transactions between one of the parties and a third person as tending to prove that he made the same bargain or proposal in the litigated situation. Slough, Relevancy Unraveled, 6 Kan.L.Rev. 38–41 (1957). Nor are they inconsistent with such cases as Whittemore v. Lockheed Aircraft Corp., 65 Cal.App. 2d 737, 151 P.2d 670 (1944), upholding the admission of evidence that plaintiff's intestate had on four other occasions flown planes from defendant's factory for delivery to his employer airline, offered to prove that he was piloting rather than a guest on a plane which crashed and killed all on board while en route for delivery.

A considerable body of authority has required that evidence of the routine practice of an organization be corroborated as a condition precedent to its admission in evidence. Slough, Relevancy Unraveled, 5 Kan.L.Rev. 404, 449 (1957). This requirement is specifically rejected by the rule on the ground that it relates to the sufficiency of the evidence rather than admissibility. A similar position is taken in New Jersey Rule 49. The rule also rejects the requirement of the absence of eyewitnesses, sometimes encountered with respect to admitting habit evidence to prove freedom from contributory negligence in wrongful death cases. For comment critical of the requirements see Frank, J., in Cereste v. New York, N.H. & H.R. Co., 231 F.2d 50 (2d Cir.1956), cert. denied 351 U.S. 951, 76 S.Ct. 848, 100 L.Ed. 1475, 10 Vand.L.Rev. 447 (1957); McCormick § 162, p. 342. The omission of the requirement from the California Evidence Code is said to have effected its elimination. Comment, Cal.Ev.Code § 1105.

Report of House Committee on the Judiciary

House Comm. on Judiciary, Fed. Rules of Evidence, H.R. Rep. No. 650, 93d Cong., 1st Sess., p. 5 (1973); 1974 U.S.Code Cong.& Ad. News 7075, 7079

Rule 406 as submitted to Congress contained a subdivision (b) providing that the method of proof of habit or routine practice could be "in the form of an opinion or by specific instances of conduct sufficient in number to warrant a finding that the habit existed or that the practice was routine." The Committee deleted this subdivision believing that the method of proof of habit and routine practice should be left to the courts to deal with on a case-by-case basis. At the same time, the Committee does not intend that its action be construed as sanctioning a general authorization of opinion evidence in this area.

Rule 407. Subsequent Remedial Measures

When, after an event, measures are taken which, if taken previously, would have made the event less likely to occur, evidence of the subsequent measures is not admissible to prove negligence or culpable conduct in connection with the event. This rule does not require the exclusion of evidence of subsequent measures when offered for another purpose, such as proving ownership, control, or feasibility of precautionary measures, if controverted, or impeachment.

Section references, McCormick 4th ed.

§ 267

Note by Federal Judicial Center

The rule enacted by the Congress is the rule prescribed by the Supreme Court without change.

Advisory Committee's Note
56 F.R.D. 183, 225

The rule incorporates conventional doctrine which excludes evidence of subsequent remedial measures as proof of an admission of fault. The rule rests on two grounds. (1) The conduct is not in fact an admission, since the conduct is equally consistent with injury by mere accident or through contributory negligence. Or, as Baron Bramwell put it, the rule rejects the notion that "because the world gets wiser as it gets older, therefore it was foolish before." Hart v. Lancashire & Yorkshire Ry. Co., 21 L.T.R. N.S. 261, 263 (1869). Under a liberal theory of relevancy this ground alone would not support exclusion as

the inference is still a possible one. (2) The other, and more impressive, ground for exclusion rests on a social policy of encouraging people to take, or at least not discouraging them from taking, steps in furtherance of added safety. The courts have applied this principle to exclude evidence of subsequent repairs, installation of safety devices, changes in company rules, and discharge of employees, and the language of the present rule is broad enough to encompass all of them. See Falknor, Extrinsic Policies Affecting Admissibility, 10 Rutgers L.Rev. 574, 590 (1956).

The second sentence of the rule directs attention to the limitations of the rule. Exclusion is called for only when the evidence of subsequent remedial measures is offered as proof of negligence or culpable conduct. In effect it rejects the suggested inference that fault is admitted. Other purposes are, however, allowable, including ownership or control, existence of duty, and feasibility of precautionary measures, if controverted, and impeachment. 2 Wigmore § 283; Annot., 64 A.L.R.2d 1296. Two recent federal cases are illustrative. Boeing Airplane Co. v. Brown, 291 F.2d 310 (9th Cir.1961), an action against an airplane manufacturer for using an allegedly defectively designed alternator shaft which caused a plane crash, upheld the admission of evidence of subsequent design modification for the purpose of showing that design changes and safeguards were feasible. And Powers v. J.B. Michael & Co., 329 F.2d 674 (6th Cir.1964), an action against a road contractor for negligent failure to put out warning signs, sustained the admission of evidence that defendant subsequently put out signs to show that the portion of the road in question was under defendant's control. The requirement that the other purpose be controverted calls for automatic exclusion unless a genuine issue be present and allows the opposing party to lay the groundwork for exclusion by making an admission. Otherwise the factors of undue prejudice, confusion of issues, misleading the jury, and waste of time remain for consideration under Rule 403.

For comparable rules, see Uniform Rule 51; California Evidence Code § 1151; Kansas Code of Civil Procedure § 60–451; New Jersey Evidence Rule 51.

Rule 408. Compromise and Offers to Compromise

Evidence of (1) furnishing or offering or promising to furnish, or (2) accepting or offering or promising to accept, a valuable consideration in compromising or attempting to compromise a claim which was disputed as to either validity or amount, is not admissible to prove liability for or invalidity of the claim or its amount. Evidence of conduct or statements made in compromise negotiations is likewise not admissible. This rule does not require the exclusion of any evidence otherwise discoverable merely because it is presented in the course of compromise negotiations. This rule also does not require exclusion when the evidence is offered for another purpose, such as proving bias or prejudice of a witness, negativing a contention of undue delay, or proving an effort to obstruct a criminal investigation or prosecution.

Section references, McCormick 4th ed.

§ 267

Note by Federal Judicial Center

The rule enacted by the Congress is the rule prescribed by the Supreme Court, amended by the insertion of the third sentence. Other amendments, proposed by the House bill, were not enacted, for reasons stated in the Report of the Senate Committee on the Judiciary and in the Conference Report, set forth below.

Advisory Committee's Note

56 F.R.D. 183, 226

As a matter of general agreement, evidence of an offer to compromise a claim is not receivable in evidence as an admission of, as the case may be, the validity or invalidity of the claim. As with evidence of subsequent remedial measures, dealt with in Rule 407, exclusion may be based on two grounds. (1) The evidence is irrelevant, since the offer may be motivated by a desire for peace rather than from any concession of weakness of position. The validity of this position will vary as the amount of the offer varies in relation to the size of the claim and may also be influenced by other circumstances. (2) A more consistently impressive ground is promotion of the public policy favoring the compromise and settlement of disputes. McCormick §§ 76, 251. While the rule is ordinarily phrased in terms of offers of compromise, it is apparent that a similar attitude must be taken with respect to completed compromises when offered against a party thereto. This latter situation will not, of course, ordinarily occur except when a party to the present litigation has compromised with a third person.

The same policy underlies the provision of Rule 68 of the Federal Rules of Civil Procedure that evidence of an unaccepted offer of judgment is not admissible except in a proceeding to determine costs.

The practical value of the common law rule has been greatly diminished by its inapplicability to admissions of fact, even though made in the course of compromise negotiations, unless hypothetical, stated to be "without prejudice," or so connected with the offer as to be inseparable from it. McCormick § 251, pp. 540–541. An inevitable effect is to inhibit freedom of communication with respect to compromise, even among lawyers. Another effect is the generation of controversy over whether a given statement falls within or without the protected area. These considerations account for the expansion of the rule herewith to include evidence of conduct or statements made in compromise negotiations, as well as the offer or completed compromise itself. For similar provisions see California Evidence Code §§ 1152, 1154.

The policy considerations which underlie the rule do not come into play when the effort is to induce a creditor to settle an admittedly due amount for a lesser sum. McCormick § 251, p. 540. Hence the rule requires that the claim be disputed as to either validity or amount.

The final sentence of the rule serves to point out some limitations upon its applicability. Since the rule excludes only when the purpose is proving the validity or invalidity of the claim or its amount, an offer for another purpose is not within the rule. The illustrative situations mentioned in the rule are supported by the authorities. As to proving bias or prejudice of a witness, see Annot., 161 A.L.R. 395, contra, Fenberg v. Rosenthal, 348 Ill.App. 510, 109 N.E.2d 402 (1952), and negativing a contention of lack of due diligence in presenting a claim, 4 Wigmore § 1061. An effort to "buy off" the prosecution or a prosecuting witness in a criminal case is not within the policy of the rule of exclusion. McCormick § 251, p. 542.

For other rules of similar import, see Uniform Rules 52 and 53; California Evidence Code §§ 1152, 1154; Kansas Code of Civil Procedure §§ 60–452, 60–453; New Jersey Evidence Rules 52 and 53.

Report of House Committee on the Judiciary

House Comm. on Judiciary, Fed.Rules of Evidence, H.R.Rep. No. 650, 93d Cong., 1st Sess., p. 8 (1973); 1974 U.S.Code Cong. & Ad. News 7075, 7081

Under existing federal law evidence of conduct and statements made in compromise negotiations is admissible in subsequent litigation between the parties. The second sentence of Rule 408 as submitted by the Supreme Court proposed to reverse that doctrine in the interest of further promoting non-judicial settlement of disputes. Some agencies of government expressed the view that the Court formulation was likely to impede rather than assist efforts to achieve settlement of disputes. For one thing, it is not always easy to tell when compromise negotiations begin, and informal dealings end. Also, parties dealing with government agencies would be reluctant to furnish factual information at preliminary meetings; they would wait until "compromise negotiations" began and thus hopefully effect an immunity for themselves with respect to the evidence supplied. In light of these considerations, the Committee recast the Rule so that admissions of liability or opinions given during compromise negotiations continue inadmissible, but evidence of unqualified factual assertions is admissible. The latter aspect of the Rule is drafted, however, so as to preserve other possible objections to the introduction of such evidence. The Committee intends no modification of current law whereby a party may protect himself from future use of his statements by couching them in hypothetical conditional form.

Report of Senate Committee on the Judiciary

Senate Comm. on Judiciary, Fed. Rules of Evidence, S.Rep. No. 1277, 93d Cong., 2d Sess., p. 10 (1974); 1974 U.S.Code Cong. & Ad. News 7051, 7056

This rule as reported makes evidence of settlement or attempted settlement of a disputed claim inadmissible when offered as an admission of liability or the amount of liability. The purpose of this rule is to encourage settlements which would be discouraged if such evidence were admissible.

Under present law, in most jurisdictions, statements of fact made during settlement negotiations, however, are excepted from this ban and are admissible. The only escape from admissibility of statements of fact made in a settlement negotiation is if the declarant or his representative expressly states that the statement is hypothetical in nature or is made without prejudice. Rule 408 as submitted by the Court reversed the traditional rule. It would have brought statements of fact within the ban and made them, as well as an offer of settlement, inadmissible.

The House amended the rule and would continue to make evidence of facts disclosed during compromise negotiations admissible. It thus reverted to the traditional rule. The House committee report states that the committee intends to preserve current law under which a party may protect himself by couching his statements in hypothetical form.[1] The real impact of this amendment, however, is to deprive the rule of much of its salutary effect. The exception for factual admissions was believed by the Advisory Committee to hamper free communication between parties and thus to constitute an unjustifiable restraint upon efforts to negotiate settlements—the encouragement of which is the purpose of the rule. Further, by protecting hypothetically phrased statements, it constituted a preference for the sophisticated, and a trap for the unwary.

Three States which had adopted rules of evidence patterned after the proposed rules prescribed by the Supreme Court opted for versions of rule 408 identical with the Supreme Court draft with respect to the inadmissibility of conduct or statements made in compromise negotiations.[2]

For these reasons, the committee has deleted the House amendment and restored the rule to the version submitted by the Supreme Court with one additional amendment. This amendment adds a sentence to insure that evidence, such as documents, is not rendered inadmissible merely because it is presented in the course of compromise negotiations if the evidence is otherwise discoverable. A party should not be able to immunize from admissibility documents otherwise discoverable merely by offering them in a compromise negotiation.

Conference Report

H.R., Fed. Rules of Evidence, Conf. Rep. No. 1597, 93d Cong., 2d Sess., p. 6 (1974); 1974 U.S.Code Cong. & Ad. News 7098, 7099

The House bill provides that evidence of admissions of liability or opinions given during compromise negotiations is not admissible, but that evidence of facts disclosed during compromise negotiations is not inadmissible by virtue of having been first disclosed in the compromise negotiations. The Senate amendment provides that evidence of conduct or statements made in compromise negotiations is not admissible. The Senate amendment also provides that the rule does not require the exclusion of any evidence otherwise discoverable merely because it is presented in the course of compromise negotiations.

The House bill was drafted to meet the objection of executive agencies that under the rule as proposed by the Supreme Court, a party could present a fact during compromise negotiations and thereby prevent an opposing party from offering evidence of that fact at trial even though such evidence was obtained from independent sources. The Senate amendment expressly precludes this result.

The Conference adopts the Senate amendment.

1. See Report No. 93–650, dated November 15, 1973.

2. Nev.Rev.Stats. § 48.105; N.Mex. Stats.Anno. (1973 Supp.) § 20–4–408;

West's Wis.Stats.Anno. (1973 Supp.) § 904.08.

Rule 409. Payment of Medical and Similar Expenses

Evidence of furnishing or offering or promising to pay medical, hospital, or similar expenses occasioned by an injury is not admissible to prove liability for the injury.

Section references, McCormick 4th ed.

§ 267

Note by Federal Judicial Center

The rule enacted by the Congress is the rule prescribed by the Supreme Court without change.

Advisory Committee's Note

56 F.R.D. 183, 228

The considerations underlying this rule parallel those underlying Rules 407 and 408, which deal respectively with subsequent remedial measures and offers of compromise. As stated in Annot., 20 A.L.R.2d 291, 293:

"[G]enerally, evidence of payment of medical, hospital, or similar expenses of an injured party by the opposing party, is not admissible, the reason often given being that such payment or offer is usually made from humane impulses and not from an admission of liability, and that to hold otherwise would tend to discourage assistance to the injured person."

Contrary to Rule 408, dealing with offers of compromise, the present rule does not extend to conduct or statements not a part of the act of furnishing or offering or promising to pay. This difference in treatment arises from fundamental differences in nature. Communication is essential if compromises are to be effected, and consequently broad protection of statements is needed. This is not so in cases of payments or offers or promises to pay medical expenses, where factual statements may be expected to be incidental in nature.

For rules on the same subject, but phrased in terms of "humanitarian motives," see Uniform Rule 52; California Evidence Code § 1152; Kansas Code of Civil Procedure § 60–452; New Jersey Evidence Rule 52.

Rule 410. Inadmissibility of Pleas, Plea Discussions, and Related Statements

Except as otherwise provided in this rule, evidence of the following is not, in any civil or criminal proceeding, admissible against the defendant who made the plea or was a participant in the plea discussions:

(1) a plea of guilty which was later withdrawn;

(2) a plea of nolo contendere;

(3) any statement made in the course of any proceedings under Rule 11 of the Federal Rules of Criminal Procedure or comparable state procedure regarding either of the foregoing pleas; or

(4) any statement made in the course of plea discussions with an attorney for the prosecuting authority which do not result in a plea of guilty or which result in a plea of guilty later withdrawn.

However, such a statement is admissible (i) in any proceeding wherein another statement made in the course of the same plea or plea discussions has been introduced and the statement ought in fairness be considered contemporaneously with it, or (ii) in a criminal proceeding for perjury or false statement if the statement was made by the defendant under oath, on the record and in the presence of counsel.

(As amended by P.L. 94–149, § 1(9), Dec. 12, 1975, 89 Stat. 805; Apr. 30, 1979, eff. Dec. 1, 1980.

Section references, McCormick 4th ed.

§ 42, § 159, § 257, § 266

Rule 410 as originally enacted

Editorial Note

When first enacted together with the other Federal Rules of Evidence, Rule 410 read as follows:

Except as otherwise provided by Act of Congress, evidence of a plea of guilty, later withdrawn, or a plea of nolo contendere, or of an offer to plead guilty or nolo contendere to the crime charged or any other crime, or of statements made in connection with any of the foregoing pleas or offers, is not admissible in any civil or criminal action, case, or proceeding against the person who made the plea or offer. This rule shall not apply to the introduction of voluntary and reliable statements made in court on the record in connection with any of the foregoing pleas or offers where offered for impeachment purposes or in a subsequent prosecution of the declarant for perjury or false statement.

This rule shall not take effect until August 1, 1975, and shall be superseded by any amendment to the Federal Rules of Criminal Procedure which is inconsistent with this rule, and which takes effect after the date of the enactment of the Act establishing these Federal Rules of Evidence.

As prescribed by the Supreme Court, the rule had consisted only of the first sentence, without the clause "Except as otherwise provided by Act of Congress". That clause and the remaining language were added by congressional amendment. The theory of the Supreme Court's rule is explained in the Advisory Committee's Note set forth immediately below, and the reasons for the amendments are stated in the congressional reports which follow it. In addition to these latter reports, see Chairman Hungate's explanation. 120 Cong.Rec. 40890 (1974); 1975 U.S.Code Cong. & Ad.News 7108, 7109.

Advisory Committee's Note

56 F.R.D. 183, 228

Withdrawn pleas of guilty were held inadmissible in federal prosecutions in Kercheval v. United States, 274 U.S. 220, 47 S.Ct. 582, 71 L.Ed. 1009 (1927). The Court pointed out that to admit the withdrawn plea would effectively set at naught the allowance of withdrawal and place the accused in a dilemma utterly inconsistent with the decision to award him a trial. The New York Court of Appeals, in People v. Spitaleri, 9 N.Y.2d 168, 212 N.Y.S.2d 53, 173 N.E.2d 35 (1961), reexamined and overturned its earlier decisions which had allowed admission. In addition to the reasons set forth in Kercheval, which was quoted at length, the court pointed out that the effect of admitting the plea was to compel defendant to take the stand by way of explanation and to open the way for the prosecution to call the lawyer who had represented him at the time of entering the plea. State court decisions for and against admissibility are collected in Annot., 86 A.L.R.2d 326.

Pleas of *nolo contendere* are recognized by Rule 11 of the Rules of Criminal Procedure, although the law of numerous States is to the contrary. The present rule gives effect to the principal traditional characteristic of the *nolo* plea, i.e. avoiding the admission of guilt which is inherent in pleas of guilty. This position is consistent with the construction of Section 5 of the Clayton Act, 15 U.S.C. § 16(a), recognizing the inconclusive and compromise nature of judgments based on *nolo* pleas. General Electric Co. v. City of San Antonio, 334 F.2d 480 (5th Cir.1964); Commonwealth Edison Co. v. Allis-Chalmers Mfg. Co., 323 F.2d 412 (7th Cir.1963), cert. denied 376 U.S. 939, 84 S.Ct. 794, 11 L.Ed. 2d 659; Armco Steel Corp. v. North Dakota, 376 F.2d 206 (8th Cir.1967); City of Burbank v. General Electric Co., 329 F.2d 825 (9th Cir.1964). See also state court decisions in Annot., 18 A.L.R.2d 1287, 1314.

Exclusion of offers to plead guilty or *nolo* has as its purpose the promotion of disposition of criminal cases by compromise. As pointed out in McCormick § 251, p. 543.

> "Effective criminal law administration in many localities would hardly be possible if a large proportion of the charges were not disposed of by such compromises."

See also People v. Hamilton, 60 Cal.2d 105, 32 Cal.Rptr. 4, 383 P.2d 412 (1963), discussing legislation designed to achieve this result. As with compromise offers generally, Rule 408, free communication is needed, and security against having an offer of compromise or related statement admitted in evidence effectively encourages it.[1]

Limiting the exclusionary rule to use against the accused is consistent with the purpose of the rule, since the possibility of use for or against other persons will not impair the effectiveness of withdrawing pleas or the freedom of discussion which the rule is designed to foster. See A.B.A. Standards Relating to Pleas of Guilty § 2.2 (1968). See also the narrower provisions of New Jersey Evidence Rule 52(2) and the unlimited exclusion provided in California Evidence Code § 1153.

Report of House Committee on the Judiciary

House Comm. on Judiciary, Fed. Rules of Evidence, H.R.Rep. No. 650, 93d Cong., 1st Sess., p. 8 (1973); 1974 U.S.Code Cong. & Ad. News 7075, 7082

The Committee added the phrase "Except as otherwise provided by Act of Congress" to Rule 410 as submitted by the Court in order to preserve particular congressional policy judgments as to the effect of a plea of guilty or of nolo

---

1. The rule as enacted, it should be noted, allows use of the statements for impeachment or in a subsequent prosecution for perjury or false statement.

contendere. See 15 U.S.C. 16(a). The Committee intends that its amendment refers to both present statutes and statutes subsequently enacted.

Report of Senate Committee on the Judiciary

Senate Comm. on Judiciary, Fed. Rules of Evidence, S. Rep. No. 1277, 93d Cong., 2d Sess., p. 10 (1974); 1974 U.S.Code Cong. & Ad. News 7051, 7057

As adopted by the House, rule 410 would make inadmissible pleas of guilty or nolo contendere subsequently withdrawn as well as offers to make such pleas. Such a rule is clearly justified as a means of encouraging pleading. However, the House rule would then go on to render inadmissible for any purpose statements made in connection with these pleas or offers as well.

The committee finds this aspect of the House rule unjustified. Of course, in certain circumstances such statements should be excluded. If, for example, a plea is vitiated because of coercion, statements made in connection with the plea may also have been coerced and should be inadmissible on that basis. In other cases, however, voluntary statements of an accused made in court on the record, in connection with a plea, and determined by a court to be reliable should be admissible even though the plea is subsequently withdrawn. This is particularly true in those cases where, if the House rule were in effect, a defendant would be able to contradict his previous statements and thereby lie with impunity.[2] To prevent such an injustice, the rule has been modified to permit the use of such statements for the limited purposes of impeachment and in subsequent perjury or false statement prosecutions.

Conference Report

H.R., Fed. Rules of Evidence, Conf. Rep. No. 1597, 93d Cong., 2d Sess., p. 6 (1974); 1974 U.S.Code Cong. & Ad. News 7098, 7100

The House bill provides that evidence of a guilty or nolo contendere plea, of an offer of either plea, or of statements made in connection with such pleas or offers of such pleas, is inadmissible in any civil or criminal action, case or proceeding against the person making such plea or offer. The Senate amendment makes the rule inapplicable to a voluntary and reliable statement made in court on the record where the statement is offered in a subsequent prosecution of the declarant for perjury or false statement.

The issues raised by Rule 410 are also raised by proposed Rule 11(e)(6) of the Federal Rules of Criminal Procedure presently pending before Congress. This proposed rule, which deals with the admissibility of pleas of guilty or nolo contendere, offers to make such pleas, and statements made in connection with such pleas, was promulgated by the Supreme Court on April 22, 1974, and in the absence of congressional action will become effective on August 1, 1975. The conferees intend to make no change in the presently-existing case law until that date, leaving the courts free to develop rules in this area on a case-by-case basis.

The Conferees further determined that the issues presented by the use of guilty and nolo contendere pleas, offers of such pleas, and statements made in connection with such pleas or offers, can be explored in greater detail during

2. See Harris v. New York, 401 U.S. 222 (1971).

Congressional consideration of Rule 11(e)(6) of the Federal Rules of Criminal Procedure. The Conferees believe, therefore, that it is best to defer its effective date until August 1, 1975. The Conferees intend that Rule 410 would be superseded by any subsequent Federal Rule of Criminal Procedure or Act of Congress with which it is inconsistent, if the Federal Rule of Criminal Procedure or Act of Congress takes effect or becomes law after the date of the enactment of the act establishing the rules of evidence.

The conference adopts the Senate amendment with an amendment that expresses the above intentions.

Rule 410 as amended in 1975

Editorial Note

In 1975 the Congress amended Rule 11(e)(6) of the Federal Rules of Criminal Procedure, P.L. 94-64, July 31, 1975, 89 Stat. 371, and then amended Evidence Rule 410 to conform to it. Amended Rule 410 read:

> Except as otherwise provided in this rule, evidence of a plea of guilty, later withdrawn, or a plea of nolo contendere, or of an offer to plead guilty or nolo contendere to the crime charged or any other crime, or of statements made in connection with, and relevant to, any of the foregoing pleas or offers, is not admissible in any civil or criminal proceeding against the person who made the plea or offer. However, evidence of a statement made in connection with, and relevant to, a plea of guilty, later withdrawn, a plea of nolo contendere, or an offer to plead guilty or nolo contendere to the crime charged or any other crime, is admissible in a criminal proceeding for perjury or false statement if the statement was made by the defendant under oath, on the record, and in the presence of counsel. P.L. 94-149, Dec. 12, 1975, 89 Stat. 805.

Report of House Committee on the Judiciary

House Comm. on Judiciary, Fed. Rules of Criminal Procedure, H.R. Rep. No. 247, 94th Cong., 1st Sess. (1975); 1975 U.S.Code Cong. & Ad. News 674, 679

The Committee added an exception to subdivision (e)(6). That subdivision provides:[1]

> Evidence of a plea of guilty, later withdrawn, or a plea of nolo contendere, or of an offer to plead guilty or nolo contendere to the crime charged or any other crime, or of statements made in connection with any of the foregoing pleas or offers, is not admissible in any civil or criminal proceeding against the person who made the plea or offer.

The Committee's exception permits the use of such evidence in a perjury or false statement prosecution where the plea, offer, or related statement was made by the defendant on the record, under oath and in the presence of counsel. The Committee recognizes that even this limited exception may discourage defendants from being completely candid and open during plea negotiations and may even result in discouraging the reaching of plea agreements. However, the Committee believes that, on balance, it is more

---

1. As prescribed by the Supreme Court and transmitted to the Congress.

important to protect the integrity of the judicial process from willful deceit and untruthfulness. [The Committee does not intend its language to be construed as mandating or encouraging the swearing-in of the defendant during proceedings in connection with the disclosure and acceptance or rejection of a plea agreement.] The Committee recast the language of Rule 11(c), which deals with the advice given to a defendant before the court can accept his plea of guilty or nolo contendere. The Committee acted in part because it believed that the warnings given to the defendant ought to include those that Boykin v. Alabama, 395 U.S. 238 (1969), said were constitutionally required. In addition, and as a result of its change in subdivision (e)(6), the Committee thought it only fair that the defendant be warned that his plea of guilty (later withdrawn) or nolo contendere, or his offer of either plea, or his statements made in connection with such pleas or offers, could later be used against him in a perjury trial if made under oath, on the record, and in the presence of counsel.

Conference Report

H.R., Fed. Rules of Criminal Procedure, Conf. Rep. No. 414, 94th Cong., 1st Sess., (1975); 1976 U.S.Code Cong. & Ad.News 713, 714

Rule 11(e)(6) deals with the use of statements made in connection with plea agreements. The House version permits a limited use of pleas of guilty, later withdrawn, or nolo contendere, offers of such pleas, and statements made in connection with such pleas or offers. Such evidence can be used in a perjury or false statement prosecution if the plea, offer, or related statement was made under oath, on the record, and in the presence of counsel. The Senate version permits evidence of voluntary and reliable statements made in court on the record to be used for the purpose of impeaching the credibility of the declarant or in a perjury or false statement prosecution.

The Conference adopts the House version with changes. The Conference agrees that neither a plea nor the offer of a plea ought to be admissible for any purpose. The Conference-adopted provision, therefore, like the Senate provision, permits only the use of statements made in connection with a plea of guilty, later withdrawn, or a plea of nolo contendere, or in connection with an offer of a guilty or nolo contendere plea.

Rule 410 as revised in 1980

Editorial Note

The Supreme Court adopted and on April 30, 1979, transmitted to the Congress a revision of Rule 11(e)(6) of the Federal Rules of Criminal Procedure, which was to operate also as a revision of Evidence Rule 410. The Congress suspended the effective date of the revision to December 1, 1980, absent congressional action otherwise. P.L. 96–42, July 31, 1979, 93 Stat. 326. Congress having taken no action, the rule as revised became effective on December 1, 1980, and is the present Rule 410, printed at the beginning of these comments.

Advisory Committee's Note

77 F.R.D. 507, 533

The major objective of the amendment to rule 11(e)(6) transmitted by the Supreme Court on April 30, 1979 is to describe more precisely, consistent with the original purpose of the provision, what evidence relating to pleas or plea discussions is inadmissible. The present language is susceptible to interpretation which would make it applicable to a wide variety of statements made under various circumstances other than within the context of those plea discussions authorized by rule 11(e) and intended to be protected by subdivision (e)(6) of the rule. See United States v. Herman, 544 F.2d 791 (5th Cir.1977), discussed herein.

Fed.R.Ev. 410, as originally adopted by Pub.L. 93–595, provided in part that "evidence of a plea of guilty, later withdrawn, or a plea of nolo contendere, or of an offer to plead guilty or nolo contendere to the crime charged or any other crime, or of statements made in connection with any of the foregoing pleas or offers, is not admissible in any civil or criminal action, case, or proceeding against the person who made the plea or offer." (This rule was adopted with the proviso that it "shall be superseded by any amendment to the Federal Rules of Criminal Procedure which is inconsistent with this rule.") As the Advisory Committee Note explained: "Exclusion of offers to plead guilty or nolo has as its purpose the promotion of disposition of criminal cases by compromise." The amendment of Fed.R.Crim.P. 11, transmitted to Congress by the Supreme Court in April 1974, contained a subdivision (e)(6) essentially identical to the rule 410 language quoted above, as a part of a substantial revision of rule 11. The most significant feature of this revision was the express recognition given to the fact that the "attorney for the government and the attorney for the defendant or the defendant when acting pro se may engage in discussions with a view toward reaching" a plea agreement. Subdivision (e)(6) was intended to encourage such discussions. As noted in H.R.Rep. No. 94–247, 94th Cong., 1st Sess. 7 (1975), the purpose of subdivision (e)(6) is to not "discourage defendants from being completely candid and open during plea negotiations." Similarly, H.R.Rep. No. 94–414, 94th Cong., 1st Sess. 10 (1975), states that "Rule 11(e)(6) deals with the use of statements made in connection with plea agreements." (Rule 11(e)(6) was thereafter enacted, with the addition of the proviso allowing use of statements in a prosecution for perjury, and with the qualification that the inadmissible statements must also be "relevant to" the inadmissible pleas or offers. Pub.L. 94–64; Fed.R.Ev. 410 was then amended to conform. Pub.L. 94–149.)

While this history shows that the purpose of Fed.R.Ev. 410 and Fed.R.Crim. P. 11(e)(6) is to permit the unrestrained candor which produces effective plea discussions between the "attorney for the government and the attorney for the defendant or the defendant when acting pro se," given visibility and sanction in rule 11(e), a literal reading of the language of these two rules could reasonably lead to the conclusion that a broader rule of inadmissibility obtains. That is, because "statements" are generally inadmissible if "made in connection with, and relevant to" an "offer to plead guilty," it might be thought that an otherwise voluntary admission to law enforcement officials is rendered inadmissible merely because it was made in the hope of obtaining leniency by a plea. Some decisions interpreting rule 11(e)(6) point in this direction. See United States v. Herman, 544 F.2d 791 (5th Cir.1977) (defendant in custody of two postal inspectors during continuance of removal hearing instigated conversation with them and at some point said he would plead guilty to armed robbery if the murder charge was dropped; one inspector stated they were not "in position" to make any deals in this regard; held, defendant's statement inadmissible under rule 11(e)(6) because the defendant "made the statements during the course of a conversation in which he sought concessions from the government in return for a guilty plea"); United States v. Brooks, 536 F.2d 1137 (6th Cir.1976) (defendant telephoned postal inspector and offered to plead guilty if he got 2-year maximum; statement inadmissible).

The amendment makes inadmissible statements made "in the course of any proceedings under this rule regarding" either a plea of guilty later withdrawn or a plea of nolo contendere, and also statements "made in the course of plea discussions with an attorney for the government which do not result in a plea of guilty or which result in a plea of guilty later withdrawn." It is not limited to statements by the defendant himself, and thus would cover statements by defense counsel regarding defendant's incriminating admissions to him. It thus fully protects the plea discussion process authorized by rule 11 without attempting to deal with confrontations between suspects and law enforcement agents, which involve problems of quite different dimensions. See, e.g., ALI Model Code of Pre-Arraignment Procedure, art. 140 and § 150.2(8) (Proposed Official Draft, 1975) (latter section requires exclusion if "a law enforcement officer induces any person to make a statement by promising leniency"). This change, it must be emphasized, does not compel the conclusion that statements made to law enforcement agents, especially when the agents purport to have authority to bargain, are inevitably admissible. Rather, the point is that such cases are not covered by the per se rule of 11(e)(6) and thus must be resolved by that body of law dealing with police interrogations.

If there has been a plea of guilty later withdrawn or a plea of nolo contendere, subdivision (e)(6)(C) makes inadmissible statements made "in the course of any proceedings under this rule" regarding such pleas. This includes, for example, admissions by the defendant when he makes his plea in court pursuant to rule 11 and also admissions made to provide the factual basis pursuant to subdivision (f). However, subdivision (e)(6)(C) is not limited to statements made in court. If the court were to defer its decision on a plea agreement pending examination of the presentence report, as authorized by subdivision (e)(2), statements made to the probation officer in connection with the preparation of that report would come within this provision.

This amendment is fully consistent with all recent and major law reform efforts on this subject. ALI Model Code of Pre-Arraignment Procedure § 350.7 (Proposed Official Draft, 1975), and ABA Standards Relating to Pleas of Guilty § 3.4 (Approved Draft, 1968) both provide:

> Unless the defendant subsequently enters a plea of guilty or nolo contendere which is not withdrawn, the fact that the defendant or his counsel and the prosecuting attorney engaged in plea discussions or made a plea agreement should not be received in evidence against or in favor of the defendant in any criminal or civil action or administrative proceedings.

The Commentary to the latter states:

> The above standard is limited to discussions and agreements with the prosecuting attorney. Sometimes defendants will indicate to the police their willingness to bargain, and in such instances these statements are sometimes admitted in court against the defendant. State v. Christian, 245 S.W.2d 895 (Mo.1952). If the police initiate this kind of discussion, this may have some bearing on the admissibility of the defendant's statement. However, the policy considerations relevant to this issue are better dealt with in the context of standards governing in-custody interrogation by the police.

Similarly, Unif.R.Crim.P. 441(d) (Approved Draft, 1974), provides that except under limited circumstances "no discussion between the parties or statement by the defendant or his lawyer under this Rule," i.e., the rule providing "the parties may meet to discuss the possibility of pretrial diversion . . . or of a plea agreement," are admissible. The amendment is likewise consistent with the typical state provision on this subject; see, e.g., Ill.S.Ct. Rule 402(f).

The language of the amendment identifies with more precision than the present language the necessary relationship between the statements and the plea or discussion. See the dispute between the majority and concurring opinions in United States v. Herman, 544 F.2d 791 (5th Cir.1977), concerning the meanings and effect of the phrases "connection to" and "relevant to" in the present rule. Moreover, by relating the statements to "plea discussions" rather than "an offer to plead," the amendment ensures "that even an attempt to open plea bargaining [is] covered under the same rule of inadmissibility." United States v. Brooks, 536 F.2d 1137 (6th Cir.1976).

The last sentence of Rule 11(e)(6) is amended to provide a second exception to the general rule of nonadmissibility of the described statements. Under the amendment, such a statement is also admissible "in any proceeding wherein another statement made in the course of the same plea or plea discussions has been introduced and the statement ought in fairness be considered contemporaneously with it." This change is necessary so that, when evidence of statements made in the course of or as a consequence of a certain plea or plea discussions are introduced under circumstances not prohibited by this rule (e.g., not "against" the person who made the plea), other statements relating to the same plea or plea discussions may also be admitted when relevant to the matter at issue. For example, if a defendant upon a motion to dismiss a prosecution on some ground were able to admit certain statements made in aborted plea discussions in his favor, then other relevant statements made in the same plea discussions should be admissible against the defendant in the interest of determining the truth of the matter at issue. The language of the amendment follows closely that in Fed.R.Evid. 106, as the considerations involved are very similar.

The phrase "in any civil or criminal proceeding" has been moved from its present position, following the word "against" for purposes of clarity. An ambiguity presently exists because the word "against" may be read as referring either to the kind of proceeding in which the evidence is offered or the purpose for which it is offered. The change makes it clear that the latter construction is correct. No change is intended with respect to provisions making evidence rules inapplicable in certain situations. See, e.g., Fed.R.Evid. 104(a) and 1101(d).

Unlike ABA Standards Relating to Pleas of Guilty § 3.4 (Approved Draft, 1968), and ALI Model Code of Pre-Arraignment Procedure § 350.7 (Proposed Official Draft, 1975), rule 11(e)(6) does not also provide that the described evidence is inadmissible "in favor of" the defendant. This is not intended to suggest, however, that such evidence will inevitably be admissible in the defendant's favor. Specifically, no disapproval is intended of such decisions as United States v. Verdoorn, 528 F.2d 103 (8th Cir.1976), holding that the trial judge properly refused to permit the defendants to put into evidence at their trial the fact the prosecution had attempted to plea bargain with them, as "meaningful dialogue between the parties would, as a practical matter, be impossible if either party had to assume the risk that plea offers would be admissible in evidence."

Rule 411. Liability Insurance

Evidence that a person was or was not insured against liability is not admissible upon the issue whether the person acted negligently or otherwise wrongfully. This rule does not require the exclusion of evidence of insurance against liability when offered for another purpose, such as proof of agency, ownership, or control, or bias or prejudice of a witness.

(As amended Mar. 2, 1987, eff. Oct. 1, 1987.)

Section references, McCormick 4th ed.

§ 201

Note by Federal Judicial Center

The rule enacted by the Congress is the rule prescribed by the Supreme Court without change.

Advisory Committee's Note
56 F.R.D. 183, 230

The courts have with substantial unanimity rejected evidence of liability insurance for the purpose of proving fault, and absence of liability insurance as proof of lack of fault. At best the inference of fault from the fact of insurance coverage is a tenuous one, as is its converse. More important, no doubt, has been the feeling that knowledge of the presence or absence of liability insurance would induce juries to decide cases on improper grounds. McCormick § 168; Annot., 4 A.L.R.2d 761. The rule is drafted in broad terms so as to include contributory negligence or other fault of a plaintiff as well as fault of a defendant.

The second sentence points out the limits of the rule, using well established illustrations. Id.

For similar rules see Uniform Rule 54; California Evidence Code § 1155; Kansas Code of Civil Procedure § 60–454; New Jersey Evidence Rule 54.

1987 Amendment. The amendment is technical. No substantive change is intended.

Rule 412. Rape Cases; Relevance of Victim's Past Behavior

(a) Notwithstanding any other provision of law, in a criminal case in which a person is accused of rape or of assault with intent to commit rape, reputation or opinion evidence of the past sexual behavior of an alleged victim of such rape or assault is not admissible.

(b) Notwithstanding any other provision of law, in a criminal case in which a person is accused of rape or of assault with intent to commit rape, evidence of a victim's past sexual behavior other than reputation or opinion evidence is also not admissible, unless such evidence other than reputation or opinion evidence is—

(1) admitted in accordance with subdivisions (c)(1) and (c)(2) and is constitutionally required to be admitted; or

(2) admitted in accordance with subdivision (c) and is evidence of—

(A) past sexual behavior with persons other than the accused, offered by the accused upon the issue of whether the accused was or was not, with respect to the alleged victim, the source of semen or injury; or

(B) past sexual behavior with the accused and is offered by the accused upon the issue of whether the alleged victim consented to the sexual behavior with respect to which rape or assault is alleged.

(c)(1) If the person accused of committing rape or assault with intent to commit rape intends to offer under subdivision (b) evidence of specific instances of the alleged victim's past sexual behavior, the accused shall make a written motion to offer such evidence not later than fifteen days before the date on which the trial in which such evidence is to be offered is scheduled to begin, except that the court may allow the motion to be made at a later date, including during trial, if the court determines either that the evidence is newly discovered and could not have been obtained earlier through the exercise of due diligence or that the issue to which such evidence relates has newly arisen in the case. Any motion made under this paragraph shall be served on all other parties and on the alleged victim.

(2) The motion described in paragraph (1) shall be accompanied by a written offer of proof. If the court determines that the offer of proof contains evidence described in subdivision (b), the court shall order a hearing in chambers to determine if such evidence is admissible. At such hearing the parties may call witnesses, including the alleged victim, and offer relevant evidence. Notwithstanding subdivision (b) of rule 104, if the relevancy of the evidence which the accused seeks to offer in the trial depends upon the fulfillment of a condition of fact, the court, at the hearing in chambers or at a subsequent hearing in chambers scheduled for such purpose, shall accept evidence on the issue of whether such condition of fact is fulfilled and shall determine such issue.

(3) If the court determines on the basis of the hearing described in paragraph (2) that the evidence which the accused seeks to offer is relevant and that the probative value of such evidence outweighs the danger of unfair prejudice, such evidence shall be admissible in the trial to the extent an order made by the court specifies evidence which may be offered and areas with respect to which the alleged victim may be examined or cross-examined.

(d) For purposes of this rule, the term "past sexual behavior" means sexual behavior other than the sexual behavior with respect to which rape or assault with intent to commit rape is alleged.

(Added P.L. 95–540, § 2(a), Oct. 28, 1978, 92 Stat. 2046; amended Nov. 18, 1988; Pub.L. 100–690, Title VII, § 7046(a), 102 Stat. 4400.)

Section references, McCormick 4th ed.

§ 43, § 44, § 193

House of Representatives

120 Cong.Rec. 34912 (1978)

Mr. Mann. . . .

Mr. Speaker, for many years in this country, evidentiary rules have permitted the introduction of evidence about a rape victim's prior sexual conduct. Defense lawyers were permitted great latitude in bringing out intimate details about a rape victim's life. Such evidence quite often serves no real purpose and only results in embarrassment to the rape victim and unwarranted public intrusion into her private life.

The evidentiary rules that permit such inquiry have in recent years come under question; and the States have taken the lead to change and modernize their evidentiary rules about evidence of a rape victim's prior sexual behavior. The bill before us similarly seeks to modernize the Federal evidentiary rules.

The present Federal Rules of Evidence reflect the traditional approach. If a defendant in a rape case raises the defense of consent, that defendant may then offer evidence about the victim's prior sexual behavior. Such evidence may be in the form of opinion evidence, evidence of reputation, or evidence of specific instances of behavior. Rule 404(a)(2) of the Federal Rules of Evidence permits the introduction of evidence of a "pertinent character trait." The advisory committee note to that rule cites, as an example of what the rule covers, the character of a rape victim when the issue is consent. Rule 405 of the Federal Rules of Evidence permits the use of opinion or reputation evidence or the use of evidence of specific behavior to show a character trait.

Thus, Federal evidentiary rules permit a wide ranging inquiry into the private conduct of a rape victim, even though that conduct may have at best a tenuous connection to the offense for which the defendant is being tried.

H.R. 4727 amends the Federal Rules of Evidence to add a new rule, applicable only in criminal cases, to spell out when, and under what conditions, evidence of a rape victim's prior sexual behavior can be admitted. The new rule provides that reputation or opinion evidence about a rape victim's prior sexual behavior is not admissible. The new rule also provides that a court cannot admit evidence of specific instances of a rape victim's prior sexual conduct except in three circumstances.

The first circumstance is where the Constitution requires that the evidence be admitted. This exception is intended to cover those infrequent instances where, because of an unusual chain of circumstances, the general rule of inadmissibility, if followed, would result in denying the defendant a constitutional right.

The second circumstance in which the defendant can offer evidence of specific instances of a rape victim's prior sexual behavior is where the defendant raises the issue of consent and the evidence is of sexual behavior with the defendant. To admit such evidence, however, the court must find that the evidence is relevant and that its probative value outweighs the danger of unfair prejudice.

The third circumstance in which a court can admit evidence of specific instances of a rape victim's prior sexual behavior is where the evidence is of behavior with someone other than the defendant and is offered by the defendant on the issue of whether or not he was the source of semen or injury. Again, such evidence will be admitted only if the court finds that the evidence is relevant and that its probative value outweighs the danger of unfair prejudice.

The new rule further provides that before evidence is admitted under any of these exceptions, there must be an in camera hearing—that is, a proceeding that takes place in the judge's chambers out of the presence of the jury and the general public. At this hearing, the defendant will present the evidence he intends to offer and be able to argue why it should be admitted. The prosecution, of course, will be able to argue against that evidence being admitted.

The purpose of the in camera hearing is twofold. It gives the defendant an opportunity to demonstrate to the court why certain evidence is admissible and ought to be presented to the jury. At the same time, it protects the privacy of the rape victim in those instances when the court finds that evidence is inadmissible. Of course, if the court finds the evidence to be admissible, the evidence will be presented to the jury in open court.

The effect of this legislation, therefore, is to preclude the routine use of evidence of specific instances of a rape victim's prior sexual behavior. Such evidence will be admitted only in clearly and narrowly defined circumstances and only after an in camera hearing. In determining the admissibility of such evidence, the court will consider all of the facts and circumstances surrounding the evidence, such as the amount of time that lapsed between the alleged prior act and the rape charged in the prosecution. The greater the lapse of time, of course, the less likely it is that such evidence will be admitted.

Mr. Speaker, the principal purpose of this legislation is to protect rape victims from the degrading and embarrassing disclosure of intimate details about their private lives. It does so by narrowly circumscribing when such evidence may be admitted. It does not do so, however, by sacrificing any constitutional right possessed by the defendant. The bill before us fairly balances the interests involved—the rape victim's interest in protecting her private life from unwarranted public exposure; the defendant's interest in being able adequately to present a defense by offering relevant and probative evidence; and society's interest in a fair trial, one where unduly prejudicial evidence is not permitted to becloud the issues before the jury.

(Proceedings of the Senate leading to passage of the bill are reported in 124 Cong.Rec. 36255 (1978).)

ARTICLE V.   PRIVILEGES

Rule
501.   General Rule.

Rule 501.   General Rule

Except as otherwise required by the Constitution of the United States or provided by Act of Congress or in rules prescribed by the Supreme Court pursuant to statutory authority, the privilege of a witness, person, government, State, or political subdivision thereof shall be governed by the principles of the common law as they may be interpreted by the courts of the United States in the light of reason and experience.   However, in civil actions and proceedings, with respect to an element of a claim or defense as to which State law supplies the rule of decision, the privilege of a witness, person, government, State, or political subdivision thereof shall be determined in accordance with State law.

Section references, McCormick 4th ed.

§ 9, § 53, § 66, § 75, § 76, § 78

Note by Federal Judicial Center

The rules enacted by the Congress substituted the single Rule 501 in place of the 13 rules dealing with privilege prescribed by the Supreme Court as Article V. . . .   The reasons given in support of the congressional action are stated in the Report of the House Committee on the Judiciary, the Report of the Senate Committee on the Judiciary, and Conference Report, set forth below.

Report of House Committee on the Judiciary

House Comm. of Judiciary, Fed. Rules of Evidence, H.R.Rep. No. 650, 93d Cong., 1st Sess., p. 8 (1973); 1974 U.S.Code Cong. & Ad.News 7075, 7082

Article V as submitted to Congress contained thirteen Rules.   Nine of those Rules defined specific non-constitutional privileges which the federal courts must recognize (i.e. required reports, lawyer-client, psychotherapist-patient, husband-wife, communications to clergymen, political vote, trade secrets, secrets of state and other official information, and identity of informer).   Another Rule provided that only those privileges set forth in Article V or in some other Act of Congress could be recognized by the federal courts.   The three remaining Rules addressed collateral problems as to waiver of privilege by voluntary disclosure, privileged matter disclosed under compulsion or without opportunity to claim privilege, comment upon or inference from a claim of privilege, and jury instruction with regard thereto.

The Committee amended Article V to eliminate all of the Court's specific Rules on privileges.   Instead, the Committee, through a single Rule, 501, left the law of privileges in its present state and further provided that privileges shall continue to be developed by the courts of the United States under a uniform standard applicable both in civil and criminal cases. That standard, derived from Rule 26 of the Federal Rules of Criminal Procedure, mandates the application of the principles of the common law as interpreted by the courts of the United States in the light of reason and experience. The words "person, government, State, or political subdivision thereof" were added by the Committee to the lone term "witnesses" used in Rule 26 to make clear that, as under present law, not only witnesses may have privileges. The Committee also included in its amendment a proviso modeled after Rule 302 and similar to language added by the Committee to Rule 601 relating to the competency of witnesses. The proviso is designed to require the application of State privilege law in civil actions and proceedings governed by Erie R. Co. v. Tompkins, 304 U.S. 64 (1938), a result in accord with current federal court decisions. See Republic Gear Co. v. Borg-Warner Corp., 381 F.2d 551, 555–556 n. 2 (2nd Cir. 1967). The Committee deemed the proviso to be necessary in the light of the Advisory Committee's view (see its note to Court Rule 501) that this result is not mandated under *Erie*.

The rationale underlying the proviso is that federal law should not supersede that of the States in substantive areas such as privilege absent a compelling reason. The Committee believes that in civil cases in the federal courts where an element of a claim or defense is not grounded upon a federal question, there is no federal interest strong enough to justify departure from State policy. In addition, the Committee considered that the Court's proposed Article V would have promoted forum shopping in some civil actions, depending upon differences in the privilege law applied as among the State and federal courts. The Committee's proviso, on the other hand, under which the federal courts are bound to apply the State's privilege law in actions founded upon a State-created right or defense, removes the incentive to "shop".

Report of Senate Committee on the Judiciary

Senate Comm. on Judiciary, Fed. Rules of Evidence, S.Rep. No. 1277, 93d Cong., 2d Sess., p. 11 (1974); 1974 U.S.Code Cong. & Ad.News 7051, 7058

Article V as submitted to Congress contained 13 rules. Nine of those rules defined specific nonconstitutional privileges which the Federal courts must recognize (i.e., required reports, lawyer-client, psychotherapist-patient, husband-wife, communications to clergymen, political vote, trade secrets, secrets of state and other official information, and identity of informer). Many of these rules contained controversial modifications or restrictions upon common law privileges. As noted supra, the House amended article V to eliminate all of the Court's specific rules on privileges. Through a single rule, 501, the House provided that privileges shall be governed by the principles of the common law as interpreted by the courts of the United States in the light of reason and experience (a standard derived from rule 26 of the Federal Rules of Criminal Procedure) except in the case of an element of a civil claim or defense as to which State law supplies the rule of decision in which event state privilege law was to govern.

The committee agrees with the main thrust of the House amendment: that a federally developed common law based on modern reason and experience shall apply except where the State nature of the issues renders deference to State privilege law the wiser course, as in the usual diversity case. The

committee understands that thrust of the House amendment to require that
State privilege law be applied in "diversity" cases (actions on questions of State
law between citizens of different States arising under 28 U.S.C. § 1332). The
language of the House amendment, however, goes beyond this in some respects,
and falls short of it in others: State privilege law applies even in nondiversity,
Federal question civil cases, where an issue governed by State substantive law
is the object of the evidence (such issues do sometimes arise in such cases); and,
in all instances where State privilege law is to be applied, e.g., on proof of a
State issue in a diversity case, a close reading reveals that State privilege law is
not to be applied unless the matter to be proved is an element of that state
claim or defense, as distinguished from a step along the way in the proof of it.

The committee is concerned that the language used in the House amendment could be difficult to apply. It provides that "in civil actions . . . with
respect to an element of a claim or defense as to which State law supplies the
rule of decision," State law on privilege applies. The question of what is an
element of a claim or defense is likely to engender considerable litigation. If
the matter in question constitutes an element of a claim, State law supplies the
privilege rule; whereas if it is a mere item of proof with respect to a claim,
then, even though State law might supply the rule of decision, Federal law on
the privilege would apply. Further, disputes will arise as to how the rule
should be applied in an antitrust action or in a tax case where the Federal
statute is silent as to a particular aspect of the substantive law in question, but
Federal cases had incorporated State law by reference to State law.[1] Is a claim
(or defense) based on such a reference a claim or defense as to which federal or
State law supplies the rule of decision?

Another problem not entirely avoidable is the complexity or difficulty the
rule introduces into the trial of a Federal case containing a combination of
Federal and State claims and defenses, e.g. an action involving Federal antitrust and State unfair competition claims. Two different bodies of privilege
law would need to be consulted. It may even develop that the same witness-
testimony might be relevant on both counts and privileged as to one but not the
other.[2]

The formulation adopted by the House is pregnant with litigious mischief.
The committee has, therefore, adopted what we believe will be a clearer and
more practical guideline for determining when courts should respect State rules
of privilege. Basically, it provides that in criminal and Federal question civil
cases, federally evolved rules on privilege should apply since it is Federal policy
which is being enforced.[3] Conversely, in diversity cases where the litigation in
question turns on a substantive question of State law, and is brought in the
Federal courts because the parties reside in different States, the committee
believes it is clear that State rules of privilege should apply unless the proof is
directed at a claim or defense for which Federal law supplies the rule of
decision (a situation which would not commonly arise.)[4] It is intended that the

1. For a discussion of reference to State substantive law, see note on Federal Incorporation by Reference of State Law, Hart & Wechsler, The Federal Courts and the Federal System, pp. 491–94 (2d ed. 1973).

2. The problems with the House formulation are discussed in Rothstein, The Proposed Amendments to the Federal Rules of Evidence, 62 Georgetown University Law

Journal 125 (1973) at notes 25, 26 and 70–74 and accompanying text.

3. It is also intended that the Federal law of privileges should be applied with respect to pendant State law claims when they arise in a Federal question case.

4. While such a situation might require use of two bodies of privilege law, federal and state, in the same case, nevertheless

State rules of privilege should apply equally in original diversity actions and diversity actions removed under 28 U.S.C. § 1441(b).

Two other comments on the privilege rule should be made. The committee has received a considerable volume of correspondence from psychiatric organizations and psychiatrists concerning the deletion of rule 504 of the rule submitted by the Supreme Court. It should be clearly understood that, in approving this general rule as to privileges, the action of Congress should not be understood as disapproving any recognition of a psychiatrist-patient, or husband-wife, or any other of the enumerated privileges contained in the Supreme Court rules. Rather, our action should be understood as reflecting the view that the recognition of a privilege based on a confidential relationship and other privileges should be determined on a case-by-case basis.

Further, we would understand that the prohibition against spouses testifying against each other is considered a rule of privilege and covered by this rule and not by rule 601 of the competency of witnesses.

Conference Report

H.R., Fed. Rules of Evidence, Conf.Rep. No. 1597, 93d Cong., 2d Sess., p. 7 (1974); 1974 U.S.Code Cong. & Ad.News 7098, 7100

Rule 501 deals with the privilege of a witness not to testify. Both the House and Senate bills provide that federal privilege law applies in criminal cases. In civil actions and proceedings, the House bill provides that state privilege law applies "to an element of a claim or defense as to which State law supplies the rule of decision." The Senate bill provides that "in civil actions and proceedings arising under 28 U.S.C. § 1332 or 28 U.S.C. § 1335, or between citizens of different States and removed under 28 U.S.C. § 1441(b) the privilege of a witness, person, government, State or political subdivision thereof is determined in accordance with State law, unless with respect to the particular claim or defense, Federal law supplies the rule of decision."

The wording of the House and Senate bills differs in the treatment of civil actions and proceedings. The rule in the House bill applies to evidence that relates to "an element of a claim or defense." If an item of proof tends to support or defeat a claim or defense, or an element of a claim or defense, and if state law supplies the rule of decision for that claim or defense, then state privilege law applies to that item of proof.

Under the provision in the House bill, therefore, state privilege law will usually apply in diversity cases. There may be diversity cases, however, where a claim or defense is based upon federal law. In such instances, federal privilege law will apply to evidence relevant to the federal claim or defense. See Sola Electric Co. v. Jefferson Electric Co., 317 U.S. 173 (1942).

the occasions on which this would be required are considerably reduced as compared with the House version, and confined to situations where the Federal and State interests are such as to justify application of neither privilege law to the case as a whole. If the rule proposed here results in two conflicting bodies of privilege law applying to the same piece of evidence in the same case, it is contemplated that the rule favoring reception of the evidence should be applied. This policy is based on the present rule 43(a) of the Federal Rules of Civil Procedure which provides: In any case, the statute or rule which favors the reception of the evidence governs and the evidence shall be presented according to the most convenient method prescribed in any of the statutes or rules to which reference is herein made.

In nondiversity jurisdiction civil cases, federal privilege law will generally apply. In those situations where a federal court adopts or incorporates state law to fill interstices or gaps in federal statutory phrases, the court generally will apply federal privilege law. As Justice Jackson has said:

> A federal court sitting in a non-diversity case such as this does not sit as a local tribunal. In some cases it may see fit for special reasons to give the law of a particular state highly persuasive or even controlling effect, but in the last analysis its decision turns upon the law of the United States, not that of any state.

D'Oench, Duhme & Co. v. Federal Deposit Insurance Corp., 315 U.S. 447, 471 (1942) (Jackson, J., concurring). When a federal court chooses to absorb state law, it is applying the state law as a matter of federal common law. Thus, state law does not supply the rule of decision (even though the federal court may apply a rule derived from state decisions), and state privilege law would not apply. See C.A. Wright, Federal Courts 251–252 (2d ed. 1970); Holmberg v. Armbrecht, 327 U.S. 392 (1946); DeSylva v. Ballentine, 351 U.S. 570, 581 (1956); 9 Wright & Miller, Federal Rules and Procedure § 2408.

In civil actions and proceedings, where the rule of decision as to a claim or defense or as to an element of a claim or defense is supplied by state law, the House provision requires that state privilege law apply.

The Conference adopts the House provision.

ARTICLE VI. WITNESSES

Rule 601. General Rule of Competency

Every person is competent to be a witness except as otherwise provided in these rules. However, in civil actions and proceedings, with respect to an element of a claim or defense as to which State law supplies the rule of decision, the competency of a witness shall be determined in accordance with State law.

Section references, McCormick 4th ed.

§ 9, § 44, § 53, § 62, § 63, § 65, § 66, § 68, § 70, § 71, § 253

Note by Federal Judicial Center

The first sentence of the rule enacted by the Congress is the entire rule prescribed by the Supreme Court, without change. The second sentence was added by congressional action.

Advisory Committee's Note

56 F.R.D. 183, 262

This general ground-clearing eliminates all grounds of incompetency not specifically recognized in the succeeding rules of this Article. Included among the grounds thus abolished are religious belief, conviction of crime, and connection with the litigation as a party or interested person or spouse of a party or interested person. With the exception of the so-called Dead Man's Acts, American jurisdictions generally have ceased to recognize these grounds.

The Dead Man's Acts are surviving traces of the common law disqualification of parties and interested persons. They exist in variety too great to convey conviction of their wisdom and effectiveness. These rules contain no provision of this kind. . . .

No mental or moral qualifications for testifying as a witness are specified. Standards of mental capacity have proved elusive in actual application. A leading commentator observes that few witnesses are disqualified on that ground. Weihofen, Testimonial Competence and Credibility, 34 Geo.Wash.L. Rev. 53 (1965). Discretion is regularly exercised in favor of allowing the testimony. A witness wholly without capacity is difficult to imagine. The question is one particularly suited to the jury as one of weight and credibility, subject to judicial authority to review the sufficiency of the evidence. 2 Wigmore §§ 501, 509. Standards of moral qualification in practice consist essentially of evaluating a person's truthfulness in terms of his own answers about it. Their principal utility is in affording an opportunity on voir dire examination to impress upon the witness his moral duty. This result may, however, be accomplished more directly, and without haggling in terms of legal standards, by the manner of administering the oath or affirmation under Rule 603.

Admissibility of religious belief as a ground of impeachment is treated in Rule 610. Conviction of crime as a ground of impeachment is the subject of Rule 609. Marital relationship is the basis for privilege under Rule 505. Interest in the outcome of litigation and mental capacity are, of course, highly relevant to credibility and require no special treatment to render them admissible along with other matters bearing upon the perception, memory, and narration of witnesses.

Report of House Committee on the Judiciary

House Comm. on Judiciary, Fed. Rules of Evidence, H.R.Rep. No. 650, 93d Cong., 1st Sess., p. 9 (1973); 1974 U.S.Code Cong. & Ad.News 7075, 7083

Rule 601 as submitted to the Congress provided that "Every person is competent to be a witness except as otherwise provided in these rules." One effect of the Rule as proposed would have been to abolish age, mental capacity, and other grounds recognized in some State jurisdictions as making a person incompetent as a witness. The greatest controversy centered around the Rule's rendering inapplicable in the federal courts the so-called Dead Man's Statutes which exist in some States. Acknowledging that there is substantial disagreement as to the merit of Dead Man's Statutes, the Committee nevertheless believed that where such statutes have been enacted they represent State policy which should not be overturned in the absence of a compelling federal interest. The Committee therefore amended the Rule to make competency in civil actions determinable in accordance with State law with respect to elements of claims or defenses as to which State law supplies the rule of decision. Cf. Courtland v. Walston & Co., Inc., 340 F.Supp. 1076, 1087–1092 (S.D.N.Y.1972).

Report of Senate Committee on the Judiciary

Senate Comm. on Judiciary, Fed. Rules of Evidence, S.Rep. No. 1277, 2d Sess., p. 13 (1974); 1974 U.S.Code Cong. & Ad.News 7051, 7059

The amendment to rule 601 parallels the treatment accorded rule 501 discussed immediately above.

Conference Report

H.R., Fed. Rules of Evidence, Conf.Rep. No. 1597, 93d Cong., 2d Sess., p. 8 (1974); 1975 U.S.Code Cong. & Ad.News 7098, 7101

Rule 601 deals with competency of witnesses. Both the House and Senate bills provide that federal competency law applies in criminal cases. In civil actions and proceedings, the House bill provides that state competency law applies "to an element of a claim or defense as to which State law supplies the rule of decision." The Senate bill provides that "in civil actions and proceedings arising under 28 U.S.C. § 1332 or 28 U.S.C. § 1335, or between citizens of different States and removed under 28 U.S.C. § 1441(b) the competency of a witness, person, government, State or political subdivision thereof is determined in accordance with State law, unless with respect to the particular claim or defense, Federal law supplies the rule of decision."

The wording of the House and Senate bills differs in the treatment of civil actions and proceedings. The rule in the House bill applies to evidence that relates to "an element of a claim or defense." If an item of proof tends to support or defeat a claim or defense, or an element of a claim or defense, and if state law supplies the rule of decision for that claim or defense, then state competency law applies to that item of proof.

For reasons similar to those underlying its action on Rule 501, the Conference adopts the House provision.

Rule 602. Lack of Personal Knowledge

A witness may not testify to a matter unless evidence is introduced sufficient to support a finding that the witness has personal knowledge of the matter. Evidence to prove personal knowledge may, but need not, consist of the witness' own testimony. This rule is subject to the provisions of rule 703, relating to opinion testimony by expert witnesses.

(As amended Mar. 2, 1987, eff. Oct. 1, 1987; Apr. 25, 1988, eff. Nov. 1, 1988.)

Section references, McCormick 4th ed.

§ 10, § 11, § 43, § 44, § 71

Note by Federal Judicial Center

The rule enacted by the Congress is the rule prescribed by the Supreme Court without change.

Advisory Committee's Note

56 F.R.D. 183, 263

". . . [T]he rule requiring that a witness who testifies to a fact which can be perceived by the senses must have had an opportunity to observe, and must have actually observed the fact" is a "most pervasive manifestation" of the common law insistence upon "the most reliable sources of information." McCormick § 10, p. 19. These foundation requirements may, of course, be furnished by the testimony of the witness himself; hence personal knowledge is not an absolute but may consist of what the witness thinks he knows from personal perception. 2 Wigmore § 650. It will be observed that the rule is in fact a specialized application of the provisions of Rule 104(b) on conditional relevancy.

This rule does not govern the situation of a witness who testifies to a hearsay statement as such, if he has personal knowledge of the making of the statement. Rules 801 and 805 would be applicable. This rule would, however, prevent him from testifying to the subject matter of the hearsay statement, as he has no personal knowledge of it.

The reference to Rule 703 is designed to avoid any question of conflict between the present rule and the provisions of that rule allowing an expert to express opinions based on facts of which he does not have personal knowledge.

1987 Amendment. The amendments are technical. No substantive change is intended.

1988 Amendment. The amendment is technical. No substantive change is intended.

Rule 603. Oath or Affirmation

Before testifying, every witness shall be required to declare that the witness will testify truthfully, by oath or affirmation administered in a form calculated to awaken the witness' conscience and impress the witness' mind with the duty to do so.

(As amended Mar. 2, 1987, eff. Oct. 1, 1987.)

Section references, McCormick 4th ed.

§ 44, § 46, § 63, § 71, § 245

Note by Federal Judicial Center

The rule enacted by the Congress is the rule prescribed by the Supreme Court without change.

Advisory Committee's Note

56 F.R.D. 183, 263

The rule is designed to afford the flexibility required in dealing with religious adults, atheists, conscientious objectors, mental defectives, and children. Affirmation is simply a solemn undertaking to tell the truth; no special verbal formula is required. As is true generally, affirmation is recognized by federal law. "Oath" includes affirmation, 1 U.S.C. § 1; judges and clerks may administer oaths and affirmations, 28 U.S.C. §§ 459, 953; and affirmations are acceptable in lieu of oaths under Rule 43(d) of the Federal Rules of Civil Procedure. Perjury by a witness is a crime, 18 U.S.C. § 1621.

1987 Amendment. The amendments are technical. No substantive change is intended.

Rule 604. Interpreters

An interpreter is subject to the provisions of these rules relating to qualification as an expert and the administration of an oath or affirmation to make a true translation.

(As amended Mar. 2, 1987, eff. Oct. 1, 1987.)

Section references, McCormick 4th ed.

None

Note by Federal Judicial Center

The rule enacted by the Congress is the rule prescribed by the Supreme Court without change.

Advisory Committee's Note

56 F.R.D. 183, 264

The rule implements Rule 43(f) of the Federal Rules of Civil Procedure and Rule 28(b) of the Federal Rules of Criminal Procedure, both of which contain provisions for the appointment and compensation of interpreters.

1987 Amendment. The amendment is technical. No substantive change is intended.

Rule 605. Competency of Judge as Witness

The judge presiding at the trial may not testify in that trial as a witness. No objection need be made in order to preserve the point.

Section references, McCormick 4th ed.

§ 62, § 68, § 70, § 71

Note by Federal Judicial Center

The rule enacted by the Congress is the rule prescribed by the Supreme Court without change.

Advisory Committee's Note

56 F.R.D. 183, 264

In view of the mandate of 28 U.S.C. § 455 that a judge disqualify himself in "any case in which he . . . is or has been a material witness," the likelihood that the presiding judge in a federal court might be called to testify in the trial over which he is presiding is slight. Nevertheless the possibility is not totally eliminated.

The solution here presented is a broad rule of incompetency, rather than such alternatives as incompetency only as to material matters, leaving the matter to the discretion of the judge, or recognizing no incompetency. The choice is the result of inability to evolve satisfactory answers to questions which arise when the judge abandons the bench for the witness stand. Who rules on objections? Who compels him to answer? Can he rule impartially on the weight and admissibility of his own testimony? Can he be impeached or cross-examined effectively? Can he, in a jury trial, avoid conferring his seal of approval on one side in the eyes of the jury? Can he, in a bench trial, avoid an involvement destructive of impartiality? The rule of general incompetency has substantial support. See Report of the Special Committee on the Propriety of Judges Appearing as Witnesses, 36 A.B.A.J. 630 (1950); cases collected in Annot. 157 A.L.R. 311; McCormick § 68, p. 147; Uniform Rule 42; California Evidence Code § 703; Kansas Code of Civil Procedure § 60–442; New Jersey Evidence Rule 42. Cf. 6 Wigmore § 1909, which advocates leaving the matter to the discretion of the judge, and statutes to that effect collected in Annot., 157 A.L.R. 311.

The rule provides an "automatic" objection. To require an actual objection would confront the opponent with a choice between not objecting, with the result of allowing the testimony, and objecting, with the probable result of excluding the testimony but at the price of continuing the trial before a judge likely to feel that his integrity had been attacked by the objector.

Rule 606. Competency of Juror as Witness

(a) At the trial. A member of the jury may not testify as a witness before that jury in the trial of the case in which the juror is sitting. If the juror is called so to testify, the opposing party shall be afforded an opportunity to object out of the presence of the jury.

(b) Inquiry into validity of verdict or indictment. Upon an inquiry into the validity of a verdict or indictment, a juror may not testify as to any matter or statement occurring during the course of the jury's deliberations or to the effect of anything upon that or any other juror's mind or emotions as influencing the juror to assent to or dissent from the verdict or indictment or concerning the juror's mental processes in connection therewith, except that a juror may testify on the question whether extraneous prejudicial information was improperly brought to the jury's attention or whether any outside influence was improperly brought to bear upon any juror. Nor may a juror's affidavit or evidence of any statement by the juror concerning a matter about which the juror would be precluded from testifying be received for these purposes.

(As amended P.L. 94–149, § 1(10), Dec. 12, 1975, 89 Stat. 805; Mar. 2, 1987, eff. Oct. 1, 1987.)

Section references, McCormick 4th ed.

Generally § 71

(a). § 62, § 68, § 70

(b). § 68

Note by Federal Judicial Center

The rule enacted by the Congress is the rule prescribed by the Supreme Court, amended only by the addition of the concluding phrase "for these purposes." The bill originally passed by the House did not contain in the first sentence the prohibition as to matters or statements during the deliberations or the clause beginning "except."

Advisory Committee's Note

56 F.R.D. 183, 265

Subdivision (a). The considerations which bear upon the permissibility of testimony by a juror in the trial in which he is sitting as juror bear an obvious similarity to those evoked when the judge is called as a witness. See Advisory Committee's Note to Rule 605. The judge is not, however in this instance so involved as to call for departure from usual principles requiring objection to be made; hence the only provision on objection is that opportunity be afforded for its making out of the presence of the jury. Compare Rule 605.

Subdivision (b). Whether testimony, affidavits, or statements of jurors should be received for the purpose of invalidating or supporting a verdict or indictment, and if so, under what circumstances, has given rise to substantial differences of opinion. The familiar rubric that a juror may not impeach his own verdict, dating from Lord Mansfield's time, is a gross oversimplification. The values sought to be promoted by excluding the evidence include freedom of deliberation, stability and finality of verdicts, and protection of jurors against annoyance and embarrassment. McDonald v. Pless, 238 U.S. 264, 35 S.Ct. 785, 59 L.Ed. 1300 (1915). On the other hand, simply putting verdicts beyond effective reach can only promote irregularity and injustice. The rule offers an accommodation between these competing considerations.

The mental operations and emotional reactions of jurors in arriving at a given result would, if allowed as a subject of inquiry, place every verdict at the mercy of jurors and invite tampering and harassment. See Grenz v. Werre, 129 N.W.2d 681 (N.D.1964). The authorities are in virtually complete accord in excluding the evidence. Fryer, Note on Disqualification of Witnesses, Selected Writings on Evidence and Trial 345, 347 (Fryer ed. 1957); Maguire, Weinstein, et al., Cases on Evidence 887 (5th ed. 1965); 8 Wigmore § 2349 (McNaughton Rev.1961). As to matters other than mental operations and emotional reactions of jurors, substantial authority refuses to allow a juror to disclose irregularities which occur in the jury room, but allows his testimony as to irregularities occurring outside and allows outsiders to testify as to occurrences both inside and out. 8 Wigmore § 2354 (McNaughton Rev.1961). However, the door of the jury room is not necessarily a satisfactory dividing point, and the Supreme Court has refused to accept it for every situation. Mattox v. United States, 146 U.S. 140, 13 S.Ct. 50, 36 L.Ed. 917 (1892).

Under the federal decisions the central focus has been upon insulation of the manner in which the jury reached its verdict, and this protection extends to each of the components of deliberation, including arguments, statements, discussions, mental and emotional reactions, votes, and any other feature of the process. Thus testimony or affidavits of jurors have been held incompetent to show a compromise verdict, Hyde v. United States, 225 U.S. 347, 382 (1912); a quotient verdict, McDonald v. Pless, 238 U.S. 264 (1915); speculation as to insurance coverage, Holden v. Porter, 405 F.2d 878 (10th Cir. 1969), Farmers Coop. Elev. Ass'n v. Strand, 382 F.2d 224, 230 (8th Cir. 1967), cert. denied 389 U.S. 1014; misinterpretation of instructions, Farmers Coop. Elev. Ass'n v. Strand, supra; mistake in returning verdict, United States v. Chereton, 309 F.2d 197 (6th Cir. 1962); interpretation of guilty plea by one defendant as implicating others, United States v. Crosby, 294 F.2d 928, 949 (2d Cir. 1961). The policy does not, however, foreclose testimony by jurors as to prejudicial extraneous information or influences injected into or brought to bear upon the deliberative process. Thus a juror is recognized as competent to testify to statements by the bailiff or the introduction of a prejudicial newspaper account into the jury room, Mattox v. United States, 146 U.S. 140 (1892). See also Parker v. Gladden, 385 U.S. 363 (1966).

This rule does not purport to specify the substantive grounds for setting aside verdicts for irregularity; it deals only with the competency of jurors to testify concerning those grounds.

See also Rule 6(e) of the Federal Rules of Criminal Procedure and 18 U.S.C. § 3500, governing the secrecy of grand jury proceedings. The present rule does not relate to secrecy and disclosure but to the competency of certain witnesses and evidence.

Report of House Judiciary Committee

House Comm. on Judiciary, Fed. Rules of Evidence, H.R.Rep. No. 650,
93d Cong., 1st Sess., p. 9 (1973); 1974 U.S.Code Cong. & Ad.News
7075, 7083

As proposed by the Court, Rule 606(b) limited testimony by a juror in the course of an inquiry into the validity of a verdict or indictment. He could testify as to the influence of extraneous prejudicial information brought to the jury's attention (e.g. a radio newscast or a newspaper account) or an outside influence which improperly had been brought to bear upon a juror (e.g. a threat to the safety of a member of his family), but he could not testify as to other irregularities which occurred in the jury room. Under this formulation a quotient verdict could not be attacked through the testimony of a juror, nor could a juror testify to the drunken condition of a fellow juror which so disabled him that he could not participate in the jury's deliberations.

The 1969 and 1971 Advisory Committee drafts would have permitted a member of the jury to testify concerning these kinds of irregularities in the jury room. The Advisory Committee note in the 1971 draft stated that ". . . the door of the jury room is not a satisfactory dividing point, and the Supreme Court has refused to accept it." The Advisory Committee further commented that—

> The trend has been to draw the dividing line between testimony as to mental processes, on the one hand, and as to the existence of conditions or occurrences of events calculated improperly to influence the verdict, on the other hand, without regard to whether the happening is within or without the jury room. . . . The jurors are the persons who know what really happened. Allowing them to testify as to matters other than their own reactions involves no particular hazard to the values sought to be protected. The rule is based upon this conclusion. It makes no attempt to specify the substantive grounds for setting aside verdicts for irregularity.

Objective jury misconduct may be testified to in California, Florida, Iowa, Kansas, Nebraska, New Jersey, North Dakota, Ohio, Oregon, Tennessee, Texas, and Washington.

Persuaded that the better practice is that provided for in the earlier drafts, the Committee amended subdivision (b) to read in the text of those drafts.

Report of Senate Judiciary Committee

Senate Comm. on Judiciary, Fed. Rules of Evidence, S.Rep. No. 1277,
93d Cong., 2d Sess., p. 13 (1974); 1974 U.S.Code Cong. & Ad.News
7051, 7060

As adopted by the House, this rule would permit the impeachment of verdicts by inquiry into, not the mental processes of the jurors, but what happened in terms of conduct in the jury room. This extension of the ability to impeach a verdict is felt to be unwarranted and ill-advised.

The rule passed by the House embodies a suggestion by the Advisory Committee of the Judicial Conference that is considerably broader than the final version adopted by the Supreme Court, which embodied long-accepted Federal law. Although forbidding the impeachment of verdicts by inquiry into the jurors' mental processes, it deletes from the Supreme Court version the proscription against testimony "as to any matter or statement occurring during the course of the jury's deliberations." This deletion would have the effect of opening verdicts up to challenge on the basis of what happened during the jury's internal deliberations, for example, where a juror alleged that the jury refused to follow the trial judge's instructions or that some of the jurors did not take part in deliberations.

Permitting an individual to attack a jury verdict based upon the jury's internal deliberations has long been recognized as unwise by the Supreme Court. In McDonald v. Pless, the Court stated:

. . .

> [L]et it once be established that verdicts solemnly made and publicly returned into court can be attacked and set aside on the testimony of those who took part in their publication and all verdicts could be, and many would be, followed by an inquiry in the hope of discovering something which might invalidate the finding. Jurors would be harassed and beset by the defeated party in an effort to secure from them evidence of facts which might establish misconduct sufficient to set aside a verdict. If evidence thus secured could be thus used, the result would be to make what was intended to be a private deliberation, the constant subject of public investigation—to the destruction of all frankness and freedom of discussion and conference.[2]

. . .

As it stands then, the rule would permit the harassment of former jurors by losing parties as well as the possible exploitation of disgruntled or otherwise badly-motivated ex-jurors.

Public policy requires a finality to litigation. And common fairness requires that absolute privacy be preserved for jurors to engage in the full and free debate necessary to the attainment of just verdicts. Jurors will not be able to function effectively if their deliberations are to be scrutinized in post-trial litigation. In the interest of protecting the jury system and the citizens who make it work, rule 606 should not permit any inquiry into the internal deliberations of the jurors.

Conference Report

H.R., Fed.Rules of Evidence, Conf.Rep. No. 1597, 93d Cong., 2d Sess., p. 8 (1974); 1974 U.S.Code Cong. & Ad.News 7098, 7102

Rule 606(b) deals with juror testimony in an inquiry into the validity of a verdict or indictment. The House bill provides that a juror cannot testify about his mental processes or about the effect of anything upon his or another juror's mind as influencing him to assent to or dissent from a verdict or indictment. Thus, the House bill allows a juror to testify about objective matters occurring during the jury's deliberation, such as the misconduct of another juror or the reaching of a quotient verdict. The Senate bill does not permit juror testimony about any matter or statement occurring during the course of the jury's deliberations. The Senate bill does provide, however, that a juror may testify on the question whether extraneous prejudicial information was improperly brought to the jury's attention and on the question whether any outside influence was improperly brought to bear on any juror.

2. 238 U.S. 264, at 267 (1914).

The Conference adopts the Senate amendment. The Conferees believe that jurors should be encouraged to be conscientious in promptly reporting to the court misconduct that occurs during jury deliberations.

1987 Amendment. The amendments are technical. No substantive change is intended.

Rule 607. Who May Impeach

The credibility of a witness may be attacked by any party, including the party calling the witness.

(As amended Mar. 2, 1987, eff. Oct. 1, 1987.)

Section references, McCormick 4th ed.

§ 23, § 38, § 39

Note by Federal Judicial Center

The rule enacted by the Congress is the rule prescribed by the Supreme Court without change.

Advisory Committee's Note

56 F.R.D. 183, 266

The traditional rule against impeaching one's own witness is abandoned as based on false premises. A party does not hold out his witnesses as worthy of belief, since he rarely has a free choice in selecting them. Denial of the right leaves the party at the mercy of the witness and the adversary. If the impeachment is by a prior statement, it is free from hearsay dangers and is excluded from the category of hearsay under Rule 801(d)(1). Ladd, Impeachment of One's Own Witness—New Developments, 4 U.Chi.L.Rev. 69 (1936); McCormick § 38; 3 Wigmore §§ 896–918. The substantial inroads into the old rule made over the years by decisions, rules, and statutes are evidence of doubts as to its basic soundness and workability. Cases are collected in 3 Wigmore § 905. Revised Rule 32(a)(1) of the Federal Rules of Civil Procedure allows any party to impeach a witness by means of his deposition, and Rule 43(b) has allowed the calling and impeachment of an adverse party or person identified with him. Illustrative statutes allowing a party to impeach his own witness under varying circumstances are Ill.Rev.Stats.1967, c. 110, § 60; Mass.Laws Annot. 1959, c. 233 § 23; 20 N.M.Stats. Annot. 1953, § 20–2–4; N.Y. CPLR § 4514 (McKinney 1963); 12 Vt.Stats. Annot. 1959, §§ 1641a, 1642. Complete judicial rejection of the old rule is found in United States v. Freeman, 302 F.2d 347 (2d Cir.1962). The same result is reached in Uniform Rule 20; California Evidence Code § 785; Kansas Code of Civil Procedure § 60–420. See also New Jersey Evidence Rule 20.

1987 Amendment. The amendment is technical. No substantive change is intended.

Rule 608. Evidence of Character and Conduct of Witness

(a) Opinion and reputation evidence of character. The credibility of a witness may be attacked or supported by evidence in the form of opinion or reputation, but subject to these limitations: (1) the evidence may refer only to character for truthfulness or untruthfulness, and (2) evidence of truthful character is admissible only after the character of the witness for truthfulness has been attacked by opinion or reputation evidence or otherwise.

(b) Specific instances of conduct. Specific instances of the conduct of a witness, for the purpose of attacking or supporting the witness' credibility, other than conviction of crime as provided in rule 609, may not be proved by extrinsic evidence. They may, however, in the discretion of the court, if probative of truthfulness or untruthfulness, be inquired into on cross-examination of the witness (1) concerning the witness' character for truthfulness or untruthfulness, or (2) concerning the character for truthfulness or untruthfulness of another witness as to which character the witness being cross-examined has testified.

The giving of testimony, whether by an accused or by any other witness, does not operate as a waiver of the accused's or the witness' privilege against self-incrimination when examined with respect to matters which relate only to credibility.

(As amended Mar. 2, 1987, eff. Oct. 1, 1987; Apr. 25, 1988, eff. Nov. 1, 1988.)

Section references, McCormick 4th ed.

Generally § 25

(a). § 43, § 44, § 47

(b). § 41, § 45, § 47

Note by Federal Judicial Center

The rule enacted by the Congress is the rule prescribed by the Supreme Court, changed only by amending the second sentence of subdivision (b). The sentence as prescribed by the Court read: "They may, however, if probative of truthfulness or untruthfulness and not remote in time, be inquired into on cross-examination of the witness himself or on cross-examination of a witness who testifies to his character for truthfulness or untruthfulness." The effect of the amendments was to delete the phrase "and not remote in time," to add the phrase "in the discretion of the court," and otherwise only to clarify the meaning of the sentence. The reasons for the amendments are stated in the Report of the House Committee on the Judiciary, set forth below. See also Note to Rule 405(a) by Federal Judicial Center, supra.

Advisory Committee's Note

56 F.R.D. 183, 268

Subdivision (a). In Rule 404(a) the general position is taken that character evidence is not admissible for the purpose of proving that the person acted in conformity therewith, subject, however, to several exceptions, one of which is character evidence of a witness as bearing upon his credibility. The present rule develops that exception.

In accordance with the bulk of judicial authority, the inquiry is strictly limited to character for veracity, rather than allowing evidence as to character generally. The result is to sharpen relevancy, to reduce surprise, waste of time, and confusion, and to make the lot of the witness somewhat less unattractive. McCormick § 44.

The use of opinion and reputation evidence as means of proving the character of witnesses is consistent with Rule 405(a). While the modern practice has purported to exclude opinion, witnesses who testify to reputation seem in fact often to be giving their opinions, disguised somewhat misleadingly as reputation. See McCormick § 44. And even under the modern practice, a common relaxation has allowed inquiry as to whether the witnesses would believe the principal witness under oath. United States v. Walker, 313 F.2d 236 (6th Cir.1963), and cases cited therein; McCormick § 44, pp. 94–95, n. 3.

Character evidence in support of credibility is admissible under the rule only after the witness' character has first been attacked, as has been the case at common law. Maguire, Weinstein, et al., Cases on Evidence 295 (5th ed. 1965); McCormick § 49, p. 105; 4 Wigmore § 1104. The enormous needless consumption of time which a contrary practice would entail justifies the limitation. Opinion or reputation that the witness is untruthful specifically qualifies as an attack under the rule, and evidence of misconduct, including conviction of crime, and of corruption also fall within this category. Evidence of bias or interest does not. McCormick § 49; 4 Wigmore §§ 1106, 1107. Whether evidence in the form of contradiction is an attack upon the character of the witness must depend upon the circumstances. McCormick § 49. Cf. 4 Wigmore §§ 1108, 1109.

As to the use of specific instances on direct by an opinion witness, see the Advisory Committee's Note to Rule 405, supra.

Subdivision (b). In conformity with Rule 405, which forecloses use of evidence of specific incidents as proof in chief of character unless character is an issue in the case, the present rule generally bars evidence of specific instances of conduct of a witness for the purpose of attacking or supporting his credibility. There are, however, two exceptions: (1) specific instances are provable when they have been the subject of criminal conviction, and (2) specific instances may be inquired into on cross-examination of the principal witness or of a witness giving an opinion of his character for truthfulness.

(1) Conviction of crime as a technique of impeachment is treated in detail in Rule 609, and here is merely recognized as an exception to the general rule excluding evidence of specific incidents for impeachment purposes.

(2) Particular instances of conduct, though not the subject of criminal conviction, may be inquired into on cross-examination of the principal witness himself or of a witness who testifies concerning his character for truthfulness. Effective cross-examination demands that some allowance be made for going into matters of this kind, but the possibilities of abuse are substantial. Consequently safeguards are erected in the form of specific requirements that the instances inquired into be probative of truthfulness or its opposite . . . . Also, the overriding protection of Rule 403 requires that probative value not be outweighed by danger of unfair prejudice, confusion of issues or misleading the jury, and that of Rule 611 bars harassment and undue embarrassment.

The final sentence constitutes a rejection of the doctrine of such cases as People v. Sorge, 301 N.Y. 198, 93 N.E.2d 637 (1950), that any past criminal act relevant to credibility may be inquired into on cross-examination, in apparent disregard of the privilege against self-incrimination. While it is clear that an ordinary witness cannot make a partial disclosure of incriminating matter and then invoke the privilege on cross-examination, no tenable contention can be made that merely by testifying he waives his right to foreclose inquiry on cross-examination into criminal activities for the purpose of attacking his credibility. So to hold would reduce the privilege to a nullity. While it is true that an accused, unlike an ordinary witness, has an option whether to testify, if the option can be exercised only at the price of opening up inquiry as to any and all criminal acts committed during his lifetime, the right to testify could scarcely be said to possess much vitality. In Griffin v. California, 380 U.S. 609, 85 S.Ct. 1229, 14 L.Ed.2d 106 (1965), the Court held that allowing comment on the election of an accused not to testify exacted a constitutionally impermissible price, and so here. While no specific provision in terms confers constitutional status on the right of an accused to take the stand in his own defense, the existence of the right is so completely recognized that a denial of it or substantial infringement upon it would surely be of due process dimensions. See Ferguson v. Georgia, 365 U.S. 570, 81 S.Ct. 756, 5 L.Ed.2d 783 (1961); McCormick § 131; 8 Wigmore § 2276 (McNaughton Rev.1961). In any event, wholly aside from constitutional considerations, the provision represents a sound policy.

Report of House Committee on the Judiciary

House Comm. on Judiciary, Fed.Rules of Evidence, H.R.Rep. No. 650, 93d Cong., 1st Sess., p. 10 (1973); 1974 U.S.Code Cong. & Ad.News 7075, 7084

The second sentence of Rule 608(b) as submitted by the Court permitted specific instances of misconduct of a witness to be inquired into on cross-examination for the purpose of attacking his credibility, if probative of truthfulness or untruthfulness, "and not remote in time." Such cross-examination could be of the witness himself or of another witness who testifies as to "his" character for truthfulness or untruthfulness.

The Committee amended the Rule to emphasize the discretionary power of the court in permitting such testimony and deleted the reference to remoteness in time as being unnecessary and confusing (remoteness from time of trial or remoteness from the incident involved?). As recast, the Committee amendment also makes clear the antecedent of "his" in the original Court proposal.

1987 Amendment. The amendments are technical. No substantive change is intended.

1988 Amendment. The amendment is technical. No substantive change is intended.

Rule 609. Impeachment by Evidence of Conviction of Crime

(a) **General rule.** For the purpose of attacking the credibility of a witness,

(1) evidence that a witness other than an accused has been convicted of a crime shall be admitted, subject to Rule 403, if the crime was punishable by death or imprisonment in excess of one year under the law under which the witness was convicted, and evidence that an accused has been convicted of such a crime shall

be admitted if the court determines that the probative value of admitting this evidence outweighs its prejudicial effect to the accused; and

(2) evidence that any witness has been convicted of a crime shall be admitted if it involved dishonesty or false statement, regardless of the punishment.

(b) Time limit. Evidence of a conviction under this rule is not admissible if a period of more than ten years has elapsed since the date of the conviction or of the release of the witness from the confinement imposed for that conviction, whichever is the later date, unless the court determines, in the interests of justice, that the probative value of the conviction supported by specific facts and circumstances substantially outweighs its prejudicial effect. However, evidence of a conviction more than 10 years old as calculated herein, is not admissible unless the proponent gives to the adverse party sufficient advance written notice of intent to use such evidence to provide the adverse party with a fair opportunity to contest the use of such evidence.

(c) Effect of pardon, annulment, or certificate of rehabilitation. Evidence of a conviction is not admissible under this rule if (1) the conviction has been the subject of a pardon, annulment, certificate of rehabilitation, or other equivalent procedure based on a finding of the rehabilitation of the person convicted, and that person has not been convicted of a subsequent crime which was punishable by death or imprisonment in excess of one year, or (2) the conviction has been the subject of a pardon, annulment, or other equivalent procedure based on a finding of innocence.

(d) Juvenile adjudications. Evidence of juvenile adjudications is generally not admissible under this rule. The court may, however, in a criminal case allow evidence of a juvenile adjudication of a witness other than the accused if conviction of the offense would be admissible to attack the credibility of an adult and the court is satisfied that admission in evidence is necessary for a fair determination of the issue of guilt or innocence.

(e) Pendency of appeal. The pendency of an appeal therefrom does not render evidence of a conviction inadmissible. Evidence of the pendency of an appeal is admissible.

(As amended Mar. 2, 1987, eff. Oct. 1, 1987; Jan. 26, 1990, eff. Dec. 1, 1990.)

Section references, McCormick 4th ed.

Generally § 42

(a). § 42

(b). § 42

(c). § 42

(d). § 42

(e). § 42

Note by Federal Judicial Center

Subdivision (a) of the rule prescribed by the Supreme Court was revised successively in the House, in the Senate, and in the Conference. The nature of the rule prescribed by the Court, the various amendments, and the reasons therefor are stated in the Report of the House Committee on the Judiciary, the Report of the Senate Committee on the Judiciary, and the Conference Report, set forth below.

Subdivision (b) of the rule prescribed by the Supreme Court was also revised successively in the House, in the Senate, and in the Conference. The nature of the rule prescribed by the Court, those amendments and the reasons therefor are likewise stated in the Report of the House Committee on the Judiciary, the Report of the Senate Committee on the Judiciary, and the Conference Report, set forth below.

Subdivision (c) enacted by the Congress is the subdivision prescribed by the Supreme Court, with amendments and reasons therefor stated in the Report of the House Committee on the Judiciary, set forth below.

Subdivision (d) enacted by the Congress is the subdivision prescribed by the Supreme Court, amended in the second sentence by substituting "court" in place of "judge" and by adding the phrase "in a criminal case."

Subdivision (e) enacted by the Congress is the subdivision prescribed by the Supreme Court without change.

Advisory Committee's Note

56 F.R.D. 183, 270

As a means of impeachment, evidence of conviction of crime is significant only because it stands as proof of the commission of the underlying criminal act. There is little dissent from the general proposition that at least some crimes are relevant to credibility but much disagreement among the cases and commentators about which crimes are usable for this purpose. See McCormick § 43; 2 Wright, Federal Practice and Procedure: Criminal § 416 (1969). The weight of traditional authority has been to allow use of felonies generally, without regard to the nature of the particular offense, and of *crimen falsi* without regard to the grade of the offense. This is the view accepted by Congress in the 1970 amendment of § 14–305 of the District of Columbia Code, P.L. 91–358, 84 Stat. 473. Uniform Rule 21 and Model Code Rule 106 permit only crimes involving "dishonesty or false statement." Others have thought that the trial judge should have discretion to exclude convictions if the probative value of the evidence of the crime is substantially outweighed by the danger of unfair prejudice. Luck v. United States, 121 U.S.App.D.C. 151, 348 F.2d 763 (1965); McGowan, Impeachment of Criminal Defendants by Prior Convictions, 1970 Law & Soc. Order 1. . . .

The proposed rule incorporates certain basic safeguards, in terms applicable to all witnesses but of particular significance to an accused who elects to testify. These protections include the imposition of definite time limitations, giving effect to demonstrated rehabilitation, and generally excluding juvenile adjudications.

Subdivision (a). For purposes of impeachment, crimes are divided into two categories by the rule: (1) those of what is generally regarded as felony grade, without particular regard to the nature of the offense, and (2) those involving dishonesty or false statement, without regard to the grade of the offense. Provable convictions are not limited to violations of federal law. By reason of our constitutional structure, the federal catalog of crimes is far from being a complete one, and resort must be had to the laws of the states for the specification of many crimes. For example, simple theft as compared with theft from interstate commerce. Other instances of borrowing are the Assimilative Crimes Act, making the state law of crimes applicable to the special territorial and maritime jurisdiction of the United States, 18 U.S.C. § 13, and the provision of the Judicial Code disqualifying persons as jurors on the grounds of state as well as federal convictions, 28 U.S.C. § 1865. For evaluation of the crime in terms of seriousness, reference is made to the congressional measurement of felony (subject to imprisonment in excess of one year) rather than adopting state definitions which vary considerably. See 28 U.S.C. § 1865, supra, disqualifying jurors for conviction in state or federal court of crime punishable by imprisonment for more than year.

Report of the House Committee on the Judiciary

House Comm. on Judiciary, Fed.Rules of Evidence, H.R.Rep. No. 650, 93d Cong., 1st Sess., p. 11 (1973); 1974 U.S.Code Cong. & Ad.News 7075, 7084

Rule 609(a) as submitted by the Court was modeled after Section 133(a) of Public Law 91–358, 14 D.C.Code 305(b)(1), enacted in 1970. The Rule provided that:

> For the purpose of attacking the credibility of a witness, evidence that he has been convicted of a crime is admissible but only if the crime (1) was punishable by death or imprisonment in excess of one year under the law under which he was convicted or (2) involved dishonesty or false statement regardless of the punishment.

As reported to the Committee by the Subcommittee, Rule 609(a) was amended to read as follows:

> For the purpose of attacking the credibility of a witness, evidence that he has been convicted of a crime is admissible only if the crime (1) was punishable by death or imprisonment in excess of one year, unless the court determines that the danger of unfair prejudice outweighs the probative value of the evidence of the conviction, or (2) involved dishonesty or false statement.

In full committee, the provision was amended to permit attack upon the credibility of a witness by prior conviction only if the prior crime involved dishonesty or false statement. While recognizing that the prevailing doctrine in the federal courts and in most States allows a witness to be impeached by evidence of prior felony convictions without restriction as to type, the Committee was of the view that, because of the danger of unfair prejudice in such practice and the deterrent effect upon an accused who might wish to testify, and even upon a witness who was not the accused, cross-examination by evidence of prior conviction should be limited to those kinds of convictions bearing directly on credibility, i.e., crimes involving dishonesty or false statement.

Report of the Senate Committee on the Judiciary

Senate Comm. on Judiciary, Fed.Rules of Evidence, S.Rep. No. 1277, 93d Cong., 2d Sess., p. 14 (1974); 1974 U.S.Code Cong. & Ad.News 7051, 7060

As proposed by the Supreme Court, the rule would allow the use of prior convictions to impeach if the crime was a felony or a misdemeanor if the misdemeanor involved dishonesty or false statement. As modified by the House, the rule would admit prior convictions for impeachment purposes only if the offense, whether felony or misdemeanor, involved dishonesty or false statement.

The committee has adopted a modified version of the House-passed rule. In your committee's view, the danger of unfair prejudice is far greater when the accused, as opposed to other witnesses, testifies, because the jury may be prejudiced not merely on the question of credibility but also on the ultimate question of guilt or innocence. Therefore, with respect to defendants, the committee agreed with the House limitation that only offenses involving false statement or dishonesty may be used. By that phrase, the committee means crimes such as perjury or subornation of perjury, false statement, criminal fraud, embezzlement or false pretense, or any other offense, in the nature of crimen falsi the commission of which involves some element of untruthfulness, deceit or falsification bearing on the accused's propensity to testify truthfully.

With respect to other witnesses, in addition to any prior conviction involving false statement or dishonesty, any other felony may be used to impeach if, and only if, the court finds that the probative value of such evidence outweighs its prejudicial effect against the party offering that witness.

Notwithstanding this provision, proof of any prior offense otherwise admissible under rule 404 could still be offered for the purposes sanctioned by that rule. Furthermore, the committee intends that notwithstanding this rule, a defendant's misrepresentation regarding the existence or nature of prior convictions may be met by rebuttal evidence, including the record of such prior convictions. Similarly, such records may be offered to rebut representations made by the defendant regarding his attitude toward or willingness to commit a general category of offense, although denials or other representations by the defendant regarding the specific conduct which forms the basis of the charge against him shall not make prior convictions admissible to rebut such statement.

In regard to either type of representation, of course, prior convictions may be offered in rebuttal only if the defendant's statement is made in response to defense counsel's questions or is made gratuitously in the course of cross-examination. Prior convictions may not be offered as rebuttal evidence if the prosecution has sought to circumvent the purpose of this rule by asking questions which elicit such representations from the defendant.

One other clarifying amendment has been added to this subsection, that is, to provide that the admissibility of evidence of a prior conviction is permitted only upon cross-examination of a witness. It is not admissible if a person does not testify. It is to be understood, however, that a court record of a prior conviction is admissible to prove that conviction if the witness has forgotten or denies its existence.

Conference Report

H.R., Fed.Rules of Evidence, Conf.Rep. No. 1597, 93d Cong., 2d Sess.,
p. 9 (1974); 1974 U.S.Code Cong. & Ad.News 7098, 7102

The House bill provides that the credibility of a witness can be attacked by proof of prior conviction of a crime only if the crime involves dishonesty or false statement. The Senate amendment provides that a witness' credibility may be attacked if the crime (1) was punishable by death or imprisonment in excess of one year under the law under which he was convicted or (2) involves dishonesty or false statement, regardless of the punishment.

The Conference adopts the Senate amendment with an amendment. The Conference amendment provides that the credibility of a witness, whether a defendant or someone else, may be attacked by proof of a prior conviction but only if the crime: (1) was punishable by death or imprisonment in excess of one year under the law under which he was convicted and the court determines that the probative value of the conviction outweighs its prejudicial effect to the defendant; or (2) involved dishonesty or false statement regardless of the punishment.

By the phrase "dishonesty and false statement" the Conference means crimes such as perjury or subornation of perjury, false statement, criminal fraud, embezzlement, or false pretense, or any other offense in the nature of crimen falsi, the commission of which involves some element of deceit, untruthfulness, or falsification bearing on the accused's propensity to testify truthfully.

The admission of prior convictions involving dishonesty and false statement is not within the discretion of the Court. Such convictions are peculiarly probative of credibility and, under this rule, are always to be admitted. Thus, judicial discretion granted with respect to the admissibility of other prior convictions is not applicable to those involving dishonesty or false statement.

With regard to the discretionary standard established by paragraph (1) of rule 609(a), the Conference determined that the prejudicial effect to be weighed against the probative value of the conviction is specifically the prejudicial effect *to the defendant*. The danger of prejudice to a witness other than the defendant (such as injury to the witness' reputation in his community) was considered and rejected by the Conference as an element to be weighed in determining admissibility. It was the judgment of the Conference that the danger of prejudice to a nondefendant witness is outweighed by the need for the trier of fact to have as much relevant evidence on the issue of credibility as possible. Such evidence should only be excluded where it presents a danger of improperly influencing the outcome of the trial by persuading the trier of fact to convict the defendant on the basis of his prior criminal record.

Advisory Committee's Note

56 F.R.D. 183, 271

Subdivision (b). Few statutes recognize a time limit on impeachment by evidence of conviction. However, practical considerations of fairness and relevancy demand that some boundary be recognized. See Ladd, Credibility Tests—Current Trends, 89 U.Pa.L.Rev. 166, 176–177 (1940). This portion of the rule is derived from the proposal advanced in Recommendation Proposing an

Evidence Code, § 788(5), p. 142, Cal.Law Rev.Comm'n (1965), though not adopted. See California Evidence Code § 788.

Report of the House Committee
on the Judiciary

House Comm. on Judiciary, Fed.Rules of Evidence, H.R.Rep. No. 650,
93d Cong., 1st Sess, p. 11 (1973); 1974 U.S.Code Cong. & Ad.News
7075, 7085

Rule 609(b) as submitted by the Court was modeled after Section 133(a) of Public Law 91–358, 14 D.C.Code 305(b)(2)(B), enacted in 1970. The Rule provided:

> Evidence of a conviction under this rule is not admissible if a period of more than ten years has elapsed since the date of the release of the witness from confinement imposed for his most recent conviction, or the expiration of the period of his parole, probation, or sentence granted or imposed with respect to his most recent conviction, whichever is the later date.

Under this formulation, a witness' entire past record of criminal convictions could be used for impeachment (provided the conviction met the standard of subdivision (a)), if the witness had been most recently released from confinement, or the period of his parole or probation had expired, within ten years of the conviction.

The Committee amended the Rule to read in the text of the 1971 Advisory Committee version to provide that upon the expiration of ten years from the date of a conviction of a witness, or of his release from confinement for that offense, that conviction may no longer be used for impeachment. The Committee was of the view that after ten years following a person's release from confinement (or from the date of his conviction) the probative value of the conviction with respect to that person's credibility diminished to a point where it should no longer be admissible.

Report of the Senate Committee
on the Judiciary

Senate Comm. on Judiciary, Fed.Rules of Evidence, S.Rep. No. 1277,
93d Cong., 2d Sess., p. 15 (1974); 1974 U.S.Code Cong. & Ad.News
7051, 7061

Although convictions over ten years old generally do not have much probative value, there may be exceptional circumstances under which the conviction substantially bears on the credibility of the witness. Rather than exclude all convictions over 10 years old, the committee adopted an amendment in the form of a final clause to the section granting the court discretion to admit convictions over 10 years old, but only upon a determination by the court that the probative value of the convictions supported by specific facts and circumstances, substantially outweighs its prejudicial effect.

It is intended that convictions over 10 years old will be admitted very rarely and only in exceptional circumstances. The rules provide that the decision be supported by specific facts and circumstances thus requiring the court to make specific findings on the record as to the particular facts and circumstances it has considered in determining that the probative value of the conviction substantially outweighs its prejudicial impact. It is expected that, in fairness, the court will give the party against whom the conviction is introduced a full and adequate opportunity to contest its admission.

Conference Report

H.R., Fed.Rules of Evidence, Conf.Rep. No. 1597, 93d Cong., 2d Sess., p. 10 (1974); 1974 U.S.Code Cong. & Ad.News 7098, 7103

The House bill provides in subsection (b) that evidence of conviction of a crime may not be used for impeachment purposes under subsection (a) if more than ten years have elapsed since the date of the conviction or the date the witness was released from confinement imposed for the conviction, whichever is later. The Senate amendment permits the use of convictions older than ten years, if the court determines, in the interests of justice, that the probative value of the conviction, supported by specific facts and circumstances, substantially outweighs its prejudicial effect.

The Conference adopts the Senate amendment with an amendment requiring notice by a party that he intends to request that the court allow him to use a conviction older than ten years. The Conferees anticipate that a written notice, in order to give the adversary a fair opportunity to contest the use of the evidence, will ordinarily include such information as the date of the conviction, the jurisdiction, and the offense or statute involved. In order to eliminate the possibility that the flexibility of this provision may impair the ability of a party-opponent to prepare for trial, the Conferees intend that the notice provision operate to avoid surprise.

Advisory Committee's Note

56 F.R.D. 183, 271

Subdivision (c). A pardon or its equivalent granted solely for the purpose of restoring civil rights lost by virtue of a conviction has no relevance to an inquiry into character. If, however, the pardon or other proceeding is hinged upon a showing of rehabilitation the situation is otherwise. The result under the rule is to render the conviction inadmissible. The alternative of allowing in evidence both the conviction and the rehabilitation has not been adopted for reasons of policy, economy of time, and difficulties of evaluation.

A similar provision is contained in California Evidence Code § 788. Cf. A.L.I. Model Penal Code, Proposed Official Draft § 306.6(3)(e) (1962), and discussion in A.L.I. Proceedings 310 (1961).

Pardons based on innocence have the effect, of course, of nullifying the conviction *ab initio.*

Report of House Committee on the Judiciary

House Comm. on Judiciary, Fed.Rules of Evidence, H.R.Rep. No. 650, 93d Cong., 1st Sess., p. 12 (1973); 1974 U.S.Code Cong. & Ad.News 7075, 7085

Rule 609(c) as submitted by the Court provided in part that evidence of a witness' prior conviction is not admissible to attack his credibility if the conviction was the subject of a pardon, annulment, or other equivalent procedure, based on a showing of rehabilitation, and the witness has not been convicted of a subsequent crime. The Committee amended the Rule to provide that the "subsequent crime" must have been "punishable by death or imprisonment in excess of one year", on the ground that a subsequent conviction of an offense not a felony is insufficient to rebut the finding that the witness has been rehabilitated. The Committee also intends that the words "based on a finding of the rehabilitation of the person convicted" apply not only to "certificate of rehabilitation, or other equivalent procedure", but also to "pardon" and "annulment."

Advisory Committee's Note

56 F.R.D. 183, 271

Subdivision (d). The prevailing view has been that a juvenile adjudication is not usable for impeachment. Thomas v. United States, 74 App.D.C. 167, 121 F.2d 905 (1941); Cotton v. United States, 355 F.2d 480 (10th Cir.1966). This conclusion was based upon a variety of circumstances. By virtue of its informality, frequently diminished quantum of required proof, and other departures from accepted standards for criminal trials under the theory of *parens patriae,* the juvenile adjudication was considered to lack the precision and general probative value of the criminal conviction. While In re Gault, 387 U.S. 1, 87 S.Ct. 1428, 18 L.Ed.2d 527 (1967), no doubt eliminates these characteristics insofar as objectionable, other obstacles remain. Practical problems of administration are raised by the common provisions in juvenile legislation that records be kept confidential and that they be destroyed after a short time. While *Gault* was skeptical as to the realities of confidentiality of juvenile records, it also saw no constitutional obstacles to improvement. 387 U.S. at 25, 87 S.Ct. 1428. See also Note, Rights and Rehabilitation in the Juvenile Courts, 67 Colum.L.Rev. 281, 289 (1967). In addition, policy considerations much akin to those which dictate exclusion of adult convictions after rehabilitation has been established strongly suggest a rule of excluding juvenile adjudications. Admittedly, however, the rehabilitative process may in a given case be a demonstrated failure, or the strategic importance of a given witness may be so great as to require the overriding of general policy in the interests of particular justice. See Giles v. Maryland, 386 U.S. 66, 87 S.Ct. 793, 17 L.Ed.2d 737 (1967). Wigmore was outspoken in his condemnation of the disallowance of juvenile adjudications to impeach, especially when the witness is the complainant in a case of molesting a minor. 1 Wigmore § 196; 3 id. §§ 924a, 980. The rule recognizes discretion in the judge to effect an accommodation among these various factors by departing from the general principle of exclusion. In deference to the general pattern and policy of juvenile statutes, however, no discretion is accorded when the witness is the accused in a criminal case.

Subdivision (e). The presumption of correctness which ought to attend judicial proceedings supports the position that pendency of an appeal does not preclude use of a conviction for impeachment. United States v. Empire Packing Co., 174 F.2d 16 (7th Cir.1949), cert. denied 337 U.S. 959, 69 S.Ct. 1534, 93 L.Ed. 1758; Bloch v. United States, 226 F.2d 185 (9th Cir.1955), cert. denied 350 U.S. 948, 76 S.Ct. 323, 100 L.Ed. 826 and 353 U.S. 959, 77 S.Ct. 868, 1 L.Ed. 2d 910; and see Newman v. United States, 331 F.2d 968 (8th Cir.1964). Contra, Campbell v. United States, 85 U.S.App.D.C. 133, 176 F.2d 45 (1949). The pendency of an appeal is, however, a qualifying circumstance properly considerable.

1987 Amendment. The amendments are technical. No substantive change is intended.

1990 Amendment. The amendment to Rule 609(a) makes two changes in the rule. The first change removes from the rule the limitation that the conviction may only be elicited during cross-examination, a limitation that virtually every circuit has found to be inapplicable. It is common for witnesses to reveal on direct examination their convictions to "remove the sting" of the impeachment. See e.g., United States v. Bad Cob, 560 F.2d 877 (8th Cir.1977). The amendment does not contemplate that a court will necessarily permit proof of prior convictions through testimony, which might be time-consuming and more prejudicial than proof through a written record. Rules 403 and 611(a) provide sufficient authority for the court to protect against unfair or disruptive methods of proof.

The second change effected by the amendment resolves an ambiguity as to the relationship of Rules 609 and 403 with respect to impeachment of witnesses other than the criminal defendant. See, Green v. Bock Laundry Machine Co., 109 S.Ct. ___, ___ U.S. ___ (1989). The amendment does not disturb the special balancing test for the criminal defendant who chooses to testify. Thus, the rule recognizes that, in virtually every case in which prior convictions are used to impeach the testifying defendant, the defendant faces a unique risk of prejudice—i.e., the danger that convictions that would be excluded under Fed.R. Evid. 404 will be misused by a jury as propensity evidence despite their introduction solely for impeachment purposes. Although the rule does not forbid all use of convictions to impeach a defendant, it requires that the government show that the probative value of convictions as impeachment evidence outweighs their prejudicial effect.

Prior to the amendment, the rule appeared to give the defendant the benefit of the special balancing test when defense witnesses other than the defendant were called to testify. In practice, however, the concern about unfairness to the defendant is most acute when the defendant's own convictions are offered as evidence. Almost all of the decided cases concern this type of impeachment, and the amendment does not deprive the defendant of any meaningful protection, since Rule 403 now clearly protects against unfair impeachment of any defense witness other than the defendant. There are cases in which a defendant might be prejudiced when a defense witness is impeached. Such cases may arise, for example, when the witness bears a special relationship to the defendant such that the defendant is likely to suffer some spill-over effect from impeachment of the witness.

The amendment also protects other litigants from unfair impeachment of their witnesses. The danger of prejudice from the use of prior convictions is not confined to criminal defendants. Although the danger that prior convictions will be misused as character evidence is particularly acute when the defendant is impeached, the danger exists in other situations as well. The amendment reflects the view that it is desirable to protect all litigants from the unfair use of prior convictions, and that the ordinary balancing test of Rule 403, which provides that evidence shall not be excluded unless its prejudicial effect substantially outweighs its probative value, is appropriate for assessing the admissibility of prior convictions for impeachment of any witness other than a criminal defendant.

The amendment reflects a judgment that decisions interpreting Rule 609(a) as requiring a trial court to admit convictions in civil cases that have little, if anything, to do with credibility reach undesirable results. See, e.g., Diggs v. Lyons, 741 F.2d 577 (3d Cir.1984), cert. denied, 105 S.Ct. 2157 (1985). The amendment provides the same protection against unfair prejudice arising from prior convictions used for impeachment purposes as the rules provide for other evidence. The amendment finds support in decided cases. See, e.g., Petty v. Ideco, 761 F.2d 1146 (5th Cir.1985); Czaka v. Hickman, 703 F.2d 317 (8th Cir. 1983).

Fewer decided cases address the question whether Rule 609(a) provides any protection against unduly prejudicial prior convictions used to impeach government witnesses. Some courts have read Rule 609(a) as giving the government no protection for its witnesses. See, e.g., United States v. Thorne, 547 F.2d 56 (8th Cir.1976); United States v. Nevitt, 563 F.2d 406 (9th Cir.1977), cert. denied, 444 U.S. 847 (1979). This approach also is rejected by the amendment. There are cases in which impeachment of government witnesses with prior convictions that have little, if anything, to do with credibility may result in unfair prejudice to the government's interest in a fair trial and unnecessary embarrassment to a witness. Fed.R.Evid. 412 already recognizes this and excluded certain evidence of past sexual behavior in the context of prosecutions for sexual assaults.

The amendment applies the general balancing test of Rule 403 to protect all litigants against unfair impeachment of witnesses. The balancing test protects civil litigants, the government in criminal cases, and the defendant in a criminal case who calls other witnesses. The amendment addresses prior convictions offered under Rule 609, not for other purposes, and does not run afoul, therefore, of Davis v. Alaska, 415 U.S. 308 (1974). Davis involved the use of a prior juvenile adjudication not to prove a past law violation, but to prove bias. The defendant in a criminal case has the right to demonstrate the bias of a witness and to be assured a fair trial, but not to unduly prejudice a trier of fact. See generally Rule 412. In any case in which the trial court believes that confrontation rights require admission of impeachment evidence, obviously the Constitution would take precedence over the rule.

The probability that prior convictions of an ordinary government witness will be unduly prejudicial is low in most criminal cases. Since the behavior of the witness is not the issue in dispute in most cases, there is little chance that the trier of fact will misuse the convictions offered as impeachment evidence as propensity evidence. Thus, trial courts will be skeptical when the government objects to impeachment of its witnesses with prior convictions. Only when the government is able to point to a real danger of prejudice that is sufficient to outweigh substantially the probative value of the conviction for impeachment purposes will the conviction be excluded.

The amendment continues to divide subdivision (a) into subsections (1) and (2) thus facilitating retrieval under current computerized research programs which distinguish the two provisions. The Committee recommended no substantive change in subdivision (a)(2), even though some cases raise a concern about the proper interpretation of the words "dishonesty or false statement." These words were used but not explained in the original Advisory Committee Note accompanying Rule 609. Congress extensively debated the rule, and the Report of the House and Senate Conference Committee states that "[b]y the phrase 'dishonesty and false statement,' the Conference means crimes such as perjury, subornation of perjury, false statement, criminal fraud, embezzlement, or false pretense, or any other offense in the nature of *crimen falsi*, commission of which involves some element of deceit, untruthfulness, or falsification bearing on the accused's propensity to testify truthfully." The Advisory

Committee concluded that the Conference Report provides sufficient guidance to trial courts and that no amendment is necessary, notwithstanding some decisions that take an unduly broad view of "dishonesty," admitting convictions such as for bank robbery or bank larceny. Subsection (a)(2) continues to apply to any witness, including a criminal defendant.

Finally, the Committee determined that it was unnecessary to add to the rule language stating that, when a prior conviction is offered under Rule 609, the trial court is to consider the probative value of the prior conviction *for impeachment*, not for other purposes. The Committee concluded that the title of the rule, its first sentence, and its placement among the impeachment rules clearly establish that evidence offered under Rule 609 is offered only for purposes of impeachment.

Rule 610. Religious Beliefs or Opinions

Evidence of the beliefs or opinions of a witness on matters of religion is not admissible for the purpose of showing that by reason of their nature the witness' credibility is impaired or enhanced.

(As amended Mar. 2, 1987, eff. Oct. 1, 1987.)

Section references, McCormick 4th ed.

§ 46

Note by Federal Judicial Center

The rule enacted by the Congress is the rule prescribed by the Supreme Court without change.

Advisory Committee's Note

56 F.R.D. 183, 272

While the rule forecloses inquiry into the religious beliefs or opinions of a witness for the purpose of showing that his character for truthfulness is affected by their nature, an inquiry for the purpose of showing interest or bias because of them is not within the prohibition. Thus disclosure of affiliation with a church which is a party to the litigation would be allowable under the rule. Cf. Tucker v. Reil, 51 Ariz. 357, 77 P.2d 203 (1938). To the same effect, though less specifically worded, is California Evidence Code § 789. See 3 Wigmore § 936.

1987 Amendment. The amendment is technical. No substantive change is intended.

Rule 611. Mode and Order of Interrogation and Presentation

(a) **Control by court.** The court shall exercise reasonable control over the mode and order of interrogating witnesses and presenting evidence so as to (1) make the interrogation and presentation effective for the ascertainment of the truth, (2) avoid needless consumption of time, and (3) protect witnesses from harassment or undue embarrassment.

(b) **Scope of cross-examination.** Cross-examination should be limited to the subject matter of the direct examination and matters affecting the credibility of the witness. The court may, in the exercise of discretion, permit inquiry into additional matters as if on direct examination.

(c) Leading questions. Leading questions should not be used on the direct examination of a witness except as may be necessary to develop the witness' testimony. Ordinarily leading questions should be permitted on cross-examination. When a party calls a hostile witness, an adverse party, or a witness identified with an adverse party, interrogation may be by leading questions.

(As amended Mar. 2, 1987, eff. Oct. 1, 1987.)

Section references, McCormick 4th ed.

Generally § 4, § 5, § 16, § 25, § 36, § 56, § 57, § 60

(a). § 4, § 5, § 6, § 7, § 16, § 29, § 32, § 40, § 41, § 42, § 44, § 51, § 52, § 55, § 56, § 58

(b). § 20, § 21, § 22, § 23, § 24, § 25, § 26, § 27, § 29, § 33, § 40, § 134

(c). § 6, § 20, § 25, § 26

Note by Federal Judicial Center

Subdivision (a) of the rule enacted by the Congress is the subdivision prescribed by the Supreme Court, amended only by substituting "court" in place of "judge."

Subdivision (b) of the rule enacted by the Congress is substantially different from the subdivision prescribed by the Supreme Court. The nature of the changes and the reasons therefor are stated in the Report of the House Committee on the Judiciary, set forth below.

The first two sentences of subdivision (c) of the rule enacted by the Congress are the same as prescribed by the Supreme Court. The third sentence has been amended in the manner and for the reasons stated in the Report of the House Committee on the Judiciary, set forth below.

Advisory Committee's Note

56 F.R.D. 183, 273

Subdivision (a). Spelling out detailed rules to govern the mode and order of interrogating witnesses and presenting evidence is neither desirable nor feasible. The ultimate responsibility for the effective working of the adversary system rests with the judge. The rule sets forth the objectives which he should seek to attain.

Item (1) restates in broad terms the power and obligation of the judge as developed under common law principles. It covers such concerns as whether testimony shall be in the form of a free narrative or responses to specific questions, McCormick § 5, the order of calling witnesses and presenting evidence, 6 Wigmore § 1867, the use of demonstrative evidence, McCormick § 179, and the many other questions arising during the course of a trial which can be solved only by the judge's common sense and fairness in view of the particular circumstances.

Item (2) is addressed to avoidance of needless consumption of time, a matter of daily concern in the disposition of cases. A companion piece is found in the discretion vested in the judge to exclude evidence as a waste of time in Rule 403(b).

Item (3) calls for a judgment under the particular circumstances whether interrogation tactics entail harassment or undue embarrassment. Pertinent circumstances include the importance of the testimony, the nature of the inqury, its relevance to credibility, waste of time, and confusion. McCormick § 42. In Alford v. United States, 282 U.S. 687, 694, 51 S.Ct. 218, 75 L.Ed. 624 (1931), the Court pointed out that, while the trial judge should protect the witness from questions which "go beyond the bounds of proper cross-examination merely to harass, annoy or humiliate," this protection by no means forecloses efforts to discredit the witness. Reference to the transcript of the prosecutor's cross-examination in Berger v. United States, 295 U.S. 78, 55 S.Ct. 629, 79 L.Ed. 1314 (1935), serves to lay at rest any doubts as to the need for judicial control in this area.

The inquiry into specific instances of conduct of a witness allowed under Rule 608(b) is, of course, subject to this rule.

Subdivision (b) *. The tradition in the federal courts and in numerous state courts has been to limit the scope of cross-examination to matters testified to on direct, plus matters bearing upon the credibility of the witness. Various reasons have been advanced to justify the rule of limited cross-examination. (1) A party vouches for his own witness but only to the extent of matters elicited on direct. Resurrection Gold Mining Co. v. Fortune Gold Mining Co., 129 Fed. 668, 675 (8th Cir.1904), quoted in Maguire, Weinstein, et al., Cases on Evidence 277, n. 38 (5th ed. 1965). But the concept of vouching is discredited, and Rule 6–07[607] rejects it. (2) A party cannot ask his own witness leading questions. This is a problem properly solved in terms of what is necessary for a proper development of the testimony rather than by a mechanistic formula similar to the vouching concept. See discussion under subdivision (c). (3) A practice of limited cross-examination promotes orderly presentation of the case. Finch v. Weiner, 109 Conn. 616, 145 Atl. 31 (1929). In the opinion of the Advisory Committee this latter reason has merit. It is apparent, however, that the rule of limited cross-examination thus viewed becomes an aspect of the judge's general control over the mode and order of interrogating witnesses and presenting evidence, to be administered as such. The matter is not one in which involvement at the appellate level is likely to prove fruitful. See, for example, Moyer v. Aetna Life Ins. Co., 126 F.2d 141 (3rd Cir.1942); Butler v. New York Central R. Co., 253 F.2d 281 (7th Cir.1958); United States v. Johnson, 285 F.2d 35 (9th Cir.1960); Union Automobile Indemnity Ass'n v. Capitol Indemnity Ins. Co., 310 F.2d 318 (7th Cir.1962). In view of these considerations, the rule is phrased in terms of a suggestion rather than a mandate to the trial judge.

The qualification "as if on direct examination," applicable when inquiry into additional matters is allowed is designed to terminate at that point the asking of leading questions as a matter of right and to bring into operation subdivision (c) of the rule.

The rule does not purport to determine the extent to which an accused who elects to testify thereby waives his privilege against self-incrimination. The question is a constitutional one, rather than a mere matter of administering the

* The Advisory Committee's Note to sub-division (b) is from the 1969 Preliminary Draft. 46 F.R.D. 161, 304.—Federal Judicial Center.

trial. Under United States v. Simmons, 390 U.S. 377 (1968), no general waiver occurs when the accused testifies on such preliminary matters as the validity of a search and seizure or the admissibility of a confession. Rule 1–04(d) [104(d)], supra. When he testifies on the merits, however, can he foreclose inquiry into an aspect or element of the crime by avoiding it on direct? The affirmative answer given in Tucker v. United States, 5 F.2d 818 (8th Cir.1925), is inconsistent with the description of the waiver as extending to "all other relevant facts" in Johnson v. United States, 318 U.S. 189, 195 (1943). See also Brown v. United States, 356 U.S. 148 (1958). The situation of an accused who desires to testify on some but not all counts of a multiple-count indictment is one to be approached, in the first instance at least, as a problem of severance under Rule 14 of the Federal Rules of Criminal Procedure. Cross v. United States, 335 F.2d 987 (D.C.Cir.1964). Cf. United States v. Baker, 262 F.Supp. 657, 686 (D.D.C.1966). In all events, the extent of the waiver of the privilege against self-incrimination ought not to be determined as a by-product of a rule on scope of cross-examination.

Report of House Committee on the Judiciary

House Comm. on Judiciary, Fed.Rules of Evidence, H.R.Rep. No. 650, 93d Cong., 1st Sess., p. 12 (1973); 1974 U.S.Code Cong. & Ad.News 7075, 7085

As submitted by the Court, Rule 611(b) provided:

A witness may be cross-examined on any matter relevant to any issue in the case, including credibility. In the interests of justice, the judge may limit cross-examination with respect to matters not testified to on direct examination.

The Committee amended this provision to return to the rule which prevails in the federal courts and thirty-nine State jurisdictions. As amended, the Rule is in the text of the 1969 Advisory Committee draft. It limits cross-examination to credibility and to matters testified to on direct examination, unless the judge permits more, in which event the cross-examiner must proceed as if on direct examination. This traditional rule facilitates orderly presentation by each party at trial. Further, in light of existing discovery procedures, there appears to be no need to abandon the traditional rule.

Report of Senate Committee on the Judiciary

Senate Comm. on Judiciary, Fed.Rules of Evidence, S.Rep. No. 1277, 93d Cong., 2d Sess., p. 25 (1974); 1974 U.S.Code Cong. & Ad.News 7051, 7071

Rule 611(b) as submitted by the Supreme Court permitted a broad scope of cross-examination: "cross-examination on any matter relevant to any issue in the case" unless the judge, in the interests of justice, limited the scope of cross-examination.

The House narrowed the Rule to the more traditional practice of limiting cross-examination to the subject matter of direct examination (and credibility), but with discretion in the judge to permit inquiry into additional matters in situations where that would aid in the development of the evidence or otherwise facilitate the conduct of the trial.

The committee agrees with the House amendment. Although there are good arguments in support of broad cross-examination from perspectives of developing all relevant evidence, we believe the factors of insuring an orderly and predictable development of the evidence weigh in favor of the narrower rule, especially when discretion is given to the trial judge to permit inquiry into additional matters. The committee expressly approves this discretion and believes it will permit sufficient flexibility allowing a broader scope of cross-examination whenever appropriate.

The House amendment providing broader discretionary cross-examination permitted inquiry into additional matters only as if on direct examination. As a general rule, we concur with this limitation, however, we would understand that this limitation would not preclude the utilization of leading questions if the conditions of subsection (c) of this rule were met, bearing in mind the judge's discretion in any case to limit the scope of cross-examination.[1]

Further, the committee has received correspondence from Federal judges commenting on the applicability of this rule to section 1407 of title 28. It is the committee's judgment that this rule as reported by the House is flexible enough to provide sufficiently broad cross-examination in appropriate situations in multidistrict litigation.

Advisory Committee's Note

56 F.R.D. 183, 275

Subdivision (c). The rule continues the traditional view that the suggestive powers of the leading question are as a general proposition undesirable. Within this tradition, however, numerous exceptions have achieved recognition: The witness who is hostile, unwilling, or biased; the child witness or the adult with communication problems; the witness whose recollection is exhausted; and undisputed preliminary matters. 3 Wigmore §§ 774–778. An almost total unwillingness to reverse for infractions has been manifested by appellate courts. See cases cited in 3 Wigmore § 770. The matter clearly falls within the area of control by the judge over the mode and order of interrogation and presentation and accordingly is phrased in words of suggestion rather than command.

The rule also conforms to tradition in making the use of leading questions on cross-examination a matter of right. The purpose of the qualification "ordinarily" is to furnish a basis for denying the use of leading questions when the cross-examination is cross-examination in form only and not in fact, as for example the "cross-examination" of a party by his own counsel after being called by the opponent (savoring more of re-direct) or of an insured defendant who proves to be friendly to the plaintiff.

The final sentence deals with categories of witnesses automatically regarded and treated as hostile. Rule 43(b) of the Federal Rules of Civil Procedure has included only "an adverse party or an officer, director, or managing agent of a public or private corporation or of a partnership or association which is an adverse party." This limitation virtually to persons whose statements would stand as admissions is believed to be an unduly narrow concept of those who may safely be regarded as hostile without further demonstration. See, for example, Maryland Casualty Co. v. Kador, 225 F.2d 120 (5th Cir.1955), and

---

1. See McCormick on Evidence, §§ 24–26 (especially 24) (2d ed. 1972).

Degelos v. Fidelity and Casualty Co., 313 F.2d 809 (5th Cir.1963), holding despite the language of Rule 43(b) that an insured fell within it, though not a party in an action under the Louisiana direct action statute. The phrase of the rule, "witness identified with" an adverse party, is designed to enlarge the category of persons thus callable.

Report of House Committee on the Judiciary

House Comm. on Judiciary, Fed.Rules of Evidence, H.R.Rep. No. 650, 93d Cong., 1st Sess., p. 12 (1973); 1974 U.S.Code Cong. & Ad.News 7075, 7086

The third sentence of Rule 611(c) as submitted by the Court provided that:

In civil cases, a party is entitled to call an adverse party or witness identified with him and interrogate by leading questions.

The Committee amended this Rule to permit leading questions to be used with respect to any hostile witness, not only an adverse party or person identified with such adverse party. The Committee also substituted the word "When" for the phrase "In civil cases" to reflect the possibility that in criminal cases a defendant may be entitled to call witnesses identified with the government, in which event the Committee believed the defendant should be permitted to inquire with leading questions.

Report of Senate Committee on the Judiciary

Senate Comm. on Judiciary, Fed.Rules of Evidence, S.Rep. No. 1277, 93d Cong., 2d Sess., p. 25 (1974); 1974 U.S.Code Cong. & Ad.News 7051, 7072

As submitted by the Supreme Court, the rule provided: "In civil cases, a party is entitled to call an adverse party or witness identified with him and interrogate by leading questions."

The final sentence of subsection (c) was amended by the House for the purpose of clarifying the fact that a "hostile witness"—that is a witness who is hostile in fact—could be subject to interrogation by leading questions. The rule as submitted by the Supreme Court declared certain witnesses hostile as a matter of law and thus subject to interrogation by leading questions without any showing of hostility in fact. These were adverse parties or witnesses identified with adverse parties. However, the wording of the first sentence of subsection (c) while generally prohibiting the use of leading questions on direct examination, also provides "except as may be necessary to develop his testimony." Further, the first paragraph of the Advisory Committee note explaining the subsection makes clear that they intended that leading questions could be asked of a hostile witness or a witness who was unwilling or biased and even though that witness was not associated with an adverse party. Thus, we question whether the House amendment was necessary.

However, concluding that it was not intended to affect the meaning of the first sentence of the subsection and was intended solely to clarify the fact that leading questions are permissible in the interrogation of a witness, who is hostile in fact, the committee accepts that House amendment.

The final sentence of this subsection was also amended by the House to cover criminal as well as civil cases. The committee accepts this amendment, but notes that it may be difficult in criminal cases to determine when a witness is "identified with an adverse party," and thus the rule should be applied with caution.

1987 Amendment. The amendment is technical. No substantive change is intended.

Rule 612. Writing Used to Refresh Memory

Except as otherwise provided in criminal proceedings by section 3500 of title 18, United States Code, if a witness uses a writing to refresh memory for the purpose of testifying, either—

(1) while testifying, or

(2) before testifying, if the court in its discretion determines it is necessary in the interests of justice,

an adverse party is entitled to have the writing produced at the hearing, to inspect it, to cross-examine the witness thereon, and to introduce in evidence those portions which relate to the testimony of the witness. If it is claimed that the writing contains matters not related to the subject matter of the testimony the court shall examine the writing in camera, excise any portions not so related, and order delivery of the remainder to the party entitled thereto. Any portion withheld over objections shall be preserved and made available to the appellate court in the event of an appeal. If a writing is not produced or delivered pursuant to order under this rule, the court shall make any order justice requires, except that in criminal cases when the prosecution elects not to comply, the order shall be one striking the testimony or, if the court in its discretion determines that the interests of justice so require, declaring a mistrial.

(As amended Mar. 2, 1987, eff. Oct. 1, 1987.)

Section references, McCormick 4th ed.

§ 9, § 93, § 97

Note by Federal Judicial Center

The rule enacted by the Congress is the rule prescribed by the Supreme Court, amended by substituting "court" in place of "judge," with appropriate pronominal change, and in the first sentence, by substituting "the writing" in place of "it" before "produced," and by substituting the phrase "(1) while testifying, or (2) before testifying if the court in its discretion determines it is necessary in the interests of justice" in place of "before or while testifying." The reasons for the latter amendment are stated in the Report of the House Committee on the Judiciary, set forth below.

Advisory Committee's Note

56 F.R.D. 183, 277

The treatment of writings used to refresh recollection while on the stand is in accord with settled doctrine. McCormick § 9, p. 15. The bulk of the case law has, however, denied the existence of any right to access by the opponent when the writing is used prior to taking the stand, though the judge may have discretion in the matter. Goldman v. United States, 316 U.S. 129, 62 S.Ct. 993, 86 L.Ed. 1322 (1942); Needelman v. United States, 261 F.2d 802 (5th Cir.1958), cert. dismissed 362 U.S. 600, 80 S.Ct. 960, 4 L.Ed.2d 980, rehearing denied 363 U.S. 858, 80 S.Ct. 1606, 4 L.Ed.2d 1739, Annot., 82 A.L.R.2d 473, 562 and 7 A.L.R.3d 181, 247. An increasing group of cases has repudiated the distinction, People v. Scott, 29 Ill.2d 97, 193 N.E.2d 814 (1963); State v. Mucci, 25 N.J. 423, 136 A.2d 761 (1957); State v. Hunt, 25 N.J. 514, 138 A.2d 1 (1958); State v. Deslovers, 40 R.I. 89, 100 A. 64 (1917), and this position is believed to be correct. As Wigmore put it, "the risk of imposition and the need of safeguard is just as great" in both situations. 3 Wigmore § 762, p. 111. To the same effect is McCormick § 9, p. 17.

The purpose of the phrase "for the purpose of testifying" is to safeguard against using the rule as a pretext for wholesale exploration of an opposing party's files and to insure that access is limited only to those writings which may fairly be said in fact to have an impact upon the testimony of the witness.

The purpose of the rule is the same as that of the *Jencks* statute, 18 U.S.C. § 3500: to promote the search of credibility and memory. The same sensitivity to disclosure of government files may be involved; hence the rule is expressly made subject to the statute, subdivision (a) of which provides: "In any criminal prosecution brought by the United States, no statement or report in the possession of the United States which was made by a Government witness or prospective Government witness (other than the defendant) shall be the subject of subpena, discovery, or inspection until said witness has testified on direct examination in the trial of the case." Items falling within the purview of the statute are producible only as provided by its terms, Palermo v. United States, 360 U.S. 343, 351 (1959), and disclosure under the rule is limited similarly by the statutory conditions. With this limitation in mind, some differences of application may be noted. The *Jencks* statute applies only to statements of witnesses; the rule is not so limited. The statute applies only to criminal cases; the rule applies to all cases. The statute applies only to government witnesses; the rule applies to all witnesses. The statute contains no requirement that the statement be consulted for purposes of refreshment before or while testifying; the rule so requires. Since many writings would qualify under either statute or rule, a substantial overlap exists, but the identity of procedures makes this of no importance.

The consequences of nonproduction by the government in a criminal case are those of the *Jencks* statute, striking the testimony or in exceptional cases a mistrial. 18 U.S.C. § 3500(d). In other cases these alternatives are unduly limited, and such possibilities as contempt, dismissal, finding issues against the offender, and the like are available. See Rule 16(g) of the Federal Rules of Criminal Procedure and Rule 37(b) of the Federal Rules of Civil Procedure for appropriate sanctions.

Report of House Committee on the Judiciary

House Comm. on Judiciary, Fed.Rules of Evidence, H.R.Rep. No. 650, 93d Cong., 1st Sess., p. 13 (1973); 1974 U.S.Code Cong. & Ad.News 7075, 7086

As submitted to Congress, Rule 612 provided that except as set forth in 18 U.S.C. § 3500, if a witness uses a writing to refresh his memory for the purpose of testifying, "either before or while testifying," an adverse party is entitled to have the writing produced at the hearing, to inspect it, to cross-examine the witness on it, and to introduce in evidence those portions relating to the witness' testimony. The Committee amended the Rule so as still to require the production of writings used by a witness while testifying, but to render the production of writings used by a witness to refresh his memory before testifying discretionary with the court in the interests of justice, as is the case under existing federal law. See Goldman v. United States, 316 U.S. 129 (1942). The Committee considered that permitting an adverse party to require the production of writings used before testifying could result in fishing expeditions among a multitude of papers which a witness may have used in preparing for trial.

The Committee intends that nothing in the Rule be construed as barring the assertion of a privilege with respect to writings used by a witness to refresh his memory.

1987 Amendment. The amendment is technical. No substantive change is intended.

Rule 613. Prior Statements of Witnesses

(a) **Examining witness concerning prior statement.** In examining a witness concerning a prior statement made by the witness, whether written or not, the statement need not be shown nor its contents disclosed to the witness at that time, but on request the same shall be shown or disclosed to opposing counsel.

(b) **Extrinsic evidence of prior inconsistent statement of witness.** Extrinsic evidence of a prior inconsistent statement by a witness is not admissible unless the witness is afforded an opportunity to explain or deny the same and the opposite party is afforded an opportunity to interrogate the witness thereon, or the interests of justice otherwise require. This provision does not apply to admissions of a party-opponent as defined in rule 801(d)(2).

(As amended Mar. 2, 1987, eff. Oct. 1, 1987; Apr. 25, 1988, eff. Nov. 1, 1988.)

Section references, McCormick 4th ed.

Generally § 34, § 37, § 39

(a). § 28, § 37, § 39

(b). § 37

Note by Federal Judicial Center

The rule enacted by the Congress is the rule prescribed by the Supreme Court, amended only by substituting "nor" in the place of "or" in subdivision (a).

Advisory Committee's Note

56 F.R.D. 183, 278

Subdivision (a). The Queen's Case, 2 Br. & B. 284, 129 Eng.Rep. 976 (1820), laid down the requirement that a cross-examiner, prior to questioning the witness about his own prior statement in writing, must first show it to the witness. Abolished by statute in the country of its origin, the requirement nevertheless gained currency in the United States. The rule abolishes this useless impediment, to cross-examination. Ladd, Some Observations on Credibility: Impeachment of Witnesses, 52 Cornell L.Q. 239, 246–247 (1967); McCormick § 28; 4 Wigmore §§ 1259–1260. Both oral and written statements are included.

The provision for disclosure to counsel is designed to protect against unwarranted insinuations that a statement has been made when the fact is to the contrary.

The rule does not defeat the application of Rule 1002 relating to production of the original when the contents of a writing are sought to be proved. Nor does it defeat the application of Rule 26(b)(3) of the Rules of Civil Procedure, as revised, entitling a person on request to a copy of his own statement, though the operation of the latter may be suspended temporarily.

Subdivision (b). The familiar foundation requirement that an impeaching statement first be shown to the witness before it can be proved by extrinsic evidence is preserved but with some modifications. See Ladd, Some Observations on Credibility: Impeachment of Witnesses, 52 Cornell L.Q. 239, 247 (1967). The traditional insistence that the attention of the witness be directed to the statement on cross-examination is relaxed in favor of simply providing the witness an opportunity to explain and the opposite party an opportunity to examine on the statement, with no specification of any particular time or sequence. Under this procedure, several collusive witnesses can be examined before disclosure of a joint prior inconsistent statement. See Comment to California Evidence Code § 770. Also, dangers of oversight are reduced. See McCormick § 37, p. 68.

In order to allow for such eventualities as the witness becoming unavailable by the time the statement is discovered, a measure of discretion is conferred upon the judge. Similar provisions are found in California Evidence Code § 770 and New Jersey Evidence Rule 22(b).

Under principles of *expression unius* the rule does not apply to impeachment by evidence of prior inconsistent conduct. The use of inconsistent statements to impeach a hearsay declaration is treated in Rule 806.

1987 Amendment. The amendments are technical. No substantive change is intended.

1988 Amendment. The amendment is technical. No substantive change is intended.

Rule 614. Calling and Interrogation of Witnesses by Court

(a) Calling by court. The court may, on its own motion or at the suggestion of a party, call witnesses, and all parties are entitled to cross-examine witnesses thus called.

(b) Interrogation by court. The court may interrogate witnesses, whether called by itself or by a party.

(c) Objections. Objections to the calling of witnesses by the court or to interrogation by it may be made at the time or at the next available opportunity when the jury is not present.

Section references, McCormick 4th ed.

§ 8

Note by Federal Judicial Center

The rule enacted by the Congress is the rule prescribed by the Supreme Court, amended only by substituting "court" in place of "judge," with conforming pronominal changes.

Advisory Committee's Note

56 F.R.D. 183, 279

Subdivision (a). While exercised more frequently in criminal than in civil cases, the authority of the judge to call witnesses is well established. McCormick § 8, p. 14; Maguire, Weinstein, et al., Cases on Evidence 303–304 (5th ed. 1965); 9 Wigmore § 2484. One reason for the practice, the old rule against impeaching one's own witness, no longer exists by virtue of Rule 607, supra. Other reasons remain, however, to justify the continuation of the practice of calling court's witnesses. The right to cross-examine, with all it implies, is assured. The tendency of juries to associate a witness with the party calling him, regardless of technical aspects of vouching, is avoided. And the judge is not imprisoned within the case as made by the parties.

Subdivision (b). The authority of the judge to question witnesses is also well established. McCormick § 8, pp. 12–13; Maguire, Weinstein, et al., Cases on Evidence 737–739 (5th ed. 1965); 3 Wigmore § 784. The authority is, of course, abused when the judge abandons his proper role and assumes that of advocate, but the manner in which interrogation should be conducted and the proper extent of its exercise are not susceptible of formulation in a rule. The omission in no sense precludes courts of review from continuing to reverse for abuse.

Subdivision (c). The provision relating to objections is designed to relieve counsel of the embarrassment attendant upon objecting to questions by the judge in the presence of the jury, while at the same time assuring that objections are made in apt time to afford the opportunity to take possible corrective measures. Compare the "automatic" objection feature of Rule 605 when the judge is called as a witness.

Rule 615. Exclusion of Witnesses

At the request of a party the court shall order witnesses excluded so that they cannot hear the testimony of other witnesses and it may make the order of its own motion. This rule does not authorize exclusion of (1) a party who is a natural person, or (2) an officer or employee of a party which is not a natural person designated as its representative by its attorney, or (3) a person whose presence is shown by a party to be essential to the presentation of the party's cause.

(As amended Mar. 2, 1987, eff. Oct. 1, 1987; Apr. 25, 1988, eff. Nov. 1, 1988; Nov. 18, 1988, Pub.L. 100–690, Title VII, § 7075(a), 102 Stat. 4405.)

Section references, McCormick 4th ed.

§ 50

Note by Federal Judicial Center

The rule enacted by the Congress is the rule prescribed by the Supreme Court, amended only by substituting "court," in place of "judge," with conforming pronominal changes.

Advisory Committee's Note

56 F.R.D. 183, 280

The efficacy of excluding or sequestering witnesses has long been recognized as a means of discouraging and exposing fabrication, inaccuracy, and collusion. 6 Wigmore §§ 1837–1838. The authority of the judge is admitted, the only question being whether the matter is committed to his discretion or one of right. The rule takes the latter position. No time is specified for making the request.

Several categories of persons are excepted. (1) Exclusion of persons who are parties would raise serious problems of confrontation and due process. Under accepted practice they are not subject to exclusion. 6 Wigmore § 1841. (2) As the equivalent of the right of a natural-person party to be present, a party which is not a natural person is entitled to have a representative present. Most of the cases have involved allowing a police officer who has been in charge of an investigation to remain in court despite the fact that he will be a witness. United States v. Infanzon, 235 F.2d 318 (2d Cir.1956); Portomene v. United States, 221 F.2d 582 (5th Cir.1955); Powell v. United States, 208 F.2d 618 (6th Cir.1953); Jones v. United States, 252 F.Supp. 781 (W.D.Okl.1966). Designation of the representative by the attorney rather than by the client may at first glance appear to be an inversion of the attorney-client relationship, but it may be assumed that the attorney will follow the wishes of the client, and the solution is simple and workable. See California Evidence Code § 777. (3) The category contemplates such persons as an agent who handled the transaction being litigated or an expert needed to advise counsel in the management of the litigation. See 6 Wigmore § 1841, n. 4.

Report of Senate Committee on the Judiciary

Senate Comm. on Judiciary, Fed.Rules of Evidence, S.Rep. No. 1277, 93d Cong., 2d Sess., p. 26 (1974); 1974 U.S.Code Cong. & Ad.News 7051, 7072

Many district courts permit government counsel to have an investigative agent at counsel table throughout the trial although the agent is or may be a witness. The practice is permitted as an exception to the rule of exclusion and compares with the situation defense counsel finds himself in—he always has the client with him to consult during the trial. The investigative agent's presence may be extremely important to government counsel, especially when the case is complex or involves some specialized subject matter. The agent, too, having lived with the case for a long time, may be able to assist in meeting trial surprises where the best-prepared counsel would otherwise have difficulty. Yet, it would not seem the Government could often meet the burden under rule

615 of showing that the agent's presence is essential.   Furthermore, it could be dangerous to use the agent as a witness as early in the case as possible, so that he might then help counsel as a nonwitness, since the agent's testimony could be needed in rebuttal.   Using another, nonwitness agent from the same investigative agency would not generally meet government counsel's needs.

This problem is solved if it is clear that investigative agents are within the group specified under the second exception made in the rule, for "an officer or employee of a party which is not a natural person designated as its representative by its attorney."   It is our understanding that this was the intention of the House committee.   It is certainly this committee's construction of the rule.

1987 Amendment.   The amendment is technical.   No substantive change is intended.

1988 Amendment.   The amendment is technical.   No substantive change is intended.

ARTICLE VII.   OPINIONS AND EXPERT TESTIMONY

Rule
701.   Opinion Testimony by Lay Witnesses.
702.   Testimony by Experts.
703.   Bases of Opinion Testimony by Experts.
704.   Opinion on Ultimate Issue.
705.   Disclosure of Facts or Data Underlying Expert Opinion.
706.   Court Appointed Experts.
    (a) Appointment.
    (b) Compensation.
    (c) Disclosure of Appointment.
    (d) Parties' Experts of Own Selection.

Rule 701. Opinion Testimony by Lay Witnesses

If the witness is not testifying as an expert, the witness' testimony in the form of opinions or inferences is limited to those opinions or inferences which are (a) rationally based on the perception of the witness and (b) helpful to a clear understanding of the witness' testimony or the determination of a fact in issue.

(As amended Mar. 2, 1987, eff. Oct. 1, 1987.)

Section references, McCormick 4th ed.

§ 11, § 12, § 14, § 35, § 43, § 313

Note by Federal Judicial Center

The rule enacted by the Congress is the rule prescribed by the Supreme Court without change.

Advisory Committee's Note

56 F.R.D. 183, 281

The rule retains the traditional objective of putting the trier of fact in possession of an accurate reproduction of the event.

Limitation (a) is the familiar requirement of first-hand knowledge or observation.

Limitation (b) is phrased in terms of requiring testimony to be helpful in resolving issues. Witnesses often find difficulty in expressing themselves in language which is not that of an opinion or conclusion. While the courts have made concessions in certain recurring situations, necessity as a standard for permitting opinions and conclusions has proved too elusive and too unadaptable to particular situations for purposes of satisfactory judicial administration. McCormick § 11. Moreover, the practical impossibility of determining by rule what is a "fact," demonstrated by a century of litigation of the question of what is a fact for purposes of pleading under the Field Code, extends into evidence also. 7 Wigmore § 1919. The rule assumes that the natural characteristics of the adversary system will generally lead to an acceptable result, since the detailed account carries more conviction than the broad assertion, and a lawyer can be expected to display his witness to the best advantage. If he fails to do so, cross-examination and argument will point up the weakness. See Ladd, Expert Testimony, 5 Vand.L.Rev. 414, 415–417 (1952). If, despite these considerations, attempts are made to introduce meaningless assertions which amount to little more than choosing up sides, exclusion for lack of helpfulness is called for by the rule.

The language of the rule is substantially that of Uniform Rule 56(1). Similar provisions are California Evidence Code § 800; Kansas Code of Civil Procedure § 60–456(a); New Jersey Evidence Rule 56(1).

1987 Amendment. The amendments are technical. No substantive change is intended.

Rule 702. Testimony by Experts

If scientific, technical, or other specialized knowledge will assist the trier of fact to understand the evidence or to determine a fact in issue, a witness qualified as an expert by knowledge, skill, experience, training, or education, may testify thereto in the form of an opinion or otherwise.

Section references, McCormick 4th ed.

§ 12, § 13, § 14, § 202, § 203

Note by Federal Judicial Center

The rule enacted by the Congress is the rule prescribed by the Supreme Court without change.

Advisory Committee's Note

56 F.R.D. 183, 282

An intelligent evaluation of facts is often difficult or impossible without the application of some scientific, technical, or other specialized knowledge. The most common source of this knowledge is the expert witness, although there are other techniques for supplying it.

Most of the literature assumes that experts testify only in the form of opinions. The assumption is logically unfounded. The rule accordingly recognizes that an expert on the stand may give a dissertation or exposition of scientific or other principles relevant to the case, leaving the trier of fact to apply them to the facts. Since much of the criticism of expert testimony has centered upon the hypothetical question, it seems wise to recognize that opinions are not indispensable and to encourage the use of expert testimony in nonopinion form when counsel believes the trier can itself draw the requisite inference. The use of opinions is not abolished by the rule, however. It will continue to be permissible for the expert to take the further step of suggesting the inference which should be drawn from applying the specialized knowledge to the facts. See Rules 703 to 705.

Whether the situation is a proper one for the use of expert testimony is to be determined on the basis of assisting the trier. "There is no more certain test for determining when experts may be used than the common sense inquiry whether the untrained layman would be qualified to determine intelligently and to the best possible degree the particular issue without enlightenment from those having a specialized understanding of the subject involved in the dispute." Ladd, Expert Testimony, 5 Vand.L.Rev. 414, 418 (1952). When opinions are excluded, it is because they are unhelpful and therefore superfluous and a waste of time. 7 Wigmore § 1918.

The rule is broadly phrased. The fields of knowledge which may be drawn upon are not limited merely to the "scientific" and "technical" but extend to all "specialized" knowledge. Similarly, the expert is viewed, not in a narrow sense, but as a person qualified by "knowledge, skill, experience, training, or education." Thus within the scope of the rule are not only experts in the strictest sense of the word, e.g. physicians, physicists, and architects, but also the large group sometimes called "skilled" witnesses, such as bankers or landowners testifying to land values.

Rule 703. Bases of Opinion Testimony by Experts

The facts or data in the particular case upon which an expert bases an opinion or inference may be those perceived by or made known to the expert at or before the hearing. If of a type reasonably relied upon by experts in the particular field in forming opinions or inferences upon the subject, the facts or data need not be admissible in evidence.

(As amended Mar. 2, 1987, eff. Oct. 1, 1987.)

Section references, McCormick 4th ed.

§ 10, § 13, § 14, § 15, § 203, § 208, § 324.3

Note by Federal Judicial Center

The rule enacted by the Congress is the rule prescribed by the Supreme Court without change.

Advisory Committee's Note

56 F.R.D. 183, 283

Facts or data upon which expert opinions are based may, under the rule, be derived from three possible sources. The first is the firsthand observation of the witness, with opinions based thereon traditionally allowed. A treating physician affords an example. Rheingold, The Basis of Medical Testimony, 15 Vand.L.Rev. 473, 489 (1962). Whether he must first relate his observations is treated in Rule 705. The second source, presentation at the trial, also reflects existing practice. The technique may be the familiar hypothetical question or having the expert attend the trial and hear the testimony establishing the facts. Problems of determining what testimony the expert relied upon, when the latter technique is employed and the testimony is in conflict, may be resolved by resort to Rule 705. The third source contemplated by the rule consists of presentation of data to the expert outside of court and other than by his own perception. In this respect the rule is designed to broaden the basis for expert opinions beyond that current in many jurisdictions and to bring the judicial practice into line with the practice of the experts themselves when not in court. Thus a physician in his own practice bases his diagnosis on information from numerous sources and of considerable variety, including statements by patients and relatives, reports and opinions from nurses, technicians and other doctors, hospital records, and X rays. Most of them are admissible in evidence, but only with the expenditure of substantial time in producing and examining various authenticating witnesses. The physician makes life-and-death decisions in reliance upon them. His validation, expertly performed and subject to cross-examination, ought to suffice for judicial purposes. Rheingold, supra, at 531; McCormick § 15. A similar provision is California Evidence Code § 801(b).

The rule also offers a more satisfactory basis for ruling upon the admissibility of public opinion poll evidence. Attention is directed to the validity of the techniques employed rather than to relatively fruitless inquiries whether hearsay is involved. See Judge Feinberg's careful analysis in Zippo Mfg. Co. v. Rogers Imports, Inc., 216 F.Supp. 670 (S.D.N.Y.1963). See also Blum et al., The Art of Opinion Research: A Lawyer's Appraisal of an Emerging Service, 24 U.Chi.L.Rev. 1 (1956); Bonynge, Trademark Surveys and Techniques and Their Use in Litigation, 48 A.B.A.J. 329 (1962); Zeisel, The Uniqueness of Survey Evidence, 45 Cornell L.Q. 322 (1960); Annot., 76 A.L.R.2d 919.

If it be feared that enlargement of permissible data may tend to break down the rules of exclusion unduly, notice should be taken that the rule requires that the facts or data "be of a type reasonably relied upon by experts in the particular field." The language would not warrant admitting in evidence the opinion of an "accidentologist" as to the point of impact in an automobile collision based on statements of bystanders, since this requirement is not satisfied. See Comment, Cal.Law Rev.Comm'n, Recommendation Proposing an Evidence Code 148–150 (1965).

1987 Amendment. The amendment is technical. No substantive change is intended.

Rule 704. Opinion on Ultimate Issue

(a) Except as provided in subdivision (b), testimony in the form of an opinion or inference otherwise admissible is not objectionable because it embraces an ultimate issue to be decided by the trier of fact.

(b) No expert witness testifying with respect to the mental state or condition of a defendant in a criminal case may state an opinion or inference as to whether the defendant did or did not have the mental state or condition constituting an element of the crime charged or of a defense thereto. Such ultimate issues are matters for the trier of fact alone.

(As amended Pub.L. 98–473, Title II, § 406, Oct. 12, 1984, 98 Stat. 2067.)

Section references, McCormick 4th ed.

§ 12, § 14, § 206, § 313

Editorial Note

Subdivision (a) is the entire rule prescribed by the Supreme Court and enacted without change by the Congress when it enacted the Rules of Evidence in 1974, except for the addition of the matter preceding the comma, which was added by the Congress in 1984.

Subdivision (b) was added by the Congress in 1984 as a part of the Insanity Defense Reform Act of 1984. P.L. 98–473, Title II, ch. IV, § 406.

Advisory Committee's Note

56 F.R.D. 183, 284

Subdivision (a).

The basic approach to opinions, lay and expert, in these rules is to admit them when helpful to the trier of fact. In order to render this approach fully effective and to allay any doubt on the subject, the so-called "ultimate issue" rule is specifically abolished by the instant rule.

The older cases often contained strictures against allowing witnesses to express opinions upon ultimate issues, as a particular aspect of the rule against opinions. The rule was unduly restrictive, difficult of application, and generally served only to deprive the trier of fact of useful information. 7 Wigmore §§ 1920, 1921; McCormick § 12. The basis usually assigned for the rule, to prevent the witness from "usurping the province of the jury," is aptly characterized as "empty rhetoric." 7 Wigmore § 1920, p. 17. Efforts to meet the felt needs of particular situations led to odd verbal circumlocutions which were said not to violate the rule. Thus a witness could express his estimate of the criminal responsibility of an accused in terms of sanity or insanity, but not in terms of ability to tell right from wrong or other more modern standard. And in cases of medical causation, witnesses were sometimes required to couch their opinions in cautious phrases of "might or could," rather than "did," though the result was to deprive many opinions of the positiveness to which they were entitled, accompanied by the hazard of a ruling of insufficiency to support a verdict. In other instances the rule was simply disregarded, and, as concessions to need, opinions were allowed upon such matters as intoxication, speed, handwriting, and value, although more precise coincidence with an ultimate issue would scarcely be possible.

Many modern decisions illustrate the trend to abandon the rule completely. People v. Wilson, 25 Cal.2d 341, 153 P.2d 720 (1944), whether abortion necessary to save life of patient; Clifford-Jacobs Forging Co. v. Industrial Comm., 19 Ill.2d 236, 166 N.E.2d 582 (1960), medical causation; Dowling v. L.H. Shattuck, Inc., 91 N.H. 234, 17 A.2d 529 (1941), proper method of shoring ditch; Schweiger v. Solbeck, 191 Or. 454, 230 P.2d 195 (1951), cause of landslide. In each instance the opinion was allowed.

The abolition of the ultimate issue rule does not lower the bars so as to admit all opinions. Under Rules 701 and 702, opinions must be helpful to the trier of fact, and Rule 403 provides for exclusion of evidence which wastes time. These provisions afford ample assurances against the admission of opinions which would merely tell the jury what result to reach, somewhat in the manner of the oath-helpers of an earlier day. They also stand ready to exclude opinions phrased in terms of inadequately explored legal criteria. Thus the question, "Did T have capacity to make a will?" would be excluded, while the question, "Did T have sufficient mental capacity to know the nature and extent of his property and the natural objects of his bounty and to formulate a rational scheme of distribution?" would be allowed. McCormick § 12.

For similar provisions see Uniform Rule 56(4); California Evidence Code § 805; Kansas Code of Civil Procedure § 60–456(d); New Jersey Evidence Rule 56(3).

Report of House Committee on the Judiciary

H.R. Report 98–1030, 98th Cong., 2d Sess., p. 230; 1984 U.S.Code Cong. & Ad.News 232 (Legislative History)

Subdivision (b).

The purpose of this amendment is to eliminate the confusing spectacle of competing expert witnesses testifying to directly contradictory conclusions as to the ultimate legal issue to be found by the trier of fact. Under this proposal, expert psychiatric testimony would be limited to presenting and explaining their diagnosis, such as whether the defendant had a severe mental disease or defect and what the characteristics of such a disease or defect, if any, may have been. * * *

Rule 705. Disclosure of Facts or Data Underlying Expert Opinion

The expert may testify in terms of opinion or inference and give reasons therefor without prior disclosure of the underlying facts or data, unless the court requires otherwise. The expert may in any event be required to disclose the underlying facts or data on cross-examination.

(As amended Mar. 2, 1987, eff. Oct. 1, 1987.)

Section references, McCormick 4th ed.

§ 13, § 14, § 15, § 16, § 31, § 324.3

Note by Federal Judicial Center

The rule enacted by the Congress is the rule prescribed by the Supreme Court, amended only by substituting "court" in place of "judge."

Advisory Committee's Note

56 F.R.D. 183, 285

The hypothetical question has been the target of a great deal of criticism as encouraging partisan bias, affording an opportunity for summing up in the middle of the case, and as complex and time consuming. Ladd, Expert Testimony, 5 Vand.L.Rev. 414, 426–427 (1952). While the rule allows counsel to make disclosure of the underlying facts or data as a preliminary to the giving of an expert opinion, if he chooses, the instances in which he is required to do so are reduced. This is true whether the expert bases his opinion on data furnished him at secondhand or observed by him at firsthand.

The elimination of the requirement of preliminary disclosure at the trial of underlying facts or data has a long background of support. In 1937 the Commissioners on Uniform State Laws incorporated a provision to this effect in their Model Expert Testimony Act, which furnished the basis for Uniform Rules 57 and 58. Rule 4515, N.Y.CPLR (McKinney 1963), provides:

> "Unless the court orders otherwise, questions calling for the opinion of an expert witness need not be hypothetical in form, and the witness may state his opinion and reasons without first specifying the data upon which it is based. Upon cross-examination, he may be required to specify the data . . . ."

See also California Evidence Code § 802; Kansas Code of Civil Procedure §§ 60–456, 60–457; New Jersey Evidence Rules 57, 58.

If the objection is made that leaving it to the cross-examiner to bring out the supporting data is essentially unfair, the answer is that he is under no compulsion to bring out any facts or data except those unfavorable to the opinion. The answer assumes that the cross-examiner has the advance knowledge which is essential for effective cross-examination. This advance knowledge has been afforded, though imperfectly, by the traditional foundation requirement. Rule 26(b)(4) of the Rules of Civil Procedure, as revised, provides for substantial discovery in this area, obviating in large measure the obstacles which have been raised in some instances to discovery of findings, underlying data, and even the identity of the experts. Friedenthal, Discovery and Use of an Adverse Party's Expert Information, 14 Stan.L.Rev. 455 (1962).

These safeguards are reinforced by the discretionary power of the judge to require preliminary disclosure in any event.

1987 Amendment. The amendment is technical. No substantive change is intended.

Rule 706. Court Appointed Experts

(a) **Appointment.** The court may on its own motion or on the motion of any party enter an order to show cause why expert witnesses should not be appointed, and may request the parties to submit nominations. The court may appoint any expert witnesses agreed upon by the parties, and may appoint expert witnesses of its own selection. An expert witness shall not be appointed by the court unless the witness consents to act. A witness so appointed shall be informed of the witness' duties by the court in writing, a copy of which shall be filed with the clerk, or at a conference in which the parties shall have opportunity to participate. A witness so appointed shall advise the parties of the witness' findings, if any; the witness' deposition may be taken by any party; and the witness may be called to testify by the court or any party. The witness shall be subject to cross-examination by each party, including a party calling the witness.

(b) **Compensation.** Expert witnesses so appointed are entitled to reasonable compensation in whatever sum the court may allow. The compensation thus fixed is payable from funds which may be provided by law in criminal cases and civil actions and proceedings involving just compensation under the fifth amendment. In other civil actions and proceedings the compensation shall be paid by the parties in such proportion and at such time as the court directs, and thereafter charged in like manner as other costs.

(c) **Disclosure of appointment.** In the exercise of its discretion, the court may authorize disclosure to the jury of the fact that the court appointed the expert witness.

(d) **Parties' experts of own selection.** Nothing in this rule limits the parties in calling expert witnesses of their own selection.

(As amended Mar. 2, 1987, eff. Oct. 1, 1987.)

Section references, McCormick 4th ed.

§ 8, § 17

Note by Federal Judicial Center

The rule enacted by the Congress is the rule prescribed by the Supreme Court, amended by substituting "court" in place of "judge," with conforming pronominal changes, and, in subdivision (b), by substituting the phrase "and civil actions and proceedings" in place of "and cases" before "involving" in the second sentence.

Advisory Committee's Note

56 F.R.D. 183, 286

The practice of shopping for experts, the venality of some experts, and the reluctance of many reputable experts to involve themselves in litigation, have been matters of deep concern. Though the contention is made that court appointed experts acquire an aura of infallibility to which they are not entitled,

Levy, Impartial Medical Testimony—Revisited, 34 Temple L.Q. 416 (1961), the trend is increasingly to provide for their use. While experience indicates that actual appointment is a relatively infrequent occurrence, the assumption may be made that the availability of the procedure in itself decreases the need for resorting to it. The ever-present possibility that the judge *may* appoint an expert in a given case must inevitably exert a sobering effect on the expert witness of a party and upon the person utilizing his services.

The inherent power of a trial judge to appoint an expert of his own choosing is virtually unquestioned. Scott v. Spanjer Bros., Inc., 298 F.2d 928 (2d Cir.1962); Danville Tobacco Assn. v. Bryant-Buckner Associates, Inc., 333 F.2d 202 (4th Cir.1964); Sink, The Unused Power of a Federal Judge to Call His Own Expert Witnesses, 29 S.Cal.L.Rev. 195 (1956); 2 Wigmore § 563, 9 id. § 2484; Annot., 95 A.L.R.2d 383. Hence the problem becomes largely one of detail.

The New York plan is well known and is described in Report by Special Committee of the Association of the Bar of the City of New York: Impartial Medical Testimony (1956). On recommendation of the Section of Judicial Administration, local adoption of an impartial medical plan was endorsed by the American Bar Association. 82 A.B.A.Rep. 184–185 (1957). Descriptions and analyses of plans in effect in various parts of the country are found in Van Dusen, A United States District Judge's View of the Impartial Medical Expert System, 32 F.R.D. 498 (1963); Wick and Kightlinger, Impartial Medical Testimony Under the Federal Civil Rules: A Tale of Three Doctors, 34 Ins. Counsel J. 115 (1967); and numerous articles collected in Klein, Judicial Administration and the Legal Profession 393 (1963). Statutes and rules include California Evidence Code §§ 730–733; Illinois Supreme Court Rule 215(d), Ill.Rev.Stat. 1969, c. 110A, § 215(d); Burns Indiana Stats.1956, § 9–1702; Wisconsin Stats. Annot.1958, § 957.27.

In the federal practice, a comprehensive scheme for court appointed experts was initiated with the adoption of Rule 28 of the Federal Rules of Criminal Procedure in 1946. The Judicial Conference of the United States in 1953 considered court appointed experts in civil cases, but only with respect to whether they should be compensated from public funds, a proposal which was rejected. Report of the Judicial Conference of the United States 23 (1953). The present rule expands the practice to include civil cases.

Subdivision (a) is based on Rule 28 of the Federal Rules of Criminal Procedure, with a few changes, mainly in the interest of clarity. Language has been added to provide specifically for the appointment either on motion of a party or on the judge's own motion. A provision subjecting the court appointed expert to deposition procedures has been incorporated. The rule has been revised to make definite the right of any party, including the party calling him, to cross-examine.

Subdivision (b) combines the present provision for compensation in criminal cases with what seems to be a fair and feasible handling of civil cases, originally found in the Model Act and carried from there into Uniform Rule 60. See also California Evidence Code §§ 730–731. The special provision for Fifth Amendment compensation cases is designed to guard against reducing constitutionally guaranteed just compensation by requiring the recipient to pay costs. See Rule 71A(*l*) of the Rules of Civil Procedure.

Subdivision (c) seems to be essential if the use of court appointed experts is to be fully effective. Uniform Rule 61 so provides.

Subdivision (d) is in essence the last sentence of Rule 28(a) of the Federal Rules of Criminal Procedure.

1987 Amendment. The amendments are technical. No substantive change is intended.

ARTICLE VIII. HEARSAY

Advisory Committee's Note

INTRODUCTORY NOTE: THE HEARSAY PROBLEM

The factors to be considered in evaluating the testimony of a witness are perception, memory, and narration. Morgan, Hearsay Dangers and the Application of the Hearsay Concept, 62 Harv.L.Rev. 177 (1948), Selected Writings on Evidence and Trial 764, 765 (Fryer ed. 1957); Shientag, Cross-Examination—A Judge's Viewpoint, 3 Record 12 (1948); Strahorn, A Reconsideration of the Hearsay Rule and Admissions, 85 U.Pa.L.Rev. 484, 485 (1937), Selected Writings, supra, 756, 757; Weinstein, Probative Force of Hearsay, 46 Iowa L.Rev. 331 (1961). Sometimes a fourth is added, sincerity, but in fact it seems merely to be an aspect of the three already mentioned.

In order to encourage the witness to do his best with respect to each of these factors, and to expose any inaccuracies which may enter in, the Anglo-American tradition has evolved three conditions under which witnesses will ideally be required to testify: (1) under oath, (2) in the personal presence of the trier of fact, (3) subject to cross-examination.

(1) Standard procedure calls for the swearing of witnesses. While the practice is perhaps less effective than in an earlier time, no disposition to relax the requirement is apparent, other than to allow affirmation by persons with scruples against taking oaths.

(2) The demeanor of the witness traditionally has been believed to furnish trier and opponent with valuable clues. Universal Camera Corp. v. N.L.R.B., 340 U.S. 474, 495–496, 71 S.Ct. 456, 95 L.Ed. 456 (1951); Sahm, Demeanor Evidence: Elusive and Intangible Imponderables, 47 A.B.A.J. 580 (1961), quoting numerous authorities. The witness himself will probably be impressed with the solemnity of the occasion and the possibility of public disgrace. Willingness to falsify may reasonably become more difficult in the presence of the person against whom directed. Rules 26 and 43(a) of the Federal Rules of Criminal and Civil Procedure, respectively, include the general requirement that testimony be taken orally in open court. The Sixth Amendment right of confrontation is a manifestation of these beliefs and attitudes.

(3) Emphasis on the basis of the hearsay rule today tends to center upon the condition of cross-examination. All may not agree with Wigmore that cross-examination is "beyond doubt the greatest legal engine ever invented for the discovery of truth," but all will agree with his statement that it has become a "vital feature" of the Anglo-American system. 5 Wigmore, § 1367, p. 29. The belief, or perhaps hope, that cross-examination, is effective in exposing imperfections of perception, memory, and narration is fundamental. Morgan, Foreword to Model Code of Evidence 37 (1942).

The logic of the preceding discussion might suggest that no testimony be received unless in full compliance with the three ideal conditions. No one advocates this position. Common sense tells that much evidence which is not given under the three conditions may be inherently superior to much that is. Moreover, when the choice is between evidence which is less than best and no evidence at all, only clear folly would dictate an across-the-board policy of doing without. The problem thus resolves itself into effecting a sensible accommodation between these considerations and the desirability of giving testimony under the ideal conditions.

The solution evolved by the common law has been a general rule excluding hearsay but subject to numerous exceptions under circumstances supposed to furnish guarantees of trustworthiness. Criticisms of this scheme are that it is bulky and complex, fails to screen good from bad hearsay realistically, and inhibits the growth of the law of evidence.

Since no one advocates excluding all hearsay, three possible solutions may be considered: (1) abolish the rule against hearsay and admit all hearsay; (2) admit hearsay possessing sufficient probative force, but with procedural safeguards; (3) revise the present system of class exceptions.

(1) Abolition of the hearsay rule would be the simplest solution. The effect would not be automatically to abolish the giving of testimony under ideal conditions. If the declarant were available, compliance with the ideal conditions would be optional with either party. Thus the proponent could call the declarant as a witness as a form of presentation more impressive than his hearsay statement. Or the opponent could call the declarant to be cross-examined upon his statement. This is the tenor of Uniform Rule 63(1), admitting the hearsay declaration of a person "who is present at the hearing and available for cross-examination." Compare the treatment of declarations of available declarants in Rule 801(d)(1) of the instant rules. If the declarant were unavailable, a rule of free admissibility would make no distinctions in terms of degrees of noncompliance with the ideal conditions and would exact no quid pro quo in the form of assurances of trustworthiness. Rule 503 of the Model Code did exactly that, providing for the admissibility of any hearsay declaration by an unavailable declarant, finding support in the Massachusetts act of 1898, enacted at the instance of Thayer, Mass.Gen.L.1932, c. 233 § 65, and in the English act of 1938, St.1938, c. 28, Evidence. Both are limited to civil cases. The draftsmen of the Uniform Rules chose a less advanced and more conventional position. Comment, Uniform Rule 63. The present Advisory Committee has been unconvinced of the wisdom of abandoning the traditional requirement of some particular assurance of credibility as a condition precedent to admitting the hearsay declaration of an unavailable declarant.

In criminal cases, the Sixth Amendment requirement of confrontation would no doubt move into a large part of the area presently occupied by the hearsay rule in the event of the abolition of the latter. The resultant split between civil and criminal evidence is regarded as an undesirable development.

(2) Abandonment of the system of class exceptions in favor of individual treatment in the setting of the particular case, accompanied by procedural safeguards, has been impressively advocated. Weinstein, The Probative Force of Hearsay, 46 Iowa L.Rev. 331 (1961). Admissibility would be determined by weighing the probative force of the evidence against the possibility of prejudice, waste of time, and the availability of more satisfactory evidence. The bases of the traditional hearsay exceptions would be helpful in assessing probative force. Ladd, The Relationship of the Principles of Exclusionary Rules of Evidence to the Problem of Proof, 18 Minn.L.Rev. 506 (1934). Procedural safeguards would consist of notice of intention to use hearsay, free comment by the judge on the weight of the evidence, and a greater measure of authority in both trial and appellate judges to deal with evidence on the basis of weight. The Advisory Committee has rejected this approach to hearsay as involving too great a measure of judicial discretion, minimizing the predictability of rulings, enhancing the difficulties of preparation for trial, adding a further element to the already over-complicated congeries of pretrial procedures, and requiring sub-

stantially different rules for civil and criminal cases. The only way in which the probative force of hearsay differs from the probative force of other testimony is in the absence of oath, demeanor, and cross-examination as aids in determining credibility. For a judge to exclude evidence because he does not believe it has been described as "altogether atypical, extraordinary. . . ." Chadbourn, Bentham and the Hearsay Rule—A Benthamic View of Rule 63(4)(c) of the Uniform Rules of Evidence, 75 Harv.L.Rev. 932, 947 (1962).

(3) The approach to hearsay in these rules is that of the common law, i.e., a general rule excluding hearsay, with exceptions under which evidence is not required to be excluded even though hearsay. The traditional hearsay exceptions are drawn upon for the exceptions, collected under two rules, one dealing with situations where availability of the declarant is regarded as immaterial and the other with those where unavailability is made a condition to the admission of the hearsay statement. Each of the two rules concludes with a provision for hearsay statements not within one of the specified exceptions "but having comparable [equivalent] circumstantial guarantees of trustworthiness." Rules 803(24) and 804(b)(6)[5]. This plan is submitted as calculated to encourage growth and development in this area of the law, while conserving the values and experience of the past as a guide to the future.

CONFRONTATION AND DUE PROCESS

Until very recently, decisions invoking the confrontation clause of the Sixth Amendment were surprisingly few, a fact probably explainable by the former inapplicability of the clause to the states and by the hearsay rule's occupancy of much the same ground. The pattern which emerges from the earlier cases invoking the clause is substantially that of the hearsay rule, applied to criminal cases: an accused is entitled to have the witnesses against him testify under oath, in the presence of himself and trier, subject to cross-examination; yet considerations of public policy and necessity require the recognition of such exceptions as dying declarations and former testimony of unavailable witnesses. Mattox v. United States, 156 U.S. 237, 15 S.Ct. 337, 39 L.Ed. 409 (1895); Motes v. United States, 178 U.S. 458, 20 S.Ct. 993, 44 L.Ed. 1150 (1900); Delaney v. United States, 263 U.S. 586, 44 S.Ct. 206, 68 L.Ed. 462 (1924). Beginning with Snyder v. Massachusetts, 291 U.S. 97, 54 S.Ct. 330, 78 L.Ed. 674 (1934), the Court began to speak of confrontation as an aspect of procedural due process, thus extending its applicability to state cases and to federal cases other than criminal. The language of *Snyder* was that of an elastic concept of hearsay. The deportation case of Bridges v. Wixon, 326 U.S. 135, 65 S.Ct. 1443, 89 L.Ed. 2103 (1945), may be read broadly as imposing a strictly construed right of confrontation in all kinds of cases or narrowly as the product of a failure of the Immigration and Naturalization Service to follow its own rules. In re Oliver, 333 U.S. 257, 68 S.Ct. 499, 92 L.Ed. 682 (1948), ruled that cross-examination was essential to due process in a state contempt proceeding, but in United States v. Nugent, 346 U.S. 1, 73 S.Ct. 991, 97 L.Ed. 1417 (1953), the court held that it was not an essential aspect of a "hearing" for a conscientious objector under the Selective Service Act. Stein v. New York, 346 U.S. 156, 196, 73 S.Ct. 1077, 97 L.Ed. 1522 (1953), disclaimed any purpose to read the hearsay rule into the Fourteenth Amendment, but in Greene v. McElroy, 360 U.S. 474, 79 S.Ct. 1400, 3 L.Ed.2d 1377 (1959), revocation of security clearance without confrontation and cross-examination was held unauthorized, and a similar result was reached in Willner v. Committee on Character, 373 U.S. 96, 83 S.Ct. 1175, 10 L.Ed.2d 224 (1963). Ascertaining the constitutional dimensions of the confrontation-hearsay aggregate against the background of these cases is a matter of some difficulty, yet the general pattern is at least not inconsistent with that of the hearsay rule.

In 1965 the confrontation clause was held applicable to the states. Pointer v. Texas, 380 U.S. 400, 85 S.Ct. 1065, 13 L.Ed.2d 923 (1965). Prosecution use of former testimony given at a preliminary hearing where petitioner was not represented by counsel was a violation of the clause. The same result would have followed under conventional hearsay doctrine read in the light of a constitutional right to counsel, and nothing in the opinion suggests any difference in essential outline between the hearsay rule and the right of confrontation. In the companion case of Douglas v. Alabama, 380 U.S. 415, 85 S.Ct. 1074, 13 L.Ed.2d 934 (1965), however, the result reached by applying the confrontation clause is one reached less readily via the hearsay rule. A confession implicating petitioner was put before the jury by reading it to the witness in portions and asking if he made that statement. The witness refused to answer on grounds of self-incrimination. The result, said the Court, was to deny cross-examination, and hence confrontation. True, it could broadly be said that the confession was a hearsay statement which for all practical purposes was put in evidence. Yet a more easily accepted explanation of the opinion is that its real thrust was in the direction of curbing undesirable prosecutorial behavior, rather than merely applying rules of exclusion, and that the confrontation clause was the means selected to achieve this end. Comparable facts and a like result appeared in Brookhart v. Janis, 384 U.S. 1, 86 S.Ct. 1245, 16 L.Ed.2d 314 (1966).

The pattern suggested in *Douglas* was developed further and more distinctly in a pair of cases at the end of the 1966 term. United States v. Wade, 388 U.S. 218, 87 S.Ct. 1926, 18 L.Ed.2d 1149 (1967), and Gilbert v. California, 388 U.S. 263, 87 S.Ct. 1951, 18 L.Ed.2d 1178 (1967), hinged upon practices followed in identifying accused persons before trial. This pretrial identification was said to be so decisive an aspect of the case that accused was entitled to have counsel present; a pretrial identification made in the absence of counsel was not itself receivable in evidence and, in addition, might fatally infect a courtroom identification. The presence of counsel at the earlier identification was described as a necessary prerequisite for "a meaningful confrontation at trial." United States v. Wade, supra, 388 U.S. at p. 236, 87 S.Ct. at p. 1937. *Wade* involved no evidence of the fact of a prior identification and hence was not susceptible of being decided on hearsay grounds. In *Gilbert*, witnesses did testify to an earlier identification, readily classifiable as hearsay under a fairly strict view of what constitutes hearsay. The Court, however, carefully avoided basing the decision on the hearsay ground, choosing confrontation instead. 388 U.S. 263, 272, n. 3, 87 S.Ct. 1951. See also Parker v. Gladden, 385 U.S. 363, 87 S.Ct. 468, 17 L.Ed.2d 420 (1966), holding that the right of confrontation was violated when the baliff made prejudicial statements to jurors, and Note, 75 Yale L.J. 1434 (1966).

Under the earlier cases, the confrontation clause may have been little more than a constitutional embodiment of the hearsay rule, even including traditional exceptions but with some room for expanding them along similar lines. But under the recent cases the impact of the clause clearly extends beyond the confines of the hearsay rule. These considerations have led the Advisory Committee to conclude that a hearsay rule can function usefully as an adjunct to the confrontation right in constitutional areas and independently in nonconstitutional areas. In recognition of the separateness of the confrontation clause and the hearsay rule, and to avoid inviting collisions between them or between the hearsay rule and other exclusionary principles, the exceptions set forth in Rules 803 and 804 are stated in terms of exemption from the general exclusionary mandate of the hearsay rule, rather than in positive terms of admissibility. See Uniform Rule 63(1) to (31) and California Evidence Code §§ 1200–1340.

Rule 801. Definitions

The following definitions apply under this article:

(a) Statement. A "statement" is (1) an oral or written assertion or (2) nonverbal conduct of a person, if it is intended by the person as an assertion.

(b) Declarant. A "declarant" is a person who makes a statement.

(c) Hearsay. "Hearsay" is a statement, other than one made by the declarant while testifying at the trial or hearing, offered in evidence to prove the truth of the matter asserted.

(d) Statements which are not hearsay. A statement is not hearsay if—

(1) Prior statement by witness. The declarant testifies at the trial or hearing and is subject to cross-examination concerning the statement, and the statement is (A) inconsistent with the declarant's testimony, and was given under oath subject to the penalty of perjury at a trial, hearing, or other proceeding, or in a deposition, or (B) consistent with the declarant's testimony and is offered to rebut an express or implied charge against the declarant of recent fabrication or improper influence or motive, or (C) one of identification of a person made after perceiving the person; or

(2) Admission by party-opponent. The statement is offered against a party and is (A) the party's own statement, in either an individual or a representative capacity or (B) a statement of which the party has manifested an adoption or belief in its truth, or (C) a statement by a person authorized by the party to make a statement concerning the subject, or (D) a statement by the party's agent or servant concerning a matter within the scope of the agency or employment, made during the existence of the relationship, or (E) a statement by a coconspirator of a party during the course and in furtherance of the conspiracy.

(As amended Pub.L. 94–113, § 1, Oct. 16, 1975, 89 Stat. 576; Mar. 2, 1987, eff. Oct. 1, 1987.)

Section references, McCormick 4th ed.

General. § 246

(a). § 250

(c). § 245

(d)(1). § 34, § 36, § 37, § 36, § 251, § 324.1, § 326

    (A). § 50, § 324.3

    (B). § 47, § 324.3

    (C). § 251

(d)(2). § 35, § 144, § 160, § 254, § 255, § 256

    (A). § 251, § 263, § 264, § 265

    (B). § 251, § 259, § 261, § 262

    (C). § 251, § 259

    (D). § 255, § 259

    (E). § 53, § 259

Note by Federal Judicial Center

The rule enacted by the Congress is the rule prescribed by the Supreme Court, with [an] amendment[s] to subdivision (d)(1). The amendment[s] inserted in item (A), after "testimony," [adds] the phrase "and was given under oath subject to the penalty of perjury at a trial, hearing, or other proceeding, or in a deposition." The reasons for [the] amendment[s] are stated in the Report of the House Committee on the Judiciary, the Report of the Senate Committee on the Judiciary, and the Conference Report, set forth below.

Advisory Committee's Note

56 F.R.D. 183, 293

Subdivision (a). The definition of "statement" assumes importance because the term is used in the definition of hearsay in subdivision (c). The effect of the definition of "statement" is to exclude from the operation of the hearsay rule all evidence of conduct, verbal or nonverbal, not intended as an assertion. The key to the definition is that nothing is an assertion unless intended to be one.

It can scarcely be doubted that an assertion made in words is intended by the declarant to be an assertion. Hence verbal assertions readily fall into the category of "statement." Whether nonverbal conduct should be regarded as a statement for purposes of defining hearsay requires further consideration. Some nonverbal conduct, such as the act of pointing to identify a suspect in a lineup, is clearly the equivalent of words, assertive in nature, and to be regarded as a statement. Other nonverbal conduct, however, may be offered as evidence that the person acted as he did because of his belief in the existence of the condition sought to be proved, from which belief the existence of the condition may be inferred. This sequence is, arguably, in effect an assertion of the existence of the condition and hence properly includable within the hearsay concept. See Morgan, Hearsay Dangers and the Application of the Hearsay Concept, 62 Harv.L.Rev. 177, 214, 217 (1948), and the elaboration in Finman, Implied Assertions as Hearsay: Some Criticisms of the Uniform Rules of

Evidence, 14 Stan.L.Rev. 682 (1962). Admittedly evidence of this character is untested with respect to the perception, memory, and narration (or their equivalents) of the actor, but the Advisory Committee is of the view that these dangers are minimal in the absence of an intent to assert and do not justify the loss of the evidence on hearsay grounds. No class of evidence is free of the possibility of fabrication, but the likelihood is less with nonverbal than with assertive verbal conduct. The situations giving rise to the nonverbal conduct are such as virtually to eliminate questions of sincerity. Motivation, the nature of the conduct, and the presence or absence of reliance will bear heavily upon the weight to be given the evidence. Falknor, The "Hear-Say" Rule as a "See-Do" Rule: Evidence of Conduct, 33 Rocky Mt.L.Rev. 133 (1961). Similar considerations govern nonassertive verbal conduct and verbal conduct which is assertive but offered as a basis for inferring something other than the matter asserted, also excluded from the definition of hearsay by the language of subdivision (c).

When evidence of conduct is offered on the theory that it is not a statement, and hence not hearsay, a preliminary determination will be required to determine whether an assertion is intended. The rule is so worded as to place the burden upon the party claiming that the intention existed; ambiguous and doubtful cases will be resolved against him and in favor of admissibility. The determination involves no greater difficulty than many other preliminary questions of fact. Maguire, The Hearsay System: Around and Through the Thicket, 14 Vand.L.Rev. 741, 765–767 (1961).

For similar approaches, see Uniform Rule 62(1); California Evidence Code §§ 225, 1200; Kansas Code of Civil Procedure § 60–459(a); New Jersey Evidence Rule 62(1).

Subdivision (c). The definition follows along familiar lines in including only statements offered to prove the truth of the matter asserted. McCormick § 225; 5 Wigmore § 1361, 6 id. § 1766. If the significance of an offered statement lies solely in the fact that it was made, no issue is raised as to the truth of anything asserted, and the statement is not hearsay. Emich Motors Corp. v. General Motors Corp., 181 F.2d 70 (7th Cir.1950), rev'd on other grounds 340 U.S. 558, 71 S.Ct. 408, 95 L.Ed. 534, letters of complaint from customers offered as a reason for cancellation of dealer's franchise, to rebut contention that franchise was revoked for refusal to finance sales through affiliated finance company. The effect is to exclude from hearsay the entire category of "verbal acts" and "verbal parts of an act," in which the statement itself affects the legal rights of the parties or is a circumstance bearing on conduct affecting their rights.

The definition of hearsay must, of course, be read with reference to the definition of statement set forth in subdivision (a).

Testimony given by a witness in the course of court proceedings is excluded since there is compliance with all the ideal conditions for testifying.

Subdivision (d). Several types of statements which would otherwise literally fall within the definition are expressly excluded from it:

(1) *Prior statement by witness.* Considerable controversy has attended the question whether a prior out-of-court statement by a person now available for cross-examination concerning it, under oath and in the presence of the trier of fact, should be classed as hearsay. If the witness admits on the stand that he made the statement and that it was true, he adopts the statement and there is no hearsay problem. The hearsay problem arises when the witness on the

stand denies having made the statement or admits having made it but denies its truth. The argument in favor of treating these latter statements as hearsay is based upon the ground that the conditions of oath, cross-examination, and demeanor observation did not prevail at the time the statement was made and cannot adequately be supplied by the later examination. The logic of the situation is troublesome. So far as concerns the oath, its mere presence has never been regarded as sufficient to remove a statement from the hearsay category, and it receives much less emphasis than cross-examination as a truth-compelling device. While strong expressions are found to the effect that no conviction can be had or important right taken away on the basis of statements not made under fear of prosecution for perjury, Bridges v. Wixon, 326 U.S. 135, 65 S.Ct. 1443, 89 L.Ed. 2103 (1945), the fact is that, of the many common law exceptions to the hearsay rule, only that for reported testimony has required the statement to have been made under oath. [It should be noted, however, that rule 801(d)(1)(A), as enacted by the Congress, requires that a prior inconsistent statement have been made under oath.] Nor is it satisfactorily explained why cross-examination cannot be conducted subsequently with success. The decisions contending most vigorously for its inadequacy in fact demonstrate quite thorough exploration of the weaknesses and doubts attending the earlier statement. State v. Saporen, 205 Minn. 358, 285 N.W. 898 (1939); Ruhala v. Roby, 379 Mich. 102, 150 N.W.2d 146 (1967); People v. Johnson, 68 Cal.2d 646, 68 Cal.Rptr. 599, 441 P.2d 111 (1968). In respect to demeanor, as Judge Learned Hand observed in Di Carlo v. United States, 6 F.2d 364 (2d Cir.1925), when the jury decides that the truth is not what the witness says now, but what he said before, they are still deciding from what they see and hear in court. The bulk of the case law nevertheless has been against allowing prior statements of witnesses to be used generally as substantive evidence. Most of the writers and Uniform Rule 63(1) have taken the opposite position.

The position taken by the Advisory Committee in formulating this part of the rule is founded upon an unwillingness to countenance the general use of prior prepared statements as substantive evidence, but with a recognition that particular circumstances call for a contrary result. The judgment is one more of experience than of logic. The rule requires in each instance, as a general safeguard, that the declarant actually testify as a witness, and it then enumerates three situations in which the statement is excepted from the category of hearsay. Compare Uniform Rule 63(1) which allows any out-of-court statement of a declarant who is present at the trial and available for cross-examination.

(A) Prior inconsistent statements traditionally have been admissible to impeach but not as substantive evidence. Under the rule they are substantive evidence. As has been said by the California Law Revision Commission with respect to a similar provision:

"Section 1235 admits inconsistent statements of witnesses because the dangers against which the hearsay rule is designed to protect are largely nonexistent. The declarant is in court and may be examined and cross-examined in regard to his statements and their subject matter. In many cases, the inconsistent statement is more likely to be true than the testimony of the witness at the trial because it was made nearer in time to the matter to which it relates and is less likely to be influenced by the controversy that gave rise to the litigation. The trier of fact has the declarant before it and can observe his demeanor and the nature of his testimony as he denies or tries to explain away the inconsistency. Hence, it is in as good a position to determine the truth or falsity of the prior statement as it is to determine the truth or falsity of the

inconsistent testimony given in court. Moreover, Section 1235 will provide a party with desirable protection against the 'turncoat' witness who changes his story on the stand and deprives the party calling him of evidence essential to his case." Comment, California Evidence Code § 1235. See also McCormick § 39. The Advisory Committee finds these views more convincing than those expressed in People v. Johnson, 68 Cal.2d 646, 68 Cal.Rptr. 599, 441 P.2d 111 (1968). The constitutionality of the Advisory Committee's view was upheld in California v. Green, 399 U.S. 149, 90 S.Ct. 1930, 26 L.Ed.2d 489 (1970). Moreover, the requirement that the statement be inconsistent with the testimony given assures a thorough exploration of both versions while the witness is on the stand and bars any general and indiscriminate use of previously prepared statements. [It should be noted that the rule as enacted by the Congress also requires that the prior inconsistent statement have been made under oath.]

Report of House Committee on the Judiciary

House Comm. on Judiciary, Fed.Rules of Evidence, H.R.Rep. No. 650, 93d Cong., 1st Sess., p. 13 (1973); 1975 U.S. Code Cong. & Ad.News 7075, 7086

Present federal law, except in the Second Circuit, permits the use of prior inconsistent statements of a witness for impeachment only. Rule 801(d)(1) as proposed by the Court would have permitted all such statements to be admissible as substantive evidence, an approach followed by a small but growing number of State jurisdictions and recently held constitutional in California v. Green, 399 U.S. 149 (1970). Although there was some support expressed for the Court Rule, based largely on the need to counteract the effect of witness intimidation in criminal cases, the Committee decided to adopt a compromise version of the Rule similar to the position of the Second Circuit. The Rule as amended draws a distinction between types of prior inconsistent statements (other than statements of identification of a person made after perceiving him which are currently admissible, see United States v. Anderson, 406 F.2d 719, 720 (4th Cir.), cert. denied, 395 U.S. 967 (1969)) and allows only those made while the declarant was subject to cross-examination at a trail [trial] or hearing or in a deposition, to be admissible for their truth. Compare United States v. DeSisto, 329 F.2d 929 (2nd Cir.), cert. denied, 377 U.S. 979 (1964); United States v. Cunningham, 446 F.2d 194 (2nd Cir.1971) (restricting the admissibility of prior inconsistent statements as substantive evidence to those made under oath in a formal proceeding, but not requiring that there have been an opportunity for cross-examination). The rationale for the Committee's decision is that (1) unlike in most other situations involving unsworn or oral statements, there can be no dispute as to whether the prior statement was made; and (2) the context of a formal proceeding, an oath, and the opportunity for cross-examination provide firm additional assurances of the reliability of the prior statement.

Report of Senate Committee on the Judiciary

Senate Comm. on Judiciary, Fed.Rules of Evidence, S.Rep. No. 1277, 93d Cong., 2d Sess., p. 15 (1974); 1974 U.S. Code Cong. & Ad.News 7051, 7062

Rule 801 defines what is and what is not hearsay for the purpose of admitting a prior statement as substantive evidence. A prior statement of a witness at a trial or hearing which is inconsistent with his testimony is, of course, always admissible for the purpose of impeaching the witness' credibility.

As submitted by the Supreme Court, subdivision (d)(1)(A) made admissible as substantive evidence the prior statement of a witness inconsistent with this present testimony.

The House severely limited the admissibility of prior inconsistent statements by adding a requirement that the prior statement must have been subject to cross-examination, thus precluding even the use of grand jury statements. The requirement that the prior statement must have been subject to cross-examination appears unnecessary since this rule comes into play only when the witness testifies in the present trial. At that time, he is on the stand and can explain an earlier position and be cross-examined as to both.

The requirement that the statement be under oath also appears unnecessary. Notwithstanding the absence of an oath contemporaneous with the statement, the witness, when on the stand, qualifying or denying the prior statement, is under oath. In any event, of all the many recognized exceptions to the hearsay rule, only one (former testimony) requires that the out-of-court statement have been made under oath. With respect to the lack of evidence of the demeanor of the witness at the time of the prior statement, it would be difficult to improve upon Judge Learned Hand's observation that when the jury decides that the truth is not what the witness says now but what he said before, they are still deciding from what they see and hear in court.[1]

The rule as submitted by the Court has positive advantages. The prior statement was made nearer in time to the events, when memory was fresher and intervening influences had not been brought into play. A realistic method is provided for dealing with the turncoat witness who changes his story on the stand.[2]

New Jersey, California, and Utah have adopted a rule similar to this one; and Nevada, New Mexico, and Wisconsin have adopted the identical Federal rule.

For all of these reasons, we think the House amendment should be rejected and the rule as submitted by the Supreme Court reinstated.[3]

Conference Report

H.R., Fed.Rules of Evidence, Conf.Rep. No. 1597, 93d Cong., 2d Sess., p. 10 (1974); 1974 U.S. Code Cong. & Ad.News 7098, 7104

The House bill provides that a statement is not hearsay if the declarant testifies and is subject to cross-examination concerning the statement and if the statement is inconsistent with his testimony and was given under oath subject to cross-examination and subject to the penalty of perjury at a trial or hearing or in a deposition. The Senate amendment drops the requirement that the

1. Di Carlo v. United States, 6 F.2d 364 (2d Cir.1925).

2. See Comment, California Evidence Code § 1235; McCormick, Evidence, § 38 (2nd ed. 1972).

3. It would appear that some of the opposition to this Rule is based on a concern that a person could be convicted solely upon evidence admissible under this Rule. The Rule, however, is not addressed to the question of the sufficiency of evidence to send a case to the jury, but merely as to its admissibility. Factual circumstances could well arise where, if this were the sole evidence, dismissal would be appropriate.

prior statement be given under oath subject to cross-examination and subject to the penalty of perjury at a trial or hearing or in a deposition.

The Conference adopts the Senate amendment with an amendment, so that the rule now requires that the prior inconsistent statement be given under oath subject to the penalty of perjury at a trial, hearing, or other proceeding, or in a deposition. The rule as adopted covers statements before a grand jury. Prior inconsistent statements may, of course, be used for impeaching the credibility of a witness. When the prior inconsistent statement is one made by a defendant in a criminal case, it is covered by Rule 801(d)(2).

Advisory Committee's Note

56 F.R.D. 183, 296

(B) Prior consistent statements traditionally have been admissible to rebut charges of recent fabrication or improper influence or motive but not as substantive evidence. Under the rule they are substantive evidence. The prior statement is consistent with the testimony given on the stand and, if the opposite party wishes to open the door for its admission in evidence, no sound reason is apparent why it should not be received generally.

Editorial Note

Subdivision (d)(1)(C) was included in the rule as prescribed by the Supreme Court but was deleted by the Congress in enacting the rules, as indicated in the Conference Report above. However, the subdivision was restored by Act effective Oct. 31, 1975. Therefore the Advisory Committee's Note to the subdivision is now reprinted below.

Advisory Committee's Note

56 F.R.D. 183, 296

(C) The admission of evidence of identification finds substantial support, although it falls beyond a doubt in the category of prior out-of-court statements. Illustrative are People v. Gould, 54 Cal.2d 621, 7 Cal.Rptr. 273, 354 P.2d 865 (1960); Judy v. State, 218 Md. 168, 146 A.2d 29 (1958); State v. Simmons, 63 Wash.2d 17, 385 P.2d 389 (1963); California Evidence Code § 1238; New Jersey Evidence Rule 63(1)(c); N.Y.Code of Criminal Procedure § 393–b. Further cases are found in 4 Wigmore § 1130. The basis is the generally unsatisfactory and inconclusive nature of courtroom identifications as compared with those made at an earlier time under less suggestive conditions. The Supreme Court considered the admissibility of evidence of prior identification in Gilbert v. California, 388 U.S. 263, 87 S.Ct. 1951, 18 L.Ed.2d 1178 (1967). Exclusion of lineup identification was held to be required because the accused did not then have the assistance of counsel. Significantly, the Court carefully refrained from placing its decision on the ground that testimony as to the making of a prior out-of-court identification ("That's the man") violated either the hearsay rule or the right of confrontation because not made under oath, subject to immediate cross-examination, in the presence of the trier. Instead the Court observed:

> "There is a split among the States concerning the admissibility of prior extra-judicial identifications, as independent evidence of identity, both by the witness and third parties present at the prior identification. See 71

A.L.R.2d 449. It has been held that the prior identification is hearsay, and, when admitted through the testimony of the identifier, is merely a prior consistent statement. The recent trend, however, is to admit the prior identification under the exception that admits as substantive evidence a prior communication by a witness who is available for cross-examination at the trial. See 5 A.L.R.2d Later Case Service 1225–1228. . . ." 388 U.S. at 272, n. 3, 87 S.Ct. at 1956.[1]

(2) *Admissions.* Admissions by a party-opponent are excluded from the category of hearsay on the theory that their admissibility in evidence is the result of the adversary system rather than satisfaction of the conditions of the hearsay rule. Strahorn, A Reconsideration of the Hearsay Rule and Admissions, 85 U.Pa.L.Rev. 484, 564 (1937); Morgan, Basic Problems of Evidence 265 (1962); 4 Wigmore § 1048. No guarantee of trustworthiness is required in the case of an admission. The freedom which admissions have enjoyed from technical demands of searching for an assurance of trustworthiness in some against-interest circumstance, and from the restrictive influences of the opinion rule and the rule requiring firsthand knowledge, when taken with the apparently prevalent satisfaction with the results, calls for generous treatment of this avenue to admissibility.

The rule specifies five categories of statements for which the responsibility of a party is considered sufficient to justify reception in evidence against him:

(A) A party's own statement is the classic example of an admission. If he has a representative capacity and the statement is offered against him in that capacity, no inquiry whether he was acting in the representative capacity in making the statement is required; the statement need only be relevant to representative affairs. To the same effect is California Evidence Code § 1220. Compare Uniform Rule 63(7), requiring a statement to be made in a representative capacity to be admissible against a party in a representative capacity.

(B) Under established principles an admission may be made by adopting or acquiescing in the statement of another. While knowledge of contents would ordinarily be essential, this is not inevitably so: "X is a reliable person and knows what he is talking about." See McCormick § 246, p. 527, n. 15. Adoption or acquiescence may be manifested in any appropriate manner. When silence is relied upon, the theory is that the person would, under the circumstances, protest the statement made in his presence, if untrue. The decision in each case calls for an evaluation in terms of probable human behavior. In civil cases, the results have generally been satisfactory. In criminal cases, however, troublesome questions have been raised by decisions holding that failure to deny is an admission: the inference is a fairly weak one, to begin with; silence may be motivated by advice of counsel or realization that "anything you say may be used against you"; unusual opportunity is afforded to manufacture evidence; and encroachment upon the privilege against self-incrimination seems inescapably to be involved. However, recent decisions of the Supreme Court relating to custodial interrogation and the right to counsel appear to resolve these difficulties. Hence the rule contains no special provisions concerning failure to deny in criminal cases.

(C) No authority is required for the general proposition that a statement authorized by a party to be made should have the status of an admission by the party. However, the question arises whether only statements to third persons

---

1. See also 121 Cong.Rec. 19752 and 31866 (1975) for action reinstating item (C).

should be so regarded, to the exclusion of statements by the agent to the principal. The rule is phrased broadly so as to encompass both. While it may be argued that the agent authorized to make statements to his principal does not speak for him, Morgan, Basic Problems of Evidence 273 (1962), communication to an outsider has not generally been thought to be an essential characteristic of an admission. Thus a party's books or records are usable against him, without regard to any intent to disclose to third persons. 5 Wigmore § 1557. See also McCormick § 78, pp. 159–161. In accord is New Jersey Evidence Rule 63(8)(a). Cf. Uniform Rule 63(8)(a) and California Evidence Code § 1222 which limit status as an admission in this regard to statements authorized by the party to be made "for" him, which is perhaps an ambiguous limitation to statements to third persons. Falknor, Vicarious Admissions and the Uniform Rules, 14 Vand.L.Rev. 855, 860–861 (1961).

(D) The tradition has been to test the admissibility of statements by agents, as admissions, by applying the usual test of agency. Was the admission made by the agent acting in the scope of his employment? Since few principals employ agents for the purpose of making damaging statements, the usual result was exclusion of the statement. Dissatisfaction with this loss of valuable and helpful evidence has been increasing. A substantial trend favors admitting statements related to a matter within the scope of the agency or employment. Grayson v. Williams, 256 F.2d 61 (10th Cir.1958); Koninklijke Luchtvaart Maatschappij N.V. KLM Royal Dutch Airlines v. Tuller, 110 U.S.App.D.C. 282, 292 F.2d 775, 784 (1961); Martin v. Savage Truck Lines, Inc., 121 F.Supp. 417 (D.D.C.1954) , and numerous state court decisions collected in 4 Wigmore, 1964 Supp., pp. 66–73, with comments by the editor that the statements should have been excluded as not within scope of agency. For the traditional view see Northern Oil Co. v. Socony Mobile [sic] Oil Co., 347 F.2d 81, 85 (2d Cir.1965) and cases cited therein. Similar provisions are found in Uniform Rule 63(9)(a), Kansas Code of Civil Procedure § 60–460(i)(1), and New Jersey Evidence Rule 63(9)(a).

(E) The limitation upon the admissibility of statements of co-conspirators to those made "during the course and in furtherance of the conspiracy" is in the accepted pattern. While the broadened view of agency taken in item (iv) might suggest wider admissibility of statements of co-conspirators, the agency theory of conspiracy is at best a fiction and ought not to serve as a basis for admissibility beyond that already established. See Levie, Hearsay and Conspiracy, 52 Mich.L.Rev. 1159 (1954); Comment, 25 U.Chi.L.Rev. 530 (1958). The rule is consistent with the position of the Supreme Court in denying admissibility to statements made after the objectives of the conspiracy have either failed or been achieved. Krulewitch v. United States, 336 U.S. 440, 69 S.Ct. 716, 93 L.Ed. 790 (1949); Wong Sun v. United States, 371 U.S. 471, 490, 83 S.Ct. 407, 9 L.Ed.2d 441 (1963). For similarly limited provisions see California Evidence Code § 1223 and New Jersey Rule 63(9)(b). Cf. Uniform Rule 63(9)(b).

Report of Senate Committee on the Judiciary

Senate Comm. on Judiciary, Fed.Rules of Evidence, S.Rep. No. 1277, 93d Cong., 2d Sess., p. 26 (1974); 1974 U.S. Code Cong. & Ad.News 7051, 7073

The House approved the long-accepted rule that "a statement by a coconspirator of a party during the course and in furtherance of the conspiracy" is not hearsay as it was submitted by the Supreme Court. While the rule refers to a coconspirator, it is this committee's understanding that the rule is meant to carry forward the universally accepted doctrine that a joint venturer is considered as a coconspirator for the purposes of this rule even though no conspiracy has been charged. United States v. Rinaldi, 393 F.2d 97, 99 (2d Cir.), cert. denied 393 U.S. 913 (1968); United States v. Spencer, 415 F.2d 1301, 1304 (7th Cir.1969).

1987 Amendment. The amendments are technical. No substantive change is intended.

Rule 802. Hearsay Rule

Hearsay is not admissible except as provided by these rules or by other rules prescribed by the Supreme Court pursuant to statutory authority or by Act of Congress.

Section references, McCormick 4th ed.

§ 246, § 299

Note by Federal Judicial Center

The rule enacted by the Congress is the rule prescribed by the Supreme Court, amended by substituting "prescribed" in place of "adopted" and by inserting the phrase "pursuant to statutory authority."

Advisory Committee's Note

56 F.R.D. 183, 299

The provision excepting from the operation of the rule hearsay which is made admissible by other rules adopted by the Supreme Court or by Act of Congress continues the admissibility thereunder of hearsay which would not qualify under these Evidence Rules. The following examples illustrate the working of the exception:

FEDERAL RULES OF CIVIL PROCEDURE

Rule 4(g): proof of service by affidavit.

Rule 32: admissibility of depositions.

Rule 43(e): affidavits when motion based on facts not appearing of record.

Rule 56: affidavits in summary judgment proceedings.

Rule 65(b): showing by affidavit for temporary restraining order.

FEDERAL RULES OF CRIMINAL PROCEDURE

Rule 4(a): affidavits to show grounds for issuing warrants.

Rule 12(b)(4): affidavits to determine issues of fact in connection with motions.

ACTS OF CONGRESS

10 U.S.C. § 7730: affidavits of unavailable witnesses in actions for damages caused by vessel in naval service, or towage or salvage of same, when taking of testimony or bringing of action delayed or stayed on security grounds.

29 U.S.C. § 161(4): affidavit as proof of service in NLRB proceedings.

38 U.S.C. § 5206: affidavit as proof of posting notice of sale of unclaimed property by Veterans Administration.

Rule 803. Hearsay Exceptions; Availability of Declarant Immaterial

The following are not excluded by the hearsay rule, even though the declarant is available as a witness:

(1) Present sense impression. A statement describing or explaining an event or condition made while the declarant was perceiving the event or condition, or immediately thereafter.

(2) Excited utterance. A statement relating to a startling event or condition made while the declarant was under the stress of excitement caused by the event or condition.

(3) Then existing mental, emotional, or physical condition. A statement of the declarant's then existing state of mind, emotion, sensation, or physical condition (such as intent, plan, motive, design, mental feeling, pain, and bodily health), but not including a statement of memory or belief to prove the fact remembered or believed unless it relates to the execution, revocation, identification, or terms of declarant's will.

(4) Statements for purposes of medical diagnosis or treatment. Statements made for purposes of medical diagnosis or treatment and describing medical history, or past or present symptoms, pain, or sensations, or the inception or general character of the cause or external source thereof insofar as reasonably pertinent to diagnosis or treatment.

(5) Recorded recollection. A memorandum or record concerning a matter about which a witness once had knowledge but now has insufficient recollection to enable the witness to testify fully and accurately, shown to have been made or adopted by the witness when the matter was fresh in the witness' memory and to reflect that knowledge correctly. If admitted, the memorandum or record may be read into evidence but may not itself be received as an exhibit unless offered by an adverse party.

(6) Records of regularly conducted activity. A memorandum, report, record, or data compilation, in any form, of acts, events, conditions, opinions, or diagnoses, made at or near the time by, or from information transmitted by, a person with knowledge, if kept in the course of a regularly conducted business activity, and if it was the regular practice of that business activity to make the memorandum, report, record, or data compilation, all as shown by the testimony of the custodian or other qualified witness, unless the source of information or the method or circumstances of preparation indicate lack of trustworthiness. The term "business" as used in this paragraph includes business, institution, association, profession, occupation, and calling of every kind, whether or not conducted for profit.

(7) Absence of entry in records kept in accordance with the provisions of paragraph (6). Evidence that a matter is not included in the memoranda, reports, records, or data compilations, in any form, kept in accordance with the provisions of paragraph (6), to prove the nonoccurrence or nonexistence of the matter, if the matter was of a kind of which a memorandum, report, record, or data compilation was regularly made and preserved, unless the sources of information or other circumstances indicate lack of trustworthiness.

(8) Public records and reports. Records, reports, statements, or data compilations, in any form, of public offices or agencies, setting forth (A) the activities of the office or agency, or (B) matters observed pursuant to duty imposed by law as to which matters there was a duty to report, excluding, however, in criminal cases matters observed by police officers and other law enforcement personnel, or (C) in civil actions and proceedings and against the Government in criminal cases, factual findings resulting from an investigation made pursuant to authority granted by law, unless the sources of information or other circumstances indicate lack of trustworthiness.

(9) Records of vital statistics. Records or data compilations, in any form, of births, fetal deaths, deaths, or marriages, if the report thereof was made to a public office pursuant to requirements of law.

(10) Absence of public record or entry. To prove the absence of a record, report, statement, or data compilation, in any form, or the nonoccurrence or nonexistence of a matter of which a record, report, statement, or data compilation, in any form, was regularly made and preserved by a public office or agency, evidence in the form of a certification in accordance with rule 902, or testimony, that diligent search failed to disclose the record, report, statement, or data compilation, or entry.

(11) Records of religious organizations. Statements of births, marriages, divorces, deaths, legitimacy, ancestry, relationship by blood or marriage, or other similar facts of personal or family history, contained in a regularly kept record of a religious organization.

(12) Marriage, baptismal, and similar certificates. Statements of fact contained in a certificate that the maker performed a marriage or other ceremony or administered a sacrament, made by a clergyman, public official, or other person authorized by the rules or practices of a religious organization or by law to perform the act certified, and purporting to have been issued at the time of the act or within a reasonable time thereafter.

(13) Family records. Statements of fact concerning personal or family history contained in family Bibles, genealogies, charts, engravings on rings, inscriptions on family portraits, engravings on urns, crypts, or tombstones, or the like.

(14) Records of documents affecting an interest in property. The record of a document purporting to establish or affect an interest in property, as proof of the content of the original recorded document and its execution and delivery by each person by whom it purports to have been executed, if the record is a record of a public office and an applicable statute authorizes the recording of documents of that kind in that office.

(15) Statements in documents affecting an interest in property. A statement contained in a document purporting to establish or affect an interest in property if the matter stated was relevant to the purpose of the document, unless dealings with the property since the document was made have been inconsistent with the truth of the statement or the purport of the document.

(16) Statements in ancient documents. Statements in a document in existence twenty years or more the authenticity of which is established.

(17) Market reports, commercial publications. Market quotations, tabulations, lists, directories, or other published compilations, generally used and relied upon by the public or by persons in particular occupations.

(18) Learned treatises. To the extent called to the attention of an expert witness upon cross-examination or relied upon by the expert witness in direct examination, statements contained in published treatises, periodicals, or pamphlets on a subject of history, medicine, or other science or art, established as a reliable authority by the testimony or admission of the witness or by other expert testimony or by judicial notice. If admitted, the statements may be read into evidence but may not be received as exhibits.

(19) Reputation concerning personal or family history. Reputation among members of a person's family by blood, adoption, or marriage, or among a person's associates, or in the community, concerning a person's birth, adoption, marriage, divorce, death, legitimacy, relationship by blood, adoption, or marriage, ancestry, or other similar fact of his personal or family history.

(20) Reputation concerning boundaries or general history. Reputation in a community, arising before the controversy, as to boundaries of or customs affecting lands in the community, and reputation as to events of general history important to the community or State or nation in which located.

(21) Reputation as to character. Reputation of a person's character among associates or in the community.

(22) Judgment of previous conviction. Evidence of a final judgment, entered after a trial or upon a plea of guilty (but not upon a plea of nolo contendere), adjudging a person guilty of a crime punishable by death or imprisonment in excess of one year, to prove any fact essential to sustain the judgment, but not including, when offered by the Government in a criminal prosecution for purposes other than impeachment, judgments against persons other than the accused. The pendency of an appeal may be shown but does not affect admissibility.

(23) Judgment as to personal, family, or general history, or boundaries. Judgments as proof of matters of personal, family or general history, or boundaries, essential to the judgment, if the same would be provable by evidence of reputation.

(24) Other exceptions. A statement not specifically covered by any of the foregoing exceptions but having equivalent circumstantial guarantees of trustworthiness, if the court determines that (A) the statement is offered as evidence of a material fact; (B) the statement is more probative on the point for which it is offered than any other evidence which the proponent can procure through reasonable efforts; and (C) the general purposes of these rules and the interests of justice will best be served by admission of the statement into evidence. However, a statement may not be admitted under this exception unless the proponent of it makes known to the adverse party sufficiently in advance of the trial or hearing to provide the adverse party with a fair opportunity to prepare to meet it, the proponent's intention to offer the statement and the particulars of it, including the name and address of the declarant.

(As amended P.L. 94–149, § 1(11), Dec. 12, 1975, 89 Stat. 805; Mar. 2, 1987, eff. Oct. 1, 1987.)

Section references, McCormick 4th ed.

Generally *§ 253*, § 326

(1). § 271

(2). § 272

(3). § 273, § 274, § 275, § 276

(4). § 277, § 278, § 324.3

(5). § 144, § 279, § 281, § 282, § 283

(6). § 250, § 286, § 287, § 288, § 289, § 290, § 291, § 292, § 293, § 294, § 296, § 324.1

(7). § 287

(8). § 288, § 295

    (A). § 296

    (B). § 296, § 297

    (C). § 296, § 297

(9). § 297

(10). § 300

(11). § 288, § 299

(12). § 299

(13). § 322

(14). § 323

(15). § 323

(16). § 323

(17). § 321

(18). § 321

(19). § 322

(20). § 324

(21). § 191

(22). § 42, § 252, § 257, § 298

(23). § 322

(24). § 208, § 324, § 324.3, § 353

Note by Federal Judicial Center

The rule enacted by the Congress retains the 24 exceptions set forth in the rule prescribed by the Supreme Court. Three of the exceptions, numbered (6), (8), and (24) have been amended in respects that may fairly be described as substantial. Others, numbered (5), (7), (14), and (16), have been amended in lesser ways. The remaining 17 are unchanged. The amendments are, in numerical order, as follows.

Exception (5) as prescribed by the Supreme Court was amended by inserting after "made" the phrase "or adopted by the witness."

Exception (6) as prescribed by the Supreme Court was amended by substituting the phrase, "if kept in the course of a regularly conducted business activity, and if it was the regular practice of that business activity to make the memorandum, report, record, or data compilation, all," in place of "all in the course of a regularly conducted activity"; by substituting "source" in place of "sources"; by substituting the phrase, "the method or circumstances of preparation," in place of "other circumstances"; and by adding the second sentence.

Exception (7) as prescribed by the Supreme Court was amended by substituting the phrase, "kept in accordance with the provisions of paragraph (6)," in place of "of a regularly conducted activity." The exception prescribed by the Supreme Court included a comma after "memoranda," while the congressional enactment does not.

Exception (8) as prescribed by the Supreme Court was amended by inserting in item (B) after "law" the phrase, "as to which matters there was a duty to report, excluding, however, in criminal cases matters observed by police officers and other law enforcement personnel," and by substituting in item (C) the phrase "civil actions and proceedings," in place of "civil cases."

Exception (14) as prescribed by the Supreme Court was amended by substituting "authorizes" in place of "authorized."

Exception (16) as prescribed by the Supreme Court was amended by substituting the phrase, "the authenticity of which," in place of "whose authenticity."

Exception (24) as prescribed by the Supreme Court was amended by substituting "equivalent" in place of "comparable," and adding all that appears after "trustworthiness" in the exception as enacted by the Congress.

Advisory Committee's Note

56 F.R.D. 183, 303

The exceptions are phrased in terms of nonapplication of the hearsay rule, rather than in positive terms of admissibility, in order to repel any implication that other possible grounds for exclusion are eliminated from consideration.

The present rule proceeds upon the theory that under appropriate circumstances a hearsay statement may possess circumstantial guarantees of trustworthiness sufficient to justify nonproduction of the declarant in person at the trial even though he may be available. The theory finds vast support in the many exceptions to the hearsay rule developed by the common law in which unavailability of the declarant is not a relevant factor. The present rule is a synthesis of them, with revision where modern developments and conditions are believed to make that course appropriate.

In a hearsay situation, the declarant is, of course, a witness, and neither this rule nor Rule 804 dispenses with the requirement of firsthand knowledge. It may appear from his statement or be inferable from circumstances. See Rule 602.

Exceptions (1) and (2). In considerable measure these two [exceptions] overlap, though based on somewhat different theories. The most significant practical difference will lie in the time lapse allowable between event and statement.

The underlying theory of Exception (1) is that substantial contemporaneity of event and statement negative the likelihood of deliberate or conscious misrepresentation. Moreover, if the witness is the declarant, he may be examined on the statement. If the witness is not the declarant, he may be examined as to the circumstances as an aid in evaluating the statement. Morgan, Basic Problems of Evidence 340–341 (1962).

The theory of Exception (2) is simply that circumstances may produce a condition of excitement which temporarily stills the capacity of reflection and produces utterances free of conscious fabrication. 6 Wigmore § 1747, p. 135. Spontaneity is the key factor in each instance, though arrived at by somewhat different routes. Both are needed in order to avoid needless niggling.

While the theory of Exception (2) has been criticized on the ground that excitement impairs accuracy of observation as well as eliminating conscious fabrication, Hutchins and Slesinger, Some Observations on the Law of Evidence: Spontaneous Exclamations, 28 Colum.L.Rev. 432 (1928), it finds support in cases without number. See cases in 6 Wigmore § 1750; Annot., 53 A.L.R.2d 1245 (statements as to cause of or responsibility for motor vehicle accident); Annot., 4 A.L.R.3d 149 (accusatory statements by homicide victims). Since unexciting events are less likely to evoke comment, decisions involving Exception (1) are far less numerous. Illustrative are Tampa Elec. Co. v. Getrost, 151 Fla. 558, 10 So.2d 83 (1942); Houston Oxygen Co. v. Davis, 139 Tex. 1, 161 S.W.2d 474 (1942); and cases cited in McCormick § 273, p. 585, n. 4.

With respect to the *time element,* Exception (1) recognizes that in many, if not most, instances precise contemporaneity is not possible, and hence a slight lapse is allowable. Under Exception (2) the standard of measurement is the duration of the state of excitement. "How long can excitement prevail? Obviously there are no pat answers and the character of the transaction or event will largely determine the significance of the time factor." Slough,

Spontaneous Statements and State of Mind, 46 Iowa L.Rev. 224, 243 (1961); McCormick § 272, p. 580.

Participation by the declarant is not required: a non-participant may be moved to describe what he perceives, and one may be startled by an event in which he is not an actor. Slough, supra; McCormick, supra; 6 Wigmore § 1755; Annot., 78 A.L.R.2d 300.

Whether *proof of the startling event* may be made by the statement itself is largely an academic question, since in most cases there is present at least circumstantial evidence that something of a startling nature must have occurred. For cases in which the evidence consists of the condition of the declarant (injuries, state of shock), see Insurance Co. v. Mosely, 75 U.S. (8 Wall.) 397, 19 L.Ed. 437 (1869); Wheeler v. United States, 93 U.S.App.D.C. 159, 211 F.2d 19 (1953), cert. denied 347 U.S. 1019, 74 S.Ct. 876, 98 L.Ed. 1140; Wetherbee v. Safety Casualty Co., 219 F.2d 274 (5th Cir.1955); Lampe v. United States, 97 U.S.App.D.C. 160, 229 F.2d 43 (1956). Nevertheless, on occasion the only evidence may be the content of the statement itself, and rulings that it may be sufficient are described as "increasing," Slough, supra at 246, and as the "prevailing practice," McCormick § 272, p. 579. Illustrative are Armour & Co. v. Industrial Commission, 78 Colo. 569, 243 P. 546 (1926); Young v. Stewart, 191 N.C. 297, 131 S.E. 735 (1926). Moreover, under Rule 104(a) the judge is not limited by the hearsay rule in passing upon preliminary questions of fact.

Proof of declarant's perception by his statement presents similar considerations when declarant is identified. People v. Poland, 22 Ill.2d 175, 174 N.E.2d 804 (1961). However, when declarant is an unidentified bystander, the cases indicate hesitancy in upholding the statement alone as sufficient, Garrett v. Howden, 73 N.M. 307, 387 P.2d 874 (1963); Beck v. Dye, 200 Wash. 1, 92 P.2d 1113 (1939), a result which would under appropriate circumstances be consistent with the rule.

Permissible *subject matter* of the statement is limited under Exception (1) to description or explanation of the event or condition, the assumption being that spontaneity, in the absence of a startling event, may extend no farther. In Exception (2), however, the statement need only "relate" to the startling event or condition, thus affording a broader scope of subject matter coverage. 6 Wigmore §§ 1750, 1754. See Sanitary Grocery Co. v. Snead, 67 App.D.C. 129, 90 F.2d 374 (1937), slip-and-fall case sustaining admissibility of clerk's statement, "That has been on the floor for a couple of hours," and Murphy Auto Parts Co., Inc. v. Ball, 101 U.S.App.D.C. 416, 249 F.2d 508 (1957), upholding admission, on issue of driver's agency, of his statement that he had to call on a customer and was in a hurry to get home. Quick, Hearsay, Excitement, Necessity and the Uniform Rules: A Reappraisal of Rule 63(4), 6 Wayne L.Rev. 204, 206–209 (1960).

Similar provisions are found in Uniform Rule 63(4)(a) and (b); California Evidence Code § 1240 (as to Exception (2) only); Kansas Code of Civil Procedure § 60–460(d)(1) and (2); New Jersey Evidence Rule 63(4).

Exception (3) is essentially a specialized application of Exception (1), presented separately to enhance its usefulness and accessibility. See McCormick §§ 265, 268.

The exclusion of "statements of memory or belief to prove the fact remembered or believed" is necessary to avoid the virtual destruction of the hearsay rule which would otherwise result from allowing state of mind, provable by a hearsay statement, to serve as the basis for an inference of the happening of the event which produced the state of mind. Shepard v. United States, 290 U.S. 96, 54 S.Ct. 22, 78 L.Ed. 196 (1933); Maguire, The Hillmon Case—Thirty-three Years After, 38 Harv.L.Rev. 709, 719–731 (1925); Hinton, States of Mind and the Hearsay Rule, 1 U.Chi.L.Rev. 394, 421–423 (1934). The rule of Mutual Life Ins. Co. v. Hillmon, 145 U.S. 285, 12 S.Ct. 909, 36 L.Ed. 706 (1892), allowing evidence of intention as tending to prove the doing of the act intended, is, of course, left undisturbed.

The carving out, from the exclusion mentioned in the preceding paragraph, of declarations relating to the execution, revocation, identification, or terms of declarant's will represents an *ad hoc* judgment which finds ample reinforcement in the decisions, resting on practical grounds of necessity and expediency rather than logic. McCormick § 271, pp. 577–578; Annot., 34 A.L.R.2d 588, 62 A.L.R.2d 855. A similar recognition of the need for and practical value of this kind of evidence is found in California Evidence Code § 1260.

Report of House Committee on the Judiciary

House Comm. on Judiciary, Fed.Rules of Evidence, H.R.Rep. No. 650,
93d Cong., 1st Sess., p. 13 (1973); 1974 U.S.Code
Cong. & Ad.News 7075, 7087

Rule 803(3) was approved in the form submitted by the Court to Congress. However, the Committee intends that the Rule be construed to limit the doctrine of Mutual Life Insurance Co. v. Hillmon, 145 U.S. 285, 295–300 (1892), so as to render statements of intent by a declarant admissible only to prove his future conduct, not the future conduct of another person.

Advisory Committee's Note

56 F.R.D. 183, 306

Exception (4). Even those few jurisdictions which have shied away from generally admitting statements of present condition have allowed them if made to a physician for purposes of diagnosis and treatment in view of the patient's strong motivation to be truthful. McCormick § 266, p. 563. The same guarantee of trustworthiness extends to statements of past conditions and medical history, made for purposes of diagnosis or treatment. It also extends to statements as to causation, reasonably pertinent to the same purposes, in accord with the current trend, Shell Oil Co. v. Industrial Commission, 2 Ill.2d 590, 119 N.E.2d 224 (1954); McCormick § 266, p. 564; New Jersey Evidence Rule 63(12)(c). Statements as to fault would not ordinarily qualify under this latter language. Thus a patient's statement that he was struck by an automobile would qualify but not his statement that the car was driven through a red light. Under the exception the statement need not have been made to a physician. Statements to hospital attendants, ambulance drivers, or even members of the family might be included.

Conventional doctrine has excluded from the hearsay exception, as not within its guarantee of truthfulness, statements to a physician consulted only for the purpose of enabling him to testify. While these statements were not admissible as substantive evidence, the expert was allowed to state the basis of his opinion, including statements of this kind. The distinction thus called for was one most unlikely to be made by juries. The rule accordingly rejects the limitation. This position is consistent with the provision of Rule 703 that the facts on which expert testimony is based need not be admissible in evidence if of a kind ordinarily relied upon by experts in the field.

Report of House Committee on the Judiciary

House Comm. on Judiciary, Fed.Rules of Evidence, H.R.Rep. No. 650,
93d Cong., 1st Sess., p. 14 (1973); 1974 U.S.Code
Cong. & Ad.News 7075, 7087

After giving particular attention to the question of physical examination made solely to enable a physician to testify, the Committee approved Rule 803(4) as submitted to Congress, with the understanding that it is not intended in any way to adversely affect present privilege rules or those subsequently adopted.

Report of Senate Committee on the Judiciary

Senate Comm. on Judiciary, Fed.Rules of Evidence, S.Rep. No. 1277,
93d Cong., 2d Sess., p. 27 (1974); 1974 U.S.Code Cong.
& Ad.News 7051, 7073

The House approved this rule as it was submitted by the Supreme Court "with the understanding that it is not intended in any way to adversely affect present privilege rules." We also approve this rule, and we would point out with respect to the question of its relation to privileges, it must be read in conjunction with rule 35 of the Federal Rules of Civil Procedure which provides that whenever the physical or mental condition of a party (plaintiff or defendant) is in controversy, the court may require him to submit to an examination by a physician. It is these examinations which will normally be admitted under this exception.

Advisory Committee's Note

56 F.R.D. 183, 306

Exception (5). A hearsay exception for recorded recollection is generally recognized and has been described as having "long been favored by the federal and practically all the state courts that have had occasion to decide the question." United States v. Kelly, 349 F.2d 720, 770 (2d Cir.1965), citing numerous cases and sustaining the exception against a claimed denial of the right of confrontation. Many additional cases are cited in Annot., 82 A.L.R.2d 473, 520. The guarantee of trustworthiness is found in the reliability inherent in a record made while events were still fresh in mind and accurately reflecting them. Owens v. State, 67 Md. 307, 316, 10 A. 210, 212 (1887).

The principal controversy attending the exception has centered, not upon the propriety of the exception itself, but upon the question whether a preliminary requirement of impaired memory on the part of the witness should be imposed. The authorities are divided. If regard be had only to the accuracy of the evidence, admittedly impairment of the memory of the witness adds nothing to it and should not be required. McCormick § 277, p. 593; 3 Wigmore § 738, p. 76; Jordan v. People, 151 Colo. 133, 376 P.2d 699 (1962), cert. denied 373 U.S. 944, 83 S.Ct. 1553, 10 L.Ed.2d 699; Hall v. State, 223 Md. 158, 162 A.2d 751 (1960); State v. Bindhammer, 44 N.J. 372, 209 A.2d 124 (1965). Nevertheless, the absence of the requirement, it is believed, would encourage the use of statements carefully prepared for purposes of litigation under the supervision of attorneys, investigators, or claim adjusters. Hence the example includes a requirement that the witness not have "sufficient recollection to enable him to testify fully and accurately." To the same effect are California Evidence Code § 1237 and New Jersey Rule 63(1)(b), and this has been the position of the federal courts. Vicksburg & Meridian R.R. v. O'Brien, 119 U.S. 99, 7 S.Ct. 118, 30 L.Ed. 299 (1886); Ahern v. Webb, 268 F.2d 45 (10th Cir.1959); and see N.L. R.B. v. Hudson Pulp and Paper Corp., 273 F.2d 660, 665 (5th Cir.1960); N.L.R.B. v. Federal Dairy Co., 297 F.2d 487 (1st Cir.1962). But cf. United States v. Adams, 385 F.2d 548 (2d Cir.1967).

No attempt is made in the exception to spell out the method of establishing the initial knowledge or the contemporaneity and accuracy of the record, leaving them to be dealt with as the circumstances of the particular case might indicate. Multiple person involvement in the process of observing and recording, as in Rathbun v. Brancatella, 93 N.J.L. 222, 107 A. 279 (1919), is entirely consistent with the exception.

Locating the exception at this place in the scheme of the rules is a matter of choice. There were two other possibilities. The first was to regard the statement as one of the group of prior statements of a testifying witness which are excluded entirely from the category of hearsay by Rule 801(d)(1). That category, however, requires that declarant be "subject to cross-examination," as to which the impaired memory aspect of the exception raises doubts. The other possibility was to include the exception among those covered by Rule 804. Since unavailability is required by that rule and lack of memory is listed as a species of unavailability by the definition of the term in Rule 804(a)(3), that treatment at first impression would seem appropriate. The fact is, however, that the unavailability requirement of the exception is of a limited and peculiar nature. Accordingly, the exception is located at this point rather than in the context of a rule where unavailability is conceived of more broadly.

Report of House Committee on the Judiciary

House Comm. on Judiciary, Fed.Rules of Evidence, H.R.Rep. No. 650,
93d Cong., 1st Sess., p. 14 (1973); 1974 U.S.Code
Cong. & Ad.News 7075, 7087

Rule 803(5) as submitted by the Court permitted the reading into evidence of a memorandum or record concerning a matter about which a witness once had knowledge but now has insufficient recollection to enable him to testify accurately and fully, "shown to have been made when the matter was fresh in his memory and to reflect that knowledge correctly." The Committee amended this Rule to add the words "or adopted by the witness" after the phrase "shown to have been made", a treatment consistent with the definition of "statement" in the Jencks Act, 18 U.S.C. 3500. Moreover, it is the Committee's understanding that a memorandum or report, although barred under this Rule, would nonetheless be admissible if it came within another hearsay exception. This last stated principle is deemed applicable to all the hearsay rules.

Report of Senate Committee on the Judiciary

Senate Comm. on Judiciary, Fed.Rules of Evidence, S.Rep. No. 1277,
93d Cong., 2d Sess., p. 27 (1974); 1974 U.S.Code
Cong. & Ad.News 7051, 7073

Rule 803(5) as submitted by the Court permitted the reading into evidence of a memorandum or record concerning a matter about which a witness once had knowledge but now has insufficient recollection to enable him to testify accurately and fully, "shown to have been made when the matter was fresh in his memory and to reflect that knowledge correctly." The House amended the rule to add the words "or adopted by the witness" after the phrase "shown to have been made," language parallel to the Jencks Act.[1]

The committee accepts the House amendment with the understanding and belief that it was not intended to narrow the scope of applicability of the rule. In fact, we understand it to clarify the rule's applicability to a memorandum adopted by the witness as well as one made by him. While the rule as submitted by the Court was silent on the question of who made the memorandum, we view the House amendment as a helpful clarification, noting, however, that the Advisory Committee's note to this rule suggests that the important thing is the accuracy of the memorandum rather than who made it.

The committee does not view the House amendment as precluding admissibility in situations in which multiple participants were involved.

When the verifying witness has not prepared the report, but merely examined it and found it accurate, he has adopted the report, and it is therefore admissible. The rule should also be interpreted to cover other situations involving multiple participants, e.g., employer dictating to secretary, secretary making memorandum at direction of employer, or information being passed along a chain of persons, as in Curtis v. Bradley.[2]

The committee also accepts the understanding of the House that a memorandum or report, although barred under this rule, would nonetheless be admissible if it came within another hearsay exception. We consider this principle to be applicable to all the hearsay rules.

Advisory Committee's Note

56 F.R.D. 183, 307

Exception (6) represents an area which has received much attention from those seeking to improve the law of evidence. The Commonwealth Fund Act was the result of a study completed in 1927 by a distinguished committee under the chairmanship of Professor Morgan. Morgan et al., The Law of Evidence: Some Proposals for its Reform 63 (1927). With changes too minor to mention, it was adopted by Congress in 1936 as the rule for federal courts. 28 U.S.C. § 1732. A number of states took similar action. The Commissioners on Uniform State Laws in 1936 promulgated the Uniform Business Records as Evidence Act, 9A U.L.A. 506, which has acquired a substantial following in the states. Model Code Rule 514 and Uniform Rule 63(13) also deal with the

---

1. 18 U.S.C. § 3500.

2. 65 Conn. 99, 31 Atl. 591 (1894). See also, Rathbun v. Brancatella, 93 N.J.L. 222,

107 Atl. 279 (1919); see also McCormick on Evidence, § 303 (2d ed. 1972).

subject. Difference of varying degrees of importance exist among these various treatments.

These reform efforts were largely within the context of business and commercial records, as the kind usually encountered, and concentrated considerable attention upon relaxing the requirement of producing as witnesses, or accounting for the nonproduction of, all participants in the process of gathering, transmitting, and recording information which the common law had evolved as a burdensome and crippling aspect of using records of this type. In their areas of primary emphasis on witnesses to be called and the general admissibility of ordinary business and commercial records, the Commonwealth Fund Act and the Uniform Act appear to have worked well. The exception seeks to preserve their advantages.

On the subject of what witnesses must be called, the Commonwealth Fund Act eliminated the common law requirement of calling or accounting for all participants by failing to mention it. United States v. Mortimer, 118 F.2d 266 (2d Cir.1941); La Porte v. United States, 300 F.2d 878 (9th Cir.1962); McCormick § 290, p. 608. Model Code Rule 514 and Uniform Rule 63(13) did likewise. The Uniform Act, however, abolished the common law requirement in express terms, providing that the requisite foundation testimony might be furnished by "the custodian or other qualified witness." Uniform Business Records as Evidence Act, § 2; 9A U.L.A. 506. The exception follows the Uniform Act in this respect.

The element of unusual reliability of business records is said variously to be supplied by systematic checking, by regularity and continuity which produce habits of precision, by actual experience of business in relying upon them, or by a duty to make an accurate record as part of a continuing job or occupation. McCormick §§ 281, 286, 287; Laughlin, Business Entries and the Like, 46 Iowa L.Rev. 276 (1961). The model statutes and rules have sought to capture these factors and to extend their impact by employing the phrase "regular course of business," in conjunction with a definition of "business" far broader than its ordinarily accepted meaning. The result is a tendency unduly to emphasize a requirement of routineness and repetitiveness and an insistence that other types of records be squeezed into the fact patterns which give rise to traditional business records. . . .

Amplification of the kinds of activities producing admissible records has given rise to problems which conventional business records by their nature avoid. They are problems of the source of the recorded information, of entries in opinion form, of motivation, and of involvement as participant in the matters recorded.

Sources of information presented no substantial problem with ordinary business records. All participants, including the observer or participant furnishing the information to be recorded, were acting routinely, under a duty of accuracy, with employer reliance on the result, or in short "in the regular course of business." If, however, the supplier of the information does not act in the regular course, an essential link is broken; the assurance of accuracy does not extend to the information itself, and the fact that it may be recorded with scrupulous accuracy is of no avail. An illustration is the police report incorporating information obtained from a bystander: the officer qualifies as acting in the regular course but the informant does not. The leading case, Johnson v. Lutz, 253 N.Y. 124, 170 N.E. 517 (1930), held that a report thus prepared was inadmissible. Most of the authorities have agreed with the decision. Gencarella v. Fyfe, 171 F.2d 419 (1st Cir.1948); Gordon v. Robinson, 210 F.2d 192 (3d Cir. 1954); Standard Oil Co. of California v. Moore, 251 F.2d 188, 214 (9th Cir.1957), cert. denied 356 U.S. 975, 78 S.Ct. 1139, 2 L.Ed.2d 1148; Yates v. Bair Transport, Inc., 249 F.Supp. 681 (S.D.N.Y.1965); Annot., 69 A.L.R.2d 1148. Cf. Hawkins v. Gorea Motor Express, Inc., 360 F.2d 933 (2d Cir.1966). Contra, 5 Wigmore § 1530a, n. 1, pp. 391–392. The point is not dealt with specifically in the Commonwealth Fund Act, the Uniform Act, or Uniform Rule 63(13). However, Model Code Rule 514 contains the requirement "that it was the regular course of that business for one with personal knowledge . . . to make such a memorandum or record or to transmit information thereof to be included in such a memorandum or record . . .." The rule follows this lead in requiring an informant with knowledge acting in the course of the regularly conducted activity.

Entries in the form of opinions were not encountered in traditional business records in view of the purely factual nature of the items recorded, but they are now commonly encountered with respect to medical diagnoses, prognoses, and test results, as well as occasionally in other areas. The Commonwealth Fund Act provided only for records of an "act, transaction, occurrence, or event," while the Uniform Act, Model Code Rule 514, and Uniform Rule 63(13) merely added the ambiguous term "condition." The limited phrasing of the Commonwealth Fund Act, 28 U.S.C. § 1732, may account for the reluctance of some federal decisions to admit diagnostic entries. New York Life Ins. Co. v. Taylor, 79 U.S.App.D.C. 66, 147 F.2d 297 (1945); Lyles v. United States, 103 U.S.App.D.C. 22, 254 F.2d 725 (1957), cert. denied 356 U.S. 961, 78 S.Ct. 997, 2 L.Ed.2d 1067; England v. United States, 174 F.2d 466 (5th Cir.1949); Skogen v. Dow Chemical Co., 375 F.2d 692 (8th Cir.1967). Other federal decisions, however, experienced no difficulty in freely admitting diagnostic entries. Reed v. Order of United Commercial Travelers, 123 F.2d 252 (2d Cir.1941); Buckminster's Estate v. Commissioner of Internal Revenue, 147 F.2d 331 (2d Cir.1944); Medina v. Erickson, 226 F.2d 475 (9th Cir.1955); Thomas v. Hogan, 308 F.2d 355 (4th Cir.1962); Glawe v. Rulon, 284 F.2d 495 (8th Cir.1960). In the state courts, the trend favors admissibility. Borucki v. MacKenzie Bros. Co., 125 Conn. 92, 3 A.2d 224 (1938); Allen v. St. Louis Public Service Co., 365 Mo. 677, 285 S.W.2d 663, 55 A.L.R.2d 1022 (1956); People v. Kohlmeyer, 284 N.Y. 366, 31 N.E.2d 490 (1940); Weis v. Weis, 147 Ohio St. 416, 72 N.E.2d 245 (1947). In order to make clear its adherence to the latter position, the rule specifically includes both diagnoses and opinions, in addition to acts, events, and conditions, as proper subjects of admissible entries.

Problems of the motivation of the informant have been a source of difficulty and disagreement. In Palmer v. Hoffman, 318 U.S. 109, 63 S.Ct. 477, 87 L.Ed. 645 (1943), exclusion of an accident report made by the since deceased engineer, offered by defendant railroad trustees in a grade crossing collision case, was upheld. The report was not "in the regular course of business," not a record of the systematic conduct of the business as a business, said the Court. The report was prepared for use in litigating, not railroading. While the opinion mentions the motivation of the engineer only obliquely, the emphasis on records of routine operations is significant only by virtue of impact on motivation to be accurate. Absence of routineness raises lack of motivation to be accurate. The opinion of the Court of Appeals had gone beyond mere lack of motive to be accurate: the engineer's statement was "dripping with motivations to misrepresent." Hoffman v. Palmer, 129 F.2d 976, 991 (2d Cir.1942). The direct introduction of motivation is a disturbing factor, since absence of motive to misrepresent has not traditionally been a requirement of the rule; that records might be self-serving has not been a ground for exclusion. Laughlin, Business Records and the Like, 46 Iowa L.Rev. 276, 285 (1961). As Judge Clark said in his dissent, "I submit that there is hardly a grocer's account book which could not be excluded on that basis." 129 F.2d at 1002. A physician's evaluation report of a personal injury litigant would appear to be in the routine of his business. If the report is offered by the party at whose instance it was made, however, it has been held inadmissible, Yates v. Bair Transport, Inc., 249 F.Supp. 681 (S.D.N.Y.1965), otherwise if offered by the opposite party, Korte v. New York, N.H. & H.R. Co., 191 F.2d 86 (2d Cir.1951), cert. denied 342 U.S. 868, 72 S.Ct. 108, 96 L.Ed. 652.

The decisions hinge on motivation and which party is entitled to be concerned about it. Professor McCormick believed that the doctor's report or the accident report were sufficiently routine to justify admissibility. McCormick § 287, p. 604. Yet hesitation must be experienced in admitting everything which is observed and recorded in the course of a regularly conducted activity. Efforts to set a limit are illustrated by Hartzog v. United States, 217 F.2d 706 (4th Cir.1954), error to admit worksheets made by since deceased deputy collector in preparation for the instant income tax evasion prosecution, and United States v. Ware, 247 F.2d 698 (7th Cir.1957), error to admit narcotics agents' records of purchases. See also Exception (8), infra, as to the public record aspects of records of this nature. Some decisions have been satisfied as to motivation of an accident report if made pursuant to statutory duty, United States v. New York Foreign Trade Zone Operators, 304 F.2d 792 (2d Cir.1962); Taylor v. Baltimore & O.R. Co., 344 F.2d 281 (2d Cir.1965), since the report was oriented in a direction other than the litigation which ensued. Cf. Matthews v. United States, 217 F.2d 409 (5th Cir.1954). The formulation of specific terms which would assure satisfactory results in all cases is not possible. Consequently the rule proceeds from the base that records made in the course of a regularly conducted activity will be taken as admissible but subject to authority to exclude if "the sources of information or other circumstances indicate lack of trustworthiness."

Occasional decisions have reached for enhanced accuracy by requiring involvement as a participant in matters reported. Clainos v. United States, 82 U.S.App.D.C. 278, 163 F.2d 593 (1947), error to admit police records of convictions; Standard Oil Co. of California v. Moore, 251 F.2d 188 (9th Cir.1957), cert. denied 356 U.S. 975, 78 S.Ct. 1139, 2 L.Ed.2d 1148, error to admit employees' records of observed business practices of others. The rule includes no requirement of this nature. Wholly acceptable records may involve matters merely observed, e.g. the weather.

The form which the "record" may assume under the rule is described broadly as a "memorandum, report, record, or data compilation, in any form." The expression "data compilation" is used as broadly descriptive of any means of storing information other than the conventional words and figures in written or documentary form. It includes, but is by no means limited to, electronic computer storage. The term is borrowed from revised Rule 34(a) of the Rules of Civil Procedure.

Report of House Committee on the Judiciary

House Comm. on Judiciary, Fed.Rules of Evidence, H.R.Rep. No. 650,
93d Cong., 1st Sess., p. 14 (1973); 1974 U.S.Code
Cong. & Ad.News 7075, 7087

Rule 803(6) as submitted by the Court permitted a record made "in the course of a regularly conducted activity" to be admissible in certain circumstances. The Committee believed there were insufficient guarantees of reliability in records made in the course of activities falling outside the scope of "business" activities as that term is broadly defined in 28 U.S.C. 1732. Moreover, the Committee concluded that the additional requirement of Section 1732 that it must have been the regular practice of a business to make the record is a necessary further assurance of its trustworthiness. The Committee accordingly amended the Rule to incorporate these limitations.

Report of Senate Committee on the Judiciary

Senate Comm. on Judiciary, Fed.Rules of Evidence, S.Rep. No. 1277,
93d Cong., 2d Sess., p. 16 (1974); 1974 U.S.Code
Cong. & Ad.News 7051, 7063

Rule 803(6) as submitted by the Supreme Court permitted a record made in the course of a regularly conducted activity to be admissible in certain circumstances. This rule constituted a broadening of the traditional business records hearsay exception which has been long advocated by scholars and judges active in the law of evidence.

The House felt there were insufficient guarantees of reliability of records not within a broadly defined business records exception. We disagree. Even under the House definition of "business" including profession, occupation, and "calling of every kind," the records of many regularly conducted activities will, or may be, excluded from evidence. Under the principle of ejusdem generis, the intent of "calling of every kind" would seem to be related to work-related endeavors—e.g., butcher, baker, artist, etc.

Thus, it appears that the records of many institutions or groups might not be admissible under the House amendments. For example, schools, churches, and hospitals will not normally be considered businesses within the definition. Yet, these are groups which keep financial and other records on a regular basis in a manner similar to business enterprises. We believe these records are of equivalent trustworthiness and should be admitted into evidence.

Three states, which have recently codified their evidence rules, have adopted the Supreme Court version of rule 803(6), providing for admission of memoranda of a "regularly conducted activity." None adopted the words "business activity" used in the House amendment.[3]

Therefore, the committee deleted the word "business" as it appears before the word "activity". The last sentence then is unnecessary and was also deleted.

It is the understanding of the committee that the use of the phrase "person with knowledge" is not intended to imply that the party seeking to introduce

3. See Nev.Rev.Stats. § 15.135; N.Mex.
Stats. (1973 Supp.) § 20–4–803(6); West's
Wis.Stats.Anno. (1973 Supp.) § 908.03(6).

the memorandum, report, record, or data compilation must be able to produce, or even identify, the specific individual upon whose first-hand knowledge the memorandum, report, record or data compilation was based. A sufficient foundation for the introduction of such evidence will be laid if the party seeking to introduce the evidence is able to show that it was the regular practice of the activity to base such memorandums, reports, records, or data compilations upon a transmission from a person with knowledge, e.g., in the case of the content of a shipment of goods, upon a report from the company's receiving agent or in the case of a computer printout, upon a report from the company's computer programmer or one who has knowledge of the particular record system. In short, the scope of the phrase "person with knowledge" is meant to be coterminous with the custodian of the evidence or other qualified witness. The committee believes this represents the desired rule in light of the complex nature of modern business organizations.

Conference Report

H.R., Fed.Rules of Evidence, Conf.Rep. No. 1597, 93d Cong., 2d Sess., p. 11 (1974); 1974 U.S.Code Cong. & Ad.News 7098, 7104

The House bill provides in subsection (6) that records of a regularly conducted "business" activity qualify for admission into evidence as an exception to the hearsay rule. "Business" is defined as including "business, profession, occupation and calling of every kind." The Senate amendment drops the requirement that the records be those of a "business" activity and eliminates the definition of "business." The Senate amendment provides that records are admissible if they are records of a regularly conducted "activity."

The Conference adopts the House provision that the records must be those of a regularly conducted "business" activity. The Conferees changed the definition of "business" contained in the House provision in order to make it clear that the records of institutions and associations like schools, churches and hospitals are admissible under this provision. The records of public schools and hospitals are also covered by Rule 803(8), which deals with public records and reports.

Advisory Committee's Note

56 F.R.D. 183, 311

Exception (7). Failure of a record to mention a matter which would ordinarily be mentioned is satisfactory evidence of its nonexistence. Uniform Rule 63(14), Comment. While probably not hearsay as defined in Rule 801, supra, decisions may be found which class the evidence not only as hearsay but also as not within any exception. In order to set the question at rest in favor of admissibility, it is specifically treated here. McCormick § 289, p. 609; Morgan, Basic Problems of Evidence 314 (1962); 5 Wigmore § 1531; Uniform Rule 63(14); California Evidence Code § 1272; Kansas Code of Civil Procedure § 60–460(n); New Jersey Evidence Rule 63(14).

Report of House Committee on the Judiciary

House Comm. on Judiciary, Fed.Rules of Evidence, H.R.Rep. No. 650,
93d Cong., 1st Sess., p. 14 (1973); 1974 U.S.Code
Cong. & Ad.News 7075, 7088

Rule 803(7) as submitted by the Court concerned the *absence* of entry in the records of a "regularly conducted activity." The Committee amended this Rule to conform with its action with respect to Rule 803(6).

Advisory Committee's Note

56 F.R.D. 183, 311

Exception (8). Public records are a recognized hearsay exception at common law and have been the subject of statutes without number. McCormick § 291. See, for example, 28 U.S.C. § 1733, the relative narrowness of which is illustrated by its nonapplicability to non-federal public agencies, thus necessitating resort to the less appropriate business record exception to the hearsay rule. Kay v. United States, 255 F.2d 476 (4th Cir.1958). The rule makes no distinction between federal and nonfederal offices and agencies.

Justification for the exception is the assumption that a public official will perform his duty properly and the unlikelihood that he will remember details independently of the record. Wong Wing Foo v. McGrath, 196 F.2d 120 (9th Cir.1952), and see Chesapeake & Delaware Canal Co. v. United States, 250 U.S. 123, 39 S.Ct. 407, 63 L.Ed. 889 (1919). As to items (A) and (B), further support is found in the reliability factors underlying records of regularly conducted activities generally. See Exception (6), supra.

(A) Cases illustrating the admissibility of records of the office's or agency's own activities are numerous. Chesapeake & Delaware Canal Co. v. United States, 250 U.S. 123, 39 S.Ct. 407, 63 L.Ed. 889 (1919), Treasury records of miscellaneous receipts and disbursements; Howard v. Perrin, 200 U.S. 71, 26 S.Ct. 195, 50 L.Ed. 374 (1906), General Land Office records; Ballew v. United States, 160 U.S. 187, 16 S.Ct. 263, 40 L.Ed. 388 (1895), Pension Office records.

(B) Cases sustaining admissibility of records of matters observed are also numerous. United States v. Van Hook, 284 F.2d 489 (7th Cir.1960), remanded for resentencing 365 U.S. 609, 81 S.Ct. 823, 5 L.Ed.2d 821, letter from induction officer to District Attorney, pursuant to army regulations, stating fact and circumstances of refusal to be inducted; T'Kach v. United States, 242 F.2d 937 (5th Cir.1957), affidavit of White House personnel officer that search of records showed no employment of accused, charged with fraudulently representing himself as an envoy of the President; Minnehaha County v. Kelley, 150 F.2d 356 (8th Cir.1945); Weather Bureau records of rainfall; United States v. Meyer, 113 F.2d 387 (7th Cir.1940), cert. denied 311 U.S. 706, 61 S.Ct. 174, 85 L.Ed. 459, map prepared by government engineer from information furnished by men working under his supervision.

(C) The more controversial area of public records is that of the so-called "evaluative" report. The disagreement among the decisions has been due in part, no doubt, to the variety of situations encountered, as well as to differences in principle. Sustaining admissibility are such cases as United States v. Dumas, 149 U.S. 278, 13 S.Ct. 872, 37 L.Ed. 734 (1893), statement of account certified by Postmaster General in action against postmaster; McCarty v.

United States, 185 F.2d 520 (5th Cir.1950), reh. denied 187 F.2d 234, Certificate of Settlement of General Accounting Office showing indebtedness and letter from Army official stating Government had performed, in action on contract to purchase and remove waste food from Army camp; Moran v. Pittsburgh-Des Moines Steel Co., 183 F.2d 467 (3d Cir.1950), report of Bureau of Mines as to cause of gas tank explosion; Petition of W——, 164 F.Supp. 659 (E.D.Pa.1958), report by Immigration and Naturalization Service investigator that petitioner was known in community as wife of man to whom she was not married. To the opposite effect and denying admissibility are Franklin v. Skelly Oil Co., 141 F.2d 568 (10th Cir.1944), State Fire Marshal's report of cause of gas explosion; Lomax Transp. Co. v. United States, 183 F.2d 331 (9th Cir.1950), Certificate of Settlement from General Accounting Office in action for naval supplies lost in warehouse fire; Yung Jin Teung v. Dulles, 229 F.2d 244 (2d Cir.1956), "Status Reports" offered to justify delay in processing passport applications. . . . Various kinds of evaluative reports are admissible under federal statutes: 7 U.S.C. § 78, findings of Secretary of Agriculture prima facie evidence of true grade of grain; 7 U.S.C. § 210(f), findings of Secretary of Agriculture prima facie evidence in action for damages against stockyard owner; 7 U.S.C. § 292, order by Secretary of Agriculture prima facie evidence in judicial enforcement proceedings against producers association monopoly; 7 U.S.C. § 1622(h), Department of Agriculture inspection certificates of products shipped in interstate commerce prima facie evidence; 8 U.S.C. § 1440(c), separation of alien from military service on conditions other than honorable provable by certificate from department in proceedings to revoke citizenship; 18 U.S.C. § 4245, certificate of Director of Prisons that convicted person has been examined and found probably incompetent at time of trial prima facie evidence in court hearing on competency; 42 U.S.C. § 269(b), bill of health by appropriate official prima facie evidence of vessel's sanitary history and condition and compliance with regulations; 46 U.S.C. § 679, certificate of consul presumptive evidence of refusal of master to transport destitute seamen to United States. While these statutory exceptions to the hearsay rule are left undisturbed, Rule 802, the willingness of Congress to recognize a substantial measure of admissibility for evaluative reports is a helpful guide.

Factors which may be of assistance in passing upon the admissibility of evaluative reports include: (1) the timeliness of the investigation, McCormick, Can the Courts Make Wider Use of Reports of Official Investigations? 42 Iowa L.Rev. 363 (1957); (2) the special skill or experience of the official, *id.,* (3) whether a hearing was held and the level at which conducted, Franklin v. Skelly Oil Co., 141 F.2d 568 (10th Cir.1944); (4) possible motivation problems suggested by Palmer v. Hoffman, 318 U.S. 109, 63 S.Ct. 477, 87 L.Ed. 645 (1943). Others no doubt could be added.

The formulation of an approach which would give appropriate weight to all possible factors in every situation is an obvious impossibility. Hence the rule, as in Exception (6), assumes admissibility in the first instance but with ample provision for escape if sufficient negative factors are present. In one respect, however, the rule with respect to evaluative reports under item (C) is very specific: they are admissible only in civil cases and against the government in criminal cases in view of the almost certain collision with confrontation rights which would result from their use against the accused in a criminal case.

Report of House Committee on the Judiciary

House Comm. on Judiciary, Fed.Rules of Evidence, H.R.Rep. No. 650,
93d Cong., 1st Sess., p. 14 (1973); 1974 U.S.Code
Cong. & Ad.News 7075, 7088

The Committee approved Rule 803(8) without substantive change from the form in which it was submitted by the Court. The Committee intends that the phrase "factual findings" be strictly construed and that evaluations or opinions contained in public reports shall not be admissible under this Rule.

House of Representatives

Feb. 6, 1974, 120 Cong.Rec. 2387 (1974)

Amendment offered by Ms. Holtzman

Ms. HOLTZMAN. Mr. Chairman, I offer an amendment.

The Clerk read as follows:

> Amendment offered by Ms. Holtzman: On page 94, line 11, after the word "law" and before the comma, insert the following: "as to which matters there was a duty to report".

Ms. HOLTZMAN. Mr. Chairman, I will try to be very brief, because it is late in the day.

My amendment is offered to clarify and narrow a provision on the hearsay rule (Rule 803(8)(B)). This rule now provides that if any Government employee in the course of his duty observes something—in fact, anything—and makes a report of that observation, that report can be entered into evidence at a trial whether criminal or civil, without the opportunity to cross-examine the author of the report.

While I respect Government employees, I think we would all concede that they are fallible, exactly like every other human. We do not provide such broad exceptions to the hearsay rule for ordinary mortals.

My amendment makes it crystal clear that random observations by a Government employee cannot be introduced as an exception to the hearsay rule and be insulated from cross-examination. My amendment would allow reports of "matters observed" by a public official only if he had a duty to report about such matters. One operating under such a duty is far more likely to observe and report accurately.

I urge adoption of this amendment in order to narrow and restrict the broad exception to the hearsay rule in the bill.

Mr. HUNGATE. Mr. Chairman, I rise in opposition to the amendment.

This is a matter that was considered in the subcommittee, and we decided to stay with the language as presented to the House here, which states as follows:

> Records, reports, statements, or data compilations, in any form, of public offices or agencies, setting forth (A) the activities of the office or agency, or (B) matters observed pursuant to duty imposed by law. . . .

Mr. Chairman, this is where the point of disagreement occurred. We stayed with that version of the bill, and I would recommend that version to the Committee of the Whole House.

Mr. DANIELSON. Mr. Chairman, I rise in support of the amendment offered by the gentlewoman from New York (Ms. Holtzman).

I think if we leave this language in the proposed bill, we are opening the door to a host of problems, the like of which we have probably never seen in a trial court.

I think the proper approach, in order to eliminate this, is simply to adopt the gentlewoman's amendment, and eliminate this provision, simply because there is absolutely no restriction on the sort of material which could come in under the language as proposed.

I urge the adoption of the gentlewoman's amendment.

Mr. DENNIS. Mr. Chairman, I rise in support of the gentlewoman's amendment.

So that the committee will know what we are talking about here, this permits the introduction in evidence as an exception to the hearsay rule of public records and reports, statements, or data compilations in any form of matters observed pursuant to duty imposed by law. The gentlewoman would add "as to which matters there was a duty to report."

Again it is a matter of judgment, but the difference would be this: Supposing you had a divorce case and you tried to put in a report of a social worker, rather than putting the social worker on the stand; under the committee's language anything she said in the report which would be observed by her pursuant to her general duties would be admissible. Under the amendment, only those things as to which she had some duty to make a report would be admissible.

If the law required her to observe and report certain things about a condition in the home, that could come in, but if she put in a lot of other stuff there, she could not put that in without calling her as a witness and giving the opposition a chance to cross-examine her.

On the whole I think the amendment improves the bill, and I support it.

The CHAIRMAN. The question is on the amendment offered by the gentlewoman from New York (Ms. Holtzman).

The amendment was agreed to.

Amendment offered by Mr. Dennis

Mr. DENNIS. Mr. Chairman, I offer an amendment.

The Clerk read as follows:

Amendment offered by Mr. Dennis: On page 94, line 11 of the bill, after the word "law", insert the words "excluding, however, in criminal cases matters observed by police officers and other law enforcement personnel".

Mr. DENNIS. Mr. Chairman, this goes to the same subject matter as the last amendment. It deals with official statements and reports.

What I am saying here is that in a criminal case, only, we should not be able to put in the police report to prove your case without calling the policeman. I think in a criminal case you ought to have to call the policeman on the beat and give the defendant the chance to cross examine him, rather than just reading the report into evidence, that is the purpose of this amendment.

Ms. HOLTZMAN. Mr. Chairman, I rise in support of the amendment.

I will be very brief again.

I commend my colleague for raising this point. Again his purpose is to restrict the possible abuse of hearsay evidence.

I think the gentleman's amendment is very valuable and reaffirms the right of cross-examination to the accused. It also permits those engaged in civil trials the right of cross-examination. Cross-examination guarantees due process of law and a fair trial.

(Ms. HOLTZMAN asked and was given permission to revise and extend her remarks.)

Mr. SMITH of New York. Mr. Chairman, I rise in opposition to the amendment.

Mr. Chairman, in reading this amendment it seems to me that the effect of the gentleman's amendment is to treat police officers and other law enforcement officers as second-class citizens, because we have already agreed that we are going to allow in as exceptions to the hearsay rule matters observed pursuant to duty imposed by law. The gentleman from Indiana would exclude from that as follows: "Excluding however, in criminal cases, matters observed by police officers and other law enforcement personnel." This would be so even though they were matters observed pursuant to a duty imposed by law.

I just think we are treading in an area the impact of which will be very unfortunate and the effect of which is to make police officers and law enforcement officers second-class citizens and persons less trustworthy than social workers or garbage collectors.

. . .

Mr. DENNIS. Mr. Chairman, I would like to say on that point that of course that is not my idea. I think the point is that we are dealing here with criminal cases, and in a criminal case the defendant should be confronted with the accuser to give him the chance to cross-examine. This is not any reflection on the police officer, but in a criminal case that is the type of report with which, in fact, one is going to be concerned.

. . .

Mr. JOHNSON of Colorado. Mr. Chairman, as an ex-prosecutor I cannot imagine that the gentleman would be advocating that a policeman's report could come in to help convict a man, and not have the policeman himself subject to cross-examination.

Is that what the gentleman is advocating?

Mr. SMITH of New York. That is what I am advocating in that the policeman's report, if he is not available, should be admissible when it is made pursuant to a duty imposed on that law enforcement officer by law. This is the amendment we have just adopted, and for other public officers these police reports ought to be admissible, whatever their probative value might be.

Mr. JOHNSON of Colorado. Mr. Chairman, if the gentleman will yield further, as I said, I was a prosecutor in a State court, and there were so many cases where good cross-examination indicated a lack of investigative ability on the part of the man who made the report that I became more and more convinced that good cross-examination was one of the principal elements in any criminal trial. If the officer who made the investigation is not available for cross-examination, then you cannot have a fair trial.

I cannot believe the gentleman would be saying that we should be able to convict people where the police officer's statement is not subject to cross-examination.

Mr. SMITH of New York. All I am saying to the gentleman from Colorado is that—and I will concede that the gentleman has probably had greater experience in this field than I have had—all I am saying is that it seems to me that it should be allowed for the jury to consider such a report, together with all of the other aspects of the case, if this report was made by a police officer pursuant to a duty imposed upon that police officer by law.

I will have to admit to the gentleman from Colorado that it is not the best evidence.

Mr. JOHNSON of Colorado. If the gentleman will yield still further, I will have to say that in my opinion the Supreme Court would have to ultimately declare that kind of a rule unconstitutional if we did pass it, and that the present amendment is one that would have to be passed if we are going to preserve the rights and traditions of individuals that have been in existence since 1066—I think that is when it started.

Mr. BRASCO. Mr. Chairman, I move to strike the requisite number of words.

(Mr. BRASCO asked and was given permission to revise and extend his remarks.)

Mr. BRASCO. Mr. Chairman, I would like to ask the author of the amendment, the gentleman from Indiana (Mr. Dennis) a question. I am deeply disturbed and troubled about these rules that have been brought out today.

It seems to me that many critical areas have been overlooked.

One of the basic tenets of our law is that one should be confronted by one's accuser and be able to cross-examine the accuser.

There are many, many exceptions to the hearsay rule here.

As I understand it the gentleman from New York (Mr. Smith) is advocating, in opposition to the amendment offered by the gentleman from Indiana (Mr. Dennis) that if a police officer made a report that he saw Mr. X with a gun on such and such an occasion, and then thereafter that police officer is unavailable that that statement could be used in a criminal trial against Mr. X without the defense attorney having the opportunity to cross-examine the officer with respect to his position with relation to Mr. X, the time of the day, whether he was under a light, or whether there was no light, how much time did he have in which to see the gun, and all other observations relevant to the case.

Mr. DENNIS. Mr. Chairman, I would say in answer to the question raised by the gentleman from New York (Mr. Brasco) that if the statements of the police officer in his report would, in the language of this bill, be "matters observed pursuant to a duty imposed by law, and as to which he was under a duty to make a report," and I rather think they might be, that then what the gentleman says is true, and would be true.

I am trying to remove that possibility, by saying that the rule will not apply in the case the gentleman is talking about.

Mr. BRASCO. I support the gentleman. I am just standing up talking, because I cannot believe that we would for one moment entertain any other rule. I would hope we would do it with all cases of hearsay.

. . .

Mr. HUNT. I had no intention of getting into this argument, but when the gentleman brings in the word "investigator," then I have to get in.

Mr. BRASCO. I did not say it.

Mr. HUNT. I know the gentleman from New York did not, but it was discussed. The only time I can recall in my 34 years of law enforcement that a report of an investigator was admissible in court was to test the credibility of an officer. We would never permit a report to come in unchallenged. We would never even think about bringing in a report in lieu of the officer being there to have that officer cross-examined; but reports were admitted as evidentiary fact for the purpose of testing the officer's credibility and perhaps to refresh his memory. That has always been the rule of law in the State of New Jersey, and I hope it will always remain that way—and even the Federal canons.

Mr. BRASCO. I do not think that the gentleman's amendment interferes with that at all. I think what he is talking about is that the prosecution could use this to prove its case in chief with the possibility of no other evidence being presented.

Mr. HUNT. He is talking about bringing the report in in lieu of an officer, and that certainly is not the case.

Mr. DENNIS. Mr. Chairman, will the gentleman yield?

Mr. BRASCO. I yield to the gentleman from Indiana.

Mr. DENNIS. I thank the gentleman for yielding. I certainly agree this amendment has nothing to do with what my friend, the gentleman from New Jersey, is talking about. This applies only to a hearsay exception, where it would be attempted to bring this report in instead of the officer to prove one's case in chief, which one could do if we do not pass this amendment; but we could still use the report to contradict him and cross-examine him.

Mr. HUNT. Certainly, but the gentleman is speaking of the best evidence available then in lieu of the direct evidence.

Mr. DENNIS. I say we should bring in the man who saw it and put him on the stand.

Mr. HUNT. Certainly, the gentleman is right.

The CHAIRMAN. The question is on the amendment offered by the gentleman from Indiana (Mr. Dennis).

The amendment was agreed to.

Report of Senate Committee on the Judiciary

Senate Comm. on Judiciary, Fed.Rules of Evidence, S.Rep. No. 1277,
93d Cong., 2d Sess., p. 17 (1974); 1974 U.S.Code
Cong. & Ad.News 7051, 7064

The House approved rule 803(8), as submitted by the Supreme Court, with one substantive change. It excluded from the hearsay exception reports containing matters observed by police officers and other law enforcement personnel in criminal cases. Ostensibly, the reason for this exclusion is that observations by police officers at the scene of the crime or the apprehension of the defendant are not as reliable as observations by public officials in other cases because of the adversarial nature of the confrontation between the police and the defendant in criminal cases.

The committee accepts the House's decision to exclude such recorded observations where the police officer is available to testify in court about his observation. However, where he is unavailable as unavailability is defined in rule 804(a)(4) and (a)(5), the report should be admitted as the best available evidence. Accordingly, the committee has amended rule 803(8) to refer to the provision of rule 804(b)(5), which allows the admission of such reports, records or other statements where the police officer or other law enforcement officer is unavailable because of death, then existing physical or mental illness or infirmity, or not being successfully subject to legal process. [This version of rule 804(b)(5) was not included in the rules as enacted.]

The House Judiciary Committee report contained a statement of intent that "the phrase 'factual findings' in subdivision (c) be strictly construed and that evaluations or opinions contained in public reports shall not be admissible under this rule." The committee takes strong exception to this limiting understanding of the application of the rule. We do not think it reflects an understanding of the intended operation of the rule as explained in the Advisory Committee notes to this subsection. The Advisory Committee notes on subsection (c) of this subdivision point out that various kinds of evaluative reports are now admissible under Federal statutes. 7 U.S.C. § 78, findings of Secretary of Agriculture prima facie evidence of true grade of grain; 42 U.S.C. § 269(b), bill of health by appropriate official prima facie evidence of vessel's sanitary history and condition and compliance with regulations. These statutory exceptions to the hearsay rule are preserved. Rule 802. The willingness of Congress to recognize these and other such evaluative reports provides a helpful guide in determining the kind of reports which are intended to be admissible under this rule. We think the restrictive interpretation of the House overlooks the fact that while the Advisory Committee assumes admissibility in the first instance of evaluative reports, they are not admissible if, as the rule states, "the sources of information or other circumstances indicate lack of trustworthiness."

The Advisory Committee explains the factors to be considered:

* * *

Factors which may be assistance in passing upon the admissibility of evaluative reports include: (1) the timeliness of the investigation, McCormick, Can the Courts Make Wider Use of Reports of Official Investigations? 42 Iowa L.Rev. 363 (1957); (2) the special skill or experience of the official, id.; (3) whether a hearing was held and the level at which conducted, Franklin v. Skelly Oil Co., 141 F.2d 568 (19th Cir.1944): (4) possible motivation problems suggested by Palmer v. Hoffman, 318 U.S. 109, 63 S.Ct. 477, 87 L.Ed. 645 (1943). Others no doubt could be added.[4]

* * *

The committee concludes that the language of the rule together with the explanation provided by the Advisory Committee furnish sufficient guidance on the admissibility of evaluative reports.

4. Advisory Committee's notes, to rule 803(8)(c).

Conference Report

H.R., Fed.Rules of Evidence, Conf.Rep. No. 1597, 93d Cong., 2d Sess.,
p. 11 (1974); 1974 U.S.Code Cong. & Ad.News 7098, 7104

The Senate amendment adds language, not contained in the House bill, that refers to another rule that was added by the Senate in another amendment (Rule 804(b)(5)—Criminal law enforcement records and reports).

In view of its action on Rule 804(b)(5) (Criminal law enforcement records and reports), the Conference does not adopt the Senate amendment and restores the bill to the House version.

Advisory Committee's Note

56 F.R.D. 183, 313

Exception (9). Records of vital statistics are commonly the subject of particular statutes making them admissible in evidence, Uniform Vital Statistics Act, 9C U.L.A. 350 (1957). The rule is in principle narrower than Uniform Rule 63(16) which includes reports required of persons performing functions authorized by statute, yet in practical effect the two are substantially the same. Comment Uniform Rule 63(16). The exception as drafted is in the pattern of California Evidence Code § 1281.

Exception (10). The principle of proving nonoccurrence of an event by evidence of the absence of a record which would regularly be made of its occurrence, developed in Exception (7) with respect to regularly conducted [business] activities, is here extended to public records of the kind mentioned in Exceptions (8) and (9). 5 Wigmore § 1633(6), p. 519. Some harmless duplication no doubt exists with Exception (7). For instances of federal statutes recognizing this method of proof, see 8 U.S.C. § 1284(b), proof of absence of alien crewman's name from outgoing manifest prima facie evidence of failure to detain or deport, and 42 U.S.C. § 405(c)(3), (4)(B), (4)(C), absence of HEW record prima facie evidence of no wages or self-employment income.

The rule includes situations in which absence of a record may itself be the ultimate focal point of inquiry, e.g. People v. Love, 310 Ill. 558, 142 N.E. 204 (1923), certificate of Secretary of State admitted to show failure to file documents required by Securities Law, as well as cases where the absence of a record is offered as proof of the non-occurrence of an event ordinarily recorded.

The refusal of the common law to allow proof by certificate of the lack of a record or entry has no apparent jusitification, 5 Wigmore § 1678(7), p. 752. The rule takes the opposite position, as do Uniform Rule 63(17); California Evidence Code § 1284; Kansas Code of Civil Procedure § 60–460(c); New Jersey Evidence Rule 63(17). Congress has recognized certification as evidence of the lack of a record. 8 U.S.C. § 1360(d), certificate of Attorney General or other designated officer that no record of Immigration and Naturalization Service of specified nature or entry therein is found, admissible in alien cases.

Exception (11). Records of activities of religious organizations are currently recognized as admissible at least to the extent of the business records exception to the hearsay rule, 5 Wigmore § 1523, p. 371, and Exception (6) would be applicable. However, both the business record doctrine and Exception (6) require that the person furnishing the information be one in the business or activity. The result is such decisions as Daily v. Grand Lodge, 311 Ill. 184, 142

N.E. 478 (1924), holding a church record admissible to prove fact, date, and place of baptism, but not age of child except that he had at least been born at the time. In view of the unlikelihood that false information would be furnished on occasions of this kind, the rule contains no requirement that the informant be in the course of the activity. See California Evidence Code § 1315 and Comment.

Exception (12). The principle of proof by certification is recognized as to public officials in Exceptions (8) and (10), and with respect to authentication in Rule 902. The present exception is a duplication to the extent that it deals with a certificate by a public official, as in the case of a judge who performs a marriage ceremony. The area covered by the rule is, however, substantially larger and extends the certification procedure to clergymen and the like who perform marriages and other ceremonies or administer sacraments. Thus certificates of such matters as baptism or confirmation, as well as marriage, are included. In principle they are as acceptable evidence as certificates of public officers. See 5 Wigmore § 1645, as to marriage certificates. When the person executing the certificate is not a public official, the self-authenticating character of documents purporting to emanate from public officials, see Rule 902, is lacking and proof is required that the person was authorized and did make the certificate. The time element, however, may safely be taken as supplied by the certificate, once authority and authenticity are established, particularly in view of the presumption that a document was executed on the date it bears.

For similar rules, some limited to certificates of marriage, with variations in foundation requirements, see Uniform Rule 63(18); California Evidence Code § 1316; Kansas Code of Civil Procedure § 60–460(p); New Jersey Evidence Rule 63(18).

Exception (13). Records of family history kept in family Bibles have by long tradition been received in evidence. 5 Wigmore §§ 1495, 1496, citing numerous statutes and decisions. See also Regulations, Social Security Administration, 20 C.F.R. § 404.703(c), recognizing family Bible entries as proof of age in the absence of public or church records. Opinions in the area also include inscriptions on tombstones, publicly displayed pedigrees, and engravings on rings. Wigmore, supra. The rule is substantially identical in coverage with California Evidence Code § 1312.

Report of House Committee on the Judiciary

House Comm. on Judiciary, Fed.Rules of Evidence, H.R.Rep. No. 650, 93d Cong., 1st Sess., p. 15 (1973); 1974 U.S.Code Cong. & Ad.News 7075, 7088

The Committee approved this Rule in the form submitted by the Court, intending that the phrase "Statements of fact concerning personal or family history" be read to include the specific types of such statements enumerated in Rule 803(11).

Advisory Committee's Note

56 F.R.D. 183, 315

Exception (14). The recording of title documents is a purely statutory development. Under any theory of the admissibility of public records, the records would be receivable as evidence of the contents of the recorded document, else the recording process would be reduced to a nullity. When, however, the record is offered for the further purpose of proving execution and delivery, a problem of lack of first-hand knowledge by the recorder, not present as to contents, is presented. This problem is solved, seemingly in all jurisdictions, by qualifying for recording only those documents shown by a specified procedure, either acknowledgement or a form of probate, to have been executed and delivered. 5 Wigmore §§ 1647–1651. Thus what may appear in the rule, at first glance, as endowing the record with an effect independently of local law and inviting difficulties of an *Erie* nature under Cities Service Oil Co. v. Dunlap, 308 U.S. 208, 60 S.Ct. 201, 84 L.Ed. 196 (1939), is not present, since the local law in fact governs under the example [exception].

Exception (15). Dispositive documents often contain recitals of fact. Thus a deed purporting to have been executed by an attorney in fact may recite the existence of the power of attorney, or a deed may recite that the grantors are all the heirs of the last record owner. Under the rule, these recitals are exempted from the hearsay rule. The circumstances under which dispositive documents are executed and the requirement that the recital be germane to the purpose of the document are believed to be adequate guarantees of trustworthiness, particularly in view of the nonapplicability of the rule if dealings with the property have been inconsistent with the document. The age of the document is of no significance, though in practical application the document will most often be an ancient one. See Uniform Rule 63(29), Comment.

Similar provisions are contained in Uniform Rule 63(29); California Evidence Code § 1330; Kansas Code of Civil Procedure § 60–460(aa); New Jersey Evidence Rule 63(29).

Exception (16). Authenticating a document as ancient, essentially in the pattern of the common law, as provided in Rule 901(b)(8), leaves open as a separate question the admissibility of assertive statements contained therein as against a hearsay objection. 7 Wigmore § 2145a. Wigmore further states that the ancient document technique of authentication is universally conceded to apply to all sorts of documents, including letters, records, contracts, maps, and certificates, in addition to title documents, citing numerous decisions. Id. § 2145. Since most of these items are significant evidentially only insofar as they are assertive, their admission in evidence must be as a hearsay exception. But see 5 id. § 1573, p. 429, referring to recitals in ancient deeds as a "limited" hearsay exception. The former position is believed to be the correct one in reason and authority. As pointed out in McCormick § 298, danger of mistake is minimized by authentication requirements, and age affords assurance that the writing antedates the present controversy. See Dallas County v. Commercial Union Assurance Co., 286 F.2d 388 (5th Cir.1961), upholding admissibility of 58-year-old newspaper story. Cf. Morgan, Basic Problems of Evidence 364 (1962), but see id. 254.

For a similar provision, but with the added requirement that "the statement has since generally been acted upon as true by persons having an interest in the matter," see California Evidence Code § 1331.

Exception (17). Ample authority at common law supported the admission in evidence of items falling in this category. While Wigmore's text is narrowly oriented to lists, etc., prepared for the use of a trade or profession, 6 Wigmore § 1702, authorities are cited which include other kinds of publications, for example, newspaper market reports, telephone directories, and city directories. Id. §§ 1702–1706. The basis of trustworthiness is general reliance by the public or by a particular segment of it, and the motivation of the compiler to foster reliance by being accurate.

For similar provisions, see Uniform Rule 63(30); California Evidence Code § 1340; Kansas Code of Civil Procedure § 60–460(bb); New Jersey Evidence Rule 63(30). Uniform Commercial Code § 2–724 provides for admissibility in evidence of "reports in official publications or trade journals or in newspapers or periodicals of general circulation published as the reports of such [established commodity] market."

Exception (18). The writers have generally favored the admissibility of learned treatises, McCormick § 296, p. 621; Morgan, Basic Problems of Evidence 366 (1962); 6 Wigmore § 1692, with the support of occasional decisions and rules, City of Dothan v. Hardy, 237 Ala. 603, 188 So. 264 (1939); Lewandowski v. Preferred Risk Mut. Ins. Co., 33 Wis.2d 69, 146 N.W.2d 505 (1966), 66 Mich.L.Rev. 183 (1967); Uniform Rule 63(31); Kansas Code of Civil Procedure § 60–460(cc), but the great weight of authority has been that learned treatises are not admissible as substantive evidence though usable in the cross-examination of experts. The foundation of the minority view is that the hearsay objection must be regarded as unimpressive when directed against treatises since a high standard of accuracy is engendered by various factors: the treatise is written primarily and impartially for professionals, subject to scrutiny and exposure for inaccuracy, with the reputation of the writer at stake. 6 Wigmore § 1692. Sound as this position may be with respect to trustworthiness, there is, nevertheless, an additional difficulty in the likelihood that the treatise will be misunderstood and misapplied without expert assistance and supervision. This difficulty is recognized in the cases demonstrating unwillingness to sustain findings relative to disability on the basis of judicially noticed medical texts. Ross v. Gardner, 365 F.2d 554 (6th Cir.1966); Sayers v. Gardner, 380 F.2d 940 (6th Cir.1967); Colwell v. Gardner, 386 F.2d 56 (6th Cir.1967); Glendenning v. Ribicoff, 213 F.Supp. 301 (W.D.Mo.1962); Cook v. Celebrezze, 217 F.Supp. 366 (W.D.Mo.1963); Sosna v. Celebrezze, 234 F.Supp. 289 (E.D.Pa.1964); and see McDaniel v. Celebrezze, 331 F.2d 426 (4th Cir.1964). The rule avoids the danger of misunderstanding and misapplication by limiting the use of treatises as substantive evidence to situations in which an expert is on the stand and available to explain and assist in the application of the treatise if desired. The limitation upon receiving the publication itself physically in evidence, contained in the last sentence, is designed to further this policy.

The relevance of the use of treatises on cross-examination is evident. This use of treatises has been the subject of varied views. The most restrictive position is that the witness must have stated expressly on direct his reliance upon the treatise. A slightly more liberal approach still insists upon reliance but allows it to be developed on cross-examination. Further relaxation dispenses with reliance but requires recognition as an authority by the witness, developable on cross-examination. The greatest liberality is found in decisions allowing use of the treatise on cross-examination when its status as an authority is established by any means. Annot., 60 A.L.R.2d 77. The exception is hinged upon this last position, which is that of the Supreme Court, Reilly v. Pinkus, 338 U.S. 269, 70 S.Ct. 110, 94 L.Ed. 63 (1949), and of recent well considered state court decisions, City of St. Petersburg v. Ferguson, 193 So.2d 648 (Fla.App.1967), cert. denied Fla., 201 So.2d 556; Darling v. Charleston Memorial Community Hospital, 33 Ill.2d 326, 211 N.E.2d 253 (1965); Dabroe v. Rhodes Co., 64 Wash.2d 431, 392 P.2d 317 (1964).

In Reilly v. Pinkus, supra, the Court pointed out that testing of professional knowledge was incomplete without exploration of the witness' knowledge of and attitude toward established treatises in the field. The process works equally well in reverse and furnishes the basis of the rule.

The rule does not require that the witness rely upon or recognize the treatise as authoritative, thus avoiding the possibility that the expert may at the outset block cross-examination by refusing to concede reliance or authoritativeness. Dabroe v. Rhodes Co., supra. Moreover, the rule avoids the unreality of admitting evidence for the purpose of impeachment only, with an instruction to the jury not to consider it otherwise. The parallel to the treatment of prior inconsistent statements will be apparent. See Rules 613(b) and 801(d)(1).

Exceptions (19), (20), and (21). Trustworthiness in reputation evidence is found "when the topic is such that the facts are likely to have been inquired about and that persons having personal knowledge have disclosed facts which have thus been discussed in the community; and thus the community's conclusion, if any has been formed, is likely to be a trustworthy one." 5 Wigmore § 1580, p. 444, and see also § 1583. On this common foundation, reputation as to land boundaries, customs, general history, character, and marriage have come to be regarded as admissible. The breadth of the underlying principle suggests the formulation of an equally broad exception, but tradition has in fact been much narrower and more particularized, and this is the pattern of these exceptions in the rule.

Exception (19) is concerned with matters of personal and family history. Marriage is universally conceded to be a proper subject of proof by evidence of reputation in the community. 5 Wigmore § 1602. As to such items as legitimacy, relationship, adoption, birth, and death, the decisions are divided. Id. § 1605. All seem to be susceptible to being the subject of well founded repute. The "world" in which the reputation may exist may be family, associates, or community. This world has proved capable of expanding with changing times from the single uncomplicated neighborhood, in which all activities take place, to the multiple and unrelated worlds of work, religious affiliation, and social activity, in each of which a reputation may be generated. People v. Reeves, 360 Ill. 55, 195 N.E. 443 (1935); State v. Axilrod, 248 Minn. 204, 79 N.W.2d 677 (1956); Mass.Stat.1947, c. 410, M.G.L.A. c. 233 § 21A; 5 Wigmore § 1616. The family has often served as the point of beginning for allowing community reputation. 5 Wigmore § 1488. For comparable provisions see Uniform Rule 63(26), (27)(c); California Evidence Code §§ 1313, 1314; Kansas Code of Civil Procedure § 60–460(x), (y)(3); New Jersey Evidence Rule 63(26), (27)(c).

The first portion of Exception (20) is based upon the general admissibility of evidence of reputation as to land boundaries and land customs, expanded in this country to include private as well as public boundaries. McCormick § 299, p. 625. The reputation is required to antedate the controversy, though not to be ancient. The second portion is likewise supported by authority, id., and is designed to facilitate proof of events when judicial notice is not available. The historical character of the subject matter dispenses with any need that the reputation antedate the controversy with respect to which it is offered. For similar provisions see Uniform Rule 63(27)(a), (b); California Evidence Code §§ 1320–1322; Kansas Code of Civil Procedure § 60–460(y), (1), (2); New Jersey Evidence Rule 63(27)(a), (b).

Exception (21) recognizes the traditional acceptance of reputation evidence as a means of proving human character. McCormick §§ 44, 158. The exception deals only with the hearsay aspect of this kind of evidence. Limitations upon admissibility based on other grounds will be found in Rules 404, relevancy of character evidence generally, and 608, character of witness. The exception is in effect a reiteration, in the context of hearsay, of Rule 405(a). Similar provisions are contained in Uniform Rule 63(28); California Evidence Code § 1324; Kansas Code of Civil Procedure § 60–460(z); New Jersey Evidence Rule 63(28).

Exception (22). When the status of a former judgment is under consideration in subsequent litigation, three possibilities must be noted: (1) the former judgment is conclusive under the doctrine of res judicata, either as a bar or a collateral estoppel; or (2) it is admissible in evidence for what it is worth; or (3) it may be of no effect at all. The first situation does not involve any problem of evidence except in the way that principles of substantive law generally bear upon the relevancy and materiality of evidence. The rule does not deal with the substantive effect of the judgment as a bar or collateral estoppel. When, however, the doctrine of res judicata does not apply to make the judgment either a bar or a collateral estoppel, a choice is presented between the second and third alternatives. The rule adopts the second for judgments of criminal conviction of felony grade. This is the direction of the decisions, Annot., 18 A.L.R.2d 1287, 1299, which manifest an increasing reluctance to reject *in toto* the validity of the law's factfinding processes outside the confines of res judicata and collateral estoppel. While this may leave a jury with the evidence of conviction but without means to evaluate it, as suggested by Judge Hinton, Note 27 Ill.L.Rev. 195 (1932), it seems safe to assume that the jury will give it substantial effect unless defendant offers a satisfactory explanation, a possibility not foreclosed by the provision. But see North River Ins. Co. v. Militello, 104 Colo. 28, 88 P.2d 567 (1939), in which the jury found for plaintiff on a fire policy despite the introduction of his conviction for arson. For supporting federal decisions see Clark, J., in New York & Cuba Mail S.S. Co. v. Continental Cas. Co., 117 F.2d 404, 411 (2d Cir.1941); Connecticut Fire Ins. Co. v. Farrara, 277 F.2d 388 (8th Cir.1960).

Practical considerations require exclusion of convictions of minor offenses, not because the administration of justice in its lower echelons must be inferior, but because motivation to defend at this level is often minimal or nonexistent. Cope v. Goble, 39 Cal.App.2d 448, 103 P.2d 598 (1940); Jones v. Talbot, 87 Idaho 498, 394 P.2d 316 (1964); Warren v. Marsh, 215 Minn. 615, 11 N.W.2d 528 (1943); Annot., 18 A.L.R.2d 1287, 1295–1297; 16 Brooklyn L.Rev. 286 (1950); 50 Colum.L.Rev. 529 (1950); 35 Cornell L.Q. 872 (1950). Hence the rule includes only convictions of felony grade, measured by federal standards.

Judgments of conviction based upon pleas of *nolo contendere* are not included. This position is consistent with the treatment of *nolo* pleas in Rule 410 and the authorities cited in the Advisory Committee's Note in support thereof.

While these rules do not in general purport to resolve constitutional issues, they have in general been drafted with a view to avoiding collision with constitutional principles. Consequently the exception does not include evidence of the conviction of a third person, offered against the accused in a criminal prosecution to prove any fact essential to sustain the judgment of conviction. A contrary position would seem clearly to violate the right of confrontation.

Kirby v. United States, 174 U.S. 47, 19 S.Ct. 574, 43 L.Ed. 890 (1899), error to convict of possessing stolen postage stamps with the only evidence of theft being the record of conviction of the thieves. The situation is to be distinguished from cases in which conviction of another person is an element of the crime, e.g. 15 U.S.C. § 902(d), interstate shipment of firearms to a known convicted felon, and, as specifically provided, from impeachment.

For comparable provisions see Uniform Rule 63(20); California Evidence Code § 1300; Kansas Code of Civil Procedure § 60–460(r); New Jersey Evidence Rule 63(20).

Exception (23). A hearsay exception in this area was originally justified on the ground that verdicts were evidence of reputation. As trial by jury graduated from the category of neighborhood inquests, this theory lost its validity. It was never valid as to chancery decrees. Nevertheless the rule persisted, though the judges and writers shifted ground and began saying that the judgment or decree was as good evidence as reputation. See City of London v. Clerke, Carth. 181, 90 Eng.Rep. 710 (K.B. 1691); Neill v. Duke of Devonshire, 8 App.Cas. 135 (1882). The shift appears to be correct, since the process of inquiry, sifting, and scrutiny which is relied upon to render reputation reliable is present in perhaps greater measure in the process of litigation. While this might suggest a broader area of application, the affinity to reputation is strong, and paragraph (23) goes no further, not even including character.

The leading case in the United States, Patterson v. Gaines, 47 U.S. (6 How.) 550, 599, 12 L.Ed. 553 (1847), follows in the pattern of the English decisions, mentioning as illustrative matters thus provable: manorial rights, public rights of way, immemorial custom, disputed boundary, and pedigree. More recent recognition of the principle is found in Grant Bros. Construction Co. v. United States, 232 U.S. 647, 34 S.Ct. 452, 58 L.Ed. 776 (1914), in action for penalties under Alien Contract Labor Law, decision of board of inquiry of Immigration Service admissible to prove alienage of laborers, as a matter of pedigree; United States v. Mid-Continent Petroleum Corp., 67 F.2d 37 (10th Cir.1933), records of commission enrolling Indians admissible on pedigree; Jung Yen Loy v. Cahill, 81 F.2d 809 (9th Cir.1936), board decisions as to citizenship of plaintiff's father admissible in proceeding for declaration of citizenship. Contra, In re Estate of Cunha, 49 Haw. 273, 414 P.2d 925 (1966).

Exception (24). The preceding 23 exceptions of Rule 803 and the first five [four] exceptions of Rule 804(b), infra, are designed to take full advantage of the accumulated wisdom and experience of the past in dealing with hearsay. It would, however, be presumptuous to assume that all possible desirable exceptions to the hearsay rule have been catalogued and to pass the hearsay rule to oncoming generations as a closed system. Exception (24) and its companion provision in Rule 804(b)(6)[5] are accordingly included. They do not contemplate an unfettered exercise of judicial discretion, but they do provide for treating new and presently unanticipated situations which demonstrate a trustworthiness within the spirit of the specifically stated exceptions. Within this framework, room is left for growth and development of the law of evidence in the hearsay area, consistently with the broad purposes expressed in Rule 102. See Dallas County v. Commercial Union Assur. Co., 286 F.2d 388 (5th Cir. 1961).

Report of House Committee on the Judiciary

House Comm. on Judiciary, Fed.Rules of Evidence, H.R.Rep. No. 650,
93d Cong., 1st Sess., p. 5 (1973); 1974 U.S.Code
Cong. & Ad.News 7075, 7079

The proposed Rules of Evidence submitted to Congress contained identical provisions in Rules 803 and 804 (which set forth the various hearsay exceptions), to the effect that the federal courts could admit any hearsay statement not specifically covered by any of the stated exceptions, if the hearsay statement was found to have "comparable circumstantial guarantees of trustworthiness."

The Committee deleted these provisions (proposed Rules 803(24) and 804(b) (6)) as injecting too much uncertainty into the law of evidence and impairing the ability of practitioners to prepare for trial. It was noted that Rule 102 directs the courts to construe the Rules of Evidence so as to promote "growth and development." The Committee believed that if additional hearsay exceptions are to be created, they should be by amendments to the Rules, not on a case-by-case basis.

Report of Senate Committee on the Judiciary

Senate Comm. on Judiciary, Fed.Rules of Evidence, S.Rep. No. 1277,
93d Cong., 2d Sess., p. 18 (1974); 1974 U.S.Code
Cong. & Ad.News 7051, 7065

The proposed Rules of Evidence submitted to Congress contained identical provisions in rules 803 and 804 (which set forth the various hearsay exceptions), admitting any hearsay statement not specifically covered by any of the stated exceptions, if the hearsay statement was found to have "comparable circumstantial guarantees of trustworthiness." The House deleted these provisions (proposed rules 803(24) and 804(b)(6)) as injecting "too much uncertainty" into the law of evidence and impairing the ability of practitioners to prepare for trial. The House felt that rule 102, which directs the courts to construe the Rules of Evidence so as to promote growth and development, would permit sufficient flexibility to admit hearsay evidence in appropriate cases under various factual situations that might arise.

We disagree with the total rejection of a residual hearsay exception. While we view rule 102 as being intended to provide for a broader construction and interpretation of these rules, we feel that, without a separate residual provision, the specifically enumerated exceptions could become tortured beyond any reasonable circumstances which they were intended to include (even if broadly construed). Moreover, these exceptions, while they reflect the most typical and well recognized exceptions to the hearsay rule, may not encompass every situation in which the reliability and appropriateness of a particular piece of hearsay evidence make clear that it should be heard and considered by the trier of fact.

The committee believes that there are certain exceptional circumstances where evidence which is found by a court to have guarantees of trustworthiness equivalent to or exceeding the guarantees reflected by the presently listed exceptions, and to have a high degree of probativeness and necessity could properly be admissible.

The case of Dallas County v. Commercial Union Assoc. Co., Ltd., 286 F.2d 388 (5th Cir.1961) illustrates the point. The issue in that case was whether the tower of the county courthouse collapsed because it was struck by lightning (covered by insurance) or because of structural weakness and deterioration of the structure (not covered). Investigation of the structure revealed the presence of charcoal and charred timbers. In order to show that lightning may not have been the cause of the charring, the insurer offered a copy of a local newspaper published over 50 years earlier containing an unsigned article describing a fire in the courthouse while it was under construction. The Court found that the newspaper did not qualify for admission as a business record or an ancient document and did not fit within any other recognized hearsay exception. The court concluded, however, that the article was trustworthy because it was inconceivable that a newspaper reporter in a small town would report a fire in the courthouse if none had occurred. See also United States v. Barbati, 284 F.Supp. 409 (E.D.N.Y.1968).

Because exceptional cases like the *Dallas County* case may arise in the future, the committee has decided to reinstate a residual exception for rules 803 and 804(b).

The committee, however, also agrees with those supporters of the House version who felt that an overly broad residual hearsay exception could emasculate the hearsay rule and the recognized exceptions or vitiate the rationale behind codification of the rules.

Therefore, the committee has adopted a residual exception for rules 803 and 804(b) of much narrower scope and applicability than the Supreme Court version. In order to qualify for admission, a hearsay statement not falling within one of the recognized exceptions would have to satisfy at least four conditions. First, it must have "equivalent circumstantial guarantees of trustworthiness." Second, it must be offered as evidence of a material fact. Third, the court must determine that the statement "is more probative on the point for which it is offered than any other evidence which the proponent can procure through reasonable efforts." This requirement is intended to insure that only statements which have high probative value and necessity may qualify for admission under the residual exceptions. Fourth, the court must determine that "the general purposes of these rules and the interests of justice will best be served by admission of the statement into evidence."

It is intended that the residual hearsay exceptions will be used very rarely, and only in exceptional circumstances. The committee does not intend to establish a broad license for trial judges to admit hearsay statements that do not fall within one of the other exceptions contained in rules 803 and 804(b). The residual exceptions are not meant to authorize major judicial revisions of the hearsay rule, including its present exceptions. Such major revisions are best accomplished by legislative action. It is intended that in any case in which evidence is sought to be admitted under these subsections, the trial judge will exercise no less care, reflection and caution than the courts did under the common law in establishing the now-recognized exceptions to the hearsay rule.

In order to establish a well-defined jurisprudence, the special facts and circumstances which, in the court's judgment, indicates that the statement has a sufficiently high degree of trustworthiness and necessity to justify its admission should be stated on the record. It is expected that the court will give the opposing party a full and adequate opportunity to contest the admission of any statement sought to be introduced under these subsections.

Conference Report [1]

H.R., Fed.Rules of Evidence, Conf.Rep. No. 1597, 93d Cong., 2d Sess.,
p. 11 (1974); 1974 U.S.Code Cong. & Ad.News 7098, 7105

The Senate amendment adds a new subsection, (24), which makes admissible a hearsay statement not specifically covered by any of the previous twenty-three subsections, if the statement has equivalent circumstantial guarantees of trustworthiness and if the court determines that (A) the statement is offered as evidence of a material fact; (B) the statement is more probative on the point for which it is offered than any other evidence the proponent can procure through reasonable efforts; and (C) the general purposes of these rules and the interests of justice will best be served by admission of the statement into evidence.

The House bill eliminated a similar, but broader, provision because of the conviction that such a provision injected too much uncertainty into the law of evidence regarding hearsay and impaired the ability of a litigant to prepare adequately for trial.

The Conference adopts the Senate amendment with an amendment that provides that a party intending to request the court to use a statement under this provision must notify any adverse party of this intention as well as of the particulars of the statement, including the name and address of the declarant. This notice must be given sufficiently in advance of the trial or hearing to provide any adverse party with a fair opportunity to prepare to contest the use of the statement.

1987 Amendment. The amendments are technical. No substantive change is intended.

Rule 804. Hearsay Exceptions; Declarant Unavailable

(a) Definition of unavailability. "Unavailability as a witness" includes situations in which the declarant—

(1) is exempted by ruling of the court on the ground of privilege from testifying concerning the subject matter of the declarant's statement; or

(2) persists in refusing to testify concerning the subject matter of the declarant's statement despite an order of the court to do so; or

(3) testifies to a lack of memory of the subject matter of the declarant's statement; or

(4) is unable to be present or to testify at the hearing because of death or then existing physical or mental illness or infirmity; or

(5) is absent from the hearing and the proponent of statement has been unable to procure the declarant's attendance (or in the case of a hearsay exception under subdivision (b)(2), (3), or (4), the declarant's attendance or testimony) by process or other reasonable means.

---

1. The Conference Report contains a
like provision with regard to Rule 804(b)
(5).—Ed.

A declarant is not unavailable as a witness if exemption, refusal, claim of lack of memory, inability, or absence is due to the procurement or wrongdoing of the proponent of a statement for the purpose of preventing the witness from attending or testifying.

(b) Hearsay exceptions. The following are not excluded by the hearsay rule if the declarant is unavailable as a witness:

(1) Former testimony. Testimony given as a witness at another hearing of the same or a different proceeding, or in a deposition taken in compliance with law in the course of the same or another proceeding, if the party against whom the testimony is now offered, or, in a civil action or proceeding, a predecessor in interest, had an opportunity and similar motive to develop the testimony by direct, cross, or redirect examination.

(2) Statement under belief of impending death. In a prosecution for homicide or in a civil action or proceeding, a statement made by a declarant while believing that the declarant's death was imminent, concerning the cause or circumstances of what the declarant believed to be impending death.

(3) Statement against interest. A statement which was at the time of its making so far contrary to the declarant's pecuniary or proprietary interest, or so far tended to subject the declarant to civil or criminal liability, or to render invalid a claim by the declarant against another, that a reasonable person in the declarant's position would not have made the statement unless believing it to be true. A statement tending to expose the declarant to criminal liability and offered to exculpate the accused is not admissible unless corroborating circumstances clearly indicate the trustworthiness of the statement.

(4) Statement of personal or family history. (A) A statement concerning the declarant's own birth, adoption, marriage, divorce, legitimacy, relationship by blood, adoption, or marriage, ancestry, or other similar fact of personal or family history, even though declarant had no means of acquiring personal knowledge of the matter stated; or (B) a statement concerning the foregoing matters, and death also, of another person, if the declarant was related to the other by blood, adoption, or marriage or was so intimately associated with the other's family as to be likely to have accurate information concerning the matter declared.

(5) Other exceptions. A statement not specifically covered by any of the foregoing exceptions but having equivalent circumstantial guarantees of trustworthiness, if the court determines that (A) the statement is offered as evidence of a material fact; (B) the statement is more probative on the point for which it is offered than any other evidence which the proponent can procure through reasonable efforts; and (C) the general purposes of these rules and the interests of justice will best be served by admission of the statement into evidence. However, a statement may not be admitted under this exception unless the proponent of it makes known to the adverse party sufficiently in advance of the trial or hearing to provide the adverse party with a fair opportunity to prepare to meet it, the proponent's intention to offer the statement and the particulars of it, including the name and address of the declarant.

(As amended P.L. 94–149, § 1(12), (13), Dec. 12, 1975, 89 Stat. 806; Mar. 2, 1987, eff. Oct. 1, 1987; Nov. 18, 1988, P.L. 100–690, Title VII, § 7075(b), 102 Stat. 4405.)

Section references, McCormick 4th ed.

Generally, § 253, § 326

(a). § 253

(b). § 320

(1). § 301, § 302, § 303, § 304, § 308

(2). § 310, § 311, § 312, § 313, § 315

(3). § 254, § 316, § 317, § 318, § 319, § 271

(4). § 322

(5). § 324, § 324.3, § 353

Note by Federal Judicial Center

The rule prescribed by the Supreme Court was amended by the Congress in a number of respects as follows:

Subdivision (a). Paragraphs (1) and (2) were amended by substituting "court" in place of "judge," and paragraph (5) was amended by inserting "(or in the case of a hearsay exception under subdivision (b)(2), (3), or (4), his attendance or testimony)".

Subdivision (b). Exception (1) was amended by inserting "the same or" after "course of," and by substituting the phrase "if the party against whom the testimony is now offered, or, in a civil action or proceeding, a predecessor in interest, had an opportunity and similar motive to develop the testimony by direct, cross, or redirect examination" in place of "at the instance of or against a party with an opportunity to develop the testimony by direct, cross, or redirect examination, with motive and interest similar to those of the party against whom now offered."

Exception (2) as prescribed by the Supreme Court, dealing with statements of recent perception, was deleted by the Congress.

. . . Exception (2) as enacted by the Congress is Exception (3) prescribed by the Supreme Court, amended by inserting at the beginning, "In a prosecution for homicide or in a civil action or proceeding".

Exception (3) as enacted by the Congress is Exception (4) prescribed by the Supreme Court, amended in the first sentence by deleting, after "another," the phrase "or to make him an object of hatred, ridicule, or disgrace," and amended in the second sentence by substituting, after "unless," the phrase, "corroborating circumstances clearly indicate the trustworthiness of the statement," in place of "corroborated."

Exception (4) as enacted by the Congress is Exception (5) prescribed by the Supreme Court without change.

Exception (5) as enacted by the Congress is Exception (6) prescribed by the Supreme Court, amended by substituting "equivalent" in place of "comparable" and by adding all after "trustworthiness."

Advisory Committee's Note

56 F.R.D. 183, 322

As to firsthand knowledge on the part of hearsay declarants, see the introductory portion of the Advisory Committee's Note to Rule 803.

Subdivision (a). The definition of unavailability implements the division of hearsay exceptions into two categories by Rules 803 and 804(b).

At common law the unavailability requirement was evolved in connection with particular hearsay exceptions rather than along general lines. For example, see the separate explications of unavailability in relation to former testimony, declarations against interest, and statements of pedigree, separately developed in McCormick §§ 234, 257, and 297. However, no reason is apparent for making distinctions as to what satisfies unavailability for the different exceptions. The treatment in the rule is therefore uniform although differences in the range of process for witnesses between civil and criminal cases will lead to a less exacting requirement under item (5). See Rule 45(e) of the Federal Rules of Civil Procedure and Rule 17(e) of the Federal Rules of Criminal Procedure.

Five instances of unavailability are specified:

(1) Substantial authority supports the position that exercise of a claim of privilege by the declarant satisfies the requirement of unavailability (usually in connection with former testimony). Wyatt v. State, 35 Ala.App. 147, 46 So.2d 837 (1950); State v. Stewart, 85 Kan. 404, 116 P. 489 (1911); Annot., 45 A.L.R.2d 1354; Uniform Rule 62(7)(a); California Evidence Code § 240(a)(1); Kansas Code of Civil Procedure § 60–459(g)(1). A ruling by the judge is required, which clearly implies that an actual claim of privilege must be made.

(2) A witness is rendered unavailable if he simply refuses to testify concerning the subject matter of his statement despite judicial pressures to do so, a position supported by similar considerations of practicality. Johnson v. People, 152 Colo. 586, 384 P.2d 454 (1963); People v. Pickett, 339 Mich. 294, 63 N.W.2d 681, 45 A.L.R.2d 1341 (1954). Contra, Pleau v. State, 255 Wis. 362, 38 N.W.2d 496 (1949).

(3) The position that a claimed lack of memory by the witness of the subject matter of his statement constitutes unavailability likewise finds support in the cases, though not without dissent. McCormick § 234, p. 494. If the claim is successful, the practical effect is to put the testimony beyond reach, as in the other instances. In this instance, however, it will be noted that the lack of memory must be established by the testimony of the witness himself, which clearly contemplates his production and subjection to cross-examination.

Report of House Committee on the Judiciary

House Comm. on Judiciary, Fed.Rules of Evidence, H.R.Rep. No. 650, 93d Cong., 1st Sess., p. 15 (1973); 1974 U.S.Code Cong. & Ad.News 7075, 7088

Rule 804(a)(3) was approved in the form submitted by the Court. However, the Committee intends no change in existing federal law under which the court may choose to disbelieve the declarant's testimony as to his lack of memory. See United States v. Insana, 423 F.2d 1165, 1169–1170 (2nd Cir.), cert. denied, 400 U.S. 841 (1970).

Advisory Committee's Note

56 F.R.D. 183, 322

(4) Death and infirmity find general recognition as grounds. McCormick §§ 234, 257, 297; Uniform Rule 62(7)(c); California Evidence Code § 240(a)(3); Kansas Code of Civil Procedure § 60–459(g)(3); New Jersey Evidence Rule 62(6) (c). See also the provisions on use of depositions in Rule 32(a)(3) of the Federal Rules of Civil Procedure and Rule 15(e) of the Federal Rules of Criminal Procedure.

(5) Absence from the hearing coupled with inability to compel attendance by process or other reasonable means also satisfies the requirement. McCormick § 234; Uniform Rule 62(7)(d) and (e); California Evidence Code § 240(a)(4) and (5); Kansas Code of Civil Procedure § 60–459(g)(4) and (5); New Jersey Rule 62(6)(b) and (d). See the discussion of procuring attendance of witnesses who are nonresidents or in custody in Barber v. Page, 390 U.S. 719, 88 S.Ct. 1318, 20 L.Ed.2d 255 (1968).

If the conditions otherwise constituting unavailability result from the procurement or wrongdoing of the proponent of the statement, the requirement is not satisfied. . . .

Report of House Committee on the Judiciary

House Comm. on Judiciary, Fed.Rules of Evidence, H.R.Rep. No. 650, 93d Cong., 1st Sess., p. 15 (1973); 1974 U.S.Code Cong. & Ad.News 7075, 7088

Rule 804(a)(5) as submitted to the Congress provided, as one type of situation in which a declarant would be deemed "unavailable", that he be "absent from the hearing and the proponent of his statement has been unable to procure his attendance by process or other reasonable means." The Committee amended the Rule to insert after the word "attendance" the parenthetical expression "(or, in the case of a hearsay exception under subdivision (b)(2), (3), or (4), his attendance or testimony)". The amendment is designed primarily to require that an attempt be made to depose a witness (as well as to seek his attendance) as a precondition to the witness being deemed unavailable. The Committee, however, recognized the propriety of an exception to this additional requirement when it is the declarant's former testimony that is sought to be admitted under subdivision (b)(1).

Report of Senate Committee on the Judiciary

Senate Comm. on Judiciary, Fed.Rules of Evidence, S.Rep. No. 1277, 93d Cong., 2d Sess., p. 20 (1974); 1974 U.S.Code Cong. & Ad.News 7051, 7066

Subdivision (a) of rule 804 as submitted by the Supreme Court defined the conditions under which a witness was considered to be unavailable. It was amended in the House.

The purpose of the amendment, according to the report of the House Committee on the Judiciary, is "primarily to require that an attempt be made to depose a witness (as well as to seek his attendance) as a precondition to the witness being unavailable."[1]

Under the House amendment, before a witness is declared unavailable, a party must try to depose a witness (declarant) with respect to dying declarations, declarations against interest, and declarations of pedigree. None of these situations would seem to warrant this needless, impractical and highly restrictive complication. A good case can be made for eliminating the unavailability requirement entirely for declarations against interest cases.[2]

In dying declaration cases, the declarant will usually, though not necessarily, be deceased at the time of trial. Pedigree statements which are admittedly and necessarily based largely on word of mouth are not greatly fortified by a deposition requirement.

Depositions are expensive and time-consuming. In any event, deposition procedures are available to those who wish to resort to them. Moreover, the deposition procedures of the Civil Rules and Criminal Rules are only imperfectly adapted to implementing the amendment. No purpose is served unless the deposition, if taken, may be used in evidence. Under Civil Rule (a)(3) and Criminal Rule 15(e), a deposition, though taken, may not be admissible, and under Criminal Rule 15(a) substantial obstacles exist in the way of even taking a deposition.

For these reasons, the committee deleted the House amendment.

The committee understands that the rule as to unavailability, as explained by the Advisory Committee "contains no requirement that an attempt be made to take the deposition of a declarant." In reflecting the committee's judgment, the statement is accurate insofar as it goes. Where, however, the proponent of the statement, with knowledge of the existence of the statement, fails to confront the declarant with the statement at the taking of the deposition, then the proponent should not, in fairness, be permitted to treat the declarant as "unavailable" simply because the declarant was not amenable to process compelling his attendance at trial. The committee does not consider it necessary to amend the rule to this effect because such a situation abuses, not conforms to, the rule. Fairness would preclude a person from introducing a hearsay statement on a particular issue if the person taking the deposition was aware of the issue at the time of the deposition but failed to depose the unavailable witness on that issue.

Conference Report

H.R., Fed.Rules of Evidence, Conf.Rep. No. 1597, 93d Cong., 2d Sess., p. 12 (1974); 1974 U.S.Code Cong. & Ad. News 7098, 7105

Subsection (a) defines the term "unavailability as a witness". The House bill provides in subsection (a)(5) that the party who desires to use the statement must be unable to procure the declarant's attendance by process or other reasonable means. In the case of dying declarations, statements against interest and statements of personal or family history, the House bill requires that the proponent must also be unable to procure the declarant's *testimony*

---

1. H.Rept. 93–650, at p. 15.   2. Uniform rule 63(10); Kan.Stat.Anno. 60–460(j); 2A N.J.Stats.Anno. 84–63(10).

(such as by deposition or interrogatories) by process or other reasonable means. The Senate amendment eliminates this latter provision.

The Conference adopts the provision contained in the House bill.

Advisory Committee's Note
56 F.R.D. 183, 323

Subdivision (b). Rule 803, supra, is based upon the assumption that a hearsay statement falling within one of its exceptions possesses qualities which justify the conclusion that whether the declarant is available or unavailable is not a relevant factor in determining admissibility. The instant rule proceeds upon a different theory: hearsay which admittedly is not equal in quality to testimony of the declarant on the stand may nevertheless be admitted if the declarant is unavailable and if his statement meets a specified standard. The rule expresses preferences: testimony given on the stand in person is preferred over hearsay, and hearsay, if of the specified quality, is preferred over complete loss of the evidence of the declarant. The exceptions evolved at common law with respect to declarations of unavailable declarants furnish the basis for the exceptions enumerated in the proposal. The term "unavailable" is defined in subdivision (a).

Exception [1]. Former testimony does not rely upon some set of circumstances to substitute for oath and cross-examination, since both oath and opportunity to cross-examine were present in fact. The only missing one of the ideal conditions for the giving of testimony is the presence of trier and opponent ("demeanor evidence"). This is lacking with all hearsay exceptions. Hence it may be argued that former testimony is the strongest hearsay and should be included under Rule 803, supra. However, opportunity to observe demeanor is what in a large measure confers depth and meaning upon oath and cross-examination. Thus in cases under Rule 803 demeanor lacks the significance which it possesses with respect to testimony. In any event, the tradition, founded in experience, uniformly favors production of the witness if he is available. The exception indicates continuation of the policy. This preference for the presence of the witness is apparent also in rules and statutes on the use of depositions, which deal with substantially the same problem.

Under the exception, the testimony may be offered (1) against the party *against* whom it was previously offered or (2) against the party *by* whom it was previously offered. In each instance the question resolves itself into whether fairness allows imposing, upon the party against whom now offered, the handling of the witness on the earlier occasion. (1) If the party against whom now offered is the one against whom the testimony was offered previously, no unfairness is apparent in requiring him to accept his own prior conduct of cross-examination or decision not to cross-examine. Only demeanor has been lost, and that is inherent in the situation. (2) If the party against whom now offered is the one *by* whom the testimony was offered previously, a satisfactory answer becomes somewhat more difficult. One possibility is to proceed somewhat along the line of an adoptive admission, i.e. by offering the testimony proponent in effect adopts it. However, this theory savors of discarded concepts of witnesses' belonging to a party, of litigants' ability to pick and choose witnesses, and of vouching for one's own witnesses. Cf. McCormick § 246, pp. 526–527; 4 Wigmore § 1075. A more direct and acceptable approach is simply to recognize direct and redirect examination of one's own witness as the equivalent of cross-examining an opponent's witness. Falknor, Former Testimony and the Uniform Rules: A Comment, 38 N.Y.U.L.Rev. 651, n. 1 (1963); McCormick § 231, p. 483. See also 5 Wigmore § 1389. Allowable techniques for dealing with hostile, double-crossing, forgetful, and mentally deficient witnesses leave no substance to a claim that one could not adequately develop his own witness at the former hearing. An even less appealing argument is presented when failure to develop fully was the result of a deliberate choice.

The common law did not limit the admissibility of former testimony to that given in an earlier trial of the same case, although it did require identity of issues as a means of insuring that the former handling of the witness was the equivalent of what would now be done if the opportunity were presented. Modern decisions reduce the requirement to "substantial" identity. McCormick § 233. Since identity of issues is significant only in that it bears on motive and interest in developing fully the testimony of the witness, expressing the matter in the latter terms is preferable. Id. Testimony given at a preliminary hearing was held in California v. Green, 399 U.S. 149, 90 S.Ct. 1930, 26 L.Ed.2d 489 (1970), to satisfy confrontation requirements in this respect.

As a further assurance of fairness in thrusting upon a party the prior handling of the witness, the common law also insisted upon identity of parties, deviating only to the extent of allowing substitution of successors in a narrowly construed privity. Mutuality as an aspect of identity is now generally discredited, and the requirement of identity of the offering party disappears except as it might affect motive to develop the testimony. Falknor, supra, at 652; McCormick § 232, pp. 487–488. The question remains whether strict identity, or privity, should continue as a requirement with respect to the party against whom offered. . . .

Report of House Committee on the Judiciary

House Comm. on Judiciary, Fed.Rules of Evidence, H.R.Rep. No. 650,
93d Cong., 1st Sess., p. 15 (1973); 1974 U.S.Code
Cong. & Ad.News 7075, 7088

Rule 804(b)(1) as submitted by the Court allowed prior testimony of an unavailable witness to be admissible if the party against whom it is offered or a person "with motive and interest similar" to his had an opportunity to examine the witness. The Committee considered that it is generally unfair to impose upon the party against whom the hearsay evidence is being offered responsibility for the manner in which the witness was previously handled by another party. The sole exception to this, in the Committee's view, is when a party's predecessor in interest in a civil action or proceeding had an opportunity and similar motive to examine the witness. The Committee amended the Rule to reflect these policy determinations.

Advisory Committee's Note

56 F.R.D. 183, 326

Exception [2]. The exception is the familiar dying declaration of the common law, expanded somewhat beyond its traditionally narrow limits. While the original religious justification for the exception may have lost its conviction for some persons over the years, it can scarcely be doubted that powerful psychological pressures are present. See 5 Wigmore § 1443 and the classic statement of Chief Baron Eyre in Rex v. Woodcock, 1 Leach 500, 502, 168 Eng.Rep. 352, 353 (K.B.1789).

The common law required that the statement be that of the victim, offered in a prosecution for criminal homicide. Thus declarations by victims in prosecutions for other crimes, e.g. a declaration by a rape victim who dies in childbirth, and all declarations in civil cases were outside the scope of the exception. An occasional statute has removed these restrictions, as in Colo.R.S. § 52–1–20, or has expanded the area of offenses to include abortions, 5 Wigmore § 1432, p. 224, n. 4. Kansas by decision extended the exception to civil cases. Thurston v. Fritz, 91 Kan. 468, 138 P. 625 (1914). While the common law exception no doubt originated as a result of the exceptional need for the evidence in homicide cases, the theory of admissibility applies equally in civil cases . . .. The same considerations suggest abandonment of the limitation to circumstances attending the event in question, yet when the statement deals with matters other than the supposed death, its influence is believed to be sufficiently attenuated to justify the limitation. Unavailability is not limited to death. See subdivision (a) of this rule. Any problem as to declarations phrased in terms of opinion is laid at rest by Rule 701, and continuation of a requirement of first-hand knowledge is assured by Rule 602.

Comparable provisions are found in Uniform Rule 63(5); California Evidence Code § 1242; Kansas Code of Civil Procedure § 60–460(e); New Jersey Evidence Rule 63(5).

Report of House Committee on the Judiciary

House Comm. on Judiciary, Fed.Rules of Evidence, H.R.Rep. No. 650, 93d Cong., 1st Sess., p. 15 (1973); 1974 U.S.Code Cong. & Ad.News 7075, 7089

Rule 804(b)(3) as submitted by the Court (now Rule 804(b)(2) in the bill) proposed to expand the traditional scope of the dying declaration exception (i.e. a statement of the victim in a homicide case as to the cause or circumstances of his believed imminent death) to allow such statements in all criminal and civil cases. The Committee did not consider dying declarations as among the most reliable forms of hearsay. Consequently, it amended the provision to limit their admissibility in criminal cases to homicide prosecutions, where exceptional need for the evidence is present. This is existing law. At the same time, the Committee approved the expansion to civil actions and proceedings where the stakes do not involve possible imprisonment, although noting that this could lead to forum shopping in some instances.

Advisory Committee's Note

46 F.R.D. 183, 327

Exception [3]. The circumstantial guaranty of reliability for declarations against interest is the assumption that persons do not make statements which are damaging to themselves unless satisfied for good reason that they are true. Hileman v. Northwest Engineering Co., 346 F.2d 668 (6th Cir.1965). If the statement is that of a party, offered by his opponent, it comes in as an admission, Rule 803(d)(2), and there is no occasion to inquire whether it is against interest, this not being a condition precedent to admissibility of admissions by opponents.

The common law required that the interest declared against be pecuniary or proprietary but within this limitation demonstrated striking ingenuity in discovering an against-interest aspect. Higham v. Ridgway, 10 East 109, 103 Eng.Rep. 717 (K.B.1808); Reg. v. Overseers of Birmingham, 1 B. & S. 763, 121 Eng.Rep. 897 (Q.B.1861); McCormick, § 256, p. 551, nn. 2 and 3.

The exception discards the common law limitation and expands to the full logical limit. One result is to remove doubt as to the admissibility of declarations tending to establish a tort liability against the declarant or to extinguish one which might be asserted by him, in accordance with the trend of the decisions in this country. McCormick, § 254, pp. 548–549. . . . And finally, exposure to criminal liability satisfies the against-interest requirement. The refusal of the common law to concede the adequacy of a penal interest was no doubt indefensible in logic, see the dissent of Mr. Justice Holmes in Donnelly v. United States, 228 U.S. 243, 33 S.Ct. 449, 57 L.Ed. 820 (1913), but one senses in the decisions a distrust of evidence of confessions by third persons offered to exculpate the accused arising from suspicions of fabrication either of the fact of the making of the confession or in its contents, enhanced in either instance by the required unavailability of the declarant. Nevertheless, an increasing amount of decisional law recognizes exposure to punishment for crime as a sufficient stake. People v. Spriggs, 60 Cal.2d 868, 36 Cal.Rptr. 841, 389 P.2d 377 (1964); Sutter v. Easterly, 354 Mo. 282, 189 S.W.2d 284 (1945); Band's Refuse Removal, Inc. v. Fairlawn Borough, 62 N.J.Super. 522, 163 A.2d 465 (1960); Newberry v. Commonwealth, 191 Va. 445, 61 S.E.2d 318 (1950); Annot., 162 A.L.R. 446. The requirement of corroboration is included in the rule in order to effect an accommodation between these competing considerations. When the statement is offered by the accused by way of exculpation, the resulting situation is not adapted to control by rulings as to the weight of the evidence, and hence the provision is cast in terms of a requirement preliminary to admissibility. Cf. Rule 406(a). The requirement of corroboration should be construed in such a manner as to effectuate its purpose of circumventing fabrication.

Ordinarily the third-party confession is thought of in terms of exculpating the accused, but this is by no means always or necessarily the case: it may include statements implicating him, and under the general theory of declarations against interest they would be admissible as related statements. Douglas v. Alabama, 380 U.S. 415, 85 S.Ct. 1074, 13 L.Ed.2d 934 (1965), and Bruton v. United States, 389 U.S. 818, 88 S.Ct. 126, 19 L.Ed.2d 70 (1968), both involved confessions by codefendants which implicated the accused. While the confession was not actually offered in evidence in *Douglas,* the procedure followed effectively put it before the jury, which the Court ruled to be error. Whether the confession might have been admissible as a declaration against penal interest was not considered or discussed. *Bruton* assumed the inadmissibility, as against the accused, of the implicating confession of his codefendant, and centered upon the question of the effectiveness of a limiting instruction. These decisions, however, by no means require that all statements implicating another person be excluded from the category of declarations against interest. Whether a statement is in fact against interest must be determined from the circumstances of each case. Thus a statement admitting guilt and implicating another person, made while in custody, may well be motivated by a desire to curry favor with the authorities and hence fail to qualify as against interest. See the dissenting opinion of Mr. Justice White in *Bruton.* On the other hand, the same words spoken under different circumstances, e.g., to an acquaintance, would have no difficulty in qualifying. The rule does not purport to deal with questions of the right of confrontation.

The balancing of self-serving against disserving aspects of a declaration is discussed in McCormick § 256.

For comparable provisions, see Uniform Rule 63(10); California Evidence Code § 1230; Kansas Code of Civil Procedure § 60–460(j); New Jersey Evidence Rule 63(10).

Report of House Committee on the Judiciary

House Comm. on Judiciary, Fed.Rules of Evidence, H.R.Rep. No. 650,
93d Cong., 1st Sess., p. 16 (1973); 1974 U.S.Code
Cong. & Ad.News 7075, 7089

Rule 804(b)(4) as submitted by the Court (now Rule 804(b)(3) in the bill) provided as follows:

> *Statement against interest.*—A statement which was at the time of its making so far contrary to the declarant's pecuniary or proprietary interest or so far tended to subject him to civil or criminal liability or to render invalid a claim by him against another or to make him an object of hatred, ridicule, or disgrace, that a reasonable man in his position would not have made the statement unless he believed it to be true. A statement tending to exculpate the accused is not admissible unless corroborated.

The Committee determined to retain the traditional hearsay exception for statements against pecuniary or proprietary interest. However, it deemed the Court's additional references to statements tending to subject a declarant to civil liability or to render invalid a claim by him against another to be redundant as included within the scope of the reference to statements against pecuniary or proprietary interest. See Gichner v. Antonio Triano Tile and Marble Co., 410 F.2d 238 (D.C.Cir.1968). Those additional references were accordingly deleted.

The Court's Rule also proposed to expand the hearsay limitation from its present federal limitation to include statements subjecting the declarant to criminal liability and statements tending to make him an object of hatred, ridicule, or disgrace. The Committee eliminated the latter category from the subdivision as lacking sufficient guarantees of reliability. See United States v. Dovico, 380 F.2d 325, 327 nn. 2, 4 (2nd Cir.), cert. denied, 389 U.S. 944 (1967). As for statements against penal interest, the Committee shared the view of the Court that some such statements do possess adequate assurances of reliability and should be admissible. It believed, however, as did the Court, that statements of this type tending to exculpate the accused are more suspect and so should have their admissibility conditioned upon some further provision insuring trustworthiness. The proposal in the Court Rule to add a requirement of simple corroboration was, however, deemed ineffective to accomplish this purpose since the accused's own testimony might suffice while not necessarily increasing the reliability of the hearsay statement. The Committee settled upon the language "unless corroborating circumstances clearly indicate the trustworthiness of the statement" as affording a proper standard and degree of discretion. It was contemplated that the result in such cases as Donnelly v. United States, 228 U.S. 243 (1912), where the circumstances plainly indicated reliability, would be changed. The Committee also added to the Rule the final sentence from the 1971 Advisory Committee draft, designed to codify the doctrine of Bruton v. United States, 391 U.S. 123 (1968). The Committee does not intend to affect the existing exception to the *Bruton* principle where the codefendant takes the stand and is subject to cross-examination, but believed there was no need to make specific provision for this situation in the Rule, since in that event the declarant would not be "unavailable".

Report of Senate Committee on the Judiciary

Senate Comm. on Judiciary, Fed.Rules of Evidence, S.Rep. No. 1277,
93d Cong., 2d Sess., p. 21 (1974); 1974 U.S.Code
Cong. & Ad.News 7051, 7067

The rule defines those statements which are considered to be against interest and thus of sufficient trustworthiness to be admissible even though hearsay. With regard to the type of interest declared against, the version submitted by the Supreme Court included inter alia, statements tending to subject a declarant to civil liability or to invalidate a claim by him against another. The House struck these provisions as redundant. In view of the conflicting case law construing pecuniary or proprietary interests narrowly so as to exclude, e.g., tort cases, this deletion could be misconstrued.

Three States which have recently codified their rules of evidence have followed the Supreme Court's version of this rule, i.e., that a statement is against interest if it tends to subject a declarant to civil liability.[3]

The committee believes that the reference to statements tending to subject a person to civil liability constitutes a desirable clarification of the scope of the rule. Therefore, we have reinstated the Supreme Court language on this matter.

The Court rule also proposed to expand the hearsay limitation from its present federal limitation to include statements subjecting the declarant to statements tending to make him an object of hatred, ridicule, or disgrace. The House eliminated the latter category from the subdivision as lacking sufficient guarantees of reliability. Although there is considerable support for the admissibility of such statements (all three of the State rules referred to supra, would admit such statements), we accept the deletion by the House.

The House amended this exception to add a sentence making inadmissible a statement or confession offered against the accused in a criminal case, made by a codefendant or other person implicating both himself and the accused. The sentence was added to codify the constitutional principle announced in Bruton v. United States, 391 U.S. 123 (1968). *Bruton* held that the admission of the extrajudicial hearsay statement of one codefendant inculpating a second codefendant violated the confrontation clause of the sixth amendment.

The committee decided to delete this provision because the basic approach of the rules is to avoid codifying, or attempting to codify, constitutional evidentiary principles, such as the fifth amendment's right against self-incrimination and, here, the sixth amendment's right of confrontation. Codification of a constitutional principle is unnecessary and, where the principle is under development, often unwise. Furthermore, the House provision does not appear to recognize the exceptions to the *Bruton* rule, e.g. where the codefendant takes the stand and is subject to cross examination; where the accused confessed, see

3. Nev.Rev.Stats. § 51.345; N.Mex. Stats. (1973 Supp.) § 20–4–804(4); West's Wis.Stats.Anno. (1973 Supp.) § 908.045(4).

United States v. Mancusi, 404 F.2d 296 (2d Cir.1968), cert. denied 397 U.S. 942 (1907); where the accused was placed at the scene of the crime, see United States v. Zelker, 452 F.2d 1009 (2d Cir.1971). For these reasons, the committee decided to delete this provision.

Conference Report

H.R., Fed.Rules of Evidence, Conf.Rep. No. 1597, 93d Cong., 2d Sess.,
p. 12 (1974); 1974 U.S.Code Cong. & Ad.News 7098, 7105

The Senate amendment to subsection (b)(3) provides that a statement is against interest and not excluded by the hearsay rule when the declarant is unavailable as a witness, if the statement tends to subject a person to civil or criminal liability or renders invalid a claim by him against another. The House bill did not refer specifically to civil liability and to rendering invalid a claim against another. The Senate amendment also deletes from the House bill the provision that subsection (b)(3) does not apply to a statement or confession, made by a codefendant or another, which implicates the accused and the person who made the statement, when that statement or confession is offered against the accused in a criminal case.

The Conference adopts the Senate amendment. The Conferees intend to include within the purview of this rule, statements subjecting a person to civil liability and statements rendering claims invalid. The Conferees agree to delete the provision regarding statements by a codefendant, thereby reflecting the general approach in the Rules of Evidence to avoid attempting to codify constitutional evidentiary principles.

Advisory Committee's Note

56 Fed.R.Evid. 183, 328

Exception [4]. The general common law requirement that a declaration in this area must have been made *ante litem motam* has been dropped, as bearing more appropriately on weight than admissibility. See 5 Wigmore § 1483. Item (i) specifically disclaims any need of firsthand knowledge respecting declarant's own personal history. In some instances it is self-evident (marriage) and in others impossible and traditionally not required (date of birth). Item (ii) deals with declarations concerning the history of another person. As at common law, declarant is qualified if related by blood or marriage. 5 Wigmore, § 1489. In addition, and contrary to the common law, declarant qualifies by virtue of intimate association with the family. Id., § 1487. The requirement sometimes encountered that when the subject of the statement is the relationship between two other persons the declarant must qualify as to both is omitted. Relationship is reciprocal. Id., § 1491.

For comparable provisions, see Uniform Rule 63(23), (24), (25); California Evidence Code §§ 1310, 1311; Kansas Code of Civil Procedure § 60–460(u), (v), (w); New Jersey Evidence Rules 63(23), 63(24), 63(25).

Exception [5]. In language and purpose, this exception is identical with Rule 803(24). See the Advisory Committee's Note to that provision.

Reports of House and Senate Committees on the Judiciary

[This exception and its companion exception in rule 803(24) are discussed together in the congressional committee reports. The reports are set forth under rule 803(24), supra.]

Conference Report [1]

The Senate amendment adds a new subsection, (b)(6), [2] which makes admissible a hearsay statement not specifically covered by any of the five [four] previous subsections, if the statement has equivalent circumstantial guarantees of trustworthiness and if the court determines that (A) the statement is offered as evidence of a material fact; (B) the statement is more probative on the point for which it is offered than any other evidence the proponent can procure through reasonable efforts; and (C) the general purposes of these rules and the interests of justice will best be served by admission of the statement into evidence.

The House bill eliminated a similar, but broader, provision because of the conviction that such a provision injected too much uncertainty into the law of evidence regarding hearsay and impaired the ability of a litigant to prepare adequately for trial.

The Conference adopts the Senate amendment with an amendment that renumbers this subsection and provides that a party intending to request the court to use a statement under this provision must notify any adverse party of this intention as well as of the particulars of the statement, including the name and address of the declarant. This notice must be given sufficiently in advance of the trial or hearing to provide any adverse party with a fair opportunity to prepare to contest the use of the statement.

1987 Amendment. The amendments are technical. No substantive change is intended.

Rule 805. Hearsay Within Hearsay

Hearsay included within hearsay is not excluded under the hearsay rule if each part of the combined statements conforms with an exception to the hearsay rule provided in these rules.

Section references, McCormick 4th ed.

§ 255, § 324.1

Note by Federal Judicial Center

The rule enacted by the Congress is the rule prescribed by the Supreme Court without change.

1. The Conference Report contains a like provision with respect to Rule 803(24).—Ed.

2. Numbered (b)(5) as finally enacted.—Ed.

Advisory Committee's Note

56 F.R.D. 183, 329

On principle it scarcely seems open to doubt that the hearsay rule should not call for exclusion of a hearsay statement which includes a further hearsay statement when both conform to the requirements of a hearsay exception. Thus a hospital record might contain an entry of the patient's age based on information furnished by his wife. The hospital record would qualify as a regular entry except that the person who furnished the information was not acting in the routine of the business. However, her statement independently qualifies as a statement of pedigree (if she is unavailable) or as a statement made for purposes of diagnosis or treatment, and hence each link in the chain falls under sufficient assurances. Or, further to illustrate, a dying declaration may incorporate a declaration against interest by another declarant. See McCormick § 290, p. 611.

Rule 806. Attacking and Supporting Credibility of Declarant

When a hearsay statement, or a statement defined in Rule 801(d) (2), (C), (D), or (E), has been admitted in evidence, the credibility of the declarant may be attacked, and if attacked may be supported, by any evidence which would be admissible for those purposes if declarant had testified as a witness. Evidence of a statement or conduct by the declarant at any time, inconsistent with the declarant's hearsay statement, is not subject to any requirement that the declarant may have been afforded an opportunity to deny or explain. If the party against whom a hearsay statement has been admitted calls the declarant as a witness, the party is entitled to examine the declarant on the statement as if under cross-examination.

(As amended Mar. 2, 1987, eff. Oct. 1, 1987.)

Section references, McCormick 4th ed.

§ 37, § 324.2

Note by Federal Judicial Center

The rule enacted by the Congress is the rule prescribed by the Supreme Court, amended by inserting the phrase "or a statement defined in Rule 801(d) (2), (C), (D), or (E)."

Advisory Committee's Note

56 F.R.D. 183, 329

The declarant of a hearsay statement which is admitted in evidence is in effect a witness. His credibility should in fairness be subject to impeachment and support as though he had in fact testified. See Rules 608 and 609. There are however, some special aspects of the impeaching of a hearsay declarant which require consideration. These special aspects center upon impeachment by inconsistent statement, arise from factual differences which exist between the use of hearsay and an actual witness and also between various kinds of hearsay, and involve the question of applying to declarants the general rule disallowing evidence of an inconsistent statement to impeach a witness unless he is afforded an opportunity to deny or explain. See Rule 613(b).

The principal difference between using hearsay and an actual witness is that the inconsistent statement will in the case of the witness almost inevitably of necessity in the nature of things be a *prior* statement, which it is entirely possible and feasible to call to his attention, while in the case of hearsay the inconsistent statement may well be a *subsequent* one, which practically precludes calling it to the attention of the declarant. The result of insisting upon observation of this impossible requirement in the hearsay situation is to deny the opponent, already barred from cross-examination, any benefit of this important technique of impeachment. The writers favor allowing the subsequent statement. McCormick, § 37, p. 69; 3 Wigmore § 1033. The cases, however, are divided. Cases allowing the impeachment include People v. Collup, 27 Cal.2d 829, 167 P.2d 714 (1946); People v. Rosoto, 58 Cal.2d 304, 23 Cal.Rptr. 779, 373 P.2d 867 (1962); Carver v. United States, 164 U.S. 694, 17 S.Ct. 228, 41 L.Ed. 602 (1897). Contra, Mattox v. United States, 156 U.S. 237, 15 S.Ct. 337, 39 L.Ed. 409 (1895); People v. Hines, 284 N.Y. 93, 29 N.E.2d 483 (1940). The force of *Mattox*, where the hearsay was the former testimony of a deceased witness and the denial of use of a subsequent inconsistent statement was upheld, is much diminished by *Carver*, where the hearsay was a dying declaration and denial of use of a subsequent inconsistent statement resulted in reversal. The difference in the particular brand of hearsay seems unimportant when the inconsistent statement is a *subsequent* one. True, the opponent is not totally deprived of cross-examination when the hearsay is former testimony or a deposition but he is deprived of cross-examining on the statement or along lines suggested by it. Mr. Justice Shiras, with two justices joining him, dissented vigorously in *Mattox*.

When the impeaching statement was made *prior* to the hearsay statement, differences in the kinds of hearsay appear which arguably may justify differences in treatment. If the hearsay consisted of a simple statement by the witness, e.g. a dying declaration or a declaration against interest, the feasibility of affording him an opportunity to deny or explain encounters the same practical impossibility as where the statement is a subsequent one, just discussed, although here the impossibility arises from the total absence of anything resembling a hearing at which the matter could be put to him. The courts by a large majority have ruled in favor of allowing the statement to be used under these circumstances. McCormick § 37, p. 69; 3 Wigmore § 1033. If, however, the hearsay consists of former testimony or a deposition, the possibility of calling the prior statement to the attention of the witness or deponent is not ruled out, since the opportunity to cross-examine was available. It might thus be concluded that with former testimony or depositions the conventional foundation should be insisted upon. Most of the cases involve depositions, and Wigmore describes them as divided. 3 Wigmore § 1031. Deposition procedures at best are cumbersome and expensive, and to require the laying of the foundation may impose an undue burden. Under the federal practice, there is no way of knowing with certainty at the time of taking a deposition whether it is merely for discovery or will ultimately end up in evidence. With respect to both former testimony and depositions the possibility exists that knowledge of the statement might not be acquired until after the time of the cross-examination. Moreover, the expanded admissibility of former testimony and depositions under Rule 804(b)(1) calls for a correspondingly expanded approach to impeachment. The rule dispenses with the requirement

in all hearsay situations, which is readily administered and best calculated to lead to fair results.

Notice should be taken that Rule 26(f) of the Federal Rules of Civil Procedure, as originally submitted by the Advisory Committee, ended with the following:

> ". . . and, without having first called them to the deponent's attention, may show statements contradictory thereto made at any time by the deponent."

This language did not appear in the rule as promulgated in December, 1937. See 4 Moore's Federal Practice ¶¶ 26.01[9], 26.35 (2d ed. 1967). In 1951, Nebraska adopted a provision strongly resembling the one stricken from the federal rule:

> "Any party may impeach any adverse deponent by self-contradiction without having laid foundation for such impeachment at the time such deposition was taken." R.S.Neb. § 25–1267.07.

For similar provisions, see Uniform Rule 65; California Evidence Code § 1202; Kansas Code of Civil Procedure § 60–462; New Jersey Evidence Rule 65.

The provision for cross-examination of a declarant upon his hearsay statement is a corollary of general principles of cross-examination. A similar provision is found in California Evidence Code § 1203.

Report of Senate Committee on the Judiciary

Senate Comm. on Judiciary, Fed.Rules of Evidence, S.Rep. No. 1277, 93d Cong., 2d Sess., p. 22 (1974); 1974 U.S.Code Cong. & Ad.News 7051, 7068

Rule 906 [806], as passed by the House and as proposed by the Supreme Court provides that whenever a hearsay statement is admitted, the credibility of the declarant of the statement may be attacked, and if attacked may be supported, by any evidence which would be admissible for those purposes if the declarant had testified as a witness. Rule 801 defines what is a hearsay statement. While statements by a person authorized by a party-opponent to make a statement concerning the subject, by the party-opponent's agent or by a coconspirator of a party—see rule 801(d)(2)(c), (d) and (e)—are traditionally defined as exceptions to the hearsay rule, rule 801 defines such admission by a party-opponent as statements which are not hearsay. Consequently, rule 806 by referring exclusively to the admission of hearsay statements, does not appear to allow the credibility of the declarant to be attacked when the declarant is a coconspirator, agent or authorized spokesman. The committee is of the view that such statements should open the declarant to attacks on his credibility. Indeed, the reason such statements are excluded from the operation of rule 806 is likely attributable to the drafting technique used to codify the hearsay rule, viz. some statements, instead of being referred to as exceptions to the hearsay rule, are defined as statements which are not hearsay. The phrase "or a statement defined in rule 801(d)(2)(c), (d) and (e)" is added to the rule in order to subject the declarant of such statements, like the declarant of hearsay statements, to attacks on his credibility.[1]

1. The committee considered it unnecessary to include statements contained in rule 801(d)(2)(A) and (B)—the statement by the party-opponent himself or the statement of which he has manifested his adoption—because the credibility of the party-

Conference Report

H.R., Fed.Rules of Evidence, Conf.Rep. No. 1597, 93d Cong., 2d Sess.,
p. 13 (1974); 1974 U.S.Code Cong. & Ad.News 7098, 7106

The Senate amendment permits an attack upon the credibility of the declarant of a statement if the statement is one by a person authorized by a party-opponent to make a statement concerning the subject, only by an agent of a party-opponent, or one by a coconspirator of the party-opponent, as these statements are defined in Rules 801(d)(2)(C), (D) and (E). The House bill has no such provision.

The Conference adopts the Senate amendment. The Senate amendment conforms the rule to present practice.

1987 Amendment. The amendments are technical. No substantive change is intended.

ARTICLE IX. AUTHENTICATION AND IDENTIFICATION

Rule
901. Requirement of Authentication or Identification.
    (a) General Provision.
    (b) Illustrations.
902. Self-Authentication.
903. Subscribing Witness' Testimony Unnecessary.

Rule 901. Requirement of Authentication or Identification

(a) General provision. The requirement of authentication or identification as a condition precedent to admissibility is satisfied by evidence sufficient to support a finding that the matter in question is what its proponent claims.

(b) Illustrations. By way of illustration only, and not by way of limitation, the following are examples of authentication or identification conforming with the requirements of this rule:

(1) Testimony of witness with knowledge. Testimony that a matter is what it is claimed to be.

(2) Nonexpert opinion on handwriting. Nonexpert opinion as to the genuineness of handwriting, based upon familiarity not acquired for purposes of the litigation.

(3) Comparison by trier or expert witness. Comparison by the trier of fact or by expert witnesses with specimens which have been authenticated.

(4) Distinctive characteristics and the like. Appearance, contents, substance, internal patterns, or other distinctive characteristics, taken in conjunction with circumstances.

opponent is always subject to an attack on
his credibility.

(5) Voice identification. Identification of a voice, whether heard firsthand or through mechanical or electronic transmission or recording, by opinion based upon hearing the voice at any time under circumstances connecting it with the alleged speaker.

(6) Telephone conversations. Telephone conversations, by evidence that a call was made to the number assigned at the time by the telephone company to a particular person or business, if (A) in the case of a person, circumstances, including self-identification, show the person answering to be the one called, or (B) in the case of a business, the call was made to a place of business and the conversation related to business reasonably transacted over the telephone.

(7) Public records or reports. Evidence that a writing authorized by law to be recorded or filed and in fact recorded or filed in a public office, or a purported public record, report, statement, or data compilation, in any form, is from the public office where items of this nature are kept.

(8) Ancient documents or data compilation. Evidence that a document or data compilation, in any form, (A) is in such condition as to create no suspicion concerning its authenticity, (B) was in a place where it, if authentic, would likely be, and (C) has been in existence 20 years or more at the time it is offered.

(9) Process or system. Evidence describing a process or system used to produce a result and showing that the process or system produces an accurate result.

(10) Methods provided by statute or rule. Any method of authentication or identification provided by Act of Congress or by other rules prescribed by the Supreme Court pursuant to statutory authority.

Section references, McCormick 4th ed.

Generally § 207, § 218

(a). § 222, § 224, § 227

(b)(1). § 214, § 219

(2). § 221

(3). § 221

(4). § 222, § 225

(5). § 226

(6). § 226

(7). § 224

(8). § 223, § 323

(9). § 214, § 293

Note by Federal Judicial Center

The rule enacted by the Congress is the rule prescribed by the Supreme Court, amended in subdivison (b)(10) by substituting "prescribed" in place of "adopted," and by adding "pursuant to statutory authority."

Advisory Committee's Note

56 F.R.D. 183, 332

Subdivison (a). Authentication and identification represent a special aspect of relevancy. Michael and Adler, Real Proof, 5 Vand.L.Rev. 344, 362 (1952); McCormick §§ 179, 185; Morgan, Basic Problems of Evidence 378 (1962). Thus a telephone conversation may be irrelevant because on an unrelated topic or because the speaker is not identified. The latter aspect is the one here involved. Wigmore describes the need for authentication as "an inherent logical necessity." 7 Wigmore § 2129, p. 564.

This requirement of showing authenticity or identity falls in the category of relevancy dependent upon fulfillment of a condition of fact and is governed by the procedure set forth in Rule 104(b).

The common law approach to authentication of documents has been criticized as an "attitude of agnosticism," McCormick, Cases on Evidence 388, n. 4 (3rd ed. 1956), as one which "departs sharply from men's customs in ordinary affairs," and as presenting only a slight obstacle to the introduction of forgeries in comparison to the time and expense devoted to proving genuine writings which correctly show their origin on their face, McCormick § 185, pp. 395, 396. Today, such available procedures as requests to admit and pretrial conference afford the means of eliminating much of the need for authentication or identification. Also, significant inroads upon the traditional insistence on authentication and identification have been made by accepting as at least prima facie genuine items of the kind treated in Rule 902, infra. However, the need for suitable methods of proof still remains, since criminal cases pose their own obstacles to the use of preliminary procedures, unforeseen contingencies may arise, and cases of genuine controversy will still occur.

Subdivision (b). The treatment of authentication and identification draws largely upon the experience embodied in the common law and in statutes to furnish illustrative applications of the general principle set forth in subdivision (a). The examples are not intended as an exclusive enumeration of allowable methods but are meant to guide and suggest, leaving room for growth and development in this area of the law.

The examples relate for the most part to documents, with some attention given to voice communications and computer print-outs. As Wigmore noted, no special rules have been developed for authenticating chattels. Wigmore, Code of Evidence § 2086 (3rd ed. 1942).

It should be observed that compliance with requirements of authentication or identification by no means assures admission of an item into evidence, as other bars, hearsay for example, may remain.

Example (1) contemplates a broad spectrum ranging from testimony of a witness who was present at the signing of a document to testimony establishing narcotics as taken from an accused and accounting for custody through the period until trial, including laboratory analysis. See California Evidence Code § 1413, eyewitness to signing.

Example (2) states conventional doctrine as to lay identification of handwriting, which recognizes that a sufficient familiarity with the handwriting of another person may be acquired by seeing him write, by exchanging correspondence, or by other means, to afford a basis for identifying it on subsequent occasions. McCormick § 189. See also California Evidence Code § 1416. Testimony based upon familiarity acquired for purposes of the litigation is reserved to the expert under the example which follows.

Example (3). The history of common law restrictions upon the technique of proving or disproving the genuineness of a disputed specimen of handwriting through comparison with a genuine specimen, by either the testimony of expert witnesses or direct viewing by the triers themselves, is detailed in 7 Wigmore §§ 1991–1994. In breaking away, the English Common Law Procedure Act of 1854, 17 and 18 Vict., c. 125, § 27, cautiously allowed expert or trier to use exemplars "proved to the satisfaction of the judge to be genuine" for purposes of comparison. The language found its way into numerous statutes in this country, e.g., California Evidence Code §§ 1417, 1418. While explainable as a measure of prudence in the process of breaking with precedent in the handwriting situation, the reservation to the judge of the question of the genuiness of exemplars and the imposition of an unusually high standard of persuasion are at variance with the general treatment of relevancy which depends upon fulfillment of a condition of fact. Rule 104(b). No similar attitude is found in other comparison situations, e.g., ballistics comparison by jury, as in Evans v. Commonwealth, 230 Ky. 411, 19 S.W.2d 1091 (1929), or by experts, Annot., 26 A.L.R.2d 892, and no reason appears for its continued existence in handwriting cases. Consequently Example (3) sets no higher standard for handwriting specimens and treats all comparison situations alike, to be governed by Rule 104(b). This approach is consistent with 28 U.S.C. § 1731: "The admitted or proved handwriting of any person shall be admissible, for purposes of comparison, to determine genuineness of other handwriting attributed to such person."

Precedent supports the acceptance of visual comparison as sufficiently satisfying preliminary authentication requirements for admission in evidence. Brandon v. Collins, 267 F.2d 731 (2d Cir.1959); Wausau Sulphate Fibre Co. v. Commissioner of Internal Revenue, 61 F.2d 879 (7th Cir.1932); Desimone v. United States, 227 F.2d 864 (9th Cir.1955).

Example (4). The characteristics of the offered item itself, considered in the light of circumstances, afford authentication techniques in great variety. Thus a document or telephone conversation may be shown to have emanated from a particular person by virtue of its disclosing knowledge of facts known peculiarly to him; Globe Automatic Sprinkler Co. v. Braniff, 89 Okl. 105, 214 P. 127 (1923); California Evidence Code § 1421; similarly, a letter may be authenticated by content and circumstances indicating it was in reply to a duly authenticated one. McCormick § 192; California Evidence Code § 1420. Language patterns may indicate authenticity or its opposite. Magnuson v. State, 187 Wis. 122, 203 N.W. 749 (1925); Arens and Meadow, Psycholinguistics and the Confession Dilemma, 56 Colum.L.Rev. 19 (1956).

Example (5). Since aural voice identification is not a subject of expert testimony, the requisite familiarity may be acquired either before or after the particular speaking which is the subject of the identification, in this respect resembling visual identification of a person rather than identification of handwriting. Cf. Example (2), supra, People v. Nichols, 378 Ill. 487, 38 N.E.2d 766 (1942); McGuire v. State, 200 Md. 601, 92 A.2d 582 (1952); State v. McGee, 336 Mo. 1082, 83 S.W.2d 98 (1935).

Example (6). The cases are in agreement that a mere assertion of his identity by a person talking on the telephone is not sufficient evidence of the authenticity of the conversation and that additional evidence of his identity is required. The additional evidence need not fall in any set pattern. Thus the content of his statements or the reply technique, under Example (4), supra, or voice identification under Example (5), may furnish the necessary foundation. Outgoing calls made by the witness involve additional factors bearing upon authenticity. The calling of a number assigned by the telephone company reasonably supports the assumption that the listing is correct and that the number is the one reached. If the number is that of a place of business, the mass of authority allows an ensuing conversation if it relates to business reasonably transacted over the telephone, on the theory that the maintenance of the telephone connection is an invitation to do business without further identification. Matton v. Hoover Co., 350 Mo. 506, 166 S.W.2d 557 (1942); City of Pawhuska v. Crutchfield, 147 Okl. 4, 293 P. 1095 (1930); Zurich General Acc. & Liability Ins. Co. v. Baum, 159 Va. 404, 165 S.E. 518 (1932). Otherwise, some additional circumstance of identification of the speaker is required. The authorities divide on the question whether the self-identifying statement of the person answering suffices. Example (6) answers in the affirmative on the assumption that usual conduct respecting telephone calls furnish adequate assurances of regularity, bearing in mind that the entire matter is open to exploration before the trier of fact. In general, see McCormick § 193; 7 Wigmore § 2155; Annot., 71 A.L.R. 5, 105 id. 326.

Example (7). Public records are regularly authenticated by proof of custody, without more. McCormick § 191; 7 Wigmore §§ 2158, 2159. The example extends the principle to include data stored in computers and similar methods, of which increasing use in the public records area may be expected. See California Evidence Code §§ 1532, 1600.

Example (8). The familiar ancient document rule of the common law is extended to include data stored electronically or by other similar means. Since the importance of appearance diminishes in this situation, the importance of custody or place where found increases correspondingly. This expansion is necessary in view of the widespread use of methods of storing data in forms other than conventional written records.

Any time period selected is bound to be arbitrary. The common law period of 30 years is here reduced to 20 years, with some shift of emphasis from the probable unavailability of witnesses to the unlikeliness of a still viable fraud after the lapse of time. The shorter period is specified in the English Evidence Act of 1938, 1 & 2 Geo. 6, c. 28, and in Oregon R.S.1963, § 41.360(34). See also the numerous statutes prescribing periods of less than 30 years in the case of recorded documents. 7 Wigmore § 2143.

The application of Example (8) is not subject to any limitation to title documents or to any requirement that possession, in the case of a title document, has been consistent with the document. See McCormick § 190.

Example (9) is designed for situations in which the accuracy of a result is dependent upon a process or system which produces it. X rays afford a familiar instance. Among more recent developments is the computer, as to which see Transport Indemnity Co. v. Seib, 178 Neb. 253, 132 N.W.2d 871 (1965); State v. Veres, 7 Ariz.App. 117, 436 P.2d 629 (1968); Merrick v. United States Rubber Co., 7 Ariz.App. 433, 440 P.2d 314 (1968); Freed, Computer Print-Outs as Evidence, 16 Am.Jur.Proof of Facts 273; Symposium, Law and Computers in the Mid-Sixties, ALI–ABA (1966); 37 Albany L.Rev. 61 (1967). Example (9) does not, of course, foreclose taking judicial notice of the accuracy of the process or system.

Example (10). The example makes clear that methods of authentication provided by Act of Congress and by the Rules of Civil and Criminal Procedure or by Bankruptcy Rules are not intended to be superseded. Illustrative are the provisions for authentication of official records in Civil Procedure Rule 44 and Criminal Procedure Rule 27, for authentication of records of proceedings by court reporters in 28 U.S.C. § 753(b) and Civil Procedure Rule 80(c), and for authentication of depositions in Civil Procedure Rule 30(f).

Rule 902. Self-Authentication

Extrinsic evidence of authenticity as a condition precedent to admissibility is not required with respect to the following:

(1) **Domestic public documents under seal.** A document bearing a seal purporting to be that of the United States, or of any State, district, Commonwealth, territory, or insular possession thereof, or the Panama Canal Zone, or the Trust Territory of the Pacific Islands, or of a political subdivision, department, officer, or agency thereof, and a signature purporting to be an attestation or execution.

(2) **Domestic public documents not under seal.** A document purporting to bear the signature in the official capacity of an officer or employee of any entity included in paragraph (1) hereof, having no seal, if a public officer having a seal and having official duties in the district or political subdivision of the officer or employee certifies under seal that the signer has the official capacity and that the signature is genuine.

(3) **Foreign public documents.** A document purporting to be executed or attested in an official capacity by a person authorized by the laws of a foreign country to make the execution or attestation, and accompanied by a final certification as to the genuineness of the signature and official position (A) of the executing or attesting person, or (B) of any foreign official whose certificate of genuineness of signature and official position relates to the execution or attestation or is in a chain of certificates of genuineness of signature and official position relating to the execution or attestation. A final certification may be made by a secretary of embassy or legation, consul general, consul, vice consul, or consular agent of the United States, or a diplomatic or consular official of the foreign country assigned or accredited to the United States. If reasonable opportunity has been given to all parties to investigate the authenticity and accuracy of official documents, the court may, for good cause shown, order that they be treated as presumptively authentic without final certification or permit them to be evidenced by an attested summary with or without final certification.

(4) **Certified copies of public records.** A copy of an official record or report or entry therein, or of a document authorized by law to be recorded or filed and actually recorded or filed in a public office, including data compilations in any form, certified as correct by the custodian or other person authorized to make the certification, by certificate complying with paragraph (1), (2), or (3) of this rule or

complying with any Act of Congress or rule prescribed by the Supreme Court pursuant to statutory authority.

(5) Official publications. Books, pamphlets, or other publications purporting to be issued by public authority.

(6) Newspapers and periodicals. Printed materials purporting to be newspapers or periodicals.

(7) Trade inscriptions and the like. Inscriptions, signs, tags, or labels purporting to have been affixed in the course of business and indicating ownership, control, or origin.

(8) Acknowledged documents. Documents accompanied by a certificate of acknowledgment executed in the manner provided by law by a notary public or other officer authorized by law to take acknowledgments.

(9) Commercial paper and related documents. Commercial paper, signatures thereon, and documents relating thereto to the extent provided by general commercial law.

(10) Presumptions under Acts of Congress. Any signature, document, or other matter declared by Act of Congress to be presumptively or prima facie genuine or authentic.

(As amended Mar. 2, 1987, eff. Oct. 1, 1987; Apr. 25, 1988, eff. Nov. 1, 1988.)

Section references, McCormick 4th ed.

Generally § 218

(1). § 228

(2). § 228

(3). § 228

(4). § 228, § 300

(5). § 228

(6). § 228

(7). § 218, § 228

(8). § 228

Note by Federal Judicial Center

The rule enacted by the Congress is the rule prescribed by the Supreme Court, amended as follows:

Paragraph (4) was amended by substituting "prescribed" in place of "adopted," and by adding "pursuant to statutory authority."

Paragraph (8) was amended by substituting "in the manner provided by law by" in place of "under the hand and seal of."

Advisory Committee's Note

56 F.R.D. 183, 337

Case law and statutes have, over the years, developed a substantial body of instances in which authenticity is taken as sufficiently established for purposes of admissibility without extrinsic evidence to that effect, sometimes for reasons of policy but perhaps more often because practical considerations reduce the possibility of unauthenticity to a very small dimension. The present rule collects and incorporates these situations, in some instances expanding them to occupy a larger area which their underlying considerations justify. In no instance is the opposite party foreclosed from disputing authenticity.

Paragraph (1). The acceptance of documents bearing a public seal and signature, most often encountered in practice in the form of acknowledgments or certificates authenticating copies of public records, is actually of broad application. Whether theoretically based in whole or in part upon judicial notice, the practical underlying considerations are that forgery is a crime and detection is fairly easy and certain. 7 Wigmore § 2161, p. 638; California Evidence Code § 1452. More than 50 provisions for judicial notice of official seals are contained in the United States Code.

Paragraph (2). While statutes are found which raise a presumption of genuineness of purported official signatures in the absence of an official seal, 7 Wigmore § 2167; California Evidence Code § 1453, the greater ease of effecting a forgery under these circumstances is apparent. Hence this paragraph of the rule calls for authentication by an officer who has a seal. Notarial acts by members of the armed forces and other special situations are covered in paragraph (10).

Paragraph (3) provides a method for extending the presumption of authenticity to foreign official documents by a procedure of certification. It is derived from Rule 44(a)(2) of the Rules of Civil Procedure but is broader in applying to public documents rather than being limited to public records.

Paragraph (4). The common law and innumerable statutes have recognized the procedure of authenticating copies of public records by certificate. The certificate qualifies as a public document, receivable as authentic when in conformity with paragraph (1), (2), or (3). Rule 44(a) of the Rules of Civil Procedure and Rule 27 of the Rules of Criminal Procedure have provided authentication procedures of this nature for both domestic and foreign public records. It will be observed that the certification procedure here provided extends only to public records, reports, and recorded documents, all including data compilations, and does not apply to public documents generally. Hence documents provable when presented in original form under paragraphs (1), (2), or (3) may not be provable by certified copy under paragraph (4).

Paragraph (5). Dispensing with preliminary proof of the genuineness of purportedly official publications, most commonly encountered in connection with statutes, court reports, rules, and regulations, has been greatly enlarged by statutes and decisions. 5 Wigmore § 1684. Paragraph (5), it will be noted, does not confer admissibility upon all official publications; it merely provides a means whereby their authenticity may be taken as established for purposes of admissibility. Rule 44(a) of the Rules of Civil Procedure has been to the same effect.

Paragraph (6). The likelihood of forgery of newspapers or periodicals is slight indeed. Hence no danger is apparent in receiving them. Establishing the authenticity of the publication may, of course, leave still open questions of authority and responsibility for items therein contained. See 7 Wigmore § 2150. Cf. 39 U.S.C. § 4005(b), public advertisement prima facie evidence of agency of person named, in postal fraud order proceeding; Canadian Uniform Evidence Act, Draft of 1936, printed copy of newspaper prima facie evidence that notices or advertisements were authorized.

Paragraph (7). Several factors justify dispensing with preliminary proof of genuineness of commercial and mercantile labels and the like. The risk of forgery is minimal. Trademark infringement involves serious penalties. Great efforts are devoted to inducing the public to buy in reliance on brand names, and substantial protection is given them. Hence the fairness of this treatment finds recognition in the cases. Curtiss Candy Co. v. Johnson, 163 Miss. 426, 141 So. 762 (1932), Baby Ruth candy bar; Doyle v. Continental Baking Co., 262 Mass. 516, 160 N.E. 325 (1928), loaf of bread; Weiner v. Mager & Throne, Inc., 167 Misc. 338, 3 N.Y.S.2d 918 (1938), same. And see W.Va.Code 1966, § 47-3-5, trade-mark on bottle prima facie evidence of ownership. Contra, Keegan v. Green Giant Co., 150 Me. 283, 110 A.2d 599 (1954); Murphy v. Campbell Soup Co., 62 F.2d 564 (1st Cir.1933). Cattle brands have received similar acceptance in the western states. Rev.Code Mont.1947, § 46–606; State v. Wolfley, 75 Kan. 406, 89 P. 1046 (1907); Annot., 11 L.R.A.(N.S.) 87. Inscriptions on trains and vehicles are held to be prima facie evidence of ownership or control. Pittsburgh, Ft. W. & C. Ry. v. Callaghan, 157 Ill. 406, 41 N.E. 909 (1895); 9 Wigmore § 2510a. See also the provision of 19 U.S.C. § 1615(2) that marks, labels, brands, or stamps indicating foreign origin are prima facie evidence of foreign origin of merchandise.

Paragraph (8). In virtually every state, acknowledged title documents are receivable in evidence without further proof. Statutes are collected in 5 Wigmore § 1676. If this authentication suffices for documents of the importance of those affecting titles, logic scarcely permits denying this method when other kinds of documents are involved. Instances of broadly inclusive statutes are California Evidence Code § 1451 and N.Y.CPLR 4538, McKinney's Consol. Laws 1963.

Report of House Committee on the Judiciary

House Comm. on Judiciary, Fed.Rules of Evidence, H.R.Rep. No. 650,
93d Cong., 1st Sess., p. 17 (1973); 1974 U.S.Code
Cong. & Ad.News 7075, 7090

Rule 902(8) as submitted by the Court referred to certificates of acknowledgment "under the hand and seal of" a notary public or other officer authorized by law to take acknowledgments. The Committee amended the Rule to eliminate the requirement, believed to be inconsistent with the law in some States, that a notary public must affix a seal to a document acknowledged before him. As amended the Rule merely requires that the document be executed in the manner prescribed by State law.

Advisory Committee's Note

56 F.R.D. 183, 339

Paragraph (9). Issues of the authenticity of commercial paper in federal courts will usually arise in diversity cases, will involve an element of a cause of action or defense, and with respect to presumptions and burden of proof will be controlled by Erie Railroad Co. v. Tompkins, 304 U.S. 64, 58 S.Ct. 817, 82 L.Ed 1188 (1938). Rule 302, supra. There may, however, be questions of authenticity involving lesser segments of a case or the case may be one governed by federal common law. Clearfield Trust Co. v. United States, 318 U.S. 363, 63 S.Ct. 573, 87 L.Ed. 838 (1943). Cf. United States v. Yazell, 382 U.S. 341, 86 S.Ct. 500, 15 L.Ed.2d 404 (1966). In these situations, resort to the useful authentication provisions of the Uniform Commercial Code is provided for. While the phrasing is in terms of "general commercial law," in order to avoid the potential complications inherent in borrowing local statutes, today one would have difficulty in determining the general commercial law without referring to the Code. See Williams v. Walker-Thomas Furniture Co., 121 U.S.App.D.C. 315, 350 F.2d 445 (1965). Pertinent Code provisions are sections 1–202, 3–307, and 3–510, dealing with third-party documents, signatures on negotiable instruments, protests, and statements of dishonor.

Report of House Committee on the Judiciary

House Comm. on Judiciary, Fed.Rules of Evidence, H.R.Rep. No. 650,
93d Cong., 1st Sess., p. 17 (1973); 1974 U.S.Code
Cong. & Ad.News 7075, 7090

The Committee approved Rule 902(9) as submitted by the Court. With respect to the meaning of the phrase "general commercial law", the Committee intends that the Uniform Commercial Code, which has been adopted in virtually every State, will be followed generally, but that federal commercial law will apply where federal commercial paper is involved. See Clearfield Trust Co. v. United States, 318 U.S. 363 (1943). Further, in those instances in which the issues are governed by Erie R. Co. v. Tompkins, 304 U.S. 64 (1938), State law will apply irrespective of whether it is the Uniform Commercial Code.

Advisory Committee's Note

56 F.R.D. 183, 340

Paragraph (10). The paragraph continues in effect dispensations with preliminary proof of genuineness provided in various Acts of Congress. See, for example, 10 U.S.C. § 936, signature, without seal, together with title, prima facie evidence of authenticity of acts of certain military personnel who are given notarial powers; 15 U.S.C. § 77f(a), signature on SEC registration presumed genuine; 26 U.S.C. § 6064, signature to tax return prima facie genuine.

1987 Amendment. The amendments are technical. No substantive change is intended.

1988 Amendment. Two sentences were inadvertently eliminated from the 1987 amendment. The amendment is technical. No substantive change is intended.

Rule 903. Subscribing Witness' Testimony Unnecessary

The testimony of a subscribing witness is not necessary to authenticate a writing unless required by the laws of the jurisdiction whose laws govern the validity of the writing.

Section references, McCormick 4th ed.

§ 218, § 220

Note by Federal Judicial Center

The rule enacted by the Congress is the rule prescribed by the Supreme Court without change.

Advisory Committee's Note

56 F.R.D. 183, 340

The common law required that attesting witnesses be produced or accounted for. Today the requirement has generally been abolished except with respect to documents which must be attested to be valid, e.g. wills in some states. McCormick § 188. Uniform Rule 71; California Evidence Code § 1411; Kansas Code of Civil Procedure § 60–468; New Jersey Evidence Rule 71; New York CPLR Rule 4537.

ARTICLE X. CONTENTS OF WRITINGS, RECORDINGS, AND PHOTOGRAPHS

Rule

Rule 1001. Definitions

For purposes of this article the following definitions are applicable:

(1) **Writings and recordings.** "Writings" and "recordings" consist of letters, words, or numbers, or their equivalent, set down by handwriting, typewriting, printing, photostating, photographing, magnetic impulse, mechanical or electronic recording, or other form of data compilation.

(2) **Photographs.** "Photographs" include still photographs, X-ray films, video tapes, and motion pictures.

(3) **Original.** An "original" of a writing or recording is the writing or recording itself or any counterpart intended to have the same effect by a person executing or issuing it. An "original" of a photo-

graph includes the negative or any print therefrom. If data are stored in a computer or similar device, any printout or other output readable by sight, shown to reflect the data accurately, is an "original".

(4) Duplicate. A "duplicate" is a counterpart produced by the same impression as the original, or from the same matrix, or by means of photography, including enlargements and miniatures, or by mechanical or electronic re-recording, or by chemical reproduction, or by other equivalent technique which accurately reproduces the original.

Section references, McCormick 4th ed.

Generally § 236

(1). § 232

(2). § 232

(3). § 230, § 236

(4). § 236

Note by Federal Judicial Center

The rule enacted by the Congress is the rule prescribed by the Supreme Court, amended in paragraph (2) by inserting "video tapes."

Advisory Committee's Note

56 F.R.D. 183, 341

In an earlier day, when discovery and other related procedures were strictly limited, the misleading named "best evidence rule" afforded substantial guarantees against inaccuracies and fraud by its insistence upon production of original documents. The great enlargement of the scope of discovery and related procedures in recent times has measurably reduced the need for the rule. Nevertheless important areas of usefulness persist: discovery of documents outside the jurisdiction may require substantial outlay of time and money; the unanticipated document may not practically be discoverable; criminal cases have built-in limitations on discovery. Cleary and Strong, The Best Evidence Rule: An Evaluation in Context, 51 Iowa L.Rev. 825 (1966).

Paragraph (1). Traditionally the rule requiring the original centered upon accumulations of data and expressions affecting legal relations set forth in words and figures. This meant that the rule was one essentially related to writings. Present day techniques have expanded methods of storing data, yet the essential form which the information ultimately assumes for usable purposes is words and figures. Hence the considerations underlying the rule dictate its expansion to include computers, photographic systems, and other modern developments.

Paragraph (2).

Report of House Committee on the Judiciary

House Comm. on Judiciary, Fed.Rules of Evidence, H.R.Rep. No. 650,
93d Cong., 1st Sess., p. 17 (1973); 1974 U.S.Code
Cong. & Ad.News 7075, 7090

The Committee amended this Rule expressly to include "video tapes" in the definition of "photographs."

Advisory Committee's Note

56 F.R.D. 183, 341

Paragraph (3). In most instances, what is an original will be self-evident and further refinement will be unnecessary. However, in some instances particularized definition is required. A carbon copy of a contract executed in duplicate becomes an original, as does a sales ticket carbon copy given to a customer. While strictly speaking the original of a photograph might be thought to be only the negative, practicality and common usage require that any print from the negative be regarded as an original. Similarly, practicality and usage confer the status of original upon any computer printout. Transport Indemnity Co. v. Seib, 178 Neb. 253, 132 N.W.2d 871 (1965).

Paragraph (4). The definition describes "copies" produced by methods possessing an accuracy which virtually eliminates the possibility of error. Copies thus produced are given the status of originals in large measure by Rule 1003, infra. Copies subsequently produced manually, whether handwritten or typed, are not within the definition. It should be noted that what is an original for some purposes may be a duplicate for others. Thus a bank's microfilm record of checks cleared is the original as a record. However, a print offered as a copy of a check whose contents are in controversy is a duplicate. This result is substantially consistent with 28 U.S.C. § 1732(b). Compare 26 U.S.C. § 7513(c), giving full status as originals to photographic reproductions of tax returns and other documents, made by authority of the Secretary of the Treasury, and 44 U.S.C. § 399(a), giving original status to photographic copies in the National Archives.

Rule 1002. Requirement of Original

To prove the content of a writing, recording, or photograph, the original writing, recording, or photograph is required, except as otherwise provided in these rules or by Act of Congress.

Note by Federal Judicial Center

The rule enacted by the Congress is the rule prescribed by the Supreme Court without change.

Section references, McCormick 4th ed.

§ 230

Advisory Committee's Note

56 F.R.D. 183, 342

The rule is the familiar one requiring production of the original of a document to prove its contents, expanded to include writings, recordings, and photographs, as defined in Rule 1001(1) and (2), supra.

Application of the rule requires a resolution of the question whether contents are sought to be proved. Thus an event may be proved by nondocumentary evidence, even though a written record of it was made. If, however, the event is sought to be proved by the written record, the rule applies. For example, payment may be proved without producing the written receipt which was given. Earnings may be proved without producing books of account in which they are entered. McCormick § 198; 4 Wigmore § 1245. Nor does the rule apply to testimony that books or records have been examined and found not to contain any reference to a designated matter.

The assumption should not be made that the rule will come into operation on every occasion when use is made of a photograph in evidence. On the contrary, the rule will seldom apply to ordinary photographs. In most instances a party *wishes* to introduce the item and the question raised is the propriety of receiving it in evidence. Cases in which an offer is made of the testimony of a witness as to what he saw in a photograph or motion picture, without producing the same, are most unusual. The usual course is for a witness on the stand to identify the photograph or motion picture as a correct representation of events which he saw or of a scene with which he is familiar. In fact he adopts the picture as his testimony, or, in common parlance, uses the picture to illustrate his testimony. Under these circumstances, no effort is made to prove the contents of the picture, and the rule is inapplicable. Paradis, The Celluloid Witness, 37 U.Colo.L.Rev. 235, 249–251 (1965).

On occasion, however, situations arise in which contents are sought to be proved. Copyright, defamation, and invasion of privacy by photograph or motion picture falls in this category. Similarly as to situations in which the picture is offered as having independent probative value, e.g. automatic photograph of bank robber. See People v. Doggett, 83 Cal.App.2d 405, 188 P.2d 792 (1948), photograph of defendants engaged in indecent act; Mouser and Philbin, Photographic Evidence—Is There a Recognized Basis for Admissibility? 8 Hastings L.J. 310 (1957). The most commonly encountered of this latter group is of course, the X-ray, with substantial authority calling for production of the original. Daniels v. Iowa City, 191 Iowa 811, 183 N.W. 415 (1921); Cellamare v. Third Ave. Transit Corp., 273 App.Div. 260, 77 N.Y.S.2d 91 (1948); Patrick & Tilman v. Matkin, 154 Okl. 232, 7 P.2d 414 (1932); Mendoza v. Rivera, 78 P.R.R. 569 (1955).

It should be noted, however, that Rule 703, supra, allows an expert to give an opinion based on matters not in evidence, and the present rule must be read as being limited accordingly in its application. Hospital records which may be admitted as business records under Rule 803(6) commonly contain reports interpreting X rays by the staff radiologist, who qualifies as an expert, and these reports need not be excluded from the records by the instant rule.

The references to Acts of Congress is made in view of such statutory provisions as 26 U.S.C. § 7513, photographic reproductions of tax returns and documents, made by authority of the Secretary of the Treasury, treated as originals, and 44 U.S.C. § 399(a), photographic copies in National Archives treated as originals.

Rule 1003. Admissibility of Duplicates

A duplicate is admissible to the same extent as an original unless (1) a genuine question is raised as to the authenticity of the original or (2) in the circumstances it would be unfair to admit the duplicate in lieu of the original.

Section references, McCormick 4th ed.

§ 231, § 236, § 243, § 354

Note by Federal Judicial Center

The rule enacted by the Congress is the rule prescribed by the Supreme Court without change.

Advisory Committee's Note

56 F.R.D. 183, 343

When the only concern is with getting the words or other contents before the court with accuracy and precision, then a counterpart serves equally as well as the original, if the counterpart is the product of a method which insures accuracy and genuineness. By definition in Rule 1001(4), supra, a "duplicate" possesses this character.

Therefore, if no genuine issue exists as to authenticity and no other reason exists for requiring the original, a duplicate is admissible under the rule. This position finds support in the decisions, Myrick v. United States, 332 F.2d 279 (5th Cir.1964), no error in admitting photostatic copies of checks instead of original microfilm in absence of suggestion to trial judge that photostats were incorrect; Johns v. United States, 323 F.2d 421 (5th Cir.1963), not error to admit concededly accurate tape recording made from original wire recording; Sauget v. Johnston, 315 F.2d 816 (9th Cir.1963), not error to admit copy of agreement when opponent had original and did not on appeal claim any discrepancy. Other reasons for requiring the original may be present when only a part of the original is reproduced and the remainder is needed for cross-examination or may disclose matters qualifying the part offered or otherwise useful to the opposing party. United States v. Alexander, 326 F.2d 736 (4th Cir. 1964). And see Toho Bussan Kaisha, Ltd. v. American President Lines, Ltd., 265 F.2d 418, 76 A.L.R.2d 1344 (2d Cir.1959).

Report of House Committee on the Judiciary

House Comm. on Judiciary, Fed.Rules of Evidence, 93d Cong., 1st Sess., p. 17 (1973); 1974 U.S.Code Cong. & Ad.News 7075, 7090

The Committee approved this Rule in the form submitted by the Court, with the expectation that the courts would be liberal in deciding that a "genuine question is raised as to the authenticity of the original."

Rule 1004. Admissibility of Other Evidence of Contents

The original is not required, and other evidence of the contents of a writing, recording, or photograph is admissible if—

(1) Originals lost or destroyed. All originals are lost or have been destroyed, unless the proponent lost or destroyed them in bad faith; or

(2) Original not obtainable. No original can be obtained by any available judicial process or procedure; or

(3) Original in possession of opponent. At a time when an original was under the control of the party against whom offered, that party was put on notice, by the pleadings or otherwise, that the contents would be a subject of proof at the hearing, and that party does not produce the original at the hearing; or

(4) Collateral matters. The writing, recording, or photograph is not closely related to a controlling issue.

(As amended Mar. 2, 1987, eff. Oct. 1, 1987.)

Section references, McCormick 4th ed.

Generally § 236, § 241

(1). § 237

(2). § 238

(3). § 239

(4). § 234

Note by Federal Judicial Center

The rule enacted by the Congress is the rule prescribed by the Supreme Court without change.

Advisory Committee's Note

56 F.R.D. 183, 344

Basically the rule requiring the production of the original as proof of contents has developed as a rule of preference: if failure to produce the original is satisfactorily explained, secondary evidence is admissible. The instant rule specifies the circumstances under which production of the original is excused.

The rule recognizes no "degrees" of secondary evidence. While strict logic might call for extending the principle of preference beyond simply preferring the original, the formulation of a hierarchy of preferences and a procedure for making it effective is believed to involve unwarranted complexities. Most, if not all, that would be accomplished by an extended scheme of preferences will, in any event, be achieved through the normal motivation of a party to present the most convincing evidence possible and the arguments and procedures available to his opponent if he does not. Compare McCormick § 207.

Paragraph (1). Loss or destruction of the original, unless due to bad faith of the proponent, is a satisfactory explanation of nonproduction. McCormick § 201.

Report of House Committee on the Judiciary

House Comm. on Judiciary, Fed.Rules of Evidence, H.R.Rep. No. 650,
93d Cong., 1st Sess., p. 17 (1973); 1974 U.S.Code
Cong. & Ad.News 7075, 7090

The Committee approved Rule 1004(1) in the form submitted to Congress. However, the Committee intends that loss or destruction of an original by another person at the instigation of the proponent should be considered as tantamount to loss or destruction in bad faith by the proponent himself.

Advisory Committee's Note

56 F.R.D. 183, 344

Paragraph (2). When the original is in the possession of a third person, inability to procure it from him by resort to process or other judicial procedure is a sufficient explanation of nonproduction. Judicial procedure includes subpoena duces tecum as an incident to the taking of a deposition in another jurisdiction. No further showing is required. See McCormick § 202.

Paragraph (3). A party who has an original in his control has no need for the protection of the rule if put on notice that proof of contents will be made. He can ward off secondary evidence by offering the original. The notice procedure here provided is not to be confused with orders to produce or other discovery procedures, as the purpose of the procedure under this rule is to afford the opposite party an opportunity to produce the original, not to compel him to do so. McCormick § 203.

Paragraph (4). While difficult to define with precision, situations arise in which no good purpose is served by production of the original. Examples are the newspaper in an action for the price of publishing defendant's advertisement, Foster-Holcomb Investment Co. v. Little Rock Publishing Co., 151 Ark. 449, 236 S.W. 597 (1922), and the streetcar transfer of plaintiff claiming status as a passenger, Chicago City Ry. Co. v. Carroll, 206 Ill. 318, 68 N.E. 1087 (1903). Numerous cases are collected in McCormick § 200, p. 412, n. 1.

1987 Amendment. The amendments are technical. No substantive change is intended.

Rule 1005. Public Records

The contents of an official record, or of a document authorized to be recorded or filed and actually recorded or filed, including data compilations in any form, if otherwise admissible, may be proved by copy, certified as correct in accordance with rule 902 or testified to be correct by a witness who has compared it with the original. If a copy which complies with the foregoing cannot be obtained by the exercise of reasonable diligence, then other evidence of the contents may be given.

Section references, McCormick 4th ed.

§ 240, § 300

Note by Federal Judicial Center

The rule enacted by the Congress is the rule prescribed by the Supreme Court without change.

Advisory Committee's Note

56 F.R.D. 183, 345

Public records call for somewhat different treatment. Removing them from their usual place of keeping would be attended by serious inconvenience to the public and to the custodian. As a consequence judicial decisions and statutes commonly hold that no explanation need be given for failure to produce the original of a public record. McCormick § 204; 4 Wigmore §§ 1215–1228. This blanket dispensation from producing or accounting for the original would open the door to the introduction of every kind of secondary evidence of contents of public records were it not for the preference given certified or compared copies. Recognition of degrees of secondary evidence in this situation is an appropriate *quid pro quo* for not applying the requirement of producing the original.

The provisions of 28 U.S.C. § 1733(b) apply only to departments or agencies of the United States. The rule, however, applies to public records generally and is comparable in scope in this respect to Rule 44(a) of the Rules of Civil Procedure.

Rule 1006. Summaries

The contents of voluminous writings, recordings, or photographs which cannot conveniently be examined in court may be presented in the form of a chart, summary, or calculation. The originals, or duplicates, shall be made available for examination or copying, or both, by other parties at reasonable time and place. The court may order that they be produced in court.

Section references, McCormick 4th ed.

§ 233

Note by Federal Judicial Center

The rule enacted by the Congress is the rule prescribed by the Supreme Court without change.

Advisory Committee's Note

56 F.R.D. 183, 346

The admission of summaries of voluminous books, records, or documents offers the only practicable means of making their contents available to judge and jury. The rule recognizes this practice, with appropriate safeguards. 4 Wigmore § 1230.

Rule 1007. Testimony or Written Admission of Party

Contents of writings, recordings, or photographs may be proved by the testimony or deposition of the party against whom offered or by that party's written admission, without accounting for the nonproduction of the original.

(As amended Mar. 2, 1987, eff. Oct. 1, 1987.)

Section references, McCormick 4th ed.

§ 242

Note by Federal Judicial Center

The rule enacted by the Congress is the rule prescribed by the Supreme Court without change.

Advisory Committee's Note

56 F.R.D. 183, 356

While the parent case, Slatterie v. Pooley, 6 M. & W. 664, 151 Eng.Rep. 579 (Exch.1840), allows proof of contents by evidence of an oral admission by the party against whom offered, without accounting for nonproduction of the original, the risk of inaccuracy is substantial and the decision is at odds with the purpose of the rule giving preference to the original. See 4 Wigmore § 1255. The instant rule follows Professor McCormick's suggestion of limiting this use of admissions to those made in the course of giving testimony or in writing. McCormick § 208, p. 424. The limitation, of course, does not call for excluding evidence of an oral admission when nonproduction of the original has been accounted for and secondary evidence generally has become admissible. Rule 1004, supra.

A similar provision is contained in New Jersey Evidence Rule 70(1)(h).

1987 Amendment. The amendment is technical. No substantive change is intended.

Rule 1008. Functions of Court and Jury

When the admissibility of other evidence of contents of writings, recordings, or photographs under these rules depends upon the fulfillment of a condition of fact, the question whether the condition has been fulfilled is ordinarily for the court to determine in accordance with the provisions of rule 104. However, when an issue is raised (a) whether the asserted writing ever existed, or (b) whether another writing, recording, or photograph produced at the trial is the original, or (c) whether other evidence of contents correctly reflects the contents, the issue is for the trier of fact to determine as in the case of other issues of fact.

Section references, McCormick 4th ed.

§ 53, § 54

Note by Federal Judicial Center

The rule enacted by the Congress is the rule prescribed by the Supreme Court, amended by substituting "court" in place of "judge," and by adding at the end of the first sentence the phrase "in accordance with the provisions of rule 104."

Advisory Committee's Note

56 F.R.D. 183, 347

Most preliminary questions of fact in connection with applying the rule preferring the original as evidence of contents are for the judge, under the general principles announced in Rule 104, supra. Thus, the question whether the loss of the originals has been established, or of the fulfillment of other conditions specified in Rule 1004, supra, is for the judge. However, questions may arise which go beyond the mere administration of the rule preferring the original and into the merits of the controversy. For example, plaintiff offers secondary evidence of the contents of an alleged contract, after first introducing evidence of loss of the original, and defendant counters with evidence that no such contract was ever executed. If the judge decides that the contract was never executed and excludes the secondary evidence, the case is at an end without ever going to the jury on a central issue. Levin, Authentication and Content of Writings, 10 Rutgers L.Rev. 632, 644 (1956). The latter portion of the instant rule is designed to insure treatment of these situations as raising jury questions. The decision is not one for uncontrolled discretion of the jury but is subject to the control exercised generally by the judge over jury determinations. See Rule 104(b), supra.

For similar provisions, see Uniform Rule 70(2); Kansas Code of Civil Procedure § 60–467(b); New Jersey Evidence Rule 70(2), (3).

ARTICLE XI. MISCELLANEOUS RULES

Rule
1101. Applicability of Rules.
    (a) Courts and Magistrates.
    (b) Proceedings Generally.
    (c) Rule of Privilege.
    (d) Rules Inapplicable.
    (e) Rules Applicable in Part.
1102. Amendments.
1103. Title.

Rule 1101. Applicability of Rules

(a) **Courts and magistrates.** These rules apply to the United States district courts, the District Court of Guam, the District Court of the Virgin Islands, the District Court for the Northern Mariana Islands, the United States courts of appeals, the United States Claims Court, and to United States bankruptcy judges and United States magistrates, in the actions, cases, and proceedings and to the extent hereinafter set forth. The terms "judge" and "court" in these rules include United States bankruptcy judges and United States magistrates.

(b) Proceedings generally. These rules apply generally to civil actions and proceedings, including admiralty and maritime cases, to criminal cases and proceedings, to contempt proceedings except those in which the court may act summarily, and to proceedings and cases under title 11, United States Code.

(c) Rule of privilege. The rule with respect to privileges applies at all stages of all actions, cases, and proceedings.

(d) Rules inapplicable. The rules (other than with respect to privileges) do not apply in the following situations:

(1) Preliminary questions of fact. The determination of questions of fact preliminary to admissibility of evidence when the issue is to be determined by the court under rule 104.

(2) Grand jury. Proceedings before grand juries.

(3) Miscellaneous proceedings. Proceedings for extradition or rendition; preliminary examinations in criminal cases; sentencing, or granting or revoking probation; issuance of warrants for arrest, criminal summonses, and search warrants; and proceedings with respect to release on bail or otherwise.

(e) Rules applicable in part. In the following proceedings these rules apply to the extent that matters of evidence are not provided for in the statutes which govern procedure therein or in other rules prescribed by the Supreme Court pursuant to statutory authority: the trial of minor and petty offenses by United States magistrates; review of agency actions when the facts are subject to trial de novo under section 706(2)(F) of title 5, United States Code; review of orders of the Secretary of Agriculture under section 2 of the Act entitled "An Act to authorize association of producers of agricultural products" approved February 18, 1922 (7 U.S.C. 292), and under sections 6 and 7(c) of the Perishable Agricultural Commodities Act, 1930 (7 U.S.C. 499f, 499g(c)); naturalization and revocation of naturalization under sections 310–318 of the Immigration and Nationality Act (8 U.S.C. 1421–1429); prize proceedings in admiralty under sections 7651–7681 of title 10, United States Code; review of orders of the Secretary of the Interior under section 2 of the Act entitled "An Act authorizing associations of producers of aquatic products" approved June 25, 1934 (15 U.S.C. 522); review of orders of petroleum control boards under section 5 of the Act entitled "An Act to regulate interstate and foreign commerce in petroleum and its products by prohibiting the shipment in such commerce of petroleum and its products produced in violation of State law, and for other purposes", approved February 22, 1935 (15 U.S.C. 715d); actions for fines, penalties, or forfeitures under part V of title IV of the Tariff Act of 1930 (19 U.S.C. 1581–1624), or under the Anti-Smuggling Act (19 U.S.C. 1701–1711); criminal libel for condemnation, exclusion of imports, or other proceedings under the Federal Food, Drug, and Cosmetic Act (21 U.S.C. 301–392); disputes between seamen under sections 4079, 4080, and 4081 of the Revised Statutes (22 U.S.C. 256–258); habeas corpus under sections 2241–2254 of title 28, United States Code; motions to vacate, set aside or correct sentence under section 2255 of title 28, United States Code; actions for penalties for refusal to transport destitute seamen under section 4578 of the Revised Statutes (46 U.S.C. 679); actions against the United States under the Act entitled "An Act authorizing suits against the United States in admiralty for damage caused by and salvage service rendered to public vessels belonging to the United States, and for other purposes", approved March 3, 1925 (46 U.S.C. 781–790), as implemented by section 7730 of title 10, United States Code.

(As amended P.L. 94–149, § 1(14), Dec. 12, 1975, 89 Stat. 806; P.L. 95–598, Title II, § 251, Nov. 6, 1978, 92 Stat. 2673; P.L. 97–164, Title I, § 142, Apr. 2, 1982, 96 Stat. 45; Mar. 2, 1987, eff. Oct. 1, 1987; Apr. 25, 1988, eff. Nov. 1, 1988; Nov. 18, 1988, Pub.L. 100–690, Title VII, § 7075(c), 102 Stat. 4405.)

Section references, McCormick 4th ed.

None

Note by Federal Judicial Center

The rule enacted by the Congress is the rule prescribed by the Supreme Court, amended as follows:

Subdivision (a) was amended in the first sentence by inserting "the Court of Claims" and by inserting "actions, cases, and." It was amended in the second sentence by substituting "terms" in place of "word," by inserting the phrase "and 'court'," and by adding "commissioners of the Court of Claims."

Subdivision (b) was amended by substituting "civil actions and proceedings" in place of "civil actions," and by substituting "criminal cases and proceedings" in place of "criminal proceedings."

Subdivision (c) was amended by substituting "rule" in place of "rules" and by changing the verb to the singular.

Subdivision (d) was amended by deleting "those" after "other than" and by substituting "Rule 104" in place of "Rule 104(a)."

Subdivision (e) was amended by substituting "prescribed" in place of "adopted" and by adding "pursuant to statutory authority." The form of the statutory citations was also changed.

Advisory Committee's Note

56 F.R.D. 183, 348

Subdivision (a). [This portion of the Advisory Committee's Note discussed the courts for which the various enabling acts granted the Supreme Court power to prescribe rules. Congressional enactment of the rules has rendered the discussion moot. The enabling acts did not include the Court of Claims which the Congress added to Rule 1101(a)].

Report of House Committee on the Judiciary

House Comm. on Judiciary, Fed.Rules of Evidence, H.R.Rep. No. 650,
93d Cong., 1st Sess., p. 17 (1973); 1974 U.S.Code
Cong. & Ad.News 7075, 7090

Subdivision (a) as submitted to the Congress, in stating the courts and judges to which the Rules of Evidence apply, omitted the Court of Claims and commissioners of that Court. At the request of the Court of Claims, the Committee amended the Rule to include the Court and its commissioners within the purview of the Rules.

Advisory Committee's Note

56 F.R.D. 183, 351

Subdivision (b) is a combination of the language of the enabling acts, supra, with respect to the kinds of proceedings in which the making of rules is authorized. It is subject to the qualifications expressed in the subdivisions which follow.

Subdivision (c), singling out the rules of privilege for special treatment, is made necessary by the limited applicability of the remaining rules.

Subdivision (d). The rule is not intended as an expression as to when due process or other constitutional provisions may require an evidentiary hearing. Paragraph (1) restates, for convenience, the provisions of the second sentence of Rule 104(a), supra. See Advisory Committee's Note to that rule.

(2) While some states have statutory requirements that indictments be based on "legal evidence," and there is some case law to the effect that the rules of evidence apply to grand jury proceedings, 1 Wigmore § 4(5), the Supreme Court has not accepted this view. In Costello v. United States, 350 U.S. 359, 76 S.Ct. 406, 100 L.Ed. 397 (1965), the Court refused to allow an indictment to be attacked, for either constitutional or policy reasons, on the ground that only hearsay evidence was presented.

> "It would run counter to the whole history of the grand jury institution, in which laymen conduct their inquiries unfettered by technical rules. Neither justice nor the concept of a fair trial requires such a change." Id. at 364.

The rule as drafted does not deal with the evidence required to support an indictment.

(3) The rule exempts preliminary examinations in criminal cases. Authority as to the applicability of the rules of evidence to preliminary examinations has been meagre and conflicting. Goldstein, The State and the Accused: Balance of Advantage in Criminal Procedure, 69 Yale L.J. 1149, 1168, n. 53 (1960); Comment, Preliminary Hearings on Indictable Offenses in Philadelphia, 106 U. of Pa.L.Rev. 589, 592–593 (1958). Hearsay testimony is, however, customarily received in such examinations. Thus in a Dyer Act case, for example, an affidavit may properly be used in a preliminary examination to prove ownership of the stolen vehicle, thus saving the victim of the crime the hardship of having to travel twice to a distant district for the sole purpose of testifying as to ownership. It is believed that the extent of the applicability of the Rules of Evidence to preliminary examinations should be appropriately

dealt with by the Federal Rules of Criminal Procedure which regulate those proceedings.

Extradition and rendition proceedings are governed in detail by statute. 18 U.S.C. §§ 3181–3195. They are essentially administrative in character. Traditionally the rules of evidence have not applied. 1 Wigmore § 4(6). Extradition proceedings are accepted from the operation of the Rules of Criminal Procedure. Rule 54(b)(5) of Federal Rules of Criminal Procedure.

The rules of evidence have not been regarded as applicable to sentencing or probation proceedings, where great reliance is placed upon the presentence investigation and report. Rule 32(c) of the Federal Rules of Criminal Procedure requires a presentence investigation and report in every case unless the court otherwise directs. In Williams v. New York, 337 U.S. 241, 69 S.Ct. 1079, 93 L.Ed. 1337 (1949), in which the judge overruled a jury recommendation of life imprisonment and imposed a death sentence, the Court said that due process does not require confrontation or cross-examination in sentencing or passing on probation, and that the judge has broad discretion as to the sources and types of information relied upon. Compare the recommendation that the substance of all derogatory information be disclosed to the defendant, in A.B.A. Project on Minimum Standards for Criminal Justice, Sentencing Alternatives and Procedures § 4.4, Tentative Draft (1967, Sobeloff, Chm.). Williams was adhered to in Specht v. Patterson, 386 U.S. 605, 87 S.Ct. 1209, 18 L.Ed.2d 326 (1967), but not extended to a proceeding under the Colorado Sex Offenders Act, which was said to be a new charge leading in effect to punishment, more like the recidivist statutes where opportunity must be given to be heard on the habitual criminal issue.

Warrants for arrest, criminal summonses, and search warrants are issued upon complaint or affidavit showing probable cause. Rules 4(a) and 41(c) of the Federal Rules of Criminal Procedure. The nature of the proceedings makes application of the formal rules of evidence inappropriate and impracticable.

Criminal contempts are punishable summarily if the judge certifies that he saw or heard the contempt and that it was committed in the presence of the court. Rule 42(a) of the Federal Rules of Criminal Procedure. The circumstances which preclude application of the rules of evidence in this situation are not present, however, in other cases of criminal contempt.

Proceedings with respect to release on bail or otherwise do not call for application of the rules of evidence. The governing statute specifically provides:

> "Information stated in, or offered in connection with, any order entered pursuant to this section need not conform to the rules pertaining to the admissibility of evidence in a court of law." 18 U.S.C.A. § 3146(f).

This provision is consistent with the type of inquiry contemplated in A.B.A. Project on Minimum Standards for Criminal Justice, Standards Relating to Pretrial Release, § 4.5(b), (c), p. 16 (1968). The references to the weight of the evidence against the accused, in Rule 46(a)(1), (c) of the Federal Rules of Criminal Procedure and in 18 U.S.C.A. § 3146(b), as a factor to be considered, clearly do not have in view evidence introduced at a hearing under the rules of evidence.

The rule does not exempt habeas corpus proceedings. The Supreme Court held in Walker v. Johnston, 312 U.S. 275, 61 S.Ct. 574, 85 L.Ed. 830 (1941), that the practice of disposing of matters of fact on affidavit, which prevailed in some circuits, did not "satisfy the command of the statute that the judge shall proceed 'to determine the facts of the case, by hearing the testimony and arguments.'" This view accords with the emphasis in Townsend v. Sain, 372 U.S. 293, 83 S.Ct. 745, 9 L.Ed.2d 770 (1963), upon trial-type proceedings, id. 311, 83 S.Ct. 745, with demeanor evidence as a significant factor, id. 322, 83 S.Ct. 745, in applications by state prisoners aggrieved by unconstitutional detentions. Hence subdivision (e) applies the rules to habeas corpus proceedings to the extent not inconsistent with the statute.

Subdivision (e). In a substantial number of special proceedings, *ad hoc* evaluation has resulted in the promulgation of particularized evidentiary provisions, by Act of Congress or by rule adopted by the Supreme Court. Well adapted to the particular proceedings, though not apt candidates for inclusion in a set of general rules, they are left undisturbed. Otherwise, however, the rules of evidence are applicable to the proceedings enumerated in the subdivision.

Report of House Committee on the Judiciary

House Comm. on Judiciary, Fed.Rules of Evidence, H.R.Rep. No. 650, 93d Cong., 1st Sess., p. 17 (1973); 1974 U.S.Code Cong. & Ad.News 7075, 7090

Subdivision (b)[E] was amended merely to substitute positive law citations for those which were not.

1987 Amendment. Subdivision (a) is amended to delete the reference to the District Court for the District of the Canal Zone, which no longer exists, and to add the District Court for the Northern Mariana Islands. The United States bankruptcy judges are added to conform the subdivision with Rule 1101(b) and Bankruptcy Rule 9017.

1988 Amendment. The amendment is technical. No substantive change is intended.

Note by Federal Judicial Center

This rule was not included among those prescribed by the Supreme Court. The rule prescribed by the Court as 1102 now appears as 1103.

Rule 1102. Amendments

Amendments to the Federal Rules of Evidence may be made as provided in section 2072 of title 28 of the United States Code.

(As amended Apr. 30, 1991, eff. Dec. 1, 1991.)

Rule 1103. Title

These rules may be known and cited as the Federal Rules of Evidence.

Note by Federal Judicial Center

The rule enacted by the Congress is the rule prescribed by the Supreme Court as Rule 1102 without change.

Sec. 2. (a) Title 28 of the United States Code is amended—

(1) by inserting immediately after section 2075 the following new section:

"§ 2076. Rules of evidence

"The Supreme Court of the United States shall have the power to prescribe amendments to the Federal Rules of Evidence. Such amendments shall not take effect until they have been reported to Congress by the Chief Justice at or after the beginning of a regular session of Congress but not later than the first day of May, and until the expiration of one hundred and eighty days after they have been so reported; but if either House of Congress within that time shall by resolution disapprove any amendment so reported it shall not take effect. The effective date of any amendment so reported may be deferred by either House of Congress to a later date or until approved by Act of Congress. Any rule whether proposed or in force may be amended by Act of Congress. Any provision of law in force at the expiration of such time and in conflict with any such amendment not disapproved shall be of no further force or effect after such amendment has taken effect. Any such amendment creating, abolishing, or modifying a privilege shall have no force or effect unless it shall be approved by act of Congress"; and

(2) by adding at the end of the table of sections of chapter 131 the following new item:

"2076. Rules of evidence."

(b) Section 1732 of title 28 of the United States Code is amended by striking out subsection (a), and by striking out "(b)".

(c) Section 1733 of title 28 of the United States Code is amended by adding at the end thereof the following new subsection:

"(c) This section does not apply to cases, actions, and proceedings to which the Federal Rules of Evidence apply."

Approved Jan. 2, 1975.

APPENDIX
OF
DELETED AND SUPERSEDED MATERIALS

Rule 105.

SUMMING UP AND COMMENT BY JUDGE
[Not enacted.]

After the close of the evidence and arguments of counsel, the judge may fairly and impartially sum up the evidence and comment to the jury upon the weight of the evidence and the credibility of the witnesses, if he also instructs the jury that they are to determine for themselves the weight of the evidence and the credit to be given to the witnesses and that they are not bound by the judge's summation or comment.

Note by Federal Judicial Center

The foregoing rule prescribed by the Supreme Court was deleted from the rules enacted by the Congress.

Advisory Committee's Note

The rule states the present rule in the federal courts. Capital Traction Co. v. Hof, 174 U.S. 1, 13–14, 19 S.Ct. 580, 43 L.Ed. 873 (1899). The judge must, of course, confine his remarks to what is disclosed by the evidence. He cannot convey to the jury his purely personal reaction to credibility or to the merits of the case; he can be neither argumentative nor an advocate. Quercia v. United States, 289 U.S. 466, 469, 53 S.Ct. 698, 77 L.Ed. 1321 (1933); Billeci v. United States, 87 U.S.App.D.C. 274, 184 F.2d 394, 402, 24 A.L.R.2d 881 (1950). For further discussion see the series of articles by Wright, The Invasion of Jury: Temperature of the War, 27 Temp.L.Q. 137 (1953), Instructions to the Jury: Summary Without Comment, 1954 Wash.U.L.Q. 177, Adequacy of Instructions to the Jury, 53 Mich.L.Rev. 505, 813 (1955); A.L.I. Model Code of Evidence, Comment to Rule 8; Maguire, Weinstein, et al., Cases and Materials on Evidence 737–740 (5th ed. 1965); Vanderbilt, Minimum Standards of Judicial Administration 224–229 (1949).

Report of the House Committee on the Judiciary

Rule 105 as submitted by the Supreme Court concerned the issue of summing up and comment by the judge. It provided that after the close of the evidence and the arguments of counsel, the presiding judge could fairly and impartially sum up the evidence and comment to the jury upon its weight and the credibility of the witnesses, if he also instructed the jury that it was not bound thereby and must make its own determination of those matters. The Committee recognized that the Rule as submitted is consistent with long standing and current federal practice. However, the aspect of the Rule dealing with the authority of a judge to comment on the weight of the evidence and the credibility of witnesses—an authority not granted to judges in most State courts—was highly controversial. After much debate the Committee determined to delete the entire Rule, intending that its action be understood as reflecting no conclusion as to the merits of the proposed Rule and that the subject should be left for separate consideration at another time.

Report of Senate Committee on the Judiciary

This rule as submitted by the Supreme Court permitted the judge to sum up and comment on the evidence. The House struck the rule.

The committee accepts the House action with the understanding that the present Federal practice, taken from the common law, of the trial judge's discretionary authority to comment on and summarize the evidence is left undisturbed.

Rule 301.

PRESUMPTIONS IN GENERAL [As prescribed by Supreme Court]

In all cases not otherwise provided for by Act of Congress or by these rules a presumption imposes on the party against whom it is directed the burden of proving that the nonexistence of the presumed fact is more probable than its existence.

Rule 301.

PRESUMPTIONS IN GENERAL IN CIVIL ACTIONS AND PROCEEDINGS [As passed by House of Representatives]

In all civil actions and proceedings not otherwise provided for by Act of Congress or by these rules, a presumption imposes on the party against whom it is directed the burden of going forward with the evidence, and, even though met with contradicting evidence, a presumption is sufficient evidence of the fact presumed, to be considered by the trier of the facts.

Note by Federal Judicial Center

Neither of the above versions of Rule 301 was enacted.

Advisory Committee's Note

This rule governs presumptions generally. See Rule 302 for presumptions controlled by state law and Rule 303 for those against an accused in a criminal case.

Presumptions governed by this rule are given the effect of placing upon the opposing party the burden of establishing the nonexistence of the presumed fact, once the party invoking the presumption establishes the basic facts giving rise to it. The same considerations of fairness, policy, and probability which dictate the allocation of the

burden of the various elements of a case as between the prima facie
case of a plaintiff and affirmative defenses also underlie the creation of
presumptions. These considerations are not satisfied by giving a lesser
effect to presumptions. Morgan and Maguire, Looking Backward and
Forward at Evidence, 50 Harv.L.Rev. 909, 913 (1937); Morgan, Instructing the Jury upon Presumptions and Burden of Proof, 47
Harv.L.Rev. 59, 82 (1933); Cleary, Presuming and Pleading: An Essay
on Juristic Immaturity, 12 Stan.L.Rev. 5 (1959).

The so-called "bursting bubble" theory, under which a presumption vanishes upon the introduction of evidence which would support a
finding of the nonexistence of the presumed fact, even though not
believed, is rejected as according presumptions too "slight and evanescent" an effect. Morgan and Maguire, *supra,* at p. 913.

In the opinion of the Advisory Committee, no constitutional infirmity attends this view of presumptions. In Mobile, J. & K. C. R. Co. v.
Turnipseed, 219 U.S. 35, 31 S.Ct. 136, 55 L.Ed. 78 (1910), the Court
upheld a Mississippi statute which provided that in actions against
railroads proof of injury inflicted by the running of trains should be
prima facie evidence of negligence by the railroad. The injury in the
case had resulted from a derailment. The opinion made the points (1)
that the only effect of the statute was to impose on the railroad the
duty of producing some evidence to the contrary, (2) that an inference
may be supplied by law if there is a rational connection between the
fact proved and the fact presumed, as long as the opposite party is not
precluded from presenting his evidence to the contrary, and (3) that
considerations of public policy arising from the character of the business justified the application in question. Nineteen years later, in
Western & Atlantic R. Co. v. Henderson, 279 U.S. 639, 49 S.Ct. 445, 73
L.Ed. 884 (1929), the Court overturned a Georgia statute making
railroads liable for damages done by trains, unless the railroad made it
appear that reasonable care had been used, the presumption being
against the railroad. The declaration alleged the death of plaintiff's
husband from a grade crossing collision, due to specified acts of
negligence by defendant. The jury were instructed that proof of the
injury raised a presumption of negligence; the burden shifted to the
railroad to prove ordinary care; and unless it did so, they should find
for plaintiff. The instruction was held erroneous in an opinion stating
(1) that there was no rational connection between the mere fact of
collision and negligence on the part of anyone, and (2) that the statute
was different from that in *Turnipseed* in imposing a burden upon the
railroad. The reader is left in a state of some confusion. Is the
difference between a derailment and a grade crossing collision of no
significance? Would the *Turnipseed* presumption have been bad if it
had imposed a burden of persuasion on defendant, although that would
in nowise have impaired its "rational connection"? If *Henderson*
forbids imposing a burden of persuasion on defendants, what happens
to affirmative defenses?

Two factors serve to explain *Henderson.* The first was that it was
common ground that negligence was indispensable to liability. Plaintiff thought so, drafted her complaint accordingly, and relied upon the
presumption. But how in logic could the same presumption establish
her alternative grounds of negligence that the engineer was so blind he

could not see decedent's truck and that he failed to stop after he saw it? Second, take away the basic assumption of no liability without fault, as *Turnipseed* intimated might be done ("considerations of public policy arising out of the character of the business"), and the structure of the decision in *Henderson* fails. No question of logic would have arisen if the statute had simply said: a prima facie case of liability is made by proof of injury by a train; lack of negligence is an affirmative defense, to be pleaded and proved as other affirmative defenses. The problem would be one of economic due process only. While it seems likely that the Supreme Court of 1929 would have voted that due process was denied, that result today would be unlikely. See, for example, the shift in the direction of absolute liability in the consumer cases. Prosser, The Assault upon the Citadel (Strict Liability to the Consumer), 69 Yale L.J. 1099 (1960).

Any doubt as to the constitutional permissibility of a presumption imposing a burden of persuasion of the nonexistence of the presumed fact in civil cases is laid at rest by Dick v. New York Life Ins. Co., 359 U.S. 437, 79 S.Ct. 921, 3 L.Ed.2d 935 (1959). The Court unhesitatingly applied the North Dakota rule that the presumption against suicide imposed on defendant the burden of proving that the death of insured, under an accidental death clause, was due to suicide.

"Proof of coverage and of death by gunshot wound shifts the burden to the insurer to establish that the death of the insured was due to his suicide." 359 U.S. at 443, 79 S.Ct. at 925.

"In a case like this one, North Dakota presumes that death was accidental and places on the insurer the burden of proving that death resulted from suicide." *Id.* at 446, 79 S.Ct. at 927.

The rational connection requirement survives in criminal cases, Tot v. United States, 319 U.S. 463, 63 S.Ct. 1241, 87 L.Ed. 1519 (1943), because the Court has been unwilling to extend into that area the greater-includes-the-lesser theory of Ferry v. Ramsey, 277 U.S. 88, 48 S.Ct. 443, 72 L.Ed. 796 (1928). In that case the Court sustained a Kansas statute under which bank directors were personally liable for deposits made with their assent and with knowledge of insolvency, and the fact of insolvency was prima facie evidence of assent and knowledge of insolvency. Mr. Justice Holmes pointed out that the state legislature could have made the directors personally liable to depositors in every case. Since the statute imposed a less stringent liability, "the thing to be considered is the result reached, not the possibly inartificial or clumsy way of reaching it." *Id.* at 94, 48 S.Ct. at 444. Mr. Justice Sutherland dissented: though the state could have created an absolute liability, it did not purport to do so; a rational connection was necessary, but lacking, between the liabililty created and the prima facie evidence of it; the result might be different if the basis of the presumption were being open for business.

The Sutherland view has prevailed in criminal cases by virtue of the higher standard of notice there required. The fiction that everyone is presumed to know the law is applied to the substantive law of crimes as an alternative to complete unenforceability. But the need does not extend to criminal evidence and procedure, and the fiction does not encompass them. "Rational connection" is not fictional or artificial, and so it is reasonable to suppose that Gainey should have known that his presence at the site of an illicit still could convict him of being connected with (carrying on) the business, United States v. Gainey, 380 U.S. 63, 85 S.Ct. 754, 13 L.Ed.2d 658 (1965), but not that Romano should have known that his presence at a still could convict him of possessing it, United States v. Romano, 382 U.S. 136, 86 S.Ct. 279, 15 L.Ed.2d 210 (1965).

In his dissent in Gainey, Mr. Justice Black put it more artistically:

"It might be argued, although the Court does not so argue or hold, that Congress if it wished could make presence at a still a crime in itself, and so Congress should be free to create crimes which are called 'possession' and 'carrying on an illegal distillery business' but which are defined in such a way that unexplained presence is sufficient and indisputable evidence in all cases to support conviction for those offenses. See Ferry v. Ramsey, 277 U.S. 88, 48 S.Ct. 443, 72 L.Ed. 796. Assuming for the sake of argument that Congress could make unexplained presence a criminal act, and ignoring also the refusal of this Court in other cases to uphold a statutory presumption on such a theory, see Heiner v. Donnan, 285 U.S. 312, 52 S.Ct. 358, 76 L.Ed. 772, there is no indication here that Congress intended to adopt such a misleading method of draftsmanship, nor in my judgment could the statutory provisions if so construed escape condemnation for vagueness, under the principles applied in Lanzetta v. New Jersey, 306 U.S. 451, 59 S.Ct. 618, 83 L.Ed. 888, and many other cases." 380 U.S. at 84, n. 12, 85 S.Ct. at 766.

And the majority opinion in *Romano* agreed with him:

"It may be, of course, that Congress has the power to make presence at an illegal still a punishable crime, but we find no clear indication that it intended to so exercise this power. The crime remains possession, not presence, and with all due deference to the judgment of Congress, the former may not constitutionally be inferred from the latter." 382 U.S. at 144, 86 S.Ct. at 284.

The rule does not spell out the procedural aspects of its application. Questions as to when the evidence warrants submission of a presumption and what instructions are proper under varying states of fact are believed to present no particular difficulties.

Report of House Committee on the Judiciary

Rule 301 as submitted by the Supreme Court provided that in all cases a presumption imposes on the party against whom it is directed the burden of proving that the nonexistence of the presumed fact is more probable than its existence. The Committee limited the scope of Rule 301 to "civil actions and proceedings" to effectuate its decision not to deal with the question of presumptions in criminal cases. (See note on Rule 303 in discussion of Rules deleted). With respect to the weight to be given a presumption in a civil case, the Committee agreed with the judgment implicit in the Court's version that the so-called "bursting bubble" theory of presumptions, whereby a presumption vanishes upon the appearance of any contradicting evidence by the other party, gives to presumptions too slight an effect. On the other hand, the Committee believed that the Rule proposed by the Court, whereby a presumption permanently alters the burden of persuasion, no matter how much contradicting evidence is introduced—a view shared by only a few courts—lends too great a force to presumptions. Accordingly, the Committee amended the Rule to adopt an intermediate position under which a presumption does not vanish upon the introduction of contradicting evidence, and does not change the burden of persuasion; instead it is merely deemed sufficient evidence of the fact presumed, to be considered by the jury or other finder of fact.

Rule 303.

PRESUMPTIONS IN CRIMINAL CASES
[Not enacted.]

(a) Scope. Except as otherwise provided by Act of Congress, in criminal cases, presumptions against an accused, recognized at common law or created by statute, including statutory provisions that certain facts are prima facie evidence of other facts or of guilt, are governed by this rule.

(b) Submission to jury. The judge is not authorized to direct the jury to find a presumed fact against the accused. When the presumed fact establishes guilt or is an element of the offense or negatives a defense, the judge may submit the question of guilt or of the existence of the presumed fact to the jury, if, but only if, a reasonable juror on the evidence as a whole, including the evidence of the basic facts, could find guilt or the presumed fact beyond a reasonable doubt. When the presumed fact has a lesser effect, its existence may be submitted to the jury if the basic facts are supported by substantial evidence, or are otherwise established, unless the evidence as a whole negatives the existence of the presumed fact.

(c) Instructing the jury. Whenever the existence of a presumed fact against the accused is submitted to the jury, the judge shall give an instruction that the law declares that the jury may regard the basic facts as sufficient evidence of the presumed fact but does not require it to do so. In addition, if the presumed fact establishes guilt or is an element of the offense or negatives a defense, the judge shall instruct the jury that its existence must, on all the evidence, be proved beyond a reasonable doubt.

Note by Federal Judicial Center

The foregoing rule prescribed by the Supreme Court was deleted from the rules enacted by the Congress.

Advisory Committee's Note

Subdivision (a). This rule is based largely upon A.L.I. Model Penal Code § 1.12(5) P.O.D. (1962) and United States v. Gainey, 380 U.S. 63, 85 S.Ct. 754, 13 L.Ed.2d 658 (1965). While the rule, unlike the Model Penal Code provision, spells out the effect of common law presumptions as well as those created by statute, cases involving the latter are no doubt of more frequent occurrence. Congress has enacted numerous provisions to lessen the burden of the prosecution, principally though not exclusively in the fields of narcotics control and taxation of liquor. Occasionally, in the pattern of the usual common law treatment of such matters as insanity, they take the form of assigning to the defense the responsibility of raising specified matters as affirmative defenses, which are not within the scope of these rules. See Comment, A.L.I. Model Penal Code § 1.13, T.D. No. 4 (1955). In other instances they assume a variety of forms which are the concern of this rule. The provision may be that proof of a specified fact (possession or presence) is sufficient to authorize conviction. 26 U.S.C. § 4704(a), unlawful to buy or sell opium except from original stamped package— absence of stamps from package prima facie evidence of violation by person in possession; 26 U.S.C. § 4724(c), unlawful for person who has not registered and paid special tax to possess narcotics—possession presumptive evidence of violation. Sometimes the qualification is added, "unless the defendant explains the possession [presence] to the satisfaction of the jury." 18 U.S.C. § 545, possession of unlawfully imported goods sufficient for conviction of smuggling, unless explained; 21 U.S.C. § 174, possession sufficient for conviction of buying or selling narcotics known to have been imported unlawfully, unless explained. See also 26 U.S.C. § 5601(a)(1), (a)(4), (a)(8), (b)(1), (b)(2), (b)(4), relating to distilling operations. Another somewhat different pattern makes possession evidence of a particular element of the crime. 21 U.S.C. § 176b, crime to furnish unlawfully imported heroin to juveniles— possession sufficient proof of unlawful importation, unless explained; 50 U.S.C.A. App. § 462(b), unlawful to possess draft card not lawfully issued to holder, with intent to use for purposes of false identification— possession sufficient evidence of intent, unless explained. See also 15 U.S.C. § 902(f), (i).

Differences between the permissible operation of presumptions against the accused in criminal cases and in other situations prevent the formulation of a comprehensive definition of the term "presumption," and none is attempted. Nor do these rules purport to deal with problems of the validity of presumptions except insofar as they may be found reflected in the formulation of permissible procedures.

The presumption of innocence is outside the scope of the rule and unaffected by it.

Subdivisions (b) and (c). It is axiomatic that a verdict cannot be directed against the accused in a criminal case, 9 Wigmore § 2495, p. 312, with the corollary that the judge is without authority to direct the jury to find against the accused as to any element of the crime, A.L.I. Model Penal Code § 1.12(1) P.O.D. (1962). Although arguably the judge could direct the jury to find against the accused as to a lesser fact, the tradition is against it, and this rule makes no use of presumptions to remove any matters from final determination by the jury.

The only distinction made among presumptions under this rule is with respect to the measure of proof required in order to justify submission to the jury. If the effect of the presumption is to establish guilt or an element of the crime or to negative a defense, the measure of proof is the one widely accepted by the Courts of Appeals as the standard for measuring the sufficiency of the evidence in passing on motions for directed verdict (now judgment of acquittal): an acquittal should be directed when reasonable jurymen must have a reasonable doubt. Curley v. United States, 81 U.S.App.D.C. 389, 160 F.2d 229 (1947), cert. denied 331 U.S. 837, 67 S.Ct. 1511, 91 L.Ed. 1850; United States v. Honeycutt, 311 F.2d 660 (4th Cir.1962); Stephens v. United States, 354 F.2d 999 (5th Cir.1965); Lambert v. United States, 261 F.2d 799 (5th Cir.1958); United States v. Leggett, 292 F.2d 423 (6th Cir.1961); Cape v. United States, 283 F.2d 430 (9th Cir.1960); Cartwright v. United States, 335 F.2d 919 (10th Cir.1964). Cf. United States v. Gonzales Castro, 228 F.2d 807 (2d Cir.1956); United States v. Masiello, 235 F.2d 279 (2d Cir.1956), cert. denied Stickel v. United States, 352 U.S. 882, 77 S.Ct. 100, 1 L.Ed.2d 79; United States v. Feinberg, 140 F.2d 592 (2d Cir.1944). But cf. United States v. Arcuri, 282 F.Supp. 347 (E.D.N.Y.1968), aff'd. 405 F.2d 691, cert. denied 395 U.S. 913; United States v. Melillo, 275 F.Supp. 314 (E.D.N.Y.1968). If the presumption operates upon a lesser aspect of the case than the issue of guilt itself or an element of the crime or negativing a defense, the required measure of proof is the less stringent one of substantial evidence, consistently with the attitude usually taken with respect to particular items of evidence. 9 Wigmore § 2497, p. 324.

The treatment of presumptions in the rule is consistent with United States v. Gainey, 380 U.S. 63, 85 S.Ct. 754, 13 L.Ed.2d 658 (1965), where the matter was considered in depth. After sustaining the validity of the provision of 26 U.S.C. § 5601(b)(2) that presence at the site is sufficient to convict of the offense of carrying on the business of distiller without giving bond, unless the presence is explained to the satisfaction of the jury, the Court turned to procedural considerations and reached several conclusions. The power of the judge to withdraw a case from the jury for insufficiency of evidence is left unimpaired; he may submit the case on the basis of presence alone, but he is not required to do so. Nor is he precluded from rendering judgment notwithstanding the verdict. It is proper to tell the jury about the "statutory inference," if they are told it is not conclusive. The jury may still acquit, even if it finds defendant present and his presence is unexplained. [Compare the mandatory character of the instruction condemned in Bollenbach v. United States, 326 U.S. 607, 66 S.Ct. 402, 90 L.Ed. 350 (1945).] To avoid any implication that the statutory language relative to explanation be taken as directing attention to failure of the accused to testify, the better practice, said the Court, would be to instruct the jury that they may draw the inference unless the evidence provides a satisfactory explanation of defendant's presence, omitting any explicit reference to the statute.

The Final Report of the National Commission on Reform of Federal Criminal Laws § 103(4) and (5) (1971) contains a careful formulation of the consequences of a statutory presumption with an alternative formulation set forth in the Comment thereto, and also of the effect of a prima facie case. In the criminal code there proposed, the terms "presumption" and "prima facie case" are used with precision and with reference to these meanings. In the federal criminal law as it stands today, these terms are not used with precision. Moreover, common law presumptions continue. Hence it is believed that the rule here proposed is better adapted to the present situation until such time as the Congress enacts legislation covering the subject, which the rule takes into account. If the subject of common law presumptions is not covered by legislation, the need for the rule in that regard will continue.

Report of House Committee on the Judiciary

Rule 303, as submitted by the Supreme Court was directed to the issues of when, in criminal cases, a court may submit a presumption to a jury and the type of instruction it should give. The Committee deleted this Rule since the subject of presumptions in criminal cases is addressed in detail in bills now pending before the Committee to revise the federal criminal code. The Committee determined to consider this question in the course of its study of these proposals.

Rule 406.

HABIT; ROUTINE PRACTICE
[Subdivision (b) not enacted.]

(b) Method of proof. Habit or routine practice may be proved by testimony in the form of an opinion or by specific instances of conduct sufficient in number to warrant a finding that the habit existed or that the practice was routine.

Advisory Committee's Note

* * *

Subdivision (b). Permissible methods of proving habit or routine conduct include opinion and specific instances sufficient in number to warrant a finding that the habit or routine practice in fact existed. Opinion evidence must be "rationally based on the perception of the witness" and helpful, under the provisions of Rule 701. Proof by specific instances may be controlled by the overriding provisions of Rule 403 for exclusion on grounds of prejudice, confusion, misleading the jury, or waste of time. Thus the illustrations following A.L.I. Model Code of Evidence Rule 307 suggests the possibility of admitting testimony by W that on numerous occasions he had been with X when X crossed a railroad track and that on each occasion X had first stopped and looked in both directions, but discretion to exclude offers of 10 witnesses, each testifying to a different occasion.

Similar provisions for proof by opinion or specific instances are found in Uniform Rule 50 and Kansas Code of Civil Procedure § 60–450. New Jersey Rule 50 provides for proof by specific instances but is silent as to opinion. The California Evidence Code is silent as to methods of proving habit, presumably proceeding on the theory that any method is relevant and all relevant evidence is admissible unless otherwise provided. Tentative Recommendation and a Study Relating to the Uniform Rules of Evidence (Art. VI. Extrinsic Policies Affecting Admissibility), Rep., Rec. & Study, Cal. Law Rev. Comm'n, 620 (1964).

Report of House Committee on the Judiciary

[Reasons for deleting subdivision (b) are stated in the report, which is set forth in the main text under rule 406, supra.]

ARTICLE V. PRIVILEGES

Note by Federal Judicial Center

The 13 rules numbered 501–513 prescribed by the Supreme Court as Article V were replaced by a single rule 501 in the rules enacted by the Congress. The rules are included here for informational purposes only.

Rule 501.

PRIVILEGES RECOGNIZED ONLY AS PROVIDED
[Not enacted.]

Except as otherwise required by the Constitution of the United States or provided by Act of Congress, and except as provided in these rules or in other rules adopted by the Supreme Court, no person has a privilege to:

(1) Refuse to be a witness; or

(2) Refuse to disclose any matter; or

(3) Refuse to produce any object or writing; or

(4) Prevent another from being a witness or disclosing any matter of producing any object or writing.

Advisory Committee's Note

No attempt is made in these rules to incorporate the constitutional provisions which relate to the admission and exclusion of evidence, whether denominated as privileges or not. The grand design of these provisions does not readily lend itself to codification. The final reference must be the provisions themselves and the decisions construing them. Nor is formulating a rule an appropriate means of settling unresolved constitutional questions.

Similarly, privileges created by act of Congress are not within the scope of these rules. These privileges do not assume the form of broad principles; they are the product of resolving particular problems in particular terms. Among them are included such provisions as 13 U.S.C. § 9, generally prohibiting official disclosure of census information and conferring a privileged status on retained copies of census reports; 42 U.S.C. § 2000e–5(a), making inadmissible in evidence anything said or done during Equal Employment Opportunity conciliation proceeding; 42 U.S.C. § 2240, making required reports of incidents by nuclear facility licensees inadmissible in actions for damages; 45 U.S.C. §§ 33, 41, similarly as to reports of accidents by railroads; 49 U.S.C. § 1441(e), declaring C.A.B. accident investigation reports inadmissible in actions for damages. The rule leaves them undisturbed.

The reference to other rules adopted by the Supreme Court makes clear that provisions relating to privilege in those rules will continue in operation. See, for example, the "work product" immunity against discovery spelled out under the Rules of Civil Procedure in Hickman v. Taylor, 329 U.S. 495, 67 S.Ct. 385, 91 L.Ed. 451 (1947), now formalized in revised Rule 26(b)(3) of the Rules of Civil Procedure, and the secrecy of grand jury proceedings provided by Criminal Rule 6.

With respect to privileges created by state law, these rules in some instances grant them greater status than has heretofore been the case by according them recognition in federal criminal proceedings, bankruptcy, and federal question litigation. See Rules 502 and 510. There is, however, no provision generally adopting state-created privileges.

In federal criminal prosecutions the primacy of federal law as to both substance and procedure has been undoubted. See, for example, United States v. Krol, 374 F.2d 776 (7th Cir.1967), sustaining the admission in a federal prosecution of evidence obtained by electronic eavesdropping, despite a state statute declaring the use of these devices unlawful and evidence obtained therefrom inadmissible. This primacy includes matters of privilege. As stated in 4 Barron, Federal Practice and Procedure § 2151, p. 175 (1951):

"The determination of the question whether a matter is privileged is governed by federal decisions and the state statutes or rules of evidence have no application."

In Funk v. United States, 290 U.S. 371, 54 S.Ct. 212, 78 L.Ed. 369 (1933), the Court had considered the competency of a wife to testify for her husband and concluded that, absent congressional action or direction, the federal courts were to follow the common law as they saw it "in accordance with present day standards of wisdom and justice." And in Wolfle v. United States, 291 U.S. 7, 54 S.Ct. 279, 78 L.Ed. 617 (1934), the Court said with respect to the standard appropriate in determining a claim of privilege for an alleged confidential communication between spouses in a federal criminal prosecution:

"So our decision here, in the absence of Congressional legislation on the subject, is to be controlled by common law principles, not by local statute." *Id.*, 13, 54 S.Ct. at 280.

On the basis of *Funk* and *Wolfle*, the Advisory Committee on Rules of Criminal Procedure formulated Rule 26, which was adopted by the Court. The pertinent part of the rule provided:

"The . . . privileges of witnesses shall be governed, except when an act of Congress or these rules otherwise provide, by the principles of the common law as they may be interpreted . . . in the light of reason and experience."

As regards bankruptcy, section 21(a) of the Bankruptcy Act provides for examination of the bankrupt and his spouse concerning the acts, conduct, or property of the bankrupt. The Act limits examination of the spouse to business transacted by her or to which she is a party but provides "That the spouse may be so examined, any law of the United States or of any State to the contrary notwithstanding." 11 U.S.C. § 44(a). The effect of the quoted language is clearly to override any conflicting state rule of incompetency or privilege against spousal testimony. A fair reading would also indicate an overriding of any contrary state rule of privileged confidential spousal communications. Its validity has never been questioned and seems most unlikely to be. As to other privileges, the suggestion has been made that state law applies, though with little citation of authority, 2 Moore's Collier on Bankruptcy ¶ 21.13, p. 297 (14th ed. 1961). This position seems to be contrary to the expression of the Court in McCarthy v. Arndstein, 266 U.S. 34, 39, 45 S.Ct. 16, 69 L.Ed. 158 (1924), which speaks in the pattern of Rule 26 of the Federal Rules of Criminal Procedure:

"There is no provision [in the Bankruptcy Act] prescribing the rules by which the examination is to be governed. These are, impliedly, the general rules governing the admissibility of evidence and the competency and compellability of witnesses."

With respect to federal question litigation, the supremacy of federal law may be less clear, yet indications that state privileges are inapplicable preponderate in the circuits. In re Albert Lindley Lee Memorial Hospital, 209 F.2d 122 (2d Cir.1953), cert. denied Cincotta v. United States, 347 U.S. 960, 74 S.Ct. 709, 98 L.Ed. 1104; Colton v. United States, 306 F.2d 633 (2d Cir.1962); Falsone v. United States, 205 F.2d 734 (5th Cir.1953); Fraser v. United States, 145 F.2d 139 (6th Cir.1944), cert. denied 324 U.S. 849, 65 S.Ct. 684, 89 L.Ed. 1409; United States v. Brunner, 200 F.2d 276 (6th Cir.1952). *Contra*, Baird v. Koerner, 279 F.2d 623 (9th Cir.1960). Additional decisions of district courts are collected in Annot., 95 A.L.R.2d 320, 336. While a number of the cases arise from administrative income tax investigations, they nevertheless support the broad proposition of the inapplicability of state privileges in federal proceedings.

In view of these considerations, it is apparent that, to the extent that they accord state privileges standing in federal criminal cases, bankruptcy, and federal question cases, the rules go beyond what previously has been thought necessary or proper.

On the other hand, in diversity cases, or perhaps more accurately cases in which state law furnishes the rule of decision, the rules avoid giving state privileges the effect which substantial authority has thought necessary and proper. Regardless of what might once have been thought to be the command of Erie R. Co. v. Tompkins, 304 U.S. 64, 58 S.Ct. 817, 82 L.Ed. 1188 (1938), as to observance of state created privileges in diversity cases, Hanna v. Plumer, 380 U.S. 460, 85 S.Ct. 1136, 14 L.Ed.2d 8 (1965), is believed to locate the problem in the area of choice rather than necessity. Wright, Procedural Reform: Its Limitations and Its Future, 1 Ga.L.Rev. 563, 572–573 (1967). Contra, Republic Gear Co. v. Borg-Warner Corp., 381 F.2d 551, 555, n. 2 (2d Cir.1967), and see authorities there cited. Hence all significant policy factors need to be considered in order that the choice may be a wise one.

The arguments advanced in favor of recognizing state privileges are: a state privilege is an essential characteristic of a relationship or status created by state law and thus is substantive in the *Erie* sense; state policy ought not to be frustrated by the accident of diversity; the allowance or denial of a privilege is so likely to affect the outcome of litigation as to encourage forum selection on that basis, not a proper function of diversity jurisdiction. There are persuasive answers to these arguments.

(1) As to the question of "substance," it is true that a privilege commonly represents an aspect of a relationship created and defined by a State. For example, a confidential communications privilege is often an incident of marriage. However, in litigation involving the relationship itself, the privilege is not ordinarily one of the issues. In fact, statutes frequently make the communication privilege inapplicable in cases of divorce. McCormick § 88, p. 177. The same is true with respect to the attorney-client privilege when the parties to the relationship have a falling out. The reality of the matter is that privilege is called into operation, not when the relation giving rise to the privilege is being litigated, but when the litigation involves something substantively devoid of relation to the privilege. The appearance of privilege in the case is quite by accident, and its effect is to block off the tribunal from a source of information. Thus its real impact is on the method of proof in the case, and in comparison any substantive aspect appears tenuous.

(2) By most standards, criminal prosecutions are attended by more serious consequences than civil litigation, and it must be evident that the criminal area has the greatest sensitivity where privilege is concerned. Nevertheless, as previously noted, state privileges traditionally have given way in federal criminal prosecutions. If a privilege is denied in the area of greatest sensitivity, it tends to become illusory as a significant aspect of the relationship out of which it arises. For example, in a state having by statute an accountant's privilege, only the most imperceptible added force would be given the privilege by putting the accountant in a position to assure his client that, while he could not block disclosure in a federal criminal prosecution, he could do so in diversity cases as well as in state court proceedings. Thus viewed, state interest in privilege appears less substantial than at first glance might seem to be the case.

Moreover, federal interest is not lacking. It can scarcely be contended that once diversity is invoked the federal government no longer has a legitimate concern in the quality of judicial administration conducted under its aegis. The demise of conformity and the adoption of the Federal Rules of Civil Procedure stand as witness to the contrary.

(3) A large measure of forum shopping is recognized as legitimate in the American judicial system. Subject to the limitations of jurisdiction and the relatively modest controls imposed by venue provisions and the doctrine of forum non conveniens, plaintiffs are allowed in general a free choice of forum. Diversity jurisdiction has as its basic purpose the giving of a choice, not only to plaintiffs but, in removal situations, also to defendants. In principle, the basis of the choice is the supposed need to escape from local prejudice. If the choice were tightly confined to that basis, then complete conformity to local procedure as well as substantive law would be required. This, of course, is not the case, and the choice may in fact be influenced by a wide range of factors. As Dean Ladd has pointed out, a litigant may select the federal court "because of the federal procedural rules, the liberal

discovery provisions, the quality of jurors expected in the federal court, the respect held for federal judges, the control of federal judges over a trial, the summation and comment upon the weight of evidence by the judge, or the authority to grant a new trial if the judge regards the verdict against the weight of the evidence." Ladd, Privileges, 1969 Ariz.St.L.J. 555, 564. Present Rule 43(a) of the Civil Rules specifies a broader range of admissibility in federal than in state courts and makes no exception for diversity cases. Note should also be taken that Rule 26(b)(2) of the Rules of Civil Procedure, as revised, allows discovery to be had of liability insurance, without regard to local state law upon the subject.

When attention is directed to the practical dimensions of the problem, they are found not to be great. The privileges affected are few in number. Most states provide a physician-patient privilege; the proposed rules limit the privilege to a psychotherapist-patient relationship. See Advisory Committee's Note to Rule 504. The area of marital privilege under the proposed rules is narrower than in most states. See Rule 505. Some states recognize privileges for journalists and accountants; the proposed rules do not.

Physician-patient is the most widely recognized privilege not found in the proposed rules. As a practical matter it was largely eliminated in diversity cases when Rule 35 of the Rules of Civil Procedure became effective in 1938. Under that rule, a party physically examined pursuant to court order, by requesting and obtaining a copy of the report or by taking the deposition of the examiner, waives any privilege regarding the testimony of every other person who has examined him in respect of the same condition. While waiver may be avoided by neither requesting the report nor taking the examiner's deposition, the price is one which most litigant-patients are probably not prepared to pay.

Rule 502.

REQUIRED REPORTS PRIVILEGED BY STATUTE
[Not enacted.]

A person, corporation, association, or other organization or entity, either public or private, making a return or report required by law to be made has a privilege to refuse to disclose and to prevent any other person from disclosing the return or report, if the law requiring it to be made so provides. A public officer or agency to whom a return or report is required by law to be made has a privilege to refuse to disclose the return or report if the law requiring it to be made so provides. No privilege exists under this rule in actions involving perjury, false statements, fraud in the return or report, or other failure to comply with the law in question.

Advisory Committee's Note

Statutes which require the making of returns or reports sometimes confer on the reporting party a privilege against disclosure, commonly coupled with a prohibition against disclosure by the officer to whom the report is made. Some of the federal statutes of this kind are mentioned in the Advisory Committee's Note to Rule 501, *supra*. See also the Note to Rule 402, *supra*. A provision against disclosure may be included in a statute for a variety of reasons, the chief of which are probably assuring the validity of the statute against claims of self-incrimination, honoring the privilege against self-incrimination, and encouraging the furnishing of the required information by assuring privacy.

These statutes, both state and federal, may generally be assumed to embody policies of significant dimension. Rule 501 insulates the federal provisions against disturbance by these rules; the present rule reiterates a result commonly specified in federal statutes and extends its application to state statutes of similar character. Illustrations of the kinds of returns and reports contemplated by the rule appear in the cases, in which a reluctance to compel disclosure is manifested. In re Reid, 155 F. 933 (E.D.Mich.1906), assessor not compelled to produce bankrupt's property tax return in view of statute forbidding disclosure; In re Valecia Condensed Milk Co., 240 F. 310 (7th Cir.1917), secretary of state tax commission not compelled to produce bankrupt's income tax returns in violation of statute; Herman Bros. Pet Supply, Inc. v. N. L. R. B., 360 F.2d 176 (6th Cir.1966), subpoena denied for production of reports to state employment security commission prohibited by statute, in proceeding for back wages. And see the discussion of motor vehicle accident reports in Krizak v. W. C. Brooks & Sons, Inc., 320 F.2d 37, 42–43 (4th Cir.1963). Cf. In re Hines, 69 F.2d 52 (2d Cir.1934).

Rule 503.

LAWYER–CLIENT PRIVILEGE
[Not enacted.]

(a) **Definitions.** As used in this rule:

(1) A "client" is a person, public officer, or corporation, association, or other organization or entity, either public or private, who is rendered professional legal services by a lawyer, or who consults a lawyer with a view to obtaining professional legal services from him.

(2) A "lawyer" is a person authorized, or reasonably believed by the client to be authorized, to practice law in any state or nation.

(3) A "representative of the lawyer" is one employed to assist the lawyer in the rendition of professional legal services.

(4) A communication is "confidential" if not intended to be disclosed to third persons other than those to whom disclosure is in furtherance of the rendition of professional legal services to the client or those reasonably necessary for the transmission of the communication.

(b) **General rule of privilege.** A client has a privilege to refuse to disclose and to prevent any other person from disclosing confidential communications made for the purpose of facilitating the rendition of professional legal services to the client, (1) between himself or his representative and his lawyer or his lawyer's representative, or (2) between his lawyer and the lawyer's representative, or (3) by him or his lawyer to a lawyer representing another in a matter of common interest, or (4) between representatives of the client or between the client and a representative of the client, or (5) between lawyers representing the client.

(c) Who may claim the privilege. The privilege may be claimed by the client, his guardian or conservator, the personal representative of a deceased client, or the successor, trustee, or similar representative of a corporation, association, or other organization, whether or not in existence. The person who was the lawyer at the time of the communication may claim the privilege but only on behalf of the client. His authority to do so is presumed in the absence of evidence to the contrary.

(d) Exceptions. There is no privilege under this rule:

(1) Furtherance of crime or fraud. If the services of the lawyer were sought or obtained to enable or aid anyone to commit or plan to commit what the client knew or reasonably should have known to be a crime or fraud; or

(2) Claimants through same deceased client. As to a communication relevant to an issue between parties who claim through the same deceased client, regardless of whether the claims are by testate or intestate succession or by *inter vivos* transaction; or

(3) Breach of duty by lawyer or client. As to a communication relevant to an issue of breach of duty by the lawyer to his client or by the client to his lawyer; or

(4) Document attested by lawyer. As to a communication relevant to an issue concerning an attested document to which the lawyer is an attesting witness: or

(5) Joint clients. As to a communication relevant to a matter of common interest between two or more clients if the communication was made by any of them to a lawyer retained or consulted in common, when offered in an action between any of the clients.

Advisory Committee's Note

Subdivision (a). (1) The definition of "client" includes governmental bodies, Connecticut Mutual Life Ins. Co. v. Shields, 18 F.R.D. 448 (S.D.N.Y.1955); People ex rel. Department of Public Works v. Glen Arms Estate, Inc., 230 Cal.App.2d 841, 41 Cal.Rptr. 303 (1965); Rowley v. Ferguson, 48 N.E.2d 243 (Ohio App.1942); and corporations, Radiant Burners, Inc. v. American Gas Assn., 320 F.2d 314 (7th Cir.1963). *Contra*, Gardner, A Personal Privilege for Communications of Corporate Clients—Paradox or Public Policy, 40 U.Det.L.J. 299, 323, 376 (1963). The definition also extends the status of client to one consulting a lawyer preliminarily with a view to retaining him, even though actual employment does not result. McCormick, § 92, p. 184. The client need not be involved in litigation; the rendition of legal service or advice under any circumstances suffices. 8 Wigmore § 2294 (Mc-

Naughton Rev.1961). The services must be professional legal services; purely business or personal matters do not qualify. McCormick § 92, p. 184.

The rule contains no definition of "representative of the client." In the opinion of the Advisory Committee, the matter is better left to resolution by decision on a case-by-case basis. The most restricted position is the "control group" test, limiting the category to persons with authority to seek and act upon legal advice for the client. See, *e.g.,* City of Philadelphia v. Westinghouse Electric Corp., 210 F.Supp. 483 (E.D.Pa.1962), mandamus and prohibition denied *sub nom.* General Electric Co. v. Kirkpatrick, 312 F.2d 742 (3d Cir.), cert. denied 372 U.S. 943; Garrison v. General Motors Corp., 213 F.Supp. 515 (S.D.Cal.1963); Hogan v. Zletz, 43 F.R.D. 308 (N.D.Okla.1967), aff'd *sub nom.* Natta v. Hogan, 392 F.2d 686 (10th Cir.1968); Day v. Illinois Power Co., 50 Ill.App.2d 52, 199 N.E.2d 802 (1964). Broader formulations are found in other decisions. See, *e.g.,* United States v. United Shoe Machinery Corp., 89 F.Supp. 357 (D.Mass.1950); Zenith Radio Corp. v. Radio Corp. of America, 121 F.Supp. 792 (D.Del.1954); Harper & Row Publishers, Inc. v. Decker, 423 F.2d 487 (7th Cir.1970), aff'd without opinion by equally divided court 400 U.S. 955 (1971), reh. denied 401 U.S. 950; D. I. Chadbourne, Inc. v. Superior Court, 60 Cal.2d 723, 36 Cal.Rptr. 468, 388 P.2d 700 (1964). Cf. Rucker v. Wabash R. Co., 418 F.2d 146 (7th Cir.1969). See generally, Simon, The Attorney-Client Privilege as Applied to Corporations, 65 Yale L.J. 953, 956–966 (1956); Note, Attorney-Client Privilege for Corporate Clients: The Control Group Test, 84 Harv.L.Rev. 424 (1970).

The status of employees who are used in the process of communicating, as distinguished from those who are parties to the communication, is treated in paragraph (4) of subdivision (a) of the rule.

(2) A "lawyer" is a person licensed to practice law in any state or nation. There is no requirement that the licensing state or nation recognize the attorney-client privilege, thus avoiding excursions into conflict of laws questions. "Lawyer" also includes a person reasonably believed to be a lawyer. For similar provisions, see California Evidence Code § 950.

(3) The definition of "representative of the lawyer" recognizes that the lawyer may, in rendering legal services, utilize the services of assistants in addition to those employed in the process of communicating. Thus the definition includes an expert employed to assist in rendering legal advice. United States v. Kovel, 296 F.2d 918 (2d Cir.1961) (accountant). Cf. Himmelfarb v. United States, 175 F.2d 924 (9th Cir.1949). It also includes an expert employed to assist in the planning and conduct of litigation, though not one employed to testify as a witness. Lalance & Grosjean Mfg. Co. v. Haberman Mfg. Co., 87 F. 563 (S.D.N.Y.1898), and see revised Civil Rule 26(b)(4). The definition does not, however, limit "representative of the lawyer" to experts. Whether his compensation is derived immediately from the lawyer or the client is not material.

(4) The requisite confidentiality of communication is defined in terms of intent. A communication made in public or meant to be relayed to outsiders or which is divulged by the client to third persons

can scarcely be considered confidential. McCormick § 95. The intent is inferable from the circumstances. Unless intent to disclose is apparent, the attorney-client communication is confidential. Taking or failing to take precautions may be considered as bearing on intent.

Practicality requires that some disclosure be allowed beyond the immediate circle of lawyer-client and their representatives without impairing confidentiality. Hence the definition allows disclosure to persons "to whom disclosure is in furtherance of the rendition of professional legal services to the client," contemplating those in such relation to the client as "spouse, parent, business associate, or joint client." Comment, California Evidence Code § 952.

Disclosure may also be made to persons "reasonably necessary for the transmission of the communication," without loss of confidentiality.

Subdivision (b) sets forth the privilege, using the previously defined terms: client, lawyer, representative of the lawyer, and confidential communication.

Substantial authority has in the past allowed the eavesdropper to testify to overheard privileged conversations and has admitted intercepted privileged letters. Today, the evolution of more sophisticated techniques of eavesdropping and interception calls for abandonment of this position. The rule accordingly adopts a policy of protection against these kinds of invasion of the privilege.

The privilege extends to communications (1) between client or his representative and lawyer or his representative, (2) between lawyer and lawyer's representative, (3) by client or his lawyer to a lawyer representing another in a matter of common interest, (4) between representatives of the client or the client and a representative of the client, and (5) between lawyers representing the client. All these communications must be specifically for the purpose of obtaining legal services for the client; otherwise the privilege does not attach.

The third type of communication occurs in the "joint defense" or "pooled information" situation, where different lawyers represent clients who have some interests in common. In Chahoon v. Commonwealth, 62 Va. 822 (1871), the court said that the various clients might have retained one attorney to represent all; hence everything said at a joint conference was privileged, and one of the clients could prevent another from disclosing what the other had himself said. The result seems to be incorrect in overlooking a frequent reason for retaining different attorneys by the various clients, namely actually or potentially conflicting interests in addition to the common interest which brings them together. The needs of these cases seem better to be met by allowing each client a privilege as to his own statements. Thus if all resist disclosure, none will occur. Continental Oil Co. v. United States, 330 F.2d 347 (9th Cir.1964). But, if for reasons of his own, a client wishes to disclose his own statements made at the joint conference, he should be permitted to do so, and the rule is to that effect. The rule does not apply to situations where there is no common interest to be promoted by a joint consultation, and the parties meet on a purely adversary basis. Vance v. State, 190 Tenn. 521, 230 S.W.2d 987 (1950), cert. denied 339 U.S. 988, 70 S.Ct. 1010, 94 L.Ed. 1389. Cf. Hunydee v. United States, 355 F.2d 183 (9th Cir.1965).

Subdivision (c). The privilege is, of course, that of the client, to be claimed by him or by his personal representative. The successor of a dissolved corporate client may claim the privilege. California Evidence Code § 953; New Jersey Evidence Rule 26(1). *Contra,* Uniform Rule 26(1).

The lawyer may not claim the privilege on his own behalf. However, he may claim it on behalf of the client. It is assumed that the ethics of the profession will require him to do so except under most unusual circumstances. American Bar Association, Canons of Professional Ethics, Canon 37. His authority to make the claim is presumed unless there is evidence to the contrary, as would be the case if the client were now a party to litigation in which the question arose and were represented by other counsel. Ex parte Lipscomb, 111 Tex. 409, 239 S.W. 1101 (1922).

Subdivision (d) in general incorporates well established exceptions.

(1) The privilege does not extend to advice in aid of future wrongdoing. 8 Wigmore § 2298 (McNaughton Rev.1961). The wrongdoing need not be that of the client. The provision that the client knew or reasonably should have known of the criminal or fraudulent nature of the act is designed to protect the client who is erroneously advised that a proposed action is within the law. No preliminary finding that sufficient evidence aside from the communication has been introduced to warrant a finding that the services were sought to enable the commission of a wrong is required. Cf. Clark v. United States, 289 U.S. 1, 15–16, 53 S.Ct. 465, 77 L.Ed. 993 (1933); Uniform Rule 26(2)(a). While any general exploration of what transpired between attorney and client would, of course, be inappropriate, it is wholly feasible, either at the discovery stage or during trial, so to focus the inquiry by specific questions as to avoid any broad inquiry into attorney-client communications. Numerous cases reflect this approach.

(2) Normally the privilege survives the death of the client and may be asserted by his representative. Subdivision (c), *supra.* When, however, the identity of the person who steps into the client's shoes is in issue, as in a will contest, the identity of the person entitled to claim the privilege remains undetermined until the conclusion of the litigation. The choice is thus between allowing both sides or neither to assert the privilege, with authority and reason favoring the latter view. McCormick § 98; Uniform Rule 26(2)(b); California Evidence Code § 957; Kansas Code of Civil Procedure § 60–426(b)(2); New Jersey Evidence Rule 26(2)(b).

(3) The exception is required by considerations of fairness and policy when questions arise out of dealings between attorney and client, as in cases of controversy over attorney's fees, claims of inadequacy of representation, or charges of professional misconduct. McCormick § 95; Uniform Rule 26(2)(c); California Evidence Code § 958; Kansas Code of Civil Procedure § 60–426(b)(3); New Jersey Evidence Rule 26(2)(c).

(4) When the lawyer acts as attesting witness, the approval of the client to his so doing may safely be assumed, and waiver of the privilege as to any relevant lawyer-client communications is a proper result. McCormick § 92, p. 184; Uniform Rule 26(2)(d); California Evidence Code § 959; Kansas Code of Civil Procedure § 60–426(b)(d) [*sic*].

(5) The subdivision states existing law. McCormick § 95, pp. 192–193. For similar provisions, see Uniform Rule 26(2)(e); California Evidence Code § 962; Kansas Code of Civil Procedure § 60–426(b)(4); New Jersey Evidence Rule 26(2). The situation with which this provision deals is to be distinguished from the case of clients with a common interest who retain different lawyers. See subdivision (b)(3) of this rule, *supra*.

Rule 504.

PSYCHOTHERAPIST–PATIENT PRIVILEGE
[Not enacted.]

(a) Definitions.

(1) A "patient" is a person who consults or is examined or interviewed by a psychotherapist.

(2) A "psychotherapist" is (A) a person authorized to practice medicine in any state or nation, or reasonably believed by the patient so to be, while engaged in the diagnosis or treatment of a mental or emotional condition, including drug addiction, or (B) a person licensed or certified as a psychologist under the laws of any state or nation, while similarly engaged.

(3) A communication is "confidential" if not intended to be disclosed to third persons other than those present to further the interest of the patient in the consultation, examination, or interview, or persons reasonably necessary for the transmission of the communication, or persons who are participating in the diagnosis and treatment under the direction of the psychotherapist, including members of the patient's family.

(b) General rule of privilege. A patient has a privilege to refuse to disclose and to prevent any other person from disclosing confidential communications, made for the purposes of diagnosis or treatment of his mental or emotional condition, including drug addiction, among himself, his psychotherapist, or persons who are participating in the diagnosis or treatment under the direction of the psychotherapist, including members of the patient's family.

(c) Who may claim the privilege. The privilege may be claimed by the patient, by his guardian or conservator, or by the personal representative of a deceased patient. The person who was the psychotherapist may claim the privilege but only on behalf of the patient. His authority so to do is presumed in the absence of evidence to the contrary.

(d) Exceptions.

(1) Proceedings for hospitalization.   There is no privilege under this rule for communications relevant to an issue in proceedings to hospitalize the patient for mental illness, if the psychotherapist in the course of diagnosis or treatment has determined that the patient is in need of hospitalization.

(2) Examination by order of judge.   If the judge orders an examination of the mental or emotional condition of the patient, communications made in the course thereof are not privileged under this rule with respect to the particular purpose for which the examination is ordered unless the judge orders otherwise.

(3) Condition an element of claim or defense.   There is no privilege under this rule as to communications relevant to an issue of the mental or emotional condition of the patient in any proceeding in which he relies upon the condition as an element of his claim or defense, or, after the patient's death, in any proceeding in which any party relies upon the condition as an element of his claim or defense.

Advisory Committee's Note

The rules contain no provision for a general physician-patient privilege. While many states have by statute created the privilege, the exceptions which have been found necessary in order to obtain information required by the public interest or to avoid fraud are so numerous as to leave little if any basis for the privilege. Among the exclusions from the statutory privilege, the following may be enumerated; communications not made for purposes of diagnosis and treatment; commitment and restoration proceedings; issues as to wills or otherwise between parties claiming by succession from the patient; actions on insurance policies; required reports (venereal diseases, gunshot wounds, child abuse); communications in furtherance of crime or fraud; mental or physical condition put in issue by patient (personal injury cases); malpractice actions; and some or all criminal prosecutions. California, for example, excepts cases in which the patient puts his condition in issue, all criminal proceedings, will and similar contests, malpractice cases, and disciplinary proceedings, as well as certain other situations, thus leaving virtually nothing covered by the privilege. California Evidence Code §§ 990–1007. For other illustrative statutes see Ill.Rev.Stat.1967, c. 51, § 5.1; N.Y.C.P.L.R. § 4504; N.C.Gen.Stat.1953, § 8–53. Moreover, the possibility of compelling gratuitous disclosure by the physician is foreclosed by his standing to raise the question of relevancy. See Note on "Official Information" Privilege following Rule 509, *infra.*

The doubts attendant upon the general physician-patient privilege are not present when the relationship is that of psychotherapist and patient. While the common law recognized no general physician-patient privilege, it had indicated a disposition to recognize a psychotherapist-patient privilege, Note, Confidential Communications to a Psychotherapist: A New Testimonial Privilege, 47 Nw.U.L.Rev. 384 (1952), when legislatures began moving into the field.

The case for the privilege is convincingly stated in Report No. 45, Group for the Advancement of Psychiatry 92 (1960):

"Among physicians, the psychiatrist has a special need to maintain confidentiality. His capacity to help his patients is completely dependent upon their willingness and ability to talk freely. This makes it difficult if not impossible for him to function without being able to assure his patients of confidentiality and, indeed, privileged communication. Where there may be exceptions to this general rule * * *, there is wide agreement that confidentiality is a *sine qua non* for successful psychiatric treatment. The relationship may well be likened to that of the priest-penitent or the lawyer-client. Psychiatrists not only explore the very depths of their patients' conscious, but their unconscious feelings and attitudes as well. Therapeutic effectiveness necessitates going beyond a patient's awareness and, in order to do this, it must be possible to communicate freely. A threat to secrecy blocks successful treatment."

A much more extended exposition of the case for the privilege is made in Slovenko, Psychiatry and a Second Look at the Medical Privilege, 6 Wayne L.Rev. 175, 184 (1960), quoted extensively in the careful Tentative Recommendation and Study Relating to the Uniform Rules of Evidence (Article V. Privileges), Cal.Law Rev. Comm'n, 417 (1964). The conclusion is reached that Wigmore's four conditions needed to justify the existence of a privilege are amply satisfied.

Illustrative statutes are Cal.Evidence Code §§ 1010–1026; Ga.Code § 38–418 (1961 Supp.); Conn.Gen.Stat., § 52–146a (1966 Supp.); Ill.Rev.Stat.1967, c. 51, § 5.2.

While many of the statutes simply place the communications on the same basis as those between attorney and client, 8 Wigmore § 2286, n. 23 (McNaughton Rev.1961), basic differences between the two relationships forbid resorting to attorney-client save as a helpful point of departure. Goldstein and Katz, Psychiatrist-Patient Privilege: The GAP Proposal and the Connecticut Statute, 36 Conn.B.J. 175, 182 (1962).

Subdivision (a). (1) The definition of patient does not include a person submitting to examination for scientific purposes. Cf. Cal.Evidence Code § 1101. Attention is directed to 42 U.S.C. 242(a)(2), as amended by the Drug Abuse and Control Act of 1970, P.L. 91–513, authorizing the Secretary of Health, Education, and Welfare to withhold the identity of persons who are the subjects of research on the use and effect of drugs. The rule would leave this provision in full force. See Rule 501.

(2) The definition of psychotherapist embraces a medical doctor while engaged in the diagnosis or treatment of mental or emotional conditions, including drug addiction, in order not to exclude the general practitioner and to avoid the making of needless refined distinctions concerning what is and what is not the practice of psychiatry. The requirement that the psychologist be in fact licensed, and not merely be believed to be so, is believed to be justified by the number of persons, other than psychiatrists, purporting to render psychotherapeutic aid and the variety of their theories. Cal.Law Rev. Comm'n, *supra,* at pp. 434–437.

The clarification of mental or emotional condition as including drug addiction is consistent with current approaches to drug abuse problems. See, *e.g.*, the definition of "drug dependent person" in 42 U.S.C. 201(q), added by the Drug Abuse Prevention and Control Act of 1970, P.L. 91–513.

(3) Confidential communication is defined in terms conformable with those of the lawyer-client privilege. Rule 503(a)(4), *supra*, with changes appropriate to the difference in circumstance.

Subdivisions (b) and (c). The lawyer-client rule is drawn upon for the phrasing of the general rule of privilege and the determination of those who may claim it. See Rule 503(b) and (c).

The specific inclusion of communications made for the diagnosis and treatment of drug addiction recognizes the continuing contemporary concern with rehabilitation of drug dependent persons and is designed to implement that policy by encouraging persons in need thereof to seek assistance. The provision is in harmony with Congressional actions in this area. See 42 U.S.C. § 260, providing for voluntary hospitalization of addicts or persons with drug dependence problems and prohibiting use of evidence of admission or treatment in any proceeding against him, and 42 U.S.C. § 3419 providing that in voluntary or involuntary commitment of addicts the results of any hearing, examination, test, or procedure used to determine addiction shall not be used against the patient in any criminal proceeding.

Subdivision (d). The exceptions differ substantially from those of the attorney-client privilege, as a result of the basic differences in the relationships. While it has been argued convincingly that the nature of the psychotherapist-patient relationship demands complete security against legally coerced disclosure in all circumstances, Louisell, The Psychologist in Today's Legal World: Part II, 41 Minn.L.Rev. 731, 746 (1957), the committee of psychiatrists and lawyers who drafted the Connecticut statute concluded that in three instances the need for disclosure was sufficiently great to justify the risk of possible impairment of the relationship. Goldstein and Katz, Psychiatrist-Patient Privilege: The GAP Proposal and the Connecticut Statute, 36 Conn.B.J. 175 (1962). These three exceptions are incorporated in the present rule.

(1) The interests of both patient and public call for a departure from confidentiality in commitment proceedings. Since disclosure is authorized only when the psychotherapist determines that hospitalization is needed, control over disclosure is placed largely in the hands of a person in whom the patient has already manifested confidence. Hence damage to the relationship is unlikely.

(2) In a court ordered examination, the relationship is likely to be an arm's length one, though not necessarily so. In any event, an exception is necessary for the effective utilization of this important and growing procedure. The exception, it will be observed, deals with a court ordered examination rather than with a court appointed psychotherapist. Also, the exception is effective only with respect to the particular purpose for which the examination is ordered. The rule thus conforms with the provisions of 18 U.S.C. § 4244 that no statement made by the accused in the course of an examination into

competency to stand trial is admissible on the issue of guilt and of 42 U.S.C. § 3420 that a physician conducting an examination in a drug addiction commitment proceeding is a competent and compellable witness.

(3) By injecting his condition into litigation, the patient must be said to waive the privilege, in fairness and to avoid abuses. Similar considerations prevail after the patient's death.

Rule 505.

HUSBAND–WIFE PRIVILEGE
[Not enacted.]

(a) General rule of privilege. An accused in a criminal proceeding has a privilege to prevent his spouse from testifying against him.

(b) Who may claim the privilege. The privilege may be claimed by the accused or by the spouse on his behalf. The authority of the spouse to do so is presumed in the absence of evidence to the contrary.

(c) Exceptions. There is no privilege under this rule (1) in proceedings in which one spouse is charged with a crime against the person or property of the other or of a child of either, or with a crime against the person or property of a third person committed in the course of committing a crime against the other, or (2) as to matters occurring prior to the marriage, or (3) in proceedings in which a spouse is charged with importing an alien for prostitution or other immoral purpose in violation of 8 U.S.C. § 1328, with transporting a female in interstate commerce for immoral purposes or other offense in violation of 18 U.S.C. §§ 2421–2424, or with violation of other similar statutes.

Advisory Committee's Note

Subdivision (a). Rules of evidence have evolved around the marriage relationship in four respects: (1) incompetency of one spouse to testify for the other; (2) privilege of one spouse not to testify against the other; (3) privilege of one spouse not to have the other testify against him; and (4) privilege against disclosure of confidential communications between spouses, sometimes extended to information learned by virtue of the existence of the relationship. Today these matters are largely governed by statutes.

With the disappearance of the disqualification of parties and interested persons, the basis for spousal incompetency no longer existed, and it, too, virtually disappeared in both civil and criminal actions. Usually reached by statute, this result was reached for federal courts by the process of decision. Funk v. United States, 290 U.S. 371, 54 S.Ct. 212, 78 L.Ed. 369 (1933). These rules contain no recognition of incompetency of one spouse to testify for the other.

While some 10 jurisdictions recognize a privilege not to testify against one's spouse in a criminal case, and a much smaller number do so in civil cases, the great majority recognizes no privilege on the part of the testifying spouse, and this is the position taken by the rule. Compare Wyatt v. United States, 362 U.S. 525, 80 S.Ct. 901, 4 L.Ed.2d

931 (1960), a Mann Act prosecution in which the wife was the victim. The majority opinion held that she could not claim privilege and was compellable to testify. The holding was narrowly based: The Mann Act presupposed that the women with whom it dealt had no independent wills of their own, and this legislative judgment precluded allowing a victim-wife an option whether to testify, lest the policy of the statute be defeated. A vigorous dissent took the view that nothing in the Mann Act required departure from usual doctrine, which was conceived to be one of allowing the injured party to claim or waive privilege.

About 30 jurisdictions recognize a privilege of an accused in a criminal case to prevent his or her spouse from testifying. It is believed to represent the one aspect of marital privilege the continuation of which is warranted. In Hawkins v. United States, 358 U.S. 74, 79 S.Ct. 136, 3 L.Ed.2d 125 (1958) it was sustained. Cf. McCormick § 66; 8 Wigmore § 2228 (McNaughton Rev.1961): Comment, Uniform Rule 23(2).

The rule recognizes no privilege for confidential communications. The traditional justifications for privileges not to testify against a spouse and not to be testified against by one's spouse have been the prevention of marital dissension and the repugnancy of requiring a person to condemn or be condemned by his spouse. 8 Wigmore §§ 2228, 2241 (McNaughton Rev.1961). These considerations bear no relevancy to marital communications. Nor can it be assumed that marital conduct will be affected by a privilege for confidential communications of whose existence the parties in all likelihood are unaware. The other communication privileges, by way of contrast, have as one party a professional person who can be expected to inform the other of the existence of the privilege. Moreover, the relationships from which those privileges arise are essentially and almost exclusively verbal in nature, quite unlike marriage. See Hutchins and Slesinger, Some Observations on the Law of Evidence: Family Relations, 13 Minn.L.Rev. 675 (1929). Cf. McCormick § 90; 8 Wigmore § 2337 (McNaughton Rev.1961). The parties are not spouses if the marriage was a sham, Lutwak v. United States, 344 U.S. 604 (1953), or they have been divorced, Barsky v. United States, 339 F.2d 180 (9th Cir.1964), and therefore the privilege is not applicable.

Subdivision (b). This provision is a counterpart of Rules 503(c), 504(c), and 506(c). Its purpose is to provide a procedure for preventing the taking of the spouse's testimony notably in grand jury proceedings, when the accused is absent and does not know that a situation appropriate for a claim of privilege is presented. If the privilege is not claimed by the spouse, the protection of Rule 512 is available.

Subdivision (c) contains three exceptions to the privilege against spousal testimony in criminal cases.

(1) The need of limitation upon the privilege in order to avoid grave injustice in cases of offenses against the other spouse or a child of either can scarcely be denied. 8 Wigmore § 2239 (McNaughton Rev.1961). The rule therefore disallows any privilege against spousal testimony in these cases and in this respect is in accord with the result reached in Wyatt v. United States, 362 U.S. 525, 80 S.Ct. 901, 4 L.Ed.2d

FEDERAL RULES OF EVIDENCE

FEDERAL RULES OF EVIDENCE

FEDERAL RULES OF EVIDENCE   **769**
931 (1960), a Mann Act prosecution, denying the accused the privilege of excluding his wife's testimony, since she was the woman who was transported for immoral purposes.

(2) The second exception renders the privilege inapplicable as to matters occurring prior to the marriage. This provision eliminates the possibility of suppressing testimony by marrying the witness.

(3) The third exception continues and expands established Congressional policy. In prosecutions for importing aliens for immoral purposes, Congress has specifically denied the accused any privilege not to have his spouse testify against him. 8 U.S.C. § 1328. No provision of this nature is included in the Mann Act, and in Hawkins v. United States, 358 U.S. 74, 79 S.Ct. 136, 3 L.Ed.2d 125 (1958), the conclusion was reached that the common law privilege continued. Consistency requires similar results in the two situations. The rule adopts the Congressional approach, as based upon a more realistic appraisal of the marriage relationship in cases of this kind, in preference to the specific result in *Hawkins*. Note the common law treatment of pimping and sexual offenses with third persons as exceptions to marital privilege. 8 Wigmore § 2239 (McNaughton Rev.1961).

With respect to bankruptcy proceedings, the smallness of the area of spousal privilege under the rule and the general inapplicability of privileges created by state law render unnecessary any special provision for examination of the spouse of the bankrupt, such as that now contained in section 21(a) of the Bankruptcy Act. 11 U.S.C. § 44(a).

For recent statutes and rules dealing with husband-wife privileges, see California Evidence Code §§ 970–973, 980–987; Kansas Code of Civil Procedure §§ 60–423(b), 60–428; New Jersey Evidence Rules 23(2), 28.

Rule 506.

COMMUNICATIONS TO CLERGYMEN
[Not enacted.]

(a) Definitions. As used in this rule:

(1) A "clergyman" is a minister, priest, rabbi, or other similar functionary of a religious organization, or an individual reasonably believed so to be by the person consulting him.

(2) A communication is "confidential" if made privately and not intended for further disclosure except to other persons present in furtherance of the purpose of the communication.

(b) General rule of privilege. A person has a privilege to refuse to disclose and to prevent another from disclosing a confidential communication by the person to a clergyman in his professional character as spiritual adviser.

(c) Who may claim the privilege. The privilege may be claimed by the person, by his guardian or conservator, or by his personal representative if he is deceased. The clergyman may claim the privilege on behalf of the person. His authority so to do is presumed in the absence of evidence to the contrary.

Advisory Committee's Note

The considerations which dictate the recognition of privileges generally seem strongly to favor a privilege for confidential communications to clergymen. During the period when most of the common law privileges were taking shape, no clear-cut privilege for communications between priest and penitent emerged. 8 Wigmore § 2394 (McNaughton Rev.1961). The English political climate of the time may well furnish the explanation. In this country, however, the privilege has been recognized by statute in about two-thirds of the states and occasionally by the common law process of decision. *Id.,* § 2395; Mullen v. United States, 105 U.S.App.D.C. 25, 263 F.2d 275 (1959).

Subdivision (a). Paragraph (1) defines a clergyman as a "minister, priest, rabbi, or other similar functionary of a religious organization." The concept is necessarily broader than that inherent in the ministerial exemption for purposes of Selective Service. See United States v. Jackson, 369 F.2d 936 (4th Cir.1966). However, it is not so broad as to include all self-denominated "ministers." A fair construction of the language requires that the person to whom the status is sought to be attached be regularly engaged in activities conforming at least in a general way with those of a Catholic priest, Jewish rabbi, or minister of an established Protestant denomination, though not necessarily on a full-time basis. No further specification seems possible in view of the lack of licensing and certification procedures for clergymen. However, this lack seems to have occasioned no particular difficulties in connection with the solemnization of marriages, which suggests that none may be anticipated here. For similar definitions of "clergyman" see California Evidence Code § 1030; New Jersey Evidence Rule 29.

The "reasonable belief" provision finds support in similar provisions for lawyer-client in Rule 503 and for psychotherapist-patient in Rule 504. A parallel is also found in the recognition of the validity of marriages performed by unauthorized persons if the parties reasonably believed them legally qualified. Harper and Skolnick, Problems of the Family 153 (Rev.Ed.1962).

(2) The definition of "confidential" communication is consistent with the use of the term in Rule 503(a)(5) for lawyer-client and in Rule 504(a)(3) for psychotherapist-patient, suitably adapted to communications to clergymen.

Subdivision (b). The choice between a privilege narrowly restricted to doctrinally required confessions and a privilege broadly applicable to all confidential communications with a clergyman in his professional character as spiritual adviser has been exercised in favor of the latter. Many clergymen now receive training in marriage counseling and the handling of personality problems. Matters of this kind fall readily into the realm of the spirit. The same considerations which underlie the psychotherapist-patient privilege of Rule 504 suggest a broad application of the privilege for communications to clergymen.

State statutes and rules fall in both the narrow and the broad categories. A typical narrow statute proscribes disclosure of "a confession * * * made * * * in the course of discipline enjoined by the church to which he belongs." Ariz.Rev.Stats.Ann.1956, § 12–2233. See also California Evidence Code § 1032; Uniform Rule 29. Illustrative of the broader privilege are statutes applying to "information communicated to him in a confidential manner, properly entrusted to him in his professional capacity, and necessary to enable him to discharge the functions of his office according to the usual course of his practice or discipline, wherein such person so communicating * * * is seeking spiritual counsel and advice," Fla.Stats.Ann.1960, § 90.241, or to any "confidential communication properly entrusted to him in his professional capacity, and necessary and proper to enable him to discharge the functions of his office according to the usual course of practice or discipline," Iowa Code Ann.1950, § 622.10. See also Ill.Rev.Stats.1967, c. 51, § 48.1; Minn.Stats.Ann.1945, § 595.02(3); New Jersey Evidence Rule 29.

Under the privilege as phrased, the communicating person is entitled to prevent disclosure not only by himself but also by the clergyman and by eavesdroppers. For discussion see Advisory Committee's Note under lawyer-client privilege, Rule 503(b).

The nature of what may reasonably be considered spiritual advice makes it unnecessary to include in the rule a specific exception for communications in furtherance of crime or fraud, as in Rule 503(d)(1).

Subdivision (c) makes clear that the privilege belongs to the communicating person. However, a prima facie authority on the part of the clergyman to claim the privilege on behalf of the person is recognized. The discipline of the particular church and the discreetness of the clergyman are believed to constitute sufficient safeguards for the absent communicating person. See Advisory Committee's Note to the similar provision with respect to attorney-client in Rule 503(c).

Rule 507.

POLITICAL VOTE
[Not enacted.]

Every person has a privilege to refuse to disclose the tenor of his vote at a political election conducted by secret ballot unless the vote was cast illegally.

Advisory Committee's Note

Secrecy in voting is an essential aspect of effective democratic government, insuring free exercise of the franchise and fairness in elections. Secrecy after the ballot has been cast is as essential as secrecy in the act of voting. Nutting, Freedom of Silence: Constitutional Protection Against Governmental Intrusion in Political Affairs, 47 Mich.L.Rev. 181, 191 (1948). Consequently a privilege has long been recognized on the part of a voter to decline to disclose how he voted. Required disclosure would be the exercise of "a kind of inquisitorial power unknown to the principles of our government and constitution, and might be highly injurious to the suffrages of a free people, as well as tending to create cabals and disturbances between contending parties in popular elections." Johnston v. Charleston, 1 Bay 441, 442 (S.C.1795).

The exception for illegally cast votes is a common one under both statutes and case law, Nutting, *supra*, at p. 192; 8 Wigmore § 2214, p. 163 (McNaughton Rev.1961). The policy considerations which underlie the privilege are not applicable to the illegal voter. However, nothing in the exception purports to foreclose an illegal voter from invoking the privilege against self-incrimination under appropriate circumstances.

For similar provisions, see Uniform Rule 31; California Evidence Code § 1050; Kansas Code of Civil Procedure § 60–431; New Jersey Evidence Rule 31.

Rule 508.

TRADE SECRETS
[Not enacted.]

A person has a privilege, which may be claimed by him or his agent or employee, to refuse to disclose and to prevent other persons from disclosing a trade secret owned by him, if the allowance of the privilege will not tend to conceal fraud or otherwise work injustice. When disclosure is directed, the judge shall take such protective measure as the interests of the holder of the privilege and of the parties and the furtherance of justice may require.

Advisory Committee's Note

While sometimes said not to be a true privilege, a qualified right to protection against disclosure of trade secrets has found ample recognition, and, indeed, a denial of it would be difficult to defend. 8 Wigmore § 2212(3) (McNaughton Rev.1961). And see 4 Moore's Federal Practice ¶¶ 30.12 and 34.15 (2nd ed. 1963 and Supp.1965) and 2A Barron and Holtzoff, Federal Practice and Procedure § 715.1 (Wright ed. 1961). Congressional policy is reflected in the Securities Exchange Act of 1934, 15 U.S.C. § 78x, and the Public Utility Holding Company Act of 1933, *id.* § 79v, which deny the Securities and Exchange Commission authority to require disclosure of trade secrets or processes in applications and reports. See also Rule 26(c) (7) of the Rules of Civil Procedure, as revised, mentioned further hereinafter.

Illustrative cases raising trade-secret problems are: E.I. Du Pont de Nemours Powder Co. v. Masland, 244 U.S. 100, 37 S.Ct. 575, 61 L.Ed. 1016 (1917), suit to enjoin former employee from using plaintiff's secret processes, countered by defense that many of the processes were well known to the trade: Segal Lock & Hardware Co. v. FTC, 143 F.2d 935 (2d Cir.1944), question whether expert locksmiths employed by FTC should be required to disclose methods used by them in picking petitioner's "pick-proof" locks; Dobson v. Graham, 49 F. 17 (E.D.Pa.1889), patent infringement suit in which plaintiff sought to elicit from former employees now in the hire of defendant the respects in which defendant's machinery differed from plaintiff's patented machinery: Putney v. Du Bois Co., 240 Mo.App. 1075, 226 S.W.2d 737 (1950), action for injuries allegedly sustained from using defendant's secret formula dishwashing compound. See 8 Wigmore § 2212(3) (Mc-Naughton Rev.1961); Annot., 17 A.L.R.2d 383; 49 Mich.L.Rev. 133 (1950). The need for accommodation between protecting trade secrets, on the one hand, and eliciting facts required for full and fair presentation of a case, on the other hand, is apparent. Whether disclosure should be required depends upon a weighing of the competing interests involved against the background of the total situation, including consideration of such factors as the dangers of abuse, good faith, adequacy of protective measures, and the availability of other means of proof.

The cases furnish examples of the bringing of judicial ingenuity to bear upon the problem of evolving protective measures which achieve a degree of control over disclosure. Perhaps the most common is simply to take testimony *in camera*. Annot., 62 A.L.R.2d 509. Other possibilities include making disclosure to opposing counsel but not to his client, E. I. Du Pont de Nemours Powder Co. v. Masland, 244 U.S. 100, 37 S.Ct. 575, 61 L.Ed. 1016 (1917); making disclosure only to the judge (hearing examiner), Segal Lock & Hardware Co. v. FTC, 143 F.2d 935 (2d Cir.1944); and placing those present under oath not to make disclosure, Paul v. Sinnott, 217 F.Supp. 84 (W.D.Pa.1963).

Rule 26(c) of the Rules of Civil Procedure, as revised, provides that the judge may make "any order which justice requires to protect a party or person from annoyance, embarrassment, oppression, or undue burden or expense, including one or more of the following: * * * (7) that a trade secret or other confidential research, development, or commercial information not be disclosed or be disclosed only in a designated way * * *." While the instant evidence rule extends this underlying policy into the trial, the difference in circumstances between discovery stage and trial may well be such as to require a different ruling at the trial.

For other rules recognizing privilege for trade secrets, see Uniform Rule 32; California Evidence Code § 1060; Kansas Code of Civil Procedure § 60–432; New Jersey Evidence Rule 32.

Rule 509.

SECRETS OF STATE AND OTHER OFFICIAL INFORMATION
[Not enacted.]

(a) Definitions.

(1) Secret of state. A "secret of state" is a governmental secret relating to the national defense or the international relations of the United States.

(2) Official information. "Official information" is information within the custody or control of a department or agency of the government the disclosure of which is shown to be contrary to the public interest and which consists of: (A) intragovernmental opinions or recommendations submitted for consideration in the performance of

decisional or policymaking functions, or (B) subject to the provisions of 18 U.S.C. § 3500, investigatory files compiled for law enforcement purposes and not otherwise available, or (C) information within the custody or control of a governmental department or agency whether initiated within the department or agency or acquired by it in its exercise of its official responsibilities and not otherwise available to the public pursuant to 5 U.S.C. § 552.

(b) General rule of privilege. The government has a privilege to refuse to give evidence and to prevent any person from giving evidence upon a showing of reasonable likelihood of danger that the evidence will disclose a secret of state or official information, as defined in this rule.

(c) Procedures. The privilege for secrets of state may be claimed only by the chief officer of the government agency or department administering the subject matter which the secret information sought concerns, but the privilege for official information may be asserted by any attorney representing the government. The required showing may be made in whole or in part in the form of a written statement. The judge may hear the matter in chambers, but all counsel are entitled to inspect the claim and showing and to be heard thereon, except that, in the case of secrets of state, the judge upon motion of the government, may permit the government to make the required showing in the above form *in camera*. If the judge sustains the privilege upon a showing *in camera*, the entire text of the government's statements shall be sealed and preserved in the court's records in the event of appeal. In the case of privilege claimed for official information the court may require examination *in camera* of the information itself. The judge may take any protective measure which the interests of the government and the furtherance of justice may require.

(d) Notice to government. If the circumstances of the case indicate a substantial possibility that a claim of privilege would be appropriate but has not been made because of oversight or lack of knowledge, the judge shall give or cause notice to be given to the officer entitled to claim the privilege and shall stay further proceedings a reasonable time to afford opportunity to assert a claim of privilege.

(e) Effect of sustaining claim. If a claim of privilege is sustained in a proceeding to which the government is a party and it appears that another party is thereby deprived of material evidence, the judge shall make any further orders which the interests of justice require, including striking the testimony of a witness, declaring a mistrial, finding against the government upon an issue as to which the evidence is relevant, or dismissing the action.

Advisory Committee's Note

Subdivision (a). (1) The rule embodies the privilege protecting military and state secrets described as "well established in the law of evidence," United States v. Reynolds, 345 U.S. 1, 6, 73 S.Ct. 528, 97

L.Ed. 727 (1953), and as one "the existence of which has never been doubted," 8 Wigmore § 2378, p. 794 (McNaughton Rev.1961).

The use of the term "national defense," without attempt at further elucidation, finds support in the similar usage in statutory provisions relating to the crimes of gathering, transmitting, or losing defense information, and gathering or delivering defense information to aid a foreign government. 18 U.S.C. §§ 793, 794. See also 5 U.S.C. § 1002; 50 U.S.C.App. § 2152(d). In determining whether military or state secrets are involved, due regard will, of course, be given to classification pursuant to executive order.

(2) The rule also recognizes a privilege for specified types of official information and in this respect is designed primarily to resolve questions of the availability to litigants of data in the files of governmental departments and agencies. In view of the lesser danger to the public interest than in cases of military and state secrets, the official information privilege is subject to a generally overriding requirement that disclosure would be contrary to the public interest. It is applicable to three categories of information.

(A) Intergovernmental opinions or recommendations submitted for consideration in the performance of decisional or policy making functions. The policy basis of this aspect of the privilege is found in the desirability of encouraging candor in the exchange of views within the government. Kaiser Aluminum & Chemical Corp. v. United States, 141 Ct.Cl. 38, 157 F.Supp. 939 (1958); Davis v. Braswell Motor Freight Lines, Inc., 363 F.2d 600 (5th Cir.1966); Ackerly v. Ley, 420 F.2d 1336 (D.C.Cir.1969). A privilege of this character is consistent with the Freedom of Information Act, 5 U.S.C. § 552(b)(5), and with the standing of the agency to raise questions of relevancy, though not a party, recognized in such decisions as Boeing Airplane Co. v. Coggeshall, 108 U.S.App.D.C. 106, 280 F.2d 654, 659 (1960) (Renegotiation Board) and Freeman v. Seligson, 132 U.S.App.D.C. 56, 405 F.2d 1326, 1334 (1968) (Secretary of Agriculture).

(B) Investigatory files compiled for law enforcement purposes. This category is expressly made subject to the provisions of the Jencks Act, 18 U.S.C. § 3500, which insulates prior statements or reports of government witnesses in criminal cases against subpoena, discovery, or inspection until the witness has testified on direct examination at the trial but then entitles the defense to its production. Rarely will documents of this nature be relevant until the author has testified and thus placed his credibility in issue. Further protection against discovery of government files in criminal cases is found in Criminal Procedure Rule 16(a) and (b). The breadth of discovery in civil cases, however, goes beyond ordinary bounds of relevancy and raises problems calling for the exercise of judicial control, and in making provision for it the rule implements the Freedom of Information Act, 18 U.S.C. § 552(b)(7).

(C) Information exempted from disclosure under the Freedom of Information Act, 5 U.S.C. § 552. In 1958 the old "housekeeping" statute which had been relied upon as a foundation for departmental regulations curtailing disclosure was amended by adding a provision that it did not authorize withholding information from the public. In

1966 the Congress enacted the Freedom of Information Act for the purpose of making information in the files of departments and agencies, subject to certain specified exceptions, available to the mass media and to the public generally. 5 U.S.C. § 552. These enactments are significant expressions of Congressional policy. The exceptions in the Act are not framed in terms of evidentiary privilege, thus recognizing by clear implication that the needs of litigants may stand on somewhat different footing from those of the public generally. Nevertheless, the exceptions are based on values obviously entitled to weighty consideration in formulating rules of evidentiary privilege. In some instances in these rules, exceptions in the Act have been made the subject of specific privileges, *e.g.*, military and state secrets in the present rule and trade secrets in Rule 508. The purpose of the present provision is to incorporate the remaining exceptions of the Act into the qualified privilege here created, thus subjecting disclosure of the information to judicial determination with respect to the effect of disclosure on the public interest. This approach appears to afford a satisfactory resolution of the problems which may arise.

Subdivision (b). The rule vests the privileges in the government where they properly belong rather than a party or witness. See United States v. Reynolds, *supra*, p. 7, 73 S.Ct. 528. The showing required as a condition precedent to claiming the privilege represents a compromise between complete judicial control and accepting as final the decision of a departmental officer. See Machin v. Zuckert, 114 U.S.App.D.C. 335, 316 F.2d 336 (1963), rejecting in part a claim of privilege by the Secretary of the Air Force and ordering the furnishing of information for use in private litigation. This approach is consistent with *Reynolds*.

Subdivision (c). In requiring the claim of privilege for state secrets to be made by the chief departmental officer, the rule again follows *Reynolds*, insuring consideration by a high-level officer. This provision is justified by the lesser participation by the judge in cases of state secrets. The full participation by the judge in official information cases, on the contrary, warrants allowing the claim of privilege to be made by a government attorney.

Subdivision (d) spells out and emphasizes a power and responsibility on the part of the trial judge. An analogous provision is found in the requirement that the court certify to the Attorney General when the constitutionality of an act of Congress is in question in an action to which the government is not a party. 28 U.S.C. § 2403.

Subdivision (e). If privilege is successfully claimed by the government in litigation to which it is not a party, the effect is simply to make the evidence unavailable, as though a witness had died or claimed the privilege against self-incrimination, and no specification of the consequences is necessary. The rule therefore deals only with the effect of a successful claim of privilege by the government in proceedings to which it is a party. Reference to other types of cases serves to illustrate the variety of situations which may arise and the impossibility of evolving a single formula to be applied automatically to all of them. The privileged materials may be the statement of government witness, as under the *Jencks* statute, which provides that, if the government elects not to produce the statement, the judge is to strike the testimony of the witness, or that he may declare a mistrial if the interests of justice so require. 18 U.S.C. § 3500(d). Or the privileged materials may disclose a possible basis for applying pressure upon witnesses. United States v. Beekman, 155 F.2d 580 (2d Cir.1946). Or they may bear directly upon a substantive element of a criminal case, requiring dismissal in the event of a successful claim of privilege. United States v. Andolschek, 142 F.2d 503 (2d Cir.1944); and see United States v. Reynolds, 345 U.S. 1, 73 S.Ct. 528, 97 L.Ed. 727 (1953). Or they may relate to an element of a plaintiff's claim against the government, with the decisions indicating unwillingness to allow the government's claim of privilege for secrets of state to be used as an offensive weapon against it. United States v. Reynolds, *supra*; Republic of China v. National Union Fire Ins. Co., 142 F.Supp. 551 (D.Md.1956).

Rule 510.

IDENTITY OF INFORMER
[Not enacted.]

(a) Rule of privilege. The government or a state or subdivision thereof has a privilege to refuse to disclose the identity of a person who has furnished information relating to or assisting in an investigation of a possible violation of law to a law enforcement officer or member of a legislative committee or its staff conducting an investigation.

(b) Who may claim. The privilege may be claimed by an appropriate representative of the government, regardless of whether the information was furnished to an officer of the government or of a state or subdivision thereof. The privilege may be claimed by an appropriate representative of a state or subdivision if the information was furnished to an officer thereof, except that in criminal cases the privilege shall not be allowed if the government objects.

(c) Exceptions.

(1) Voluntary disclosure; informer a witness. No privilege exists under this rule if the identity of the informer or his interest in the subject matter of his communication has been disclosed to those who would have cause to resent the communication by a holder of the privilege or by the informer's own action, or if the informer appears as a witness for the government.

(2) Testimony on merits. If it appears from the evidence in the case or from other showing by a party that an informer may be able to give testimony necessary to a fair determination of the issue of guilt or innocence in a criminal case or of a material issue on the merits in a civil case to which the government is a party, and the government invokes the privilege, the judge shall give the government an opportunity to show *in camera* facts relevant to determining whether the informer can, in fact, supply that testimony. The showing will ordinarily be in the form of affidavits, but the judge may direct that testimony

be taken if he finds that the matter cannot be resolved satisfactorily upon affidavit. If the judge finds that there is a reasonable probability that the informer can give the testimony, and the government elects not to disclose his identity, the judge on motion of the defendant in a criminal case shall dismiss the charges to which the testimony would relate, and the judge may do so on his own motion. In civil cases, he may make any order that justice requires. Evidence submitted to the judge shall be sealed and preserved to be made available to the appellate court in the event of an appeal, and the contents shall not otherwise be revealed without consent of the government. All counsel and parties shall be permitted to be present at every stage of proceedings under this subdivision except a showing *in camera,* at which no counsel or party shall be permitted to be present.

(3) Legality of obtaining evidence. If information from an informer is relied upon to establish the legality of the means by which evidence was obtained and the judge is not satisfied that the information was received from an informer reasonably believed to be reliable or credible, he may require the identity of the informer to be disclosed. The judge shall, on request of the government, direct that the disclosure be made *in camera.* All counsel and parties concerned with the issue of legality shall be permitted to be present at every stage of proceedings under this subdivision except a disclosure *in camera,* at which no counsel or party shall be permitted to be present. If disclosure of the identity of the informer is made *in camera,* the record thereof shall be sealed and preserved to be made available to the appellate court in the event of an appeal, and the contents shall not otherwise be revealed without consent of the government.

Advisory Committee's Note

The rule recognizes the use of informers as an important aspect of law enforcement, whether the informer is a citizen who steps forward with information or a paid undercover agent. In either event, the basic importance of anonymity in the effective use of informers is apparent, Bocchicchio v. Curtis Publishing Co., 203 F.Supp. 403 (E.D.Pa.1962), and the privilege of withholding their identity was well established at common law. Roviaro v. United States, 353 U.S. 53, 59, 77 S.Ct. 623, 1 L.Ed.2d 639 (1957); McCormick § 148; 8 Wigmore § 2374 (McNaughton Rev.1961).

Subdivision (a). The public interest in law enforcement requires that the privilege be that of the government, state, or political subdivision, rather than that of the witness. The rule blankets in as an informer anyone who tells a law enforcement officer about a violation of law without regard to whether the officer is one charged with enforcing the particular law. The rule also applies to disclosures to legislative investigating committees and their staffs, and is sufficiently broad to include continuing investigations.

Although the tradition of protecting the identity of informers has evolved in an essentially criminal setting, noncriminal law enforcement situations involving possibilities of reprisal against informers fall within the purview of the considerations out of which the privilege originated. In Mitchell v. Roma, 265 F.2d 633 (3d Cir.1959), the privilege was given effect with respect to persons informing as to violations of the Fair Labor Standards Act, and in Wirtz v. Continental Finance & Loan Co., 326 F.2d 561 (5th Cir.1964), a similar case, the privilege was recognized, although the basis of decision was lack of relevancy to the issues in the case.

Only identity is privileged; communications are not included except to the extent that disclosure would operate also to disclose the informer's identity. The common law was to the same effect. 8 Wigmore § 2374, at p. 765 (McNaughton Rev.1961). See also Roviaro v. United States, supra, 353 U.S. at p. 60, 77 S.Ct. 623; Bowman Dairy Co. v. United States, 341 U.S. 214, 221, 71 S.Ct. 675, 95 L.Ed. 879 (1951).

The rule does not deal with the question whether presentence reports made under Criminal Procedure Rule 32(c) should be made available to an accused.

Subdivision (b). Normally the "appropriate representative" to make the claim will be counsel. However, it is possible that disclosure of the informer's identity will be sought in proceedings to which the government, state, or subdivision, as the case may be, is not a party. Under these circumstances effective implementation of the privilege requires that other representatives be considered "appropriate." See, for example, Bocchicchio v. Curtis Publishing Co., 203 F.Supp. 403 (E.D.Pa.1962), a civil action for libel, in which a local police officer not represented by counsel successfully claimed the informer privilege.

The privilege may be claimed by a state or subdivision of a state if the information was given to its officer, except that in criminal cases it may not be allowed if the government objects.

Subdivision (c) deals with situations in which the informer privilege either does not apply or is curtailed.

(1) If the identity of the informer is disclosed, nothing further is to be gained from efforts to suppress it. Disclosure may be direct, or the same practical effect may result from action revealing the informer's interest in the subject matter. See, for example, Westinghouse Electric Corp. v. City of Burlington, 122 U.S.App.D.C. 65, 351 F.2d 762 (1965), on remand City of Burlington v. Westinghouse Electric Corp., 246 F.Supp. 839 (D.D.C.1965), which held that the filing of civil antitrust actions destroyed as to plaintiffs the informer privilege claimed by the Attorney General with respect to complaints of criminal antitrust violations. While allowing the privilege in effect to be waived by one not its holder, *i.e.* the informer himself, is something of a novelty in the law of privilege, if the informer chooses to reveal his identity, further efforts to suppress it are scarcely feasible.

The exception is limited to disclosure to "those who would have cause to resent the communication," in the language of Roviaro v. United States, 353 U.S. 53, 60, 77 S.Ct. 623, 1 L.Ed.2d 639 (1957), since disclosure otherwise, *e.g.* to another law enforcing agency, is not calculated to undercut the objects of the privilege.

If the informer becomes a witness for the government, the interests of justice in disclosing his status as a source of bias or possible support are believed to outweigh any remnant of interest in nondisclosure which then remains. See Harris v. United States, 371 F.2d 365 (9th Cir.1967), in which the trial judge permitted detailed inquiry into the relationship between the witness and the government. Cf. Attorney General v. Briant, 15 M. & W. 169, 153 Eng.Rep. 808 (Exch.1846). The purpose of the limitation to witnesses for the government is to avoid the possibility of calling persons as witnesses as a means of discovery whether they are informers.

(2) The informer privilege, it was held by the leading case, may not be used in a criminal prosecution to suppress the identity of a witness when the public interest in protecting the flow of information is outweighed by the individual's right to prepare his defense. Roviaro v. United States, *supra*. The rule extends this balancing to include civil as well as criminal cases and phrases it in terms of "a reasonable probability that the informer may be able to give testimony necessary to a fair determination of the issue of guilt or innocence in a criminal case or of a material issue on the merits in a civil case." Once the privilege is invoked a procedure is provided for determining whether the informer can in fact supply testimony of such nature as to require disclosure of his identity, thus avoiding a "judicial guessing game" on the question. United States v. Day, 384 F.2d 464, 470 (3d Cir.1967). An investigation *in camera* is calculated to accommodate the conflicting interests involved. The rule also spells out specifically the consequences of a successful claim of the privilege in a criminal case; the wider range of possibilities in civil cases demands more flexibility in treatment. See Advisory Committee's Note to Rule 509(e), *supra*.

(3) One of the acute conflicts between the interest of the public in nondisclosure and the avoidance of unfairness to the accused as a result of nondisclosure arises when information from an informer is relied upon to legitimate a search and seizure by furnishing probable cause for an arrest without a warrant or for the issuance of a warrant for arrest or search. McCray v. Illinois, 386 U.S. 300, 87 S.Ct. 1056, 18 L.Ed.2d 62 (1967), rehearing denied 386 U.S. 1042. A hearing *in camera* provides an accommodation of these conflicting interests. United States v. Jackson, 384 F.2d 825 (3d Cir.1967). The limited disclosure to the judge avoids any significant impairment of secrecy, while affording the accused a substantial measure of protection against arbitrary police action. The procedure is consistent with McCray and the decisions there discussed.

Rule 511.

WAIVER OF PRIVILEGE BY VOLUNTARY DISCLOSURE
[Not enacted.]

A person upon whom these rules confer a privilege against disclosure of the confidential matter or communication waives the privilege if he or his predecessor while holder of the privilege voluntarily discloses or consents to disclosure of any significant part of the matter or communication. This rule does not apply if the disclosure is itself a privileged communication.

Advisory Committee's Note

The central purpose of most privileges is the promotion of some interest or relationship by endowing it with a supporting secrecy or confidentiality. It is evident that the privilege should terminate when the holder by his own act destroys this confidentiality. McCormick §§ 87, 97, 106; 8 Wigmore §§ 2242, 2327–2329, 2374, 2389–2390 (McNaughton Rev.1961).

The rule is designed to be read with a view to what it is that the particular privilege protects. For example, the lawyer-client privilege covers only communications, and the fact that a client has discussed a matter with his lawyer does not insulate the client against disclosure of the subject matter discussed, although he is privileged not to disclose the discussion itself. See McCormick § 93. The waiver here provided for is similarly restricted. Therefore a client, merely by disclosing a subject which he had discussed with his attorney, would not waive the applicable privilege; he would have to make disclosure of the communication itself in order to effect a waiver.

By traditional doctrine, waiver is the intentional relinquishment of a known right. Johnson v. Zerbst, 304 U.S. 458, 464, 58 S.Ct. 1019, 82 L.Ed. 1461 (1938). However, in the confidential privilege situations, once confidentiality is destroyed through voluntary disclosure, no subsequent claim of privilege can restore it, and knowledge or lack of knowledge of the existence of the privilege appears to be irrelevant. California Evidence Code § 912; 8 Wigmore § 2327 (McNaughton Rev.1961).

Rule 512.

PRIVILEGED MATTER DISCLOSED UNDER COMPULSION OR WITHOUT OPPORTUNITY TO CLAIM PRIVILEGE
[Not enacted.]

Evidence of a statement or other disclosure of privileged matter is not admissible against the holder of the privilege if the disclosure was (a) compelled erroneously or (b) made without opportunity to claim the privilege.

Advisory Committee's Note

Ordinarily a privilege is invoked in order to forestall disclosure. However, under some circumstances consideration must be given to the status and effect of a disclosure already made. Rule 511, immediately prceding, gives voluntary disclosure the effect of a waiver, while the present rule covers the effect of disclosure made under compulsion or without opportunity to claim the privilege.

Confidentiality, once destroyed, is not susceptible of restoration, yet some measure of repair may be accomplished by preventing use of the evidence against the holder of the privilege. The remedy of exclusion is therefore made available when the earlier disclosure was compelled erroneously or without opportunity to claim the privilege.

With respect to erroneously compelled disclosure, the argument may be made that the holder should be required in the first instance to assert the privilege, stand his ground, refuse to answer, perhaps incur a judgment of contempt, and exhaust all legal recourse, in order to sustain his privilege. See Fraser v. United States, 145 F.2d 139 (6th Cir.1944), cert. denied 324 U.S. 849, 65 S.Ct. 684, 89 L.Ed. 1409; United States v. Johnson, 76 F.Supp. 538 (M.D.Pa.1947), aff'd 165 F.2d 42 (3d Cir.1947), cert. denied 332 U.S. 852, 68 S.Ct. 355, 92 L.Ed. 422, reh. denied 333 U.S. 834, 68 S.Ct. 457, 92 L.Ed. 1118. However, this exacts of the holder greater fortitude in the face of authority than ordinary individuals are likely to possess, and assumes unrealistically that a judicial remedy is always available. In self-incrimination cases, the writers agree that erroneously compelled disclosures are inadmissible in a subsequent criminal prosecution of the holder, Maguire, Evidence of Guilt 66 (1959); McCormick § 127; 8 Wigmore § 2270 (McNaughton Rev.1961), and the principle is equally sound when applied to other privileges. The modest departure from usual principles of res judicata which occurs when the compulsion is judicial is justified by the advantage of having one simple rule, assuring at least one opportunity for judicial supervision in every case.

The second circumstance stated as a basis for exclusion is disclosure made without opportunity to the holder to assert his privilege. Illustrative possibilities are disclosure by an eavesdropper, by a person used in the transmission of a privileged communication, by a family member participating in psychotherapy, or privileged data improperly made available from a computer bank.

Rule 513.

COMMENT UPON OR INFERENCE FROM CLAIM OF PRIVILEGE; INSTRUCTION
[Not enacted.]

(a) **Comment or inference not permitted.** The claim of a privilege, whether in the present proceeding or upon a prior occasion, is not a proper subject of comment by judge or counsel. No inference may be drawn therefrom.

(b) **Claiming privilege without knowledge of jury.** In jury cases, proceedings shall be conducted, to the extent practicable, so as to facilitate the making of claims of privilege without the knowledge of the jury.

(c) **Jury instruction.** Upon request, any party against whom the jury might draw an adverse inference from a claim of privilege is entitled to an instruction that no inference may be drawn therefrom.

Advisory Committee's Note

Subdivision (a). In Griffin v. California, 380 U.S. 609, 614, 85 S.Ct. 1229, 14 L.Ed.2d 106 (1965), the Court pointed out that allowing comment upon the claim of a privilege "cuts down on the privilege by making its assertion costly." Consequently it was held that comment upon the election of the accused not to take the stand infringed upon his privilege against self-incrimination so substantially as to constitute a constitutional violation. While the privileges governed by these rules are not constitutionally based, they are nevertheless founded upon important policies and are entitled to maximum effect. Hence the present subdivision forbids comment upon the exercise of a privilege, in accord with the weight of authority. Courtney v. United States, 390 F.2d 521 (9th Cir.1968); 8 Wigmore §§ 2243, 2322, 2386; Barnhart, Privilege in the Uniform Rules of Evidence, 24 Ohio St.L.J. 131, 137–138 (1963). Cf. McCormick § 80.

Subdivision (b). The value of a privilege may be greatly depreciated by means other than expressly commenting to a jury upon the fact that it was exercised. Thus, the calling of a witness in the presence of the jury and subsequently excusing him after a sidebar conference may effectively convey to the jury the fact that a privilege has been claimed, even though the actual claim has not been made in their hearing. Whether a privilege will be claimed is usually ascertainable in advance and the handling of the entire matter outside the presence of the jury is feasible. Destruction of the privilege by innuendo can and should be avoided. Tallo v. United States, 344 F.2d 467 (1st Cir.1965); United States v. Tomaiolo, 249 F.2d 683 (2d Cir.1957); San Fratello v. United States, 343 F.2d 711 (5th Cir.1965); Courtney v. United States, 390 F.2d 521 (9th Cir.1968); 6 Wigmore § 1808, pp. 275–276; 6 U.C.L.A.Rev. 455 (1959). This position is in accord with the general agreement of the authorities that an accused cannot be forced to make his election not to testify in the presence of the jury. 8 Wigmore § 2268, p. 407 (McNaughton Rev.1961).

Unanticipated situations are, of course, bound to arise, and much must be left to the discretion of the judge and the professional responsibility of counsel.

Subdivision (c). Opinions will differ as to the effectiveness of a jury instruction not to draw an adverse inference from the making of a claim of privilege. See Bruton v. United States, 389 U.S. 818, 88 S.Ct. 126, 19 L.Ed.2d 70 (1968). Whether an instruction shall be given is left to the sound judgment of counsel for the party against whom the adverse inference may be drawn. The instruction is a matter of right, if requested. This is the result reached in Bruno v. United States, 308 U.S. 287, 60 S.Ct. 198, 84 L.Ed. 257 (1939), holding that an accused is entitled to an instruction under the statute (now 18 U.S.C. § 3481) providing that his failure to testify creates no presumption against him.

The right to the instruction is not impaired by the fact that the claim of privilege is by a witness, rather than by a party, provided an adverse inference against the party may result.

Rule 804.

HEARSAY EXCEPTIONS: DECLARANT UNAVAILABLE
[Subdivision (b)(2) not enacted.]

* * *

(b) Hearsay exceptions. The following are not excluded by the hearsay rule if the declarant is unavailable as a witness:

* * *

(2) *Statement of recent perception.* A statement, not in response to the instigation of a person engaged in investigating, litigating, or settling a claim, which narrates, describes, or explains an event or condition recently perceived by the declarant, made in good faith, not in contemplation of pending or anticipated litigation in which he was interested, and while his recollection was clear.

Note by Federal Judicial Center

Hearsay exception (b)(2) is set forth above as prescribed by the Supreme Court. It was not included in the rules enacted by the Congress but is reproduced here for such value as it may have for purposes of interpretation.

Advisory Committee's Note

Exception (2). The rule finds support in several directions. The well known Massachusetts Act of 1898 allows in evidence the declaration of any deceased person made in good faith before the commencement of the action and upon personal knowledge. Mass.G.L., c. 233, § 65. To the same effect is R.I.G.L. § 9–19–11. Under other statutes, a decedent's statement is admissible on behalf of his estate in actions against it, to offset the presumed inequality resulting from allowing a surviving opponent to testify. California Evidence Code § 1261; Conn.G.S., § 52–172; and statutes collected in 5 Wigmore § 1576. See also Va.Code § 8–286, allowing statements made when capable by a party now incapable of testifying.

In 1938 the Committee on Improvements in the Law of Evidence of the American Bar Association recommended adoption of a statute similar to that of Massachusetts but with the concept of unavailability expanded to include, in addition to death, cases of insanity or inability to produce a witness or take his deposition. 63 A.B.A. Reports 570, 584, 600 (1938). The same year saw enactment of the English Evidence Act of 1938, allowing written statements made on personal knowledge, if declarant is deceased or otherwise unavailable or if the court is satisfied that undue delay or expense would otherwise be caused, unless declarant was an interested person in pending or anticipated relevant proceedings. Evidence Act of 1938, 1 & 2 Geo. 6, c. 28; Cross on Evidence 482 (3rd ed. 1967).

Model Code Rule 503(a) provided broadly for admission of any hearsay declaration of an unavailable declarant. No circumstantial guarantees of trustworthiness were required. Debate upon the floor of the American Law Institute did not seriously question the propriety of the rule but centered upon what should constitute unavailability. 18 A.L.I. Proceedings 90–134 (1941).

The Uniform Rules draftsman took a less advanced position, more in the pattern of the Massachusetts statute, and invoked several assurances of accuracy: recency of perception, clarity of recollection, good faith, and antecedence to the commencement of the action. Uniform Rule 63(4)(c).

Opposition developed to the Uniform Rule because of its countenancing of the use of statements carefully prepared under the tutelage of lawyers, claim adjusters, or investigators with a view to pending or prospective litigation. Tentative Recommendation and a Study Relating to the Uniform Rules of Evidence (Art. VIII. Hearsay Evidence), Cal.Law Rev.Comm'n, 318 (1962); Quick, Excitement, Necessity and the Uniform Rules: A Reappraisal of Rule 63(4), 6 Wayne L.Rev. 204, 219–224 (1960). To meet this objection, the rule excludes statements made at the instigation of a person engaged in investigating, litigating, or setting a claim. It also incorporates as safeguards the good faith and clarity of recollection required by the Uniform Rule and the exclusion of a statement by a person interested in the litigation provided by the English act.

With respect to the question whether the introduction of a statement under this exception against the accused in a criminal case would violate his right of confrontation, reference is made to the last paragraph of the Advisory Committee's Note under Exception (1), *supra*.

Report of House Committee on the Judiciary

Rule 804(b)(2), a hearsay exception submitted by the Court, titled "Statement of recent perception," read as follows:

A statement, not in response to the instigation of a person engaged in investigating, litigating, or settling a claim, which narrates, describes, or explains an event or condition recently perceived by the declarant, made in good faith, not in contemplation of pending or anticipated litigation in which he was interested, and while his recollection was clear.

The Committee eliminated this Rule as creating a new and unwarranted hearsay exception of great potential breadth. The Committee did not believe that statements of the type referred to bore sufficient guarantees of trustworthiness to justify admissibility.

INDEX
TO
FEDERAL RULES OF EVIDENCE

ADMISSIONS
Party opponent, hearsay, extrinsic evidence of prior inconsistent statement of witness, applicability, provisions respecting, Rule 613.

Writings, recordings or photographs, contents of proved by, Rule 1007.

ADOPTION
Hearsay exception,
Reputation concerning, Rule 803.
Statement of declarant concerning, Rule 804.

ADVERSE PARTIES
See Parties, this index.

AFFIRMATIONS
See Oaths and Affirmations, generally, this index.

AGENCIES
Federal Agencies and Instrumentalities, generally, this index.

Records and reports, hearsay exception, Rule 803.

AGENTS
See Principal and Agent, generally, this index.

AGRICULTURAL PRODUCTS OR COMMODITIES
Associations of producers, monopolizing or restraining trade, cease and desist orders, review, rules applicable in part, Rule 1101.

AIRPLANES OR AIRCRAFT
Prize, applicability of rules in part, Rule 1101.

AMENDMENTS
Method of, Rule 1102.

Rules of Criminal Procedure, provisions concerning offer to plead guilty, nolo contendere, etc., Rule 410.

ANCIENT DOCUMENTS
Authentication and identification, conformity with requirements, Rule 901.

Statements in, hearsay exception, Rule 803.

ANNULMENT
Conviction, subject of, impeachment of witness by evidence of conviction of crime, effect, Rule 609.

ANTI–SMUGGLING ACT
Fines, penalties and forfeitures, action for, applicability of rules in part, Rule 1101.

APPEAL AND REVIEW
Admissibility of evidence, pendency of appeal, impeachment of witness by evidence of conviction of crime, Rule 609.

Agricultural products, association of producers, monopolizing or restraining trade, cease and desist orders, rules applicable in part, Rule 1101.

Aliens, action respecting naturalization and revocation thereof, rules applicable in part, Rule 1101.

Aquatic products, cease and desist orders, restraint of trade by association engaged in catching, etc. applicability of rules in part, Rule 1101.

Availability to appellate court, withheld portion of writing used to refresh memory, Rule 612.

Federal agency actions set aside by reviewing court, facts subject to trial de novo, rules applicable in part, Rule 1101.

Pendency of appeal,
As not rendering evidence of conviction inadmissible, impeachment by evidence of conviction of crime, Rule 609.
Judgment of previous conviction, admissibility, hearsay exception, Rule 803.

Perishable agricultural products, unfair conduct, reparation order respecting, rules applicable in part, Rule 1101.

Petroleum products, application for certificate of clearance for shipment in interstate commerce, order denying, applicability of rules in part, Rule 1101.

APPEARANCE
Authentication and identification, conformity with requirements, Rule 901.

AQUATIC PRODUCTS
Cease and desist orders, restraint of trade by association engaged in catching, etc., applicability of rules in part, Rule 1101.

ARREST
Warrants, issuance, proceedings for, inapplicability, Rule 1101.

ARTS
Learned treatises, statements in, hearsay exception, Rule 803.

ATTACKING CREDIBILITY OF WITNESSES
See Credibility of Witnesses, this index.

ATTORNEYS AND COUNSELORS
Officer or employee of party not natural person designated as representative by attorney, exclusion, provisions governing exclusion of witnesses as not authorizing, Rule 615.

CONTENTS
See specific index headings.

CONTROL
Inscriptions, signs, etc., purporting to be affixed in course of business and indicating, self-authentication, Rule 902.
Insurance against liability, admissibility for purpose of proving, Rule 411.
Subsequent remedial measures, admissibility to prove, Rule 407.

CONVICTION
Impeachment of witness, evidence of conviction of crime, Rule 609.
Judgment of previous conviction, hearsay exception, Rule 803.

COSMETICS
Criminal libel for condemnation, exclusion of imports or other proceedings, applicability of rules in part, Rule 1101.

COUNSELORS
See Attorneys and Counselors, generally, this index.

COURT OF CLAIMS
Applicability of rules, Rule 1101.
Commissioners,
    "Court" as including, applicability of rules, Rule 1101.
    "Judge" as including, applicability of rules, Rule 1101.

COURTS
Calling and interrogation of witnesses, Rule 614.
Court of Claims, generally, this index.
Defined, applicability of rules, Rule 1101.
Discretion of Court, generally, this index.
Experts, appointment, Rule 706.
Judges and Justices, generally, this index.
Mode and order of interrogating witnesses and presenting evidence, control of, Rule 611.
Orders of Court, generally, this index.
Own motion, exclusion of witnesses so that other witnesses cannot be heard, Rule 615.
Rules as governing proceedings in, Rule 101.
Supreme Court, generally, this index.
Writings, recordings, or photographs,
    Contents, functions repecting, Rule 1008.
    Voluminous, production, Rule 1006.

COURTS OF APPEALS
Applicability of rules, Rule 1101.

CREDIBILITY OF WITNESSES
Attacking or supporting,
    By evidence in form of opinion or reputation, Rule 608.

CREDIBILITY OF WITNESSES—Cont'd
Credibility of declarant, hearsay statements, Rule 806.
Cross-examination, scope limited to matters affecting, Rule 610.
Impeachment,
    By evidence of conviction of crime, Rule 609.
    Persons who may impeach, Rule 607.
Preliminary questions, rule concerning as not limiting right of party to introduce evidence respecting, Rule 104.
Religious beliefs or opinions, admissibility to impair or enhance, Rule 610.
Self-incrimination privilege not waived when accused or other witness examined respecting matters relating only to, Rule 608.
Specific instances of conduct to attack or support, Rule 608.
Supporting. Attacking or supporting, generally, ante, this heading.
Who may impeach, Rule 607.

CRIMES AND OFFENSES
Character evidence, evidence of other crimes, admissibility, Rule 404.
Conviction, generally, this index.
Homicide, generally, this index.
Investigations of. Criminal Investigations, generally, this index.
Perjury, generally, this index.

CRIMINAL ACTIONS AND PROCEDURE
Applicability of rules, Rule 1101.
Character of victim, homicide case, Rule 404.
Federal Food, Drug and Cosmetic Act, criminal libel for condemnation, exclusion of imports, or other proceedings under, applicability of rules in part, Rule 1101.
Judicial notice, instructions to jury, Rule 201.
Jury, generally, this index.
Obstruction of criminal prosecution, compromise and offers to compromise claims, admissibility of evidence respecting to prove, Rule 408.
Plea of Guilty, generally, this index.
Plea of Nolo Contendere, generally this index.
Police officers and law enforcement personnel, matters observed by, hearsay, public records and reports, exception and exclusion, Rule 803.
Preliminary examination, inapplicability of rules, Rule 1101.
Summonses, issuance, inapplicability, Rule 1101.
Writing used to refresh memory, failure to produce or deliver, striking of testimony or declaration of mistrial, Rule 612.

CRIMINAL INVESTIGATIONS
Factual findings resulting from, hearsay exception, Rule 803.
Obstruction, compromise and offers to compromise claims, admissibility to prove effort respecting, Rule 408.

CROSS-EXAMINATION
Accused testifying on preliminary matter, examination as to other issues in case, Rule 104.
Conviction of crime, impeachment, credibility of witness by evidence of, Rule 609.
Court, witnesses called by, Rule 614.
Disclosure of facts or data underlying expert opinion, Rule 705.
Experts appointed by court, Rule 706.
Hearsay statements, examination of declarant by party against whom admitted, Rule 806.
Leading questions, Rule 611.
Relevant specific instances of conduct, methods of proving character of person, Rule 405.
Scope of, mode and order of interrogation and presentation of evidence, Rule 611.
Writing used to refresh memory, witness using, Rule 612.

CRYPTS
Hearsay exception, statements concerning engravings on, Rule 803.

CULPABILITY
Conduct, subsequent remedial measures, admissibility to prove, Rule 407.

CUMULATIVE EVIDENCE
Exclusion of relevant evidence due to needless presentation of, Rule 403.

CUSTOMS DUTIES
Fines and penalties, actions for, application of rules in part, Rule 1101.
Searches, seizures, and forfeitures, actions for, applicability of rules in part, Rule 1101.

DATA
Compilation,
   Regularly conducted activity, hearsay exception, Rule 803.
   "Writings" and "recordings" as including, contents of writings, etc., Rule 1001.

DEATH
Hearsay, this index.

DEATH PENALTY
Impeachment, credibility of witness, evidence of conviction of crime punishable by death, court determination, probative value, Rule 609.
Judgment of previous conviction of crime punishable by death, evidence of, hearsay exception, Rule 803.

DECREES
See Judgments and Decrees, generally, this index.

DEFENSES
Character or trait of character as essential element, proof of specific instances of conduct, Rule 405.
Competency of witness, state law as determining unless federal law supplies rule of decision, Rule 601.
Privilege of witness, person, etc., state law as determining unless federal law supplies rule of decision respecting, Rule 501.

DEFINITIONS
Declarant, hearsay, Rule 801.
Duplicate, contents of, Rule 1001.
Hearsay, Rule 801.
Judge, applicability of rules, Rule 1101.
Original of writing or recording, contents, Rule 1001.
Photographs, contents of, Rule 1001.
Recordings, contents of, Rule 1001.
Relevant evidence, Rule 401.
Statements, hearsay, Rule 801.
Statements which are not hearsay, Rule 801.
Unavailability as a witness, hearsay exceptions, Rule 804.
Writings, contents of, Rule 1001.

DELAY
Compromise and offers to compromise claims, admission of evidence negativing contention of undue delay, Rule 408.
Elimination of unjustifiable delay, purpose and construction of rules, Rule 102.
Exclusion of relevant evidence on grounds of undue delay or waste of time, Rule 403.

DEPOSITIONS
Court appointed experts, Rule 706.
Writings, recordings or photographs, proof of contents, Rule 1007.

DESIGN
Hearsay exceptions, statements respecting, Rule 803.

HEARSAY—Cont'd

Death,

Declarant unable to be present or to testify at hearing because of, "unavailability as witness" as including, exception, Rule 804.

Records of, exception, Rule 803.

Statement under belief of impending death, exception, Rule 804.

Declarant, defined, Rule 801.

Definitions, Rule 801.

Design, statements respecting, exception, Rule 803.

Divorce,

Records of, exception, Rule 803.

Statement of declarant concerning, exception, Rule 804.

Engravings, rings, urns, crypts or tombstones, statements concerning, exception, Rule 803.

Exceptions, enumeration of, Rules 803, 804.

Excited utterance, statement relating to, exception, Rule 803.

Existing mental, emotional, or physical condition, statement respecting, exception, Rule 803.

Factual findings resulting from investigation, civil actions and criminal cases, public records and reports, exception, Rule 803.

Family bibles, statements of personal or family history in, exception, Rule 803.

Family history or records,

Reputation concerning, exception, Rule 803.

Statement of, exception, Rule 804.

Fetal deaths, records of, exception, Rule 803.

Former testimony, exception, Rule 804.

Genealogies, statement of personal or family history contained in, exception, Rule 803.

General listing, reputation concerning or judgment as to, exception, Rule 803.

Impending death, statement under belief of, exception, Rule 804.

Inability of declarant to be present or testify at hearing because of death, etc., "unavailability as witness" as including, exceptions, Rule 804.

Intent, statements respecting, exception, Rule 803.

Interest, statement against, exception, Rule 804.

Judgment,

As to personal, family or general history or boundaries, exception, Rule 803.

Previous convictions, exception, Rule 803.

Lack of memory of subject matter of his statement, declarant testifying to, "unavailability as witness" as including, exceptions, Rule 804.

HEARSAY—Cont'd

Learned treatises, exception, Rule 803.

Legitimacy, statement of declarant concerning, exception, Rule 804.

Market reports, exception, Rule 803.

Marriage,

Records of, exception, Rule 803.

Statement of declarant concerning, exception, Rule 804.

Matters not excluded by hearsay rule, declarant,

Available as witness, Rule 803.

Unavailable as witness, Rule 804.

Medical diagnosis or treatment, statements for purposes of, exception, Rule 803.

Memoranda, recollections, exception, Rule 803.

Motive, statements respecting, exception, Rule 803.

Pain, statements respecting, exception, Rule 803.

Personal history. Family history or records, generally, ante, this heading.

Police officers and law enforcement personnel, matters observed by, public records and reports, exception and exclusion, Rule 803.

Present sense impression, statement describing, etc., exception, Rule 803.

Previous conviction, judgment of, exception, Rule 803.

Procurement or wrongdoing of proponent of statement, declarant not available as witness if his exemption, refusal, etc., is due to, exception, Rule 804.

Property, record of or statements in documents affecting an interest in, exception, Rule 803.

Public records and reports, exceptions, Rule 803.

Recorded recollection, exception, Rule 803.

Refusing to testify concerning subject matter of statement despite court order to do so, declarant persisting in, "unavailability as witness" as including exceptions, Rule 804.

Regularly conducted activity, records of, exception, Rule 803.

Relationship by blood or marriage, records of religious organizations, exception, Rule 803.

Religious organizations, records of, exception, Rule 803.

Reputation,

As to character, exception, Rule 803.

Concerning boundaries or general history, exception, Rule 803.

Ruling of court, declarant exempted by on ground of privilege from testifying concerning subject matter of his statement, "unavailability as witness" as including, exception, Rule 804.

Statements,

Defined, Rule 801.

ISSUES—Cont'd
Opinion testimony by lay witnesses, Rule 701.
Ultimate issue, opinion on, Rule 704.

JUDGES AND JUSTICES
Bankruptcy, applicability of rules, Rule 1101.
Scope, Rule 101.
Competency as witness, Rule 605.
Defined, applicability of rules, Rule 1101.

JUDGMENTS AND DECREES
Hearsay exception,
Personal, family or general history, or boundaries, judgment as proof of, Rule 803.
Previous conviction judgment, evidence of, Rule 803.

JUDICIAL NOTICE
Adjudicative facts, Rule 201.
Learned treatises, statements in, hearsay exception, Rule 803.

JUDICIAL REVIEW
See Appeal and Review, generally, this index.

JURY
Calling and interrogation of witnesses by court, objection to made when jury not present, Rule 614.
Comparison by with specimens which have been authenticated, Rule 901.
Competency of juror as witness, Rule 606.
Disclosure to, court appointment, expert witnesses, Rule 706.
Extraneous prejudicial information improperly brought to jury's attention, testimony of juror respecting, Rule 606.
Hearing,
Admissibility of confessions, conducting out of presence of, Rule 104.
Rulings on evidence, Rule 103.
Inquiry into validity of indictment, testimony of juror, restriction and exception, Rule 606.
Instructions to Jury, generally, this index.
Misleading, exclusion of relevant evidence on grounds of, Rule 403.
Outside influence improperly brought to bear on juror, testimony of juror respecting, Rule 606.
Writings, recordings or photographs, admissibility of evidence of contents, functions respecting, Rule 1008.

JUSTICES
See Judges and Justices, generally, this index.

JUVENILE DELINQUENTS AND OFFENDERS
Adjudication, impeachment of witness by evidence of, admissibility, Rule 609.

KNOWLEDGE
Lack of personal knowledge, testimony of witness, Rule 602.
Proof of, admissibility of evidence of other crimes, wrongs or acts, Rule 404.
Recorded recollection, hearsay exception, Rule 803.
Scientific, technical or specialized, testimony by experts, Rule 702.
Testimony of witness with, authentication and identification, conformity with requirements, Rule 901.

LABELS
Purporting to be affixed in course of business and indicating ownership, control or origin, self-authentication, Rule 902.

LAW ENFORCEMENT PERSONNEL
Matters observed by, public records and reports, hearsay exception, Rule 803.

LAWYERS
See Attorneys and Counselors, generally, this index.

LEADING QUESTIONS
Witnesses, Rule 611.

LEGITIMACY AND ILLEGITIMACY
Hearsay exception,
Records of, Rule 803.
Statement of declarant concerning, Rule 804.

LISTS
Use and reliance on by public or persons in particular occupations, hearsay exception, Rule 803.

LOSS
Originals of records, writings or photographs, admissibility, other evidence of contents, Rule 1004.

MAGISTRATES
See United States Magistrates, generally, this index.

MAGNETIC IMPULSE
"Writings" and "recordings" as including, contents of writings, etc., Rule 1001.

MARITIME CASES
See Admiralty, generally, this index.

MARITIME PRIZE
Applicability of rules in part, Rule 1101.

MARKET QUOTATIONS
Hearsay exception, Rule 803.

RECORDS AND RECORDING—Cont'd
Testimony or deposition or written admission of party, proof by, Rule 1007.
Voluminous recordings, summaries of, Rule 1006.
Family history or records. Hearsay, generally, this index.
Hearsay, generally, this index.
Offer of proof and ruling on, Rule 103.
Statements, remainder or part of, introduction, Rule 106.
Summaries, contents of voluminous recordings, Rule 1006.

REFEREES
Bankruptcy, this index.

REHABILITATION
Certificate of, conviction subject of, impeachment of witness by evidence of conviction of crime, effect, Rule 609.

RELATIVES
Blood or marriage, relationship by, records of religious organizations, hearsay exception, Rule 803.

RELEVANT EVIDENCE
See, also, Admissibility of Evidence, generally, this index.
Character Evidence, generally, this index.
Defined, Rule 401.
Exclusion on grounds of prejudice, confusion, waste of time or needless presentation of cumulative evidence, Rule 403.
Fulfillment, condition of fact, relevancy of evidence dependent upon, admission, Rule 104.
Generally admissible, Rule 402.
Habit of person, Rule 406.
Irrelevant evidence inadmissible, Rule 402.
Subsequent remedial measures, Rule 407.

RELIGIOUS BELIEFS OR OPINIONS
Credibility of witness, admissibility to impair or enhance, Rule 610.

RELIGIOUS ORGANIZATIONS
Records of, hearsay exception, Rule 803.

REMOVAL OF CAUSES
Without regard to citizenship of parties, competency of witnesses, state law as determining, exception, Rule 601.

REPORTS
Authentication and identification, conformity with requirements, Rule 901.
Hearsay exception,
Public reports, Rule 803.
Regularly conducted activity, Rule 803.

REPUTATION
Hearsay, this index.

REQUESTS
Judicial notice, opportunity to be heard as to propriety of taking, Rule 201.
Limited admissibility of evidence, Rule 105.
Prior statements of witnesses, showing or disclosing to opposing counsel, Rule 613.

REVIEW
See Appeal and Review, generally, this index.

RINGS
Engravings, statements concerning, hearsay exception, Rule 803.

ROUTINE PRACTICE
Organizations, relevant evidence, Rule 406.

RULES OF CRIMINAL PROCEDURE
Supersedure of provisions concerning offer to plead guilty, nolo contendere, etc., by amendment to, Rule 410.

RULINGS ON EVIDENCE
Generally, Rule 103.

SCIENCES
Learned treatises, statements in, hearsay exception, Rule 803.

SCOPE OF RULES
Generally, Rule 101.
Judicial notice, adjudicative facts, rule respecting, Rule 201.

SEALS
Domestic public documents under or not under, extrinsic evidence of authenticity as condition precedent to admissibility not required, Rule 902.

SEAMEN
Destitute seamen, transportation to U.S., actions for penalties for refusal of, applicability of rules in part, Rule 1101.
Foreign diplomatic and consular officers, disputes between seamen, applicability of rules in part, Rule 1101.

SEARCHES AND SEIZURES
Warrants, issuance, proceedings for, inapplicability, Rule 1101.

SELF–INCRIMINATION
Not waived by accused or other witness when examined respecting matters relating only to credibility, Rule 608.

SENSATION
Hearsay exceptions, statement respecting, Rule 803.

SUPREME COURT—Cont'd

Relevant evidence admissible except as otherwise prescribed by, Rule 402.

SYSTEM

Used to produce result, etc., authentication and identification, conformity with requirements, Rule 901.

TABULATIONS

Use and reliance on by public or persons in particular occupations, hearsay exception, Rule 803.

TAGS

Purporting to be affixed in course of business and indicating ownership, control or origin, self-authentication Rule 902.

TELEGRAPHS AND TELEPHONES

Authentication and identification, telephone conversations, conformity with requirements, Rule 901.

TERRITORIES

Documents of under or not under seal, self-authentication, Rule 902.

TESTIMONY

See specific index headings.

TIME

Judicial notice, taking, Rule 201.

Limit, impeachment by evidence of conviction of crime, Rule 609.

Needless consumption of, court control of mode and order of interrogating witnesses and presenting evidence to avoid, Rule 611.

Waste of, exclusion of relevant evidence on grounds of, Rule 403.

TOMBSTONES

Engravings on, statements concerning, hearsay exceptions, Rule 803.

TRADE INSCRIPTIONS

Purporting to be affixed in course of business and indicating ownership, control or origin, self-authentication, Rule 902.

TREATISES

Learned, statements in, hearsay exception, Rule 803.

TRIAL

Jury, generally, this index.

Writing used to refresh memory, criminal cases, failure to produce or deliver, ground for mistrial, Rule 612.

TRIAL DE NOVO

Federal agency actions set aside, facts subject to, rules applicable in part, Rule 1101.

TRIER OF FACT

See Jury, generally, this index.

TRUST TERRITORY OF PACIFIC ISLANDS

Documents of under or not under seal, self-authentication, Rule 902.

TYPEWRITING

"Writings" and "recordings" as including, contents of writings etc., Rule 1001.

UNITED STATES

Documents of under or not under seal, self-authentication, Rule 902.

UNITED STATES MAGISTRATES

Applicability of rules, Rules 101, 1101.

"Court" as including, applicability of rules, Rule 1101.

"Judge" as including, applicability of rules, Rule 1101.

Minor and petty offenses, trial of, applicability of rules in part, Rule 1101.

Rules as governing proceedings before, Rules 101, 1101.

URNS

Hearsay exception, statement concerning inscriptions on, Rule 803.

VERDICT

Inquiry into validity, testimony of juror in connection with, restriction and exception, Rule 606.

VESSELS

Prize, applicability of rules in part, Rule 1101.

VICTIMS

Character evidence, Rule 404.

VIDEO TAPES

"Photographs" as including, contents of photographs, etc., Rule 1001.

VIRGIN ISLANDS

District court, applicability of rules, Rule 1101.

VITAL STATISTICS

Records of, hearsay exception, Rule 803.

VOICES

Identification, authentication and identification, conformity with requirements, Rule 901.

WEIGHT OF EVIDENCE

Preliminary questions, rule concerning as not limiting right of party to introduce evidence respecting, Rule 104.

WILLS

Statement of memory or belief relating to execution, revocation, etc., hearsay, exclusion, Rule 803.

WITNESSES

Attacking or supporting credibility. Credibility of Witnesses, this index.

Bias or Prejudice, generally, this index.

Calling and interrogation of by court, Rule 614.

Character evidence, Rules 404, 607 to 609.

Competency,
    Generally, Rule 601.
  Judge, Rule 605.
  Jurors, Rule 606.

Credibility of Witnesses, generally, this index.

Cross-Examination, generally, this index.

Examination, prior statements of, Rule 613.

Exclusion of, Rule 615.

Extrinsic evidence of prior inconsistent statement of, Rule 613.

Harassment or undue embarrassment, control by court of mode and order of interrogating witnesses and presenting evidence to protect from, Rule 611.

Hostile witnesses, interrogation by leading questions, Rule 611.

Impeachment of Witnesses, generally, this index.

Interrogation, mode and order of, control by court, Rule 611.

Lack of personal knowledge, Rule 602.

Leading questions, Rule 611.

Oaths and affirmations, Rule 603.
  Interpreters, Rule 604.

Opinions and Expert Testimony, generally, this index.

Perjury, generally, this index.

Personal knowledge, evidence to prove, Rule 602.

Prior statements of, examination concerning, Rule 613.

Privileges, generally, this index.

Qualification, preliminary questions concerning, court determination, Rule 104.

Subscribing witness, testimony of unnecessary to authenticate writing, exception, Rule 903.

WORDS AND PHRASES

See Definitions, generally, this index.

WRITINGS

Containing matter not related to subject matter of testimony, excising and ordering delivery of remainder to party entitled thereto, refreshing memory, Rule 612.

Contents of,
  Collateral matters, other evidence of contents, Rule 1004.
  Copies of, duplicates, admissibility of, Rule 1003.
  Definitions, Rule 1001.
  Duplicates, defined, Rule 1001.
  Functions of court and jury, Rule 1008.
  Loss or destruction of originals, other evidence of contents, Rule 1004.
  Opponent, original in possession of, other evidence of contents, Rule 1004.
  Original,
    Defined, Rule 1001.
    Not obtainable other evidence of contents, Rule 1004.
  Other evidence of admissibility, Rule 1004.
  Proof of, requirement of original, exception, Rule 1002.
  Testimony, deposition or written admission of party, proof by, Rule 1007.
  Voluminous writings, summaries of, Rule 1006.
  Writings, defined, Rule 1001.

Examination by court in camera, writing used to refresh memory, Rule 612.

Nonexpert opinion on handwriting, authentication and identification, conformity with requirements, Rule 901.

Remainder or part of, introduction, Rule 106.

Subscribing witness, testimony of unnecessary to authenticate, exception, Rule 903.

Summaries of voluminous writings, Rule 1006.

Use to refresh memory, Rule 612.

X–RAYS

"Photographs" as including, contents of photographs, etc., Rule 1001.

Appendix B

EVIDENCE LAW
RESEARCH ON WESTLAW

Analysis

Section 1. Introduction

The discussion of the law of evidence in this text provides a strong base for analyzing evidence problems. Analyzing an evidence problem can be a complex task, requiring the examination of case law, statutes, court rules and orders, administrative materials and commentary. Along with West books, WESTLAW is an excellent source of research materials.

WESTLAW evidence databases contain rules, commentaries, statutes, cases and administrative materials. Each database is assigned an identifier, which you use to access the database. You can find identifiers for all WESTLAW databases in the WESTLAW Directory and in the *WESTLAW Database List*. When you need to know more detailed information about a database, use the SCOPE command. SCOPE displays unique commands and related databases for each WESTLAW database and service.

You can retrieve documents on WESTLAW by accessing a database and entering a query; by using FIND, a one-step document retrieval service; or by using such services as Insta–Cite ®, Shepard's ®, Shepard's PreView ™ and Quick*Cite* ™. You can also use West's menu-driven research system, EZ ACCESS ™, for additional help.

Additional Resources

If you have not used WESTLAW or have questions not addressed in this appendix, see the *WESTLAW Reference Manual* or contact the West Reference Attorneys at 1–800–688–6363.

Section 2. Evidence Law Databases

Because new information is continually being added to WESTLAW, you should check the WESTLAW Directory for any new database information.

Database Description	Database Iden- tifier	Coverage
Federal Databases		
U.S. Supreme Court Cases	SCT	From 1945 [1]
U.S. Courts of Appeals Cases	CTA	From 1945 [1]
Individual Courts of Appeals	CTA1–CTA11 CTADC CTAF	See SCOPE for the specific court.
U.S. District Courts Cases [2]	DCT	See SCOPE for the specific court.
U.S. Code Annotated	USCA	Current
U.S. Public Laws	US–PL	Current [3]
Federal Rules	US–RULES	Current
Federal Orders	US–ORDERS	Current
Federal Register	FR	From July 1980
Code of Federal Regulations	CFR	Current [3]
State Databases		
Case Law from all 50 states and the District of Columbia	ALLSTATES	From 1945 [1]
Individual State Cases [3]	XX–CS	See SCOPE for the specific state.
State Statutes—Annotated Statutes and annotations from all available states, the District of Columbia, Puerto Rico and the Virgin Islands	ST–ANN–ALL	See SCOPE for the specific state.

Database Description	Database Identifier	Coverage
State Statutes—Unannotated Unannotated statutes from all available states, the District of Columbia, Puerto Rico and the Virgin Islands	STAT–ALL	See SCOPE for the specific state.
Individual State Statutes—Annotated [4]	XX–ST–ANN	See SCOPE for the specific state.
Individual State Statutes—Unannotated [4]	XX–ST	See SCOPE for the specific state.
Multistate Legislative Service Documents passed by the legislative bodies from all available states, the District of Columbia, Puerto Rico and the Virgin Islands	LEGIS–ALL	See SCOPE for the specific state.
Individual State Legislative Service [3] Documents passed by the legislative bodies of each state, district or territory	XX–LEGIS	See SCOPE for the specific state.
Individual State Statutes [3] General index references for the statutes and constitutions of all available states and the District of Columbia	XX–ST–IDX	See SCOPE for the specific state.
Individual State Attorney General Opinions [3] Attorney general opinions from 49 states	XX–AG	See SCOPE for the specific state.
Individual State Court Rules [4] State court rules from all available states, Puerto Rico and the Virgin Islands	XX–RULES	See SCOPE for the specific state.
Individual State Court Orders [4] State court orders from all available states	XX–ORDERS	See SCOPE for the specific state.

SPECIALIZED MATERIALS

Database Description	Database Identifier	Coverage
Federal Military Law—Manual for Courts–Martial	FMIL–MCM	From 1941
Military Criminal Law Evidence	MCLE	From July 1987
WESTLAW Topical Highlights—Federal Practice and Procedure	WTH–FPP	Current

| | Database Iden- | |
| Database Description | tifier | Coverage |

Texts & Treatises

| Federal Rules Decisions [5] (articles) | FEDRDTP | From 1986 |

(1) Cases dated before 1945 are contained in databases whose identifiers end with the suffix—OLD. For example, the identifier for the U.S. Supreme Court Cases—Before 1945 database is SCT–OLD. Coverage for federal databases whose identifiers end with the suffix—OLD is 1789–1944. Coverage for the ALLSTATES–OLD database varies by state.

(2) Case law from the *Federal Rules Decisions* ® reporter can be found in the U.S. District Courts Cases database (DCT).

(3) To search for historical versions of the C.F.R. or U.S. Public Laws, access the appropriate database by typing **db cfrxx** or **db us-plxx**, where xx is the last two digits of a year. For example, to access the C.F.R. as it existed in 1986, type **db cfr86**. To access U.S. Public Laws for 1990, type **db us-pl90**.

(4) XX is a state's two-letter postal abbreviation.

(5) Case law from the *Federal Rules Decisions* reporter can be found in the U.S. District Courts Cases database (DCT), articles from the *Federal Rules Decisions* reporter can be found in the Federal Rules Decisions database (FEDRDTP).

Section 3. EZ ACCESS ™

EZ ACCESS is West Publishing company's menu-driven research system. It is ideal for new or infrequent WESTLAW users because it requires no experience or training on WESTLAW.

EZ ACCESS assists you in performing the following research tasks on WESTLAW:

1. Retrieving a document using its citation or title

2. Retrieving cases using a West topic or key number

3. Retrieving documents using significant words

4. Retrieving references to a document using Insta–Cite ®, Shepard's ® Citations, Shepard's PreView ™ and WESTLAW as a citator.

To access EZ ACCESS, type **ez**. Whenever you are unsure of the next step, or if the choice you want is not listed, simply type **ez**; additional choices will be displayed. Once you retrieve documents with EZ ACCESS, use standard WESTLAW commands to browse your documents. For more information on EZ ACCESS, see the *Guide to EZ ACCESS*. For more information on browsing documents, see the browsing commands listed later in this appendix or Section 9 of the *WESTLAW Reference Manual*.

Section 4. FIND

Overview: FIND is a WESTLAW service that allows you to retrieve a document by entering its citation. FIND allows you to retrieve documents from anywhere in WESTLAW without accessing or changing databases or losing your search result. FIND is available for many documents including federal court rules, case law (federal and state), state statutes, *United States Code Annotated ®, Code of Federal Regulations* and *Federal Register* materials, and state and federal public laws.

☐ To use FIND, type **fi** followed by the document citation.

☐ When you are finished using FIND, you have several options. You can access other services, such as Insta–Cite, Shepard's Citations, Shepard's PreView or Quick*Cite* ™. You can also return to the last database or service accessed before using FIND by typing **gb** or **map**.

To FIND This Document	Type
Jones v. Goodyear Tire & Rubber Co., 1991 WL 128474	**fi 1991 wl 128474**
Wardwell v. United States, 758 F.Supp. 769	**fi 758 fsupp 769**
United States Public Law ** 102–40	**fi us pl 102–40**
Federal Rules of Evidence Rule 803	**fi fre rule 803**
137 Cong.Rec. S8486 (daily ed. June 24, 1991) (statement of Sen. Grassley)	**fi 137 cr s8486**

Section 5. Query Formulation

Overview: A query is a request you make to WESTLAW specifying the information you wish to retrieve. The terms in a query are words or numbers that you include in your request so that WESTLAW will retrieve documents containing those words or numbers. These terms are linked together by connectors, which specify the relationship in which the terms must appear.

5.1 Terms

Plurals and Possessives: Plurals are automatically retrieved when you enter the singular form of a term. This is true for both regular and irregular plurals (e.g., **child** retrieves *children*). If you do not want to retrieve the plural form, you can turn off the automatic pluralizer by typing the # symbol in front of the singular form. If you enter the plural form of a term, you will not retrieve the signular form.

If you enter the non-possessive form of a term, WESTLAW automatically retrieves the possessive form as well. However, if you enter the possessive form, only the possessive form is retrieved.

** FIND retrieves public laws from the current congressional session. To search for historical versions of U.S. public laws, access the appropriate database by typing **db us-plxx,** where xx is the last two digits of a year. For example, to access the United States Public Laws—1990 database (US–PL90), type **db us-pl90.**

Automatic Equivalencies: Some terms have alternative forms or equivalencies; for example, *5* and *five* are equivalent terms. WESTLAW automatically retrieves equivalent terms.

Compound Words and Acronyms: When a compound word is one of your search terms, use a hyphen to retrieve all forms of the word. For example, the term **cross-examination** retrieves *cross-examination, cross examination* and *crossexamination.*

When using an acronym as a search term, place a period after each of the letters in the acronym to retrieve any of its forms. For example, the term **a.p.a.** retrieves *apa, a.p.a., a p a* and *a. p. a.*

Root Expander and Universal Character: Placing a root expander (!) at the end of a root term generates ALL other terms with that root. For example, adding the ! symbol to the root *confess* in the query

confess! /s miranda

instructs WESTLAW to retrieve such words as *confess, confesses, confessed, confessing, confession,* and *confessions.*

The universal character (*) stands for one character and can be inserted in the middle or at the end of a term. For example, the term

withdr*w

will retrieve *withdraw* and *withdrew.* More than one universal character can be used in a term. But adding only two asterisks to the root *jur* in the query

jur*

instructs WESTLAW to retrieve all forms of the root with up to two additional characters. Terms like *jury* or *juror* are retrieved by this query. However, terms with more than two letters following the root, such as *jurisdiction,* are not retrieved. Plurals are always retrieved, even if more than two letters follow the root.

Phrase Searching: To search for a phrase on WESTLAW, place it within quotation marks. For example, to search for references to the doctrine of *res gestae,* type **"res gestae"**. You should use phrase searching only when you are certain that the phrase will not appear in any other form.

5.2 Alternative Terms

After selecting the terms for your query, consider which alternative terms are necessary. For example, if you are searching for the term *custody,* you might also want to search for the terms *detain!* and *detention.* You should consider both synonyms and antonyms as alternative terms.

5.3 Connectors

After selecting terms and alternative terms for your query, use connectors to specify the relationship that should exist between search terms in your retrieved documents. The connectors you can use are described below:

Connector	Meaning	Example
or (space)	Retrieves documents containing either term or both terms.	**coerc! force***
& (and)	Retrieves documents containing both terms.	**waiver & privilege**
/p	Retrieves documents containing both terms in the same paragraph.	**withdr*w /p plea**
/s	Retrieves documents containing both terms in the same sentence.	**refresh! /s recollection**
+s	Retrieves documents in which the first term precedes the second within the same sentence.	**marital +s privilege**
/n	Retrieves documents in which terms are within a specified number of terms of each other.	**business /3 record**
+n	Retrieves documents in which the first term precedes the second by no more than the specified number of terms.	**parol +2 evidence**
% (but not)	Excludes all documents containing the term(s) following the % symbol.	**los* /3 evidence % to (110)**

5.4 Restricting Your Search by Field

Documents in each WESTLAW database consist of several segments, or fields. One field may contain the citation, another the title, another the synopsis, and so forth. A query can be formulated to retrieve only those documents that contain search terms in a specified field. Not all databases contain the same fields. Also, depending on the database, fields of the same name may contain different types of information.

To view the fields and field content for a specific database, type **f** while in the database. Note that in some databases, not every field is available for every document. To restrict your search to a specific field, type the field name or its two-letter abbreviation followed by search terms enclosed in parentheses.

The following fields are available in some WESTLAW databases you might use for evidence law research:

Digest and Synopsis Fields: The digest and synopsis fields, available in cases published by West Publishing Company, summarize the main points of a case. A search in these fields is useful because it retrieves only cases in which a search term was significant enough to be included in a summary.

Consider restricting your search to one or both of these fields if

☐ you are searching for common terms or terms with more than one meaning, and you need to narrow your search; or

☐ you cannot narrow your search by moving to a smaller database.

For example, suppose you want to retrieve cases that discuss whether parol evidence is admissible in a contract dispute to explain ambiguity in the contract. Access an appropriate database, such as the Connecticut Cases database (CT–CS) and type a query like the following:

sy,di(parol extrinsic /p ambigui! /s contract agreement)

Headnote Field: You can also restrict your search to the headnote field. The headnote field, which is part of the digest field, does not include the topic number, the key number, the citation or the title. A headnote field search is useful when you are searching for references to specific code sections or rule numbers.

For example, to retrieve cases that discuss rule 803(24) of the Federal Rules of Evidence, access a database such as the U.S. Court of Appeals for the Fifth Circuit Cases database (CTA5), and type a query like the following:

he(803(24))

Topic Field: The topic field includes the West digest topic number, topic name, key number and text of the key line for each key number. You should restrict your search to the topic field in a case law database if

☐ a digest field search retrieves too many documents; or

☐ you want to retrieve cases with digest paragraphs classified under more than one topic.

For example, the topic *Evidence* has the topic number 157. To retrieve Illinois cases that discuss the work product doctrine, access the Illinois Cases database (IL–CS) and type a query like the following:

to(157) /p work-product

To retrieve West headnotes classified under more than one topic, search for the topic name in the topic field.

For example, to search for Illinois cases that discuss privilege and the work product doctrine, access the Illinois Cases database (IL–CS) and type a query like the following:

to(privilege!) /p work-product

Be aware that cases from slip opinions and looseleaf services do not contain the digest, synopsis, headnote or topic fields.

Prelim and Caption Fields: Restrict your search to the prelim and caption fields in a database containing statutes, rules or regulations to retrieve documents where your terms are important enough to appear in the heading or name of a statute or rule.

For example, to retrieve the federal rules of evidence discussing character evidence, access the Federal Rules database (US–RULES) and type

pr,ca(character & evidence)

☐ To look at sections surrounding those your query retrieved, use the DOCUMENTS IN SEQUENCE command. When you are viewing rule 404 you can retrieve the section preceding it by typing **d-**. To retrieve the section immediately following a retrieved document, type **d.** To cancel this command and return to your original search result, type **xd.**

☐ To see if a rule has been amended or repealed, use the UPDATE service. Simply type **update** while viewing the rule to display any court order that amends or repeals the rule.

5.5 Restricting Your Search by Date

You can instruct WESTLAW to retrieve documents decided or issued before, after, or on a specified date, as well as within a range of dates. The following are examples of queries that contain date restrictions:

da(bef 1991   &   aft 1986)   &   los* /3 evidence

da(1990)   &   los* /3 evidence

da(1988 1989)   &   los* /3 evidence

da(4/26/90) & los* /3 evidence

da(april 26, 1990)   &   los* /3 evidence

da(aft 1–1–89)   &   los* /3 evidence

You can also instruct WESTLAW to retrieve documents added to a database on or after a specified date, as well as within a range of dates. The following are examples of queries that contain added date restrictions:

ad(5–10–91)   &   los* /3 evidence

ad(aft 1–1–89)   &   los* /3 evidence

ad(aft 2–1–91 & bef 3–1–91)   &   los* /3 evidence

Section 6. Insta–Cite ®

Overview: Insta–Cite is West Publishing Company's case history and citation verification service. It is the most current case history service available. Insta–Cite provides the following types of information about a citation:

Direct History: In addition to reversals and affirmances, Insta–Cite gives you the complete reported history of a litigated matter including any related cases. Insta–Cite provides direct history for federal cases from 1754 and for state cases from 1879.

Related References: Related references are cases that involve the same parties and facts as your case, but deal with different legal issues. Insta–Cite provides related references from 1983 to date.

Negative Indirect History: Insta–Cite lists subsequent cases that have a substantial negative impact on your case, including cases overruling your case or calling it into question. Cases affected by decisions from 1972 to date will be displayed on Insta–Cite. To retrieve negative indirect history prior to 1972, use Shepard's Citations (discussed in Section 7).

Secondary Source References: Insta–Cite also provides references to secondary sources that cite your case. These secondary sources presently include legal encyclopedias such as *Corpus Juris Secundum* ®.

Parallel Citations: Insta–Cite provides parallel citations for cases including citations to *Callaghan's Federal Rules Service, Federal Rules Decisions* (cases only), and many other looseleaf reporters.

Citation Verification: Insta–Cite confirms that you have the correct volume and page number for a case. Citation verification information is available from 1754 for federal cases and from 1920 for state cases.

Commands

The following commands can be used in Insta–Cite:

ic xxx or **ic**   Retrieves an Insta–Cite result when followed by a case citation (where xxx is the citation), or when entered from a displayed case, Shepard's result or Shepard's PreView result.

pubs   Displays a list of publications and publication abbreviations available in Insta–Cite.

sc   Displays the scope of Insta–Cite coverage.

expand   Displays the Insta–Cite result with chronological case history. (LOCATE is not available in an expanded Insta–Cite result.)

Loc xxx	Restricts an Insta–Cite result to direct or indirect history or to secondary source references when followed by the appropriate code. For example, **Loc dir** restricts the Insta–Cite result to direct history, including related references.
xLoc	Cancels your LOCATE request.
Loc auto xxx	Automatically restricts subsequent Insta–Cite results according to your LOCATE request (where **XXX** is a LOCATE request).
xLoc auto	Cancels your LOCATE AUTO request.
gb or **map2**	Returns you to your previous service or search result, if one exists.

Section 7. Shepard's Citations ®

Overview: Shepard's provides a comprehensive list of cases and publications that have cited a particular case. Shepard's also includes explanatory analysis to indicate how the citing cases have treated the case, e.g., "followed," "explained."

In addition to citations from federal, state, and regional citators, Shepard's on WESTLAW includes citations from specialized citators, such as *Civil Procedure Reports, Federal Rules Decisions* (cases only), and many other looseleaf reporters.

Commands

The following commands can be used in Shepard's:

sh xxx or **sh**	Retrieves a Shepard's result when followed by a case citation (where xxx is the citation), or when entered from a displayed case, Insta–Cite result or Shepard's PreView result.
pubs	Displays a list of publications that can be Shepardized ® and their publication abbreviations.
sc xxx	Displays the scope of coverage for a specific publication in Shepard's, where xxx is the publication abbreviation (e.g., **sc civ. proc. n.s.**).
cmds	Displays a list of Shepard's commands.
Loc	Restricts a Shepard's result to a specific category when followed by the analysis code, headnote number, or state/circuit or publication abbreviation to which you want the display restricted. For example, **Loc 5** restricts the Shepard's result to cases discussing the point of law contained in headnote number five of the cited case. Type **xLoc** to cancel LOCATE.
gb or **map2**	Leaves Shepard's and returns you to your previous service or search result, if one exists.

Section 8. Shepard's PreView ™

Overview: Shepard's PreView gives you a preview of citing references from West's ® National Reporter System ® that will appear in Shepard's Citations. Depending on the citation, Shepard's PreView provides citing information days, weeks or even months before the same information appears in Shepard's online. Use Shepard's PreView to update your Shepard's results.

Commands

The following commands can be used in Shepard's PreView:

sp xxx or **sp**   Retrieves a Shepard's PreView result when followed by a case citation (where xxx is the citation), or when entered from a displayed case, Insta–Cite result or Shepard's result.

pubs   Displays a list of publications and publication abbreviations that are available in Shepard's PreView.

sc xxx   Displays the scope of citing references.

cmds   Displays a list of Shepard's PreView commands.

Loc xxx   Restricts a Shepard's PreView result by date, publication or jurisdiction, where xxx is the abbreviation.

gb or **map2**   Leaves Shepard's PreView and returns you to your previous service or search result, if one exists.

Section 9. Quick*Cite* ™

Overview: Quick*Cite* is a citator service on WESTLAW that enables you to retrieve the most recent citing cases, including slip opinions, automatically.

There is a four- to six-week gap between citing cases listed in Shepard's PreView and the most recent citing cases available on WESTLAW. This gap occurs because cases go through an editorial process at West before they are added to Shepard's PreView. To retrieve the most recent citing cases, therefore, you need to search case law databases on WESTLAW for references to your case; this search technique is known as using WESTLAW as a citator. Quick*Cite* makes using WESTLAW as a citator automatic.

After you've checked your case in the other citator services on WESTLAW, type **qc** to display the Quick*Cite* screen. From this screen, you can press **ENTER** to retrieve the most recent citing cases on WESTLAW, including slip opinions. You can also type **qc** and the citation to display the Quick*Cite* screen, e.g., **qc 96 sct 1569.**

Quick*Cite* formulates a query using the title, the case citation(s), and an added date restriction to retrieve cases more recent than those listed in Shepard's PreView. Quick*Cite* then accesses the appropriate database, either ALLSTATES or ALLFEDS, and runs the query for you.

QuickCite also allows you to choose a different date range and database for your query so you can tailor it to your specific research needs.

Commands

The following commands can be used in Quick *Cite:*

qc xxx or qc   Retrieves a Quick*Cite* result when followed by a case citation (where **xxx** is the citation), or when entered from a displayed case, Insta–Cite result, Shepard's result or Shepard's PreView result.

scope   Displays the scope of Quick*Cite* coverage.

Press ENTER   Updates Shepard's and Shepard's PreView by re-trieving documents added to ALLFEDS within the last three months that cite this decision.

all   Retrieves all ALLFEDS documents that cite this decision.

Database
  Identifier   Retrieves documents added to WESTLAW within the last three months that cite this decision in the selected database.

q   Displays the Quick*Cite* query for editing in ALLFEDS.

map1   Leaves your Quick*Cite* result and returns you to the WESTLAW Directory.

Quick*Cite* is designed to retrieve documents that cite cases. To retrieve citing references to other documents, such as statutes and law review articles, use WESTLAW as a citator.

Section 10. WESTLAW as a Citator

Using WESTLAW as a citator, you can search for documents citing a specific statute, regulation, rule or agency decision. To retrieve documents citing Miss.R.Evid. 804(b), *Hearsay exceptions,* access the Mississippi Cases database (MS–CS) and search for the citation alone:

804(b)

If the citation is not a unique term, add descriptive terms. For example, to retrieve documents citing Miss.R.Evid. 404, discussing character evidence, type a query like the following:

404 /p character /3 evidence

Section 11. Research Examples

1.   A colleague refers you to a periodical article surveying the federal law of privileges. How can you retrieve the article on WESTLAW?

Solutions

☐ If you know the publication in which the article appeared, in this case, *Litigation,* check the WESTLAW Directory to see if the publication is online and find the database identifier.

Access the database by typing **db litig.** At the Enter Query screen, type a query like the following:

evidence /p privilege

☐ If you know that the title of the article is *The Federal Law of Privileges,* but you don't know the journal in which it appears, access the Journals & Law Reviews database (JLR). Search for key terms in the title field:

ti(federal /s law /s privilege)

☐ If you know that the article citation is 16 Litigation 32 (1989), access the Litigation database (LITIG). Search for terms from the citation in the citation field:

ci(16 +5 32)

2. Your client, who lives in Oregon, is charged with a sex crime against a child. You need to retrieve court rules governing the competency of children as witnesses.

Solution

☐ Access the Oregon Rules database (OR–RULES) and type a query like the following:

child /p witness /p competen!

☐ To see if a rule has been amended or repealed, use the UPDATE service. Simply type **update** while viewing the rule to display any court orders that amend or repeal the rule.

To run your original query in the Oregon Criminal Justice Cases database (ORCJ–CS), type **sdb orcj-cs.**

3. Your client is injured in an automobile accident with an out of state driver. You have brought the action in federal court because of diversity of parties. The defendant has indicated that pursuant to Fed.R.Evid. 609, he intends to impeach the plaintiff by introducing evidence of the plaintiff's past conviction for issuing a bad check with the intent to defraud.

☐ When you know the citation for a specific rule, use FIND to retrieve it. For example, to retrieve Fed.R.Evid. 609, *Impeachment by Evidence of Conviction of Crime,* type the following:

fi fre 609

☐ To view preceding and subsequent rules, use the DOCUMENTS IN SEQUENCE command. To view Fed.R.Evid. 608, type **d-.** To view Rule 610, type **d.**

☐ To see if a rule has been amended or repealed, use the UPDATE service. Simply type **update** while viewing the rule to display any court orders that amend or repeal the rule.

When you retrieve Fre.R.Evid. 609, you also retrieve historical and statutory notes, advisory committee notes, cross references, references to law review commentaries and notes of decisions. Use the LOCATE command to quickly zero in on any annotations in Fed.R.

Evid. 609 that discuss bad checks. Type Loc and your query, e.g., **Loc check.**

One of the cases noted is *Petty v. Ideco, Div. of Dresser Industries, Inc.,* 761 F.2d 1146 (5th Cir.1985). Use FIND to retrieve this case by typing **fi 761 f2d 1146.**

You wish to see if this case is still good law and if other cases have cited this case.

Solution

☐ Use Insta–Cite to retrieve the direct and negative indirect history of *Petty.* While viewing the case, type **ic.**

☐ You want to Shepardize ® *Petty.* Type **sh.**

Limit your Shepard's result to decisions containing a reference to a specific headnote, such as headnote 12. Type **Loc 12.**

☐ Check Shepard's PreView for more current cases citing *Petty.* Type **sp.**

☐ Check QuickCite for the most current cases citing *Petty.* Type **qc** and follow the online instructions.

4. In a personal injury action, you want to introduce thermographic evidence to substantiate your client's chiropractor's diagnosis and treatment. You have not found any cases on this subject. How can you retrieve cases discussing the admissibility of thermographic evidence?

Solution

☐ Access the ALLSTATES database and type a query like the following:

thermogra! /p admiss! admit! inadmissib!

5. Your client is chemically dependent and at times forgets to feed her children and clean the house. She went to a social worker for family therapy. Her ex-spouse has commenced an action for change in custody and intends to call the social worker to testify about your client's problems. There are physician-patient and psychotherapist privileges in New York, but you are unsure if these privileges cover social workers or other mental health therapists and counselors engaged in marriage and family therapy.

Solution

☐ Access the New York Cases database (NY–CS), and type a query like the following:

sy,di(privilege* /p social mental family /3 worker counselor therapist)

6. With the advent of computer simulations, it is now possible to display the movement of a car under specified conditions and in

compliance with the laws of physics based on mathematical calculations.

While driving in her car, your client's spouse was hit and run over by a semi-truck, killing her instantly. The truck apparently was forced into the spouse's lane when the road narrowed and a red Corvette passed the truck on the right.

Your accident reconstruction expert has a computer-generated simulation that graphically demonstrates, based on the skid marks and the speed of the vehicles, that the truck driver lost control of his vehicle and literally ran over your client's car. How can you get this simulation admitted into evidence?

Solution

☐ Access the Pennsylvania Cases database (PA–CS), and type a query like the following:

computer! /s animat! simulat! /p evidence admiss! admit! inadmissib!

☐ If you don't retrieve any cases in your jurisdiction, you will want to run the same query in the ALLSTATES database by typing **sdb allstates**.

☐ Run the same query in the Journals & Law Reviews database (JLR) by typing **sdb jlr**. The JLR database contains articles from law reviews, Continuing Legal Education course handbooks and bar journals.

7. As a new associate in the firm, you are expected to keep up with and summarize recent legal developments in the area of evidence. How can you monitor developments in evidence efficiently?

Solution

☐ One of the easiest ways to stay abreast of recent developments in evidence is by regularly accessing the WESTLAW Topical Highlights—Federal Practice and Procedure database (WTH–FPP). The WTH–FPP database summarizes recent legal developments, including court decisions, legislation and materials released by administrative agencies that pertain to the issues of jurisdiction, evidence, the rules of civil and appellate procedure, limitations and the mechanics of practicing law in the federal courts.

☐ To access the database, type **db wth-fpp**. You automatically retrieve a list of documents added to the database in the last two weeks. To read a summary of a document listed, type its corresponding number.

☐ You can also search this database. To display the Enter Query screen, type **s** from anywhere in the database. At the Enter Query screen, type your query. For example, to retrieve references discussing evidence and discovery of business records, type a query like the following:

business   /3   record file

Section 12.   WESTLAW Commands

General Commands

ez	Accesses the EZ ACCESS system; when entered from EZ ACCESS, displays additional choices.
help	Displays explanatory messages.
scope	Displays a database description when followed by a database identifier or when entered from a database; displays the scope of coverage when entered from a service, such as Insta–Cite.
time	Displays the amount of chargeable time used in your research session.
off	Signs off WESTLAW.
pr	Displays the Offline Printing and Downloading Menu.
opd	Displays the Offline Print Directory.
client	Allows you to change your client identifier.
options	Displays the WESTLAW Options Directory.

Search Commands

s	New search—displays the Enter Query screen.
q	Edit query—displays the last query for editing.
x	Cancels a search in progress.
db	Returns to the WESTLAW Directory from a database; accesses a database when followed by a database identifier: **db sct**.
sdb xxx	Runs the same query in a different database, where **xxx** is the database identifier: **sdb allfeds**.
qdb xxx	Displays the query for editing in a different database, where **xxx** is the database identifier: **qdb allstates**.
read	In selected databases, retrieves the most recent documents when entered at the Enter Query screen.
List	In selected databases, retrieves a list of the most recent documents when entered at the Enter Query screen.

Browsing Commands

t	Term mode—displays the next page containing the terms in the requested relationship; **t-** displays the previous page containing the terms in the requested relationship.

p   Page mode—displays the next page of a document; **p-** displays the previous page of a document. To display a specific page, type **p** followed by the page number: **p5**.

Loc   LOCATE—locates selected terms in retrieved documents; also restricts a Shepard's display to selected categories, such as history and treatment codes, headnote numbers and citing publications.

LLoc   Retrieves a citations list of LOCATE documents.

xLoc   Cancels a LOCATE command.

r   Displays the next ranked document; displays a specific document when followed by the document's rank number: **r3**.

L   Displays a citations list.

Lr#   Displays a citations list beginning with a specific rank number: **Lr8**.

g   Search summary—displays the query and the number of documents retrieved by it.

h+   Advances one half page in a document.

h−   Moves back one half page in a document.

d   DOCUMENTS IN SEQUENCE—displays sections preceding or following the retrieved document: **d+#, d−#**.

xd   Cancels DOCUMENTS IN SEQUENCE and displays the document you were viewing when you entered the DOCUMENTS IN SEQUENCE command.

f   Displays a list of fields in a database; restricts your display to a selected field or fields when followed by the field name: **f opinion**.

xf   Cancels your command to restrict your display by field.

Service Commands

fi   FIND—retrieves a document when followed by its citation: **fi 93 sct 2357**.

ic   Retrieves an Insta–Cite result when followed by the case citation, **ic 93 sct 2357**, or when entered from a displayed case, Shepard's result or Shepard's PreView result.

sh   Retrieves a Shepard's result when followed by the case citation, **sh 93 sct 2357**, or when entered from a displayed case, Insta–Cite result or Shepard's PreView result.

sp   Retrieves a Shepard's PreView result when followed by the case citation, **sp 93 sct 2357**, or when entered from a displayed case, Insta–Cite result or Shepard's result.

qc	Retrieves a QuickCite result when followed by the case citation, **qc 93 sct 2357**, or when entered from a displayed case, Insta–Cite result, Shepard's result or Shepard's PreView result.
pdq	Personal Directory of Queries—displays a list of saved queries for selection and update.
di	Enters the Black's Law Dictionary ® service or displays a definition when followed by the word or phrase: **di presumption**.
update	Displays any document amending or repealing the statute, rule or regulation you are viewing.
rm	Displays the Related Materials Directory for a statute, legislative service document, rule or order.
gm	Displays General Materials, which are references and tables applicable to the entire title, chapter and subchapter containing the displayed statute.
annos	Displays annotations (Notes of Decisions) for the displayed statute.
refs	Displays references to the unannotated statutory document you are viewing.
st-ann	Displays the annotated statute(s) amended or repealed by the displayed document.
stat	Displays the unannotated statute(s) amended or repealed by the displayed document.
rules	Displays the court rule(s) affected by the displayed court order.
gb	GO BACK—returns to a previous location in WESTLAW from a service, e.g., Insta–Cite, Shepard's, FIND.
map	Displays a list containing the most recent database and services accessed and allows you to return to them.
map1	Returns to the WESTLAW Directory.
map2	Returns to your search result, if one exists.

*

McCormick in the Courts

This table lists cases decided since January 1, 1984 which cite the 3rd Edition of McCormick on evidence as authority. It refers the practitioner to recent caselaw bearing on the contents of each hornbook section. The primary purpose of the table is to afford ready access to the prevailing local rule or, where local precedent is inadequate, to other judicial authority.

All citing cases are listed under the section number of the 4th Edition which deals with the same subject matter as in the 3rd Edition. With some exceptions, the section numbers are the same. An explanatory note indicates each instance in which the subject matter appeared under a different section number in the 3rd Edition.

Under each section, U.S. Supreme Court cases are listed first, followed by decisions of the United States Courts of Appeal, the United States District Courts (including United States Bankruptcy Courts) and finally, the state appellate court decisions ordered with the most recent decision first.

To obtain citations to earlier editions of McCormick than the 3rd Edition, check WESTLAW by entering a query similar to the following: MCCORMICK /S EVIDENCE + 5 n + 5 2ND 1972 (where n is the section number being searched).

Some of these cites are only available on WESTLAW and not in the bound volumes. They are indicated by a "W.L." in the citation (e.g., 1984 WL 573). Before citing or relying upon these opinions, the researcher would be well advised to refer to the appropriate local law (court rules, statutes, etc.) limiting the purposes for which these opinions may be cited.

Note: An asterisk (*) following a citation to an unpublished opinion indicates that the full-text is available on WESTLAW.

CHAPTER 1. PREPARING AND PRESENTING THE EVIDENCE

§ 1. Planning and Preparation of Proof as Important as the Rules of Evidence

§ 2. Preparation for Trial on the Facts, Without Resort to the Aid of the Court

C.A.7 (Ill.)1989. Lenea v. Lane 882 F.2d 1171.

§ 3. Invoking the Aid of the Court in Preparing for Trial: Right to Interview Witnesses: Discovery and Depositions: Requests for Admission: Pretrial Conferences

§ 4. The Order of Presenting Evidence at the Trial

N.C.App., 1991. Harris v. Miller 407

S.E.2d 556, 103 N.C.App. 312.

Conn.1991.   Shaham v. Capparelli 591 A.2d 1269, 219 Conn. 133.

Minn.App.1990.   State v. Rasinski 464 N.W.2d 517.

Conn.1987.   State v. Coleman 519 A.2d 1201, 202 Conn. 86.

N.Y.A.D. 2 Dept.1987.   People v. Brown 511 N.Y.S.2d 86, 126 A.D.2d 657.

CHAPTER 2.   THE FORM OF QUESTIONS ON DIRECT: THE JUDGE'S WITNESSES: REFRESHING MEMORY

§ 5.   The Form of Questions: (a) Questions Calling for a Free Narrative Versus Specific Questions

§ 6.   The Form of Questions: (b) Leading Questions

Utah 1989.   State v. Ireland 773 P.2d 1375.

Ohio App., 1987.   State v. Bradley 1987 WL 17303.

N.Y.A.D. 2 Dept.1986.   People v. Walker 510 N.Y.S.2d 203, 125 A.D.2d 732.

§ 7.   The Form of Questions: (c) Misleading and Argumentative Questions

La.App. 1 Cir.1986.   State v. Ducksworth 496 So.2d 624.

§ 8.   The Judge May Examine and Call Witnesses

D.C.N.Y.1985.   Larsen v. A.C. Carpenter, Inc. 620 F.Supp. 1084.

S.C., 1991.   State v. Anderson 406 S.E.2d 152.

Fla.1991.   Shere v. State 579 So.2d 86.

Vt.1988.   In re Nash 556 A.2d 88, 151 Vt. 1.

Vt.1988.   Auger v. Auger 546 A.2d 1373, 149 Vt. 559.

Ind.App. 2 Dist 1985.   Jones v. State 477 N.E.2d 353.

§ 9.   Refreshing Recollection

C.A.10 (Kan.)1985.   U.S. v. Rinke 778 F.2d 581.

Alaska 1990.   Matomco Oil Co., Inc. v. Arctic Mechanical, Inc. 796 P.2d 1336.

Ga.App.1988.   Miller v. State 376 S.E.2d 901, 189 Ga.App. 587.

Miss.1988.   Livingston v. State 525 So.2d 1300.

Tenn.App., 1986.   Martin v. Caution, Inc. 1986 WL 2868.

Fla.App. 3 Dist.1985.   Peoples Gas System, Inc. v. Hotel Ocean 71 Associates, Ltd. 479 So.2d 203.

Md.App.1985.   Newman v. State 499 A.2d 492, 65 Md.App. 85.

Pa.Super.1985.   Dean Witter Reynolds, Inc. v. Genteel 499 A.2d 637, 346 Pa.Super. 336.

D.C.App.1985.   Yeager v. Greene 502 A.2d 980.

Idaho 1985.   Matter of Contempt of Wright 700 P.2d 40, 108 Idaho 418.

CHAPTER 3.   THE REQUIREMENT OF FIRSTHAND KNOWLEDGE: THE OPINION RULE: EXPERT TESTIMONY

§ 10.   The Requirement of Knowledge From Observation

C.A.9 (Cal.)1986.   U.S. v. Owens 789 F.2d 750.

C.A.5 (Miss.)1986.   U.S. v. Davis 792 F.2d 1299.

S.D.N.Y.1990.   Folio Impressions, Inc. v. Byer California 752 F.Supp. 583.

D.Utah 1988.   Bocage v. Litton Systems, Inc. 702 F.Supp. 846.

W.D.Wis.1988.   Moyer v. Dunn County 691 F.Supp. 164.

Ark.App., 1990.   Yingling v. State 1990 WL 212806.

Tex.App. Fort Worth 1990. Middlebrook v. State 803 S.W.2d 355.

D.C.App.1990. Smith v. U.S. 583 A.2d 975.

Neb.1989. State v. McSwine 438 N.W.2d 778, 231 Neb. 886.

Pa.Super.1988. Kearns by Kearns v. De-Haas 546 A.2d 1226, 377 Pa.Super. 200.

N.Y.A.D. 2 Dept.1985. People v. Womble 489 N.Y.S.2d 521, 111 A.D.2d 283.

Ohio App., 1985. State v. Johnson. 1985 WL 9452.

§ 11. The Evolution of the Rule Against Opinions: Opinions of Laymen

U.S.Fla.1988. Beech Aircraft Corp. v. Rainey 109 S.Ct. 439, 488 U.S. 153, 102 L.Ed.2d 445.

Pa.Super.1988. Kearns by Kearns v. De-Haas 546 A.2d 1226, 377 Pa.Super. 200.

Miss.1988. Whittington v. State 523 So.2d 966.

N.C.1987. State v. Davis 361 S.E.2d 724, 321 N.C. 52.

Okl.Cr.1987. Whittmore v. State 742 P.2d 1154.

Tex.App. Texarkana 1987. Gross v. State 730 S.W.2d 104.

Mo.App.1987. State v. Gray 731 S.W.2d 275.

Md.1986. Bloodsworth v. State 512 A.2d 1056, 307 Md. 164.

D.C.App.1986. Jones v. U.S. 512 A.2d 253.

Okl.Cr.1985. Green v. State 713 P.2d 1032.

Idaho 1985. Matter of Contempt of Wright 700 P.2d 40, 108 Idaho 418.

§ 12. The Relativity of the Opinion Rule: Opinions on the Ultimate Issue

C.A.9 (Cal.)1989. Miller v. Fairchild Industries, Inc. 885 F.2d 498.

C.A.10 (Colo.)1988. Specht v. Jensen 853 F.2d 805.

C.A.2 (N.Y.)1988. U.S. v. Scop 846 F.2d 135.

Mo.App., 1991. American Family Mutual Ins. Co. v. Lacy 1991 WL 137332.

Md.App.1990. Cook v. State 578 A.2d 283, 84 Md.App. 122.

Mont.1990. Heltborg v. Modern Machinery 795 P.2d 954, 244 Mont. 24.

N.J.Super.A.D.1989. State v. Grimes 561 A.2d 647, 235 N.J.Super. 75.

Ariz.1989. Dunham v. Pima County 778 P.2d 1200, 161 Ariz. 304.

Conn.1989. State v. Spigarolo 556 A.2d 112, 210 Conn. 359.

La.App. 5 Cir.1988. Burk v. Illinois Cent. Gulf R. Co. 529 So.2d 515.

Tex.1988. Louder v. De Leon 754 S.W.2d 148.

Conn.1988. State v. Vilalastra 540 A.2d 42, 207 Conn. 35.

Miss.1988. Whittington v. State 523 So.2d 966.

Ind.1987. Greene v. State 515 N.E.2d 1376.

La.App. 1 Cir.1987. Schwamb v. Delta Air Lines, Inc. 516 So.2d 452.

Tex.App.Texarkana 1987. Gross v. State 730 S.W.2d 104.

Colo.1986. People v. Collins (Two Cases) 730 P.2d 293.

Iowa 1986. State v. Myers 382 N.W.2d 91.

Mo.App.1986. State v. Willis 706 S.W.2d 265.

Mass.App.1985. Com. v. Mendrala 480 N.E.2d 1039, 20 Mass.App. 398.

Idaho 1985. Matter of Contempt of Wright 700 P.2d 40, 108 Idaho 418.

Ala.Cr.App.1985. Meadows v. State 473 So.2d 582.

§ 13. Expert Witnesses: Subjects of Expert Testimony: Qualifications: Cross–Examination

C.A.5 (Tex.)1989. Peteet v. Dow Chemical Co. 868 F.2d 1428.

E.D.Pa., 1989. Mateer v. U.S. Aluminum 1989 WL 60442.

M.D.N.C., 1987. Peterson v. Air Line Pilots Ass'n 1987 WL 16435.

Idaho App., 1990. State v. Rodgers 812 P.2d 1227.

Tenn.Cr.App., 1990. State v. Armitage 1990 WL 93850.

Neb.1990. State v. Reynolds 457 N.W.2d 405, 235 Neb. 662.

Mich.1990. People v. Beckley 456 N.W.2d 391, 434 Mich. 691.

N.J.Super.A.D.1990. Rubanick v. Witco Chemical Corp. 576 A.2d 4, 242 N.J.Super. 36.

Colo.1990. People v. Williams 790 P.2d 796.

La.App. 3 Cir.1990. Jaffarzad v. Jones Truck Lines, Inc. 561 So.2d 144.

W.Va.1990. State v. Dietz 390 S.E.2d 15.

D.C.App.1990. District of Columbia v. Bethel 567 A.2d 1331.

D.C.App.1989. In re Melton 565 A.2d 635.

La.App. 5 Cir.1988. Burk v. Illinois Cent. Gulf R. Co. 529 So.2d 515.

Wis.App., 1988. Local Government Property Ins. Fund v. HSR Associates, Inc. 428 N.W.2d 561 (Table), 145 Wis.2d 895, Unpublished Disposition.(*)

Mich.1987. People v. Gambrell 415 N.W.2d 202, 429 Mich. 401.

La.App. 1 Cir.1987. Schwamb v. Delta Air Lines, Inc. 516 So.2d 452.

D.C.App.1987. Ford v. U.S. 533 A.2d 617.

N.C.1987. State v. Goodwin 357 S.E.2d 639, 320 N.C. 147.

Miss.1987. Brown v. Mladineo 504 So.2d 1201.

D.C.App.1986. Gant v. U.S. 518 A.2d 103.

Mich.1986. People v. Smith 387 N.W.2d 814, 425 Mich. 98.

N.Y.A.D. 1 Dept.1986. Christoforou v. Lown 502 N.Y.S.2d 184, 120 A.D.2d 387.

Conn.1986. State v. Kemp 507 A.2d 1387, 199 Conn. 473.

Conn.App.1985. Campbell v. Pommier 496 A.2d 975, 5 Conn.App. 29.

Wyo.1985. Krucheck v. State 702 P.2d 1267.

§ 14. Grounds for Expert Opinion: Hypothetical Questions

C.A.2 (N.Y.)1988. U.S. v. Scop 846 F.2d 135.

Tenn.App., 1990. Evans v. Wilson 1990 WL 84578.

Tenn.1989. Evans v. Wilson 776 S.W.2d 939.

S.C.App.1987. Harris v. Campbell 358 S.E.2d 719, 293 S.C. 85.

Mass.1986. Department of Youth Services v. A Juvenile 499 N.E.2d 812, 398 Mass. 516.

Pa.Super.1986. Pascone v. Thomas Jefferson University 516 A.2d 384, 357 Pa.Super. 524.

Idaho App.1985. State v. Garza 704 P.2d 944, 109 Idaho 40.

Idaho App.1984. State v. Crabb 688 P.2d 1203, 107 Idaho 298.

§ 15. Expert's Opinion Based on Reports of Others and Inadmissible or Unadmitted Data and Facts

D.C.Conn.1985. Reardon v. Manson 617 F.Supp. 932.

N.J.1990. Ryan v. KDI Sylvan Pools, Inc. 579 A.2d 1241, 121 N.J. 276.

Ala.Cr.App.1989. Wesley v. State 575 So.2d 108.

Pa.Super.1989. In re Glosser Bros., Inc. 555 A.2d 129, 382 Pa.Super. 177.

Del.Super., 1988. Ramada Inns, Inc. v. Dow Jones & Co., Inc. 1988 WL 25375.

D.C.App.1987. Clifford v. U.S. 532 A.2d 628.

Wis.App.1986. Bagnowski v. Preway, Inc. 405 N.W.2d 746, 138 Wis.2d 241.

D.C.App.1986. Matter of Samuels 507 A.2d 150.

Idaho App.1985. Long v. Hendricks 705 P.2d 78, 109 Idaho 73.

§ 16. Should the Hypothetical Question Be Retained?

Wis.1988. State v. Jensen 432 N.W.2d 913, 147 Wis.2d 240.

D.C.App.1987. Clifford v. U.S. 532 A.2d 628.

Pa.1987. Kozak v. Struth 531 A.2d 420, 515 Pa. 554.

§ 17. Proposals for Improvement of the Practice Relating to Expert Testimony

E.D.N.Y.,1991. Joint Eastern and Southern District Asbestos Litigation v. Blinken 129 B.R. 710.

Del.Ch., 1990. Matter of Shell Oil Co. 1990 WL 201390.

Wis.1988. State v. Jensen 432 N.W.2d 913, 147 Wis.2d 240.

Del.Ch., 1985. Kahn v. United States Sugar Corporation 1985 WL 4449.

§ 18. Application of the Opinion Rule to Out-of-Court Statements

C.A.9 (Cal.)1986. U.S. v. Owens 789 F.2d 750.

Or.1990. Washington v. Taseca Homes, Inc. 802 P.2d 70, 310 Or. 783.

CHAPTER 4. CROSS–EXAMINATION AND SUBSEQUENT EXAMINATIONS

§ 19. The Right of Cross–Examination: Effect of Deprivation of Opportunity to Cross-Examine

Cl.Ct.1989. Clark v. Secretary of the Dept. of Health and Human Services 19 Cl.Ct. 113.

Wis.App.1990. Matter of Guardianship of R.S. 454 N.W.2d 1, 154 Wis.2d 706.

Mass.1989. Com. v. Kirouac 542 N.E.2d 270, 405 Mass. 557.

La.1988. State ex rel. Nicholas v. State 520 So.2d 377.

Mass.1987. Roche v. Massachusetts Bay Transp. Authority 508 N.E.2d 614, 400 Mass. 217.

N.C.1985. State v. Burgin 329 S.E.2d 653, 313 N.C. 404.

§ 20. Form of Interrogation

C.A.6 (Ky.)1987. U.S. v. Slone 833 F.2d 595.

Md.App.1991. Lancaster v. State 585 A.2d 274, 86 Md.App. 74.

§ 21. Scope of Cross–Examination: Restriction to Matters Opened Up on Direct: The Various Rules

U.S.S.C.1989. Perry v. Leeke 109 S.Ct. 594, 488 U.S. 272, 102 L.Ed.2d 624.

Tenn.App., 1989. Frye v. Frye 1989 WL 79160.

Wis.App., 1986. State v. Platek 395 N.W.2d 832 (Table), 133 Wis.2d 480, Unpublished Disposition.(*)

§ 22. Cross–Examination to Impeach Not Limited to the Scope of the Direct

D.C.App.1991. 2101 Wisconsin Associates v. District of Columbia Dept. of Employment Services 586 A.2d 1221.

Me.1986. Colony Cadillac & Oldsmobile, Inc. v. Yerdon 505 A.2d 98.

Mo.1985. State v. Johnson 700 S.W.2d 815.

§ 23. Practical Consequences of the Restrictive Rules: Effect on Order of Proof: Side–Effects

§ 24. The Scope of the Judge's Discretion Under the Wide–Open and Restrictive Rules

C.A.7 (Ill.)1990. U.S. v. Carter 910 F.2d 1524.

§ 25. Application of Wide–Open and Restrictive Rules to the Cross–Examination of Parties—(a) Civil Parties

§ 26. Application of Wide–Open and Restrictive Rules to the Cross–Examination of Parties—(b) The Accused in a Criminal Case

U.S.S.C.1989. Perry v. Leeke 109 S.Ct. 594, 488 U.S. 272, 102 L.Ed.2d 624.

§ 27. Merits of the Systems of Wide–Open and Restricted Cross–Examination

Md., 1991. Domingues v. Johnson 593 A.2d 1133.

§ 28. Cross–Examination About Witness's Inconsistent Past Writings: Must Examiner Show the Writing to the Witness Before Questioning About Its Contents?

§ 29. The Standard of Relevancy as Applied on Cross–Examination: Trial Judge's Discretion

Mich.1990. People v. Cetlinski 460 N.W.2d 534, 435 Mich. 742.

La.App. 2 Cir.1990. State v. Harrison 560 So.2d 450.

Or.App.1987. State v. Hart 733 P.2d 469, 84 Or.App. 160.

§ 30. The Cross–Examiner's Art

C.A.7 (Wis.)1985. U.S. v. Cerro 775 F.2d 908.

Colo.1986. People v. Collins (Two Cases) 730 P.2d 293.

§ 31. Cross–Examination Revalued

N.H.1989. Petition of Sprague 564 A.2d 829, 132 N.H. 250.

§ 32. Redirect and Subsequent Examinations

Ohio App., 1989. Stachura v. Doctors Hosp., Inc. 1989 WL 75748.

Vt.1988. State v. Recor 549 A.2d 1382, 150 Vt. 40.

Conn.1987. State v. Jones 534 A.2d 1199, 205 Conn. 638.

Wis.App., 1987. State v. Mayr 414 N.W.2d 320 (Table), 141 Wis.2d 976, Unpublished Disposition.(*)

Pa.Super.1986. Com. v. Johnson 512 A.2d 1242, 355 Pa.Super. 123.

Conn.1986. State v. Graham 509 A.2d 493, 200 Conn. 9.

Pa.Super.1986. Hawthorne v. Dravo Corp., Keystone Div. 508 A.2d 298, 352 Pa.Super. 359.

CHAPTER 5. IMPEACHMENT AND SUPPORT

§ 33. Introductory: The Stages of Impeachment and the Modes of Attack

C.A.9 (Nev.)1987. U.S. v. Behanna 814 F.2d 1318.

D.C.App., 1991. R. & G. Orthopedic Appliances and Prosthetics, Inc., v. Curtin, —— A.2d ——, 1991 WL 165284.

Colo.1990. People v. Williams 790 P.2d 796.

Del.Super., 1990. Wilkerson v. Chevrier 1990 WL 35275.

Ind.App. 4 Dist 1990. Brinegar v. Robertson Corp. 550 N.E.2d 812.

Ind.App. 1 Dist 1989. Spaulding v. State 533 N.E.2d 597.

Miss.1988. Wyeth Laboratories, Inc. v. Fortenberry 530 So.2d 688.

Ill.1988. People v. James 528 N.E.2d 723, 123 Ill.2d 523, 124 Ill.Dec. 35.

N.C.App.1988. State v. Anderson 364 S.E.2d 163, 88 N.C.App. 545.

Ind.App. 1 Dist 1987. Hughes v. State 508 N.E.2d 1289.

Pa.Super.1987. Bolus v. United Penn Bank (Two Cases) 525 A.2d 1215, 363 Pa.Super. 247.

Pa.1987. Williams v. McClain 520 A.2d 1374, 513 Pa. 300.

Pa.Super.1987. Dion v. Graduate Hosp. of University of Pennsylvania 520 A.2d 876, 360 Pa.Super. 416.

D.C.App.1986. Bassil v. U.S. 517 A.2d 714.

Ind.App. 1 Dist 1986. Summers v. State 495 N.E.2d 799.

Ohio App., 1985. State v. York 1985 WL 8502.

Md.App.1985. Cordovi v. State 492 A.2d 1328, 63 Md.App. 455.

Pa.Super.1985. Com. v. Shands 487 A.2d 973, 338 Pa.Super. 296.

§ 34. Prior Inconsistent Statements: Degree of Inconsistency Required

C.A.9 (Nev.)1989. U.S. v. Van Griffin 874 F.2d 634.

Colo.1990. Burlington Northern R. Co. v. Hood 802 P.2d 458.

Minn.1990. Hunt v. Regents of University of Minnesota 460 N.W.2d 28.

Conn.1990. State v. Alvarez 579 A.2d 515, 216 Conn. 301.

Minn.1990. State v. Gray 456 N.W.2d 251.

N.Y.1990. People v. Hults 557 N.Y.S.2d 270, 76 N.Y.2d 190, 556 N.E.2d 1077.

Conn.1989. State v. Torres 556 A.2d 1013, 210 Conn. 631.

N.Y.A.D. 4 Dept. 1988. Carriage House Motor Inn, Inc. (Motel Property) v. City of Watertown 524 N.Y.S.2d 930, 136 A.D.2d 895.

Colo.1987. Montoya v. People 740 P.2d 992.

Nev.1986. Summers v. State 718 P.2d 676, 102 Nev. 195.

Ohio App., 1986. State v. Buck 1986 WL 2993.

Fla.App. 3 Dist.1985. Green v. State 475 So.2d 1294, 10 Fla.L.Week. 2165.

§ 35. Prior Inconsistent Statements: Opinion in Form

Conn.App.1988. Hartmann v. Black & Decker Mfg. Co. 547 A.2d 38, 16 Conn. App. 1.

§ 36. Prior Inconsistent Statements: Extrinsic Evidence: Previous Statements as Substantive Evidence of the Facts Stated

[Treated in §§ 36 and 39 in the 3rd Ed.]

C.A.10 (Okl.)1991. U.S. v. Walker 930 F.2d 789.

Minn.1990. State v. Gray 456 N.W.2d 251.

Del.Supr., 1989. Wei v. State 571 A.2d 788 (Table), Unpublished Disposition.(*)

Pa.Super.1989. In re Glosser Bros., Inc. 555 A.2d 129, 382 Pa.Super. 177.

La.1987. State v. Fernandez 513 So.2d 1185.

Conn.1986. State v. O'Neill 511 A.2d 321, 200 Conn. 268.

Tenn.Cr.App., 1986. State v. Daly 1986 WL 828.

§ 37. Prior Inconsistent Statements: Requirement of Preliminary Questions on Cross–Examination as "Foundation" for Proof by Extrinsic Evidence

C.A.10 (Wyo.)1987. U.S. v. Soundingsides 820 F.2d 1232.

Tenn.App., 1991. Belew v. Gilmer 1991 WL 45396.

Fla.App. 1 Dist.1990. Annis v. First Union Nat. Bank of Florida 566 So.2d 273.

W.Va.1990. State v. King 396 S.E.2d 402.

D.C.App.1988. Chaabi v. U.S. 544 A.2d 1247.

Conn.1988. State v. Butler 543 A.2d 270, 207 Conn. 619.

Colo.1987. Montoya v. People 740 P.2d 992.

La.1986. State v. Davis 498 So.2d 723.

§ 38. Prior Inconsistent Statements: Rule Against Impeaching One's Own Witness

C.A.5 (La.)1990. Herbert v. Wal–Mart Stores, Inc. 911 F.2d 1044.

Tex.Cr.App., 1990. Johnson v. State 1990 WL 208091.

Tex.Cr.App.1990. Russeau v. State 785 S.W.2d 387.

S.C.1989. State v. Bailey 377 S.E.2d 581, 298 S.C. 1.

La.1987. State v. Fernandez 513 So.2d 1185.

Tex.App. Eastland 1987. Stills v. State 728 S.W.2d 422.

Conn.1986. State v. Whelan 513 A.2d 86, 200 Conn. 743.

Mich.1986. People v. Standifer 390 N.W.2d 632, 425 Mich. 543.

Conn.1986. State v. Jasper 508 A.2d 1387, 200 Conn. 30.

Mo.1985. Rowe v. Farmers Ins. Co., Inc. 699 S.W.2d 423.

§ 39. Partiality

[Treated in § 40 in the 3rd Ed.]

W.D.N.C., 1991. U.S. v. Stamper 766 F.Supp. 1396.

C.A.2 (N.Y.) 1991. U.S. v. Weiss 930 F.2d 185.

C.A.4 (N.C.), 1988. U.S. v. Johnson 850 F.2d 690 (Table), 25 Fed.R.Evid.Serv. 1444, Unpublished Disposition.(*)

U.S.1984. U.S. v. Abel 105 S.Ct. 465, 469 U.S. 45, 83 L.Ed.2d 450.

R.I., 1991. State v. Texter 594 A.2d 376.

Tenn.Cr.App., 1991. State v. Williams 1991 WL 89844.

Mo.App.1990. State v. Hedrick 797 S.W.2d 823.

Minn.1990. State v. Bergeron 452 N.W.2d 918.

Ind.App. 1 Dist 1990. Lenover v. State 550 N.E.2d 1328.

Minn.App.1989. Hunt v. Regents of University of Minnesota 446 N.W.2d 400.

Minn.1989. State v. Blasus 445 N.W.2d 535.

Conn.1989. State v. Oehman 562 A.2d 493, 212 Conn. 325.

Md.1989. Pettie v. State 560 A.2d 577, 316 Md. 509.

N.Y.1988. People v. Hudy 538 N.Y.S.2d 197, 73 N.Y.2d 40, 535 N.E.2d 250.

Ohio App.1988. State v. Williams 573 N.E.2d 704, 61 Ohio App.3d 594.

Ark.1988. Bowden v. State 761 S.W.2d 148, 297 Ark. 160.

Wis.App., 1987. State v. Gross 419 N.W.2d 574 (Table), 142 Wis.2d 946, Unpublished Disposition.(*)

Okl.Cr.1987. Croney v. State 748 P.2d 34.

Ark.1987. Smith v. State 722 S.W.2d 853, 291 Ark. 163.

Ariz.1986. Dombey v. Phoenix Newspapers, Inc. 724 P.2d 562, 150 Ariz. 476.

Or.App.1986. State v. Barfield 720 P.2d 394, 79 Or.App. 688.

D.C.App.1985. Matter of C.B.N. 499 A.2d 1215.

D.C.App.1985. Washington v. U.S. 499 A.2d 95.

Ariz.1985. State v. Bracy 703 P.2d 464, 145 Ariz. 520.

§ 40. Character: In General

[Treated in § 41 in the 3rd Ed.]

Mo.App., 1991. State v. Watts 1991 WL 152989.

Tenn.Cr.App., 1988. State v. Mathis 1988 WL 23938.

Mo.1985. State v. Johnson 700 S.W.2d 815.

Neb.1985. State v. Williams 365 N.W.2d 414, 219 Neb. 587.

§ 41. Character: Misconduct, for Which There Has Been No Criminal Conviction

[Treated in § 42 in the 3rd Ed.]

C.A.10 (Okl.)1990. U.S. v. Bowie 892 F.2d 1494.

S.D., 1991. Larson v. Kreiser's, Inc. 472 N.W.2d 761.

Ark.App., 1989. Mullins v. State 1989 WL 64190.

Nev.1988. Berner v. State 765 P.2d 1144, 104 Nev. 695.

Vt.1988. State v. Larose 554 A.2d 227, 150 Vt. 363.

Nev.1988. Bostic v. State 760 P.2d 1241, 104 Nev. 367.

N.Y.1987. People v. Betts 520 N.Y.S.2d 370, 70 N.Y.2d 289, 514 N.E.2d 865.

Conn.App.1987. State v. McIntosh 530 A.2d 191, 12 Conn.App. 179.

Conn.1986. State v. Martin 513 A.2d 116, 201 Conn. 74.

Conn.App.1986. State v. Horton 513 A.2d 168, 8 Conn.App. 376.

N.M.App.1985. State v. Vigil 711 P.2d 28, 103 N.M. 583.

Pa.Super.1985. Com. v. Pacell 497 A.2d 1375, 345 Pa.Super. 203.

Neb.1985. State v. Williams 365 N.W.2d 414, 219 Neb. 587.

S.C.App.1985. State v. Hale 326 S.E.2d 418, 284 S.C. 348.

§ 42. Character: Conviction of Crime

[Treated in § 43 in the 3rd Ed.]

U.S.1989. Green v. Bock Laundry Mach. Co. 109 S.Ct. 1981, 490 U.S. 504, 104 L.Ed.2d 557.

C.A.7 (Ill.)1987. Campbell v. Greer 831 F.2d 700.

C.A.8 (Mo.) 1986. U.S. v. Brown 794 F.2d 365.

C.A.7 (Ill.) 1985. U.S. v. Fountain 768 F.2d 790.

Cal.App. 2 Dist.1991. People v. Wheeler 281 Cal.Rptr. 758, 230 Cal.App.3d 1406.

N.M.App., 1991. State v. Mares 812 P.2d 1341.

Md.1990. State v. Watson 580 A.2d 1067, 321 Md. 47.

Alaska 1990. State v. Wickham 796 P.2d 1354.

Wash.1989. State v. Brown 782 P.2d 1013, 113 Wash.2d 520.

Utah 1989. State v. Bruce 779 P.2d 646.

Vt.1989. State v. Goodrich 564 A.2d 1346, 151 Vt. 367.

Mich.1988. People v. Finley 431 N.W.2d 19, 431 Mich. 506.

Md.App.1988. Brown v. State 547 A.2d 1099, 76 Md.App. 630.

N.J.Super.A.D.1988. State v. Onysko 545 A.2d 226, 226 N.J.Super. 599.

Wash.1988. State v. Brown 761 P.2d 588, 111 Wash.2d 124.

Miss.1988. Johnson v. State 529 So.2d 577.

Md.1988. Prout v. State 535 A.2d 445, 311 Md. 348.

Okl.Cr.1987. Croney v. State 748 P.2d 34.

Mo.App.1987. State v. Arney 731 S.W.2d 36.

Tenn.App., 1987. Copley v. Davis 1987 WL 9161.

Conn.1987. State v. Crumpton 520 A.2d 226, 202 Conn. 224.

Minn.App.1987. State v. Yeager 399 N.W.2d 648.

Wyo.1985. Vaupel v. State 708 P.2d 1248.

Md.1985. Foster v. State 499 A.2d 1236, 304 Md. 439.

Me.1985. State v. Chase 490 A.2d 208.

Tex.App. 4 Dist. 1985. Texas Employers' Ins. Ass'n v. Olivarez 694 S.W.2d 92.

Cal.1985. People v. Castro 211 Cal.Rptr. 719, 38 Cal.3d 301, 696 P.2d 111.

Ariz.App.1984. Wilson v. Riley Whittle, Inc. 701 P.2d 575, 145 Ariz. 317.

Or.1984. State v. McClure 692 P.2d 579, 298 Or. 336.

§ 43. Character: Impeachment by Proof of Opinion or Bad Reputation

[Treated in § 44 in the 3rd Ed.]

C.A.D.C.1984. Ollman v. Evans 750 F.2d 970, 242 U.S.App.D.C. 301.

Conn.App.1988. State v. Petterson 551 A.2d 763, 17 Conn.App. 174.

Tex.Cr.App.1985. Nethery v. State 692 S.W.2d 686.

§ 44. Defects of Capacity: Sensory or Mental

[Treated in § 45 in the 3rd Ed.]

Ohio App., 1991. State v. Boggs 1991 WL 13735.

Fla.1989. Edwards v. State 548 So.2d 656.

D.C.App.1988. Durant v. U.S. 551 A.2d 1318.

Tenn.App., 1988. Gotwald v. Gotwald 1988 WL 120778.

Tenn.App.1988. Gotwald v. Gotwald 768 S.W.2d 689.

Minn.App.1988. Seelye v. State 429 N.W.2d 669.

R.I.1987. State v. Carrera 528 A.2d 331.

R.I.1987. State v. Burke 522 A.2d 725.

N.Y.Sup.1987. People v. Fappiano 512 N.Y.S.2d 301, 134 Misc.2d 693.

N.J.Super.A.D.1987. State v. Johnson 524 A.2d 826, 216 N.J.Super. 588.

Kan.1986. State v. Hicks 729 P.2d 1146, 240 Kan. 302.

Ohio App., 1986. State v. Meeker 1986 WL 9077.

§ 45. Impeachment by "Contradiction"

[Treated in § 47 in the 3rd Ed.]

C.A.2 (N.Y.)1991. Berkovich v. Hicks 922 F.2d 1018.

C.A.5 (La.)1988. Roussell v. Jeane 842 F.2d 1512.

C.A.2 (N.Y.)1988. Rosario v. Kuhlman 839 F.2d 918.

C.A.S.D.1985. U.S. v. LeAmous 754 F.2d 795.

Ark.App., 1991. Sanchez v. State 1991 WL 39880.

Fla.App. 1 Dist.1990. Faucher v. R.C.F. Developers 569 So.2d 794.

D.C.App.1990. Patterson v. U.S. 580 A.2d 1319.

D.C.App.1990. Ware v. U.S. 579 A.2d 701.

Conn.1988. Demers v. State 547 A.2d 28, 209 Conn. 143.

Neb.1988. State v. Watkins 419 N.W.2d 660, 227 Neb. 677.

Miss.1987. Clark v. State 514 So.2d 1221.

Wis.App., 1987. State v. Stomner 414 N.W.2d 318 (Table), 141 Wis.2d 973, Unpublished Disposition.(*)

Colo.1986. Banek v. Thomas 733 P.2d 1171.

Idaho App.1986. State v. Howard 730 P.2d 1030, 112 Idaho 110.

Me.1986. State v. Leonard 513 A.2d 1352.

Mo.App.1986. State v. Willis 706 S.W.2d 265.

N.H.1986. State v. Dukette 506 A.2d 699, 127 N.H. 540.

N.H.1985. State v. Brooks 495 A.2d 1258, 126 N.H. 618.

Md.App.1985. Cordovi v. State 492 A.2d 1328, 63 Md.App. 455.

Mich.App.1984. McMiddleton v. Otis Elevator Co. 362 N.W.2d 812, 139 Mich.App. 418.

§ 46. Beliefs Concerning Religion

[Treated in § 48 in the 3rd Ed.]

§ 47. Supporting the Witness

[Treated in § 49 in the 3rd Ed.]

C.A.3 (Pa.)1991. U.S. v. Gambino 926 F.2d 1355.

C.A.4 (N.C.)1990. U.S. v. Bolick 917 F.2d 135.

C.A.2 (N.Y.)1988. U.S. v. Cosentino 844 F.2d 30.

Wis.App.1991. State v. Anderson 471 N.W.2d 279.

Tex.Cr.App.1990. Duckett v. State 797 S.W.2d 906.

Md.App.1990. Cole v. State 574 A.2d 326, 83 Md.App. 279.

Pa.Super.1989. Com. v. Smith 567 A.2d 1080, 389 Pa.Super. 626.

La.1989. State v. Smith 554 So.2d 676.

Ohio App., 1989. State v. Blunt 1989 WL 101050.

Wis.1989. State v. Johnson 439 N.W.2d 122, 149 Wis.2d 418.

Tex.Cr.App.1989. Beathard v. State 767 S.W.2d 423.

Ill.App. 2 Dist.1989. People v. Chambers 534 N.E.2d 554, 179 Ill.App.3d 565.

Idaho App.1989. Pierson v. Brooks 768 P.2d 792, 115 Idaho 529.

Wis.App., 1988. State v. Cetnarowski 434 N.W.2d 623 (Table), 147 Wis.2d 884, Unpublished Disposition.(*)

Wis.App., 1988. State v. Johnson 430 N.W.2d 379 (Table), 145 Wis.2d 905, Unpublished Disposition.(*)

Mich.1988. People v. Straight 424 N.W.2d 257, 430 Mich. 418.

Ark.App.1988. Pennington v. State 749 S.W.2d 680, 24 Ark.App. 70.

D.C.App.1988. Sweat v. U.S. 540 A.2d 460.

Ind.1988. Fox v. State 520 N.E.2d 429.

Conn.App.1987. State v. Daley 526 A.2d 14, 11 Conn.App. 185.

Or.1986. State v. Carr 725 P.2d 1287, 302 Or. 20.

Ala.Cr.App.1986. Varner v. State 497 So.2d 1135.

Ark.1986. Rock v. State 708 S.W.2d 78, 288 Ark. 566.

Ark.App.1985. Maples v. State 698 S.W.2d 807, 16 Ark.App. 175.

Neb.1985. State v. Johnson 370 N.W.2d 136, 220 Neb. 392.

§ 48. Attacking the Supporting Character Witness

[This § new in 4th Ed.]

§ 49. Contradiction: Collateral and Non–Collateral Matters: Good Faith Basis

[This § new in 4th Ed.]

§ 50. Exclusion and Separation of Witnesses

[This § new in 4th Ed.]

CHAPTER 6. THE PROCEDURE OF ADMITTING AND EXCLUDING EVIDENCE

§ 51. Presentation of Evidence: Offer of Proof

U.S.Fla.1988. Beech Aircraft Corp. v. Rainey 109 S.Ct. 439, 488 U.S. 153.

C.A.4 (Md.), 1987. U.S. v. Orekyeh 812 F.2d 1402 (Table), Unpublished Disposition.(*)

C.A.Or.1984. Paddack v. Dave Christensen, Inc. 745 F.2d 1254.

Wis.1991. Milwaukee Rescue Mission, Inc. v. Redevelopment Authority of City of Milwaukee 468 N.W.2d 663, 161 Wis.2d 472.

Conn.App.1990. Streicher v. Resch 570 A.2d 230, 20 Conn.App. 714.

La.1989. State v. Adams 550 So.2d 595.

S.C.1989. Roberts v. Roberts 384 S.E.2d 719, 299 S.C. 315.

N.Y.A.D. 4 Dept.1988. Benderson Development Co., Inc. v. State 529 N.Y.S.2d 50, 139 A.D.2d 927.

Ind.1986. Reames v. State 497 N.E.2d 559.

Me.1986. State v. Zadakis 511 A.2d 1074.

Ariz.1986. State v. Bay 722 P.2d 280, 150 Ariz. 112.

§ 52. Objections

C.A.9 (Nev.), 1990. Minato v. Scenic Airlines, Inc. 908 F.2d 977 (Table), Unpublished Disposition.(*)

C.A.9 (Cal.)1990. U.S. v. Gomez–Norena 908 F.2d 497.

Bkrtcy.D.Mass.1988. In re Lewis 94 B.R. 789.

C.A.5 (La.)1985. U.S. v. Marshall 762 F.2d 419.

D.C.App., 1991. Hill v. United States ___ A.2d ___, 1991 WL 108356.

Idaho App.1991. State v. Johnson 810 P.2d 1138, 119 Idaho 852.

D.C.App.1990. Wilkins v. U.S. 582 A.2d 939.

N.J.Super.A.D.1990. State In Interest of J.H. 581 A.2d 1347, 244 N.J.Super. 207.

N.C.App.1990. Webster v. Powell 391 S.E.2d 204, 98 N.C.App. 432.

D.C.App.1990. Mack v. U.S. 570 A.2d 777.

Tex.App. Tyler 1989. White v. State 784 S.W.2d 453.

Tex.1989. State Bar of Texas v. Evans 774 S.W.2d 656.

Md.App.1989. Turgut v. Levine 556 A.2d 720, 79 Md.App. 279.

Md.App.1988. Hickman v. State 543 A.2d 870, 76 Md.App. 111.

Md.1988. Prout v. State 535 A.2d 445, 311 Md. 348.

Ohio App., 1987. Stepp v. Ray 1987 WL 14654.

Conn.App.1987. Cohen v. Cohen 527 A.2d 245, 11 Conn.App. 241.

Del.Super., 1987. Good v. Bautista 1987 WL 12439.

Tex.Cr.App.1987. Polk v. State 729 S.W.2d 749.

Md.App.1987. In re Owen F. 523 A.2d 627, 70 Md.App. 678.

Ark.App., 1987. Johnson v. State 1987 WL 8912.

Neb.1987. State v. Roggenkamp 402 N.W.2d 682, 224 Neb. 914.

Idaho App.1986. Davidson v. Beco Corp. 733 P.2d 781, 112 Idaho 560.

Ind.1986. Reames v. State 497 N.E.2d 559.

D.C.App.1986. Crooks v. Williams 508 A.2d 912.

§ 53. Preliminary Questions of Fact Arising on Objections

C.A.10, 1991. Burke v. Board of Governors ___ F.2d ___, 1991 WL 140169.

U.S.Ohio 1987. Bourjaily v. U.S. 107 S.Ct. 2775, 483 U.S. 171, 97 L.Ed.2d 144.

D.Mass.1987. U.S. v. Dray 659 F.Supp. 1426.

C.A.D.C.1985. U.S. v. Singleton 759 F.2d 176, 245 U.S.App.D.C. 156.

N.H., 1991. Riverwood Commercial Properties, Inc. v. Cole 1991 WL 135955.

Or.1991. State v. Carlson 808 P.2d 1002, 311 Or. 201.

Wis.1990. State v. DeSantis 456 N.W.2d 600, 155 Wis.2d 774.

Kan.1990. State v. Butterworth 792 P.2d 1049, 246 Kan. 541.

Neb.1990. In re Interest of M.L.S. 452 N.W.2d 39, 234 Neb. 570.

Mich.1989. People v. Burton 445 N.W.2d 133, 433 Mich. 268.

Md.1989. Kosmas v. State 560 A.2d 1137, 316 Md. 587.

N.Y.City Crim.Ct.1989. People v. Serrano 539 N.Y.S.2d 845, 142 Misc.2d 1087.

Wyo.1987. Burke v. State 746 P.2d 852.

Colo.1987. People v. Romero 745 P.2d 1003.

Colo.1984. People v. Gallegos 692 P.2d 1074.

Mass.App.Ct.1986. Com. v. Allen 494 N.E.2d 55, 22 Mass.App.Ct. 413.

§ 54. Availability as Proof of Evidence Admitted Without Objection

C.A.5 (La.)1989. U.S. v. Yamin 868 F.2d 130.

C.A.1 (R.I.)1988. Willco Kuwait (Trading) S.A.K. v. deSavary (Two Cases) 843 F.2d 618.

M.D.La.1989. Walsh v. City Mortg. Services, Inc. 102 B.R. 502.

Tex.Cr.App.1991. Fernandez v. State 805 S.W.2d 451.

Conn.App.1987. Cohen v. Cohen 527 A.2d 245, 11 Conn.App. 241.

Fla.App. 1 Dist.1986. Tri-State Systems, Inc. v. Department of Transp. 500 So.2d 212.

Fla.App. 3 Dist.1985. Southeastern Fire Ins. Co. v. King's Way Mortg. Co. 481 So.2d 530.

Ind.App. 3 Dist.1985. Porter Memorial Hosp. v. Malak 484 N.E.2d 54.

Me.1985. State v. Liberty 498 A.2d 257.

§ 55. Waiver of Objection

D.C.App.1988. Howard University v. Best 547 A.2d 144.

Ohio App., 1987. State v. Malcolm 1987 WL 19243.

Ark.App., 1987. Johnson v. State 1987 WL 8912.

Me.1985. State v. Liberty 498 A.2d 257.

§ 56. The Effect of the Introduction of Part of a Writing or Conversation

C.A.4 (Md.)1988. Merrick v. Mercantile Safe Deposit & Trust Co. 855 F.2d 1095.

Wyo.1987. Ramirez v. State 739 P.2d 1214.

Ind.1987. Duff v. State 508 N.E.2d 17.

Neb.1987. Chirnside By and Through Waggoner v. Lincoln Tel. & Tel. Co. 401 N.W.2d 489, 224 Neb. 784.

Ill.1985. People v. Williams 487 N.E.2d 613, 109 Ill.2d 327.

Mich.1985. Moody v. Pulte Homes, Inc. 378 N.W.2d 319, 423 Mich. 150.

Md.App.1985. Newman v. State 499 A.2d 492, 65 Md.App. 85.

§ 57. Fighting Fire With Fire: Inadmissible Evidence as Opening the Door

C.A.D.C.1990. U.S. v. Brown 921 F.2d 1304.

C.A.9 (Cal.)1988. U.S. v. Whitworth 856 F.2d 1268.

D.C.Pa.1984. Pearsall v. Emhart Industries, Inc. 599 F.Supp. 207.

Iowa, 1991. State v. Jones 471 N.W.2d 833.

Pa.Super.1989. Com. v. Hoyman 561 A.2d 756, 385 Pa.Super. 439.

Iowa 1988. Lala v. Peoples Bank & Trust Co. of Cedar Rapids 420 N.W.2d 804.

Utah 1988. State v. Speer 750 P.2d 186.

R.I.1987. State v. Burke 529 A.2d 621.

Ark.1986. McFadden v. State 717 S.W.2d 812, 290 Ark. 177.

D.C.App.1986. Lampkins v. U.S. 515 A.2d 428.

Md.1986. Booth v. State 507 A.2d 1098, 306 Md. 172.

Mass.App.1985. Com. v. Ruffen 485 N.E.2d 190, 21 Mass.App. 90.

§ 58. Admissibility of Evidence Dependent on Proof of Other Facts: "Connecting Up"

Okl.Cr.1988. McClellan v. State 762 P.2d 281.

Neb.1987. State v. Copple 401 N.W.2d 141, 224 Neb. 672.

§ 59. Evidence Admissible for One Purpose, Inadmissible for Another: "Limited Admissibility"

C.A.9 (Nev.), 1990. Minato v. Scenic Airlines, Inc. 908 F.2d 977 (Table), Unpublished Disposition.(*)

C.A.3 (Pa.) 1989. U.S. v. Parcel of Real Property Known as 6109 Grubb Road, Millcreek Tp., Erie County, Pa. 886 F.2d 618.

Ill.App. 1 Dist.1989. People v. Leaks 534 N.E.2d 491, 179 Ill.App.3d 231.

Vt.1988. State v. Fortier 547 A.2d 1327, 149 Vt. 599.

Mich.App.1988. Bonelli v. Volkswagen of America, Inc. 421 N.W.2d 213, 166 Mich. App. 483.

§ 60. Admission and Exclusion of Evidence in Trials Without a Jury

C.A.3 (Pa.)1989. U.S. v. Parcel of Real Property Known as 6109 Grubb Road, Millcreek Tp., Erie County, Pa. 886 F.2d 618.

C.A.7 (Ill.)1987. Greycas, Inc. v. Proud 826 F.2d 1560.

N.Y.A.D. 4 Dept.1991. People v. Di Fabio 566 N.Y.S.2d 172.

Del.Super., 1990. Hynson v. Autoport, Inc. 1990 WL 18325.

Mich.1988. People v. Adams 425 N.W.2d 437, 430 Mich. 679.

Fla.App. 3 Dist.1985. Southeastern Fire Ins. Co. v. King's Way Mortg. Co. 481 So.2d 530.

CHAPTER 7. THE COMPETENCY OF WITNESSES

§ 61. In General

C.A.10 (Utah)1990. U.S. v. Bedonie 913 F.2d 782.

§ 62. Mental Incapacity and Immaturity: Oath or Affirmation

C.A.8 (S.D.)1989. U.S. v. Spotted War Bonnet 882 F.2d 1360.

R.I.1989. State v. Girouard 561 A.2d 882.

Mich.App.1989. People v. Kosters 438 N.W.2d 651, 175 Mich.App. 748.

Pa.Super.1988. Com. v. Anderson 552 A.2d 1064, 381 Pa.Super. 1.

Mo.1987. State v. Williams 729 S.W.2d 197.

Pa.Super.1987. Com. v. Stohr 522 A.2d 589, 361 Pa.Super. 293.

Fla.App. 3 Dist.1986. Zabrani v. Riveron 495 So.2d 1195.

Md.1985. Evans v. State 499 A.2d 1261, 304 Md. 487.

D.C.App.1985. In re A.H.B. 491 A.2d 490.

R.I.1985. State v. Pettis 488 A.2d 704.

W.Va.1984. Burdette v. Lobban 323 S.E.2d 601.

§ 63. Religious Belief

§ 64. Conviction of Crime

Md.1985. Evans v. State 499 A.2d 1261, 304 Md. 487.

§ 65. Parties and Persons Interested: The Dead Man Statutes

Minn.1990. State v. Bergeron 452 N.W.2d 918.

W.Va.1989. Cross v. State Farm Mut. Auto. Ins. Co. 387 S.E.2d 556.

W.Va.1988. Moore v. Goode 375 S.E.2d 549.

Or.1988. Equitable Life Assur. Soc. of the U.S. v. McKay 760 P.2d 871, 306 Or. 493.

Vt.1988. In re Estate of Farr 552 A.2d 387, 150 Vt. 196.

Ariz.App.1986. Imperial Litho/Graphics v. M.J. Enterprises 730 P.2d 245, 152 Ariz. 68.

§ 66. Husbands and Wives of Parties

D.Colo.1987. In re Grand Jury 851 666 F.Supp. 196.

Conn.1989. State v. James 560 A.2d 426, 211 Conn. 555.

Wash.App.1988. State v. Wood 758 P.2d 530, 52 Wash.App. 159.

Pa.1987. Com. v. Scott 532 A.2d 426, 516 Pa. 346.

Mich.1986. People v. Love 391 N.W.2d 738, 425 Mich. 691.

§ 67. Incompetency of Husband and Wife to Give Testimony on Non–Access

§ 68. Judges, Jurors, and Lawyers

Colo.1990. Ravin v. Gambrell 788 P.2d 817.

Del.Super.1988. McLain v. General Motors Corp. 586 A.2d 647.

Neb.1988. State v. Barker 420 N.W.2d 695, 227 Neb. 842.

Neb.1987. Rahmig v. Mosley Machinery Co. 412 N.W.2d 56, 226 Neb. 423.

Colo.1987. People v. Tippett 733 P.2d 1183.

§ 69. Firsthand Knowledge and Expertness

C.A.D.C.1989. U.S. v. Burnett 890 F.2d 1233, 281 U.S.App.D.C. 428.

Ind.App. 3 Dist 1991. Osborne v. Wenger 572 N.E.2d 1343.

Pa.Super.1986. Hawthorne v. Dravo Corp., Keystone Div. 508 A.2d 298, 352 Pa.Super. 359.

§ 70. The Procedure of Disqualification

§ 71. Probable Future of the Rules of Competency

CHAPTER 8. THE SCOPE AND EFFECT OF THE EVIDENTIARY PRIVILEGES

§ 72. The Purposes of Rules of Privilege

C.A.9 (Cal.)1988. Gubiensio-Ortiz v. Kanahele 857 F.2d 1245, 57 U.S.L.W. 2136.

C.A.6 (Tenn.),1988. U.S. v. Harris 852 F.2d 569 (Table), Unpublished Disposition.(*)

Mich.1989. People v. Hamacher 438 N.W.2d 43, 432 Mich. 157.

Ill.1988. People v. Foggy 521 N.E.2d 86, 121 Ill.2d 337, 118 Ill.Dec. 18.

Ala., 1987. Handley v. Richards 518 So.2d 682.

Ill.App. 4 Dist.1987. Illinois Educational Labor Relations Bd. v. Homer Community Consol. School Dist. No. 208 514 N.E.2d 465, 160 Ill.App.3d 730, 112 Ill. Dec. 802.

Tex.App. Fort Worth 1987. Tarrant County Hosp. Dist. v. Hughes 734 S.W.2d 675.

Mo.App.1987. Hester v. Barnett 723 S.W.2d 544.

Ala.1987. Ex parte Rudder 507 So.2d 411.

D.C.App.1986. Arnold v. U.S. 511 A.2d 399.

§ 73. Procedural Recognition of Rules of Privilege

Ala.Cr.App.1986. Watson v. State 504 So.2d 339.

§ 74. Limitations on the Effectiveness of Privileges

Ill.1988. People v. Foggy 521 N.E.2d 86, 121 Ill.2d 337, 118 Ill.Dec. 18.

Ala.Cr.App.1987. Thornton v. State 527 So.2d 143.

Mass.1986. Com. v. Two Juveniles 491 N.E.2d 234, 397 Mass. 261.

Colo.1985. Williams v. District Court, El Paso County 700 P.2d 549.

§ 75. The Sources of Privilege

Mass.1988. Babets v. Secretary of Executive Office of Human Services 526 N.E.2d 1261, 403 Mass. 230.

§ 76. The Current Pattern of Privilege

Idaho 1985. Matter of Contempt of Wright 700 P.2d 40, 108 Idaho 418.

§ 77. The Future of Privilege

Ala.1987. Ex parte Rudder 507 So.2d 411.

CHAPTER 9. THE PRIVILEGE FOR
MARITAL COMMUNICATIONS

§ 78. History and Background
and Kindred Rules

E.D.Pa., 1990. Fallowfield Development Corp. v. Strunk 1990 WL 52749.

Mont.1988. State v. Nettleton 760 P.2d 733, 233 Mont. 308.

§ 79. What Is Privileged: Communications Only, or Acts and Facts?

Minn.1990. State v. Hannuksela 452 N.W.2d 668.

Vt.1989. State v. Wright 581 A.2d 720, 154 Vt. 512.

Ind.1988. Kindred v. State 524 N.E.2d 279.

Ill.1988. People v. Foggy 521 N.E.2d 86, 121 Ill.2d 337.

§ 80. The Communication Must Be Confidential

Mich.1989. People v. Hamacher 438 N.W.2d 43, 432 Mich. 157.

Mich.1989. People v. Vermeulen 438 N.W.2d 36, 432 Mich. 32.

§ 81. The Time of Making the Communication: Marital Status

Mich.1989. People v. Vermeulen 438 N.W.2d 36, 432 Mich. 32.

Okl.Cr.1988. Blake v. State 765 P.2d 1224.

§ 82. Hazards of Disclosure to Third Persons Against the Will of the Communicating Spouse

Ala.Cr.App.1990. Ellis v. State 570 So.2d 744.

Mich.1989. People v. Hamacher 438 N.W.2d 43, 432 Mich. 157.

Mo.1986. State v. Heistand 708 S.W.2d 125.

§ 83. Who Is the Holder of the Privilege? Enforcement and Waiver

Mich.1989. People v. Hamacher 438 N.W.2d 43, 432 Mich. 157.

Conn.1988. State v. Pierson 546 A.2d 268, 208 Conn. 683.

§ 84. Controversies in Which the Privilege Is Inapplicable

§ 85. If the Communication Was Made During the Marriage, Does Death or Divorce End the Privilege?

§ 86. Policy and Future of the Privilege

C.A.6 (Tenn.),1988. U.S. v. Harris 852 F.2d 569 (Table), Unpublished Disposition.(*)

Mich.1989. People v. Hamacher 438 N.W.2d 43, 432 Mich. 157.

Wash.App.1988. State v. Wood 758 P.2d 530, 52 Wash.App. 159.

Tex.App.Dallas 1988. Pope v. State 756 S.W.2d 401.

CHAPTER 10. THE CLIENT'S PRIVILEGE:
COMMUNICATIONS BETWEEN
CLIENT AND LAWYER

§ 87. Background and Policy of the Privilege

C.A.Mo.1984. Pritchard–Keang Nam Corp. v. Jaworski 751 F.2d 277.

N.D.Ill.1987. Abbott Laboratories v. Baxter Travenol Laboratories, Inc. 676 F.Supp. 831.

Fla.App. 3 Dist.1990. Adelman v. Adelman 561 So.2d 671.

McCormick, Evidence 4th Ed. Vol. 2 PT—28

N.Y.1989. Rossi v. Blue Cross and Blue Shield of Greater New York 542 N.Y.S.2d 508, 73 N.Y.2d 588, 540 N.E.2d 703.

Tex.App. Dallas 1989. Manning v. State 766 S.W.2d 551.

Wash.1988. State v. Maxon 756 P.2d 1297, 110 Wash.2d 564.

La.1987. Succession of Bilwood Smith v. Kavanaugh, Pierson & Talley 513 So.2d 1138.

Ala.1987. Ex parte Rudder 507 So.2d 411.

Del.Super.1986. Ramada Inns, Inc. v. Dow Jones & Co., Inc. 523 A.2d 968.

Hawaii 1986. DiCenzo v. Izawa 723 P.2d 171.

§ 88.   The Professional Relationship

C.A.10 (Kan.) 1989. Wylie v. Marley Co. 891 F.2d 1463.

N.J.1991. State v. Marshall 586 A.2d 85, 123 N.J. 1.

Wyo.1990. Brooks v. Zebre 792 P.2d 196.

Mo.App.1990. State v. Longo 789 S.W.2d 812.

Ariz.App.1989. Foulke v. Knuck 784 P.2d 723, 162 Ariz. 517.

N.J.Super.A.D.1989. In re Maraziti 559 A.2d 447, 233 N.J.Super. 488.

Ariz.1988. Matter of Pappas 768 P.2d 1161, 159 Ariz. 516.

N.Y.A.D. 2 Dept.1987. Seeley v. Seeley 514 N.Y.S.2d 110, 129 A.D.2d 625.

La.1986. Louisiana State Bar Ass'n v. Bosworth 481 So.2d 567, Rehearing Denied.

Wash.App.1985. Intercapital Corp. of Oregon v. Intercapital Corp. of Washington 700 P.2d 1213.

Mo.App.1984. St. Louis Little Rock Hosp., Inc. v. Gaertner 682 S.W.2d 146.

§ 89.   Subject–Matter of the Privilege— (a) Communications

W.D.N.C., 1991. U.S. v. Stamper 766 F.Supp. 1396.

E.D.Pa., 1989. Lipson v. Snyder 1989 WL 79779.

La.1987. State v. Taylor 502 So.2d 537.

La.1986. State v. Green 493 So.2d 1178.

La., 1986. State v. Taylor 502 So.2d 534, Rehearing Granted.

Ariz.1986. Bishop v. Superior Court, In and For Pima County 724 P.2d 23, 150 Ariz. 404.

Pa.Super.1985. In re Gartley 491 A.2d 851, 341 Pa.Super. 350.

§ 90.   Subject Matter of the Privilege— (b) Fact of Employment and Identity of the Client

C.A.11 (Fla.)1990. In re Grand Jury Proceedings 896 F.2d 1267.

C.A.9 (Ariz.)1986. In re Grand Jury Subpoenas 803 F.2d 493.

Or.App.1988. State v. Keenan 756 P.2d 51, 91 Or.App. 481.

Tenn.App., 1986. Anderson v. Anderson 1986 WL 14442.

§ 91.   The Confidential Character of the Communications: Presence of Third Persons and Agents: Joint Consultations and Employments: Controversies Between Client and Attorney

C.A.3 (Pa.)1989. U.S. v. Furst 886 F.2d 558.

S.D.N.Y., 1988. Solomon v. Scientific American, Inc. 125 F.R.D. 34.

N.D.Ill.1987. In re Consolidated Litigation Concerning Intern. Harvester's Disposition of Wisconsin Steel 666 F.Supp. 1148.

C.A.D.C.1984. Eureka Inv. Corp., N.V. v. Chicago Title Ins. Co. 743 F.2d 932.

Ill., 1991. Waste Management, Inc. v. International Surplus Lines Ins. Co. 1991 WL 80956.

Mass.App.Ct.1989. Com. v. Anolik 542 N.E.2d 327.

Wyo.1987. Oil, Chemical and Atomic Workers Intern. Union v. Sinclair Oil Corp. 748 P.2d 283.

Utah 1985. Hofmann v. Conder 712 P.2d 216.

Or.1985. State v. Miller 709 P.2d 225, 300 Or. 203.

§ 92.   The Client as the Holder of the Privilege: Who May Assert, and Who Complain on Appeal of Its Denial?

C.A.N.J.1984. Klitzman, Klitzman and Gallagher v. Krut 744 F.2d 955.

Conn.App.1991. In re Sean H. 586 A.2d 1171, 24 Conn.App. 135.

Idaho App.1988. State v. Guinn 752 P.2d 632, 114 Idaho 30.

Wash.App.1986. Olson v. Haas 718 P.2d 1.

§ 93. Waiver

N.D.Ill.1987. In re Consolidated Litigation Concerning Intern. Harvester's Disposition of Wisconsin Steel 666 F.Supp. 1148.

N.D.Ill., 1986. Brainerd & Bridges v. Weingeroff Enterprise, Inc. 1986 WL 10638.

Mass.App.Ct.1988. Com. v. Woodberry 530 N.E.2d 1260.

Mont.1987. State v. Statczar 743 P.2d 606, 228 Mont. 446.

La.1987. Succession of Bilwood Smith v. Kavanaugh, Pierson & Talley 513 So.2d 1138.

N.Y.1985. People v. Wilkins 490 N.Y.S.2d 759, 65 N.Y.2d 172, 480 N.E.2d 373.

Fla.App. 3 Dist.1984. Hoyas v. State 456 So.2d 1225.

§ 94. The Effect of the Death of the Client

§ 95. Consultation in Furtherance of Crime or Fraud

C.A.11 (Fla.)1991. In re Federal Grand Jury Proceedings, 89–10 (MIA) 938 F.2d 1578.

D.C.Pa.1988. U.S. v. Moscony 697 F.Supp. 888.

C.A.2 1986. In re Grand Jury Subpoenas Duces Tecum 798 F.2d 32.

C.A.Mo.1984. Pritchard–Keang Nam Corp. v. Jaworski 751 F.2d 277.

Alaska 1990. Central Const. Co. v. Home Indem. Co. 794 P.2d 595.

Del.Super.1988. Tackett v. State Farm Fire and Cas. 558 A.2d 1098.

Wash.App.1986. Whetstone v. Olson 732 P.2d 159.

§ 96. Protective Rules Relating to Materials Collected for Use of Counsel in Preparation for Trial: Reports of Employees, Witness–Statements, Experts' Reports, and the Like

Bkrtcy.N.D.Ill.1989. In re Grabill Corp. 103 B.R. 996.

Mo.App.1985. May Dept. Stores Co. v. Ryan 699 S.W.2d 134.

Mo.App.1984. St. Louis Little Rock Hosp., Inc. v. Gaertner 682 S.W.2d 146.

§ 97. Discovery in Criminal Cases: Statements by Witnesses

Fla.App. 3 Dist.1990. Adelman v. Adelman 561 So.2d 671.

Mo.App.1987. State ex rel. Missouri Highway and Transp. Com'n v. Dooley 738 S.W.2d 457.

CHAPTER 11. THE PRIVILEGE FOR CONFIDENTIAL INFORMATION SECURED IN THE COURSE OF THE PHYSICIAN–PATIENT RELATIONSHIP

§ 98. The Statement of the Rule and Its Purpose

Mich.1990. People v. Perlos 462 N.W.2d 310, 436 Mich. 305.

N.Y.1989. Dillenbeck v. Hess 539 N.Y.S.2d 707, 73 N.Y.2d 278, 536 N.E.2d 1126.

Wis.App.1985. State ex rel. Klieger v. Alby 373 N.W.2d 57, 125 Wis.2d 468.

Tex.1985. Ginsberg v. Fifth Court of Appeals 686 S.W.2d 105.

Or.1984. State ex rel. Grimm v. Ashmanskas 690 P.2d 1063, 298 Or. 206.

§ 99. Relation of Physician and Patient

C.A.10 (Wyo.)1989. Harvey By and Through Harvey v. General Motors Corp. 873 F.2d 1343.

Kan.App.1985. State v. Pitchford 697 P.2d 896.

§ 100. Subject Matter of the Privilege: Information Acquired in Attending the Patient and Necessary for Prescribing

La., 1990. State v. McElroy 568 So.2d 1016.

Vt.1988. Ley v. Dall 553 A.2d 562, 150 Vt. 383.

Ark.App.1984. Horne v. State 677 S.W.2d 856.

§ 101. The Confidential Character of the Disclosure: Presence of Third Persons and Members of Family: Information Revealed to Nurses and Attendants: Public Records

La., 1990. State v. McElroy 568 So.2d 1016.

Minn.App.1990. State v. Kunz 457 N.W.2d 265.

La.1989. State v. McElroy 553 So.2d 456.

Ariz.App.1988. Hospital Corp. of America v. Superior Court of Pima County 755 P.2d 1198, 157 Ariz. 210.

Mo.App.1987. State v. Shirley 731 S.W.2d 49.

Or.1985. State v. Miller 709 P.2d 225, 300 Or. 203.

Ark.App.1984. Horne v. State 677 S.W.2d 856.

§ 102. Rule of Privilege, Not Incompetency: Privilege Belongs to the Patient, Not to an Objecting Party as Such: Effect of the Patient's Death

Wash.App.1990. Sauter v. Mount Vernon School Dist. No. 320, Skagit County 791 P.2d 549.

Ariz.1989. State v. Dumaine 783 P.2d 1184, 162 Ariz. 392.

Wis.App.1989. State v. Echols 449 N.W.2d 320, 152 Wis.2d 725.

§ 103. What Constitutes a Waiver of the Privilege?

Colo.App.1989. People v. Silva 782 P.2d 846.

Ariz.App.1987. Danielson v. Superior Court of State of Ariz. In and For Maricopa County 754 P.2d 1145, 157 Ariz. 41.

§ 104. Kinds of Proceedings Exempted From the Application of the Privilege

§ 105. The Policy and Future of the Privilege

Wyo.1990. Gale v. State 792 P.2d 570.

Vt.1989. State v. Chenette 560 A.2d 365, 151 Vt. 237.

N.Y.1989. Dillenbeck v. Hess 539 N.Y.S.2d 707, 73 N.Y.2d 278, 536 N.E.2d 1126.

Ark.1989. Oxford v. Hamilton 763 S.W.2d 83, 297 Ark. 512.

Del.Super.1985. Green v. Bloodsworth 501 A.2d 1257.

CHAPTER 12. PRIVILEGES FOR GOVERNMENTAL SECRETS

§ 106. Other Principles Distinguished

Md.App.1989. Laws v. Thompson 554 A.2d 1264, 78 Md.App. 665.

§ 107. The Common Law Privileges for Military or Diplomatic Secrets and Other Facts the Disclosure of Which Would Be Contrary to the Public Interest

C.A.D.C.1984. Northrop Corp. v. McDonnell Douglas Corp. 751 F.2d 395.

§ 108. Qualified Privileges for Government Information: The Constitutional Presidential Privilege: Common Law Privileges for Agency Deliberations and Law Enforcement Files

Del.Super., 1989. Lefferts v. J.C. Penney Co. 1989 WL 89652.

N.Y.1989. Dillenbeck v. Hess 539 N.Y.S.2d 707, 73 N.Y.2d 278, 536 N.E.2d 1126.

§ 109. Effect of the Presence of the Government as a Litigant

S.D.N.Y.1991. Department of Economic Development v. Arthur Andersen & Co. v. Fetherston, — F.R.D. —, 1991 WL 217882.

§ 110. The Scope of the Judge's Function in Determining the Validity of the Claim of Privilege

Mass.App.1985. Cleary v. Commission of Public Welfare 485 N.E.2d 955, 21 Mass. App. 140.

§ 111. The Privilege Against the Disclosure of the Identity of an Informer

Fla.App. 3 Dist.1989. State v. Villar 554 So.2d 576.

N.J.1986. Grodjesk v. Faghani 514 A.2d 1328, 104 N.J. 89.

§ 112. Statutory Privileges for Certain Reports of Individuals to Government Agencies: Accident Reports, Tax Returns, etc.

§ 113. The Secrecy of Grand Jury Proceedings: (a) Votes and Expressions of Grand Jurors: (b) Testimony of Witnesses

Md.App.1989. Laws v. Thompson 554 A.2d 1264, 78 Md.App. 665.

CHAPTER 13. THE PRIVILEGE AGAINST SELF–INCRIMINATION

§ 114. The History of the Privilege: (a) Origin of the Common Law Privilege

C.A.Cal.1985. U.S. v. Flores 753 F.2d 1499.

§ 115. The History of the Privilege: (b) Development of the Privilege in America

§ 116. The History of the Privilege: (c) Development of the Two Branches of the Privilege—The Privilege of an Accused in a Criminal Proceeding and the Privilege of a Witness

[Treated in §§ 116 and 135 in the 3rd Ed.]

Kan.App., 1988. State v. Bates 761 P.2d 335 (Table).(*)

Tex.Cr.App.1988. Marroquin v. State 746 S.W.2d 747.

Fla.App. 5 Dist.1987. M.S.S. by Blackwell v. DeMaio 503 So.2d 1384.

S.D.1986. State v. Helling 391 N.W.2d 648.

Ohio App., 1986. Matter of Kuhn 1986 WL 2992.

§ 117. The History of the Privilege: (d) Current Status of the Privilege

Md.1989. Adkins v. State 557 A.2d 203, 316 Md. 1.

§ 118. Policy Foundations of the Modern Privilege

Md.1987. Adams v. Mallory 520 A.2d 371, 308 Md. 453.

§ 119. Procedural Manner of Effectuating the Privilege

§ 120. Personal Nature of the Privilege

Ill.App. 1 Dist.1986. People v. Johnson 502 N.E.2d 304, 150 Ill.App.3d 1075, 104 Ill.Dec. 41.

§ 121. General Scope of the Privilege: (a) Protection Against Criminal Liability

Minn.App.,1990. State v. Bland 1990 WL 81404.

§ 122. General Scope of the Privilege: (b) Requirement of a "Real and Appreciable" Risk of Incrimination

[Treated in § 123 in the 3rd Ed.]

D.C.App.1985. Yeager v. Greene 502 A.2d 980.

§ 123. General Scope of the Privilege: (c) Incrimination Under the Laws of Another Jurisdiction

[Treated in § 122 in the 3rd Ed.]

D.C.App.1985. Yeager v. Greene 502 A.2d 980.

§ 124. General Scope of the Privilege: (d) Activity Compelled Must Be "Testimonial"

Pa.Super.1986. Com. v. Romesburg 509 A.2d 413, 353 Pa.Super. 215.

D.C.App.1985. Yeager v. Greene 502 A.2d 980.

§ 125. General Scope of the Privilege: (e) Compulsion

§ 126. General Scope of the Privilege: (f) Burdens on Exercise of the Privilege

[This § new in 4th Ed.]

§ 127. The Privilege as Related to Documents and Tangible Items: (a) Limits on Use of "Private" Papers

§ 128. The Privilege as Related to Documents and Tangible Items: (b) Compulsory Production

[Treated in § 126 in the 3rd Ed.]

§ 129. The Privilege as Related to Corporations, Associations, and Their Agents: (a) The Privilege of the Organization

[Treated in § 128 in the 3rd Ed.]

§ 130. The Privilege as Related to Corporations, Associations, and Their Agents: (b) Agents' Ability to Invoke Their Personal Privilege

[Treated in § 129 in the 3rd Ed.]

§ 131. The Privilege of an Accused in a Criminal Proceeding: (a) Definition of an Accused in a Criminal Proceeding

[Treated in § 130 in the 3rd Ed.]

C.A.10 1986. Roach v. National Transp. Safety Bd. 804 F.2d 1147.

Conn.App.1990. State v. Lynch 574 A.2d 230.

N.J.Super.A.D.1988. State v. Bogus 538 A.2d 1278.

§ 132. The Privilege of an Accused in a Criminal Proceeding: (b) Inferences From and Comment Upon the Accused's Reliance Upon the Privilege

[Treated in § 131 in the 3rd Ed.]

Md.1989. Hardaway v. State 562 A.2d 1234, 317 Md. 160.

Mass.App.Ct.1987. Com. v. Sherick 502 N.E.2d 156.

§ 133. The Privilege of an Accused in a Criminal Proceeding: (c) Instructing the Jury Regarding the Privilege

[This § new in 4th Ed.]

§ 134. The Privilege of an Accused in a Criminal Proceeding: (d) "Waiver" of the Privilege by Voluntary Testimony

[Treated in § 132 in the 3rd Ed.]

N.M.App., 1991. State v. Delgado 815 P.2d 631.

Mo.App.1988. State ex rel. Imboden v. Romines 760 S.W.2d 130.

§ 135. Special Problems: (a) Limits on Compelled Defense Disclosure to the Prosecution Imposed by the Privilege

[Treated in § 133 in the 3rd Ed.]

§ 136. Special Problems: (b) Psychiatric Examinations of the Criminal Defendant

[Treated in § 134 in the 3rd Ed.]

§ 137. The Privilege of a Witness: (a) Invoking the Privilege

[Treated in § 136 in the 3rd Ed.]

C.A.10 1991. Burke v. Board of Governors of Federal Reserve System 940 F.2d 1360.

E.D.Pa., 1990. General Elec. Capital Corp. v. Alden 1990 WL 40853.

E.D.Mich.1988. Fireman's Fund Ins. Companies v. ExCello Corp. 702 F.Supp. 1317.

C.A.10 1986. Roach v. National Transp. Safety Bd. 804 F.2d 1147.

C.A.6 (Mich.)1985. Rogers v. Webster 776 F.2d 607.

Kan.App., 1988. State v. Bates 761 P.2d 335 (Table).(*)

§ 138. The Privilege of a Witness: (b) The Right to Be Warned and to Counsel

[Treated in § 137 in the 3rd Ed.]

§ 139. The Privilege of a Witness: (c) Determination Whether a Specific Response Would Be Incriminatory

[Treated in §§ 138 and 139 in the 3rd Ed.]

Bkrtcy.E.D.Pa.1988. In re J.M.V., Inc. 90 B.R. 737.

Md.1989. Adkins v. State 557 A.2d 203, 316 Md. 1.

Kan.App., 1988. State v. Bates 761 P.2d 335 (Table).(*)

Colo.App.1986. Union Ins. Co. v. RCA Corp. 724 P.2d 80.

§ 140. The Privilege of a Witness: (d) "Waiver" by Disclosure of Incriminating Facts

Bkrtcy.E.D.Pa.1988. In re J.M.V., Inc. 90 B.R. 737.

Kan.App., 1988. State v. Bates 761 P.2d 335 (Table).(*)

Tex.App.Austin 1988. Chandler v. State 744 S.W.2d 341.

Wis.App.1987. State v. Whiting 402 N.W.2d 723, 136 Wis.2d 400.

N.J.Super.A.D.1986. State v. Kobrin Securities, Inc. 516 A.2d 1130, 213 N.J.Super. 161.

N.Y.1986. People v. Chin 499 N.Y.S.2d 638, 67 N.Y.2d 22, 490 N.E.2d 505.

Okl.Cr.1985. Roubideaux v. State 707 P.2d 35.

Tex.Cr.App.1984. Grayson v. State 684 S.W.2d 691.

§ 141. Agreement to Waive the Privilege

§ 142. The "Required Records" Exception

§ 143. Removing the Danger of Incrimination: Immunity and Immunity Statutes

CHAPTER 14. CONFESSIONS

§ 144. "Confessions" and Admissibility

C.A.3 (Virgin Islands)1991. Government of Virgin Islands v. Harris 938 F.2d 401.

Wash.1986. City of Bremerton v. Corbett 723 P.2d 1135, 106 Wash.2d 569.

Va.1986. Caminade v. Com. 338 S.E.2d 846, 230 Va. 505.

W.Va.1985. State v. Clark 331 S.E.2d 496.

§ 145. Corroboration and Independent Proof of the *Corpus Delicti.*

C.A.3 (Virgin Islands)1991. Government of Virgin Islands v. Harris 938 F.2d 401.

C.A.10 (Utah)1989. U.S. v. Shunk 881 F.2d 917.

C.A.7 (Wis.)1988. U.S. v. Kerley 838 F.2d 932.

Ill.1990. People v. Furby 563 N.E.2d 421, 138 Ill.2d 434, 150 Ill.Dec. 534.

Ind.1990. Willoughby v. State 552 N.E.2d 462.

Ark.1990. Hart v. State 783 S.W.2d 40, 301 Ark. 200.

Mo.App.1989. Hooker v. State 775 S.W.2d 303.

Or.1988. State v. Manzella 759 P.2d 1078, 306 Or. 303.

Wash.1986. City of Bremerton v. Corbett 723 P.2d 1135, 106 Wash.2d 569.

N.C.1985. State v. Parker 337 S.E.2d 487, 315 N.C. 222.

Pa.Super.1985. Com. v. McCabe 498 A.2d 933, 345 Pa.Super. 495.

Ind.App. 2 Dist 1985. Groves v. State 479 N.E.2d 626.

§ 146. Voluntariness (a) The Common Law Rule

§ 147. Voluntariness (b) Modern Standards

[This § name is new in 4th Ed, but covers same material as in 3rd Ed.]

§ 148. Self–Incrimination Standards (a) *Miranda* Requirements

[Treated in §§ 150, 152, 153 and 154 in the 3rd Ed.]

Iowa App.1989. State v. McKowen 447 N.W.2d 546.

Tenn.Cr.App., 1989. State v. Mudrich 1989 WL 21799.

§ 149. Self–Incrimination Requirements (b) Applicability of *Miranda*

[Treated in § 151 in the 3rd Ed.]

§ 150. Self–Incrimination Requirements (c) Prohibition Against Interrogation

[Treated in § 152 in the 3rd Ed.]

Tenn.Cr.App., 1989. State v. Mudrich 1989 WL 21799.

§ 151. Self–Incrimination Requirements (d) Voluntariness of Waivers

[Treated in § 153 in the 3rd Ed.]

§ 152. Self–Incrimination Requirements (e) Intelligence of Waivers

[Treated in § 153 in the 3rd Ed.]

Iowa App.1989. State v. McKowen 447 N.W.2d 546.

§ 153. General Right to Counsel Requirements

[Treated in § 155 in the 3rd Ed.]

§ 154. Promises Made to Suspects

[Treated in §§ 148 and 153 in the 3rd Ed.]

§ 155. Deception of Suspects

[Treated in §§ 149 and 153 in the 3rd Ed.]

§ 156. Delay in Presenting Arrested Person Before Magistrate

§ 157. Confessions as "Fruit" of Improper Arrests or Detentions

§ 158. Evidence Obtained as Result of Inadmissible Confessions

§ 159. Judicial Confessions, Guilty Pleas, and Admissions Made in Plea Bargaining

W.Va.1988. State v. Bennett 370 S.E.2d 120.

Idaho App.1987. State v. Simonson 732 P.2d 689, 112 Idaho 451.

§ 160. "Tacit" and "Adoptive" Confessions and Admissions

Md.App.1990. Wills v. State 573 A.2d 80, 82 Md.App. 669.

Conn.App.1989. State v. Daniels 556 A.2d 1040, 18 Conn.App. 134.

Conn.1988. State v. Walker 537 A.2d 1021, 206 Conn. 300.

Conn.1986. State v. Leecan 504 A.2d 480, 198 Conn. 517.

CHAPTER 15. THE PRIVILEGE CONCERNING IMPROPERLY OBTAINED EVIDENCE

§ 177. **Admissibility of Evidence With An "Independent Source"**

[Treated in § 176 in the 3rd Ed.]

N.Y.1985. People v. Johnson 497 N.Y.S.2d 618, 66 N.Y.2d 398.

§ 178. **Effect of Illegality Upon "Jurisdiction" Over Criminal Defendants**

[Treated in § 176 in the 3rd Ed.]

§ 179. **Exceptions to Exclusion (a) Attenuation of Taint**

[Treated in § 176 in the 3rd Ed.]

§ 180. **Exceptions to Exclusion (b) Inevitable Discovery**

[Treated in § 176 in the 3rd Ed.]

§ 181. **Exceptions to Exclusion (c) "Good Faith"**

[Treated in § 177 in the 3rd Ed.]

§ 182. **Exceptions to Exclusion (d) Use of Illegally Obtained Evidence to Impeach Testifying Defendant**

[Treated in § 178 in the 3rd Ed.]

§ 183. **Enforcement of the Right to Exclusion**

[Treated in §§ 180, 181 and 182 in the 3rd Ed.]

Hawaii 1989. State v. Kirn 767 P.2d 1238.

CHAPTER 16. RELEVANCE

§ 184. **Relevance as the Presupposition of Admissibility**

Ind.1989. Mitchell v. State 535 N.E.2d 498.

Ark.App.1984. Dooley v. Cecil Edwards Const. Co., Inc. 681 S.W.2d 399.

§ 185. **The Meaning of Relevancy and the Counterweights**

U.S.Wash.1985. U.S. v. Bagley 105 S.Ct. 3375, 473 U.S. 667, 87 L.Ed.2d 481.

C.A.3 (Pa.)1990. Bhaya v. Westinghouse Elec. Corp. 922 F.2d 184.

C.A.1 (Puerto Rico)1990. U.S. v. Maravilla 907 F.2d 216.

C.A.10 (Kan.)1989. U.S. v. Porter 881 F.2d 878.

C.A.9 (Cal.)1989. Miller v. Fairchild Industries, Inc. 876 F.2d 718.

C.A.9 (Cal.)1989. Miller v. Fairchild Industries, Inc. 885 F.2d 498.

C.A.4 (N.C.)1988. U.S. v. Workman 860 F.2d 140.

C.A.9 (Cal.)1988. U.S. v. Bowen 857 F.2d 1337.

C.A.6 (Mich.)1988. U.S. v. Schrock 855 F.2d 327.

C.A.7 (Ill.)1987. Sherrod v. Berry 827 F.2d 195.

C.A.6 (Tenn.)1986. U.S. v. Dunn 805 F.2d 1275.

C.A.10 (Colo.)1986. Hill v. Bache Halsey Stuart Shields Inc. 790 F.2d 817.

N.D.Ill.1988. Randle v. LaSalle Telecommunications, Inc. 697 F.Supp. 1474.

E.D.Tenn., 1987. Oody v. Aetna Cas. & Sur. Co. 1987 WL 43116.

C.D.Ill.1986. Jones v. Greer 627 F.Supp. 1481.

Neb., 1991. State v. Messersmith 473 N.W.2d 83, 238 Neb. 924.

D.C.App., 1991. Eric M. Collins, Appellant, v. United States, Appellee. ___ A.2d ___, 1991 WL 150179.

Md.App., 1991. Billman v. State of Md. Deposit Ins. Fund Corp. 593 A.2d 684, 88 Md.App. 79.

Tex.Cr.App., 1991. Mayes v. State 1991 WL 87589.

Md.1991. Krauss v. State 587 A.2d 1102, 322 Md. 376.

Fla.1991. Gillion v. State 573 So.2d 810.

Neb.1990. State v. Baltimore 463 N.W.2d 808, 236 Neb. 736.

Or.1990. State v. Clowes 801 P.2d 789, 310 Or. 686.

D.C.App.1990. Roundtree v. U.S. 581 A.2d 315.

Md.App.1990. Cook v. State 578 A.2d 283.

Ga.1990. McEachern v. McEachern 394 S.E.2d 92, 260 Ga. 320.

Pa.Super.1990. Com. v. Foy 576 A.2d 366, 394 Pa.Super. 442.

N.J.Super.A.D.1990. State v. Hutchins 575 A.2d 35, 241 N.J.Super. 353.

Wis.App., 1990. State v. Johnson (To be reported at: 458 N.W.2d 389 (Table), 156 Wis.2d 468 Unpublished Disposition.(*)

Md.App.1989. Harris v. State 567 A.2d 476.

La.1989. State v. Rogers 553 So.2d 453.

Ala.Cr.App.1989. Watley v. State 568 So.2d 852.

Md.1989. Wilson v. Morris 563 A.2d 392, 317 Md. 284.

Tenn.App.1989. Keith v. Murfreesboro Livestock Market, Inc. 780 S.W.2d 751.

N.J.1989. State v. Pitts 562 A.2d 1320, 116 N.J. 580.

R.I.1989. State v. Chiellini 557 A.2d 1195.

Ind.1989. Henson v. State 535 N.E.2d 1189.

Mich.1989. People v. LaLone 437 N.W.2d 611, 432 Mich. 103.

Ind.1989. Games v. State 535 N.E.2d 530.

N.Y.1988. People v. Hudy 538 N.Y.S.2d 197, 73 N.Y.2d 40, 535 N.E.2d 250.

Pa.Super.1988. Com. v. Copeland 554 A.2d 54, 381 Pa.Super. 382.

Md.1988. State v. Joynes 549 A.2d 380, 314 Md. 113.

Pa.Super.1988. Kearns by Kearns v. De-Haas 546 A.2d 1226, 377 Pa.Super. 200.

Del.Super., 1988. State v. Callaway 1988 WL 90541.

Fla.1988. State v. McClain 525 So.2d 420.

Neb.1988. State v. Oliva 422 N.W.2d 53, 228 Neb. 185.

Tex.App.Hous. (14 Dist.) 1988. Ahlschlager v. Remington Arms Co., Inc. 750 S.W.2d 832.

Wis.App., 1988. City Glass Co. v. Walia 423 N.W.2d 884 (Table), 143 Wis.2d 904, Unpublished Disposition.(*)

Wash.1988. State v. Ciskie 751 P.2d 1165.

Ga.1988. Polito v. Holland 365 S.E.2d 273, 258 Ga. 54.

Del.Supr.1988. Getz v. State 538 A.2d 726.

Ga.1988. Reynolds v. State 363 S.E.2d 249, 257 Ga. 725.

Mass.1987. Massachusetts Auto. Rating and Acc. Prevention Bureau v. Commissioner of Ins. 516 N.E.2d 1132, 401 Mass. 282.

Vt.1987. State v. Raymond 538 A.2d 164, 148 Vt. 617.

Pa.Super.1987. Com. v. McNeely 534 A.2d 778, 368 Pa.Super. 517.

Pa.1987. Lewis v. Coffing Hoist Div., Duff–Norton Co., Inc. 528 A.2d 590, 515 Pa. 334.

Del.Super., 1987. American Communications Installations Ltd. v. Emory 1987 WL 12429.

Idaho App.1987. State v. Winkler 736 P.2d 1371, 112 Idaho 917.

D.C.App.1987. Curry v. U.S. 520 A.2d 255.

Neb.1987. State v. Clancy 398 N.W.2d 710, 224 Neb. 492.

Md.1986. State v. Allewalt 517 A.2d 741, 308 Md. 89.

Utah 1986. State v. Smith 728 P.2d 1014.

Colo.App.1986. People v. Lucero 724 P.2d 1374.

Tenn.Cr.App., 1986. State v. Crawford 1986 WL 6638.

Hawaii 1986. Kaeo v. Davis 719 P.2d 387, 68 Haw. 447.

N.J.Super.A.D.1985. State v. Allison 504 A.2d 1184, 208 N.J.Super. 9.

Idaho App.1985. State v. Garza 704 P.2d 944, 109 Idaho 40.

Md.1985. Ellsworth v. Sherne Lingerie, Inc. 495 A.2d 348, 303 Md. 581.

Tex.Cr.App.1985. Plante v. State 692 S.W.2d 487.

Md.App.1985. Eiler v. State 492 A.2d 1320, 63 Md.App. 439.

Md.App.1985. Brittingham v. State 492 A.2d 354, 63 Md.App. 164.

Fla.App. 3 Dist. 1985. Stambor v. One Hundred Seventy–Second Collins Corp. 465 So.2d 1296.

Ark.App.1984. Dooley v. Cecil Edwards Const. Co., Inc. 681 S.W.2d 399, 13 Ark. App. 170.

CHAPTER 17. CHARACTER AND HABIT

§ 186. Character: In General

D.C.App.1989. Rogers v. U.S. 566 A.2d 69.

Pa.Super.1985. Carlson Min. Co. v. Titan Coal Co., Inc. 494 A.2d 1127, 343 Pa.Super. 364.

Pa.Super.1989. Butler v. FloRon Vending Co. 557 A.2d 730, 383 Pa.Super. 633.

Pa.Super.1988. Com. v. Norman 549 A.2d 981, 379 Pa.Super. 212.

Wyo.1987. Coleman v. State 741 P.2d 99.

Mich.App.1985. People v. Anderson 383 N.W.2d 186, 147 Mich.App. 789.

Tex.Cr.App.1989. James v. State 772 S.W.2d 84.

§ 187. Character in Issue

C.A.7 (Ill.)1988. U.S. v. Manos 848 F.2d 1427.

Wis.1991. State v. Daniels 465 N.W.2d 633, 160 Wis.2d 85.

Wis.App.1989. State v. Pence 442 N.W.2d 540, 150 Wis.2d 759.

Pa.Super.1985. Carlson Min. Co. v. Titan Coal Co., Inc. 494 A.2d 1127, 343 Pa.Super. 364.

§ 188. Character as Circumstantial Evidence: General Rule of Exclusion

Idaho App.1990. State v. Rodriguez 801 P.2d 1299, 118 Idaho 948.

Mo.App.1989. LaGue v. Farmers and Merchants Ins. Co. 779 S.W.2d 14.

Mass.1989. Com. v. De La Cruz 540 N.E.2d 168, 405 Mass. 269.

Minn.App.1989. Aitkin County Family Service Agency on Behalf of Wiebrand v. Gangl 441 N.W.2d 814.

Pa.Super.1988. Com. v. Norman 549 A.2d 981, 379 Pa.Super. 212.

Mo.App.1988. Williams v. Bailey 759 S.W.2d 394.

Mass.App.Ct.1987. Com. v. Doherty 504 N.E.2d 681.

Hawaii App.1986. Meyer v. City and County of Honolulu 729 P.2d 388, 6 Haw. App. 505.

Mich.1986. People v. Whitfield 388 N.W.2d 206, 425 Mich. 116.

N.C.App.1985. State v. McKoy 337 S.E.2d 666, 78 N.C.App. 531.

Ariz.1985. State v. Smith 707 P.2d 289, 146 Ariz. 491.

Pa.Super.1985. Carlson Min. Co. v. Titan Coal Co., Inc. 494 A.2d 1127, 343 Pa.Super. 364.

§ 189. Character for Care in Civil Cases

Tenn.App., 1987. Copley v. Davis 1987 WL 9161.

Fla.App. 1 Dist. 1985. Chambliss v. White Motor Corp. 481 So.2d 6.

Pa.Super.1985. Carlson Min. Co. v. Titan Coal Co., Inc. 494 A.2d 1127, 343 Pa.Super. 364.

§ 190. Bad Character as Evidence of Criminal Conduct: Other Crimes

C.A.5 (Miss.)1990. U.S. v. Brookins 919 F.2d 281.

C.A.8 (Mo.)1990. U.S. v. Drew 894 F.2d 965.

C.A.10 (Kan.)1989. U.S. v. Porter 881 F.2d 878.

C.A.3 (Pa.)1989. Lesko v. Owens 881 F.2d 44.

C.A.7 (Ill.)1989. U.S. v. Connelly 874 F.2d 412.

C.A.8 (Mo.)1988. Mercer v. Armontrout 844 F.2d 582.

C.A.11 (Ga.)1987. Brooks v. Scheib 813 F.2d 1191.

C.A.D.C.1985. U.S. v. Daniels 770 F.2d 1111, 248 U.S.App.D.C. 198.

C.A.D.C.1985. U.S. v. Lavelle 751 F.2d 1266, 243 U.S.App.D.C. 47.

C.A.N.Y.1984. U.S. v. Sliker 751 F.2d 477.

D.Del.1986. U.S. v. Hill 629 F.Supp. 493.

N.C., 1991. State v. Stager 406 S.E.2d 876.

Fla.App. 1 Dist., 1991. Flanagan v. State of Florida 1991 WL 133574.

Mont.1991. State v. Matt 814 P.2d 52.

Conn.App.1991. State v. Jenkins 588 A.2d 648, 24 Conn.App. 330.

Neb.1991. State v. Stephens 466 N.W.2d 781, 237 Neb. 551.

Md.App.1991. Kearney v. State 586 A.2d 746, 86 Md.App. 247.

Or.1991. State v. Pinnell 806 P.2d 110, 311 Or. 98.

Conn.App.1990. State v. Plaza 583 A.2d 925, 23 Conn.App. 543.

Utah App.1990. State v. Morrell 803 P.2d 292.

Idaho App.1990. State v. Rodriguez 801 P.2d 1299, 118 Idaho 948.

Minn.App.1990. State v. Cichon 458 N.W.2d 730.

W.Va.1990. State v. Gilbert 399 S.E.2d 851.

Tex.Cr.App.1990. Montgomery v. State 810 S.W.2d 372.

Fla.App. 3 Dist.1990. Lazarowicz v. State 561 So.2d 392.

Wash.1990. State v. Bythrow 790 P.2d 154, 114 Wash.2d 713.

Mich.1990. People v. Engelman 453 N.W.2d 656, 434 Mich. 204.

Ark.App.1990. Flowers v. State 785 S.W.2d 242, 30 Ark.App. 204.

Md.App.1990. McKinney v. State 570 A.2d 360, 82 Md.App. 111.

N.J.Super.A.D.1990. Burbridge v. Paschal 570 A.2d 1250, 239 N.J.Super. 139.

Utah App.1990. State v. Cox 787 P.2d 4.

Utah App.1990. State v. Moore 788 P.2d 525.

Md.App.1989. Harris v. State 567 A.2d 476, 81 Md.App. 247.

Mo.App.1989. State v. Burgess 780 S.W.2d 688.

Ill.1989. People v. McCarthy 547 N.E.2d 459, 132 Ill.2d 331, 138 Ill.Dec. 292.

Ill.1989. People v. Kokoraleis 547 N.E.2d 202, 132 Ill.2d 235, 138 Ill.Dec. 233.

Pa.Super.1989. Com. v. Newman 564 A.2d 1308, 388 Pa.Super. 146.

Wyo.1989. Pena v. State 780 P.2d 316.

Idaho App.1989. State v. Gauna 785 P.2d 647, 117 Idaho 83.

Ill.App. 4 Dist.1989. People v. Connolly 542 N.E.2d 517, 186 Ill.App.3d 429, 134 Ill.Dec. 338.

Hawaii 1989. State v. Pinero 778 P.2d 704, 70 Haw. 509.

Wyo.1989. Garcia v. State 777 P.2d 1091.

S.D.1989. State v. Perkins 444 N.W.2d 34.

N.J.1989. State v. Stevens 558 A.2d 833, 115 N.J. 289.

Mass.1989. Com. v. Cordle 537 N.E.2d 130, 404 Mass. 733.

Ind.1989. Clark v. State 536 N.E.2d 493.

R.I.1989. State v. Lassor 555 A.2d 339.

Hawaii 1989. State v. Austin 769 P.2d 1098, 70 Haw. 300.

Wis.App.1988. State v. Bedker 440 N.W.2d 802, 149 Wis.2d 257.

Md.1989. State v. Faulkner 552 A.2d 896, 314 Md. 630.

Wis.App.1989. State v. Kaster 436 N.W.2d 891, 148 Wis.2d 789.

Ala.1988. Bowden v. State 538 So.2d 1226.

D.C.App.1988. Williams v. U.S. 549 A.2d 328.

Or.App.1988. State v. Zybach 761 P.2d 1334, 93 Or.App. 218.

N.J.1988. State v. Schumann 545 A.2d 168, 111 N.J. 470.

Pa.1988. Com. v. Perkins 546 A.2d 42, 519 Pa. 149.

D.C.App.1988. Thompson v. U.S. 546 A.2d 414.

R.I.1988. State v. Mastracchio 546 A.2d 165.

Utah 1988. State v. Shickles 760 P.2d 291.

Conn.App.1988. State v. Perry 541 A.2d 1245, 14 Conn.App. 526.

Hawaii 1988. State v. Castro 756 P.2d 1033, 69 Haw. 633.

Ga.1988. Boyce v. State 366 S.E.2d 684, 258 Ga. 171.

Del.Super.,1988. Starkey v. HuntMadani Professional Associates, P.A. 1988 WL 33561.

Del.Supr.1988. Getz v. State 538 A.2d 726.

Ga.1988. Jones v. State 363 S.E.2d 529, 257 Ga. 753.

Tex.App.—Hous. (14 Dist.)1987. Dickerson v. State 745 S.W.2d 401.

D.C.App.1987. Easton v. U.S. 533 A.2d 904.

Va.App.1987. Marshall v. Com. 361 S.E.2d 634, 5 Va.App. 248.

Tex.App.—Hous. [14 Dist.],1987. Magic v. State 1987 WL 18794.

Tex.App.—Hous. [14 Dist.], 1987. Dickerson v. State 1987 WL 17689.

Miss.1987. Lockett v. State 517 So.2d 1317.

Conn.App.1987. State v. Carsetti 530 A.2d 1095, 12 Conn.App. 375.

Ala.Cr.App.1987. Watson v. State 538 So.2d 1216.

Ill.App. 1 Dist.1987. People v. Dougherty 513 N.E.2d 946, 160 Ill.App.3d 870, 112 Ill.Dec. 337.

D.C.App.1987. Bartley v. U.S. 530 A.2d 692.

Pa.1987. Com. v. Bryant 530 A.2d 83, 515 Pa. 473.

Wyo.1987. Coleman v. State 741 P.2d 99.

Vt.1987. State v. Catsam 534 A.2d 184, 148 Vt. 366.

Ill.App. 1 Dist.1987. People v. Bryan 511 N.E.2d 1289, 159 Ill.App.3d 46, 110 Ill. Dec. 969.

N.J.1987. State v. Weeks 526 A.2d 1077, 107 N.J. 396.

Wis.1987. State v. Evers 407 N.W.2d 256, 139 Wis.2d 424.

Wash.App.1987. State v. Bowen 738 P.2d 316, 48 Wash.App. 187.

Mo.App.1987. State v. Peters 732 S.W.2d 227.

W.Va.1987. State v. Smith 358 S.E.2d 188.

Colo.App.1987. People v. Adrian 744 P.2d 768.

Tenn.Cr.App., 1987. State v. Wilson 1987 WL 10404.

Mo.App.1987. State v. Rose 727 S.W.2d 919.

Ill.App. 4 Dist.1987. People v. Taylor 506 N.E.2d 321, 153 Ill.App.3d 710, 106 Ill. Dec. 614.

Idaho App.1987. State v. Simonson 732 P.2d 689, 112 Idaho 451.

Wis.1987. State v. Friedrich 398 N.W.2d 763, 135 Wis.2d 1.

Ark.1986. Snell v. State 721 S.W.2d 628, 290 Ark. 503.

R.I.1986. State v. Cruz 517 A.2d 237.

Wash.App.1986. State v. Gogolin 727 P.2d 683, 45 Wash.App. 640.

Mo.App.1986. State v. Chance 719 S.W.2d 108.

Wis.App., 1986. State v. Haley 392 N.W.2d 848 (Table), 132 Wis.2d 479, Unpublished Disposition.(*)

S.D.1986. State v. Helling 391 N.W.2d 648.

W.Va.1986. State v. Dolin 347 S.E.2d 208.

Wash.App.1986. State v. Holmes 717 P.2d 766, 43 Wash.App. 397.

Md.1986. Grandison v. State 506 A.2d 580, 305 Md. 685.

Me.1986. State v. DeLong 505 A.2d 803.

N.C.1986. State v. Morgan 340 S.E.2d 84, 315 N.C. 626.

Pa.Super.1985. Com. v. Vedam 502 A.2d 1383, 349 Pa.Super. 270.

Va.App.1985. Sutphin v. Com. 337 S.E.2d 897, 1 Va.App. 241.

Ariz.1985. State v. Smith 707 P.2d 289, 146 Ariz. 491.

R.I.1985. State v. Lemon 497 A.2d 713.

Conn.App.1985. State v. Gilnite 496 A.2d 525, 4 Conn.App. 676.

Pa.1985. Com. v. Claypool 495 A.2d 176, 508 Pa. 198.

Pa.Super.1985. Carlson Min. Co. v. Titan Coal Co., Inc. 494 A.2d 1127, 343 Pa.Super. 364.

Pa.Super.1985. Com. v. Campbell 493 A.2d 101, 342 Pa.Super. 438.

Md.1985. State v. Werner 489 A.2d 1119, 302 Md. 550.

Neb.1985. State v. Craig 361 N.W.2d 206, 219 Neb. 70.

Ariz.1984. State v. Roscoe 700 P.2d 1312, 145 Ariz. 212.

Mo.App.1984. State v. Perkins 680 S.W.2d 331.

§ 191. Good Character as Evidence of Lawful Conduct: Proof by the Accused and Rebuttal by the Government

C.A.10 (Kan.)1990. U.S. v. Daily 921 F.2d 994.

D.Kan., 1991. U.S. v. Leeseberg 767 F.Supp. 1091.

Vt.1991. State v. McCarthy 589 A.2d 869.

Md.1990. State v. Watson 580 A.2d 1067, 321 Md. 47.

Ark.App.1989. Lee v. State 770 S.W.2d 148, 27 Ark.App. 198.

Mass.App.Ct.1989. Com. v. Montanino 535 N.E.2d 617, 27 Mass.App.Ct. 130.

Colo.1988. People v. Pratt 759 P.2d 676.

Ga.1988. Boyce v. State 366 S.E.2d 684, 258 Ga. 171.

Tenn.Cr.App., 1988. State v. Mathis 1988 WL 23938.

Tenn.1988. State v. Sims 746 S.W.2d 191.

R.I.1987. State v. Oliviera 534 A.2d 867.

La.App. 1 Cir.1987. State v. Moten 510 So.2d 55.

W.Va.1987. State v. Banjoman 359 S.E.2d 331.

Wis.App., 1987. State v. Chiolino 407 N.W.2d 566 (Table), 139 Wis.2d 856, Unpublished Disposition.(*)

Idaho App.1986. State v. Lawrence 730 P.2d 1069, 112 Idaho 149.

Ill.App. 2 Dist. 1986. People v. Randle 498 N.E.2d 732, 147 Ill.App.3d 621, 101 Ill. Dec. 408.

Mass.App.1985. Com. v. Piedra 478 N.E.2d 1284, 20 Mass.App. 155.

Mo.1984. State v. Byrd 676 S.W.2d 494.

§ 192. Character in Civil Cases Where Crime Is in Issue

C.A.10 (Okl.)1986. Perrin v. Anderson 784 F.2d 1040.

Pa.Super.1985. Bell v. City of Philadelphia 491 A.2d 1386, 341 Pa.Super. 534.

§ 193. Character of Victims in Cases of Assault, Murder, and Rape

Wis.App., 1991. State v. Merriweather 1991 WL 150519, Unpublished Disposition.(*)

Wis.App., 1991. State v. Clifton 472 N.W.2d 247 (Table), Unpublished Disposition.(*)

Wis.1991. State v. Daniels 465 N.W.2d 633, 160 Wis.2d 85.

D.C.App.1990. District of Columbia v. Thompson 570 A.2d 277.

W.Va.1989. State v. Woodson 382 S.E.2d 519.

Mich.1989. People v. LaLone 437 N.W.2d 611, 432 Mich. 103.

Wis.App.1988. State v. Herndon 426 N.W.2d 347, 145 Wis.2d 91.

Miss.1987. Tolbert v. State 511 So.2d 1368.

Idaho 1985. State v. Dallas 710 P.2d 580, 109 Idaho 670.

§ 194. Evidence of Character to Impeach a Witness

C.A.6 (Mich.) 1988. Sparks v. Foltz 848 F.2d 194 (Table), Unpublished Disposition.(*)

Idaho 1990. Hake v. DeLane 793 P.2d 1230, 117 Idaho 1058.

§ 195. Habit and Custom as Evidence of Conduct on a Particular Occasion

C.A.7 (Ill.)1985. U.S. v. Mascio 774 F.2d 219.

La.App. 2 Cir.1991. State v. Flowers 574 So.2d 448.

Mass.App.Ct.1990. Com. v. Mandell 562 N.E.2d 111, 29 Mass.App.Ct. 504.

W.Va.1990. Rodgers v. Rodgers 399 S.E.2d 664.

Idaho 1990. Hake v. DeLane 793 P.2d 1230, 117 Idaho 1058.

Or.1990. State v. Nefstad 789 P.2d 1326, 309 Or. 523.

Ind.1990. Phillips v. State 550 N.E.2d 1290.

N.J.Super.A.D.1989. State v. Radziwil 563 A.2d 856, 235 N.J.Super. 557.

W.Va.1989. State v. Marrs 379 S.E.2d 497.

Vt.1988. State v. Larose 554 A.2d 227, 150 Vt. 363.

Wash.App.1987. State v. Young 739 P.2d 1170, 48 Wash.App. 406.

Or.1986. Charmley v. Lewis 729 P.2d 567, 302 Or. 324.

Ala.Cr.App.1984. Calhoun v. State 460 So.2d 868.

CHAPTER 18. SIMILAR HAPPENINGS AND TRANSACTIONS

§ 196. Other Claims, Suits or Defenses of a Party

C.A.10 (N.M.)1991. Owens v. International Business and Mercantile Reassurance Co. 1991 WL 137603 Unpublished Disposition.(*)

C.A.2 (N.Y.)1988. Outley v. City of New York 837 F.2d 587.

C.A.2 (N.Y.)1985. Raysor v. Port Authority of New York and New Jersey 768 F.2d 34.

D.C.App.1990. Roundtree v. U.S. 581 A.2d 315.

§ 197. Other Misrepresentation and Frauds

Tenn.App.1989. Keith v. Murfreesboro Livestock Market, Inc. 780 S.W.2d 751.

Ill.App. 4 Dist.1987. Bond v. Noble 517 N.E.2d 319, 163 Ill.App.3d 1067, 115 Ill. Dec. 117.

§ 198. Other Contracts and Business Transactions

Colo.1989. Adrian v. People 770 P.2d 1243.

§ 199. Other Sales of Similar Property as Evidence of Value

Ill.App. 2 Dist.1986. People v. Randle 498 N.E.2d 732, 147 Ill.App.3d 621, 101 Ill. Dec. 408.

Pa.Super.1986. Com. v. Rounds 514 A.2d 630, 356 Pa.Super. 317.

N.Y.A.D. 2 Dept.1985. People v. James 489 N.Y.S.2d 527, 111 A.D.2d 254.

§ 200. Other Accidents and Injuries

C.A.6 (Tenn.),1989. Broome v. Dazey Corp. 885 F.2d 871 (Table), Unpublished Disposition.(*)

C.A.6 (Ky.),1988. Bryan v. Emerson Elec. Co., Inc. 856 F.2d 192 (Table), Unpublished Disposition.(*)

C.A.6 (Ky.)1988. Hines v. Joy Mfg. Co. 850 F.2d 1146.

C.A.7 (Wis.)1988. Nachtsheim v. Beech Aircraft Corp. 847 F.2d 1261.

Vt.1990. Mobbs v. Central Vermont Ry., Inc. 583 A.2d 566.

Mo.App.1990. Eagleburger v. Emerson Elec. Co. 794 S.W.2d 210.

Conn.1990. Hall v. Burns 569 A.2d 10, 213 Conn. 446.

Mo.App.1989. Luthy v. Denny's, Inc. 782 S.W.2d 661.

N.Y.1989. Putnam Rolling Ladder Co., Inc. v. Manufacturers Hanover Trust Co. 547 N.Y.S.2d 611, 74 N.Y.2d 340, 546 N.E.2d 904.

Mo.1989. Pierce v. PlatteClay Elec. Co-op., Inc. 769 S.W.2d 769.

Mo.App.1989. McJunkins v. Windham Power Lifts, Inc. 767 S.W.2d 95.

Iowa 1988.   Cook v. State 431 N.W.2d 800.

Me.1988.   Marois v. Paper Converting Machine Co. 539 A.2d 621.

Pa.Super.1987.   Vernon v. Stash (Two Cases) 532 A.2d 441, 367 Pa.Super. 36.

Miss.1987.   Mitcham v. Illinois Cent. Gulf R. Co. 515 So.2d 852.

Mo.App.1987.   Welkener v. Kirkwood Drug Store Co. 734 S.W.2d 233.

Nev.1986.   Galloway v. McDonalds Restaurants of Nevada, Inc. 728 P.2d 826, 102 Nev. 534.

Idaho 1986.   Sliman v. Aluminum Co. of America 731 P.2d 1267, 112 Idaho 277.

Idaho App.1986.   Harmston v. Agro–West, Inc. 727 P.2d 1242, 111 Idaho 814.

Idaho 1985.   Fish Breeders of Idaho, Inc. v. Rangen, Inc. 700 P.2d 1, 108 Idaho 379.

Ariz.1985.   Jones v. Pak–Mor Mfg. Co. 700 P.2d 819, 145 Ariz. 121.

Ohio 1984.   Drake v. Caterpillar Tractor Co. 474 N.E.2d 291.

CHAPTER 19.   INSURANCE AGAINST LIABILITY

§ 201.   Insurance Against Liability

Mo.1990.   Ballinger v. Gascosage Elec. Co-op. 788 S.W.2d 506.

Md.1989.   Allstate Ins. Co. v. Miller 553 A.2d 1268, 315 Md. 182.

Pa.Super.1987.   Phillips v. Schoenberger 534 A.2d 1075, 369 Pa.Super. 52.

Wyo.1987.   Clarke v. Vandermeer 740 P.2d 921.

D.C.App.1986.   Felton v. Wagner 512 A.2d 291.

CHAPTER 20.   EXPERIMENTAL AND SCIENTIFIC EVIDENCE

§ 202.   Pretrial Experiments

C.A.6 (Ky.)1985.   U.S. v. Metzger 778 F.2d 1195.

N.Y.A.D. 4 Dept.1989.   Goldner v. Kemper Ins. Co. 544 N.Y.S.2d 396, 152 A.D.2d 936.

Pa.Super.1989.   Leonard by Meyers v. Nichols Homeshield, Inc. 557 A.2d 743, 384 Pa.Super. 1.

Mo.App.1988.   School Dist. of City of Independence, Mo., No. 30 v. U.S. Gypsum Co. 750 S.W.2d 442.

Iowa 1987.   State v. Barrett 401 N.W.2d 184.

Fla.App. 3 Dist.1986.   Rindfleisch v. Carnival Cruise Lines, Inc. 498 So.2d 488.

Ariz.App.1986.   Volz v. Coleman Co., Inc. 748 P.2d 1187, 155 Ariz. 563.

Wis.App.1985.   Maskrey v. Volkswagenwerk Aktiengesellschaft 370 N.W.2d 815, 125 Wis.2d 145.

Mo.App.1985.   Lawson v. Schumacher & Blum Chevrolet, Inc. 687 S.W.2d 947.

§ 203.   Scientific Tests in General: Admissibility and Weight

C.A.11 (Fla.)1989.   U.S. v. Piccinonna 885 F.2d 1529.

C.A.6 (Ky.), 1989.   U.S. v. Walker 865 F.2d 1269 (Table), Unpublished Disposition.(*)

C.A.D.C.1988.   Kropinski v. World Plan Executive Council—US 853 F.2d 948.

C.A.6 (Mich.)1987.   U.S. v. Kozminski 821 F.2d 1186.

Idaho App.1991.   State v. Van Sickle 813 P.2d 910.

N.Y.1990.   People v. Mooney 560 N.Y.S.2d 115, 76 N.Y.2d 827, 559 N.E.2d 1274.

N.J.Super.A.D.1990.   Rubanick v. Witco Chemical Corp. 576 A.2d 4, 242 N.J.Super. 36.

Ala.Cr.App., 1990.   Bird v. State 1990 WL 44301.

Minn.1989.   State v. Schwartz 447 N.W.2d 422.

Utah 1989.   State v. Rimmasch 775 P.2d 388.

Fla.App. 5 Dist. 1988.   Andrews v. State 533 So.2d 841.

Mich.1986. People v. Young 391 N.W.2d 270, 425 Mich. 470.

Mass.1986. Com. v. Cifizzari 492 N.E.2d 357, 397 Mass. 560.

R.I.1985. State v. Wheeler 496 A.2d 1382.

N.C.1984. State v. Bullard 322 S.E.2d 370, 312 N.C. 129.

§ 204. Particular Tests: Physics and Electronics: Speed Detection and Recording

Va.App.1990. Myatt v. Com. 397 S.E.2d 275, 11 Va.App. 163.

§ 205. Particular Tests: Biology and Medicine: Drunkenness, Blood, Tissue and DNA Typing

Tenn.App.,1990. McIntrye v. Balentine 1990 WL 126206.

Wash.App.1988. State v. Watson 756 P.2d 177, 51 Wash.App. 947.

Tex.1988. In Interest of S.C.V. 750 S.W.2d 762.

N.Y.A.D. 2 Dept.1988. Nyack Hosp. v. Government Employees Ins. Co. 526 N.Y.S.2d 614, 139 A.D.2d 515.

Conn.1987. State v. Pollitt 531 A.2d 125, 205 Conn. 132.

N.C.1987. State v. Jackson 358 S.E.2d 679, 320 N.C. 452.

Mich.App.1987. People v. Lewis 413 N.W.2d 48, 162 Mich.App. 558.

Or.1986. State v. Jancsek 730 P.2d 14, 302 Or. 270.

N.Y.1986. People v. Mertz 506 N.Y.S.2d 290, 68 N.Y.2d 136, 497 N.E.2d 657.

Tenn.Cr.App.1986. State v. Johnson 717 S.W.2d 298.

Pa.Super.1986. Com. v. Speights 509 A.2d 1263, 353 Pa.Super. 258.

N.Y.1985. People v. Mountain 495 N.Y.S.2d 944, 66 N.Y.2d 197, 486 N.E.2d 802.

Ind.App. 2 Dist. 1985. Davis v. State 476 N.E.2d 127.

Tenn.App.1984. Knapp v. Holiday Inns, Inc. 682 S.W.2d 936.

§ 206. Particular Tests: Psychology: Eyewitness Testimony, Lie Detection, Drugs, Hypnosis, and Profiles

C.A.9 (Cal.)1990. Toussaint v. McCarthy 918 F.2d 752.

C.A.9 (Cal.)1990. Toussaint v. McCarthy 926 F.2d 800.

Fla.App. 1 Dist., 1991. Flanagan v. State 1991 WL 133574.

N.Y.1990. People v. Mooney 560 N.Y.S.2d 115, 76 N.Y.2d 827, 559 N.E.2d 1274.

Mich.1988. People v. Lee 450 N.W.2d 883, 434 Mich. 59.

La.App. 2 Cir.1989. State v. Woodfin 539 So.2d 645.

Pa.1988. Com. v. Gallagher 547 A.2d 355, 519 Pa. 291.

Alaska App.1988. Haakanson v. State 760 P.2d 1030.

Conn.1987. State v. Miller 522 A.2d 249, 202 Conn. 463.

Ark.1986. Rock v. State 708 S.W.2d 78, 288 Ark. 566, 54 U.S.L.W. 2611.

Fla.App. 1 Dist. 1985. Hawthorne v. State 470 So.2d 770.

Okl.Cr.1985. Harmon v. State 700 P.2d 212.

§ 207. Particular Tests: Criminalistics: Identifying Persons and Things

Del.Supr.1988. Thompson v. State 539 A.2d 1052.

N.J.Super.A.D.1986. Windmere, Inc. v. International Ins. Co. 506 A.2d 834, 208 N.J.Super. 697.

Me.1986. State v. Thompson 503 A.2d 689.

§ 208. Statistical Studies: Surveys and Opinion Polls

Cal.App. 2 Dist.1990. Leighton v. Old Heidelberg, Ltd. 268 Cal.Rptr. 647, 219 Cal. App.3d 1062.

Ariz.App.1985. Gosewisch v. American Honda Motor Co., Inc. 737 P.2d 365, 153 Ariz. 389.

§ 209. Statistical Studies: Correlations and Causes: Statistical Evidence of Discrimination

§ 210. Probabilities as Evidence: Identification Evidence Generally

Wyo.1991. Pearson v. State 811 P.2d 704.

Fla.App. 5 Dist.1989. Martinez v. State 549 So.2d 694.

Mass.1988. Com. v. Gomes 526 N.E.2d 1270, 403 Mass. 258.

Minn.1987. State v. Joon Kyu Kim 398 N.W.2d 544.

§ 211. Probabilities as Evidence: Paternity Testing

Del.Supr.1990.

Allen v. Division of Child Support Enforcement ex rel. Ware 575 A.2d 1176.

N.J.Super.A.D.1989. State v. Spann 563 A.2d 1145, 236 N.J.Super. 13.

Wis.1988. In re Paternity of M.J.B. 425 N.W.2d 404, 144 Wis.2d 638.

Utah 1987. Kofford v. Flora 744 P.2d 1343.

N.C.1987. State v. Jackson 358 S.E.2d 679, 320 N.C. 452.

Or.1987. Plemel v. Walter 735 P.2d 1209, 303 Or. 262.

Va.App.1986. Bridgeman v. Com. 351 S.E.2d 598, 3 Va.App. 523.

Or.App.1986. Plemel v. Walter 721 P.2d 474, 80 Or.App. 250.

Me.1986. State v. Thompson 503 A.2d 689.

Ind.App. 2 Dist.1985. Davis v. State 476 N.E.2d 127.

CHAPTER 21. DEMONSTRATIVE EVIDENCE

§ 212. Demonstrative Evidence in General

C.A.4 (Va.), 1991. U.S. v. Taylor 935 F.2d 1288 (Table), Unpublished Disposition.(*)

C.A.9 (Or.),1990. Steele v. Maass 905 F.2d 1541 (Table), Unpublished Disposition.(*)

C.A.10 (N.M.)1989. U.S. v. Cardenas 864 F.2d 1528.

C.A.3 (Virgin Islands)1986. Government of Virgin Islands v. Brathwaite 782 F.2d 399.

Ala.Cr.App.1989. Pardue v. State 571 So.2d 320.

W.Va.1989. State v. Hardway 385 S.E.2d 62.

Wis.App.,1988. State v. Calderio 423 N.W.2d 882 (Table), 143 Wis.2d 901, Unpublished Disposition.(*)

Miss.1987. Murriel v. State 515 So.2d 952.

N.C.App.1987. FCX, Inc. v. Caudill 354 S.E.2d 767, 85 N.C.App. 272.

Hawaii 1986. Monlux v. General Motors Corp. 714 P.2d 930, 68 Haw. 358.

Me.1986. State v. Thompson 503 A.2d 689.

Utah 1985. State v. Royball 710 P.2d 168.

§ 213. Maps, Models, and Duplicates

Tenn.Cr.App., 1991. State v. Sterna 1991 WL 135006 (Tenn.Cr.App.).

Okl.Cr.1990. Moore v. State 788 P.2d 387.

Md.1986. Grandison v. State 506 A.2d 580, 305 Md. 685.

Md.1985. Evans v. State 499 A.2d 1261, 304 Md. 487.

§ 214. Photographs, Movies, and Sound Recordings

Me.1991. State v. Cyran 586 A.2d 1238.

Mass.App.Ct.1991. Com. v. Nadworny 566 N.E.2d 625, 30 Mass.App.Ct. 912.

N.J.Super.A.D.1988. State v. Nemesh 550 A.2d 757, 228 N.J.Super. 597.

Ala.Cr.App.1988. Molina v. State 533 So.2d 701.

Miss.1988. George v. State 521 So.2d 1287.

Va.App.1986. Saunders v. Com. 339 S.E.2d 550, 1 Va.App. 396.

Utah 1985. State v. Purcell 711 P.2d 243.

Mass.App.1985. Rosenthal v. Weckstein 473 N.E.2d 202, 19 Mass.App. 944.

Mich.App.1984. McMiddleton v. Otis Elevator Co. 362 N.W.2d 812, 139 Mich.App. 418.

§ 215. Bodily Demonstrations: Experiments in Court

C.A.10 (N.M.)1986. U.S. v. Wanoskia 800 F.2d 235.

R.I.1990. State v. Perry 574 A.2d 149.

R.I.1989. State v. Wiley 567 A.2d 802.

D.C.App.1989. Irick v. U.S. 565 A.2d 26.

Mo.App.1986.   State v. Marks 721 S.W.2d 51.

§ 216.   Views

D.Or.1987.   Oregon Natural Resources Council, Inc. v. U.S. Forest Service 659 F.Supp. 1441.

D.C.App.1989.   Dailey v. District of Columbia 554 A.2d 339.

Idaho App.1987.   Gilbert v. City of Caldwell 732 P.2d 355, 112 Idaho 386.

R.I.1985.   Matter of Blackstone Valley Dist. Com'n 490 A.2d 974.

§ 217.   Exhibits in the Jury Room

Wis.1988.   State v. Jensen 432 N.W.2d 913, 147 Wis.2d 240.

CHAPTER 22.   AUTHENTICATION

§ 218.   General Theory: No Assumption of Authenticity

Wis.App.,1989.   Peterson v. Hartland Cicero Mut. Ins. Co. 439 N.W.2d 644 (Table), 149 Wis.2d 399, Unpublished Disposition.(*)

Mo.App.1987.   Collins v. West Plains Memorial Hosp. 735 S.W.2d 404.

D.C.App.1986.   Adams v. U.S. 502 A.2d 1011.

§ 219.   Authentication by Direct Proof: (a) In General

Fla.App. 3 Dist.1991.   Buchanan v. State 575 So.2d 704.

Conn.App.1988.   Kraus v. Newton 542 A.2d 1163, 14 Conn.App. 561.

N.C.App.1988.   U.S. Leasing Corp. v. Everett, Creech, Hancock, and Herzig 363 S.E.2d 665, 88 N.C.App. 418.

Ind.App. 3 Dist 1986.   Ruth v. First Federal Sav. and Loan Ass'n of LaPorte County 492 N.E.2d 1105.

Pa.Super.1985.   City of Philadelphia v. Watkins 494 A.2d 1135, 343 Pa.Super. 380.

§ 220.   Authentication by Direct Proof: (b) Requirement of Production of Attesting Witnesses

§ 221.   Authentication by Direct Proof: (c) Proof of Handwriting

C.A.9 (Cal.),1990.   U.S. v. Ates 896 F.2d 1370 (Table), Unpublished Disposition.(*)

C.A.9 (Guam)1988.   People v. Cepeda 851 F.2d 1564.

Minn.App.1990.   State v. Glidden 459 N.W.2d 136.

Pa.Super.1986.   Com. v. Brooks 508 A.2d 316, 352 Pa.Super. 394.

§ 222.   Authentication by Circumstantial Evidence: (a) Generally

Conn.App.1986.   State v. Jones 512 A.2d 932, 8 Conn.App. 177.

§ 223.   Authentication by Circumstantial Evidence: (b) Ancient Documents

Ohio App.,1985.   In re Estate of Cannon 1985 WL 3701.

§ 224.   Authentication by Circumstantial Evidence: (c) Custody

Wis.App.1990.   Matter of Guardianship of R.S. 454 N.W.2d 1, 154 Wis.2d 706.

§ 225.   Authentication by Circumstantial Evidence: (d) Knowledge: Reply Letters and Telegrams

Tenn.Cr.App.1990.   State v. Lewis 803 S.W.2d 260.

Tenn.Cr.App., 1989.   State v. Farmer 1989 WL 137899.

Conn.App.1987.   Presnick v. DeRosa 532 A.2d 1309, 12 Conn.App. 554.

§ 226.   Authentication by Circumstantial Evidence; (e) Telephone Messages and Other Oral Communications

C.A.5 (Tex.)1990.   First State Bank of Denton v. Maryland Cas. Co. 918 F.2d 38.

Mo.App.1990.   State v. Cody 801 S.W.2d 430.

Ind.1990.   King v. State 560 N.E.2d 491.

R.I.1988.   State v. Messa 542 A.2d 1071.

Pa.Super.1988. Com. v. Sullivan 538 A.2d 1363, 372 Pa.Super. 88.

W.Va.1987. State v. Smith 358 S.E.2d 188.

Conn.App.1986. Hartford Nat. Bank and Trust Co. v. DiFazio 506 A.2d 1069, 6 Conn.App. 576.

§ 227. Functions of Judge and Jury in Authentication

R.I.1988. State v. Messa 542 A.2d 1071.

N.C.App.1988. U.S. Leasing Corp. v. Everett, Creech, Hancock, and Herzig 363 S.E.2d 665, 88 N.C.App. 418.

Va.App.1986. Duncan v. Com. 347 S.E.2d 539, 2 Va.App. 717.

§ 228. Escapes from the Requirements of Producing Evidence of Authenticity: Modern Theory and Practice

Tex.App. Dallas 1990. Handspur v. State 792 S.W.2d 239.

Fla.App. 3 Dist.1989. Sunnyvale Maritime Co., Inc. v. Gomez 546 So.2d 6.

Miss.1987. Monroe v. State 515 So.2d 860.

Pa.Super.1986. Com. v. Brooks 508 A.2d 316, 352 Pa.Super. 394.

CHAPTER 23. THE REQUIREMENT OF THE PRODUCTION OF THE ORIGINAL WRITING AS THE "BEST EVIDENCE"

§ 229. The "Best Evidence" Rule

N.J.Super.A.D.1988. Nerney v. Garden State Hosp. 550 A.2d 1003, 229 N.J.Super. 37.

§ 230. Original Document Rule

C.A.9 (Cal.)1986. Seiler v. Lucasfilm, Ltd. 797 F.2d 1504.

Conn.App.1990. State v. Comollo 572 A.2d 1037, 21 Conn.App. 210.

Pa.Super.1988. Com. v. Shiffler 541 A.2d 780, 373 Pa.Super. 497.

Pa.Super.1987. Panko v. Alessi 524 A.2d 930, 362 Pa.Super. 384.

Mo.App.1987. State v. Foulk 725 S.W.2d 56.

Conn.App.1986. Morales v. Saint Francis Hosp. and Medical Center 519 A.2d 86, 9 Conn.App. 379.

§ 231. The Reasons for the Rule

C.A.9 (Cal.)1986. Seiler v. Lucasfilm, Ltd. 797 F.2d 1504.

C.A.9 (Cal.)1986. Seiler v. Lucasfilm, Ltd. 808 F.2d 1316.

Pa.Super.1991. Hamill–Quinlan, Inc. v. Fisher 591 A.2d 309.

§ 232. What Are Writings? Application to Objects Inscribed and Uninscribed

Tenn.1987. State v. Coker 746 S.W.2d 167.

Mo.App.1987. State v. Welty 729 S.W.2d 594.

§ 233. What Constitutes Proving the Terms

C.A.5 (Tex.)1987. U.S. v. Fagan 821 F.2d 1002.

Minn.App., 1990. State v. Gehrke 1990 WL 101505.

Ark.1987. Ward v. Gerald E. Prince Const., Inc. 732 S.W.2d 163, 293 Ark. 59.

Mo.App.1987. State v. Welty 729 S.W.2d 594.

Okl.Cr.1985. Anderson v. State 704 P.2d 499.

§ 234. Writings Involved Only Collaterally

Idaho App.1986. State v. Rosencrantz 714 P.2d 93, 110 Idaho 124.

§ 235. Which Is the "Writing Itself" That Must Be Produced? Telegrams, Counterparts

Del.Supr., 1986. Dalton v. State 514 A.2d 413 (Table), Unpublished Disposition.(*)

Colo.1985. Banks v. People 696 P.2d 293.

§ 236. Reproductions: Carbons: Printed and Multigraph Copies: Photo and Xerographic Copies

Tenn.Cr.App.1989. State v. Chance 778 S.W.2d 457.

Cal.App. 2 Dist.1988. People v. Garcia 247 Cal.Rptr. 94, 201 Cal.App.3d 324.

Del.Supr., 1986. Dalton v. State 514 A.2d 413 (Table), Unpublished Disposition.(*)

§ 237. Excuses for Nonproduction of the Original Writing: (a) Loss or Destruction

Tenn.Cr.App., 1987. State v. Moore 1987 WL 6377.

§ 238. Excuses for Nonproduction of the Original Writing: (b) Possession by a Third Person

§ 239. Excuses for Nonproduction of the Original Writing: (c) Failure of Adversary Having Possession to Produce After Notice

§ 240. Excuses for Nonproduction of the Original Writing: (d) Public Records

§ 241. Preferences Among Copies and Between Copies and Oral Testimony

§ 242. Adversary's Admission as to the Terms of a Writing

§ 243. Review of Rulings Admitting Secondary Evidence

CHAPTER 24.   THE HEARSAY RULE

§ 244. The History of the Rule Against Hearsay

§ 245. The Reasons for the Rule Against Hearsay: Exceptions to the Rule

C.A.2 (N.Y.)1991. U.S. v. Salerno 937 F.2d 797.

C.A.7 (Wis.)1986. U.S. v. Norwood 798 F.2d 1094.

Fla.App. 3 Dist.1991. Metropolitan Dade County v. Yearby 580 So.2d 186.

Ind.1991. Banks v. State 567 N.E.2d 1126.

Tex.Cr.App.1991. Fernandez v. State 805 S.W.2d 451.

La.1989. State v. Adams 550 So.2d 595.

Pa.Super.1988. Com. v. Fanelli 547 A.2d 1201, 377 Pa.Super. 555.

Hawaii 1988. In Interest of Doe 761 P.2d 299, 70 Haw. 32.

Va.App.1988. Penny v. Com. 370 S.E.2d 314, 6 Va.App. 494.

Conn.1987. State v. Vinal 534 A.2d 613, 205 Conn. 507.

Md.1987. Wildermuth v. State 530 A.2d 275, 310 Md. 496.

Ariz.1987. State v. Robinson 735 P.2d 801, 153 Ariz. 191.

Wash.1987. State v. Anderson 733 P.2d 517, 107 Wash.2d 745.

Pa.Super.1987. Com. v. Joraskie 519 A.2d 1010, 360 Pa.Super. 97.

Neb.1986. Alliance Nat. Bank & Trust Co. v. State Sur. Co. 390 N.W.2d 487, 223 Neb. 403.

§ 246. A Definition of Hearsay

C.A.1 (Mass.)1987. U.S. v. Cintolo 818 F.2d 980.

Pa., 1991. Commonwealth v. Ludwig 594 A.2d 281.

Or.1991. State v. Carlson 808 P.2d 1002, 311 Or. 201.

N.J.1990. State v. Hill 578 A.2d 370, 121 N.J. 150.

Ala.1990. Ex Parte Snell 565 So.2d 271.

Ga.App.1990. Hurston v. State 390 S.E.2d 119, 194 Ga.App. 226.

Wash.1989. State v. Monson 784 P.2d 485, 113 Wash.2d 833.

Ala.Cr.App.1989. McLemore v. State 562 So.2d 639.

Mass.1989. Com. v. Cordle 537 N.E.2d 130, 404 Mass. 733.

Ala.Cr.App.1989. Snell v. State 565 So.2d 265.

Tenn.App.1988. Lance Productions, Inc. v. Commerce Union Bank 764 S.W.2d 207.

Ala.1988. Turner v. Wean United, Inc. 531 So.2d 827.

Tenn.Cr.App., 1988. State v. Pate 1988 WL 81000.

Pa.Super.1988. Niles v. Fall Creek Hunting Club, Inc. 545 A.2d 926, 376 Pa.Super. 260.

La.1988. State v. Vigee 518 So.2d 501.

Pa.Super.1987. Com. v. Michaux 520 A.2d 1177, 360 Pa.Super. 452.

Mo.App.1986. M___ E___ v. M___ E___ E___ 715 S.W.2d 572.

R.I.1985. Craig v. Pare 497 A.2d 316.

N.C.1985. State v. Craven 324 S.E.2d 599, 312 N.C. 580.

§ 247. Distinction Between Hearsay Rule and Rule Requiring Firsthand Knowledge

Mo.App.1990. Stallings v. Washington University 794 S.W.2d 264.

§ 248. Instances of the Application of the Hearsay Rule

§ 249. Some Out-of-Court Utterances Which Are Not Hearsay

C.A.6 (Ky.)1990. U.S. v. Martin 897 F.2d 1368.

C.A.2 (N.Y.)1989. New Era Publications Intern., ApS v. Henry Holt and Co., Inc. 873 F.2d 576.

C.A.1 (Mass.)1987. U.S. v. Cintolo 818 F.2d 980.

C.A.7 (Wis.)1986. U.S. v. Norwood 798 F.2d 1094.

C.A.9 (Cal.)1986. U.S. v. Makhlouta 790 F.2d 1400.

S.D.N.Y., 1990. Nobler v. Beth Israel Medical Center 735 F.Supp. 65.

Tex.App.–Hous. (1 Dist.), 1991. Webb v. State 1991 WL 137382.

La.App. 1 Cir., 1991. State v. Veal 1991 WL 119722.

Tex.App.–Dallas, 1991. Davis v. Household Intern., Inc. 1991 WL 110042.

Tex.App.–Dallas, 1991. Roy, Appellant, v. The State of Texas, Appellee. 813 S.W.2d 532.

Del.Supr.1991. Johnson v. State 587 A.2d 444.

Wis.App.1991. State v. Wilson 467 N.W.2d 130, 160 Wis.2d 774.

Md.App.1990. McCray v. State 581 A.2d 45, 84 Md.App. 513.

Conn.1990. State v. Alvarez 579 A.2d 515, 216 Conn. 301.

Ill.App. 1 Dist.1990. Harry W. Kuhn, Inc. v. State Farm Mut. Auto. Ins. Co. 559 N.E.2d 45, 201 Ill.App.3d 395, 147 Ill. Dec. 45.

Miss.1990. Cooper v. State Farm Fire & Cas. Co. 568 So.2d 687.

La.1990. Buckbee v. United Gas Pipe Line Co., Inc. 561 So.2d 76.

Wash.App.1990. State v. Aaron 787 P.2d 949, 57 Wash.App. 277.

La.1990. State v. Jones 558 So.2d 546.

La.1990. State v. Wille 559 So.2d 1321, Rehearing Denied.

R.I.1990. State v. Braxter 568 A.2d 311.

Ill.App. 4 Dist.1989. People v. Cameron 546 N.E.2d 259, 189 Ill.App.3d 998, 137 Ill.Dec. 505.

Tex.Cr.App.1989. Schaffer v. State 777 S.W.2d 111.

Pa.Cmwlth.1989. Cleland Simpson Co. v. W.C.A.B. (Decker and Moosic Borough) 562 A.2d 981, 128 Pa.Cmwlth. 62.

Mass.App.Ct.1989. Com. v. Perez 540 N.E.2d 697, 27 Mass.App.Ct. 550.

R.I.1989. In re Jean Marie W. 559 A.2d 625.

R.I.1989. State v. Lassor 555 A.2d 339.

Pa.1989. Com. v. Palsa 555 A.2d 808, 521 Pa. 113.

Fla.1988. State v. Welker 536 So.2d 1017.

Pa.Cmwlth.1988. Hoffmaster v. County of Allegheny 550 A.2d 1023, 121 Pa. Cmwlth. 266.

W.Va.1988. State v. Murray 375 S.E.2d 405.

Md.1988. Su v. Weaver 545 A.2d 692, 313 Md. 370.

R.I.1988. State v. Mastracchio 546 A.2d 165.

N.M.App.1988. Matter of Estate of Bergman 761 P.2d 452, 107 N.M. 574.

Ga.1988. Holiday v. State 369 S.E.2d 241, 258 Ga. 393.

Vt.1988. In re R.M. 549 A.2d 1050, 150 Vt. 59.

La.App. 4 Cir.1988. Jackson v. Tyson 526 So.2d 398.

Wis.App., 1988. FPC Securities Corp. v. Hemmings 423 N.W.2d 882 (Table), 143 Wis.2d 901, Unpublished Disposition.(*)

Pa.1988. Matter of Cunningham 538 A.2d 473, 517 Pa. 417.

Pa.Super.1987. Com. v. Blough 535 A.2d 134, 369 Pa.Super. 230.

Fla.1987. Koon v. State 513 So.2d 1253.

Fla.App. 1 Dist.1987. Welker v. State 504 So.2d 802.

Va.App.1986. Johnson v. Com. 347 S.E.2d 163, 2 Va.App. 598.

Mo.App.1985. State v. Hendrix 699 S.W.2d 779.

Pa.Super.1985. Com. v. Underwood 500 A.2d 820, 347 Pa.Super. 256.

Mass.App.1985. Fahey v. Rockwell Graphic Systems, Inc. 482 N.E.2d 519, 20 Mass. App. 642.

Fla.1985. Florida Patient's Compensation Fund v. Von Stetina 474 So.2d 783.

Ark.1985. Hall v. State 689 S.W.2d 524, 286 Ark. 52.

Hawaii 1985. Shea v. City and County of Honolulu 692 P.2d 1158, 67 Haw. 499.

Minn.1984. State v. Hardy 354 N.W.2d 21.

§ 250. Conduct as Hearsay: "Implied Assertions"

C.A.1 (Mass.)1987. U.S. v. Figueroa 818 F.2d 1020.

D.C.Md.1990. Wilson v. Clancy 747 F.Supp. 1154.

Colo.1990. People v. Bowers 801 P.2d 511.

Wash.1989. State v. Mejia 766 P.2d 454, 111 Wash.2d 892.

Ky.1988. Sanborn v. Com. 754 S.W.2d 534.

Tenn.Cr.App., 1988. State v. Rutherford 1988 WL 23569.

N.C.App.1988. State v. Peek 365 S.E.2d 320, 89 N.C.App. 123.

N.M.App.1987. Jim v. Budd 760 P.2d 782, 107 N.M. 489.

N.C.App.1986. State v. Parker 344 S.E.2d 330, 81 N.C.App. 443.

Or.App.1986. State v. Harmon 714 P.2d 271, 77 Or.App. 705.

Mo.App.1985. State v. Meyer 694 S.W.2d 853.

§ 251. Prior Statements of Witnesses as Substantive Evidence

D.C.App.1991. Carr v. U.S. 585 A.2d 158.

D.C.App.1990. Matter of T.M. 577 A.2d 1149.

Mich.1990. Solomon v. Shuell 457 N.W.2d 669, 435 Mich. 104.

W.Va.,1990. State v. Collins. —— S.E.2d ——, 1990 WL 303091.

Minn.1990. State v. Gray 456 N.W.2d 251.

Ala.1990. Ex Parte Snell 565 So.2d 271.

Md.App.1990. Joiner v. State 571 A.2d 844, 82 Md.App. 282.

Wis.App.,1989. State v. Lamb 449 N.W.2d 336 (Table), 152 Wis.2d 403, Unpublished Disposition.(*)

Ark.1989. Johnson v. State 770 S.W.2d 128, 298 Ark. 617.

Or.1989. Powers v. Cheeley 771 P.2d 622, 307 Or. 585.

Ala.Cr.App.1989. Snell v. State 565 So.2d 265.

Pa.Super.1989. Com. v. Doa 553 A.2d 416, 381 Pa.Super. 181.

Ohio App.,1988. State v. Newlin 1988 WL 66755.

Mo.App.1988. State v. Lloyd 750 S.W.2d 589.

N.J.Super.A.D.1987. State v. Bryant 524 A.2d 1291, 217 N.J.Super. 72.

Conn.App.1987. State v. Harris 522 A.2d 323, 10 Conn.App. 217.

Conn.1986. State v. Whelan 513 A.2d 86, 200 Conn. 743.

Mo.1986. State v. Harris 711 S.W.2d 881.

Utah 1986. State v. Speer 718 P.2d 383.

Mo.1985. Rowe v. Farmers Ins. Co., Inc. 699 S.W.2d 423.

Pa.1985. Com. v. Floyd 498 A.2d 816, 508 Pa. 393.

Mo.App.1985. State v. Henderson 700 S.W.2d 105.

Ariz.App.1985. State v. Moran 728 P.2d 243, 151 Ariz. 373.

W.Va.1985. Rowan v. Barker 334 S.E.2d 630.

N.J.Super.A.D.1985. State v. Burgos 490 A.2d 316, 200 N.J.Super. 6.

Mass.App.1984. Com. v. Kirby 469 N.E.2d 499, 18 Mass.App. 960.

§ 252. Constitutional Problems of Hearsay: Confrontation and Due Process

C.A.10 (Kan.)1990. Myatt v. Hannigan 910 F.2d 680.

C.A.3 (Pa.)1985. U.S. v. Caputo 758 F.2d 944.

C.A.Mont.1984. Creekmore v. District Court of Eighth Judicial Dist. of State of Mont. In and For Cascade County 745 F.2d 1236.

N.C.1991. State v. Roper 402 S.E.2d 600, 328 N.C. 337.

Mass.1989. Opinion of the Justices To the Senate 547 N.E.2d 8, 406 Mass. 1201.

Md.App.1988. In re Rachel T. 549 A.2d 27, 77 Md.App. 20.

Pa.Super.1988. Com. v. Fanelli 547 A.2d 1201, 377 Pa.Super. 555.

Md.1988. State v. Garlick 545 A.2d 27, 313 Md. 209.

Ariz.App.1987. State v. Spinks 752 P.2d 8, 156 Ariz. 355.

Md.1987. State v. Fuller 520 A.2d 1315, 308 Md. 547.

Ill.App. 4 Dist.1986. In Interest of K.L.M. 496 N.E.2d 1262, 146 Ill.App.3d 489, 100 Ill.Dec. 197.

N.Y.1986. People v. Nieves 501 N.Y.S.2d 1, 67 N.Y.2d 125, 492 N.E.2d 109.

N.Y.A.D. 2 Dept.1984. People v. Klein 481 N.Y.S.2d 743, 105 A.D.2d 805.

§ 253. The Hearsay Exceptions: Unavailability of the Declarant

U.S.Ill.1986. Lee v. Illinois 106 S.Ct. 2056, 476 U.S. 530, 90 L.Ed.2d 514.

C.A.7 (Wis.)1989. Sahagian v. Murphy 871 F.2d 714.

C.A.D.C.1984. U.S. v. Houser 746 F.2d 55, 241 U.S.App.D.C. 62.

Pa.,1991. Commonwealth v. Ludwig 594 A.2d 281.

Fla.App. 3 Dist.1991. Metropolitan Dade County v. Yearby 580 So.2d 186.

Or.App.1991. State v. Logan 806 P.2d 137, 105 Or.App. 556.

Neb.1991. State v. Johnson 464 N.W.2d 167, 236 Neb. 831.

La.App. 2 Cir.1990. Tutorship of Price v. Standard Life Ins. Co. 569 So.2d 261.

Vt.1990. State v. Roberts 574 A.2d 1248, 154 Vt. 59.

Wash.1989. State v. Monson 784 P.2d 485, 113 Wash.2d 833.

Cal.App. 5 Dist.1989. People v. Allen 263 Cal.Rptr. 826, Ordered Not Published, (Rule 976, Cal. Rules of Ct.).(*)

Wyo.1989. King v. State 780 P.2d 943.

Ala.Cr.App.1989. Rouse v. State 548 So.2d 643.

Mich.1988. People v. Dye 427 N.W.2d 501, 431 Mich. 58.

Ariz.1986. Mister Donut of America, Inc. v. Harris 723 P.2d 670, 150 Ariz. 321.

Ariz.App.1985. Mister Donut of America, Inc. v. Harris 723 P.2d 696, 150 Ariz. 347.

Ind.App. 2 Dist.1984. Baker v. Wagers 472 N.E.2d 218.

CHAPTER 25. ADMISSIONS OF A PARTY–OPPONENT

[Formerly chapter 26 in the 3rd Ed.]

§ 254. Nature and Effect

[Treated in § 262 in the 3rd Ed.]

U.S.Ohio 1987. Bourjaily v. U.S. 107 S.Ct. 2775, 483 U.S. 171, 97 L.Ed.2d 144.

Bkrtcy.S.D.N.Y.1987. In re Fill 68 B.R. 923.

Md.App.1991. Kitchen v. State 589 A.2d 575, 87 Md.App. 299.

Va.App.1991. Alatishe v. Com. 404 S.E.2d 81.

Conn.1991. State v. Rosado 588 A.2d 1066, 218 Conn. 239.

Fla.App. 3 Dist.1991. Metropolitan Dade County v. Yearby 580 So.2d 186.

Md.1991. Briggeman v. Albert 586 A.2d 15, 322 Md. 133.

Colo.1990. Burlington Northern R. Co. v. Hood 802 P.2d 458.

Or.1990. Washington v. Taseca Homes, Inc. 802 P.2d 70, 310 Or. 783.

Wyo.1990. Pena v. State 792 P.2d 1352.

Mich.1989. Shields v. Reddo 443 N.W.2d 145, 432 Mich. 761.

Pa.Super.1989. Com. v. Hoyman 561 A.2d 756, 385 Pa.Super. 439.

S.D.1988. State v. Stuck 434 N.W.2d 43.

Fla.1988. Swafford v. State 533 So.2d 270.

Pa.Super.1988. Schwarcz v. Schwarcz 548 A.2d 556, 378 Pa.Super. 170.

N.Y.A.D. 2 Dept.1988. People v. Hills 532 N.Y.S.2d 269, 140 A.D.2d 71.

Pa.Super.1988. Durkin v. Equine Clinics, Inc. 546 A.2d 665, 376 Pa.Super. 557.

Okl.Cr.1988. Phillips v. State 756 P.2d 604.

Tenn.App.1986. Curtis by Tedder v. Van Dusen 723 S.W.2d 648.

Minn.App.1986. Wagner v. Thomas J. Obert Enterprises 384 N.W.2d 477.

R.I.1986. Martin v. Lilly 505 A.2d 1156.

Colo.1985. People v. Sabell 708 P.2d 463.

Md.App.1984. Nisos v. Nisos 483 A.2d 97, 60 Md.App. 368.

§ 255. Testimonial Qualifications: Mental Competency; Personal Knowledge

[Treated in § 263 in the 3rd Ed.]

Fla.App. 3 Dist.1991. Metropolitan Dade County v. Yearby 580 So.2d 186.

Mont.1990. Heltborg v. Modern Machinery 795 P.2d 954, 244 Mont. 24.

Idaho App.1990. McGill v. Frasure 790 P.2d 379, 117 Idaho 598.

Pa.Super.1988. Com. v. Reardon 542 A.2d 572, 374 Pa.Super. 212.

Wis.App., 1985. Miller v. Bartel 368 N.W.2d 846 (Table), 123 Wis.2d 544, Unpublished Disposition.(*)

§ 256. Admissions in Opinion Form; Conclusions of Law

[Treated in § 264 in the 3rd Ed.]

C.A.1 (N.H.)1990. Brookover v. Mary Hitchcock Memorial Hosp. 893 F.2d 411.

C.A.8 (Mo.)1985. Crues v. KFC Corp. 768 F.2d 230.

§ 257. Admissions in Pleadings; Pleas of Guilty

[Treated in § 265 in the 3rd Ed.]

C.A.9 (Cal.),1990. Katz v. Cohn 900 F.2d 262 (Table), Unpublished Disposition.(*)

C.A.Fed.1988. Water Technologies Corp. v. Calco, Ltd. 850 F.2d 660.

C.A.10 (Kan.)1987. Romine v. Parman 831 F.2d 944.

D.Mass.1987. Avemco Ins. Co. v. Aerotech, Ltd. 677 F.Supp. 35.

Bkrtcy.D.Del.1991. Matter of Continental Airlines, Inc. 125 B.R. 415.

Bkrtcy.N.D.Ill.1991. In re Cooper 125 B.R. 777.

D.C.App.1991. Morris v. Rasque 591 A.2d 459.

Md.1991. Briggeman v. Albert 586 A.2d 15, 322 Md. 133.

Mich.1990. Lichon v. American Universal Ins. Co. 459 N.W.2d 288, 435 Mich. 408.

Md.App.1990. Briggeman v. Albert 568 A.2d 865, 81 Md.App. 482.

W.Va.1988. Moore v. Goode 375 S.E.2d 549.

Tenn.App.1987. Pankow v. Mitchell 737 S.W.2d 293.

Del.Ch.,1986. Wilmington Sav. Fund Soc. v. Tucker 1986 WL 3136.

Del.Ch.,1986. Debbs v. Berman 1986 WL 1243.

§ 258. Testimony by the Party as an Admission

[Treated in § 266 in the 3rd Ed.]

N.D.Ill.1989. Price v. Highland Community Bank 722 F.Supp. 454.

E.D.Wis.1988. Nelson v. Ferrey 688 F.Supp. 1304.

Ga.App.1991. Cameron v. Moore 406 S.E.2d 133, 199 Ga.App. 800.

Ohio App.,1985. Thompson v. Ron's Waste Service & Co., Inc. 1985 WL 7262.

§ 259. Representative Admissions; Coconspirator Statements

[Treated in § 267 in the 3rd Ed.]

U.S.Ohio 1987. Bourjaily v. U.S. 107 S.Ct. 2775, 483 U.S. 171, 97 L.Ed.2d 144.

C.A.4 (Va.)1989. U.S. v. Gregory 871 F.2d 1239.

C.A.8 (Mo.)1988. U.S. v. Townsley 843 F.2d 1070.

D.Puerto Rico 1986. U.S. v. Panzardi–Alvarez 646 F.Supp. 1158.

Md.App.1990. B & K Rentals & Sales Co., Inc. v. Universal Leaf Tobacco Co. 578 A.2d 274, 84 Md.App. 103.

N.Y.A.D. 2 Dept.1989. Niesig v. Team I 545 N.Y.S.2d 153, 149 A.D.2d 94.

Wyo.1989. Bigelow v. State 768 P.2d 558.

Mass.App.Ct.1988. Gage v. City of Westfield 532 N.E.2d 62, 26 Mass.App.Ct. 681.

Pa.Super.1988. Durkin v. Equine Clinics, Inc. 546 A.2d 665, 376 Pa.Super. 557.

Md.1987. State v. Rivenbark 533 A.2d 271, 311 Md. 147.

Iowa 1987. State v. Florie 411 N.W.2d 689.

S.C.App.1987. Yaeger v. Murphy 354 S.E.2d 393, 291 S.C. 485.

Md.App.1986. Rivenbark v. State 504 A.2d 647, 66 Md.App. 378.

Neb.1986. Bump v. Firemens Ins. Co. of Newark, N.J. 380 N.W.2d 268, 221 Neb. 678.

Idaho App.1985. State v. Caldero 705 P.2d 85, 109 Idaho 80.

§ 260. Declarations by "Privies in Estate," Joint Tenants, Predecessors in Interest Joint Obligors, and Principals Against Surety

[Treated in § 268 in the 3rd Ed.]

§ 261. Admissions by Conduct: (a) Adoptive Admissions

[Treated in § 269 in the 3rd Ed.]

R.I.1987. State v. Brennan 527 A.2d 654.

W.Va.1985. State v. Howerton 329 S.E.2d 874.

Or.1985. State v. Severson 696 P.2d 521, 298 Or. 652.

§ 262. Admissions by Conduct: (b) Silence

[Treated in § 270 in the 3rd Ed.]

C.A.10 (Kan.)1989. New England Mut. Life Ins. Co. v. Anderson 888 F.2d 646.

C.A.7 (Ill.)1986. Benson v. Allphin 786 F.2d 268.

Md.1991. Briggeman v. Albert 586 A.2d 15, 322 Md. 133.

Va.App.1990. Weinbender v. Com. 398 S.E.2d 106.

D.C.App.1990. Holmes v. U.S. 580 A.2d 1259.

Md.App.1990. Wills v. State 573 A.2d 80, 82 Md.App. 669.

Ill.App. 1 Dist.1989. People v. Maldonado 550 N.E.2d 1011, 193 Ill.App.3d 1062, 140 Ill.Dec. 886.

N.Y.A.D. 2 Dept.1988. People v. Robinson 528 N.Y.S.2d 676, 140 A.D.2d 644.

N.Y.1987. People v. Lourido 522 N.Y.S.2d 98, 70 N.Y.2d 428, 516 N.E.2d 1212.

Md.1986. Booth v. State 507 A.2d 1098, 306 Md. 172.

Md.App.1985. Duncan v. State 494 A.2d 235, 64 Md.App. 45.

§ 263. Admissions by Conduct: (c) Flight and Similar Acts

[Treated in § 271 in the 3rd Ed.]

C.A.6 (Ohio)1989. U.S. v. Dillon 870 F.2d 1125.

Md.1990. State v. Edison 569 A.2d 657, 318 Md. 541.

Md.1989. Bedford v. State 566 A.2d 111, 317 Md. 659.

Md.1989. Sorrell v. State 554 A.2d 352, 315 Md. 224.

Mont.1988. State v. Burk 761 P.2d 825, 234 Mont. 119.

Wis.App., 1988. State v. Johnson 430 N.W.2d 379 (Table), 145 Wis.2d 905, Unpublished Disposition.(*)

Ark.App.1988. Kidd v. State 748 S.W.2d 38, 24 Ark.App. 55.

Md.1988. Hunt v. State 540 A.2d 1125, 312 Md. 494.

§ 264. Admissions by Conduct: (d) Failure to Call Witnesses or Produce Evidence; Refusal to Submit to a Physical Examination

[Treated in § 272 in the 3rd Ed.]

C.A.5 (La.)1990. Herbert v. Wal–Mart Stores, Inc. 911 F.2d 1044.

C.A.9 (Cal.),1988. Osborne v. City of Long Beach 865 F.2d 264 (Table), Unpublished Disposition.(*)

C.A.2 (N.Y.)1988. U.S. v. Torres 845 F.2d 1165.

C.A.6 (Ohio),1987. Yuk Shau Mui v. Wing 822 F.2d 1089 (Table), Unpublished Disposition.(*)

E.D.Pa.,1990. Mack v. City of Philadelphia 1990 WL 67218.

D.C.App.,1991. Mills v. United States —— A.2d ——, 1991 WL 163116.

Ill.App. 4 Dist.1991. Board of Regents of Regency Universities v. Illinois Educational Labor Relations Bd. 566 N.E.2d 963, 208 Ill.App.3d 220, 153 Ill.Dec. 113.

D.C.App.1990. Allen v. U.S. 579 A.2d 225.

N.Y.A.D. 2 Dept.1989. People v. Boyajian 539 N.Y.S.2d 683, 148 A.D.2d 740.

Mass.App.Ct.1988. Com. v. Groce 517 N.E.2d 1297, 25 Mass.App.Ct. 327.

D.C.App.1987. Carr v. U.S. 531 A.2d 1010.

Ark.App.,1987. Sandlin v. Kochman 1987 WL 17736.

Ark.App.,1987. Murphy v. Bank of Dardanelle 1987 WL 17036.

N.Y.1986. People v. Gonzalez 509 N.Y.S.2d 796, 68 N.Y.2d 424, 502 N.E.2d 583.

Mass.App.Ct.1986. Com. v. Schatvet 499 N.E.2d 1208, 23 Mass.App.Ct. 130.

§ 265. Admissions by Conduct: (e) Misconduct Constituting Obstruction of Justice

[Treated in § 273 in the 3rd Ed.]

C.A.5 (Tex.)1991. U.S. v. Farias–Farias 925 F.2d 805.

C.A.5 (Tex.)1988. U.S. v. Richardson 848 F.2d 509.

C.A.6 (Ky.)1988. Welsh v. U.S. 844 F.2d 1239.

C.A.Cal.1984. Handgards, Inc. v. Ethicon, Inc. 743 F.2d 1282.

N.D.Ill., 1986. Empire Gas Corp. v. American Bakeries Co. 1986 WL 6945.

N.D.Ill., 1986. Empire Gas Corp. v. American Bakeries Co. 646 F.Supp. 269.

D.C.App.1990. Battocchi v. Washington Hosp. Center 581 A.2d 759.

Ark.App.1990. Flowers v. State 785 S.W.2d 242, 30 Ark.App. 204.

Conn.1990. State v. Walker 571 A.2d 686, 214 Conn. 122.

Ill.App. 2 Dist.1989. People v. Chambers 534 N.E.2d 554, 179 Ill.App.3d 565, 128 Ill.Dec. 372.

Ill.App. 4 Dist.1986. People v. Houston 497 N.E.2d 784, 146 Ill.App.3d 982, 100 Ill.Dec. 606.

Conn.App.1986. State v. Waterman 509 A.2d 518, 7 Conn.App. 326.

Ariz.App.1985. State v. Rea 701 P.2d 6, 145 Ariz. 298.

§ 266. Admissions by Conduct: (f) Offers to Compromise Disputed Claim in Civil Suits and Plea Negotiations in Criminal Cases

[Treated in § 274 in the 3rd Ed.]

C.A.2 (N.Y.) 1990. American Soc. of Composers, Authors and Publishers v. Showtime/The Movie Channel, Inc. 912 F.2d 563.

C.A.9 (Wash.)1987. Cassino v. Reichhold Chemicals, Inc. 817 F.2d 1338.

C.A.5 (Tex.)1986. Kennon v. Slipstreamer, Inc. 794 F.2d 1067.

S.D.N.Y., 1989. U.S. v. American Soc. of Composers, Authors and Publishers 1989 WL 222654.

N.C.App.1991. Carter v. Foster 404 S.E.2d 484, 103 N.C.App. 110.

Idaho, 1991. Fitzgerald v. Walker 1991 WL 1258.

Mich.1990. Lichon v. American Universal Ins. Co. 459 N.W.2d 288, 435 Mich. 408.

D.C.App.1990. Beckman v. Farmer 579 A.2d 618.

Wash.1989. Bulaich v. AT & T Information Systems 778 P.2d 1031, 113 Wash.2d 254.

Ark.App., 1989. Williams v. Williams 1989 WL 10063.

D.C.App.1988. Goon v. Gee Kung Tong, Inc. 544 A.2d 277.

Mass.App.Ct.1988. Bedford v. Trustees of Boston University 518 N.E.2d 874, 25 Mass.App.Ct. 372.

Iowa 1987. Gail v. Clark 410 N.W.2d 662.

Wis.App., 1987. Marso v. Ulma 409 N.W.2d 670 (Table), 140 Wis.2d 859, Unpublished Disposition.(*)

D.C.App.1985. Pyne v. Jamaica Nutrition Holdings Ltd. 497 A.2d 118.

Idaho 1985. Rojas v. Lindsay Mfg. Co. 701 P.2d 210, 108 Idaho 590.

§ 267. Admissions by Conduct: (g) Safety Measure After an Accident; Payment of Medical Expenses

[Treated in § 275 in the 3rd Ed.]

La.1991. Northern Assur. Co. v. Louisiana Power & Light Co. 580 So.2d 351, Rehearing Denied.

Mo.App., 1990. Schaefer v. Yellow Freight Systems, Inc. 1990 WL 12072.

Md.1989. Wilson v. Morris 563 A.2d 392, 317 Md. 284.

Mo.App.1989. State ex rel. Kawasaki Motors Corp., U.S.A. v. Ryan 777 S.W.2d 247.

Tenn.App.1988. Howard v. Abernathy 751 S.W.2d 432.

Tenn.App.1988. Thompson v. Thompson 749 S.W.2d 468.

Neb.1987. Rahmig v. Mosley Machinery Co. 412 N.W.2d 56, 226 Neb. 423.

Miss.1987. Mitcham v. Illinois Cent. Gulf R. Co. 515 So.2d 852.

Md.App.1986. University Nursing Home, Inc. v. R.B. Brown & Associates, Inc. 506 A.2d 268, 67 Md.App. 48.

Mich.App.1985. Hadley v. Trio Tool Co. 372 N.W.2d 537, 143 Mich.App. 319.

Mich.1984. Downie v. Kent Products, Inc. 362 N.W.2d 605, 420 Mich. 197.

CHAPTER 26. SPONTANEOUS STATEMENTS

[Formerly Chapter 29 in the 3rd Ed.]

§ 268. Res Gestae and the Hearsay Rule

[Treated in § 288 in the 3rd Ed.]

La.App., 1991. State v. Moran 1991 WL 116850.

Wis.App., 1991. State v. Hoyt 472 N.W.2d 248 (Table), Unpublished Disposition.(*)

Wash.App.1990. State v. Heath 792 P.2d 558, 58 Wash.App. 320.

Ala.Cr.App.1989. Cheriogotis v. State 555 So.2d 1147.

Tenn.Cr.App.1989. State v. Carpenter 773 S.W.2d 1.

Miss.1988. Sayre v. State 533 So.2d 464.

N.Y.Sup.1987. People v. Luke 519 N.Y.S.2d 316, 136 Misc.2d 733.

Ind.1987. Riley v. State 506 N.E.2d 476.

La.App. 1 Cir.1986. State v. Yochim (Two Cases) 496 So.2d 596.

Ala.Cr.App.1986. Lovett v. State 491 So.2d 1034.

Md.App.1985. Booth v. State 488 A.2d 195, 62 Md.App. 26.

§ 269. Spontaneous Statement as Nonhearsay: Circumstantial Proof of a Fact in Issue

[Treated in § 289 in the 3rd Ed.]

Pa.1986. Com. v. Peterkin 513 A.2d 373, 511 Pa. 299.

§ 270. "Self–Serving" Aspects of Spontaneous Statements

[Treated in § 290 in the 3rd Ed.]

§ 271. Unexcited Statements of Present Sense Impressions

[Treated in § 298 in the 3rd Ed.]

E.D.N.Y.1985. U.S. v. Obayagbona 627 F.Supp. 329.

Pa.Super.1989. Lira v. Albert Einstein Medical Center 559 A.2d 550, 384 Pa.Super. 503.

Tenn.Cr.App.1989. State v. Carpenter 773 S.W.2d 1.

Md.1987. State v. Jones 532 A.2d 169, 311 Md. 23.

N.Y.Sup.1987. People v. Luke 519 N.Y.S.2d 316, 136 Misc.2d 733.

W.Va.1987. State v. Smith 358 S.E.2d 188.

Pa.1986. Com. v. Peterkin 513 A.2d 373, 511 Pa. 299.

Md.1986. Booth v. State 508 A.2d 976, 306 Md. 313, 54 U.S.L.W. 2642.

Md.App.1985. Jones v. State 499 A.2d 511, 65 Md.App. 121.

§ 272. Excited Utterances

[Treated in § 297 in the 3rd Ed.]

C.A.4 (Va.)1988. Morgan v. Foretich (Two Cases) 846 F.2d 941.

C.A.1 (Mass.)1987. U.S. v. Bailey 834 F.2d 218.

C.D.Ill.1986. Jones v. Greer 627 F.Supp. 1481.

E.D.N.Y.1985. U.S. v. Obayagbona 627 F.Supp. 329.

Fla.App. 1 Dist.,1991. Flanagan v. State 1991 WL 133574.

Colo.App.,1991. People v. Hulsing 1991 WL 131994.

La.App. 2 Cir.1991. State v. Bean 582 So.2d 947.

Wis.App.,1991. State v. La Porte 472 N.W.2d 247 (Table), Unpublished Disposition.(*)

Tex.App.–Eastland, 1991. Texas Utilities Elec. Co. v. Gold Kist, Inc. 1991 WL 186885.

Md.App.1990. Cole v. State 574 A.2d 326, 83 Md.App. 279.

Fla.App. 3 Dist.,1990. Hernandez v. State 556 So.2d 1165.

Fla.App. 3 Dist.1990. Sunn v. Colonial Penn Ins. Co. 556 So.2d 1156.

Ind.1989. Williams v. State 546 N.E.2d 1198.

Mich.1989. People v. Burton 445 N.W.2d 133, 433 Mich. 268.

Tenn.Cr.App.1989. State v. Payton 782 S.W.2d 490.

Tenn.Cr.App.1989. State v. Person 781 S.W.2d 868.

Wis.1989. State v. Martinez 440 N.W.2d 783, 150 Wis.2d 62.

N.H.1989. Wilder v. City of Keene 557 A.2d 636, 131 N.H. 599.

Idaho App.1989. State v. Burton 772 P.2d 1248, 115 Idaho 1154.

Mont.1988. State v. J.C.E. 767 P.2d 309, 235 Mont. 264.

D.C.App.1988. Price v. U.S. 545 A.2d 1219.

Mich.1988. People v. Straight 424 N.W.2d 257, 430 Mich. 418.

Fla.1988. State v. Jano 524 So.2d 660.

N.J.Super.A.D.1988. State v. J.S. 536 A.2d 769, 222 N.J.Super. 247.

Ind.1987. Matthews v. State 515 N.E.2d 1105.

N.Y.1987. People v. Brown 522 N.Y.S.2d 837, 70 N.Y.2d 513, 517 N.E.2d 515.

Vt.1987. State v. Ayers 535 A.2d 330, 148 Vt. 421.

Va.App.1987. Martin v. Com. 358 S.E.2d 415, 4 Va.App. 438.

Pa.Super.1987. Com. v. Rhoades 527 A.2d 148, 364 Pa.Super. 54.

W.Va.1987. State v. Smith 358 S.E.2d 188.

Mich.App.1987. People v. Kent 404 N.W.2d 668, 157 Mich.App. 780.

Idaho 1986. State v. Parker 730 P.2d 921, 112 Idaho 1.

La.App. 1 Cir.1986. State v. Yochim (Two Cases) 496 So.2d 596.

N.C.1985. State v. Smith 337 S.E.2d 833, 315 N.C. 76.

N.H.1985. State v. Bonalumi 503 A.2d 786, 127 N.H. 485.

Ind.1985. Holmes v. State 480 N.E.2d 916.

Mo.App.1985. State v. Meyer 694 S.W.2d 853.

N.J.Super.,1985. State v. Ramos 496 A.2d 386, 203 N.J.Super. 197.

Nev.1984. Dearing v. State 691 P.2d 419, 100 Nev. 590.

§ 273. Statements of Physical or Mental Condition: (a) Bodily Feelings, Symptoms, and Condition

[Treated in § 291 in the 3rd Ed.]

Mo.App.1990. Koenke v. Eldenburg 803 S.W.2d 68.

Pa.Super.1989. Hreha v. Benscoter 554 A.2d 525, 381 Pa.Super. 556.

Okl.Cr.1988. Phillips v. State 756 P.2d 604.

§ 274. Statements of Physical or Mental Condition: (b) Statements of Present Mental or Emotional State to Show a State of Mind or Emotion in Issue

[Treated in § 294 in the 3rd Ed.]

C.A.8 (Minn.) 1990. U.S. v. French 900 F.2d 1300.

Bkrtcy.S.D.N.Y.1987. In re Fill 68 B.R. 923.

Mo.App.1991. State v. Buckner 810 S.W.2d 354.

D.C.App.1988. Jackson v. Young 546 A.2d 1009.

Md.App.1988. Kirkland v. State 540 A.2d 490, 75 Md.App. 49.

Pa.1987. Com. v. Jermyn 533 A.2d 74, 516 Pa. 460.

Md.App.1987. Nash v. State 519 A.2d 769, 69 Md.App. 681.

Pa.Super.1986. Reimer v. Tien 514 A.2d 566, 356 Pa.Super. 192.

Colo.1986. People v. Haymaker 716 P.2d 110.

N.J.Super.A.D.1986. State v. Downey 502 A.2d 1171, 206 N.J.Super. 382.

Pa.Super.1985. Spotts v. Reidell 497 A.2d 630, 345 Pa.Super. 37.

§ 275. Statements of Physical or Mental Condition: (c) Statements of Intention Offered to Show Subsequent Acts of Declarant

[Treated in § 295 in the 3rd Ed.]

C.A.9 (Wash.)1986. U.S. v. Washington Water Power Co. 793 F.2d 1079.

La.1990. State v. Brown 562 So.2d 868, Rehearing Denied.

Minn.App.,1989. State v. Goodmund 1989 WL 49260.

Conn.1987. State v. Santangelo 534 A.2d 1175, 205 Conn. 578.

Mo.App.1987. State v. Peters 732 S.W.2d 227.

Mich.App.1987. People v. Furman 404 N.W.2d 246, 158 Mich.App. 302.

Md.1985. McCray v. State 501 A.2d 856, 305 Md. 126.

Tex.App. 8 Dist.1985. Howlett v. State 700 S.W.2d 751.

Mo.App.1985. State v. Newman 699 S.W.2d 29.

Wash.App.1985. State v. Bernson 700 P.2d 758, 40 Wash.App. 729.

§ 276. Statements of Physical or Mental Condition: (d) Statements of State of Mind to Show Memory or Belief as Proof of Previous Happenings

[Treated in § 296 in the 3rd Ed.]

Mass.App.Ct.1991. Com. v. Williams 571 N.E.2d 29, 30 Mass.App.Ct. 543.

Pa.Super.1989. Hreha v. Benscoter 554 A.2d 525, 381 Pa.Super. 556.

La.App. 1 Cir.1988. State v. Riley 532 So.2d 1174.

Mass.1986. Com. v. Pope 491 N.E.2d 240, 397 Mass. 275.

Ark.1986. Vasquez v. State 702 S.W.2d 411, 287 Ark. 468.

CHAPTER 27. STATEMENTS FOR THE PURPOSE OF MEDICAL DIAGNOSIS OR TREATMENT

[This chapter is new in 4th Ed.]

§ 277. Statements of Bodily Feelings, Symptoms, and Condition: (a) Statements Made to Physicians Consulted for Treatment

[Treated in § 292 in the 3rd Ed.]

C.A.5 (Tex.)1991. Wilson v. Zapata Off-Shore Co. 939 F.2d 260.

C.A.11 (Ga.)1989. Jones v. Miles Laboratories, Inc. 887 F.2d 1576.

E.D.Pa., 1986. Brown v. Frame, et al. 1986 WL 1211.

N.J.1991. R.S. v. Knighton 592 A.2d 1157, 125 N.J. 79.

Mont.1991. State v. Harris 808 P.2d 453.

W.Va.1990. State v. Edward Charles L. 398 S.E.2d 123.

Miss.1989. Hall v. State 539 So.2d 1338.

Wis.1987. State v. Nelson 406 N.W.2d 385, 138 Wis.2d 418.

Ill.App. 4 Dist.1987. People v. Taylor 506 N.E.2d 321, 153 Ill.App.3d 710, 106 Ill. Dec. 614.

Colo.1986. Oldsen v. People 732 P.2d 1132.

N.C.1986. State v. Aguallo 350 S.E.2d 76, 318 N.C. 590.

§ 278. Statements of Bodily Feelings, Symptoms, and Condition: (b) Statements Made to Physicians Consulted Only to Testify

[Treated in § 293 in the 3rd Ed.]

Mich.App.1990. People v. Hackney 455 N.W.2d 358, 183 Mich.App. 516.

Mich.1989. People v. LaLone 437 N.W.2d 611, 432 Mich. 103.

Ala.1987. Seaboard System R.R., Inc. v. Keen 514 So.2d 1018.

CHAPTER 28. RECORDS OF PAST RECOLLECTION

[Formerly Chapter 30 in 3rd Ed.]

§ 279. History and Theory of the Exception

[Treated in § 299 in the 3rd Ed.]

§ 280. Firsthand Knowledge

[Treated in § 300 in the 3rd Ed.]

C.A.9 (Cal.)1986. U.S. v. Owens 789 F.2d 750.

D.C.App.1986. Roberts v. U.S. 508 A.2d 110.

Idaho App.1986. State v. Rosencrantz 714 P.2d 93, 110 Idaho 124.

§ 281. Written Statement Made While the Witness' Memory Was Clear

[Treated in § 301 in the 3rd Ed.]

R.I.1988. State v. Mastracchio 546 A.2d 165.

§ 282. Impairment of Recollection

[Treated in § 302 in the 3rd Ed.]

Md.App.1986. Sanders v. State 505 A.2d 557, 66 Md.App. 590.

Ind.App. 2 Dist 1986. Blinn v. State 487 N.E.2d 462.

§ 283. Proving the Accuracy of the Written Statement; Multi–Party Situations

[Treated in § 303 in the 3rd Ed.]

D.C.App.1985. Eldridge v. U.S. 492 A.2d 879.

CHAPTER 29. RECORDS OF REGULARLY KEPT RECORDS

[Formerly Chapter 31 in 3rd Ed.]

§ 284. Admissibility of Regularly Kept Records

[Treated in § 304 in the 3rd Ed.]

C.A.5 (La.)1985. U.S. v. Marshall 762 F.2d 419.

N.J.Super.A.D.1990. State In Interest of J.H. 581 A.2d 1347, 244 N.J.Super. 207.

§ 285. The Origin of the Regularly Kept Records Exception and the Shopbook Vestige

[Treated in § 305 in the 3rd Ed.]

Mich.1990. Solomon v. Shuell 457 N.W.2d 669, 435 Mich. 104.

Md.1988. State v. Garlick 545 A.2d 27, 313 Md. 209.

§ 286. The Regularly Kept Records Exception in General

[Treated in § 306 in the 3rd Ed.]

C.A.5 (La.)1991. Rock v. Huffco Gas & Oil Co., Inc. 922 F.2d 272.

C.A.7 (Ill.)1990. Datamatic Services, Inc. v. U.S. 909 F.2d 1029.

Ark.App., 1988. Woolford v. State 1988 WL 124769.

Pa.Super.1988. Com. v. Sullivan 538 A.2d 1363, 372 Pa.Super. 88.

N.Y.1986. People v. Kennedy 510 N.Y.S.2d 853, 68 N.Y.2d 569, 503 N.E.2d 501.

Ark.App.1986. Wildwood Contractors v. Thompson–Holloway Real Estate Agency 705 S.W.2d 897, 17 Ark.App. 169.

Pa.Super.1985. Ganster v. Western Pennsylvania Water Co. 504 A.2d 186, 349 Pa.Super. 561.

§ 287. Types of Records; Opinions; Absence of Entry

[Treated in § 307 in the 3rd Ed.]

Ark.App., 1988. Woolford v. State 1988 WL 124769.

§ 288. Made in the Routine of a "Business"; Accident Reports

[Treated in § 308 in the 3rd Ed.]

C.A.5 (La.)1991. Rock v. Huffco Gas & Oil Co., Inc. 922 F.2d 272.

C.A.2 (N.Y.)1988. U.S. v. Freidin 849 F.2d 716.

C.A.Or.1984. Paddack v. Dave Christensen, Inc. 745 F.2d 1254.

S.D.N.Y., 1987. U.S. v. Freidin 1987 WL 9442.

Mich.1990. Solomon v. Shuell 457 N.W.2d 669, 435 Mich. 104.

Tex.App.–Hous. [14 Dist.], 1987. Interstate Maintenance Co. v. Floyd West & Co. 1987 WL 25855.

Fla.App. 3 Dist.1985. Stambor v. One Hundred Seventy–Second Collins Corp. 465 So.2d 1296.

§ 289. Made at or Near the Time of the Transaction Recorded

[Treated in § 309 in the 3rd Ed.]

Neb.1986. Crowder v. Aurora Co-op. Elevator Co. 393 N.W.2d 250, 223 Neb. 704.

N.Y.A.D. 2 Dept.1984. People v. Klein 481 N.Y.S.2d 743, 105 A.D.2d 805.

§ 290. Personal Knowledge; All Participants in Regular Course of Business

[Treated in § 310 in the 3rd Ed.]

C.A.11 (Fla.)1991. T. Harris Young & Associates, Inc. v. Marquette Electronics, Inc. 931 F.2d 816.

E.D.Pa.1989. In re Fleet 95 B.R. 319.

Colo.1990. Schmutz v. Bolles 800 P.2d 1307.

Pa.Super.1987. Wilkerson v. Allied Van Lines, Inc. 521 A.2d 25, 360 Pa.Super. 523.

D.C.App.1986. In re D.M.C. 503 A.2d 1280.

§ 291. Unavailability

[Treated in § 311 in the 3rd Ed.]

§ 292. Proof; Who Must Be Called to Establish Admissibility

[Treated in § 312 in the 3rd Ed.]

Ark.App.,1988. Woolford v. State 1988 WL 124769.

Ind.App. 3 Dist 1988. Getha v. State 524 N.E.2d 325.

Ind.App. 3 Dist 1986. Wilson v. Jenga Corp. 490 N.E.2d 375.

N.Y.A.D. 2 Dept.1985. Walker v. State 488 N.Y.S.2d 793, 111 A.D.2d 164.

§ 293. Special Situations: (a) Hospital Records

[Treated in § 313 in the 3rd Ed.]

C.A.9 (Or.)1987. U.S. v. Simmons 812 F.2d 561.

E.D.Pa.,1986. Brown v. Frame 1986 WL 1211.

La.,1990. State v. McElroy 568 So.2d 1016.

Tenn.Cr.App.,1990. State v. Draper 1990 WL 90940.

La.1989. State v. McElroy 553 So.2d 456.

Mass.1987. Com. v. McDonough 511 N.E.2d 551, 400 Mass. 639.

N.H.1987. Aubert v. Aubert 529 A.2d 909, 129 N.H. 422.

Minn.App.1986. Wagner v. Thomas J. Obert Enterprises 384 N.W.2d 477.

Mo.1984. Breeding v. Dodson Trailer Repair, Inc. 679 S.W.2d 281.

§ 294. Special Situations: (b) Computer Records

[Treated in § 314 in the 3rd Ed.]

C.A.Pa.1985. U.S. v. Downing 753 F.2d 1224.

Pa.Super.1991. Com. v. Corradino 588 A.2d 936, 403 Pa.Super. 251.

CHAPTER 30. PUBLIC RECORDS, REPORTS, AND CERTIFICATES

[Formerly Chapter 32 in 3rd Ed.]

§ 295. The Exception for Public Records and Reports: (a) In General

[Treated in § 315 in the 3rd Ed.]

C.A.11 (Ala.)1988. Gholston v. Jones 848 F.2d 1156.

Tex.Cr.App.,1990. Cole v. State 1990 WL 176357.

Wash.1989. State v. Monson 784 P.2d 485, 113 Wash.2d 833.

Wash.App.1989. State v. Monson 771 P.2d 359, 53 Wash.App. 854.

D.C.App.1988. Giles v. District of Columbia 548 A.2d 48.

Va.App.1986. Ingram v. Com. 338 S.E.2d 657, 1 Va.App. 335.

Md.1985. Ellsworth v. Sherne Lingerie, Inc. 495 A.2d 348, 303 Md. 581.

§ 296. The Exception for Public Records and Reports: (b) Activities of the Office; Matters Observed; Investigative Reports; Restrictions on Prosecutorial Use

[Treated in § 316 in the 3rd Ed.]

C.A.5 (La.)1990. Federal Deposit Ins. Corp. v. Mmahat 907 F.2d 546.

D.Colo.1989. In re Air Crash Disaster at Stapleton Intern. Airport, Denver, Colo., on Nov. 15, 1987 720 F.Supp. 1493.

U.S.Fla.1988. Beech Aircraft Corp. v. Rainey 109 S.Ct. 439, 488 U.S. 153, 102 L.Ed.2d 445.

C.A.3 (Pa.)1987. Trustees of University of Pennsylvania v. Lexington Ins. Co. 815 F.2d 890.

Ill.App. 1 Dist.,1991. People v. Garrett 159 Ill.Dec. 662, 576 N.E.2d 331.

Mich.1990. Solomon v. Shuell 457 N.W.2d 669, 435 Mich. 104.

Or.App.1988. State v. Scally 758 P.2d 365, 92 Or.App. 149.

Md.1985. Ellsworth v. Sherne Lingerie, Inc. 495 A.2d 348, 303 Md. 581.

§ 297. The Exception for Public Records and Reports: (c) Vital Statistics

[Treated in § 317 in the 3rd Ed.]

W.Va.1988. Moore v. Goode 375 S.E.2d 549.

§ 298. The Exception for Public Records and Reports: (d) Judgments in Previous Cases, Especially Criminal Convictions Offered in Subsequent Civil Cases

[Treated in § 318 in the 3rd Ed.]

C.A.6 (Mich.),1991. U.S. v. Cohen ___ F.2d ___, 1991 WL 199439, Unpublished Disposition.*

2. C.A.7 (Ill.)1987. Greycas, Inc. v. Proud 826 F.2d 1560.

3. C.A.3 (Pa.)1987. Trustees of University of Pennsylvania v. Lexington Ins. Co. 815 F.2d 890.

N.M.App., 1991. State v. Hoeffel 815 P.2d 654.

N.J.Super.L.1990. Yelder v. Zuvich 585 A.2d 434, 245 N.J.Super. 331.

Ark.1989. Ruiz v. State 772 S.W.2d 297, 299 Ark. 144.

W.Va.1988. Moore v. Goode 375 S.E.2d 549.

Tenn.App., 1988. Sullivan v. Forbis 1988 WL 23913.

Ohio App., 1988. State v. Bunfill 1988 WL 3214.

Idaho 1986. Anderson v. City of Pocatello 731 P.2d 171, 112 Idaho 176.

Minn.App.1986. Regents of University of Minnesota v. Medical Inc. 382 N.W.2d 201.

§ 299. The Exception for Official Certificates: (a) In General

[Treated in § 319 in the 3rd Ed.]

§ 300. The Exception for Official Certificates: (b) Certified Copies or Summaries of Official Records; Absence of Record

[Treated in § 320 in the 3rd Ed.]

N.J.Super.A.D.1990. State In Interest of J.H. 581 A.2d 1347, 244 N.J.Super. 207.

D.C.App.1988. Giles v. District of Columbia 548 A.2d 48.

CHAPTER 31. TESTIMONY TAKEN AT A FORMER HEARING OR IN ANOTHER ACTION

[Formerly Chapter 25 in 3rd Ed.]

§ 301. Introduction; Is It Hearsay? Scope of Statutes and Rules

[Treated in § 254 in the 3rd Ed.]

Pa.Super.1987. Com. v. McGrogan 532 A.2d 1203, 367 Pa.Super. 394.

Ind.App. 2 Dist 1986. Blinn v. State 487 N.E.2d 462.

Md.1985. Huffington v. State 500 A.2d 272, 304 Md. 559.

Ariz.1985. State v. Williams 698 P.2d 724, 144 Ariz. 479.

§ 302. The Requirement of Oath and Opportunity for Cross–Examination; Confrontation and Unavailability

[Treated in § 255 in the 3rd Ed.]

Md.App.1990. Traverso v. State 574 A.2d 923, 83 Md.App. 389.

Md.App.1990. Board of Educ. of Charles County v. Plymouth Rubber Co. 569 A.2d 1288, 82 Md.App. 9.

W.Va.1989. King v. Kayak Mfg. Corp. 387 S.E.2d 511.

Md.1985. Huffington v. State 500 A.2d 272, 304 Md. 559.

§ 303. Identity of Parties; "Predecessor in Interest"

[Treated in § 256 in the 3rd Ed.]

Pa.Super.1986. Estate of Keefauver 518 A.2d 1263, 359 Pa.Super. 336.

Mo.App.1986. Maxwell v. City of Springfield 705 S.W.2d 90.

§ 304. Identity of Issues; Motive to Cross–Examine

[Treated in § 257 in the 3rd Ed.]

Mich.App.1986. People v. Vera 395 N.W.2d 339, 153 Mich.App. 411.

Va.1986. Gray v. Graham 341 S.E.2d 153, 231 Va. 1.

§ 305. The Character of the Tribunal and of the Proceedings in Which the Former Testimony Was Taken

[Treated in § 258 in the 3rd Ed.]

§ 306. Objections and Their Determination

[Treated in § 259 in the 3rd Ed.]

Mich.1989. People v. Hamacher 438 N.W.2d 43, 432 Mich. 157.

S.C.App.1985. Clark v. Ross 328 S.E.2d 91, 284 S.C. 543.

§ 307. Methods and Scope of Proof

[Treated in § 260 in the 3rd Ed.]

Miss.1986. Brumfield v. Mississippi State Bar Ass'n 497 So.2d 800.

N.C.App.1985. State v. West 333 S.E.2d 522, 76 N.C.App. 459.

§ 308. Possibilities of Improving Existing Practice

[Treated in § 261 in the 3rd Ed.]

CHAPTER 32. DYING DECLARATIONS

[Formerly Chapter 28 in 3rd Ed.]

§ 309. Introduction

[Treated in § 281 in the 3rd Ed.]

N.Y.1986. People v. Nieves 501 N.Y.S.2d 1, 67 N.Y.2d 125, 492 N.E.2d 109.

§ 310. Requirements That Declarant Must Have Been Conscious of Impending Death and That Declarant Must Be Dead or Otherwise Unavailable

[Treated in § 282 in the 3rd Ed.]

§ 311. Limitation to the Use in Criminal Homicide Cases, and Other Arbitrary Limitations

[Treated in § 283 in the 3rd Ed.]

N.Y.1986. People v. Nieves 501 N.Y.S.2d 1, 67 N.Y.2d 125, 492 N.E.2d 109.

§ 312. Admissible on Behalf of Accused as Well as for Prosecution

[Treated in § 284 in the 3rd Ed.]

Fla.App. 4 Dist.1990. State v. Weir 569 So.2d 897.

§ 313. Application of Other Evidentiary Rules: Personal Knowledge; Opinion; Rules About Writings

[Treated in § 285 in the 3rd Ed.]

Fla.App. 4 Dist.1990. State v. Weir 569 So.2d 897.

§ 314. Instructions regarding the Weight to Be Given to Dying Declarations

[Treated in § 286 in the 3rd Ed.]

§ 315. Decisional and Statutory Extensions of Common Law Admissibility

[Treated in § 287 in the 3rd Ed.]

CHAPTER 33. DECLARATIONS AGAINST INTEREST

[Formerly Chapter 27 in 3rd Ed.]

§ 316. General Requirements; Distinction Between Declarations Against Interest and Admissions

[Treated in § 276 in the 3rd Ed.]

Md.App.1985. Muir v. State 498 A.2d 666, 64 Md.App. 648.

§ 317. Declarations Against Pecuniary or Proprietary Interest; Declarations Affecting Claim or Liability for Damages

[Treated in § 277 in the 3rd Ed.]

Ga.1987. Hamrick v. Greenway 357 S.E.2d 580, 257 Ga. 287.

Pa.Super.1985. Heddings v. Steele 496 A.2d 1166, 344 Pa.Super. 399.

§ 318. Penal Interest; Interest of Prestige or Self–Esteem

[Treated in § 278 in the 3rd Ed.]

U.S.Ill.1986. Lee v. Illinois 106 S.Ct. 2056, 476 U.S. 530, 90 L.Ed.2d 514.

Wyo.1989. King v. State 780 P.2d 943.

Utah 1988. State v. Worthen 765 P.2d 839.

Mass.App.Ct.1988. Com. v. Marple 524 N.E.2d 863, 26 Mass.App.Ct. 150.

Md.1987. State v. Standifur 526 A.2d 955, 310 Md. 3.

Conn.1987. State v. Bryant 523 A.2d 451, 202 Conn. 676.

Iowa 1985. Conner v. State 362 N.W.2d 449.

§ 319. Determining What Is Against Interest; Confrontation Problems

[Treated in § 279 in the 3rd Ed.]

D.C.Pa.1988. U.S. v. Green 694 F.Supp. 107.

Ala.Cr.App., 1990. Turner v. State 1990 WL 187036.

Utah App.1990. State v. Drawn 791 P.2d 890.

Md.1987. State v. Standifur 526 A.2d 955, 310 Md. 3.

Md.App.1985. Standifur v. State 497 A.2d 1164, 64 Md.App. 570.

Idaho 1984. State v. Hoak 692 P.2d 1174, 107 Idaho 742.

§ 320. Unavailability of the Declarant

[Treated in § 280 in the 3rd Ed.]

CHAPTER 34. VARIOUS OTHER EXCEPTIONS AND THE FUTURE OF THE RULES ABOUT HEARSAY

[Formerly chapter 33 in 3rd Ed.]

§ 321. Learned Writings, Industry Standards, and Commercial Publications

N.C.App.,1991. The Rowan County Board of Education v. United States Gypsum Company 407 S.E.2d 860, 103 N.C.App. 288.

Pa.Super.1988. Majdic v. Cincinnati Mach. Co. 537 A.2d 334, 370 Pa.Super. 611.

La.App. 1 Cir.1987. State v. Schrader 506 So.2d 866.

§ 322. Statements and Reputation as to Pedigree and Family History, Land Boundaries, and General History

§ 323. Recitals in Ancient Writings and Documents Affecting an Interest in Property

S.C.App.1990. Johnson v. Pritchard 395 S.E.2d 191.

W.Va.1988. Moore v. Goode 375 S.E.2d 549.

§ 324. The Residual Hearsay Exceptions

Ind.1991. Miller v. State 575 N.E.2d 272.

Or.1991. State v. Pinnell 806 P.2d 110, 311 Or. 98.

Ill.App. 2 Dist.1989. People v. Chambers 534 N.E.2d 554, 179 Ill.App.3d 565, 128 Ill.Dec. 372.

Tenn.App.1989. West End Recreation, Inc. v. Hodge 776 S.W.2d 101.

N.C.1988. State v. Deanes 374 S.E.2d 249, 323 N.C. 508.

Tenn.App.,1988. Breedlove v. Tennessee Farmers Mut. Ins. Co. 1988 WL 67167.

Idaho App.1988. State v. Boehner 756 P.2d 1075, 114 Idaho 311.

Pa.Super.1987. Wilkerson v. Allied Van Lines, Inc. 521 A.2d 25, 360 Pa.Super. 523.

Md.App.1987. Nash v. State 519 A.2d 769, 69 Md.App. 681.

Pa.Super.1986. Maravich v. Aetna Life and Cas. Co. 504 A.2d 896, 350 Pa.Super. 392.

N.C.1985. State v. Smith 337 S.E.2d 833, 315 N.C. 76.

Or.1985. State v. Campbell 705 P.2d 694, 299 Or. 633.

Tenn.App.1985. Butler v. Ballard 696 S.W.2d 533.

Mo.App.1985. Killian Const. Co. v. Tri-City Const. Co. 693 S.W.2d 819.

Ark.App.1985. Arkansas State Highway Com'n v. Schell 683 S.W.2d 618, 13 Ark. App. 293.

§ 325. Evaluation of the Present Rules

§ 326. Basic Shifts in the Contemporary Pattern

§ 327. The Future of Hearsay

CHAPTER 35. JUDICIAL NOTICE

§ 328. The Need for and the Effect of Judicial Notice

C.A.9 1985. Lawrence v. Commodity Futures Trading Com'n 759 F.2d 767.

Tex.Cr.App.1987. Chapa v. State 729 S.W.2d 723.

Idaho App.1986. Brazier v. Brazier 726 P.2d 1143, 111 Idaho 692.

§ 329. Matters of Common Knowledge

Mass.App.Ct.1989. Com. v. Green 543 N.E.2d 424, 27 Mass.App.Ct. 762.

Neb.1989. State v. Vejvoda 438 N.W.2d 461, 231 Neb. 668.

Mo.App.1987. Hammond v. Missouri Property Ins. Placement Facility 731 S.W.2d 360.

Md.App.1986. Trusty v. State 508 A.2d 1018, 67 Md.App. 620.

Minn.App.1986. State v. Pilla 380 N.W.2d 207.

§ 330. Facts Capable of Certain Verification

Neb.1990. Gottsch v. Bank of Stapleton 458 N.W.2d 443, 235 Neb. 816.

Mass.App.Ct.1989. Com. v. Green 543 N.E.2d 424, 27 Mass.App.Ct. 762.

§ 331. Social and Economic Data Used in Judicial Law-Making: "Legislative" Facts

Wis.1990. State v. Rewolinski 464 N.W.2d 401, 159 Wis.2d 1.

Tex.Cr.App.1987. Chapa v. State 729 S.W.2d 723.

Minn.App.1986. State v. Pilla 380 N.W.2d 207.

§ 332. The Uses of Judicial Notice

§ 333. Procedural Incidents

C.A.10 (Kan.)1990. Clemmons v. Bohannon 918 F.2d 858.

§ 334. Trends in the Development of Judicial Notice of Facts

§ 335. The Judge's Task as Law-Finder: Judicial Notice of Law

C.A.7 (Ill.)1987. Justice v. Elrod 832 F.2d 1048.

C.A.7 (Ill.)1986. Benson v. Allphin 786 F.2d 268.

Vt.,1991. State v. Metivier 596 A.2d 352.

Or.1986. Warm Springs Forest Products Industries, Div. of Confederated Tribes of Warm Springs Reservation of Oregon v. Employee Benefits Ins. Co. 716 P.2d 740, 300 Or. 617.

Mass.App.1985. Rice v. James Hanrahan & Sons 482 N.E.2d 833, 20 Mass.App. 701.

CHAPTER 36. THE BURDENS OF PROOF AND PRESUMPTIONS

§ 336. The Burdens of Proof: The Burden of Producing Evidence and the Burden of Persuasion

C.A.7 (Ill.)1989. Fallon v. State of Ill. 882 F.2d 1206.

C.A.Fed.1988. Yamaha Intern. Corp. v. Hoshino Gakki Co., Ltd. 840 F.2d 1572.

C.A.9 (Cal.)1986. Lew v. Moss 797 F.2d 747.

C.A.D.C.1984. City of Winnfield, La. v. F.E.R.C. 744 F.2d 871.

E.D.Mich.1988. Fireman's Fund Ins. Companies v. ExCello Corp. 702 F.Supp. 1317.

Bkrtcy.D.R.I.,1991. In re Max Sugarman Funeral Home Inc., 130 B.R. 119.

Bkrtcy.D.Vt.1988. In re Mayo 94 B.R. 315.

Bkrtcy.D.Vt.1985. In re Trail's End Lodge, Inc. 54 B.R. 898.

Wash.App.1991. In re Dependency of C.B. 810 P.2d 518, 61 Wash.App. 280.

Tex.App.Dallas 1991. Alford v. State 806 S.W.2d 581.

Mo.App.,1990. State v. Tipton 1990 WL 121243.

Miss.1989. Clardy v. National Bank of Commerce of Mississippi 555 So.2d 64.

Md.1989. Kassap v. Seitz 553 A.2d 714, 315 Md. 155.

Alaska App.1988. Davis v. State 766 P.2d 41.

Pa.Super.1988. Mitzelfelt v. Kamrin 549 A.2d 935, 379 Pa.Super. 121.

Ga.1988. Miller v. Miller 366 S.E.2d 682, 258 Ga. 168.

Md.1988. Harris v. State 539 A.2d 637, 312 Md. 225.

Alaska App.1988. Selig v. State 750 P.2d 834.

Md.1987. Commodities Reserve Corp. v. Belt's Wharf Warehouses, Inc. 529 A.2d 822, 310 Md. 365.

Okl.1987. McKellips v. Saint Francis Hosp., Inc. 741 P.2d 467.

Mich.1987. McKinstry v. Valley Obstetrics–Gynecology Clinic, P.C. 405 N.W.2d 88, 428 Mich. 167.

Mo.App.1986. Martin v. Prier Brass Mfg. Co. 710 S.W.2d 466.

Md.1985. Evans v. State 499 A.2d 1261, 304 Md. 487.

D.C.App.1985. Green v. District of Columbia Dept. of Employment Services 499 A.2d 870.

§ 337. Allocating the Burdens of Proof

C.A.Fed.1990. Wright v. Department of Transp. 900 F.2d 1541.

C.A.9 (Or.),1988. Jeldness v. Watson 857 F.2d 1478 (Table), Unpublished Disposition.(*)

C.A.6 (Ky.)1988. Welsh v. U.S. 844 F.2d 1239.

D.Del.1988. Elmer v. Tenneco Resins, Inc. 698 F.Supp. 535.

Bkrtcy.E.D.Mich.1990. In re Premo 116 B.R. 515.

Bkrtcy.W.D.Ark.1988. In re Circle J Dairy, Inc. 92 B.R. 832.

Md.,1991. Newell v. Richards, Jr. 594 A.2d 1152.

La.,1991. Hare v. Hodgins. __ So.2d __, 1991 WL 173200.

Conn.1991. B.A. Ballou and Co., Inc. v. Citytrust 591 A.2d 126, 218 Conn. 749.

Wash.App.1991. In re Dependency of C.B. 810 P.2d 518, 61 Wash.App. 280.

La.App. 2 Cir.1991. Succession of Harvey 573 So.2d 1304.

D.C.App.1990. Riggs Nat. Bank of Washington, D.C. v. District of Columbia 581 A.2d 1229.

D.C.App.1990. Teamsters Local Union 1714 v. Public Employee Relations Bd. 579 A.2d 706.

Miss.1989. Clardy v. National Bank of Commerce of Mississippi 555 So.2d 64.

Vt.1989. State v. St. Francis 563 A.2d 249, 151 Vt. 384.

Md.1989. Kassap v. Seitz 553 A.2d 714, 315 Md. 155.

Tenn.App.,1988. Advantage Leasing Co., Inc. v. Shepperd 1988 WL 136667.

La.1988. In re J.M.P. 528 So.2d 1002.

N.J.Super.A.D.1987. Monsen Engineering Co. v. Tami–Githens, Inc. 530 A.2d 313, 219 N.J.Super. 241.

N.C.1986. Alford v. Shaw 349 S.E.2d 41, 318 N.C. 289.

D.C.App.1986. District of Columbia v. Savoy Const. Co., Inc. 515 A.2d 698.

Md.1986. Everett v. Baltimore Gas and Elec. Co. 513 A.2d 882, 307 Md. 286.

Idaho 1986. Pace v. Hymas 726 P.2d 693, 111 Idaho 581.

§ 338. Satisfying the Burden of Producing Evidence

Bkrtcy.D.Vt.1988. In re Mayo 94 B.R. 315.

Cl.Ct.1990. Loveladies Harbor, Inc. v. U.S. 21 Cl.Ct. 153.

Cl.Ct.1989. Pratt & Whitney Canada, Inc. v. U.S. 17 Cl.Ct. 777.

Miss.1989. Clardy v. National Bank of Commerce of Mississippi 555 So.2d 64.

N.M.App.1988. Matter of Estate of Gonzales 775 P.2d 1300, 108 N.M. 583.

Vt.1988. Fidelity & Deposit Co. of Maryland v. Wu 552 A.2d 1196, 150 Vt. 225.

Neb.1986. In re Estate of Price 388 N.W.2d 72, 223 Neb. 12.

§ 339. Satisfying the Burden of Persuasion: (a) The Measure of Persuasion in Civil Cases Generally

D.C.Pa.1988. Pinizzotto v. Parsons Brinkerhoff Quade and Douglas, Inc. 697 F.Supp. 886.

Cl.Ct.,1991. McClendon v. Secretary of Dept. of Health and Human Services 1991 WL 133602.

Cl.Ct.1991. McClendon v. Secretary of Dept. of Health and Human Services 23 Cl.Ct. 191.

Cl.Ct.1989. Clark By and Through Clark v. Secretary of the Dept. of Health and Human Services 19 Cl.Ct. 113.

Nev.1991. Brown v. State 807 P.2d 1379, 107 Nev. 164.

W.Va.1990. Lutz v. Orinick 401 S.E.2d 464.

Mich.1990. Falcon v. Memorial Hosp. 462 N.W.2d 44, 436 Mich. 443.

D.C.App.1990. Rowan Heating–Air Conditioning–Sheet Metal, Inc. v. Williams 580 A.2d 583.

N.J.Super.A.D.1989. Middlesex County Bd. of Social Services on Behalf of Y.G. v. G.G. 567 A.2d 1019, 237 N.J.Super. 322.

Miss.1989. Clardy v. National Bank of Commerce of Mississippi 555 So.2d 64.

Hawaii 1989. Masaki v. General Motors Corp. 780 P.2d 566, 71 Haw. 1.

Miss.1989. McClendon v. State 539 So.2d 1375.

Md.App.1988. Weisman v. Connors 547 A.2d 636, 76 Md.App. 488.

Ariz.1987. Hawkins v. Allstate Ins. Co. 733 P.2d 1073, 152 Ariz. 490.

D.C.App.1985. Petition of D.I.S. 494 A.2d 1316.

§ 340. Satisfying the Burden of Persuasion: (b) Requirement of Clear and Convincing Proof

D.C.Pa.1988. Pinizzotto v. Parsons Brinkerhoff Quade and Douglas, Inc. 697 F.Supp. 886.

D.Mass.1989. In re King 96 B.R. 413.

Bkrtcy.E.D.Mich.1988. In re Watkins 90 B.R. 848.

D.Mass.1987. Kwiat v. Doucette 81 B.R. 184.

Bkrtcy.C.D.Cal.1987. In re Drayman 77 B.R. 773.

C.A.9 (Or.)1987. Wilcox v. First Interstate Bank of Oregon, N.A. 815 F.2d 522.

La.,1991. Chatelain v. State Department of Transportation and Development, 586 So.2d 1373.

Conn.1991. Kilduff v. Adams, Inc. 593 A.2d 478, 219 Conn. 314.

W.Va.1990. Lutz v. Orinick 401 S.E.2d 464.

N.H.1990. Drucker's Case 577 A.2d 1198, 133 N.H. 326.

Fla.App. 1 Dist.1990. In Interest of D.J.S. 563 So.2d 655.

La.1989. Louisiana State Bar Ass'n v. Edwins 540 So.2d 294, Rehearing Denied.

Miss.1989. McClendon v. State 539 So.2d 1375.

Md.App.1988. Weisman v. Connors 547 A.2d 636, 76 Md.App. 488.

Ariz.1988. State v. King 763 P.2d 239, 158 Ariz. 419.

Ariz.App.1987. State v. Renforth 746 P.2d 1315, 155 Ariz. 385.

Idaho App.1986. Thompson v. Thompson 714 P.2d 62, 110 Idaho 93.

Pa.Cmwlth.1984. Sheibley v. W.C.A.B. (ARA Food Services Co.) 483 A.2d 593.

§ 341. Satisfying the Burden of Persuasion: (c) Proof Beyond a Reasonable Doubt

Alaska App.1988. Davis v. State 766 P.2d 41.

N.H.1988. In re Sanborn 545 A.2d 726, 130 N.H. 430.

La.1988. State v. Mussall 523 So.2d 1305.

La.1988. State v. Spooner 520 So.2d 336, Rehearing Denied.

Conn.1987. State v. McDonough 533 A.2d 857, 205 Conn. 352.

§ 342. Presumptions: In General

C.A.Fed.1988. Demaco Corp. v. F. Von Langsdorff Licensing Ltd. 851 F.2d 1387.

C.A.4 1986. Stapleton v. Westmoreland Coal Co. 785 F.2d 424.

Md.1991. Williams v. State 585 A.2d 209, 322 Md. 35.

Ind.App. 3 Dist.1990. Matter of Estate of Borom 562 N.E.2d 772.

La.App. 3 Cir.1990. Lucas v. St. Frances Cabrini Hosp. 562 So.2d 999.

La.1989. Cangelosi v. Our Lady of the Lake Regional Medical Center 564 So.2d 654.

Md.1989. Ristaino v. Flannery 564 A.2d 790, 317 Md. 452.

Kan.App.1987. State v. Larson 737 P.2d 880, 12 Kan.App.2d 198.

Or.App.1987. State ex rel. Juvenile Dept. of Deschutes County v. Merritt 732 P.2d 46, 83 Or.App. 378.

Colo.App.1986. Union Ins. Co. v. RCA Corp. 724 P.2d 80.

Mass.App.1984. Com. v. Kane 472 N.E.2d 1343, 19 Mass.App. 129.

§ 343. Reasons for the Creation of Presumptions: Illustrative Presumptions

U.S.1990. N.L.R.B. v. Curtin Matheson Scientific, Inc. 110 S.Ct. 1542, 494 U.S. 775, 108 L.Ed.2d 801.

C.A.1 (Mass.)1987. Whyte v. Connecticut Mut. Life Ins. Co. (Two Cases) 818 F.2d 1005.

D.C.App.1991. Abdulshakur v. District of Columbia 589 A.2d 1258.

N.M.1991. Salandre v. State 806 P.2d 562, 111 N.M. 422.

D.C.App.1990. Eilers v. District of Columbia Bureau of Motor Vehicles Services 583 A.2d 677.

R.I.1990. Witt v. Moran 572 A.2d 261.

Fla.1990. State v. Rolle 560 So.2d 1154.

Wash.1989. State v. Jackson 774 P.2d 1211, 112 Wash.2d 867.

Colo.1989. Moreno v. People 775 P.2d 1184.

Vt.1988. Brennen v. Mogul Corp. 557 A.2d 870, 151 Vt. 91.

La.1988. Succession of Talbot 530 So.2d 1132, Rehearing Denied.

Vt.1988. Lamoureux v. Chromalloy Farm Systems, Inc. 549 A.2d 649, 150 Vt. 156.

La.App. 3 Cir.1987. Safeco Ins. Co. v. Baker 515 So.2d 655.

La.App. 3 Cir.1987. Felice v. Valleylab, Inc. 520 So.2d 920.

La.1987. Bloxom v. Bloxom 512 So.2d 839.

Neb.1987. Gordman Properties Co. v. Board of Equalization of Hall County 403 N.W.2d 366, 225 Neb. 169.

Pa.Super.1986. Lynn v. Cepurneek 508 A.2d 308, 352 Pa.Super. 379.

§ 344. The Effect of Presumptions in Civil Cases

C.A.10 (Colo.)1989. Tafoya v. Sears Roebuck and Co. 884 F.2d 1330.

C.A.8 (Mo.)1987. Monger v. Cessna Aircraft Co. 812 F.2d 402.

C.A.4 1986. Stapleton v. Westmoreland Coal Co. 785 F.2d 424.

N.J.1991. Feldman v. Lederle Laboratories, a Div. of American Cyanamid Co. 592 A.2d 1176, 125 N.J. 117.

Del.Super.1990. Staats by Staats v. Lawrence 576 A.2d 663.

Ga.1988. Miller v. Miller 366 S.E.2d 682, 258 Ga. 168.

N.H.1987. Cunningham v. City of Manchester Fire Dept. 525 A.2d 714, 129 N.H. 232.

Ohio App.,1986. Wagner v. White 1986 WL 12971.

Pa.1986. Waddle v. Nelkin 515 A.2d 909, 511 Pa. 641.

Pa.Super.1986. Lynn v. Cepurneek 508 A.2d 308, 352 Pa.Super. 379.

§ 345. Constitutional Questions in Civil Cases

C.A.D.C.1985. United Scenic Artists, Local 829, Broth. of Painters and Allied Trades, AFL-CIO v. N.L. 762 F.2d 1027.

N.Y.1987. Casse v. New York State Racing and Wagering Bd. 523 N.Y.S.2d 423, 70 N.Y.2d 589, 517 N.E.2d 1309.

§ 346. Affirmative Defenses and Presumptions in Criminal Cases: (a) Terminology

Cl.Ct.1989. Pratt & Whitney Canada, Inc. v. U.S. 17 Cl.Ct. 777.

Colo.1987. Barnes v. People 735 P.2d 869.

Pa.Super.1985. Com. v. Bryant 491 A.2d 181, 341 Pa.Super. 123.

Pa.Super.1985. Com. v. Karl 490 A.2d 887, 340 Pa.Super. 493.

§ 347. Affirmative Defenses and Presumptions in Criminal Cases: (b) Constitutionality

C.A.11 (Ga.)1985. Brooks v. Kemp 762 F.2d 1383.

Kan.App.1990. State v. Kershner 801 P.2d 68, 15 Kan.App.2d 17.

Hawaii App.1987. State v. Arakaki 744 P.2d 783, 7 Haw.App. 48.

§ 348. Affirmative Defenses and
Presumptions in Criminal Cases:
(c) Special Problems

C.A.4 (W.Va.)1985. U.S. v. Boggs 775 F.2d
582.

§ 349. Choice of Law

La.App. 1 Cir.1991. Dupre v. Joe's River-
side Seafood, Inc. 578 So.2d 158.

CHAPTER 37. ADMINISTRATIVE EVIDENCE

§ 350. Introduction to Administrative
Adjudication

§ 351. Law Governing Administrative
Evidence

§ 352. Admissibility of Evidence

Tenn.App., 1986. Davis v. Yount 1986 WL
8590.

R.I.1985. Craig v. Pare 497 A.2d 316.

§ 353. Evaluation of Evidence

Iowa App.1990. Schmitz v. Iowa Dept. of
Human Services 461 N.W.2d 603.

Me.1990. Elvin v. City of Waterville 573
A.2d 381.

§ 354. The Substantial Evidence Rule

Vt.1991. Watker v. Vermont Parole Board
596 A.2d 1277.

Colo.1989. Industrial Claims Appeals Office v. Flower Stop Marketing Corp. 782
P.2d 13.

D.C.App.1987. Martin v. District of Columbia Police and Firefighters' Retirement and Relief Bd. 532 A.2d 102.

§ 355. Opinion Evidence and
Expert Testimony

§ 356. Privilege in Administrative
Proceedings

§ 357. Presentation of Case: Burden
of Proof and Presumptions

Wyo.1987. Willadsen v. Christopulos 731
P.2d 1181.

Idaho App.1984. Intermountain Health
Care, Inc. v. Board of County Com'rs of
Blaine County, Idaho 688 P.2d 260, 107
Idaho 248.

§ 358. Presentation of Case—Written
Evidence and Cross–Examination

§ 359. Official Notice

*

Table of Cases

Tables

Table of Statutes and Rules

UNITED STATES

UNITED STATES CONSTITUTION

Amend.	This Work Sec.	Note
1	63	9
	76.2	
	76.2	21
4	124	13
	127	
	128	
	149	
	156	33
	157	
	158	
	164	
	166	
	167	
	167	5
	168	
	168	23
	171	
	171	26
	173	
	173	12
	173	30
	174	
	175	
	175	44
	176	
	176	18
	177	
	179	
	179	21
	179	22
	180	7
	181	
	181	24
	182	
	183	
	183	1
5	19	25
	26	
	31	
	115	
	116	
	117	
	118	
	119	
	121	
	123	

UNITED STATES CONSTITUTION

Amend.	This Work Sec.	Note
5 (Cont'd)	123	11
	124	
	124	15
	124	33
	124	59
	125	
	126	
	126	34
	127	
	128	
	129	
	130	
	130	5
	130	17
	131	
	131	7
	132	
	132	39
	135	
	135	6
	136	
	136	17
	137	
	138	
	139	
	139	24
	140	
	142	
	143	
	143	20
	143	39
	143	41
	145	
	147	
	148	
	148	2
	149	
	150	
	152	
	153	
	153	30
	154	
	155	
	155	30
	156	
	157	
	158	
	161	
	161	13
	161	21

UNITED STATES CONSTITUTION

Amend.	This Work Sec.	Note
5 (Cont'd)	162	
	163	
	166	
	166	5
	166	11
	168	
	176	
	262	8
	302	7
	356	
6	19	
	31	
	50	12
	59	
	137	
	143	
	148	2
	149	2
	153	
	153	3
	153	10
	153	12
	153	24
	153	30
	153	35
	153	45
	154	
	155	
	155	30
	156	
	161	
	166	
	166	23
	168	
	180	
	182	
	216	16
	251	5
	252	
8	348	
14	31	
	63	9
	135	
	147	
	155	
	158	
	161	21
	162	
	163	
	168	
	216	16

UNITED STATES CODE ANNOTATED

5 U.S.C.A.—Government Organization and Employees

Sec.	This Work Sec.	Note
301	108	6
551—559	351	1

UNITED STATES CODE ANNOTATED

5 U.S.C.A.—Government Organization and Employees

Sec.	This Work Sec.	Note
551(7)	350	4
552	108	8
	356	33
552(b)(5)	108	11
552(b)(7)	108	11
	108	30
554	350	4
556(d)	351	8
	352	2
	356	3
	357	1
	358	10
	358	12
	359	2
556(e)	350	15
	359	7
701—706	351	1
706(2)(E)	351	10
822	108	4
3105	351	1
3344	351	1
5362	351	1
7521	351	1

8 U.S.C.A.—Aliens and Nationality

Sec.	This Work Sec.	Note
1252(b)	351	9

15 U.S.C.A.—Commerce and Trade

Sec.	This Work Sec.	Note
45(c)	351	3

18 U.S.C.A.—Crimes and Criminal Procedure

Sec.	This Work Sec.	Note
17	12	28
2510 et seq.	170	3
2510(11)	175	32
2515	170	4
	173	25
3481	132	4
3500	9	
	9	22
	97	3
	97	7
	113	23
3501	147	58
	148	
	148	37
	156	
	156	9
	156	15
	156	25
3501(a)	147	2

UNITED STATES CODE ANNOTATED
18 U.S.C.A.—Crimes and Criminal Procedure

18 U.S.C.A.App.—Crimes and Criminal Procedure

28 U.S.C.A.—Judiciary and Judicial Procedure

29 U.S.C.A.—Labor

44 U.S.C.A.—Public Printing and Documents

45 U.S.C.A.—Railroads

UNITED STATES CODE ANNOTATED
49 U.S.C.A.—Transportation

STATUTES AT LARGE

POPULAR NAME ACTS

ADMINISTRATIVE PROCEDURE ACT

LABOR MANAGEMENT RELATIONS ACT

STATE STATUTES

ALASKA STATUTES

ALASKA RULES OF CRIMINAL PROCEDURE

ALASKA RULES OF EVIDENCE

Rule	This Work Sec.	Note
410(b)	159	40
412	161	28
	171	
	173	24
503(a)(2)	87	20
503(d)(7)	104	5
903	220	17

ARIZONA REVISED STATUTES

Sec.	This Work Sec.	Note
12–2233	76.2	8
12–2251	65	6
13–3988	148	37
	156	25
28–692.03(A)	205	

ARIZONA RULES OF CIVIL PROCEDURE

Rule	This Work Sec.	Note
9(i)6	228	3

ARIZONA RULES OF CRIMINAL PROCEDURE

Rule	This Work Sec.	Note
12.6	138	25

ARIZONA RULES OF EVIDENCE

Rule	This Work Sec.	Note
410	159	24
611(b)	21	2

ARKANSAS CODE ANNOTATED

Sec.	This Work Sec.	Note
16–89–111(d)	145	5

ARKANSAS STATUTES

Sec.	This Work Sec.	Note
28–109	335	20
62–1601	343	20

ARKANSAS RULES OF CRIMINAL PROCEDURE

Rule	This Work Sec.	Note
16.2(1)	183	4

ARKANSAS RULES OF EVIDENCE

Rule	This Work Sec.	Note
301	344	66

WEST'S ANNOTATED CALIFORNIA CONSTITUTION

Art.	This Work Sec.	Note
I, § 4	63	4
I, § 15	135	
I, § 24	135	23
I, § 28	168	24
I, § 30	135	23

WEST'S ANNOTATED CALIFORNIA BUSINESS AND PROFESSIONS CODE

Sec.	This Work Sec.	Note
6068	40	2

WEST'S ANNOTATED CALIFORNIA CODE OF CIVIL PROCEDURE

Sec.	This Work Sec.	Note
1881(4)	98	

WEST'S ANNOTATED CALIFORNIA EVIDENCE CODE

Sec.	This Work Sec.	Note
5	78	10
240	253	47
403	53	10
404	139	17
405	53	13
451	335	1
	335	3
	335	7
452	335	20
600	344	34
600 et seq.	343	10
600(a)	342	8
603—604	344	57
605—606	344	56
621	343	23
643	223	10
664	343	11
704	68	13
730—733	17	8
770	37	26
771	9	19
785	38	14
787	41	7
788	42	5
	42	29
	42	34
801(b)	14	5

WEST'S ANNOTATED CALIFORNIA EVIDENCE CODE

Sec.	This Work Sec.	Note
802	14	4
	16	5
804	14	5
805	12	10
912(a)	83	5
913	74.1	12
916	55	22
918	73.1	11
954	72.1	4
	74	9
	92	8
956	92	8
	95	10
980	82	13
	83	4
981	79	15
994	102	6
995	102	6
996	103	10
998	104	5
1010	99	1
1014(c)	102	2
1040	107	8
	108	37
1153	159	22
	257	35
1202	37	17
1252	274	6
1451	228	4
1505	241	6
	241	7
1881, subd. 2	88	3

WEST'S ANNOTATED CALIFORNIA GOVERNMENT CODE

Sec.	This Work Sec.	Note
11513	352	1

WEST'S ANNOTATED CALIFORNIA LABOR CODE

Sec.	This Work Sec.	Note
5708	351	15
5709	351	15

WEST'S ANNOTATED CALIFORNIA PENAL CODE

Sec.	This Work Sec.	Note
25(a)	12	31
28	12	31
29	12	31
631(c)	74	8
632(d)	74	8
1112	44	23
1324	143	23

WEST'S ANNOTATED CALIFORNIA PENAL CODE

Sec.	This Work Sec.	Note
1324.1	143	23
1538.5(f)	174	17
1538.5(h)	183	7
1538.5(m)	183	38

WEST'S ANNOTATED CALIFORNIA VEHICLE CODE

Sec.	This Work Sec.	Note
17150	343	15

WEST'S COLORADO REVISED STATUTES ANNOTATED

Sec.	This Work Sec.	Note
16–5–204(4)(d)	138	25

COLORADO RULES OF CRIMINAL PROCEDURE

Rule	This Work Sec.	Note
41(e)	183	7
41(g)	183	7

CONNECTICUT CONSTITUTION

Art.	This Work Sec.	Note
I, § 8	124	55

CONNECTICUT GENERAL STATUTES ANNOTATED

Sec.	This Work Sec.	Note
52–145	42	3
52–182	343	16
52–208	58	17
	60	9
54–84(b)	133	7

DELAWARE CONSTITUTION

Art.	This Work Sec.	Note
I, § 7	153	

DELAWARE RULES OF EVIDENCE

Rule	This Work Sec.	Note
803(5)	279	17

DISTRICT OF COLUMBIA CODE

Sec.	This Work Sec.	Note
4–140	156	8
14	63	6
14–104	38	10
14–305	42	59

WEST'S FLORIDA CONSTITUTION

Art.	This Work Sec.	Note
I, § 12	168	22
	168	23
	182	38

WEST'S FLORIDA STATUTES ANNOTATED

Sec.	This Work Sec.	Note
75.071	216	8
90.410	159	40

WEST'S FLORIDA RULES OF CRIMINAL PROCEDURE

Rule	This Work Sec.	Note
3.210	17	9

OFFICIAL CODE OF GEORGIA ANNOTATED

Sec.	This Work Sec.	Note
24–3–10	304	5

GEORGIA CODE

Sec.	This Work Sec.	Note
3A–116(a)	352	1
	353	6
3A–116(b)	353	19
38–1205	41	19
38–1801	38	10
38–1803	28	8

HAWAII CONSTITUTION

Art.	This Work Sec.	Note
I, § 8	148	39

HAWAII REVISED STATUTES

Sec.	This Work Sec.	Note
91–10(2)	353	19

HAWAII RULES OF EVIDENCE

Rule	This Work Sec.	Note
306	348	18

IDAHO CODE

Sec.	This Work Sec.	Note
9–203(4)	104	5
9–203(4)(B)	104	13
9–1210	28	8
9–1302	41	7

IDAHO RULES OF CIVIL PROCEDURE

Rule	This Work Sec.	Note
43(b)(6)	42	5

IDAHO RULES OF EVIDENCE

Rule	This Work Sec.	Note
803(24)	252	28

ILLINOIS CONSTITUTION

Art.	This Work Sec.	Note
I, § 3	63	5

This Work

ILLINOIS SMITH–HURD ANNOTATED

Ch.	This Work Sec.	Note
38, para. 14–5	74	8
38, para. 109–3(e)	174	17
47, para. 9	216	8
51, para. 5.2	99	1
57, para. 48a	335	11
116, para. 207(f)	108	25

ILLINOIS SUPREME COURT RULES

Rule	This Work Sec.	Note
212(c)	56	5

INDIANA CODE

Sec.	This Work Sec.	Note
34–1–14–13	43	9
34–14–15	38	8
35–35–3–4	159	22
35–37–4–2	43	9

INDIANA ACTS

Year	This Work Sec.	Note
1969, c. 312	156	25

INDIANA RULES OF APPELLATE PROCEDURE

Rule	This Work Sec.	Note
7.2(A)(3)(b)	212	13

IOWA CODE ANNOTATED

Sec.	This Work Sec.	Note
321.493	343	15
622.18	43	9
675.41	211	
780.17	68	14
813.2	68	14
	113	20

IOWA RULES OF CRIMINAL PROCEDURE

Rule	This Work Sec.	Note
13	113	20
20(4)	145	5

KANSAS STATUTES ANNOTATED

Sec.	This Work Sec.	Note
60–420	38	14
60–427(b)	104	6
60–437(b)(5)	79	15
60–445	185	31
60–456	14	4
60–456—60–458	16	5
60–456(a)	11	12
60–457	14	4
60–460(f)	154	20

KENTUCKY REVISED STATUTES

Sec.	This Work Sec.	Note
61.878(h)	108	25
422.100	228	4

KENTUCKY RULES OF CRIMINAL PROCEDURE

Rule	This Work Sec.	Note
5.16	113	20

LOUISIANA CONSTITUTION

Art.	This Work Sec.	Note
I, § 5	175	38

LOUISIANA STATUTES ANNOTATED— CODE OF CRIMINAL PROCEDURE

Art.	This Work Sec.	Note
230.1(D)	156	25
703(E)(2)	134	22

LOUISIANA EVIDENCE CODE

Art.	This Work Sec.	Note
803(6)	291	8

MAINE REVISED STATUTES ANNOTATED

Tit.	This Work Sec.	Note
15, § 1205(1)	253	47

MAINE RULES OF EVIDENCE

Rule	This Work Sec.	Note
301	344	66
611(b)	21	2

MARYLAND ANNOTATED CODE

Art.	This Work Sec.	Note
41, § 252(b)	353	19

MARYLAND CODE, COURTS AND JUDICIAL PROCEEDINGS

Sec.	This Work Sec.	Note
9–107	117	2
10–905	42	5
10–912	156	25

MASSACHUSETTS CONSTITUTION

Art.	This Work Sec.	Note
12, Pt. 1	143	20
14	182	41

MASSACHUSETTS GENERAL LAWS ANNOTATED

Ch.	This Work Sec.	Note
30A, § 11(2)	351	15
30A, § 11(4)	353	19
210, § 3(b)	104	14
233, § 23A	255	3
233, § 65	276	12
	326	2
233, § 70	335	20
	335	30

MASSACHUSETTS GENERAL LAWS ANNOTATED

Ch.	This Work Sec.	Note
233, § 70 (Cont'd)	335	41
277, § 14A	138	25

MASSACHUSETTS ACTS & RESOLVES

Year	This Work Sec.	Note
1898, c. 535	326	2
1913, c. 746	112	4

MASSACHUSETTS RULES OF CIVIL PROCEDURE

Rule	This Work Sec.	Note
44.1	335	30

MICHIGAN COMPILED LAWS ANNOTATED

Sec.	This Work Sec.	Note
3.560(175)	353	6
3.560(176)	353	19
9.2101	343	16

MICHIGAN RULES OF EVIDENCE

Rule	This Work Sec.	Note
410	159	18
803(6)	293	19

MINNESOTA STATUTES ANNOTATED

Sec.	This Work Sec.	Note
14.60	353	19
169.09, subd. 13	112	3

MINNESOTA RULES OF EVIDENCE

Rule	This Work Sec.	Note
410	159	24

VERNON'S ANNOTATED MISSOURI STATUTES

Sec.	This Work Sec.	Note
491.070	21	8
536.070(8)	352	1
542.296	183	35
546.260	21	8
	26	5
552.020.12	136	29
552.030.5	136	29

MONTANA CODE ANNOTATED

Sec.	This Work Sec.	Note
45–5–111	145	40
46–14–401	136	29

NEBRASKA REVISED STATUTES

Sec.	This Work Sec.	Note
27–503(e)	104	12
27–509	108	37
29–2261.02	170	5
84–914(3)	353	19

NEVADA REVISED STATUTES

Sec.	This Work Sec.	Note
27–410	159	40
27–410(1)	159	18
50–095	42	5

NEW HAMPSHIRE REVISED STATUTES ANNOTATED

Sec.	This Work Sec.	Note
516:24	38	12

NEW JERSEY CONSTITUTION

Art.	This Work Sec.	Note
I, § 4	63	5

NEW JERSEY STATUTES ANNOTATED

Sec.	This Work Sec.	Note
2A:84A–22.2	101	15
3A:40–1	343	20

NEW JERSEY RULES OF EVIDENCE

Rule	This Work Sec.	Note
8(2)	53	10
20	38	14
22	41	7
22(b)	37	26
25	117	3
39	74.1	12
57	14	4
	16	5
58	14	4
	16	5
63(12)	274	6

NEW MEXICO STATUTES ANNOTATED

Sec.	This Work Sec.	Note
20–1–12	83	4

OHIO RULES OF EVIDENCE

Rule	This Work Sec.	Note
601	62	12
607	38	10
	38	11

OKLAHOMA CONSTITUTION

Art.	This Work Sec.	Note
2, § 30	173	28

OKLAHOMA STATUTES ANNOTATED

Sec.	This Work Sec.	Note
12, § 2403	185	31
75, § 310(1)	356	39
75, § 310(2)	353	19

OREGON REVISED STATUTES

Sec.	This Work Sec.	Note
133.683	176	41
	179	2
	180	35
183.450(2)	353	19
813.320	170	7

OREGON RULES OF EVIDENCE

Rule	This Work Sec.	Note
309	348	18
608(1)(b)	41	7

PENNSYLVANIA STATUTES

Tit.	This Work Sec.	Note
28, § 312	63	4
28, § 328	103	12
42, § 5919	42	61

PENNSYLVANIA RULES OF CRIMINAL PROCEDURE

Rule	This Work Sec.	Note
323(b)	183	7
323(e)	183	13
323(f)	183	2
323(h)	183	35

RHODE ISLAND GENERAL LAWS 1956

Sec.	This Work Sec.	Note
9–17–19	17	8
9–19–11	276	12

RHODE ISLAND GENERAL LAWS 1956

Sec.	This Work Sec.	Note
9–19–25	173	24
42–35–10	353	6
42–35–10(a)	352	1
42–35–10(b)	353	19

RHODE ISLAND RULES OF EVIDENCE

Rule	This Work Sec.	Note
410(4)	159	24

SOUTH DAKOTA CODIFIED LAWS

Sec.	This Work Sec.	Note
19–12–12	159	18

TENNESSEE CODE ANNOTATED

Sec.	This Work Sec.	Note
24–1–201	79	3

VERNON'S ANNOTATED TEXAS CONSTITUTION

Art.	This Work Sec.	Note
I, § 5	63	4
I, § 10	117	6

VERNON'S ANNOTATED TEXAS CIVIL STATUTES

Art.	This Work Sec.	Note
5561h	100	6

VERNON'S ANNOTATED CODE OF CRIMINAL PROCEDURE

Art.	This Work Sec.	Note
1.05	117	2
18.20, § 2	170	5
18.20, § 14(b)	170	5
20.17	138	24
38.11	84	11
38.21	147	2
38.22	161	29
38.22, § 1	144	7
38.23	170	1
	182	45
38.23(b)	181	43
38.28	38	8
43.07	38	8

VERNON'S ANNOTATED RULES OF CIVIL EVIDENCE

Rule	This Work Sec.	Note
511	103	5
803(24)	320	1

VERNON'S ANNOTATED RULES OF CRIMINAL EVIDENCE

Rule	This Work Sec.	Note
803(24)	320	1

UTAH CONSTITUTION

Art.	This Work Sec.	Note
I, § 7	124	57
I, § 12	117	6

UTAH CODE ANNOTATED

Sec.	This Work Sec.	Note
78–24–9	41	19
	121	2

UTAH RULES OF EVIDENCE

Rule	This Work Sec.	Note
20	38	14

VERMONT STATUTES ANNOTATED

Tit.	This Work Sec.	Note
12, § 1642	38	7

VIRGINIA CODE 1950

Sec.	This Work Sec.	Note
8–292	38	7

VIRGIN ISLANDS CODE

Tit.	This Work Sec.	Note
5, § 885	185	

WEST'S REVISED CODE OF WASHINGTON ANNOTATED

Sec.	This Work Sec.	Note
9.73	175	42
	175	43
9A.44.120	272.1	12
34.04.100(2)	353	19

WASHINGTON RULES OF EVIDENCE

Rule	This Work Sec.	Note
613(a)	28	9
801(d)(2)(iv)	259	5

WEST VIRGINIA CODE

Sec.	This Work Sec.	Note
29A–5–2(a)	352	1
	353	6

WISCONSIN STATUTES ANNOTATED

Sec.	This Work Sec.	Note
227.08	352	
885.235(2a)	205	
902.03	335	10
904.12	255	3
905.04(4)(d)	104	7
905.09	108	36
971.16	17	9
971.31(5)(b)	174	17

WYOMING RULES OF EVIDENCE

Rule	This Work Sec.	Note
301	344	66

UNIFORM COMMERCIAL CODE

Sec.	This Work Sec.	Note
1–205(2) to 1–205(6)	198	
2–723	199	
2–724	321	19
7–403(1)	343	17
7–403(1)(b)	343	17

UNIFORM INTERSTATE AND INTER-NATIONAL PROCEDURE ACT

Sec.	This Work Sec.	Note
Art. IV	335	
	335	30
4.01	335	25
4.02	335	25
4.03	335	25
4.04	335	25
5.03	335	36

CODE OF FEDERAL REGULATIONS

Tit.	This Work Sec.	Note
1, § 305.70–4	358	23
14, § 302.24(m)(1)	359	20

CODE OF FEDERAL REGULATIONS

Tit.	This Work Sec.	Note
16, § 3.40	357	13
16, § 3.45	356	31
20, §§ 404.715–404.728	322	18
29, § 18.44	351	21
29, § 18.803(a)(26)—(30)	351	27
29, § 18.1101	351	25
29, § 2200.72	351	21
43, § 4.122	351	21
46, § 502.226	359	20
47, § 1.351	351	21
49, § 1100.45	358	5
49, § 1100.49	358	5
49, § 1100.50	358	5
49, § 1100.53	358	5
49, § 1114.1	351	21

FEDERAL REGISTER

Vol.	This Work Sec.	Note
55, p. 13219	351	26

FEDERAL RULES OF CIVIL PROCEDURE

Rule	This Work Sec.	Note
8(c)	337	11
8(e)(2)	257	21
9(c)	337	15
15(a)	257	26
15(b)	54	15
	54	16
	54	17
	185	3
16	3	20
	228	
26	96	23
26—37	3	12
	96	7
26(b)	96	28
26(b)(1)	3	14
	96	10
	109	8
26(b)(3)	96	
	96	28
26(b)(4)	16	7
	96	
	96	28
	96	39
26(b)(4)(B)	89	15
26(c)	96	23
	253	35
26.2	97	
30	3	13
30(b)	96	
30(b)(6)	259	2
30(c)	19	5
30(d)	253	35
32(a)	302	14
32(a)(1)	3	23
	301	13

FEDERAL RULES OF CIVIL PROCEDURE

Rule	This Work Sec.	Note
32(a)(2)	3	22
	259	2
	301	13
32(a)(3)	3	23
	253	36
32(a)(4)	56	5
	307	3
32(b)	52	9
	52	10
32(c)	38	12
32(d)	52	9
	52	10
32(d)(3)	306	5
33	3	15
34	3	16
	96	
	96	28
35	3	17
	264	6
36	3	18
37	109	8
37(b)	264	6
37(b)(2)(B)	164	1
	185	31
44.1	335	43
45(e)(1)	253	23
46	51	13
	51	17
	52	60
53	17	24
56	358	6

FEDERAL RULES OF CRIMINAL PROCEDURE

Rule	This Work Sec.	Note
5(a)	156	
	156	10
5.1	174	
5.1(a)	174	4
6(d)	113	9
6(e)	113	2
6(e)(1)	113	21
6(e)(3)(C)(i)	113	13
9	159	
10	156	10
11	257	30
11(e)(6)	159	17
	159	23
	257	35
	266	36
11(e)(6)(D)	159	21
12	183	
12(b)	183	5
12(c)	183	5
12(f)	183	6
12(i)	97	
	97	19
15	52	9
15(a)	253	39

FEDERAL RULES OF CRIMINAL PROCEDURE

FEDERAL RULES OF EVIDENCE

FEDERAL RULES OF EVIDENCE

*

Index

References are to pages. II indicates reference to volume II.

1007

MOTION TO STRIKE
Evidence not "connected up," 233, 234.
Liability insurance, reference to, 856.
Testimony not subject to cross-examination, 78–81.
When appropriate, 200.

NEWSPAPERS
Authentication of, II–56.
Original writing rule applied to, II–73.
Reliability of, II–518.

NOLO CONTENDERE PLEA
See, also, Impeachment
Compromise, protected as, II–199.

NOTICE
See, also, particular topics
Intent to offer secondary evidence, II–80.
Other accidents, to prove, 848, 849.
Statements revealing as non-hearsay, II–113, 114.

OATH
Value of, II–94.

OATH OR AFFIRMATION
Competency, 244–246.
Form of, 249.
Self-incrimination, role in history of, 421–425.
Value, II–94.

OBJECTIONS
Generally, 200 et seq.
Deposition testimony, 202.
Evidence not "connected up," form, 233–235.
General, 204, 213.
Judge, exclusion of evidence without, 224, 225.
Plain error, 211, 212.
Renewed, as to evidence not "connected up," 235.
Repetition, 208.
Specific, 204–208.
Portions of documents, 207.
Specificity required, 197, 204–208.
Status of inadmissible evidence not objected to, 217.
Tactics, 209, 210.
Timing of, 195, 200, 201.
Waiver, 221–225.
Earlier trial, at, 202.
Failure to object as, 15, 163, 164, 221.
Failure to object to like evidence, 222, 223.
Inspection of demanded writing, 221, 222.
Introduction of inadmissible evidence, 229–232.
Offer of like evidence, 208, 223, 224.

OBSERVATION
See, Firsthand Knowledge.

OBSTRUCTION OF JUSTICE
Admission of party, as, II–190–194.
Tort remedies for, II–193.

OFFER OF COMPROMISE
Generally, II–194–200.
Acceptance of, effect, II–198.
Admitted claims, II–195.
Criminal cases,
Victim, with, II–198.
Distinguished from rule of privilege, 271.
Negotiations preceeding, II–195.
Policies favoring exclusion, II–194.

OFFER OF PROOF
Generally, 194–200.
Admissible portions of documents, 199.
Jury excused during, 196, 197.
Multiple witnesses, 199, 200.
Necessity for on appeal, 197–200.
Reasons for requiring, 195, 196.

OFFICIAL NOTICE
See Administrative Adjudications; Judicial Notice

OFFICIAL RECORDS
See, also, Public Records
Authentication of, II–48.

OFFICIAL WRITTEN STATEMENTS
See, Public Records

OPINION POLLS
Generally, 935–943.
Confidence intervals, 941–943.
Hearsay status of, 936.
Methodology, 938, 939.
Sources of error in, 939, 940.

OPINIONS
See, also, Expert Witnesses
Generally, 41 et seq.
Administrative adjudications, II–523, 524.
Admissions in form of, II–146.
Character, of, 788.
Dying declarations, in, II–331.
Legal conclusions, 50, 51.
Mental state constituting element of crime, 52.
Modern rules relating to, 44, 45.
Out-of-court statements, 75, 76.
Ultimate issue, on, 47–51.

ORDER OF PRESENTATION
Court control of, 10, 223.
Role of counsel, 233.

ORDER OF PROOF
Generally, 8.
Scope of cross-examination as affecting, 87–89.

ORIGINAL WRITING RULE
Generally, II–59 et seq.
Admissions, terms, II–85, 86.
Appellate review, II–86, 87.

PHYSICIANS—Cont'd
Statements of bodily condition to, II–246–252.
  Cause of condition, II–247.
  Child sex abuse cases, II–251, 252.
  Consultation for treatment, II–246–249.
  Preparation to testify, II–249–252.

PLAIN ERROR
  Generally, 211, 212.
Excuse for failure to object, 201.

PLEA BARGAINS
Compromises, protected as, II–198, 199.

PLEADINGS
Admissions in, effect, II–142.
Admissions of fact in, II–147, 148.
Allocation of burden of, II–427, 428.
Character placed in issue by, 790.

PLEAS
  See, also, Plea Bargains
Guilty pleas as judicial admissions, II–147, 148.

POLICE FILES
See Government Secrets

POLICE INVESTIGATIONS
See Government Secrets

POLICE REPORTS
Multiple hearsay, in, II–368.
Public records, as, II–292–294.
Regularly kept records, as, II–272, 274, 275.

POLYGRAPH
  See, also, Lie Detection; Scientific Evidence
Self-incrimination, testing as, 452.

PRELIMINARY HEARING
Former testimony, hearsay exception, II–316.

PRELIMINARY QUESTIONS OF FACT
  Generally, 212 et seq.
Bigamy, in cases concerning, 217.
Coconspirators' statements, affecting, 217, 218.
Competency of witnesses, 217.
Determined by court, 213.
Determined by jury, 215.
Dying declarations, affecting, 216, 217.
Lost writing, 217, 218.
Original writing rule, raised by, 217, 218.
Standards of proof for determining, 218, 219.

PREPARATION FOR TRIAL
  See also, Depositions; Discovery; Refreshing Recollection; Witnesses
  Generally, 2 et seq.
Refreshing recollection of witnesses, 28.

PRESENT SENSE IMPRESSIONS
Hearsay exception for, II–211–215.

PRESERVATION OF TESTIMONY
Statutory provisions for, 8.

PRESUMPTIONS
  See, also, Burden of Proof
  Generally, II–449 et seq.
Affirmative criminal defenses compared, II–479–481.
Burden of persuasion, transfer by, II–470–476.
"Bursting bubble" theory of, II–462–476.
  Deviations from, II–462–476.
    Conflicting presumptions, II–465, 466.
    Instructions to jury, II–467–469.
Choice of Law, II–494–497.
Classification of, II–471, 344, 345.
Conclusive presumption, distinguished, II–451.
Conflicting, II–465, 466.
Constitutionality,
  Civil cases, II–476–479.
  Criminal cases, II–481–490.
Creation, reasons for, II–340–344.
Criminal cases, in,
  Affirmative defenses compared, II–492.
  Constitutionality, 489–499.
    Instructing the jury, II–493, 494.
    Instructions as affecting, II–488, 489.
    Mandatory presumptions, II–488, 493.
    Permissive presumptions, II–488, 493.
    Rational connection test, II–485.
    Reasonable doubt standard, II–486.
    Submission to jury of issue involving, II–493.
Defined, II–449.
Effect,
  Burden of persuasion, II–470–476.
  Burden of producing evidence, transfer of, II–449, 450.
  Civil cases, II–460–476.
    "Bursting bubble" theory, II–462–476.
    Differentiated, II–471.
  Criminal cases, II–451.
    Affirmative defenses compared, II–480, 481.
Erie rule affecting, II–494–497.
Examples, II–455–460.
Failure to produce evidence, raising, II–188.
Illustration, II–455–460.
Improvement of, II–475, 476.
Inferences distinguished, II–450, 451.
Innocence, presumption of, distinguished, II–452, 453.
Intoxication, from blood alcohol, 888.
Mandatory presumptions,
  Defined, II–481.

STAR CHAMBER
Self-incrimination, role in history of privilege against, 423.

STARTLED UTTERANCES
See, Excited Utterances

STATEMENTS
See, Prior Consistent Statements; Prior Inconsistent Statements

STATEMENTS AGAINST INTEREST
See, Declarations Against Interest

STIPULATIONS
Effects of, II-142.
Pretrial, 3.

STUDIES
See, Scientific Techniques

SUBPOENA DUCES TECUM
Original writings, use to obtain, II-80.

SUBSEQUENT REMEDIAL MEASURE
Distinguished from rule of privilege, 271.

SUICIDE
Attempted, as admission, II-182, 183.
Death certificate indicating, II-295.
Presumption against, II-460.
Spontaneous statements to prove, II-238.

SURVEYS
Administrative adjudication, in, II-520.

SYMPTOMS
See, Excited Utterances

TENANTS IN COMMON
Admissions of party opponent by, II-169.

TESTAMENTARY CAPACITY
Opinion of, 50, 51.
Psychiatric testimony concerning, 164, 165.

TESTS
See, Experiments; Scientific Techniques

TITLE DOCUMENTS
Hearsay exception, II-361.
Recordation, effect, II-361.

ULTIMATE ISSUES
See Opinions

UNIFORM ACTS
Uniform Act to Secure Attendance of Witnesses from Without a State, II-134.

UNIFORM RULES OF CRIMINAL PROCEDURE
Self-incrimination, immunity provisions, 542.

VIDEOTAPE
Child sex abuse cases, use in, II-225.
Child witness, sex offense, II-137, 138.
Demonstrative evidence, II-17, 18, 25–28.

VIEWS
Evidentiary status of, II-27, 28.

VITAL STATISTICS
Public records, hearsay exception, II-294–296.
State statute, regulation by, II-295.

WAIVER
See, particular topics

WITHDRAWAL OF EVIDENCE
Generally, 210, 211.

WITNESSES
See, also, Expert Witnesses; Firsthand Knowledge.
Attesting, II-39–41.
Calling by court, 23.
Character, 816.
Cross-examination of, 816, 817.
To impeach, 137 et seq.
Children,
Confrontation of, II-137, 138.
Sex offenses against, II-224–226.
Provisions for testimony in, II-225.
Competency, 242–266.
Defects of capacity for impeachment, 160–168.
Eyewitnesses,
Habit evidence, as affecting admissibility of, 828.
Scientific evidence concerning reliability, 903–907.
Hearsay declarants as, II-371.
Compulsory process to obtain, II-371.
Hostile,
Cross-examination, Scope of, 91.
Records of past recollection, II-260.
Ordinary conditions required, II-93.
Party as, effect of testimony, II-153–156.
Planning use of, 4.
Preparation for trial, 4.
Protection from harassment, 141.
Psychiatric examination of, 164–168.
Psychiatric examination to determine competency, 264.
Psychiatric testing of, impeachment, 164, 165.
Right to interview, 4, 5.
Self-incrimination privilege available to, 510–529.
Separation of, 188–192.
Violation of order, 191, 192.
When appropriate, 188–192.

WORK PRODUCT
See, also, Attorney–Client Privilege
Attorney-client privilege, 353–360.
Criminal cases,
Jencks Act, 363–366.
History of doctrine, 356–360.

WORKERS' COMPENSATION
Nature of as affecting admissibility evidence, II-519, 520.